Introduction to Business

Introduction to Business

JULIAN E. GASPAR
Director, Center for International Business Education and Research

LEONARD BIERMAN
Professor of Management

JAMES W. KOLARI
Professor of Finance

RICHARD T. HISE
Professor of Marketing

L. MURPHY SMITH
Professor of Accounting

ANTONIO ARREOLA-RISA
Associate Professor of Information and Operations Management

BEN WELCH, Editorial Advisor
Senior Lecturer for Introduction to Business

All of Mays Business School at Texas A&M University

Houghton Mifflin Company

Boston   New York

| *Dedications*

To Jayanthi, Philip, and Jeremy
—Julian E. Gaspar

To Risa, Joshua, and David
—Leonard Bierman

To Karie and Wes
—James W. Kolari

To Carol, Amy, and Emily
—Richard T. Hise

To Mary Katherine, Tracy, Jacob, and Hannah
—L. Murphy Smith

To Cecivon, Cecivonita, Tony, Maui, and Alex
—Antonio Arreola-Risa

Editor-in-Chief: George Hoffman

Associate Sponsoring Editor/Developmental Manager: Susan M. Kahn

Senior Project Editor: Rachel D'Angelo Wimberly

Editorial Assistant: Sage Anderson

Art/Design Coordinator: Jill Haber

Photo Editor: Jennifer Meyer Dare

Composition Buyer: Sarah Ambrose

Senior Manufacturing Coordinator: Chuck Dutton

Executive Marketing Manager: Steven W. Mikels

Marketing Associate: Lisa E. Boden

Cover Image: © Andy Whale/Getty Images

Printed in the U.S.A.

Library of Congress Control Number: 2004111273

ISBN —

Student text: 0–618–30636–6

Exam copy: 0–618–56848–4

1 2 3 4 5 6 7 8 9 — WC — 09 08 07 06 05

Brief Contents

Part One

The Nature of Contemporary Business   1

1 What Is Business?   2
2 The Environment of Business   49
3 Business Governance, Ethics, and Social Responsibility   94
4 Small Business and Entrepreneurship   127

Part Two

Managing Business Behavior   161

5 Managing and Organizing Business   162
6 Human Resources Management   194
7 Motivating and Leading Employees   227

Part Three

Marketing   273

8 Marketing Basics   274
9 Developing the Product and Pricing Mixes   308
10 Developing the Promotion and Distribution Mixes   340

Part Four

Accounting   377

11 Accounting for Decision Making   378
12 Financial Reporting   407

Part Five

Finance   441

13 Financial Management of the Firm and Investment Management   442
14 Understanding the Financial System, Money, and Banking   476
15 Personal Financial Planning   518

Part Six

Managing Business Operations, Management Information Systems, and the Digital Enterprise   555

16 Managing Business Operations   556
17 Management Information Systems   590
18 The Digital Enterprise   615

Appendix

Case in Point Company Profiles   A-1

Contents

Preface *xiv*

Part One
The Nature of Contemporary Business 1

1 What Is Business? 2

Introduction *4*
  Defining Business and Profit *4*
  The Evolution of Business in the United States *5*
  The New Society of Knowledge Workers *8*
Types of Economic Systems and Their Impact on Business *10*
  The Free Enterprise, or Capitalist, System *10*
  The Command, or Planned, Economic System *17*
  The Mixed Economic System *17*
  The Transition Economies *18*
Production of Goods and Services *19*
Measuring Business Performance *21*
  Maximizing Profit and Shareholder Wealth *21*
  Maximizing Stakeholder Wealth *22*
Ethics in Business *Corporate Profits Versus Corporate Ethics* *23*
  Minimizing Unemployment and Income Inequalities *24*
  Not-for-Profit Organizations *24*
Demand for Goods and Services *25*
  Measuring Consumer Confidence *25*
  The Consumer Knows Best *26*
  Consumer Demographics and Psychographics *26*
  Cultural Diversity *27*
Case in Point *McDonald's Corporation: Ronald Goes to France* *29*
  Measuring Gross National Product, Gross National Income, and Gross Domestic Product *30*
  Purchasing Power Parity *33*
  Business Cycles *34*
The Digital Era *35*

E-Business *35*
  Impact of IT on Globalization, Culture, Society, and Politics *38*
Careers in Business *39*

Summary 40 Chapter Questions 43 Interpreting Business News 44 Web Assignments 44 Portfolio Projects 45 Test Prepper 47

2 The Environment of Business 49

Introduction *50*
Evaluating the Business Environment *51*
  Major Goals of Economic Management *52*
  Policy Tools to Manage the Economy *53*
The Global Nature of Business *56*
  Why Do Countries Trade or Invest Overseas? *56*
Global Business *India: A Star Global Outsourcing Center* *57*
  Theory of Absolute and Comparative Advantage in Trade *59*
  Barriers to International Trade and Investments *61*
  The Foreign Exchange Market and the Exchange Rate *64*
The Rise in Globalization *66*
  The World Trade Organization *66*
  Regional Trading Blocs *67*
Going International *76*
  Export-Import Business *77*
  Licensing and Franchising *78*
  International Joint Ventures and Strategic Alliances *79*
  Multinational Enterprises *80*
Case in Point *DaimlerChrysler: Expanding Its Technological Reach* *81*
  Careers in International Business *85*

Summary 87 Chapter Questions 90 Interpreting Business News 90 Web Assignments 90 Portfolio Projects 91 Test Prepper 92

3
Business Governance, Ethics, and Social Responsibility 94

Introduction   95

Technology and Business *E-mail, AT&T, and Jack Grubman*   96

Business Governance Structures   97
  Sole Proprietorships   97
  Partnerships   98
  Corporations   98

Shareholder Model of Business Governance   102
  Separation of Ownership and Control and Potential Conflicts of Interest   103
  Addressing Separation of Ownership and Control-Related Conflicts of Interest   106

Stakeholder Model of Business Governance   112
  Business and Local Communities   112
  Creditors   114
  Suppliers   114
  Distributors   114
  Customers   115
  Employees   115

Case in Point *The Supervisory Board at DaimlerChrysler*   116
  Shareholders   116

Societal Responsibility Model of Business Governance   116

Business Ethics   117
  Defining Business Ethics   117
  Business Codes of Ethics   119
  Dealing with Business Ethical Breaches   119
  Penalties for Business Ethical Breaches   119
  Business Ethics Training   120
  Business Ethics on Campus   120

Careers in Business Governance, Ethics, and Social Responsibility   120

Summary   121   Chapter Questions   122   Interpreting Business News   123   Web Assignments   123   Portfolio Projects   124   Test Prepper   125

What Is the Role of Small Business Firms?   129
  Creative Destruction   129
  Invention and Innovation   130
  Job Opportunities   132
  Globalization   132

Global Business *Global Small Business and Information Technology Products*   133

Government Support of Small Business   134

Who Is an Entrepreneur?   135
  Personal Qualities   135
  Education and Training   136
  Women in Small Business   137
  Ethnic and Immigrant Small Business   138

Developing a Business Plan   139
  Essential Components   139
  Business Ideas   140
  Seed Money   141
  Initial Production and Sales   142
  Creating Value   142

Forms of Small Business Organizations   142
  Sole Proprietorships and Partnerships   142
  Corporations and Franchises   143

Case in Point *Franchising: A Way for Small Business and Large Business to Work Together*   145

Small Business Management Decisions   147
  Hiring Employees   147
  Ethics in Entrepreneurship   148
  Running a Family Business   149
  Going Public Versus Staying Private   150
  Controlling Business Risks   151

Careers in Small Business   154

Summary   155   Chapter Questions   156   Interpreting Business News   156   Web Assignments   157   Portfolio Projects   157   Test Prepper   158

Part Two
Managing Business Behavior 161

4
Small Business and Entrepreneurship 127

Introduction   128
What Is a Small Business?   128

5
Managing and Organizing Business 162

Introduction   163
Understanding Management   163

The Management Process   *164*
  Planning   *164*
  Organizing   *170*

Global Business *Pushing Pills Around the World* *172*
  Directing   *182*
  Controlling   *182*

Kinds of Managers   *183*
  Levels of Management   *184*
  Areas of Management   *184*

Management Skills   *185*
  Technical Skills   *186*
  Conceptual Skills   *186*
  Human Relations Skills   *186*
  International Skills   *186*

Case in Point *Managerial Human Relations Skills and the Success of the Sony Corporation* *187*

Careers in Management   *187*

Summary *188* *Chapter Questions* *189* *Interpreting Business News* *190* *Web Assignments* *190* *Portfolio Projects* *191* *Test Prepper* *192*

International Labor Relations   *213*

Legal Environment of Human Resources Management   *213*
  Employment-at-Will Revisited   *213*
  Federal Legislation After 1960   *215*
  State Regulation   *217*

Ethics in Business *Workplace Ethics: The Issue of Coworker Dating* *218*

Workplace Diversity   *218*

Case in Point *Workforce Diversity at McDonald's* *219*
  Advantages and Challenges of a Diverse Workforce   *219*
  Equal Employment Opportunity Versus Affirmative Action   *219*
  University of Michigan Affirmative Action Cases   *220*
  Workforce Diversity After 9/11   *220*

Careers in Human Resources Management   *221*

Summary *221* *Chapter Questions* *223* *Interpreting Business News* *223* *Web Assignments* *224* *Portfolio Projects* *224* *Test Prepper* *225*

6
Human Resources Management   194

Introduction   *195*
  What Do Human Resources Managers Do?   *196*
  Technology and Human Resources Management   *196*

Human Resources Planning   *197*
  Job Analysis   *197*
  Forecasting Human Resources Demand   *197*
  Forecasting Human Resources Supply   *198*
  Matching Supply with Demand   *198*

Organizational Staffing   *199*
  Recruiting   *199*
  Selection   *200*
  Orientation   *201*

Compensation and Benefits   *201*
  Wages and Salaries   *201*
  Benefits   *203*

Developing an Effective Workforce   *205*
  Needs Analyses   *205*
  Methods for Developing an Effective Workforce   *205*
  Feedback and Performance Appraisal and Evaluation   *206*

Labor-Management Relations   *208*
  Historical Overview   *208*
  Collective Bargaining   *210*
  The Decline of Unions   *212*

7
Motivating and Leading Employees   227

Introduction   *228*

What Is Motivation?   *229*

Traditional Motivational Theories   *231*
  Classical Theory: Taylor's Scientific Management Theory   *231*
  Behavior Theory: The Hawthorne Studies   *235*
  Maslow's Hierarchy of Needs   *236*
  Herzberg's Motivation-Hygiene Theory   *237*
  McGregor's Theories X and Y   *238*
  Ouchi's Theory Z   *239*

Contemporary Motivation Theories   *240*
  Expectancy Theory   *240*
  Equity Theory   *241*
  Reinforcement Theory   *242*

Enhancing Employee Performance and Job Satisfaction   *243*
  Management by Objective   *244*
  Use of Teams by Firms   *245*
  Participative Management and Employee Empowerment   *246*
  Job Enrichment and Redesign   *247*

Work-Life Programs   *249*
  Flextime Programs   *250*
  Part-Time Work   *251*

Work-Share Programs *251*
Self-Managing Teams *252*
Telecommuting and Alternative Work Styles *252*

What Is Leadership? *253*

Ethics in Business *Goodbye to an Ethicist* *254*

Major Leadership Theories *255*
Servant Leadership *255*
Transactional and Transformational Leadership *255*
Charismatic Leadership *256*
Contingency Theories of Leadership *256*
Chaos Theory *257*

The Practice of Leadership *257*
Autocratic Style *259*
Democratic Style *260*
Free-Rein Style *261*
The Contingency Approach to Leadership *261*

Case in Point *Sony: Preparing Tomorrow's Leaders* *262*

Careers in Motivation and Leadership *263*

Summary 264   Chapter Questions 267   Interpreting Business News 268   Web Assignments 268   Portfolio Projects 269   Test Prepper 270

Part Three
Marketing   273

8
Marketing Basics   274

Introduction *275*

The Definition of Marketing *276*

Markets *277*
Consumer Market *277*

Global Business *Starbucks Seeks Growth Overseas* *278*

Business-to-Business Market *281*
Government Market *282*
International Markets *283*

Case in Point *Sony Decides to Enter the China Market* *283*

The Marketing Environment *284*
Competition *285*
Technology *285*
The Economy *286*
The Legal and Political Environment *287*
Culture *288*

Obtaining Information About Markets and the Environment *288*
Marketing Information Systems *288*
Marketing Research *290*
Databases *291*

Objectives *292*

Strategies *294*

Technology and Business *Michelin Uses High Tech in Its Quest to Become the Leading Tire Manufacturer* *295*

Managing Customers *298*
Analyzing Customers *298*
Customer Satisfaction *299*
Customer Service *300*

Case in Point *McDonald's Grapples with Poor Service Levels* *301*

Careers in Marketing *302*

Summary 303   Chapter Questions 304   Interpreting Business News 304   Web Assignments 305   Portfolio Projects 305   Test Prepper 306

9
Developing the Product and Pricing Mixes   308

Introduction *309*

Guidelines for Developing the Marketing Mix *310*

Developing the Product Mix *310*
Product Elements *310*

Case in Point *DaimlerChrysler Relies on Product Design to Escape Performance Doldrums* *311*

Developing New Products *314*

Case in Point *Sony's Product Lines Are an Important Asset as It Considers Merger and Acquisition Possibilities* *315*

Managing Existing Products *325*

Technology and Business *Electric Toy Trains Make a Comeback* *326*

Developing the Pricing Mix *329*
Pricing Objectives *329*
Pricing Concepts *330*
Setting Prices for New Products *330*

Case in Point *McDonald's Offers a $1-Item Menu* *331*

Changing Prices for Existing Products *331*
Pricing Decisions for Products Sold Internationally *333*
Retailers' Pricing Decisions *333*

Global Business *Fuji Film Accused of Dumping in the U.S. Market* *333*

Ethics in Business *Companies Charge Fees Because They Can't Raise Prices   334*

Careers in Brand Management   *335*

Summary   335   Chapter Questions   336   Interpreting Business News   336   Web Assignments   337   Portfolio Projects   337   Test Prepper   338

10
Developing the Promotion and Distribution Mixes   340

Introduction   *341*

The Promotion Mix   *342*
   Advertising   *343*
   Sales Promotion   *345*
   Personal Selling   *350*

Ethics in Business *The Use of Incentives by Pharmaceutical Companies   354*

   Publicity   *355*

The Distribution Mix   *356*
   Channels of Distribution   *356*
   Logistics   *362*

Technology and Business *Logistics Relies on Technology to Cut Cost and Provide Better Levels of Customer Service   367*

Case in Point *McDonald's Good at Distribution—But Problems Elsewhere   368*

Careers in Promotion   *368*

Careers in Distribution   *369*

Summary   370   Chapter Questions   371   Interpreting Business News   372   Web Assignments   372   Portfolio Projects   373   Test Prepper   374

Part Four
Accounting   377

11
Accounting for Decision Making   378

Introduction   *379*

Accounting Information System   *379*
   Management Accounting   *380*
   Financial Accounting and External Users of Accounting Information   *380*

Accounting Literature: Generally Accepted Accounting Principles   *381*

Information Role of the Accounting Information System Within the Management Information System   *383*

Accounting for International Trade   *384*
   International Information Flow   *385*
   International Accounting Standards Board   *385*
   International Financial Reporting Standards   *386*
   International Auditing and Assurance Standards Board   *388*
   International Standards on Auditing   *388*

Importance of Ethical Accounting Practices   *390*

Case in Point *McDonald's Works to Improve Health   392*

   Can Ethics Be Taught?   *392*
   Role of Professional Organizations   *393*

Computer Crime   *394*

Internal Control   *395*
   Types of Controls   *395*
   Role of the Auditor   *396*
   Foreign Corrupt Practices Act   *397*
   Computer Security of Accounting Information   *398*
   Computer Contingency Planning for Accounting Information   *399*

Careers in Accounting   *400*

Ethics in Business *How Do You Measure Success?   401*

Summary   402   Chapter Questions   403   Interpreting Business News   403   Web Assignments   403   Portfolio Projects   404   Test Prepper   405

12
Financial Reporting   407

Introduction   *408*

The Purpose of Financial Reporting   *408*

The Four Financial Statements   *409*
   Income Statement   *409*
   Statement of Retained Earnings   *411*
   Balance Sheet   *412*
   Statement of Cash Flows   *414*
   Relationships Among Financial Statements   *415*

Case in Point *DaimlerChrysler: Accounting for Costs and Benefits of Technology and Innovation   416*

Auditing the Financial Statements   *416*
   External or Financial Statement Audit   *417*
   Audit Steps   *417*
   Audit Evidence   *418*
   Impact of Computerization   *419*

Foreign Currency Translation *422*
Current Rate Method *423*
Temporal Rate Method *423*
The Impact of Technology *423*
Technology and Business *Timeline of Major Events Regarding Accounting and Information Processing* *425*
American Institute of CPAs Top Ten Technologies *426*
Accounting and Auditing Resources on the Web *427*
Careers in Accounting *435*
Summary *435* *Chapter Questions* *436* *Interpreting Business News* *436* *Web Assignments* *436* *Portfolio Projects* *437* *Test Prepper* *438*

Part Five
Finance 441

13
Financial Management of the Firm and Investment Management 442

Introduction *443*
Key Financial Concepts *444*
Owners Versus Managers *444*
Accounting Profits Versus Economic Profits *445*
Role of the Financial Manager *445*
Time Value of Money and Interest Rates *446*
Technology and Business *The Time Value of Money: How Money Grows* *448*
Firm Financial Decision Making *450*
Net Present Value and Capital Budgeting Decisions *450*
Technology and Business *Capital Budgeting Decisions for Multiple-Year Investments* *452*
Sources of Funds and Financing Decisions *452*
Managing Cash Within the Firm *457*
Matching Assets and Liabilities *458*
The Role of Investment Managers *459*
Ethics in Business *Trust in Investment Services* *460*
Balancing Returns and Risks *461*
Measuring Returns *461*
Counting the Risks *463*
Case in Point *Market Risk and the Stock Performance of DaimlerChrysler, McDonald's, and Sony* *464*
Managing Investment Risks *465*
Making Investment Choices *467*

Careers in Financial and Investment Management *469*
Summary *470* *Chapter Questions* *471* *Interpreting Business News* *471* *Web Assignments* *472* *Portfolio Projects* *472* *Test Prepper* *474*

14
Understanding the Financial System, Money, and Banking 476

Introduction *477*
The Financial System *478*
Components of the Financial System *478*
Case in Point *Are the Golden Arches Turning Red?* *480*
Structure of Financial Systems *482*
Financial Systems and the Economy *486*
Money and Banking *487*
What Is Money? *487*
Central Banks and Monetary Policy *492*
Monetary Policy Framework *495*
Financial Institutions *501*
Depository Institutions *503*
Technology and Business *Online Banking* *505*
Nondepository Institutions *505*
Managing a Financial Institution *510*
Careers in the Financial System *512*
Summary *512* *Chapter Questions* *513* *Interpreting Business News* *514* *Web Assignments* *514* *Portfolio Projects* *515* *Test Prepper* *516*

15
Personal Financial Planning 518

Introduction *519*
The Purpose of Personal Financial Planning *519*
Key Concepts *520*
Computing Net Worth *520*
Setting Financial Goals *522*
Evaluating Spending Patterns *523*
Identifying Your Stage in Life *525*
Turning to Experts *525*
Managing Income *527*
Budgeting *527*
The Envelope Budget *529*

Checkbook Management *530*
Financial Planning Software *532*
Web Resources *533*
Insurance *534*
Living on One Income *536*
Investing *538*
Managing Investments *539*

Global Business *Buying Stock in Multinational Companies Is a Way to Diversify Your Investment Portfolio* *540*
Fixed-Income Investments *541*
Equity Investments *541*

Case in Point *Financial Information Available to Investors on the Web Regarding Sony Corporation* *542*
Your Home *543*
Retirement and Estate Planning *545*
Social Security *545*
IRAs and 401(k) Plans *546*
A Will *546*
Tax Planning *547*
Ethics of Financial Planning *547*
Giving *548*
Repaying Debts *548*
Paying Taxes *548*
Providing for Your Family *549*
Planning for Future Needs *549*
Keep Money in Perspective *549*
Careers in Personal Financial Planning *550*

Summary 550 Chapter Questions 551 Interpreting Business News 552 Web Assignments 552 Portfolio Projects 552 Test Prepper 553

Part Six

Managing Business Operations, Management Information Systems, and the Digital Enterprise   555

16
Managing Business Operations   556

Introduction *557*
What Is Operations Management? *557*
Goods and Services *559*
Operations Management and Competitiveness *560*

Historical Development of Operations Management *561*
What Do Operations Managers Do? *563*
Design Decisions *564*
Product *564*
Process *566*
Capacity *567*
Location *569*
Layout *570*

Technology and Business *McDonald's Looks for Competitive Advantage with Its New High-Tech Kitchen Layout* *572*
Planning Decisions *572*
Production Rate *573*
Material Requirements *574*
Purchasing *576*
Inventory *577*

Case in Point *Operations Management Is a Powerful Competitive Weapon* *578*
Control Decisions *580*
Scheduling *580*
Quality *581*
Careers in Operations Management *583*

Summary 585 Chapter Questions 586 Interpreting Business News 586 Web Assignments 586 Portfolio Projects 587 Test Prepper 588

17
Management Information Systems   590

Introduction *592*
What Are Management Information Systems? *592*
Computer Hardware *593*
Computer Software *595*
Databases *597*
Telecommunications Networks *598*
Classification of Information Systems *600*
Information Systems for Operations Managers *600*
Information Systems for Middle Managers *601*
Information Systems for Senior Managers *602*
Marketing Information Systems *603*
Production Information Systems *603*
Accounting Information Systems *603*
Financial Information Systems *603*
Human Resources Information Systems *604*
Developing Information Systems *604*
Global Information Systems *605*

Case in Point *Information Systems Development at McDonald's   606*

Information Systems Controls   *608*

Ethics in Business *Computer Monitoring   608*

Careers in Information Systems   *609*

Summary   610   Chapter Questions   611   Interpreting Business News   611   Web Assignments   611   Portfolio Projects   612   Test Prepper   613

18
The Digital Enterprise 615

Introduction   *616*

Information Technology Infrastructure for the Digital Enterprise   *617*

Enterprise Resource Planning Systems   *618*
   Benefits and Costs of ERP Systems   *620*
   ERP Software Vendors   *621*
   Implementing ERP Systems   *624*

Supply Chain Management   *625*
   Economic Impact of Supply Chain Management   *627*
   Supply Chain Management Strategies   *627*

E-Business   *628*

Case in Point *Supply Chain Management at DaimlerChrysler   629*

Global Business *Global Supply Chains   630*

   Electronic Payment Systems   *631*
   Opportunities and Challenges   *632*

Ethics in Business *Information Technology and Privacy   633*

Careers in the Digital Enterprise   *634*
   Information Technology Infrastructure for the Digital Enterprise   *634*
   ERP Systems   *634*
   Supply Chain Management   *634*
   E-Business   *635*

Summary   635   Chapter Questions   637   Interpreting Business News   637   Web Assignments   637   Porfolio Projects   637   Test Prepper   638

Appendix:
Case in Point
Company Profiles A-1

Glossary   *G-1*

Test Prepper Answers   *T-1*

Notes   *N-1*

Photo Credits   *P-1*

Name Index   *I-1*

Subject Index   *I-6*

Preface

Opening the door to the world of business involves many challenges for both instructors and students. The goal of this text is to provide the keys to success that will lead to a rewarding educational experience and set the stage for pursuing a business career.

Any business, big or small, is fraught with risk, and unless students have a clear understanding of contemporary business principles, they will be taking unnecessary risk, and such risk could lead to failure. Understanding today's fundamental pillars of the business environment—globalization, technology, and ethics—is also crucial to success. The purpose of this book is to introduce students to these principles—the art and science of managing a business—and in a way that is interesting, relevant, and engaging, in the hope that they may develop a successful business career.

A Team of Experts Can Make a Difference

The introduction to business course covers a lot of ground, touching on all the major functional areas of business. We recognize that it is a challenge for students to understand how all the different functional areas are interrelated, and it is a challenge for an instructor to cover all these areas with equal amounts of enthusiasm and expertise. Other introduction to business texts are written by authors who have expertise in one, two, or perhaps three functional areas. One thing that makes our book unique is our author team of six functional area experts. For more than two years, we have met weekly as a team to share ideas, review manuscript, examine market feedback, and make sure that we created a cohesive, comprehensive, authoritative presentation of business that is unparalleled in the market. Helping us all the way in this process—making sure that the material is presented consistently and clearly—has been our editorial advisor. He has taught thousands of introduction to business students and understands the challenges they and you, the instructor, face.

Goals and Themes of the Book

Throughout the planning and writing of *Introduction to Business*, we have sought and listened to the advice of instructors across the country who have taught this course for many years. We have also sought student feedback to be sure the content is appealing and relevant to students. As a result, the features of this book have been carefully designed to respond to both student and instructor needs.

Key Themes

Anyone who listens to the news and follows current business events knows that contemporary business, regardless of where it is conducted, is heavily influenced by rapid globalization, advances in technology, and enforcement of ethical standards. With globalization, the notion of the purely domestic firm has become a myth. Similarly, progress in technology, in the form of electronic commerce, operations, supply chain management, electronic banking, etc., is quickly transforming the way businesses operate to be successful. There is hardly any business that is "technology insensitive." Finally, firms need to be ethically managed if they are to survive, deliver value to investors and customers alike, and be successful in the long term. To be successful in business—today and in the foreseeable future—students need a text that fully integrates these three themes within all aspects of business. That is why we have embraced these concepts through numerous in-text examples as well as boxed features throughout.

A Focus on Integrated Examples

Another unique feature of this text is weaving the strategies and operations of three major global companies—DaimlerChrysler, McDonald's, and Sony—throughout the text so that students can follow how the topics at hand, across different functional areas, relate to these real-world examples. These three companies, which students have already heard of, reflect three dynamic regions of the world: Europe (DaimlerChrysler), North America (McDonald's), and Asia (Sony). Also, these three companies are following extremely challenging and interesting business strategies in order to maintain leadership in their fields. *Case in Point* boxed features throughout the book follow these three companies. Many of the boxes also touch on the themes of globalization, technology, and ethics. A brief background and overview of each of these companies appears in the Appendix.

Accessible, Relevant Text

Since this is an introductory business text, we have aimed to keep the narrative conversational and concise. Reviewers have commented positively about the readability of the text. We hope this text will be "user-friendly" so that students will read the chapters and come to class prepared. Every aspect of *Introduction to Business* aims at getting the reader to think deeply about the subject—the contemporary environment of business as well as the functional areas and operations of business. Our primary goal is to help the reader fully appreciate business fundamentals and pursue a career in business—either as an owner or as an employee.

New Material on Up-to-Date Topics

To make the text relevant and interesting, keeping abreast of current issues is vital. Examples of new business trends or issues that we have identified and included are:

- The important role knowledge workers play in contemporary business
- Why transition economies are a source of business opportunity
- The measurement and impact of consumer confidence on business
- The importance of understanding consumer demographics and psychographics in business
- How to manage cultural diversity to enhance business performance
- How to utilize purchasing power parity to determine business opportunity
- How the digital era is changing the business world
- Why trade is better than no trade for society as a whole
- The rationale behind a country's choice of exchange rate regimes
- The evolution of globalization and its impact on business
- The increasing importance of shareholder proposals and institutional investors in corporate governance

- The Sarbanes-Oxley Act, Regulation FD, and other recent governmental regulations in corporate governance area
- Business ethics training and the impact of recent business ethics scandals on college campuses
- Crisis and contingency planning in the post-9/11 era
- Current military and foreign policy examples to help teach organizational structure material
- Six sigma initiatives recently adopted by General Electric and other leading companies as control mechanisms
- The impact of technological advances in HRM
- Recent U.S. Supreme Court – University of Michigan affirmative action cases and the impact of 9/11 on workforce diversity
- Off-duty conduct statutes and other state-level regulation of HRM
- How to develop a small business plan to increase your chances of success
- The impact of innovation and invention in the creation of small business enterprises
- The pros and cons of contemporary work-life programs
- How major leadership theories impact leadership styles
- Why share of wallet is being increasingly used as a measure of customer purchasing patterns
- Determining the level of total satisfaction customers are experiencing
- The greater emphasis companies are placing on maximizing the value of their brand equity
- The increasing attention being paid to materials management as firms seek to improve their logistic capabilities
- Key elements of the financial process for making business investment decisions
- Advice on how to wisely invest your money in the financial markets
- Electronic money and how to protect yourself from identity theft
- Information on central banks and their effects on the economy, businesses, and individuals
- The crucial role that operations management plays in creating a competitive advantage
- The recently gained importance of service operations
- How management information systems can create value for businesses and customers
- The continually evolving impact of information technology on business operations
- The increasing ubiquity of enterprise resource planning systems
- The redefinition of business competition via supply chain management
- The emergence of digital enterprises

The Features that Are the Keys to Success

Part and Chapter Openers

Each part gives students an overview of what they are about to cover and helps link the different parts together. Each chapter begins with an *outline* and a list of *learn-*

ing objectives to help direct student reading. The learning objectives are repeated in the margins of the text so that students can map their progress through the chapter. The chapter summary is also organized by the learning objectives to help students retain their focus on key points.

Chapter Opening Vignettes

Each chapter opens with a short but interesting story—something that students can relate to easily—that corresponds to the chapter's topic. Within the chapter, reference is made to the chapter openers to connect the opening story to chapter content.

Case in Point and Theme Boxed Features

Each chapter includes at least one *Case in Point* box featuring DaimlerChrysler, McDonald's, or Sony. Each chapter also includes at least one box that deals with one of the three themes, *Global Business* ,*Technology and Business* , and *Ethics in Business,* that is relevant to that chapter. Every box concludes with questions that encourage students to think about what they've read and can lead to interesting in-class discussion.

Graphics, Color, and Real Examples

The layout of the book has been designed for clarity, with an uncluttered, sophisticated look. At the same time, this streamlined approach is enhanced with color and graphics meant to heighten interest in the topics and focus the reader's attention on the most important business concepts. Real-world examples are used throughout the text to show how the topic at hand impacts big and small businesses. The important role that globalization, technology, and ethics play in the future of business should stand out because of these features.

Margin Notes

The introduction to business course is chock-full of terms that are new to students. To make this new vocabulary more accessible, all key terms appear in bold type in the chapters and are defined clearly in the text, margin notes, and the comprehensive glossary at the end of the text.

Reality Check

Each learning objective section ends with a Reality Check, a question that asks students how that section's learning objective impacts him or her. By bringing business issues to a personal level, students are more likely to be engaged in the subject.

End-of-Chapter Pedagogy

The end-of-chapter pedagogy carefully reinforces the relevance of chapter content as well as the learning of terminology, concepts, business environment, and operations. A menu of assignments allows instructors to choose which activities are most appropriate for their course.

Careers Before the summary for each chapter, there is a section devoted to career opportunities in that chapter's field. Students are informed about the various job possibilities that are available in that area of business and provided with tips on how to go about the job search.

Chapter Summary Each chapter summary is organized according to the learning objectives. By the time students finish going through the summary, they will have read the learning objectives at least three times and, hopefully, will know where to find the required information related to them.

Chapter Questions Some fifteen *Chapter Questions* help students recall business concepts, understand how these concepts are applied, and challenge students to use judgment when developing their answers.

Interpreting Business News Based on typical and/or current business news items that readers would find in periodicals such as The *Wall Street Journal, Financial Times, Business Week*, etc., students are required to interpret what the news item means using their understanding of the material covered in that chapter.

Web Assignment Students are directed to visit the websites of specific companies to extract the information necessary for answering chapter-based business questions.

Portfolio Projects To help students build their own business portfolio, one or both of the *Portfolio Projects* may be assigned as individual or group activities that span the course. The objective of *Exploring Your Own Case in Point* is to encourage and enable students to conduct a comprehensive analysis of a large company (e.g., a *Fortune 500* company). Students select a company that is publicly traded and obtain information that is readily available on the Web and from library sources. By answering chapter-specific questions in these sections, students will have conducted a comprehensive analysis of the company by the end of the course. The questions in *Starting Your Own Business* are intended to provide students with the opportunity to put together a comprehensive business plan—the first step in the start-up of a new enterprise. The objective here is to enable students to become successful entrepreneurs by helping them to establish clear business goals, strategies, and methods of operation.

Test Prepper Professors and students alike have lauded this feature as one that is unique and truly adds value to the book. Without having to purchase an extra study guide, students can test their comprehension of a chapter's subject matter by using these true/false and multiple-choice questions.

Organization and Topical Coverage of the Text

The contents of the text have been arranged so that each chapter builds on the substance of previous chapters. In addition, each topic is covered by explaining business fundamentals carefully before getting into examples and other details. The logical sequence of the parts and chapters is given below.

Part One, The Nature of Contemporary Business, provides a four-chapter introduction to what business—large and small—is all about. Chapter 1, *What Is Business?* defines business in terms of for-profit and not-for-profit organizations and how they operate in different types of economic systems. We explain concepts such as inputs, outputs, and how business performance is measured in a consumer-driven market economy that operates in the digital era. In Chapter 2, *The Environment of Business*, we explain carefully why business is global in nature regardless of the type and location of business activity. We show that with falling trade and investment barriers, and advances in information technology, we live in a global village where outsourcing of goods and services is the norm and where ethical businesses will thrive. Chapter 3, *Business Governance, Ethics, and Social Responsibility*, takes an up-to-date look at business governance structures and the potential conflicts of interest that exist within these structures. It also examines business codes of ethics and how companies are seeking to promote better ethical behavior on the part of their employees. In Chapter 4, *Small Business and Entrepreneurship*, we discuss the critical role of small business in the economy, government support for small business, what kind of individuals become successful entrepreneurs, how to develop a viable business plan and set up a small business organization, and key management decisions of small businesses. This chapter is geared toward providing ingredients essential to starting a small business and includes many real-world examples of entrepreneurs and their small business operations.

Part Two, Managing Business Behavior, includes three chapters and examines the specifics of managing business—since all firms need to be managed. In Chapter 5, *Managing and Organizing Business*, students will learn about the basic managerial functions of planning, organizing, directing, and controlling. This chapter also discusses the different types of managers and management skills that are needed to run a business successfully. In Chapter 6, *Human Resources Management*, the management of people in organizations is explored. Issues such as recruiting employees, setting their wages and benefits, the legal environment of HRM, and workplace diversity in the post-9/11 era are all discussed. In Chapter 7, *Motivating and Leading Employees*, we focus on the crucial role motivation and leadership play in business success. After defining motivation, we examine major motivation theories from the perspective of how employee job satisfaction and performance can be enhanced. Special attention is also given to how businesses can implement work-life programs, which can allow employees to best balance present-day work with family lives. This part concludes with a comprehensive analysis and a discussion of major leadership theories and leadership styles, along with an examination of the importance that ethics plays in this function.

Part Three, Marketing, provides the student with a three-chapter introduction to this important business responsibility. Chapter 8, *Marketing Basics*, describes the various types of markets that companies can elect to serve, what comprises the marketing environment, how information is gathered about markets and the environment, what objectives marketing executives pursue, what strategies they might employ to achieve those objectives, and how to effectively manage customers. Chapter 9, *Developing the Product and Pricing Mixes*, deals with the product and pricing elements of the marketing mix. It familiarizes students with the basic aspects of products. The new product development process is presented. Ways to effectively manage existing products are provided. Pricing objectives are presented, along with basic pricing concepts. Chapter 10, *Developing the Promotion and Distribution Mixes*, provides coverage of the other marketing mix elements, promotion and distribution. It contains a discussion of the promotion mix. Integrated marketing promotion programs are emphasized, as are the advantages and disadvantages of using or not using channels of distribution. The importance of direct marketing is also identified, and the increasing attention being paid to logistics by the business world is discussed.

Part Four, Accounting, consisting of two chapters, describes the role of accounting to people within and outside the business firm. Chapter 11, *Accounting for Decision Making,* describes how the accounting information system contributes to developing a sound organizational structure, ensures that employees are held responsible for their actions, and maintains cost-effective business operations. Outside the firm, financial statements are used by such external users as investors and lending institutions, to make investment and loan decisions, respectively. In Chapter 12, *Financial Reporting,* we focus on the four financial statements: the income statement, the statement of retained earnings, the balance sheet, and the statement of cash flows. Together, the four financial statements represent a business firm in financial terms. These statements provide information that people need to make effective business decisions.

Part Five, Finance, includes three chapters that review important elements of finance applicable to business firms, investors, and individuals. In Chapter 13, *Financial Management of the Firm and Investment Management,* we consider how companies raise funds for investment and evaluate the best way to invest those funds. We also consider how investors who purchase the debt and equity of firms seek to assess how well financial managers are performing their duties. Chapter 14, *Understanding the Financial System, Money, and Banking,* looks at the bigger picture of the financial system as a whole. The financial system is comprised of financial markets, institutions, and instruments. We show how financial systems affect the lives of individuals and the success of business firms. Chapter 15, *Personal Financial Planning,* covers important principles of personal financial planning. Financial planning involves gathering all your financial and personal data, analyzing that data, and creating a financial plan for the future. This hands-on chapter can help any individual to achieve a sound personal financial plan.

Part Six, Managing Business Operations, Management Information Systems, and the Digital Enterprise, includes three independent yet interrelated chapters. In Chapter 16, *Managing Business Operations,* the student is exposed to the operations function and to how good management of this function leads to competitive advantage for the firm and to value creation for the firm's customers. We explain the key operations management decisions in regard to product, process, capacity, location, layout, production rate, material requirements, purchasing, inventory, scheduling, and quality. In Chapter 17, *Management Information Systems,* the student is introduced to the management information systems function. We first present the major elements of contemporary MIS: computer hardware, computer software, databases, and telecommunications networks. Management information systems are then classified by the type of manager or the business function that they serve. The chapter also addresses the development of information systems, the strategies for the globalization of information systems, and the activities that firms perform to ensure the security and accuracy of their information systems. In Chapter 18, *The Digital Enterprise,* we share with the student attempts by companies to digitally integrate across business functions via enterprise resource planning systems, across firms via supply chain management, and with their customers and partners via e-business. This chapter offers evidence to the student that for the digital enterprise, the future is already here.

Additional Keys to Making Teaching and Learning Easier

We have created a robust package of supplements to support both students and instructors as they use this book. This package was shaped with the help of our editorial advisor, as well as the help of our reviewers and both student and instructor focus group participants.

For Instructors

For the convenience of instructors, we offer most of the instructor supplements content in a variety of formats, in traditional print form as well as on CD and the Web.

Instructor's Resource Manual Created by Carmen Powers of Monroe Community College, the *Instructor's Resource Manual* includes detailed lecture outlines as well as a variety of teaching tips and suggestions, summaries of all the boxed features, suggested answers to all the questions in the text, and suggestions for in-class exercises.

Test Bank With more than one thousand questions, the *Test Bank* provides essay, true/false, and multiple-choice items that are keyed to the text's learning objectives. The questions test both knowledge and application of concepts, and page references to the main text are provided.

ClassPrep with HMTesting This Instructor's CD provides a variety of teaching resources in electronic format, allowing for easy customization to meet specific instructional needs. Files on the disk include the *PowerPoint*® slides, Word files of the Instructor's Resource Manual, and Word files of the Test Bank. HMTesting, also on the CD, is a testing program that allows instructors to generate and change tests easily and create multiple versions of tests. An online testing feature enables instructors to administer tests via a local area network or over the Web. It also has a grade feature that lets users set up sections and record and track grades.

Instructor Website The instructor website includes many of the same resources as the ClassPrep CD (except testing content) so that instructors have their choice of how to get this material. In addition, the instructor website includes sample syllabi, regular updates to text content, and new, current examples that instructors can bring to class.

PowerPoint Slides Created by Milton Pressley of the University of New Orleans, the *PowerPoint* slides present complete lecture outlines for every chapter that incorporate key exhibits from the text as well as additional exercises, figures, and links to the Web.

Support for Online Instruction BlackBoard and WebCT courses are populated with the text's learning objectives, chapter outlines, the *PowerPoint* slides, questions from the textbook with suggested answers, and test bank items. Powerful, customizable, and interactive, Eduspace®, powered by Blackboard™, is

Houghton Mifflin's online learning tool. It is populated with the same content that we provide in our Blackboard and WebCT courses. Plus it includes unique student quizzing content, as well as unique video clip exercises. Instructors can choose to use the content as is, modify it, or even add their own content.

Videos Developed specifically for use with business texts, these videos highlight a variety of companies and illustrate how key concepts in the text are applied in the real world. An accompanying video guide gives an overview of the video for each chapter, as well as suggested discussion questions. The videos are available in both VHS and DVD formats. In addition to the chapter videos, there is footage supporting the Case in Point feature in the text.

Transparencies Key exhibits from the text are reproduced in this traditional format for instructors to use during class presentation.

For Students

In addition to the Test Prepper, built directly into the text, we provide these additional supplements to help students succeed in this course.

Business Bonus Pack: Your Guide to an 'A' Packaged automatically with every new text, this supplement provides study tips and guidance on how to use the various pieces of the student support package for the best results. Available only with the Bonus Pack, the HM eStudy CD provides additional questions, similar to those presented in the Test Prepper, and chapter outline and learning objective worksheets that can be used for self-study. Also on the eStudy CD are Portfolio Project Extensions, worksheets, and hints for completing the end-of-chapter Exploring Your Own Case in Point and Starting Your Own Business projects.

Student Website The student website includes even more study and research aids including ACE Self-Tests (with unique question content), glossaries, flashcards for reviewing all the text's key terms, the Web Assignments from the text (updated as URLs may change), and links to all the companies featured in the text.

Acknowledgments

This textbook owes a debt of gratitude to Texas A&M University's Center for International Business Education and Research (CIBER), which played an important role in motivating the three critical business themes of our book: globalization, technology, and ethics. We would also like to acknowledge support from Dean Jerry Strawser of Mays Business School, who provided the collegial and scholarly environment necessary to fulfill such an ambitious project.

We benefited from corporate information provided by three major multinational companies: DaimlerChrysler, McDonald's, and Sony. Their business stories are weaved throughout the text to help demonstrate modern business practices.

In addition, many professors provided us with constructive criticisms throughout the writing process. We would like to express special thanks to Dr. Ben Welch, who provided invaluable guidance in his role as editorial advisor, based on his many years of teaching experience in the introduction to business course at Mays Business School. Also, numerous professors acted as reviewers and Advisory Board members, contributing constructive comments that have improved the quality of our text:

Gary Amundson
Montana State University–Billings

Steven McHugh
Centenary College

Charlene Barker
Spokane Falls Community College

Lawrence Overlan
Stonehill College

Joe Bell
University of Northern Colorado

Carmen Powers
Monroe Community College

Gary Donnelly
Casper College

Gary Reinke
University of Phoenix

William Flood
Capitol College

Marianne Sebok
Community College of Southern Nevada

Leatrice Freer
Pitt Community College

James Smith
Rocky Mountain College

Selena Griswold
The University of Toledo

William Steiden
Jefferson Community College

Starla Haislip
Boise State University

Mary Thibodeaux
University of North Texas

Karen Hawkins
Miami Dade College

Shafi Ullah
University of Central Oklahoma

Mary Higby
University of Detroit—Mercy

Mary Williams
Community College of Southern Nevada

Scott Homan
Purdue University

Finally, George Hoffman, Editor-in-Chief, and the editorial staff at Houghton Mifflin Company worked tirelessly to produce this quality textbook. In particular, editors Susan Kahn and Rachel D'Angelo Wimberly played a critical role in all stages of writing and revisions to chapters. Their attention to organization, content, and mundane details is much appreciated by all of the authors. Likewise, Sage Anderson, Steven Mikels, Lisa Boden, Katie Huha, Sarah Ambrose, Jill Haber, and Chuck Dutton helped to ensure a smooth publishing process.

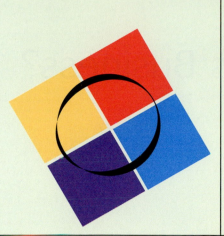

The Nature of Contemporary Business

CHAPTER 1
What Is Business?

CHAPTER 2
The Environment of Business

CHAPTER 3
Business Governance, Ethics, and Social Responsibility

CHAPTER 4
Small Business and Entrepreneurship

PART ONE

Why study business? You see businesses—small, medium, and large—all around you, and they affect your everyday life. Just as you make decisions every day—about how hard you are going to work, how you are going to spend your scarce time and money, and what you are going to do tomorrow to achieve your goals for the future—businesses make similar choices, but on a global scale and with a profit motive. Events that happen around the world, such as scandalous news stories about certain business executives' practices and reassuring stories about business executives who contribute to society, and the pervasiveness of technology and the Internet have direct impacts on business success or failure that touch you every day. All of these are important reasons to study business—to make you more aware of the world around you and of how business affects you as a consumer, an employee, or an employer.

In this text you will learn the fundamentals of all the major functional areas of business—management, marketing, accounting, finance, and operations management. You will come to understand how these areas are interrelated and how they are all affected by globalization, technology, and ethics. We hope that this text will help you decide which functional area of business you may want to major in. But if you decide that a business major is not for you, you will still gain valuable commercial insights that will help you succeed in any job you take in the future.

Part One sets the stage by examining the nature of contemporary business. It starts with a definition of business and goes on to explore the environmental factors that influence business. It then analyzes and studies the importance of business ethics and social responsibility. Finally, it examines the vigorous world of small business and entrepreneurship.

1

1

What Is Business?

Introduction

Defining Business and Profit

The Evolution of Business in the United States

The New Society of Knowledge Workers

Types of Economic Systems and Their Impact on Business

The Free Enterprise, or Capitalist, System

The Command, or Planned, Economic System

The Mixed Economic System

The Transition Economies

Production of Goods and Services

Measuring Business Performance

Maximizing Profit and Shareholder Wealth

Maximizing Stakeholder Wealth

Minimizing Unemployment and Income Inequalities

Not-for-Profit Organizations

Demand for Goods and Services

Measuring Consumer Confidence

The Consumer Knows Best

Consumer Demographics and Psychographics

Cultural Diversity

Measuring Gross National Product, Gross National Income, and Gross Domestic Product

Purchasing Power Parity

Business Cycles

The Digital Era

E-Business

Impact of IT on Globalization, Culture, Society, and Politics

Careers in Business

Learning Objectives

After studying this chapter, you should be able to

1 Identify the three major factors that are impacting business today and discuss the roles of for-profit and not-for-profit organizations in an economy.

2 Summarize the evolution of business in the United States and explain the key issues that are impacting its outlook for the future.

3 Explain the fundamental features of the free enterprise, or capitalist, system that make it efficient and dynamic.

4 Discuss what is meant by *market structure*, and explain why most industries fall under the banner of monopolistic competition.

5 Discuss the rationale for countries wanting to choose other forms (rather than capitalism) of economic systems and explain what direction most countries are moving toward.

6 Explain how the factors of production impact the supply of goods and services in an economy.

7 Discuss how business performance is measured in a capitalist system versus a socialist system and how the objectives of for-profit businesses differ from the objectives of state-owned enterprises and of not-for-profit organizations.

8 Explain the important role consumers play in determining corporate performance and show how businesses try to identify consumer needs.

9 Discuss why and how national output is measured and consider the rationale for using output based on purchasing power parity (PPP) when comparing countries.

10 Evaluate the impact of the digital revolution on global businesses, governments, and societies.

Silicon Valley: The Keys to Business Success

California's Silicon Valley is known for the start-up of several dynamic and successful U.S. companies, especially in such fields as electronics, semiconductors, information technology (IT), the Internet, and software development. However, behind the valley's success stories are numerous companies that failed. It is the willingness on the part of entrepreneurs and investors alike to take risk that has led to major business innovations with global implications. The bulk of business activities taking place in Silicon Valley (and in other similar centers within the United States and in faraway technology centers like Bangalore, Dublin, Singapore, and Tel Aviv) are based more on human knowledge skills than on manufacturing.

The origins of the Internet revolution can be traced to the invention of the World Wide Web in 1989 by British technologist Tim Berners-Lee (working for CERN, a physics research lab on the French-Swiss border). Its commercialization began in northern California's Silicon Valley. The 1990s was a period of unprecedented excitement and growth in the information technology industry, and that euphoria spread like wildfire across the globe impacting all sectors of economies, especially in the United States, in the form of hundreds of dotcom firms. The demand for IT talent was so fierce that sign-up bonuses became a norm. To attract these skilled knowledge workers, some companies, for example Enron and PricewaterhouseCoopers, provided flexible work hours, lax dress codes, on-site health facilities, free meals or snacks, and so on, with little regard for cost control.

This new environment was so contagious that some economists and Wall Street finance gurus saw the beginning of a new era where standard measurements of business performance such as profits, dividends, and consumer demand no longer seemed to matter. To most entrepreneurs in Silicon Valley, the future was just rosy and filled with high expectations. Ordinary citizens with some savings saw the opportunity to make money. They ploughed their savings and retirement funds into these stocks, and thus helped to perpetuate the boom. Stock prices of many of these companies took on a momentum of their own, with share prices of companies like Yahoo.com jumping by $20 or more in a single day. Only in 2000 to 2002 did it become apparent that some of the stock analysts, as well as some corporate executives, were unethical and were misleading investors on the companies' business prospects. The collapse of dotcom share prices started in 2000, and many dotcoms saw their shares trading in 2002 to 2003 at 3 percent of their peak values. Quite a few of the dotcoms vanished.

The economic implications of the collapse of dotcom shares are serious, since several of these companies participated in unethical accounting and financial practices. With the bursting of the technology bubble and the losses at supporting financial institutions, hundreds of thousands of white-collar technology workers and bankers lost their jobs, bringing the stock market down along with them. In his new book, Harvard business professor Quinn Mills points out that financial bubbles are engineered by professional players who take advantage of public excitement and ineffective government regulations to realize profit opportunities.[1] New York attorney general Eliot Spitzer took charge in early 2002 to remove Wall Street's corporate abuses and bring greater investor confidence in the United States' premiere financial center. It is interesting to note the similarities with the 1930s; for example, soon after the Great Depression, William O. Douglas, one of the first Securities and Exchange

Commission (SEC) chairpersons, clashed with Wall Street as the agency brought enforcement actions over that era's excesses.

Introduction

LEARNING OBJECTIVE 1
Identify the three major factors that are impacting business today and discuss the roles of for-profit and not-for-profit organizations in an economy.

Business is *global* in nature regardless of where you live. Also, we live in an *information technology* age, where developments—scientific or commercial—in one part of the world can and will be transmitted across national boundaries instantaneously via data networks. As illustrated in the opening story, entrepreneurs who can identify opportunities and commercialize them are bound to do well, provided they stick to some fundamental principles of business and *ethics* as discussed in Part One of this text. Yet, there will always be winners and losers in business.

Defining Business and Profit

When you ask yourself the question, "What is business?" as you commute to class, the first things that you may recall are the stores and billboards that you see on your route. These may include gasoline stations such as Exxon and Shell; fast-food establishments like McDonald's and Burger King; car dealerships like Ford, DaimlerChrysler, and Toyota; airlines like American, AeroMexico, and Cathay Pacific; retailing giants like Wal-Mart and Auchan; personal computer manufacturers like Dell and Sony; even a hairstylist or a Salvation Army store. In technical terms, these operations—big and small—are called **businesses.** There is one thing common to all these operations: they are all trying to create value for their customers.

businesses Those organizations that try to create value for the customer

Peter Drucker, an Austrian-American and world-renowned management professor and guru, defines businesses as just that, those organizations that create value for the customer. If businesses did not create value, that is, if they did not meet a customer's unsatisfied need, they would cease to exist.

Basically, there are two types of businesses. The first type, which comprises the vast majority of businesses in the world today, exists to make a **profit.** Simply put, profit is the difference between revenue (income or sales) and expenditure (cost of goods or services sold). This means that these businesses produce goods (for example, gasoline, burgers, cars, and computers) or services (for example, haircutting, laundering, and banking) for a profit.

profit The difference between revenue (income or sales) and expenditure (cost of goods or services sold)

The businesses that make up the second type are called **not-for-profit organizations.** Examples are the Salvation Army, Goodwill Industries, educational institutions, and the like. Their primary objective is to provide goods and services to society without the goal of making a profit. Some of these not-for-profit organizations may charge a nominal amount for their goods and services, but this is meant to cover basic business cost even if some of the items are donated. While not-for-profit organizations play an extremely important role in society worldwide, we will focus more attention on "for profit" businesses.

not-for-profit organizations Organizations whose primary objective is to provide goods and services to society without the goal of making a profit

For-profit businesses provide a whole array of goods and services to society. Did you ever wonder why businesses are so eager to sell their goods and services? Surely it is not to make themselves feel good. It is for profit! The more goods and services that businesses sell, the more profit they hope to make. The more profit they make, the greater is the income to the owners of these businesses. Is this fair? Sure! These business people have invested their money and time and have taken a **risk** to cre-

risk The probability that the business will fail

ate goods and services that they hope consumers will buy. Risk is nothing but the probability that the business will fail. When a person takes a risk by investing his or her money and time setting up a business, he or she expects to be rewarded for it. The reward, which is profit, is never guaranteed. Why? Well, it depends on the consumer. If the consumer does not see the need for the product (or service) or does not like the product for whatever reason, then the consumer will not buy it. Consumers all over the world behave in a similar fashion, although for cultural reasons they may have dissimilar tastes. If consumers do not purchase goods and services provided by businesses, profits will not be realized and businesses will crease to grow or they may even fail. Only when people see the potential to make profits will they be willing to invest their savings in these firms so that the company may grow and generate even greater profits for investors. This growth helps the whole country, since when business grows, more people (including high school and college graduates) will be hired to take on the new jobs being generated. As employment increases, tax (federal and state income taxes, state sales tax, and property taxes) collection increases, and that will lead to more or better public services (schools, roads, and police). In addition, as employment increases, people will want to buy houses, cars, and other necessities and luxuries of life. This in turn will boost the economy even further. That's one of the main reasons why a country's economic and financial managers and professional investors pay such close attention to corporate profits. The level and rate of growth of corporate profits is a bellwether that indicates the health of business and the economy as a whole.

Goods donated by businesses and the public are sorted out by volunteers, who also tag and price these items for sale at Salvation Army stores.

reality CHECK *What are the major not-for-profit organizations in your community? Do you think they play an important role in the community?*

The Evolution of Business in the United States

LEARNING OBJECTIVE 2
Summarize the evolution of business in the United States and explain the key issues that are impacting its outlook for the future.

The origin of business in the United States is fascinating and can be traced to the time when settlers from Europe crossed the Atlantic Ocean. The business climate reflected a combination of different government policies, the availability of abundant land and diverse natural resources, and a constant and growing inflow of migrants and capital, initially from Europe. All these factors helped fuel the growth of American cities and founded and developed important industries. (The whole evolution of U.S. business is summarized in Exhibit 1.1 on p. 6.)

EXHIBIT 1.1

The Evolution of Business in the United States

1800	1825	1850	1875	1900	1925	1950	Present

The Industrial Revolution
- Birth of the factory system
- Introduction of labor-saving equipment

The Railroad Era
- Coast to coast business expansion
- Growth of monopolies and introduction of antitrust laws

The Assembly Line Era
- Introduction of scientific management in manufacturing
- Birth of labor laws and labor unions

The Globalization Era
- Liberalization of international trade and investment regulations
- Innovations in IT and the Internet
- Tightening of corporate governance regulations and ethics

1815   1875   1913   1944

The Industrial Revolution and the Growth of the Factory System in the United States.

During the 60 years between 1815 and 1875, the Industrial Revolution, which began in Great Britain, transformed the United States from an agrarian economy into an industrial giant. Britain's Industrial Revolution had its spillover effects in such areas as railways, roads, harbors, electric power plants, and telephone and telegraph systems.[2] The United States, with its continental-sized land mass, large mineral deposits, relatively scarce but growing labor force, and individualist philosophy, offered profit-seeking businesspeople the opportunity to earn a high return on their investment. Agriculture in the United States was very profitable and led to rising farm incomes and a strong demand for standardized consumer products.

The Industrial Revolution brought with it new technologies that facilitated mass production of standardized items beneath one roof—the **factory system.** Under the factory system of mass production, raw materials, machinery, and labor were brought together in large volumes in one location to produce goods less expensively. Since production was on a large scale, raw materials and machinery could be purchased in bulk and at lower cost. However, the growing demand for mass-produced goods led to labor shortages in factories. This caused labor cost to rise, and this in turn forced businesses to invent and adopt labor-saving equipment and manufacturing techniques that became a unique feature of "Yankee ingenuity." The new machines were capable of producing goods faster, cheaper, and more uniformly (and of better quality) than those produced by hand. Over time, this type of manufacturing process led to the **specialization of labor;** that is, employees were grouped together on the basis of their skills and factory demand and were increasingly assigned to specific tasks.

The Railroad Era.

In the early 1870s, the railroad drove economic expansion, encouraged massive speculation, and created fabulous wealth. Continental railroads turned the United States into a unified market from coast to coast. Retailers expanded to serve immigrants (including Chinese) who worked on building the railroad system. Land values soared along the rail routes, and cargo that took weeks to travel by boat and wagon could now be moved in days. The railroad era, like the dotcom era of the late 1990s and early 2000, was riddled with speculation, corruption, and miscalculation. Rail barons worked political connections to obtain federal land grants, and speculators grew rich. During this period, the advanced technologies developed by U.S. business made the United States the most important country among the industrialized nations of the world. For example, during the 1875 to 1913 period, the U.S. share of world manufactures rose from 23 to almost 36 percent while Britain's declined from nearly 32 to only 14 percent.

factory system A method of mass production in which raw materials, machinery, and labor are brought together in large volumes in one location to produce goods less expensively than in dispersed locations

specialization of labor Grouping employees to work on assigned tasks on the basis of their specific skills and factory demand

This largely reflected the rapid growth of the relatively young country and the **laissez-faire** system followed by the nation at that time. The principle of laissez faire advocates total government inaction in business; that is, businesses are free to do what and as they please. Key contributing factors to U.S. economic growth were a steady natural increase in domestic population supplemented by a large immigration (including imported slaves) inflow and a high rate of business investment. Businesses exploited the buoyant economic conditions, which supported a rising standard of living for most Americans. This period also saw one of the most rapid growths in the number and size of companies in the United States. A side effect of the laissez-faire system was that it encouraged companies to consolidate (merge) and dominate the market. **Market domination** was established through either acquiring competitors or colluding with companies that resisted acquisition. As their size grew, some of these firms became so powerful that they dominated the market by controlling product prices and preventing competitors from entering the market. Consumers as well as affected businesses protested this unregulated laissez-faire system. This ultimately led the U.S. government to institute **antitrust policies**—laws designed to break up monopolies and control monopoly abuses—in 1890 and 1914. Antitrust laws set limits on firm behavior by prohibiting certain kinds of anticompetitive practices (like price fixing, market sharing, predatory pricing, and exclusionary activities).

laissez faire The economic doctrine that advocates total government inaction in business, so businesses are free to do what and as they please

market domination A strategy of either acquiring competitors or colluding with them to control product prices and prevent new competitors from entering the market

antitrust policies Government laws designed to break up monopolies and control monopoly abuses by business

The Assembly Line Era and the Great Depression.

A new era in manufacturing began in 1913 when the Ford Motor Company started mass production of Model T cars at its Highland Park, Michigan, plant in the United States. Ford used an assembly line where the factory worker remained in one spot and the car came to the worker to be assembled. This system of production was based on studies to determine the most efficient approach to production. The idea was to avoid unnecessary movement on the part of the worker to complete a specific job. By bringing an incomplete car on an assembly line track to a worker, the time and effort needed to perform a specific task is minimized as compared with a system where the car's position was fixed and workers had to spend a lot of time moving around it. The net result was that the assembly line reduced production cost and made cars more affordable, thereby encouraging sales. The assembly line is still used in several industries today, although the techniques for using it have been further refined. The drawback of this system is the monotony that it creates for the worker and the ever-increasing pressure to perform better and faster. Assembly line employees complained about the rigors of working under those conditions. This contributed to the formation of labor unions that strove to protect workers' rights. The government's role increasingly became one of a mediator between labor (preventing exploitation of workers) and business (preventing unreasonable demands on firms that could lead to their financial ruin).

The Post–World War II Period: The Globalization Era.

Europe was physically devastated after World War II, while the United States' infrastructure was relatively unharmed. In order to rebuild Europe, the United States instituted and paid for the Marshall Plan. In addition, several important international institutions were set up to develop new rules for facilitating international trade, foreign investment, and global economic growth. Key among these international financial institutions were the International Monetary Fund (IMF) and the World Bank, both headquartered in Washington, D.C. The IMF's role was essentially to facilitate and support stable exchange rates (of currencies) and the flow of capital (money) between countries so that countries could invest and trade with each other without being too concerned about the value of their currencies. The World Bank was set up as an international development institution whose primary role was to provide financial and technical assistance to rebuild Europe. Only countries that were members of the United Nations could choose to become members of the IMF and the World Bank. Member countries provided aid money to the World Bank for distribution to needy members on relatively easy repayment terms, while some funds were disbursed as interest-free grants. Although World Bank funds were initially geared to rebuilding Europe, rapid recovery in Europe soon led to the diversion of development funds to other poorer countries of the world.

To facilitate trade, the General Agreement on Tariffs and Trade (GATT) was established in 1947. The GATT sets rules of conduct for international trade policy and is headquartered in Geneva. Much of the multilateral tariff reduction that has taken place since World War II has been accomplished under the GATT (now renamed the World Trade Organization [WTO]). Over the years several rounds of trade policy liberalization have taken place. Each trade liberalization step has led to the accelerating **globalization** of business, because tariffs have been lowered further and quotas eliminated. This, in turn, has given a boost to international competition through the increased exports of goods and services as well as capital flows between countries. Globalization is the process of integrating the market for goods and services worldwide. One could argue that the globalization of business, which began after World War II, has led to the worldwide economic and social advances that we are witnessing today.

> **globalization** The process of integrating the market for goods and services worldwide

The New Society of Knowledge Workers[3]

The society that we currently live in is already diverging from that of the twentieth century, which saw the rapid decline of the agriculture sector that had dominated society for thousands of years. In 1913 farm products accounted for 70 percent of world trade, whereas now their share is at most 17 percent. In the early years of the twentieth century, agriculture in most developed countries was the largest single contributor to a country's production of goods and services; now in rich countries its contribution has dwindled to the point of becoming marginal. And the farm population is down to a tiny proportion of the total.

Manufacturing has traveled a long way down the same road as well. Since World War II, manufacturing output in the developed world has tripled in volume, but inflation-adjusted manufacturing prices have fallen steadily. Manufacturing employment in the United States has fallen from 35 percent of the workforce in the 1950s to less than half that now, without causing much social disruption. However, such a transition in countries such as Japan or Germany, where manufacturing workers still make up 25 to 30 percent of the labor force, is proving difficult. Furthermore, the cost of services, especially prime knowledge products—health care and education—has tripled (even adjusted for inflation) since World War II.

While the **new economy,** an economy largely driven by developments in information technology and the Internet, may or may not materialize, one thing sure to happen is that the next successful society will comprise **knowledge workers**—people whose jobs require good formal and advanced schooling. In the developed as well as the developing countries of the world, the role that knowledge workers play, especially by using information technology (IT) tools, will be more important than information technology or the Internet itself.

> **new economy** An economy largely driven by developments in information technology and the Internet
>
> **knowledge workers** Employees whose jobs require formal and advanced schooling

Knowledge (using more brains than brawn; see Exhibit 1.2) will be a key resource, and knowledge workers will be the dominant group in the future workforce. The main characteristics of the knowledge workforce will be

- Borderless, because knowledge travels even more effortlessly than money

- Upwardly mobile, since knowledge will enable everyone who has acquired a good formal education to move up
- Offered the potential for success

Together, these three characteristics will make the global society highly competitive for businesses and individuals alike. This effect is already illustrated clearly by the volume of knowledge-based services that are being outsourced to India.

Information technology, although only one (the others include biotechnology and nanotechnology) of many features of the new society, is already having a tremendous effect: It is allowing knowledge to spread near-instantly and making it accessible to everyone. Given the ease and speed at which information travels, every institution in the knowledge society—not only businesses but also schools, universities, hospitals, and, increasingly, government agencies too—will need to become globally competitive, even though most organizations will continue to be local in their activities and in their markets. This is because the Internet will keep customers everywhere informed about what is available and at what price anywhere in the world. This new economy will rely heavily on knowledge workers, which at present describes people with considerable theoretical knowledge and learning: doctors, engineers, scientists, and teachers. The most striking growth, however, is anticipated in knowledge technologists: computer technicians, software designers, clinical lab analysts, manufacturing technologists, and paralegals. Just as skilled manufacturing workers were the dominant social and political force in the twentieth century, knowledge technologists are likely to become the dominant social, and perhaps also political, force over the next decades.

reality CHECK *Have you seen any changes in business activity in your hometown over the past five years? If yes, what is the cause of these changes?*

EXHIBIT 1.2

Brains, Not Brawn

Distribution of total employment by occupation, United States (percent)

	1988	1998	2008*
Executive and managerial	10.3	10.5	10.7
Professional	12.5	14.1	15.6
Technicians	3.2	3.5	3.8
Marketing or sales	10.3	10.9	11.0
Administrative support	18.5	17.4	16.6
Services	15.5	16.0	16.4
Agriculture	3.5	3.2	2.8
Production, craft, and repair	11.9	11.1	10.5
Operators, fabricators, and laborers	14.2	13.2	12.7

*Forecast.

Types of Economic Systems and Their Impact on Business

economic resources Land, labor, capital, and technology that are scarce

Economic resources (land, labor, capital, and technology) are scarce, and no matter how much we have of them, we continue to face a shortage—the inability to have as much as we want at a price that we are willing to pay. Countries have adopted different approaches to allocate these scarce resources among competing demands in order to generate economic growth. The economic system adopted by any particular country depends basically on the following factors:

- Ownership of the factors of production (private versus government)
- Method of resource allocation
- Transparency of economic policies
- Availability of functioning institutions

These factors have a profound effect on the efficiency of resource allocation, business development, economic evolution, and growth. The country with the most open (ease of entry into and exit out of industry) type of economic system will tend to have the most efficient system of resource allocation and rapid business growth.

The Free Enterprise, or Capitalist, System

LEARNING OBJECTIVE 3
Explain the fundamental features of the free enterprise, or capitalist, system that make it efficient and dynamic.

capitalism The economic system that is based on private property rights, the free market system, the pursuit of self-interest, the freedom to choose, and the ability to borrow money

The economic system practiced in the United States is **capitalism** (also called the free enterprise or free market system), which is based on private property rights, a free market system, the pursuit of self-interest (profit or wealth maximization), the freedom to choose, and the ability to borrow money. Far from the popular image of a haven for "corporate fat cats," a capitalist economy crowns the consumer as king, and the system provides for the public's well-being.[4]

In the free enterprise system, the key players are consumers and producers. Consumers like you and me are in the market to buy all sorts of goods (books, clothes, toiletries, food, etc.) and services (airline tickets, concert tickets, season passes for ball games, etc.). Some of these goods and services that we purchase may be imported (e.g., Heineken beer from Holland or a Singapore Airlines ticket). In the

free market system The economic system in which consumers demand certain goods and services and are willing to pay a price based on their budget, and producers are willing to supply the goods and services on the basis of a price that will cover their costs and provide a profit margin

free market system, consumers demand certain products or services and are willing to pay a certain price for them based on their usefulness and the consumers' budget. The producer, on the other hand, is willing to supply the goods or services to the consumer at some price, which will depend on the cost of the inputs used in producing the goods or services and a profit margin. The United States is the largest economy in the world and essentially practices a free market system. Most European countries, as well as other industrialized countries and regions like Japan, South Korea, Taiwan, Singapore, Hong Kong (now a Special Administrative Region of China), Chile, and so on, are also essentially free enterprise systems. The relationship between the economic system and business is very close, and unless you understand how a particular economic system works, you may not be able to conduct business in that country successfully. This section explains the fundamentals of the free market system, which show how private investors identify opportunities for profits on the basis of a simple demand and supply analysis and the degree of competition in a market.

Demand, Supply, and Price. Consumers create a *demand* for goods and services, and the quantity demanded depends on the price of the product or service as well as on how much money the consumer has at her or his disposal. Literally, there are thousands of goods and services that people consume to maintain their lifestyle. When they consume any one of these goods and services, they create a separate demand for each product and service. As a general rule, you will have noticed that when the price of a particular product or service falls, you tend to purchase more of it. This is the idea behind the "special sale" advertisements that you see promoted in newspapers, on TV, and on the radio. Businesses know that when they lower prices, consumers will tend to demand (purchase) more of their product. This behavior has led to what is called the **theory** or **law of demand:** Consumers will buy more when prices fall and less when prices rise. Just imagine what you would do if the price of gasoline were doubled. You would at once try to carpool with your friends to school or work and cut down on your cruising habits too! What you are essentially doing is reducing your demand for gasoline. Just remember, you are not the only one who will cut down on gasoline consumption when prices rise. Your friends and neighbors will do the same as well. In fact, the whole society will do the same thing, and the net impact will be a drop in the demand for gasoline in the whole country. The opposite happens when the price of gasoline goes down. Lower gasoline prices encourage consumption and increase gasoline demand. We can represent this behavior with the help of a diagram.

> **theory** or **law of demand** The statement, which appears to hold, that consumers will buy more when prices fall and less when prices increase

Exhibit 1.3(a) on p. 12 shows that when the price of gasoline drops, say, from $2.00 to $1.50 per gallon, the quantity of gasoline demanded by a particular consumer increases from 5 to 8 gallons per week. Or, if the price of gasoline increases from $1.50 to $2.00 per gallon, the amount of gasoline that a consumer would purchase decreases from 8 to 5 gallons per week. The line *AB* is called the **demand curve,** which shows the relationship between the quantity of gasoline demanded and the price of gasoline for a particular customer. If there were, say, 10,000 students on campus, we could derive the demand curve for each student in a similar fashion. We could then aggregate (total) all the individual demand curves and determine the total number of gallons of gasoline that the 10,000 students would demand at different prices. In a similar manner, we could determine the demand curve for any product or service for the whole city or country, for that matter. It's that simple. The slope (steepness) of the demand curve is heavily influenced by the consumer's budget for that product or service and by the consumer's taste (spending priority). When the slope of the demand curve is steep, economists characterize the demand represented as **price inelastic demand.** For example, a significant increase in the price of cigarettes will have little effect on the quantity of cigarettes demanded. On the other hand, when the slope of the demand curve is very gentle, then the demand represented is **price elastic demand.** For example, a relatively small change in the price of DVDs will have a significant impact on the quantity demanded. In the real world, some products and services, like medical services, are price inelastic. When you get sick and need to see a physician, you are not likely to think twice about the high cost of doctor fees! However, if the price of Levi's jeans goes up sharply, you probably will be able to get by without purchasing a new pair of jeans for some time. The demand for jeans is price elastic.

> **demand curve** The curve that shows the relationship between the quantity demanded and the price of a product or service for a particular customer, group of consumers, or even a whole country (It is downward sloping.)

> **price inelastic demand** The demand where significant increases in the price of a product or service will have little effect on the quantity of the product or service demanded

> **price elastic demand** The demand where a small change in the price will have a significant impact on the quantity demanded of a product or service

Just as the consumer creates the demand for goods and services, the *supply* of goods and services comes from producers. Producers are willing to supply goods and services at a price that will cover their production costs and generate a reasonable profit. The higher the price, the more goods and services the producer is willing to supply. As prices go up, producers see the opportunity to make greater profits and are therefore willing to supply more goods and services. This behavior on the part of producers is generalized in the **theory** or **law of supply:** Producers will

> **theory** or **law of supply** The statement, which appears to hold, that producers will be willing to sell more when prices rise and less when prices fall

EXHIBIT 1.3

The Demand and Supply Curves

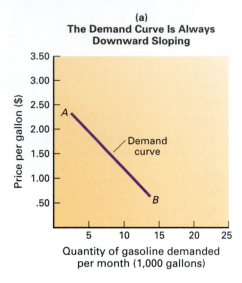

(a)
The Demand Curve Is Always Downward Sloping

Quantity of gasoline demanded per month (1,000 gallons)

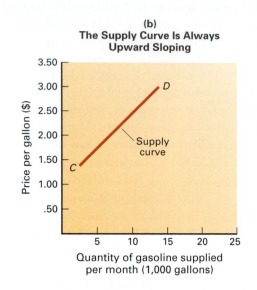

(b)
The Supply Curve Is Always Upward Sloping

Quantity of gasoline supplied per month (1,000 gallons)

be willing to sell more when prices rise and less when prices fall. In the gasoline case that we just discussed, if the price of gasoline doubled, gas stations would be willing to sell more gasoline so that they could earn greater profits. Low gasoline prices would discourage gas stations from selling gasoline and instead encourage them to sell more items from the convenience stores that are generally attached to the gas stations these days. The producer's behavior can also be explained with the help of the same diagram.

Exhibit 1.3(b) shows what happens when the price of gasoline rises, say, from $1.50 to $2.00 per gallon. The quantity of gasoline that your local gas station will be willing to supply may increase from 5000 to 7000 gallons per month. The upward-sloping **supply curve** *CD* clearly shows that as prices rise the producer is willing to sell more of the product (gasoline in our case). Again, the steepness of the supply curve carries important meaning. If the supply curve is steep, the implication is that large changes in the price will have little impact on the quantity of goods supplied by the producer. For example, electricity has a **price inelastic supply.** On the other hand, when the supply curve slopes gently upward, a relatively small increase in price will bring about significant increases in supply. For example, a product like beef has a **price elastic supply.** One point to remember is that the producer does not just supply one consumer but a whole bunch of consumers in a given market or region. Also, there may be several producers for a single product, in which case an aggregate (total) supply curve can be developed. The aggregate supply curve is also called the market supply curve.

In countries that follow the free market system, the prices that consumers pay for goods and service are determined by the collective interaction of total consumer demand and cumulative producer supply. The intersection of the market demand and supply curves provides us with the **market clearing, or equilibrium, price,** the price at which supply will equal demand and there will be no unsold goods or services. This situation can also be shown with the help of a diagram.

In a free market system, price will always tend to move toward the equilibrium price so that the market clears—that is, everything that is produced is sold. From Exhibit 1.4 it is clear that if price falls below the equilibrium level, the quantity demanded (represented by the demand curve) will be greater than the quantity supplied by producers (represented by the supply curve). When price is such that demand exceeds supply, then we have a **shortage.** When there is a shortage, price will keep rising, so demand will shrink, and the shortage will become smaller and smaller until it vanishes. You will notice that the shortage vanishes when the price reaches the equilibrium or market clearing price. In the opposite case, when market supply exceeds market demand, we have a **surplus.**

Private Property and Property Rights.
Capitalism has been defined as that form of private property economy in which innovations are carried out with the help

supply curve The curve that shows the relationship between the quantity supplied and the price of a product or service (It is upward sloping.)

price inelastic supply The supply where a large change in the price will have little impact on the quantity of a good or service supplied by the producer

price elastic supply The supply where a small change in the price will bring about significant increases in the quantity of a product or service supplied by the producer

market clearing, or **equilibrium, price** The price at which supply will equal demand

shortage The amount of a good or service that will not be available when the price of the good or service is set below the equilibrium price (Demand will exceed supply.)

surplus The amount of a good or service that will not be sold when the price of the good or service is set above the equilibrium price (Supply will exceed demand.)

EXHIBIT 1.4

Market Clearing Price and Quantity

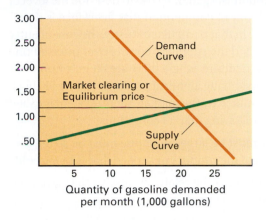

Quantity of gasoline demanded per month (1,000 gallons)

of borrowed money.[5] Capitalism is a system based on private property, which does not just imply land but also includes all types of personal property that you see, such as your house, car, furniture, books, stereos, CDs, and so on. In the capitalist system, along with private property comes property rights, that is, your rights to buy, own, use, and sell your property as you see fit. Private property and property rights are things that Americans take for granted. However, in communist countries like China (where property rights are changing very slowly) or in countries that have very recently gained independence from the former Soviet Union (like Kazakhstan, Kyrgyzstan, Tajikistan, Turkmenistan, and Uzbekistan in Central Asia), private property, especially land title, still belongs to the state and there are severe restrictions on what citizens in these countries can do with their land (the house that they build on the land may belong to them, but not the land!). This lack of property rights severely restricts innovation and business, since people do not have the freedom of choice to do what they want and make a profit. There is little or no incentive to invest in property when people know that the government may take away their land at any time. Private property rights are crucial for success in a free market system.

reality CHECK *How has the price of a typical personal computer performed over the past three years? Why?*

LEARNING OBJECTIVE 4
Discuss what is meant by *market structure,* and explain why most industries fall under the banner of monopolistic competition.

Degrees of Competition.

What is competition, and why does it matter? By the time you finish reading this section, you will begin to appreciate the importance of competition, especially as it relates to the price, quantity, and quality of the products and services that are produced and consumed in an economy. Most firms are founded to satisfy consumers' unfulfilled needs and, in so doing, to earn profit before the product or service they are selling becomes obsolete. All firms have a life cycle that begins with the introduction of a new, better, or cheaper product. At this stage, firms tend to be most profitable before competitors have had the time to enter the market with a cheaper, better alternative. The potential for profit motivates new entrants into the marketplace, and as the number of firms providing similar goods and services increases, the level of competition intensifies and prices fall. Unless the original firm increases its efficiency (by cutting production costs and "doing things right") and effectiveness (by introducing new products, markets, and business models, i.e., "doing the right things"), it will become less profitable and then obsolete and fade away. That is the fundamental reason why firms that do not change with time do not exist forever. Just as perceived profits attract business, in the **product life cycle,** competition forces firms to become efficient, invest, and outsource products and services abroad or to go out of business. In the capitalist system, the law of the corporate jungle is clear: compete—restructure—or die.

product life cycle theory The theory that explains the different stages—introduction, growth, maturity, and decline—that a product goes through before it fades away

market structure The organization of an industry determined by the level of competition within the industry

pure competition The industry market structure where there are a large number of suppliers that produce essentially identical products, which are sold at a price determined by the market

monopoly The industry market structure where there is essentially a single supplier of goods or services that has the power to set prices

imperfect competition The industry market structure where the industry's output of goods or services is supplied by a relatively small number of firms and price is largely determined by market forces

firm concentration ratios The percentage of total industry output that can be accounted for by the four largest firms and so a measure of the sellers' market power

This is called the process of "creative destruction." The degree of competition that firms face can vary from industry to industry and from country to country.

Market structure is the term that economists generally use to describe the level of competition within an industry. The amount of competition that firms face is determined by the number of firms that operate in that particular industry, the ease of entry into that industry, product homogeneity, and the supplier's control over price. At one end of the industrial spectrum we have agriculture, where there are literally hundreds of thousands of suppliers who produce essentially identical products (e.g., milk, beef, chicken, etc.) that are sold at a price determined by the market. Such a system is called **pure competition,** and it must meet the following market conditions:

1. The number of firms in the industry must be large, and none must be so big as to have undue influence on the price of the product or service that is being sold.

2. Entry into and exit out of this industry must be relatively easy so that firms can get in and out of this business if they so desire.

3. Each firm must produce a product or service identical to that of the other firms so that consumers cannot differentiate between the products.

4. The price for the product must be determined by the overall market demand and supply, and neither a single supplier nor a single customer must be able to influence prices.

At the other extreme, one could witness a utility (electricity) company that services a large region of a country all by itself. In this case we would have a **monopoly,** that is, a single firm supplying electricity to a large area of customers. This company then behaves like a monopolist (derived from the Greek words *mono* for "one" and *polist* for "seller"). Since this electric utility is the only game in town with no close substitutes for its service, it will be inclined to set prices as high as the market will bear. That is why we have utilities regulated by the government: to make sure that these firms do not make excessive profits, often called monopoly profits. On the basis of the four criteria indicated above, you will notice that entry into and exit out of the utility industry is neither easy nor inexpensive.

Not all industries are identical in their configuration. In fact, the real world contains a significant mixture of monopoly imperfections along with elements of competition. We can then classify the real world for the most part as having the market structure of **imperfect competition,** one that is neither perfectly competitive nor perfectly monopolistic. Imperfect competition arises when the total industry's output of goods or services is supplied by a small number of firms at market-determined prices. This leads to a consideration of **firm concentration ratios,** the percentage of the total industry output that is accounted for by the largest firms. Normally, four-firm concentration ratios, defined as the percentage of total industry output that is accounted for by the four largest firms in the industry, are used to measure the monopolistic nature of an industry. In 2000, about one-fifth of total manufacturing in the United States occurred in highly concentrated industries with four-firm concentration ratios above 60 percent.[6]

The differences in market structure arise from variations in cost composition between industries as well as from barriers to competition. In some industries, production will need to be on a large scale in order to make economic sense. Take, for example, the automobile industry. Given the huge investment in plant and equipment that will be needed, the thousands of parts required to assemble a car, the spare parts inventory, and the personnel that will be required to manage and operate the plant, average production cost will continue to decline as the number of cars produced increases. Hence, there are significant economies of scale in automobile production that could essentially wipe out small-volume car producers that will invariably have higher average costs. Unless the market for cars is large, it will not make sense nor will it be profitable to build mini auto plants. That's a major reason why you don't see automobile plants in countries with a small car market. It would make more sense to import cars than to build them in these countries.

Barriers to competition, also sometimes called barriers to entry, arise when certain legal restrictions are imposed on an industry or when suppliers themselves try to differentiate their products or services. Examples of legal restrictions to competition include patent protection, licensing, and tariffs. **Patents** are awarded to companies or individuals by governments to protect their inventions (intellectual property). Patents provide exclusive rights to the owner to produce goods (e.g., pharmaceuticals) or services (e.g., software) for a set period of time, thereby preventing others from doing so during that period. A patent awards exclusivity, or monopoly rights, to the owner for a given period of time so that the inventor can recoup the research and development cost of the invention and also earn a certain profit for the effort. **Licensing** operates in a similar manner and is more prevalent in developing countries where governments select certain investors to operate a particular type of businesses (cement manufacturing, steel production, etc.). Licensing restricts entry into an industry, thereby reducing competition. Finally, **tariffs,** which are taxes on imports, raise the price of imports and boost prices to domestic consumers. Domestic producers of import-competing products are therefore provided relief from overseas competition (from lower-cost imports).

barriers to competition Barriers that arise when certain legal restrictions (patent protection, licensing, and tariffs) that reduce the level of competition are imposed on an industry

patents Awards to companies or individuals by governments to protect their inventions (intellectual property) by providing exclusive rights to the owner to produce the goods (e.g., pharmaceutical products) or services (e.g., software or operating systems) for a set period of time, thereby preventing others from doing so during that time period

licensing The practice by governments of selecting investors to operate certain types of businesses, thereby restricting entry into those businesses and reducing competition

tariffs Taxes on imports that raise the price of imports and consequently enable domestic competitors to raise prices as well

OLIGOPOLY.   How imperfect can imperfect competition get? At one extreme is the monopolist, or single seller. **Oligopoly** implies "few sellers," that is, an industry in which a few sellers cater to the needs of the whole market. An oligopolist is one of these few sellers who produces and sells identical (or almost identical) products like cement, steel, copper, and so on, or services like airlines. On the basis of the four conditions of market structure that were discussed earlier, you will find that oligopolists are generally large producers, so only a few of them are needed to supply the whole market. Since the products or services sold by oligopolists are quite similar, when an oligopolist lowers prices, consumers will at once switch to the lower-price seller. In order not to lose market share, the other oligopolists will be forced to match the lower prices or go out of business. If you use commercial airlines, you will understand what we mean. For example, if American Airlines lowers its fare between any two cities, at once other carriers that cater to that pair of cities will lower their prices as well and will match American's fare; otherwise, customers will flock to American Airlines. Unlike a monopolist, the oligopolist does not control prices, but each can have a great effect on market price, especially downward.

oligopoly The industry market structure where a few producers of almost identical products cater to the needs of the whole market

MONOPOLISTIC COMPETITION.   The key characteristic of monopolistic competition is **product differentiation.** Although there are quite a few sellers in this type of market structure, each firm will try to make its product sound or appear different from the rest. Although the number of producers remains large (not as large as in pure competition), each firm will try to advertise and promote its products as if they are unique. Take, for example, jeans, which are a common product. However, through the creation of brand awareness, brands like Polo, Calvin Klein, Levi's, Wrangler, Lee's, Rustler, and so on, the companies try to give the consumer the impression that their jeans are something out of the ordinary—in a class by themselves. Each company tries to convey to the consumer that its jeans are unique— one of a kind—in the market, and it wants to behave like a monopolist in the market for its jeans. This way it can try to charge a monopoly price. While some consumers may say that jeans are jeans and go for the ones that cost the least, there

product differentiation A strategy that firms employ to make their product seem different from those of their competitors

are others who are convinced that "there is nothing between me and my Calvins" and are willing to pay a high price for a pair of Calvin Klein jeans.

Since product differentiation is such an important part of monopolistic competition, firms in this industry spend a tremendous amount of money on advertising to convince the consumer that their product is truly different. Other industry examples of differentiated products include perfumes, soda pop, toothpaste, detergents, makeup, sneakers, gasoline, and so on. While the utility value of all the products within a category may be about the same, the aura of the specific product enables the supplier to charge a higher price and reap some monopoly profit.

Exhibit 1.5 summarizes the basics of market structure in a capitalist system. The degree of competition varies from pure competition with numerous sellers of identical products, to a large number of sellers of differentiated products, to a system of few sellers of almost identical products, to the limiting case of a single seller—a monopolist. Each structure is associated with a particular pricing mechanism, which is of significant importance to businesses and consumers.

reality CHECK   *Identify a company that is a monopolist in your hometown.*

LEARNING OBJECTIVE 5
Discuss the rationale for countries wanting to choose other forms (rather than capitalism) of economic systems and explain what direction most countries are moving toward.

EXHIBIT 1.5

Market Structure

Most industries fall in the category of monopolistic competition.

	Pure Competition	Monopolistic Competition	Oligopoly	Monopoly
Where prevalent	Agricultural products, e.g., corn, rice, wheat	Retail trade, e.g., fast food, gasoline	Airlines, autos, construction materials, e.g., cement, steel	Utilities, e.g., cable TV, telephone, electricity
Number of producers	Numerous	Many but not as numerous	Few	Single producer
Product differentiation	Identical products	Perceived differences in product	Some difference in product	Unique product with no close substitutes
Barriers to entry	None	Relatively easy	Relatively difficult	Regulated by government
Degree of control over price	None	Some	Some	Considerable
Methods of market promotion	Minimal promotion	Heavy advertising to differentiate product	Advertise heavily to promote perceived quality	Advertise service, quality, and reliability

The Command, or Planned, Economic System

Capitalism is a system based on profits and efficient resource allocation along with the primary goal of satisfying consumer demand. At the other end of the spectrum of global economic systems is the **command,** or **planned, economic system,** in which ownership and control of all the factors of production are totally in the hands of the government and not the private citizens. The concept of private property does not exist in this system, and the government makes all decisions on which goods and services will be produced, where they will be produced, how much of those goods and services will be produced, and at what price they will be sold. As you can see, the consumer has little say in such a system. In the command economic system, the government plans (hence it is sometimes called the planned economic system) production on the basis of national goals and an elaborate analysis of sources and uses of resources available to the economy. The government's objectives are to

- Utilize as much of domestic resources as possible, since these countries invariably focus on domestic self-sufficiency and not on international trade.
- Employ whoever is willing to work in order to solve unemployment and poverty.
- Minimize income inequality among workers by diminishing wage differentials.
- Provide limited choice to workers in terms of where to work and what type of work they can undertake.

The command economic system is based on the assumptions that the government knows what is best for the consumer and the country and that it should try to eliminate wasteful conspicuous consumption. The consumer certainly is not the king in the command economic system. While the command economic system seeks to minimize the exploitation of workers, it does so at a great expense to efficiency and consumer choice (for example, in the former Soviet bloc countries and in present-day Cuba and North Korea). In the long run, countries that follow the command economic system invariably end up bankrupt. The market mechanism is not allowed to operate and there are no incentives for earning profits. In general, a curious thing to notice in command economies is the almost total lack of quality consumer goods. When goods are available, there is not much of a choice and the goods are of poor quality. If a product happens to be appealing to consumers, it will invariably be in short supply, since prices are not based on supply and demand—the government sets them! Furthermore, the concepts of competition and private property do not exist. All of these elements contribute to the production of a whole bunch of goods that consumers do not want and also lead to an acute scarcity of other goods that consumers really do want.

Firms that produce goods and services in a command economic system are run by the government and are called **state enterprises.** State enterprises are essentially inefficient bureaucracies that employ far more workers than needed for efficient production. Prior to 1978, when China was a command economy, most Chinese consumers wore gray drab outfits and had little to look forward to in terms of consumer goods and choices. With the introduction of a free enterprise system in China in 1978 and the nascent reform of state enterprises, China is rapidly becoming a capitalist country with communist roots.

The Mixed Economic System

Very few economies in the world practice pure capitalism. Hong Kong, now a Special Administrative Region of China, is closest to a pure capitalist system. However, even in Hong Kong, several types of services, such as mass transportation

command, or **planned, economic system** The economic system in which the ownership and control of the factors of production are totally in government hands

state enterprises Government-owned firms that produce goods and services, generally in command and mixed economic systems

and utilities, are still provided by the government. A number of services (defense, social services, Amtrak, the Tennessee Valley Authority, etc.) in the United States are also provided by the government. Most economies are mixed economic systems.

mixed economic system The economic system that exhibits elements of both the capitalist and the command economic systems

A **mixed economic system** is one that exhibits elements of both the capitalist system and the command system. Not all services (e.g., defense and social welfare) can be provided by the private sector; hence the government plays a crucial role in providing these services while at the same time procuring goods (fighter aircrafts, naval fleet, ammunition, etc.) from private companies. Not all mixed economies are alike. In some countries public sector (government-owned or state-owned) enterprises play a much larger role than in others. In the industrialized countries of Europe, for example, France, the government owns (now partially) several companies like Air France and SNCF (the French railroad system). In many developing countries, for example, China and India, several companies in the manufacturing and service sectors are owned by their governments. The Indian government owns several steel, fertilizer, petrochemical, oil and gas, machinery, and electronics firms as well as services like airlines, railways, and shipping.

The larger the role state enterprises play in an economy, the greater the prospect for economic inefficiency. State enterprises are inherently overstaffed with underperforming employees who have little motivation to work hard or efficiently, since their salaries are generally not tied to productivity. All employees get paid more or less the same and salaries are normally based on seniority—number of years of service with the state agency. If you have traveled to France or India, you will readily see for yourself how the United States compares with them in terms of efficiency in the production of goods and services. Countries that are dominated by private sector enterprises generally exhibit dynamic business and economic growth. The trend these days in mixed economies like France and India is to move away from state enterprises to private businesses. This is being achieved through the sale of state enterprises to private entrepreneurs—a process called **privatization.**

privatization The process of selling state enterprises to private entrepreneurs

As countries privatize state enterprises, their economies are bound to grow faster and productive employees will become richer. Governments can then focus their attention on providing services like social welfare and defense that generally cannot be provided by private firms. While the mixed economy is bound to stay with us for a very long time, the role of government in running businesses is destined to diminish.

The Transition Economies

economic transition The move from a command economic system to a capitalist economic system (in the direction of competitive, market-oriented economics) that is aimed at ending the inefficiencies of central planning

In 1989, after years of state control of all productive assets in the Soviet bloc, the Berlin Wall fell and the Soviet Union broke up. This led to the start of market-oriented reforms in Russia and the former communist economies of Central and Eastern Europe and Central Asia. This move, from central planning to capitalism (in the direction of competitive, market-oriented, open trade economics), is called **economic transition** and is aimed at ending the inefficiencies of central planning. Privatizing state-owned enterprises is also designed to free resources and talent that could be used productively by the private sector, thereby raising the living standards of these people. While economists generally refer to the former Soviet Union countries as transition economies, China in 1978 was the first major economy to embark on the reform from state control to capitalism. China is implementing market-oriented reforms that are introducing profit incentives to rural enterprises and private businesses, liberalizing foreign trade and investment regulations, relaxing state control over some prices, and investing in industrial infrastructure and the education of its workforce. By encouraging the growth of rural enterprises and not focusing exclusively on the urban industrial sector, China has successfully moved millions of workers off farms and into factories without creating an urban crisis. Finally, China's relatively open-door policy has spurred massive foreign direct investment in the country, creating new jobs and linking the Chinese economy with international markets.[7]

The experience of transition economies (China and the former Soviet Union countries) clearly shows the important link between private sector development and economic growth, and the fact that privatized enterprises invariably outperform state-run companies. Research on transition economies shows that firms that started from scratch with new management performed best, followed by newly privatized firms run by outsiders, either local or foreign. Privatized firms managed by insiders were found to be least efficient and productive, but even these firms did better than state enterprises. If transition economies are to grow and develop rapidly, they must ensure that the proper economic environment—institutions that support property rights, the rule of law, a competitive market structure and prices, and attention to consumer demand—is in place.[8]

 **reality CHECK** *Are you aware of any government-operated business in your city or state?*

Production of Goods and Services

The performance of the U.S. economy is primarily measured in terms of how many and how efficiently goods and services are produced in the country. These goods, such as cars, gasoline, TVs, computers, breakfast cereals, and so on, as well as services like haircutting, dry cleaning, banking, consulting, and transportation, are all called **outputs.** In other words, outputs consist of a wide array of useful goods or services that are either consumed or used for further production. The primary role of businesses, regardless of in which country they are located, is to produce goods or services that consumers need.

> **outputs** A wide array of useful goods or services that are either consumed or used for further production in business

LEARNING OBJECTIVE 6
Explain how the factors of production impact the supply of goods and services in an economy.

Every output requires two or more **inputs.** Economists define inputs as factors of production, that is, commodities or services that are used by firms in their production processes. The final result of the production process is outputs. For example, when we consume French fries, the potatoes, the oil, the frying pot, the oven heat, and the chef's time are all inputs. The crisp fries are the output. Traditionally, factors of production have been divided into four major categories: land (and the natural resources beneath it), labor (of all types), capital (money and capital goods like machinery), and technology.

> **inputs** Factors of production (land, labor, capital, and technology), that is, commodities or services that are used by firms in their production processes

Land consists of the ground used for agriculture or under factories or railroads (or airports, automobile roads, etc.); natural resources include nonrenewable resources like coal, crude oil, and iron ore and renewable resources like trees used in the production of lumber and paper. Nonrenewable natural resources are provided by nature and are in fixed supply.

Labor consists of human time spent in productive activities, for example, running a farm, working in an automobile factory, teaching, conducting research, consulting, or running a business. Today's economic environment has led to tremendous specialization

entrepreneurs People with initiative who seize opportunities as they see them to get things done or make things happen, generally for profit

eBay founder Pierre Omidyar and CEO Meg Whitman are entrepreneurs who are responsible for creating the world's first, largest, and most profitable online person-to-person trading, using the auction format.

capital goods Finished goods like machinery and equipment that can be used as inputs for further production of goods and services

of labor. We have engineers and scientists in various disciplines who constantly work on enhancing and inventing new technologies that can be used for improving business processes. We have **entrepreneurs,** people with initiative who seize opportunities as they see them to get things done or make things happen for a profit. While an entrepreneur does not invent things, he or she exploits in novel ways what has already been invented and brings into existence new products or services or a new business or industry. Entrepreneurs are a class of specialized labor not unlike engineers and scientists. Pierre Omidyar changed the face of Internet commerce in 1995 when he created eBay (**www.ebay.com**), the world's first online marketplace. Looking for a way to create an efficient market, he pioneered the auction format for online person-to-person trading. Entrepreneurs, as you can see, play an important role in business creation and development. The supply of human resources is generally not a response to economic conditions, but is determined by social and biological factors. Land and labor are generally called *primary* factors of production because their supplies are not determined by the economic system; that is, neither land nor labor is regarded as an output in the business sense.

Capital comes in two major forms. First, money (also called financial capital) is utilized to start businesses and run operations (paying salaries and buying raw materials). Sources of money for entrepreneurs are their personal savings, loans from banks, and the issuance of bonds (IOUs) and stocks. A second, equally important type of capital (called **capital goods** or physical capital) consists of durable goods produced by the economy in order to produce yet other goods. These durable goods include machinery, construction equipment, trucks, factories, computers, software, and so on, that you see every day. Unlike land and labor, which are primary factors of production, capital goods are produced goods that can be used as inputs for the further production of more goods and services.

Technology makes the production process more efficient through the introduction of better and cheaper ways of getting things done (providing goods and services). The information technology (IT) industry, for example, utilizes fiber-optic cables or wireless telephone and broadband networks to relay data, information, and audio and video messages within companies and across national boundaries instantaneously. Developments in information technology and the Internet are something unique. They are like the birth of electricity, the railroad, the telephone, and the telegraph years ago, each of which brought about massive changes in business and economic growth. These marvelous developments are constantly being used by business to improve production management. Companies like SAP in Germany and I-2 Technologies and Oracle in the United States are world famous suppliers of software that helps improve planning, production efficiency, and inventory control, thereby bringing down the cost of the final output to the customer.

What factor of production is most abundant in your state?

Measuring Business Performance

> **LEARNING OBJECTIVE 7**
> Discuss how business performance is measured in a capitalist system versus a socialist system, and how the objectives of for-profit businesses differ from the objectives of state-owned enterprises and of not-for-profit organizations.

In the free market system, businesses exist to meet specific consumer needs (either for products or services). In other words, businesses must provide value to the customers. In this process, businesses must be profitable to survive. The exception is not-for-profit organizations like the Public Broadcasting System, **www.pbs.org,** or National Public Radio, **www.npr.org,** whose objectives are to provide balanced reporting and educate people. These and similar not-for-profit organizations depend on contributions from "viewers like you" and on some government and corporate support. In the private sector of the United States as well as most industrialized and industrializing countries of the world, firms are owned either by individuals (like small businesses) or by major investors who have put in a lot of their own money as well as people like you and me who have bought company stock. All **investors** who have a financial stake in a business, be it small or large, expect to receive a return on their invested capital; otherwise, they might as well put their money in a bank and earn a small but decent amount of interest. So, how would you as an investor figure out whether you would be better off keeping your money in a bank or investing your savings in a company? To answer this, we need to analyze business performance, which is the subject of discussion in this section. We briefly look into how business performance is narrowly defined and measured and how not-for-profit organizations and different societies evaluate business performance.

> **investors** Those who have a financial stake in a business, small or large, and expect to receive a return on their invested capital

Maximizing Profit and Shareholder Wealth

All firms, small or big, need to make a profit to remain in business. Profit is the difference between revenue (sales of goods or services) and the cost of the goods or services sold. **Revenue** is the sum of the quantities of all goods and services sold times their price.

> **revenue** The sum of the quantities of all goods or services sold times their price

> Revenue = (quantities of all goods sold) × (their price) + (quantities of all services sold) × (their price)

Thus, the revenue generated by a McDonald's outlet is the sum of the quantities of all the items that McDonald's sells (Big Macs, Chicken McNuggets, French fries, cola, etc.) times their price (the price of the Big Mac, Chicken McNuggets, French fries, cola, etc.). The cost to the McDonald's outlet includes what the owner of the outlet pays for the various inputs, that is, the buns, burgers, chicken, frozen fries, cooking oil, cola, and so on. In addition, the outlet's cost includes the salaries and benefits paid to its employees, the maintenance cost of the outlet, the rent for space, and the fee (called the franchise fee) paid to McDonald's Corporation for using the McDonald's brand name and the services that McDonald's Corporation provides to the owner of the outlet. When you add up all these costs and subtract the sum from the revenue, you can determine the profit for the McDonald's outlet (see Exhibit 1.6 on p. 22). So, if you were considering owning a McDonald's outlet, you could figure out on the basis of the anticipated profit to be generated by the outlet whether you would be better off investing your money in the business or keeping your savings in a bank. Most rational investors who start a business want to generate as much revenue as possible and at the *same time* want to keep expenses under control. That is, investors want to maximize

EXHIBIT 1.6

Relationship Between Revenue, Expenses, and Profit

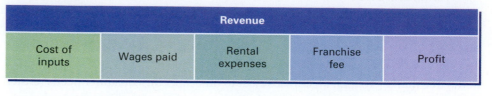

Revenue				
Cost of inputs	Wages paid	Rental expenses	Franchise fee	Profit

revenue and minimize expenses. Since profit is the difference between revenue and expenses, what investors want to do is to *maximize profit*. When revenue is less than costs, the firm incurs a loss.

In large corporations like Ford Motor Company, even the Ford family is unable to come up with the huge investment (for building factories, installing various equipment, maintaining stocks of steel, etc.) needed to run the company. Although Ford may be able to borrow some money from banks to meet the expenses associated with building automobiles, trucks, and so on, banks will lend only a certain amount of money. So the rest of the funds will have to come from investors (people with savings) who will purchase stocks issued by Ford Motor Company. While Ford will not be able to guarantee a return (income, or dividends) to investors (called stockholders) on its stocks, Ford's management will try to maximize profit. Part of the profit will be distributed to Ford's stockholders in the form of **dividends.** Thus the more profit Ford generates, the more dividends the stockholders will likely receive while Ford reinvests some of the remaining profit—called **retained earnings**—into the company to generate additional profit in the future. In essence, what Ford tries to do is to maximize **shareholder wealth** (dividends plus the increase in the stock prices over time). By purchasing Ford Motor Company's stocks, the Ford stockholder puts her or his money and faith in Ford's management. Ford's management believes that its obligation is to maximize shareholder wealth. The greater the dividends that Ford shareholders receive and the higher that Ford stock prices rise, the happier the investors are and the more willing they will be to buy and hold Ford stocks.

dividends The portion of profits distributed to stockholders

retained earnings The portion of profits not distributed as dividends but reinvested back into the company to generate additional profits in the future

increasing shareholder wealth Increasing dividends and stock prices

Maximizing Stakeholder Wealth

In the United States, employees (labor) at firms and corporations are generally looked on as a factor of production just like land and capital. When the U.S. economy slows or a company is not doing well for various reasons, the U.S. norm is to lay off workers (shed excess labor) to reduce cost until profits improve. Despite unemployment compensation benefits paid by the government, laid-off workers and their families go through tremendous economic and psychological stress and hardship. The Europeans and Japanese do not like the U.S. approach. They believe that the U.S. system of laying off workers is too ruthless (which it is!) since from their point of view, employees are more than mere factors of production—they are humans—and therefore need to be treated better. Many European managers believe in a broader corporate objective than maximizing shareholder wealth. Supported by European public opinion, these business leaders would like to maximize stakeholder wealth and move toward a stakeholder society rather than a shareholder society. There is tremendous debate in Europe and Asia, and to a lesser extent in the United States (except during various global meetings, e.g., the IMF, World Bank, and WTO meetings), on the merits of a **stakeholder company**—one that does not focus exclusively on shareholder wealth maximization and its short-term interests but

stakeholder company A business that takes into consideration the interests of all its partners, including its customers, management, employees, suppliers, and society

Ethics in Business

Corporate Profits Versus Corporate Ethics

The U.S. business system focuses on maximizing short-term profits; stock analysts as well as investors continually focus on the quarterly profit performance of companies. Corporate managers (whose salaries and bonuses are often tied to corporate performance) in turn try their best to meet short-term expectations—maximizing corporate profits and boosting stock prices! Recent events, especially in corporate America, have brought the issue of **business ethics** to the forefront. Business ethics deals with questions about whether certain business practices (some of which may be legal) are morally acceptable, especially when they have a detrimental impact on consumers, investors, or employees—compromising long-term wealth maximization for short-term gain by encouraging various forms of corporate (especially accounting and financial) scandals. For example, since early in 2000, investors have been hit with a wide array of scandals that have tarnished the reputations of some of the United States' largest corporations and financial institutions. While the facts in each case have varied, the downfall of several major companies (e.g., Arthur Anderson, Enron, Global Crossing, HealthSouth, IM Clone, Lucent Technologies, Rite Aid, Worldcom, etc.) can be attributed to a common thread: unethical behavior of key corporate executives that had been tolerated for years, often with regulators and industry insiders looking the other way. These corporate scandals were generally the result of executives boosting short-term revenues and artificially inflating their corporation's stock prices.

These developments, which have had significant detrimental effects on investors (especially retirees and those with retirement plans) as well as employees of those companies, led to a public outcry and an investigation by Eliot Spitzer, the New York attorney general. In April 2003, ten well-known Wall Street investment banks (Citigroup, Credit Suisse First Boston, Bear Stearns, Goldman Sachs, J. P. Morgan Chase, Lehman Brothers, Morgan Stanley, UBS Warburg, US Bancorp Piper Jaffray, and Merrill Lynch) were reprimanded and settled (for a total of $1.4 billion in fines) investigations into whether their research analysts misled the public by touting stocks publicly that they denigrated privately in order to win lucrative investment banking business from those corporations. These events have raised serious discussions in Congress and in academia about the need to improve corporate ethics (social responsibility) and curtail white-collar crime.

Source: D. Quinn Mills, "Buy, Lie, and Sell High: How Investors Lost Out on Enron and the Internet Bubble" (NJ: *Financial Times,* Prentice-Hall, 2002).

Questions

1. Should corporations regulate themselves? Or can market forces rectify the situation? Or is better government regulation and supervision needed? Is this a case of a few rotten apples, or is the problem systemic?
2. Why do you think so many well-known U.S. firms have been involved in unethical behavior, especially when compared with the relatively few cases in Europe and Japan?

---

that takes into consideration the welfare of all its constituents: customers, management, employees, suppliers, and society. While maximizing shareholder wealth is relatively straightforward, measuring stakeholder wealth and maximizing it can get a bit difficult. For example, in the latter case, companies are obliged to keep retraining their employees and sharing some of society's cost. Europeans believe strongly that in the long term, such a socially responsible company will be better off than businesses that are exclusively based on shareholder wealth creation. In stakeholder-oriented companies, employees are considered more than a factor of production and they cannot be hired or fired easily. As a comparison of equity, the ratio of salary paid to the chief executive of a company to that of an average factory worker is close to 50:1 in Europe and Japan, as compared with 400:1 in the United States. As Warren Buffet, the Sage of Omaha, indicated in Berkshire Hathway's 2003 annual letter (March 7, 2004) to shareholders, "In judging whether corporate America is

business ethics The principles governing whether certain business practices are morally acceptable, especially when they have a detrimental impact on consumers, investors, or employees

serious about reforming itself, CEO pay remains the acid test. To date, the results aren't encouraging."

Minimizing Unemployment and Income Inequalities

In several developing countries of Africa, Asia, the former Soviet bloc, and Latin America, the primary objective of many large companies is to keep people employed. Invariably, these companies are government-owned state enterprises. While many of these state enterprises, especially in China and India, are currently being sold to private entrepreneurs in the process called privatization, a significant number of state enterprises still exist in the Middle East, Central Asia, and Latin America. Most governments consider state enterprises a source of employment generation. As a result, state enterprises tend to be overstaffed, and the employees are invariably underpaid. Also, the productivity of state enterprise employees is generally very low. This creates a vicious cycle. Because the employees are poorly paid, they do not work hard. Since they do not work hard (they hardly work in many cases!), **productivity** (dollar output of goods and services per dollar input of labor) is low and they are entitled only to low wages. There is generally a total lack of motivation on the part of these employees and managers to work hard and perform well, since employees and management are not rewarded on the basis of profits. The tendency of workers and managers alike is to do the minimum needed to get by.

> **productivity** The dollar output of goods and services per dollar input of labor

A related objective of state enterprises is to minimize income inequalities. In the free enterprise system, anyone with a good business idea can start a firm and operate it within the rule of law. Those with ideas, initiative, and resources can become rich while those with no ideas, initiative, or resources are likely to be left behind. Thus in the free market system, we can see that those who work hard are likely to succeed and earn a decent living while those who do not work hard may not be well off. Politicians in some countries do not consider this to be appropriate (since the rich seem to get richer and the poor, poorer) and have used state enterprises, where most employees are paid almost the same, as a tool to bridge the gap between the rich and poor, thereby minimizing income inequalities among workers. The drawback of this system is that it focuses too much effort on income distribution and not much emphasis on generating profits and economic growth.

Not-for-Profit Organizations

The primary objective of these organizations is to serve society. Since these organizations are not-for-profit, they are exempt from paying corporate taxes. Not-for-profit organizations have an extremely important role to play in an economy. They provide goods and services that would otherwise not be made available and without which society as a whole would be worse off. There are hundreds of local (Boy Scouts and Girl Scouts), state (Adapt of Texas), national (United Way), and international (Catholic Relief Services) not-for-profit organizations that are vital for the well-being of society.

Take educational institutions, for example. Although one may think or feel that these schools or universities are out to make a profit, that is not true. Public schools are funded by taxpayer dollars, and there is a constant challenge for governments to manage within state-allocated budgets. State universities receive some government funding, which is generally not adequate, and universities charge students tuition and fees to cover the cost of instruction, lab equipment, and campus facilities. Universities also use income from endowments (donations from alumni or corporations) to defray some costs. Private universities operate in a similar fashion to public universities. All these institutions try to manage within their budgets, and when there is a surplus (not a profit), those monies are reserved for emergencies or for future capital (campus) improvements. There are numerous other national and international not-for-profit charitable organizations. These include the international not-for-profit agencies like UNICEF, Doctors Without Borders, and World Vision. These charities reach out to people who need help and improve their quality of life.

reality CHECK *Do you feel that the rich are getting richer and the poor are getting poorer in your country? Why?*

Demand for Goods and Services

LEARNING OBJECTIVE 8
Explain the important role consumers play in determining corporate performance and show how businesses try to identify consumer needs.

Firms are in the business of producing goods or providing services for customers. Without customers, businesses will cease to exist and unemployment will increase. Consumers, therefore, are extremely important for business success as well as for the well-being of the country as a whole. Approximately 70 percent of the U.S. economy is based on private consumption. So when the U.S. consumer curtails her or his spending habits, the demand for goods and services is at once negatively affected and private consumption shrinks; this leads to **inventory**—unsold goods— buildup. When inventory buildup reaches a certain level, businesses cut down production and lay off workers, and the economy contracts. The role of the consumer, regardless of the country under consideration, is paramount for business growth and profitability. Businesses constantly try to identify consumer needs in order to develop products and services that can be sold profitably.

inventory Unsold goods in stock

Measuring Consumer Confidence

Given the crucial role consumers play in an economy, businesses are eager to know how positive consumers feel about themselves and their environment. If consumers feel great about their jobs, their job security, their salaries, and their general home environment, they are likely to spend freely on all types of items, thereby boosting business revenue and economic growth. Government policymakers are always happy to see their economy grow for several simple reasons. Steady economic growth implies that businesses are doing well and are generating profits. When businesses do well, they employ more people and also pay more corporate taxes. The resulting high rate of employment in turn generates more income taxes for the government and also reduces unemployment benefits and social problems like crime. For these reasons, businesses as well as economists are interested in knowing the level of consumer confidence, that is, how satisfied consumers feel about themselves, the economy, and their spending habits.

A closely watched measure of consumer confidence is the **Consumer Confidence Index,** which is put out monthly by the Conference Board, **www. conferenceboard.org,** in New York. The Conference Board is a not-for-profit organization that works as a global, independent membership organization serving the public interest. The Consumer Confidence Index is based on the Consumer Confidence Survey, **www.consumerresearchcenter.org,** which samples 5000 U.S. households monthly. For example, that index, which remained virtually unchanged in May 2004, increased sharply in June 2004 and stood at 101.9 (1985 = 100) up from 93.1 in

Consumer Confidence Index An indicator that measures the self-assurance of consumers and is crucial in determining consumer spending habits that have a direct impact on business prospects and the economy

May 2004. When the index rises, it indicates that consumers are more confident about *current* business conditions. This implies that consumers may continue spending, and this in turn could affect business revenues and earnings. A drop in the Consumer Confidence Index sends a message to firms that they should not be optimistic about the immediate business environment and may want to curb investment or expansion plans. Economists get very concerned, since these actions may raise unemployment and reduce corporate profits and income tax revenues. A related index put out by the Conference Board is the Expectations Index, which measures the consumer outlook for the short term. When this index rises, it indicates that overall, consumers are optimistic about the short-term outlook for the U.S. economy.

The Consumer Knows Best

Given the fact that businesses depend heavily on consumers for their survival, the questions in every businessperson's mind are, Who is the consumer? Are all consumers alike? Do culture, income, demographics, national boundaries, and so on impact a consumer's purchasing habits and purchasing power? If so, how and why? Properly identifying, understanding, and serving customer needs is key to business success. Regardless of what businesspeople think, it is ultimately the consumer who calls the shots. Quite often businesses come up with a relatively novel product or service, but the consumer may not be ready for it. The consumer may find the particular product or service to be of little value to him or her, and this may result in that business's failure. The test of business success is in the market, and in the market the consumer rules!

Consumer Demographics and Psychographics

The United States is the largest consumer market in the world. It is also the world's largest economy with one of the lowest unemployment rates. In addition, the United States is the world's largest importer and exporter of goods and services. According to the U.S. Census Bureau, for example, 51 percent of the U.S. population of some 285 million in 2004 (and projected to increase to 300 million by the end

American Eagle Outfitters is a typical specialty store that primarily tries to cater to the changing desires and needs of American teenagers.

of the decade) is female; 13 percent is African American and 13 percent is Hispanic; approximately 7 percent of the population is in the 15-to-19-year age group, 14 percent is in the 25-to-34-year age group, 16 percent (highest concentration) is in the 35-to-44 year age group, and 14 percent is in the 45-to-54-year age group. Furthermore, currently 23 percent of the U.S population is over 55 years old, and this population group is expected to increase to 25 percent by 2010 and to 31 percent by 2050.[9] And, the Hispanic population is projected to rise to 24 percent by 2050. What do all these statistics mean to business? Does anyone care? Yes, these statistics reflect the diversity of U.S. consumers and are of great interest to businesses as they try to determine what to produce and for whom. For example, magazine publishers in the United States have analyzed this information to come up with such magazines as *Black Enterprise, Golf for Women, Latina Magazine, Seventeen,* and *Sports Illustrated for Kids* to cater precisely to the needs of specific audiences. Among the wealth of statistics available from the Census Bureau is information on where and how the U.S. population is distributed. That information enables businesses to identify the right location for manufacturing and marketing different products and services.

We all know for sure that not all consumers are alike. People have different tastes (and therefore different needs for goods and services), which might depend on various demographic and social characteristics like *gender, age, race, national origin, income, education, employment, physical location or residence, sexual orientation,* and *marital status.* However, a group of people can be identified who have similar tastes and who for all practical purposes can be lumped together as one of several target groups that businesses may want to cater to. Depending on the type and number of consumers in it, the target group may have a critical mass, a size that makes business viable. A **target group** could be U.S. teenagers in the 15-to-19 year age group (7 percent of the U.S. population), who more or less have similar consumption habits like eating at fast-food restaurants, listening to certain types of pop music, and wearing certain types of clothes. Here, what businesses are trying to do is to break up the consumer population on the basis of *age* to see which goods and services could be sold to each age group.

target group A population segment whose members have more or less similar consumption habits

Mercedes Benz cars, for example, have traditionally been purchased by a specific segment of the U.S. population, that is, those with relatively *high income* and around *middle age.* Income and age are some of the demographic characteristics that DaimlerChrysler may use for **market segmentation.** Depending on the product or service that is being considered, businesses may include product-specific demographics. **Psychographics,** on the other hand, deals with an analysis and understanding of the consumer's mind to identify likes, dislikes, or preferences and develop commercials that try to manipulate the recipient's mind to create a desire for certain goods or services. Here businesses try to go across demographics to identify and arouse certain consumer tastes to sell their products.

market segmentation The breakdown of target consumers into categories on the basis of age, gender, education, ethnic background, or other criteria to determine the products or services that could be made to suit the segments' specific needs

psychographics The analysis and understanding of the consumer's mind to identify consumer likes, dislikes, or preferences and develop commercials that manipulate the recipient's mind to create a need for certain new goods or services

Cultural Diversity

Culture plays an extremely important role in business, especially in such functional areas as human resource management and marketing. Domestic and international companies that have been successful in identifying, designing, and implementing strategies that take into consideration cultural differences in their business environments are the ones that are most likely to succeed. Businesses, big and small, are slowly recognizing that to succeed, they must please individual customers of many national origins with many different national cultures.

culture The behavior patterns, beliefs, and institutions that underpin all human activities, explain much of our behavior, create an awareness for learning, and vary by social grouping

The challenge with culture is that it is as easy to grasp as a wet frog. Yet, cultural awareness is paramount to business success. Culture underpins all human activities, explains much of our behavior, and creates awareness for learning. Cultural differences exist not only between countries but also within them. While it is true that cultural differences between nations are wide and varied, we should not ignore the fact that even people within a country like the United States vary in their beliefs and behavior and they must be treated equitably. As a nation of immigrants, the United States has always accepted people from abroad who meet specific requirements (immediate relatives, refugees, and employment-based immigrants) to settle in the country and to spur economic growth and enrich the national landscape. Approximately 7.5 million immigrants entered the United States legally during the 1980s and 1990s from all continents of the world. Approximately 42 percent of these immigrants came from Mexico, Central America, and the Caribbean. Another 32 percent came from Asia, 14 percent from Europe, 6 percent from South America, and 4 percent from Africa. The United States is truly a multicultural society, an amalgamation of peoples of different ethnic background, religion, and social class all living in one economic environment.

The challenges and opportunities for businesses get more complex when they take into consideration cultural diversity in a global business environment. For example, in a conservative country like Saudi Arabia, McDonald's restaurants have separate service lines for "ladies" and "gentlemen" and provide customized menus (serving McArabia Sandwiches, for example) to reflect local tastes.

The primary role of business is to serve the customer. Unless a business is able to identify the cultural background of the consumer, the firm may not be in a position to identify consumer requirements and satisfy that particular need. Depending on their cultural background, customers will like to acquire different types of food, shelter, clothing, and entertainment. With increased globalization, consumer tastes and behavior will change across cultures more rapidly as foreign cultural norms permeate open societies. However, while some cultures may be willing to readily accept and adapt to foreign cultures, others may resist them to maintain their national identity. This is particularly true in the way people dress, eat, and entertain. McDonald's, for example, has tried to adapt its menus to meet the needs of different cultures while maintaining its relatively unique fast-food service quality. Since questions were raised about the nutritional value of its food (in terms of portion size and fat and carbohydrate content), the company has taken major positive steps like revamping its menu to make it healthier. To suit American taste, DaimlerChrysler manufactures in Alabama the Mercedes M-class SUVs, which it does not produce or sell (or rarely sells) in Europe. Cross-cultural understanding and competency is crucial not only for successful global management and marketing but also for human relationships. Lack of cultural sensitivity can lead to declining profits and stock prices, new-product disasters, and litigation.

Instituting cultural diversity in the workplace can lead to innovation, new-product development, and increased corporate profits. At one time, hiring employees of different backgrounds was considered good corporate citizenship. However, the globalization of business is now making it imperative for firms to have a diverse workforce at all levels to achieve corporate success. Employees of different backgrounds help bring new perspectives on products, services, and markets that otherwise might have gone untapped. Along with diversity come sensitivity to cultural differences and an understanding of what motivates consumers to choose one product over another. Firms can no longer use a "one-size-fits-all" approach in business if they are to be financially viable. Coca-Cola, for example, under the direction of its former CEO Douglas Daft, had stressed the importance of promoting some of the major local brands it had acquired overseas rather than abandoning them and imposing Coca-Cola products. In India, with a population of a billion,

Case in Point

McDonald's Corporation: Ronald Goes to France

In a country known for its exquisite cuisine and proud culture, the entry of a U.S. fast-food icon could have been a shock to the French. Yet, McDonald's has been pretty profitable in its French operations. Since setting foot in France in 1972, McDonald's has been quite successful in marrying its basic fast-food philosophy to French palates. Currently, McDonald's has some 930 outlets with some 35,000 employees in France. For the French, eating out is a way of life—an experience in culture. The tradition-oriented French believe that food is to be savored at leisure, not "gobbled down." Those of you who have visited France will have realized that the French do take long meal breaks. It is part of their culture to enjoy food with a glass of wine (sometimes beer) and discuss lofty private, local, and world events in a comfortable setting for hours on end.

When we think of McDonald's, what comes to mind is relatively inexpensive food (with no alcoholic beverages) served in decent portions, quick service, a clean restaurant environment, and above all the familiar Golden Arches, which are visible from a distance in the United States. In addition, quite a few McDonald's restaurants in the United States have drive-thru windows. Finally, most of the customers visiting McDonald's restaurants in the United States do not spend too much time there beyond eating.

Although McDonald's has been in France for over 30 years, this has not been without incidents. Resentful of McDonald's incursion into French culture, Mr. Jose Bove, a militant French farmer, became a national hero in 1999 after driving his tractor into a McDonald's restaurant in southern France. Although Mr. Bove was convicted, the message was clear: globalization requires adaptation in order to achieve success. What works in the United States may not work abroad! Understand your customer and deliver value! McDonald's generally adapts its menus to reflect local tastes. In the French case, it became apparent to McDonald's that customers were willing to pay a premium for the ambiance and the more expensive food items, including beer and espresso, that were added to the menu. This way, the French were able to enjoy their meal, beer, and espresso in comfort without being rushed.

To address the issue of ambiance, almost one-half of the 930 McDonald's outlets in France have been upgraded to a level that will be unrecognizable to an American. The Golden Arches are almost invisible; hardwood floors, exposed bricks, and armchairs are the norm. Furthermore, in order to blend in with the physical environment of the local area, McDonald's has adopted different themes. For example, the largest and most-frequented French McDonald's outlet is on the Champs Elysees with a cozy Parisian atmosphere, the McDonald's outlet on the Basque coast has a surfing theme, and the one located in the heart of the skiing area in Briancon features large stones, beams, and big heavy tables.

As they say, when in Rome, do as the Romans do—but don't sacrifice your business principles!

Source: Adapted from "McHaute Cuisine: Armchairs, TVs, and Espresso—Is It McDonald's?" *The Wall Street Journal*, August 30, 2002; pp. A1, A6 and **www.mcdonalds.com**.

Questions

1. What was McDonald's business strategy in France? Was it successful? How?
2. If you were to open a McDonald's franchise in India, what are some of the major factors that you would consider before making that investment?

Coca-Cola decided to boost profits by reactivating the sale of Limca, a popular Indian lemonade drink that it had acquired, rather than force Coca-Cola down the throats of Indians! Businesses today need employees at all levels to be open to varying ideas and viewpoints, and that can only be brought about by practicing cultural diversity. The success of companies like Samsung, Sony, Toyota, VW, Microsoft, IBM, GE, Lockheed Martin, Merck, Johnson & Johnson, Procter & Gamble, and so on can be largely attributed to their commitment to and appreciation of cultural diversity at work and in the marketplace. The key to the success of these companies is their willingness to adapt goods and services to meet local demand.

In the United States, federal laws require organizations to practice nondiscriminatory policies with regard to personnel recruitment, and this produces a diverse workforce (for example, visit **www.DiversityInc.com**) in terms of race, sex, and national origin. Texas A&M University, for example, is committed to Equal Employment Opportunity and Affirmative Action for minorities, women, veterans, and individuals with disabilities. The university's Affirmative Action Program can be viewed at **http://hr.tamu.edu/employment/action.html** on its Human Resources Department home page. The program's objective is to recruit, select, promote, pay, and take all personnel actions on the basis of professional abilities and qualifications. Companies that treated employees unfairly have paid a heavy price. For example, Home Depot agreed to pay $104 million in 1997 to settle a class action suit on behalf of 25,000 women who claimed they were denied promotions because they were female. Coca-Cola and Texaco, now part of ChevronTexaco, each paid well over $100 million to settle race discrimination cases in 2000. More recently, the largest ever class action suit related to gender discrimination was filed against Wal-Mart Corporation in July 2004 by all the female employees of that company.

reality CHECK   *By looking at the businesses around you, would you say that your hometown is culturally diverse?*

Measuring Gross National Product, Gross National Income, and Gross Domestic Product

LEARNING OBJECTIVE 9
Discuss why and how national output is measured and consider the rationale for using output based on purchasing power parity (PPP) when comparing countries.

Another equally important factor that impacts consumer behavior and business performance is income level, which when measured on a national scale is a country's **gross national product (GNP).** The GNP is the value of all *final* goods and services produced by a country's factors of production (regardless of where these factors are located) and sold on the market at current prices over a given time period, usually a year. The GNP is a summary measure of all goods, for example food, clothing, books, cars, and so on, and services, for example education, consulting, dry cleaning, haircutting, airlines, and so on, that a country's factors of production are capable of producing. It is also a measure of a country's living standard, including its health status and educational attainment. The output of goods and services is not possible without the help of factor inputs. The expenditures (*income* earned) tied to the employment of each factor—land, labor, capital, and technology—are called **gross national income (GNI)** and are equal to GNP.

Economists generally divide GNP among the four main uses for which a country's output of goods and services is purchased. These include

- **Consumption** (the expenditures of private domestic residents)
- **Investment** (the spending by private firms to build plant and equipment for future production)
- **Government expenditure** (the amount spent by the government)
- **Net exports** (the amount of goods and services sold overseas less the amount of goods and services bought from abroad)

The term *national income accounts* is used to describe this fourfold classification because a country's income, that is, its GNI, in fact equals its GNP. The reason for this equality is that every dollar used to purchase goods or services automatically ends up as somebody's income. A visit to your local hairstylist provides a sim-

gross national product (GNP) The value of all final goods and services produced in an economy and measured at current prices over a given time period, usually a year

gross national income (GNI) The expenditures that make up GNP and are equal to the income that the factors of production (land, labor, capital, and technology) receive

consumption The amount used by private domestic residents

investment The amount spent by private firms on new plant and equipment for future production and profit

government expenditure The amount spent by the government

net exports Exports minus imports of goods and services

ple example of how an increase in national output (in services) raises national income by the same amount. The $15 you pay the hairstylist for a haircut represents the market value of the service that he or she provides you, so your visit to the hairstylist raises GNP by $15. But the $15 you pay the hairstylist also raises his or her income by that amount. So national income GNI rises by $15 as well.

Countries these days report **gross domestic product (GDP)** rather than GNP as their primary measure of national economic performance. The GDP measures the total dollar value of all *final* goods and services produced each year *within* a country's borders regardless of who owns the resources (see Exhibit 1.7). For example, a Mexican migrant worker who works on a California farm will increase U.S. GDP, although she or he is not a U.S. citizen. On the other hand, GDP does not include profits earned by U.S. companies *overseas* or the goods and services produced by Americans overseas, since those products and services were produced abroad, not in the United States. Thus, GNP (or GNI) equals GDP plus *net receipts* of factor income from the rest of the world. These receipts are what domestic residents earn on the wealth they hold in other countries less the payments made to foreign owners of wealth located at home.

> **gross domestic product (GDP)** The total dollar value of all final goods and services produced each year within a country's borders

By breaking down GDP into its components, one could analyze how, for example, consumption is affected by a recession and the important role consumers play in the U.S. economy. This approach (as well as by utilizing the *World Development Report* as a source) allows for comparisons across countries and also provides evidence about why consumers in some countries are rich while others are not. A major drawback of GDP/GNP/GNI analysis is that these indicators do not include nonmarket (unpaid) activities such as housework, yard work, or volunteering. Therefore, when a person quits doing housework and hires a maid, or you quit doing your own yard work and hire a landscaper to mow your lawn, GDP, GNP, and GNI will increase.

The ultimate measure of economic success is a country's ability to generate a high *level* of and steady *growth* in the output of goods and services regardless of whether we use the GNP, GNI, or GDP standard. The higher the *level* and faster the *growth rate* of an economy, the richer and better off the consumers of that country are. The GNI, GNP, or GDP can be measured in current prices; this is called **nominal GNI, GNP, or GDP.** One can also measure GNI, GNP, or GDP on an inflation-adjusted basis; this is called **real GNI, GNP, or GDP.** Inflation basically moves the general price level up. Economists use a price index number to "deflate" a current, or nominal, GNI, GNP, or GDP to a real GNI, GNP, or GDP using a certain base year (the International Monetary Fund [IMF] currently uses 1995 as the base year; that is, the GDP deflator is 100 for 1995). (See Exhibit 1.8 on p. 32 for details.)

> **nominal GNI, GNP,** or **GDP** Economic output measured in current prices
>
> **real GNI, GNP,** or **GDP** Economic output measured on an inflation-adjusted basis

$$\text{Real GDP} = \frac{\text{nominal GDP}}{\text{GDP deflator}}$$

EXHIBIT 1.7

The Components of U.S. GDP, 2001

GDP 100%			
Private consumption 68%	Investment 21%	Government expenditures 14%	

Net exports –3%

Note: figures may not add up to 100% because of rounding error.

Source: World Bank, *World Development Report,* 2003.

For example,

$$\text{U.S. real GDP in 2001} = \frac{\text{U.S. nominal GDP in 2001}}{\text{GDP deflator in 2001}} = \frac{\text{U.S. \$10,082.2 billion}}{1.101}$$

$$= \text{U.S. \$9,157.3 billion in 1995 prices (real GDP in 1995 prices)}$$

When financial media like the *Financial Times* or *The Wall Street Journal* report economic growth in the United States or Japan or in any other country, the reference is to *real* GDP growth and not *nominal* GDP growth. Changes in nominal economic growth will include inflation for the period under consideration. Nominal GDP growth rates will provide a distorted view of GDP growth, especially for countries with high inflation rates.

EXHIBIT 1.8

U.S. Nominal and Real GDP, 1985—2001 (US$ billions)
Nominal GDP grows faster than real GDP because of inflation.

	Nominal GDP	GDP Deflator	Real GDP
1985	4,213.0	75.1	5,609.9
1986	4,452.9	76.8	5,798.0
1987	4,742.5	79.1	5,995.6
1988	5,108.3	81.8	6,244.9
1989	5,489.1	84.9	6,465.4
1990	5,803.2	88.2	6,579.6
1991	5,986.2	91.4	6,549.5
1992	6,318.9	93.6	6,751.0
1993	6,642.3	95.9	6,926.3
1994	7,054.3	97.9	7,205.6
1995	7,400.5	100.0	7,400.5
1996	7,813.2	101.9	7,667.5
1997	8,318.4	103.9	8,006.2
1998	8,781.5	105.2	8,347.4
1999	9,274.3	106.7	8,691.9
2000	9,824.6	108.6	9,046.6
2001	10,082.2	110.1	9,157.3

Source: International Monetary Fund, *International Financial Statistics Yearbook*, 2002.

Purchasing Power Parity

As you can infer from the preceding discussion, annual GNI per capita is an important measure of how well consumers of a country are doing in that particular year. It is determined by dividing a country's nominal GNI by the country's population for that year.

Exhibit 1.9 lists the world's ten largest economies in terms of their nominal GNI levels (after converting local currency GNI into U.S. dollars) in 2001. The third data column of the table provides the midyear population in 2001, and the GNI per capita is computed in column four. This table clearly brings home the fact that both the size of an economy and its per capita income are important factors that businesses must consider. Because nominal exchange rates of foreign currencies with respect to the U.S. dollar do not always reflect differences in inflation rates between the country under consideration and the United States, a country's GNI needs to be converted into international dollars using **purchasing power parity (PPP)** conversion factors.

At the PPP rate, one international dollar will have the same purchasing power in any country as one U.S. dollar has in the United States. Hence, when foreign country GNI is converted to the PPP basis, it allows for the comparison of GNIs among countries. The PPP approach is a true measure of the economic well-being of the citizens of a country. Exhibit 1.10 (on p. 34) lists the world's top ten countries in terms of their GNI based on PPP. When you carefully evaluate Exhibit 1.10, you will understand why businesspeople consider Brazil, China, India, and Russia to be important markets and competitors for the future. The greater the GNI per capita (PPP basis) in a country, the greater the purchasing power of the citizens in that country. The GNI (PPP basis) of the country as a whole is also important, since it gives businesses a feel for the country's potential market size.

purchasing power parity (PPP) The purchasing power of an international dollar, which will have the same purchasing power in any country as the U.S. dollar has in the United States

EXHIBIT 1.9

World's Ten Largest Economies, U.S. dollars 2001

Country	GNI (US$ billions)	Percentage of World GNI	Population (millions)	GNI per Capita (US$)
United States	9,900.70	31.43	284.0	34,870
Japan	4,574.20	14.52	127.1	35,990
Germany	1,948.00	6.18	82.2	23,700
United Kingdom	1,451.40	4.61	59.9	24,230
France	1,377.40	4.37	59.2	22,690
China	1,131.00	3.59	1271.9	890
Italy	1,123.50	3.57	57.7	19,470
Canada	661.90	2.10	31.0	21,340
Spain	586.90	1.86	39.5	14,860
Mexico	550.50	1.75	99.4	5,540
Others	8,194.50	26.01	4020.9	2,030
World Total	31,500.00	100.00	6132.8	5,140

Source: World Bank, *World Development Report,* 2003.

EXHIBIT 1.10

World's Ten Largest Economies, PPP Basis, U.S. dollars 2001

Country	PPP GNI (US$ billions)	Percentage of World PPP GNI	Population (millions)	PPP GNI per Capita (US$)
United States	9,900.70	21.34	284	34,870
China	5,415.00	11.67	1,272	4,260
Japan	3,487.00	7.51	127	27,430
India	2,530.00	5.45	1,033	2,450
Germany	2,098.00	4.52	82	25,530
France	1,495.00	3.22	59	25,280
United Kingdom	1,466.00	3.16	60	24,460
Italy	1,404.00	3.03	58	24,340
Brazil	1,286.00	2.77	173	7,450
Russia	1,255.00	2.70	145	8,660
Others	16,066.30	34.62	2,840	5,650
World Total	46,403.00	100.00	6,133	8,660

Note: The PPP conversion factors used here are from the World Bank's *World Development Report,* 2003, and are derived from the most recent round of price surveys conducted by the International Comparison Program, a joint project of the World Bank and the regional economic commissions of the United Nations.
Source: World Bank, *World Development Report,* 2003.

Business Cycles

business cycles The up- and downswings in real GNI, GNP, or GDP levels over time

The up- and downswings in real GNI, GNP, or GDP levels over time are called **business cycles.** These swings in real national output are not uniform or timely, and often they are erratic. The long economic boom of the 1990s in the United States made some people think that the business cycle was dead, but the collapse of the dotcom and tech companies in 2001 and 2002 proved otherwise. Business cycles are a regular feature of the capitalist system, but over the long run, real output always tends to show a steady increase. During the upswing, or expansion phase, output, employment, and investment all tend to rise, indicating a period of prosperity. Inflation, especially in the later stages of an economic upswing, tends to accelerate before the economy peaks (firms operate at close to full capacity). The country then begins the contraction phase when output, employment, investment, and inflation begin to fall, reflecting a period of hard times. The economy must reach the bottom, or trough, before a new cycle of expansion can begin. Economists have been studying—by establishing the causal linkages among various economic activities—business cycles for a long time in order to identify turning points so that appropriate policies could be implemented to prevent the boom and bust periods and smooth out the cycles. This has not been easy, especially since the turning points are apparent only after the fact.

 What companies in your area are involved in the export of goods or services?

The Digital Era

LEARNING OBJECTIVE 10
Evaluate the impact of the digital revolution on global businesses, governments, and societies.

What is the **digital era?** Innovations in information technology (IT—computers, software, telecommunications, and the Internet) are radically changing the way people live, communicate, and work. You have probably noticed that essentially everything we do in our daily lives, at home, at school, at play, and at work, is going through fundamental change. This period of transformation—adjusting our lifestyle to make the Internet and related technologies a part of our everyday lives— is called the digital era. While some of us like a slow pace of change, today's realities are different. New information technologies, of which the Internet is by far the most publicly visible form, are turning the world upside down as access to the technology spreads rapidly around the globe. The capacity and speed of communications networks has increased tremendously. As **bandwidth** (the amount of data and other information that can be transferred in a second over the Internet) expands and as communications costs fall, more and more computers (and people) will be linked together. The benefits of online communication will increase exponentially with the number of such connections. Increasingly, as networks take hold, they will reshape the way people (all over the world) live, entertain, communicate, and work. The fact is, those same technological changes that are transforming the business world now will also revolutionize the way government does its business, as well as the nature of our public life.

digital era The period of transformation within our lifestyle to make the Internet and related technologies a part of our everyday lives

bandwidth The amount of data and other information that can be transferred in a second via the Internet

E-Business

To understand why and how organizations in our economic system will be profoundly affected by the IT revolution, it is useful first to examine the enormous impact of the digital economy on business.

Women, even in villages of many developing countries, use the cell phone to determine current market price and demand for their products. Transacting small business with traders in metropolitan cities via the phone, these women can save valuable time and money by not commuting through traffic.

Internet-worked technologies are spawning new business models that are radically changing the basic operating structure in firms that have served the marketplace well for decades. For example, you can purchase music, videos, books, and a whole variety of things online from your home computer without having to visit a retail store. A whole set of companies like Amazon.com and eBay have entered the business scene to cater to such needs. The value of IT and the Internet lies in their capacity to store, retrieve, analyze, and communicate information instantly, anywhere, at negligible cost. If IT and the Internet are to be placed in the same league as previous technological revolutions (like the Industrial Revolution and the introduction of the railroad system in particular), three major questions must be addressed.[10]

- How radically does the technology change day-to-day life?
- How much does it require businesses to reorganize their production processes to become more consumer-friendly and efficient?
- What is the impact of the new technology on business across the whole economy, either by allowing existing products to be made more efficiently or by creating entirely new products?

Around the globe, commercial enterprises are scrambling to avoid being left behind in terms of efficiency as suppliers and customers latch on to Internet-related ways of doing business. Today, by virtue of Internet-worked communications, the transaction costs of many business activities (buying, selling, sourcing) are falling close to zero as the reach and speed of communications technologies increase exponentially and tools become more robust. E-commerce is only the tip of the iceberg that is remaking the rules of business. Several key trends are emerging.[11]

1. Companies are being transformed on a massive scale. Established businesses are undergoing a radical overhaul in strategy, structure, and process to meet the needs of the digital economy. For example, almost all automobile dealerships in the United States have introduced Internet sales managers, whose role is to quote a price up-front over the Internet to customers who are seeking to buy specific automobiles and to have a no-hassle buying experience.

2. Customers are becoming smarter and more demanding. With the vast amount of information readily available to them and with their improved ability to share knowledge, consumers are empowered as never before. Consumers expect—even demand—the customization of goods and services to meet their individual needs, and they want it right away. Again, in the automobile industry, several companies like Autobytel (**www.autobytel.com**) have evolved. One could sit by a computer terminal and connect with Autobytel to research, buy, or sell automobiles on the basis of customized specifications.

3. Business is becoming more nimble. More than ever before, agility and flexibility drive competitive advantage in business. Authoritarian management structures and bureaucratic decision-making processes—in large or small businesses—are all likely to suffer in the digital economy. For example, Dell computer's manufacturing philosophy is based on a system of flexible, customized production, which enables Dell to dominate the PC market. Dell is able to maintain very low inventories, offer attractive prices, and also adjust production to changing consumer demand along and the constant introduction of new and powerful computer chips (and related components).

4. Knowledge is the key asset. The abundance of information and the speed of communication imply that innovation based on this knowledge and speed will be the key to business success. Because of its quality higher-education system, India has an abundant supply of talented IT professionals who can provide world-class IT services at competitive rates. Several Indian companies like

Tata Consulting Services, Infosys, and Wipro have successfully utilized their IT and software expertise along with their knowledge of the United States' corporate needs to attract outsourcing business to India. Companies in the United States will be forced to compete by focusing attention on developing next-generation industries in biotechnology, nanotechnology, and digital media.

5. Transparency and openness are crucial for business success. Increasingly, customers and markets demand openness (as opposed to secrecy and a strong emphasis on turf protection) in company culture and transparency in company information (especially accounting and financial). As companies move into the digital era, they discover a competitive advantage in making information and knowledge available to their networked partners. In the airline industry, for example, special discounted fares were in the past disclosed only to travel agents who charged a fee to the customer. Now, discount fares are made readily available on the airline's website or with online travel services like Travelocity.com, Orbitz.com, Cheapfares.com, and Expedia.com for easy access by all customers.

In the emerging business models, success will be achieved by those businesses that involve their suppliers, their infrastructure providers, and—perhaps most importantly—their customers in a network in which they can build value together. The idea of partnership is very real in the new e-business world.[12]

Within the e-business environment, there are several specialized sub-e-businesses that deal with certain segments of the economy. Most customers, students in particular, have quite a bit of experience purchasing goods (like CDs, books, stereos, etc.) directly from online retailers like Amazon.com, **www.amazon.com.** Transactions between Amazon.com (the business) and you (the customer) are called **B2C** (business-to-consumer) e-commerce. Similarly, when Amazon.com (the business) purchases this textbook from Houghton Mifflin (this book's publisher) and sells it to you, the transaction between Amazon.com and Houghton Mifflin is called **B2B** (business-to-business) e-commerce. By improving the flow, accuracy, and timeliness of information, secure Internet-enabled systems provide greater transparency and efficiency at all points along the supply chain. Simply put, the Internet is a continuation of technological improvements that deliver information faster and cheaper, reduce search and transaction costs in online markets, and improve the management of product transportation and inventories. These savings come from both cheaper information and cheaper inputs (through increased competition).[13]

B2C Business–to-consumer electronic commerce

B2B Business-to-business electronic commerce

EXHIBIT 1.11

The Supply Chain

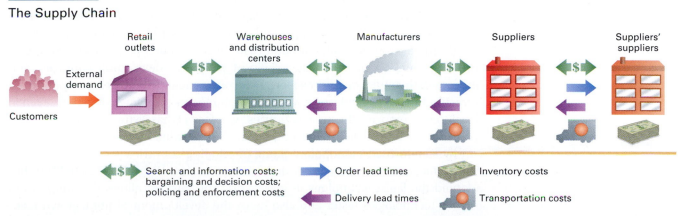

Source: From Thomas F. Siems, "B2B E-Commerce: Why the New Economy Lives," *Southwest Economy,* Federal Reserve Bank of Dallas, July–August 2001, p. 3. Reprinted with permission.

The Internet is of tremendous importance, but it is only a small segment of a nation's economic output. However, the fact that the Internet is important does not imply that it must be profitable. The bursting of the Internet bubble in 2000 clearly exposed the common misconception that importance equals profitability.[14] As we have noted, there are many similarities between the IT-enabled technologies (especially fiber-optic cable and related business) of 2000 and the United States' railway mania of the 1870s. In the 1870s, would-be rail millionaires raised vast sums of money on the stock market to finance proposed railway lines by misleading investors on their companies' business prospects. Most railway companies never paid a penny to shareholders, and many went bust (just like Global Crossings, Worldcom, and the dotcoms of the early 2000s in the United States), largely because irrational exuberance and overinvestment created excess capacity. Even so, the railways brought huge economic benefits to the U.S. economy long after their share prices crashed. The lesson is that although the IT and Internet bubbles burst in 2000, these may still produce long-term economic gains. Many investors, however, will have lost their shirts in the bargain! It is a sobering thought that 99 percent of the 5000 railway companies that once existed in the United States are no longer around. The same is true of 2000 car firms that once existed in the United States. According to a study by investment bankers Goldman Sachs, profits and share prices of the early electricity firms in the United States were disappointing, despite the industry's profound effect on the economy.[15]

Despite the collapse of many IT and dotcom firms and the failure of many e-marketplaces, the fundamentals behind B2B e-commerce remain strong. A major risk that has emerged since September 11, 2001, in B2B e-commerce is the impact of terrorism (especially on transportation systems) along the supply chain. Efficiency improvements and cost savings achieved through B2B e-commerce have already led to higher productivity growth and lower costs and prices, which should allow Internet-enabled economies to grow faster with low inflation. While most of the gains will occur between businesses, the greatest long-term beneficiaries of B2B e-commerce will be the consumers, who will enjoy lower prices and higher living standards.

Impact of IT on Globalization, Culture, Society, and Politics

Although developing countries are widely thought to be losing out from ever-faster technological change, the Internet and related technologies are getting cheaper all the time, making timely information available instantaneously and globally. For example, *A Better Life Foundation* (**www.ablf.org**), a not-for-profit European organization, ships older PCs (as they get replaced by their sophisticated European owners) to African countries like Burkina Faso for reuse. Such programs of computer recycling enhance the computer skills of people in developing countries and improve their employment prospects. Everyone benefits. Countries with poor fixed infrastructure need not despair. Mobile telephones are popular everywhere, even in developing countries. In poor countries, wireless IT has extra advantages, since fixed-line telephones in these countries are woefully inadequate and inefficiently run by state-owned monopolies. Some developing countries have created better communications infrastructures than rich countries, since they started late but adopted the latest technology at lower cost. The Internet allows the adoption of outside technologies faster and also helps the development of homegrown technologies that often use open-source (free, e.g., Linux) software. It also enables closer collaboration within and among countries. Governments need to remove obstacles and pursue transparent policies that encourage foreign investment and competition.

The IT revolution has barely started, yet its impact is being felt globally. Unlike changes brought about by such technological revolutions as electricity and the railroad, which took decades to spread around the globe, the IT revolution has been almost instantaneous. This reinforces the fact that IT and globalization are closely related. By reducing communications costs, IT has helped to globalize production and has encouraged a freer flow of goods and services, including capital, across national boundaries. In fact, IT acts as a catalyst in the globalization process by bringing down operating costs.

Internet and related technologies make many societies (especially political authorities in such societies as China, Central Asia, and the Middle East) uneasy. Political authorities in some societies, especially in nondemocratic ones, wonder if uncensored information from countries abroad will corrupt local cultures and bring about social and political instability. Advances in communications technology could also shift the balance of power between ordinary people and their government and make dissent and tax avoidance safer. Internet-related communications help make societies and corporations less hierarchical because of greater access to everyone concerned. However, it is unlikely that Internet and related technologies will remain or even thrive completely free of government interference. Most people like what modern technology has to offer. Developing countries are now making the same transition that the United States, Europe, and Japan made earlier, only they're making it faster and cheaper. In the transition period, this could cause political strain, especially in nondemocratic societies. Failure to adapt is bound to hurt some countries more than others. As current technologies get cheaper, they will spread the world over. While some governments will hold their countries back, the vast majority will move them forward.[16]

reality CHECK   *How has the Internet changed your daily life?*

Careers in Business

Just as the study of business is fascinating, so are careers in business, and they are as varied as the topics of study and as rewarding as the study itself. Successful completion of an undergraduate degree in business opens up a world of challenges and opportunities for motivated graduates. Careers in business are well-paying, especially in countries that practice the free enterprise system. Professional opportunities for business graduates occur in the private sector and in the public and not-for-profit sectors of an economy.

In the private sector, careers can be developed in publicly held corporations, in privately held businesses, or in small businesses as an entrepreneur. In the public and not-for-profit sectors, career opportunities exist in federal, state, and local government agencies; in not-for-profit organizations or nongovernmental organizations (NGOs); and in colleges and universities. As you can see, business careers span the whole spectrum—domestic and international as well as public and private. Yet, for those of you who are enterprising and those who crave personal and financial freedom, starting a small business with all its challenges may provide you with the greatest chance for fulfilling the dream of doing what you want and achieving financial independence. Whatever the dream, starting your own business, one that meets your long-term goals and consumer demand, calls for hard work and dedication.

Your success can be measured by the personal freedom, financial well-being, and job satisfaction that come with being an entrepreneur.

At the end of each chapter of this text, there is a brief write-up on career opportunities in the area of business (accounting, consulting, finance, information systems, international business, management, and marketing) considered in that chapter. So, the focus of these write-ups is on institutions that offer business career opportunities. For those of you who would enjoy working for large corporations like GE, IBM, Ford, and so on, either domestically or internationally, the first thing you may want to do is to identify the firm that interests you. The 500 largest U.S. corporations are called the *Fortune 500* companies and the list is published by *Fortune* magazine each year. If you are interested in working for any of the world's largest 500 corporations, you may want to look into the *Financial Times Global 500,* which is published by the *Financial Times* newspaper of London. Details of the activities of all these companies can be found on their corporate websites, and most of them also list career opportunities there as well. Major privately held businesses, although few in number (e.g., Bechtel, **www.bechtel.com**), also have their own websites that you can surf to identify job opportunities. Not-for-profit organizations, domestic and international, offer challenging opportunities for business graduates as well. Organizations like the Red Cross, the United Way, and CARE offer interesting and fulfilling business career opportunities. International institutions like the United Nations offer absorbing career opportunities with attractive (tax-free) salaries; however, the work environment can be quite demanding, especially when one works overseas. Finally, federal, state, and local governments also offer interesting and stable career opportunities. Since government agencies are not driven by profits or competition, they generally tend not to lay off employees. However, while careers in government do offer job security, salary levels may not match those of the private sector.

There are numerous websites that focus on business careers. One site that you may want to visit is Careers in Business, **www.careers-in-business.com,** which has a number of very useful links as well as an excellent list of "Recommended Books on Jobs in Business," which could prove to be a valuable tool as you seek to identify the business career of your choice.

Summary

In this introductory chapter, the objective is to acquaint you with the basic concepts of business operations.

LEARNING OBJECTIVE 1

Identify the three major factors that are impacting business today and discuss the roles of for-profit and not-for-profit organizations in an economy.

The three major issues that are significantly impacting business today, which are the themes of this textbook, are *globalization*, *technology*, and *ethics*. As more countries adopt open trading systems, business is becoming increasingly global in nature. Rapid advances in information technology and the Internet are encouraging the growth of new business, and also changing the way business is done. Finally, firms must be ethically managed if they are to survive and deliver value to investors and customers alike, and also be successful in the long term. The primary role of business is to create value for the customer and meet the consumer's unmet needs in a profitable manner. If a firm is not profitable, it will not be able to remain in business. However, not all firms have a profit motive. The primary objective of not-for-profit organizations like educational institutions and charitable organizations is to serve the public. Even not-for-profit organizations need to cover costs, or they will be forced to shrink or close down operations.

LEARNING OBJECTIVE 2

Summarize the evolution of business in the United States and explain the key issues that are impacting its outlook for the future.

The evolution of business in the United States can be traced from the time when the first settlers from Europe crossed the Atlantic Ocean. The initial business climate largely reflected a free market, or laissez-faire, system, coupled with the availability of abundant land (and natural resources) and a constant and growing inflow of labor and capital, in the beginning from Europe. The Industrial Revolution (1815–1875) transformed the United States from an agrarian economy to an industrial giant that fostered the growth of the factory system, which involved efficient mass production of standardized products under one roof. Business prospects accelerated with the introduction of the railroad (1875–1913), which led to the westward (coast-to-coast) expansion of the United States and increased the need for goods and services. This was also an era of mergers and acquisitions that resulted in the growth of huge companies, which dominated the U.S. market. Public concern enabled the introduction of antitrust policies to curb anticompetitive business practices. A new era (1913–1944) of manufacturing began in 1913 when the Ford Motor Company initiated assembly line manufacturing using scientific management techniques. Finally, at the end of World War II, the United States and other major nations of the world saw the need to work together to increase trade and investment among countries as a way to propel global business growth. Several international organizations were set up to facilitate the process, and this started the globalization era—the first major element impacting the outlook for U.S. business.

The two other major elements are technology and ethics. Advances in technology have moved the United States from an agrarian to a manufacturing to a service and now to a knowledge-based economy. The future of U.S. business will be heavily influenced by the successful evolution of its knowledge workers and by how ethically its managers function in the global economy.

LEARNING OBJECTIVE 3

Explain the fundamental features of the free enterprise, or capitalist, system that make it efficient and dynamic.

The free market system, also called the laissez-faire or capitalist system, is based on private property rights, the pursuit of profits, and the freedom to choose. The system espouses two major principles. First, it calls for minimum government intervention in the marketplace; that is, entrepreneurs should be allowed to participate in any commercial venture they see fit with ease of entry into and exit out of the industry. Since entrepreneurs take a risk by investing their time and resources to

develop business and profits, the role of government is to ensure that these enterprises do not get involved in illegal (drugs, money laundering, environmental pollution, employee discrimination) or anticompetitive activities. Second, the free market system operates on the basis of supply and demand, where consumers are the source of demand and producers are the source of supply. In the marketplace, supply and demand interact to determine the price of goods and services. The free market system is efficient because supply will always (in the medium term) equal demand and there will be no surplus or shortage. In the short term, if there is a surplus (supply exceeding demand), price will fall until the surplus vanishes. Similarly, if there is a shortage (demand exceeding supply), price will rise until the shortage vanishes. From the above discussion it is clear that the free market system is both efficient and dynamic.

LEARNING OBJECTIVE 4

Discuss what is meant by *market structure,* and explain why most industries fall under the banner of monopolistic competition.

Market structure describes the level of competition (number of producers of goods or services) within an industry. In the free enterprise system there are four different forms of market structure—pure competition, monopolistic competition, oligopoly, and monopoly. In pure competition there are several producers of identical products, in monopolistic competition there are several producers of similar (not identical) products, in oligopoly there are few producers of similar products who supply a significant share of the market demand, and in monopoly there is only one producer who supplies the whole market. Producers can have an influence over prices, depending on the level of competition in the industry. The monopolist has the power to set market prices, while a producer under pure competition will not be able to influence market prices at all. In the real world, most of the goods and services that are produced are not identical; they are similar, and that is the reason why most industries fall in the category of monopolistic competition. While pure competition is best for society as a whole, in practice, firm concentration ratios (especially in the United States) seem to indicate that most industries fall within the monopolistic competition framework.

LEARNING OBJECTIVE 5

Discuss the rationale for countries wanting to choose other forms (rather than capitalism) of economic systems and explain what direction most countries are moving toward.

Apart from the free market system, the other major economic systems today are the command, or planned, economic system; the mixed economic system; and the transition economic system. In the command economic system, the government plans the production of goods and services on the basis of national goals and an elaborate analysis of sources and uses of resources available to the economy. The government's objectives are to utilize as many domestic resources as possible, employ whoever is willing to work in order to solve unemployment and poverty, and minimize income inequality among workers by diminishing wage differentials. In so doing it provides little choice to workers about where to work and what type of work they can undertake. The command economic system is based on the elimination of wasteful conspicuous consumption. The government decides how much of the goods and services that are produced consumers can purchase and at what prices. While the command economic system seeks to minimize the exploitation of workers, it does so at great expense to efficiency and consumer choice.

A mixed economic system is one that exhibits elements of both the capitalist and the planned (or command) systems. Not all services (e.g., defense and social welfare) will be provided in a purely capitalist system; in the mixed economic system the government plays a crucial role in providing these services while at the same time procuring goods (fighter aircraft, naval fleets, ammunition, etc.) from private companies. The trend these days in mixed economies is to gradually move away from state enterprises to private businesses. This is being achieved through the sale of state enterprises to private entrepreneurs—a process called privatization. In 1989, after years of state control of all productive assets, the Soviet Union broke up. This started market-oriented reforms in Russia and the former communist economies of Central and Eastern Europe and Central Asia. The move from central planning to market-oriented, open trade economies is called economic transition and is aimed at ending the inefficiencies of central planning.

LEARNING OBJECTIVE 6
Explain how the factors of production impact the supply of goods and services in an economy.

Every output of goods and services requires two or more inputs. Economists define inputs as factors of production that are used by firms in their production processes. Traditionally, the factors of production have been divided into four major categories. First there is land and the natural resources beneath it. The quality of the land and the resources beneath it determine how productive it can be. Second is labor, which consists of human time spent in productive activities. Entrepreneurs play an important role in business creation and development. Third is capital, which comes in two major forms: money that is utilized to set up a business and pay for its operation (paying salaries and buying raw materials), and durable goods like machinery that are produced by the economy in order to make yet other

goods. Finally, there is technology, which makes the production process more efficient through the introduction of better and cheaper ways of getting things done.

LEARNING OBJECTIVE 7
Discuss how business performance is measured in a capitalist system versus a socialist system and how the objectives of for-profit businesses differ from the objectives of state-owned enterprises and of not-for-profit organizations.

In the free market system, businesses exist to meet specific consumer needs and to maximize profits. In addition, firms try to maximize shareholder wealth (dividends plus increase in stock prices) over time. Many socialist managers believe in a broader corporate objective than just maximizing shareholder wealth. These business leaders would like to maximize stakeholder wealth, which encompasses the welfare of all a business's constituents: customers, management, employees, suppliers, and society.

In several developing countries, governments consider state enterprises a source of employment generation. A related objective of these governments is to minimize income inequalities. In state enterprises, most employees are paid about the same.

The primary objective of not-for-profit organizations is to serve society. They provide goods and services that would otherwise not be made available and without which society as a whole would be worse off.

LEARNING OBJECTIVE 8
Explain the important role consumers play in determining corporate performance and show how businesses try to identify consumer needs.

Firms are in the business of providing goods and services to customers for profit. Without customers, businesses will cease to exist. Businesses constantly try to identify consumer needs in order to develop products and services that can be sold profitably. Given the crucial role consumers play in an economy, businesses are eager to know how positive consumers feel about themselves and their environment. Businesses also spend significant amounts of money to research and analyze consumer cultural diversity, demographics, and psychographics to identify the needs of specific consumer groups and to study the minds of consumers to influence their perception of those needs.

LEARNING OBJECTIVE 9
Discuss why and how national output is measured and consider the rationale for using output based on purchasing power parity (PPP) when comparing countries.

An important factor that impacts business performance is income level, which when measured on a national scale is a country's gross national product (GNP). The GNP is the value of all *final* goods and services produced by a country's factors of production (regardless of where these factors are located) and sold on the market at current prices over a given time period, usually a year. It is also a measure of a country's living standard, including its health status and educational attainment. By breaking GNP down into its components, one could analyze how, for example, consumption is affected by a recession and the importance of the role consumers play in an economy. The higher the *level* and faster the *growth rate* of an economy, the richer and better off the consumers of that country are. At the PPP rate, one international dollar will have the same purchasing power in any country as one U.S. dollar has in the United States. Hence, when foreign country GNI (equal to GNP) is converted to the PPP basis, it allows for the comparison of GNIs among countries. The PPP approach is a true measure of the economic well-being of the citizens of a country. The greater the GNI per capita (PPP basis) of a country, the greater is the purchasing power of the citizens of that country. The GNI (PPP basis) of the country as a whole is also important, since it gives businesses a feel for the country's potential market size.

LEARNING OBJECTIVE 10
Evaluate the impact of the digital era on global businesses, governments, and societies.

Innovations in information technology (IT—computers, software, telecommunications, and the Internet) are radically changing the way people live, communicate, and work. This period of transformation— adjusting our lifestyle to make the Internet and related technologies a part of our everyday lives—is called the digital era. Information technologies, of which the Internet is by far the most publicly visible form, are turning the world upside down as access to the technologies spreads rapidly around the globe. These technologies are having an enormous impact on business, spawning new business models that are radically changing the basic operating structure in firms that have served the marketplace well for decades. Several key trends are emerging: companies are being transformed on a massive scale; customers are becoming smarter and more demanding; business is becoming more nimble; knowledge is becoming a key asset; and transparency and openness are becoming crucial for business success. In the emerging business models, success will be achieved by those businesses that involve their suppliers, their infrastructure providers, and—perhaps most importantly—their customers in a network where they can build value together.

The Internet and related technologies are not only here to stay; they will also play an extremely important role as an engine of economic growth and development in countries. The key issue is how fast Internet and related technologies diffuse across national boundaries from developed to developing countries. With information technology advancing in leaps and bounds, and the price of semiconductor chips and software falling all the time, developing countries that have just started investing in IT are obtaining a lot more for each dollar invested in this technology than did countries that invested earlier. The impact of these technologies on education, family planning, and health care, as well as business, in developing countries is remarkable. The Internet will help bridge the gap between the developed and developing countries, but the latter will need to keep their markets open and allow new technologies to come in while at the same time implementing reforms that raise the level of education in their countries.

The success of Internet and related technologies depends on how effectively and widely these technologies can be put to use by businesses to boost efficiency and growth. Countries with open economic and political systems will see big gains overall. The IT industry's rapid growth in any country will have to go hand in hand with minimal government controls and regulations.

Chapter Questions

1. What is profit? How might you try to improve profits if your company is not doing as well as you think it should?

2. Historically, business evolved in the United States through four distinct periods. List the periods and mention one or two key factors that influenced business development during each. Pick one of the periods and explain in detail what type of business development took place then.

3. What is globalization, and what are the origins and effects of globalization on U.S. business?

4. What is capitalism? How are resources allocated in a free market system? Is this an efficient system for business?

5. Why is a "purely competitive" market structure best for consumers and society alike? Is it good for business as well?

6. What is a monopoly, and why are consumers and governments opposed to having monopolies in their economies?

7. What are the major flaws of the command economic system? Explain how this system essentially led to the downfall of economies like the Soviet Union.

8. Although many countries claim to be capitalist, none of the countries practice pure capitalism. Why? So, what system do the majority of countries practice? Where do the transition economies fit in the scheme of things?

9. Explain what the major factors of production are. Which factor do you think will play a crucial role in the United States' business future, and why?

10. Compare shareholder wealth maximization with stakeholder wealth maximization. Which approach do you prefer, and why?

11. What are the pros and cons of keeping state-owned enterprises? Would you suggest that all state-owned enterprises be privatized? Why?

12. Not-for-profit organizations play extremely important roles in countries. Pick a not-for-profit organization that you are familiar with and determine its primary objectives, its organization, and its recent performance.

13. Culture's role in business is extremely important, both domestically and internationally. Identify a product that you use or see every day and trace the role of culture in its design, development, and promotion (advertising).

14. What are the four major components of GDP? Which component drives U.S. economic growth, and why? What is the "bellwether" indicator that businesses closely watch to determine the outlook for their industry?

15. Pick any Latin American country and develop a table like Exhibit 1.8. Graph nominal and real GDP over time for that country. How does the country's real GDP compare with its nominal GDP, and why?

16. In the current global business environment, if you are considering exporting a particular item, will you look at nominal GNI or PPP-based GNI of countries to decide which country to export to? Why? What would your top five countries of choice to export to be?

17. Explain and analyze the impact of the Internet on business.

18. We have seen a number of e-businesses come and go. Why do you think that some of these companies failed? Do you see any challenges that e-commerce is likely to face? How may they be overcome?

Interpreting Business News

1. Business newspapers such as the *Financial Times* and *The Wall Street Journal* may at times state that "Consumer confidence is at [say] a 5-year low: Signs of crumbling faith in the U.S. economy fuel prospect for interest rate cut by Fed." How will a cut in interest rates help businesses and consumers?

2. Because business is global, you will come across reports from companies indicating that they anticipate rising sales revenue but at the same time expect profits to decline. What do you think is going on in the marketplace?

3. On several occasions, Federal Reserve Bank chair Allan Greenspan has expressed confidence that U.S. productivity growth will continue because of corporate spending on technology. What does *productivity growth* mean? How does technology spending by companies help productivity growth?

Web Assignments

1. Visit McDonald's website, **www.mcdonalds.com,** surf that website, and go to some of the company's country sites and study their menus. What can you say about McDonald's menus in foreign countries? Pick a particular non-U.S. and non-European country where McDonald's does business and explain that country's menu.

2. Visit Coca-Cola's home page, **www.cocacola.com,** select a foreign brand product Coca-Cola has acquired, and write a one-page (double-spaced) report on that product. Did you know that Coca-Cola owns and sells many foreign brands that you have never heard of in the United States?

3. The *Economic Report of the President*, which is an annual report on the state of the U.S. economy, is prepared by the President's Council of Economic Advisors and delivered by the president to the U.S. Congress. It is an extremely important document with a lot of facts and figures. Thanks to the Internet, issues of this document are now available on the Web at **http://www.gpoaccess.gov/eop/ index.html.** Pick the section that deals with the United States in the international economy. What are the key factors contributing to increased integration of the U.S. economy into the rest of the world?

4. Visit Panasonic's homepage, **www.panasonic.com,** which shows Panasonic electronic gadgets you see and use every day. Where is Panasonic's corporate headquarters? Visit their corporate site and write a one-page report (double spaced) on Panasonic's corporate philosophy. What is the type of consumer most important to Panasonic?

Portfolio Projects

Exploring Your Own Case in Point

Throughout this text you will find many examples of real companies to help illustrate how the concepts you are learning about are applied in real business situations. In particular, we will follow three companies—Sony, McDonald's, and DaimlerChrysler—in detail through the Case in Point boxed features. The Portfolio Project at the end of every chapter takes that Case in Point concept to the next step by helping you explore a company of your own choosing and enhancing your understanding of basic business principles.

The objective of this project is to enable you to conduct an independent comprehensive analysis of a large company (e.g., a Fortune 500 company). Select a company that you admire, a company that intrigues you, or a company that you always wanted to know more about. Select a company that is publicly traded (such as one listed on the New York Stock Exchange), so that various types of information (financial and otherwise) are readily available. You should be able to obtain information from web searches and from your library. Library sources include *The International Directory of Company Histories* (Chicago: St. James Press), company annual reports, and reports from rating agencies such as Standard & Poor's, Moody's, and Value Line. By answering questions at the end of each chapter, you should be able to understand your company better. Each chapter focuses on a specific topic and the end-of-chapter questions will encourage you to analyze how that particular topic relates to your company. You will follow your company through every chapter of the book, and by the time you have completed Chapter 18, you will have learned almost everything about your chosen company! (Hint: Be sure to keep a bibliography of all the sources you use —both print and electronic. This bibliography will provide useful resources as you answer questions in later chapters. Also, your instructor may require a complete bibliography as part of this assignment.)

After reading this chapter you should be prepared to answer some basic questions related to the type and nature of company that you have chosen to follow.

1. Determine when and where your company was established and its line of business. What are the major products and services provided by your company?

2. Is your company a private, public, or state-owned firm? How is business performance measured in your company? Is your company a for-profit or not-for-profit company?

3. What is the market structure of the industry in which your company operates? How did you come to that conclusion? How has information technology impacted your company?

4. Who is the target audience of your company? How would you break down your company's consumers based on demographics?

Starting Your Own Business

Many students who take an introductory business course do so because they are thinking about starting their own business. Many instructors use a business planning project as a way to help students understand the interrelatedness of all the topics that are covered during the course. An essential first step to starting a new enterprise is developing a business plan. The business plan reflects the goals, strategies, and daily operations of the firm. Business plans are comprised of a number of components. Following the organization of your text, these broad components could include: the nature of contemporary business (Chapters 1–4), which covers issues related to the macro- and microeconomic environments in which your business will operate; management (Chapters 5–7), which delves into firm-level organizational issues; marketing (Chapters 8–10), which addresses the selling of goods and services; accounting (Chapters 11–12), which emphasizes the importance of bookkeeping in a firm; finance (Chapters 13–15), which identifies the various funding options available to firms; and operations and information technology (Chapters 16–18), which explores the role of information technology in facilitating day-to-day business operations.

The Portfolio Project at the end of every chapter includes questions on Starting Your Own Business. These questions are intended to provide you with the opportunity to compile your own business plan. In addition, Chapter 4 is devoted to addressing issues related to small businesses and entrepreneurship. Furthermore, you can find web-based information on how to compose a business plan by connecting to the Small Business Administration's website (**www.sba.gov**) and clicking on "Starting Your Business."

Before you begin this project, think about a business that you would like to start. Perhaps you have an idea for a completely new product or service; or maybe you have thought of a way to improve on an existing one. Whatever your business idea might be, these exercises will help you think it through in detail. Perhaps you too could be an entrepreneur!

After reading this chapter you should be able to address some basic issues related to the input and output of your firm, the firm's performance measures, and the impact of technology.

1. Describe the major inputs that will be used by your firm and the sources of these resources. Is the supply of inputs stable or is it volatile? What is your strategy for maintaining an uninterrupted supply of inputs at relatively stable prices?

2. How will you determine the market for your products or services? Will you analyze consumer diversity and demographics? What are the factors that will help you decide on an ideal location for your business?

3. Is yours a for-profit or not-for-profit business? Will your business be private or public? How do you plan to reinvest and grow your business? How will you determine success or failure in your business? How would you handle business failure, i.e., what is your exit strategy? What ethical standards have you set for your business?

4. Describe how you will use information technology to make your business efficient.

Test Prepper

You've read the chapter, studied the key terms, and the exam is any day now. Think you are ready to ace it? Take this sample test to gauge your comprehension of chapter material. You can check your answers at the back of the book.

True/False Questions

Please indicate if the following statements are true or false:

_____ 1. Business is global in nature.

_____ 2. The goal of every business is to make a profit.

_____ 3. Profit is the difference between revenue and expenses.

_____ 4. When companies merge, the level of competition in the industry increases.

_____ 5. The economic system followed by the United States is called democratic socialism.

_____ 6. The transition economies are economies that are moving away from a system of free markets toward greater government control of productive assets.

_____ 7. Business ethics is not an issue as long as companies conduct business legally.

_____ 8. Selling products and services at a low price is more important than understanding consumer needs for business to be successful.

_____ 9. It does matter whether business uses nominal GNI or PPP-based GNI to determine market potential in countries.

_____ 10. The digital era is a fad and is unlikely to impact how business is conducted today or in the future.

Multiple-Choice Questions

Choose the best answer.

_____ 1. Peter Drucker defined business as organizations that create

  a. profit.
  b. goods and services.
  c. risk.
  d. value for the customer.
  e. revenue.

_____ 2. Which of the following statements is *not* true about the U.S. economy?

  a. The Industrial Revolution transformed the United States from an agrarian economy to an industrial giant.
  b. The factory system led to specialization of labor.

  c. The railroad era turned the U.S. into a unified market from coast to coast, leading to antitrust issues.
  d. The assembly line era became incompatible with the formation of labor unions.
  e. The post–World War II era started the age of globalization.

_____ 3. The free market system is based on all of the following *except*

  a. the theory of supply and demand.
  b. the notion of private property.
  c. the freedom to choose and enter into and exit out of industry.
  d. the assumption that the government knows best.
  e. the notion of property rights.

_____ 4. The key issues that affect the market structure include all of the following *except*

  a. the number of firms that operate in that industry.
  b. the ease of entry into that industry.
  c. the suppliers' control over prices in that industry.
  d. the similarity of products or services in that industry.
  e. the ownership of businesses in the industry.

_____ 5. Which of the following statements regarding the command economic system is *not* true?

  a. The government decides what, how much, and at what price goods and services are to be provided.
  b. The government's goal is to employ whoever is willing to work.
  c. The government allocates resources efficiently.
  d. The government tries to minimize income inequality.
  e. Consumers have little say in the system.

_____ 6. Which of the following is *not* a factor of production?

  a. Land and the natural resources beneath it
  b. Labor, including entrepreneurs
  c. Money and capital goods
  d. Government regulations
  e. Technology

_____ 7. Several countries would like business to maximize stakeholder wealth for all the following reasons *except*

    a. it takes into consideration the welfare of all business's constituents: customers, employees, suppliers, and society.

    b. it focuses more on long-term benefits than maximizing shareholder wealth does.

    c. it treats labor as more than a mere factor of production.

    d. it means that employees can be hired and fired easily.

    e. it is more responsible than maximizing shareholder wealth.

_____ 8. Business success depends heavily on understanding the consumer, whose consumption pattern depends on all of the following *except*

    a. how positive consumers feel about themselves and their jobs.

    b. population demographics.

    c. cultural diversity.

    d. inventory levels.

    e. psychographics.

_____ 9. PPP-based national income level is important for all of the following reasons *except*

    a. it is a good measure for comparing potential business opportunities across countries.

    b. it is a true measure of the size of an economy.

    c. it is a realistic measure of the wealth of the citizens of a country.

    d. it identifies the value of all goods and services produced by a country.

    e. it allows for comparison of GNI between countries.

_____ 10. The impact of the digital era on business is apparent from all of the following facts *except*

    a. companies are being transformed on a massive scale.

    b. customers are becoming smarter by using the Internet.

    c. business is becoming more nimble.

    d. developing countries have been able to adopt the latest technology at lower cost.

    e. developing countries are being left behind.

Want more questions? Visit the student website at **http://college.hmco.com/business/student/** (select Gaspar, *Introduction to Business*) and take the ACE quizzes for more practice.

2

The Environment of Business

| Introduction

| **Evaluating the Business Environment**
  Major Goals of Economic Management
  Policy Tools to Manage the Economy

| **The Global Nature of Business**
  Why Do Countries Trade or Invest Overseas?
  Theory of Absolute and Comparative Advantage in Trade
  Barriers to International Trade and Investments
  The Foreign Exchange Market and the Exchange Rate

| **The Rise of Globalization**
  The World Trade Organization
  Regional Trading Blocs

| **Going International**
  Export-Import Business
  Licensing and Franchising
  International Joint Ventures and Strategic Alliances
  Multinational Enterprises

| Careers in International Business

Learning Objectives

After studying this chapter, you should be able to

1 Define the major goals of effective economic management.

2 Summarize the key policy tools available to manage an economy.

3 Explain why trade is better than no trade for society as a whole.

4 Evaluate the different forms of trade and foreign investment barriers and their impact on business, consumers, and governments.

5 Compare the rationales behind countries' choices of exchange rate regimes.

6 Describe the evolution of globalization.

7 Summarize the stages of regional integration and explain its pros and cons.

8 Identify the major regional trading blocs and explain why some have succeeded while others have not.

9 Define and summarize the various methods of conducting business internationally.

10 Explain the major strategic reasons why multinational enterprises go abroad.

From Garlic to Biomedical Science: Adapting Business to Environmental Change

Although garlic is used primarily as a food-flavoring herb today, it has historically been a remedy for a wide variety of health conditions and diseases. Studies by the U.S. Department of Agriculture indicate that garlic has become a popular nutrition item in the United States, and has also gained scientific credibility as a significant contributor to good health. Garlic consumption in the United States soared in the 1990s, with per capita use increasing to 3.1 pounds in 1999, three times the 1989 level. The strong surge in demand can be attributed to two main factors. First, globalization has led to a rise in popularity of ethnic cuisine as consumers seek out new tastes and experiences. Second, garlic's perceived healing qualities (historically, garlic was valued as a medicinal herb by the Chinese, Egyptians, and Indians) created a demand in the health supplement industry.

To satisfy the growing demand, U.S. garlic production increased from 16,000 acres in 1989 to 41,000 acres (output valued at $200 million) in 1999, with imports accounting for another 20 percent. Garlic production is concentrated both internationally and domestically (in the United States). China is the world's largest producer with 66 percent of world output, followed by India and South Korea producing 5 percent each and the United States producing 3 percent. Within the United States, California accounts for 84 percent of U.S. garlic acreage. Gilroy in Santa Clara County is billed as the garlic capital of the United States because a significant volume of California's fresh-market garlic, which is hand harvested, is shipped from there. However, rising U.S. production costs (higher cost of labor, water, etc.) and China's entry into the World Trade Organization (WTO) are rapidly shifting the garlic production scene. Since the early 1990s, major U.S. garlic producers like Christopher Ranch in Gilroy and the Garlic Company have lobbied local and national politicians to retain tariffs and trade restrictions like quotas to ward of competition from China. Yet, with China's entry into WTO, which will dismantle trade barriers against China soon, U.S. garlic producers are being forced to give up hiding behind tariff protection. The issue for U.S. garlic producers is to compete effectively on the basis of competitive advantage and efficiency, that is, doing the right things or else! Having given up on lowering garlic production costs, Gilroy now hopes to transform itself from an agricultural backwater to a biomedical center with affordable land for technology parks—a sea change in the business environment.

Introduction

The wedge between purely domestic and international business has narrowed drastically with open trade and advances in information technology. As the opening story illustrates, the business environment has become truly global. Even as students, you tend to consume goods and services that are produced both domestically and overseas. When you purchase music CDs or DVDs, invariably you are paying for a service (music or a movie provided by a singer or a movie producer like Disney or Sony) produced domestically, in the United States. When you purchase an automobile like Toyota Celica, Hyundai Tiburon, or Ford Mustang, do you ever wonder the type of business environment in which these companies operate? The

Celica is manufactured in Japan, the Tiburon in South Korea, and the Mustang in the United States. Do you think the business systems in all these countries are the same? If not, why are the systems different, and how? And why should that matter? And how does this affect the way that one conducts business in a particular country? Do you know why the United States exports products like airplanes and soybeans and imports items like cars, shoes, stereos, and wine from other countries? Also, if you decide to get involved in the export/import business after you graduate, do you realize what you need to know in order to manage your firm successfully? In this chapter we will explore these interesting issues carefully and in a very fundamental way, since a company's options will always be limited by what is going on in the world around it. There are some basic economic reasons and theories that explain why countries export and import certain goods and services. The environment in which businesses operate is fascinating, and the more you understand the business setting, domestic and global, the better prepared you will be to manage a firm. This chapter will provide you with a fundamental understanding of why and how countries exchange goods and services, and the challenges and opportunities that businesses face operating in different economic systems. Economics deals with the allocation of scarce resources (factors of production that we studied in the previous chapter) among consumers and producers. In business, we utilize economics to help provide us with insight into something that we are all interested in—creating wealth and having the freedom to enjoy it.

Evaluating the Business Environment

For much of the nineteenth and early-twentieth centuries, countries did little to directly manage their economies. This contributed to business cycles. With advances in macroeconomic theory and practice, governments have come to a better understanding of what major economic policy goals ought to be and what economic policy tools governments could use to stabilize or smooth out economic performance. Exhibit 2.1 lists the major goals and tools for managing an economy to facilitate business development and growth.[1]

EXHIBIT 2.1

Major Goals and Tools of Managing the Economy

Goals	Tools
Output	Fiscal policy
High levels of GDP	Government expenditure
Rapid growth of real GDP	Taxation policies
Employment	Monetary policy
Low unemployment	Control of money supply
	Interest rate policy
Inflation	Incomes policies
Low and stable prices	Wage and price guidelines
Exchange rate stability	Trade and exchange rate policies
Market-determined rates	Liberalized trade policies
	Flexible exchange rates

Major Goals of Economic Management

LEARNING OBJECTIVE 1
Define the major goals of effective economic management.

The ultimate objective of sound economic management is to achieve

- High levels of output coupled with rapid rate of real GDP growth
- High levels of employment with unemployment close to the involuntary rate
- Low rates of inflation with free markets
- Stable exchange rates with relatively free trade

Any country that can consistently achieve most of these objectives is bound to have a solid economy with a booming business environment. While most countries try to achieve these goals, corruption and the lack of political will or institutions to implement appropriate policies are factors that lead to poor economic performance and a weak business environment. Business will flourish in countries where economic policy goals are well defined and achievable.

Output. The best measure of economic success in a country is the generation of high levels of output (GDP), coupled with rapid, sustainable real GDP growth. Achieving this goal implies rising individual income and consumption levels. Consumption in countries with high per capita income will boost the demand for goods and services and opportunities for business. In developing countries with high rates of real GDP growth, the number of middle-class consumers will tend to grow. Middle-class consumers are generally the key market segment targeted by business for the sale of goods and services. In addition, they are the major taxpayers in most countries. For example, China's middle class is estimated to be about 400 million, and India's 300 million, market segments that are of great importance to foreign multinational corporations.

Employment. Countries try to generate as many jobs as possible to keep the economy buoyant yet stable. However, the jobs that are created must pay well and be relatively easy to obtain. Society is better off with high employment, since the crime rate will remain low and unemployment benefit payments will remain small. In addition, the employed will pay taxes, which could go toward the provision of better public services. High employment levels will lead to a large demand for goods and services and excellent business opportunities. The labor force in any country includes the employed as well as the unemployed, but it excludes involuntary unemployment, that is, those who are unemployed and are not actively looking for work. Ever since the Great Depression of the 1930s, when U.S. unemployment averaged around 30 percent, the United States' economic policies have focused on keeping unemployment as low as possible while tolerating higher inflation.

Inflation. Another important economic policy objective is price stability; that is, countries like to see that prices do not increase or fall too rapidly. **Inflation** is the rate of price level increase in an economy from one period to another (monthly, quarterly, or annually). Countries that manage their economies well generally have annual inflation in the 0 to 2 percent per year range. It is important to remember that while unemployment affects only those out of work, inflation affects everyone in an economy. Ever since the hyperinflation of the late 1930s and early 1940s in Germany, its government has followed a low-inflation economic policy. For this reason, unlike the United States, Germany has been willing to accept a higher rate of unemployment for low inflation.

inflation The rate of price level increase in an economy from one period to another (monthly, quarterly, or annually)

Stable Exchange Rates. The exchange rate is nothing but a price. It is the price of one currency compared with another currency and is generally determined by the demand and supply for the currencies in the foreign exchange market. Countries try to maintain a **stable currency,** a currency with a value that does not fluctuate wildly, while maintaining an unrestricted trading system by exporting and importing goods and services from other countries. Unless a country has a stable currency, foreign businesses may not be willing to deal with or invest in that country, since the business risk associated with unstable currencies is great. Currency stability is extremely important in international business transactions.

Achieving all four goals of economic management is a daunting task, and very few countries are able to meet these goals in a consistent manner. Countries that are rich or are progressing well are the ones that (over time) have been able to meet most of these economic policy objectives in a relatively successful manner. Well-managed countries continually try to grow rapidly while maintaining low inflation by utilizing various economic policy tools.

> **reality CHECK** *Visit your local car dealership and ask the manager if she or he prefers a stable dollar or a strong dollar and why.*

stable currency A currency with a value that does not fluctuate wildly

Policy Tools to Manage the Economy

LEARNING OBJECTIVE 2
Summarize the key policy tools available to manage an economy.

Now that we understand the major goals of economic management, our next step is to identify ways of achieving those goals. Fortunately, governments have some important direct and indirect policy tools or instruments at their disposal to help them meet those objectives. These include fiscal policy, monetary policy, incomes policy, and trade and exchange rate policies. To use an analogy, your goal may be to get to Sydney, Australia. The tools or instruments may be a jet aircraft (or ship), the speed of travel, and the route you take. So depending on the policy tool you chose, you may or may not achieve your goal within the time frame under consideration.

Fiscal Policy. The two major elements of **fiscal policy** are government expenditures and taxation. **Government expenditure** is the purchase of goods and services by government to serve the needs of the general public. The federal government spends a significant amount of money on defense and national security by purchasing big-ticket items like fighter airplanes, battleships, and missiles, by financing important services like Medicare and social security, and by building highways, dams, and harbors. Federal, state, and local governments spend money by providing citizens services through agencies like the police, the FBI, the CIA, and the IRS. In most economies (especially the advanced countries), public services are made available by governments with the help of private companies. However, in some countries, governments also actively run commercial enterprises, for example, the oil industry, the power sector, mining, and manufacturing. In the United States, the government is very rarely involved in commercial operations. On the basis of the composition of GDP (see Exhibit 1.7 in Chapter 1), it is clear that as the size of federal expenditure increases, the relative size of private consumption or investment must decrease.

Taxes play an important role in an economy. As we have just seen, without the help of taxes, governments will not be able to spend money on social programs and defense. Public services like police and fire protection can only be provided by

fiscal policy A government policy of using expenditures and taxation to guide the economy to meet economic goals (related to output, employment, inflation, and the exchange rate)

government expenditure The purchase of goods and services by government to serve the needs of the general public

National security, particularly after the events of September 11, 2001, has been greatly enhanced through various types of government expenditures, including the funding of vehicle searches to detect transport of illegal substances and ammunition.

government through taxes, since private investors will not supply them. What we need to ask ourselves is, how do taxes affect economic goals such as real GDP growth, inflation, employment, and exchange rate stability? Income taxes reduce a person's **disposable income,** which is the money left over after taxes are taken out of a person's paycheck. As disposable income is reduced, you are forced to spend less; this in turn reduces consumption expenditure at the national level and lowers GDP growth. A lower GDP growth rate means business will hire fewer additional workers. Reduced consumption will cause inflation to drop. Conversely, if taxes are lowered, economic growth and employment will increase. More specifically, if taxes on businesses are lowered, business people will want to invest more in plant and equipment to produce more goods and services, thereby increasing GDP level and growth. From this brief discussion it is clear that fiscal policy (i.e., government expenditure and taxes) has a significant impact on economic goals and business performance. Depending on which economic goal the government wants to impact, fiscal policy can be designed to have the appropriate effect.

disposable income The money left over after taxes are taken out of a person's paycheck

monetary policy A policy followed by the central bank (the Fed in the United States) to control the money supply in an economy, and hence to manage inflation, economic growth, employment, and the exchange rate

Monetary Policy.   The second major tool of macroeconomic management is **monetary policy.** Simply put, monetary policy deals with the control of money supply in an economy. Central banks in various countries (the Federal Reserve System in the United States, the Bank of Japan in Japan, or the European Central Bank in the case of the European Union) work through their commercial banking system to control or manage their country's money supply. A central bank's primary objective is to make sure that there is sufficient money (currency, checking deposits, and savings deposits) available in the economy to promote economic (GDP) growth with low inflation. When the money supply is excessive, interest rates will fall in the short term and consumers and investors alike will be induced to borrow and spend freely on stereos, furniture, cars, houses, plant, and equipment. This could become inflationary—too much money chasing too few goods—in the long term. When the U.S. Federal Reserve (Fed) wants to stamp out inflation, it will tighten (reduce the U.S. money supply) monetary policy; this will raise interest rates in the short term and curb borrowing by consumers and business. This will slow consumption and investment expenditure (and so will slow GDP growth), reduce inflation, and also cause unemployment to rise. A major objective of central banks in developed economies is to keep inflation under control (i.e., low). Countries with low inflation will have stable currencies, which will make investors, domestic and foreign, happy since they reduce foreign exchange risk and increase investors' confidence in that economy. Germany is an excellent example of a country that has consistently followed tight monetary policy, which has resulted in low inflation and a stable currency. The nature of monetary policy—the impact of money supply on output, employment, inflation, and exchange rate—is a fascinating area of research for economists and policymakers. Another monetary policy tool available to central banks is the direct control over interest rates. The central bank could raise or lower key interest rates in order to impact private consumption, business investment, the exchange rate, and GDP growth.

Incomes Policies.

If the economic environment is such that the unemployment rate is already high and we need to cut inflation as well, some policymakers will recommend **incomes policies**—strategies based on wage and price controls. Some countries try to implement incomes policies through labor-union-supported voluntary wage controls and price freezes by business. This approach is generally difficult to achieve, except in times of national emergencies. In other countries, labor unions and businesses are coerced to freeze wages and prices during hard times. Depending on the type of political system (from shades of democracy to authoritarian regimes) in a country, the success of incomes policies will vary. The results of incomes policies have been mixed at best. Most economists oppose incomes policies, as they go against the basic principle of free markets, where prices and wages are determined by market supply and demand. Furthermore, even in cases where incomes policies have been relatively successful in the immediate short run, the moment incomes policies are eliminated, large spikes in wages and prices follow. It is therefore debatable whether incomes policies as a tool are capable of achieving any of our economic goals, that is, solid economic growth, low inflation and unemployment, or exchange rate stability on a sustained basis.

incomes policies Strategies based on wage and price controls that are used by governments to curb inflation and at the same time maintain employment and keep economic output stable

Trade and Exchange Rate Policies.

Given the global nature of business and the close integration of economies worldwide, **trade** and **exchange rate policies** are playing an extremely important role in achieving macroeconomic objectives. Since the creation of the United Nations and the Bretton Woods institutions (the World Bank and the International Monetary Fund) in 1944, the world has become increasingly globalized. The World Trade Organization (WTO), a sister institution of the United Nations, is armed with the responsibility of bringing about liberalized (freer) trade among member nations, whereas the International Monetary Fund (IMF) is responsible for advising and helping countries achieve stable exchange rates. As we noted in Chapter 1, since 1944 global trade and investment policies have been liberalized on a regular basis through the elimination of quotas on imports and the reduction of tariffs (taxes on imported goods). While some quotas and tariffs still remain in the agricultural sector, most other industries have seen a significant drop in tariffs, which has boosted trade (exports and imports) between countries. Increased exports lead to rising GDP and economic growth, which in turn generate employment. Countries are better off with open trade systems since they are generally able to export goods and services that they are competitive at producing and to import quality goods at attractive prices from abroad. Competition from imports will also help keep domestic inflation under control.

trade policy Government policy implemented primarily through changes in tariff rates or quotas with the objective of encouraging exports or discouraging imports

exchange rate policy A policy of managing the country's exchange rate, to improve the country's balance of payments position

Exchange rate policy is a second and equally important international economic policy tool. However, manipulating (normally trying to keep a currency weak) the exchange rate could lead to short-term gain but long-term economic pain. Some countries try to keep their currency weak to boost exports and reduce imports. This way they hope to increase domestic production (hence employment as well) and exports, thereby raising GDP growth. When a country manipulates its exchange rate, other countries that get hurt by this policy will tend to retaliate, producing reduced trade and economic growth in the countries concerned. Businesses, especially those in the export and import sector, are negatively impacted in the bargain. In a similar manner, countries that try to maintain an artificially strong currency will see imports getting a boost at the expense of exports (which involve domestic production) and growth. As you can see, trade and exchange rate policy tools are very potent in achieving economic policy goals.

In conclusion, countries have a wide range of economic policy tools that can be used to achieve economic goals. Some of these policy tools may work against each other. Hence the role of economic policymakers is to coordinate policies that reinforce each other to arrive at the right goal. To revert back to our analogy, if your goal is to get to Sydney, you will need to use the right combination of transportation tools to get there as quickly and safely as you can.

reality CHECK   *How will you know whether the federal government is living beyond its means?*

The Global Nature of Business

What is happening in China and India today illustrates how globalization is impacting blue-collar and white-collar workers alike in wealthy countries such as the United States, as low-skill factory jobs as well as high-skill service jobs migrate overseas. Business is becoming increasingly global in nature. What do we mean by that statement? Businesses, big and small, depend to an extent on inputs of goods and services from abroad. This is true not only in the United States but also in most foreign countries, especially those that do not follow the command economic system. When you visit Wal-Mart or any retail store close by and check a product's label, you will find out where the product is manufactured. You will notice that quite a few products that you often purchase are manufactured or assembled in different parts of the world. Even some of the vegetables displayed in your grocery store have been harvested with the help of foreign labor, not to speak of the Australian, Chilean, French, German, and Italian wines that you often see on your grocery or liquor store shelf. Since some 60 percent of crude oil consumed in the United States comes from abroad, it is highly likely that the gasoline that you buy to fill your car's gas tank is of foreign origin. For that matter, even your car is probably of international origin. Since the mid-1990s, the service sector in the United States has become increasingly global as U.S. companies accelerated their offshore outsourcing strategy to remain competitive. For example, some of the telemarketing calls you receive (typically during dinner time!) regarding getting credit cards or switching to different long-distance telephone carriers originate from call centers of U.S. companies located in India or the Philippines. Furthermore, as U.S. and European companies have grown more familiar with the expertise of their Indian outsourcing partners, they have increased the complexity of the work (such as software development, supply chain management, and company or stock analysis) that they are willing to hand over to them. Most businesses that you interact with on a daily basis are directly or indirectly associated with their international counterparts.

Why Do Countries Trade or Invest Overseas?

international trade The import or export of goods or services from or to other countries by individuals, firms, or governments

imports Goods or services that are purchased from abroad

exports Goods or services that are sold to citizens abroad

LEARNING OBJECTIVE 3
Explain why trade is better than no trade for society as a whole.

International trade occurs when individuals, firms, or governments import or export goods or services. **Imports** are goods or services that are purchased from abroad (outside national boundaries). Similarly, **exports** are goods or services that

Global Business

India: A Star Global Outsourcing Center

Unlike the United States, which is a service economy, India is an agrarian economy with a solid manufacturing sector. Yet, when one analyzes India's balance of trade in goods and services, it becomes apparent that growth has been most remarkable in its services exports. Most notable among India's services exports is software and business process outsourcing (also called off-shoring)—Internet-driven outsourcing. In fact, India's Information Technology (IT)-enabled services grew by 25 percent in 2001 to $10 billion, of which $8 billion was exported. Its IT revenues and exports have been growing at that rate ever since. There is more to India's IT than meets the eye. India's strategic location has made the linkage between service sectors in the United States and India both complementary and competitive. Depending on the particular time zone that one is in in the United States, India is roughly one-half a day ahead of the United States. Just when Americans get ready to leave their workplace to go home, Indians are getting ready to leave home for work. A large segment of India's middle class (estimated to be between 250 and 300 million) is educated and most speak English—a cultural heritage. Furthermore, India's higher education system churns out several hundred thousand talented engineers, scientists, and software programmers each year, thereby keeping their labor cost relatively stable and at a fraction of U.S. levels. These factors have made India a major outsourcing center for U.S.- and Europe-based companies. For example, the time difference enables U.S. companies to beam software and programming problems to India via satellite before the end of the U.S. workday. Indian software engineers have a full workday to complete the project before beaming it back to the United States for delivery to the U.S. customer the very next day. It is as if the solution to the problem was worked on the whole night in the U.S. itself. Similarly, in order to provide U.S. consumers with 24-hour personal service (to avoid listening to Beethoven or Mozart), customer service call centers have been established in India (where Indians are trained to flatten their accents by religiously watching U.S. sitcoms!) along with medical records transcription service and the like. All these services are provided at a fraction of the U.S.

cost, along with efficiencies associated with time difference. Outsourcing to India has been a win-win situation for most global companies as well as for the Indian employees. Global competition is forcing an increasing number of U.S. firms to pursue cost-cutting strategies to boost profits, retain higher-level positions, and continue R&D investment at home. India is making the most of its competitive advantage by winning a larger slice of the outsourcing pie. About half the number of companies in *Financial Times 500's World's Largest Companies* contract IT and related services to India.

Now India's outsourcing industry is moving upscale from software development to biotech research to equity analysis for investment banks. The latter is particularly timely given the intense pressure U.S. investment banks currently face to separate financial research from investment banking business. Although cost savings are the key, increasingly it is the value added and efficiency that are gaining demand. Some of the most successful Indian outsourcing companies include Wipro, Tata Consultancy, and Infosys. Once global companies find outsourcing to India's IT firms reliable, foreign companies tend to continue the relationship for the long term. What does all this mean? It heralds a fundamental restructuring of rich-world economies. Like the globalization of manufacturing in the 1980s that affected blue-collar workers, the rapid globalization of outsourcing (trade in services) started in the 1990s and is having its impact on white-collar workers in rich-world countries who will need to find alternate jobs as they move up the technology ladder. Also, India is likely to remain one of the few developing countries that will have a growing surplus in services balance exports without having its nationals leave the country.

Questions

1. Identify two major issues that are responsible for the rapid growth of global outsourcing of service sector jobs.
2. Explain why outsourcing to India is inevitable, frequently makes business sense, and can even be beneficial to multinational enterprises.

are sold to other countries. In a **free trade regime,** imports and exports of goods or services take place voluntarily (without government coercion or support), based on a system of open markets. Countries gain from free trade, since it leads them to specialize in the production of goods and services in which they perform comparatively well. Also, at the firm level, some companies may choose to go overseas as producers rather than as exporters of goods and services. We need to ask ourselves: What are the benefits of trade? Unless there is concrete evidence that trade benefits consumers, businesses will not participate in international trade. International trade benefits consumers in three major ways by providing

- A greater amount of choice in the availability of goods and services
- Lower prices for goods and services consumed
- Higher living standards

Greater Amount of Choice.

When a country opens up to international trade, domestic firms (as well as individuals and governments) are allowed to import raw materials (oil, natural gas, coffee beans, etc.), semifinished products (silicon chips, auto parts, etc.), and final goods (cars, stereos, DVD players, camcorders, apparel, etc.) as well as use services (foreign air carriers, insurance, business processing, etc.) from abroad. This increases the choice that domestic consumers have, and they can decide whether to purchase a purely domestic good or an international product. The increase in choice enhances consumer satisfaction and welfare. Just take a look at the items that you own like clothes, shoes, TVs, CD players, cars, etc. Where were all those products made? If you set aside all those goods that were produced overseas, what are you left with? How satisfied will you be without those imports? As you can see, many products that we consume on a day-to-day basis are produced in other countries, and we purchase them voluntarily because of their perceived or real value to us.

Lower Prices to the Consumer.

Because of imports, the level of competition in the domestic market increases. For example, the competition that U.S. car manufacturers like Ford and General Motors face domestically increases with the number of cars imported from firms like Toyota, Honda, Nissan, Hyundai, BMW, Mercedes Benz, VW, and so on, from abroad. Imports benefit consumers in two major ways. First, the increased number of suppliers raises the level of domestic competition, and this helps keep a lid on price increases. Second, increased competition leads to better quality products. From a producer's point of view, open trade allows domestic firms to penetrate foreign markets through exports. As domestic firms expand production, manufacturing efficiency and profits increase.

Higher Living Standards.

International trade raises people's living standards primarily because of increased choice and lower prices that we just discussed. On a relative (with respect to a case without international trade) basis all consumers (both in the exporting and importing countries) will be better off; that is, trade is better than no trade. This fact is based on the *assumption* that all countries practice free market and open trade systems, and governments do not hinder international commerce. Domestic firms will increase production to meet overseas demand, thereby generating new jobs as well as higher wages at home. All these factors will improve the overall quality of life and standard of living in countries that practice open trade. However, for countries to gain from trade, all trade partners must honestly practice open trade. Otherwise, some countries will gain at the expense of others. Citizens in countries that do not practice open trade are generally worse off than those in countries that do have open trade systems. All you need to do is to read about the living standards of folks in the former Soviet bloc to get a feel for their life prior to 1990. Even to this day, people in these transition economies are not as well off as people in free market or emerging market economies, although they are slowly getting there.

Theory of Absolute and Comparative Advantage in Trade

At the heart of international trade theory is the fact that trade encourages countries to specialize in the production of goods and services that they turn out most efficiently. There are two basic theories that try to explain this behavior: the theory of absolute advantage in production and the theory of comparative advantage in production. These theories are best explained with the help of examples.

Theory of Absolute Advantage. Let's take two countries, Brazil and the United States, in a hypothetical example and try to determine what each of these countries would export if they opened their countries to free trade. Let us assume that because of soil and climatic conditions, Brazil is more efficient (measured in pounds of coffee beans produced per acre of farmland) in the production of coffee than the United States. Let's further assume that for the same reason (soil and climate), the United States is more efficient than Brazil in the production of corn. From this it is obvious that it will make more sense for Brazil to concentrate on coffee production only. Part of the coffee that is produced will be kept for local consumption and the remainder exported to the United States. The United States, on the other hand, can do the same by concentrating on corn production, saving some for domestic consumption and exporting the rest to Brazil. The gains from trade are obvious. Citizens from both Brazil and the United States will enjoy the benefits of lower-cost coffee and corn because of trade. If there were no trade, the United States would have to produce its own coffee, which could be expensive, and Brazil would have to grow its own corn, which would be inefficient and at a high cost to its citizens. In the language of international trade, we will say that Brazil has an **absolute advantage** in coffee production and the United States has an absolute advantage in corn production. An absolute advantage exists when one country can produce a good—such as coffee or corn—more efficiently than the other.

> **absolute advantage** The ability of one country to produce a good or service more efficiently than another

Theory of Comparative Advantage. Now suppose that one country has an absolute advantage over another in the production of two (or more) products. Should trade between these two countries occur? The answer is yes! Let's analyze the rationale behind this assertive answer.

Let's continue with the Brazil-U.S. case that we just explored. Let's now make two small changes and *assume* that Brazil can produce both coffee and corn more efficiently (again, measured in terms of pounds of coffee or corn per acre of farmland) than the United States, and that Brazil can produce five times more coffee than the United States but only two times more corn than the United States, using the same quantity of resources. Brazil has an absolute advantage over the United States in the production of both coffee and corn. However, in which commodity, coffee or corn, does Brazil have a greater production advantage than the United States? It is in the production of coffee, because Brazil can produce five times as much, compared with only twice as much corn. So, what should Brazil do? Well, Brazil should produce the commodity in which it has the greatest advantage, that is, coffee. You will notice that Brazil not only has an absolute advantage in coffee production, it also has a **comparative advantage** in coffee production over corn

> **comparative advantage** The ability of one country that has an absolute advantage in the production of two or more goods (or services) to produce one of them relatively more efficiently than the other

production. Despite the fact that Brazil has an absolute advantage over the United States in the production of both coffee and corn, free trade will ensure that both countries will have a higher standard of living if Brazil concentrates its efforts in the production of coffee and the United States utilizes its resources in corn production. A country has a comparative advantage in the production of a good or service when it has the greater advantage over another country. It is important to remember that resources in all countries are scarce. That is why countries must choose the most efficient use of their scare resources. When all countries specialize in the production of the goods and services in which they enjoy a comparative advantage, they not only use their resources most efficiently, but they also increase the total output and welfare of the world!

World Trade and World Trade Patterns.   Based on the competitive advantages of countries in terms of both resource endowment and production efficiency and on the demands of a growing world population, global trade has increased tremendously over the years. World exports in 2001 stood at $6.1 trillion and imports were $6.4 trillion, bringing total trade (exports plus imports) to $12.5 trillion. Exhibit 2.2 provides an overview (in U.S. dollar terms) of world exports and imports to and from the different regions of the globe during 1997 to 2001.

The information for 2001 is provided graphically in Exhibit 2.3 in the form of percent trade distribution. Notice that industrialized countries account for the lion's share of world trade, exporting and importing almost two-thirds of the total. Among developing countries, Asian economies (excluding industrialized countries like Japan and South Korea) are the largest and fastest growing suppliers of world imports, averaging some 20 percent of the total. The Middle East's supply of world imports hovers around 4 percent, whereas the Western Hemisphere south of the United States accounts for some 6 percent of the total. While studying international trade, it is always important to understand which countries (or group of countries) are major exporters or importers to analyze what goods are traded and why. This will provide you with insights into where global business opportunities exist.

EXHIBIT 2.2

World Trade of Goods by Regions and Industrialization (in billions of U.S. dollars)

	Exports					Imports				
	1997	1998	1999	2000	2001	1997	1998	1999	2000	2001
World Total	5523	5400	5668	6379	6143	5593	5527	5821	6612	6365
Industrial countries	3528	3610	3867	4243	4078	3622	3706	3954	4373	4219
Developing countries	1921	1731	1752	2084	2006	1967	1817	1862	2235	2140
Africa	98	102	98	105	110	107	109	108	114	120
Asia	1020	826	904	1121	1041	1058	878	958	1195	1081
Europe	320	311	278	324	327	312	313	283	327	339
Middle East	169	170	163	174	180	154	159	163	191	198
Western Hemisphere	315	323	309	361	348	337	358	350	409	402
Other countries n.i.e.*	4	4	4	4	5	4	4	4	5	6
Other countries/areas**	78	57	45	48	53	53	45	41	51	62

* "Not included elsewhere"; refers to Cuba and North Korea.
**Unreported trade primarily among developing countries.
Source: IMF, *Direction of Trade Statistics Yearbook,* 2002, pp. 2–6.

EXHIBIT 2.3

World Trade of Goods: Distribution by Regions and Industrialization, 2001

World Exports for 2001

DEVELOPING COUNTRIES:
Western Hemisphere 6%
Middle East 3%
Europe 5%
Asia 18%
Africa 2%
INDUSTRIAL COUNTRIES 66%

World Imports for 2001

DEVELOPING COUNTRIES:
Western Hemisphere 6%
Middle East 3%
Europe 5%
Asia 17%
Africa 2%
INDUSTRIAL COUNTRIES 66%

Source: IMF, *Direction of Trade Statistics Yearbook*, 2002, pp. 2–6, derived from Exhibit 2.2.

reality CHECK   *Do you think that you are benefitting from free trade? Why or why not?*

Barriers to International Trade and Investments

LEARNING OBJECTIVE 4
Evaluate the different forms of trade and foreign investment barriers and their impact on business, consumers, and governments.

Trade theory clearly shows how free trade has a positive effect on the economic welfare of all trading partners by essentially improving the standard of living of people in those countries. Free trade also has positive effects on business, since it provides opportunities for entrepreneurs to be directly involved in the export-import business (of goods and services). Also, the volume of domestic business is enhanced through the domestic sales of imported products (and services) and exports of domestic goods (and services). Apart from business opportunities generated through exports and imports, trade also encourages domestic businesses to explore the possibility of investing in plant and equipment abroad in order to either serve that market or even export from the international location. This type of investment is called **foreign direct investment (FDI).** There are literally hundreds of thousands of companies, domestic as well as foreign, that are involved in FDI. McDonald's of the United States, Sony of Japan, and DaimlerChrysler of Germany are good examples of companies that have massive FDI.

While free trade is the best form of conducting business with partners overseas, quite often countries try to restrict trade as well as FDI for various political reasons. When a government tries to restrict trade by creating barriers to trade through various mechanisms, it is called **protection.** Whom is the government trying to protect, and why? Obviously, it is the domestic producer (e.g., the U.S. textile or sugar industries that have lost comparative advantage over the years, but are politically well connected) that the government is trying to shield from international competition. Barriers to trade have a cost and also distort market-based trade patterns. While domestic firms (for example, textile firms in the United States) gain because the competitive pressure from abroad is reduced through protection (and domestic firms can conduct business less efficiently), the person who ultimately pays for this inefficiency, in the form of higher prices or lower-quality goods or services

foreign direct investment (FDI) An overseas investment in plant and equipment to produce goods or services for local consumption or for exports

protection The government practice of imposing trade barriers (e.g., tariffs) to shield domestic producers from international competition

purchased, is the domestic consumer. Despite the fact that protection reduces consumer welfare, politically powerful business groups (e.g., steel, textile, sugar, and auto producers in the United States and farmers in the U.S. and especially in the European Union) are able to influence their governments to impose trade restrictions. The bad thing about protection is the detrimental impact it has on the more efficient overseas producers who are invariably located in developing countries. For example, catfish farmers in Vietnam, sugar cane producers in the Philippines, steel mill owners in Brazil, and textile manufacturers in Bangladesh, China, India, and Pakistan are forced to curtail their competitive exports to the United States. Protectionist policies in developed countries have severe negative effects on developing countries' production, employment, and economic growth. In a nutshell, protection penalizes consumers in the importing country and producers in the exporting country.

There are five major types of trade barriers—tariffs, quotas, voluntary restraints, counter trade, and embargoes—that we will briefly discuss in this section to give you an appreciation for what trade barriers are, who benefits, and at what cost to society.

tariffs Taxes on imports

Tariffs. **Tariffs** are taxes on imports. Generally, it is the domestic producers who seek government help in the form of tariff protection to enable them to continue with their high-cost (and uncompetitive) operation or to restructure their firms and stay in business. Take, for example, the U.S. steel industry in 2002. Several executives of U.S. steel companies sought government protection, claiming that competition from foreign steel companies was literally driving them out of business. They said that overseas steel companies were competing unfairly. However, a major structural problem with some U.S. steel manufacturers was their uncompetitive cost structure and high-cost pension program liabilities. The U.S. government (International Trade Commission) conducted a study and decided to impose a temporary (for three years) import tariff of some 10 to 30 percent on different types of imported steel to allow the U.S. steel companies to restructure and operate in the competitive international environment. Steel exporters in Asia, Brazil, and Europe were not very happy (since they had to curtail their exports to the United States) with that decision, and some countries retaliated by imposing tariffs on certain U.S. agricultural exports. When the U.S. government imposes a 30 percent tariff on imported steel, imported steel will cost 30 percent more in the United States. This in turn will enable domestic (U.S.) steel producers to raise their domestic prices to match those of the higher-cost imported steel. When the price of steel rises, the U.S. automobile industry, for example, will also raise car prices to offset the increased cost of steel input. Ultimately, it is the consumer who will bear the cost of tariffs, and the beneficiary is the domestic steel industry (both the efficient as well as the less efficient producers). The other group that loses is the foreign steel producers whose exports to the United States will be reduced.

quantitative restrictions (QRs) Quotas that limit the amount of imports that can come into a country

Quotas. Also called **quantitative restrictions (QRs),** quotas are one of the worst forms of trade barriers. While a tariff, which is basically a tax on imports, makes imports more expensive by the amount of the tariff, quotas limit the amount of imports that can come into a country. Thus, depending on the domestic demand for the imported product, its price could literally go through the roof. Let's assume, for example, that in order to protect the domestic sports car industry, the U.S. government limits the import of German (e.g., Porsche) sports cars to the United States to 1,000 units a year. Let's further assume that there are some 5000 Americans who want to buy Porsches each year. What do you think will happen? Well, since U.S. demand for Porsches far exceeds the restricted supply of imports, the price of Porsches will shoot up and Porsches could possibly end up selling for double or triple the free trade price. Again it is the consumer who loses out in the bargain! Many developing countries impose quotas on various goods that result in a high cost for the domestic consumer and fat profits for domestic producers of import-competing products as well as importers. The Multi Fiber Arrangement (MFA) deals with global trade in textiles and apparel and sets import quotas (gradually eliminated starting in 2005) for various products exported to industrialized countries in Europe and the United States. The net result is that apparel is a lot more expensive in Europe and the United States than in the developing world where it is produced. Global trade in textile and apparel is anything but free! This contributes to stagnant income levels in many developing countries.

Voluntary Restraints.

Self-imposed quotas by exporters (or the exporting country) are called **voluntary restraints.** For political reasons, some countries that are very competitive in the manufacture of certain products will voluntarily limit their exports of specific goods to another country for a set period of time. The philosophy behind these voluntary restraints is to provide some breathing time for domestic producers to retool and restructure operations and adjust to the realities of import competition. An excellent example of voluntary restraint is the restrictions that Japan imposed on its car exporters to the United States in the early 1980s. Japan, as you probably know, has a comparative advantage in the production of competitively priced, well-built, relatively small, fuel-efficient cars. In 1980, soon after the Iranian revolution (which led to the doubling of crude oil prices), gasoline prices in the United States shot up and the U.S. consumers' appetite for fuel-efficient, well-built Japanese cars increased tremendously as the consumers moved away from the "gas guzzlers" produced by Detroit. The U.S. automobile manufacturers were losing market share and had huge inventories of unsold cars. They appealed to the U.S. government. In the early 1980s Japan's government came to an agreement with the U.S. government to limit car exports to the United States (to 1.68 million cars per year). Because of this voluntary restraint quota, Japanese cars, which were in great demand, commanded premium prices. Just as in the case of quotas, it was the consumer (the U.S. consumer in this case) who ended up paying a high price for Japanese cars. As you can see, voluntary restraints operate similarly to quotas. By the mid-1980s President Ronald Reagan lifted the voluntary restraint and allowed open trade in automobiles. Since that time, Japanese automobile companies like Toyota and Honda have been setting the global benchmark for automobile value.

voluntary restraints Self-imposed export quotas on specific sensitive products (autos, steel, etc.), to a specific country or countries for a set period of time

Counter Trade.

During the Cold War period (and even today in several countries of the former Soviet bloc and in some developing countries) the Soviet bloc countries practiced **counter trade**—a barter system of exchange. As you can imagine, counter trade is an extremely inefficient form of trade between countries. Countries participate in counter trade especially when they do not have adequate amounts of foreign currency (e.g., the U.S. dollar, the euro, etc.) to pay for their imports. Another reason why countries pursue counter trade is that they may not be capable of producing goods of international quality to sell and earn the needed foreign exchange for imports. Generally, under a system of counter trade, countries exchange one substandard product for another. Obviously, consumers in both countries would be better off with a system of open trade. During the Soviet days, the government of India imported Soviet fighter jets and other defense hardware in exchange for Indian-made consumer goods. The terms of trade (number of copy machines or tubes of toothpaste per fighter aircraft!) are generally worked out between the countries. However, achieving balanced trade between counter trade partners is always a challenge.

counter trade A barter system of exchange in which trade between specific countries is conducted without the use of monetary transactions

Since 1990, both the Russian and Indian governments have moved to relatively open trade systems and the volume of counter trade has fallen drastically. Yet, despite its inefficiency, counter trade continues to be practiced in many developing countries. In fact, several multinational companies have been forced to participate in counter trade in order to sell their goods or services to some of these developing countries in return for valuable natural resources like oil or minerals.

embargoes Trade sanctions that are imposed on a country and that restrict trade with that country

Embargoes.   When sanctions are imposed on a country, they basically restrict trade with that country. These disruptions of trade are called **embargoes.** Embargoes, which may not be universally enforced, are generally meant to punish a country for perceived unacceptable international behavior. Trade embargoes have been used—largely for political reasons—against several countries over time. The United States has had a trade embargo against communist Cuba for over 40 years. The objective is to put pressure on the Cuban government to change its ways and bring about economic and political freedom in Cuba. However, foreign policy experts question whether the embargo has achieved its objective and suggest that it has just hurt the average Cuban consumer. The embargo's failure partly reflects the fact that the sanction has been implemented largely on a bilateral (U.S.-Cuba) basis and not multilaterally (by all countries) against Cuba. Prior to 1990, the United States had imposed an embargo on shipment of grains (especially wheat) to the Soviet Union at various times when the United States felt the Soviets had misbehaved, for example, when the Soviets invaded Afghanistan in 1979.

reality CHECK   *How does the U.S. trade embargo against Cuba impact U.S. smokers?*

The Foreign Exchange Market and the Exchange Rate

LEARNING OBJECTIVE 5
Compare the rationales behind countries' choices of exchange rate regimes.

In 2001, world merchandise trade totaled almost $12.5 trillion, which was greater than the U.S. GDP of $10 trillion. In fact, U.S. exports alone in 2001 were $731 billion with imports running at $1.18 trillion. There are currently 191 countries in

A U.S. trade embargo against Cuba has resulted in difficult times for Cuban taxi owners, and they are sometimes forced to improvise spare parts that they cannot import for their old American cars.

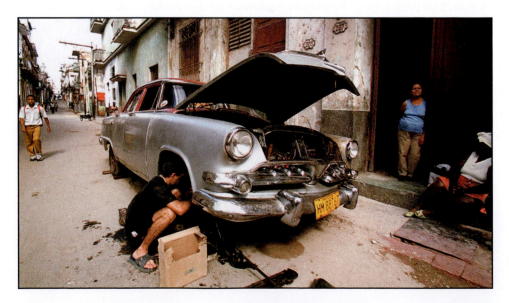

the world and most of them trade with each other, and many have their own currencies as well. Most of these countries would like to use their own currencies to transact international trade. The question is, with so many currencies in circulation, where does the exchange of currencies take place and how are currency values determined?

Foreign Exchange Markets.

The exchange of currencies takes place in **foreign exchange markets,** that is, financial centers where a network of international banks (exporters and importers work with these banks), central banks (that want to buy or sell currencies to manage exchange rates), and currency traders (who buy, sell, or speculate on currencies) transact business. There is no central bank or financial institution that controls this network. Almost $1.9 trillion worth of currencies are traded each day at the various foreign exchange markets globally. The three largest foreign exchange markets are in London, New York, and Tokyo, followed by Hong Kong and Singapore. Each of these centers caters to the foreign exchange needs of certain regions of the world. For historical reasons, and largely serving Europe, the Middle East, and Africa, London is the largest foreign exchange market and handles some 32 percent of the world's daily transactions. Second is New York, which handles some 19 percent of the global transactions and caters to the needs of the Western Hemisphere. Tokyo ranks third with some 9 percent of world transactions and serves Asia along with other strong competitors like Hong Kong and Singapore. Then there are smaller foreign exchange markets in almost all countries (generally located at their key commercial centers). The foreign exchange market is a 24-hour market, and the various financial institutions in these centers are connected by means of sophisticated telecommunications systems that enable instant, real-time exchange rate quotations. The function of the foreign exchange market is to facilitate international trade in goods and services and investment (FDI, portfolio investment, as well as short-term capital flows); this in turn helps determine exchange rates.

foreign exchange markets Financial centers where a network of international banks and currency traders (people who buy, sell, or speculate on currencies) transact business

The Exchange Rate.

What is the exchange rate, and how are exchange rates currently determined? An **exchange rate** is nothing but the price of one currency compared with that of another currency. As you already know, in a free market system price is determined by the interaction of demand and supply. Similarly, in a free-market-oriented foreign exchange market, currency values are determined by the demand for and supply of currencies—called the **floating exchange rate system.** The value of the world's major currencies, namely, the U.S. dollar, the euro, and the yen, is market determined. The U.S. dollar plays a major role in foreign exchange markets all over the world. A contributing factor to the dollar's dominant role is that a number of important commodities (crude oil, steel, etc.) and goods are priced in U.S. dollars; this in turn creates a massive demand for dollars in the world's foreign exchange markets. The value of some currencies (e.g., the Indonesian rupiah, Thai baht, Russian ruble, Indian rupee, and Singapore dollar) is determined partly by demand and supply in the foreign exchange market and partly by active government intervention (central bank purchases and sales of their own currencies by countries to manage their currency values) in the foreign exchange market—called the **managed floating exchange rate system.** Furthermore, since some countries conduct the bulk of their international transactions with a few major trade partners, they link their currencies (e.g., the Hong Kong dollar, Chinese yuan, Malaysian ringgit, and Saudi Arabian riyal) to those of their major trade partners. The reason for doing this is simple. These countries do not want their trade flows to be disrupted by changing exchange rates, especially since the major trade partner is well identified. Such a system is called the **fixed exchange rate system,** one in which the country pegs (fixes)

exchange rate The price of one currency compared with that of another currency

floating exchange rate system The system in which currency values are determined by the demand for and supply of currencies in a foreign exchange market

managed floating exchange rate system A floating exchange rate system in which the values of some currencies are partly determined by active government intervention (central bank purchases and sales of their own currencies)

fixed exchange rate system The system in which a country pegs (fixes) its currency value (formally or de facto) at a fixed rate to a major currency or a basket of currencies

its currency's value (formally or de facto) to that of a major currency or a basket of currencies (if it trades with a couple of major countries) and the exchange rate fluctuates within a narrow margin around a central rate.

reality *If you were involved in the business of international trade, would you*
CHECK *prefer a fixed or a floating exchange rate system?*

The Rise of Globalization

◆ LEARNING OBJECTIVE 6
Describe the evolution of globalization.

globalization The process of eliminating trade, investment, cultural, and even political barriers across countries, which in turn could lead to freer movement of goods, services, labor, capital, technology, and companies across international borders

Imagine yourself sitting relaxed on a leather couch in your house or apartment, sipping a cup of hot coffee or tea, and watching a TV show on the Discovery Channel. Chances are high that the leather couch you are seated on was made in Italy, the cup was made by Corning of the United States, the coffee came from Brazil but was processed by Nestlés of Switzerland or the tea came from India and was processed by Lipton's of the United Kingdom, the Sony TV was produced in Japan, and the Discovery Channel program was being beamed live from Masai Mara in Kenya, not to speak of the clothes from China that you may be wearing. All these advances have been made possible by **globalization,** i.e., the process of eliminating trade, investment, cultural, and even political barriers that separate countries. It reflects the growing commercial links among people, communities, and economies around the world. Globalization has made it possible for goods, services, and capital to cross national borders; this in turn has allowed for the movement of labor and companies across international borders. It is reasonable to conclude that globalization is facilitated when barriers across national borders are brought down and the process is accelerated as a result of lower communications and transactions costs brought about through rapid development in information technology and the Internet.

The news media might give you the impression that globalization is a recent phenomenon. Unfortunately, that's not the case. The dawn of globalization can be traced back to the fifteenth century when the Portuguese navigator and explorer Vasco de Gamma made voyages to Kerala State, on India's west coast, in search of spices to satisfy European palates. It was about the same time when Arabs and Chinese traders were making similar voyages to facilitate trade in spices and silk. Goods, people, and ideas have been traveling across the globe ever since that time. More recently, globalization began to accelerate after World War II, starting in 1944 with the creation of such international institutions as the World Bank (**www.worldbank.org**), the International Monetary Fund (**www.imf.org**), and later the General Agreement on Tariffs and Trade (GATT), now called the World Trade Organization (**www.wto.org**). While globalization may be good for all concerned, much depends on how the "rules of the game," that is, fair trade and investment policies and harnessing the Internet, are implemented.

The World Trade Organization

In 1947, a couple of years after the end of World War II, the General Agreement on Tariffs and Trade (GATT) was set up to oversee and liberalize multilateral trade arrangements. The GATT was established as the world's most important trade policy institution, whose primary objective was to increase trade and economic welfare among member countries. To achieve this goal, countries were encouraged to lower their tariff barriers, as well as eliminate quotas and subsidies on merchandise exports and imports. The successive lowering of tariff and nontariff barriers (like product specification, size, etc.) was done through successive rounds of multilateral trade negotiations. Every five years or so, a new round of trade negotiations is started among GATT members with the objective of further lowering tariff barriers and increasing global trade—accelerating the globalization process. Since the creation of GATT in 1947, world trade has increased by an average of some 6 percent per year (see Exhibit 2.2 for growth in trade since 1997). The last round of trade negotiations began in 2001 in Doha (Qatar) and is called the Doha round of trade talks. A key goal of the Doha round is to reduce farm subsidies on agricultural production, especially in the European Union and the United States. When agricultural subsidies are reduced, the production of surplus (which is dumped in the international market) agricultural products, especially in Europe and the United States, will decrease. This, in turn, will raise the world price (to the theoretical equilibrium price) of agricultural products, and this will encourage developing countries to increase domestic production and attain greater food self-sufficiency. The GATT was renamed the World Trade Organization (WTO) on January 1, 1995 and it currently has 148 members. The WTO was established to include trade in agriculture and services, and investment liberalization. The vast majority of WTO members are developing countries, which still maintain relatively high tariff rates. On the other hand, the industrialized countries, although few in number, account for almost two-thirds of the world's merchandise trade (see Exhibit 2.3) and have brought down tariff barriers gradually over the past 55 years. With each new round of trade negotiations, both the developed and the developing countries have lowered their trade and investment barriers. Each reduction has led to the further globalization of business. While globalization is here to stay, the process could always be slowed if some or all countries either refrain from further tariff or investment liberalization or resort to preferential bilateral (between two countries) or regional (a group of countries within a region of the world) trade agreements at the expense of multilateral trade agreements under the auspices of the WTO.

reality CHECK *How have you been personally affected by globalization?*

Regional Trading Blocs

LEARNING OBJECTIVE 7
Summarize the stages of regional integration and explain its pros and cons.

The WTO is an international organization within which multiple national groups, corporations, and governments cooperate on matters—such as increasing international trade and investment—of mutual interest. This can lead to a greater volume of trade and investment across countries, faster economic growth, job creation, tax receipts, increased competition, and increased consumer welfare. Despite the fact that global trade and investment liberalization lead to global benefits, some countries prefer to work more closely within a regional setting. We need to ask ourselves: What are the motives for regional integration? Why do certain countries want to work more closely with one another while others do not? Are all regional trading blocs based on identical principles?

Stages of Regional Integration. Countries may have economic, social, or political reasons for regional integration. For the most part, countries generally begin working together with some form of economic integration, for example, to promote trade and investment among themselves. Economic integration occurs when two or more countries join together to form a larger economic bloc. The main objectives here are economic gain, that is, to increase economic growth and efficiency (through economies of scale) by working together rather than separately, to raise employment opportunities and the quality of life for the citizens of the region, and to promote peace and harmony within the region. As shown in Exhibit 2.4, while some groups of countries may stop with regional trade and investment integration, others may go further with the goal of having greater economic and social union such that the members of those groups will have similar shared economic and social values. In the ultimate case, some countries that share similar economic and political systems may choose to form a union to fend off foreign aggression or threat.

Economic integration can take several forms, representing varying degrees of integration.[2] However, if a logical progression could be outlined along functional lines, it could look something like this.[3]

free trade area An area in which two or more countries agree to eliminate all barriers to trade such as tariffs, quotas, and nontariff barriers like border restrictions, while at the same time they keep their own external tariffs (usually within WTO guidelines) against nonmembers

First, two or more countries may create a **free trade area** by eliminating all barriers to trade such as tariffs, quotas, and nontariff barriers like border restrictions, while at the same time keeping their own external (against nonmembers) tariffs, usually within WTO guidelines.

customs union A group of free trade member countries that have adopted a common external tariff with nonmember countries

Second, when countries within a free trade area have differential external tariffs, imports will largely enter the free trade area through the country that has the lowest external tariffs and trade restrictions, thereby causing other free trade member countries to lose out on import business. This may lead to the creation of a **customs union,** in which all free trade member countries will adopt a common external tariff with nonmember countries.

Third, within the member countries of the customs union, investment (hence business and job opportunities) will flow to the countries that have the best labor productivity and low capital cost. This in turn may encourage the removal of barriers to the free movement of capital and labor within the customs union, thereby creating a **common market** or **single market.**

common market or **single market** A market formed when member countries of a customs union remove all barriers to the movement of capital and labor within the customs union

economic and monetary union A union formed when members of a common market agree to implement common social programs (on education, employee benefits and retraining, health care, etc.) and coordinated macroeconomic policies (such as fiscal and monetary policies) that would lead to the creation of a single regional currency and an apex central bank

Fourth, within the common market, the free movement of labor and capital may encourage member states to implement common social programs (on education, employee benefits and retraining, health care, retirement programs, etc.) and coordinated macroeconomic policies (such as common fiscal and monetary policies) that could lead to the creation of a single regional currency and an **economic and monetary union.** Finally, since member countries of the economic and monetary union will work closely with each other on all major business and economic issues, the urge to have common policies in other fields like defense and foreign policies may lead to the creation of a **political union,** i.e., a group of countries that will behave as a single country.

political union The union created when member countries of an economic and monetary union work closely with each other to arrive at common defense and foreign policies and behave as a single country

Pros and Cons of Regional Integration.
The benefits and costs of regional integration depend crucially on the level of integration achieved by the countries in

EXHIBIT 2.4

Form and Stages of Regional Integration

Stage of Integration	Abolition of Tariffs and Quotas Among Members	Common External Tariff and Quota System	Abolition of Restrictions on Factor Movements	Harmonization and Unification of Economic Policies and Institutions
Free trade area	Yes	No	No	No
Customs union	Yes	Yes	No	No
Common market	Yes	Yes	Yes	No
Economic union	Yes	Yes	Yes	Yes

the group. While the motives of the member countries may be similar (not identical)—creation of greater business opportunities, increased value (better choice, price, and service) for consumers, shared values, peace within the region, and common security against threat—the degree of success of the integrated group will largely depend on how well they implement the agreed-on economic policies. The effect of regional integration will depend on the net impact of the benefits and costs listed below.

The benefits of regional integration include

- Creating a large pool of consumers with growing incomes, similar culture, tastes, and social values
- Encouraging economies of scale in production and increasing the level of competition and economic growth through investment flows
- Freeing the flow of capital and labor to the most productive regions
- Increasing cooperation, peace, and security among countries in the region
- Encouraging member states to enhance their level of social welfare to that of the most progressive states

The costs of regional integration include

- Undermining the most-favored-nation status rule, an essential principle of the WTO (The lowest tariff applicable to one member must be extended to all members.)
- Imposing uniform laws and regulations that at times do not take into account national economic, cultural, and social differences
- Eliminating jobs and increasing unemployment in protected industries
- Losing sovereignty, national independence, and identity
- Reducing the powers of the national government
- Rising crime associated with drugs and terrorism (because of ease of cross-border labor movement)

reality CHECK   *Are you concerned that greater regional integration will hurt rather than help the United States? Why?*

LEARNING OBJECTIVE 8
Identify the major regional trading blocs and explain why some have succeeded while others have not.

Major Regional Integration Blocs.   Groups of countries in all continents of the world have formed various forms of cooperation agreements, primarily to enhance issues of mutual interest. Each step up the economic integration ladder leads to closer integration of the countries involved, and the final stage (economic union) will lead to the transfer of some sovereignty to supranational organizations (e.g., the European Commission). As countries clamor for bilateral or regional trade agreements, economists are concerned that the prospects of creating a truly open *global* economic system may recede. Some governments may sign trade pacts (the proposed U.S.–Middle East free trade area) to cement diplomatic or security ties that risk slowing the momentum behind multilateral trade liberalization. Described briefly below are the major regional economic blocks that are of importance to business.

THE EUROPEAN UNION (EU).   The EU (**www.eurunion.org** and **http://europa.eu.int**), headquartered in Brussels, Belgium, is the most highly evolved example of regional integration in the world. It is already in the fourth stage of the economic integration process and is moving toward the final step that calls for political union with common defense and foreign policy institutions. After the devastation of infrastructure in Europe during World War II, the United States chose to help rebuild Europe through the Marshall Plan. In addition, the World Bank (especially the International

Bank for Reconstruction and Development) was established in 1944 to help stabilize European economies. The ultimate objective of all these initiatives was to create a strong, independent, and united Europe based on free market principles and economic cooperation.

The origins of the EU can be traced to the creation of the European Coal and Steel Community (ECSC) in 1952 which established a common market in coal, steel, and iron ore and included the six nations of France, West Germany, Italy, Belgium, the Netherlands, and Luxembourg. The second big step was their approval of the Treaty of Rome in 1957 establishing the European Economic Community (EEC). In 1960, the European Free Trade Association (EFTA) was formed by the United Kingdom, Denmark, Sweden, Finland, Switzerland, Austria, and Portugal. Although the United Kingdom, Ireland, and Denmark applied to join the EEC in August 1961, these countries were allowed to enter the EEC only in 1973 (bringing its membership to nine) primarily because of French president Charles de Gaulle's resistance to the United Kingdom's joining the EEC. Greece joined the EEC in 1981 followed by Spain and Portugal in 1986, bringing its membership to 12. Until then, the focus of the EEC was the establishment of a common market with free movement of goods, labor, and capital, that is, the factors of production. However, by 1992, the European Economic Community decided to become a full economic union, the European Union (EU), by incorporating (harmonization and unification) the fiscal, monetary, and social policies of its member countries. In January 1995 Austria, Sweden, and Finland joined the European Union, bringing its membership to 15. In May 2004, 10 new countries (eight from the former Soviet block, and Cyprus and Malta)–the Accession Candidates—were admitted to the EU, bringing the EU membership to the present 25 (see Exhibit 2.5). The case of three "candidate" countries, that is, Bulgaria, Romania and Turkey is to be considered in 2007.

The introduction of the euro, the EU's common (or single) currency that is currently used in 12 (excluding Denmark, Sweden, and the United Kingdom which have opted to stay out of the euro area till a later date) of the 15 eligible original EU member countries, is considered by many as the crowning success of the EU's plans to integrate the economies of Europe. The focus of the EU currently is to deepen (strengthen) institutional (economic, political, social, and defense) linkages; this

EXHIBIT 2.5

The European Union

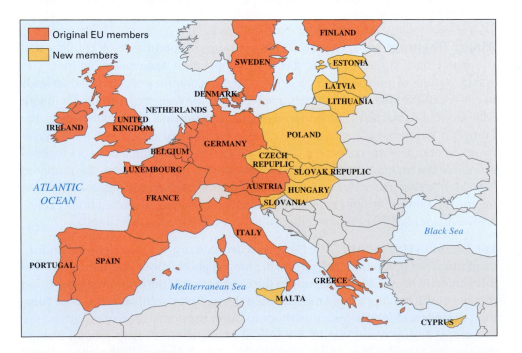

will enable the EU to act like one country with the economic and political power that will effectively compete (both in terms of GNI and population; see Exhibit 2.6) with the United States. The EU's massive eastward expansion reflects a common past. It also opens new opportunities for some industries in the ten new EU countries while at the same time increased competition will be faced by others. The enlarged EU will offer tremendous challenges and opportunities for businesspeople in nonmember countries who seek to penetrate the expanded EU.

EXHIBIT 2.6

The United States and the Enlarged European Union: A Comparison

	Population (million)	Surface Area (thousand sq km)	Population Density (people per sq km)	Gross National Income ($ billion 2001)	Gross National Income per Capita ($ 2001)	PPP Gross National Income ($ billion 2001)	PPP Gross National Income per Capita ($ 2001)
United States	285	9629	31	9,780.8	34,280	9,780.8	34,280
Original EU members (15)							
Austria	8	84	98	194.7	23,940	215.0	26,380
Belgium	10	31	313	245.3	23,850	269.0	26,150
Denmark	5	43	126	164.0	30,600	153.0	28,490
Finland	5	338	17	123.4	23,780	125.0	24,030
France	59	552	108	1,380.7	22,730	1,425.0	24,080
Germany	82	357	231	1,939.6	23,560	2,078.0	25,240
Greece	11	132	82	121.0	11,430	186.0	17,520
Ireland	4	70	55	87.7	22,850	104.0	27,170
Italy	58	301	197	1,123.8	19,390	1,422.0	24,530
Luxembourg	0.44	2	220	17.1	38,740	16.9	38,330
Netherlands	16	42	473	390.3	24,330	439.0	27,390
Portugal	10	92	110	109.3	10,900	178.0	17,710
Spain	41	506	82	588.0	14,300	816.0	19,860
Sweden	9	450	22	225.9	25,400	212.0	23,800
United Kingdom	59	243	244	1,476.8	25,120	1,431.0	24,340
The EU 15	377.44	3243	116	8,187.6	21,692	9,069.9	24,030
New members (10)							
Cyprus	0.76	9	84	8.1	10,380	12.0	15,750
Czech Republic	10	79	132	54.3	5,310	146.0	14,320
Estonia	1	45	32	5.3	3,870	13.0	9,650
Hungary	10	93	110	49.2	4,830	122.0	11,990
Latvia	2	65	38	7.6	3,230	18.0	7,760
Lithuania	3	65	54	11.7	3,350	29.0	8,350
Malta	0.39	0.3	1,300	3.4	8,720	3.2	8,110
Poland	39	323	127	163.6	4,230	362.0	9,370
Slovak Republic	5	49	112	20.3	3,760	64.0	11,780
Slovania	2	20	99	19.4	9,760	34.0	17,060
The New EU 10	73.15	748.3	98	342.9	4,688	803.2	10,980
The current EU 25	450.59	3991.3	113	8,530.5	18,932	9,873.1	21,911

Source: World Bank, *World Development Indicators,* 2003, pp. 14–16; European Commission.

NORTH AMERICAN FREE TRADE AGREEMENT (NAFTA). You will notice in Exhibit 2.7 that the United States' top two trade partners are its neighbors, Canada and Mexico. In 2001, U.S. trade with Canada was $384 billion, and with Mexico it was $235 billion. Historically, Canada has always been the United States' largest trade partner and Mexico has ranked either second or third (after Japan). With such close trade linkages with its northern and southern neighbors, it made sense for the United States to explore more formal trade linkages with its strategic neighbors. It is always prudent to implement progressive economic (especially trade and investment) policies that enable your neighboring countries to grow and prosper along with you. It is like living in a place where your neighbors are employed and are enjoying an improved standard of living. You will feel safe, since everyone's standard of living and quality of life is being enhanced, as opposed to having unemployed neighbors who are likely to relieve you of your prized possessions!

NAFTA (see Exhibit 2.8) is a comprehensive trade agreement among Canada, the United States, and Mexico that deals with issues ranging from phased reduction (and finally elimination) of trade barriers to protection of workers' rights and the environment (see Exhibit 2.8). NAFTA (**www.nafta-sec-alena.org/DefaultSite/index.htm**) negotiations began in the early 1990s; the agreement was signed by the three

EXHIBIT 2.7

United States: Exports and Imports of Goods to and from Top Ten Trade Partners (in billions of U.S. dollars)

	Exports				
	1997	1998	1999	2000	2001
World total	688	680	691	772	731
Canada	150	154	163	175	164
Mexico	71	79	86	109	102
Japan	66	58	58	65	58
United Kingdom	36	39	39	41	41
Germany	25	27	27	29	30
South Korea	25	17	22	27	22
France	17	18	19	20	20
Netherlands	20	19	19	22	20
China (X. Hong Kong)	13	14	13	16	19
Singapore	18	16	16	17	18

	Imports				
	1997	1998	1999	2000	2001
World total	899	845	1048	1238	1180
Canada	171	178	199	229	220
Mexico	87	96	110	135	133
Japan	124	125	134	150	130
China (X. Hong Kong)	66	75	87	106	109
Germany	44	51	56	60	61
United Kingdom	34	36	40	44	42
South Korea	24	25	32	41	37
France	21	25	27	30	31
Italy	20	22	23	26	25
Malaysia	19	20	22	26	23

Source: IMF, *Direction of Trade Statistics Yearbook*, 2002, pp. 480–482.

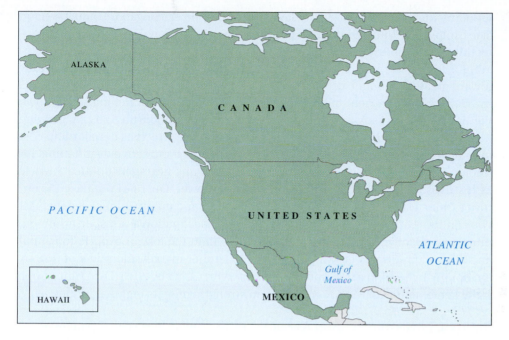

EXHIBIT 2.8
NAFTA

governments in December 1992, ratified by the legislatures of the three countries, and came into effect on January 1, 1994. The idea of integrating the economies of North America gained strength with the success of the Canada-U.S. Free Trade Agreement, which was signed in 1988 and took effect in 1989. NAFTA has three major objectives. First is the expansion of trade in goods and services through the phased elimination of barriers to trade, including tariffs, quotas, and licensing restrictions, among the parties. Second is the protection of intellectual property rights (enforcement of patent and copyright laws for software, music recordings, etc.). Third is the creation of institutions to deal with potential problems (unfair trade practices, disputes between firms or governments, environmental protection, worker's rights, competition policies, and the implementation of NAFTA rules and regulations). Two side agreements dealing with Mexican labor laws and environmental quality were signed by the United States and Mexico to make sure that Mexico did not practice unfair labor laws and enforced agreed-on environmental quality standards.

While the structure of NAFTA is relatively complex, its institutions are not as far reaching as those of the European Union, which include institutions set up to coordinate political, legal, foreign, and defense policies.[4] Because of its close economic ties with the United States, Mexico's economic prospects are heavily influenced by the performance of its northern neighbor. When the U.S. economy slides into a recession, the impact on Mexico is severe, as can be seen by the volume of Mexican exports to the United States. Mexico has tried to deal with this problem by signing a free trade agreement with the European Union in 1999. Since then Mexican trade with the EU has been steadily increasing and bilateral trade with Spain, in particular, has surged from some $2.3 billion in 1999 to almost $4.5 billion in 2002. Although the United States remains Mexico's largest trade partner, trade and foreign investment diversification (especially with the EU) will be necessary for Mexico to maintain economic growth as low-cost manufacturing gets diverted to China by the United States.

ASSOCIATION OF SOUTH EAST ASIAN NATIONS (ASEAN). ASEAN (**www.aseansec.org**), headquartered in Jakarta, Indonesia, was established in August 1967 by the five founding members: Indonesia, Malaysia, the Philippines, Singapore, and Thailand (see Exhibit 2.9). With an initial interest in addressing regional security issues (protecting the region from big power rivalry and the spread of communism and creating a forum for resolving intraregional disputes), ASEAN has moved steadily toward greater economic cooperation with a goal of establishing a free trade area by 2007. ASEAN's current membership stands at ten with Brunei joining in 1984, Vietnam in 1995, Laos and Burma in 1977, and Cambodia in 1999. A growing ASEAN concern is the economic ascendancy of China, which as a major low-cost manufacturing center has been one of the world's most attractive destinations for foreign investment. China is embracing capitalism and flexing its political muscle as it strives to become the world's second superpower. For 18 of the past 20 centuries China was the largest economy in the world, and many Chinese see the past two centuries of underdevelopment and colonial occupation as an aberration that must be overcome. To prevent the loss of jobs (and the loss of exports to China) and also to tap China's growing domestic consumer market, members of ASEAN are hoping to develop a free trade agreement with China by 2010. For China, a free trade agreement with ASEAN would mean strengthening its regional influence.

REGIONAL INTEGRATION IN LATIN AMERICA. Latin America has seen a patchwork of constantly changing regional trade and investment agreements (see Exhibit 2.10). This is a result of unrealistic integration goals, political paralysis, and poor economic policies that have undermined implementation of most trade agreements so far, forcing participating countries to regularly change their alliances, objectives, and approaches. The first step toward free trade in Latin America was taken with the signing of the Treaty of Montevideo in 1960, creating the Latin American Free Trade

EXHIBIT 2.9

ASEAN

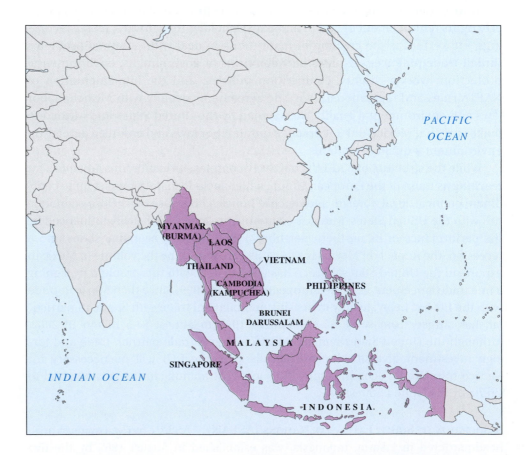

Association (LAFTA). Seven countries—Argentina, Brazil, Chile, Mexico, Paraguay, Peru, and Uruguay—indicated their intention to create a free trade zone by 1972, but got derailed because members were unable to agree on the timetable and the phased lowering of tariff barriers.

EXHIBIT 2.10

Latin America

In 1969, frustrated by the lack of progress in LAFTA, Bolivia, Chile, Colombia, Ecuador, and Peru joined in creating the Andean Group, which aimed at economic integration through reduced taxes, a common external tariff, and investment in poorer industrial areas of their countries. Argentina and Brazil, on the other hand, began discussions on bilateral trade liberalization in 1985 that led to the signing of the Treaty of Asuncion in 1991 among Argentina, Brazil, Paraguay, and Uruguay, creating the Southern Cone Common Market, or *Mercosur* (*Mercado Comun del Sur*). That treaty called for progressive tariff reduction, the adoption of sectoral agreements, a common external tariff, and the ultimate creation of a common market by 2005. Much remains to materialize in *Mercosur* given the economic uncertainties in Argentina and Brazil.

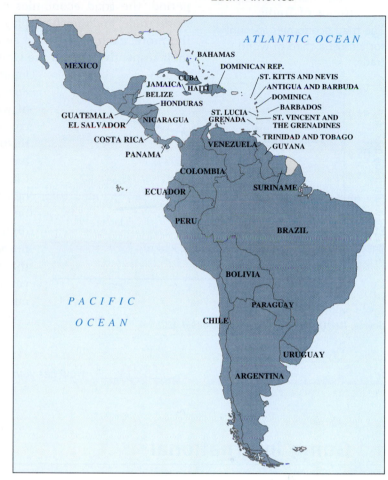

With the apparent success of NAFTA, formal discussions to establish a Free Trade Area of the Americas (FTAA), an idea initiated by the 34-nation (all countries of Latin America excluding Cuba) Summit of the Americas in 1994, began under the Clinton administration. The United States hopes to meet the 2005 deadline for the FTAA agreement that would encompass 800 million people and a $13 trillion regional economy. The region accounts for some 37 percent of all U.S. trade and $155 billion in U.S. FDI. However, before FTAA is established, numerous issues similar to those discussed during NAFTA negotiations will need to be addressed. These include clarification of rules and procedures for reducing or eliminating trade barriers; enforcement of FTAA; and measures for addressing environmental, labor, and related issues.

After formally signing a free trade agreement with Chile on June 6, 2003, the Bush administration began free trade talks with five Central American countries (Costa Rica, El Salvador, Guatemala, Honduras, and Nicaragua) as a means to push NAFTA south of Mexico. Although U.S.–Central American bilateral trade was around $20 billion in 2001, or roughly 9 percent of U.S.–Mexico trade during the same year, the United States' and Central America's economies are relatively complementary, with the United States having a competitive advantage in producing grains (cereals) and Central America being a low-cost producer of tropical fruits, ornamental plants, and sugar. A major challenge that will need to be overcome is Central America's access to the highly protected U.S. sugar market (a protection strongly supported by politically powerful U.S. "sugar barons").

THE TRIAD ECONOMIES. A close look at world trade flows, Exhibit 2.11, (on p. 76) shows the dominant role played by three major market economies—the United States, Japan, and Germany—also known as the triad economies. The United States,

EXHIBIT 2.11

The Triad Economies: The Importance of Trade

The triad economies account for almost a third of world trade.

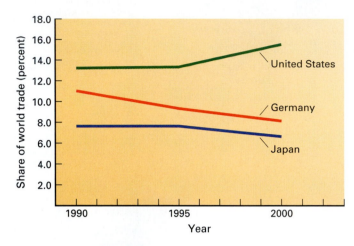

Source: *IMF, Direction of Trade Statistics, 1997, 2002.*

Japan, and Germany are the world's three largest (GDP in nominal terms) economies and the world's largest traders as well. During the 1990 to 2000 period, the triad economies consistently accounted for almost one-third of world trade, and they have played a major role in globalization of business. Furthermore, each of the triad economies is a leader of trade and investment in their respective region, the United States leading in the North America region, Japan leading in Asia, and Germany leading in the European Union. They represent the tripolarization of world trade. The triad economies are generally considered the "engine of growth" of their respective regions, although Japan's performance since 1990 has been disappointing and is overshadowed by China's booming economy. Although the discussion here is restricted to international trade, the same can be said about international investment (foreign direct investment as well as portfolio investment) flows among the triad economies. The net effect is that the triad economies are the epicenters for innovation, new product or service development, and entrepreneurship.

reality CHECK   *How has your state been affected by NAFTA?*

Going International

LEARNING OBJECTIVE 9

Define and summarize the various methods of conducting business internationally.

risk profile The potential loss that entrepreneurs are willing to take in a business

There are several ways that businesses could participate in and profit from international operations, and much will depend on the amount of risk that entrepreneurs are willing to take. A fundamental fact of life in business is the risk-return trade-off. In general, the greater the risk (loss of capital invested) entrepreneurs are willing to take, the greater the rewards (profits) they are likely to reap. The converse is also true: The lower the business risk, the lower the rewards (return on investment). Thus when firms decide to go international (either willingly or unwillingly), a wide range of opportunities is available and entrepreneurs can choose the approach that suits their **risk profile,** the amount of potential loss they are willing to take. When domestic firms refrain from entering overseas markets because of concerns such as uncertainty and unfamiliarity with foreign cultures, foreign firms may take that opportunity to enter the domestic market. Global competition in a free enterprise system cannot be avoided and businesses must seek to explore opportunities both at home and abroad simultaneously in order to succeed. Conducting business internationally is rewarding both financially and emotionally. In the ensuing approaches to going international, the amount of business risk that firms will need to take increases as we go along. But, as we discussed earlier, with increased risk the opportunity to make greater profit also increases.

Export-Import Business

As seen in Exhibit 2.2, the value of global merchandise trade (exports plus imports) in 2001 was approximately $12.5 trillion. International trade offers tremendous opportunities to firms interested in penetrating foreign markets (by exporting) or importing merchandise at competitive prices for domestic consumption. The **export-import business** is a relatively low-risk operation given the fact that capital is not tied up and it is relatively easy to enter or exit out of this business. Furthermore, there are well-established techniques for financing international trade (called trade finance) that are aimed at facilitating trade on the one hand and minimizing financial risk on the other. Simply stated, in trade finance, the exporter is assured of receiving payment soon after the importer receives the stated merchandise in good condition. This is accomplished with the help of documents (export invoice, insurance on goods, shipping documents, customs clearance documents at foreign ports, etc.) that are made available to the importer's banks prior to payment. When the importer receives the stated documents, she or he can take delivery of the merchandise only after making payment (to the bank) for the imported goods. The importer's bank then transfers the payment to the exporter. There is, therefore, hardly any risk in this business, and banks play an important role in facilitating international trade.

Firms can conduct export-import business with as little as three or four employees, as in the case of importing spices, groceries, or handicrafts from abroad. At the other extreme, large trading companies (especially Japanese trading firms like Mitsui & Company) may employ hundreds or thousands of workers, since they trade in high-cost and high-volume consumer durables (cars, washing machines, appliances, consumer electronics, etc.) and industrial products (chemicals, minerals, crude oil, etc.). In the United States, companies like Cargill, ADM, and Conagra are major exporters of agricultural products. Furthermore, large corporations like Boeing, General Electric, and Intel conduct their own export-import businesses. Still, some 20 percent of U.S. international trade is conducted by small business.

The opportunity to participate in export-import business is significant, and various government and nongovernmental agencies offer specialized seminars and programs on how to identify overseas markets and sell merchandise there. For example, certification from the U.S. Department of Commerce can be obtained for individuals enrolling in the Global Market Series Export Certificate Program (**www.exportimport.com**). In order to facilitate and encourage small- and medium-sized firms to penetrate emerging overseas markets, the U.S. government (U.S. Agency for International Development) has set up the Global Technology Network (**www.usgtn.org**), which is a network of domestic and international partners. Furthermore, the U.S. government provides a wealth of information (**www.ita.doc.gov/td/industry/otea**) on business conditions in various foreign countries that can help entrepreneurs identify potential business opportunities overseas. With the advent of the Internet, conducting international trade has become even easier and more exciting. Companies, big and small, have installed their own websites that detail all the products and services that they provide. Product catalogs with detailed specifications, pictures, prices, shipping details, and so on are made available on the website for the whole world to see and order from. The websites are constantly updated so that interested customers are made fully aware of what is available. The Internet has largely eliminated the need for printing brochures, which invariably become outdated the moment they are printed! Also, once orders are placed, both the buyer and seller can readily identify the location of the product as it moves along the supply chain. However, since it is relatively easy

export-import business A relatively low-risk operation that involves penetrating foreign markets (by exporting) or importing merchandise (of all kinds) at competitive prices for domestic consumption

to participate in the export-import business, competition is generally keen and the profit margins may not be very high.

Licensing and Franchising

In international trade, the relationship between the exporter and the importer is at arms length; that is, the two parties may not even know or meet with each other. Merchandise is shipped and payment is received; it is that straightforward. However, in licensing and franchising, the relationship with the overseas partner is closer. The company that is providing the license or franchise will need to properly evaluate, understand, and trust the overseas partner, since those relationships generally last for several years, if not longer. Licensing and franchising involve slightly more risk than pure international trade business. In **licensing,** a company or individual provides the foreign partner the technology (patented technology, copyright, process, trademark, etc.) to manufacture and sell its products in return for an annual license fee. The license fee could be based on a percentage of final sales revenue or the number of units sold. The understanding is that the foreign partner will use the patented technology as agreed to produce and sell products that meet the licensor's standards (to avoid sales of substandard products, which could ruin the licensor's global reputation). For example, when Mercedes Benz provided Tata (a major industrial group in India) a license to manufacture Mercedes-Benz trucks, Tata agreed to maintain quality control to Mercedes-Benz specifications and also to provide a license fee depending on sales volume. Drug manufacturers like Merck, Eli Lilly, Aventis, and so on frequently license their technology to foreign firms (e.g., Ranbaxy in India) for a fee to produce certain drugs and sell them in the local market. Why do firms license their technology to foreign partners rather than export the drug to the country or manufacture the product overseas themselves? The reason is quite simple. If the market for a particular drug in a country is huge, it may make sense to manufacture the product there (to take advantage of lower labor and raw material costs) rather than depend on exports. Also, the licensor may not have the resources needed for making the overseas investment in plant and equipment or the licensor may have better uses for those resources. At times, a firm may provide its license to a foreign partner to manufacture and sell the patented product not only locally but also to other countries in the region as well. A major point of concern to the licensor is the fact that at times unscrupulous licensees may manufacture the licensed product and sell it under a different brand name. In this case, the licensor will lose some of the patent fees (because of sales diversion) and sales (because of competition from the local brand).

Franchising, on the other hand, obligates the parent firm to provide specialized equipment and/or service (e.g., product, price, promotion, and distribution strategy), and even some seed money, to the foreign franchisee in return for an annual fee. The fast-food industry is best known for franchises, domestically and internationally. Some of the well-known fast-food franchises include McDonald's, Burger King, Pizza Hut, Domino's, Popeye's, KFC, and Subway. Most of these franchises, domestically and internationally, are owned and operated by local residents who generally obtain capital locally. As in the case of licensing, franchising essentially leads to penetration of international markets without significant capital investment abroad. In return for the franchise fee, the fast-food franchisee receives help in the layout of the outlet, the equipment that is required to run the operation, training on how to manage the franchise, and so on, so that customers visiting a McDonald's outlet in Australia, for example, can expect to

licensing The practice in which a company or individual provides the foreign partner the technology (patented technology, copyright, process, trademark, etc.) to manufacture and sell products or services for an annual license fee

franchising The practice in which a firm is obligated to provide specialized equipment and service support (e.g., training, product, price, promotion, and distribution strategy), and at times even some seed money, in return for an annual fee from the franchisee

receive quality of product and service comparable to that they would receive in the United States, France, or Singapore. Along with the spread of MTV culture, fast-food and related franchises have spread all over the world. For example, Yum! Brands (**www.yum.com/about/default.htm**), which is based in Louisville, Kentucky, is organized around its five core constituents, KFC, Pizza Hut, Taco Bell, A&W All American Food Restaurants, and Long John Silver's. International profits have been the key to Yum! Brands' success. For example, profits in 2001 grew by 39 percent in China, 33 percent in the United Kingdom, and 20 percent in South Korea. In 2001, Yum! Brands added more than 1000 new outlets internationally (**www.yum.com/international/default.htm**), mostly with franchisees. That's almost three new restaurants being opened somewhere outside the United States every day of the year. China is Yum! Brands' fastest-growing and most profitable market (outside the United States); 500 KFC and 60 Pizza Hut restaurants were opened there in 2001.

International Joint Ventures and Strategic Alliances

When firms find the domestic market saturated (reflected by the high degree of domestic competition and low profit margins) and opportunities for sales and profits overseas are significant, some of these firms may consider making major investments abroad in order to expand their business. Since the profit potential is significant, these firms may be willing to take on more financial risk to reap greater profits. Yet, these firms may not quite be willing to take on the risk of completely owning and operating a plant overseas. They may prefer to share the risk as well as the return with another corporate entity. That's what joint ventures are all about. An **international joint venture** is a business that is jointly owned (implies shared equity) and operated by two or more firms (usually one from the host country and the other from another country) that pool their resources (labor, capital, technology, and management) to penetrate host country markets, generate (and share) profits, and share the commercial risk. For example, several oil companies that compete in their respective domestic markets may form a joint venture together with the Saudis to explore for oil and gas in Saudi Arabia in order to set up a gas-gathering system that would produce petrochemicals and also generate electricity for the Saudis. The formation of a joint venture would make sense because the investment needs will be so huge (billions of dollars) that no single company in the joint venture would be willing to come up with all the needed funds. Furthermore, even if one company had the capital to invest, it would be unwilling to risk all its capital in one venture; that is, firms will want to diversify to reduce risk. Furthermore, international joint ventures enable each partner to utilize its comparative advantage for the betterment of the joint operation. In most cases, international joint ventures will include at least one local firm (a firm that resides in the foreign country). The reason is simple. The local partner will be most knowledgeable about the domestic economic, cultural, and political environment. Hence, the local partner will be able to "get things done" overseas in an efficient manner. International joint ventures with local firms often lead to the transfer of management and technical expertise in the long run. In addition, some of the corporate profits generated there will remain in the domestic economy. The automobile industry, which is highly capital intensive, is an excellent example of an international joint venture. DaimlerChrysler, for example, has a joint venture operation with Mitsubishi Motors of Japan in order to gain a foothold in Japan. Some of the Daimler Benz engines will be shipped and used in Mitsubishi cars. Similarly, DaimlerChrysler has a joint venture with Hyundai

international joint venture A business that is jointly owned (implies shared equity) and operated by two or more firms (usually one from the host country and the other from another country) that pool their resources (capital, technology, and management) to penetrate host country markets, generate (and share) profits, and share the commercial risk

Motors of Korea (Hyundai sells cars in Asia, Europe, and the United States). Ford has joint ventures with Mazda of Japan, Volvo of Sweden, and Kia of South Korea. General Motors has joint ventures in South Korea and China. The ultimate objective of most of these joint ventures is to use joint production and sales distribution networks to generate increased revenue (also market share) and profits. Coca-Cola, for example, has 31 bottling plants and two concentrate manufacturing plants with three separate joint venture partners in China alone. With about $1.1 billion invested in China, Coca-Cola employs some 20,000 workers there and has been profitable for the past eight years.

strategic alliances Marriages of convenience between two or more firms that do not involve the creation of a separate entity with joint ownership (nonequity arrangements) and in which the firms stand to gain through cooperation with each other for specific purposes and for a given period of time

Although similar to joint ventures in many ways, **strategic alliances** differ from joint ventures in one major characteristic: they involve nonequity arrangements. Strategic alliances do not involve the creation of a separate entity with joint ownership. They are marriages of convenience between two or more firms that stand to gain through cooperation with each other for specific reasons and for a given period of time. Thus one could consider strategic alliances to be cooperative ventures rather than joint ventures.

Since strategic alliances are based on cooperative arrangements, there are numerous ways that firms from different countries can cooperate to form them. For example, companies in different parts of the world may cooperate in the field of biotechnology with one focusing on genetically modified rice and the other focusing on genetically modified corn or wheat. These companies could pool their research findings to help each other. Similarly, companies could form strategic alliances in production, where each partner manufactures a specific component in which it has comparative advantage and later swaps those components with the other partners (e.g., automobile manufacturers). Firms could also form strategic alliances in marketing when each alliance partner has a niche market. A good example is the Star Alliance system (**www.star-alliance.com**) in the airline industry. Star Alliance members can code-share flights (e.g., Lufthansa Flight 11 could be designated as United Flight 2011); this enables each member airline to make reservations on the other's flight. It helps passengers in a couple of ways. First, passengers traveling between two cities (in different countries) could complete some of their flight segments using United Airlines and the remaining segments using Lufthansa Airlines. Although United might not have flights to the final destination, Lufthansa will. Second, passengers who are members of United's frequent flyer program will receive mileage credit for the Lufthansa segments as well. The same applies to passengers who are members of Lufthansa's frequent flyer program. Members of the Star Alliance stand to gain as well, since they will be able to better utilize their seating capacity. Strategic alliance in the airline industry is aimed at maximizing capacity utilization of all flights with the ultimate goal of keeping member airlines profitable. A challenge facing strategic alliances is the fact that any member could prematurely quit the alliance, producing a negative impact on some or all of the other partners. Choosing the right partner with whom to cooperate is a key to the success of strategic alliances.

Multinational Enterprises

multinational enterprises Firms that have a home base in one country, but own and control plants (factories) or other businesses in one or more foreign countries

Multinational enterprises (MNEs) are firms that have a home base in one country, but own and control plants (factories) or other businesses overseas. General Electric (United States), IBM (United States), Microsoft (United States), Sony (Japan), BMW (Germany), Shell (United Kingdom–Netherlands), and BP (United Kingdom) are some of the hundreds of large MNEs that are based in one country but own and operate plants in other countries.

Case in Point

DaimlerChrysler: Expanding Its Technological Reach

In June 2000, DaimlerChrysler of Germany and Hyundai Motor Company of South Korea announced the formation of a 50-50 joint venture for the production of commercial vehicles and engines in Chonju, South Korea. This venture was made possible through DaimlerChrysler's acquisition of a 10.5 percent stake in Hyundai Motor Company for U.S. $428 million. Together with the existing DaimlerChrysler–Mitsubishi Motors Corporation partnership, the DaimlerChrysler–Mitsubishi–Hyundai Motor Company partnership hoped to become one of the strongest alliances in the automotive industry. As part of the agreement, the trio planned to jointly develop and produce a range of world-class, high-quality gasoline engines for small cars and commercial vehicles to compete in key *global* markets such as Asia, NAFTA, Latin America, and Europe. Juergen E. Schrempp, chairman of DaimlerChrysler AG, said, "Hyundai Motor Company is an ideal partner to expand DaimlerChrysler's growing presence in Asia. Hyundai is successful, profitable, and by far the strongest player in the Korean automotive market. It has an excellent distribution network throughout Asia and in particular the fast-growing ASEAN countries. The commercial vehicle joint venture will also further strengthen our position as the number one commercial vehicle producer in the world."

Under the terms of the commercial vehicle joint venture, Hyundai agreed to provide its state-of-the-art commercial vehicle plant in Chonju and Daimler-Chrysler was to contribute its innovative technology, thereby creating an ideal platform for the production of commercial vehicles for the global market. However, since commencement of the strategic alliance in 2000, DaimlerChrysler's financial performance has been below expectations, which resulted in a re-prioritization of both companies' strategic objectives. On May 12, 2004, the two companies agreed to terminate plans regarding the commercial vehicle joint venture in South Korea and move forward with the joint development and manufacture of a family of four-cylinder gasoline engines, with a focus on project-by-project collaborative efforts and without a shareholding relationship. To achieve cost efficiencies, DaimlerChrysler and Hyundai will also cooperate in R&D, joint procurement activities, and *global supply chain* management. The joint venture will utilize the companies' respective *global* distribution network to increase market share. As part of the strategic alliance realignment, DaimlerChrysler sold its 10.5 percent stake in Hyundai Motor at a profit of several hundred million dollars.

Source: www.daimlerchrysler.com/new/top/2002; www.daimlerchrysler.com/homepage/homepage_e.htm.

Questions

1. Does the DaimlerChrysler joint venture with Hyundai Motor Company make business sense? Why?
2. What are some potential challenges that these two companies could face as they move forward?

In general, MNEs are large corporations with a significant amount of resources (capital, management talent, and technology) at their disposal. Given these assets, MNEs are willing and able to take on the risk needed to operate internationally. Exhibit 2.12 (on p. 82) provides a list of the top ten MNEs in the world (in 2003) in terms of valuation (company stock price times the number of stocks outstanding in the world market). The *Financial Times* annually publishes the list of the world's largest 500 companies (**www.ft.com/ft500**). In 2003, U.S. MNEs continued to dominate the *Financial Times* Global 500 list with 240 companies ranked in the top 500, followed by Japan with 47 companies and the United Kingdom with 34 companies. Multinational enterprises are also sometimes called multinational corporations (MNCs) or transnational corporations (TNCs).

While the emergence of MNEs can be traced to the early part of the twentieth century, their growth greatly accelerated only after World War II, when various international organizations (and international rules of the game) were established and

DaimlerChrysler AG, a German multinational enterprise with dual headquarters in Stuttgart, Germany and Auburn Hills, Michigan, has factories worldwide. This plant in Sao Bernardo is one of two manufacturing plants in Brazil. It produces Mercedes-Benz trucks and buses sold primarily in the Latin American market.

international trade and investment rules and regulations began a process of liberalization. In the early part of the twentieth century, the profit-motivated MNEs were primarily raw material seekers. Most of them were from the industrialized countries of Europe and North America and were in search of primary products like crude oil and minerals (iron ore, copper, bauxite, gold, coal, etc.), which were largely to be found in such developing regions as the Middle East, Africa, Asia, Latin America, and Australia. With the introduction of assembly line production by Ford in 1903, U.S. companies like Ford and General Motors sought to actively penetrate the European market by acquiring (purchasing) some of the small car companies in Europe and expanding their operations. Although U.S. MNEs still play a dominant

EXHIBIT 2.12

The World's Ten Largest Companies (2003)

  The United States' MNEs dominate the world business scene.

Rank	Company	Sector	Country	Market Value ($ billion)
1	Microsoft	Software	United States	264
2	General Electric	Electrical equipment	United States	260
3	Exxon Mobil	Oil & gas	United States	241
4	Wal-Mart	Retailing	United States	234
5	Pfizer	Pharmaceuticals/biotech	United States	196
6	Citigroup	Banking/finance	United States	184
7	Johnson & Johnson	Pharmaceuticals/Biotech	United States	170
8	Royal Dutch/Shell	Oil & gas	Netherlands/ United Kingdom	149
9	British Petroleum	Oil & gas	United Kingdom	144
10	IBM	Computers & software	United States	139

Source: "FT Global 500: How the Corporate Titans Line Up," *Financial Times,* May 28, 2004. Special Report, p.13.

role in the world economy, since the early 1960s, the dynamic growth of European, Japanese, and South Korean MNEs has changed the competitive nature of global business. Increasingly, MNEs are sprouting from many developing countries of Asia and Latin America in some niche areas of operation.

reality CHECK *What form of international business is most prevalent in your business community?*

LEARNING OBJECTIVE 10
Explain the major strategic reasons why multinational enterprises go abroad.

There are several reasons why MNEs go international, all of which are based on the urge to earn higher profits by utilizing the MNE's competitive advantage. Some of the major reasons why MNEs invest abroad include

1. Acquiring essential raw materials: MNEs generally use raw materials in the production of goods and services and quite often these raw materials are located overseas. In order to have a reliable supply of these resources, MNEs choose to invest abroad. For example, the oil majors (ExxonMobil, Chevron-Texaco, Shell, BP, Total, etc.) have invested tremendous amounts of capital in the oil-rich regions of the world such as the Middle East, Central Asia, Russia, Southeast Asia, and Latin America. This is because much of crude oil consumption is in developed countries, whereas the oil reserves are found largely in developing countries. DeBeers (the diamond cartel) has acquired or operates most of the large diamond mines in Africa. Alcoa has heavy investment in bauxite (aluminum ore) mines in Latin America, enabling it to produce aluminum ingots.

2. Maximizing production efficiency: MNEs are always looking for the least-cost method of production, utilizing low-cost raw material inputs, employing productive labor, obtaining capital at attractive rates, and utilizing appropriate technology. Since a large amount of quality inexpensive labor is readily available in China, many MNEs have set up operations in that country to manufacture all sorts of products like Toastmaster ovens, Sony DVD players, Sanyo TVs, and so on. Motorola, for example, is one of the largest foreign investors in China with some $3.4 billion invested in two plants manufacturing mobile phones, cellular networks, and semiconductors (recently sold to Chinese partners). Similarly, India has a large pool of talented, relatively inexpensive software engineers; hence companies like Microsoft, Oracle, Texas Instruments, Alcatel, and so on have set up operations in India's technology centers like Bangalore and Hyderabad to develop and market software.

3. Expanding market share: When the domestic market is saturated, which is reflected in a high level of competition and low profit margins, MNEs seek to explore overseas markets where competition may not be that fierce or the consumer market is large. For example, there are quite a few foreign MNEs with manufacturing plants in the United States. Honda has several plants in Ohio, Toyota has production facilities in California, Hyundai is building a plant in Alabama, Mercedes Benz has a plant in Alabama as well, and BMW has a plant in South Carolina. The market for automobiles in the *United States* is large, and foreign MNEs want to manufacture cars close to the market. Similarly, given China's 1.3 billion consumers with growing income levels, many MNEs have successfully penetrated that market as well. China is now Eastman Kodak's second largest market after the United States, and its sales in China are growing faster than anywhere else. With a total investment of some $1.2

billion in five manufacturing plants for cameras, chemicals, and film, Kodak has more than 8000 stores in China. Also, Groupe Danone (France) has successfully manufactured and marketed biscuits, beverages, and dairy products in China. Procter & Gamble (United States) and Siemens (Germany) have been success stories in China and India.

4. Minimizing compliance cost: Industrialized countries generally impose stringent regulations, especially as they relate to environmental quality, worker protection (safety and health), minimum wage, zoning, and so on. In addition, corporate tax rates may be high in the home countries of MNEs. All these factors add to the cost of conducting business in industrialized countries. For these reasons some MNEs relocate operations to developing countries where the regulatory environment is less rigorous and enforcement of regulations may be lax. Several U.S.-based MNEs have been accused of taking advantage of Mexico's lax environmental standards by investing in **maquiladoras** along the U.S.-Mexico border. These issues have become contentious, and various nongovernmental organizations (NGOs) like Greenpeace have resorted to massive protests and economic disruption in recent years whenever there is an international gathering or conference that deals with globalization (e.g., IMF, World Bank, or WTO meetings). At times these protests have turned violent. The perception of these organizations is that MNEs (e.g., Nike) are exploiting workers (using child labor, providing unsafe working conditions, and paying substandard wages) in poor countries and polluting the environment (and the health of citizens) in developing countries.[5,6] Such protests are likely to continue until these concerns are adequately addressed.

5. Pursuing a politically safe business environment: Like all businesses, MNEs dislike uncertainty, since uncertainty, implies risks. When MNEs venture overseas, they are more prone to invest in countries that have a stable political environment, that is, where the "rule of law" is transparent and enforcement is swift and evenhanded. MNEs try to shy away from countries that are prone to coups and where political succession is not well defined. They prefer to invest in countries where the risk of expropriation (government takeover of assets without compensation) and nationalization (government acquisition of MNEs without adequate compensation) are minimal. Industrialized countries and others with well-established legal systems and professional law enforcement agencies, for example, Singapore, Malaysia, and Chile, attract sizable numbers of MNEs.

maquiladoras The Maquiladora program allowed factories (primarily on the Mexican border to the U.S.) to temporarily import supplies, parts, machinery, and equipment necessary to produce goods and services in Mexico duty-free, as long as the output was exported back to the United States

The two main avenues by which MNEs enter foreign countries are **mergers and acquisitions** of existing operations, and the establishment of new subsidiaries.

mergers and acquisitions The process of identifying, valuing, and taking over a foreign firm to meet a company's growth objectives

Cross-Border Mergers and Acquisitions.   Multinational enterprises often enter foreign markets by merging or acquiring (buying) well-established firms overseas. The advantages are obvious. An existing firm in a host country may already have a well-developed production or marketing operation along with a good distribution network or valuable technology. By merging activities with the host country firm, the new firm will become more competitive internationally. In **acquisitions,** the home country firm will buy the host country firm outright and implement its own international business strategy (as the acquiring company sees fit). However, in mergers, the management of both companies will play an active role in business development. Cross-border mergers and acquisitions will enable MNEs to have instant access to foreign markets that fit their global strategy. Along with the acquired company comes goodwill and market share. When Coca-Cola acquired

acquisitions Purchase of established firms abroad with the goal of utilizing the existing production, marketing, and distribution networks and of having instant access to foreign markets that fit the purchasing firm's global strategy

Parle's in India, it instantly had access to Parle's huge national bottling and distribution network. All that Coca-Cola had to do was to upgrade existing production facilities and manufacture Coca-Cola products, which were then ready to be sold through Parle's distribution network. It is important for MNEs to make sure that the company being acquired is well established and has a good reputation in the local market. As compared with other types of foreign market entry discussed so far, acquisitions are relatively risky because a significant amount of capital may be needed to acquire and upgrade facilities. Also, cultural differences may inhibit the integration of the two organizations of different nationality, customs, and values. If for some unfortunate reason (e.g., labor problems) the new firm performs poorly and the MNE wants to dispose of its assets, serious thought must be given to its exit strategy—how to get out of the country and at the same time sell the company at a reasonable price without incurring significant loss.

Establishment of New Subsidiaries. As an alternative to acquisitions, MNEs frequently decide to build and operate their own new facilities (also called "green field" plants) overseas. These **subsidiaries** of MNEs require a large capital investment. Yet, the new subsidiaries will most likely be modern, efficient, environmentally sound, and designed to contemporary international standards, which will enable them to handle the latest in supply chain management. For these reasons subsidiaries are sometimes preferred to acquisitions because they can be tailored to meet the MNE's needs. However, subsidiaries will require major marketing efforts to penetrate the international market because of cultural differences and the fact that the entrant is relatively unknown. A new customer base needs to be established through a well-orchestrated marketing campaign.

> **subsidiaries** New facilities built and operated overseas by MNEs that require large investment of capital given the fact that these new establishments are tailored to the exact needs of the MNEs

reality CHECK *Name a U.S. multinational enterprise that you are familiar with and identify the main strategic reason for its going abroad.*

Careers in International Business

International business careers cover a broad spectrum of opportunities and can be challenging, fascinating, and rewarding. While most careers in international business require a certain amount of international travel, advances in information technology and the Internet have reduced that need somewhat. Furthermore, there are quite a few international business jobs that are home based. Rapid developments in communications and IT have made ours a "small world after all." A professional career in international business will invariably require the following three major traits, in descending order of importance: First is a functional area (accounting, finance, information systems, management, or marketing) of expertise coupled with a strong international business knowledge that could be obtained through an undergraduate business degree. Second is a passion for and ability to work in diverse cultural environments. Finally is knowledge of (or the willingness to learn) a foreign language. With the rapid globalization of business, the outlook for graduates with an international perspective is very bright. Employment opportunities for students interested in international business can be found in three major sectors of the economy: the private business sector, government agencies, and international organizations.

Within the private sector, international careers can be developed by working with small- or medium-sized companies, large multinational enterprises and banks, or the service sector (e.g., teaching, translation or interpretation, tourism and hospitality, etc.). Next, government agencies offer challenging opportunities in such fields as foreign service (foreign policy, economics and commerce, development, research, and translation), intelligence, and teaching. Finally, international organizations offer a host of opportunities, especially for extremely well qualified graduates. Most large corporations do not assign employees who are freshly graduated to their international or overseas division until they have a comprehensive understanding of the business. They must also prove themselves in domestic assignments and come to understand the global nature of the business. It is therefore important for business majors to have some functional expertise and also take courses in international business and culture. Most international organizations, like the United Nations, the IMF, the WTO, and the World Bank, however, require employees to have advanced degrees in international business or economics.

The Internet is an excellent source for identifying opportunities in international business. A google.com search of "international business careers" will provide you with a wealth of information. Some of the information indicated here can be found in International Business Careers (**www.sc.maricopa.edu/ibs/internat.htm**), Careers in International Business (**www.ibes.utoledo.edu/careers.htm**), and the Career Center of the University of California at Berkeley (**career.berkeley.edu/Icareers/Icareers.stm**. An undergraduate with a strong interest in international business could find the following entry-level positions interesting:

Careers with Small- or Medium-Sized Firms.

Following are opportunities with companies in the export-import business, transportation and insurance, travel agencies, and so on. Their duties and responsibilities could include

- Researching and evaluating overseas customers and distributors
- Preparing invoices, contracts, letters of credit, and shipping and customs documents
- Maintaining customer relations and service
- Searching for the most attractive fares for international travel and providing visa service
- Traveling abroad at times to meet with customers or clients

Careers with Multinational Enterprises (MNEs).

The best way to identify job opportunities with MNEs is to first identify those companies that generate a sizeable portion of their revenue from international operations. An entry-level job will invariably start with a domestic assignment before the employee works her or his way to the international division of the firm. A career in international business could start in any functional area mentioned before, such as accounting, auditing, taxes, financial analysis, investment analysis, banking, corporate finance, human resource management, planning, product management, sales, advertising, retailing, foreign exchange trading, international cash management, or trade finance.

Careers with the Government.

Unlike jobs with MNEs, entry-level international business positions are readily found with government agencies. Some positions, like those with the U.S. Foreign Service, require potential employees to pass an examination like the Foreign Service Examination. Other positions, like those with the U.S. Department of Commerce or Treasury, will require an undergraduate business degree with a strong aptitude for international business along with international cultural sensitivity. A useful link is *FedWorld*, which lists overseas job opportunities with the U.S. government.

Careers with the Service Industry. Broadly categorized as the hospitality and tourism sector, this industry includes the airlines, shipping, cruise lines, hotels, entertainment, national parks, and so on. The service industry requires close interacting with customers and meeting customer needs. Cultural sensitivity and foreign language proficiency could be crucial requirements for successful careers in this business sector.

Summary

The focus of this chapter is the contemporary business environment, and the most important fact to remember is that business is global in nature.

LEARNING OBJECTIVE 1
Define the major goals of effective economic management.

The primary goals of sound economic management are a high rate of real GDP growth; low levels of unemployment; low rates of inflation with free markets; and stable exchange rates with relatively open trade. A country that can consistently achieve most of these objectives is bound to have a solid economy with a booming business environment.

LEARNING OBJECTIVE 2
Summarize the key policy tools available to manage an economy.

Governments have some important direct and indirect policy tools to help them achieve their economic goals. These instruments include fiscal policy, monetary policy, incomes policies, and trade and exchange rate policies. Fiscal policy consists of government expenditures and taxation. Governments purchase goods and services to serve the needs of the general public. Taxes are the source of government revenue, without which governments would not be able to spend money on social programs and defense. Monetary policy deals with the control of the money supply in an economy. A central bank's primary objective is to make sure that there is sufficient money in the economy to promote economic growth with low inflation. Incomes policies consist of wage and price controls that are usually implemented during periods of hard economic times. Finally, trade and exchange rate policies involve the elimination of quotas and tariffs on the one hand and the maintenance of stable exchange rates on the other. The objective is to increase trade, investment, and global economic growth. Countries therefore have a wide range of economic policy tools that they can use to achieve economic goals. Yet, some of these policy tools may work against each other. The role of economic policymakers is to coordinate policies that reinforce each other to arrive at the right economic goal.

LEARNING OBJECTIVE 3
Explain why trade is better than no trade for society as a whole.

Countries gain from free trade, since on the supply side, it leads them to specialize in the production of goods and services in which they perform comparatively well. Equally important, on the demand side, international trade benefits consumers by providing a greater amount of choice in the availability of goods and services, competitive prices for those goods and services, and higher living standards. It is a win-win situation for society as a whole.

LEARNING OBJECTIVE 4
Evaluate the different forms of trade and foreign investment barriers and their impact on business, consumers, and government.

While free trade is the best form of conducting business with partners overseas, quite often countries try to restrict trade as well as FDI for various political reasons. Barriers to trade have a cost, and they also distort market-based trade patterns. While domestic firms gain because the competitive pressure from abroad is reduced through protection (and domestic firms could conduct business less efficiently), the person who ultimately pays for this inefficiency is the domestic consumer in the form of higher prices or lower-quality goods or services purchased. Protectionist policies in developed countries have severe negative effects on developing countries' production, employment, and economic growth. There are five major types of trade barriers: tariffs, quotas, voluntary restraints, counter trade, and embargoes. Protection penalizes consumers in the importing country and producers in the exporting country.

LEARNING OBJECTIVE 5

Compare the rationales behind countries' choices of exchange rate regimes.

An exchange rate is nothing but the price of one currency compared with that of another currency; the exchange of currencies takes place in foreign exchange markets. In a free market system, currency values are determined by the demand for and supply of currencies; this is called the floating exchange rate system. The values of the world's major currencies, namely, the U.S. dollar, the euro, and the yen, are largely market determined. The values of some currencies are partly determined by demand and supply in the foreign exchange market and partly by active government (central bank) intervention (purchases and sales of their own currency to manage the exchange rate) in the foreign exchange market; this is called the managed floating exchange rate system. The reason for central bank intervention is to keep the country's currency stable and encourage exports and foreign investment inflows. The central banks of major countries at times also intervene in the foreign exchange market. Some countries conduct the bulk of their international transactions with a major trade partner or in a major currency, so they link their currency's value to that of the major trade partner. Such a system is called the fixed exchange rate system.

LEARNING OBJECTIVE 6

Describe the evolution of globalization.

The dawn of globalization can be traced back to the fifteenth century, when Portuguese navigator and explorer Vasco de Gamma made voyages to Kerala State, on India's west coast, in search of spices to satisfy European palates. It was about the same time when Arabs and Chinese traders were making similar voyages to facilitate trade in spices and silk. Goods, people, and ideas have been traveling across the globe ever since. Globalization began to accelerate after World War II, starting in 1944 with the implementation of free and open economic policies by such multilateral institutions as the World Bank, the International Monetary Fund, and later the General Agreement on Tariffs and Trade (GATT), now called the World Trade Organization (WTO). While globalization is good for all concerned, much depends on how the "rules of the game"—fair trade and investment policies and harnessing the Internet—are implemented.

LEARNING OBJECTIVE 7

Summarize the stages of regional integration and explain its pros and cons.

Economic integration occurs when two or more countries join together to form a larger economic bloc. Countries have economic, social, or political reasons for regional integration. They generally begin with some form of economic integration to promote trade and investment within a group of countries. The main objectives here are economic gain—to increase economic growth and efficiency, to raise employment opportunities and the quality of life for citizens of the region, and to promote peace and harmony within the region.

Economic integration could involve the following sequence of events: First, two or more countries may create a free trade area by eliminating all barriers to trade among them. Second, these countries may form a customs union in which all free trade member countries will adopt a common external tariff with nonmember countries. Third, the countries in the customs union may remove barriers to the free movement of capital and labor within the customs union, thereby creating a common market. Fourth, the member states of the common market may choose to implement common social programs and coordinated economic policies that would lead to the creation of a single regional currency and an economic and monetary union. Finally, since member countries of the economic and monetary union would work closely with each other on all major business and economic issues, the urge to have common policies in other fields like defense and foreign policies may lead to the creation of a political union—a group of countries that will behave as a single country.

The benefits of regional integration include creating a large pool of somewhat similar consumers; encouraging economies of scale in production; freeing the flow of capital and labor; increasing cooperation, peace, and security in the region; and encouraging member states to enhance their level of social welfare to that of the most progressive states. The costs of regional integration include undermining the most-favored-nation status rule that the lowest tariff applicable to one member must be extended to all members; imposing uniform laws and regulations that at times do not take into account national economic, cultural, and social differences; losing sovereignty, national independence, and identity; and rising crime because of the ease of the cross-border movement of labor.

LEARNING OBJECTIVE 8

Identify the major regional trading blocs and explain why some have succeeded while others have not.

Regions in all continents of the world have entered into various forms of cooperation agreements, primarily to enhance issues of mutual interest. Following are some of the major regional economic blocs of importance to business: The European Union (EU) is the most highly evolved example of regional integration in the world, since it is already in the fourth stage of the economic integration process and is quickly moving toward the final step, which calls for political union with common defense and foreign policy institutions. The North American Free Trade Agreement (NAFTA) is a comprehensive trade agreement that deals with issues ranging from the phased reduction (and finally elimination) of trade barriers to the protection of workers' rights and the environment among Canada, the United States, and Mexico. While the structure of NAFTA is relatively complex, its institutions are not as far reaching as those of the European Union. With an initial interest in addressing regional security issues, the Association of South East Asian Nations (ASEAN) has moved steadily toward greater economic cooperation with a goal of establishing a free trade area by 2007. ASEAN's current membership stands at ten. To prevent loss of jobs (and loss of exports to China) and also to tap China's growing domestic consumer market, members of ASEAN are hoping to develop a free trade agreement with China by 2010. Regional integration in Latin America has seen a patchwork of constantly changing regional trade and investment agreements. This is a result of unrealistic integration goals, political paralysis, and poor economic policies that have undermined the implementation of most trade agreements, forcing participating countries to regularly change their alliances, objectives, and approaches. The first step toward free trade in Latin America was taken with the signing of the Treaty of Montevideo in 1960, creating the Latin American Free Trade Association (LAFTA). In 1969, frustrated by the lack of progress in LAFTA, Bolivia, Chile, Colombia, Ecuador, and Peru joined in creating the Andean Group, which aimed at economic integration through reduced taxes, a common external tariff, and investment in the poorer industrial areas of their countries. The Treaty of Asuncion in 1991 among Argentina, Brazil, Paraguay, and Uruguay created the Southern Cone Common Market, or *Mercosur* (*Mercado Comun del Sur*). That treaty called for progressive tariff reduction, the adoption of sectoral agreements, a common external tariff, and the creation of a common market by 2005. With the apparent success of NAFTA, formal discussions to establish a Free Trade Area of the Americas (FTAA), an idea initiated by a 34-nation (all countries of Latin America excluding Cuba) Summit of the Americas in 1994, begun during the Clinton administration. The United States hopes to meet the 2005 deadline for the FTAA agreement that would encompass 800 million people and a $13 trillion regional economy.

LEARNING OBJECTIVE 9

Define and summarize the various methods of conducting business internationally.

There are several ways that businesses could participate in and profit from international operations and much will depend on the amount of risk that entrepreneurs are willing to take. The approaches to going international that follow are ordered from less to more business risk that they entail. First, export-import business is a relatively low-risk operation given the fact that capital is not tied up and it is relatively easy to enter into or exit out of this business. Furthermore, there are well-established techniques of trade finance that are aimed at facilitating trade on the one hand and minimizing financial risk on the other. Second, in licensing and franchising, the relationship with the overseas partner is closer. The company that is providing the license or franchise will need to properly evaluate, understand, and trust the overseas partner, since such relationships last for several years. Licensing and franchising involve slightly more risk than international trade. In licensing, a company or individual provides the foreign partner the technology to manufacture and sell its products in return for an annual license fee. Franchising, on the other hand, obligates the parent firm to provide specialized sales and service support, and sometimes even some seed money, to the foreign franchisee in return for an annual fee. As in the case of licensing, franchising essentially leads to the penetration of international markets without significant capital investment abroad. Third, an international joint venture is a business that is jointly owned (implies shared equity) and operated by two or more firms (usually one from the host country) that pool their resources to penetrate foreign markets, generate (and share) profits, and share the commercial risk. Fourth, strategic alliances differ from joint ventures in one major characteristic: they involve nonequity arrangements. Strategic alliances do not involve the creation of a separate entity with joint ownership. They are a marriage of convenience between two or more firms that stand to gain through cooperation with each other for specific reasons and for a given period of time. Finally, multinational enterprises (MNEs) play a dominant role in this last, relatively high-risk (with corresponding high reward) area. Multinational enterprises are firms that have a home base in one country, but own and control plants (factories) or other businesses overseas.

LEARNING OBJECTIVE 10

Explain the major strategic reasons why multinational enterprises go abroad.

There are several reasons why MNEs go international, all of which are based on the urge to earn higher profits by utilizing the MNE's competitive advantage. Some of the major reasons why MNEs invest abroad include acquiring essential raw materials, maximizing production efficiency, expanding market share, minimizing compliance cost, and pursuing a politically safe business environment. Two major avenues by which MNEs enter overseas markets are mergers and acquisitions of existing operations, and the establishment of new subsidiaries.

Chapter Questions

1. Should business really care what a government's economic policy goals are? Why? What are the implications for business?
2. Four major policy tools to manage the economy are discussed in this chapter. Each policy tool has its own implications to business. Analyze in detail.
3. Explain the three major reasons why consumers would prefer to live in countries that participate in free trade.
4. Compare the theories of absolute and comparative advantage.
5. Given the fact that free trade is the best form of transacting business between countries, why do countries impose trade barriers? What are the major forms of barriers to trade? Explain fully.
6. What is the difference between foreign direct investment and foreign portfolio investment?
7. What is the foreign exchange market? What is an exchange rate and how is it determined in a free market system? Differentiate between the floating, managed floating, and fixed exchange rate systems.
8. Trace the history of globalization from the fifteenth century.
9. Explain the stages of regional integration and highlight the major pros and cons of regional integration.
10. Explain the major ways for firms to get involved in international business. What is the trade-off firms should consider before they get involved with any particular form of international business activity, and why should they consider it?
11. What are multinational enterprises (MNEs)? What are the factors that motivate MNEs to venture overseas? Describe two major avenues by which MNEs expand their overseas operations.

Interpreting Business News

1. We often hear on the radio and TV and read in business newspapers that, "Retail gasoline prices are rising in the U.S. as OPEC decides to curb crude oil output." What is OPEC? How does a cut in OPEC's output impact U.S. gasoline prices?
2. Airbus, the European aircraft manufacturer, has strengthened its lead over Boeing for leadership in the global civil aerospace industry by winning more aircraft orders. What is Airbus's nationality, and what is the most daring venture it is currently undertaking? What is Boeing's response to Airbus's venture?
3. Wal-Mart, the world's largest company in terms of sales revenue, is on a global expansion spree. Wal-Mart either builds brand new stores or purchases existing stores overseas to meet its growth ambitions. What is this form of international business activity called? How would you rationalize Wal-Mart's strategic move?

Web Assignments

1. Visit O.I. Corporation's website, **www.oico.com,** surf that website, and determine what size business it is, what types of products it makes, and where its major markets are located. How competitive is O.I. Corporation and what intrigues you most about O.I. Corporation?
2. Visit Unilever's home page, **www.unilever.com,** and determine the nationality of this company. What is Unilever's major business? List the various brands of products (by category) that it sells in the United States.
3. Visit Cemex's website, **www.cemex.com,** surf that website, and determine the line of business of this company, the company's main business strategy, and how this company managed to become the most efficient and profitable in its industry.
4. Visit Infosys's homepage, **www.infosys.com,** and answer the following questions: Where are Infosys's corporate and U.S. headquarters located? What is the company's main line of business and where (which country) does its major source of revenue come from? What type of industry is this MNE venturing in and how successful has this company been over the years? How would you measure Infosys's success?

Portfolio Projects

Exploring Your Own Case in Point

In this chapter we focused on the setting in which businesses operate. We found that business is global in nature, and advances in information technology are making our world smaller all the time. Yet businesses are heavily influenced by domestic economic policies as well. Answers to the following questions will enable you to understand the surroundings in which your company operates.

1. What economic policy goals are most important for your company's successful operation?

2. Does your company sell any of its goods and services overseas? If yes, what is the percentage of overseas sales, and to which countries are the products and services sold and why? Do any of these overseas countries impose trade barriers on your company's products? If yes, what types of trade barriers?

3. If your company does business with foreign countries, what are the major currencies that it gets involved with and what type of exchange rate system do those currencies follow?

4. What is the type of foreign market penetration selected by your company? Why? Would you consider your company to be an MNE? If yes, what was the chosen mode of foreign venture?

Starting Your Own Business

After reading this chapter, your business plan should answer questions related to the global business environment within which your firm will operate.

1. Where will your outputs be sold? Is your market domestic, regional, or international? Will sales of your output face overseas competition? If so, from which countries and why? How will NAFTA and developments in the European Union affect your business?

2. Will trade barriers impact your business? How? What is your strategy for handling such situations?

3. What is the competitive advantage of your business? Is this likely to diminish over time because of globalization and offshoring? Have you considered offshoring?

4. What aspects of domestic economic policies will likely have a negative effect on your business? What strategies do you have in place to overcome these challenges when they appear?

Test Prepper

You've read the chapter, studied the key terms, and the exam is any day now. Think you are ready to ace it? Take this sample test to gauge your comprehension of chapter material. You can check your answers at the back of the book.

True/False Questions

Please indicate if the following statements are true or false:

_____ 1. As in the nineteenth century, policymakers in government today can do little to effectively manage the economy.

_____ 2. Trying to keep inflation and unemployment very low simultaneously is a difficult task.

_____ 3. Trade theory is based on the fact that in a free enterprise and open economic system, countries will specialize in the production and export of the goods and services that they turn out most efficiently.

_____ 4. Quotas are the worst form of barriers to international trade.

_____ 5. In a free market system, the exchange rate is a price—the price of one currency compared with that of another currency.

_____ 6. Globalization has nothing to do with the elimination of barriers to trade, investment, and information flow.

_____ 7. Regional integration occurs because groups of countries may have similar economic, social, or political objectives.

_____ 8. U.S. sugar producers are not protectionists, although they are politically powerful (provide massive campaign contributions to both the Democratic and Republican parties).

_____ 9. When domestic firms refrain from entering overseas markets because of unfamiliarity with foreign cultures, foreign firms may take that opportunity to enter the domestic market.

_____ 10. Multinational enterprises are firms that have no home base, but own and control operations in other countries.

Multiple-Choice Questions

Choose the best answer.

_____ 1. Which of the following statements is not true in a free market economic system? The primary goal(s) of the government is(are) to

a. achieve rapid growth of real GDP with low unemployment.

b. maintain low inflation with stable exchange rates.

c. maintain a strong currency.

d. achieve rapid growth with low inflation.

e. achieve low inflation and unemployment at the same time.

_____ 2. Which of the following is *not* an economic policy tool that countries have at their disposal to meet their economic goals?

a. taxation and government spending policies

b. incomes policies

c. trade and exchange rate policies

d. interest rate and money supply policies

e. mergers and acquisitions policies

_____ 3. Trade is better than no trade for consumers in countries that practice free trade. Which of the following statements is not true?

a. Consumers will enjoy a greater amount of choice in goods and services that they buy.

b. Consumers will pay lower prices for imports and import-competing domestic goods and services.

c. Consumers will enjoy a higher standard of living.

d. Domestically produced goods will become expensive.

e. Consumers will have access to better quality goods.

_____ 4. The worst barrier to international trade is

a. tariffs.

b. quotas.

c. counter trade.

d. low wage rates.

e. inadequate or non-existent infrastructure (roads, etc.).

_____ 5. The U.S. Federal Reserve Bank sometimes intervenes in the foreign exchange market to control the value of the dollar. The dollar therefore follows

a. the fixed exchange rate system.

b. the floating exchange rate system.

c. the managed floating exchange rate system.

d. the gold standard system.

e. the Bretton Woods system.

_____ 6. Globalization does not

    a. reflect the process of eliminating trade, investment, cultural, and even political barriers between countries.

    b. reflect the growing links among people, communities, and economies around the world.

    c. make it possible for goods, services, and capital to cross national borders.

    d. allow for the movement of labor and companies across international borders.

    e. force countries to live in harmony and peace.

_____ 7. Regional integration does not include

    a. creating a large pool of consumers with growing incomes and similar culture, tastes, and social values.

    b. encouraging economies of scale in production and increasing the level of competition in industries.

    c. freeing the flow of capital and labor to the most productive areas.

    d. increasing cooperation, peace, and security among member countries.

    e. developing a common official language.

_____ 8. Which of the following statements is *not* true when you compare the United States with the 25-member European Union (EU)?

    a. The U.S. population is less than the EU population.

    b. U.S. income (PPP-based GNI) is less than the corresponding EU income.

    c. U.S. per capita income (PPP-based GNI) is greater than EU per capita income.

    d. U.S. land surface area is greater than the EU's.

    e. U.S. income (nominal GNI) is less than the corresponding EU income.

_____ 9. Which of the following statements is *not* true regarding conducting international business?

    a. A wider range of opportunities is available for entrepreneurs.

    b. Firms generally refrain from entering overseas markets because of unfamiliarity with foreign cultures and business practices.

    c. Conducting business internationally is not rewarding, both financially and emotionally.

    d. The risk involved in international business is greater than in domestic business.

    e. The risk-reward tradeoff depends crucially on the type of international business activity the firm chooses.

_____ 10. Which of the following is *not* a reason why MNEs invest abroad?

    a. To seek control of essential raw materials

    b. To expand market and profits

    c. To maximize production efficiency

    d. To minimize control of their operations

    e. To have access to foreign technology and skills

Want more questions? Visit the student website at **http://college.hmco.com/business/student/** (select Gaspar, *Introduction to Business*) and take the ACE quizzes for more practice.

3

Business Governance, Ethics, and Social Responsibility

| Introduction |
| **Business Governance Structures** |
| Sole Proprietorships |
| Partnerships |
| Corporations |

Shareholder Model of Business Governance

Separation of Ownership and Control and Potential Conflicts of Interest

Addressing Separation of Ownership and Control-Related Conflicts of Interest

Stakeholder Model of Business Governance

Businesses and Local Communities

Creditors

Suppliers

Distributors

Customers

Employees

Shareholders

Societal Responsibility Model of Business Governance

Business Ethics

Defining Business Ethics

Business Codes of Ethics

Dealing with Business Ethical Breaches

Penalties for Business Ethical Breaches

Business Ethics Training

Business Ethics on Campus

Careers in Business Governance, Ethics, and Social Responsibility

Learning Objectives

After studying this chapter, you should be able to

1. Describe the differences among sole proprietorships, partnerships, and corporations.

2. Explain the basic roles of corporate boards of directors and officers.

3. Discuss the basic dynamics of the shareholder model of business governance, and the problems engendered in major corporations today because of the separation of ownership and control.

4. Analyze different methods of solving the problems and conflicts of interest engendered by the separation of ownership and control in major corporations.

5. Discuss the stakeholder model of business governance.

6. Describe the societal responsibility model of business governance.

7. Explain the basic parameters of business ethics.

8. Discuss the development of business codes of ethics and business ethics training.

The Underground Economy

Recent estimates are that close to 9 percent of the U.S. gross domestic product is "underground," or "off the books." On the basis of studies of overall economic activity, it appears that the amount of unreported income in the United States more than doubled during the 1990s, reaching $1.25 trillion in 2000. Thousands of unrecorded cash business transactions are conducted in the United States daily, with all levels of taxation being avoided. Similarly, the growth of the U.S. service economy has created a situation where literally millions of child-care, lawn-care, domestic help, and other workers toil completely off the books. Unrecorded barter transactions, such as an orthodontist providing a neighbor's son free braces in exchange for a free racing bicycle from the bicycle store the neighbor owns, are also not uncommon. The trillion dollars plus annual U.S. underground economy involves a wide range of significant governance, social responsibility, and ethical issues and presents a situation where at times hard-working tax-paying citizens are supporting government services for working citizens who pay no or little taxes.[1]

Introduction

To say that issues of business governance, social responsibility, and ethics have recently commanded a lot of public attention is, of course, to put it mildly. From Martha Stewart, to Enron, to Tyco Corporation's Dennis Koslowski, to Arthur Andersen, news of corporate scandals has been front and center in the media.[2] For its 2002 Persons of the Year, *Time* magazine chose three **whistleblowers.** Two of these were Sherron Watkins, who early on questioned the accounting practices at Enron Corporation, and Cynthia Cooper, an accountant at WorldCom Corporation who in June of 2002 alerted WorldCom's Board of Directors to accounting trickery that inflated 2001 and 2002 profits by $3.5 billion.[3]

whistleblowers Employees who inform the appropriate authorities about an employer's wrongdoing

Sometimes stories of corporate misdeeds are quite straightforward; for example, executives stole money directly from the company. Usually, however, matters are far more complex, and discerning "right from wrong" can be far more complicated.

As we see, business ethical, governance, and social responsibility issues can arise in a wide variety of contexts. In addition, improved computer technologies such as permanently saved e-mails have vastly increased the ability of government agencies and others to monitor business activities in this regard. In this chapter we will examine a variety of business governance structures, as well as various types of possible conflicts of interest that can arise between shareholders/owners of businesses and the managers of said businesses. We will also discuss new developments in the area of governmental regulation of business governance, and new ways businesses are working to prevent ethical problems from arising at their enterprises.

The case of former Salomon Smith Barney star stock research analyst Jack Grubman illustrates some of the pressures that may lead to issues involving questionable ethics. It also shows the role of Internet technology in investigating possible corporate misdeeds.

Technology and Business

E-mail, AT&T, and Jack Grubman

You might assume that once you delete e-mails from your computer, they are forever gone from the world. This is, though, as even computer guru Bill Gates of Microsoft Corporation ironically learned during the government's antitrust case against his company, simply *not* the case. Computer servers save everything, including deleted e-mails. Jack Grubman is another high-level executive to fall victim to e-mail technology.

Grubman was formerly a star stock research analyst at the Salomon Smith Barney brokerage and investment banking unit of Citigroup. His intensive research of AT&T had given him a long-held negative view of the company's stock. In November of 1999, however, he abruptly changed his research rating of AT&T to "buy."

A series of saved e-mails purportedly revealed, however, that Grubman may have been pressured to change his stock rating on AT&T by Citigroup's chief executive Sanford I. Weil. Weil wanted to be in AT&T's good graces for a couple of reasons. First, Citigroup wished to do investment banking business for AT&T, especially with respect to its sale of public shares in its wireless division scheduled for April 2000. Second, Weil sought political support from C. Michael Armstrong, the CEO of AT&T and a member of Citigroup's Board of Directors, in his bid to "nuke" intracompany rival John Reed, Citigroup's co-chairperson.

Saved e-mails also appear to reveal that Weil, to help grease the skids with Grubman, made on behalf of Citigroup a $1 million donation to a very high-class New York City nursery school. Grubman had been trying to get his children admitted to this nursery school and had, despite his $20 million per year salary, been unsuccessful until the Citigroup philanthropy. A lesson from all this: Never write anything in an e-mail you wouldn't want published on the front page of the newspaper!

Source: Charles Gasparino, "Fallout from Grubman E-Mails Adds a Twist to Wall Street Probe," *The Wall Street Journal,* November 14, 2002, p. 1; Emily Nelson and Laurie P. Cohen, "Why Jack Grubman Was So Keen to Get His Twins into the Y," *The Wall Street Journal,* November 15, 2002, p. 1; Gretchen Morgenson and Patrick McGeehan, "Wall St. and the Nursery School: A New York Story," *New York Times—Online,* November 14, 2002.

Questions

1. What are some other ways e-mail has had a profound impact on the way business is conducted, beyond the saving of past communication records?
2. What are some other new technologies that help employers monitor and keep better historical track of employee activities?
3. Are there ways charities can better make sure corporate gifts won't present any conflicts of interest?

The above discussion illustrates some of the kinds of competitive pressures facing top business executives today, pressures which may at times force even the heads of leading corporations like Citigroup to arguably tread the line between ethical and unethical behavior. Citigroup chief executive Sanford I. Weil felt competitive pressure externally in that he feared that AT&T's investment banking business might go to a Citigroup competitor like Merrill Lynch Corporation. He also felt competitive pressure within the firm from the company's co-chairman, John Reed. Nevertheless, the actions Mr. Weil may have taken with respect to pressuring Mr. Grubman to change his recommendation on AT&T stock appear to be inappropriate. Moreover, the $1 million donation Mr. Weil made to a ritzy New York City nursery school may not have represented the best possible use of shareholder money.

Business Governance Structures

Sole Proprietorships

You don't need to form a large corporation like Citigroup in order to go into business. The vast majority of businesses operating in the United States operate as **sole proprietorships.** Indeed, roughly 18 million Americans do business as unincorporated sole proprietors, who are solely responsible for running the business. These individuals report the revenues, expenses, and profits or losses of their business on their personal tax return, assuming that all business is transacted "on the books."[4]

sole proprietorships Individually operated unincorporated businesses

There are a number of advantages to operating a sole proprietorship. For one, you can do business in your own personal name and pay taxes on earnings only once at your personal income tax rate (doing business under an "assumed name" is only slightly more complicated).

There are, however, some important disadvantages. The most important is probably liability; that is, as a sole proprietor you are personally liable for any claims against your business. Various forms of insurance can provide considerable liability protection, but it is very difficult to completely insure against all forms of liability. Another potential disadvantage is in raising capital for your business. You may be relying on your own personal financial statement as the basis on which to raise capital, and investors may be skeptical about putting money into a "one person show."

In sum, sole proprietorships are the simplest way to operate a business, but may not be the best governance structure in terms of potential liability and the need to raise capital. Exhibit 3.1 gives an overview of different forms of business governance.

EXHIBIT 3.1

Characteristics of Different Business Structures

	Formation	Funding	Taxation	Liability
Sole proprietorship	Very easy to form	May be difficult to raise capital	Earnings taxed on personal income tax form, no double taxation	Personal liability for business, can insure against some liabilities
Partnership	Need partnership agreement, somewhat harder to form than sole proprietorship	Capital contributions from different partners; outside funding possibly easier to obtain than with sole proprietorship	Income and losses reported on personal tax form, no double taxation	Complicated liability issues: general liability for actions of other partners and for business, but some partners are liable just to extent of capital contributions
Traditional corporation	Generally more difficult to form than sole proprietorships and partnerships	Capital formation generally easier than with sole proprietorship or partnership; able to float public shares	Separate tax entity; separate individual taxation of dividends paid to shareholders although at special low tax rates	No personal liability for shareholders except in very rare cases of fraud, etc.

Partnerships

partnerships Unincorporated businesses run by two or more individuals

Partnerships involve two or more people running a business. The partners share the assets, liabilities, and profits of the business. Business partnerships are more difficult to form than sole proprietorships, and while they do provide the business with multiple financial statements on which to raise capital, they also can raise fairly complicated issues in terms of liability. Technically, in a partnership each partner is liable for the obligations of the other partner made in the course of doing business. Thus, if one partner purchases goods for the business, the entire partnership, that is, each of the other partners, is liable for paying for these goods, even if the other partners didn't know about the purchase.

partnership agreement An agreement spelling out the organizational details of a partnership

general partners Partners who run the partnership's business and who are liable for its actions

limited partners Partners whose liability is limited to the amount of money they invested in the partnership and who generally aren't involved in running the business

Ownership in partnerships does not have to be equal; partnership shares can be divided in any way the parties so desire. Details on this and other issues are generally set forth in a **partnership agreement.** In most partnerships, key partners are usually **general partners,** who share in running the business and are liable for the partnership's actions. It may be possible, though, for some partners in a business to have a lesser degree of involvement with it. For example, **limited partners** are partners whose liability is generally limited to only the amount of money they invested in the partnership. There is always the possibility of conflict among partners with respect to how to run the business, although hopefully the original partnership agreement is written with enough detail to help avoid potential conflicts.[5] Many professional service and related firms operate on a partnership basis. For tax purposes, partnership income (or losses) flow directly through to the individual partners who report that income on their individual tax returns and pay taxes on it based on their personal tax rate.

Corporations

corporations Legal "persons," or entities, established for the purpose of doing business and distinct from their owners in terms of liability

Corporations are a completely different form of business organization than sole proprietorships or partnerships. The key difference is that the corporation itself is a legal "person," or entity, completely separate from the individuals involved in setting it up or running it. Once a corporation is formally established, a wall, often referred to as a "corporate veil," goes up between the corporation and its shareholders, or owners. This means that the corporate entity itself is responsible for its own debts or liabilities or, put another way, the shareholders of the corporation are not personally liable for the debts of the corporation. This feature of **limited liability** is an extremely important part of the corporate structure and distinguishes it considerably from sole proprietorships or partnerships where the owners of the business are generally personally liable for the debts of the business. Shareholders in corporations are similar to limited partners in partnerships in that the extent of loss they can suffer due to their business investment is limited to the dollar amount invested in the business. This limited liability feature is, for obvious reasons, enormously helpful to corporations in raising capital. For example, in the late 1990s individuals invested hundreds of millions of dollars in corporations involved with the Internet. A significant number of these corporations went into bankruptcy, owing others millions of dollars. The investors in these corporations likely lost all of their investments, but they were not in any way personally liable for the corporation's still-pending debts. One negative aspect of traditional corporations, however, is that the corporate entity must file a separate corporate tax return and pay a corporate income tax. Any dividends paid by the corporation to its shareholders are then also taxed, although currently at a rate much lower than that applied to other personal income. (Special tax rules apply to some corporations with very limited numbers of shareholders, known as S corporations or Chapter S corporations.) While a relatively small percentage of all businesses in the United States (no more

limited liability The principle that shareholders are not generally liable for the debts or actions of the corporation

than 20 percent) exist in corporate form, these businesses do the vast majority of dollar volume business in the country.

Historically, corporations did not dominate early American commerce. In the eighteenth and early nineteenth centuries, high transportation costs limited the size of the markets factories and other businesses could serve. This, in turn, led to relatively small local businesses with relatively low needs for capital. But new technology in the form of the steam-powered railroad locomotive dramatically lowered the cost of land transportation and led to the growth of far larger factories and businesses. These new larger businesses needed capital, and the corporate organizational form with its limited liability and opportunities for anonymous investment (no one has to know in what businesses someone owns shares) was ideally suited to the needs of these new larger business entities. In 1837, the state of Connecticut passed the first general incorporation law in the United States, giving anyone who met certain basic requirements the right to form a corporation in that state. Nearly all other states in the United States passed similar legislation shortly thereafter, and today each state in the country has its own incorporation laws.

Place of Incorporation.   A corporation is created by filing a certificate of incorporation in a given state. Different states have different laws regarding corporations, and they impose different taxes on corporate entities. The most popular state in the United States in which to incorporate is the state of Delaware. Over 300,000 companies are incorporated in Delaware, including more than one-half of the nation's 500 largest corporations (the so-called *Fortune 500*). Why Delaware? For one, Delaware has established a special, and now very respected, court known as the Chancery Court, which devotes itself to corporate issues. This court has developed a comprehensive body of corporate law precedents and has been known to interpret the law in a flexible manner that is responsive to corporate needs. In addition, this corporate-oriented court is also known for the timeliness of its decisions and its impartiality.[6]

Indeed, not only do a good number of companies initially incorporate in Delaware, some even switch their incorporation to that state from another state. Recently, for example, a major California telecommunications company named Surewest Communications switched its incorporation from California to Delaware (while now formally incorporated in Delaware, it still does nearly all its business in its original "home" state of California). These were the main reasons it gave for wanting to reincorporate in Delaware.

> *Prominence, Predictability, and Flexibility of Delaware Law.* For many years Delaware has followed a policy of encouraging incorporation in that state and . . . has been a leader in adopting, construing and implementing comprehensive, flexible corporate laws responsive to the legal and business needs of corporations organized under its laws. . . . [B]oth the legislature and courts in Delaware have demonstrated an ability and a willingness to act quickly and effectively to meet changing business needs. The Delaware courts have developed considerable expertise in dealing with corporate issues, and a substantial body of case law has developed construing Delaware law and establishing public policies with respect to corporate legal affairs.
>
> *Well-Established Principles of Corporate Governance.* There is substantial judicial precedent in the Delaware courts as to the legal principles applicable to measures that may be taken by a corporation and as to the conduct of the Board of Directors such as under the business judgment rule and other standards. The Company believes that its shareholders will benefit from the well-established principles of corporate governance that Delaware law affords.[7]

In addition, and far more controversially than incorporating in Delaware, some U.S. companies incorporate or reincorporate offshore in countries like Bermuda, the Bahamas, the Cayman Islands, Aruba, and Barbados. The Enron Corporation formerly had 43 subsidiaries legally established in the tiny island republic of Mauritius off the coast of Africa. The main draw of offshore incorporation is tax savings. Companies argue that the corporate tax burden in the United States is too high, and by incorporating or reincorporating in places like Bermuda, they can save millions of dollars annually. These additional earnings go right to the bottom line and help the company's stock price and shareholders. For example, when a company called the Stanley Works of New Britain, Connecticut, was recently thinking about reincorporating to Bermuda, it estimated it could save $30 million annually in taxes, thus increasing its earnings per share by about 35 cents annually, which would result in a projected increase in its stock of about 11.5 percent.[8] While a company's reincorporation in a tax haven like Bermuda may potentially be good for company shareholders, it obviously has a negative impact on other individuals (e.g., other taxpayers now have to carry a higher load). Incidentally, because of public pressure from unions and other constituencies, the Stanley Works Corporation ultimately scrapped its plan to reincorporate in Bermuda.

Classes of Stock.   One key advantage in forming a corporation is the capital-raising flexibility involved in issuing shares, or stock, in the company. In some companies there exists only one class, or type, of regular common stock. Other companies, however, have a wide range of stock offerings including, for example, preferred stock, which is generally a type of stock that pays a high rate of interest but confers no voting rights on its holder. One increasingly common trend for family-owned businesses now incorporating and going public is to issue two classes of common stock, usually Class A and Class B. These two types of common stock are identical except that one of the classes has far superior voting rights to the other class; they are **supravoting shares.** The founding family issues a large number of regular common shares (Class A) to the general public, but by issuing itself supravoting shares, it is often able to keep voting control of the company even though it is now a public corporation.

> **supravoting shares** Shares of a corporation's stock that have superior voting rights

For example, the William Wrigley Corporation, a large chewing gum company founded by the Wrigley family of Chicago, has just over 225 million shares outstanding. Of these 225 million shares, a little over 180 million are regular common Class A shares owned by the general public, each share having one vote. The company's remaining 45 million Class B shares, however, are supravoting shares, each, having 10 votes per share. The clear majority of these votes are in the possession, even today, of the Wrigley family. There is thus little doubt that the Wrigley family still controls the Wrigley Corporation even though it has evolved from a small family business run as a sole proprietorship into a major worldwide corporation doing close to $3 billion a year in business.

Piercing the Corporate Veil.   A key advantage to incorporation is that a wall, or "veil," is created between the corporation's shareholders and the business itself. Thus, the corporation's shareholders are not personally liable for the corporation's liabilities or debts. If a corporation, however, does not follow proper legal requirements, that is, hold annual meetings and so on, or if large shareholders make personal use of corporate property and otherwise act as if they personally are the corporation, the legal wall between the corporation and the shareholders will come crumbling down. Put another way, in such situations those owed money by the corporation may be able to **pierce the corporate veil** and reach the personal assets of company shareholders.

> **pierce the corporate veil** The situation where creditors of a corporation are able to break down the legal wall separating the corporation and its shareholders and reach the assets of its shareholders

 *Do you know the organizational form of your family physician's office? To what kind of organization do you make your payments payable?*

LEARNING OBJECTIVE 2
Explain the basic roles of corporate boards of directors and officers.

Boards of Directors. The legal governing body of all corporations is its **board of directors.** State incorporation laws generally require that there be at least three members of the board and that it meet at least once a year. In practice, most large corporations have a larger board of directors (20 or so members is not uncommon), with board meetings scheduled quarterly or more. Boards of directors are responsible for all major policy decisions of the corporation, including the hiring (and sometimes firing!) of corporate officials.

Traditionally, boards of directors have had two general types of members—**inside directors** and **outside directors.** Inside directors are individuals from inside the corporation, such as its chief executive officer (CEO) and other top officers, that sit on the board. Outside directors are individuals who are not employed as officers of the company and are thus outside of the firm. Outside directors are typically prestigious individuals such as university presidents, CEOs of other corporations, attorneys, accountants, and so on, who are named to help run the corporation.

At times, though, the distinction between inside and outside directors is blurred, for example, in the case of former employees still sitting on the board. Because of this, the New York Stock Exchange and other entities have begun distinguishing between **independent outside directors** and those outside directors not deemed to be independent. For example, an attorney whose law firm has as a major client the company on whose board of directors the attorney is sitting would not be viewed as an independent outside director. Similarly, an outside director who in addition to her or his director's fee also is employed by the company as a $200,000 per year marketing consultant would not be truly independent of the company. General Electric (GE) has recently adopted very stringent requirements in this regard, stating that its goal is to have two-thirds of its board of directors be truly independent outside directors. GE has defined *independence* to mean that the outside director and any other entities he or she is involved with cannot have any meaningful ties to the company beyond the given directorship service. GE will consider as meaningful in the case of directors who are executives of other companies the fact that either sells to or purchases from GE total of 1 percent or more of the revenues of the companies where the individuals are executive officers. Put another way, executives at companies that do a lot of business with General Electric will not be regarded as independent outside directors by GE.[9]

Boards of directors of all corporations (as well as corporate officers) operate under a legal doctrine known as the **business judgment rule.** This essentially means that directors in carrying out their duties must act in good faith and exercise at least the level of care that an ordinary prudent person would exercise in similar circumstances. In short, they must give their work as a corporate director their best business judgment. This means directors cannot properly come to meetings drunk or take actions for which there was no rational basis. They must continually try to fulfill their key role of aligning the interests of the corporation's top management and its shareholders.

It is very important, though, to note that the business judgment rule does not require that corporate directors always make the "right" decisions. It is well understood that corporate boards of directors are often faced with very complex decisions in very complex business environments. Thus, shareholders, courts, government regulators, and so on are not allowed to second-guess, or "Monday morning quarterback," corporate boards so long as the directors made their decisions in good faith using their (at the given time) best judgment.

board of directors The governing board of a corporation, which generally must have at least three members

inside directors Corporate board of directors members employed full-time by the company, for example, the CEO or other corporate officers

outside directors Corporate board of directors members not employed full-time by the company

independent outside directors Outside directors who do not have any financial or other relationship with the corporation beyond their service as a director

business judgment rule The requirement that corporate directors and officers act in good faith and exercise at least an ordinary prudent person's judgment in making business decisions

Officers. While a corporation's board of directors has ultimate policy-making power over the business, the day-to-day affairs of most larger corporations are handled by corporate officers hired by the board. The corporation's top officer is usually its **chief executive officer (CEO),** who is responsible to the board for the firm's overall performance. The CEO is generally given authority to hire other executives for the corporation. Virtually all major corporations also have a **chief financial officer (CFO),** who is responsible for accounting and general financial matters at the firm. See Exhibit 3.2 for the typical organization of a corporation.

chief executive officer (CEO) The top officer of a corporation

chief financial officer (CFO) The top corporate financial officer

EXHIBIT 3.2

Typical Corporate Governance Structure

reality CHECK *Does anyone you know serve on a corporate board, like the board of your local bank? How does he or she view that role?*

Shareholder Model of Business Governance

LEARNING OBJECTIVE 3
Discuss the basic dynamics of the shareholder model of business governance, and the problems engendered in major corporations today because of the separation of ownership and control.

shareholder model of business governance The business governance model operating from the premise that the purpose of the business is to maximize financial returns to shareholders

The **shareholder model of business governance** operates from the basic premise that the purpose of a business is to maximize financial returns for its owners, or in the case of corporations, shareholders. Of course, many other groups of individuals (and indeed society as a whole) may tangentially benefit from the running of a successful corporation (e.g., the local community collects property and other taxes, suppliers get paid, employees earn wages), but pursuant to this model of governance, a corporation exists for the benefit of its shareholders. The Nobel laureate economist Milton Friedman, a proponent of this viewpoint, has noted that the role of corporate officials is simply "to make as much money for their shareholders as possible."[10]

For example, under this model of governance, if it is legal for a corporation to reincorporate from, say, California to Delaware, Bermuda, or the Cayman Islands, and such a move will clearly help the pocketbooks of the company's shareholders, the corporation should make such a move. The fact that the state of California will lose some tax revenues or even that some employees may lose their jobs because of this action is not really relevant under this governance model. The purpose of the corporation is to legally maximize profits for its shareholders. Similarly, if laws are changed and it becomes harmful to company shareholders for a company to be incorporated in Bermuda, the Cayman Islands, and so on, the corporation then has a responsibility to change its place of incorporation.

However, what if the overall impact of a company's reincorporation in Bermuda is neutral or even slightly negative for company shareholders (this actually may be the case in some situations, since such reincorporation may trigger some additional shareholder taxes that offset shareholder benefits from increased company profits or stock price gains) but extremely beneficial for the corporation's CEO who likes to vacation in that country and who recently purchased a vacation home there right on the ocean? In such a situation, the corporation's CEO may by pursuing Bermuda reincorporation be acting in her or his own self-interest but not necessarily in the best interests of the company's shareholders. This example highlights the key issue and problem in the shareholder model of governance—potential conflicting interests of shareholders on the one hand and directors and corporate executive officers on the other.

Separation of Ownership and Control and Potential Conflicts of Interest

Corporate governance today, particularly in the case of large, publicly-held corporations, is built on a variety of principal-agent relationships. The owners of corporations—their shareholders—are the **principals.** These principals elect a corporate board of directors to act as their **agents** and to set policy and govern the corporation in the principals' best interests. The board of directors then hires more agents, the corporation's officers, to run the corporation on a day-to-day basis.

Today's major public corporations have very large numbers of shares outstanding and very large numbers of shareholders. General Electric (GE), for example, has approximately 10 billion shares of common stock outstanding and well over 500,000 shareholders. GE shareholders are dispersed all over the world, and it is virtually impossible for any individual shareholder or even shareholder group to own any sort of controlling stake in the business. Purchasing even 1 percent of GE's common stock would involve billions of dollars of investment. The upshot of all this is that in most prominent corporations today (the Wrigley Corporation noted above being a rare exception) there is a **separation of ownership and control.** The corporation's ownership lies in the hands of hundreds of thousands of widely dispersed shareholders, each owning a very small stake in the business, while control of the corporation rests with its board of directors, and perhaps even more so with its corporate officers. While technically corporate officers and directors are agents reporting to the corporation's shareholders, the fractured nature of most corporate ownership today affords shareholders relatively little monitoring power over the officers and directors. This lack of adequate monitoring of corporate officers and directors has helped lead to a wide variety of recent corporate scandals, as at Enron, Tyco, and WorldCom. In these and a wide variety of other situations, corporate officers or directors arguably acted in their own self-interest, rather than in the best interests of their principals, the shareholders. There are a number of key areas where important potential principal-agent conflicts exist in the corporate world today. They include

- Takeover bids
- Short-term versus long-term orientation
- Empire-building
- Informational access

Takeover Bids. Mergers and acquisitions are a regular part of corporate life today, and even some of the nation's formerly largest companies (e.g., Mobil Corporation, recently bought by Exxon Corporation to form Exxon-Mobil Corporation) have in recent years been acquired by other firms. Moreover, in some industries such as banking, legal restrictions on corporate mergers have dramatically fallen in recent years (e.g., past restrictions on interstate banking have collapsed and banks are now free to acquire other banks anywhere in the United States). So, what happens if a company receives a **takeover bid,** or offer to be acquired, from another company at a 50 percent premium to its present stock price? Obviously, from the perspective of the to-be-acquired company's shareholders, this is probably a wonderful thing.

What about from the perspective of the company's officers? For many of them such an acquisition may not be such a good thing, since they will likely lose their

principals Owners—shareholders—of a business

agents People working for the owners of the business

separation of ownership and control The fact that the shareholders of major corporations generally do not have much control with respect to the corporation

takeover bid An offer made by another company to acquire a company

jobs, and they may not own enough stock or have that good a severance package to offset this loss. Moreover, even if they do own a decent amount of stock or have a good severance package, many top corporate officers don't want to lose the power and prestige of being a CEO or other top executive of a major corporation. Somewhat similarly, corporate directors may not want to lose their lucrative directorships (total director compensation at many big companies today approaches $100,000 per year) and the power, prestige, and networking opportunities that go with the directorship. Thus, corporate officers and directors may be more reluctant to entertain takeover bids than the ordinary shareholder of the corporation—creating a potential conflict of interest.

Short-Term Versus Long-Term Orientation. Investors (as opposed to speculators) in shares of major corporations frequently have a rather long-term focus. Shareholders may intend to own shares of quality companies literally for decades. As a result, they may not be particularly concerned with a company's current profitability if current profits are suffering because the company is investing positively for the future. The classic "buy-and-hold" investor is mostly concerned not with a company's present stock price but with what that company's stock price is going to be in thirty years (perhaps when the investor is planning to retire). The long-run success and profitability of the corporation is what such individuals are interested in.

In contrast, many corporate officers (and even boards of directors) have recently been criticized for their highly short-term focus and orientation. Today, the tenure of many corporate CEOs is less than five years, and such corporate officers often pull out all the stops to make sure that the company is a raving success during their tenure in office. Such an approach may have a variety of benefits for given CEOs and other top corporate officers. First, executive officer bonuses are generally based on annual corporate profits. Second, stock options for executives usually have a relatively short fuse (certainly nothing like a twenty or thirty year duration), and it thus is important financially for CEOs and other top executives to keep the company's short- to medium-term stock price high. Third, high current profitability and a high current stock price help keep speculators in a company's stock happy and off the backs of the CEO and other corporate officers. Finally, running a highly profitable and successful business helps increase the marketability of the CEO and other officers should they for whatever reasons seek employment with another corporation.

The area of corporate research and development (R&D) is one area where this long-term versus short-term orientation conflict comes to the foreground. A long-term investor in a company's stock wants the company to invest heavily (even at the price of high current profitability) in new product and other research and development, so as to enhance the company's posture thirty years hence. A corporate CEO planning to leave the company in two years may, in contrast, slash the company's R&D budget in order to sharply boost current company profits. While such an action is legal, and certainly is expedient for the given CEO, it is also possibly deleterious to the long-term interests of the shareholders the CEO is supposed to be serving.

Moreover, in recent years the pressure from CEOs and other corporate officers for high current earnings has arguably led to actions far beyond just perhaps inappropriately cutting R&D budgets. Indeed, a variety of prominent companies have during the past few years illegally "cooked" their books. For example, the Enron Corporation through a variety of schemes inflated its income by $586 million, Sunbeam Corporation overstated its 1997 income by $71.1 million, and WorldCom Corporation inflated its earnings by a whopping $3.8 billion. In all three cases, top corporate officers reaped millions of dollars in performance bonuses and exercised stock option gains due to the inflated earnings, although their actions in this regard also ultimately led all three companies into bankruptcy and wiped out over $200 billion in shareholder value. Incidentally, highly reputable accounting firms signed off on all these inflated accounting reports—but that involves another sort of conflict of interest. Enron's accounting firm, Arthur Andersen, for example, was receiving $52 million in fees annually from Enron, and was thus very reluctant to raise the company's wrath by questioning what it was doing.[11]

Empire Building. Another area where a potential conflict of interest arises between the shareholders of a corporation and those who control it on a day-to-day basis, its executive officers and its directors, is with respect to the growth of the company—empire building. CEOs in particular are often interested in expanding the business via acquisitions or other methods. Part of the reason for this is the fact that CEOs (and other corporate officers) typically get paid on the basis of the size of the operation they run; the CEO of a manufacturing company generating $2 billion in annual sales will generally be paid considerably more than the CEO of a manufacturing company generating $900 million in annual sales. Also, running a larger corporation enhances the CEO's power and prestige in the business community, and likely his or her marketability on the executive job market.

However, while corporate acquisitions are almost always good for the shareholders of the firm being acquired (who usually receive a nice premium for their stock), the impact on the long-term shareholders of the firm doing the acquiring is frequently far less sanguine. Many corporate acquisitions don't, for a wide variety of reasons (e.g., purported synergies are not achieved, corporate cultures don't mesh), work out and indeed ultimately end up doing harm to the acquiring company long after the CEO who engineered the acquisition has retired. In sum, while empire building may be good for company executives, it isn't always good over the long run for company shareholders.

Information Access. The separation of ownership and control in today's large modern public corporation also results in large disparities in access to information about the company among principals, shareholders, agents, and corporate

© Mike Peters, Dayton Daily News, March 17, 2002. Reprinted with special permission of King Features Syndicate.

boards of directors and officers. The company's CEO and her or his lieutenants obviously know, or should know, virtually everything that's going on in the corporation. Moreover, the CEO should be sharing all important information with the board of directors, although this may not always be the case (e.g., in some recent corporate scandal situations various directors have argued that they were never fully informed about what was going on by the CEO, and thus they should not be held responsible for any misdeeds).

Where do the owners of the company, its shareholders, fit in this scenario? Shareholders are invited to the corporation's annual meeting (but only a very small number actually attend) and receive annual and quarterly reports regarding corporate developments. The advent of the Internet also permits shareholders to access any corporate press releases or governmental filings fairly easily. In general, though, shareholders do not have any better access to information about the company they own than nonowner general members of the public.

asymmetry of corporate information An imbalance among different people regarding information or what's going on at a corporation

What kind of mischief can this imbalance of information, or so-called **asymmetry of corporate information,** breed? Suppose the CEO of a corporation knows good news that is not yet publicly known about the company. Putting legal issues aside, the CEO can then go out and buy shares in the company from an existing shareholder, who would not be paid what the shares were really worth, and also might well not even be selling the shares if he or she had the information the CEO possessed. Conversely, the CEO might be selling shares, as some prominent former CEOs have recently been convicted of doing, if he or she knew bad information about the company before the general public.[12] Under current laws, these actions by a CEO would be blatantly illegal insider trading, as would be any trading by the CEO's friends or relatives based on his or her tips. Nevertheless, on occasion such actions continue to occur.

reality CHECK   *Do you or anyone you know own stock in a corporation? Do you know anyone who has ever attended a company's annual meeting?*

LEARNING OBJECTIVE 4
Analyze different methods of solving the problems and conflicts of interest engendered by the separation of ownership and control in major corporations.

Addressing Separation of Ownership and Control-Related Conflicts of Interest

There are a wide variety of ways to address and possibly solve some of the myriad conflicts of interest that result because of the separation of ownership and control in today's large public corporations. None of these possible solutions is perfect. Nevertheless, they do represent a good start. These potential solutions are either private solutions or public government solutions.

Private Solutions.

ALIGNMENT OF FINANCIAL INTERESTS.   One way of addressing the principal–agent problems in corporate governance is by better aligning the financial interests of corporate executive officers and directors with those of shareholders. If shareholders (again, as opposed to stock speculators) are concerned with the long-term appreciation of their stock, why not strongly tie executive and even board member compensation to this criterion? Granting executives and directors stock options is in general a way to accomplish this, but as typically granted, such options do not usually achieve the desired financial alignment goals.

For example, a typical company might grant its CEO on January 1, 2005, the right to buy 40,000 shares of its stock at the then-current price of $40 per share. The right to purchase all of these shares might vest immediately or perhaps over a few years (e.g., 10,000 shares vest immediately and an additional 10,000 shares vest annually on January 1, 2006, on January 1, 2007, and January 1, 2008). These stock options can be exercised any time during the six-year period between January 1, 2005 and January 1, 2011. This stock option scheme thus gives the CEO a lot of flexibility with respect to exercising her or his options and then immediately selling, or "flipping," the stock.

For example, in January, 2002, the Tenet Healthcare Corporation CEO Jeffrey C. Barbakow cashed out options and immediately sold company stock worth $111 million shortly after calling the company's business sensational and increasing its profit forecast. Tenet Corporation ended up having a terrible year, missing profit projections, and being subject to FBI and other investigations. Its stock closed the year at around $16 per share, down approximately 60 percent from the $43.35 price received by its CEO when he sold his stock in January. Tenet's stock was also down over 25 percent from its price five years previously.[13]

In response to the developments regarding Mr. Barbakow and other top executives reaping tremendous rewards flipping stock options, numerous observers have called for tying stock options and other stock compensation more firmly to *long-term corporate performance*. The Pennsylvania State Employees Retirement System's chief investment officer Peter M. Gilbert has, for example, said that the stock option "system has just distorted itself."[14] Similarly, Richard E. Cavanagh, the chief executive of the Conference Board, a major business research group, has said that you "can always dress up a company to make it look good" for a short period of time and that as a result, long holding periods for company stock are needed to "focus executives on long-term results."[15]

Because of these concerns, a number of major companies, including GE and WorldCom, now prohibit executives from exercising stock options and then immediately selling the stock. Indeed, WorldCom's CEO must hold (not sell) 75 percent of all stock he or she receives from exercising options or otherwise until at least six months after he or she leaves the company.[16]

Another way to perhaps even better align executives' and directors' financial interests with shareholders' financial interests is to make **restricted stock** payments a very significant part of their overall compensation. Such a procedure involves giving top executives and directors company stock as remuneration but severally restricting its sale in a variety of ways; for example, the stock cannot be sold for a period of at least 10 or 15 years, unless the company gets purchased.

restricted stock Corporate stock that has some restrictions on it, for example, regarding when it can be sold

Restricted stock grants work well, in terms of better aligning shareholder and executive and director interests, from a number of perspectives. First, executives and directors now become large shareholders (as opposed to stock-option-flipping speculators) in the business. Moreover, by restricting the sale of the stock for a very long time, these individuals now become more concerned with long-term company performance. In addition, by adding the proviso that the stock can be sold at any time if the company is purchased, these individuals may now also be less averse to a takeover bid for the company.

STRONGER INDEPENDENT OUTSIDE BOARDS OF DIRECTORS. Hypothetically, a company's board of directors supervises and monitors the company's CEO, preventing her or him from empire building and making sure that takeover bids and other shareholder enhancing items get careful attention. Unfortunately, this isn't always how things have worked in the real world.

First, in some companies the number of inside directors, that is, high-level corporate officers, may equal or outnumber the outside directors. Second, in many situations the chairperson of the company's board is also the CEO (e.g., Merck and Company's CEO Raymond Gilmartin also serves as its board chairperson). In such situations the CEO or board chairperson obviously has a major and directive role in setting the board of directors' policy. Finally, even when the CEO is not also the chairperson of the board, the CEO frequently has considerable power and influence over who is appointed to the board and to what extent board members might also receive consulting contracts, use of the company plane, contributions to the organizations where they work if they are from the not-for-profit sector (e.g., university presidents, medical center directors), and so on. The upshot of all this is that many corporate board members are to some extent frequently beholden to the CEO in one way or another, thus making it difficult to effectively monitor her or him.

For example, the former CEO of Enron, Kenneth Lay, also served as the company's chairperson of the board, and he handpicked many members of the company's board of directors. He was also very generous (with the company's money!) to various directors with respect to awarding them side consulting contracts, giving large sums of money to the medical centers and other not-for-profit organizations they headed or were involved with, and so forth. Enron's board was very loyal to Ken Lay—so loyal that they didn't ask very many questions about the company's use of special purpose entities and other unusual accounting vehicles. But boards of directors ultimately owe a fiduciary duty to the company's shareholders, not to the company's CEO, and as former U.S. Securities and Exchange Commission (SEC) chairperson Arthur Levitt has asserted, Enron's board arguably failed the "smell test."[17]

It seems obvious that one possible positive step for corporations to take in addressing separation of ownership and control-related conflicts of interest is to separate the roles of company board chairperson and CEO. Having one person doing both of these jobs is somewhat akin to having the fox guarding the chicken coop.

In addition, boards need to have more outside directors, and more clearly independent outside directors. Moreover, new independent outside directors should be selected by a committee of their peers, not by the CEO. Finally, the general power and independence of the board of directors should be increased so that it has and exercises real oversight and monitoring authority and is not merely a sort of rubber stamp for management actions.

SHAREHOLDER PROPOSALS AND INSTITUTIONAL INVESTORS.   Shareholders do have one direct way of monitoring actions by corporate executives and directors, and this is through the **shareholder proposal process.** Shareholders generally make proposals a number of months in advance of the firm's annual meeting, so that they can be included in the company's annual proxy materials. These proxy materials are then distributed to all shareholders, and shareholders vote on the various items contained therein. These votes are then tabulated and announced at the company's annual meeting.

shareholder proposal process The process by which shareholders make proposals a number of months before a firm's annual meeting, so that they can be included in the company's annual proxy materials

Shareholders can and do bring proposals on a wide range of issues (e.g., executive compensation, corporate ethics, corporate workforce diversity). There are, however, some limits on the types of topics shareholders can bring proposals on. For example, shareholders cannot bring proposals involving personal grievances against the company or generally on matters involving mundane day-to-day management of the corporation.

Shareholders gather in Fayetteville, Arkansas for the Wal-Mart Corporation's 2004 annual meeting. In addition to conducting company business, attendants were entertained by singers Patti LaBelle and Paula Abdul, among others.

More significantly, shareholder proposals not supported by the management of the company are rarely very successful, with many getting less than 20 percent of the shareholder vote. In addition, even if they are very successful and garner a majority of shareholder support, in almost all cases (because of the way corporate bylaws are written) they are *not* binding. Instead, votes on shareholder proposals are virtually always advisory or precatory to the company's board of directors. Company boards are generally free to ignore such votes, although there are at the least some public relations and other problems involved when a board ignores majority shareholder votes.

Although individual shareholders sometimes bring shareholder proposals, they are most frequently brought by **institutional investors.** The term *institutional investor* is generally used to describe a large, professionally managed investor source of capital such as a pension fund, mutual fund, or insurance company. While it is generally not worth the time and effort of an individual investor owning, say, $3000 worth of a company's stock to closely monitor corporate activities and make shareholder proposals, institutional investors often have literally billions of dollars at stake and thus close monitoring of a given company's activities may be very much worth their time and effort. The nation's largest pension fund, the California Public Employees Retirement System (CalPERS), has over $140 billion in assets and has taken a very aggressive stance with respect to monitoring the actions of the companies in which it invests, bringing shareholder proposals, and so on. Close monitoring and positive actions by large institutional shareholders like CalPERS obviously benefit all shareholders and help keep the interests of shareholders and management in better alignment.

> **institutional investors** Large, professionally managed sources of capital

CONTRACTUAL INFORMATION PROTECTION. Corporations frequently have key executives and directors enter into **confidentiality agreements.** Confidentiality agreements are contractual agreements whereby the signatory party agrees to keep confidential trade secrets and other sensitive information learned through his or her employment that is potentially damaging to the company if released. Confidentiality agreements are generally strictly enforced by the courts.

> **confidentiality agreements** Agreements by employees to keep confidential trade secrets or other sensitive information learned by working at a company

Companies also sometimes have their top executives sign **covenants not to compete.** These agreements, which can come in various shapes and forms, prohibit

> **covenants not to compete** Agreements by employees not to compete with their former employer

the executive for a certain period of time from opening or joining a competing business, perhaps within a certain geographic area. For example, a bank might have a covenant not to compete with its CEO that prohibits the CEO from opening a new bank within a 100-mile radius of the bank *for a period of at least three years after leaving the organization.* This agreement prevents the CEO from using information gained about customers and so on at his or her old bank and opening a directly competitive new bank, which would likely damage the old bank and its customers.

golden parachute agreements
Severance payment agreements, often fairly lucrative, to be received by corporate executives if their corporation is acquired

Most major corporations have **golden parachute agreements** with their top executives that provide special, often fairly lucrative severance payments to them should they be forced to leave the company in the event of a takeover of the company by another firm. Often these agreements are coupled with covenants not to compete for a certain period of time. Ostensibly, these agreements should make top executives more amenable to takeover bids that enhance shareholders value. Younger CEOs, though, may not find these agreements as lucrative as staying in office. Moreover, younger CEOs may not want to be forced into retirement (due to the accompanying covenants not to compete) with its accompanying loss of power at a relatively young age. Thus it seems unlikely that golden parachutes, unless ridiculously exorbitant, will completely produce proper alignments of shareholder and executive interests in takeover bid situations, especially in the case of relatively young top executives. Properly constructed restricted stock grants probably are one way to provide more positive alignments in such situations.

Public and Governmental Solutions.

Sarbanes-Oxley Act Federal corporate governance legislation increasing the duties and liabilities of corporate officers and directors

SARBANES-OXLEY ACT.   The federal **Sarbanes-Oxley Act** became effective in 2003 and adds a new panoply of legal regulation (far beyond the business judgment rule) with respect to corporate executives and directors. The law considerably strength-

President George W. Bush, on July 30, 2002, shakes hands with Senator Paul Sarbanes (D-Md.), co-author of the Sarbanes-Oxley Act, after signing this legislation into effect. The act strengthens federal government regulation of corporate governance. The law's other co-author, Congressman Mike Oxley (R-Oh.), looks on and applauds.

ens corporate responsibility by requiring company CEOs and CFOs to be personally responsible for the accuracy of their company's financial reports. The law also strictly limits the ability of a company's auditors to provide non-auditing services to the company and requires auditors to report directly to the board of directors rather than management. Further, the law generally prohibits corporate loans to directors and executives. It appears that these and other of the law's provisions strengthen the hand of corporate boards of directors with respect to better monitoring CEO and other corporate executive actions and making sure such actions are positively aligned with shareholder interests. Moreover, by making corporate executives personally accountable (with strict penalties) for the accuracy of company financial statements, the possibility of earnings misstatements (and the possibility for executives to flip stock options in conjunction with such misstatements) appears to be reduced considerably. One negative aspect of the Sarbanes-Oxley Act, however, is that it has dramatically increased legal, accounting, investor relations, and other costs for publicly traded companies, placing significant stress in this regard on smaller public corporations.[18]

REGULATION FD. In a major step toward better addressing information asymmetry problems in the stock markets, the U.S. Securities and Exchange Commission (SEC) in late 2000 promulgated a new rule entitled **Rule FD,** or Rule Fair Disclosure. This rule went into effect on October 23, 2000, and prohibits so-called selective disclosure of material information by companies to stock analysts or certain large investors. Under the new rule, any intentional disclosure of information to selective individuals must be accompanied by simultaneous public disclosure. The intent of the rule is to increase investor confidence in the fairness and integrity of the markets and to prohibit any potential stock market trading based on the selective disclosure. This rule clearly prohibits company CEOs or CFOs from leaking important information to favored large shareholders or stock analysts. Thus, for example, the Schering-Plough Corporation drug company recently paid a $1 million fine (and its CEO a personal fine of $50,000) because of special information provided by the CEO to one of the company's large mutual fund shareholders in violation of Rule FD.[19]

Rule FD The federal fair disclosure rule prohibiting selective disclosure of corporate information to certain parties

INSIDER TRADING RULES. Rule 10(b)(5) of the SEC Act of 1934 goes beyond Rule FD to prohibit all **insider trading.** Under this rule, anyone who gains access to material nonpublic information because of his or her relationship to the corporation cannot trade on it without first making public disclosure. For example, the CEO of a company cannot sell stock on the basis of bad information only he knows without first releasing that information to the public, in which case the stock's price will likely go down and prevent the CEO from getting out of the stock at an inflated price. Insider trading rules also apply to individuals directly tipped by the CEO. Federal law provides for both civil and criminal penalties for anyone who buys or sells securities while possessing material nonpublic information. The SEC closely monitors stock trading by top corporate executives and corporate directors and has special reporting requirements for such individuals. The SEC also closely monitors unusual trading patterns in company stocks generally as a possible signal of inside information leaks.

insider trading Stock trading based on material nonpublic information

SHORT-SWING PROFITS LIABILITY. Section 16(b) of the SEC Act of 1934 takes the inside information trading prohibitions of Section 10(b)(5) a step further. This section of the law prohibits all corporate directors, officers, and 10 percent or greater shareholders from making a profit by buying and selling the company's stock within any six-month period, that is, from making what are known as **short-swing profits** in their company's stock. This rule applies even if there is absolutely no evidence that the individual traded on any sort of inside information. For example, suppose the CEO of XYZ Corporation buys 500 shares of his company's stock at $50 per share on

short-swing profits Stock trading profits made by corporate insiders within a six-month period

January 1, 2005. On May 15, 2005, he decides he's going to buy his daughter a nice new car as a college graduation present and sells his stock at $52 per share for a total of $26,000. There is absolutely no evidence of any wrongdoing or misuse of information in this situation. Nevertheless, the CEO must disgorge back to the company treasury the $1000 profit he made on the transaction. The intent behind Section 16(b) is to prevent even any appearance of impropriety in that short-term trading for a profit by a corporate officer may be automatically presumed by many to be based on inside information. Rule 16(b) thus works to reduce possible information asymmetries between top corporate officials and ordinary shareholders.

reality CHECK *What do you think about the Sarbanes-Oxley Act and all the new recently enacted regulations of corporate governance?*

Stakeholder Model of Business Governance

LEARNING OBJECTIVE 5
Discuss the stakeholder model of business governance.

stakeholder model of business governance The business governance model operating from the premise that the purpose of businesses is to benefit all groups with a meaningful stake in them

Ron Blackwell, the AFL-CIO's director of corporate affairs, argued in a recent speech that the core structure of U.S. corporations has undergone a drastic and negative change during the past twenty years. Unlike in prior times, he asserted, companies today have become "the private property of shareholders" and this results in "the needs and rights of workers being sacrificed for a greater profit margin for the shareholders." Blackwell also argued for a change in the role of CEOs so that "they serve the best interests of all parties, not just the shareholders."[20]

Blackwell is thus a proponent of what is known as the **stakeholder model of business governance.** Proponents of this model believe that businesses exist to benefit not just their shareholders but also all the various groups that have a meaningful stake in their operations. Clearly employees are one such group, and probably the most important one from Blackwell's perspective. There are, however, also a variety of other stakeholder groups. These include a company's customers, suppliers, creditors, trade associations, and so on.

The Coca-Cola Company is one company that has formally adopted a stakeholder model of corporate governance. In the corporate governance section of its website, it has a formal statement by its CEO stating "[F]undamentally, the Coca-Cola Company is built on a deep and abiding relationship of trust between it and all its constituents: bottlers, . . . customers, . . . consumers, . . . shareholders, . . . employees, . . . suppliers, . . . and the very communities of which successful companies are an integral part. That trust must be nurtured and maintained on a daily basis."[21] A diagram of the Coca-Cola Company's and its stakeholders' constituencies would look something like Exhibit 3.3.

In sum, while the shareholder view of business governance takes the view that the role of businesses is to make as much money as possible for their shareholders, the stakeholder view of business governance takes the position that businesses should be managed for the benefit of all their stakeholder groups and indeed that positive, trusting two-way relationships should exist between the businesses and those groups.

Businesses and Local Communities

Royal Dutch/Shell Group is a company that makes special efforts to consider the impact of its business operations on the local communities in which it does business. In particular, it is conspicuously sensitive about consulting

EXHIBIT 3.3

Coca-Cola Corporation and
Its Stakeholders

with local groups in the planning of new projects, such as new pipelines or oil drilling. For example, before recently building a new pipeline in the Philippines, the company aggressively consulted with local groups about how the pipeline should be routed. Ultimately, the pipeline, which was completed in the fall of 2001, was carefully routed to avoid sacred burial sites, coral beds, and fishing grounds.[22]

Shell has become concerned with local community stakeholder interests only fairly recently and in part due to public pressure. In the mid-1990s there was considerable public protest, especially in Europe, against oil drilling plans the company announced (without any local community input or consultation) for the North Atlantic and Nigeria. As a result, the company now takes a clear stakeholder approach to local communities in doing business. As Mark Wade, a Shell executive, has put it, the mid-1990s protests "triggered our understanding of the importance of building relationships."[23]

There are, of course, numerous other ways that businesses contribute to, and positively interact with, their local communities. Some companies, such as Target Stores, donate a percentage of sales to the local communities in which they do business. Other firms focus specifically on the arts and culture, perhaps sponsoring local ballet troupes or symphonies. Tate & Lyle, a large British corporation, has been particularly active in developing child reading programs in the places where it operates and ensuring that children in those communities have books in their homes.[24] Since 2000, Starbucks Corporation has designated the month of September as Make Your Mark month, during which Starbucks employees (and the customers it is able to recruit) devote thousands of hours to a wide variety of volunteer projects in the communities where the company has coffee shops.[25] Some companies that operate throughout the world vary their local community activities, depending on the country in which they're operating.

One of the most unique local community stakeholder approaches is the one taken by Atlantic Stewardship Bank of Midland Park, New Jersey, the primary subsidiary of publicly traded Stewardship Financial Corporation. The bank has a formal Tithing Program (**www.asbnow.com/tithing.htm**) whereby it tithes itself, or takes 10 percent of its *pre*tax income or profits, and shares it with local "Christian and not-for-profit organizations" chosen by its board of directors. Some of the recent recipients of monies from the bank's Tithing Program include Brookdale Christian School, Bloomfield, New Jersey; Eastern Christian High School, North

Haledon, New Jersey; Friendship Ministries, Midland Park, New Jersey; and the Waldwick Seventh Day Adventist School in Waldwick, New Jersey. Interestingly, the bank encourages tithe recipients to maintain accounts at the bank and reports that a majority of such recipients do so. The bank states that such account relationships help the bank "achieve its mission of tithing."[26]

Creditors

In the spring of 2002, a major public controversy erupted regarding what, if any, responsibilities businesses have toward individuals from whom they borrow money. William H. Gross, the manager of the world's largest bond fund at Pacific Investment Management Company (PIMCO), castigated General Electric (GE) for not disclosing enough about its operations to bond investors. Gross also announced that for the foreseeable future PIMCO will own no GE commercial debt. In essence, Gross argued that people who lend money to corporations are entitled to be treated as important stakeholders.[27]

Suppliers

Companies like the Coca-Cola Company view suppliers as an important stakeholder group. Such companies manage relations with this group with care, keeping them informed about future plans and negotiating fairly with them over prices and delivery schedules. In some situations corporations may invest in or develop other special financial relationships with their suppliers.

One common concern for a number of major corporations is increasing supplier diversity. Nordstrom Corporation, an owner of major department stores, is highly dedicated to supplier diversity and has developed a specific program encouraging minority- and woman-owned suppliers.

The issue is also a highly important one for McDonald's Corporation, which in the United States alone operates more than 12,000 restaurants. McDonald's supplier diversity policy reads in part as follows:

> McDonald's seeks to leverage the diversity within our supplier community through growing our existing supplier base, as well as developing new supplier relationships. The more diverse our customers become, the more important it is that we have a diverse suppliers group in order to channel wealth back into those respective communities in which we do business.[28]

Suppliers are clearly a very important stakeholder for many corporations.

Distributors

Many large companies do not sell their products directly to consumers. Instead, these products first go to distributors or middlepersons. For example, the Coca-Cola corporation sends its product to bottlers, who then distribute it to retail outlets. Somewhat similarly, major auto manufacturers such as General Motors, Ford, and DaimlerChrysler send their cars to auto dealerships throughout the country (and indeed the world). These distributors obviously have an important stakeholder relationship with the given corporation. For example, if General Motors antagonizes its distributor dealerships, they might not be as enthusiastic about selling GM cars.

Just as many companies have put forth considerable effort to increasing diversity among their suppliers, many companies have also put forth considerable effort to increasing diversity among the distributors of their products. DaimlerChrysler Corporation, for example, started a major minority dealership program in 1983 designed to increase the number of minority-owned dealerships selling its products. Today, an increasing number of DaimlerChrysler dealerships are minority-owned, including such dealerships as Fullerton Dodge in Fullerton, California; Cross Road Chrysler Jeep in Oklahoma City, Oklahoma; and Rainier Dodge in Olympia, Washington.

Customers

Customers are an extremely important stakeholder group for corporations. Obviously, a company that does not treat its customers properly will ultimately lose their trust and their business. If customers stop purchasing (and indeed repurchasing) the company's products, the company's existence will clearly be in question.

Customer, or consumer, stakeholders are very concerned about both product quality and product safety, and companies are increasingly making major efforts to address these concerns. Nordstrom's, for example, has built a reputation for very high-quality apparel and very good customer service. Its employees go out of their way to help customers find merchandise, and they make returning or exchanging merchandise very easy. The company is committed to the simple idea of earning the trust of its customers "one at a time."[29]

Johnson & Johnson (J&J) is another company known for its high-quality products, and especially for its high commitment to consumer safety. In 1982, someone spiked Extra-Strength Tylenol capsules with cyanide, causing seven deaths in the Chicago, Illinois, area and widespread panic throughout the country. J&J, which makes the popular painkiller, immediately pulled all Tylenol capsules from retailer shelves and alerted consumers across the country not to use any Tylenol product. The company then immediately designed new tamper-resistant, triple-seal packages. Although having to take a $100 million charge against earnings because of the Tylenol incident, J&J did not point any accusatory finger elsewhere (e.g., at the stores where the product was sold for improper monitoring). By acting forcefully and calmly to protect consumer safety, J&J eventually regained its share of the analgesic market.[30]

Today, many companies have extensive consumer education programs that emphasize product usage and safety. General Motors has been a leader in this regard. Such special efforts on behalf of customers involve businesses taking a stakeholder perspective toward this important constituency group.

Employees

In today's knowledge economy, especially, where in many industries, like computer software development, the employees themselves are the actual means of production, employees can be a very special stakeholder group. Many companies today make special efforts to have a strong two-way relationship with their employees, seeking input from them regarding the running of the business and helping them develop their careers. Nordstrom's, for example, forthrightly states that "our company is our people," and that it is "dedicated to hiring outstanding individuals and empowering them to unlock their talent and creativity."[31]

In some countries in the world, like Germany, employee input is mandated by law. Under that country's codetermination law, the boards of directors, or supervisory boards, of all major corporations must include significant employee representation.

Case in Point

The Supervisory Board at DaimlerChrysler

The supervisory board, or board of directors, at DaimlerChrysler Corporation, one of the world's largest automobile companies, has according to German codetermination law 20 members, 10 of whom are elected by the shareholders and 10 of whom represent the employees. The shareholder-elected representatives include leading academics and business executives from throughout the world, such as the chairperson of Nortel Networks Corporation, the former chairperson of Dresdner Bank, and the former CEO of Xerox Corporation. The employee members represent employees from throughout the worldwide operations of the company, including a representative from the United Autoworkers Union (UAW) in the United States and a representative from the German Metalworkers' Union in Germany.

Source: www.daimlerchrysler.de/company/supervisory/ supervisory_e.htm (accessed June 3, 2004).

Questions

1. Do you think union and other employee representatives should be members of corporate boards of directors?
2. To what extent should the DaimlerChrysler board of directors have representatives from both Germany (Daimler) and the United States (Chrysler)?
3. Why do you suppose German law is so encouraging of stakeholder representation on corporate boards?

Companies taking a stakeholder orientation toward their employees care about them and make a special effort to look after them. The classic example, perhaps, is that of Malden Mills in Methuen, Massachusetts. In 1995, a fire burned the company facility to the ground, putting 3000 people out of work. The company's owner and CEO Aaron Feuerstein, however, kept them all on the payroll with full benefits for three months. In explaining his decision, Feuerstein simply said, "I have a responsibility to the worker, both blue-collar and white-collar."[32]

Shareholders

Even under a stakeholder model of business governance, a company's shareholders remain its most important constituency. The difference between the stakeholder and shareholder governance models is that under the stakeholder model, shareholders are not the *only* important constituency.

reality CHECK *Can you think of a company you interact with that goes especially out of its way to assist its customer stakeholder group?*

Societal Responsibility Model of Business Governance

LEARNING OBJECTIVE 6
Describe the societal responsibility model of business governance.

societal responsibility model of business governance The business governance model operating from the premise that a purpose of business is to benefit society at large

The **societal responsibility model of business governance** goes a step beyond the stakeholder model and says that businesses operate for the benefit of, and have a responsibility toward, not just stakeholders but society in general. Take, for example, the case of SC Johnson Company, the family-owned company that makes such well-known household products as Johnson's Wax, Raid, Pledge, and Glade. In 1975, years before any legal ban, the company voluntarily removed all chlorofluorocarbon propellants (CFCs) from its aerosol products worldwide on the basis of preliminary evidence linking CFCs with ozone depletion.[33] S.C. Johnson's concern about ozone depletion and the worldwide environment is a good example of the societal responsibility model in action.

DaimlerChrysler Corporation is another company that has taken a strong societal responsibility position of business governance toward the global environment. In its 2002 Company Environmental Report it lists the following environmental accomplishments:

> Certified environmental management systems at the majority of our plants; a substantial improvement in the efficiency with which we use resources; and the increased use of renewable raw materials in the automobile production process are our cornerstone environmental achievements. In our development laboratories we have created new vehicles which consume less energy and emit less carbon dioxide from one generation to the next. As a result, our average fleet fuel consumption in Germany has fallen by more than 22 percent since 1995.[34]

It is also working on developing fuel cell and hybrid vehicles as well as more efficient internal combustion engines. DaimlerChrysler is clearly committed to improving the world environment.

Finally, Andersen Corporation of Bayport, Minnesota, a privately held manufacturer of patio doors and windows with $1.7 billion in annual sales, is an example of a company operating under a societal responsibility mode of governance in a different context. Andersen Corporation is a leading corporate partner of Habitat for Humanity International, a not-for-profit organization that builds homes for the less privileged. To date, Andersen Corporation has donated well over $2 million worth of its products to Habitat for Humanity for the construction of homes not only in the communities where it operates, but throughout the United States.[35] Companies like S.C. Johnson, DaimlerChrysler, and Andersen that adopt a societal responsibility model are generally ones where giving back to society as a whole has become embedded in the company's culture.

reality CHECK *Are there any companies in your community that have shown a special concern for preserving the environment?*

Business Ethics

LEARNING OBJECTIVE 7
Explain the basic parameters of business ethics.

Defining Business Ethics

What is business ethics? What is ethical behavior? The topic is in the news every day, but what does it all mean? **Ethics** involves beliefs about what is right and wrong, what is morally acceptable and what is not. **Unethical behavior** involves behavior that is either illegal or morally unacceptable to the larger community. **Business ethics** involves the application of ethical standards to business situations. The Arthur Andersen accounting firm's recent actions with respect to Enron Corporation—shredding documents and so on—were unethical by most any definition. The firm was criminally convicted of obstruction of justice.[36] But many times defining what is unethical business behavior is much more difficult. For example, there has been a fairly recent controversy over the fact that the Augusta National Golf Club in

ethics Beliefs about what is right and wrong, what is morally acceptable and what is not

unethical behavior Behavior that is either illegal or morally unacceptable to the larger community

business ethics The application of ethical standards to business situations

Augusta, Georgia (home of the famed Masters Golf Tournament) does not admit female members. Is it unethical for the CEOs of companies like Coca-Cola Company, Adolph Coors Company, and IBM to continue to be members of this golf club?[37] Is it unethical for a company incorporated in the state of Connecticut to change its place of incorporation to Bermuda or the Cayman Islands? Such a reincorporation, at least under current laws, is clearly legal, but being legal does not per se make it ethical or morally acceptable.

While some arguably unethical behavior by employees within a business organization is clearly harmful to that organization, other kinds of employee unethical behavior may be helpful to the company. For example, what if an employee lies to a government regulator calling for a certain report and tells the regulator that his or her boss is out sick with the flu, in order to buy a few more days to get the report done without any repercussions? Such an arguably unethical action is very helpful to the company and likely emanates from the fact that the employee has been treated well and feels a degree of loyalty to his or her boss or the company.

Finally, what is viewed as unethical behavior in one country, culture, or society may not be viewed the same way in another country or culture. In some countries like Haiti, Nigeria, Uganda, and Bolivia, bribery and corruption are both pervasive and very much accepted. In some of these countries, there are even published lists of the amount of bribes government and other officials need to be paid in order to influence their business decisions!

Foreign Corrupt Practices Act The federal law prohibiting U.S. companies doing business overseas from making payments to foreign officials to influence their discretionary decisions

In 1977, however, the U.S. Congress enacted the **Foreign Corrupt Practices Act** to regulate conduct in this regard by U.S. businesses engaged in commerce overseas. Under this law, payments by U.S. businesses to foreign officials to influence a discretionary decision such as the purchase of services or goods by a foreign government agency are now illegal under U.S. law. Corporations found violating this law are subject to multimillion dollar fines, and guilty individual agents can be sent to jail for up to five years or subjected to a large fine. Enforcement of this law, however, is difficult, and many companies argue it unfairly handicaps their ability to do business abroad.

© Mike Peters, Dayton Daily News, August 31, 2002. Reprinted with special permission of King Features Syndicate.

 *Have you ever been involved in what might be viewed as unethical behavior?*

LEARNING OBJECTIVE 8
Discuss the development of business codes of ethics and business ethics training.

Business Codes of Ethics

Increasingly, many companies today are adopting formal written **business codes of ethics.** These codes may deal with a wide number of topics ranging from workplace romance to the personal use of company property. Lee Enterprises, for example, is an Iowa-based company that owns 44 local daily newspapers throughout the United States. Some of the papers Lee Enterprises owns include the *Lincoln Journal Star* in Lincoln, Nebraska; the *Missoulian* in Missoula, Montana; and the *Southern Illinoisan* in Carbondale, Illinois. In 2002, the company's board of directors adopted a five-page, 11-point Code of Business Conduct and Ethics to guide its employees. This code puts special emphasis on potential employee conflicts of interest, often a very important issue in the field of journalism. The company's code very strictly limits the ability of Lee employees to accept gifts from individuals they interact with, in order to clearly prevent potential conflicts of interest from arising.[38] It is likely that more and more companies will be adopting detailed and comprehensive business ethics codes along the lines adopted by Lee Enterprises in the future.

> **business codes of ethics** Formal written documents adopted by businesses regarding ethical conduct standards

Dealing with Business Ethical Breaches

While the instinctive reaction of many top business executives when there is an ethical breach is to deny the problem and then clam up, experts today generally see this as not being the right approach to such situations. Frequently it's best, just as Johnson & Johnson did during the Tylenol crisis in the 1980s, to quickly acknowledge the existence of a problem and calmly attempt to solve it. Sometimes it may even be appropriate to issue a public apology. If a public apology is made, it should be stated clearly (plain English, no legalese, loopholes, etc.) and should definitely come from the top, that is, be issued by the company's CEO or chairperson of the board.[39]

Penalties for Business Ethical Breaches

The penalties for corporate ethical breaches obviously need to be formulated to properly fit the "crime." To date, this doesn't seem to have always been the case. While the penalties for some types of business ethical breaches—up to five years in prison for individual violations of the Foreign Corrupt Practices Act—seem to have been far too high, other ethical breaches, like accounting fraud or insider trading, have sometimes been met with only a slap on the wrist. The recently enacted Sarbanes-Oxley Act, with its increased penalties on company executives and directors for accounting misstatements and other actions, appears to be a step in the right direction in this regard. Under Section 1107 of the Sarbanes-Oxley Act, for example, corporate officers can be sent to prison for up to ten years if they intentionally act against employees who assist federal law enforcement officials in investigating certain types of corporate wrongdoing.[40]

Business Ethics Training

Increasing numbers of companies today are sending their employees to formal ethics training sessions. Sun Microsystems Corporation of Santa Clara, California, for example, has been sending thousands of its managers around the world to intense two-day training programs covering ethical issues ranging from fraud detection to new accounting practices. While Sun Microsystems has publicized its ethical guidelines to its executives since the early 1990s and two years ago created a formal business conduct office, the company felt that this was not enough.[41] Interestingly, a number of major corporations are turning to the Internet for ethics training. Pfizer Corporation, for instance, is offering scores of online ethics courses for managers, covering topics from ethical decision making to the proper use of e-mail.[42]

Business Ethics on Campus

Before its ethical downfall, the Arthur Andersen accounting firm was a generous benefactor to numerous universities. Indeed, it endowed 40 to 50 professorships to schools across the country, including the University of Southern California and Texas A&M University. Similarly, there is an endowed Enron Professorship in Economics at the University of Nebraska, Omaha, and two dealing with e-commerce and risk management at Rice University in Enron Corporation's hometown of Houston, Texas. Seton Hall University in New Jersey has a lecture hall named for the scandal-plagued former Tyco Corporation CEO Dennis Koslowski, and a gym named for the convicted money launderer Robert E. Brennan.

Should universities now take these names off the buildings and professorships? Fairfield University in Fairfield, Connecticut, did. Fairfield changed the name of a computer classroom donated by Arthur Andersen and named the Andersen Interactive Classroom the Alumni Interactive Classroom after Andersen was criminally convicted of obstruction of justice charges in the Enron case in June 2002. In making this move, the dean of the business school (where the $250,000 classroom was located) said, "[W]e are a Jesuit, Catholic institution and we take ethics and where we get the money from as seriously as the resources themselves." But is it ethical to take a company's name off something if they've already paid for it?[43] Formulating appropriate ethical standards is not always as easy as it seems.

reality CHECK   *Do you think you can teach ethics to someone, or is it something that's an innate part of individuals' personalities that can't really be changed?*

Careers in Business Governance, Ethics, and Social Responsibility

A wide and growing range of careers exists in business governance, ethics, and social responsibility. In the wake of the Sarbanes-Oxley Act and similar reforms, numerous companies have created the position of ethics officer and begun hiring individuals for these jobs. HCA, one of the nation's largest owners of hospitals and surgery centers, has established a company department of ethics, compliance, and corporate responsibility, headed by a corporate senior vice president. Similarly, Dell Computer Corporation has designated one of its vice presidents to also serve as the company's chief ethics officer. Moreover, virtually all publicly traded companies have investor relations departments that regularly hire individuals who are daily on the frontline of dealing with business governance issues. In addition, many large corporations in the United States have active philanthropic foundations, which hire employees to administer grant programs. In recent years, the General Electric Company Foundation has made annual philanthropic grants of about $46 million, while the General Motors Corporation Foundation has made annual grants of about $41 million.

Opportunities for careers in business governance, ethics, and social responsibility have also been expanding rapidly in accounting, law, and consulting firms. The Sarbanes-Oxley Act in particular has sharply increased the demand for accounting firm auditors. Finally, some governmental agencies such as the U.S. Securities and Exchange Commission have, because of Sarbanes-Oxley and other legislation, recently experienced major increases in their personnel budgets and are actively hiring employees across a wide range of functions. Top federal agencies like the SEC offer excellent long-term career opportunities or the chance to gain valuable short-term experience that then can be applied to a career in the private sector.

Summary

LEARNING OBJECTIVE 1
Describe the differences among sole proprietorships, partnerships, and corporations.

There are various forms of business governance structures. The simplest form is the sole proprietorship, where individuals are responsible for running the business. One problem with this form of business structure is that the person running the business is usually personally liable for any business debt. Partnerships are a more complicated business structure involving two or more people linked together in a partnership agreement in running the business. Personal liability issues also arise in partnerships, although it may be possible to structure partnerships so that some partners have more limited liability. Partnerships may also have an easier time obtaining funding than sole proprietorships.

The vast majority of dollar volume business in the United States is done via the corporate form of business organization. Corporations are different from other forms of business organizations in that the corporation itself is a legal "person," or entity, separate from the individuals involved in setting it up or running it. This means that the corporate entity is responsible for its own debts or liabilities and that a wall, or "veil," exists between the corporation and its shareholders, protecting them from any personal liability for company debt or activities. This limited liability feature is immensely helpful to corporations in raising capital; the most investors risk is the money they put in. Corporations, though, are treated as separate tax entities, and dividends paid to shareholders of these companies continue to be subject to some level of double taxation.

LEARNING OBJECTIVE 2
Explain the basic roles of corporate boards of directors and officers.

Once legally established, all corporations are required to have a board of directors. Boards of directors are responsible for all major policy decisions of the corporation, including the hiring of corporate officers who run the company on a day-to-day basis. Inside directors are individuals who already work for the corporation, such as the CEO, while outside directors are typically prestigious individuals not employed as officers of the company. Boards of directors and corporate officers operate under a legal doctrine known as the business judgment rule, which means that they should give their work their best business judgment. The doctrine, however, does not require corporate directors or officers to always make good decisions; they only must use their best judgment to make decisions.

LEARNING OBJECTIVE 3
Discuss the basic dynamics of the shareholder model of business governance and the problems engendered in major corporations today because of the separation of ownership and control.

The shareholder model of business governance operates from the basic premise that the purpose of a business is to maximize financial returns for its shareholders. Under this model of governance, if it's legal and best for the pocketbooks of company shareholders for the company to reincorporate in a place like the Cayman Islands, the company should take such action. In large public corporations, however, there is often a separation of ownership (which rests with hundreds of thousands of shareholders) and control (which rests with the company's CEO and a few other individuals). This fractured nature of corporate ownership frequently gives shareholders relatively limited monitoring power over company officers and directors who control the company and who may tend to act in their own self-interest rather than in the long-term interests of the shareholders. For example, a company CEO whose annual bonus depends on the maintenance of very high current levels of corporate profitability may not want to meaningfully invest in company research and development that might best benefit shareholders in the long-run but will hurt current profit levels.

LEARNING OBJECTIVE 4

Analyze different methods of solving the problems and conflicts of interest engendered by the separation of ownership and control in major corporations.

A wide range of private and public governmental mechanisms exist for addressing the potential conflicts of interest that arise between shareholders and officers or directors in large corporations. Increasingly, efforts are being made to better align the financial interests of shareholders and officers or directors by tying officer or director compensation to long-term corporate performance. Various laws and regulations, such as those that outlaw insider trading by corporate officers and directors, also help to reduce potential conflicts of interest between corporate ownership and control.

LEARNING OBJECTIVE 5

Discuss the stakeholder model of business governance.

The stakeholder model of business governance takes the perspective that businesses exist to benefit not just their shareholders but also all the various groups (e.g., customers, employees, suppliers, etc.) that have a meaningful stake in their operations. Many businesses, for example, make special efforts to help the local communities in which they operate. In some foreign countries a stakeholder model of governance is to some degree mandated by law. In Germany, all large companies are required by law to have employee representatives on their board of directors or supervisory board and to take workers directly into

account with respect to company operations in a variety of ways.

LEARNING OBJECTIVE 6

Describe the societal responsibility model of business governance.

The societal responsibility model of business governance goes a step beyond the stakeholder model and says that businesses operate for the benefit of, and have a responsibility toward, not just stakeholders but society in general. A number of large corporations have adopted a societal responsibility model toward the global environment by voluntarily reducing pollution from their operations far beyond the levels required by law.

LEARNING OBJECTIVE 7

Explain the basic parameters of business ethics.

Business ethics involves the application of ethical standards to business situations. Ethics invokes beliefs about what is right and wrong, what is morally acceptable and what is not. Unethical behavior involves behavior that is either illegal (e.g., CEO insider trading in the United States) or morally unacceptable (e.g., in some circles reincorporating a company from Connecticut to Bermuda). Standards for defining unethical business behavior vary widely throughout the world. In many countries paying government officials bribes to obtain certain types of regulatory approval is considered morally acceptable or indeed even legal. In the United States, however, this is not the case.

LEARNING OBJECTIVE 8

Discuss the development of business codes of ethics and business ethics training.

Many businesses (especially large corporations) today are adopting formal written business codes of ethics. These codes may deal with a wide number of topics ranging from workplace romance, to personal use of company property, to possible employee conflicts of interest. Companies are also increasingly developing formal business ethics training programs, including Internet online courses. Business ethics portends to be an increasingly important topic in years to come.

Chapter Questions

1. What is a whistleblower? What problems do whistleblowers face in organizations?
2. You are establishing a business renting small dormitory-sized refrigerators to fellow college students. What type of business governance structure

should you use? What factors enter into making this decision?
3. What makes a corporation such a special business entity?
4. The state of Delaware is the most popular state in the United States for large company incorporation.

What are the pros and cons of a company incorporating in Delaware?

5. You have recently taken a job at an executive search firm that has been hired by a large company to help it find two new independent outside directors. What kinds of individuals do you suggest for these positions? Any specific names to suggest?

6. Who is a principal and who is an agent in the corporate governance context?

7. What is the basic business governance conflict of interest that results from the separation of ownership and control in today's large corporations?

8. What would be some good examples of empire building on the part of corporate executives?

9. You have been hired by a large corporation as a consultant to better align the financial interests of its corporate officers with those of its shareholders. What specifically do you suggest?

10. What are some recent laws or regulations that deal with corporate governance and conflict of interest issues?

11. A CEO of a publicly traded company buys 1000 shares of the company's stock on January 1, 2005, at $40 per share and sells this stock on September 1, 2005, at $50 per share for a $10,000 profit. Assuming no trading on inside information, has the executive done anything illegal? If so, what remedy is appropriate?

12. What is the stakeholder model of business governance? Do you think this model represents a better one than the shareholder model of business governance? Why or why not?

13. Do you think the tithing approach taken by the Atlantic Stewardship Bank of New Jersey is a good one? Should other companies emulate this approach?

14. What is unethical behavior? What are some examples of unethical business behavior?

15. What is the Foreign Corrupt Practices Act? Give two examples of companies violating this act.

Interpreting Business News

1. There has been considerable recent controversy regarding the safety of hamburgers and other meat sold in the United States. Fairly recently, for example, the presence of *E. coli* bacteria in ground beef packed by ConAgra Foods Corporation resulted in one death, 38 serious illnesses, and the second-largest meat recall in U.S. history. Ground beef is harder to keep safe than roasts or other types of meat because any contamination is mixed right into the meat rather than staying on the surface where it can be killed by cooking or other methods. Obviously, ConAgra and other meat-packing companies are required to follow all U.S. Department of Agriculture (USDA) safety requirements. However, pursuant to the stakeholder model of governance, should they adopt meat safety procedures *greater than* what's required by federal law? With the average American consuming approximately 30 pounds of ground beef per year, your thoughts on the matter are *not* trivial!

2. The Home Depot Corporation recently sent a memo to its 1300 stores nationwide instructing them not to do business with the U.S. government (i.e., don't accept federal government purchase orders, federal government credit cards, etc.). The reason why the home improvement retailer doesn't want to do business with the federal government is that it doesn't want to be deemed a federal contractor. Federal contractors are under a wide array of U.S. Department of Labor reporting and affirmative action requirements. Analyze Home Depot's action from the point of view of a societal responsibility model of business governance. Do you agree with Home Depot's action? Why or why not?

Web Assignments

1. The U.S. Securities and Exchange Commission (SEC) is the primary federal governmental agency regulating corporate governance matters. Go to the SEC's webpage, **www.sec.gov,** and prepare a one-page summary regarding what the SEC primarily does. Also, find the section on the site that shows speeches and public statements and read at least one speech or public statement by a SEC official to get a better idea about some of the agency's current activities.

2. The California Public Employees Retirement System (CalPERS) is the largest pension fund in the United States, with over $140 billion in assets. CalPERS has in recent years been very active, as a major investor, in the corporate governance area. Go to the CalPERS website at **www.calpers.ca.gov** and locate the page that lists press releases. Find three press releases during the past three years dealing with the pension fund's investments or corporate governance activities. Then write a one-to two-page synopsis of the issues addressed in these three press releases.

3. General Electric (GE) has been at the vanguard of corporate governance and business ethics reforms. Go to the GE website, **www.ge.com,** and find the company's statement about its commitment to governance. Skim the provisions of this section to get an idea regarding the company's activities in this regard, and then find the company's code of conduct. Locate the section dealing with GE's integrity policy for employees. Pick any two GE employee integrity policies—fair employment practices, privacy, conflicts of interest—and write a one- to two-page paper analyzing the quality of these policies and how they might possibly be improved or why it looks as though they can't be improved.

Portfolio Projects

Exploring Your Own Case in Point

This chapter deals with the governance structure of businesses, including large publicly traded corporations. It examines governmental regulation of major corporations, as well as the ethical practices and social responsibility of corporations. Answers to the questions below will help you better understand how your company is governed and how it operates in its communities.

1. Where is your company incorporated, and what type or types of common stock does it have issued and outstanding?

2. Who are the members of the board of directors of your company? What are their backgrounds? Are there any/many female/minority directors?

3. During the past few years, has your company issued stock options to its corporate officers or directors? If so, how many shares of stock options has it issued? How many shares of stock do the company's top officers own outright versus via stock options?

4. Has your company issued a company code of ethics? If so, what are some of the key provisions of this code?

5. Is your company involved in efforts to improve its community? If so, describe some of its recent efforts. How is this involvement beneficial to your company?

Starting Your Own Business

After reading this chapter you should be able to address some issues related to the potential legal structure of your business, its possible stakeholders, and its role in your community.

1. Which business governance structure will you use? What are the advantages/disadvantages of this business form? Do you think you might change your structure as the business grows?

2. Is there any possibility that in the near future you might have partners in your business? What kind of partners (general or limited) would you be most interested in having?

3. Will you need to have creditors to fund your business? What kind of relationship with your creditors do you hope to establish?

4. Who will be some of the suppliers for your business? Do you expect to have a diverse set of suppliers?

5. How will your business interact with its community? How will you prevent unethical behavior from occurring in your business?

Test Prepper

You've read the chapter, studied the key terms, and the exam is any day now. Think you are ready to ace it? Take this sample test to gauge your comprehension of chapter material. You can check your answers at the back of the book.

True/False Questions

Please indicate if the following statements are true or false.

_____ 1. A key benefit of a sole proprietorship is limited liability.

_____ 2. Sherron Watkins is a famous whistleblower.

_____ 3. A limited partner is generally the one who runs a partnership.

_____ 4. Historically, corporations dominated early American commerce.

_____ 5. The Wrigley family maintains control of the William Wrigley Corporation by virtue of its large holding of class B stock.

_____ 6. The separation of corporate ownership and control can lead the company to have a short-term versus a long-term orientation.

_____ 7. Golden parachute agreements involve a new type of skydiving.

_____ 8. The AFL-CIO is generally supportive of the stakeholder model of business governance.

_____ 9. Andersen Corporation of Bayport, Minnesota, is a company committed to a societal responsibility model of business governance.

_____ 10. Augusta National Golf Club in Georgia has recently gotten into trouble for being a major polluter.

Multiple-Choice Questions

Choose the best answer.

_____ 1. A good example of the underground economy is

   a. high rates of pay for corporate CEOs.
   b. proxy proposals by pension funds.
   c. oil drilling by Schlumberger Corporation.
   d. not paying for dental care by providing the dentist with free legal services.
   e. making a donation to a hospital.

_____ 2. Capital formation is easiest for

   a. partnerships.
   b. corporations.
   c. sole proprietorships.
   d. limited partnerships.
   e. businesses incorporated in California.

_____ 3. The Stanley Works Corporation received considerable public attention because of

   a. its decision to pay a much higher dividend.
   b. its firing of its CEO.
   c. its attempt to reincorporate in Bermuda.
   d. its establishment of a new class of preferred stock.
   e. its new corporate directors.

_____ 4. The business judgment rule means that corporate directors must

   a. always make the right decision.
   b. hold all annual meetings in Florida.
   c. fire CEOs regularly.
   d. issue preferred stock.
   e. make decisions in good faith as ordinary prudent persons.

_____ 5. Restricted stock payments to top corporate executives and directors involve

   a. giving them company stock that cannot be sold for many years.
   b. restricting insider trading.
   c. stock option payments.
   d. giving company stock only to the CEO.
   e. illegal corporate activity.

_____ 6. CalPERS is an example of

   a. an excellent high-technology company.
   b. confidentiality agreements.
   c. a new California university.
   d. an important institutional investor.
   e. a sole proprietorship.

_____ 7. The U.S. Securities and Exchange Commissions Rule FD has recently

   a. been repealed.
   b. been enforced against the Schering-Plough corporation.
   c. led to increased short-swing corporate profits.
   d. led to more closed corporate meetings with stock analysts.
   e. led to an increase in the membership of the Federal Reserve Bank.

_____ 8. The Atlantic Stewardship Bank of New Jersey has a unique

a. checking account.
b. savings account.
c. online banking program.
d. book club program for customers.
e. tithing program.

_____ 9. Lee Enterprises' business code of ethics is geared in large measure toward

a. engineers.
b. journalists.
c. computer programmers.

d. reincorporation in Bermuda.
e. international corporations.

_____ 10. Fairfield University in Connecticut recently had to decide whether to

a. change the name of the university.
b. change the name of an Enron Corporation professorship.
c. change from being a Jesuit, Catholic institution.
d. move to New Mexico.
e. change the name of a classroom named for the Arthur Andersen accounting firm.

Want more questions? Visit the student website at **http://college.hmco.com/business/student/** (select Gaspar, *Introduction to Business*) and take the ACE quizzes for more practice.

Small Business and Entrepreneurship

4

| Introduction

| What Is a Small Business?

| What Is the Role of Small Business Firms?
Creative Destruction
Invention and Innovation
Job Opportunities
Globalization

| Government Support of Small Business

| Who Is an Entrepreneur?
Personal Qualities
Education and Training
Women in Small Business
Ethnic and Immigrant Small Business

| Developing a Business Plan
Essential Components
Business Ideas
Seed Money
Initial Production and Sales
Creating Value

| Forms of Small Business Organizations
Sole Proprietorships and Partnerships
Corporations and Franchises

| Small Business Management Decisions
Hiring Employees
Ethics in Entrepreneurship
Running a Family Business
Going Public Versus Staying Private
Controlling Business Risks

| Careers in Small Business

Learning Objectives

After studying this chapter, you should be able to

1 Explain why small business is important.

2 Discuss the ways government can support small business enterprises.

3 Describe the personal qualities and training needed to be a successful entrepreneur, including the cases of women and minorities in small business.

4 List and briefly define each of the essential components of a business plan.

5 Compare the different small business organizational forms, including sole proprietorships, partnerships, corporations, and franchises.

6 Evaluate key small business management decisions, including hiring employees, ethics issues, family business benefits and costs, going public versus staying private, and controlling internal and external business risks.

Making Dreams Come True

Margaret Rodriguez started a construction business in 1992 in Phoenix, Arizona. Her father, a Native American and former kindergarten teacher, had always wanted to start his own business, but never realized his dream. After observing economic development construction in her community over the years, she decided to open a three-person construction company. With no previous experience in construction other than watching her father build a one-room addition on their home, she sought information from the U.S. Small Business Administration on how to start the business. Although there were ups and downs in the business in its early years, she gradually increased the volume of commercial building projects. In 2001 Rodriguez's company had a landmark year; she landed a $1.9 million federal contract to renovate facilities at a nearby air force base. Nowadays, her business employs over 30 people and has multimillion dollar annual revenues. Rodriquez is proud to point out that "Our business was built because of relationships. I have surrounded myself with a good team. We have worked hard, have been up front and honest, and we do a good job."

Introduction

If you drive down a street in any city, you pass a large number and variety of businesses. Most of those stores, shops, service outlets, and producers are small business firms—the result of entrepreneurship on the part of people in the community. Undoubtedly, you will also see a smaller number of large businesses. Keep in mind that those large businesses were once small entrepreneurial enterprises. Their size is proof that they were successful endeavors that resulted in growth over time.

Small business firms, like Margaret Rodriguez's construction business, are essential to a healthy economy and nation. They are a major force for technological change, inventing and innovating new products and services. Also, small firms fill the gaps in services and products that large firms cannot possibly meet with so many customer demands by individuals, businesses, and government agencies.

In the United States, small businesses with fewer than 500 employees account for more than half of all workers and are a dominant source of job opportunities for countries around the world. The driving force behind the formation and development of small businesses is free enterprise, where businesses are subject to supply and demand forces in the marketplace, rather than government regulation and control. Of course, government plays a meaningful role in fostering the growth of the small business sector of the economy. For example, government can protect the rights of individuals to engage in free enterprise via a commercial legal system. The commercial legal system serves to advance the principles of individual liberty and equal rights among people so that everyone has access to owning and operating a small business.

What Is a Small Business?

small business A firm with fewer than 500 employees that is typically owned and managed by the same person and serves a niche market

A **small business** is a firm that employs fewer than 500 people. Such firms are typically owned and managed by a single person. Examples include computer service firms, local bread companies, construction companies, small manufacturing firms, and many farming operations. Small businesses are important to an economy in numerous ways (see Exhibit 4.1). Some experts consider a very small business with less than

EXHIBIT 4.1

Importance of Small Businesses

- Account for 99 percent of all business firms.
- Employ 51 percent of private sector workers, 51 percent of workers on public assistance, and 38 percent of workers in high-tech jobs.
- Represent almost all of the self-employed, who make up 7 percent of the workforce.
- Produce 51 percent of the private sector output of goods and services.
- Represent 96 percent of all exporters of goods.
- Obtain 33 percent of federal contract dollars.
- Are 53 percent home-based and 3 percent franchises.
- Have 45 percent women employees.
- Account for 99 percent of minority-owned businesses.
- Number over 20 million enterprises.

Source: U.S. Small Business Administration, Office of Advocacy, Washington, DC, 2002. Small business is defined as those firms with fewer than 500 employees.

five employees to be a **microbusiness.** Examples of microbusinesses are local restaurants, dry cleaners, repair shops, hair salons, doctor's offices, and gas stations.

Small businesses are the result of entrepreneurship. An **entrepreneur** is anyone who starts, owns, or runs a small business. Entrepreneurs identify unmet needs and then take it on themselves to meet those needs. The combination of profit and personal motives makes the small business entrepreneur a dynamic source for change in the business world.

microbusiness A small business with fewer than five employees

entrepreneur Anyone who starts, owns, or runs a small or large business

What Is the Role of Small Business Firms?

LEARNING OBJECTIVE 1
Explain why small business is important.

Small business contributes to the productivity of any country in a number of ways. Small firms stimulate change within the business sector—a process known as creative destruction. They are the seedbed of invention and innovation due to their ability to rapidly respond to new technology and competitive market conditions. They are major employers in most countries and open up many new job opportunities for workers. Due to the Internet and telecommunications, they are increasingly participating in the globalization of business enterprise.

Creative Destruction

Joseph Schumpeter coined the term **creative destruction** to describe the competitive process of business success and failure.[1] Small firms enter the marketplace to compete against existing larger firms. The emergence of these small firms is many times the result of new technological innovations. Inevitably, the increase in competition causes the failure of other businesses based on older technologies, some of which are large firms. Exhibit 4.2 (on p. 130) illustrates the process of creative destruction in which capitalism is a method of economic change. In recent years we have seen the collapse of Builder's Square due to competition from Lowe's and Home Depot. Microsoft and Intel developed the personal computer, which put

creative destruction The competitive process of business success and failure, whereby small firms enter the marketplace to compete against existing larger firms and cause the failure of some of those existing firms

EXHIBIT 4.2

Small Business and Creative Destruction

Technologically innovative new businesses destroy old-technology large businesses.

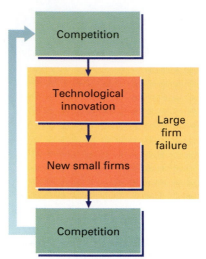

Source: Joseph A. Schumpeter, *Capitalism, Socialism, and Democracy* (New York: Harper & Row, 1942).

economies of scale The reduction in cost per unit output that occurs as a firm mass-produces a product or service

many mainframe computer firms out of business. Other examples of businesses that failed to keep up with competitive challenges over the past twenty years are Eastern Airlines, Texaco, Continental Airlines, Allied Stores, Federated Department Stores, Greyhound, R.H. Macy, Pan Am, Maxwell Communication, and Olympia & York. The destruction of large firms can certainly be disrupting. However, these failures present opportunities for new firms to prosper and grow in the future. Also, some large firms that fail are reorganized in bankruptcy and return to become successful after substantial changes in their operations. Many economists believe that competition is healthy because it leads to technological innovation and change. In turn, competition enables the business sector to increase the quantity and quality of goods and services. If countries protected business firms from competition, creative destruction could not take place, and a vibrant, healthy economy could not flourish.

Invention and Innovation

A common argument against small business firms is that they are too small to produce goods and services as efficiently as large firms. We know that mass production reduces the cost per unit output; this is known as **economies of scale.** Since smaller firms would be forced to produce the same products and services at a higher unit cost, some economists argue they cannot compete with larger firms, which can offer lower sales prices to customers. The wisdom of this logic is evident in the preponderance of extremely large firms in many industries, such as automobiles (e.g., DaimlerChrysler), electronics (Sony), fast food (McDonald's), beverages (Coca-Cola and Pepsi), computer software (Microsoft), and so on. However, each of these industries is constantly experiencing the entry of new, smaller firms. Small businesses have a substantial share of the gross domestic product (GDP) in various industries (see Exhibit 4.3).

EXHIBIT 4.3

Small Business Shares of Gross Domestic Product in Different U.S. Industries, 2001

Industry Group	Total Small Business Share (in percent)
Mining and manufacturing	30
Utilities	22
Construction	90
Trade	64
Transportation and warehousing	40
Information	25
Finance and insurance	29
Real estate, rental, and leasing	74
Professional and technical, administrative, support, etc.	65
Educational services	45
Health and social services	57
Arts, entertainment, and recreation services	76
Accommodation and food services	57
Other services	71
Total private nonfarm industries	50

Source: Joel Popkin & Company, "Small Business Shares in NAICS Industries," report no. SBAHQ-01-M-1056, submitted to the U.S. Small Business Administration, Office of Advocacy, Washington, DC, 2002.

Despite the possibility of inefficiency due to the loss of cost benefits from not achieving economies of scale, small firms do have some advantages over larger firms. Small firms can often react more rapidly to technological changes than large firms; redirecting the efforts of five or ten employees is much easier than trying to do so with 5000 employees. The computer or telecommunications industry, for example, features a myriad of small firms attempting to invent new technologies or to take existing technologies and adapt them to produce a new successful product or service. Larger firms tend to operate in established or traditional sectors of the economy, whereas small firms are well suited to excel in new technology areas.

Another advantage of small firms is that their size encourages experimentation. Large firms must focus on mass markets to cover high fixed operating costs of plant and equipment. Small firms can operate with low production expenses. Their largest expense is often employee salaries. With lower cost pressures and with more human capital as a proportion of their total assets than large firms, small businesses can more readily experiment with new ideas for products and services. Experimentation on a small scale is an effective way to test the market to find out what people want. You may have a great idea for a product, but if no one wants it, there would be little or no profit in pursuing it. Small firms are constantly churning out and testing new products and services. Simply put, small firms are more dynamic than large firms. Able to more freely experiment, invent, and innovate new business ideas, they create diversity, competition, and change that are essential to a country. Indeed, for any country to have a healthy business sector and economy, it must have dynamic and prosperous small businesses.

Of course, large businesses are the consequence of a successful small business. How can a large business retain the entrepreneurial spirit that is the hallmark of small firms? An **intrapreneur** is a person within a large corporation who has the responsibility to develop a new product through innovation and risk taking. The intrapreneur's compensation is linked to the success of the new product. Large companies need intrapreneurship to stay competitive and increase their chances of continued survival. Creative people within the organization can be lost to entrepreneurial opportunities that cause them to leave the firm. The benefits of staying with the firm are more security and more potential resources available through the firm than on their own as entrepreneurs. Intrapreneurship gives them a way to express their creativity within the firm.

intrapreneur A person within a large corporation who takes the responsibility to develop a new product through innovation and risk taking

Sytel is a small company with 300 employees headquartered in Maryland. The company specializes in delivering information technology professional services to government agencies. Some clients include the U.S. Air Force, Army, and Navy, the State, Justice, and Homeland Security departments, the NSA, and the USDA. Here we see how Sytel assisted the government in encouraging families to buy fresh fruits and vegetables from farmers markets. One beneficiary, Carletta Thompson, feeds her five-month-old son an organically grown pea at the Spokane Farmers Market.

EXHIBIT 4.4

Percentages of New Jobs Created
by Different-Sized Firms

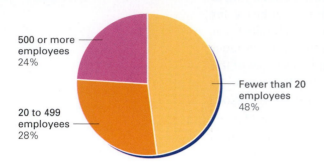

500 or more
employees
24%

Fewer than 20
employees
48%

20 to 499
employees
28%

Source: U.S. Small Business Administration, Office of Advocacy,
Washington, DC, 1997. Based on data gathered from the U.S.
Census Bureau.

home business A small business that is
operated out of a household address,
rather than out of a business office or
factory

Job Opportunities

Perhaps the most compelling reason for the importance of small business firms is that they provide jobs that people want. Does being your own boss sound good to you? Tired of the job you are in and want to design your own job? Have a great idea for a business and want to reap the profit, rather than let someone else gain that profit? Want to work at home or in an environment that you find attractive? Is there a way to combine family and business in your life? Are your close friends interested in working together? Do you see unmet needs in your community and wish someone would do something about them? If you are a woman or member of a minority group, do you want to make your own future, rather than be subject to societal pressures that seem unfair to you? These questions express the motivations for many people who start, purchase, or join a small business.

The U.S. Small Business Administration estimates that there are over 25 million small businesses in the United States. Together, they account for at least half of the jobs and total production of the nation. And, most new jobs are created in the small business sector (see Exhibit 4.4).

Computer and telecommunications technology is changing the way people work in small businesses, and its use in small business is growing (see Exhibit 4.5). For parents taking care of children, a **home business** can provide professional opportunities without sacrificing family values. Many larger firms are finding that they can plug into a network of small business professionals in their region without adding permanent employees to their payrolls. Disabled persons are also finding that they can fit into this remote business model. No longer is there an absolute need to get to a physical location and be at a desk. E-mail, Internet chat rooms, video conferencing, computers, cell phones, and pagers are connecting people to work on business problems without the necessity of everyone being at one place at one time. Also, these allow small niche businesses to rapidly adapt and change to the needs of society.

EXHIBIT 4.5

Small Office and Home Office Information
Technology (IT) Spending

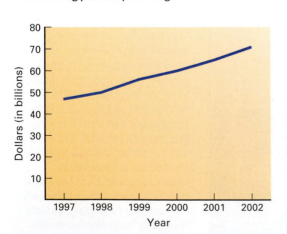

Dollars (in billions)

Year

Source: U.S. Small Business Administration, Office of Advocacy, "Small Business Expansions and Electronic Commerce," report by staff, Washington, DC, June 2000. Data gathered from IDC.

Globalization

Another trend that is changing the role of small business is globalization. The 1990s witnessed unprecedented growth in international trade. While large business firms have surely been the main beneficiaries of increased trade between countries, small businesses are learning how to participate in this growing activity. One way for small firms to get involved is by becoming part of the supply chain of larger firms. As large firms expand their reach across national boundaries, they stretch their human and physical resources and increase their demand for the incremental contributions of small firms. Alternatively, small firms can link up with other small firms in the global marketplace. Networking is a popular way for small businesses to import and export goods and services. For example, a small candy retailer could start importing candies from small, foreign producers to expand their product line and increase sales. Also, many small e-businesses operating on the Internet can market their wares around the world nowadays. Only twenty years ago, this type of global reach was simply impossible for all but the largest firms in the world.

Global Business

Global Small Business and Information Technology Products

Information technology (IT) is allowing small businesses to engage in domestic and international business in ways only dreamed about in the past. IT infrastructure consists of computers, software, Internet service providers (ISPs) or Internet access, high-speed Internet connections, and high-tech innovators who bring these technologies together. It also includes telephone communications, cable television, cellular mobile networks, satellites, broadcasting networks, and electricity distribution networks. Small businesses are participating in IT products with $106 billion in investments in Germany, France, and the United Kingdom and $450 billion worldwide in 1999. It is apparent that technology is size-neutral in that aggressive, flexible small companies can implement many aspects of IT as readily as well-established, larger firms. Importantly, technology allows small firms to break down previous barriers to exporting and reach out to customers in global markets. In doing so, small firms can increase sales and profits as well as lower business risks.

A report by the U.S. Small Business Administration (SBA) gathered the following facts about U.S. small business activity in electronic commerce:

- In 1997 there were over 4600 Internet service providers with fewer than 500 employees.
- In 2000 small businesses expected 30 percent of their annual revenue to come from online Internet sales in that year.
- In 1999 very small businesses with 5 to 99 employees invested about $9 billion in network hardware, which compares to $14 billion invested by small and medium-sized firms with 100 to 999 employees.
- About 85 percent of small businesses with fewer than 100 employees had personal computers in 1999, of which 61 percent had Internet access.
- Very small firms with fewer than ten employees invested more in IT in proportion to their total assets or size than larger firms.
- Home-based businesses invest on average about $1100 in IT, and microbusinesses with fewer than five employees invest about $1500 each year.
- About 60 percent of venture capital investments went to IT industries in 1998, most of which was allocated to small firms.

The surge in electronic commerce by small firms is creating new jobs. Indeed, most new high-tech businesses are themselves small business firms. In 1997 high-tech entrepreneurs added $134 billion to the economy and employed 2.2 million people in the United States. Data collected by the SBA on high-technology occupations (scientists, engineers, computer programmers, and analysts) reveals that about 38 percent of the 4.5 million high-tech workers are in small firms with fewer than 500 employees. Also, small firms were responsible for more than 70 percent of the new jobs in IT in the period 1992 to 1996. These statistics make a powerful case for small business as a technological leader.[2]

Some reasons why small businesses are able to expand into IT are access to capital financing, falling costs of computers and electronic equipment, and the development of the Internet. Venture capitalists and angels tend to concentrate their investments in high-tech enterprises, such as biotechnology, computer networking, and the Internet. Declining costs of computers and electronic communications are opening up IT to even microbusinesses. And most small businesses have access to the Internet. It is expected that 85 percent of small business firms will conduct business via the Internet in the near future. Surely technology is a window through which small businesses can open up a new worldwide frontier and revolutionize business practices.

Source: U.S. Small Business Administration, Office of Advocacy, "Small Business Expansions in Electronic Commerce," Washington, DC, June 2000.

Questions

1. Imagine you owned and operated a small business producing a product that could be sold on a global basis. How could you use the Internet to reach customers around the world?
2. If globalizing your business using the Internet increased the volume of orders for your product, what new computer and telecommunications needs would your growing business require, in your opinion?
3. How would the above globalization of your business operations affect your personal educational training and skills? What about the training and skills of new employees that you might hire?

Do you know of a new small business in your area that recently opened? Why is this new business needed or why isn't it?

Government Support of Small Business

LEARNING OBJECTIVE 2
Discuss the ways government can support small business enterprises.

Government can play an important role in fostering and supporting small business creation and development by providing an environment in which entrepreneurship can flourish. Some of the ways government can assist small business firms are

- Reduction of burdensome regulations
- Simplification of tax rules
- Improved access to financial resources

For example, the U.S. Small Business Administration[3] is a federal agency that provides loan guarantees to banks making loans to small business firms. Since the loans are guaranteed by the government, if the small business does not pay back the loan, the bank can obtain its loaned funds from the government. With lower risk in making such loans, banks make more loans to small businesses and make loans at lower interest rates than if no guarantees were available. Small businesses benefit from the increased access to needed financing, banks gain from new customers that will hopefully grow over time and form long-term credit relationships, and the government serves society by sowing the seeds of future economic development in communities across the country.

Another way in which government can support small business entrepreneurs is by providing essential information. In the United States the following websites are designed by the federal government to help small businesses get the information they need to succeed:

- **www.sba.gov/advo** The Small Business Administration (SBA) Office of Advocacy provides one of the premier websites for small business firms. Regulations and sources of private and government financing are among the types of information that are available. The SBA was established by the government in 1976 to "counsel, assist, and protect small businesses" and works to bridge government and private groups in supporting small business.
- **www.businesslaw.gov** Federal and state rules and regulations are covered here. The SBA and Department of Commerce are working together to expand the types of information available on this website.
- **www.dol.gov/elaws** The Department of Labor gives compliance assistance to small businesses using online legal services that can help answer questions about labor.
- **www.export.gov** The Department of Commerce helps small businesses export their products to foreign countries on this website.

The importance of public policy in the growth of small business is apparent in comparing the United States and Europe. From 1960 to 1983, the number of businesses in the United States more than doubled, but did not change on average in different countries in Europe. The economist and 1992 Nobel laureate Gary S. Becker has argued that this difference is due to regulatory barriers and high taxation in Europe that slows business job growth. The United States has sought less rigid labor and capital markets, freer competition, and lower industrial subsidies than Europe. In recent years, Europe has been moving toward a public policy more similar to that of the U.S. through the creation of the European Monetary Union

(EMU), labor and trade liberalization, privatization of large firms previously owned and operated by the government, and numerous other changes intended to reduce barriers to competition and stimulate business growth.

reality CHECK How far from you is the nearest Small Business Development Center (SBDC), which is sponsored by the U.S. Small Business Administration? What does this office offer to small businesses?

Who Is an Entrepreneur?

LEARNING OBJECTIVE 3
Describe the personal qualities and training needed to be a successful entrepreneur, including the cases of women and minorities in small business.

Entrepreneurs are people who establish new businesses with the desire to meet market demands for goods or services. With the exception of not-for-profit organizations, profit is a major incentive that offsets the risks of starting a new enterprise. Unlike employees of established firms, who work for a salary or commission from their jobs and receive regular paychecks, entrepreneurs can pay themselves both a regular salary from the proceeds of sales revenues as well as extra income from the net profit of the firm, provided the firm makes a profit. Generally speaking, entrepreneurs enjoy the challenge of solving business problems, making their own successes, and reaping the rewards of those successes.

Personal Qualities

What makes someone successful as an entrepreneur? Due to the diversity of small business firms, there is no doubt that all kinds of people can succeed. But entrepreneurs do have some common character traits. Probably the most important personal trait is a *commitment* to make the business profitable despite problems that inevitably arise. This commitment could be due to a lifelong passion for a particular product or service, or simply the stubbornness not to quit. Certainly the personal commitment or drive of an entrepreneur to make a business a success is important in itself.

Another key trait is the desire for *independence*. Entrepreneurs find that working for themselves is more fulfilling than working for someone else as an employee. By being independent, they can directly reap the rewards of their labors, build personal relationships that they want most to pursue, and undertake tasks that they choose. Yet another personal trait common in entrepreneurs is *self-confidence*. They believe that their personal talents and resources are sufficient to run the business. In this respect, some entrepreneurs could be considered to be ambitious. They want to run their own business in order to more rapidly accumulate wealth from a profitable enterprise than if they worked for someone else as a salaried employee. Finally, entrepreneurs tend to be *risk takers*. Most small business people know the feeling of "taking the plunge" and starting their business. A lot of anxiety can naturally occur about the possible failure of the business and related personal guilt of letting down their family, employees, and themselves. Despite these fears, small business entrepreneurs forge ahead, all the while trying not only to make profits but also to reduce their risk of failure. The ability to control risk is an essential part of any successful business. In this context, it is appropriate to consider entrepreneurs to be risk assessors.

Education and Training

Small business entrepreneurs have to deal with all aspects of a business enterprise. Some basic level of knowledge concerning their product or service, accounting and finance principles, marketing and management practices, production methods, taxation, and business law is necessary to succeed. Except for college graduates in business studies, few people have these diverse skills. Even for those with business degrees, the specialized nature of a business will mean that further education and training are required.

Where can you get help in managing the many different areas of a small business? Fortunately, most communities have organizations and trade groups that address small business development. The over 900 Small Business Development Centers (SBDCs) operated by the U.S. Small Business Administration (SBA) are a good place to start. They offer free counseling, access to resources, contacts to organizations and individuals in the community, training materials, and more. The Service Corps of Retired Executives (SCORE) works as a resource partner with the SBA in helping small businesses get professional counseling services. For example, Michael Stoff started a new business named Novi to build and sell Tune-Tote (a stereo system for bicycles). He was referred by the SBA to a local SCORE adviser and obtained help in developing an international marketing plan, setting up a fax to communicate with customers and distributors, and arranging bank financing of international transactions. Shane Beard worked with SCORE advisers to overcome start-up problems in the purchase of a Fastsigns franchise. While the franchise organization offered him training and support, he found that the franchise could not help him with every problem that came up. SCORE worked with him to develop a small business plan that paid off in terms of attracting bank financing, legal assistance, and accounting services. A sales tracking program revealed that most of his customers were due to referrals, rather than ads or direct-mail pieces. Information on these and other areas of business operations helped to smooth out the bumps that every new small business is bound to experience. When new small business owners come to his store to purchase signs, Shane is quick to refer them to local SCORE advisers.

Other sources of small business assistance are local charitable groups and community institutions. These local organizations can help entrepreneurs to meet many knowledgeable people who could be valuable to new businesses. Many times social and professional networks can be important as a support group. Also, the psychological benefits of talking with other small business entrepreneurs and sharing problems, discussion, and solutions are hard to measure but definitely worthwhile.

The Internet is another new and expanding source of information for new small business firms. Searching for the name of your city or town and the words *small business* will no doubt yield a number of websites to explore. Information on your intended product or service can be gathered. Even data on the financial profitability and risks of related business activities can be obtained.

Most small business owners enjoy interacting with other small business people, sharing stories and information resources, and increasing their own personal network of colleagues. Do you need legal assistance to get a patent or trademark? Help with tax questions? Recommendations on accounting software? Many of these questions can be answered by talking with other small business people. Over time it is not uncommon for friendships and alliances to deepen and later result in mergers and acquisitions, as two or more small businesses join together to grow more rapidly and compete more effectively in the marketplace.

Mills Duncan is president and CEO of Duncan Coffee Company in Houston, Texas. He has re-started from scratch the business that his grandfather originally founded and then sold to Coca-Cola Company. The small company is once again gaining a reputation for premium blends of fresh-roasted, made-to-order coffee. Duncan prefers keeping the business small so that he has complete control of the product quality.

Women in Small Business

Women accounted for only 5 percent of small businesses in the United States in 1970, but today represent about 40 percent of small business owners and managers (see Exhibit 4.6 on p. 138). Many women are choosing self-employment over working for wages as an employee of a business firm. This choice is made easier by the onset of the information age. Computers and telecommunications allow women to have home-based businesses, so many women are finding that it is possible to balance family demands and professional business careers.

Changes in laws under the Equal Credit Opportunity Act of 1975, the Affirmative Action Act of 1986, and the Equal Opportunity for Women in the Workplace Act of 1999 have increased women's ability to enter small business enterprise. The latter act established a federal agency to address employment issues of women in the workplace. In general, these acts prohibit discriminating against any worker or job applicant on the basis of gender, in addition to race, color, religion, age, national origin, ability, or veteran status. These legal changes have enabled women to increase their role in communities at all levels of society. By becoming a more integral part of communities and their leadership, women can network more effectively than in the past with business groups that assist small businesses, such as the chamber of commerce, charitable organizations, government agencies, and educational institutions. As their skills, contacts, and knowledge grow in the years to come, we can expect women to play a vital role in the dynamic small business world.

Women bring new perspectives and skills to the small business sector. An example is the unique enterprise Reflections on Vintage Clothing. Bernice Richard started this business in a small town in Massachusetts after personal problems left her with limited income. She began buying old clothes at local shops and charitable organizations and restoring them to like-new condition for her own use. When a neighbor remarked that she looked great in "vintage" clothing, she got the idea to

EXHIBIT 4.6

Woman-Operated Sole Proprietorships

- The number of women's sole proprietorships in the United States increased from 5.6 million in 1990 to 7.1 million in 1998.
- From 1990 to 1998, women's share of sole proprietorship net income (or profit) has risen from 16.9 to 21.5 percent.
- In the 1990s women sole proprietors earned almost 70 percent of their net income (or profit) in the services industries.
- About 87 percent of women's sole proprietorships were small firms with gross sales receipts less than $50,000.
- Large sole proprietorships operated by women, with at least $200,000 in gross sales receipts, represent 2.7 percent of such firms, and their number is growing.
- About two-thirds of women operators of sole proprietorships were married in the 1990s and filed joint tax returns with their husbands.
- About 53 percent of woman-operated sole proprietorships were concentrated in ten major business activities, with door-to-door sales and child daycare topping the list.

Source: U.S. Small Business Administration, Office of Advocacy, Washington, DC. Based on data gathered from the U.S. Census Bureau.

begin a small business selling refurbished clothing. Eventually, after spending many hours researching what it takes to start a business and working with the Small Business Administration, Bernice converted her hobby into a career. She attributes much of her success to surrounding herself with other women small business owners, family, and local organizations to help solve business problems and gain personal support.

Ethnic and Immigrant Small Business

Ethnic-oriented small business is widespread. For example, Harry Luna started Director's Video over a decade ago in Trenton, New Jersey, to serve the Latin American community there. Due to customer requests, he began dubbing or subtitling movies in Spanish. While the enterprise employs only a handful of people, it has been able to compete with large, national video outlets due to meeting the needs of Latinos in the area. The firm has been an inspiration to other small businesses and recently received an award from the New Jersey Chamber of Commerce. Luna says that his goal is to empower Latin businesses to assist the development of the community.

Over the past 200 years, many immigrants have clustered in U.S. communities in sections of rural areas, towns, or cities. These ethnic pockets laid the foundation for the development of a spirit of entrepreneurship among minorities, as language and cultural barriers are typically lower for ethnic-oriented businesses in these communities. The upshot has been a rich source of innovation and dynamic change that creates jobs, new products and services, and human capital. Indeed, U.S.-produced goods and services could never have grown so fast without the determination and entrepreneurial spirit of newcomers. This is true not only of the past, but continues today as an American legacy.

Many countries around the world now recognize that ethnic diversity is an important ingredient in building a more prosperous small business sector. A country whose public policies favor the entry of skilled workers will attract people who are willing to move to a new country to seek better jobs. In this way, countries can acquire human capital, rather than be dependent on internal population trends for skilled labor.

reality CHECK *What kind of small business would you like to start if you had the chance?*

Developing a Business Plan

LEARNING OBJECTIVE 4

List and briefly define each of the essential components of a business plan.

An essential step to start a new enterprise (or expand an existing one) is developing a business plan. The business plan reflects the goals, strategies, and daily operations of a firm. Most business plans are made up of marketing, operations, and financial plans (see Exhibit 4.7 on p. 140). In the event you want to start a new business, you should go to the Small Business Administration's website (**www.sba.gov**) and select "Starting your business." Here you can find further information on business plans, a start-up checklist, and other valuable information for entrepreneurs.[4]

Essential Components

A **vision,** or **mission, statement** gives the main goals of an enterprise in such a way as to capture the imagination of employees within the firm, as well as customers and suppliers outside the firm. It gives inspiration and impetus to move forward with the business plan. A vision must be realistic and easily understood to focus attention on a central objective. For example, the vision of Harry Luna's Director's Video is "to make popular movies accessible in Spanish to Latin Americans."

vision, or **mission, statement** A statement that illuminates the main goals of an enterprise

Goals are the aims that guide the future direction of the firm. Goals can include future sales, new job opportunities, greater market share, profits, and technological achievements. Goals inform employees in the firm what they are striving to achieve. For example, a goal of initial sales of $200,000 in the first year, followed by, say, 10 percent growth in sales for the next five years, lets the management team know what they are supposed to accomplish in the near future.

goals The aims that guide the future direction of a firm

Strategies are more detailed descriptions of how a goal can be achieved. Strategies for advertising, sales promotions, pricing, target market, and so on can be specified. For example, to ensure strong sales in the first year, an advertising campaign in local newspapers and on local radio stations could be implemented that would provide customers special discounts for trying out the firm's new products or services.

strategies More detailed descriptions of how a goal can be achieved

The following components should be included in a written business plan:

- *Title page.* Company name, address, telephone numbers, website address, and logo are provided. It is also common to list the primary owners and lead executives of the firm.
- *Table of contents.* Sections in the report and their corresponding page numbers are listed.
- *Executive summary.* A one- to two-page synopsis of the business.
- *Vision, or mission, statement.* A concise and brief overview of the central concept or business idea.

EXHIBIT 4.7

Key Components of a Business Plan

- *Overview of the company*. History of when and how the firm was started, motivations for establishing the firm, major accomplishments, anticipated products and services, competitive environment, perceived strengths and weaknesses, employees, suppliers, and customers.
- *Goals*. Briefly stated overall firm objectives, as well as marketing, operations, and financial objectives.
- *Products and services*. Detailed descriptions and pictures of the firm's outputs in addition to a discussion of their innovative aspects.
- *Marketing plan*. Research information about customer demand for the firm's outputs and how the firm intends to attract customers and reach sales objectives.
- *Management plan*. Organizational structure, backgrounds of key managers, employee personnel needs, and leadership responsibilities.
- *Operating plan*. Production facilities, technology, quality control, raw materials, inventory, and distribution of products and services.
- *Financial plan*. Expected (or pro forma) accounting statements, cash earnings over time (or cash flows), sources of funds to produce outputs, and profit and share value goals in the near future.
- *Appendices*. Supporting documents, data, and other materials needed to supplement the previous sections of the report.

The business plan is needed not only to give managers a document from which to work but also to attract investors and customers. Without a business plan, managers would be confused about their responsibilities and duties. Also, investors would not have critical information to evaluate potential risks and returns, and the firm would have difficulty raising funds needed to produce its products and services. Note that a business plan is not a static view of a firm. Most small firms are dynamic, fast-changing enterprises in their early years. Consequently, business plans are continually amended to accommodate change. Business plans are so important that business consultants are often hired to help develop and modify plans.

Business Ideas

Where can you find successful business ideas? Personal experiences are probably the most common source. For example, a business idea could emerge in your work as an employee for another firm: by accident you discover a new chemical compound unrelated to your employer's firm. Or, you might be frustrated with a product or service that you regularly purchase and have an idea on how to make a better version. Some people go through repeated failures and by trial-and-error eventually get the business idea right. The active pursuit of new technology is another source of new business ideas. Sometimes it is a unique mix of personalities that through brainstorming and cooperation yields a good idea for a business. New ideas also result from discussions with friends, family members, or fellow employees.

Not every good idea is feasible. You and those around you may well believe that a business idea is a sure winner. However, the ultimate test is convincing the customer that this is true. Without sales, no business can survive. For this reason, market research is desirable to gauge customer demand, complaints, possible improvements, and competition. Customer surveys and trials are used to collect data. Also, the potential size of the market is an important consideration. The key question is, Do customers really want your product or service?

Let's consider some examples of how personal experiences led to business ideas:

- Donna Mae Montgomery always enjoyed photography, ceramics, sculpture, and painting, and some of her work is exhibited in New York's Whitney Museum. In a museum bookstore she noticed a jewelry pin made out of shrink-it plastic. She got the idea to photocopy designs onto plastic and then form and bake the plastic to make jewelry pins. Her Folk Dada pins have colorful painted characters in a surreal style; other pins are in a romantic style.
- Edmund Scientific is a scientific equipment company that started when its founder noticed that damaged, chipped lenses could be sold in newspaper classified ads. Some buyers were willing to accept slightly damaged lenses at lower discounted prices. The company now employs more than 150 people selling discount lenses.
- Lillian Vernon is a mail-order business that initially sold monogrammed leather belts out of the owner's kitchen. The owner had the idea that people liked to have some items personalized with their initials or name. Expanding to other personalized gifts, toys, and games, the mail-order business now exceeds $200 million in revenues annually.
- La Bella Madonna sprang from the owner's experience of having a baby. She noticed that new mothers appreciated a basket full of small gifts and treats to reduce the stresses of dealing with a newborn child. An Internet-based home business, La Bella Madonna delights new mothers with a variety of baskets that contain information, supplies, and gifts.

These examples demonstrate that some of the best ideas for a small business arise from the everyday lives of people.

Seed Money

Most people have some personal savings to cover some of the start-up costs for a new business. But you have to think ahead to properly raise sufficient seed money to keep the business going for at least one or two years. Assume that you have enough savings to rent a property, pay for some raw materials, and cover labor expenses for a few months. Many customers want to pay later for your products and demand credit. Suppose that your new firm produced decorative pottery. Retail stores that purchase your pottery want to pay you back 60 days after you send them the pottery because they want to display and sell the pottery before they pay you. In the meantime, more orders for your pottery come in due to the word spreading about the quality and design of your pottery. Where can you get the money to keep production going?

At this early stage of a firm's development, the most likely sources of seed money are outside investors, banks, and the government. **Venture capitalists** are investors seeking higher-risk and higher-return business opportunities (e.g., annual profit rates of 60 percent or more). These investors usually want part ownership of the firm. As such, they share the net profits of the firm with the original owner-manager(s). Some venture capitalists are wealthy individuals, or so-called **angels,** while others are institutional investors, such as investment companies. Some banks are entering the venture capital business also.

Alternatively, new firms can seek credit financing at local banks. Banks are the largest financier of **working capital,** which finances raw materials, variable (as opposed to fixed) production costs, and labor needed to produce a product. In many countries, the government provides loan guarantee programs that assist

venture capitalists Investors in small business firms seeking higher-risk and higher-return business opportunities by purchasing equity ownership positions

angels Venture capitalists who are wealthy individuals and who likely were previously successful small business people

working capital Money needed to pay the short-run expenses of producing a product or service, including raw materials, variable production costs, and labor

small firms seeking bank loans. If the firm fails to pay the loan back to the bank, the government will pay it. Given the reduced risk of losing their money, banks will loan small firms more funds than they would otherwise.

Initial Production and Sales

If a person has little experience with a new product or service, how can she or he ensure the quality and quantity of production? After the fall of communism in the former Soviet Union, many new firms emerged in Russia's new free enterprise system—bakery shops, clothes cleaners, repair services, neighborhood restaurants, and so on. One typical way of ensuring quality and quantity was to buy an existing property in cooperation with employees who had previous experience in producing similar products or services. Business properties can be located through the newspaper, local government, businesses, local business organizations, and word of mouth. However, at times it is necessary to develop new property. The decision to use new or old facilities depends on their relative costs and benefits. Generally speaking, acquiring new property is much more costly than using existing plant and equipment, and therefore, the benefits must be relatively high to justify this choice.

Creating Value

Every business must create value for customers, employees, and investors. Customers demand quality products at competitive prices. Employees seek jobs with good salaries, working conditions, and benefits (e.g., health and insurance coverage and retirement plans). Investors want fair rates of return to compensate them for taking risks in giving their money to the firm. You can readily infer that creating value is not easy to accomplish. Managers and employees must work together to achieve the firm's business objectives and realize the firm's vision for the future.

An illusive but crucial factor in creating value is leadership. In most small firms, the owner-manager is highly visible to employees, customers, investors, and others. Leadership entails spreading enthusiasm and confidence, providing decision making, and communicating effectively with others. It is not enough to have a great business idea; you must follow through with personal actions that motivate others to join in the vision of the firm. Leadership can spread throughout an organization, contributing to managers and employees taking personal responsibility for their actions. Leadership can transform a business from one person's hopes, dreams, and energy to those of many people within the firm. In this way value can be created by the firm.

 Ask a local business person for a copy of his or her firm's business plan or ask your local Small Business Development Center for an example of a business plan.

Forms of Small Business Organizations

LEARNING OBJECTIVE 5
Compare the different small business organizational forms, including sole proprietorships, partnerships, corporations, and franchises.

Sole Proprietorships and Partnerships

The simplest form of business organization is the *sole proprietorship*—a business owned and operated by one person (see Exhibit 4.8). Most small firms begin as a sole proprietorship. A key advantage of this business form is that the individual has total control over the enterprise. Many times proprietorships are family businesses that are later passed on to children and relatives.

Another early stage business form is a *partnership* made up of two or more individuals. The main reasons for establishing a partnership are that more start-up capital is needed, unique and different talents are essential, personal friendships or family ties come into play, and companionship is valuable as a lifestyle choice. While these benefits are certainly reasonable, it is well known that partnerships can suffer from a number of disadvantages. Disagreements can arise between the partners in almost any area of business management. Conflicts over the firm's goals, strategy, financing, and so on are common over time. More than half of the partnerships run into such serious personal problems that the firm is either dissolved or one partner buys out the other partner.

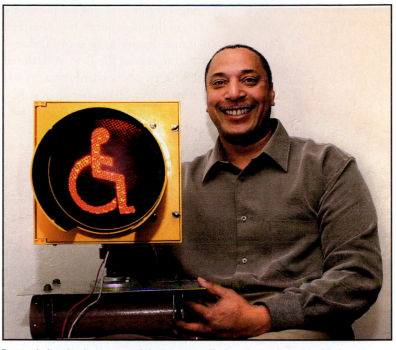

Demetris Lewis shows one of the cross-walk signals produced by his home-based business, Quantrell Enterprise. The device warns drivers of the possible presence of disabled pedestrians.

Corporations and Franchises

As small firms grow, it may be necessary to adopt the corporate form of business organization. A *corporation* is essentially an individual entity that exists only in

EXHIBIT 4.8

Characteristics of Different Kinds of Business Organizations

A sole proprietorship
- Personal taxation of business income
- Total control of the enterprise
- Problem of managing all aspects of the business
- Problem of personal liability for bank loans
- Availability of government support for financing needs

A partnership provides greater financial and human resources.
- Problem of management disagreements

A C corporation is registered within its home state.
- Corporate taxation as an individual entity
- Ability to issue common stock to raise new equity capital
- Limited liability of managers and shareholders
- Problem of double taxation of earnings (but S corporations taxed as partnerships)
- Problem of dilution of ownership control with many shareholders
- Problem of loss of entrepreneurial spirit

A franchise provides training and brand name recognition for the franchisee from the larger franchisor.
- Problem of fees and royalty payments
- Problem of loss of independence

C corporation A legal entity that is chartered under state law

legal terms and has no physical presence. A **C corporation** is the most common legal business form; it is chartered under state law. The corporate charter lists the name, location, type of business, owners, board of directors, and officers (or key managers) of the firm. A fictional individual, the corporation can live beyond the lifetimes of its current owners and managers. As such, its future survival is not dependent on the personal survival of individuals within the firm. A key advantage of corporate status is the *limited liability* of its owners and managers. In the event of the failure of the firm, owners can only lose the investment capital that they have put into the firm. Managers can only lose their jobs. The personal assets of investors or managers are generally not liable to seizure by creditors.

Another major advantage of the corporate form is that the firm can issue common shares to raise capital to expand its assets and grow. Common shareholders not only have voting rights within the firm but can receive dividends paid by the firm from its profits. **Dividends** are paid quarterly by the firm from net income after taxes. If there were 100 shareholders, the firm had net profits of $10,000, and the firm was going to retain $5,000 to invest in new equipment for producing its products, the dividend per share would be $5000 per 100 shares, or $50 per share. If you held 10 shares, you would be paid $500.

dividends Quarterly payments by the firm from net income after taxes to corporation shareholders

par value The initial value of stocks issued by a firm

stock price The market value of a share of stock issued by a firm

capital gain The difference between the price paid to purchase a share of stock and the money received when it is sold

Shareholders can also earn money from an increase in the value of the common shares. If 10,000 shares were issued for $10 **par value** to raise capital, a total of $100,000 would then be available to the firm to invest in new assets. These common shares can be sold by shareholders to other parties. If the **stock price** rose to $20 and you owned 100 shares, you would make a $10 **capital gain** on each share sold, for a total profit of $1000. Capital gain must be reported on your personal income tax forms. The value, or price, of common shares rises (or falls) depending on the profitability and riskiness of the firm over time. Shareholders and potential shareholders focus on the future expected profits and risks of the business in determining the desirability of the common stock and hence its current price.

double taxation of earnings The taxation of a corporation's profits plus the taxation of the dividends paid to shareholders from after-tax profits

The corporate form of business is not without disadvantages. One problem is the **double taxation of earnings.** The firm is taxed on its profits, and after the firm pays its taxes and disperses its net profits as dividends to shareholders, the dividends are taxed a second time as ordinary income paid to shareholders. This double taxation is under debate in the United States at the present time. There is a possibility that the personal taxation of dividends will be eliminated in whole or in part. The rationale is to increase the rewards to shareholders for investing their savings in firms and taking a risk that they might lose money if the firm is not profitable.

dilution of ownership control The loss of ownership control that occurs as more shareholders own stock, thereby reducing the percentage ownership of each individual shareholder

Another disadvantage of the corporate form is the **dilution of ownership control** as more and more shares are issued by the firm. At some point each shareholder feels somewhat powerless to use her or his votes to exercise ownership control. If you held only 10 out of 100,000 shares, you might stop voting on important business decisions. In this case managers with administrative control increase in power due to the diminishing ownership control on the part of individual shareholders.

A final disadvantage of corporations that can occur is the potential loss of entrepreneurial spirit. Managers in firms with diluted ownership control do not have the profit incentives of owners to motivate them. In an effort to overcome this potential problem, many firms offer managers **stock options** to buy common shares at a predetermined price. If they do a good job, increase the firm's profits, and stock prices rise, the managers can buy shares at the predetermined price and then sell them at the higher market price to earn capital gains.

stock options A type of compensation that gives managers the right to buy common shares of stock at a predetermined price

S corporation A hybrid form of corporation that has limited liability but is taxed as a partnership and therefore avoids double taxation of earnings; also known as a Subchapter S corporation

The **S corporation** (otherwise known as the Subchapter S corporation, due to this part of the federal income tax rules) is a hybrid form of company. The corporation has limited liability, but is taxed as a partnership and therefore avoids the double taxation of earnings. Earnings are not taxed on the corporate level; instead, they are passed through to shareholders as dividends and taxed only as their personal income. Only domestic firms with less than 75 shareholders are allowed to be S corporations in the United States, so S corporations tend to be fairly small in size.

Finally, the **limited liability company** (**LLC**) combines the corporate advantage of limited liability protection with only the personal taxation of a partnership or S corporation. LLCs are owned by their members, who are analogous to partners in a partnership or shareholders in a corporation, depending on how the LLC is set up. However, if an LLC member participates in the firm's management, profits become subject to self-employment tax.

limited liability company (LLC) A type of corporation that combines the corporate advantage of limited liability protection with the personal taxation of a partnership or S corporation

The **franchise** is another form of business corporation. A corporation can offer franchises to individuals that allow them to participate as an owner-manager in the firm. McDonald's Corporation, KFC (Kentucky Fried Chicken) Corporation, and Subway have retail food franchises; Holiday Inn Worldwide and Best Western have hotel franchises; and Jiffy Lube International, Radio Shack, and Mail Boxes Etc. are

franchise An authorization by a corporation to individuals that allows them to participate as an owner-manager of a branch entity of the corporate firm

Case in Point

Franchising: A Way for Small Business and Large Business to Work Together

Many small businesses are franchise members of larger corporations. Car dealerships are highly visible, small franchise businesses in most towns and cities. They offer a way for small local enterprises to participate within a larger corporate firm. Indeed, most car dealerships are owned and operated by local small businesspeople.

Consider the small business history of Brown Chrysler. Although a true story, we have changed the names and some details to protect privacy. In 1960 George Kinkade Sr. and James Baumgartner, long-time partners in several businesses in the local community, opened a small used car lot. Broken-down cars were towed from the surrounding region, repaired and repainted at their car lot, and then sold as used cars. Typical financing was simple; a small down payment and weekly payments of 10 to 20 dollars was enough to buy one of their cars!

In 1962 they leased an abandoned property in town and installed repair and painting facilities to expand their automobile renovation business. The next year they incorporated their firm under the name Car Repair and Sales. In the mid-1960s the corporation moved to a new location and began to stock more expensive automobiles that were financed by the local banks.

In 1972 the small corporation applied for a Chrysler franchise under the name Brown Chrysler.

Shortly thereafter, the firm was awarded a franchise by another automobile franchising organization. Expanding their local business further, the firm in recent years has benefitted from the merger of Chrysler Corporation and Daimler-Benz to form DaimlerChrysler. Changing their name to Brown DaimlerChrysler, the franchise added luxury German cars to its product line.

Kinkade and Baumgartner operated their small business franchise until 2000. At that time Kinkade's son John purchased more than 50 percent of the firm's stock from his father and his father's business partner. The family-owned business found that franchising not only reduced their business risk but allowed faster growth than otherwise possible.

Questions

1. Choose a small business franchise in your area and write a two-page report that summarizes its founder(s), owner(s), business activities, and growth over time.
2. What are the main advantages of owning and managing this franchise organization?
3. What are the main disadvantages of owning and managing this franchise organization?

other examples of franchise businesses. The corporation is the franchisor and each individual owner-manager is a franchisee. The franchise contract details the legal relationship between the franchisor and franchisee.

The key advantages of being a franchisee are training and brand name recognition. McDonald's is well known for its Hamburger University in Oak Brook, Illinois. According to McDonald's, they are the largest training organization in the United States. Restaurant employees receive about 32 hours of training in their first month with McDonald's. Both managers and employees can receive training at Hamburger University. Other franchisors are also very active in providing training to their franchisees. The training helps to assure a uniform and high-quality product or service regardless of the store location. Brand name recognition is important to advertising and consumer acceptance and helps to establish a regular customer base for the franchisee. At times franchisors offer financial assistance to their franchisees. While McDonald's does not offer financial support, it is likely that bank credit is more readily obtained by franchisees who have been approved by the corporation. Thus, franchisor reputation is valuable in obtaining financing. The U.S. Small Business Administration has established the Franchise Registry, which allows banks and other lenders to verify franchisor information. Finally, franchisors have developed proven methods of business operation that are passed along to franchisees in the form of manuals and regular information updates on taxes, health, insurance, and so on.

There are some possible disadvantages of franchising. Franchisees pay an initial franchising fee ($45,000 for McDonald's) and must come up with start-up cash (about $100,000 for McDonald's). Royalty payments on gross monthly sales (about 4 percent for McDonald's) are common. In some cases franchisors also charge 1 to 2 percent of sales to help cover corporate advertising costs. The franchisor seeks to standardize their product or service by placing a variety of restrictions on franchisees, geographic area, store appearance, products and services sold, operating details, and so on. These restrictions tend to reduce entrepreneurial independence and opportunities to some extent. Franchise management is not for everyone. Nonetheless, franchisors do lower the chance of failure and increase the ability to earn a fair profit for franchisees. For all these reasons, they are a popular corporate form that enables franchisor firms to grow rapidly and tap into the dynamic entrepreneurship of the small business sector.

An example of a franchise organization is O.I. Corporation. Founded in Oklahoma in 1963 by William W. Botts under the name Clinical Development Corporation, the firm initially was a building contractor for medical and research enterprises. It was purchased in 1969 by investors and moved to Texas as a franchise organization under the name Oceanography International Corporation (OIC). The founding of the franchise led to OIC's production of equipment to measure water quality. In 1994 the franchise acquired CMS Research Corporation (Alabama), a manufacturer of air quality testing equipment. In that year it also acquired Floyd Associates (South Carolina), a manufacturer of equipment used to prepare chemical compounds for analysis in a laboratory. More acquisitions followed: Laboratory Automation (Missouri) in 1995, ALPKEM Corporation (Oregon) in 1996, and General Analysis Corporation (Connecticut) in 1999. These acquisitions increased the franchise's product line in analytical instruments for the sample preparation, detection, and measurement of chemical compounds. The company currently employs over 150 people and has sales over $25 million, with about 20 percent of sales from international business. The franchise has become well known for its innovative products used in chemical analysis. As a dynamic franchise changing to meet market demands, OIC has strategically positioned itself to develop new products. According to president and CEO Will Botts, "We know fulfillment of our vision will require the franchise to grow internally with quality products that make us a leader in the eyes of our customers and externally through key acquisitions and partnerships that add synergistic products and markets."

reality **CHECK**   *What is the local business franchise in your area that you most frequently visit? Why do you choose to go there as a customer?*

Small Business Management Decisions

LEARNING OBJECTIVE 6
Evaluate key small business management decisions, including hiring employees, ethics issues, family business benefits and costs, going public versus staying private, and controlling internal and external business risks.

Hiring Employees

All firms seek to hire the best employees. However, there are differences between the personnel needs of small business and those of large business. Small firms offer employees a chance to gain experience and to move into responsible positions at a faster pace of advancement than large firms. Each employee in a small business is relatively more important to the business and more expensive to train than in a large business. In a small business, the president and chief executive officer may well offer employees hands-on training sessions. This type of training would be unlikely in a large firm! Another difference is that small firms have higher failure rates than large firms. For this reason, small firms must be particularly careful in recruiting employees who can do the job and maintain quality expectations of customers.

Some employees are attracted to small business job opportunities not only by the chance to move up faster but also by the flexibility of working hours, recognition of their individual efforts, and possible monetary rewards. Salary structures can be readily adapted to employee productivity using either changes in wages, commissions on sales, or stock options in the firm. Also, some employees aspire to reach managerial positions that might be more difficult to reach in a large firm. They might someday want to run their own small business or eventually take over a franchise of the existing firm.

There are many sources of potential job applicants. High schools, trade schools, colleges, and universities are major sources of young workers. State and local employment offices offer referrals of individuals seeking employment with specific job descriptions. There are also private employment offices and executive search firms that can be used, especially if professional managers are needed. Small firms can advertise that they have job opportunities available in local newspaper want ads, on Internet websites specializing in posting job applicants' resumes, and by word of mouth in their community.

Screening job candidates involves sifting through application forms in an attempt to find applicants that fit the job profile. Once a set of final candidates is identified, personal interviews are required to evaluate interpersonal skills, attitudes, and personality. It is important to carefully consider the diversity of the employee ranks. Today, more women and minorities are needed in the workplace than in the past to better meet the diverse customer base that most firms confront in the marketplace.

It is important to offer employees quality training to ensure that they are prepared to function competently in their jobs. New employees are less experienced in handling customer orders than more experienced employees. It is imperative that new employees receive assistance from the other employees, as well as continued training, to become effective workers. Some existing employees may receive added compensation for training duties to motivate and reward them for excellent work.

Ethics in Entrepreneurship

Business ethics comprise moral values, standards of behavior, cultural norms, social customs, and legal systems. A small business manager needs to understand the laws that affect the firm's activities and communicate them to the employees. Laws pertaining to discrimination, personal abuse, and human rights are especially relevant to ethical issues. People have rights as citizens that businesses must respect.

Organizational policies and procedures regarding interactions among workers, customers, and other individuals and businesses are on another level of ethical standards. Each business should create a written document that clearly states the entrepreneur's guidelines for ethical business practices. Can employees use equipment, such as phones and computers, for their personal needs? Which personal or family emergencies can be excused to allow employees to temporarily leave work? What are the privacy rights of employees in their use of e-mail messages and other forms of communication? Employees should receive a copy of the document and be advised that violation of policies and procedures with respect to ethical conduct can result in dismissal.

company credo A business philosophy that provides an ethical standard for a firm, as well as its managers and employees

Another application of ethics in business is an entrepreneur's personal philosophy about how people should be treated. It is difficult for laws as well as firm policies and procedures to cover all dimensions of such a complex concept as ethics. Sometimes a **company credo** or code is developed to highlight an ethical philosophy. What is the difference between right and wrong? What standard should be applied to ethical problems that inevitably arise in human interactions in a business firm? To which values should employees adhere in their work duties? A business philosophy can give guidance to people within the firm about how to deal with ethical challenges. One way to operationalize a business philosophy is to set out a list of principles that are consistent with the philosophy. Each principle of conduct should give a concrete example of how employees can apply the firm's philosophy to their work. For example, a common business assumption is that customers are critical to the firm's future success. As such, the principle that the "customer is king" implies that even if a customer seems unreasonable, she or he will be treated with all due respect and every effort will be made to satisfy the customer's demands. When an employee is not sure how to handle an ethical problem, the entrepreneur and employee should discuss the best course of action under the circumstances.

It is conceivable that a decent person will engage in an unethical act. The stresses of everyday life as well as competitive pressures facing the firm can cause employees to suffer lapses in ethical behavior. Also, sometimes people make mistakes because they do not foresee an ethical dilemma until it happens. These ethical blunders are bound to occur. Entrepreneurs need to be flexible and implement policies that accommodate ways of overcoming ethical mishaps. Naturally, an employee who repeatedly makes ethical mistakes should be counseled and may have to be released if counseling fails to correct lapses. When hiring employees, it is essential to discuss ethical business practices in the interview process so that they know what is expected by the entrepreneur.

Finally, ethics in business encompasses social and environmental responsibility. Today, many educated customers want to buy products and services from firms that are sensitive to community social needs (poverty, homelessness, health care, human rights, etc.) and environmental concerns (pollution, forests, animal rights, recycling, wasteful resource use, etc.). Firms that do not demonstrate social and environmental responsibility to their customers can suffer lost sales.

Running a Family Business

Most small business firms are family owned and operated. By intertwining family and business, there are costs and benefits that should be considered. Some of the costs are

- Conflicts between family members
- Management succession disagreements
- Arguments over money
- Differences in the vision and strategic planning for the firm
- Management control of family employees

Of these costs, management succession is the main reason why small firms go out of business. Accumulated wealth in a family business must at some point be transferred to the next generation. Siblings can end up in bitter battles for control of the firm and its management. Parents as founders must communicate to their children their wishes concerning who will own and manage the firm in the future. Sometimes it is necessary to select someone outside the family to assume the management reins. Obviously, management succession is an emotionally-charged issue. Founders can increase the chances of a smooth succession by being fair, open, and respectful of all family members' views in this regard.

The benefits of a family business are

- The ability to spend more time with family members
- Helping family members succeed in their work
- Sharing common family values that are incorporated in the business
- Strengthening family bonds
- Trust and mutual cooperation

Family members who do not work in a family enterprise will often end up living and working in different locations, having different types of jobs, and having limited time on vacations and holidays to be with other family members. By contrast, family businesses tend to bring family members closer to one another. Family businesses have fewer employee problems in hiring, promotion, and reward compensation. Also, family members are likely more loyal and stable workers than other employees with no personal attachment to the business.

There are many good examples of family businesses. The Duncan Coffee Company was established in 1918 by Herschel Mills Duncan in Houston, Texas. The company gained a reputation for special blends that were served in fine restaurants and hotels. After Duncan died in 1957, the company was sold to Coca-Cola. However, in 1997, great grandson H. Mills Duncan IV, 38 and a successful entrepreneur in commercial real estate, decided to reestablish the Duncan Coffee Company. Like his grandfather before him, he began marketing high-quality, fresh-roasted coffee beans to the best restaurant and hotel establishments in the Houston region. Because coffee beans lose their freshness after roasting, batches of beans were custom-roasted to order and promptly delivered to customers. The local success of the business has attracted some offers to buy and expand the company, but Duncan has resisted these offers because he feels that the quality of the coffee would suffer. Also, he would prefer that the small business stay in the family this time.

Bob's Valley Market has become a gathering place for locals in Helena, Montana. Pat Bartmess had over 35 years of retail experience before she and her husband Bob purchased a 900-square-foot country store and gas station. They obtained a Small Business Administration (SBA) loan to finance one of numerous remodeling projects. Their mission has been to "provide personal service to customers in a clean, friendly environment." In 1988 they brought a contract post office location into the store. In 1995 the SBA made another loan to help finance a ham store and carryout deli. Steve Bartmess was in charge of this facility, which was so successful that the family sought additional SBA, state, and bank financing to open an entirely new store. The new 12,000-square-foot facility has a fuel area, deli, bakery, meat department, and produce section. The store offers groceries, gasoline and diesel fuel, fish and game licenses, lotto and lottery tickets, an instant cash machine, transport permits, a post office, a deli, and a notary service. Sales have grown from $100,000 in 1973 to over $3 million today. The family-owned corporation has become a mini-supermarket that meets community needs not only for goods and services but also for community social interaction.

Going Public Versus Staying Private

Small businesses have the choice of staying private or going public. Private firms have more direct control of the business and less outside interference than public firms. The stock of private firms is held primarily by the president or founder. For a number of reasons, a private firm may seek to issue stock to the general public. One major reason is that new capital must be raised to finance growth. Demand for the firm's products is strong enough to justify the expansion or upgrading of the firm's physical facilities. Another reason is that the owner-manager can increase his or her personal wealth by issuing stock and allowing the market to set a price for the firm's stock. Due to investor interest in the firm, it is possible that the market price will be higher than the accounting (or book) value of the stock. Suppose the stock value is $10 per share as listed in a firm's accounting statements. This book value was determined at the time the stock was first issued. With a public sale, if investors were willing to pay $15 per share, the personal wealth of the owner-manager would rise $5 per share, or 50 percent.

acquisition The purchase of one firm by another for a price that is paid to the purchased firm's owner(s)

If a firm decides to go public, there are two possible avenues. Most commonly, firms are bought by another firm in an **acquisition.** The firm may be totally absorbed into the acquiring firm (known as a *merger*), or it may become a component of the acquiring firm and remain intact for the most part. In the former case, the owner-manager likely exits the firm, whereas in the latter case the owner-manager may well remain as the head of the new component or division of the acquiring firm. Another alternative is an **initial public offering (IPO).** In an IPO the owner-manager maintains the role of president and chief operating officer but sells shares of stock to people outside the firm. When going public, should the firm sell out or use an IPO? This decision is both a personal and a financial choice. Some entrepreneurs prefer the IPO to keep closer control of the firm. Other entrepreneurs choose to sellout if they no longer want to run the business. Also, when comparing a sell out versus an IPO, the price of the stock in these two situations should be compared.

initial public offering (IPO) The first public sale by a firm of its common stock

Sometimes a venture capitalist or angel can influence decisions about going public or staying private. Venture capital firms and angels typically have owned and operated successful small businesses in the past. Venture capitalists obtain a high degree of control of the firm for a specified period of time. For example, a venture capitalist contributing $1,000,000 of equity capital to the firm could demand control of the firm for five years. The entrepreneur might after five years have the option to buy out the ownership shares of stock held by the venture capitalist. At that time the firm would revert back to the complete control of the entrepreneur. However, what if the entrepreneur did not have the capital to buy out the venture capitalist? In this case the venture capitalist could assist the entrepreneur with contacts and advice regarding going public via a sellout or an IPO. With the profits from this sale of shares, the entrepreneur could buy back her or his controlling interest in the firm. However, if the firm is sold to an acquiring firm, it is likely that the entrepreneur will have only a minority ownership interest in the larger combined firm made up of the acquired and the acquiring firms. Generally speaking, it is recommended that an entrepreneur seek legal and business counseling when considering sellouts and IPOs.

Controlling Business Risks

Small businesses have relatively high failure rates compared to larger firms, especially in their early years. Risks of losses that severely cripple the business or even cause bankruptcy are known as **business risks.** As shown in Exhibit 4.9, business risks can be internal or external in origin. Internal business risks include elements under the direct control of management, such as a poor business plan, bad leadership, too much debt, inexperienced management, and marketing problems. An example of bad leadership or inexperienced management is losses due to costs rising faster than revenues. Note that the firm may well be experiencing rising sales revenues and could have all the outward appearances of a successful business. However, rising wage costs, equipment and supply costs, overhead expenses for building space and land, and taxes could more than offset increasing revenues. Or, sales may suddenly slow down with the result that revenues fall; unfortunately, many operating expenses mentioned above may be fixed or can only be decreased gradually. Again, the firm's profits could turn negative and trigger a bankruptcy if the firm cannot pay its bills on time.

Another important internal business risk concerns the potential inability to pay debt. Suppose that a firm seeks debt financing at a local bank. It will have to submit accounting and other information as part of the loan application. The bank will use this information to determine the ability of the firm to pay its debt. Firms with higher levels of debt or with sales that fluctuate considerably over time tend to be more susceptible to failure or bankruptcy risk. Also, firms with high fixed operating expenses, due to maintenance costs of a manufacturing factory building and

business risks Internal and external risks of losses that can severely cripple a business or even cause bankruptcy

EXHIBIT 4.9

Sources of Business Risks: Reasons for Small Business Failures

Internal Business Risks	External Business Risks
Poor business plan	Competitor firms
Bad leadership	Changes in customer preferences
Too much debt	
Inexperienced management	Economic downturn
Marketing problems	Catastrophic losses from property damage, personal liabilities, and legal problems

equipment, tend to have a higher failure risk than other firms. And, firms with little extra cash or financial assets to cover losses will be exposed to greater bankruptcy risk than those with more cash or financial assets.

Small business managers can overcome these internal business risks by working with an accountant or local banker on their financial condition. Accounting statements from quarter to quarter are needed to examine operating revenues and costs over time and gain a better understanding of internal business risks. Most internal business risks are controllable.

By contrast, most external business risks are uncontrollable. Any successful firm is bound to attract competition. Aware of the firm's success, other firms act to make inroads into the firm's market. The resulting loss of customers can cause sales to fall as competitive pressures increase. Or the firm may have to cut its prices to discourage competitors from entering their market. The lower prices of products will lower sales revenues even if sales levels stay the same as before.

Customer tastes and trends can impact a firm. For example, a new product may capture initial customer interest simply because it is different than other products. However, as the newness wears off, sales could drop as some customers seek out newer products or return to their old product purchases.

recessions Relatively brief slowdowns, or contractions, in economic activity within a business cycle

The business sector in free market economies is prone to cycles. Business cycles alternate between economic expansions and later economic contractions called **recessions.** Economists define recessions as two consecutive three-month periods (or quarters) in which the output of goods and services declined. Normally, economic expansions last five to eight years, while recessions are fairly brief at less than one year. Longer, more severe recessions are termed **depressions,** which can last for as long as five to ten years. Over the past 200 years, there have been only a few full-blown depressions in the United States. Small businesses are adversely affected by recessions and depressions due to the fall in consumer demand in these periods. Economic slowdowns cause business sales to fall, layoffs of workers by business firms, and an increased number of bankruptcies. What can a small business do to survive a recession? Foremost, it can stay informed about the state of the economy. News in papers, on the radio and TV, and on the Internet regularly gives data and opinions on the economy. If this information points to an economic slowdown, small businesses can take defensive actions by cutting back inventories, reducing debt expenses, lowering fixed expenses, slowing down salary raises, and working harder to make sales. These defensive actions will enable the firm to build its cash in hand and increase the chances that it can keep paying its day-to-day bills as the economy moves into a recession.

depressions Long, severe economic downturns that are particularly damaging to a business economy

property insurance Protection purchased from an insurance company against property losses due to fire, water and wind damage, lightning, crime, and so on

Lastly, small businesses need to carefully evaluate unexpected losses from property damage, personal liabilities, and legal problems. These sources of external business risk can be managed by purchasing insurance. Property losses due to fire, water and wind damage, lightning, and crime are often covered by insurance. **Property insurance** on cars, buildings, equipment, and other valuable physical assets is a way to transfer these risks to an insurance company. An **insurance premium** must be paid to the insurance company on a monthly or periodic basis to obtain coverage.

insurance premium A payment to an insurance company on a monthly or periodic basis for insurance coverage

liability insurance Insurance coverage of employees under worker compensation laws that require employers to pay health and disability costs to injured employees and liability losses in court decisions against a firm

Liability insurance covers payments to employees under worker compensation laws that require employers to pay health and disability costs to injured employees. Another area of liability loss is court decisions against the firm. One type of court decision is the violation of a contract with a supplier or customer. Another type is negligence lawsuits that claim the firm did not exercise reasonable care in protecting the safety of employees and others. Examples are a customer getting hurt by slipping on a loose stairway step, a defective product that injures a customer, and improper installation of a product. Court cases are expensive, and regardless of who wins a court decision, they can absorb considerable work hours, and result in lawyer fees and other costs of litigation.

Personal losses include expenses attributable to health problems and death. **Health insurance** is necessary to protect against the high costs of medical treatment, such as doctor and dentist visits, vision care, prescription drugs, and major medical procedures. Group plans can be purchased by a firm for all its employees under a single policy to lower the premium cost per individual. **Disability insurance** can be purchased to cover longer-term expenses resulting from a chronic medical condition that prevents a person from continuing to work. **Life insurance** is intended to pay a death benefit to a beneficiary (e.g., a family member or friend). For small businesses, the death of the owner-manager can be devastating not only to the firm but also to the spouse and heirs. An **estate plan** seeks to reduce taxes on the family level and to provide for an orderly transfer of wealth as specified in the owner-manager's will. It also can name the future leaders of the firm and, therefore, help in the problem of leadership succession. Small businesses should work with their accountant, lawyer, and insurance agent to draft an estate plan and will, in addition to reviewing their external business risks and related insurance needs. The old adage "penny-wise and pound-foolish" certainly applies to ignoring insurable external business risks to cut operating costs.

Exhibit 4.10 shows that most firms voluntarily close their doors or fail. Voluntary firm closures occur when the owners sell their firm, quit due to inadequate profits, retire and liquidate the firm, or simply lose interest in the firm. Bankruptcy is triggered by the failure to pay bills on time. If the firm cannot pay its bills, then it can be forcibly closed by creditors, suppliers, and others who have unpaid bills outstanding. It is difficult to determine the exact rates of voluntary and bankruptcy closures of small businesses due to differences between various kinds of businesses. Roughly speaking, according to the Small Business Administration (SBA), about 30 percent of new small businesses close within two years of start-up. And, about 50 percent of small businesses close within five years. After the five years, the closure rate drops sharply, as these businesses tend to survive. Again, most closures are voluntary as opposed to forced under bankruptcy. These statistics make clear that small businesses have much more failure risk than large firms. Nonetheless, there are many success stories out there. Statistics gathered by the SBA during the mid-1990s indicate that the industry survival rate was highest for firms owned by African Americans in legal services (79 percent), Hispanic and Asian Americans in health services (66 percent and 76 percent, respectively), and white non-Hispanics in oil and gas extraction (82 percent). What can small businesses do to increase their chances of success? First, it is important to recognize the internal and external business risks facing the firm. Second, managers need to take steps to control or offset these risks in order to lower the probability of failure. Third, it is useful to review typical mistakes that lead to business failures (see Exhibit 4.11).

health insurance Protection offered by insurance companies against the high costs of medical treatment, such as doctor and dentist visits, vision care, prescription drugs, and major medical procedures

disability insurance Protection offered by insurance companies against longer-term expenses resulting from a chronic medical condition that prevents a person from continuing to work

life insurance Protection offered by insurance companies intended to pay a death benefit to a beneficiary (e.g., a family member or friend)

estate plan A plan that seeks to reduce taxes on the family level and provide for an orderly transfer of wealth and leadership within a firm

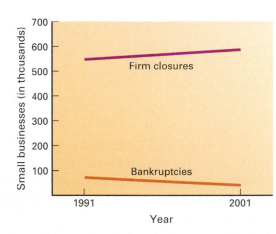

EXHIBIT 4.10

Voluntary Closures and Failures of Small Business Firms

Source: U.S. Small Business Administration, Office of Advocacy, Washington, DC, 2002. Small business is defined as those firms with less than 500 employees. Data were collected from the U.S. Census Bureau, the Bureau of Labor Statistics, and other sources.

reality CHECK *Is it ethical for a business to maximize its profits at costs to its employees, customers, community citizens, and other parties with which it interacts?*

EXHIBIT 4.11

Common Causes of Small Business Failure

- Choosing a business that is not very profitable
- Inadequate cash on hand to carry the business through the first six months or so before it starts making money
- Failure to clearly define and understand the business's market, customers, and customers' buying habits
- Failure to price the business's product or service correctly
- Failure to adequately anticipate cash flow in terms of expenses for inventory and later receipts on sales
- Failure to anticipate or react to competition, technology, or other changes in the marketplace
- Trying to do everything for everyone, which leads to spreading the business too thin and so diminishes quality
- Overdependence on a single customer
- Uncontrolled growth, as going after all possible opportunities drains the business's cash and actually reduces overall profitability
- Managers believing they can do everything themselves, instead of delegating authority to others
- Inadequate management, which commonly occurs as a company grows and individuals' abilities to manage and plan become ill suited to the new situation

Source: U.S. Small Business Administration, Office of Advocacy, Washington, DC, 2003 (**http://www.sba.gov/**).

Careers in Small Business

There are so many small business opportunities out there that it can be difficult to decide on the best choice for you. The U.S. Department of Labor has established a comprehensive database named the Occupational Information Network (O*NET) at whose website, **http://online.onetcenter.org/**, job seekers can learn about the skills required for particular occupations. Links to other valuable Internet resources are provided, including wage and occupational trend information and job accommodations for those with disabilities.

According to Assistant Secretary Emily Stover DeRocco, head of the department's Employment and Training Administration, "This tool identifies the requirements of the twenty-first century workplace so that employers and job seekers can speak the same language about job opportunities. Hiring better suited workers increases the job satisfaction of workers and retention of employers." Not sure about what occupations are right for you? O*NET allows you to explore opportunities on the basis of your personal qualities and preferences.

Another good source of information on careers is the U.S. Small Business Administration's website at **www.careers.org.** You can get career advice, distribute your resume, and check available jobs that are listed there. The website also has links to small business information by state.

Summary

LEARNING OBJECTIVE 1
Explain why small business is important.

Small businesses are vital to any country as catalysts for dynamic change in the business sector. New firms arise in a competitive business environment to replace old, outdated firms in the process of *creative destruction*. Small firms play a central role in the invention and innovation of new products and services demanded by customers. What they give up in efficient production due to a lack of scale economies compared to large firms, small firms gain back in terms of experimentation, flexibility, diversity, and change, which enable them to thrive in market niches. The small business sector is large in most developed countries, accounting for over 50 percent of employment in the United States as well as most new job creation. Technology and globalization of the business world are lending themselves to more family businesses, greater market access, and increased networking of small firms.

LEARNING OBJECTIVE 2
Discuss the ways government can support small business enterprises.

In recognition of the importance of the small business to national business development, governments in many countries offer a variety of forms of assistance to entrepreneurs. Information on how to start a business, business plans, financing, and so on is available on a number of government websites and at local government offices in many communities.

LEARNING OBJECTIVE 3
Describe the personal qualities and training needed to be a successful entrepreneur, including the cases of women and minorities in small business.

Entrepreneurs can be anyone with a business idea about something people want. Rather than working for an established firm for a regular wage, entrepreneurs set out to own and operate their own business. Some advantages are being your own boss, directly receiving the rewards of your labor, working at home or in a family business, and lifestyle benefits. Entrepreneurs tend to be people who have a commitment to make the business profitable, desire independence, have self-confidence in their personal ability, and are risk takers to some degree. Education and training are important in reducing the risk of failure. Interestingly, women and ethnic groups hold a prominent place in the small business sector due to the fact that diversity is a key

ingredient to building a prosperous small business sector.

LEARNING OBJECTIVE 4
List and briefly define each of the essential components of a business plan.

Developing a business plan is a crucial step in starting a new enterprise. Some of the components of this plan are the vision statement, goals, strategies, and products and services, as well as marketing, management, operating, and financial plans. Business ideas should be backed up with marketing research to gauge customer demand. Seed money is needed to begin initial production and keep the firm going for one to two years. Venture capitalists (including angels), banks, and the government are common sources of start-up funding. To create value, a business must contribute to its customers, employees, and investors. Leadership by the owner-manager is a necessary factor in creating value in any firm.

LEARNING OBJECTIVE 5
Compare the different small business organizational forms, including sole proprietorships, partnerships, corporations, and franchises.

Different forms of business organizations exist. The sole proprietorship and partnership are most often used at the early stage of a firm's development. As firms grow, they should consider the corporate and franchise forms of organization. These forms allow greater access to capital and faster growth. Each form has its advantages and disadvantages, which should be evaluated by the small business entrepreneur. Differences among these organizational forms are evident with respect to direct versus indirect control, manager versus firm liability, personal versus corporate taxation, and the book value versus the market value of stock.

LEARNING OBJECTIVE 6
Evaluate key small business management decisions, including hiring employees, ethics issues, family business benefits and costs, going public versus staying private, and controlling internal and external business risks.

Key small business management decisions must be made about hiring employees, ethics in entrepreneurship, running a family business, going public versus staying private, and controlling business risks. In small firms each employee is relatively more important and more expensive to train than in large firms. Small firms offer employees a chance to gain experience and get promoted to a higher position at a faster rate than large firms. Ethical issues abound in the business environment of small firms. Legal issues, organizational policies and procedures, and a business philosophy (i.e., company credo or code) are important to communicate to all employees. Many small firms are family businesses that have their own unique set of costs and benefits. At some point a small firm may decide to go public by selling out or doing an initial public offering (IPO) of its stock. This decision involves how much control is desired by the owner-manager and financial wealth implications. Issuing common stock diminishes control of the firm (as shareholders can vote on major firm decisions) but can increase the wealth of the original business owners by selling the stock for an attractive price. Finally, business risks can arise from both internal and external sources. Internal risks are directly under the control of management and relate to the firm's revenues and costs. External risks are not under the control of the firm; for example, competition from other firms and catastrophic losses from property damage and legal problems. Small firms should work with their accountant, insurance agent, and lawyer to manage external business risks.

Chapter Questions

1. How does small business affect employment in a country?
2. What is creative destruction and what role do small firms play in this process?
3. How can small firms compete with large firms that have the advantage of economies of scale?
4. What is a home business and why do some people opt for this type of small business?
5. List three things that government can do to support small business development in a country.
6. Are entrepreneurs different from other people? How? What is an intrapreneur? Why would someone prefer to be an intrapreneur rather than an entrepreneur?
7. What kind of education and training would help to prepare a person to run a small business?
8. Why are women and minorities important to maintaining a vibrant small business sector?
9. In a business plan, what are the vision, or mission, statement, goals, and strategies? Why are these important for small business firms?
10. Form groups of four people in the class. Students will meet in these groups for 30 minutes. Each group is required to propose an idea for a new business based on their own personal experiences, and explain why they believe their idea will be successful. (Note: This assignment can be completed either in class or outside of class at the discretion of the instructor.)
11. What other key components, in addition to those mentioned in question 9, should be in a good business plan?
12. Who are venture capitalists? Angels? What role do they play in the early stages of development of a growing small business?
13. How can firms create value? What is a crucial factor in successfully creating value?
14. Compare the sole proprietorship and the partnership forms of business organizations.
15. Why would a firm opt to become a C corporation? S corporation?
16. What are the advantages and disadvantages of the franchise form of corporation?
17. Form groups of four people in the class. Each group is responsible to visit a local franchise, meet with its manager or owner, and write a report on the strengths and weaknesses of the operation of the franchise.
18. What is small business ethics? Discuss legal criteria, organizational policies and procedures, and personal philosophy as dimensions of small business ethics.
19. Give two ways for a private small business firm to go public. How could a venture capitalist influence this decision?
20. What are internal versus external business risks? What can small businesses do to help control these risks?

Interpreting Business News

1. In the newspaper you read that "Creative destruction among business firms has been led by dynamic changes taking place in the small business sector." How would such changes eventually result in both increased employment and increased profitability of business firms in the future?
2. A firm issues new shares of its common stock. How might this determine who controls the firm?
3. A company's credo or code is to produce the highest quality products without cutting corners and without damaging the environment and community in the surrounding area. What kind of ethical values does this credo suggest?

Web Assignments

1. Go to the Small Business Administration's website (**www.sba.gov**) and look for a reference to starting your business. From the information there, put together a start-up checklist.
2. What kind of assistance can small business firms obtain to export their products to other countries at the U.S. Department of Commerce's website, **www.export.gov?** Give three examples of such support.
3. Use an Internet browser to explore small business support groups in your area. What kinds of organizations did you find? What kinds of support do they offer to foster the success of small businesses in your community?
4. What kind of career fits you? Go to the U.S. Department of Labor's O*NET website, **http://www.online.onetcenter.org,** and explore occupations based on your personal skills and characteristics.

Portfolio Projects

Exploring Your Own Case in Point

This chapter examines principles of small business planning and development. However, many of these principles are applicable to firms of all sizes. For your selected company, some key questions to answer in this area are as follows.

1. Does your selected firm have franchises? If not, why do you think that they are not used by the firm?
2. What is your company's credo or business philosophy? How does the firm implement this credo in practice?
3. Go to your firm's website and find its accounting and financial information. If there is no website for your firm, go to **http://finance.yahoo.com/** and search for your company's name there. What kind of data can you find? Also search for stock price information about your company. How has your company's stock been doing?

Starting Your Own Business

After reading this chapter, your business plan should contain answers to the following questions.

1. How is your new business related to your own personal experiences and life?
2. What is your vision for the new business?
3. Provide detailed descriptions of the firm's products or services in addition to discussing their innovative or new aspects.

Test Prepper

You've read the chapter, studied the key terms, and the exam is any day now. Think you are ready to ace it? Take this sample test to gauge your comprehension of chapter material. You can check your answers at the back of the book.

True/False Questions

Please indicate if the following statements are true or false:

_____ 1. The competitive process of business success and failure proposed by Joseph Schumpeter is known as creative destruction.

_____ 2. Computer and telecommunications technology is increasing the number of home businesses and opening up new working opportunities for disabled persons.

_____ 3. Entrepreneurs can earn a salary from running a small business but are not allowed to earn extra income from the net profits of the firm.

_____ 4. SCORE is an organization made up of retired executives that seeks to help small businesses get professional counseling services.

_____ 5. Ethnic diversity is an important ingredient in building a more prosperous small business sector.

_____ 6. Seed money is the net profits earned by a small business firm.

_____ 7. A company credo or code is important as a marketing jingle or catchy phrase to attract customers.

_____ 8. Risks of losses that severely cripple the business or even cause bankruptcy are known as business risks.

_____ 9. Disability insurance can be purchased to cover longer-term expenses resulting from a chronic medical condition that prevents a person from continuing to work.

_____ 10. A severe recession is known as a depression.

Multiple-Choice Questions

Choose the best answer.

_____ 1. Some experts consider a small business with less than five employees to be a

    a. partnership.
    b. microbusiness.
    c. sole proprietorship.
    d. C corporation.
    e. S corporation.

_____ 2. A person within a large corporation who takes responsibility to develop a new product through innovation and risk taking is referred to as a(an)

    a. entrepreneur.
    b. small business owner.
    c. intrapreneur.
    d. inventor.
    e. innovator.

_____ 3. Government can support small business by

    a. reducing the number of government websites.
    b. making more complex tax rules.
    c. diminishing access to financial resources.
    d. decreasing access to important information.
    e. reducing burdensome regulation.

_____ 4. Which of the following is *not* a personal quality of an entrepreneur?

    a. Commitment to make the business profitable
    b. Enjoying working for her- or himself
    c. Self-confidence to be able to run the business
    d. Fear of failure
    e. Risk taker willing to take the plunge and start a small business

_____ 5. Which of the following is *not* an essential component of a small business plan?

    a. Common stock
    b. Vision, or mission, statement
    c. Goals
    d. Strategies
    e. Overview of the company

_____ 6. Leadership entails

    a. avoiding enthusiasm and confidence.
    b. reducing decision making.
    c. decreasing effective communication with others.
    d. getting all other people to do the work.
    e. motivating others to join in the vision of the firm.

_____ 7. If you bought a share of common stock for $10 and its price rose to $15, you would earn a _____ of $5.

    a. capital gain

    b. dividend

    c. payment of interest

    d. value in exchange

    e. total value

_____ 8. A franchise has the disadvantage of

    a. training of employees and managers.

    b. brand name recognition.

    c. payment of an initial franchising fee.

    d. franchisor reputation.

    e. financial assistance from the franchisor.

_____ 9. Which of the following is an internal (as opposed to external) business risk?

    a. Competitor firms

    b. Downturn in the general economy

    c. Catastrophic losses from property damage

    d. Sudden changes in customer preferences and demand

    e. Large amounts of debt within the firm

_____ 10. Which of the following types of insurance pays a death benefit to a beneficiary?

    a. Life insurance

    b. Health insurance

    c. Liability insurance

    d. Property insurance

    e. Credit insurance

Want more questions? Visit the student website at **http://college.hmco.com/business/student/** (select Gaspar, *Introduction to Business*) and take the ACE quizzes for more practice.

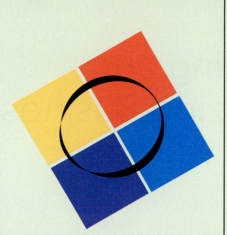

Managing Business Behavior

CHAPTER 5
Managing and Organizing Business

CHAPTER 6
Human Resources Management

CHAPTER 7
Motivating and Leading Employees

PART TWO

Once a business is established, it needs to be managed. Management involves planning, organizing, directing, and controlling an organization's resources in the manner most effective for it to meet its goals. Part Two focuses on the management function. Think about a new major league baseball franchise or a business college at a university that has just been created and now needs to be managed.

Once an organization has been established, goals need to be set for it. For a baseball team, the goal may be winning the baseball World Series; for a business college, becoming ranked in the top 20 in the country. Then an organizational infrastructure needs to be put in place to help operationalize these goals. The infrastructure will include things like establishing a chain of command and setting up various departments. Finally, managers, such as a coach or a dean, need to be hired to lead the organization, and employees, such as baseball players or professors, to work in the organization.

Managing an organization's human resources is a critical part of the management function. Not only do employees need to be hired, but compensation and benefit levels have to be set for them, labor unions dealt with, and workforce diversity addressed. Today's managers also have to be familiar with a wide range of legal regulations governing human resources management. Moreover, increasing numbers of businesses today have operations throughout the world, and this means that managers must be familiar with different employment practices in different countries. For example, in European countries employees are traditionally allotted considerably more vacation time than in the United States.

Ultimately, it is the role of managers to motivate and lead employees toward the achievement of the organization's goals. Positive employee behaviors need to be reinforced, and efforts made to keep employees satisfied with their work. A wide variety of leadership styles and techniques come into play in helping managers achieve organizational goals. Managing in the twenty-first century is not easy.

161

5

Managing and Organizing Business

| Introduction

| Understanding Management

| The Management Process
  Planning
  Organizing
  Directing
  Controlling

| Kinds of Managers
  Levels of Management
  | Areas of Management

| Management Skills
  Technical Skills
  Conceptual Skills
  Human Relations Skills
  | International Skills

| Careers in Management

Learning Objectives

After studying this chapter, you should be able to

1 Describe the strategic planning process, including the establishment of strategic goals, strategy formulation, and strategy implementation.

2 Discuss the special planning elements of succession planning, innovation planning, and contingency and crisis planning.

3 Explain chains of command, organizational charts, and job specialization.

4 Analyze and describe different types of departmentalization within organizations.

5 Describe different types of delegation of authority within organizations.

6 Explain briefly the directing and controlling functions of the management process, including the use of six sigma initiatives.

7 Describe the basic kinds of managers within organizations.

8 Analyze the different types of skills that go into making effective managers.

Bank Chief Apologizes

The Goldman Sachs Group in New York City is one of the world's leading investment banks. Recently, though, its CEO, Henry M. Paulson Jr. (who is paid $12 million plus per year), had to eat some crow. He sent a firmwide voice mail message apologizing to all employees for remarks he made at an investment conference the prior week. At the conference he said, "I don't want to sound heartless" but "in almost every one of our businesses there are 15 or 20 percent of the people that really add 80 percent of the value." He went on to say that Goldman Sachs would fire employees if economic conditions warranted: "I think we can cut a fair amount and not get into muscle and still be very well positioned for the upturn."[1]

Paulson's remarks created incredible anger and distress among employees at Goldman Sachs, particularly because the company had long been organized and managed from a teamwork perspective. Employees felt that Paulson's comments contradicted Goldman Sachs's traditional "we're all in this together" ethic. One employee said, "People here are very upset. We've always been told that it's about teamwork and not a star system."[2]

Paulson's quick response to the situation, which included statements that he was "profoundly embarrassed" by his choice of words and that his comments had "created an impression completely at odds" with his respect for the people of Goldman Sachs, helped defuse the organizational crisis his earlier statement had created.[3] Nevertheless, the sting of his initial remarks continues to reverberate within the company.

Introduction

The Goldman Sachs story touches on many of the key principles to be discussed in this chapter. This chapter is about how businesses are managed and organized. **Management** is the process of planning, organizing, directing, and controlling an organization's various resources in the manner most effective for the organization to achieve its goals. Obviously, there is some tension at Goldman Sachs regarding the best way to manage the organization. In addition, the general management skills of its CEO have recently been tested, as have his abilities to lead in a crisis situation. Hopefully, when you finish reading this chapter, you'll have ideas for Goldman Sachs regarding positively managing and organizing its business in the future.

> **management** The process of planning, organizing, directing, and controlling an organization's resources in the manner most effective for it to achieve its goals

Understanding Management

What does management involve? Sure, the definition given above, "the process of planning, organizing, directing . . . ," gives some clues, but it still leaves the concept somewhat unclear. A better way to understand the concept is to think of a management situation most everyone is familiar with—the management of sports teams. All baseball teams have **managers.** What do baseball team managers do?

Baseball team managers plan and set organizational goals. The goal of all baseball teams is to win as many games as possible, but the goal of winning the World Series may be a realistic goal for one major league team, and simply having more wins than losses a realistic goal for another team. Each team's manager must figure

> **managers** People involved in the management of organizations

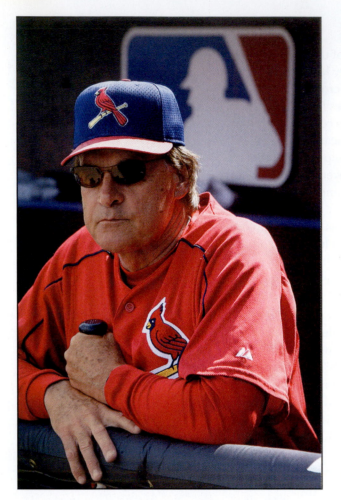

Baseball team managers, such as St. Louis Cardinals manager Tony LaRussa, have significant responsibility for the success or failure of their teams. Here LaRussa ponders team strategy while awaiting the start of a recent spring training game against the New York Mets.

out how to operationalize the goal. If the team has been losing a lot of games because of a relatively weak pitching staff, the team manager needs to think about hiring or trading for some new good pitchers. Moreover, the manager has to make the hiring decision in the context of limited resources. Hiring a couple of all-star pitchers may mean that there's not enough money left to renew the contract of a high-priced, very good, but not all-star third base player.

Putting the best possible team together, however, is only the beginning of a baseball team manager's work. The manager decides which pitchers to play in which games, and the team's batting lineup. The manager directs players regarding whether they should try to steal bases. The manager makes sure that optimal medical care, weight training equipment, and other resources are available for the players. The manager counsels and reprimands players who are arrested for drunk driving on Saturday night. The manager decides how much to invest in the team's minor league clubs and future player development.

Do good baseball team managers make a difference? Recent academic research on major league baseball teams says that the answer to this question is yes.[4] Teams with certain styles of management have been found to outperform other teams having equivalent or even better resources, players, and budgets. The Anaheim Angels baseball team, with an annual player payroll of about $65 million, won a World Series championship after beating the New York Yankees, with an annual player payroll of over $140 million, in the first round of the playoffs. The Anaheim Angels' excellent management had something to do with this success.

The Management Process

LEARNING OBJECTIVE 1
Describe the strategic planning process, including the establishment of strategic goals, strategy formulation, and strategy implementation.

There are four basic functions of the management process: planning, organizing, directing, and controlling. Managers engage in all of these activities on an ongoing basis.

Planning

planning Establishing organizational goals and deciding how best to get them achieved

Planning involves establishing organizational goals and deciding how best to achieve them. For example, it might be the goal of a 64-year-old owner of a small business to sell the business for a lot of money and retire to Aruba. The question becomes how best to plan to make this goal a reality.

Planning is the most important management function in that all the excellent management execution in the world—excellent organizing, directing, and controlling—is worthless without the right organizational strategy and goals. Or, as Intel

Corporation chair Andrew S. Grove put it, "Great execution is necessary, but not sufficient."[5] To some extent, good organizational planning involves a bit of dreaming, of thinking about how to make the future better, and then placing bets on that vision. Clearly great business leaders from Andrew Carnegie (U.S. Steel) and Henry Ford (Ford Motor Company) to Sam Walton (Wal-Mart Stores), Bill Gates (Microsoft), and Michael Dell (Dell Computer) have almost always been both superb visionaries and planners and superb hands-on managers.[6]

Companies' visions are frequently set forth in corporate **mission statements,** which are statements that spell out the basic purpose of the enterprise. For example, the mission statement of Whirlpool Corporation, the world's leading manufacturer and marketer of major home appliances with over $12 billion in annual sales, says, "Every Home . . . Everywhere. With Pride, Passion and Performance. We create the world's best home appliances, which make life easier and more enjoyable for all people."[7]

mission statement Statements spelling out the basic purpose of the enterprise

Strategic Goals.   The next step in the management planning process is translating the mission of the company into more specific long-term corporate goals, known as **strategic goals.** If you were a top manager at Whirlpool Corporation, what might be a strategic goal you would set drawing on the company's mission statement? Clearly, given the desire of the company to have Whirlpool appliances in "every home . . . everywhere," having as one strategic goal the expansion of company sales and operations into international markets appears warranted.

strategic goals Long-term goals related to an organization's mission statement

Strategy Formulation.   Having a company mission and then setting strategic goals related to this mission is wonderful, but this only becomes meaningful if some clear course of action can be established to achieve these goals. Formulating the approach to achieving the strategic goals is called **strategy formulation.**

Strategy formulation is not easy. While Whirlpool has established that it wants to go international, what does this mean? Does it mean simply manufacturing Whirlpool appliances in upstate New York and selling them in Canada, or does it involve setting up manufacturing facilities in faraway countries like India and China and selling these products there? Does Whirlpool want to make and sell a wide variety of its products—refrigerators, ovens, clothes washers—in foreign countries or concentrate on just one product? How should Whirlpool enter foreign markets, via acquisitions of foreign companies, through joint ventures or alliances with other companies, or by establishing new operations on its own in the foreign countries?

strategy formulation The formulation of the approach to achieving strategic goals

Answering these questions requires Whirlpool to do extensive environmental and organizational analyses. An **environmental analysis** involves a company scanning outside the firm, in its external environment, for both threats and opportunities. For example, in late 2001, Whirlpool Corporation executives learned that the Moulinex-Brandt Group, a large French conglomerate, had filed for bankruptcy. Whirlpool was very interested because it knew that Moulinex-Brandt owned 96 percent of the shares of a company called Polar S.A., a leading major home appliance manufacturer in Poland. Since Whirlpool was interested in expanding its operations in Poland and central Europe, this presented the company with a real opportunity. In 2002, it made a successful bid in French bankruptcy court of $43 million (including some assumption of debt) to purchase Moulinex-Brandt's controlling stake in Polar. With this purchase, Whirlpool owned the leading brand name in laundry and refrigeration appliances in Poland.[8]

environmental analysis A strategic scan by an organization for external threats and opportunities

International opportunities exist for Whirlpool throughout the world. One area that Whirlpool has recently become very interested in is China, the world's largest potential consumer appliance market with over 1 billion people and a growing middle class.

A company's environmental analysis also involves analyzing external threats to the company and its business. Whirlpool has a number of major competitors including Maytag Corporation, based in the United States, Siemens Corporation of Germany, and LG Electronics of South Korea. Before entering a new international market, Whirlpool needs to closely examine what these major competitors are up to in that market. Changing consumer tastes and new government regulations, such as new tax or antitrust laws, are also examples of possible threats to the company.

In addition to the analysis of environmental factors, managers engaged in strategy formulation need to examine internal organizational factors, that is, conduct an **organizational analysis.** An organizational analysis involves taking a close look at the company's own strengths and weaknesses, and how they interact with the company's strategic goals.

organizational analysis A strategic scan by an organization of its own strengths and weaknesses

For example, Whirlpool may want to purchase various foreign appliance makers, but it just doesn't have the spare cash to do so. Of course, it may be possible for a company to borrow some or even all of the money needed to make a foreign purchase, but this will depend on the kind of credit available to the company and on whether the company's overall financial situation can handle the additional debt and interest payments. Also, in expanding overseas, a company has to carefully examine the strengths and weaknesses of its managerial talent. Thus, in Whirlpool's case, having a cadre of highly skilled managers who speak Polish or Chinese would be a major strength, while having no such managers might be a significant weakness. One critical strength for Whirlpool in expanding internationally is the fact that a recent global marketing survey found Whirlpool to be the world's most recognized appliance brand.[9]

Finally, there may be special circumstances that any company needs to take into account in corporate strategy formulation. In the case of Whirlpool Corporation, the special circumstance has the name of Sears, Roebuck & Company. Whirlpool and Sears have a special relationship dating back to 1916, when a brand-new Whirlpool clothes washer was listed in the Sears catalog for $54.75. The relationship between the two was later cemented when Sears lent Whirlpool money for expansion, in exchange for stock in the company. For many years, Whirlpool has been the largest supplier of major home appliances to Sears, with Whirlpool-made products sold at Sears under the Kenmore brand name. Sears has sold Kenmore clothes washers in overseas locations since 1936, and Whirlpool will definitely have to check with Sears before it starts selling its regular brand products in international locations. Clearly Whirlpool does not in any way want to offend its largest customer by far, Sears, Roebuck & Company.[10]

In sum, strategy formulation is a very difficult and complicated process. It involves examining and weighing a wide range of possibilities and issues in deciding how best to pursue the company's strategic goals.

Strategy Implementation.   Once strategic goals have been set and a general strategy for achieving these goals formulated, the strategy needs to be implemented. Specific plans need to be made regarding hiring people, buying assets, forming alliances and joint ventures, and so on. **Tactical plans** are smaller-scale plans developed to implement formulated company strategic goals and usually covering one to three years. For example, Whirlpool Corporation may have a broad strategic goal to further expand its operations in Poland and

tactical plans Shorter-term (one to three years) plans formulated for achieving organizational strategic goals

may have formulated a strategy for achieving this goal by purchasing additional Polish appliance companies to add to its Polar acquisition. Now, tactical plans have to be developed specifying precisely which Polish firms Whirlpool wants to try to buy during the next few years and how exactly to go about doing this. Tactical planning generally involves both upper- and middle-level company management.

Once tactical plans are established, strategy implementation requires businesses to set **operational plans.** Operational plans are a list of what a company has to do in the very short run to achieve its strategic goals. Operational plans are usually set for one year or less and sometimes involve even just daily or weekly planning. In the case of Whirlpool Corporation in Poland, operational planning might involve deciding what newspaper, radio, and television advertisements to place for Polar products during the next three months (business quarter) in order to increase Polar's quarterly sales by 5 percent.

operational plans Very short-term (less than one year) plans formulated for achieving organizational strategic goals

Strategic Planning Review: "Whirlpool Goes to China".

Strategic planning is a multitiered and multistep process. The first part involves a company formulating its mission statement. The heart of Whirlpool Corporation's mission statement is "Every Home . . . Everywhere." To achieve this mission, Whirlpool has established a strategic goal of expanding and developing its international operations. More specifically, since the mid-1990s Whirlpool has had the strategic goal of developing its business in the world's most populous country with more than 1 billion people, China.

Formulating a strategy to achieve this goal, however, has not been easy for Whirlpool. It entered the market by way of joint ventures with a variety of Chinese electric companies and ended up losing a good part of its initial $145 million investment. In 1999, though, it decided to sell off its money-losing home refrigerator and air conditioner ventures and concentrate on its Chinese clothes washing machine business. Today, Whirlpool is breaking even or doing slightly better on its clothes washing machine business in China.

Whirlpool in recent years has also shifted gears about where in China it wants to concentrate its business efforts. Initially, Whirlpool concentrated its efforts on major affluent coastal cities like Shanghai. It found, however, competition for business in places like Shanghai to be very intense. In Shanghai, it was competing not only with homegrown Chinese appliance companies like Haier but also with other international conglomerate appliance makers like Germany's Siemens Corporation and South Korea's LG Electronics. Consequently, Whirlpool has today reformulated its strategy and is concentrating its efforts in the Chinese heartland in small rural cities like Huainan, which is about an eight-hour drive northwest of Shanghai and has 2.1 million people.

Whirlpool executives recently visited with top Chinese Communist Party officials in Huainan and discussed more investments in that city, including possibly even building a factory there (see Exhibit 5.1 on p. 168). Company plans to build a Whirlpool factory in Huainan, China, during the next one to three years would represent company tactical plans. Currently, at the Hualian commercial store in beautiful downtown Huainan, China, Whirlpool sells about 33 automatic clothes washing machines per month. Company plans involving improving the Whirlpool display at the store so that during the next few months the company can improve its monthly sales at the store by about 10 percent to 36 to 37 washing machines would represent company operational plans.[11]

EXHIBIT 5.1

Strategic Analysis: Whirlpool Goes to China

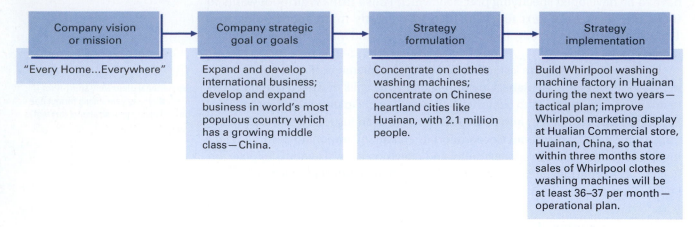

Company vision or mission	Company strategic goal or goals	Strategy formulation	Strategy implementation
"Every Home...Everywhere"	Expand and develop international business; develop and expand business in world's most populous country which has a growing middle class—China.	Concentrate on clothes washing machines; concentrate on Chinese heartland cities like Huainan, with 2.1 million people.	Build Whirlpool washing machine factory in Huainan during the next two years—tactical plan; improve Whirlpool marketing display at Hualian Commercial store, Huainan, China, so that within three months store sales of Whirlpool clothes washing machines will be at least 36–37 per month—operational plan.

If you were going to start a business selling magazine subscriptions to students at your college, what might an initial environmental analysis for this business involve?

LEARNING OBJECTIVE 2
Discuss the special planning elements of succession planning, innovation planning, and contingency and crisis planning.

Special Planning Elements. The strategic planning process contains three parts, or elements, that deserve and receive special and separate attention. They are succession planning, innovation planning, and contingency and crisis planning.

succession planning Planning related to choosing successors for top organization executives

SUCCESSION PLANNING. **Succession planning** involves planning about choosing successors for top company executives. Most companies have what the former General Electric Company CEO Jack Welch called "hit by a truck" succession plans.[12] Such plans frequently involve depth charts, much like royal orders of succession in countries with monarchies. These charts list in what order various top managers will move into the company's CEO and other top executive spots should an accident, like a plane crash, occur, killing or incapacitating the company's CEO or other top official. Some companies require that certain top executives never travel together, just as the president and vice president of the United States never fly on the same airplane together. Many companies also carry, for the benefit of the company, large life insurance policies on the lives of their CEO and other top executives.

Another, more controversial type of succession planning involves comprehensive planning regarding which individual is going to succeed the firm's top executive. Some CEOs strongly resist naming and grooming a successor and setting a specific date for their own retirement. Moreover, some boards of directors are reluctant to set up an explicit horse race for the top slot, lest it attract unnecessary publicity and promote unnecessary rivalries within the firm.

In contrast, other CEOs and corporate boards embrace a strong and explicit CEO succession planning process. Jack Welch, for example, started a comprehensive CEO succession plan at GE in 1994, seven *years* in advance of his planned 2001 retirement. The so-called NG (for New Guy) process became the biggest job of GE's senior vice president for human resources and initially involved 23 (all internal) candidates. Ultimately, the CEO horse race came down to three candidates: Jeff

Immelt, the head of GE's medical systems business; Bob Nardelli, the head of the company's power system business; and Jim McNerney, the head of the company's aircraft engine business. These three finalists spent considerable time during the last year or two of the process interacting with members of the GE board of directors and with Welch himself, as the board and Welch tried to make a decision. As Welch put it, "We had three Gold Medal winners, and only one Gold Medal to give."[13] In the end, the nod went to Jeff Immelt, who holds the CEO position at General Electric today. Within ten days, both Nardelli and McNerney, who were now told to leave GE, had new jobs—Bob Nardelli as CEO of the Home Depot Corporation, and Jim McNerney as CEO of the 3M Company.

INNOVATION PLANNING.   Increasingly, given the competitiveness of today's marketplace, companies are under considerable pressure to innovate—to come up with new business ideas. While this may come fairly naturally to fledgling small businesses, it does *not* come naturally to large, well-established corporations. More and more, however, large corporations are engaging in **innovation planning,** where they explicitly plan ways to instill more of an entrepreneurial spirit into their corporation. Innovation planning can have a wide variety of focuses. Some such planning involves formulating ways to instill more of an entrepreneurial spirit in individuals working at the company, while other such planning primarily focuses on developing a more entrepreneurial spirit in the culture and organizational systems of the firm. The idea is to plan ways for companies to be more innovative and creative and to successfully commercialize new products and other innovations that they discover.[14]

One company that has been very successful in this regard is the large pharmaceutical company Pfizer. For example, Pfizer tested the drug *sildenafil citrate* at a research center in England as a treatment for angina (heart muscle pain). Innovatively-oriented researchers saw that the drug might also be useful in successfully treating erectile dysfunction. Moreover, innovation planning at Pfizer had made

innovation planning Planning to instill more of an entrepreneurial spirit into an organization

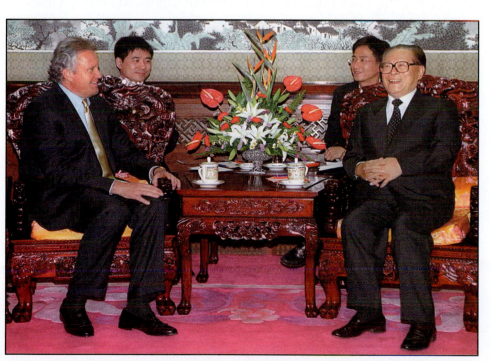

Fairly shortly after his appointment as the head of the General Electric Company (GE), Jeff Immelt (left) flew to China to meet with Chinese president Jiang Zemin (right). GE, like Whirlpool and many other American companies, is actively pursuing business in China.

sure that excellent lines of communication had been established between the company's researchers and its marketing team. Pfizer's marketers were quickly made aware of a possible new blockbuster drug for the company. Today, Viagra is one of Pfizer's best-selling products.

CONTINGENCY AND CRISIS PLANNING.   For better or worse, today's business world is not always very stable. More simply put, things change. Oil prices change, interest rates change, world politics change, and companies need to be prepared for such changes. **Contingency planning** involves planning for change and trying to identify in advance important business dynamics that are subject to change.

contingency planning Planning for change and for business dynamics that are subject to change

A number of major companies have formal organizational groups that engage in contingency planning. Many companies also use computer models and programs to help them plan for possible changes in their business environment. Royal Dutch/Shell Group, for example, in 1972 started a formal scenario planning department to help it look into and plan for possible changes in the future. The former head of this department at Royal Dutch/Shell once described his role as "hunting in a pack of wolves, being the eyes of the pack, and sending signals back to the rest."[15]

One important contingency planning issue currently facing many U.S. corporate executives is how to plan for possible significant increases in anti-U.S. sentiment in other parts of the world. Is there a possibility that consumers in other parts of the world might boycott U.S. products like Starbucks coffee, McDonald's hamburgers, and Coca-Cola soft drinks? Interestingly, McDonald's Corporation has recently sought to preempt the impact of any such general product boycott in the Middle East by launching a new product there, called McArabia, which is a chicken sandwich on special Arabian bread.[16]

crisis planning Planning for very high-magnitude, unthinkable events

Crisis planning is very similar to contingency planning, but involves planning for a very high magnitude change, for the unthinkable, for a crisis. For example, the American Express Company's international payment processing subsidiary formerly based at 7 World Trade Center in New York City had engaged in crisis planning to prepare for any major disaster that might threaten to totally shut down its vital international payment processing operations. Unfortunately, on September 11, 2001, this disaster did occur, but American Express was ready. It immediately moved 85 employees from the World Trade Center to a parallel payment processing facility it had established at a "warm site" somewhere (undisclosed!) in New Jersey. In the meantime, customers all over the world could continue to count on American Express![17]

While not a positive commentary on the state of the world, comprehensive crisis planning has now become quite common in today's business world. The well-known management consulting firm Booz Allen Hamilton, for example, recently conducted a planning exercise for its clients that involved dirty bombs being found in containers shipped to various U.S. ports. Planning for possible terrorist attacks of this kind is a good example of crisis planning.[18]

 Were any businesses in your community particularly impacted by the events of September 11, 2001?

Organizing

Once strategic plans are set, businesses need to set up organizational structures to carry out these plans. If Whirlpool wants to be in China and has formulated specific plans toward this end, it will need to establish a specific division, branch, or department within its organization to coordinate and supervise its Chinese operations.

Small sole proprietor businesses have relatively little concern with organizational structure. In 1983, when Michael Dell started selling computers out of his off-campus apartment at the University of Texas in Austin, there was one person involved in the business—him. His parents, concerned with what he was up to, showed up unannounced at his apartment in November 1983 and were not happy. His dad saw a bunch of computer boxes lying around and said to him, "You only have computer parts here; where are your books?" They made him promise that he'd stop "fooling around" with the computer business and concentrate on school. Within a few weeks, though, Michael Dell decided he couldn't keep this promise to his parents. His business of selling computers directly to customers was just going too well. He told his parents he was going to take the spring 1984 semester off, but if things in business didn't turn out as planned, he'd go back to college. He never made it back to the classroom.[19]

In 1984, Dell Computer Corporation was formed. It moved out of Michael Dell's off-campus apartment to 1000 square feet of rented space. Within short order, it moved on to even bigger space and had about 25 employees. Michael Dell, however, still ran everything, literally keeping the key to the office's Coke machine. One day someone lost a quarter in the machine and came to Dell for a refund. For Michael Dell, it was a "management moment" in that he decided he had to start delegating some authority. He handed the key to the Coke machine to the employee who had come to him and said, "From now on, you're in charge of the Coke machine."[20]

Today, Dell Computer Corporation has about 40,000 employees, does approximately $40 billion a year in business, and has nearly 25 employees on just its senior management committee. It has three major divisions: Dell Americas, which is responsible for about 70 percent of the company's business; Dell Europe/Middle East/Africa, which is responsible for about 20 percent of the company's business; and Dell Asia Pacific–Japan, which is responsible for about 10 percent of the company's business. The regional headquarters for Dell Americas, and indeed the headquarters for the entire corporation, are in Austin, Texas, not too far from the student apartment where the business started. The regional headquarters for Dell Europe, Middle East, and Africa are in Bracknell, England. The regional headquarters for Dell Asia Pacific–Japan are split between Singapore and Kawasaki, Japan. In 1996, Dell developed e-commerce capability, and it quickly became the first U.S. company to record $1 million in online sales. Today, Dell has one of the highest-volume Internet sites in the world. In 1999, Dell started Dell Ventures as a wholly-owned strategic investment and venture capital arm of Dell. Dell Ventures has invested money in a wide range of computer-related companies including Hire.com, Netstock Direct Corporation, and Zeevo.[21]

Since 1984, Michael Dell has spent a lot of time as a manager trying to figure out how best to group, arrange, and allocate Dell Corporation's resources and activities so as to most successfully build the business. From having to decide who to put in charge of the Coke machine to where to locate the company's Asian regional headquarters, Michael Dell has had a lot of important decisions to make. This is called **organizing.**

> **organizing** Setting up organizational structures to carry out strategic plans

---

LEARNING OBJECTIVE 3
Explain chains of command, organizational charts, and job specialization.

Organizations and Organizational Structure.

An **organization** is a grouping of two or more people working together to achieve certain ends. One person conducting business, like Michael Dell working out of his college apartment, is not an

> **organization** A grouping of two or more people working together to achieve certain ends

Global Business

Pushing Pills Around the World

Once a company like Pfizer, through innovation planning, discovers a drug like Viagra, it then has to sell it. While direct-to-consumer pharmaceutical advertising via television and other media is permitted in the United States, this is not the case in all countries.

The traditional focus of pharmaceutical drug marketing throughout the developed world is the personal "detail." This involves big drug companies organizing a large team of sales representatives. These sales representatives receive intensive training about the company's products and pharmaceuticals in general, and then are assigned a territory in which they regularly visit doctors and try to sell their company's drugs. The idea is that through face-to-face visits with physicians, the detailers can persuade doctors to write a lot of prescriptions for their company's products and to use their company's products rather than similar products sold by other companies.

This organizational technique for marketing pharmaceutical drugs, however, has had its problems. In Italy, for example, there have been recent investigations of 40 employees of the British drug company GlaxoSmithKline and 30 physicians for *comparaggio,* which is physicians agreeing to prescribe company drugs in exchange for free computers and other lavish gifts. Nevertheless, it's unlikely that pharmaceutical company detailers, or the free samples they bring to physicians' offices, are going to go away any time soon.

New technologies, however, may change the detailers' roles to a considerable extent. For example, the company iphysiciannet.com provides detailing to physicians via computer-based videoconferencing. A number of major pharmaceutical companies have signed up for this service, which potentially allows company sales representatives to have more daily interactions with physicians in a more monitored setting. Selling pharmaceutical drugs is a multibillion dollar per year business, and pharmaceutical companies are continually trying to figure out how to best organize and allocate resources to this endeavor.

Source: "Pushing Pills," *The Economist*, February 13, 2003, p. 61; telephone interview with Mr. Charles Van Cott, executive vice president, iphysiciannet.com, March 20, 2003.

Questions

1. How do you think the performance of pharmaceutical detailers is measured? What kind of technology is necessary?
2. Who should regulate any ethical issues that arise between detailers and physicians?
3. What disadvantages are there to Internet or computer detailing versus traditional face-to-face detailing?

---

organizational structure Specified positions within an organization and the ways they interrelate with each other

organization. But once Michael Dell hired someone, an organization was formed. All organizations have some sort of structure. More specifically, **organizational structure** involves specified positions within an organization and how they interrelate with each other. For example, major pharmaceutical companies like Pfizer, Merck, and GlaxoSmithKline have people in their organizations who do research on the market for legal drugs and the people who sell these drugs, the detailers. The detailers need to constantly interface with purchasers. For example, they need to be able to quickly inform physicians about a newly discovered use for a drug.

Different organizations need different types of organizational structures. The type of organizational structure that works best in the military, for instance, may not be at all effective in an Internet start-up company. Moreover, organizational structures may change with changing circumstances. Let's say that a major league baseball team decides that any new players it hires during the next five years are already going to have had at least some playing experience with another major league team. If the team adopts such a strategic plan, it probably will not need as many people working in its minor league organization. Similarly, an accounting firm or other business that adopts such a hiring approach, i.e., experienced employees only, can probably sharply downsize or even temporarily eliminate its college recruiting department.

In sum, once two or more people start working together to achieve common goals, an organization exists, and some sort of organizational structure needs to be established. Organizational structures will differ widely, and organizations will change their structures to meet current needs.

Chain of Command.

At the heart of all organizational structure is a **chain of command.** The chain of command is the lines of authority or reporting relationships that exist within an organization. When you hear the term *chain of command,* you may think of the military, and the U.S. Army has very explicit and strict lines of authority and reporting relationships. Lower-ranked personnel report and take orders from higher-ranked personnel, and there are strict limitations on the extent personnel at different ranks can socialize or fraternize. The rationale for this is that it might be hard for a higher-ranked individual to give certain kinds of military orders to their lower-ranked friends.

> **chain of command** The lines of authority or reporting relationships that exist within an organization

There are currently about 500,000 active duty military personnel in the U.S. Army. The chain of command starts with the president of the United States, the commander in chief, and moves through various ranks of officers into the enlisted ranks. Enlisted ranks in the U.S. Army start with the E-1 designation for buck private and go up through E-9 for the highest-level sergeant. The U.S. Army has roughly 79,000 officers and 407,000 enlisted personnel. It also has roughly 4000 cadets at West Point. The current chain of command for the organization called the U.S. Army, and the number of individuals occupying each rank, can be presented in an **organization chart.** An organization chart is simply a diagram depicting an organization's structure, including the positions and reporting relationships.

> **organization chart** A diagram depicting an organization's structure

Of course, there aren't too many organizations that are as large and have as many ranks of personnel as the U.S. Army. A more typical organization might be the local public library in a medium-sized town of 40,000 people. A possible organization chart for that organization, involving about 16 people, is shown in Exhibit 5.2.

In short, a chain of command exists in all organizations. Moreover, most organizations develop formal organizational charts that outline their organizational structure, including their chain of command.

JOB SPECIALIZATION. An important part of organizing is job specialization. **Job specialization** involves breaking down organizational activities into specific tasks and designating different people to perform those tasks. In the local library organizational chart in Exhibit 5.2, one librarian is assigned full-time to work with children in the children's department. At Dell Computer Corporation, there is one

> **job specialization** Organizational activities are broken down into specific tasks and different people designated to perform those tasks

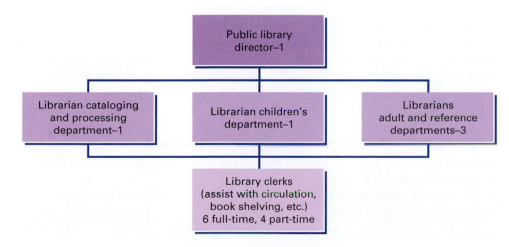

EXHIBIT 5.2

Organizational Chart: Small Local Public Library
Source: Telephone interview, reference librarian, College Station, Texas, Public Library, March 21, 2003.

employee who has been assigned the job of chief ethics officer and vice president of global diversity.

Job specialization is related to organizational growth. A very small public library in a remote town in Alaska may have only one librarian who performs all the tasks in the library. The giant main branch of the New York City Public Library may have specific librarians who specialize in working with five-to-six year olds, seven-to-eight year olds, and so on. Similarly, it's unlikely Michael Dell, when he started his company in his college apartment, ever foresaw having a specific employee working just on global diversity and corporate ethics.

The advantages of job specialization are self-evident. A librarian specializing in children's books can gain a considerable expertise in this area and do a better job for the organization than a generalist librarian who works in this area only on an intermittent basis. There can also, though, be some disadvantages to job specialization. Employees sometimes get bored doing the same specific job, year after year. To alleviate such problems, some companies use job rotation. **Job rotation** involves periodically shifting employees from one job to another. It is hoped that by giving employees a greater variety of tasks, even if this variety is limited to only a couple of other roles, they will be less likely to get bored or dissatisfied.

job rotation Periodically shifting employees from one job to another

reality CHECK *What is the chain of command at the place you've most recently worked?*

LEARNING OBJECTIVE 4
Analyze and describe different types of departmentalization within organizations.

departmentalization The process of grouping jobs into coordinated units

DEPARTMENTALIZATION. You are all familiar with the concept of **departmentalization,** which is the process of grouping jobs into coordinated units. At your school, for example, all the accounting teachers (a specialized job) will likely be grouped together into the Accounting Department. The local public library has its children's librarians and clerks grouped in the Children's Department. The terrorist attacks of September 11, 2001, led the U.S. government to create the Homeland Security Department. Departmentalization helps managers higher up in the chain of command to better monitor the organization's activities. For example, in 2002, Sears, Roebuck & Company bought Land's End Corporation. By establishing a Land's End Department within its organization, it can specifically monitor how successful its purchase of Land's End has been without getting its Land's End operations mixed up with its sales of home appliances, like its Kenmore washing machines made by Whirlpool. Today, the most common methods of organizational departmentalization are by function, product, geography, and type of customer (see Exhibit 5.3).

functional departmentalization Departmentalization based on the functions performed by that unit

Functional departmentalization is departmentalization based on the activities, or functions, performed by that unit or group. Most major corporations, for example, have a legal department, which handles the company's legal activities; a marketing department, which handles marketing activities; a human resources department, which is in charge of the human resources function; and so forth. The U.S. military is also departmentalized by function. Reduced to its most basic form (and leaving out the Coast Guard, Marines, and Special Operations Forces), the U.S. military has three departments—the army, the navy, and the air force. The function of the army is to fight on the ground, the navy to fight on the seas, and the air force to fight in the air.

product departmentalization Departmentalization based on the products or services sold

Product departmentalization is departmentalization based on products or services sold. General Electric, for example, has an aircraft engines department, a plastics department, a medical systems department, and so on, with each

EXHIBIT 5.3

Methods of Departmentalization

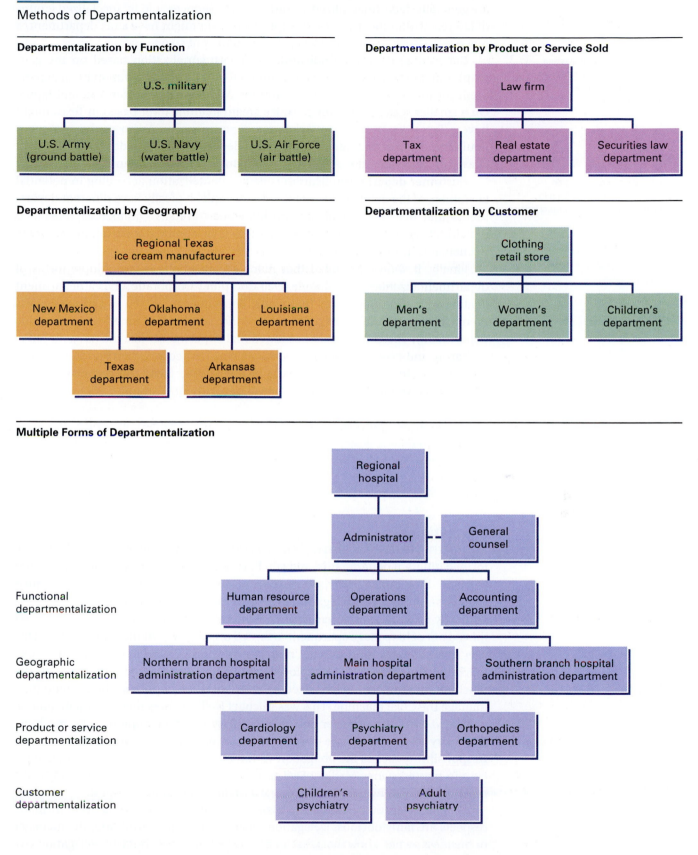

Departmentalization by Function

U.S. military
- U.S. Army (ground battle)
- U.S. Navy (water battle)
- U.S. Air Force (air battle)

Departmentalization by Product or Service Sold

Law firm
- Tax department
- Real estate department
- Securities law department

Departmentalization by Geography

Regional Texas ice cream manufacturer
- New Mexico department
- Oklahoma department
- Louisiana department
- Texas department
- Arkansas department

Departmentalization by Customer

Clothing retail store
- Men's department
- Women's department
- Children's department

Multiple Forms of Departmentalization

Regional hospital

Administrator — — General counsel

Functional departmentalization
- Human resource department
- Operations department
- Accounting department

Geographic departmentalization
- Northern branch hospital administration department
- Main hospital administration department
- Southern branch hospital administration department

Product or service departmentalization
- Cardiology department
- Psychiatry department
- Orthopedics department

Customer departmentalization
- Children's psychiatry
- Adult psychiatry

department representing a major product segment sold by GE. Similarly, law firms are generally departmentalized according to the services sold by specialized groups of lawyers within the firm. For example, a law firm might have a tax department, a real estate department, a securities department, and so on.

geographic departmentalization
Departmentalization based on the geographic areas or locations served by the organization

Geographic departmentalization is departmentalization based on the geographic areas served by the organization. Dell Computer Corporation has a department for the Americas, for Europe and the Middle East, and for Asia and Japan. On a smaller scale, a medium-sized ice cream manufacturer based in Texas might have a Texas department, an Oklahoma department, an Arkansas department, a Louisiana department, and a New Mexico department. These departments are in charge of ice cream sales and general company operations in those states.

customer departmentalization
Departmentalization according to potential customers of the organization

Customer departmentalization is departmentalization according to potential customers of the organization. Banks, for example, typically have different departments that deal with retail (private individuals) versus commercial (business) banking. Large retail stores usually have distinct clothing departments for men, women, teens, and children.

Finally, it should be noted that many organizations have multiple forms of departmentalization. For example, Dell Computer Corporation has a department dealing with corporate ethics (functional department), as well as various departments dealing with different parts of the world, such as Dell Americas (geographic department). The U.S. military has functional departments like the navy, air force, and army and geographic departments such as Centcom, which handles all military matters for Iraq and other parts of the Middle East. The regional hospital depicted in Exhibit 5.3 has a wide range of departmentalization.

reality CHECK *What is the departmental structure of your favorite retail store?*

LEARNING OBJECTIVE 5
Describe different types of delegation of authority within organizations.

Delegation.

AUTHORITY AND RESPONSIBILITY.   You've hired workers with specialized skills, you've formed different departments, and you have an organization chart, but now comes perhaps the hardest part of organizing for many managers and business founders—delegation. **Delegation** involves a manager assigning some of his or her authority or work to other employees. Remember Michael Dell and when he first moved out of his college apartment to rented office space? At that time Michael Dell was running everything at Dell Computer, including being in charge of the Coke machine. Then one day an employee came along and wanted a refund from the machine, and Michael Dell realized he had a lot more important things to do than manage the Coke machine. This was Michael Dell's management moment, and he delegated his authority over and responsibility for the company Coke machine. **Authority** means legitimate power within an organization over certain matters. **Responsibility** means the obligation within an organization to be accountable for certain matters. Once Michael Dell turned over those keys to the company Coke machine, he no longer had any power over it or was responsible for it.

delegation The assignment by a manager of some of his or her authority or work to other employees

authority Legitimate power within an organization over certain matters

responsibility Accountability within an organization for certain matters

Why is delegation so hard for many managers to do? The answers in many respects are fairly obvious. Delegation means giving up control. You, the manager or business owner, know that you can get the job done well, but with delegation you now have to trust someone else to do the job. How can anyone else ever do the job as well as you? Moreover, managers and business owners who delegate are generally ultimately responsible or accountable for what's going on in the organization. The CEO of a major *Fortune 500* corporation delegates all kinds of authority and responsibility, but if the corporation performs very poorly, the CEO knows that it is he or she whom the board of directors will fire.

Despite all the fears over delegating authority and responsibility, managers and business owners know that at the very least it is a necessary evil. Once he moved the business out of his college apartment, there was just no way for Michael Dell to keep running everything at Dell Computer Corporation. Even the hardest working micromanagers (think of the former U.S. president Jimmy Carter, who personally kept the schedule for use of the White House tennis courts) learn that it's impossible to micromanage everything. Moreover, micromanaging/fear of delegation can result in managers not focusing enough on the big picture issues before them (in former president Carter's case, things like the Iran hostage crisis). Long story short, the key to delegation is trust. Managers and business owners need to recognize that they can't do everything themselves and that they need to hire subordinates they trust to help them with their endeavors. Sometimes they are pleasantly surprised, with subordinates doing the job even better than they could ever have done it. Certainly, Michael Dell wouldn't be where he is today if he weren't an excellent delegator of authority and responsibility.

Centralization Versus Decentralization.   The degree of delegation by an organization's top management determines whether the organization is centralized or decentralized. A **centralized organization** is one where there is relatively little delegation of authority and authority is concentrated at the top. A **decentralized organization** is one where a significant amount of delegation has taken place and a good deal of authority has been spread out throughout the organization. See Exhibit 5.4.

To visualize the differences in these types of organization, let's pretend you win some money in the lottery and decide to go on a three-day vacation at a fancy hotel. You make reservations for the hotel, but when you get there they tell you that they have no record of your reservation and that they are completely booked. You start complaining, but each person you complain to says she or he has no authority to do anything about your problem. They tell you the only way to get anything done is to contact the CEO of the company, since the CEO is the only person with any authority to give you some sort of a refund or credit—or bed. This hotel has a centralized organization.

> **centralized organization** An organization where relatively little delegation of authority occurs and authority is concentrated at the top
>
> **decentralized organization** An organization where a significant amount of delegation of authority has occurred and authority is spread out

EXHIBIT 5.4

Centralized and Decentralized Organizations

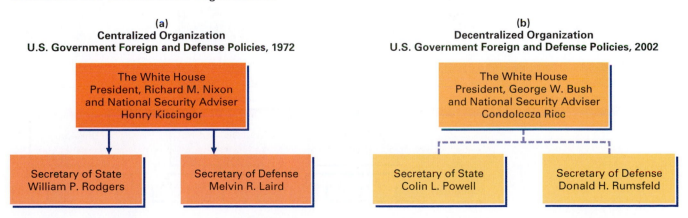

Perhaps, though, you got lucky and made your reservations at a Ritz Carlton Hotel. In the Ritz Carlton Hotel chain every employee, including junior bellhops, can spend up to $2000 on the spot to fix a guest's problems—no questions asked! At Ritz Carlton a front desk clerk quickly makes reservations for you at another nearby deluxe hotel and hands you a check for $700 to help pay for your stay at the other establishment.[22] Ritz Carlton is an example of a decentralized organization.

Issues related to centralized versus decentralized organizations also come into play in areas more weighty than mixed-up hotel reservations. In the U.S. government, the president is technically supposed to delegate foreign and defense policy authority to the heads of the two appropriate cabinet departments, the secretary of state and the secretary of defense. President Richard M. Nixon, though, did not want to delegate authority in this area. He set up a centralized organization and hired a very strong White House staff assistant, National Security Advisor Henry Kissinger, to deal with foreign and defense policies; he also appointed relatively weak secretaries of state (William P. Rodgers) and defense (Melvin R. Laird). In contrast, 30 years later, President George W. Bush decided to establish a decentralized organization for governing foreign and defense policies. He appointed very strong secretaries of state (Colin L. Powell) and defense (Donald H. Rumsfeld) and delegated primary authority to them, while maintaining a coordinating role in the top national security staffer Condoleeza Rice.

span of control The number of employees directly reporting to, or being supervised by, a given manager

SPAN OF CONTROL. The degree of delegation of authority and responsibility in an organization also directly impacts the managerial span of control. The **span of control,** also referred to as the span of management, is the number of employees directly reporting to, or being directly supervised by, a given manager (see Exhibit 5.5). A manager with a large number of direct subordinates has a wide span of control, while a manager with few direct reports has a narrow span of control.

For example, a partner in a top management consulting firm may have a dozen firm associates reporting directly to him or her. This represents a relatively wide

EXHIBIT 5.5

Span of Control

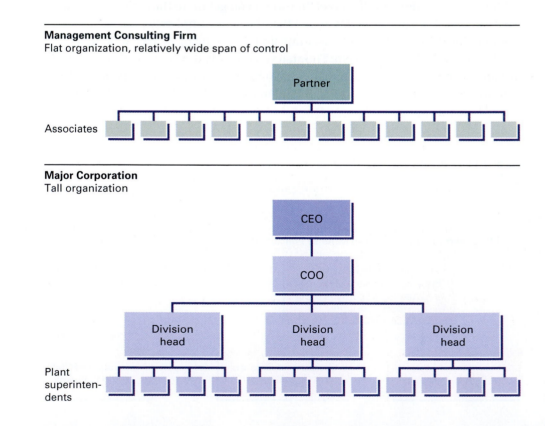

Management Consulting Firm
Flat organization, relatively wide span of control

Partner

Associates

Major Corporation
Tall organization

CEO

COO

Division head | Division head | Division head

Plant superinten-dents

span of control and results in a relatively flat organizational structure. The partner's ability to monitor the activities of each of these dozen individuals daily is limited. Wider spans of control often involve giving subordinates fairly broad autonomy.

Conversely, a manager with a narrow span of control will have relatively few direct reports, and probably more ability to regularly monitor and interact with these individuals. The CEO of a large corporation, for instance, may have only one individual reporting directly to him or her, the company's Chief Operating Officer (COO). Narrow spans of control generally lead to taller, more pyramid-like organizations. Different managerial spans of control may be appropriate for given organizations at different times.

LINE, STAFF, AND COMMITTEE AUTHORITY.   Organizing leads to different types of managerial roles, with managers having different types of organizational authority. **Line authority** involves being a part of an organization's direct chain of command and having direct responsibility for achieving the goals of the organization. Kraft Foods Corporation, for example, is one of the world's largest food companies with over $34 billion a year in sales. It makes such well-known products as Jell-O, Kraft Macaroni and Cheese, Ritz crackers, Maxwell House coffee, Oreo cookies, DiGiorno frozen pizzas, and Toblerone candies. Two clear line authority positions at Kraft Foods are corporate group vice president, Kraft cheese, meals, and enhancers, and corporate group vice president, biscuits, snacks, and confections. The first manager has overall responsibility and authority for the production of Kraft Macaroni and Cheese and other products, while the second has overall responsibility and authority for the production of Ritz crackers and other snacks. Both of the line departments supervised by these line personnel are absolutely essential to the survival and growth of Kraft.

> **line authority** The right to achieve organizational goals by being part of an organization's direct chain of command

Kraft Foods also has numerous staff authority positions. **Staff authority** involves providing advice, support, and special expertise within an organization. Kraft, for instance, has a senior vice president and general counsel, and the attorney holding this position has staff authority to provide advice to line personnel throughout the company. The company's senior vice president, human resources, also plays an important staff authority role.

> **staff authority** The right to provide advice, support, and special expertise within an organization

In some companies, especially those outside the United States like Toyota Motor Corporation, there may be more of a team or committee authority approach. **Committee authority** involves having committees or teams run the organization. A committee approach to running an organization may help bring a diversity of perspectives to problems, but may also be more time consuming than traditional organizational authority approaches.

> **committee authority** The right of committees to run an organization

It is not unusual for there to be some tension between and among individuals in different types of authority roles. In particular, individuals in staff versus line authority positions are not infrequently at odds. Staff personnel such as attorneys, human resources professionals, and ethics officers are often in internal compliance-type roles where they are telling line personnel not to do things like pay bribes to foreign officials, discriminate against disabled individuals, and so forth. Line personnel sometimes feel that staffers in their ivory towers don't understand the real world of business and what it's like to be in the trenches. That is, it may be necessary to pay some bribes in order to sell Oreo cookies in a certain foreign country, and by the way, selling Oreo cookies is the way the company pays for everything.

Virtually all organizations have both line and staff authority positions. For example, in the regional hospital illustrated in Exhibit 5.3, all the positions shown are line positions except the general counsel, which is a staff position.

reality CHECK   *In situations where you've managed things, do you generally like to delegate authority or keep strong centralized control?*

Different Forms of Organizational Structure.

We will briefly examine four types of organizational structure: functional, divisional, matrix, and network.

functional organizational structure
The structure of an organization around certain functions such as marketing, finance, and so on

FUNCTIONAL ORGANIZATIONAL STRUCTURE. **Functional organizational structure** involves structuring an organization around basic business functions such as production and operations, marketing, and finance. This organizational structure approach is frequently used by small- to medium-sized businesses and other organizations and is relatively straightforward. A diagram of a functional organizational structure is shown in Exhibit 5.6.

divisional organizational structure
The structure of an organization with various divisions operating autonomously under a broad organizational framework

DIVISIONAL ORGANIZATIONAL STRUCTURE. A corporation with a **divisional organizational structure** has various company divisions operating autonomously as businesses under a broad corporate framework. Companies with various distinct products, for example, might establish a divisional organizational structure whereby the manufacture and sale of each product is more or less conducted by a separate company under a broad corporate umbrella. The Coca-Cola Corporation, for example, might be organized in this manner. In addition to making carbonated soft drinks (Coca-Cola, Fanta, etc.), the company also makes juices and juice drinks (Minute Maid, Hi-C, etc.), sports drinks (Powerade, Aquarius, etc.), and filtered water (Dasani, Ciel, etc.). A divisional structure for Coca-Cola Corporation might be similar to the one shown in Exhibit 5.6.

matrix organizational structure
The structure of an organization around team project situations where employees report to more than one manager

MATRIX ORGANIZATIONAL STRUCTURE. A **matrix organizational structure** involves employees reporting to multiple managers in team project situations. Pfizer, for example, might establish a project team to further develop its product Viagra. The team might have a research scientist, a sales representative or detailer, an engineer, and an accountant. The project team is then assigned a project manager. In this situation the scientist, sales representative, engineer, and so on, on the project team essentially have two bosses, two reporting relationships. They have as managers both the project manager for the Viagra team and their regular manager, who may be the company chief scientist, the head of company sales, or some other manager.

Exhibit 5.6 assumes that Pfizer establishes three different teams to work on further developing three of its most important pharmaceutical drugs, Viagra, Zoloft (for the treatment of depression), and Celebrex (for the treatment of arthritis). Each project team has a project manager and is made up of a scientist, a sales representative, an engineer, and an accountant. These individuals all report to their given team project managers and to the regular heads of their functional areas. For example, scientist A reports both to his or her regular boss, the company's vice president, research/chief scientist, and to the head of Project A, the company's Viagra project. The resulting diagram of relationships, as Exhibit 5.6 shows, is a matrix.

network organizational structures
Organizational structures where the organization contracts out most functions except administration

NETWORK ORGANIZATIONAL STRUCTURE. Finally, increasing numbers of companies today are adopting what are known as **network organizational structures.** The main function performed by such organizational structures is administration, with manufacturing, distribution, and sales all contracted out to other firms. Thus, the main purpose of this structure is to administrate and coordinate agreements and contracts with other organizations that do all the producing, distributing, and selling. Some athletic shoe companies have a network organizational structure. The company designs the shoe, but then contracts with manufacturers to make the

EXHIBIT 5.6

Forms of Organizational Structure

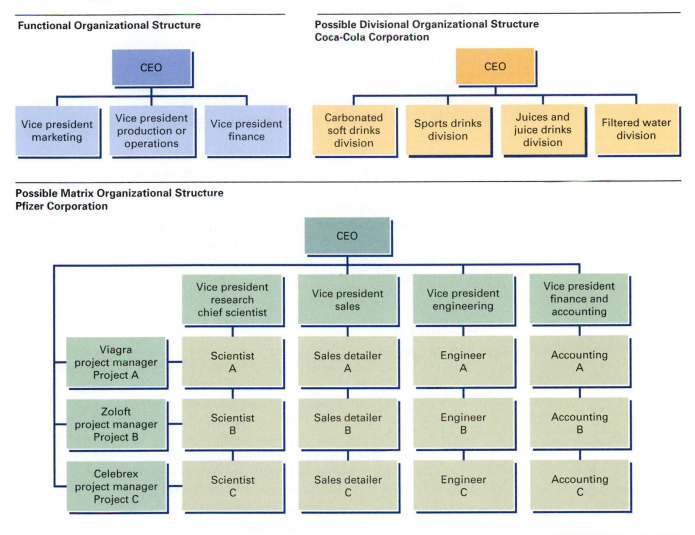

Functional Organizational Structure

**Possible Divisional Organizational Structure
Coca-Cola Corporation**

**Possible Matrix Organizational Structure
Pfizer Corporation**

Network Organizational Structure

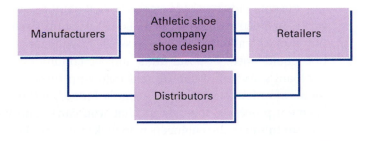

shoes, with distributors to ship the completed shoes, and with retail stores to display, advertise, and sell the shoes. Thus, the athletic shoe company is at the administrative hub of a network of other companies that make, distribute, and sell the shoes. Somewhat similarly, a company might own a convention hall but then contract out everything done in the hall, from event planning, to sale of concessions, to janitorial services.

LEARNING OBJECTIVE 6
Explain briefly the directing and controlling functions of the management process, including the use of six sigma initiatives.

Directing

An organization can have all the planning and the best organizational structure in the world and still be very ineffective in meeting its goals. Employees in the organization need to be motivated, guided, and led toward achieving what the organization wants to achieve. This is called **directing.**

directing Guiding, motivating, and leading employees toward what an organization wishes to achieve

One of the most famous quotes about the directing function is a statement made by former president Harry S Truman when former Army General Dwight D. Eisenhower (Ike) was about to be elected his successor as president. President Truman quipped, "He'll sit here all day saying do this, do that, and nothing will happen. Poor Ike, it won't be a bit like the Army. He'll find it very frustrating."[23] What President Truman was saying was that President Eisenhower was going to have a much more difficult time directing the federal government bureaucracy than he did directing the military.

Controlling

controlling Measuring, monitoring, evaluating, and regulating an organization's progress toward meeting its goals

Controlling, the final step in the management process, involves measuring, monitoring, evaluating, and regulating an organization's progress toward meeting its goals. How many prescriptions for Viagra do physicians visited by a given Pfizer detailer write per month? How many Whirlpool clothes washing machines are sold at the Hualian commercial store in Huainan, China, in a particular week? What are the precise dollar sales of Land's End products in Sears, Roebuck stores in Indiana?

The controlling function, properly implemented, has a major feedback component. Organizations establish standards, measure whether performance meets these standards, and then via feedback take corrective action as necessary. If a physician in a Pfizer detailer's territory hasn't been writing any Viagra prescriptions, the company might have the detailer bring the doctor more free samples as well as videotaped testimonials from product users saying that the product really does work.

One company that puts a great deal of emphasis on the control function is the Emerson Electric Company of St. Louis, Missouri. Emerson Electric is a major corporation with about $16 billion in sales of a wide range of electric products such as household waste disposal units and air conditioning system compressors. The company's system of control and follow-up turns on having accurate measurements of various aspects of its business. Indeed, at the heart of the company's management process is the concept that "you can't control what you can't measure." Toward this end, the engineers who make up a good part of the company's leadership spend a lot of time focusing on specific business measures such as free cash flow and return on capital.[24]

six sigma initiatives Organizational initiatives seeking to limit defects to 3.4 per million

One interesting type of control function that has received a lot of recent attention is that of **six sigma initiatives.** A number of leading companies including the Motorola Corporation, Texas Instruments Corporation, and General Electric have adopted six sigma initiatives during the past decade or so. What is a six sigma initiative? The term *sigma* is a statistical term that measures how far a given process deviates from a given norm. A six sigma procedure is one that barely deviates at all from perfection.

Let's apply the six sigma concept to that of a major airline and the problem of lost passenger luggage (see Exhibit 5.7). A perfect outcome, of course, would be one where the airline loses absolutely zero luggage. Realistically, though, all airlines lose at least some passenger luggage, as it's virtually impossible to completely prevent some loss when handling millions of pieces of passenger luggage each year. The question becomes, how much lost luggage is too much? Assuming an airline handles 1 million pieces of passenger luggage per year, a two sigma standard of control will mean that 308,537 pieces of luggage (nearly 31 percent) are lost every year—not very good. If an airline has a three sigma standard, 66,807 pieces of luggage out of a million are lost every year, or about 7 percent of the luggage handled. A four sigma standard means that only 6210 pieces of luggage out of 1 million handled annually will be lost, a five sigma standard means losing only 223 pieces of luggage, and a six sigma standard means that only *3.4* pieces of luggage out of 1 million handled annually will be lost by the airline. Implementation of a six sigma standard of control means that passengers will not lose their luggage 99.999997 percent of the time, which is probably as close to perfection as realistically possible.

Lets assume a major airline is currently operating at a three sigma defects level with respect to lost luggage; it loses about 7 percent of the luggage. But it wants to move to a six sigma standard. The company first develops plans for adopting this standard, and then organizes (e.g., six sigma councils and various other kinds of organizational structures may be necessary) for this change of approach. The company follows this up by motivating, guiding, and leading, that is, directing, employees through this change.

In terms of the final management function, controlling, the company has established a clear performance standard—six sigma—only 3.4 bags per million lost. It will then monitor whether this standard is met. If it is indeed met, things are great, everyone is happy, and ongoing company six sigma activities will likely simply just continue. What happens if 200 pieces of luggage out of a million are lost by the airline during the coming year—a performance slightly better than five sigma but not six sigma? In such a situation the airline might say this is good enough and adjust its standards a bit. Alternatively, the airline might say that a six sigma standard means a six sigma standard and that 200 pieces of luggage lost means 200 angry passengers and this is too many. In this case, the airline will have to take some corrective actions to bolster its six sigma initiative during the coming year.[25]

EXHIBIT 5.7

Airline Lost Luggage and Control Standards (per year, 1 million pieces of baggage handled)

Two sigma	308,537	bags lost
Three sigma	66,807	bags lost
Four sigma	6,210	bags lost
Five sigma	223	bags lost
Six sigma	3.4	bags lost

reality
CHECK   *Has your airline luggage or a package you've shipped ever been lost? How did the carrier respond to the loss, and what level of quality control did they appear to have?*

Kinds of Managers

LEARNING OBJECTIVE 7
Describe the basic kinds of managers within organizations.

All managers are to some extent involved with all the management functions—planning, organizing, directing, and controlling—but their involvement with these functions varies considerably depending on their area of management and their level within the organization. For example, certain financial managers in a company, such as internal auditors, may be primarily involved in a control management role, while certain operations managers, such as manufacturing plant superintendents, may spend most of their time in a directing role. Similarly, top managers in a company are probably more likely to be involved in corporate planning, while middle managers spend more time dealing with organizing issues.

Levels of Management

There are basically three levels of management in an organization, top management, middle management, and first-line management. The coordinated efforts of the managers at all these levels are necessary for an organization to achieve its goals.

top managers The people who run organizations

Top Managers.
Top managers are the people who run companies and other organizations. Common titles for top managers in the corporate world are chief executive officer (CEO), chief operating officer (COO), chief financial officer (CFO), president, vice president, and treasurer. Most major corporations list their top managers in their company annual report. Top managers have the most power and authority in an organization and are ultimately held responsible for its failure or success. In recent years, increasing numbers of women and minority group members have been moving into top corporate manager positions. In 2003, Charlene T. Begley, a 36-year-old mother of three, was named president and CEO of General Electric's multibillion dollar GE Transportation Systems unit. She thus became the first woman ever to lead a major GE unit.[26]

middle managers Managers who implement the decisions, policies, and strategies of the top managers

Middle Managers.
Most managers fall into the middle management category. **Middle managers** implement the decisions, policies, and strategies made and developed by top managers. The manager of a major 5000-employee drug manufacturing facility for Pfizer would likely be deemed a middle manager. The titles of plant manager, department head, operations manager, and division manager are commonly used to designate middle managers.

first-line managers Managers who are directly responsible for supervising and working with employees and getting the work done

First-Line Managers.
First-line managers are the ones directly responsible for supervising and working with employees and getting the necessary work done. The manager of a small (eight employees) retail store would likely be a first-line manager. This small-store manager would in all probability directly supervise the store's sales and other personnel and be responsible to middle managers, if the store is part of a larger chain, for the store's operations. Common titles for first-line managers are foreperson, supervisor, office manager, store manager, and group leader.

Areas of Management

Most large companies and other organizations have managers working in a wide variety of areas including human resources, marketing, finance, operations, information, and general administration.

human resources managers Managers who manage the people part of an organization

Human Resources Managers.
Nearly all companies have human resources managers. **Human resources managers** are involved in managing the people part of the organization. Indeed, some companies call the Human Resources Department the People Department. Among other things, human resources managers are involved in designing and administering systems for hiring, firing, training, and evaluating the performance of employees. Historically, human resources managers sometimes played something of a supervisory bean counter and record keeper role, making sure records of employee absences, sick leave, vacation time, and so on, were properly kept. Today, however, nearly all human resources record keeping functions are done by computer, freeing human resources managers to spend more time on other managerial issues.

Marketing Managers. **Marketing managers** are in charge of developing the firm's marketing strategy in areas like sales, promotion, market research, and advertising. The persons in charge of the detailers at Pfizer, for example, are marketing managers. It is not unusual for marketing managers to become the CEOs of major corporations.

Financial Managers. **Financial managers** are in charge of the money side of a business, including accounting, treasury, investments, and similar functions. Financial management is at the heart of nearly all businesses, and the top financial manager in major corporations, the CFO, is almost always among the corporation's highest-paid executives.

Operations Managers. **Operations managers** are in charge of the production of goods and services. They often manage organizations' manufacturing, quality control, and inventory processes, among other things. In a company like the Ford Motor Company, operations managers get involved with supervising the nitty-gritty of manufacturing Ford automobiles and trucks. Operations managers play a very important role in organizations, especially in companies like Ford with a strong product manufacturing focus.

Takao Yuhara is the top financial manager/chief financial officer (CFO) of Japan's giant Sony Corporation. At a recent Tokyo news conference he had the unpleasant task of announcing a quarterly decline in profits for the worldwide electronics company.

Information Managers. With the increased importance of computers and other information technology devices in running businesses has come the need for managers to supervise their use and implementation. **Information managers** are in charge of computer and other information systems within businesses. The top manager in this area is generally designated the chief information officer (CIO). CIOs are playing increasingly important roles in many major corporations.

General Managers. **General managers,** also known as administrative managers, are not associated with any specific functional area such as marketing or finance, but serve in more general managerial roles within a business. General managers, such as the general manager of a major league baseball team, coordinate and supervise the roles of various more-specialized managers. CEOs of most companies are essentially general managers.

marketing managers Managers in charge of developing firm marketing strategies

financial managers Managers in charge of the money side of an organization

operations managers Managers in charge of the production of goods and services

information managers Managers who manage computer and other information systems within an organization

general managers Managers who coordinate and supervise more-specialized managers

reality CHECK *Do you personally know any woman who has become a top manager in a business or other organization?*

Management Skills

LEARNING OBJECTIVE 8
Analyze the different types of skills that go into making effective managers.

What does it take to be a good manager? What kinds of skills are necessary? Top-flight managers generally possess a wide range of skills, although their skills in some areas may be stronger than others. Perhaps the four most important types of skills today's managers must have are technical, conceptual, human relations, and international.

Technical Skills

technical skills Specific skills needed to perform a specialized task

Technical skills are the specific skills needed to perform a specialized task. An information manager at a major corporation must have an in-depth knowledge of computers, information technology, and many other things in order to effectively supervise and manage employees working in this area. Similarly, an accounting manager for a major museum or other not-for-profit organization needs to have technical knowledge regarding tax regulation of such not-for-profit entities. Technical skills are especially important for first-line managers supervising the work of fellow professional employees, for example, an accounting manager managing the work of other accountants.

Conceptual Skills

conceptual skills Abilities to think broadly and abstractly, to see the big picture

Conceptual skills refer to an individual's ability to think broadly and abstractly, to see the big picture. Skills of this kind are especially important for managers involved in planning roles. Conceptual skills help people analyze organizational threats and opportunities. It is very important for top managers to have strong conceptual skills.

Human Relations Skills

human relations skills Abilities to get along and deal effectively with people

Human relations skills involve having the ability to get along and deal effectively with other people. Human relations skills are also known as interpersonal skills. Managers are frequently called on to use these skills both inside and outside their organization. Indeed, in recent years some observers have argued that the emotional intelligence (EQ) involved in good human relations skills is perhaps even more important to managerial success than traditional IQ conceptual thinking skills.[27] If nothing else, it is clear that skills like being able to build friendships, trust others, be adaptable, and so on, are valuable in all spheres of life. The story about the development and success of the Sony Corporation in the Case in Point illustrates the role of human relations skills.

International Skills

international skills Abilities to understand foreign cultures, markets, politics, languages, and so on

Greater globalization, particularly in the world of business, has sharply increased the need for managers to have skills in the international area. **International skills** involve having the ability to understand foreign cultures and markets, speak foreign languages, and live for extended periods of time in other parts of the world. As companies like the Whirlpool Corporation continually expand operations in faraway places like China, they need more and more managers who understand the Chinese economy, speak Chinese, appreciate Chinese culture, and are willing to live in China for at least a couple of years.

In your work experience to date, has it ever been important for you to have international skills?

Case in Point

Managerial Human Relations Skills and the Success of the Sony Corporation

What is today the giant Sony Corporation, maker of video cameras, televisions, and electronic equipment of all kinds with $70 billion per year in sales and 170,000 employees, was founded just after World War II on May 7, 1946. The company's success is due in large measure to the managerial human relations skills of its founder Masaru Ibuka. Ibuka worked well with others and made a point of staying in touch with friends. He made a special point of staying in touch with a young protégé he worked with during the war named Akio Morita and wrote Morita at his home in Kosugaya, Aichi Prefecture, to come join him in Tokyo in his new business venture. Ibuka and Morita became the "dynamic duo," leading Sony for many decades. In 1952 Ibuka made his first trip to the United States. He was anxious to expand his fledgling business into areas beyond making tape recorders and was looking for opportunities. A friend he had in the United States told him that the Western Union Corporation (then the parent of Bell Laboratories) was possibly interested in licensing its patent rights for manufacturing the transistor to other companies. Ibuka and his friend got in touch with Western Electric and, using their interpersonal skills, more or less charmed Western Electric, which was

skeptical of doing business with such a small unknown Japanese company, into giving them the transistor manufacturing license. Ibuka then worked through various friends at MITI, the Japanese government's powerful Ministry of International Trade and Industry, and got official Japanese government approval of his endeavor. In short order, Sony Corporation started manufacturing transistor radios, and Ibuka and his friend Morita were running a company successful beyond even their wildest dreams!

Source: Sony Corporation Website, **www.world.sony.com,** September 25, 2003.

Questions

1. Why are patent rights so important to high-technology companies like Sony?
2. What are some ways companies in the United States build good relationships with government agencies along the lines of the positive relationship Sony developed with MITI?
3. How has the conduct of international business changed from the time Masaru Ibuka first visited the United States in 1952?

Careers in Management

A very wide range of managerial careers are available, particularly to individuals with college course work in the field. Most major corporations and government agencies have management training programs. In many of these programs, the individuals hired will rotate among various parts of the organization for a couple of years to get a feel for where they might best fit over the long run. Most colleges and universities have some sort of career services office that can help students look for managerial positions, as well as plan long-term careers in management. Alumni of your school already placed in managerial positions can also be very helpful. In addition, the U.S. Department of Labor's Bureau of Labor Statistics, **www.bls.gov/oco,** prepares occupational outlook surveys and handbooks for various managerial careers. These government data provide comprehensive information regarding how much employment in given managerial roles is expected to increase to 2010 and beyond, as well as expected salaries for persons holding these positions. Thus, this government information can be very helpful in planning specific managerial careers.

Summary

LEARNING OBJECTIVE 1

Describe the strategic planning process, including the establishment of strategic goals, strategy formulation, and strategy implementation.

There are four basic functions in the management process: planning, organizing, directing, and controlling. Planning involves establishing organizational goals and then figuring out how best to achieve those goals. Once specific long-term business goals related to the company's mission, known as strategic goals, are established, a clear course of action must be devised for their achievement. This process, known as strategy formulation, usually involves extensive environmental and internal analyses examining such things as the company's competitors (external analysis) and the computer skills of the company's workforce (internal analysis). Once an organizational strategy has been formulated, the company then makes specific plans, for example, opening new plants or buying newspaper ads, to implement this strategy.

LEARNING OBJECTIVE 2

Discuss the special planning elements of succession planning, innovation planning, and contingency and crisis planning.

Businesses frequently face a variety of special planning elements. Succession planning, for example, involves planning related to choosing successors for top company executives. Some companies put extraordinary effort into this important process. Innovation planning involves explicit planning of ways to instill more of an entrepreneurial spirit into a business. Planning of this kind has become increasingly important in today's highly competitive marketplace. Finally, events of the kind that occurred on September 11, 2001, have led business to put greater effort into planning for abrupt changes or crises. Planning of this kind meant that some companies with numerous employees in the World Trade Center, such as American Express Corporation, were able to continue operations after September 11, 2001, without a hitch.

LEARNING OBJECTIVE 3

Explain chains of command, organizational charts, and job specialization.

Organizations have various types of structures, and at the heart of such structures are chains of command. A chain of command is the line of authority or reporting relationships within an organization. Organizational

charts are charts that lay out the chain of command or reporting relationships in an organization. Job specialization is an important part of organizing. It involves breaking down organizational activities into specific tasks and designating different people to perform those tasks.

LEARNING OBJECTIVE 4

Analyze and describe different types of departmentalization within organizations.

Departmentalization is the process of grouping jobs into coordinated units and is an important part of organizing a business. Functional departmentalization involves departmentalizing based on the functions performed by a given unit, while product departmentalization involves departmentalizing based on products or services sold by the unit. In turn, geographic departmentalization involves dividing the business up on the basis of the geographic areas or locations served by the organization, while customer departmentalization involves departmentalizing activities according to potential customers of the organization. Different types of departmentalization will work more or less effectively in different types of organizations, and many organizations will have a mix of departmental forms.

LEARNING OBJECTIVE 5

Describe different types of delegation of authority within organizations.

Michael Dell, when he started Dell Computer Corporation in his college apartment, didn't have to delegate any authority as he was the company's sole employee and so had power over all matters. As the company grew, however, he necessarily had to relinquish authority over certain functions of the company to others in the organization. Centralized organizations have most of the authority kept at the top of the organization, while decentralized organizations, such as the Ritz Carlton Hotel, have a significant amount of delegation that has taken place and authority is spread throughout the entity. The degree of delegation of authority affects the managerial span of control, the number of employees directly reporting to, or being supervised by, a manager. Some managers are delegated line authority which involves being directly responsible for a part of the company's operations. Other managers are delegated staff authority which involves providing advice and support for line managers, for example, the authority of a company's legal staff. Finally, some companies function on a committee or team approach which involves a delegation of authority to committees or teams.

LEARNING OBJECTIVE 6

Explain briefly the directing and controlling functions of the management process, including the use of six sigma initiatives.

Once organizations have planned and organized to make things happen, employees in them need to be motivated and directed toward achieving what the organization wants to achieve. Things have to be made to happen, and some monitoring or controlling of the organization's progress toward its goals becomes necessary. Most organizations have a feedback process whereby employees and others who aren't meeting organizational performance goals are informed and given the opportunity to take corrective action. Six sigma initiatives, taken in recent years by many leading corporations, are one type of control mechanism. Such initiatives set a very high standard for the quality of production, stating that out of 1 million products produced only three or four will have any quality problems.

LEARNING OBJECTIVE 7

Describe the basic kinds of managers within organizations.

Organizations have various kinds of managers. Top managers are the people that run companies and other organizations. The chief executive officer (CEO) is usually the number one manager in an organization. Middle managers implement the policies and strategies developed by top managers and run important segments of the organization. First-line managers are directly responsible for supervising and working with employees and getting the necessary work done. Moreover, most large businesses and other organizations have managers working in a wide variety of specialized areas such as human resources, marketing, and accounting.

LEARNING OBJECTIVE 8

Analyze the different types of skills that go into making effective managers.

A wide variety of skills go into making effective managers. Managers need conceptual skills enabling them to think broadly and abstractly, and often technical skills like an in-depth knowledge of computers, which help them perform a specialized task. Increasing globalization has led to a greater and greater need for managers to have international skills such as the ability to speak a foreign language. Finally, human relations skills, involving the ability to get along and deal effectively with other people, are always extremely important for managers to possess.

Chapter Questions

1. What are some arguments for the proposition that the CEO of Goldman Sachs Group, Henry Paulson, should not have apologized to company employees for the statement he made at the referenced investment conference?

2. You are the manager of a major league baseball team with the strategic goal of winning the World Series. What type of strategy would you formulate to achieve this goal, and how would you go about implementing this strategy?

3. Do you think a mission statement is necessary for a company to have? Why or why not?

4. You and a friend are thinking about starting a company that would rent dorm refrigerators at local college campuses and you need to do a strategic environmental analysis. What would an environmental analysis involve in such a situation?

5. How do tactical plans differ from operational plans?

6. What are the negatives of having public CEO succession races of the kind held by General Electric on the succession of CEO Jack Welch?

7. You graduate from school and open a company providing crisis planning consulting for businesses. What are three things you would advise companies to plan for in the event of a terrorist attack at their corporate headquarters?

8. The U.S. Army is an example of an organization with a very strict chain of command. What are some examples of organizations with looser chains of command?

9. You graduate school and are hired into a highly specialized position in an organization. After a year or two you become very bored in your job. What are some job assignment alternatives you can propose to your supervisor that don't involve your entirely giving up your current position?

10. What are some departments in the organization where you currently work or have most recently worked?

11. Why is delegating authority so hard for managers to do?

12. A matrix organizational structure is most appropriate in what kinds of situations?

13. A newspaper currently operates at the three sigma level with respect to errors in its printed stories, but wants to move to the six sigma level. What does this mean? What are three specific suggestions you might make to the newspaper's management regarding how it might best make this change?

14. It is true that probably more than an average number of CEOs were formerly marketing managers. Why do you think this is the case?

15. What are some of the kinds of international skills managers will find most useful in today's world business environment? What are some ways students can best gain these skills?

Interpreting Business News

1. The U.S. military is increasingly developing a network organizational structure, with significant military functions being contracted out to private companies. You may never have heard about companies like DynCorp, Cubic, PCI, and MPRI, but they do billions of dollars a year in business with the federal government, providing services to the military ranging from KP duty and laundry detail to enlisted personnel recruiting. The idea is that the U.S. military should focus on its core competency and leave doing laundry, slicing potatoes for dinner, and so on, to the private nonmilitary sector. Recent efforts by the U.S. Army with regard to contracting out recruiting functions to companies with human resources management expertise have enabled it to transfer back to the field hundreds of soldiers who had been working at various army recruiting stations. Do you agree with the U.S. military's increased emphasis on contracting out? What are some arguments against such contracting out with respect to recruiting and some other functions?

2. You have probably never heard of Donald Sterling. He is the very low-key owner of the Los Angeles Clippers basketball team. Sterling bought the team in 1981, when it was based in San Diego, for $12.5 million. In 1984 he moved the team to Los Angeles. Over the past two decades or so, the Clippers have had one of the very worst performance records in the National Basketball Association. While the other professional basketball team in Los Angeles, the Los Angeles Lakers, lavishes huge salaries on players like Shaquille O'Neal, the Clippers have a very low total annual player payroll of about $34 million. Donald Sterling's low-budget approach also involves hiring as few coaches as possible and trading players (such as Ron Harper and Derek Anderson) if they do well and start demanding higher pay rates. Why do you think Donald Sterling has adopted this kind of business strategy? Do you agree with his business strategy? (Hint: The Clippers post an annual operating profit of $16 million, twice the NBA average, and Sterling's initial investment in the team is now worth well over $200 million.)

Web Assignments

1. Go to the website of the Goldman Sachs Group investment bank, **www.gs.com,** and find the section on careers. Within the careers section, go to the business divisions section and then find the section that lists Goldman Sachs's 14 business principles. What are Goldman Sachs's key business principles? Write a one- to two-page paper analyzing the comments made by the company's CEO, Henry M. Paulson, in the introductory vignette of the chapter in the context of these company business principles. Specifically discuss the extent to which Mr. Paulson's comments jibe with the company's stated principles.

2. The Kraft Foods Corporation, **www.kraft.com,** formerly had a very unusual top management structure, one held by less than 1 percent of public companies in the United States. Go to the Kraft website's 2003 prior news release section and to its December 16, 2003 news release discussing management changes. What was so unique about Kraft's former management structure? Write a one-page analysis of why you think this management structure failed. Also, discuss the types of organizations or situations where you think such a management structure might operate more successfully.

3. The Coca-Cola Company is one of the world's most well-known companies, with arguably the world's most famous brand. Look up the company's website, **www.coca-cola.com.** Look for the company's beliefs and then the Coca-Cola promise, which is the company's mission statement stating why it exists. Write a one-page paper setting forth Coca-Cola Company's mission statement and analyzing (drawing on the plethora of other information on this website) whether you think the company is currently fulfilling its mission.

Portfolio Projects

Exploring Your Own Case in Point

After reading this chapter, you should understand the basic processes of corporate planning, organizing, directing, and controlling. You should also better understand the different types of corporate managers and the skills they need. Answers to the following questions will help you better understand the management process at the company you have chosen to research.

1. Has your company named an "heir apparent" to its CEO? If not, does it appear to have a CEO succession planning process in operation?

2. Was your company directly impacted by the events of September 11, 2001? If so, how did it respond?

3. What is the departmental structure of your company? What is its chain of command?

4. Has your company adopted six sigma or other quality control measures?

Starting Your Own Business

After reading this chapter, you should be able to add to your business plan answers to these questions related to the future operational structure of your business.

1. What are the short-term goals of your business?

2. What are the long-term goals of your business?

3. After you have conducted an environmental analysis, what external opportunities and threats do you see for your business? How do you plan to best mitigate these threats and capitalize on these opportunities?

4. What, if any, quality control measures, e.g., six sigma initiatives, do you plan to have for your business?

Test Prepper

You've read the chapter, studied the key terms, and the exam is any day now. Think you are ready to ace it? Take this sample test to gauge your comprehension of chapter material. You can check your answers at the back of the book.

True/False Questions

Please indicate if the following statements are true or false:

_____ 1. Baseball teams involve little management.

_____ 2. Being a dreamer is a sure way to fail in business.

_____ 3. An environmental analysis for a corporation might involve extensive analysis of its competitors.

_____ 4. Operational plans for the Whirlpool Corporation might involve deciding what newspaper advertisements to place for three months for its Polar products in Poland.

_____ 5. The events of September 11, 2001, probably increased corporate contingency planning activities.

_____ 6. Job specialization involves shifting employees from one job to another.

_____ 7. Large retail stores typically use geographic departmentalization.

_____ 8. Delegation is often hard for managers because it means giving up control.

_____ 9. A company in-house attorney has considerable line authority.

_____ 10. First-line managers are directly responsible for supervising and working with employees.

Multiple-Choice Questions

Choose the best answer.

_____ 1. In deciding its strategic moves, Whirlpool Corporation is most likely to consult with

　　a. Maytag Corporation.
　　b. Boeing Company.
　　c. Sears, Roebuck & Company.
　　d. Disney Corporation.
　　e. General Motors Corporation.

_____ 2. _____ plans are a list of what a company has to do in the very short run to achieve its strategic goals.

　　a. Strategic
　　b. Tactical
　　c. Succession

　　d. Operational
　　e. Contingency

_____ 3. The problem with *comparaggio* is that

　　a. people don't like doing business in Italy.
　　b. it creates ethical problems.
　　c. IBM Corporation is headquartered in New York.
　　d. Dell Computer Corporation is headquartered in Texas.
　　e. it makes doing business in China difficult for the Whirlpool Corporation.

_____ 4. An example of departmentalization by customer would be

　　a. the securities law department of a law firm.
　　b. Dell Computer Corporation's headquarters in Austin, Texas.
　　c. the Oklahoma department of a regional ice cream manufacturer.
　　d. the U.S. Navy.
　　e. the children's department of a clothing retail store.

_____ 5. The Ritz Carlton Hotel chain is a good example of a _____ because authority has been spread throughout the organization.

　　a. centralized organization
　　b. decentralized organization
　　c. six sigma organization
　　d. hotel chain with security problems
　　e. hotel chain with a military chain of command

_____ 6. President Harry S Truman once expressed concern that his successor, Dwight D. Eisenhower, would have a hard time with _____ because of Eisenhower's military background.

　　a. the planning aspects of the presidency
　　b. the pomp and circumstance of the presidency
　　c. the organizing aspects of the presidency
　　d. the directing aspects of the presidency
　　e. the matrix organizational structure of the presidency

_____ 7. An airline with a six sigma initiative would aim to have about how many lost bags out of 5 million handled?

   a. 1100
   b. 31,000
   c. 17
   d. 335,000
   e. 1.5 million

_____ 8. _____ managers implement the decisions, policies, and strategies made by top managers.

   a. First-line
   b. Middle
   c. Human resources
   d. Operations
   e. Technical

_____ 9. A manager with excellent human relations skills would almost definitely have

   a. a high EQ.
   b. a high IQ.
   c. a high level of computer training.
   d. military experience.
   e. training at a military institute.

_____ 10. The skills needed to perform a specialized task are called

   a. technical skills.
   b. conceptual skills.
   c. human relations skills.
   d. international skills.
   e. general skills.

Want more questions? Visit the student website at **http://college.hmco.com/business/student/** (select Gaspar, *Introduction to Business*) and take the ACE quizzes for more practice.

6

Human Resources Management

Introduction
What Do Human Resources Managers Do?
Technology and Human Resources
Management

Human Resources Planning
Job Analysis
Forecasting Human Resources Demand
Forecasting Human Resources Supply
Matching Supply with Demand

Organizational Staffing
Recruiting
Selection
Orientation

Compensation and Benefits
Wages and Salaries
Benefits

Developing an Effective Workforce
Needs Analyses
Methods for Developing an Effective
Workforce
Feedback and Performance Appraisal and
Evaluation

Labor–Management Relations
Historical Overview
Collective Bargaining
The Decline of Unions
International Labor Relations

**Legal Environment of Human Resources
Management**
Employment-at-Will Revisited
Federal Legislation After 1960
State Regulation

Workplace Diversity
Advantages and Challenges of a Diverse
Workforce
Equal Employment Opportunity Versus
Affirmative Action
University of Michigan Affirmative Action Case
Workforce Diversity After 9/11

Careers in Human Resources Management

Learning Objectives

After studying this chapter, you should be able to

1. Describe how advances in technology and other factors have led to an increasingly strategic role in organizations for human resources management.

2. Explain how human resources managers engage in planning and forecasting.

3. Discuss the process of recruiting and selecting employees for an organization.

4. Evaluate the types, value, and effectiveness of the compensation and benefit plans that organizations offer employees.

5. Analyze different methods for developing an effective workforce and providing workforce members with proper feedback.

6. Describe the role of the National Labor Relations Act in abolishing company unions, and the process by which "real" unions come into power and engage in collective bargaining.

7. Discuss how and why the field of human resources management has become so highly legally regulated, especially by the federal government, in recent decades.

8. Analyze the difference between equal employment opportunity and affirmative action, the impact of this difference on workplace diversity, and recent developments in affirmative action and workplace diversity.

Working Part-Time

With increasing frequency, many employees, especially women with children, are exploring the possibility of working part-time. This is true even of highly trained professional employees, such as lawyers. For example, an organization called Flex-Time Lawyers was recently formed in New York and Philadelphia to help lawyers get part-time jobs and to act as a support group for attorneys holding part-time positions.

Many large law firms have responded to this interest by offering part-time flexible schedules to attorneys in the firm, both at the associate attorney and partner levels. One large Philadelphia law firm recently promoted a female part-time associate to part-time partner. She works 80 percent of a full-time schedule for 80 percent compensation and generally takes Fridays off.

Technological advances have aided opportunities for part-time work, even in highly demanding fields like law. Cell phones, e-mail, and other devices enable clients and firms to be in touch with part-time attorneys at any time.

Despite these developments, however, some lawyers are reluctant to take advantage of part-time employment opportunities. They fear the stigma that taking the part-timer route means you're not really fully committed to your work.[1] Moreover, managing a part-time professional workforce presents a new and significant human resources management challenge to law firms, as well as other organizations.

Introduction

LEARNING OBJECTIVE 1
Describe how advances in technology and other factors have led to an increasingly strategic role in organizations for human resources management.

The famous Bob Dylan song goes "The times they are a-changin'."[2] In many ways, the same can be said about managing human resources. Historically, the human resources function of businesses was not viewed as highly important to the organization. The so-called personnel office was frequently relegated to handling rather mundane tasks such as monitoring employee attendance, making sure workers received their paychecks, and so on; the office played a relatively small role in the strategic operation of the business. Also, during a significant segment of the past century, labor unions played a major role in the conduct of human resources in a large number of U.S. businesses, with union-management collective bargaining agreements regulating a good deal of company–employee relations.

The times, however, have indeed been a-changin'. While labor unions continue to play an important role in the U.S. economy, their role has declined, with only about 10 percent of private sector employees currently being covered by collective bargaining agreements. This shift has been related to an overall shift in our economy away from manufacturing to service. Increased foreign trade has led to the movement of U.S. manufacturing facilities to countries like Mexico and China, where cheap manual labor can be readily found, and with such movement, hundreds of thousands of U.S. textile worker, steel worker, and other jobs have been lost. In their stead, however, hundreds of thousands of U.S. knowledge industry jobs in the computer, financial services, biotechnology, and other high-tech industries have evolved in recent years.

The impact of all of this on managing human resources should hopefully be becoming clear. Historically, employees operated various machines and other means of production. Today in the United States and other highly developed countries, however, a growing number of knowledge workers, for example, software programmers, are themselves the means of the company's production. If human resources become the means of production, successfully managing such resources becomes extraordinarily important.[3] This includes hiring the right people, motivating them, dealing with issues such as the part-time schedules mentioned in the opening vignette, staying abreast of the latest legal issues, and appreciating the value of a diverse workforce. Thus, the human resources management function in many companies today is clearly no longer second tier, and plays an extremely important role in the strategic operation of the business. Today, in many respects, all managers are human resources mangers.

What Do Human Resources Managers Do?

Southwest Airlines, based in Texas, calls its corporate human resources management department its People Department and instead of having a vice president of human resources management in charge of the department, it has a vice president of people. Southwest Airlines is correct: human resources management is all about people. Among the primary human resources management (HRM) functions are recruiting and selecting people for the organization; training and orienting selected people; evaluating the performance of these people and then tying their compensation and performance to such evaluations; when necessary, disciplining and perhaps even firing these people; and working with unions these people may form. In very small organizations, the business's owner will likely handle all or most HRM functions. In larger organizations, specific individuals will be hired to fill HRM functions. Some large organizations centralize the HRM at corporate headquarters, while other organizations have the bulk of their human resources managers working in the field as part of various corporate divisions. Somewhat similarly, some corporations hire mostly HRM generalists, and then rotate these individuals into different jobs, while others hire HRM specialists, for example, in the areas of compensation or labor relations, and expect individuals to build a career in that specialty area. Finally, many companies hire a mix of HRM generalists and specialists.

Technology and Human Resources Management

In addition to helping change the nature of work in the United States from manufacturing to service, advances in technology have also had a tremendous impact on the conduct of HRM. The Internet and companies like careerbuilder.com and monster.com have revolutionized the way many companies conduct their employee recruitment, application, and selection processes. Employee payroll and related functions, which historically had to monotonously be done by the personnel office by hand, are now almost always done by computer, and indeed are frequently outsourced to companies like Automatic Data Processing Corporation, which specialize in this area. Fax machines, employee intranets and e-mail, cell phones, and other such devices have facilitated a major shift away from traditional 9-to-5 work hours, allowing employees to design more flexible work hours and workweeks, and even in some cases mostly to work at home and telecommute. Computer forecasts allow employers to conduct better human resources planning, while online learning and simulation software have clearly helped improve staff training and development. All in all, advances in technology have had a major positive impact on the human resources function in organizations and have clearly helped human resources managers shed their role as paper pushers for a more strategic one in the companies they serve.[4]

What is the role of the human resources managers at the place you've most recently worked?

Human Resources Planning

LEARNING OBJECTIVE 2
Explain how human resources managers engage in planning and forecasting.

Organizations need to plan their human resources function. What kind of people are they going to need in the future, and to what extent are these types of people going to be available? The first step in this process involves figuring out exactly what type of person is needed to perform a particular job. This is called **job analysis.**

job analysis A systematic evaluation of the elements and requirements needed for a job

Job Analysis

An accounting department of a college's business school has recently been faced with a sharp increase in the number of students wishing to major in accounting. The problem is that almost all these new students are primarily interested in international accounting. The department knows it needs to hire more accounting faculty, but hiring just any accounting faculty is not likely to fill the demand. The department needs to do a job analysis, or a systematic evaluation of the elements required for the job and the qualities required to perform it. After doing such an analysis, the department determines that it needs international accounting professors. The department then writes up a formal **job description,** which is a list of the duties of the job, working conditions, responsibilities, people to be supervised, and so on. The department also will write up a **job specification,** which describes in detail the skills, education, experience, and other credentials required for the job. This job description and specification, which make up the job analysis, will play an important role in recruiting and selecting an individual to fill the job. They will also likely be used later in evaluating job performance, determining equitable compensation, and other aspects of HRM.

job description A list of the duties of the job, working conditions, responsibilities, people to be supervised, and so on

job specification A detailed listing of the individual qualifications needed for a job

Forecasting Human Resources Demand

Forecasting human resources (HR) demand is, of course, a tricky business. In the accounting department example, it appears right now that there is strong demand at the school for an international accounting professor, but before hiring or even redirecting existing faculty, attempts need to be made to look into the future and forecast future demand. What are the general demographic trends with respect to new college students? Will the accounting profession continue to have a high or increasing international demand? Are there any possible external events that could radically change this situation? (For

Personal trainer Sal Fichera helps Peg Warren during a 2004 workout at a gym in New York City. Government statistics forecast that the demand for health and fitness workers will grow by nearly 50 percent during the coming decade.

example, the events of September 11, 2001, clearly changed many corporate HR demand forecasts.) Is the college planning any new initiatives, such as an endowed center for international accounting, that may have an impact on this analysis? Government data and computer simulations testing various scenarios will likely help in conducting such forecasting.

Forecasting Human Resources Supply

Forecasting HR supply involves looking at both internal and external labor supply. In the accounting department example, it may be possible that individuals already working or coming to work at the college have the credentials for this job or can be retrained or redirected to do it. Conversely, it may be necessary to hire for this job from the external market. In general, employers have an easier time making forecasts about the internal supply of labor than about the external supply.

replacement charts Charts outlining possible replacements for key personnel

Internal Labor Supply Forecasts. Organizations use various techniques to try to forecast the internal supply of labor. At the managerial level, **replacement charts** of key personnel and their possible replacements already within the organization are kept. In essence, firms keep a list of replacement workers ready and able to step into top jobs in case of an unexpected event (e.g., a plane crash disabling or killing the company's CEO or CFO), resignation, retirement, and so on. Companies also frequently use computer technology to compile a **skills inventory,** which is a data bank containing information about the skills, experiences, and aspirations of all present employees. This data bank then aids both line and HR managers in identifying company personnel to fill new or newly available positions. For example, if a company is opening a new office in Lisbon, Portugal, and is looking to transfer employees who speak Portuguese to that office, the computerized skills inventory can very quickly identify possible candidates.

skills inventory A data bank listing skills, experiences, and aspirations of present employees

External Supply Forecasts. Forecasting the external availability of certain types of labor is a somewhat more difficult exercise for most businesses. Figures supplied by various government sources, such as state employment commissions, and by colleges with respect to the numbers of majors in different fields may be helpful.

Matching Supply with Demand

Once armed with the forecasts of the supply of labor, HR and other managers can begin making decisions. If it appears that the demand for personnel is going to be greater than the supply, recruiting efforts will likely be commenced. Recruitment may be for permanent employees or possibly for contingent or temporary workers—a trend that is growing. Conversely, if the labor supply is forecast to likely be greater than the demand, paring back the workforce needs to take place. Most organizations initially try to achieve such paring back by way of attrition, that is, not replacing employees when they leave. If attrition doesn't bring supply and demand into proper balance, other actions ranging from special early retirement incentive programs to layoffs may be necessary.

 What types of jobs do you think are going to be the most plentiful in your community over the next decade?

Organizational Staffing

> LEARNING OBJECTIVE 3
> Discuss the process of recruiting and selecting employees for an organization.

Recruiting

Recruiting is the process of attracting qualified job applicants for jobs as they come open. At the heart of recruiting is the development of an **applicant pool,** which is the pool of people applying for a particular job or jobs. Some companies put a high priority on developing very large applicant pools, taking the viewpoint that one never knows where there might be a diamond in the rough. In recent years Southwest Airlines has, on average, solicited and received well over 100,000 job applications per year for a few thousand or so new hires.[5] Other organizations, however, solicit and recruit job applicants more narrowly, perhaps focusing on job applicant sources that worked well for them in the past.

Internal recruiting means considering present employees (internal supply) as candidates for available positions. Such situations may involve promoting current employees to higher-level positions or transferring them from one position to another at the same level. Internal opportunities for both promotion and transfer may help increase employee morale and lessen turnover (employees leaving the organization). In many cases such opportunities for internal promotion or transfer are open, with the position being publicly posted and all applications encouraged. In some cases, though, internal staffing moves are made in a more closed manner, with managers deciding which employee will be considered for the job promotion or transfer.

External recruiting involves reaching outside the organization for new employees. Numerous different means are available for external recruiting ranging from Internet sites to union hiring halls to executive search firms to campus interviews. The means of external recruiting used will likely turn in significant measure on the type of job involved. For better or worse, word-of-mouth recruiting, that is, referrals from current employees or other individuals well known to the organization, can play a very important role in hiring. Aggressive external recruitment may cause resentment among current employees in certain situations, such as where they feel there are well-qualified employees within the organization who could be promoted to the position.

recruiting Attracting qualified job applicants

applicant pool The pool of people applying for a particular job or jobs

internal recruiting Considering present employees as candidates for available jobs

external recruiting Considering individuals outside the organization as candidates for the job

U.S. Internal Revenue Service (IRS) recruiter Doug Fuller (left) talks to Leslie Lang during a recent job fair held at Rutgers University in New Brunswick, New Jersey. The IRS is actively recruiting college business students.

Selection

selection Choosing the best individual from the applicant pool

Selection is at the heart of HRM. Once the applicant pool is established, the issue becomes one of selecting the best match for the given job. Unfortunately, this is an area where organizations sometimes run into trouble. Organizations may look to hire the person with the highest credentials, best college grade point average, and so on, even though that person may not be the best match for the given job, as defined by the job analysis. For example, a college may hire a really brainy professor with a tremendous scholarly record, but if the professor's primary role at that school is to be a great classroom teacher and the individual hired is not very good at that, the selection process did not culminate in a very good match.

Enterprise Rent-A-Car Corporation is one of the nation's largest car rental companies, with billions of dollars in annual revenues and a very strong rate of growth. It has grown by putting a very high emphasis on customer service. It hires virtually only people who have attended college, but puts little emphasis on their academic performance, instead looking for good sales skills and personalities. The company's CEO commented, "We hire from the half of the college class that makes the upper half possible. . . . We want . . . people people."[6] These types of folks are a good match for Enterprise, and having been humbled a bit in their college experience, may also be very loyal to the company that gave them an opportunity. A science student with a 4.0 grade point average and no outside activities may be a good match for a job in a scientific research laboratory, but not for a job with Enterprise Rent-A-Car. Selecting employees that are good matches is very important because if the person hired turns out not to be such a good match, there will likely be costly problems later. Traditional selection processes have a number of formal steps including application forms, employment tests or other screening, interviews, and reference checks. In certain situations, these steps may be short-circuited; for example, a corporate CEO may directly hire for a vice president slot an individual he or she knows well without any reference checks.

Applications and Resumes.   Many organizations have formal application forms that ask detailed questions about the prospective employee's education, job history, and so on. For some jobs, a one- or two-page resume, or summary of the candidate's background, prepared by the job candidate may be sufficient.

Employment Test.   Some employers administer ability, or aptitude, tests to certain job candidates. These tests must be job-related, for example, a typing test for a secretarial position. These tests must also accurately measure an individual's ability to perform a given job.

Interviews.   Employment interviews are probably the most widely used selection device. It is common for individuals to be offered positions only after having had an on-site job interview. Interviews cut both ways in that they afford job applicants the opportunity to learn more about the organization, while at the same time giving the organization the opportunity to learn more about the candidate. While job interviews are common, biases inherent in the way people evaluate others on first meeting can sometimes impact their usefulness; we may rank highly people who have something in common with us even though they may not be a good match for the job. **Structured interviews** where all applicants are asked a specific set of questions may lend more consistency to the interview process and help remove possible bias.

structured interviews Interviews where all job applicants are asked a specific set of questions

References.   Job candidates are usually asked to furnish at least one **reference,** which is someone who can provide information about the applicant's suitability for the job. Since candidates are expected to list only references who think positively of them, a negative evaluation from a reference when checked may send up a red flag to the employer.

reference Someone who can provide information about a job applicant's suitability for a job

Orientation

Many organizations have some sort of orientation program for employees once they join the firm. **Orientation** is simply the process of acquainting new employees with the organization. In some organizations, the orientation may be very simple, perhaps only a short presentation by a human resources manager of company insurance and other benefits. In other organizations, the orientation program may be quite elaborate, involving trips to company overseas offices and other activities.

orientation The process of introducing new employees to the organization

reality CHECK   *Have you ever been involved in interviewing a prospective employee? How did you decide whether you wanted to hire the individual?*

Compensation and Benefits

LEARNING OBJECTIVE 4
Evaluate the types, value, and effectiveness of the compensation benefit plans that organizations offer employees.

Designing effective organizational compensation and benefits programs is a significant and very important HRM function. To some extent, federal and state government regulations underpin this area of human resources. The federal **Fair Labor Standards Act (FLSA),** for example, mandates that there be a minimum wage throughout the country of at least, currently, $5.15 per hour, and that workers receiving the minimum wage receive time-and-a-half pay if they work overtime, generally defined as more than 40 hours per week. Professional and supervisory employees are deemed to be exempt from this law and thus do not have to receive overtime pay. Some observers have strongly criticized the federal minimum wage, stating that it does not provide people earning it with enough income to live on. In response, some state and local jurisdictions have mandated minimum wages that are much higher than the federal minimum ($10 per hour plus for employers in some counties in California). Federal laws also provide old-age pensions and health care programs—social security and Medicare—to which both employees and employers must contribute. In addition, state-administered unemployment insurance and worker's compensation insurance plans throughout the country provide insurance coverage for employees if they are, respectively, laid off or injured on the job. Beyond these government-mandated programs, employers have considerable flexibility in creating compensation and benefits programs that work best for their organization.

Fair Labor Standards Act (FLSA) A federal law passed in 1938 regulating employee wages and work hours

Wages and Salaries

Wages and salaries are the dollars paid to employees for their work. **Wages** are monies paid for time worked. A **salary** is a monetary stipend paid for fulfilling job responsibilities and is usually set forth as an amount paid per year. Companies regularly conduct **wage and salary surveys** to find out what other comparable employers are paying employees in comparable positions. Some companies establish formal policies whereby they will always pay all employees a given percentage, say

wages Monies paid to employees for time worked

salary Monies paid to employees for fulfilling job responsibilities

wage and salary surveys Data collection on prevailing wages and salaries within an industry or geographic area

15 percent, above the market average for given positions. Paying employees above-market wages helps companies retain top-quality employees and reduce employee turnover.

seniority Longevity on the job

Seniority, or longevity on the job, is also frequently a factor in setting wages and salaries, particularly under labor-management collective bargaining contracts. Proponents of seniority-based pay argue that it rewards employee loyalty. Other observers argue that pay should be tied primarily to individual performance and not merely to years on the job. In recent years there has been considerable debate about the merit and legality of **employer pay confidentiality rules,** rules adopted by employers that employees must not talk to others about their pay. About one-third of U.S. employers have such rules, even though they appear to be generally illegal under federal law.[7] Federal law also mandates, pursuant to the **Equal Pay Act,** that men and women doing essentially the same job must be paid the same. No federal law currently exists, though, with respect to the principle of **comparable worth,** which states that men and women in comparable jobs in terms of training and education required, job responsibility, and so on, should be paid the same. Proponents of this concept argue that employees in certain female-dominated fields like nursing get paid considerably less than men in comparable-type jobs in fields like accounting. Opponents of the comparable worth concept argue that market forces should determine what different jobs get paid, not the federal government.

employer pay confidentiality rules Employer rules mandating that employees not speak to others about their pay

Equal Pay Act A federal law passed in 1963 requiring equal pay for men and women doing equal work

comparable worth The principle that men and women should be paid the same for comparable work

job evaluation The process of determining the relative worth of different jobs

To the extent the doctrine of comparable worth has been adopted in parts of other countries like Canada, the concept of **job evaluation** comes into significant play. Job evaluation is considerably different from job analysis in that it involves determining the relative worth of a given job to an organization. Not infrequently, a system of points is part of a job evaluation plan. For example, all jobs in a given organization are assigned a number of points ranging from 16 to 900 depending on the responsibilities of the job, the credentials required for it, and so forth, and each employee receives a base annual salary of $1000 multiplied by the number of points assigned to his or her job. The CEO of a company likely receives 900 points, or a base annual salary of $900,000, while an entry-level accountant receives 50 points, or $50,000. An entry-level registered nurse in the company's infirmary may, when all factors of the job are evaluated, also receive 50 points, or the same $50,000 per year as the accountant. The accounting and nursing jobs are clearly not the same, but they are comparable.

Contingent, or Variable, Compensation.
Most compensation plans have both a predetermined fixed and a contingent, or variable, portion. A person who takes a nursing position may receive a base salary of $50,000 per year. This individual, though, will also likely be eligible for at least some additional, or variable, compensation contingent on certain things, such as individual or group performance.

Individually Based Contingent Compensation.
A good deal of contingent, or variable, compensation is individually based. For example, a new stockbroker may receive a base salary of $2000 per month ($24,000 per year) plus 50 percent of any commissions (from stock trading and related activities) he or she generates in a given month. This second part of the compensation package is completely variable; if the stockbroker has a very bad commission month, this part of his or her compensation may amount to far less than the $2000 base pay; while in a very good month it may far exceed this amount. In addition, this extra compensation completely turns on the individual's performance. It might be possible for an individual stockbroker to have a great commission month and make a lot of extra money even though the brokerage company as a whole is experiencing bad times, or vice versa.

MERIT PAY PLANS. **Merit pay plans** are a good example of individually-based variable compensation. Such plans involve giving individuals special pay bonuses, or money above across-the-board raises, because of the particular merit of their contribution to the organization. A professional baseball pitcher may, for example, be eligible for a $200,000 bonus if he wins more than 15 games in a season.

merit pay plans Pay plans that compensate individuals on the basis of their individual contribution to the organization

KNOWLEDGE- OR SKILL-BASED PAY. **Knowledge-** or **skill-based pay** systems are similar to individually-based contingent pay plans. Most public school districts, for example, pay school teachers an extra annual sum if they earn college degrees beyond the bachelor's level (a master's degree or even a Ph.D.). Similarly, an organization may pay individuals extra for learning additional job-related computer or other skills.

knowledge- or **skill-based pay** Pay for individuals for having or obtaining specific knowledge or skills

Group-Based Contingent Compensation.

Organizations also often offer additional parts of the compensation package that are contingent on special team, or group, performance. For example, all players on professional football teams (even the second stringers!) generally get a uniform significant bonus if the team makes it to the Super Bowl. The overall success of the team is shared by all.

PROFIT SHARING PLANS. **Profit sharing plans** involve employees sharing a part of the business's annual profits. If the company as a whole does well and has considerable profits, employees also do well, and vice versa. Some multidivision companies have been known to tie employee profit sharing to the profits of the employee's division as opposed to the company as a whole. The idea here is to more closely tie employee profit sharing to areas over which the employees have some control. Why should employees of General Electric's power systems division suffer because its NBC television division had a poor year?

profit sharing plans Pay plans that give employees some share of overall company profits

GAINSHARING PLANS. **Gainsharing plans** allow employees to share in company productivity gains or savings due to group, or team, efforts or recommendations. Typically work groups are charged with coming up with measures to lower company costs or improve company productivity, and any dollar savings or gains clearly achieved are then shared with the group.

gainsharing plans Plans for sharing company productivity gains or savings with the responsible work group

Benefits

Employee **benefits** such as health and life insurance are the nonwage or nonsalary portion of employee compensation and are today a very important and growing part of overall compensation packages. The explosive growth in employee benefits dates back to World War II. During the war, the federal government established a special War Labor Board and instituted wage controls to prevent runaway wage inflation (during this period you had a sharp increase in the demand for labor coupled with a sharp decrease in the supply of labor; millions of able-bodied men were in the military). Faced with the inability to gain significant increases in wages, employees and their unions came up with the idea of seeking comprehensive health, life, and other insurance benefits for their members. These benefits were not technically deemed to be wages and were apparently thus permissible under wartime regulations. In addition, federal tax laws gave, and continue to give, such insurance benefits very favorable treatment, generally allowing them to be treated as deductible expenses for employers but *not* as income for employees.

benefits The nonwage or nonsalary portion of employee compensation, such as health and life insurance

The upshot of all of this is that employer-paid insurance coverage, and especially comprehensive health care insurance, is today very much an important part of the total compensation package received by most employees. In addition, many employers offer employees a myriad of other benefits including vacation time, paid sick leave, child-care, pension or retirement plans, and even stock ownership or options plans. In recent years, some have argued that third-party insurance payment of employee medical care has helped lead to a surge in health care costs, and many companies like Wal-Mart are asking employees to directly pay at least a portion of health insurance costs.

Pension, or Retirement, Plans.

Recent scandals at Enron Corporation and other companies have brought considerable attention to the existence and viability of company pension benefits and plans.[8] There are basically two kinds of pension plans: **defined benefit plans** and **defined contribution plans.**

defined benefit plans Retirement plans where the benefit is based on a formula and precisely known

defined contribution plans Retirement plans where contributions are known but benefits may vary

Employee Retirement Income Security Act (ERISA) A federal law passed in 1974 to regulate employer-defined benefit plans

Pension Benefit Guaranty Corporation (PBGC) The federal agency administering the defined benefit plan insurance program

Defined benefit plans are generally fully funded by the employer and regulated by the federal government pursuant to the **Employee Retirement Income Security Act (ERISA).** The federal government, up to certain limits, insures these pension benefits even if the employee's company goes bankrupt, with the federal **Pension Benefit Guaranty Corporation (PBGC)** administering this insurance program in which employers pay insurance premiums to the PBGC. Employees receive defined benefit pensions based on the number of years they work at the employer and the wages or salaries they have received during that employment. A fairly common formula is that employees receive defined pension benefits of 2 percent per year multiplied by the employee's years of service multiplied by the average of the employee's last three years of wages or salaries. For example, if an employee worked for a company for 30 years, he or she would receive a defined annual pension for the rest of his or her life of 60 percent (2 percent times 30 years) of the average of his or her last three years' wages or salaries. If the last three years of the employee's wages or salaries averaged $50,000, the employee would receive an annual lifetime pension of $30,000. The employee bears no investment or other risk with respect to this pension. Under ERISA, all employees working for an employer with a defined benefit pension plan are generally vested in that pension plan after five to seven years on the job. Employees leaving that employer before vesting receive no retirement benefits.

Today, however, employees are probably more likely to work for an employer with a defined contribution pension plan, than for one with a defined benefit pension plan. Under defined contribution plans, a defined contribution is made into the pension plan, usually each pay period, by the employer or by the employer and employee jointly. For example, a plan may mandate that the employer contribute 8 percent of the employee's salary and the employee contribute 6 percent of her or his salary to the plan each monthly paycheck. Thus, if an employee makes $5,000 per month, $700 per paycheck ($400 from the employer and $300 from the employee) goes into the plan. The employee generally has a choice of a number of investment options for the monies (e.g., stock investments, bond investments, money market funds, etc.) and absorbs considerable risk if the investment choices turn out to be poor ones. Some companies have historically required, as Enron did, that all or a portion of the money the company contributes to the plan must be invested in the company's stock. In such situations, the investment returns of the pension plan will turn in good measure on how well the company and its stock perform.

reality CHECK *If you have a choice on a job, would you rather have a defined benefit or a defined contribution pension plan?*

stock options The right to buy company stock at a predetermined price

Stock or Stock Options.

A growing number of companies give employees company stock or **stock options** as a benefit. Stock and stock options grants are considerably different. Outright grants of stock make the employee a part owner in the company, and the value of the employee's holdings increases or decreases with the value of the company's shares. Stock options, on the other hand, give the employee the option of purchasing the company's stock at a given price. An option may give an employee the right to buy 200 shares of the company's stock at $15 a share for a period of five years. If the stock goes above $15, the employee can exercise the option and then sell the stock for a profit. If the company's stock, however, falls permanently to $5 per share, the option becomes worthless. Under this scenario, the employee has gained nothing, but he or she also has borne no risk.

Flexible, or Cafeteria, Benefit Plans. Historically, companies provided the same package of benefits to all employees. In recent years, though, there has been a growing realization by organizations that employees have different needs and that one standard benefits package may not be the best approach. In its stead, many companies have developed **flexible,** or **cafeteria, benefit plans** where each employee is generally given a set amount of dollars to spend on benefits and is then free to allocate the dollars to best meet his or her needs. A young single employee without any dependents but with considerable dental problems may, for example, decide to purchase zero life insurance and instead use this money to purchase the best dental insurance coverage possible.

> **flexible,** or **cafeteria, benefit plans** Plans giving employees considerable choice in picking the benefits they want

Developing an Effective Workforce

LEARNING OBJECTIVE 5
Analyze different methods for developing an effective workforce and providing workforce members with proper feedback.

Employee development has many aspects. Almost all organizations provide their employees with some sort of job training. This training can be on the job or off the job; indeed some large companies have even established their own universities. Virtually all organizations also help develop employees by providing feedback on their performance, more formally known as **performance appraisals.** First, though, organizations must figure out their precise needs in this area of HRM.

> **performance appraisals** Formal evaluations of the effectiveness of employees' job performance

Needs Analyses

Organizations differ, and it is important for given organizations to examine the knowledge, skills, and abilities needed to perform the organization's work effectively vis-à-vis the capabilities of the organization's existing workforce. **Needs analyses** involve making such assessments. Sometimes needs analyses can lead to pleasant surprises; for example, the current workforce is already well qualified, prepared, and motivated to effectively carry out the organization's mission. Frequently, though, needs analyses will reveal something in the capabilities of the existing workforce to be lacking, in which case the organization must figure out what types of employee development programs will best ameliorate this situation.

> **needs analyses** Assessments of an organization's job-related needs and the abilities of the current workforce

Methods for Developing an Effective Workforce

Work-Based Programs. **Work-based programs** tie employee development activities directly to the work to be done. For example, a professor who has already taught a class may be asked to assist a professor who is going to be teaching the class for the first time with developing teaching materials, and so on. In certain

> **work-based programs** Programs that tie employee development activities directly to task performance

types of jobs, particularly those involving skilled trades such as carpentry and plumbing, employees often do apprenticeships where they work closely with an experienced skilled tradesperson for a number of years in order to effectively learn the job. Some workers receive work-based training in simulated environments away from the actual workplace. For example, most major airlines use flight simulators so that pilots can effectively develop their skills. Simulated environment training of this kind is known as **vestibule training,** and it can be an extremely effective work-based human resource development method.

vestibule training Employee training provided in a simulated environment close to the actual work situation

Instructional-Based Programs.

Instructional-based programs for workforce development involve training designed to provide new knowledge or information. Some large corporations have started their own universities where students or employees of the organization attend lectures and participate in discussions. Computer software allows some of this type of employee instruction to be done at times most convenient for the employee and at his or her own pace.

instructional-based programs Teaching and learning approaches to employee development

New Workforce Development Technology.

New technology beyond the basic personal computer and computer software has been an enormous aid in helping companies develop their workforces. Interactive video, video teleconferencing, and the Internet all offer myriad ways of better training and developing employees.

Feedback and Performance Appraisal and Evaluation

A critical part of effective workforce development in an organization is having an effective program of employee feedback and performance appraisal and evaluation. Employees need to be kept regularly apprised as to how they're doing, that is, be given feedback and opportunities to correct or improve their performance where it is lacking. Employees should also be rewarded and recognized for good performance. The performance feedback and appraisal and evaluation process is in many ways analogous to receiving grades in college courses and involves many of the same complications and issues.

Objective Evaluation Methods.

Some jobs (and college classes!) lend themselves well to **objective evaluation methods.** A salesperson, for example, is likely to be evaluated on how many dollars worth of sales he or she made during a given period—an extremely straightforward method of evaluation. Similarly, a college physical education class may be graded on a pass or fail basis with attendance the only criterion for evaluation; more than one unexcused absence per semester means the student fails the class. One key advantage of objective evaluation methods is that they are easily measured and generally seen as fair. The fact that a professor or supervisor may like or dislike you has virtually no bearing: either you've sold products during the past year or not; either you are or you're not attending the class.

objective evaluation methods Performance appraisals based on specific and clear criteria such as sales mode

Subjective Evaluation Methods.

For better or worse, however, most jobs and college classes do not lend themselves to such easy objective evaluation and instead require **subjective evaluation methods.** In the classroom, for example, a professor may have to evaluate a wide variety of class presentations, term papers on different topics, and individual student class participation. Similarly, most jobs are multifaceted, with any effective performance evaluation involving looking at a

subjective evaluation methods Performance appraisals based on less-well-defined criteria.

significant number of employee activities. This is particularly true as our society has moved away from manufacturing to service. One obvious concern with the more multifaceted subjective evaluations involved in measuring things like employee service effectiveness, student class participation, and so on, is the possibility of bias on the part of the individual making the evaluation. Various civil rights laws protect employees (similar but different laws protect students) against any evaluator bias based on race, religion, gender, national origin, and so on. Nevertheless, it is probably impossible to completely prevent all elements of bias, positive or negative, from entering into subjective performance evaluations.

In the college classroom, most faculty carry out the evaluation process by giving students grades. Somewhat similar grading dynamics are generally used in the workplace. One university, for example, annually grades the overall performance of all its faculty as excellent, satisfactory, or unsatisfactory. A common issue is how many gradations there should be in the grading process. For example, some companies rank their employees' performance using six different gradations: distinguished, excellent, good, satisfactory, marginally satisfactory, and unsatisfactory; and many colleges use pluses and minuses to more fine-tune their traditional A, B, C grades.

Forced Evaluation Distributions.

In many organizations, there has been an increased use of **forced distribution methods** of evaluation in which employees are grouped into predefined distributions, or frequencies, of performance ratings. For example, the Enron Corporation, under former CEO Kenneth Lay and former president Jeffrey Skilling, force-ranked employees into one of five groups. The top-performing 15 percent of employees were placed in group 1, the next 20% in group 2, the next 25% in group 3, the next 25% in group 4, and the bottom 15% in group 5.[9] In a college course, a predetermined grading curve, where only the top 15% of the class gets an A and the bottom 15% of the class must get either a grade of D or F, would represent a similar distribution.

forced distribution methods Performance appraisals requiring a defined ranking of performance into different levels

There are obviously pros and cons to having forced evaluation distributions. Forced distributions will likely tend to make employees and students more cutthroat in their competition. Forced distributions clearly have a win-lose element to them; not all individuals can do well under a forced distribution system, even if all employees are generally performing well. Also, at times employee performance levels may be very similar, and a forced distribution system may force distinctions that don't exist to be made among employees. The good thing about forced distribution evaluation systems is that they deal very directly with the problem of grade inflation. Just as some professors give As and Bs to nearly all students in their college classes, some work supervisors also tend to grade very highly, even when all employees are not doing a spectacular job. Such grade inflation may hurt employees by not giving them accurate feedback, and it clearly hurts the organization by potentially rewarding employees who are not doing great jobs. Grade inflation may also create some resentment from employees who are working very hard and doing very good jobs, but who end up getting the same or close to the same grade as all other employees.

360-Degree Feedback.

Traditionally, performance feedback and evaluation has been top-down; that is, the boss evaluates the employee or the professor evaluates the student. Increasingly, though, organizations are using full-circle, or **360-degree, feedback,** where employees are evaluated not only by their boss but also by their peers, subordinates, and so on. Indeed, sometimes 360-degree feedback even includes evaluations from customers and others outside the organization. In the classroom

360-degree feedback Full-circle evaluation of an employee by supervisor, peers, subordinates, and so on

setting, a feedback system of this kind may involve students being evaluated regarding class participation, team project work, and so on, by other students, and students preparing teaching evaluations of the professor, in addition to the traditional model of the professor evaluating the student's work. While there are various pros and cons to 360-degree feedback, it probably is sometimes true that bosses being graded by their subordinates may be a little more gentle in grading their subordinates or professors may give students high grades in the hope that they will be evaluated highly by students. Consequently, stronger arguments may exist for forced distribution evaluation systems where 360-degree feedback mechanisms are also in place.

Feedback Frequency and Follow-Up.   In order for performance appraisal feedback programs to be effective in helping develop an effective workforce, they have to be conducted with some degree of frequency and involve follow-up. Supervisors in most organizations provide employees informal feedback on an ongoing basis, and open communication channels should be encouraged. Organizations should also have regular formal feedback where employees receive formal developmental feedback and evaluation at least once a year.

Follow-up is also extremely important if the performance appraisal process is going to be developmentally effective. For example, an employee and supervisor may be advised to develop an action plan for the employee's future. If the employee is already doing outstanding A+ work, this plan may focus on opportunities for the employee to be promoted or advanced. Most employees, though, are not A+ employees, and most feedback action plans will focus on how the given employee may be able to improve his or her performance and contribution to the organization. In situations where the employee's performance is unsatisfactory or even just marginally satisfactory, it will be important for the supervisor to discuss with the employee the possibility of disciplinary action, perhaps even discharge, if the employee does not take prompt corrective action.

reality CHECK   *Do you have any ideas for combating the grade inflation that occurs so frequently in employee performance evaluations? Have you ever received a performance evaluation that was higher than you thought you deserved?*

Labor–Management Relations

LEARNING OBJECTIVE 6
Describe the role of the National Labor Relations Act in abolishing company unions and the process by which "real" unions come into power and engage in collective bargaining.

Historical Overview

Early History.   The laissez-faire economic climate of the United States in the nineteenth century and early twentieth century was not a hospitable one for labor unions. Limited state laws protecting employees from being fired or otherwise discriminated against because of their interest in having a union were struck down by the U.S. Supreme Court as representing unconstitutional interferences with employer rights.[10] The time's emphasis on rugged individualism was encapsulated by the widespread legal adoption of the doctrine of **employment-at-will,** a doctrine first set forth in an academic treatise in 1877.[11] Under the employment-at-will doctrine, employees can quit their job at any time for any reason, and conversely, employers can fire employees at any time for any reason. Employees did not see the need for collective action via unionization during this period of free market individualism.

employment-at-will Legal rule stating that an employer can fire an employee at any time for any reason, and an employee can quit at any time

The Great Depression and the New Deal.

The stock market crash of 1929 and the ensuing Great Depression resulted in massive structural unemployment and a dramatic shift in the role of unions in the United States. With millions of individuals unable to find any sort of work, laissez-faire parity between employers and employees seemed inappropriate, and President Franklin Roosevelt's New Deal administration asked Congress to enact various pieces of pro-worker legislation. The first major piece of such legislation passed by Congress was the **Norris–La Guardia Act** of 1932. This law sharply limited the ability of employers to get judicial assistance in stopping strikes and made the **yellow dog contract** illegal. Yellow dog contracts were contracts signed by employees where they agreed not to join a union during the term of their employment with the employer.

Norris–La Guardia Act New Deal legislation of 1932 limiting employer rights

yellow dog contract Employment contract where employee agrees not to join a union

In 1935, Congress enacted the original **National Labor Relations Act (NLRA),** or Wagner Act, legislation also known as the Magna Carta of American labor. This law for the first time clearly made labor unions lawful in the United States. Indeed, this law as enacted in 1935 directly *encouraged* employee unionization and collective bargaining. The idea, at the time, was that only by grouping together and forming labor unions could employees overcome their relatively powerless situation and have parity with employers. The NLRA set forth detailed procedures whereby employees could form labor unions and engage in collective bargaining with their employers and established an administrative agency, the **National Labor Relations Board (NLRB),** to administer the law. Shortly after the enactment of the NLRA, Congress in 1938 passed the Fair Labor Standards Act, which set an initial floor on wages of 25 cents per hour as a minimum wage, limited the number of hours employees could work without overtime pay, and outlawed most child labor.

National Labor Relations Act (NLRA) A federal law of 1935 establishing employee right to unionize

National Labor Relations Board (NLRB) The federal agency with regulatory authority over U.S. labor laws

Abolishing and Preventing Company Unions.

When it legalized and encouraged unionization with the passage of the NLRA in 1935, Congress feared that employers would try to set up employer-supported unions, or so-called **company unions.** These unions, while giving employees some voice, can never engage in arms-length collective bargaining since they are supported and controlled to some extent by the employer. To abolish and prevent the existence of company unions and to encourage the establishment of "real" unions, the Wagner Act contained a specific section, Section 8(a)(2), which states that it is unlawful for an employer to "dominate or interfere with the formation or administration of any labor organization or contribute financial or other support [to] it."[12] Moreover, the law also defines the term **labor organization** quite broadly, so as to include any sort of employee committee that deals with the employer about working conditions.[13] Historically, this provision played an important role in the establishment of unionization throughout the country. More recently, though, Section 8(a)(2) has come under considerable criticism because its language can be read to outlaw employee programs established by companies such as work teams, quality circles, and so on. Efforts to date to amend the legislation, however, have been unsuccessful.

company unions Unions that are supported and dominated by the employer

labor organization Any sort of employee organization that deals with the employer about working conditions

Organizing Employees and Electing Unions.

Once the NLRA was enacted in 1935 and declared constitutional by the U.S. Supreme Court in 1937, unionization took off like a wildfire throughout the United States. The first step in the unionizing process is for a union to identify a particular group of employees it seeks to have join its ranks. For example, a union may target the employees of the Wal-Mart store in a given town. This group of employees becomes the proposed **bargaining unit,** or the designated group of employees who will be represented by the union. In order to proceed with its organizing efforts, the union must obtain signed authorization cards, that is, cards stating that the designated employees are interested in being

bargaining unit The specifically defined group of employees eligible for union representation

represented by a union, from at least 30 percent of the employees in the proposed bargaining unit. If the Wal-Mart store has 99 employees, at least 30 must sign authorization cards in order for the union to proceed to the next step. If the union gets this 30 percent show of interest, the union takes these cards to the NLRB, and the next step is for the NLRB to schedule a supervised secret ballot election in that bargaining unit.

There are numerous rules and regulations regarding what unions and employers can say and do during the organizing process and during the election campaign period, which begins when the union documents it has a 30 percent showing of interest in the designated employee group, and ends at the final tally of the NLRB supervised secret ballot election. Unions generally can not organize or campaign on the employer's property, even its parking lot. Unions are, however, permitted to organize and campaign by visiting employees at their homes, while it is unlawful for employers to do so. Neither unions nor employers can threaten employees during labor representation election campaigns, although at times it has been difficult to define what precisely is a threat. Employers obviously cannot discriminate against employees who are union supporters, that is, fire or demote them.

Majority Vote Exclusive Representation.

Union representation elections conducted by the NLRB are analogous to U.S. political elections in that majority vote governs their outcome and they involve winner-take-all scenarios. For the Wal-Mart store with 99 employees, if 50 of these employees vote for the union, the union wins and becomes the representative of *all* 99 employees. However, if only 49 employees vote for the union, the union loses and represents no one, and cannot even make another election try here for at least one year. Similarly, if a candidate for governor of Massachusetts wins 51 percent of the vote, he or she becomes governor of all the people in the state for a requisite period of time, while the losing candidate with 49 percent of the vote ends up with nothing.

A winning union at the Wal-Mart store represents all 99 employees at the store. Indeed, it now becomes the exclusive representative of all these employees; the employees are now generally required to work through the union in dealing with the employer. The union is also under a specific **duty of fair representation** to all these employees. This means that the union must fairly represent all the employees and not discriminate among employees while engaged in collective bargaining, grievance handling, and so on. For example, a union may not seek pay raises for employees who supported it and not for those who did not. A major related question, of course, is whether all 99 employees must now join or pay dues to the union given the fact that the union has the duty to work nondiscriminately on behalf of all of them. Whether employees have to pay union dues is determined by what state of the United States they live in.

> **duty of fair representation** The duty of a union to fairly represent all employees in its bargaining unit

Collective Bargaining

Winning a union representation election, while an achievement, is not the final goal of any union. The final goal is being able to successfully negotiate with the employer a favorable labor contract for the employees. The NLRA requires employers to sit down with the elected union representative of the employees and bargain in good faith regarding "wages, hours, and other terms and conditions of employment."[14] The law hopes that the parties sign a contract, but clearly does not compel either party to agree or make any concessions.

Defining **good faith bargaining** has proven somewhat problematic over the years, as has determining what subjects constitute the mandatory "wages, hours, and other terms and conditions of employment" bargaining topics. Figuring out what the "other terms and conditions of employment" that must be bargained over are has been particularly vexing. Is the price of food in the company cafeteria a

> **good faith bargaining** The duty of employers and unions to bargain with each other honestly

term and condition of employment? What about an employer decision to contract out janitorial work or hire a new advertising agency? The parties are free to negotiate or bargain over almost anything, but whether a given topic has to be bargained over is unclear and important; unions can only lawfully go on strike over mandatory bargaining issues.

The Labor Contract and "Just Cause" Protection.

If collective bargaining is successful, the parties agree to a labor contract. Such contracts are typically for a term of three years and comprehensively regulate virtually all aspects of employee–employer relations during this time period. Among the topics generally covered by labor contracts are wage rates, overtime pay rates, vacation time, rest periods, working hours, and pension plans. Most labor contracts also usually deal with standards for employee promotions and layoffs, placing considerable weight on employee seniority, or length of service with the employer, in making such determinations.

Perhaps the two most critical sections in nearly all labor contracts—the no-strike clause and the grievance procedure clause—represent something of a trade-off. These provisions address what happens when a dispute arises regarding the contract during its term. In general, if the union agrees not to go on strike over such disputes during the contract's term—the no-strike clause—the employer agrees to a defined procedure to resolve the disputes—the grievance procedure clause. In virtually all cases the last step of the labor contract's grievance procedure is **labor arbitration,** which involves calling in an independent outside party—a professor, a member of the clergy, and so on—to resolve the dispute. Decisions regarding contract interpretation by outside labor arbitrators have been uniformly held by the courts to be binding.

labor arbitration The resolution of a labor dispute by a neutral outside third party

Within a labor contract's grievance procedure, the most important section is the **just cause provision.** This provision states that under the contract the employer can discharge, suspend, or discipline an employee only for "just cause." That does not mean that employers can never fire or discipline an employee. For example, if an employee is found to have stolen goods or money from the employer, just cause for discharge certainly exists. It does mean, however, that an employer must articulate a clear business-related reason for a discharge or other disciplinary action.

just cause provision The labor contract provision stating that an employer can only fire or discharge an employee for a legitimate business reason

For example, an employer working under a labor contract with a just cause provision cannot fire an employee for wearing a green shirt to work on the grounds that the employer does not like the color green. A labor arbitrator hearing such a case would rule that the employer had no clear business-related reason, no just cause, for such an action.

Despite their general decline, labor unions still remain important in many key industries. After signing the 2003–2007 UAW-GM collective bargaining agreement for GM employees, United Auto Workers (UAW) Union president Ron Gettelfinger (left) shakes hands with General Motors Corporation (GM) president Rick Wagoner (right).

Union-negotiated labor contracts with just cause provisions represent the antithesis of the doctrine of employment-at-will. Under the employment-at-will doctrine, employers can fire or discipline employees at any time for *any* reason, including not liking the color green! The just cause protection brought to workers by unions via negotiated labor contracts has historically been a very important one indeed.

The Decline of Unions

Union power grew enormously between the enactment of the Wagner Act in 1935 and the end of World War II in 1945, with unions representing close to 40 percent of the nonagricultural workforce by the end of the war. During the war, however, unions began sowing the seeds of their own demise. Some unions ignored war labor regulations against going on strike and otherwise pushed the envelope, so that by the end of the war many in the U.S. Congress felt that the power of unions had to be cut back. This feeling led to the enactment in 1947, over multiple vetoes by President Harry S Truman, of the **Taft-Hartley Act** amending the NLRA.

Taft-Hartley Act A federal law of 1947 cutting back on the power of labor unions

The Taft-Hartley Act, known to unions as the Slave Labor Act, sharply curtailed the power of unions in the United States. Officially, these amendments to the original NLRA put the U.S. government in a neutral posture regarding whether employees should join unions, as opposed to the law's initial posture of encouraging unionization. Indeed, Section 7 of the NLRA was specifically amended to state that not only did employees have the right to join unions, but they also had the right to *refrain* from joining unions. The new amendments allowed individual states to pass **right-to-work laws,** and close to half of the states in the United States (see Exhibit 6.1) have passed such legislation. Under right-to-work laws, employees in the states with such legislation have the right to work without paying any union dues or fees, even if the union has won a bona fide representation election at their workplace. These laws operate as a disincentive for unions to organize in the states that have them because they mean that a union can win an election in those states and come under a duty to represent certain employees but that these employees do not have to pay any dues or fees to the union. In short, unions are at risk of losing considerable money when they organize in right-to-work states; in non-right-to-work states unionized employees are generally required to pay at least a service fee to the union for its representation efforts. Right-to-work states tend to be the more conservative states in the southern and western parts of the United States.

right-to-work laws Laws allowing workers represented by unions the right to be employed without paying dues to the union

EXHIBIT 6.1

Right-to-Work States

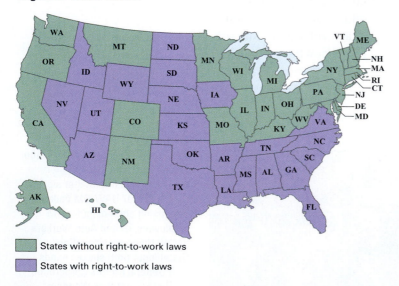

■ States without right-to-work laws

■ States with right-to-work laws

The Taft-Hartley Act also made a number of union practices unlawful and gave the president of the United States special powers to resolve union strikes, such as the October, 2002, longshore worker strikes at ports on the West Coast, deemed to be posing a national emergency. In 1959, after a series of congressional hearings revealing unethical practices by labor unions, the U.S. Congress further regulated union power with the enactment of the **Landrum Griffin Act** of 1959, which further amended the NLRA. The Landrum Griffin Act gives the U.S. Department of Labor broad supervisory power over the internal workings of labor unions. All union expenditures, for example, must be reported to the Labor Department, and the Labor Department also plays a role in supervising elections for union officers.

Landrum Griffin Act A federal law of 1959 regulating internal union activities

While the Taft-Hartley and Landrum Griffin Acts have played a role in the decline of unions, they don't tell the whole story. Shifts in the focus of the U.S. economy have also played a part in the decline of unionization in the country. Moreover, the strong resistance by some employers to unions and collective bargaining contracts has clearly not helped their situation. Finally, some observers, even in the union movement, have said that the unions themselves over the years had become too complacent in their organizing efforts. When all is said and done, though, unions over the past half century or so have gone from being a central part of human resources management in the United States to being a still important but far less significant factor.

International Labor Relations

Interestingly, the decline in the role of labor unions in the United States has not been fully emulated in various other countries with developed economies. In other countries such as Great Britain, the labor movement has historically been much more directly integrated into the political process than in the United States. Indeed, in Britain one of the two major political parties is the Labor Party, and this has clearly helped British unions gain broader cultural and community acceptance than in the United States.

Other countries, such as Germany and Canada, continue to have relatively more pro-union labor laws on their books. Under German codetermination, for example, all large employers are required to have union representatives on their company boards of directors.

One important issue that has arisen lately is the interrelationship between labor relations/laws and international free trade agreements. If countries agree to a free trade agreement or free trade zone, to what extent do the labor laws in one country apply to the other countries that are part of the agreement? Also, to what extent do free trade agreements with lower-wage-paying countries encourage the movement of jobs from the United States to those countries? These were highly contentious issues during the negotiations among the United States, Canada, and Mexico on the North American Free Trade Agreement (NAFTA). Ultimately, a special labor side agreement to NAFTA was agreed to; it provides that each country must make efforts to enforce its own labor laws and establishes a new enforcement mechanism whereby citizens and groups can complain about the lack of labor rights enforcement in the three NAFTA countries. The NAFTA labor side agreement also establishes a North America Commission on Labor Cooperation, now based in Washington, D.C., which promotes cooperative labor activities among the signatory countries. In more recent U.S. free trade agreements with countries like Chile, Singapore, and Jordan, however, the special labor side agreement model has been abandoned in favor of directly addressing labor issues in the text of the agreement itself. The loss of U.S. jobs to countries we have free trade agreements with continues to be a very important and difficult issue to address.

reality CHECK *Do you know any individuals who are members of private sector unions? What about members of public sector, or government employee unions?*

Legal Environment of Human Resources Management

LEARNING OBJECTIVE 7
Discuss how and why the field of human resources management has become so highly legally regulated, especially by the federal government, in recent decades.

Employment-at-Will Revisited

The decline of unions and collective bargaining contracts that began in 1947 with the enactment of the Taft-Hartley Act put millions of U.S. private sector workers back under the regime of employment-at-will. Whereas previously unions had negotiated with employers regarding issues like job safety, pension benefits, workplace, sick leave, the impact of plant closures, and even age, disability, and other discrimination in the workplace, these issues now came completely under the authority of the employer. Also, without the just cause protection of labor contract grievance procedures, employees could now be fired or disciplined by employers for any or no reason whatsoever.

Government, or public sector, employees are entitled to fairly broad constitutional workplace protections. In addition, in direct contrast to the private sector, the rate of unionization among these employees has increased dramatically during the past few decades. Public sector unionization is regulated by special laws and not by the NLRA.

Private sector workers, however, were not ready to accept a total return to the laissez-faire employment regulation policies of the nineteenth century and began pressing both federal and state legislative bodies for action. The result, over the past four decades, has been a virtual explosion of government, especially federal government, regulation of the workplace. The U.S. Congress has since the early 1960s, right after the anti-union Landrum Griffin Act of 1959, passed at least ten major pieces of legislation regulating or affecting human resources management. These are listed in Exhibit 6.2. Moreover, various state legislatures have also passed laws in this area, and state court judges have been particularly active in cutting back on the doctrine of employment-at-will.

EXHIBIT 6.2

Post–1960 Federal Legislation Affecting Human Resources Management

Law	Scope
Equal Pay Act (1963)	Mandates that men and women doing equal jobs must be paid the same wage
Title VII of the Civil Rights Act of 1964	Outlaws discrimination in employment practices based on race, sex, color, religion, or national origin
Age Discrimination in Employment Act (1967 and 1986)	Prohibits human resource practices that discriminate against people aged 40 and older, and 1986 amendments eliminate mandatory retirement age for most all individuals
Occupational Safety and Health Act (1970)	Regulates safety in U.S. workplaces
Employment Retirement Income Security Act (1974)	Regulates private employer defined benefit pension plans and establishes a federal insurance program for such plans
Pregnancy Discrimination Act (1978)	Prohibits discrimination against employees on the basis of their pregnancy
Worker Adjustment and Retraining Notification (WARN) Act of 1988	Requires employers to give employees 60 days notice of plant closure or layoff if 50 or more employees
Americans with Disabilities Act (1990)	Prohibits discrimination in employment practices with respect to qualified individuals with disabilities
Civil Rights Act (1991)	Expands rights of employees to sue and collect damages under the Civil Rights Act of 1964
Family and Medical Leave Act (1993)	Requires employers with 50 or more employees to provide employees with up to 12 weeks of unpaid leave for specified family or medical reasons

Federal Legislation After 1960

Equal Pay Act. The Equal Pay Act prohibits unequal pay for men and women doing equal work. Equal work means jobs that require equal skill, effort, training, and responsibility and are performed under the same working conditions. For example, this law would require that men and women graduating from the same college with a bachelor's degree in accounting and taking the same job with the same large accounting firm be paid the same. While this seems obvious today, it was not so obvious forty or so years ago. At that time it was not unknown for employers to pay female college graduates doing the same job as males less on the grounds that they weren't supporting families or that they would be leaving the workforce soon to have families. The Equal Pay Act does permit some limited exceptions to its mandates; for example, male and female pay differentials are allowed where they are based on quantity of job production. The Equal Pay Act does not address the issue of male and female pay differentials where jobs are different but deemed to be of equal worth, that is, the issue of comparable worth.

Civil Rights Act of 1964. This watershed piece of federal legislation prohibits organizations with 15 or more employees from in any way discriminating against their employees on the basis of race, sex, color, religion, or national origin. This law covers all aspects of human resources management from selection and recruitment to promotions, compensation, access to training, discipline, and discharge. This law is administered by the **Equal Employment Opportunity Commission (EEOC),** which has offices throughout the United States. The EEOC investigates employment discrimination complaints and can take cases it feels meritorious to federal court or give the complainant the authority to take his or her case to federal court on his or her own. In recent years the EEOC has placed an emphasis on trying to conciliate or mediate many of the complaints it receives, as a way of dealing with its burgeoning caseload.

Equal Employment Opportunity Commission (EEOC) The federal agency that administers U.S. employment discrimination laws

Age Discrimination Act of 1967. This law, as amended in 1986, outlaws discrimination against Americans over 40 and most company mandatory retirement policies (certain types of employees like airline pilots can still be forced to retire at

Female employees, led by Betty Dukes (right), have recently filed a major class-action lawsuit against the Wal-Mart Corporation. The suit alleges widespread company sex discrimination in violation of the Civil Rights Act of 1964. Wal-Mart is the nation's largest private sector employer and the outcome of this case will be watched closely by human resources professionals throughout the country.

certain ages). This law has become more important as the workforce has aged, and the end of mandatory retirement has had a tremendous impact on U.S. workforce demographics. Interestingly, this law does not prohibit age-based discrimination with respect to workers younger than 40, although some states like New Jersey have passed laws protecting employees of all ages against age discrimination.

Occupational Safety and Health Act of 1970. This law mandates that employers keep records regarding workplace accidents and submit to random federal government work site safety inspections. It also regulates the types of safety equipment employers must provide employees. Firms found to be in violation of federal health and safety standards can be fined or even shut down. This law is administered by the U.S. Department of Labor.

Employment Retirement Security Act of 1974. This law regulates employee defined benefit pension plans. While it does not require that employers have pension plans, it does bring existing defined benefit pension plans under strict federal government regulation. Pursuant to ERISA, employees participating in pension plans vest within a prescribed number of years and are provided insurance against the loss of benefits under the plan. The Pension Benefit Guaranty Corporation administers the insurance program. ERISA also regulates how the investment funds of the pension plans are managed and makes sure that the interests of the employee beneficiaries are the top management concern.

Pregnancy Discrimination Act of 1978. This law states that pregnant individuals are protected under U.S. discrimination laws. More specifically, the law states that pregnancy is a disability and qualifies pregnant women to receive the same benefits they would with any other type of disability.

WARN Act of 1988. This law requires employers to give employees at least 60 days notice of plant closures. Employers must also give similar notice if they are going to lay off 50 or more employees. The law was enacted in response to a rash of company plant closures and layoffs in the 1980s that were made without virtually any notice to employees. The U.S. Department of Labor now regulates these procedures.

Americans with Disabilities Act of 1990. This landmark piece of federal legislation, administered by the EEOC, prohibits employment discrimination against individuals with disabilities. It defines a person with a disability as:

> Prong One. A person with a physical or mental impairment that substantially limits one or more major life activities or
> Prong Two. A person with a record of such a physical or mental impairment or
> Prong Three. A person who is regarded as having such an impairment[15]

The Prong One definition of disability is relatively easy to understand. It applies to individuals who suffer current impairments that substantially limit their present life activities. For example, the golfer Casey Martin has a degenerative condition in his right leg that substantially limits his ability to walk. The U.S. Supreme Court, in Martin's lawsuit against the Professional Golf Association (PGA), found him to be protected by the Americans with Disabilities Act (ADA) and allowed him to use a golf cart rather than walk as required under PGA rules when participating in PGA golf tournaments.[16]

Prong Two of the ADA's definition of disability is a little more subtle in that it protects persons having records of a disability, even if they no longer have the disability. For example, the ADA prohibits not hiring or promoting an individual who previously had cancer but is now cured.

Prong Three protects people who are regarded as having an impairment even though this is not the case. For example, the ADA prohibits an employer not promoting an employee because of a rumor that the employee has been infected with the human immunodeficiency virus (HIV).

Family and Medical Leave Act of 1993.   This law passed in 1993 requires organizations with 50 or more employees to provide employees who have worked at least 1250 hours during the prior 12 months up to 12 weeks of *unpaid* leave on the birth or adoption of a child or if the employee or his or her spouse, child, or parent is seriously ill. Despite the fact that the required leave is unpaid, a number of business organizations lobbied strenuously against this legislation on the grounds that it would lead to considerable work scheduling and other problems. Even so, there have been numerous proposals to broaden the scope of the Family and Medical Leave Act (FMLA) to allow employees to take time off for family events other than births or illnesses.

State Regulation

There has also during the past few decades been an increase in state regulation of HRM. State regulation has come by way of both state laws and state court decisions.

Employment-at-Will.   During the past few decades state courts throughout the country have been chipping away at the doctrine of employment-at-will on a case-by-case basis. Indeed, today the majority of state courts recognize a public policy exception to this doctrine. For example, numerous courts have intervened where employers have fired employees for being out on jury duty; remember, under the strict employment-at-will doctrine, an employer can fire an employee for any reason at any time. In essence, these courts have held that the public policy in favor of jury trials outweighs the employer's right to fire an employee. The state of Montana has enacted a state law comprehensively protecting employees from wrongful discharge, and thus statutorily overturning the doctrine of employment-at-will in that state. The **Montana Wrongful Discharge from Employment Act** states that an employer's discharge of an employee is wrongful, or unlawful, if it was against public policy, in violation of the employer's written personnel policy, or not for good cause providing that the employee has passed the employer's workplace probationary period.[17] The good cause provision in the Montana statute is very similar to that in union labor contracts. Thus, the Montana Wrongful Discharge from Employment Act gives all employees in that state very broad protection from being fired by employers for nonlegitimate business reasons.

Montana Wrongful Discharge from Employment Act A law in the state of Montana outlawing the doctrine of employment-at-will

Off-Duty Conduct Statutes.   The vast majority of states in the United States have also passed laws protecting employees from being discriminated against by employers because of their lawful off-duty conduct. Interestingly, these **off-duty conduct statutes** started being widely enacted in the 1980s because of strong lobbying by the tobacco industry, which had become very concerned that employees were not being hired or were even being fired because they were smokers. As a result, most states today have laws that at least protect employees from any adverse employment action due to their off-duty use of tobacco and other lawful products.

off-duty conduct statutes State laws protecting in various degrees employee off-duty conduct

Ethics in Business

Workplace Ethics: The Issue of Coworker Dating

The issue of coworker dating is a very important one in today's workplace. During World War II women entered the workforce in a major way and have remained there ever since. Indeed, today around half of all U.S. workers are female. The influx of females into the workplace, coupled with later marriages, increased divorces, and long work hours, has led to a natural increase in people viewing work as a place to meet people to date. Indeed, it has been estimated that in the United States today about *one-third* of all dating relationships start at work.

But coworker dating creates a significant number of HRM and even ethical problems for employers. For one, can there ever be truly consensual dating when one of the dating parties is the other party's supervisor? Moreover, isn't it possible for even a truly consensual relationship, not marked by any power differentials between the parties, to break down and lead to strained relationships at work or even a sexual harassment claim? What about office gossip and claims of possible company favoritism toward employees engaged in certain coworker dating relationships? What about the employer's professional image? Can a high enough level of coworker dating lead external constituencies to view the given organization as being unprofessional?

All of these concerns, though, are juxtaposed against the fact that forces of nature being as they are, coworker dating is probably always going to exist. If an employer completely prohibits all coworker dating, it's likely to still continue, but now to be underground and perhaps create even more problems later. Moreover, employees do have privacy rights, some protected by state statute. For example,

in New York State all employee off-duty legal recreational activity is protected by law, and the question has thus arisen whether coworker dating represents "recreational activity"!

Some employers have responded to this complex issue by allowing all coworker dating but mandating that employees immediately disclose their relationship to the employer and sign dating waivers. Dating waivers are legal forms where the dating employees attest that their dating is truly consensual and waive their rights to bring any future sexual harassment or other claims because of the relationship. Other employers permit coworker dating, but strictly prohibit any dating between supervisors and subordinates. Finally, some employers simply outlaw, to the extent legally possible in the given states where they operate, all coworker dating. What do you think is the best approach to this difficult issue?

Sources: Stephanie Armour, "Romance at Work Tricky to Manage: Even Consensual Relationships Can Hurt Morale," *USA Today*, January 23, 1998, p. B2; Michelle Conklin, "Love on the Job: Liaisons Can Be Tricky, But Good for a Company," *Rocky Mountain News*, February 22, 1998, p. 2G; Lisa Black, "Power Imbalance Is the Key to Most Policies on Sex," *Chicago Tribune*, January 29, 1998, p. 1; *State v. Wal-Mart Stores, Inc.*, 621 N.Y. 2d 158 (N.Y. Ct. App. 1995); Andrea Minarcek, "Taboo on Office Romance Fading," June 29, 2004, Cox News Service, **www.azcentral.com.**

Questions

1. Why is it difficult for a dating relationship with a supervisor to ever be truly consensual?
2. What types of favoritism might be afforded employees engaged in workplace dating relationships? What ethical issues does such favoritism present?
3. Do you think dating waiver forms make sense?

A handful of states have gone even further and protect employees from adverse employment action because of any lawful off-duty activities.

reality CHECK *Which federal employment law enacted during the past half century has had the most impact on your working life?*

Workplace Diversity

Bob Dylan's famous lyric "The times they are a-changin'" applies more than anywhere in the area of workplace diversity. Today women constitute around half of the U.S. workforce, and the various antidiscrimination laws have played a significant role in increasing workplace participation by a wide range of minority groups.

Case in Point

Workforce Diversity at McDonald's

The McDonald's Corporation is strongly committed to workforce diversity, and indeed to diversity with respect to all its various stakeholder groups, franchisees, suppliers, and so on. Its mission with respect to corporate diversity is to "leverage the unique talents, strengths and assets of our diversity in order to be the world's best quick service restaurant experience." To achieve this mission, the company has a clear vision of ensuring that its employees "reflect and represent the diverse populations McDonald's serves around the world." The company has a wide-ranging diversity education program including special seminars on topics such as female, Hispanic, African American, and Asian career development. In fostering its workplace diversity, McDonald's has established close relationships with a wide range of groups including the National Urban League, the National

Council of La Raza, the NAACP, and the Rainbow/Push Coalition. McDonald's has won numerous awards for its workforce diversity efforts, including being named the Best Employer for Asians and as one of the Top 25 Companies for People with Disabilities.

Source: **http://www.McDonalds.com/corporatediversity**.

Questions

1. Why is workforce diversity so important to a company like McDonald's?
2. What are some financial mechanisms McDonald's might use to achieve better franchise diversity?
3. What are some specific approaches McDonald's might take to develop even closer relationships with groups like the NAACP and the National Council of La Raza?

Having a highly diverse workforce, though, arguably has both pros and cons and raises a number of important issues.

Advantages and Challenges of a Diverse Workforce

There are numerous obvious advantages to having a diverse workforce. Clearly a highly diverse workforce can bring very helpful insights into marketing goods to a highly diverse customer base. A diverse workforce may also be more creative and innovative than a more homogeneous one. On the negative side of things, however, a diverse workforce may be less cohesive and have more communication problems than a homogenous work group. In addition, there may be some mistrust and tension in a diverse workforce, especially if some colleagues are seen as having gotten their jobs through preferential treatment.

LEARNING OBJECTIVE 8
Analyze the difference between equal employment opportunity and affirmative action, the impact of this difference on workplace diversity, and recent developments in affirmative action and workplace diversity.

Equal Employment Opportunity Versus Affirmative Action

Laws such as Title VII of the Civil Rights Act of 1964 are equal employment opportunity laws; they are laws that mandate that employees of all kinds of backgrounds be treated equally in the workplace. The concept of **equal employment opportunity** is considerably different, though, from the concept of **affirmative action.** Affirmative action involves an organization taking special steps to recruit, hire, and

equal employment opportunity The principle that all groups of employees should be treated equally in the employment relationship

affirmative action The principle that some groups of employees should receive a degree of preference in the employment relationship

Executive Order 11246 The presidential executive order mandating affirmative action in employment by large federal government contractors

promote individuals from underrepresented minority groups. The primary basis for affirmative action in the U.S. workplace is a presidential executive order entitled **Executive Order 11246,** signed by President Lyndon B. Johnson in 1965 and mandating that companies that have contracts with the federal government of over $50,000 per year, which covers most large U.S. companies, develop affirmative action goals and plans with respect to their workforce.

Executive Order 11246 has been highly controversial. Some individuals and groups argue that while it has helped women, African Americans, Hispanics, and other minority groups get a toehold in the workforce, it hasn't done enough; women and minorities still hold very few top executive positions. Others, however, argue that the executive order has led employers to adopt workforce quotas for hiring different types of employees and led to some minority group members getting preferential treatment in hiring, promotions, and so on, thus helping create feelings of tension and mistrust on the part of white males and others.

University of Michigan Affirmative Action Cases

On June 23, 2003, the U.S. Supreme Court decided two cases, *Grutter v. Bollinger* and *Gratz v. Bollinger,* involving affirmative action admissions programs in the University of Michigan's graduate and undergraduate programs, respectively. In the *Grutter* case the Supreme Court upheld the university's use of race as a positive factor in its admissions process because of the compelling educational benefits that flow from having a diverse student body. In the *Gratz* case, however, the Court struck down the university's use of a quota system using race in admissions decisions. In short, the Supreme Court in the University of Michigan cases held that universities can count race or ethnicity as a plus in a particular applicant's file but that they must also consider that file on an individualized basis in competition with all other applicant files.

Over 50 major U.S. companies joined legal briefs to the Supreme Court supporting the University of Michigan's general use of affirmative action, and the Supreme Court's decision was hailed as a big victory for corporate America.[18] For example, Microsoft Corporation, which was one of the many companies joining briefs generally supporting the school's use of affirmative action, issued the following statement immediately following the Supreme Court's decision:

> Microsoft applauds the Supreme Court's decision to uphold the University's right to include race and other factors in its admissions process. We hope this ruling will help preserve the ability of our nation's institutions of higher education to develop the diverse talent many companies need to cultivate a multi-cultural workforce. At Microsoft, we believe that the ability to recruit such a diverse workforce is critical to our success in today's global marketplace, and we look forward to continuing our partnership with the University of Michigan and other institutions.[19]

In sum, the recent University of Michigan cases can be seen as a strong endorsement by the nation's highest court of the general concept of affirmative action.

Workforce Diversity After 9/11

The tragic events of September 11, 2001, have raised a variety of workplace diversity issues. One very important issue is to what extent companies should take special measures to prevent potential workplace harassment or discrimination against individuals of Arab descent or Muslim belief.[20] The EEOC has been particularly vigilant in this regard, urging employers to promote tolerance and guard against any misdirection of anger toward innocent employees because of their national origin, ethnicity, or religion. The EEOC has also brought lawsuits against employers accused of discriminating against Arab or Muslim employees.[21]

Careers in Human Resources Management

The field of human resources management offers a wide range of career opportunities. Indeed, virtually all for-profit and not-for-profit organizations in the country offer professional opportunities in this field. A wide variety of governmental agencies, such as the EEOC, NLRB, and U.S. Department of Labor, also offer excellent career opportunities in the area. In addition, many individuals use employment with government agencies as a training ground where they can gain valuable experience before moving into the private sector. Most organizations hire students for human resources professional positions with either an associate or a bachelor's degree. However, some organizations prefer the individuals they hire for these roles to have a master's degree, and a growing number of colleges and universities have started master's degree programs in human resources management. The Society for Human Resource Management (SHRM), formerly the American Society for Personnel Administration, is the world's largest association devoted to human resources management, and it provides its members with considerable information about careers in the field. Student memberships in SHRM are available at significantly discounted rates, and a number of colleges and universities have student SHRM chapters.

 ## Summary

LEARNING OBJECTIVE 1

Describe how advances in technology and other factors have led to an increasingly strategic role in organizations for human resources management.

In recent decades the U.S. economy has shifted from manufacturing to service. In a service economy, employees become the most important asset of a business, and thus the management of these employees—human resources management—plays a central role. Moreover, computer and Internet technologies have given human resources professionals the opportunity to devote less time to the traditional record-keeping and payroll-processing functions of HRM and enabled them to focus more on strategic business issues. Today, HRM is a very integral part of nearly all business organizations.

LEARNING OBJECTIVE 2

Explain how human resources managers engage in planning and forecasting.

One important strategic role human resources managers play is in human resources planning. Such planning involves ascertaining what types of people the organization is going to need in the future. Sometimes forecasting future human resources demand can be rather tricky, as unexpected events may occur. Human resources managers also plan with respect to the future availability of needed employees, that is, the human resources supply. Good HR managers look at both the internal supply, people already working in the company who can be promoted or otherwise moved into needed positions, and the external supply, people outside the organization who will have to be hired to fill needed slots. Increasingly, HR managers are recruiting employees for both permanent and temporary employment.

LEARNING OBJECTIVE 3

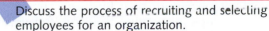 Discuss the process of recruiting and selecting employees for an organization.

Once human resources hiring plans have been formulated, a very important role of HRM becomes coordinating the recruitment and selection of these employees. At the heart of recruiting is the development of a good applicant pool, or pool of people wanting to work in a given job. Employees are then selected from this applicant pool. Employers use a variety of techniques, such as job interviews and employment tests, in selecting employees for the organization. The goal is getting the best match for the job, with the understanding that different jobs in organizations require widely different skills and personalities.

LEARNING OBJECTIVE 4
Evaluate the types, value, and effectiveness of the compensation and benefit plans that organizations offer employees.

Businesses compensate employees in a wide variety of ways. Wages and salaries, which are monies directly paid for time worked or for fulfilling job responsibilities, are generally the most important part of employee compensation. Some employers put considerable emphasis on seniority, or longevity on the job, in determining wages and salaries, while others try to pay employees on individual performance without regard to years of service. Seniority-based pay clearly rewards employee loyalty, while pay based on individual performance is probably more likely to create incentives for all employees to work their hardest. Increasing numbers of employers have developed one type or another of profit sharing plans for their employees. In recent decades, employee benefits such as health insurance have in some cases become nearly as important to employees as wages and salaries. Many employers offer employees some type of pension plan. Defined benefit pension plans are highly regulated by the government and offer employees a predetermined annual stipend when they retire. Defined contribution pension plans involve having employers and usually employees contribute certain percentages of employee pay to a pension fund which is managed by the employee. Employees enjoy far more control over their monies with a defined contribution plan, but unlike with a defined benefit plan, have no guaranty regarding future retirement income.

LEARNING OBJECTIVE 5
Analyze different methods for developing an effective workforce and providing workforce members with proper feedback.

Once employees are part of an organization, it becomes important for the organization to try and better develop their skills and give them meaningful feedback regarding their job performance. Businesses have a wide range of employee training programs. Indeed, some large companies have even established their own universities. Businesses also engage in a wide variety of employee feedback and performance appraisal methods. Some jobs lend themselves well to objective performance evaluation; a salesperson is likely to be evaluated primarily on how many dollars of goods he or she has sold, and given feedback about whether this level of sales meets employer needs. Other jobs, however, such as service positions, do not lend themselves as easily to objective evaluation methods, and thus require a more subjective evaluation approach. A continuing challenge is to try and make sure that managerial bias such as favoritism is kept out of subjective performance appraisals. Increasingly, organizations are using full-circle, or 360-degree, feedback, which involves not only supervisors evaluating employees but also employees evaluating supervisors.

LEARNING OBJECTIVE 6
Describe the role of the National Labor Relations Act in abolishing company unions, and the process by which "real" unions come into power and engage in collective bargaining.

In 1935, the U.S. Congress enacted the National Labor Relations Act, which for the first time made unions lawful in the United States. One fear when the law was enacted was that in response to the legalization of unions, employers would try and establish employer-supported unions known as company unions. To prevent this from happening, the NLRA contains a specific provision, Section 8(a)(2), which makes it unlawful for employers to play a role in forming, administering, or contributing financial support to any labor organization. Instead, the law encourages the establishment of "real" unions via secret ballot elections in designated employee bargaining units. A union is able to schedule such an election by garnering a show of interest from 30 percent of the employees in the designated bargaining unit. If the union wins a majority vote in the representation election, it becomes the exclusive representative of all employees in that bargaining unit. On winning, the union begins collective bargaining with the employer in an attempt to obtain a labor contract for these employees. Typically, labor contracts cover a wide range of employment issues and are for three-year terms.

LEARNING OBJECTIVE 7
Discuss how and why the field of human resources management has become so highly legally regulated, especially by the federal government, in recent decades.

The shift of the U.S. economy away from manufacturing has led to a sharp decline in private sector unionization in the United States. Without the protection of union labor contracts, U.S. employees were increasingly left without any legal protections from unfair or discriminatory treatment by employers. Consequently, employees throughout the country put pressure on the U.S. Congress and state legislatures to pass various types of protective employment legislation. During the past few decades the

U.S. Congress has responded by enacting a panoply of laws protecting the rights of employees to work in safe environments, take unpaid leave for family or medical reasons, not be discriminated against because of disability, and receive 60 days notice if the plant where they work is going to close.

LEARNING OBJECTIVE 8

Analyze the difference between equal employment opportunity and affirmative action, the impact of this difference on workplace diversity, and recent developments in affirmative action and workplace diversity.

Equal employment opportunity laws require that all employees be treated equally in the workplace. Title VII of the Civil Rights Act of 1964, for example, states that women must be treated equally to men in hiring and on the job. Under this law, a high-performing woman must be given the same opportunity for job advancement as an equally high-performing man. Affirmative action takes this concept a step further and states that organizations must take special steps to recruit, hire, and promote individuals from underrepresented groups. Under an affirmative action plan, a business may give a high-performing woman *preference* in obtaining promotions over an equally high-performing man. The idea behind such an approach is to help women obtain supervisory jobs of the kind they ordinarily have not had, where they have been underrepresented. In two important 2003 cases, the U.S. Supreme Court upheld the general concept of affirmative action.

Chapter Questions

1. How have increases in technology impacted the conduct of human resources management in the United States?
2. Why have labor unions experienced such a decline in private sector membership? Why do you think the same dynamics have not occurred in the public sector, that is, the government? Why would there be differences between the two sectors?
3. What government information sources are available for human resources planning? How would you use or apply these resources?
4. How can the Internet help employers with recruiting employees? Give some examples of the most useful Internet sites in this regard.
5. Why are recruitment interviews often viewed as being a bad selection device? What can be done to overcome the problems involved with interviews?
6. Is employee seniority a good criterion on which to base employee compensation and other rewards? Give the pros and cons of using seniority.
7. Describe some different types of employee compensation, and discuss their effectiveness.
8. What are stock options? Why has there been so much recent controversy regarding their use?
9. Why might employees be better off having a defined benefit pension plan as opposed to a defined contribution plan?
10. What is the doctrine of employment-at-will? What are the arguments that the application of this doctrine is good for U.S. business?
11. What topics are employers required to bargain over with unions? Give some examples of such topics.
12. Employer X fires employee Y for being seen by various people entering an adult entertainment strip club on Saturday night; the employee works only Monday through Friday. Is this discharge lawful? What different factors control this determination?
13. Why was the Family and Medical Leave Act (FMLA) so controversial when its enactment was being considered by the U.S. Congress? Should the FMLA's coverage be expanded? What are the pros and cons of such expanded coverage?
14. Describe the differences between equal employment opportunity and affirmative action. How have these concepts been applied in recent U.S. Supreme Court decisions to college and university admissions?
15. The tragic events of September 11, 2001, have impacted many things in the United States. How have they impacted human resources management, especially in the area of workplace diversity?

Interpreting Business News

1. There continues to be a major controversy regarding the lack of African American coaches in the National Football League. Since Art Shell became the first African American NFL coach (for the Oakland Raiders) in 1989, there have been only a handful of other African Americans holding these prestigious posts. NFL teams argue that they don't discriminate in hiring coaches and only try to hire the best possible coach for the team (equal employment opportunity model). Various groups, though, argue that teams should be very proactive in trying to hire African American coaches and generally have more diverse front offices (affirmative action model). Some observers have

indeed argued that teams with African American coaches should get extra draft picks, while teams without African American coaches or other clear indications of having a diverse front office should lose draft picks. Others have argued that African American players should boycott playing for teams that have not been proactive in this regard. What do you think? Any ideas for positively addressing this issue?

2. Americans work harder than employees in almost every developed country in the world. While employees in countries like Germany, Italy, and France take an average of 35 to 40 vacation days, including public holidays, per year, Americans squeeze in an average of only about 14 vacation days. Americans also tend to work as many or more hours per week. Moreover, these differences have been increased by advances in technology like cell phones and e-mail, which permit Americans to work even while on vacation. But is all this work, which many Americans wear as a badge of honor, good? Increasingly, medical studies show a correlation between a lack of vacation time and illnesses such as heart attacks. In addition, there is evidence that taking vacations leads to increased workplace productivity when on the job—that refreshed workers are better workers. What do you think? Should the United States move toward the European and Canadian models of more worker vacation time?

Web Assignments

1. The Society for Human Resource Management (SHRM) is the world's largest association devoted to HRM, with over 175,000 members. It was founded in 1948 and has more than 500 affiliated chapters in the United States and members in more than 120 countries. Go to its website at **www.shrm.org,** and find a list of the 500 affiliated chapters. Also, find and read SHRM's most recent annual report and make a list of its top priorities and initiatives. And if you're interested, look and see if they have any jobs or internships open!

2. The U.S. Equal Employment Opportunity Commission (EEOC) plays a major role in regulating today's workplace. Go to the EEOC website, **www.eeoc.gov,** and prepare short one-paragraph summaries of five current posted news items involving the EEOC. Also, write a one-page history and evaluation of the success of the EEOC's mediation program.

3. The International Labor Organization (ILO) is a branch of the United Nations dealing with the rights of workers throughout the world. Go to its website, **www.ilo.org,** and familiarize yourself with the general goals and operations of this agency. Then go to its special website for the United States at **us.ilo.org** and write a one-page analysis of the ILO's key things the ILO does and the role of the United States in this organization.

Portfolio Projects

Exploring Your Own Case in Point

In this chapter we presented a comprehensive overview of the human resource function of major corporations. Answering these questions will help you better understand this important dimension of your company's operations.

1. What types of employee staffing needs is your company going to have during the coming decade? What are some of the primary places your company recruits for new employees?

2. Does your company have pension/retirement plans for its employees? If it has a defined benefit plan, is this plan adequately funded?

3. Are any of your company's employees represented by labor unions? If so, when do its current collective bargaining agreements expire?

4. How diverse is your company's workforce? Are any of its top executives females or minority group members?

Starting Your Own Business

After reading this chapter, you should be able to add information about your company's human resources to your business plan.

1. Will your business need to hire employees? If so, what types of individuals will have to be hired initially?

2. How do you intend to recruit the initial employees your business will need? Do you already have any individuals in mind?

3. Do you plan to offer health insurance and other benefits for the employees you plan to initially hire? From what carrier(s) do you hope to obtain such insurance and other benefits?

4. Is there a chance your business might face an early union organizing drive or request for recognition by a labor union? How do you plan to react to such a unionization effort by your employees?

Test Prepper

You've read the chapter, studied the key terms, and the exam is any day now. Think you are ready to ace it? Take this sample test to gauge your comprehension of chapter material. You can check your answers at the back of the book.

True/False Questions

Please indicate if the following statements are true or false:

_____ 1. Few female attorneys have shown any interest in part-time legal employment.

_____ 2. With the increased movement of the United States toward being a knowledge economy, the human resources management function has taken on greater importance in businesses.

_____ 3. Southwest Airlines Company puts a strong emphasis on developing a very large job applicant pool.

_____ 4. Stockbrokers generally receive mostly fixed compensation.

_____ 5. The growth in employee benefit packages dates back to World War I.

_____ 6. The process of 360-degree feedback involves employees evaluating their bosses.

_____ 7. Unions are under a duty to fairly represent all employees in a given NLRB-certified collective bargaining unit, including employees who did not support the union.

_____ 8. Labor issues were not a highly controversial part of NAFTA.

_____ 9. The Equal Pay Act says that men and women must be paid the same if they are doing essentially the same work.

_____ 10. The Family and Medical Leave Act entitles employees to up to 12 weeks of paid leave in the case of family situations or illness.

Multiple-Choice Questions

Choose the best answer.

_____ 1. A job specification involves a

a. systematic evaluation of the elements required for a job.

b. list of the duties of a job.

c. detailed list of the skills, education, and other credentials needed for a job.

d. forecast of human resources demand.

e. type of employment outsourcing.

_____ 2. Enterprise Rent-A-Car Corporation likes to hire

a. high school dropouts.

b. only people from New Jersey.

c. college students ranking in the top 5 percent of their class.

d. scientists.

e. college students with average grades.

_____ 3. One problem with rewarding employees on the basis of seniority is

a. it takes away incentives for individual employee performance.

b. it rewards employee loyalty.

c. it is seen as being fair and equitable.

d. unions do not like this approach.

e. it promotes pay confidentiality.

_____ 4. An example of knowledge- or skill-based pay is

a. getting paid more for selling more of a product.

b. getting paid more for earning a master's degree at a university.

c. being paid a commission.

d. getting paid a profit sharing bonus.

e. being paid above the minimum wage.

_____ 5. In defined contribution pension plans, investment decisions are generally made by

a. the employer.

b. the PBGC.

c. ERISA.

d. the employee.

e. the NLRB.

_____ 6. In a forced distribution employment evaluation process

a. all employees get bonuses.

b. some employees are forced to earn graduate university degrees.

c. all employees can receive high performance rankings.

d. FLSA problems tend to exist.

e. some employees will receive poor performance rankings.

——— 7. The final step in a labor contract's grievance procedure is usually

    a. mediation.
    b. arbitration.
    c. fact-finding.
    d. collective bargaining.
    e. a pay raise.

——— 8. The Landrum Griffin Act deals with

    a. collective bargaining.
    b. the minimum wage.
    c. part-time employment.
    d. internal union affairs.
    e. comparable worth.

——— 9. The doctrine of employment-at-will has been chipped away at primarily by

    a. federal courts.
    b. state courts.
    c. state governors.
    d. the president of the United States.
    e. city councils.

——— 10. Executive Order 11246 is an example of

    a. an affirmative action regulation.
    b. an equal employment opportunity regulation.
    c. comparable worth in action.
    d. state employment legislation.
    e. collective bargaining regulation.

Want more questions? Visit the student website at **http://college.hmco.com/business/student/** (select Gaspar, *Introduction to Business*) and take the ACE quizzes for more practice.

Motivating and Leading Employees

7

| Introduction

| What Is Motivation?

| **Traditional Motivational Theories**
Classical Theory: Taylor's Scientific Management Theory
Behavior Theory: The Hawthorne Studies
Maslow's Hierarchy of Needs
Herzberg's Motivation-Hygiene Theory
McGregor's Theories X and Y
Ouchi's Theory Z

| **Contemporary Motivation Theories**
Expectancy Theory
Equity Theory
Reinforcement Theory

| **Enhancing Employee Performance and Job Satisfaction**
Management by Objective
Use of Teams by Firms
Participative Management and Employee Empowerment
Job Enrichment and Redesign

| **Work-Life Programs**
Flextime Programs
Part-Time Work
Work-Share Programs
Self-Managing Teams
Telecommuting and Alternative Work Styles

| **What Is Leadership?**

| **Major Leadership Theories**
Servant Leadership
Transactional and Transformational Leadership
Charismatic Leadership
Contingency Theories of Leadership
Chaos Theory

| **The Practice of Leadership**
Autocratic Style
Democratic Style
Free-Rein Style
The Contingency Approach to Leadership

| **Careers in Motivation and Leadership**

Learning Objectives

After studying this chapter, you should be able to

1. Explain what motivation is, and the importance of keeping employees motivated.

2. Discuss Frederick Taylor's scientific management theory, and explain how his pioneering work has practical value even today.

3. Compare the behavioral studies of Elton Mayo with Maslow's hierarchy of needs, and explain which theory is more meaningful today.

4. Explain why Theories X and Y are totally different from Theory Z.

5. Summarize contemporary motivation theories and describe the richness of each of the three major theories.

6. Compare management by objective with participative management and the use of teams by firms.

7. Explain why job enrichment and redesign are important and describe how they can be done to achieve corporate goals.

8. Define the objective of work-life programs, and summarize the pros and cons of the various approaches.

9. Discuss what leadership is, and summarize the major leadership theories.

10. Identify how leadership impacts corporate success, and critically discuss the various leadership styles used today.

Meditation: A Motivational Therapy for Knowledge Workers?

As the business world moves increasingly toward a knowledge-based economy, a primary issue of concern to employees and employers alike is stress in the workplace. Various forms of therapy have been tried over the years to overcome stress-related problems like pain in the lower back, neck, headaches, skin rashes, and so on. Stress-related troubles lead to decreased productivity, increased absenteeism, sloppy workmanship, and tardiness that annually cost companies worldwide billions of dollars. Increasingly, companies are resorting to meditation as a major way of relieving stress thereby enabling employees to perform tasks better. Meditation has always been part of Eastern religions, starting with the Vedic tradition of Hinduism sometime between 2000 and 3000 B.C.[1] Companies are embracing meditation as scientific studies show that it works to reduce stress-related problems, increase motivation, and enhance employee productivity. Over 10 million Americans practice meditation regularly. Meditation programs are offered by corporations as well as by some schools, hospitals, government agencies, and professional sports.

High-profile corporate executives from such firms as Ford Motor Company, Apple Computer, Yahoo!, Google, McKinsey, and Deutsche Bank regularly meditate, and an increasing number of companies have begun offering meditation classes aimed at energizing their leaders as well. Furthermore, meditation programs are inexpensive and are unlikely to get axed during periods of tight budgets.

Introduction

Creating value—providing useful products or services at reasonable prices—for the customer is crucial for business success. While shareholders are extremely important and need to be rewarded adequately for providing risk capital, their interest is only one among many others, like employees' and society's, that business must satisfy. Placing the pursuit of profits above either customers' or employees' interests will often lead to short-term gain but long-term pain. For example, the business could end up relatively profitable in the short run, but if it produces crummy products and develops an estranged workforce, it could decline in the long run.

In the present business era—one based on globalization, information technology, and ethics—human capital, that is, employees, is the greatest source, more than land, natural resources, and capital, of competitive advantage among companies and countries. Thus employee job satisfaction and welfare, as noted in the meditation vignette, are critical if firms are to provide top-notch products and customer service. However, firms need to be cautious and not go overboard, since several employee-centered organizations—primarily those based on job security, noncontributory pension plans, and elaborate employee benefits—tend to become too internally focused, cost ineffective, and complacent over time with little regard to customer satisfaction. In order to prevent this from happening, managers try to motivate employees by providing various incentives that promote job satisfaction, which in turn increases productivity, improves customer service, and ultimately accelerates profit growth. Exhibit 7.1 illustrates what it takes to achieve corporate goals.

EXHIBIT 7.1

How Leadership and Motivation Impact Corporate Goals

Good leadership will help motivate employees to keep customers satisfied.

Serving customers well can provide job satisfaction to employees and at the same time enable firms to enhance their competitive edge and profits in the global marketplace. Thus customers, employees, shareholders, and society are all well served. The key requirement is ethical leadership that can serve customer needs well while placing high priority on employee job satisfaction and motivation, which are the focus of this chapter.

Culture and ethics play an extremely important role in explaining both employee motivation and managerial leadership. Corporate leaders have long wrestled with the challenge of managing culturally diverse employees without dampening job satisfaction, motivation, customer service, and corporate objectives. Employee job satisfaction strategies, employee motivation, and leadership styles vary with culture and over time within any particular culture. Firms that deal with a culturally diverse workforce should be aware that employee incentives must reflect cultural differences to be successful, and managers should not use a "one size fits all" approach to motivate employees or to lead firms.

In this chapter, you will come to understand what motivation is and why it is so important to keep employees motivated. You will be exposed to the major traditional and contemporary motivation theories and learn how firms try to enhance employee satisfaction. Also, you will learn some fundamentals of leadership and the reasons why some business leaders succeed while others fail.

What Is Motivation?

LEARNING OBJECTIVE 1
Explain what motivation is and the importance of keeping employees motivated.

Most students want to finish college as soon as possible so that they can pursue their goals of obtaining a decent job, a new car, a house, and a family. A **motive** is a specific need or desire that arouses an individual and directs his or her behavior toward achieving a goal. Motives are triggered by some external stimulus or internal feeling. When a stimulus induces goal-directed behavior in an individual, we say that the stimulus has *motivated* that person. You may come across some classmates who are really not interested in their studies. They like to goof around and may take a decade to graduate. These students lack **motivation,** or the drive to achieve a goal in life. Psychologists generally divide drive into two categories,

motive A specific need or desire that arouses an individual and directs his or her behavior toward achieving a goal

motivation The drive to achieve a goal in life

primary drives Instinctive or unlearned motives like hunger, thirst, and sex that direct behavior that is vital to survival

secondary drives Motives that are acquired through learning, such as a work ethic

intrinsic motivation Motivation for which the reward is provided by the activity itself

extrinsic motivation Motivation for which the reward is obtained as a consequence of the activity

primary drives and secondary drives. **Primary drives** are instinctive or unlearned, are found in humans and animals alike, and motivate behavior that is vital to the survival of the individual. They include hunger, thirst, and sex. **Secondary drives,** such as a work ethic, are acquired through learning, from parents or elders, for example. They are not based on the physiological state of the individual.

Psychologists also distinguish between intrinsic and extrinsic motivations. **Intrinsic motivation** refers to rewards provided by an activity itself. Certain types of activities, like membership in a student club or working with Habitat for Humanity, are so rewarding in themselves that students are motivated to participate in these organizations with little more than moral support. Similarly, most kindergarten teachers spend a lot of time in their classrooms with their students; they obtain a lot of enjoyment working with small kids. **Extrinsic motivation** refers to rewards that are obtained not from the activity itself but as a consequence of the activity. For example, some employees may be asked to attend computer software training classes. Although not all the employees may be interested, they do realize that attending those classes may lead to wage increases or promotion.

Determining whether employee behavior is intrinsically or extrinsically motivated is of great interest to business. As you can see in Exhibit 7.1, leadership in organizations plays an extremely important role in motivating employees to perform well. Organizations expect employees to *work smart,* not just hard, but hard and intelligently and to be loyal to the company and its objectives. Employees, on the other hand, want to be treated with respect, valued for their qualifications and accomplishments, and compensated in an equitable manner. Employees also like a work environment that is harmonious, where the relationship between managers and employees is cordial. Then employee morale is high. Leadership, employee welfare and motivation, employee performance, and achieving corporate goals follow in sequence and have been the focus of much research since the late nineteenth century. During the twentieth century, labor unions became an important channel for employee involvement in business. However, since the 1980s, union membership and consultative committees have declined in the United States and Europe, prompting growth in more direct forms of involvement such as teams and problem-solving groups. Concepts such as participation, involvement, and empowerment have become common in the thinking of human resources managers these days.

In order to better understand the evolution of motivation theories, we will start with traditional theories, followed by contemporary theories and current thinking on how to enhance employee job satisfaction and performance. As a student, you may wonder why you should bother yourself with all these theories. The reasons are quite simple.

- You need to understand the history of motivation theories so that you get a feel for why and how these theories evolved over time, and you do not try to "reinvent the wheel" when you become a manager.
- You need to appreciate the fact that motivation theories are a function of culture, time, and the business environment in which companies operate, and so be aware that what worked in the past may or may not be applicable to specific industries and countries today.
- You may be required to develop motivation strategies or policies for your organization in order to make it competitive and at the same time be able to retain the people you will need in your organization.

The environment in which an organization operates largely determines which motivational theory will work and when. Cultural differences and income disparity between countries, diversity within a country, and the stage of economic development or business cycle are all crucial factors that determine how employees can or should be motivated.

reality CHECK   *What motivated you to go to college?*

Traditional Motivational Theories

Managers have always wrestled with keeping employees motivated. While some employees may be encouraged by certain incentives, others may be indifferent to them. Psychologists and industrial engineers have been studying these issues for almost a hundred years to determine how best to motivate employees and improve the work environment. The evolution of motivation theories over time is summarized in Exhibit 7.2 (on pp. 232–234).

LEARNING OBJECTIVE 2
Discuss Frederick Taylor's scientific management theory, and explain how his pioneering work has practical value even today.

Classical Theory: Taylor's Scientific Management Theory

The classical era of management lasted from 1900 to 1930, and the most-respected scholar at that time was Frederick W. Taylor, an American mechanical engineer. Frederick Taylor is often regarded as the father of **scientific management,** because of his role in dissecting factory work into its logical components and figuring out the most efficient way of getting the job done. Taylor believed in two basic principles. First, he believed that workers were interested only in money, so the more money they earned the more satisfied they would be with their jobs. Second, he believed that there was one best way to get any job done and, once that way was identified, output could be measured scientifically along with productivity and corporate goals.

scientific management Figuring out and using the best way of getting a job done by dissecting the work into its logical components

Taylor's interest in a scientific approach to management began in the early 1900s when he took one of his first jobs with Midvale Steel and Bethlehem Steel companies in Philadelphia where he noticed that employees wasted tremendous amounts of resources and time on the shop floor. He found that employees worked slowly in order to keep a steady flow of work and that management had no way to determine what optimum factory output ought to be. Convinced that there was a better way of doing business, Taylor came up with an idea whereby both workers as well as the firm would gain through changes in workplace tasks. Taylor believed that since factory workers were most concerned about money, if workers were provided with money incentives, they would be motivated to work harder, produce more steel, and earn more money. However, in order to achieve this objective, Taylor believed that the company would first have to earn more profits; this could be done through a scientific reform of the workplace task.

First, the company would have to break each job into several independent tasks. Second, it would have to identify, select, and train the best workers to perform each task efficiently with the help of appropriate machine tools. Third, it would have to promote cooperation between managers and workers to guarantee that the jobs were accomplished as planned. This approach led to the development of the

EXHIBIT 7.2
Evolution of Motivation Theories

	Traditional Motivation Theories					
	Taylor's Scientific Management	The Hawthorne Studies	Maslow's Hierarchy of Needs	Herzberg's Motivation-Hygiene Theory	McGregor's Theory X and Y	Ouchi's Theory Z
Period	1900–1930	1925–1932	1954	Late 1950s	1960	1981
Key aspect of motivation theory (What motivates employees?)	Money	Attention to work environment	The stage of the five-stage hierarchy of needs that an employee is currently in	Job-related issues and work environment	Whether employee falls in Type X, lethargic, or Type Y, hardworking and self-driven	The best management practices of Japanese and American systems
Enabler	Improve productivity by identifying the "best way" to get the job done.	Improve work environment.	Fulfill employee's physiological needs before moving up to the next stage.	Address employee's job satisfaction issues before attacking job dissatisfaction issues.	Operate the firm as if all employees are Type Y; this will motivate Type X employees as well.	Infuse best practices of American and Japanese firms and ensure close binding of employees and management.
Approach	Implement a piece-rate system of compensation.	Give employees greater control over the work environment.	After meeting an employee's physiological needs, move up the hierarchy to satisfy safety, social, esteem, and self-actualization needs.	Put more emphasis on motivation factors like wages and benefits that have a direct impact on productivity, customer service, and corporate profits.	Give Type Y employees the opportunity to achieve corporate objective, and give Type X employees additional incentives to perform satisfactorily.	Develop a new corporate culture for U.S. firms that combines lifetime employment, specialized career paths after job rotation, collective decision making, gradual wage increases, and so on.

(continued)

EXHIBIT 7.2 (Cont.)
Evolution of Motivation Theories

Application (examples)	Automobile assembly, meat packing, apparel and athletic shoe manufacturing, etc.	Many companies, large and small, allow employees to manage their own work environment within reason, e.g., schools, universities, etc.	Commonly adopted in universities and white-collar corporate jobs.	Particularly applicable to white-collar jobs since the theory was based on a study of accountants.	Civil servants will tend to fall under Type X. However, even they can be motivated to perform better using positive re-inforcements.	Japanese car transplants in the U.S., especially Honda and Toyota, have achieved much success using Theory Z approach.
Theory's Weakness	Does not hold universally, especially in developed countries.	In common work areas, the likes and dislikes of all parties need to be considered. Conflicts and security concerns must be addressed.	Not applicable worldwide, especially in developing countries where the hierarchy of needs could be different.	Distinction between motivation and hygiene factors are not universal or clear cut. One person's motivation factor may be another's hygiene factor.	It is difficult and unjust to broadly categorize people under Type X and Y.	Corporate America is generally unwilling to guarantee lifetime employment, just as American labor unions are unwilling to accept gradual wage increases.

Contemporary Motivation Theories

	Expectancy Theory	Equity Theory	Reinforcement Theory
Key aspect of motivation theory (What motivates employees?)	Employees will be motivated to work hard to achieve an identifiable award provided the prospects of receiving that reward are reasonable.	Employees are motivated to work smart and contribute to corporate success if they believe that they are treated and compensated fairly.	Employees are rewarded when they do the desired work and penalized when they don't.

(continued)

EXHIBIT 7.2 (Cont.)

Evolution of Motivation Theories

	Contemporary Motivation Theories		
	Expectancy Theory	Equity Theory	Reinforcement Theory
Enabler	The relationship between employee's effort, performance, and corporate rewards must be clearly defined to enable employees to achieve their goals.	Keep employees motivated by treating those who exhibit similar skills and performance fairly. Employees' "outcomes-to-input" ratio must be equitable.	Provide support or rewards when desired work is done well, and reprimand employees who do not do the expected work.
Approach	Employee's job performance requirements must be made clear and should be attainable. In addition, the link between performance and reward structure must be made transparent.	The outcomes (wages, benefits, promotion, and awards) of employees with similar background (education level, professional experience) and work output should be comparable.	Encourage good employee behavior (working smart, being punctual, neat, etc.) with rewards (salary increases, promotion, awards, etc.) and discourage unacceptable behavior (tardiness, sloppiness, gossiping, etc.) by reprimanding (decreased responsibilities, reduced pay, demotion, etc.) those employees.
Application (examples)	Industries where an employee's output can be quantified vis-à-vis production goals, e.g., piece-rate work.	Most companies strive to enforce equity in the workplace with the help of clearly defined job requirement and corresponding reward structure.	Both manufacturing and service companies try to handle the reinforcement issue by designing detailed job description and providing regular performance review of employees.
Theory's Weakness	In some industries, an employee's performance is not quantifiable and will depend on management's subjective evaluation.	In practice, equity issues could be manipulated by managers to make the system more subjective and less transparent.	Some managers may not be objective or impartial.

piece-rate system, where employees are paid on the basis of the number of units they produce. This system is used even today in several sectors of economies worldwide, like apparel and shoe production. Under Taylor's piece-rate system, all factory workers are paid a specific amount to produce a certain minimum number of units of goods. However, if the worker exceeds the target output, the worker is paid at a higher rate for all the units produced.

Taylor's pioneering work has had profound global impact, as countries all over the world adopted key elements of his **time-and-motion studies** (industrial engineering techniques used to determine the best approach to perform jobs efficiently) to increase production efficiency, specialization of labor, and assembly line production techniques. Taylor's scientific management theory is used today in industries such as automobile assembly and meatpacking to maximize efficiency by carefully studying the best and least-cost approach of delivering quality products to customers. Although Taylor's scientific management techniques have revolutionized production management, his assumption that increased pay would lead to rising worker motivation is relatively simplistic and not universally held. Taylor's ideas may be valid especially in developing countries of Asia, Africa, and Latin America that have low income levels and young populations, but they may not hold in affluent countries of Europe, East Asia, and North America, where the motivation-productivity relationship is more complex.

reality CHECK How would you feel about being compensated using a piece-rate system?

> **LEARNING OBJECTIVE 3**
> Compare the behavioral studies of Elton Mayo with Maslow's hierarchy of needs, and explain which theory is more meaningful today.

Behavior Theory: The Hawthorne Studies

The classical era of management, which emphasized personal economic needs as what provides job satisfaction and motivates individuals to increase productivity, was followed by the human relations era, which focused on the relationship between the effects of the physical and operational work environment on employee job satisfaction and productivity. In 1925, a group of engineers from the Hawthorne plant of Western Electric Company in Chicago conducted a study to determine the impact of changing light intensity on worker productivity. Their findings were interesting but inconclusive: They found that when light intensity in the plant was either lowered or raised, output increased. To explain this effect, the Hawthorne engineers requested Harvard professor Elton Mayo and a team of his colleagues to examine the findings. Between 1927 and 1932, Mayo and his colleagues conducted two studies. The first study was to evaluate the **Hawthorne Studies,** and the second was to determine the effect of elements of the work environment, such as job redesign, length of workday or workweek, length of break time, and the piece-rate system, on increasing the output of *groups* of workers. The results of the studies were astonishing, since they indicated that productivity increases were closely related to employee feelings. In both the lighting case and the job redesign case, employees felt that special attention was being given to them, and this encouraged them to perform better and to increase productivity. In cases where employees were given greater autonomy to control their work environment, they became even more motivated. These findings led to the development of the **Hawthorne effect,** which recognizes the important role that the work environment plays in job satisfaction,

piece-rate system A compensation method where employees are paid on the basis of the number of units they produce

time-and-motion studies Studies that measure the time taken to conduct each subactivity of a job in order to determine the best approach to performing the total job efficiently

Hawthorne Studies Studies conducted by a group of engineers at the Hawthorne plant of Western Electric Company in Chicago in 1925 to determine the impact of changing light intensity on worker productivity

Hawthorne effect The principle that when employees are given autonomy to control their work environment, they become more motivated, and this has a positive impact on employee morale, job satisfaction, and productivity

employee morale, and productivity. This implies that firms that pay attention to their employees' physical and operational work environment will likely have a motivated workforce that will perform well and be productive. Present-day human relations management functions in corporations are based on the premise that a satisfied employee is a productive employee; hence the work environment needs to be inviting. That is a major reason why most employers today provide all sorts of benefits like subsidized health care, maternity leave, retirement benefits, meditation time, and so on, for their employees.

Maslow's Hierarchy of Needs

Like the Hawthorne Studies, **Maslow's hierarchy of needs** falls in the behavioral era of human resources management. In 1954 Abraham Maslow, an American humanistic psychologist, developed a theory of motivation based on a hierarchy of human needs. He classified the motive to work by arranging needs into five distinct categories in a hierarchy, from lower to higher in importance as it relates to personal satisfaction and development.[2]

Maslow's hierarchy of needs The principle that physiological needs are basic and must be satisfied before a person is motivated to satisfy higher levels of needs that have more subtle origins

According to Maslow, *physiological needs* are basic; these most fundamental motives spring from the need to survive and include such things as food, clothing, and shelter. These basic needs are something all employers try to provide through adequate wages. Basic needs must be satisfied before employees are motivated to satisfy less basic needs that are higher up in Maslow's hierarchy. The second level consists of *safety needs,* things that we desire to have to live without anxiety, such as health insurance, meditation programs, pension plans, job security, and working conditions. The third level is *social needs*, which include a sense of belonging or acceptance by others within a group or organization at work or outside work. Informal social groups like the Women in Business Club or the International Club help meet this need as employees get a sense of togetherness.

The fourth level in Maslow's hierarchy is *esteem needs*, which are satisfied with rewards, promotion, and recognition achieved by making the best possible impression on others. For example, universities often give best teaching awards or best researcher awards to professors to keep them motivated. Some real estate firms and supermarkets give recognition to the Employee of the Month and even provide those employees with special parking privileges. Maslow believed that the highest motive in the hierarchy is *self-actualization*—the drive to realize one's full potential. Jack Welch, the former CEO of General Electric, was never content with all he had achieved in his career at GE, and he always felt that GE could do still better— the "GE Way." Maslow's hierarchy of needs is illustrated in Exhibit 7.3.

EXHIBIT 7.3

Maslow's Hierarchy of Needs

Basic needs must be largely satisfied before higher motives can emerge.

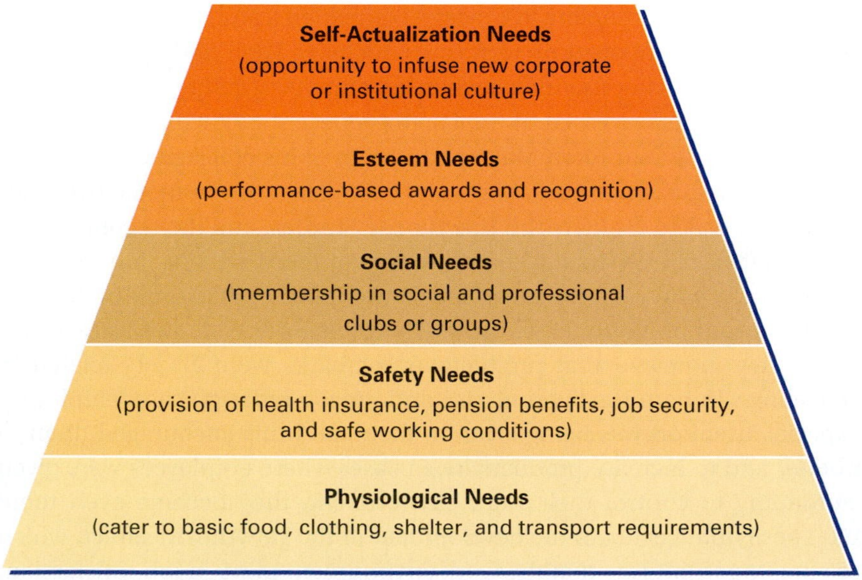

Self-Actualization Needs
(opportunity to infuse new corporate or institutional culture)

Esteem Needs
(performance-based awards and recognition)

Social Needs
(membership in social and professional clubs or groups)

Safety Needs
(provision of health insurance, pension benefits, job security, and safe working conditions)

Physiological Needs
(cater to basic food, clothing, shelter, and transport requirements)

In Maslow's theory, higher motives emerge only after the more basic ones have been largely satisfied. Hence, Maslow's model offers an appealing way to organize motives into a coherent structure, and it provides managers with a policy framework for developing employee motivation programs.

Recent research across different cultures and in countries with relatively low income levels challenges the universality of Maslow's views. Maslow's research was primarily based on observations of historic and famous individuals, the majority of whom where white males living in Western societies. In many simpler societies, people live on the very edge of survival, yet they form strong and meaningful social ties and possess a firm sense of self-esteem. In fact, the difficulty in meeting basic needs can actually foster satisfaction of higher needs; a single parent and the children she or he is struggling financially to raise may grow closer as a result of the experience.

reality CHECK *If you were to start your own business, which approach would you prefer to use to motivate your employees, Mayo's or Maslow's? Why?*

Herzberg's Motivation-Hygiene Theory

In late 1950s, American psychologist Frederick Herzberg conducted a study on a group of some 200 accountants and engineers in Pittsburgh, Pennsylvania, to determine what factors made them like (be satisfied with) their jobs and what factors did not make them like (be dissatisfied with) their jobs. The two major conclusions that he arrived at amazed him. First, he found that job satisfaction was based on a set of factors that were intrinsic to the job itself, whereas job dissatisfaction was based on a completely different set of factors that were extrinsic to the job, or related to the job environment. Second, he found that contrary to prevailing beliefs, employee satisfaction and dissatisfaction did not lie on opposite ends of the same scale, but in fact were on two different scales. One scale ranged from satisfaction to no satisfaction and the other from dissatisfaction to no dissatisfaction. Herzberg concluded that job satisfaction depended on **motivation factors,** such as the job itself, responsibility, advancement, and so on, and job dissatisfaction depended on **hygiene factors** such as the work environment. The premise that job satisfaction and dissatisfaction are not part of the same spectrum is referred to as **Herzberg's motivation-hygiene theory** (see Exhibit 7.4).

The motivation-hygiene theory has important implications. Since motivation factors are essentially related to the job itself and hygiene factors are related to the work environment, managers can develop a two-pronged approach to motivate employees. First, they can instill job satisfaction through proper work design—what is expected, how employees are promoted, how recognition is provided. Unless you are satisfied with your work, it is only a matter of time before you quit. The job needs to be rewarding. Imagine yourself working at a Mercedes plant in Stuttgart, Germany, and you are given responsibility to manage an assembly line. Your boss lets you know what is expected of you in terms of the number of cars to be assembled and the number of defects that is acceptable. You will be motivated to do a good job, since everything is spelled out clearly and you know that you will be financially rewarded for doing a good job. By manipulating

motivation factors Factors such as the job itself, responsibility, and advancement which determine job satisfaction

hygiene factors Factors that influence the work environment which determine job dissatisfaction

Herzberg's motivation-hygiene theory The theory that job satisfaction and dissatisfaction are not part of the same spectrum

EXHIBIT 7.4

Herzberg's Motivation-Hygiene Theory

Employee job satisfaction and dissatisfaction are not part of the same spectrum.

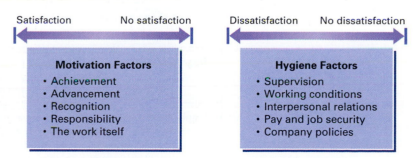

Satisfaction ←→ No satisfaction   Dissatisfaction ←→ No dissatisfaction

Motivation Factors
- Achievement
- Advancement
- Recognition
- Responsibility
- The work itself

Hygiene Factors
- Supervision
- Working conditions
- Interpersonal relations
- Pay and job security
- Company policies

motivational factors, such as assigning well-defined jobs, managers can influence job satisfaction. Second, they can minimize job dissatisfaction by improving hygiene factors such as work conditions and the communication of corporate policies. Consider, for example, working in the kitchen of a fast-food restaurant. Imagine that there was no one to clean the kitchen floor, or the air conditioning or exhaust system was not functioning well. As a student, your primary motive to work at the restaurant is to earn money to pay expenses for your studies. You will be willing to put up with a not-so-ideal work environment and remain dissatisfied. However, if management takes notice of the work environment and has someone periodically clean the kitchen floor and fixes the air conditioner, you will be less dissatisfied, and you will continue to work. According to Herzberg's theory, managers must focus more on motivational factors—wages and benefits—because they lead to job satisfaction and employee productivity, customer satisfaction, and corporate profits. To a lesser extent, hygiene factors should be attended to to minimize job dissatisfaction and prevent quitting.

Herzberg's motivation-hygiene theory has interesting implications for employee job satisfaction and productivity. However, research has shown that the distinction between motivation and hygiene factors is not universal as Herzberg thought. It is likely that one person's motivational factor may be another person's hygiene factor. There are a number of reasons why this is so—culture, income levels, the type of job, and the general economic environment itself. Despite this shortcoming, Herzberg's theory does provide important clues on how to motivate employees and improve worker productivity.

LEARNING OBJECTIVE 4
Explain why Theories X and Y are totally different from Theory Z.

McGregor's Theories X and Y

In 1960, Douglas McGregor, an American behavioral scientist and one of Maslow's students, set forth Theory X and Theory Y in a study whose goal was to show how managers perceived employee behavior.[3] McGregor came to the conclusion that managers generally classify workers into two distinct categories with almost opposite traits. Exhibit 7.5 provides a contrast of Theory X and Theory Y, based on assumptions perceived by management.

EXHIBIT 7.5

McGregor's Theory X and Theory Y

People's Traits	Theory X	Theory Y
Attitude toward work	People are lazy.	People are hardworking and diligent.
Degree of supervision	People need close supervision.	People are self-starters and seek responsibility.
Degree of inertia	People do not like change and have a low commitment to work.	People like to grow professionally and financially.
Employee prospects	People have low potential to succeed on their own.	People are bright with high potential for success.

Theory X is based on management's distrustful vision of human nature in general and of employees in particular. According to Theory X,

1. People dislike work and will try to avoid it if they can.

2. Because people dislike work, managers will need to use control, coercion, threat, and other forceful techniques to obtain work from employees in order to meet corporate objectives.

3. Since people are generally lethargic and seek security rather than responsibility, they will need to be led or directed to get the job done.

From these assumptions it is apparent that under Theory X, employees should be kept in a controlled environment, because they are subservient, reactive, and prone only to follow management's directives.

Theory Y is based on a positive view of human nature, with traits quite opposite to those perceived in Theory X. Employees are seen as self-driven and willing to take an initiative to achieve corporate goals as long as it leads to appropriate rewards. According to Theory Y,

1. People do not dislike work; in fact they enjoy it so much that they perceive work to be part of their daily activity.

2. People can be motivated to work smart and achieve corporate objectives in anticipation of receiving tangible rewards.

3. Most employees are creative and seek responsibility to do a better job, and it is management that does not try to utilize the employees' potential fully.

Managers who operate on Theory Y principles recognize that employees seek growth in job and pay and can be more productive. Also, given the opportunity, employees will play an important role in achieving corporate objectives as long as they are given proper incentives to develop and utilize their skills to full potential. McGregor stated that most managers operate on the Theory X assumption. Yet, he believed that managers operating on the Theory Y assumption were more likely to achieve corporate goals, especially since some Type X employees could be motivated to perform well using Theory Y techniques, thereby increasing productivity and output more.

> **Theory X** The theory that is based on the distrustful vision of human nature in general and employees in particular

> **Theory Y** The theory that is based on the positive view of employees

Ouchi's Theory Z

In 1981, at the height of Japan's manufacturing and economic supremacy, William Ouchi, a professor of management at the University of California, Los Angeles, conducted studies on the management practices of U.S. and Japanese companies to determine what factors influenced Japanese firms to do so well globally.[4] Ouchi found the management practices in the two countries to be very different, which to a large extent reflected their cultural differences. The Japanese are a relatively homogeneous society and they generally tend to be group-oriented, whereas Americans are more individualistic.

Ouchi labeled Japanese firms Type J firms, which had several distinctive management characteristics. Type J firms promoted lifetime employment, job rotation for most professional employees so that everyone had an appreciation for the others' jobs, collective decision making with the group being held responsible for the final outcome in terms of business performance, slow and steady salary raises for employees with due consideration given to seniority, and a total concern for employee welfare.

On analyzing U.S. companies, Ouchi labeled them Type A firms, whose management practices were radically different from the Type J firms. U.S. firms focused on short-term employment, specialized career paths, individualistic decision making

Type Z firm An ideal U.S. firm that combines the best practices of U.S. and Japanese management systems and would advocate lifetime employment, a more specialized career path, collective decision making with corresponding responsibilities for its outcomes, and gradual pay increases along with great concern for the welfare of all employees

coupled with individual responsibility for the outcomes of the decisions, quick promotion, and concern for employees only as an important factor of production.

Ouchi's Theory Z was that a hybrid firm, **Type Z,** that married the best practices of Type A and Type J firms would be the best for the United States. These firms would advocate lifetime employment, a more specialized career path (after initial job rotation), collective decision making with collective responsibilities for the outcomes, and gradual pay increases along with great concern for the welfare of all employees. A key characteristic of a Type Z firm would be a close binding of management and employees in the form of participative management. Any employee could suggest changes that could lead to job improvement and cost savings. A closer working relationship between management and labor would foster greater trust and job satisfaction along with corresponding productivity increases and profitability.

A few firms, for example, Honda Motor Company, have been able to blend Type A and Type J systems of management to develop Type Z firms in the United States. If you visit Honda's Saitama facilities in Tokyo, where many promising managers from Honda's U.S. facilities, especially those in Marysville, Ohio, are trained, you really get the feel for a Type Z firm in action. Honda nurtures teamwork between employees as well as with management—always soliciting and incorporating employee suggestions into the production process. After undergoing significant job rotation initially, employees are allowed to specialize. Job rotation and retraining enables Honda to minimize layoffs, and this leads to job security for its employees. What Honda has been doing in the United States is to blend the best elements of the Japanese management system with those of the U.S. system. Honda's success in the United States can at least partially be attributed to the practice of Theory Z.

reality CHECK *How motivated would you be in your job if Theory Z were implemented in your company?*

Contemporary Motivation Theories

LEARNING OBJECTIVE 5
Summarize contemporary motivation theories and describe the richness of each of the three major theories.

In this section, we explore three contemporary theories—expectancy theory, equity theory, and reinforcement theory—to better understand employee motivation.

Expectancy Theory

expectancy theory The theory that an individual will be motivated to work hard to achieve a coveted reward, provided the prospect of receiving that reward is reasonable, or the individual will not bother at all

One of the most researched theories of motivation is **expectancy theory,** which states that an individual will be motivated to work hard to achieve a coveted reward provided the prospects of receiving that reward are reasonable. That's one of the major reasons why people who think they can achieve their goals work hard while others who believe that the reward may not be attainable don't. Expectancy theory can be explained in terms of three important relationships as shown in Exhibit 7.6.

EXHIBIT 7.6

Expectancy Theory Model

Employee expectations play a role in motivating behavior.

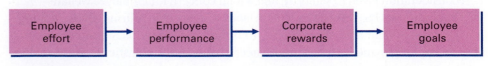

| Employee effort | → | Employee performance | → | Corporate rewards | → | Employee goals |

1. Relationship between an employee's effort and performance. The employee's expectation is that a certain amount of effort will result in the desired performance.

2. Relationship between employee performance and firm's rewards. This is a tricky relationship, since a firm's conditions for providing the reward could be opaque, making the employee's outcome uncertain.

3. Relationship between a firm's reward and an employee's goals. The expectations are clear, since the employee anticipates achieving his or her goals soon after receiving the reward.

Expectancy theory helps explain why employees in certain countries of the former Soviet bloc did not work hard. Since all employees were paid almost the same and salary increases were based on years of service, there was little motivation to work hard. Expectancy theory does provide managers with ideas of how to motivate employees. For example, making employee performance requirements clear and attainable, linking rewards to performance in a transparent manner, and tying rewards to employee goals will enable employees to respond appropriately—through increased productivity. When employers enforce a piece-rate compensation system, they are inadvertently practicing expectancy theory.

Equity Theory

Equity theory is something that most of us are familiar with in our day-to-day lives. Equity at the corporate level means fairness, justice, or evenhandedness in the workplace. All of us like to be treated in a fair manner at work, school, and play and in stores and restaurants. In countries such as the United States, the United Kingdom, France, Germany, South Africa, India, Sri Lanka, and so on, which have diverse populations, equity theory plays an extremely important role in employee satisfaction, motivation, and productivity. A major economic strength of these countries is the diversity, primarily in race, religion, and class or caste, of their populations and workforce. Unless all employees are treated fairly, employee morale will be low and the firm may face legal action. Literally thousands of lawsuits have been filed and won in the United States because employees were not treated equitably by their employers.

Equity theory states that employees are motivated to work smart and contribute to a firm's success as long as they believe that they are treated and compensated fairly relative to others with *similar*, not identical, levels of education and professional experience. How do employees determine whether they are being treated in an equitable manner? Employees first try to decide whether the employer rewards them in proportion to their input. Some of the major rewards they consider are wages, benefits, promotion, and awards—called *outcomes*. Employees then consider what they provide to the company in terms of hours worked, educational level, professional experience, and skills—called *inputs*. The employees compute the *outcomes-to-inputs* ratio to determine if they are being fairly treated by the company. The question then becomes "With whom do employees compare themselves?"

Employees generally do this in a stepwise manner. First, they try to compare themselves with employees of similar background within the organization. Second, they try to compare themselves with employees with similar background outside the organization but in a similar line of business. Finally, they compare now to their past experience with another company. After making these comparisons, if they find the outcomes-to-inputs ratios to be somewhat similar, they will feel that the treatment is fair and equitable and they will leave things alone. However, if they conclude that

equity theory The theory that employees are motivated to work smart and contribute to the success of the firm as long as they believe that they are treated and compensated fairly relative to others with *similar* levels of education and professional experience

they are not being fairly treated, they may take appropriate action. First, they may change their work habits by decreasing input, for example, reducing the hours of work or spending more time surfing the Internet instead of working, or by increasing their output but redirecting it, for example, trying to make additional money by doing other jobs on company time or to use corporate resources for personal purposes. Second, some employees may try to rationalize their inequitable outcomes-to-inputs ratio to their job itself: "My job carries more prestige than the other person's." This way the employees increase the outcomes stream in the outcomes-to-inputs ratio. Finally, some employees may depart from the situation they are in, that is, quit.

Because equity theory is very down to earth, employers can impact employee motivation by taking simple steps to make sure that all employees are treated fairly. Very rarely do you find two employees with identical backgrounds in terms of education, professional skills, attitude toward work, and so on. Yet, every effort should be made by firms to treat employees fairly, otherwise there will be a negative impact on employee morale, productivity, and corporate performance—not to speak of the class action law suits that will follow. For example, on July 12, 2004, Morgan Stanley—a Wall Street investment bank—agreed to settle with the U.S. Equal Opportunity Commission (EEOC) and pay $54 million to end a sex bias trial. The EEOC alleged that women at Morgan Stanley were systematically denied equal compensation and promotion given to men. The equal opportunity employment policy that is largely followed in the United States is based on the equity theory philosophy.

Reinforcement Theory

reinforcement theory The theory that is based on the principle that rewarding good behavior will lead to continued good performance, while penalizing unacceptable behavior will lead to reducing unacceptable conduct

Reinforcement theory is based on the principle that rewarding desired behavior will lead to continued good performance, while penalizing unacceptable behavior will lead to reduced misconduct. As a child you may have participated in the practice of reinforcement theory without knowing it. When children behave well at home, parents often reward them with a pat on the back and with such remarks as "good boy" or "good girl," and if they are lucky, the children may even receive a treat! However, if the children throw tantrums, which are unacceptable behaviors, even after an initial warning, they may end up in a "time-out" session. In the business world, managers try to reinforce employees' good behavior—working hard, meeting set goals, being punctual, being neat and tidy—by offering rewards—pay increases, promotion, awards. This type of employee reinforcement is called **positive reinforcement.** Managers also try to reduce unacceptable behavior—tardiness, sloppiness, chitchatting, web browsing at work—by reprimanding—sidelining, demoting, reducing pay, increasing workload, laying off—the employee. This type of reinforcement is called **negative reinforcement,** which managers try to avoid as much as possible because of employee resentment and its unpleasant impact on office morale and productivity. Whether it works positively or negatively, a **reinforcer** is any consequence that strengthens specific behavior.

positive reinforcement Giving of rewards by managers to try to strengthen employees' good behavior

negative reinforcement Reprimanding of an employee by a manager to reduce unacceptable behavior

reinforcer Any consequence that strengthens a specific behavior

Managers can use positive and negative reinforcers in a number of ways to achieve desired corporate objectives. The effectiveness of reinforcers on employee motivation and performance depends on what types are used, when they are used, and in what culture they are used. Employees generally prefer to have reinforcers spelled out clearly so that the rules of the game are transparent. New employees generally require positive reinforcers early in their career so that they develop a positive attitude to management and the firm. As the years pass, employees know what is expected of them. In general, positive reinforcers are the preferred approach to employee motivation, with negative reinforcement being used as sparingly as possible or even being coupled with some rewards.

The manager of a major retail store rewards an employee for working efficiently and promoting corporate goals. Coworkers cheer the employee on as he is recognized.

reality CHECK *Which of the three contemporary motivation theories do you think best describes your motivation? Why?*

Enhancing Employee Performance and Job Satisfaction

Managers of companies big and small, domestic, foreign, and international have tried to use employee motivation theories to enhance employee performance to gain corporate competitive advantage.

The general framework involved in the design of policies that are aimed at enhancing employee performance and job satisfaction may be universal in nature. However, managers should be careful not to apply the same approach in

- All companies in an industry
- All companies across the board
- All companies across international borders
- The same company all the time

The reasons are simple. Cultural diversity—gender, race, religion, custom, class, caste—within and between countries will hinder the application of a "one size fits all" approach to employee motivation. As they say, the "devil is in the details"; hence policies aimed at promoting employee job satisfaction and performance require careful planning and implementation. Also, time is an important factor. The only factor that is constant in life is change. We live in a dynamic world where things are happening faster all the time and people's lifestyles keep changing as well. So what motivated employees a decade or two ago may not motivate them anymore. Yet, managers should stay away from fads or copying the Joneses by providing a lot of freebies to motivate employees. Unless the dollar cost of motivating employees is more than offset by increased revenues through rising productivity and corporate profits, companies will fail.

LEARNING OBJECTIVE 6
Compare management by objective with participative management and the use of teams by firms.

Management by Objective

management by objective (MBO) A top-down approach to management that requires full collaboration of employees right down the line to be a success

These days, **management by objective (MBO)** is looked on as a relatively simple concept of running a successful organization. Peter Drucker in his classic work, *The Practice of Management* (1954), first argued that management must be driven by objectives if the firm is to succeed. In other words, managers should be directed and controlled by objectives, rather than dictates from the boss, and should be paid for performance. As the name suggests, the paramount issue in MBO is how to successfully achieve company objectives. To become effective, this management philosophy must be endorsed and implemented by the top management of the company. As can be seen in Exhibit 7.7, MBO is essentially a top-down approach to running a firm, and it requires full collaboration of employees right down the line to make it a success. Also, if the top managers of the company do not buy into the MBO concept, the system will fail, since middle or junior managers by themselves will not be able to implement the program. Having adopted the MBO concept, the firm will then need to follow the following steps in the sequence indicated:

1. Clearly spell out corporate goals, which are based on the company's *mission statement*. Corporate goal setting could be a time-consuming affair, since it is not restricted to financial objectives like profits and return on investment, but includes such issues as implementing diversity, affirmative action, ethics, and upward mobility in the workplace. Goal setting is a dynamic process, and it should be altered or refined as the business environment changes or if the goals are found to be unrealistic or inadequate.

2. Depending on the complexity of the organization, the manager or managers who report to the chief executive officer meet with the employee team to explain what the goals of the group as a whole are and obtain employee input. The manager tries to identify how each employee could contribute to achieving the group's objective, by which the manager and the group will be judged and compensated.

EXHIBIT 7.7

Major Stages of a Typical MBO Program

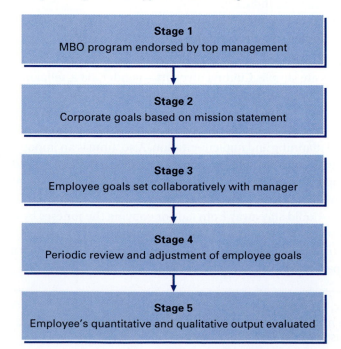

Stage 1
MBO program endorsed by top management

Stage 2
Corporate goals based on mission statement

Stage 3
Employee goals set collaboratively with manager

Stage 4
Periodic review and adjustment of employee goals

Stage 5
Employee's quantitative and qualitative output evaluated

3. The manager then meets with each employee to work out detailed yet realistic goals for each and also determine exactly *how* and *when* output will be measured. As far as possible, the output must be quantifiable and verifiable to facilitate quarterly or annual evaluation. The manager also tries to identify any additional resources that each employee will need to achieve his or her goals.

4. The manager meets with each employee periodically to review progress and make mutually acceptable changes to goals because of new developments in the business environment like a regional, national, or global economic slowdown; political instability; or a changing structure of competition caused by mergers and acquisition activity. The original goals could have become unrealistic given drastic changes in the business environment.

5. At the time of the annual evaluation, the manager meets with each employee to determine if the agreed-on goals were met. The employee's rewards—pay increase, recognition, promotion—will reflect whether he or she met the agreed-on goals.

Several companies practice MBO because it involves the joint setting of achievable goals through close communication between management and employees. The disadvantages of the MBO system are its top-down approach and the fact that top management must endorse the program; otherwise it will fail. Also, the process could be quite time-consuming, especially if reviews are to be conducted each quarter. Although managers try to be as objective as possible by using quantifiable output measures, some tasks still call for subjective evaluation, which could lead to some unpleasant outcomes. All things considered, MBO is being successfully used in many companies globally.

Use of Teams by Firms

As the workforce in a country becomes better educated and skilled, managers realize that employees can be made more productive if work is organized around groups to exploit synergies associated with teams. Teams are collections of people who must rely on group collaboration if each member is to experience the optimum of success and goal achievement.[5] Firms use teams in the workplace due to their efficiency, as measured in terms of output. Managers use the team approach in production when they realize that the output in terms of quantity and quality of work of the team is greater than the sum of the individual outputs of its members. Globalization, advances in information technology and the Internet, and increased concern over business ethics have even motivated the development of international teams in several industries. The changing environment of business is increasingly calling for the use of multicultural, multidisciplinary teams that can cater to the needs of diverse domestic and international markets. Firms in the past have successfully utilized teams in such industries as manufacturing, management consulting, project design and analysis, and new product development, including R&D. These days, firms increasingly utilize international teams in projects like customized software and business process offshoring.

Researchers have identified 17 guidelines that facilitate team success.[6]

1. Tolerating ambiguity, uncertainty, and seeming lack of structure.

2. Taking an interest in each member's achievement, as well as the group's

3. Giving and accepting feedback in a nondefensive manner

4. Being open to change, innovation, group consensus, team decision making, and creative problem solving

5. Creating a team atmosphere that is informal, relaxed, comfortable, and non-judgmental

6. Establishing intense, short-term member relations

7. Keeping group communication on target and schedule, while permitting disagreement and valuing effective listening

8. Urging a spirit of constructive criticism and authentic, nonevaluative feedback

9. Encouraging members to express feelings and to be concerned about group morale

10. Clarifying roles, relationships, assignments, and responsibilities

11. Sharing leadership functions within the group and using total member resources

12. Pausing periodically from task pursuits to reexamine and reevaluate team progress and communications

13. Fostering trust, confidence, and commitment within the group

14. Being sensitive to the team's linking function with other work units

15. Fostering a norm that members will be supportive and respectful of one another and realistic in their expectations of each other

16. Promoting an approach that is goal-directed, seeks group participation, divides the labor fairly, and synchronizes effort

17. Setting high performance standards for the group

Depending on the cultural and professional background of its members, the performance of the team will vary. Yet, firms will be justified using the team approach as long as the team as a unit is more productive than its members working separately.

Participative Management and Employee Empowerment

Managers have long wrestled with the challenge of how to involve employees in the management process and at the same time control the organization to achieve corporate objectives. **Participative management** calls for employees to actively provide input in the management decision-making process, as well as in the operation of the company. **Employee empowerment** is a proactive approach to management where workers decide what, when, and how they would like to work to achieve corporate goals. Unlike MBO, which is essentially a top-down method to management, participative management and empowerment is a bottom-up approach. The objective of participative management and employee empowerment is to motivate employees and provide them with the satisfaction that they are part of the corporate decision-making process. Rather than management directing employees on what, when, and how work is to be done, employees will now be able to share their ideas with management on how to get the job done. The sense of participation in the decisions that affect their own jobs motivates employees and provides great job satisfaction.

A good example of participative management is in the IT and software development business. Here employees are given a specific task, like developing a particular type of software for a client, along with a deadline. It is up to the employees to decide what, when, and how to accomplish the job. Companies like Microsoft (United States), SAP (Germany), Infosys (India), and others give their employees a lot of leeway in getting their jobs done. Yet, the crucial issue from a company's point of view is whether increased job satisfaction is reflected in performance, productivity increases, and rising consumer satisfaction. If employee empowerment does

participative management A management approach where employees participate in the management decision-making process as well as in the operation of the company

employee empowerment A proactive approach to management where workers decide what, when, and how they will work to achieve corporate goals

nothing more than enhance employee satisfaction, then participative management is not a panacea to the challenges faced by management.

Participative management cannot be applied to all situations. It is particularly helpful when the output of goods or service is team-driven. In situations like these, participative management can be very useful, as team members can and will be able to figure the best approach to get the job done. The Japanese have largely perfected the art of participative management, especially in the automobile industry, with what are called quality circles, groups of employees that meet regularly to discuss quality and related issues on their shop floor. Employees are encouraged to make suggestions on how to improve quality, eliminate waste and unnecessary assembly line movements, best sequence steps in the production process, and reduce the number of employees in the team to get the job done. Also, Japanese employee suggestions on how and where to automate certain operations have made Japanese auto assembly workers the most productive in the world.

Teamwork in Japan and other countries that have adopted the Japanese model has participative management having a positive effect on job satisfaction, motivation, productivity, and pay increases. Yet, whenever production and compensation are based on a piece-rate system, participative management has not worked well. This is because quick workers within a group are pulled down by the laggards who are unable or unwilling to pick up speed. This can lead to resentment among employees, job dissatisfaction, and a fall in productivity and wages.

Critics of participative management argue that employee empowerment is not useful for all organizations. Some employees may prefer to be told what to do, rather than be asked to suggest what, when, and how they should work. Some employees are not sure how their suggestions will impact corporate goals and are willing to participate only where their actions clearly add value to the firm. It is precisely for this reason that for employee participation and empowerment to work, management must be closely involved in setting goals, communicating standards by which employees will be judged, performing periodic reviews, and conducting final evaluations. If managers are to be willing to change their own behavior and employees are to become involved, organizational systems need to change as well. Reward systems, training and development, modes of communication, career paths, and processes for allocating resources all need to reinforce and support the empowerment program. This in turn will enhance employee job satisfaction, motivation, and corporate performance.[7] Several companies, Wal-Mart for one, continue to encourage participative management, especially where teamwork is the norm, in order to improve motivation.

___reality___
CHECK

Is the participative management style better than MBO for mom-and-pop stores?

LEARNING OBJECTIVE 7
Explain why job enrichment and redesign are important and describe how they can be used to achieve corporate goals.

Job Enrichment and Redesign

Management's primary objective in job enrichment and job redesign programs is to make existing jobs more satisfying for employees by incorporating motivating factors in them.

job rotation The practice where employees are periodically moved through different operations in a company to break job monotony and to provide employees the opportunity to learn different skills and obtain a feel for all the operations of the company

Job Enrichment Programs.

In order to break the monotony in certain jobs, especially those requiring repetitive action such as in an assembly line, managers generally resort to **job rotation.** For example, managers periodically move employees through different operations on an assembly line. This also provides employees the opportunity to learn different skills and to obtain a feel for all the operations of the company. It provides employees with an appreciation for what other workers in the company do as well. In some countries, job rotation is the norm, regardless of the industry or professional level of work. For example, Japanese corporations even rotate their managers from personnel to finance to marketing to manufacturing. This approach creates a whole cadre of general managers who can be moved quickly to different management functions depending on corporate need. Job rotation provides both employees and management greater flexibility in operation, especially during periods when structural changes such as greater global competition take place. Companies can move employees from areas where there is less demand for a certain type of skilled worker to divisions where demand is high, thereby minimizing the need to hire and fire workers.

job enlargement The practice where employees are assigned to manage and run related tasks that lead to job enrichment

Since the deregulation of the airline industry in the United States, most airlines have resorted to **job enlargement,** especially at smaller airports. Airline employees are assigned to manage and run related tasks that lead to job enrichment. For example, an airline employee will be issuing tickets and checking in baggage at one time and will be on the runway moments later loading baggage into the airplane or directing a pilot to park the plane. Although job enlargement may also become monotonous after some time, it does provide job enrichment and helps both the employee and the company.

Job Redesign Programs.

Employees have certain likes and dislikes about their jobs. These can be due to demographics or the academic and professional experience of the employee concerned. To help keep employees satisfied and also to enhance their creativity and performance, managers often try to redesign existing jobs with the goal of motivating employees. **Job redesign** can be accomplished through three major avenues: combining tasks, forming compatible work groups, and establishing customer relationships. The goal of combining tasks is to make the redesigned job more employee-specific by adding responsibilities that are more in line with the employee's area of interest or expertise, while at the same time deleting the more mundane job chores and delegating them to others in the organization who may be interested in doing them. Increasingly, some of these relatively mundane service jobs are being outsourced overseas (also called offshoring). Companies in industrialized countries, especially the United States, the United Kingdom, and other English-speaking countries, are moving these jobs, such as programming and systems work and loan and credit card processing work, abroad to countries like India and the Philippines that have a large pool of highly-educated, English-speaking workers. This trend will continue to accelerate in the future.[8] There are two major benefits of outsourcing jobs. First, home country employees find redesigned jobs more to their liking, since they requested the job modification in the first place. Combining tasks enriches jobs, and helps motivate employees and maintain high job satisfaction and performance. Second, outsourcing significantly increases corporate profitability since the jobs that are outsourced cost a fraction of those in the United States.[9]

job redesign Redefining jobs to keep employees satisfied and to enhance their creativity and performance

Another approach to job redesign is the development of compatible work groups in which employees with similar interests and professional background work together often as teams. As a group, they tend to have expertise in a specific area and work well with each other and the organization as a whole; these lead to accomplishing corporate goals. Hollywood is a good example of compatible work groups of various professions that come up with creative ideas.

Job redesign through the establishment of customer relationships provides employees direct access to the client, along with all the feedback that customers may provide on the company and its employees. Most companies redesign employee jobs relatively frequently as a means of giving workers greater control over their jobs and how goals are achieved. Greater control over how they carry out tasks allows employees to exploit their competitive advantage.

reality CHECK *How do professors try to enrich the courses they teach?*

Work-Life Programs

LEARNING OBJECTIVE 8
Define the objective of work-life programs, and summarize the pros and cons of the various approaches.

Companies all over the world are trying to address the personal and family needs of their employees. Companies in the United States have moved from purely performance-based objectives and policies to a more strategic approach, which is particularly aimed at meeting the needs of employees with young children. Many such initiatives are based on giving autonomy to employees about where, when, and how they work.

Companies give several reasons for supporting workers in their family or personal roles. First is, in the increasing competition for talent, there is a desire to recruit and retain the best employees. The sense that they are being helped to integrate their work and personal life increases the workers' willingness to go the extra mile for the company. As employees have become more diverse with a variety of lifestyles and family structures, companies have set up task forces and committees to help resolve work-life issues using a range of programs. Second is globalization. Offshoring has made it easy and cost-effective for firms to get certain jobs done overseas, enabling domestic employees to retain the jobs that add more value to the product or service at home. Third is technology. Internet and information technology have made alternative work styles possible. Finally, the success of work-life programs depends on ethics, how honest employees are with the more relaxed work rules. Training is often needed to ensure that employees are aware of their responsibilities and that supervisors support program implementation.

Multinational companies like Merrill Lynch and Glaxo offer programs such as childcare centers, summer camps, and flexible work arrangements. Applying a comprehensive approach to work-life initiatives is not limited to large companies. Even relatively small start-ups with limited resources realize the importance of a comprehensive **work-life program.** For example, ECS, an environmental risk management specialist in the United States, offers flexible hours, reimbursement of tuition fees, resource and referral services, extended parental leave, health programs, adoption leave, and on-site child care. Federal agencies are also adopting a comprehensive approach. Similar initiatives are also evident in academia. Implementing such flexibility is never easy. Companies continue to educate managers on the value of workplace flexibility and its compatibility with superior corporate performance. At the heart of these approaches is a respect for employee choices.[10]

work-life program Employment programs and policies aimed at meeting the needs of employees, especially those with young children

The prevalence of work-life programs is a function of the business environment. For example, if the economy is booming and unemployment is low, employers will be more willing to consider alternative work styles like flexible work schedules. However, if the economy is in a deep recession or unemployment is high, employers may not be enthused to entertain the flexible work schedules that employees may request. Two major considerations that are troubling to employers are how will the implementation of flexible schedules affect work flow, customer service, and corporate performance, and what is the work ethic of the employees who request flexible schedules? Despite these concerns, about one-third of full-time U.S. workers are on flexible schedules of some type or other. These employers see flexible schedules as a way of keeping valued employees satisfied.

Some of the most common types of work-life programs used globally include flextime programs, part-time work, work-share programs, self-managed work teams, telecommuting, and alternative work styles.

Flextime Programs

About one-third of U.S. employees work on flexible schedules. For various reasons, some workers are required to work during so-called nonpeak hours. Manufacturing plants, especially those based on continuous-flow operations in industries like chemicals, drugs, and steel, operate on a 24-hour basis, and employees working in such facilities generally work on three shifts of eight hours each. Some of these employees work on rotation and are on flexible schedules. Similarly, in the health care field, doctors, nurses, and paramedical personnel operate on flexible schedules. There are a number of other professionals, like police officers and commercial airline pilots, who work on flexible schedules. Yet, when we speak of flextime, we generally talk about people who work staggered times during regular daytime.

flextime The flexible daily work hours chosen by employees in consultation with their supervisors in addition to core time, the daily period during which all employees are expected to be at work to facilitate interactive communication and workflow

Employees on **flextime** choose their daily work hours in consultation with their supervisors. Each company has periods during the workday that it considers core time, periods during which all employees are expected to be at work to facilitate interactive communication and workflow. Generally, the core time can be any block or blocks of time between 9:00 A.M. and 5:00 P.M. when all employees are required to be present. The noncore time is the flextime, and employees are given the option of choosing the flextime most convenient for them, provided they put in a total of eight hours (core time plus flextime) each day. Sometimes, managers may allow workers to put in ten hours of work one day and six hours another day. There is no hard and fast rule on what the workweek would look like for a flextime worker. This is something that employees need to work out with their managers. Anyway, an employee will need to put in a total of 40 hours of work each week.

While flextime does provide employees freedom as far as work hours are concerned, managers face some challenges. First, since employees work on different schedules, the manager's job gets more thorny, and the manager may at times get the feeling that she or he has lost control over the job situation. Second, a good system for monitoring work hours (time cards) needs to be in place; otherwise the manager will just have to hope that the employees behave ethically. Some employees, unless they are closely supervised, may not put in their required hours. Finally, colleagues generally look on employees on flextime programs suspiciously. Fellow workers are not sure whether flextime employees show up for work, put in the required hours of work if they do show up, or do any work when they are there, since supervisors may not be present.

Part-Time Work

Most of you have either worked or know someone who has worked part-time. **Part-time work** is permanent, except the employee agrees with a firm's management to work for less than the normal 40 hours per week in the United States or 35 hours per week in much of Europe. Most part-time jobs comprise 20 hours of work per week. Employees complete their part-time work by the time the firm closes for the day, as at a restaurant or grocery store. The major financial drawback in the case of most part-time work is the area of employee benefits. Most companies do not provide benefits like retirement programs, or even health insurance coverage, unless the employee works more than 20 hours per week. Of course, there are exceptions and certain companies provide health care benefits even to employees who work 10 hours a week.

People work part-time for a number of reasons. Some employees may have family members to take care of and therefore are not available to work eight hours each day. Some are students like you, who may be taking a full load of course work in college and need to finance their studies. Then there are others who already have a full-time job, but because of financial obligations, are forced to take a second job, and part-time is sufficient. Also, there are those who are unable to find a full-time job, and are therefore compelled to take part-time jobs. Finally, there are a few who are either relatively well off or who are moving to semiretirement, as the baby boom generation may be doing in another ten years. These individuals like to keep themselves active by working part-time and to spend the rest of the time on leisure.

> **part-time work** Work that is permanent and in which the employee agrees with the firm's management to work for less than the normal 40 hours per week

Work-Share Programs

When two employees have similar professional backgrounds and are highly compatible with one another in terms of work ethic, communication, and organization, they may team together and share a job—job sharing. People share jobs when two employees cannot, for personal reasons, take full-time jobs. The advantages of **work-share programs** are that the job is permanent and yet it also offers the flexibility of part-time work. As in the case of part-time work, employees in work-share programs may not receive all the benefits, such as pension programs and health insurance coverage, that

> **work-share programs** Jobs that are permanent and in which two compatible employees with similar professional background split a job

To better meet their family obligations, these two teachers with similar professional backgrounds share daily classroom hours and duties at an elementary school.

full-time employees receive. Of course, there is no hard and fast rule regarding benefits, and much depends on the specific company and the demand for the skills of the work-share program employees. By implementing work-share programs, firms are also able to attract and retain some key personnel. The challenge is to identify the right partners for the work-share program. Often employees themselves identify their work-share partners before approaching managers with their proposal. If the partners are not compatible, work will not get done and corporate objectives will not be achieved.

There are different ways of sharing jobs. The two employees may choose to work half a day every workday of the week or to work on alternate days. Regardless of the schedule that is finally worked out between the two employees, the manager is always kept informed of their plans so that she or he knows who is doing what and when. Since job sharing calls for a strong partnership of two employees, these workers need to keep each other well informed about their daily work through effective communication, be it via telephone or e-mail. Also, work sharing will be successful only if each partner gets the feeling that the other is contributing his or her fair share of work.

Self-Managing Teams

self-managing teams Employee-formed teams that make wide range of decisions, including traditional management choices

Self-managing teams are the most successful approach to employee performance improvement and motivation in recent decades. Terms such as *self-managing teams, self-directed teams,* and *semiautonomous groups* have all been used to describe team-working practices, and names and methods vary from organization to organization. Self-managed teams make a wide range of decisions, often including traditional management choices. These may include selecting leaders, assigning jobs, training, redesigning processes, assessing internal performance, judging and managing quality, managing budgets, and liaising with other teams. Self-managing teams, therefore, are involved in a variety of activities with ample responsibilities, and this motivates employees. Furthermore, self-managing teams offer members the opportunity to rotate among jobs and broaden their professional skills. Yet, a self-managing team approach cannot be implemented in all businesses. Some 35 percent of businesses in the United Kingdom use self-managing teams. However, their prevalence varies considerably with the type of core occupational group in the workplace. Over 50 percent of British companies that have professional workers as the largest occupational group in the company use self-managing teams, as compared with only 13 percent of workplaces that have plant and machine operators as the largest occupational group.[11]

Research shows that the benefits of self-managing teams are greater than those of quality circles. Studies have also shown that when correctly implemented, self-managing teams increase employee satisfaction, improve work attitudes, reduce absenteeism, and enhance work outcomes. Yet, for self-managing teams to operate effectively, senior management must be committed to this approach and be willing to provide ongoing training and rewards for team-based performance.

Telecommuting and Alternative Work Styles

telecommuting An employee's working at home for family or physical reasons while being "virtually" at work with the help of current information technology

A growing number of people long to work from home, hoping for more personal time. The reasons why some employees prefer to work at home include eliminating commuting time, taking care of a young child or elderly parent, and needing flexible work hours. **Telecommuting**—working at home while being "virtually" at work—is a way to resolve this challenge. Companies are increasingly exploring this avenue as a means of reducing the fixed cost for office space, as long as they are able to get the same amount of work from the employees. Telecommuting is information technology driven. With constant advances in information technology, telecommunication costs keep coming down, making telecommuting even more attractive. Telepresence could effectively replace physical presence in a number of situations. In addition to lowering real estate and commuting costs, employers implementing successful telecommuting programs witness improved employee satisfaction, and productivity. In addition, employers advocating telecommuting programs will be able to attract new pools of labor, like senior citizens and disabled workers.

With telecommuting becoming more attractive to employees and employers alike, it is likely that we will see more workers telecommuting. Telecommuting employees can accomplish all their work at home with the help of high-speed data lines, phone lines, faxes, PCs, cell phones, and wireless technologies. Sony, **www.sony.com,** is in the forefront of important telecommuting technologies, and it has redoubled its R&D spending on these technologies since September 11, 2001. In telecommuting, location becomes less important as employees everywhere conduct business with customers anywhere. However, managers face challenges in monitoring employees' productivity, work activity, hours spent working, and so on. Unless an employer embraces clear, fair alternative-work policies, setting telecommuting guidelines can be challenging. Also, the employee will need to have a clear understanding of the organization's goals, to show how telecommuting can serve and enhance corporate goals.

Even if the employee has the work ethic to be a successful telecommuter, she or he will still need to muster the courage to submit a proposal. A good place for the employee to start to draft a proposal is the website run by the International Telework Association and Council, **www.workingfromanywhere.org,** a research and advocacy group.

reality CHECK *What is your perception of work-life programs? Do people abuse the freedom they offer?*

What Is Leadership?

LEARNING OBJECTIVE 9
Discuss what leadership is, and summarize the major leadership theories.

Corporate success or failure can be traced to the firm's leadership. Since 1998, the *Financial Times* and PricewaterhouseCoopers (henceforth referred to *FT*/PwC respectively) have annually published the "World's Most Respected Companies Report." In its 2003 report, *FT*/PwC identified the world's top three most-respected companies to be General Electric, Microsoft, and Toyota.[12] And, the world's top three most-respected business leaders were Bill Gates of Microsoft, Warren Buffett of Berkshire Hathaway, and Jack Welch (retired) of General Electric. Hiroshi Okuda of Toyota was ranked fifth. Is there a correlation between the world's most-respected companies and their leaders? Is this a case of "Behind every great company there is a great leader"? The *FT*/PwC report also ranks Carly Fiorina of Hewlett-Packard Compac (HPC) as the ninth most-respected business leader in the world. Fiorina was the only woman to have made it in *FT*/PwC's top 50 most-respected business leaders in world. It appears that more women (Susan Kropf of Avon Products, Colleen Barrett of Southwest Airlines, Meg Whitman of eBay, Charlene Begley of GE, and Sallie Krawcheck of Smith Barney) and minority leaders (Fred Hassan of Schering-Plough, Andrea Jung of Avon, Dick Parsons of Time Warner, and Stan O'Neill of Merrill Lynch) are likely to make it to this prestigious ranking.

The spate of financial scandals that ravaged corporate America since 2000 have intensified public distrust in capitalism and big corporations in general, and

Ethics in Business

Goodbye to an Ethicist

There is a telling story about Marvin Bower, the legendary leader of McKinsey & Co., who died on Jan. 22, 2003, at age 99. It says much about the bedrock values of this unassuming man, who was known as the father of management consulting.

In the 1950s, Bower was summoned to Los Angeles by billionaire Howard Hughes, who wanted him to study Paramount Pictures. During the visit, Hughes was in a magnanimous mood and drove the fledgling consultant around in his ancient Chevy, even giving him a late-night tour of the Spruce Goose, the massive wooden plane Hughes developed during the war.

But Bower sensed that nothing good could come of working for Hughes. He found the entrepreneur's approach to business "so unorthodox and so unusual" that he felt he would never be able to help Paramount. Instead of taking the assignment and reaping a big fee, he walked away.

The move was classic Bower. He built McKinsey into a global consulting powerhouse by insisting that values mattered more than money. He preached the notion that consulting was not a business but a profession, arguing that, like the best doctors and lawyers, consultants should put the interests of their clients first, conduct themselves ethically, and insist on telling clients the truth, not what they wanted to hear.

That was as unusual then as it is today. But so was Bower, a towering figure at McKinsey and in the larger world of consulting. At McKinsey, Bower helped to move consulting from shop-floor efficiency studies to major strategy reviews for top-tier corporations. He created one of the world's most productive leadership factories, producing hundreds of corporate CEOs and presidents. In the mid-1950s, he was the first to systematically recruit raw talent off B-school campuses, helping to give the MBA degree new cachet. He was, after all, a Harvard lawyer and MBA himself, who joined the New York office of Chicago-based James O. McKinsey & Co. in 1933, when it had only 18 professionals in two locations.

After McKinsey's death in 1937, Bower reestablished the firm in New York and served as its managing director from 1950 to 1967. His vision for McKinsey came straight from his experiences at Jones Day, where he had worked as a lawyer. He wanted to bring the professional standards of a top law firm to what was then called management engineering.

Bower also insisted that the success of his firm brought personal obligations. Louis V. Gerstner Jr., the former IBM chairman who had spent 11 years at McKinsey, remembers Bower marching into his office one day 35 years ago. "What are you going to do to give something back?" Bower asked. "Come with me." Recalls Gerstner: "We went together to a meeting on public school reform, something I'm still involved in."

In a Jan. 23 e-mail to McKinsey employees, current Managing Director Rajat K. Gupta wrote: "Many of us will continue to make choices for the rest of our professional careers based in large part on the question we often ask ourselves: 'What would Marvin have done?'" It's a good question—one any manager in the world might ask.

Source: From John A. Byrne, "Commentary: Goodbye to an Ethicist," *Business Week*. Issued February 10, 2003. Reprinted from *Business Week* by special permission. Copyright © 2003 by The McGraw-Hill Companies, Inc.

Questions

1. Marvin Bower of McKinsey & Company was a legendary leader who believed that consulting was not a business but a profession. Explain what he meant by that statement.
2. Within the context of this chapter, what does the article mean by saying that Marvin Bower moved McKinsey from "shop-floor efficiency studies" to "major strategic reviews" of corporations?

corporate leaders in particular. A number of cases that involved earnings manipulation by executives of major corporations, most notoriously John Rigas of Adelphia Communications, Joseph Beradino of the now-defunct Arthur Andersen, Kenneth Lay of Enron Corporation, and many others, have devastated shareholders and employees alike. Leaders in many of these companies were downright unethical, and several CEOs treated their firms as a gold mine, to collect the gold and leave the employees and stockholders with little or nothing.

Good **leadership** (see Exhibit 7.1) is the art of motivating employees to enhance their performance in order to achieve corporate goals ethically. Researchers have debated for years whether leaders are born or made, whether a person who lacks charisma can become a leader, and what makes some leaders succeed while others fail. Are tall people better leaders than short people? Are good-looking people better leaders than not-good-looking people? Studies have shown that one cannot explain leadership by intelligence, birth order, family wealth, nationality, economic or social environment, level of education, ethnicity, race, or gender. From one leader to another, there is an enormous variation in every one of these factors.

Four timeless and culture-independent elements of successful leadership have recently been identified.[13] First, is adaptive capacity, the ability to adapt to circumstances whether war, imprisonment, or sudden economic swings. Most leadership failures in business, the authors argue, are the result of a failure to adapt to changing circumstances. Second, is the ability to create shared meaning, to motivate people behind a common goal, even in the face of adversity. Tolerance, even encouragement of, dissent is an important factor. Third, is personal voice, authenticity, and character, founded on a strong set of principles about how people should be treated. Finally, is integrity, the delicate balance of ambition, competence, and morality. All of these factors play a crucial role in the lives of successful leaders.

> **leadership** The art of motivating employees to enhance their performance in order to achieve corporate goals ethically

Major Leadership Theories

Organizations all over the world adopt differing leadership practices or styles, which are based largely on a firm's leadership philosophy and its business environment. Leadership styles are identified in leadership theories that have evolved over time, and they have and will continue to impact organizations in the future. Summarized below are some of the major leadership theories.

Servant Leadership

This theory characterizes the leader as a steward in his or her relationship with those in the organization. The leader is obligated to enhance the material wealth and reputation of the organization and leave behind a legacy. Hence the organization's success is the foremost priority for **servant leaders,** whose role is to create a working environment that induces participants to function at their best. Leaders must provide appropriate tools (training and equipment) and opportunities (through a well-thought-out strategy) to followers so that they can be efficient (doing things right) and effective (doing the right thing). An effective servant leader's role is to create an environment that will motivate people to perform better all the time and provide them with appropriate tools for achieving the corporate vision in an ethical manner.

> **servant leadership** The leader creating a work environment that induces participants to function at their best

Transactional and Transformational Leadership

In the context of political and social movements in countries, the role of a leader is to make followers do something that they would not have done otherwise.[14] In the context of organizations, **transactional leadership** occurs when a leader takes the initiative and provides followers rewards (promotion, salary increases, and greater responsibilities) for good performance or reprimands followers for unacceptable

> **transactional leadership** The leader providing followers rewards for good performance or reprimanding followers for unacceptable performance

performance. The leader-follower relationship in transactional leadership is strictly "arms-length," and there is no mutual binding between the two to pursue and attain higher corporate goals. **Transformational leadership** goes a step further. It occurs when a leader is able to gain the trust of and inspire followers to work jointly, setting aside their self-interest, to achieve the leader's vision for the organization and to benefit the individual members of the organization.[15]

transformational leadership The leader gaining the trust of and inspiring followers to work jointly to achieve the leader's vision for the organization and to benefit the members of the organization

Charismatic Leadership

Charismatic leaders are energetic transformational leaders who are often considered heroes by the organization in their pursuit of a rosy vision for the future. Charismatic leaders are highly capable people who can change relatively weak organizations into powerful and successful enterprises. Rose Marie Bravo is an excellent example of a charismatic leader who was responsible for the successful turnaround of the ailing British retailer Burberry Group PLC. Howell and Avolio believe that charismatic leaders achieve heroic feats in organizations by "powerfully communicating a compelling vision of the future, passionately believing in their vision, relentlessly promoting their beliefs with boundless energy, pounding creative ideas, and expressing confidence in followers' abilities to achieve high standards."[16] However, a cautious distinction must be made between ethical and unethical charismatic leadership when searching for leaders who can turn around ailing companies or bureaucracies or start new corporations.

charismatic leaders Energetic transformational leaders who are often considered heroes by the organization in their pursuit of a rosy vision for the future

Ranked as the ninth most respected corporate leader in the world (2003), Hewlett-Packard Compac CEO Carly Fiorina has exhibited charismatic leadership by communicating a compelling vision of the future and successfully turning around the ailing Hewlett-Packard and Compaq through a merger.

Contigency Theories of Leadership

While there are several different **contingency theories of leadership,** all of them assert that leadership effectiveness is maximized when leaders make their behavior dependent on the characteristics of followers and the situation they are in.[17] It is a well-known fact that leaders do not interact with all followers the same way. Leaders try to interact with different followers in unique ways so as to optimize the interaction process and achieve organizational goals. The aim is to bring out the behavioral response of all followers that would maximize leadership success. Four major contingency theories of leadership are briefly discussed here. These four theories emphasize the fact that in order to be effective, leaders must make their behavior contingent on certain traits of their followers or the situation.

- The *situational leadership model* shows that some combinations of task (telling followers what to do, when to do it, how to do it, and who is to do it) and relationship (listening, encouraging, facilitating, clarifying, and providing emotional support) behaviors are more effective in certain situations than in others.[18]

- The *Vroom and Yetton model* describes the many ways that leaders can make effective decisions by incorporating the selective participation of subordinates in the decision-making process.[19] Allowing subordinates to participate in the decision-making process enhances leadership success, and the growth and development of followers as they feel a sense of inclusion. The key disadvantage of this type of leadership is it can be quite time-consuming.

- *Fiedler's contingency model* states that while leaders may be willing to adjust their behaviors toward individual subordinates, leaders themselves may have some strong behavioral tendencies.[20] Some leaders may be supportive and relationship-oriented toward subordinates, while others may be task-oriented to meet corporate goals. Fiedler's model recognizes this fact and specifies situations where certain leaders, on the basis of their behaviors, may be more effective than others.

- The *path-goal theory* focuses on how effective leaders motivate their followers to achieve corporate goals.[21] In the path-goal theory, an effective leader's actions strengthen followers' beliefs that if they exert a certain level of effort, they will most likely accomplish a task and this will lead to receiving a reward. An effective leader will ensure that followers will receive certain rewards (the "goal") if they follow the best way (the "path") to get there.

> **contingency theories of leadership**
> Theories that assert that leadership effectiveness is maximized when leaders make their behavior dependent on the characteristics of their followers and the business environment (p. 256)

Chaos Theory

Chaos theory is based on the assumption that organizations are multifaceted and complex and they operate in a disorderly environment. An external event, 9/11 for example, could shock a stable business environment lead to chaos in the short term, which could have an impact on the organization. This is especially true if an organization has several functions (accounting, finance, information technology, management, and marketing) and operates in several regions of the country or the world. Leaders in this chaotic world are called on to manage their organizations with governing principles that emphasize vision, values, and organizational beliefs.[22] When crises occur, effective leadership is exercised by enforcing agreed-on corporate governing principles, that lead to acceptable solutions.

> **chaos theory** The theory based on the assumption that organizations are multifaceted and complex and operate in a disorderly business environment

The challenge faced in all the theories is how to put leadership together in an organization to effectively and ethically attain the firm's vision, values, and goals. This may require movement away from single executive-level leadership to a multi-leadership focus, that is based on various organizational functions, purposes, and levels.

reality CHECK *What leadership theory do you think fits best with the current business environment?*

The Practice of Leadership

LEARNING OBJECTIVE 10
Identify how leadership impacts corporate success, and critically discuss the various leadership styles used today.

Almost as interesting as the leaders that predominate in the *FT*/PwC rankings are the reasons their fellow chief executives gave for nominating them. There is no single leadership style that dominates the ranking. The chief executives that made it into the top 25 (see Exhibit 7.8 on p. 258) are all very different.

Indeed, these leaders are admired precisely because of their adaptive capacity to the individual circumstances of their companies, their industries, and the global economy. **Leadership style** is the behavior that managers exhibit when dealing with their employees and professional staff. Style must be accompanied with sub-

> **leadership style** The behavior that top managers exhibit when dealing with their employees and professional staff

EXHIBIT 7.8

World's Most Respected Business Leaders, 2003

Rank	Name	Company	Country
1	Bill Gates	Microsoft	United States
2	Warren Buffet	Berkshire Hathaway	United States
3	Jack Welch (retired)	General Electric	United States
4	Carlos Ghosn	Nissan	Japan
5	Hiroshi Okuda	Toyota	Japan
6	Michael Dell	Dell	United States
7	Lou Gerstner (retired)	IBM	United States
8	Nobuyuki Idei	Sony	Japan
9	Carly Fiorina	Hewlett-Packard	United States
10	Jeffrey Immelt	General Electric	United States
11	Richard Branson	Virgin	United Kingdom
12	Jurgen Schrempp	DaimlerChrysler	Germany
13	Steve Jobs	Apple	United States
14	Wendelin Wiedeking	Porsche	Germany
15	Takeo Fukui	Honda	Japan
16	Lindsay Owen-Jones	L'Oreal	France
17	Sam Walton	Wal-Mart	United States
18	John Browne	British Petroleum	United Kingdom
19	Jack Smith (retired)	General Motors	United States
20	Rupert Murdoch	New Corporation	Australia
21	Michael Eisner	Disney	United States
22	Jong Yong Yun	Samsung	South Korea
23	Alan Greenspan	Federal Reserve	United States
24	Marco Tronchetti Provera	Pirelli	Italy
25	William Ford	Ford	United States

Source: *FT*/PwC,"World's Most Respected Companies Report," *Financial Times*, January 20, 2004.

stance if leaders and their organizations are to be respected. Bill Gates received praise and respect for "coming out of nowhere" and "creating one of the best-managed companies in the world" (see Exhibit 7.9 on p. 259). He is also praised for creating a dominating company in the midst of international antitrust regulations and respected for his charitable and philanthropic activities. Jack Welch, who retired in 2002 and later ran into personal problems that revealed the generous retirement perks GE's board had awarded him, is remembered for his ability to drive up shareholder wealth through a ruthless, results-driven corporate culture and his skill in training great managers. The survey attributes Mr. Buffett's rise to second place to "his skepticism about the dotcom world, in which he did not invest, and the chief executive's increasing appreciation of investment values—in particular, the importance he places on the quality of the managers in whose companies he invests." Leadership style is influenced by the traits of managers as well as the circumstances surrounding the company that is being managed.

In general, leadership styles fall within a spectrum that ranges from autocratic style at one end to free-rein style on the other end with participative, or democratic, style falling in between. The fourth style of leadership is the contingency style, which adopts the three styles on the basis of the business environment faced. These four leadership styles are summarized in Exhibit 7.10 (on p. 260).

EXHIBIT 7.9

World's Most Respected Companies, 2003

Rank	Name	Country	Sector
1	General Electric	United States	Electrical/electronics
2	Microsoft	United States	Information technology
3	Toyota	Japan	Engineering
4	IBM	United States	Information technology
5	Wal-Mart	United States	Retailing
6	Coca-Cola	United States	Food/beverages
7	Dell	United States	Information technology
8	Berkshire Hathaway	United States	Financial services
9	DaimlerChrysler	Germany	Engineering
10	Sony	Japan	Consumer goods
11	Nestlé	Switzerland	Food/beverages
12	General Motors	United States	Engineering
13	Disney	United States	Media/leisure
14	BMW	Germany	Engineering
15	Honda	Japan	Engineering
16	Exxon Mobil	United States	Chemicals/energy
17	3M	United States	Consumer goods
18	Johnson & Johnson	United States	Health care
19	Procter & Gamble	United States	Food/beverages
20	L'Oreal	France	Consumer goods
21	Du Pont	United States	Energy/chemicals
22	Royal Dutch/Shell	Netherlands/UK	Energy/chemicals
23	Southwest Airlines	United States	Transportation
24	Cisco Systems	United States	Information technology
25	Siemens	Germany	Electrical/electronics

Source: *FT*/PwC, "World's Most Respected Companies Report," *Financial Times*, January 20, 2004.

Autocratic Style

An **autocratic style** of leadership is a top-down approach to management where decisions are made by the top manager with little input from employees or subordinates. Autocratic leaders do not tolerate dissent and rarely seek employee participation in the decision-making process. Job satisfaction and motivation of most employees in such companies are generally low, as the threat of getting fired is the main reason for getting the job done. Also, since employees in such firms are not part of the decision-making process, company information is not passed on to workers and employee morale could remain low. Under such a management system, corporate success or failure will squarely fall on the leader, who will be held responsible for the outcome for the firm. Employees are essentially followers in such organizations, and if the leader's decisions lead to achieving corporate goals, then the leader will be held in high regard both in and outside the company. However, if autocratic leaders fail to achieve company objectives, they will be demoted or fired. Autocratic leaders are found all over the world and are generally associated with privately-held companies, family-run operations, and the military. The ruling philosophy here is "Do things my way, or you are out!" or "My way or the highway." While the decision-making process is fast in such a management system, the consequence of poor decisions could prove fatal to the firm and the leader.

autocratic style A top-down approach to management where all decisions are made by the top manager with little if any input from employees or subordinates

EXHIBIT 7.10

Leadership Styles

	Autocratic Style	Democratic Style	Free-Rein Style	Contingency Approach to Leadership
Leadership characteristic	Top-down approach with little input from employees: "My way or the high-way!"	Active participation of all members or employees: "No policy implementa-tion without representa-tion."	Employees enjoy complete freedom to accomplish agreed on task within set deadline: "laissez faire"	Managers may adopt autocratic, democratic, or free-rein leadership style on the basis of the prevailing business environment: "One size doesn't fit all."
Examples of organizations	Privately held firms Family run businesses The military	Professional service organizations Architectural firms Consulting firms Labor unions Academic associations	University professors School teachers Researchers Software engineers Lawn care services	Public/ multinational enterprises International business Businesses dealing with culturally diverse workforces

Although the trend in most large companies is generally to move away from the autocratic style of leadership, some companies continue to be managed by auto-crats. Sanford "Sandy" Weill of Citigroup, who recently announced his retirement, is known for his autocratic management style. He is said to terrorize subordinates and his organization with his in-your-face management style and ruthlessness. *Business Week* rated Sandy Weill as one of the worst managers of 2002, as the bank-ing giant that he headed landed in a series of financial scandals through its associ-ation with a string of failed companies like Enron.[23] From his early years at Cogan, Berlind, Weill & Levitt through his tumultuous tenure at American Express and sub-sequent culture clash and battle for corporate power with John Reed of Citigroup, Sandy Weill has cost shareholders billions of dollars in lost value. Also, autocratic leaders generally tend to create a cadre of sycophants who will not voice their candid opinions. It appears that Sandy Weill and Citigroup could have benefited more from a participative style of management.

Democratic Style

democratic style A bottom-up approach to management where management receives input from its members and major policies are accepted for implementation on the basis of majority vote

A purely **democratic style** of leadership is practiced in only a few types of organi-zations, most of which are professional, like consulting and architectural firms. The American Economic Association, the Academy for International Business, and the Academy of Management elect officers and vote on issues that affect their mem-bers. The management receives input from its members, and major policies are accepted for implementation on the basis of a majority vote. Leadership, policies, and practices of labor unions also use democratic leadership styles. While the advantage of such a leadership style is obviously the strong participation of all concerned—no policy implementation without representation—the drawback is the likely slowdown of the decision-making process.

A variant of a purely democratic style of management is **consultative leadership.** Consultative leaders confer with colleagues and employees before making the final decision. Although thoughts and ideas are sought from subordinates, the firm's leader, who is held responsible for corporate performance, makes the ultimate decision. The decision-making process is quicker than those in a purely democratic system. Yet, it has the advantage of worker participation, which motivates employees and enhances performance. This approach is widely used in assembly line and team operations.

consultative leadership The leader conferring with colleagues and employees before making the final decision

Free-Rein Style

In a **free-rein style** of leadership, also known as a laissez-faire (a French term that means "leave it alone") style of management, employees are given complete freedom to perform their jobs the way they want within the framework of company rules and regulations. Management informs the employees or employee teams of what is expected of them and when. Then it is left to the employees to decide on how they want to perform their jobs to meet corporate goals. The employees or employee teams are of course encouraged to consult with management if they require any guidance. This approach works well in some professions, as with professors at universities. Department heads inform professors about the number and type of courses that they will need to teach each semester, the quality and quantity of research expected, and the service they will need to provide to the department or college. Once these objectives have been clearly spelled out, the professors are given free rein to accomplish their task. If the professors meet the objectives set by the department heads, they get promoted and receive salary increases. If they don't, they remain on the same level or are not retained. The free-rein style provides unlimited freedom for people to work the way they want as long as they accomplish the task. Some professors may choose to come to work late and leave early during the week and work on Saturdays. Others may feel more productive working at night, especially in laboratories, when things are quiet. While some employees may prefer this unstructured leadership style, there are others who may not like it.

free-rein style An approach to management where employees are given complete freedom to perform their jobs the way they want within company rules and objectives

The Contingency Approach to Leadership

The *FT*/PwC report on the world's most respected companies clearly shows that for corporate success, an honest, nonconformity style of management was preferred to the conventional management styles discussed. This is primarily for two reasons. First is the attitude of the employees or subordinates to the three leadership styles. Do subordinates prefer the autocratic, participative, or free-rein style of management? There is no clear answer. Some employees resent autocratic managers since these employees don't like to be pushed around and told what to do. On the other hand, there are some who like to be told what and how things need to be done. The latter find this approach to be clear-cut and prefer managers to tell them what to do, since they believe that executives know their business better than their employees. This is typical in the fast-food industry, where employees are specifically trained to do what, when, and how as they are told.

Quite a few employees may like the participative management leadership style because they feel their ideas or suggestions are valued by management and they get

Case in Point

Sony: Preparing Tomorrow's Leaders

Ken Kutaragi, president and CEO of Sony Computer Entertainment, is credited with building Sony Corporation's $8 billion world-class video game business from scratch. His strategy, which is being emulated throughout Sony, was to use low-margin hardware to sell high-margin software. Although the creator of the *Playstation* and its derivatives, which are hits with consumers globally, Kutaragi bears a heavy burden on his shoulders as he strives to lead Sony's dominance in the convergence of three technologies, consumer electronics, multimedia, and software, to develop the next generation of world-class Sony devices. Sony's chairperson, Nobuyuki Idei, would like to see Kutaragi lead and transform Sony because of his unparalleled success with video games. He believes that the highly driven Kutaragi is the right person for the job and could soon lead Sony to commanding heights.

At a major corporate meeting in 1999, Kutaragi, in un-Japanese manner, stunned his audience by declaring that it was time for Sony's old managers to step aside and allow young up-and-coming executives to take over Sony's leadership. Kutaragi believed that a sea change was taking place in their industry and the future was moving toward a system of consumer electronics linked by wireless and Internet networks. Although many at the meeting thought Kutaragi to be audacious, Sony's corporate history shows that the company often encouraged its potential leaders to be visionaries who could say and do what they wanted, of course within reason. Many competitors and observers alike consider these traits the main reason Sony remains one of the world's most-admired and successful technology companies.

Now Sony is embarking on its logical next step by trying to develop a super microprocessor that would integrate its audiovisual and broadband networks more closely with its hardware and software business—a job cut out for Kutaragi. The challenge that Sony faces as it moves to the future is trying to straddle the consumer electronics, software, and media sectors against competition from other giants like Samsung, Microsoft, and Time Warner. If Kutaragi generates another hit, he may end up running the entire Sony Corporation soon after.

Source: Sony Corporation, http://www.sony.com/SCA/index.shtml; "The Best Managers," *Time*, January 13, 2003, p. 64.

Questions

1. What is the leadership style that is practiced at Sony Corporation? Substantiate your answer.
2. What is Ken Kutaragi's track record as an executive? Why is he likely to lead Sony Corporation in the not-too-distant future?

the sense of being closely involved in the decision-making process and its consequent impact on corporate goals. Typical examples are assembly line work and teamwork of various kinds. Again, there may be some employees who feel this style is a joke, since managers try to acquire ideas from employees only to follow their own predetermined directives. These employees are cynical of management's motives and believe that managers are basically "going through the motions" to keep employees motivated.

Professionals love the free-rein leadership approach since it clearly defines the final objectives while at the same time it provides them with flexibility to do their jobs as they see them. Yet, there are others who dislike the free-rein approach since they get a feeling of abandonment, that management does not care what they are doing or how well they are doing it. They miss the ongoing feedback and encouragement of how well they are performing. As you can see, regardless of the leadership style, the effectiveness of any particular management style crucially depends on its impact on employee morale, motivation, and performance. Much also depends on employee diversity in education, culture, gender, race, and nationality.

A second reason why an honest, nonconformity style of management is preferred to conventional management styles comes from the manager's perspective.

Each conventional management style has its own strengths and weaknesses. Most managers like to make the decision-making process short, so that they can implement their plans quickly to achieve corporate goals. The autocratic leadership style offers speed in decision making at the expense of employee participation, and the reverse is the case with the participative style of leadership. The drawback of the free-rein leadership style is that the number of companies where it can be used may not be large. Studies have shown that leadership style has to be flexible, since the reaction to certain policies or incentives in one company may not deliver similar results elsewhere, especially internationally.

For these reasons, the **contingency approach to leadership** is becoming increasingly popular. In this approach, managers study the environment in which companies operate, both at the micro and macro level, to determine the appropriate leadership style to adopt. At the micro level, the company will study its employees, especially in terms of their diversity and how they feel they are being treated by management and in comparison to how competitors treat their employees, to determine what management style it should adopt to motivate them. At the macro level, managers consider issues such as the current state of the economy, cultural differences, especially in overseas operations, and international legal systems. For example, in the United States and some Western countries, employees prefer independence; hence the free-rein style of leadership may work well there. However, the Russians appear to be more used to the autocratic style of management, and most Russian employees tend to feel lost if they are not informed what, when, and how to get things done. The Japanese and South Koreans are big on participative management, and they feel most comfortable working in groups, making suggestions for improving performance to achieve corporate goals. As you can see, a single company operating internationally may have to adopt different management styles in different countries. The contingency approach to leadership accepts the fact that companies cannot use a "one size fits all" approach to management given the complex business environments in which they operate.

contingency approach to leadership
An approach to management where managers study the environment in which their companies operate to determine the appropriate leadership style to adopt

reality CHECK *If you had your own company, what type of leadership style would you adopt? Why?*

Careers in Motivation and Leadership

Careers in motivation and leadership are in the management function. However, if you seek an analyst position that addresses employee motivation issues, one of the best places to start would be with the human resources management or HR departments of organizations. It is within the HR departments that firms develop and implement strategies for motivation, using the tools of compensation, benefits, pension programs, incentives, and so on. Medium- and large-sized firms regularly update, design, implement, and evaluate new motivational strategies to determine what is best for the company given the changing business environment. Companies try out various motivation strategies to determine which approach maximizes employee job satisfaction on the one hand and corporate cost effectiveness on the other. Analyst positions within HR departments such as benefits or compensation analyst offer interesting opportunities for business graduates. These positions require analyzing policies followed by competitors and understanding industry norms. National and international labor laws and environmental standards must also be adhered to while designing corporate motivational strategies.

To attain a leadership role in a firm, you should be willing and able to take on strategic responsibilities. While a manager's effectiveness is dependent on how he or she builds relationships with others, a leader's agenda is different. There are four basic traits that differentiate leaders from managers.[24] First, leaders have a more open-ended approach than managers and work to create a vision of the future. Second, leaders put more stress on communication. Third, leaders aim to inspire and motivate the organization. Finally, a leader's job is to create and manage change. In essence, while a manager's job is focused on execution and control, leadership deals with planning and vision. In other words, while management is about the present, leadership is about the future. Hence, to obtain a leadership position in a firm, the career path is through any management function, as long as you are an effective communicator and a visionary.

Summary

This chapter focused on two major human resources issues, employee motivation and corporate leadership, that have a paramount impact on corporate goals, customer satisfaction, and corporate profitability. When we study motivation and leadership, we must always consider these issues within the framework of globalization, information technology, and ethics.

LEARNING OBJECTIVE 1

Explain what motivation is and the importance of keeping employees motivated.

A motive is a specific need or desire that arouses an individual and directs his or her behavior toward achieving a goal. When the stimulus induces goal-directed behavior in an individual, we say that the stimulus has motivated that person. Leadership in organizations plays an extremely important role in motivating employees. High employee morale leads to job satisfaction, productivity increases, customer satisfaction, and rising corporate profits. Employees want to be treated with respect, valued for their qualifications and accomplishments, and compensated in an equitable manner. Employees also like a work environment that is harmonious—one where the relationship between managers and employees is cordial.

LEARNING OBJECTIVE 2

Discuss Frederick Taylor's scientific management theory, and explain how his pioneering work has practical value even today.

Frederick Taylor's scientific management theory involves dissecting factory work into its logical components and figuring out the most efficient way of getting the job done. Taylor believed in two basic principles. First is that workers are interested only in money, so the more money they earn the more satisfied they are with their job. Second is that there is one "best way" to get any job done and, once that is identified, output can be measured and projected to meet corporate goals. Scientific management involves breaking each job into several independent tasks; identifying, selecting, and training the best workers to perform each task efficiently with the help of appropriate machine tools; and promoting cooperation between managers and workers to guarantee that the job is accomplished as planned. This approach led to the development of the piece-rate system, where employees are paid on the basis of the number of units they produce. This system is used today in several industries worldwide such as automobile assembly and meatpacking. Although Taylor's scientific management techniques have revolutionized production management, his assumption that the prospects of increased pay would lead to rising worker motivation is not universally held.

LEARNING OBJECTIVE 3

Compare the behavioral studies of Elton Mayo with Maslow's hierarchy of needs, and explain which theory is more meaningful today.

Elton Mayo's studies found an important link between work environment and employee job satisfaction, morale, and productivity. This implied that firms that pay attention to their employees' welfare will likely have a motivated workforce that will be productive; a satisfied employee is a productive employee.

Maslow believed that an employee's motive to work was based on satisfying five distinct categories of need, which are based on an individual's circumstance. The individual could rank these needs from lower to higher in importance, with basic needs being satisfied first before an employee can be motivated to work toward the next level of need. According to Maslow, basic needs include such things as food, clothing, and shelter, which employers try to provide through adequate wages. As employees move up Maslow's hierarchy of needs, the motives become more subtle. The second level consists of safety needs, things that we desire to have to live without anxiety or pain. The third level is social needs, like the need for a sense of belonging. In the fourth level are esteem needs, which are needs for rewards, promotion, and recognition achieved by making the best possible impression on others. The final level is self-actualization. Maslow's model offers an appealing way to organize motives into a coherent structure, and it provides managers with a policy framework for developing employee motivation programs.

LEARNING OBJECTIVE 4

Explain why Theories X and Y are totally different from Theory Z.

In his study, McGregor concluded that managers generally classify workers into two categories with almost opposite traits. Theory X is based on management's distrustful vision of employees. According to Theory X, employees should be kept in a controlled environment, because they are subservient, reactive, and prone only to follow management's directives. Theory Y is based on a positive view of human nature, where employees are self-driven and are willing to take an initiative to achieve corporate goals as long as it leads to appropriate rewards.

Ouchi's Theory Z posits that in order to be globally competitive, a hybrid firm, Type Z, that married the best practices of U.S. and Japanese firms would be the best system for the United States. Type Z firms would advocate lifetime employment, a more specialized career path after initial job rotation, collective decision making with corresponding responsibilities for its outcomes, and gradual pay increases along with great concern for the welfare of all employees. A key characteristic of a Type Z firm is a close interaction between management and employees in the form of participative management.

LEARNING OBJECTIVE 5

Summarize contemporary motivation theories and describe the richness of each of the three major theories.

The three major contemporary motivation theories are expectancy theory, equity theory, and reinforcement theory. Expectancy theory predicts that an employee will be motivated to work hard to achieve a coveted reward, provided the prospects of receiving that reward are reasonable. Expectancy theory can be explained in terms of three important relationships: between an employee's effort and performance, between employee performance and firm's rewards, and between a firm's rewards and an employee's goals.

Equity theory states that employees are motivated to work smart and contribute to a firm's success as long as they believe that they are treated and compensated fairly relative to others with similar levels of education and professional experience. Because equity theory is very down to earth, employers can impact employee motivation by taking simple steps to make sure that all employees are treated fairly.

Reinforcement theory is based on the principle that rewarding desired behavior will lead to continued good performance, while penalizing unacceptable behavior will lead to reduced misconduct. Managers can therefore use positive and negative reinforcers in a number of ways to achieve desired corporate objectives. In general, positive reinforcement is the preferred approach to employee motivation with negative reinforcement being used as sparingly as possible or even being coupled with some rewards.

LEARNING OBJECTIVE 6

Compare management by objective with participative management and the use of teams by firms.

The mantra of management by objective is that managers should be directed and controlled by objectives, rather than dictates from the boss, and rewarded for performance. MBO is essentially a top-down approach to running a firm, and it requires full collaboration of employees right down the line to make the system a success. Also, it requires that top managers of the company buy into the MBO concept, or the system will fail since middle or junior managers by themselves will not be able to implement it. Companies practice MBO because it involves the joint setting of achievable goals through close communication between management and employees. Implementing MBO programs can be time-consuming.

As the workforce in countries becomes better educated and more skilled, managers realize that employees can be more productive if work is organized around teams. Teams are collections of people who must rely on group collaboration if each member is to achieve success. The changing environment of business is increasingly calling for the use of multicultural, multidisciplinary teams that can cater to the needs of diverse domestic and international markets. Depending on the cultural and professional background of its members, team performance will vary. Yet, firms will be justified using the team approach as long as the team as a unit is more productive than the sum of its individual members' outputs.

Participative management calls for employees to actively provide input in the management decision-making process, as well as in the operation of the company. Participative management is a bottom-up approach. The sense of participation in the decisions that affect their jobs provides great job satisfaction and motivates employees. Participative management cannot be applied to all situations.

LEARNING OBJECTIVE 7
Explain why job enrichment and redesign are important and describe how they can be done to achieve corporate goals.

Management's primary objective in job enrichment and job redesign programs is to make existing jobs more satisfying for employees by incorporating motivating factors like job rotation into them. This is done to break the monotony in certain jobs, especially those requiring repetitive action. Job rotation also provides employees the opportunity to learn different skills and to obtain a feel for all the operations of the company. In addition, job rotation provides both employees and management greater flexibility in operation, especially during periods when there is less demand for certain type of skilled workers.

In job enlargement, employees are assigned to manage and run related tasks. To help keep employees satisfied and also to enhance their creativity and performance, managers often try to redesign existing jobs. Job redesign can be accomplished through three major avenues: combining tasks, forming compatible work groups, and establishing customer relationships.

LEARNING OBJECTIVE 8
Define the objective of work-life programs, and summarize the pros and cons of the various approaches.

Companies all over the world have tried to address the personal and family needs of their employees by implementing various forms of work-life programs. Companies in the United States have moved from purely performance-based objectives and policies to a more strategic approach, which is particularly aimed at meeting the needs of employees with young children. Many such initiatives are based on giving autonomy to employees about where, when, and how they work. Companies give several reasons for supporting workers in their family or personal roles. First is increasing competition for talented employees. Second is globalization; outsourcing has made it easy and cost effective for firms to get certain jobs done overseas, enabling domestic employees to retain the jobs that add more value at home. Third is technology. Internet and information technology have made alternative work styles possible. Training is often needed to ensure that employees are aware of their responsibilities and that supervisors fully support program implementation. Two questions troubling to employers are how will the implementation of flexible schedules affect workflow, customer service, and corporate performance, and what is the work ethic of the employees who request

flexible schedules? Some of the most common types of work-life programs practiced globally include flextime programs, part-time work, work-share programs, self-managed work teams, telecommuting, and alternative work styles.

LEARNING OBJECTIVE 9
Discuss what leadership is, and summarize the major leadership theories.

Leadership is the art of motivating employees to enhance their performance in order to achieve corporate goals ethically. Four timeless and culture-independent elements of successful leadership are adaptive capacity, the ability to adapt to circumstances; creation of shared meaning, the ability to motivate people behind a common goal even in the face of adversity; personal voice, authenticity, and character founded on a strong set of principles about how people should be treated; and integrity, the delicate balance of ambition, competence, and morality. All these factors play a crucial role for successful leaders.

Leadership styles are described in leadership theories that have evolved over time. In servant leadership theory, the leader is obligated to enhance the material wealth and reputation of the organization and leave behind a legacy. An effective servant leader's role is to create an environment that will motivate people to perform better all the time and provide them with appropriate tools for achieving the corporate vision in an ethical manner. In transactional leadership, a leader provides followers rewards for good performance or reprimands followers for unacceptable performance. The leader-follower relationship in transactional leadership is strictly "arms-length," and there is no mutual binding between the two to pursue and attain higher corporate goals. Transformational leadership occurs when a leader inspires followers to work jointly to achieve the leader's vision for the organization and to benefit the individual members of the organization. Charismatic leadership consists of energetic transformational leaders who are highly capable people who can convert relatively weak organizations into powerful and successful enterprises. There are several different contingency theories of leadership. However, all of them assert that leadership effectiveness is maximized when leaders make their behavior dependent on the characteristics of their followers and the situation they are in.

It is a well-known fact that leaders do not interact with all followers in the same way. Leaders try to interact with different followers or groups of followers in unique ways so as to optimize the interaction process and achieve organizational goals. The aim is to bring out the behavioral response of all followers that will maximize leadership success. Chaos theory is based on the assumption that organizations are multifaceted and complex and operate in a disorderly environment. An external event can shock a stable business environment and lead to chaos in the short term, which can impact the organization. Leaders in this chaotic world are called on to manage their organizations through predetermined governing principles that emphasize vision, values, and organizational beliefs. When crises occur, effective leadership is exercised by enforcing agreed-on corporate governing principles, which should then lead to acceptable solutions.

LEARNING OBJECTIVE 10

Identify how leadership impacts corporate success, and critically discuss the various leadership styles used today.

Leaders are admired precisely because of their adaptive capacity, the way they react to the individual circumstances of their companies, their industries, and the global economy. Leadership style is the behavior that managers exhibit when dealing with their employees and professional staff. It is influenced by the character of the managers as well as the circumstances of the company that is being managed.

In general, leadership styles fall within a spectrum that ranges from autocratic style at one end to free-rein style on the other, with participative, or democratic, style falling in between. An autocratic style of leadership is a top-down approach to management with decisions made by the top manager with little input from subordinates. Autocratic leaders do not tolerate dissent and rarely seek employee participation in the decision-making process. A purely democratic style of leadership is practiced in only a few types of organizations, most of which are professional. Management receives input from its members and major policies are accepted for implementation on the basis of majority vote. While the advantage of such a leadership style is obviously the strong participation of all concerned, the drawback is the likely slowdown of the decision-making process. In the free-rein style of management, employees are given complete freedom to perform their jobs the way they want within the framework of company rules and regulations. Management informs the employees or employee teams on what is expected of them and when. Then it is left to the employees to decide on how they want to perform their jobs to meet corporate goals.

The *FT*/PwC report on the world's most respected companies clearly shows that for corporate success, an honest, nonconformity style of management is preferred to conventional management styles. This is primarily for two reasons. First is the attitude of the employees or subordinates to the three leadership styles. Second is from the manager's perspective. Each conventional management style has its own strengths and weaknesses. Most managers like to make the decision-making process short, so they can implement their plans quickly to achieve corporate goals. The autocratic leadership style offers speed in decision making at the expense of employee participation, and the reverse is the case with the participative leadership style. The drawback of the free-rein leadership style is that the number of companies where it can be used may not be large. Studies have shown that leadership style has to be flexible, since the reaction to certain policies or incentives in one company may not give similar results elsewhere, especially internationally. A single company operating internationally may have to adopt different management styles in different countries. The contingency approach to leadership accepts the fact that companies cannot use a "one size fits all" approach to management given the complex business environments in which they operate. Management styles need to be adapted to the specific circumstances of the organization.

Chapter Questions

1. What is motivation? Why do managers spend so much time designing different types of employee motivation programs?
2. Is the scientific management theory of motivation a thing of the past? Why? If it is not a theory of the past, give two examples, one domestic and the other international, where scientific management is currently used.
3. What is Maslow's hierarchy of needs? Do you agree with his study? Is the hierarchy of needs universally applicable?
4. What are Theory X and Theory Y? What do you fall under, and why?
5. Type Z firms are a hybrid of Type A and Type J firms. What type of firm would you rather manage, and why? Substantiate your case fully.
6. Why are expectancy, equity, and reinforcement theories called contemporary motivation theories? Which of these theories appeals to you most, and why?
7. Compare MBO and participative management. Which would you prefer, and why? Identify a company that fits into each category and explain fully.

8. What is the idea behind job enrichment and job redesign programs? How do these programs contribute to corporate profitability?

9. What is the guiding principle behind work-life programs? What is the difference between flextime and part-time programs? What are the benefits and costs of these programs?

10. Self-managing teams have been found to be successful when implemented properly. How does this work, and how can managers measure corporate benefits?

11. What are the challenges associated with telecommuting and alternative work styles? Are these fads, or are they likely to become more prevalent in the future?

12. What is leadership? With the help of a flow diagram, show how leadership influences corporate performance.

13. Summarize the three major leadership styles. What are the strengths and weaknesses of each? Identify a corporate leader who falls in each category and explain how that person fits that category.

14. The business environment in which firms operate is constantly changing. In your opinion, which is the leadership style that will be best suited to meet our changing corporate needs?

15. What is the leadership style and employee motivational strategy followed in communist economies?

Interpreting Business News

1. Several investment banks on Wall Street were fined millions of dollars by U.S. regulators for taking kickbacks in the early 2000s from rich investors in exchange for shares of hot initial public offerings (brand new stocks being sold in the market for the first time). On the basis of these revelations, what can you say about employee motivation, leadership, and ethics within these firms?

2. Carlos Ghosn of France's Renault company, took over a near-bankrupt Nissan Motor Company in 1999 and turned it to profitability in record time. Why was Ghosn trying to turn Nissan around? What does this say about the globalization of business and Ghosn's leadership style?

3. Since the early 1980s, the ratio of the chief executive's compensation package to that of the average production worker in the United States has risen from 42:1 to more than 400:1 (currently around 40:1 in Europe and Japan). What does this say about corporate leadership and social and ethical responsibility on the one hand and employee motivation on the other?

Web Assignments

1. Container Store, **www.containerstore.com,** a Dallas-based store, continues to offer some of the highest salaries in the retail industry. Container Store was ranked second in "*Fortune's* 100 Best Companies to Work For" (*Fortune*, January 20, 2003). Visit the company website and identify the benefits that employees of Container Store receive, which motivate the employees and make the company so great.

2. Motive Communications, **www.motive.com,** an Austin, Texas, software company, is not gunning for any best-company-to-work-for list. CEO Scott Harmon's credo is, "We're not warm and fuzzy, there's not a lot of cheerleading, and we don't give backrubs on Fridays." What does Harmon imply by saying that? Visit Motive's website and determine how that company motivates its employees.

3. Let's assume that you currently have a full-time job but you are one of those telecommuting wannabes. Visit the work-life program website **www.workoptions.com,** go over the checklist of things to do before approaching the boss, and develop your own proposal to submit to your boss so you can switch to telecommuting. To find out if you are temperamentally suited to work at home, visit AT&T's website, **www.att.com/telework/ get_started,** and the site managed by the Dallas consultant Joanne Pratt, **www.joannepratt.com/ wannabes.**

4. Coca-Cola, **www.cocacola.com,** is one of the most globalized companies in the world, with the bulk of its revenues and profits coming from abroad. The CEO of Coca-Cola would like consumers in every country it operates in to think of Coca-Cola as a local, not a U.S., company. Why, and how? Visit Coca-Cola's website, find out more about its CEO, and figure out her/his leadership style.

Portfolio Projects

Exploring Your Own Case in Point

After reading this chapter, you should be able to research the employee motivation strategies and leadership style of your chosen company.

1. Determine how management tries to motivate employees to achieve corporate objectives. Refer to specific theories discussed in this chapter. Does the company use the same motivation strategy in all its operations, domestically and internationally?

2. Does your company practice MBO? If your company uses job enrichment programs, describe the programs. How do employees feel about these programs?

3. If your company participates in work-life programs to help valued employees, describe the programs. Have they been successful?

4. What is the CEO's leadership style? How much of the firm's success or failure can be attributed to the CEO's leadership qualities? What do you think about the CEO's leadership?

Starting Your Own Business

After reading this chapter, you should appreciate the important role employee motivation and leadership play in your business's success.

1. How do you plan to motivate employees in your business? Explain why you will choose that particular approach.

2. How do you plan to keep employees in your business satisfied with their jobs? What will be the annual cost associated with this?

3. In order to retain valued employees, what types of work incentives will you have in place in your business? What type of work-life program discussed in this chapter would you develop for your business?

4. What leadership style would you choose for your business? Why? What are its implications for employee motivation and business performance?

Test Prepper

You've read the chapter, studied the key terms, and the exam is any day now. Think you are ready to ace it? Take this sample test to gauge your comprehension of chapter material. You can check your answers at the back of the book.

True/False Questions

Please indicate if the following statements are true or false:

_____ 1. Understanding what motivation is may be of great interest to a psychologist, but it is of little use in the real business world.

_____ 2. Frederick Taylor believed that there was one best way to get a job done because factory work could be broken up into its logical components, and the most efficient way of getting the job done could be figured out.

_____ 3. The Hawthorne Studies proved that better lighting in factories motivated employees to perform better.

_____ 4. Theory Z combines the best practices of Theory X and Theory Y.

_____ 5. Contemporary motivation theories take into consideration the realities of the present-day work environment to better understand employee motivation.

_____ 6. Peter Drucker believed strongly that a firm's management must be driven by a set of corporate objectives if it is to succeed, and this led to the MBO concept.

_____ 7. Management's primary objective in job enrichment and job redesign programs is to make existing jobs more complex so that employees remain alert at work.

_____ 8. Work-life programs are designed in such a way that they facilitate employees to work for life.

_____ 9. On the basis of the *FT*/PwC *World's Most Respected Companies Report,* one could argue that behind every great company there is a respected leader.

_____ 10. Employees prefer the autocratic style of leadership because they can receive quick responses to their problems.

Multiple-Choice Questions

Choose the best answer.

_____ 1. Motivating employees is a high-priority issue, especially in private firms, for all the following reasons *except*

a. employees are the greatest source of competitive advantage among companies and countries.

b. employee job satisfaction and welfare are crucial to retaining productive employees.

c. employees seem to get motivated when they are provided with certain incentives.

d. a major corporate goal is to enhance profits, which can be achieved with the help of motivated workers.

e. human capital, land, natural resources, and capital are all equally important.

_____ 2. Which of the following statements is *not* true of Frederick Taylor's scientific management theory?

a. Employees are interested only in making money.

b. There is only one best way of getting any job done and that way can and needs to be identified.

c. Specialization of labor is important in scientific management.

d. The ultimate goal of scientific management is to maximize productivity and corporate profits.

e. Cooperation should be promoted between managers and workers.

_____ 3. Which of the following statements is *not* true in Maslow's hierarchy of needs?

a. Employees have some basic needs that must be satisfied before they can be motivated to perform better and be rewarded.

b. Some of the basic needs are membership in social and professional clubs.

c. Physiological needs must be satisfied first.

d. Self-actualization is the drive to realize one's full potential.

e. Health insurance is one way to help meet employees' safety needs.

_____ 4. In Herzberg's motivation-hygiene theory,

a. employee satisfaction and dissatisfaction are part of the same spectrum.

b. motivation factors are as important as hygiene factors.

c. hygiene factors are more important than motivation factors.

d. hygiene factors include supervision, working conditions, and company policies.

e. motivation factors are related to the work environment.

_____ 5. Ouchi's Theory Z

a. is based on a comparison of Japanese and U.S. management practices.

b. advocates total adoption of Japanese business practices by American firms to succeed in the global environment.

c. is based on the fact that Japanese management practices are far superior to their U.S. counterparts.

d. is a combination of Theory X and Theory Y.

e. advocates individualistic decision making coupled with individual responsibility for the outcomes of decisions.

_____ 6. Equity theory states that

a. employees are motivated to work smart as long as they believe that they are treated fairly.

b. if employees are not treated fairly, they will work even harder until their effort is recognized by managers.

c. fair treatment of employees means that all employees must be treated identically.

d. all employees should have similar levels of education and professional experience.

e. employees will work hard if they think they can achieve their goals.

_____ 7. Management by objective is *not*

a. a management practice first advocated by the management guru Peter Drucker.

b. an approach that advocates the use of teams to meet corporate objectives.

c. a top-down approach with corporate goals set by the CEO.

d. an approach in which employee rewards will reflect whether the employee met his or her goals.

e. a system that involves goals based on the company's mission statement.

_____ 8. Which of the following statements about work-life programs is *false*?

a. They are here to stay, since they are designed to meet present-day employees' family needs.

b. They have been made possible because of globalization and the Internet.

c. They crucially depend on the ethical behavior of employees to be successful.

d. They are of concern to managers, as they may affect efficient workflow.

e. They do not reflect the true diversity of employee lifestyles and family structures.

_____ 9. A leader who uses a top-down approach to management decision making is using the _____ leadership style.

a. democratic

b. free-rein

c. consultative

d. autocratic

e. contingency

_____ 10. The contingency approach to leadership has become more prevalent for all the following reasons *except*

a. the business environment is varied and complex.

b. the workplace is increasingly diverse.

c. management can use a "one size fits all" method.

d. international business is so common.

e. different people are motivated by different things.

Want more questions? Visit the student website at **http://college.hmco.com/business/student/** (select Gaspar, *Introduction to Business*) and take the ACE quizzes for more practice.

Marketing

It has been said in the business world that "nothing happens until a sale is made." With this occurrence, companies generate revenues that they expect will exceed the cost of the product or service sold, so that a profit is produced.

It is the responsibility of a company's marketing department to develop the means whereby companies sell their products and services at a profit. While other departments—finance, production, research and development, accounting, human resources, and so on—contribute significantly to the sale of a company's products and services, marketing has the direct responsibility for contacting the market and convincing people or organizations in that market to purchase them.

Part Three of this text is concerned with companies' marketing efforts. Chapter 8 introduces the reader to some basic marketing concepts. These include the four types of markets, the marketing environment, what information is needed about markets and the environment and how it can be obtained, marketing objectives and strategies, and how companies' customers need to be managed. Chapter 9 provides general guidelines for developing a marketing mix, then deals specifically with two aspects of the marketing mix: the product mix and the pricing mix. Chapter 10 is concerned with the remaining two elements of the marketing mix: promotion and distribution.

As with the other chapters making up this text, Chapters 8, 9, and 10 reveal how companies' operations, in this case marketing operations, are affected by globalization, technology, and ethics.

CHAPTER 8
Marketing Basics

CHAPTER 9
Developing the Product and Pricing Mixes

CHAPTER 10
Developing the Promotion and Distribution Mixes

PART THREE

8

Marketing Basics

| **Introduction**

| **The Definition of Marketing**

| **Markets**
  Consumer Market
  Business-to-Business Market
  Government Market
  International Markets

| **The Marketing Environment**
  Competition
  Technology
  The Economy
  The Legal and Political Environment
  Culture

| **Obtaining Information About Markets and the Environment**
  Marketing Information Systems
  Marketing Research
  Databases

| **Objectives**

| **Strategies**

| **Managing Customers**
  Analyzing Customers
  Customer Satisfaction
  Customer Service

| **Careers in Marketing**

Learning Objectives

After studying this chapter, you should be able to

1. Explain the different aspects of the definition of marketing.

2. Explain the importance of marketing.

3. Describe the major types of markets and their importance.

4. Identify and describe the components of the marketing environment.

5. Distinguish between marketing information systems and marketing research.

6. Identify and understand companies' chief objectives.

7. Describe the concept of niche marketing and explain the advantages of employing a niche marketing strategy.

8. Discuss the importance of customer service programs and how they should be conducted.

Vinchel Must Learn to Market Its Wines

Vinchel is a winery located in Chelyabinsk, Russia, in the southeastern part of the Ural mountains. The company was founded in 1969. Anatoly Bondarev is Vinchel's general director.

For its first two decades, the firm was owned by the state because Russia was a Communist republic. Under the Soviet system, state planners determined how much wine the company could produce and what types. The government decided markets for the company's output, so there was no need for Vinchel to come up with a marketing plan.

Then, in the early 1990s, Russia threw off Communism and government control of the economy and of companies was no more. Virtually overnight, Bondarev and Vinchel's other executives were forced for the first time in the firm's history to develop a comprehensive program for marketing its wines in Russia and eventually to Western Europe and the United States.

Bondarev realized that this greater attention to marketing would require Vinchel to obtain more information about the market for wine and the new environment in which the company now had to operate. He and his executive team would have to establish objectives for the firm and develop appropriate strategies for achieving them. Understanding the basic concepts of effectively managing Vinchel's customers was an additional responsibility that would now have to be dealt with.

You will be introduced to these important topics in this first chapter concerning the marketing operations of business firms.

Introduction

Companies realize that they must be effective marketers in order to succeed. As a starting point, they focus on determining the needs and desires of their markets. Not only products are marketed; services must be marketed as well. Services are increasingly important to the U.S. economy and to other countries' economies.

Companies will sell their products and services through the development of an effective marketing mix (product, price, promotion, and distribution). Marketing touches our daily lives and is an important responsibility for companies. It is a vital component of the U.S. economy.

Companies can elect to serve any or all of four major markets: consumer, business-to-business, government, and international markets. They gather information about these markets and the environment (economy, culture, legal-political, technology, and competition). Companies also recognize the advantages and disadvantages of the three major ways to gather this information: marketing information systems, marketing research, and databases.

Marketing executives will set objectives for the marketing operation and will develop ways to achieve those objectives (strategies). Many companies are effectively employing a niche marketing strategy.

Successful marketers know how to manage their customers. They spend much time in analyzing them, they understand the importance of customer satisfaction and customer service programs, and they are skilled at handling customer complaints.

The Definition of Marketing

LEARNING OBJECTIVE 1
Explain the different aspects of the definition of marketing.

marketing The determination of the needs and desires of markets so that products and services can be developed, priced, promoted, and distributed to these markets in order to satisfy the market's needs and desires and the organization's objectives

Marketing can be defined as the determination of the needs and desires of markets so that products and services can be developed, priced, promoted, and distributed to these markets in order to satisfy the market's needs and desires and that organizational objectives can be achieved. A transaction takes place between a buyer and a seller; the buyer obtains a product or service, and the seller receives money. A wide variety of organizations (businesses, charities, art galleries, universities, governments, etc.) market their products, services, and ideas in order to achieve profit (revenues, market share, an enhanced image, acceptance of a viewpoint, etc.).

reality CHECK   *Ask two of your friends how they would define marketing. Are their definitions close to that given in the text?*

Marketers must know what the market's needs and desires are *before* products and services are produced. Companies need to give the market what it wants, not guess what it wants, in order to increase the likelihood that their products and services will be purchased. Boeri Sports USA is a distributor of Italian ski helmets. Marc Hauser, Boeri's president, hired InsightExpress to collect data over the Web about its customers. Pleased with the results, Hauser said: "We learned our potential customers' needs and wants so we can react to them. Making a commitment to tap into the wrong market could be fatal to our company. InsightExpress showed us that we needed to make a bold move without betting the farm."[1] In 2001, Thomas Ebeling was hired as chief executive officer of Novartis's pharmaceutical business. Formerly an executive at Pepsico, Ebeling feels that there is little difference between the two industries; both are extremely competitive markets and both require an in-depth knowledge of consumer behavior. When justifying interviewing 10,000 people with irritable bowel syndrome—they were asked to describe their symptoms and what they wanted from a drug—Ebeling said, "There's a name to this approach. Give the customers what they want."[2] Not only products are marketed; services are marketed too. Most people are amazed when they discover that over 80 percent of our nation's gross domestic product is accounted for by services (banking, insurance, education, health care, stocks, consulting, etc.), and 80% of jobs are located in services sectors of our economy.

marketing mix The combination of products or services, prices, promotion, and distribution used to market products or services to specific markets over a specific period of time

Entrance to Citibank, Manhattan.

Products and services must be priced, promoted, and distributed. The product, price, promotion, and distribution are collectively called the **marketing mix.**

It is important that a marketer's product or service satisfy the market. If not, customers will turn to other companies to have their needs and desires fulfilled.

How involved are you with marketing? It's all around you. When you purchase new clothes, when you see an advertisement on television or in a magazine, when a truck delivers your new furniture, when you receive a sample of soap in the mail, when an automobile dealer gives you a $1000 rebate on a new car, when you are asked over the telephone to answer a few questions about how you spend your money, you are involved with marketing.

LEARNING OBJECTIVE 2
Explain the importance of marketing.

How important is marketing? Virtually every organization, whether it be business or nonbusiness, engages in marketing. A large percentage of the final cost of goods and services is composed of marketing costs. Executives of organizations are spending more time in marketing. Companies are realizing that a greater emphasis on marketing can improve their profits. This is why DaimlerChrysler's chief executive officer, Dieter Schrempp, hired Jim Schroeder from Ford; the company wanted a greater emphasis on marketing so that it would obtain a maximum profit on each vehicle.[3] Many high-tech dotcoms, saddled with poor results, began to hire experienced marketing executives. For example, Autobytel.com, which sells automotive services over the Web, added a chief marketing executive (CME) in 2000. More and more chief marketing executives are rising to the top spot in their companies, eventually becoming the chief executive officer (CEO) or even chairperson. Companies realize that marketing factors are often the most important in mergers and acquisitions and in ensuring their success. Marketing is a key to successfully selling products and services outside the United States. The consulting firm McKinsey & Company estimates that 80 percent of the world's business by 2027 will be sold across international borders.[4] Michael Dell, CEO of Dell Computers, the world's largest maker of personal computers, confirmed the importance of the international market with *Business Week* when he said: "Then, there's globalization. We have about 22 percent share in 45 percent of the market. We have only 5 percent in the other 55 percent of the market. So there's a big opportunity to grow outside of the top four or five countries of the world."[5] And, finally, from an employment perspective, marketing offers challenging and financially rewarding careers for enthusiastic and hardworking men and women.

reality CHECK *Some people say that a society does not need marketing. How would you respond to this belief?*

Markets

LEARNING OBJECTIVE 3
Describe the major types of markets and their importance.

No marketing professional can be successful without knowledge of the various markets that his or her company is trying to reach. For firms in the twenty-first century, the most important markets are the consumer, business-to-business, government, and international markets.

Consumer Market

The **consumer market** consists of people and households. In 2000 in the United States, there were 281 million people and 103 million households. Population and household figures are important to marketers; the larger the population and

consumer market People and households that purchase consumer products and services

Global Business

Starbucks Seeks Growth Overseas

Starbucks Corporation realized that if it wanted to grow as it did in the past, it would have to increase the pace of its expansion into international markets. Starbucks had 17 coffee shops in Seattle in 1987; in 2001, it had 5689 outlets in 28 countries, with 4247 in the United States and Canada. Revenues reached $2.6 billion in 2001 and profits were $181 million, for a healthy profit margin of almost 7 percent.

Domestically, Starbucks executives believe that they are close to the saturation point. While there are eight states that do not have Starbucks, most large cities are awash with them. Seattle has a Starbucks for every 9400 people—considered to be the upper limit; 124 Starbucks are in New York City, although at 12,000 people per shop, only a slight opportunity for additional expansion exists. While executives know that flooding the market with new shops will result in a loss of 30 percent of revenues for existing outlets, this blanketing strategy is believed by company executives to result in marketing dominance. The CEO, Orin Smith, maintains that the company's clustering strategy eventually leads to sales above what could be obtained by one store and increases total revenue and market share.

Four hundred of the 1200 planned openings in 2002 are earmarked for overseas markets. Even with close to 1400 Starbucks in foreign countries, company executives feel that there is room for growth. By 2006, it expects to have close to 10,000 stores worldwide, with most growth coming from expansion overseas. On the near-term horizon are outlets in Athens, Mexico, and Puerto Rico.

Expanding overseas has its downside. Most of the international shops are operated with local partners; this means that the company's share of profits is only 20 to 50 percent.

Source: Stanley Homes and Geri Smith, "To Keep Up the Growth, It Must Go Global Quickly," *Business Week,* September 9, 2002, pp. 100–110.

Questions

1. What other problems besides lower profit margin is Starbucks likely to encounter as it goes overseas?
2. What countries should Starbucks emphasize as it goes international?
3. How might Starbucks try to obtain higher shares of profit from its overseas partners?

number of households, the greater the potential sales of a wide variety of products and services: candy bars, canned soup, automobiles, life insurance, banking services, oil changes, houses, furniture, dining out, soft drinks, clothes, shoes, and so on. Rates of growth in population are also examined. The World Bank estimates that the rate of population growth in the United States from 2000 to 2015 will be 0.8 percent. For some countries, like Italy, little growth is forecast; for others, mainly countries in Africa, large increases of over 3 percent annually are expected.

When companies analyze their markets, they examine differences, because not all people are equally interested in buying the same products or services. Frequently, they want to know where people live, how old they are, what their race is, and what gender they are.

In 2002, the seven most populous states in the United States had the following populations:

California	35.1 million
Texas	21.8 million
New York	19.2 million
Florida	16.7 million
Illinois	12.6 million
Pennsylvania	12.3 million
Ohio	11.4 million

These seven states had a combined population of 129.1 million. In other words, almost half, 45 percent, of our population is found in only a handful of our states. The cities in the United States with over 1 million population include

New York	8.0 million
Los Angeles	3.8 million
Chicago	2.9 million
Houston	2.0 million
Philadelphia	1.5 million
Phoenix	1.4 million
San Diego	1.3 million
Dallas	1.2 million
San Antonio	1.1 million

Census tracts divide cities into smaller units. Marketers find the smaller units helpful because they often contain individuals and families with similar characteristics, making it easier for marketers to reach specific market segments.

Exhibit 8.1 shows the distribution of the U.S. population by age. This is an important distinction for marketers because different age groups have different product and service needs and desires. For example, persons over 65 are heavy purchasers of prescription drugs and travel, whereas school-aged children need clothes and school supplies. Exhibit 8.1 reveals that the three most populous groups are 25 to 34, 35 to 44, and 45 to 54 years of age. Like most western European countries and Japan, the population in the United States is, on average, getting older, meaning that the market for people over 65 is becoming more important.

In 2000, 82 percent of the U.S. population was white, 13 percent was African American, 4 percent was Asian or Pacific Islander, 1 percent was Native American or Eskimo, and 12 percent was Hispanic. In 2000, 48.9 percent of the U.S. population was male, compared to 51.1 percent female. Recently, some marketers have begun aggressive efforts to target the gay and lesbian subsets of the male and female markets.

Income is another factor marketers examine, because people and households need money to acquire goods and services. Marketers of luxury goods, like Jaguars and Armani suits, are especially interested in how many high-income people there are in a given market. Income per capita in the United States was $34,100 in 2000; 21.3 percent of U.S. households earned $20,000 to $34,999 a year, 17.5 percent made $35,000 to $49,999, and 35.3 percent brought in $50,000 or more.[6]

Marketers often look beyond these demographic factors when they study the consumer market. They also look at psychological and sociological determinants of consumer behavior. Exhibit 8.2 (on p. 280) shows these factors. The inner ring shows the psychological factors, while the outer ring contains the sociological factors.

Psychological Factors.
Psychological factors affect what, why, and how individuals purchase. Much of human behavior is learned. **Learning** occurs by acquiring information, then developing preferences and habits. Learning is usually achieved by providing rewards. Marketing strategies, especially those related to

EXHIBIT 8.1

Distribution of the U.S. Population by Age, 2002

Age	Percentage of U.S. Population
Under 5 years	6.8
5 to 9 years	7.3
10 to 14 years	7.3
15 to 19 years	7.2
20 to 24 years	6.7
25 to 34 years	14.2
35 to 44 years	16.0
45 to 54 years	13.4
55 to 59 years	4.8
60 to 64 years	3.8
65 to 74 years	6.5
75 to 84 years	4.4
85 years and over	1.5
Total	100.00

Source: *Statistical Abstract of the United States,* 2003.

psychological factors Learning, perception, motives, attitudes, and self-concept that affect what, why, and how consumers purchase goods and services

learning Acquiring information, preferences, and habits that determine what, why, and how consumers purchase goods and services

EXHIBIT 8.2

Determinants of Consumer Behavior

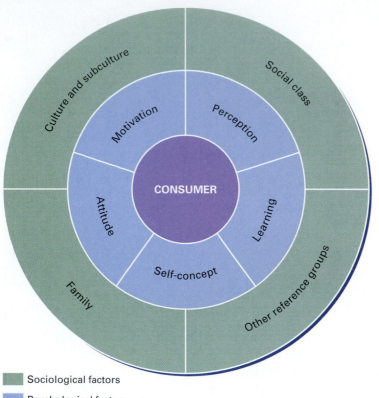

■ Sociological factors

■ Psychological factors

perception The awareness of cues or stimuli from the physical surroundings that affect what, why, and how consumers purchase goods and services

attitudes Consistent ways of acting that determine what, why, and how consumers purchase goods and services

self-concept The combination of self-image, ideal image, looking-glass self and real self that determines what, why, and how consumers purchase goods and services

sociological factors Group-related variables that affect what, why, and how consumers purchase goods and services

reference groups Groups to which consumers belong or would like to belong to that affect what, why, and how they purchase goods and services

promotion, need to understand the process through which consumers learn.

Perception refers to the cues, or stimuli, that we are exposed to from our physical surroundings and how we respond to them. Much perception is selective. For example, we seek out and notice information that interests us and ignore that which does not. An understanding of perception is important; for example, it explains why consumers are resistant to advertising that tries to get them to switch from a familiar product or service to a new one.

Motives deal with our needs. Physical needs involve survival requirements, such as food, drink, shelter, and efforts to protect ourselves from harm. Social needs involve acceptance by family and friends and trying to achieve status above others. Self needs refer to the striving for satisfaction. **Attitudes** involve our consistent way of acting toward a given object or idea. Marketers want to know what consumers' attitudes are toward their products, brands, and company.

A person's **self-concept** is made up of four components: *self-image*, the way we see ourselves; *ideal image*, the way we would like to be; *looking-glass self*, the way we think others see us; and *real self*, the way we really are. The possessions we own and the activities we pursue are a reflection of our self-concept. Marketers will try to match, through product design, pricing, advertising, packaging, and so on, the image their product has with consumers' self-images. For example, Volvo's design and marketing effort for many of its models portray a safety image that will resonate well with purchasers who regard themselves as being cautious, deliberative, and protective.

Sociological Factors. While psychological aspects of consumer markets tend to focus on individuals, **sociological factors** look at individuals in group settings. **Reference groups** are groups individuals belong to or would like to belong to. The family is probably the most important reference group for most of us and will strongly influence the attitudes, beliefs, and actions of its members. Parents will act as purchasing agents for children. Frequently, the entire family will act jointly in buying such items as housing, food, vacations, and automobiles. What we learn about consuming in a family setting often stays with us forever. Other reference groups—friends, church, teammates, coworkers, classmates—will also affect what we buy, why we buy and how we buy.

Culture is a learned way of life that a society hands down from one generation to the next. Culture is made up of shared beliefs, values, customs, and rules (standards of behavior). How we act toward others, what is important to us, what we wear, eat, and otherwise buy and consume are greatly influenced by culture. *Subcultures* are smaller groups within society that share much of the larger culture, but have their own distinct religious or racial identity. The two most important subcultures in the United States today, because of their size and significant levels of expenditures, are the African American and Hispanic communities.

The social hierarchy that exists in a country is often called **social class structure.** We have all heard of such designations as upper class, middle class, and lower class. Each tends to have certain distinctions regarding purchases. Upper classes, for example, are excellent markets for luxury products.

Consumers generally go through a specific process when they purchase (see Exhibit 8.3).

- They become aware of a problem that can be solved by a purchase.
- They hunt for information about alternative solutions, including both products or services and the sellers of these products and services.
- These products or services and vendors are evaluated on criteria important to the consumer—price, quality, durability, taste, delivery times, and so on.
- They make a purchase decision to include the specific product or service and the vendor from which the item will be purchased.
- After purchase, they evaluate the product or service and vendor. The possible outcomes include being satisfied or dissatisfied or experiencing dissonance, that is, the feeling that they have made a purchasing mistake. It is important to note that dissonance can occur after a purchase but before the product or service is even used. In order to reduce dissonance, and the possibility that the item in question may be returned, smart marketers will reassure the buyer about the choice made.

social class structure The social level in a society that affects what, why, and how consumers purchase goods and services

EXHIBIT 8.3

The Consumer's Buying Decision Process

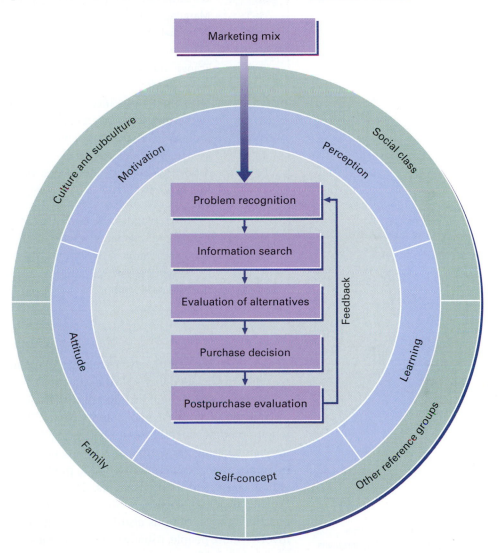

Business-to-Business Market

Many companies in the United States sell their products and services to other businesses and organizations—the **business-to-business market.** In order to identify potential customers who might be interested in purchasing what companies have to sell, the **North American Industry Classification System (NAICS)** is often used. Exhibit 8.4 (on p. 282) shows the two-digit codes for the 20 major industries included in the NAICS. The NAICS divides these industries into various subindustries through the use of three-, four- and five-digit codes. For example, one of the subindustries of manufacturing is 315, apparel. Classification 3151 designates knitting mills, and 31511 identifies hosiery and sock mills. Companies wanting to

business-to-business market The market where businesses purchase goods and services from other businesses

North American Industry Classification System (NAICS) The use of two, three, four, and five digits to classify industries and subindustries in the United States, Canada, and Mexico

EXHIBIT 8.4

The North American Industry Classification System (NAICS)
for Business Firms

Code	Industry
11	Agriculture, forestry, fishing, and hunting
21	Mining
22	Utilities
23	Construction
31–33	Manufacturing
41–43	Wholesale trade
44–46	Retail trade
48–49	Transportation and warehousing
51	Information
52	Finance and insurance
53	Real estate and rental and leasing
54	Professional, scientific, and technical services
55	Management of companies
56	Administrative and support and waste management and remediation services
61	Educational services
62	Health care and social assistance
71	Arts, entertainment, and recreation
72	Accommodation and food service
81	Other services (except public administration)
91–93	Public administration

market their products or services to any of these industries can obtain lists of companies that are included in the NAICS categories.

Marketers need to understand the differences between the ways consumers and organizations purchase goods and services. While many purchases by consumers involve modest expenditures for consumable products, organizations are more likely to be purchasing more expensive products, like machinery, that are used in making other products. Business firms tend to purchase in much larger quantities than individual consumers or households. They put more emphasis on rational buying motives such as efficiency, productivity, and cost versus value than consumers. Purchasing by organizations also involves a more complex and lengthier process and involves more people, usually trained specialists, than that by individual consumers.

It is helpful for marketers to understand the type of purchasing decisions facing organizations. **New tasks** are brand-new, first-time purchasing decisions; they require a great deal of information gathering and evaluation. A **straight rebuy** situation is routine and requires little or no time or effort. In a **modified rebuy** case, the buying firm is considering different suppliers for an item previously bought on a straight rebuy basis.

Government Market

In the United States, the **government market** involves purchases by local, state, and federal governments, which amount to about 25 percent of all purchases. Thus, the government sector is an important customer. In some countries, governments are

new tasks Brand-new, first-time purchasing decisions for organizations that require a great deal of information gathering and evaluation

straight rebuy A routine purchasing situation for organizations that requires little or no time or effort to conclude

modified rebuy The buying decision for organizations that involves the consideration of different suppliers for an item previously bought on a straight rebuy basis

government market Local, state, and federal purchasers of goods and products

even more significant purchasers. The governments of Denmark and Sweden account for about 45 percent of all purchases nationwide; and it is even higher, almost 60 percent, in Belgium and the Netherlands.

Governments buy a wide variety of products and services, including office supplies and equipment, automobiles, food, clothing, specialized military hardware, and research services. In order to successfully sell to governments, it is necessary to understand how governments buy. When standard items are being purchased by governments, marketers are normally required to submit bids that give prices for the products with the service specifications and performance requirements as stipulated by the government. In general, the lowest-priced bid will be accepted. For items like planes and warships, the government will negotiate with one or two selected suppliers, putting a great deal of emphasis on their reputation and past evidence of their being able to do the job. Because small businesses are important determinants of growth, the U.S. government sets aside funds specifically earmarked for bids submitted by them.

Government buying is open to public scrutiny and control. Thus, it is relatively easy to be aware of and understand what products and services the government needs. On the other hand, many small firms are reluctant to do business with the government because of the bureaucracy encountered and the paperwork required.

reality CHECK *Scan your local newspaper for three or four days. Are there any examples of the types of products and services your local government purchases?*

International Markets

With 95 percent of the world's population living outside the United States and 80 percent of its income there, it is not surprising that many companies are finding that **international markets** offer attractive opportunities for U.S. products and services.

international markets Markets for products and services that exist in foreign countries

Case in Point

Sony Decides to Enter the China Market

In 2002, Sony was making plans to market its *PlayStation* in China. Previously, Sony had been reluctant to enter the Chinese market due to piracy problems. Besides *PlayStation*, China has also been accused of being a source of pirated video games, DVDs, and music CDs. As part of its marketing strategy, Sony will get local talent to develop the software programs. They will also be given a stake in the business, which Sony executives believe will reduce the piracy problem.

Most *PlayStation* consoles are imported from Hong Kong. They retail in Shanghai for around $340, much higher than what is quoted on Amazon.com ($249.99, plus shipping and handling). However, at

about $1 each, pirated software retails in China at a much lower price than elsewhere. *PlayStation* is one of Sony's most profitable items, with a profit margin of 8.4 percent. It is the leader in market share over such competitors as *Sega*, *Nintendo*, and Microsoft's *Xbox*. None of these had been introduced into China by the beginning of 2003.

Questions

1. What are the advantages and disadvantages of Sony's China strategy? What areas of marketing covered in this chapter are mentioned in this article? Should Sony introduce *PlayStation* into China? Why or why not?

A country's population and income determine its attractiveness as a market. Some countries have very large populations.

China	1.3 billion
India	1.1 billion
Indonesia	210 million
Brazil	170 million
Russia	146 million
Pakistan	138 million
Bangladesh	131 million
Nigeria	127 million[7]

Others have very small populations. For example, Botswana, Estonia, Gabon, Gambia, Guinea-Bissau, Kuwait, Latvia, Lesotho, Mauritius, Mongolia, Namibia, Oman, Slovenia, Swaziland, and Trinidad and Tobago have fewer than 2 million people.

As with population, there are wide disparities in incomes. Switzerland has a per capita income of $38,140, followed by Japan with $35,620, Norway with $34,530, and Denmark with $32,230. Austria, Hong Kong, Finland, Germany, the Netherlands, Singapore, Sweden, and the United Kingdom have per capita incomes of $24,000 to $27,000. On the other hand, many countries, chiefly those in Africa, have per capita incomes of less than $300 per year.[8]

The U.S. government spends over $3 billion a year to help companies either to begin marketing their products or services overseas or to expand already existing operations. A good deal of this funding is to provide information about overseas markets.

- The National Trade Data Bank contains over 200,000 government documents dealing with international markets.
- The International Trade Administration contains both country and product experts who have information on overseas markets, as does the U.S. and Foreign Commercial Services.
- The International Data Base, located in the U.S. Department of Commerce's Bureau of the Census, helps firms identify and analyze potential foreign markets.
- U.S. Export Assistance Centers (USEACS) help identify attractive overseas target markets.

The Marketing Environment

LEARNING OBJECTIVE 4
Identify and describe the components of the marketing environment.

marketing environment Areas outside the firm (competition, technology, economy, legal and political arenas, and culture) that companies need to monitor and react to

In addition to the market, marketers need to understand what is occurring in the **marketing environment.** The marketing environment consists of competition, technology, the economy, the legal and political arenas, and culture. Developments in these areas can positively or negatively affect companies' operations. If positively affected, marketers will want to take advantage of the opportunities available; if negatively impacted, they need to decide what to do to minimize the damage. Since the marketing environment exists outside the firm, little or no control can be exerted over what happens; firms pretty much have to operate reactively.

Competition

Most large companies have established **competitor intelligence (CI)** programs to monitor their competitors. The Quaker State chairperson and CEO, Herbert M. Baum, justifies his firm's CI program like this: "I don't ever want to be in a fair fight, I want an edge everywhere I go."[9]

Companies that have installed CI programs have benefited greatly. Nutra Sweet put an $84 million advertising campaign on hold when it discovered Johnson & Johnson's Sucralose would not get quick approval by the Food and Drug Administration. (Nutra Sweet estimates that its competitor intelligence unit is worth at least $50 million annually in sales gained or revenues not lost). Marriott built a new chain of hotels, Fairfield Inn, which has an occupancy rate 10 percent higher than similar operations, when it found some travelers prefer lower-priced lodging with less amenities.[10] Texas Instruments gathered information that prompted it to acquire two firms and resulted in a "leaner and more decisive investment strategy."[11]

The first step in any CI program is to identify who the competition is. Companies that are leaders in an industry, produce and market the same products or services, and have the potential for a significant technology breakthrough are those that should be included on the list. Foreign competitors should not be ignored, particularly those that market products and services in the domestic market and in overseas markets where a firm is operating.

The next step is to determine what information about competitors is needed. Their strategies, prices, strengths and weaknesses, objectives, market shares, and new product plans are usually considered to be the most desirable information. Then, ways to collect the information have to be developed. It should be emphasized that firms need to employ ethical and legal means. Paying janitors to root through competitors' trash and planting electronic bugs in competitors' conference rooms are not acceptable. Besides, 95 percent of what is needed can be gotten by studying magazines, newspapers, annual reports, sales force reports, competitors' advertisements, and their executives' speeches. Emmanuel Kampouris, CEO of American Standard, a $5 billion manufacturer of toilets, brakes, and air conditioners, uses the press, financial reports, and market research. "I don't consider our competitors as Communists or Hitler," he said.[12]

Technology

We see the results of technology all around us—personal computers, Internet, interactive television, high-definition television (HDTV), microwave ovens, cell phones, laser surgery, more-fuel-efficient cars, and so on. **Technology** refers to the development of new products *and* processes. Companies need new products to replace existing products that have to be phased out and to help the firm to grow. New processes, such as those applied to a company's manufacturing or logistics operations, help companies to reduce their costs and operate more efficiently.

competitor intelligence (CI) Information about competitors

technology The development of new products and processes

A shopper scans her groceries in a supermarket. This technology helps customers save time.

Firms need to monitor the technology environment to keep abreast of new products and processes that are being developed. Significant new product breakthroughs can severely hurt the sales of companies, so the sooner this information is available, the quicker the threatened firm can adjust. The argument applies to new processes. It is important for companies to remember that new technology frequently originates in another industry or even in another country and is then adopted by the threatened firm's industry.

How should firms adjust to a new technology? Three courses of action are possible. First, the company can do nothing. Second, it can try to improve its existing product or process. Third, it can adopt the new technology. The existing evidence suggests that the third option is preferable. Not doing anything will result in the firm's product or process being rapidly outdated. Piecemeal efforts to improve existing technology usually are time-consuming and ineffective. Companies that quickly adopt a new technology typically do very well; they realize that all products and processes have performance limits and that all technology eventually has to be replaced.

The Economy

It is important for marketers to be knowledgeable about the status of the economy. The size of a country's gross domestic product (GDP) is often viewed as a key measure. In 2000, the ten countries with the largest GDPs were

United States	$ 9.6 trillion
Japan	$ 4.5 trillion
Germany	$ 2.1 trillion
United Kingdom	$ 1.5 trillion
France	$ 1.4 trillion
Italy	$ 1.2 trillion
China	$ 1.1 trillion
Canada	$700 billion
Brazil	$600 billion
Spain	$600 billion[13]

Marketers are also interested in what is happening to GDPs. Are they increasing or decreasing; that is, is the size of an economy growing, flat, or shrinking?

What is happening to prices is also important. If prices are increasing, inflation is occurring. If inflation is steep enough—say 20, 40, even 100 percent annually—the purchasing power of people is reduced if their incomes have not kept pace and they will probably purchase less. Some countries like Brazil, Argentina, and Israel have, unfortunately, experienced rampant inflation in recent times. Turkey's high rate of inflation has been one of the factors explaining why it has not been granted membership in the European Union.

Deflation occurs when prices are falling. Too much deflation brings its own set of problems. Companies have to keep cutting their prices in order to sell their products. Sometimes this will not be successful, and companies' revenues will decrease, along with their profits, causing them to reduce output and lay off workers. It was believed by many economists that, in the fall of 2002, the United States was in a deflationary period. Companies with lower costs than competitors would be able to absorb price cuts. For example, Southwest Airlines' expenses are 29 percent below the industry average, so it would continue to be successful with its low-fare strategy. Other companies, in order to cope, put more stress on higher-priced products directed to more affluent markets. General Electric began pushing high-end refrigerators ($2,000 prices) and Pepsico is marketing bite-sized Go Snack chips that will command higher prices.[14]

Distribution of income is of interest to marketers. A large percentage of high-income households is good for the marketer of luxury products. A large percentage of middle-income people means a sizable market for a wide range of products and services. On the other hand, a high percentage of low-income households that will have trouble affording even the basic necessities is a marketer's nightmare.

The Legal and Political Environment

Marketers need to abide by the laws that are in existence, anticipate those that might be passed, and be aware of how these laws are being administered. There are two major sets of laws that affect marketing operations. One set protects consumers. The Federal Trade Commission Act (1914) prohibits deceptive advertising and labeling. The Pure Food and Drug Act (1906) prevents the distribution of adulterated or misbranded foods, drugs, and unsafe consumer products. The Consumer Products Safety Act (1972) protects the consumer from unreasonable risk of injury from products not covered by previous legislation. The Fair Packaging and Labeling Act (1966) outlaws deceptive packaging or labeling of consumer products. The Trademark Counterfeiting Act (1980) penalizes companies that deal in counterfeit consumer goods that can threaten health or safety. The Nutritional Labeling and Education Act (1990) prohibits exaggerated health claims and requires processed foods to contain nutritional information on labels. The Telephone Consumer Protection Act (1991) places restrictions on unwanted telephone solicitations.

The second set of laws is concerned with unfair competitive practices. The most important of these are

> Sherman Antitrust Act (1890). Prohibits various activities that restrain trade. Puts restrictions on attempts to monopolize.
>
> Clayton Act (1914). An amendment to the Sherman Antitrust Act, it outlaws such specific practices as price discrimination, exclusive dealer arrangements, and tying arrangements where a customer has to buy a product from a company related to the one already being purchased from that company.
>
> Federal Trade Commission Act (1914). Created the Federal Trade Commission and gave it power to prevent unfair methods of competition.
>
> Robinson-Patman Act (1936). Prohibits price discrimination that lessens competition among wholesalers and retailers.
>
> Wheeler Lea Act (1938). Even if competition is not injured, acts and practices deemed to be unfair or deceptive are prohibited.
>
> Lanham Trademark Act (1946). Provides protection for companies' brand names, brand marks, trade names, and trademarks.

Regulatory agencies make decisions that interpret laws. Some of the major ones are the Food and Drug Administration, the Federal Trade Commission, and the Consumer Products Safety Commission. Many of the decisions by these agencies have far-reaching consequences. For example, the Food and Drug Administration did not approve a cancer-fighting drug developed by ImClone; that led to allegations of illegal insider trading being made against the company's CEO and Martha Stewart. They were accused of selling ImClone stock in advance of the FDA's ruling, which caused a sharp decline in the stock's price.

Individuals who head up regulatory agencies often bring a certain predisposition that will influence the work of the agency. A case in point is Timothy J. Murris, President

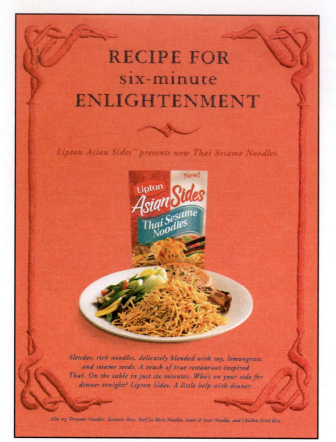

RECIPE FOR six-minute ENLIGHTENMENT

Lipton Asian Sides™ presents new Thai Sesame Noodles.

New! Lipton Asian Sides Thai Sesame Noodles

Slender, rich noodles, delicately blended with soy, lemongrass, and sesame seeds. A touch of true restaurant-inspired Thai. On the table in just six minutes. Who's on your side for dinner tonight? Lipton Sides. A little help with dinner.

Also try Teriyaki Noodles, Teriyaki Rice, Beef Lo Mein Noodles, Sweet & Sour Noodles, and Chicken Fried Rice.

This ad shows an example of the influence of foreign culture on products sold in the United States.

George W. Bush's nominee to head the Federal Trade Commission. Murris is believed to be more open to mergers than previous heads and less likely to demand concessions from the prospective partners. The previous chairperson, Robert Pitofsky, gave high-tech deals particularly close scrutiny, requiring, for example, that AOL and Time Warner agree to restrictions on their efforts on interactive television and that the pharmaceutical firm Novartis divest itself of some promising drug products. Murris believes that mergers can create huge efficiencies and is not inclined to believe that regulators can accurately predict the competitive outcomes of mergers before they occur.[15]

Culture

Marketers need to understand the culture that exists in their own countries, but more importantly, they need to recognize the culture that predominates in other countries.

Language, religion, holidays, relationships, education, work, attitudes toward time, and so on, are determined by culture. Because cultures overseas differ so much from that in the United States, companies that are ignorant of them are bound to make damaging mistakes. Chevrolet introduced the Nova car into Latin America, not realizing that "no va" in Spanish means "it won't go." Campbell Soup failed in Brazil because it didn't know that Brazilian housewives preferred to add their own ingredients to basic stock. Coca-Cola was astonished to find out that the calligraphy they used in China for Coca-Cola was translated "Bite the waxed tadpole." Many marketers doing business in Arab countries, such as Saudi Arabia, Kuwait, and Oman, offend their Arab hosts by using their left hand (the "toilet hand"), showing the soles of their shoes, asking about the host's wife, and overly praising some possession of the Arab businessman (he thinks he needs to give it to you).

reality CHECK   *Skim a recent issue of a business publication, such as, Business Week, Fortune, Forbes, or The Wall Street Journal. Record any references to the cultural dimensions of the marketing environment.*

Obtaining Information About Markets and the Environment

Companies use marketing information systems (MIS), marketing research, and databases to gather information about markets and the environment.

Marketing Information Systems

marketing information systems (MIS)
Systems that continually monitor, with heavy use of computers, a company's market, competition, customers, products, and marketing operations in order to determine if problems exist

LEARNING OBJECTIVE 5
Distinguish between marketing information systems and marketing research.

Marketing information systems (MIS) have been installed in many companies to fill the need for continuous monitoring of the market, competition, customers, products, and marketing operations. The information obtained may be internal to

EXHIBIT 8.5

Location and Type of MIS Information

Type of Information	Location of Information	
	Internal	External
Secondary	Financial or accounting data and reports Operating reports Sales force's call reports and other sales reports	Periodicals Newsletter and bulletins Published reports Syndicated reports Books, directories, encyclopedias, and handbooks Databases Organizations
Primary	Studies conducted by company's marketing research department Company's sales force and other employees Marketing databases	Trade shows, exhibits, and fairs Conventions and meetings Company's advertising agencies Company's channels of distribution Consultants

the company or external to it. In addition, the information may be secondary or primary. *Secondary information* is already available; it has been developed by someone other than the company using it. *Primary information* is information that was obtained by a company for its own use. Exhibit 8.5 provides examples of the various types of information and their sources.

reality CHECK *Go to your university or college library and scan the table of contents in the* United States Statistical Abstract. *What information does it have that would be useful to marketers of consumer products?*

The specific kinds of information that an MIS would be expected to generate are illustrated by the information Mary Kay Cosmetics wanted its MIS to obtain about its European market. The company, which uses female sales associates to sell its products via demonstrations and "parties" and has sales of over $1 billion, wanted the following information about Europe:

Industry data, especially sales and trends by product category
Attitudes, interests, and lifestyles of European women
Population and income data
Cultural, social, and economic information about European countries
Perceptions of European women about Mary Kay products and career opportunities
Employment opportunities for women
Women's use of skin care and makeup products
Legal aspects of direct selling in Europe
Daily financial information, including revenues and expenses

Mary Kay executives hoped that the MIS-Europe would result in a number of benefits, including keeping customers longer, getting additional income from them, identifying customer segments most responsive to specific types of promotional programs, reducing marketing expenses, and shortening the time required to develop new products. They will examine such performance variables as revenues, profits, market share, repeat purchases, and market penetration levels to determine the effectiveness of the MIS.

An MIS reports on a regular basis how well a firm is doing. It examines such performance variables as revenues, profits, market share, repeat purchases, and penetration levels. Company executives are especially interested when an MIS reveals that their firm's performance is not up to par. It is at this juncture that the firm will usually call on its marketing research department to find out the reasons for the poor performance. Thus, the major differences between marketing information systems and marketing research are that

- MIS focuses more on the environment; marketing research more on marketing performance.
- MIS provides information on a regular basis; marketing research as needed.
- MIS stresses the *what* of information gathering; marketing research the *why*.
- The use of MIS precedes marketing research; that is, marketing research is employed after an MIS uncovers a problem.

Marketing Research

marketing research The process whereby marketers are provided with information so that effective marketing decisions can be made

Marketing research is the process where marketers are provided with information so that effective marketing decisions can be made. Decisions in the areas of measuring market potentials, forecasting, product testing, sales analysis, market share analysis, and media research are often the focus of marketing research. The marketing research process is shown in Exhibit 8.6.

EXHIBIT 8.6

The Marketing Research Process

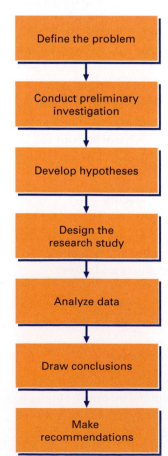

Define the problem

Conduct preliminary investigation

Develop hypotheses

Design the research study

Analyze data

Draw conclusions

Make recommendations

preliminary investigation The step in the marketing research process wherein companies try to get some idea as to what is the cause of a problem

hypothesis Marketing researchers' idea as to what is the cause of a problem

research study design A comprehensive plan for testing an hypothesis, that includes planning the sample and collecting data

Failure to accurately define the problem is disastrous because time spent on the subsequent steps will be wasted. Assuming that the problem for a floor cleaning product is that its sales have dropped 20 percent in one year, let's examine the marketing research steps.

The purpose of a **preliminary investigation** is to get some idea as to what is causing the problem. Researchers use a variety of sources in conducting the preliminary investigation, such as reading newspapers, business magazines, and trade association reports; analyzing internal company data; talking informally with key executives; and talking directly with customers.

Researchers then develop **hypotheses,** or tentative explanations, as to what is causing the problem. In the floor cleaning example, the hypothesis to be tested is that the product's offensive odor is causing its sales decline.

The **research study design** is a comprehensive plan for testing an hypothesis. It involves two major aspects: planning the sample and collecting data. It would be too expensive and time-consuming to get in touch with all of the consumers in the United States who are no longer using the floor cleaning product to find out if its odor is the problem. Fortunately, the company can get a good idea by getting in touch with only a small number of them. This is called a *sample*. Let's assume that the company decided that the sample size would be 200. The company has a variety of ways to collect the information it wants. It could use personal interviews, a mail questionnaire, or a telephone survey. We will assume that the firm elected to use telephone interviews in which skilled interviewers would question former users as to why they no longer use the product.

In *data analysis,* the major findings of the study are summarized, usually in tables. In the floor cleaning example, lets assume the following results from the 200 people interviewed over the telephone:

Reasons for Not Purchasing the Cleaning Product	Number of Respondents Indicating Reason	Percentage of Respondents Indicating Reason
The product did not do a good job of cleaning the floors.	10	5.0
The product has a bad odor.	100	50.0
The product's price was too high.	5	2.5
The product's package was too difficult to open.	25	12.5
The product's package was not attractive.	10	5.0
I found another product I liked better.	25	12.5
The product often was not available at the store where I shopped.	25	12.5
Total	200	100.0

Once the marketer has data to look at, conclusions can be drawn as to whether the hypothesis tested can be accepted. In this example, half of the people interviewed stated that the offensive odor was the reason they stopped buying the product, and all other reasons were indicated by much lower percentages of the respondents. Thus, the company can confidently conclude that the product's smell very likely explains why its sales have been dropping.

Recommendations flow from the conclusions. In this example, the marketing researchers would probably recommend that the company find some way to make the cleaning product's odor more acceptable.

Databases

Databases are banks of information companies have about their *individual* customers. They reflect the realization by many companies that they no longer can be successful by believing that all customers are equally valuable to them. Customer databases are considered to be one of a company's most important assets. As such, they are viewed as a necessary investment. While current customers are the most significant focus, prospects and former customers should also be included. Basic information that should be in the database for current customers are name, address, telephone number, products they have purchased, the value of their purchases, and whether the purchase was in response to any promotional program. With this information, companies can obtain three crucial measures of the value of customers: recency of purchase, frequency of purchase, and dollar amount of total purchases. Commonly referred to as *RFM*, recency, frequency, and dollar amount are the data needed to calculate the **lifetime value (LTV)** of customers. The higher the lifetime value, the more valuable a customer.

By knowing how specific customers have responded to previous promotions, companies can tailor future promotions to them. These data will indicate what types of products and services should be offered, whether customers should

databases Banks of information that companies have about their individual customers

lifetime value (LTV) The future value of a customer based on recency, frequency, and dollar amount of past purchases

receive a promotion, what time of the year are they most and least likely to buy, and what kind of incentive should be used.

share of wallet The percentage of a customer's spending on a product or service category that is obtained by a specific company's product or service

An increasingly important piece of information that databases provide is **share of wallet.** This refers to the percentage of a customer's spending on a product or service category that the company obtains. For example, if Ms. Smith spends $1000 annually on clothing and $300 at one store, the store's share of wallet is 30 percent. Those customers for whom a firm has a low share of wallet should be targeted, because potential exists to increase its revenues. Some examples of how companies have benefited from using their databases include

- A men's clothing store found it was overstocked with size 42 suits. The sales manager called all of its size-42 customers; 50 percent of them purchased one or more of the overstocked suits.
- Hilton Hotels got 50 percent of its frequent-guest club members to take unplanned trips that included stops at Hilton Hotels.
- Land Rover identified 4000 Range Rover owners and invited them to a special marketing event. It sold 1000 vehicles with an average price of $52,000, giving it a return on investment of $150,000.
- Fashion Bug stopped mailings to the 10 percent of customers who had spent less than $50 in the previous 18 months. It saved $90,000 a year without reducing profitability.

relationship marketing Developing long-lasting, profitable relations with customers

A company's database can be used to help it develop long-lasting relationships with its customers. Called **relationship marketing,** the database will identify those customers who are profitable for the firm and who have been customers for some time and hopefully will continue to be so in the future. This can be achieved by making a strong effort to satisfy those customers so well that they will not consider taking their business to a competitor.

Some ethical concerns have been voiced about databases and their uses. Critics allege that the information contained invades the privacy of customers who are included in the database. Another criticism is that companies will sell the information in the database to other companies, which will then begin to heavily promote their products and services to these persons, adding to the volume of junk mail that they receive. Consumers often complain that they are not treated as well as the better customers identified by the database.

Objectives

LEARNING OBJECTIVE 6
Identify and understand companies' chief objectives.

objectives Goals or targets that companies and their marketing departments establish and try to achieve

Objectives are goals or targets that companies and their marketing operations are trying to achieve. Companies' objectives usually emphasize revenues, profitability, market share, and market value. Revenues are firms' sales in dollars and are found by multiplying the number of units sold by the price customers paid. For example, if 1000 units with a price of $40 each are sold, revenue is $40,000 (1000 × $40). Often, companies will stipulate a specific revenue that they are trying to achieve, such as $60 million.

Profits are what a company has remaining after all costs for materials used to produce products, wages, utilities, rent, advertising, transportation, and so on have been deducted from revenues. If a company has $100 million in revenues and $95 million in costs, it would have earned $5 million in profits ($100 million – $95 million). Profits are important because they reward owners for their risk in investing in a company, significantly affect the price of a company's stocks, and are used to reinvest in a company so it can continue to grow. Besides trying to achieve certain numerical levels of profit, firms will also pursue objectives related to profit margin, return on assets, and return on owners' equity. **Profit margin** is calculated by dividing profit by revenues. If a firm had a profit of $5 million and revenues of $100 million, its profit margin would be 5 percent ($5 million/$100 million). If the firm used $50 million in assets (plant and equipment, cash, inventories, etc.) to obtain the $5 million in profits, its **return on assets** would be 10 percent ($5 million/$50 million). Owners' equity is the level of assets contributed to the firm by its owners. If owners' equity for the firm with the $5 million profit was $25 million, its **return on owners' equity** would be 20 percent ($5 million/$25 million).

Market share is the percentage of total units sold of a product that is accounted for by a specific company's products. For example, if there are 10 million cars sold in the United States and Ford sold 2 million of these, Ford's market share would be 20 percent (2 million/10 million). Toyota is a company that emphasizes market share as an objective. Its stated objective is to never let market share in Japan drop below 40 percent. Usually companies obtain improved profits as their market share increases. However, they often find that, at some level of market share, profits may decline because they have to spend so much to attract other firms' customers. Also, companies with high market shares may become targets of other companies or the U.S. government if it believes that that market position has been achieved unfairly.

Recently, U.S. firms have been stressing market value of their companies as an objective. **Market value,** or capitalization rate, is determined by multiplying the price of a company's stock by the number of its shares of stock. For example, if a company has 1 million shares that have a price of $40, the firm's market value is $40 million ($40 × 1 million). Following are some examples of objectives that various companies have strived to obtain:

- Skechers is a footwear company located in California. Its revenues are close to $1 billion annually. Its international sales account for 10 percent of this total. Skechers wants to increase this percentage to 20 to 50 percent in three to five years.[16]
- Michelin, the world's largest tire maker, seeks a consistent 10 percent profit margin.[17]
- eBay's CEO, Meg Whitman, wants her company to achieve $3 billion in revenues by 2005—a 50 percent annual increase.[18]
- Compaq wanted to obtain revenue growth of 6 to 8 percent.[19]
- According to Bobbie Gaunt, CEO of Ford of Canada, it is striving to be number one or number two in each vehicle segment.[20]
- Du Pont pushed to have 30 percent of its profits generated by its biotech and pharmaceutical operations.[21]

Like the overall company, the marketing department has objectives to achieve. These are related to various aspects of the marketing operation. It is expected that if these departmental objectives are achieved, they will help in obtaining the company's objectives. For example, if sales personnel reach their target of calling on so many prospects and customers, it is expected that company revenue objectives will be met. Some examples of marketing objectives that are representative of what companies might establish include

- To reduce sales force expenses by $1 million
- To increase the number of calls made by the sales force to an average of 25 a week
- To achieve a cost-per-sales call of $200
- To reduce average delivery times to customers by 1.5 days

profit margin A company's profit divided by its revenues

return on assets A company's profit divided by the assets used to obtain that profit

return on owners' equity A company's profit divided by the amount of assets contributed to the company by its owners

market share The percentage of total units sold of a product or service divided into the number of units of that product sold by a specific company

market value The price of a company's stock multiplied by the number of shares of the stock

- To reduce inventory costs by 10 percent
- To have 20 percent of readers of a magazine recall an advertisement that a company placed there
- To reduce the time the sales force spends on paperwork by 20 percent

There are various principles that companies need to recognize as they set objectives. Objectives must be realistic. Two companies that ignored this principle are Du Pont and Chrysler. When Du Pont failed to obtain profit objectives, *Business Week* said that CEO Charles O. Holiday's "grandiose ambitions have brought major disappointment."[22] *Fortune* made this comment about Chrysler's problems: "It made unrealistic projections about the future at the same time that it was spending money extravagantly."[23] Objectives must recognize company resources because these act as a constraint on the ability of a company to achieve objectives. After all, a company has a limited number of sales personnel, a limited number of delivery trucks, and a limited amount of warehouse space. Objectives need to be specific so that there will be no misunderstanding as to what is expected. Attaching a specific number to the objective helps clarify it.

reality CHECK   *Think about any full- or part-time job experience you have had. What objectives was the company trying to achieve?*

Strategies

strategies Ways that companies use to achieve their objectives

Strategies are the ways that companies use to achieve their objectives. While a wide variety of strategies can be employed, those selected should give the best chance for meeting goals. This is more likely to occur if companies have a thorough understanding of their markets and the environment, especially technology and competition, and their internal strengths and weaknesses. Here are some examples of strategies that have been deployed by major companies.

- Dell Computer delays the final configuration of its personal computers until customers call in with indications of what they want. The company uses direct sales, rather than marketing its products through stores. Growth will be internal rather than by acquiring other firms.[24]
- Exxon acquired Mobil in 1999. Almost $5 billion in cost savings were wrung out of the combined firms. The company intends to increase its output of oil and gas.[25]
- Chrysler wants to reduce its break-even point to 83 percent of plant capacity.[26]
- eBay decided to try to increase the number of customers and the number of goods traded, move into global markets, and make the user experience "more fun, exciting, and easier."[27]
- Boeing will be providing higher margin service and seeking more aggressively to increase its share of space and defense business.[28]
- James B. Adamson, Kmart's chairperson, wants to emphasize its private-label brands and position itself as a promotional discounter. It is also trying to get its best customers to shop 4 times a month instead of 3.2 times.[29]
- Gillette has traditionally relied on its engineering skills, which result in superior products that carry premium prices.[30]
- J.C. Penney closed 44 stores and laid off 5000 staff personnel.[31]
- Kohl's stores sell department store brands at discount prices. Kohl's "offers easy-to-navigate stores in accessible locations to time-strapped middle-class families."[32]
- Saks Fifth Avenue department stores expanded into smaller markets in the United States.[33]

Technology and Business

Michelin Uses High Tech in Its Quest to Become the Leading Tire Manufacturer

Tire manufacturers Michelin, Bridgestone, and Goodyear together account for about 20 percent of the world's tire market. Michelin, however, wants to become the leader, "with a comfortable lead over rivals." A high-tech strategy is at the heart of the company's plans for achieving this objective. The firm hopes to develop various new, advanced tires that will enable it to charge premium prices. One such high-tech tire—the PAX "run flat" tire—was introduced at the Paris auto show in the fall of 2000. The PAX can go for 125 miles after it has been punctured. The tire's gel-filled interior ring gives such a smooth ride that drivers are not even aware that

there is a flat; a monitor indicates that there is a problem and asks the driver to reduce speed to 50 miles per hour. Upscale models like the Audi A8 sedan and Cadillac's roadster will include the PAX on new models.

Source: Christine Tierney, "Michelin Rolls," *Business Week*, September 30, 2002, pp. 53–62.

Questions

1. Do you believe Michelin's high-tech strategy will be successful?
2. Should Michelin's high-tech tires be developed only for upscale cars?

- The new CEO of toymaker Mattel, Robert A. Eckert, wants to improve the firm's performance by emphasizing such tried-and-true products as Barbie dolls, Hot Wheels cars, and Fisher-Price toys.[34]

The marketing group of a firm needs to decide on strategies to achieve its objectives. For example, a better system of routing for the sales force might be introduced in order to reduce its travel costs as a way to obtain a 20 percent reduction in the cost-per-sales call. In order to increase the number of customers, a new advertising campaign might be developed. A lower price might be charged in order to increase revenues. There are some guidelines that many companies follow in developing their various strategies. One is the need to obtain a **sustainable competitive advantage (SCA).** An SCA is a strategy that gives a firm a significant edge over competition that can be maintained over an extended length of time. It might be a better product, a more efficient distribution system, a better trained sales force, and so on. Whatever it is, it must resonate with the firm's customers. An example of an unsuccessful attempt to obtain an SCA is Saks Fifth Avenue, which began emphasizing low-riding jeans that were targeted to women in their twenties. This strategy alienated older shoppers, causing a former Saks executive to remark, "Saks Fifth Avenue has 'been forced to look for another advantage for the customer and I don't think they've found it yet.'"[35]

Competing directly with a successful, large firm does not usually work, unless you can provide the market with a significant benefit that the entrenched company can't. Firms are becoming increasingly wary about trying to be all things to all customers. As a result, they are emphasizing a return to their **core competency,** that is, the aspects of their operations that they are best at doing. Patrick Richard, chairperson and CEO of Pernod Ricard, the U.S. subsidiary of the world's largest spirits and wine company, said, "Everyone in the world now understands the strength of staying within a core competency. Ours, obviously, is wine and spirits."[36] Often, a reemphasis on a core competency means getting rid of noncore products. For example, it has been recommended that Sony needs to get out of such noncompetitive products as computer chips and peripherals.[37]

sustainable competitive advantage (SCA) A strategy that gives a firm a significant edge over competition and can be maintained over an extended length of time

core competency The aspects of a company's operations that it is best at doing

When companies develop strategies, they often realize that their firm does not have the required experience or skills. Then, they may decide to either outsource or partner with another firm to form a strategic alliance. Outsourcing occurs when a company has another company perform an activity that it used to perform itself. Frequently, companies will turn over marketing research or advertising to specialized marketing research or advertising agencies. A recent trend is the outsourcing of distribution operations, which Sun Microsystems did, achieving seven-day-a-week, round-the-clock parts supply.[38] The potential benefits from outsourcing include lowering costs and being able to better concentrate on core competencies.

Strategic alliances are formal or informal agreements among two or more companies to pursue a common objective. They can involve domestic or foreign companies, but they are companies at the same level of the value chain, for example, manufacturers. Examples of strategic alliances include Pepsico and Lipton jointly selling canned iced tea beverages, American Express and Toys 'R' Us developing cooperative advertising and promotion, and Ford and Nissan designing and producing small cars.

Developing strategies for international markets contains some special considerations. The greater level of risk for companies than the risk in domestic markets must be kept in mind. Risk is increased because of the differences in markets and culture that exist between the domestic and international markets and the longer distances involved. Another factor is the need for international strategies to recognize a longer time horizon. DaimlerChrysler chairperson Jurgen Schrempp develops long-term global strategies; he has a time horizon of ten years.[39] It has been estimated that it took forty years for Campbell Soup to develop successful strategies for the Japanese market.[40] One expert suggests a D.U.M.B. strategy for international markets: Is the product Demonstrable, is it Unique, is it Meaningful, is it Believable? BMW cars illustrate the D.U.M.B. principle. Their ride can be demonstrated, their Bavarian engineering and styling are unique, they are meaningful to discriminating buyers, and they do what they claim and so are believable.[41]

LEARNING OBJECTIVE 7
Describe the concept of niche marketing and explain the advantages of employing a niche marketing strategy.

A major strategic consideration for companies is which target markets they should enter. The options available are shown in Exhibit 8.7. When an **undifferentiated strategy** is used, a firm will go after the entire market with the same product or service. When Henry Ford, developer of the Ford automobile, said "They can have any color they want as long as it's black," he was essentially pursuing an undifferentiated strategy. On the other hand, a **niche marketing strategy** involves different products or services being directed to various market segments. In a multiple segment approach, the marketer divides the entire market into various segments and develops an offering for each one. A one-segment strategy develops and markets a product or service to only one segment of the market. An undifferentiated strategy assumes, for the most part, that all segments of the market have similar needs and desires. A niche marketing strategy is based on the belief that various segments have different needs and desires and that these can be identified and effectively served.

Many companies have pursued niche marketing strategies and benefited significantly.

- Kiwi, a small airline with only two planes flying between Chicago, Atlanta, and Orlando, made $10 million in profits in its first year of operation.[42]

undifferentiated strategy The plan of a company to make the same product and service available to all segments of a market

niche marketing strategy The plan of a company to direct different products and services to different market segments

EXHIBIT 8.7

Alternative Target Market Strategies

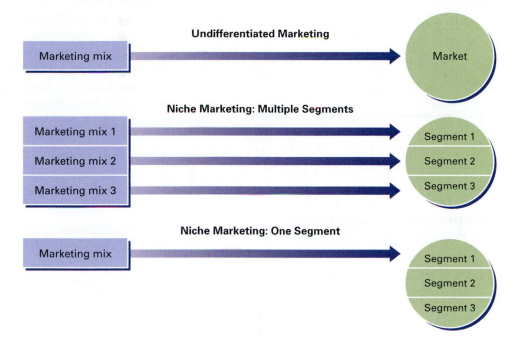

- Dial customized its soaps and detergents by geographic regions, and enjoyed annual growth rates of 8 to 12 percent and generated an outstanding return on stockholders' equity of 20 percent.[43]
- Key Corp's Society Bank, Cleveland, Ohio, inaugurated a Dino Saver Club for children 12 and under. Within four months, 20,000 accounts, with $3 million in deposits, were opened.[44]
- Natural Nectar developed FI-BAR, a low-fat, cholesterol-free, high-fiber granola snack bar, for the young adult and senior market. Revenues jumped from $5 million to $35 million.[45]
- BioCosmetics Research Labs introduced a Black Opal cosmetics line for African American women that generated $2 million in sales the first year.[46]
- Viewing of television cable channels that are directed to niche markets—the Travel Channel, Cooking Channel, History Channel, ESPN—is exceeding that of the regular networks. [47]

Niche market programs are successful for a variety of reasons. They are more closely tuned to the needs of specific markets. The closer matching can result in improved levels of customer loyalty and satisfaction, and ultimately higher sales and profits. According to John T. Schiffman, chairperson of Smith, Batchelder & Rugg, a medium-sized accounting firm located in Lebanon, New Hampshire, a niche-market strategy allowed them to concentrate on markets where they could have a "significant and lasting influence."[48] Because only one or several markets are involved, they can be served much more quickly—an important advantage as speed of response has become such a critical competitive weapon today. Niche marketing also allows companies to focus, resulting in more effective use of limited resources, such as time, money, and people. Focus provides executives with clear-cut visions of the markets they will serve, products or services to be marketed, quality levels expected, and the basis of competitive advantage. By not trying to be everything to everybody, scarce resources are not dissipated in markets that have little use for a

first mover The company that is first into a market with a new product or service

positioning Endowing a new or existing product or service with attributes deemed important by a market so that the market perceives the offering as superior to competitive products on these attributes

EXHIBIT 8.8

Positioning a New Soft Drink

company's product or service. If a company is the first to invade a niche market, it can obtain **first-mover** advantages. These include the possibility of preempting competitors, aura of leadership, initial cost advantages, and higher profits.

Another important aspect of a niche marketing strategy is positioning. **Positioning** refers to endowing an existing or new product or service with attributes that are deemed important by the market, with the market perceiving that the offering is superior to competitive products on these attributes. Let's assume that a food and beverage company is considering developing a new soft drink. In researching consumers, it discovers that taste and price are the two most important qualities affecting their choice of soft drink. The company then conducts additional research to see how their offering compares to five major brands on these qualities. Exhibit 8.8 shows that the new brand is positioned well for success, as it is the only brand that is perceived to have both low price and good taste.

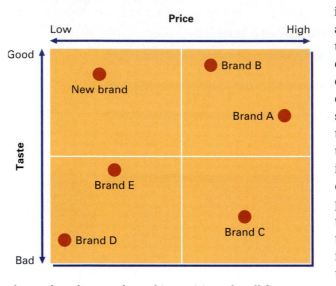

reality CHECK   *Give some examples of how political parties have pursued a niche marketing strategy.*

Managing Customers

General Electric, AT&T, Chevron, Federal Express, Hewlett-Packard, Intel, Levi Strauss, Southwest Airlines, State Farm, and Taco Bell are some of the smart companies that are putting together aggressive programs for managing their customers. They are doing this because they realize that customers may well be their most important asset. They have been rewarded handsomely for their customer management programs.

- AT&T and Intel obtained market-value-to-book-value ratios of 4.5 times or better. General Electric achieved return-on-equity to cost-of-equity ratios of better than 2.5 to 1.[49]
- State Farm obtained a 20 percent increase in average annual income for its insurance agents.
- John Deere increased its golf and turf revenues by 35 percent.[50]
- British Airways' profits jumped 61 percent in 1995 over what it earned in 1993.
- Ritz Carlton Hotel has 90 percent of its customers stay with them again.[51]

Analyzing Customers

The first step in a customer management program is to analyze your customers. The chief objective is to determine which are profitable and unprofitable. "Learning where your customers rank in terms of profitability is the future of business and companies that are doing it now have a distinct advantage over their competitors."[52]

Royal Bank of Canada determines the profitability of all of its 10 million customers on a monthly basis. In so doing, the bank found out that only 17 percent of its customers accounted for 93 percent of its profits. This means that 83 percent of its customers provided only 7 percent of its profits, calling into question the profitability of many of that 83 percent. One of the United States' largest retailers stated that it had no unprofitable customers, yet analysis found that it was directing marketing effort to those which were not profitable and never would be. "This company was actually spending money to bring in customers who were reducing the value of the firm."[53]

Profitable customers justify being provided high levels of service. Companies do not want to lose them; what companies need to do is determine their characteristics and try to get more of them to do business with the company. Efforts to increase revenues, such as mailings describing sales, can be directed to them. But such mailings would be inappropriate for unprofitable customers since any resulting business would reduce the company's profits.

The best approach for dealing with unprofitable customers is to try and serve them at a lower level of cost so that the revenue they bring in becomes profitable. This is what Fidelity Investment, the world's largest mutual funds company, did. After it discovered that many of its customers were unprofitable because they took up a lot of costly service reps' time, customers were encouraged to use automated telephone lines and the company's website. When they needed to talk to a service rep, they were routed into longer queues, allowing profitable customers to be served more quickly. This approach turned out to be a win-win situation for Fidelity: If unprofitable customers used these other contact options, they became profitable; if they balked and went to another firm, Fidelity's profits also increased.[54]

Customer Satisfaction

Companies in the United States spend close to $4 billion annually to find out how well their customers are satisfied. However, many companies do not monitor customer satisfaction. When John McDonough took over as Rubbermaid's CEO, he was flabbergasted to discover that the company was not assessing levels of customer satisfaction.[55]

Companies with satisfied customers benefit greatly. Satisfied customers are less price sensitive and more willing to pay for additional services, and purchase more frequently and in greater quantities. They are far less expensive to serve than new customers. Free publicity is obtained because satisfied customers make favorable comments to other customers and noncustomers. Satisfied customers are likely to become loyal customers. In short, customer satisfaction is associated with higher revenues, lower costs, and higher profits.

Marketers need to understand that **total satisfaction** for customers is the key to success, not anything less. Sixty to 80 percent of restaurant diners who defect to competitor establishments have indicated that they were "satisfied" or even "very satisfied" with their dining experience. Here is evidence that total satisfaction is essential.

total satisfaction The postpurchase response in which the customer has no dissatisfaction at all with the product or service accompanying the product

- In the automobile industry, completely satisfied customers are much more loyal than customers who are only "satisfied."
- Xerox found that its totally satisfied customers were six times more likely to repurchase its products over the next year and a half than were its "satisfied" customers.

A JOB WELL DONE IS A JOB THAT'S NEVER REALLY DONE.

SMITH BARNEY HAS THE HIGHEST CLIENT SATISFACTION OF
THE TOP NATIONAL FULL-SERVICE BROKERAGE FIRMS.*

A good Financial Consultant never clocks out. Markets close but the process of watching, evaluating, reading and discerning never ceases. For us at Smith Barney, building your wealth is an unending process. The goal is not a number. The goal is a tireless work ethic that doesn't wax and wane with market conditions. It is a belief shared by Financial Consultant and company alike. Maybe that's why so many of the best FCs, and clients, stay with us for so long. www.smithbarney.com **THIS IS WHO WE ARE. THIS IS HOW WE EARN IT."**

SMITHBARNEY citigroup

This Smith Barney ad shows the importance of customer satisfaction in companies' marketing programs.

- Opinion Research Corporation, Princeton, New Jersey, found that completely satisfied customers were almost 42 percent more likely than merely satisfied customers to exhibit loyalty.[56]
- Bain & Company consultant Frederick Reichheld estimates that 65 to 85 percent of customers who had defected stated that they were "satisfied" or "very satisfied" with their former supplier.[57]

There is growing acceptance that an effective way to determine how satisfied customers are is to visit personally with them. Companies that have used this concept have benefited significantly.

- The general manager of the Wireline division of Schlumberger and his top subordinates regularly visit their customers. They discovered that its shallow-well customers didn't need the division's full range of technical skills and the extra costs they had to pay for them.[58]
- Weyerhaeuser Sawmill general managers and operative personnel (Cottage Grove, Oregon) spend a week at a time as "employees" of their customers, looking, listening, and learning. Insights learned gave this sawmill the edge over others in terms of productivity, profit, and morale.[59]
- Sir Colin Marshall, chairperson of British Airways, has his service managers regularly talk to the airline's passengers. On the basis of these interactions, British Airways asked its flight crews not to pass out food and drinks and then disappear because just seeing crew members increases passengers' customer satisfaction levels.[60]
- Deere & Company has its engineers in the field for ten days or more watching their customers put prototypes to work. The results: a redesign of the transmission of its 7000 series of row-crop tractors, which allowed for a super-slow speed for garlic and other crops.[61]

LEARNING OBJECTIVE 8
Discuss the importance of customer service programs and
how they should be conducted.

Customer Service

Deliveries, processing orders, installation of machinery, helping customers with problems, explaining and honoring warranties and guarantees, checking out shoppers at department stores and supermarkets, repairs, accepting returns, providing emergency shipments—these are examples of what is involved in providing customer service. Although it is ancillary to the product itself, the importance of customer service should not be underestimated. Customer service is now perceived by many experts as the key to achieving sustainable competitive advantage. When competitors' products and services are perceived as being equal—which is often the case today, because products and prices are easily duplicated—the services offered often decide who gets the business. "When the all-important issue of customer service is examined, it has been estimated that customers are five times more likely to switch vendors because of perceived service problems than for price concerns or product quality issues."[62] By having a far higher standard of customer service, a share of wallet may be increased by as much as 80 percent.[63]

Companies must guard against providing too high a level of service. When customers do not respond in some desirable way, such as giving a vendor more business, or the costs associated with providing a higher level of customer service are high, firms may be overcommitting resources. They also need to be sure that their customer service is reliable. **Reliability** includes receiving shipments on time; order accuracy, completeness and condition; getting repairs done on time; consistency of product quality, and so on.

reliability The consistency with which a product is produced or a service rendered

An important aspect of customer service is how customer complaints are handled. The astute company welcomes complaints, because if they are handled properly, they will prevent customer defections, increase loyalty, improve sales, and result in customers spreading favorable word-of-mouth comments. Jay Narivaha, senior vice president of Technical Assistance Research Programs, a customer service consultancy, says that customers who have problems resolved are more loyal than those who don't have problems.[64] Companies should fear noncomplainers. These are customers who don't make their concerns known but defect to another vendor, leaving the previous supplier completely in the dark as to why, and with less business.

Often, it takes only a single complaint not handled fairly to result in a lower level of satisfaction and increase the probability of the customer's becoming someone else's customer.

When complaints from customers arise, the most effective strategy is to deal with them immediately. The importance of immediately responding to complaints is emphasized at British Airways. Sir Colin Marshall, British Airways' chairperson, says, "We try to make it clear to employees that we expect them to respond to customers on the spot—before a customer writes a letter or makes a phone call."[65] And

Case in Point

McDonalds's Grapples with Poor Service Levels

McDonald's hired mystery shoppers to visit its fast-food restaurants and evaluate food quality, cleanliness, and service. The results were disappointing: speed of service standards were being met only 46 percent of the time and 30 percent of customers had to wait more than four minutes. The mystery shoppers also reported rude service, unprofessional employees, and inaccurate service.

The frustration being experienced by McDonald's customers has led them to turn to competitors, like Wendy's, Burger King, and Carl's Jr. Financial problems have also occurred. Profits for 2002 were lower than those for 2001, and the company's stock closed at $18.16 on September 18, 2002—a seven-year low.

In 1999, CEO Jack M. Greenberg introduced Made-For-You kitchen configurations that use computers to make fresher sandwiches. The problem was that the better product took longer to make,

increasing customer wait time. Headquarters says that the longer wait times are fueled by the failure of the restaurants to use the new equipment properly. The franchisees claim that the equipment is poorly designed. Headquarters wants franchisees to train employees better and hire more crew members for lunch hours. The franchisees are resisting because both recommendations would increase their costs—cutting into already meager profit margins.

Source: Julie Forster, "You Deserve A Better Break Today," *Business Week,* September 30, 2002, p. 42, and "Fast Food, Slow Service," *Fortune,* September 30, 2002, p. 38.

Questions

1. Do you mind waiting more than four minutes to get your food in a fast-food restaurant?
2. Who is to blame for the longer wait times, headquarters or franchisees?
3. How can you explain the problem customers are experiencing with McDonald's employees?

British Airways follows another important tenet: Even if the effort to immediately take care of a problem is not perfect—some mistakes occur—it is better to make the effort than do nothing.[66]

Another rule of thumb: Employees should be empowered to take care of problems right away. Don't force them to have to consult with some superior, and give them enough resources so that they can make an adjustment that will be meaningful to the aggrieved customer. Employees at Ritz Carlton hotels can spend up to $2000 to address a guest's grievance on the spot.[67] Michael Kauffaman, CEO of Southwestern Bell Yellow Pages, empowered his service reps to adjust dissatisfied advertisers' bills by up to $1000.[68]

reality CHECK *Think about the last time you shopped at a department store. How would you rate their customer service? Why did you give it this rating?*

Careers in Marketing

With one-fourth to one-third of U.S. employment made up of marketing or marketing-related jobs, excellent career opportunities in marketing abound. Demand for persons trained in marketing remains strong, compensation is good, fringe benefits are attractive, work assignments are interesting and challenging, and opportunities for advancement are exceptional. Many industries require marketing personnel: manufacturing, retailing, wholesaling, services (banks, insurance, stockbrokers, consulting, universities, transportation, etc.), not-for-profits (hospitals, charities, political parties), and local, state, and federal governments. Especially appealing are careers in personal selling, retailing, advertising, product management, logistics, and public relations. For those who have been successful marketers, they may advance to the position of chief marketing executive.

Chief marketing executives (CMEs) are responsible for all of a company's marketing operations. As such, they spend a lot of time in developing marketing strategies, managing people, coordinating the various marketing functions, and evaluating how well marketing is performing. People with experience in sales, product management, and logistics are most likely to be best prepared for the CME job.

CMEs usually report to an organization's top executive, its chief executive officer. Often, a CME may be in line for this position. About 20 percent of *Fortune 500* CEOs have had most of their experience in marketing. In order to be qualified for the CEO slot, CMEs need to have knowledge and experience in a field other than marketing; finance and operations are highly desirable. As a chief marketing executive, they need to have been successful in developing strategies and must have acquired a solid knowledge of technology.[69]

The chief marketing executive is very dependent on marketing research specialists to provide her or him with the information needed to make effective decisions. Top marketing research specialists earn an average of about $55,000 with new hires making about half that amount. Marketing researchers provide their firms with information about markets, products, competitors, and their sales and other promotion activities. Besides working in-house for a manufacturer, retailer, bank, and so on, there are also excellent career opportunities with marketing research firms and government.

Marketing researchers need to be skilled in statistics, knowledgeable about all aspects of marketing, and computer literate.

Summary

LEARNING OBJECTIVE 1

Explain the different aspects of the definition of marketing.

Marketing is defined as the determination of the needs and desires of markets so that products and services can be developed, priced, promoted, and distributed to these markets in order to satisfy the market's needs and desires and organizational objectives can be achieved.

LEARNING OBJECTIVE 2

Explain the importance of marketing.

Virtually every organization engages in marketing activities. A large portion of the final cost of goods and services is composed of marketing costs. Executives of organizations are spending more time in marketing. Companies realize that marketing is an important key to improving their profits. Many marketing executives are taking over their organizations' top positions. And marketing offers challenging and rewarding careers.

LEARNING OBJECTIVE 3

Describe the major types of markets and their importance.

The major markets to be served are the consumer, business-to-business, government, and international markets. Without knowledge of the markets an organization is serving, it is difficult for the organization to achieve its objectives.

LEARNING OBJECTIVE 4

Identify and describe the components of the marketing environment.

The marketing environment consists of competition, technology, the economy, the legal and political arena, and culture. Companies need to establish competitor intelligence (CI) programs to monitor their competitors. Companies will want to be developing new technology that will better help them achieve their objectives. They need to monitor the technology environment to keep abreast of new products and processes that are being developed. Such aspects of the economy as its size, prices, and distribution of income need to be understood by marketers. Marketers need to abide by laws that are in existence, anticipate those that might be passed, and be aware of how laws are being administered. Organizations need to understand the culture in their own country but also in foreign countries to which they market their products and services.

LEARNING OBJECTIVE 5

Distinguish between marketing information systems and marketing research.

Marketing information systems continually monitor the market, competition, products, and companies' marketing operations. They tell a company how well it is performing. Marketing research is the process whereby marketers are provided with information so that effective marketing decisions can be made. Marketing research is usually done after a marketing information system has uncovered a problem.

LEARNING OBJECTIVE 6

Identify and understand companies' chief objectives.

Revenues are a company's sales expressed in dollars. Profits are what are left after all of the firm's costs are deducted from its revenues. Profit margin is calculated by dividing profits by revenues. Dividing a firm's profits by its assets yields return on assets. Return on owners' equity is found by dividing profit by the value of the owners' equity. Market share refers to the percentage of total units sold of a product that is accounted for by a specific company's products. Market value is found by multiplying the price of a company's stock by the number of its shares of stock.

LEARNING OBJECTIVE 7

Describe the concept of niche marketing and explain the advantages of employing a niche marketing strategy.

A niche marketing strategy involves different products or services being offered to different market segments. It is successful because it is closely tuned to the needs of specific markets, markets can be served more quickly, a greater level of focus is achieved, and first-mover advantages are obtained.

LEARNING OBJECTIVE 8

Discuss the importance of customer service programs and how they should be conducted.

Customer service is believed to be a key in enabling companies to obtain a sustainable competitive advantage. Effective customer service efforts do not provide too high a level of service, they stress reliability and have a specific procedure in place to handle customer complaints.

Chapter Questions

1. What aspects of marketing are included in the marketing mix? Can you think of anything else that might be included?

2. Can you think of any other problems, besides the lower share of profits, that Starbucks might encounter as it expands into international markets?

3. Besides the kinds of goods and services purchased by older people, are there any other aspects of the older-person market that marketers should know about?

4. What are the major differences between sociological and psychological dimensions of the consumer market?

5. What are the differences and similarities between consumer and business-to-business markets? How might these affect strategies used to market to them?

6. Describe the major differences between domestic and international markets. Why do you think companies that have marketed their products or services solely to the domestic market would decide to introduce them into international markets?

7. Suppose the only way you could get secret and valuable information about a major competitor was to lure away one of its high-level executives with top dollars and pump him for that information. Would you do it? Why or why not?

8. Carefully distinguish between marketing information systems (MIS) and marketing research as ways to collect information about markets and the marketing environment.

9. Some marketers believe that share of wallet is a better measure of how well a company is doing than market share. Do you agree or disagree? Why or why not?

10. Do you believe that Michelin's technology strategy will be successful? Why or why not?

11. Do you think it is okay for firms to give higher levels of service to their most profitable customers and lower levels of service to their least profitable and unprofitable customers? Why or why not?

12. How does the postpurchase experience of dissonance compare to the postpurchase experience of dissatisfaction?

13. Do you think it is ethical for McDonald's to use mystery shoppers to find out how good or bad its service is? How else might it have obtained this information?

14. Give five specific examples of marketing that you noticed yesterday.

Interpreting Business News

Miele is a German manufacturer of dishwashers, washers, dryers, and vacuum cleaners. The company's sales are concentrated chiefly in Western Europe. Its products are high quality and carry correspondingly high prices. Annual sales are about $2 billion.

Since the 1980s, Miele has been expanding outside Western Europe, with particular emphasis on Australia and the United States.

California recently elected to outlaw the use of perchloroethylene ("Perc") in the 3,500 professional dry cleaners in the Los Angeles area. Chicago and other cities are expected to follow soon with the same restriction. "Perc" is used by 85% of all dry cleaning establishments in the United States.

Miele estimates that there are 33,000 dry cleaners in the United States. Using that figure, the company believes that there is a $1.5 billion market for their washers and dryers, which do not require the use of "perc," but instead use water. This estimate is buoyed by a six percent increase in the United States for home improvement products in the previous year.

1. Do you think that this market presents a good opportunity for Miele? Why or why not?

2. What should Miele's objectives be in this market?

3. How should Miele try to achieve these objectives?

An article in the April 19, 2004, issue of *Business Week* (Andrew Park, "Dude You're Getting a Printer") discusses Dell, Inc.'s move into the printer market. It contains a number of references to Dell's objectives and strategies–two important concepts discussed in this chapter–as Dell implements this decision. These include:

- Dell views unit sales as one of its objectives. Dell's sales in 2004 were expected to reach around 3.5 million units, with revenues of about $1 billion (another objective of Dell).

- Dell's domestic market share for all-in-one inkjet printers, which scan, copy, and fax, is 14.5 percent, compared to Hewlett-Packard's leading figure of 55 percent.

- Dell has a worldwide market share of 10 percent on ink jet and monochrome laser printers; Hewlett-Packard's is around 45 percent.

- Dell does not sell printers through retail stores. Customers have to order them online or over the phone; software lets them know when the cartridges need to be replaced and Dell offers free shipping and handling.

- Dell projects that its direct sales approach will result in low costs and low prices, forcing competitor prices down. However, midway through 2004, Hewlett-Packard still was able to maintain a 16 percent profit margin.

1. Are there any other objectives discussed in this chapter not included in Dell's objectives?
2. Dell gets 80 percent of its printer business from business customers. What material in this chapter does this performance figure suggest to you?

Web Assignments

1. Go to Sony's website and see what it says about the company's charitable giving. What are the objectives of its giving program? What areas of society are targeted? Who is the recipient of Sony Music Entertainment's charitable activities? What kinds of victims has Sony helped? Do you think that Sony's charitable giving program helps its marketing effort? Why or why not?

2. McDonald's website, on October 25, 2002, contained a press release announcing the appointment of Kay Napier as the company's senior vice president of marketing. Napier had previously served as Procter & Gamble's (P&G's) Vice President of North American Pharmaceuticals and Corporate Women's Health and Vitality. In that position, she led P&G's entry into the women's health area and was responsible for P&G's U.S. and Canadian pharmaceutical efforts.

In accepting the position with McDonald's, Ms. Napier said, "I have long admired McDonald's as one of the world's greatest brands, and for what it represents to millions of customers every single day, in the restaurants and in local communities. I consider it an honor to be part of the team."

Go to McDonald's website and see if there are any announcements about executive hires. Are any of these in the marketing area? What position is involved? What is the new executive's background?

 # Portfolio Projects

Exploring Your Own Case in Point

After reading this chapter, you will be familiar with the major markets that business can serve, the marketing environment, and how to obtain information about those markets and the environment. You will understand the need for companies to decide on objectives and the strategies for achieving them. You will learn how to effectively manage your customers. By answering the following questions for your selected company, you will have a better idea of its marketing operations.

1. To what major market(s) does your company direct its products or services? Which specific segments of these markets are emphasized?

2. What objectives is your company trying to achieve? Are they financial objectives such as profits and sales? Are any of the objectives marketing objectives such as market share?

3. Does your company appear to recognize the importance of its customers? What evidence indicates that the company considers its customers to be important?

Starting Your Own Business

After reading this chapter, you should have an appreciation for the importance of marketing for a new business venture. By addressing the following concerns, you will obtain invaluable information for the business plan needed to start your own business.

1. Describe the markets that your product or service is directed to. If you have segmented your markets, indicate what criteria were used—age, gender, income, geography, etc.

2. Discuss how you will monitor competitors. What information will you want to gather about competitors?

3. Describe the information you will collect and store about customers. How will you obtain this information?

Test Prepper

You've read the chapter, studied the key terms, and the exam is any day now. Think you are ready to ace it? Take this sample test to gauge your comprehension of chapter material. You can check your answers at the back of the book.

True/False Questions

Please indicate if the following statements are true or false:

_____ 1. Services account for about 80 percent of our nation's gross domestic product.

_____ 2. Perception is a type of psychological variable.

_____ 3. The real self is the person you would like to be.

_____ 4. Culture and subculture are types of sociological variables.

_____ 5. Dissonance can occur after a purchase has been made but before it is used.

_____ 6. Governments account for about 25 percent of all purchases made in the United States.

_____ 7. Japan has the world's largest gross domestic product.

_____ 8. Inflation involves the economic situation where steep price increases are occurring.

_____ 9. Secondary information is information that is already available.

_____ 10. Databases are banks of information that companies have about their individual customers.

Multiple-Choice Questions

Choose the best answer.

_____ 1. Which of the following is *not* part of the marketing environment?

  a. Competition
  b. Colleges and universities
  c. Technology
  d. Economy
  e. Culture

_____ 2. A company makes a profit of $5 million on revenues of $50 million. By dividing $5 million by $50 million, we obtain

  a. profit margin.
  b. return on assets.
  c. return on stockholders' equity.
  d. market share.
  e. market value.

_____ 3. Which of the following does *not* explain the success of niche marketing programs?

  a. Needs of specific markets are recognized.
  b. Markets can be served quickly.
  c. Effective use of limited resources occurs.
  d. Clear-cut visions of markets to be served or not to be served are obtained.
  e. There is a lack of focus.

_____ 4. Which state has the largest population?

  a. California
  b. Texas
  c. New York
  d. Ohio
  e. Delaware

_____ 5. Which of the following refers to cues and stimuli from our physical surroundings?

  a. Learning
  b. Perception
  c. Motives
  d. Attitudes
  e. Self-concept

_____ 6. Which of the following is *not* part of a person's self-concept?

  a. Self-image
  b. Self-denial
  c. Ideal image
  d. Looking-glass self
  e. Real self

_____ 7. The most populous country in the world is

  a. Russia.
  b. the United States.
  c. China.
  d. India.
  e. Canada.

_____ 8. Most of the countries with low per capita incomes are located in

  a. South America.
  b. Europe.
  c. the Middle East.
  d. Africa.
  e. Asia.

_____ 9. The legislation that prohibits deceptive advertising and labeling is the

    a. Federal Trade Commission Act.
    b. Pure Food and Drug Act.
    c. Consumer Products Safety Act.
    d. Trademark Counterfeiting Act.
    e. Telephone Consumer Protection Act.

_____ 10. Which of the following is a characteristic of a marketing information system (MIS)?

    a. Focuses more on marketing performance than the marketing environment
    b. Provides information on a regular basis
    c. Stresses the why of information gathering
    d. Analyzes data provided by marketing research studies
    e. Relies exclusively on internal data

Want more questions? Visit the student website at **http://college.hmco.com/business/student/** (select Gaspar, *Introduction to Business*) and take the ACE quizzes for more practice.

9

Developing the Product and Pricing Mixes

| Introduction

| Guidelines for Developing
the Marketing Mix

Developing the Product Mix
  Product Elements
  Developing New Products
  Managing Existing Products

Developing the Pricing Mix
  Pricing Objectives
  Pricing Concepts
  Setting Prices for New Products
  Changing Prices for Existing Products
  Pricing Decisions for Products Sold
  Internationally
  Retailers' Pricing Decisions

| Careers in Brand Management

Learning Objectives

After studying this chapter, you should be able to

1. Explain how a marketing mix is developed.

2. Describe the basic elements of a product.

3. Describe the differences between standardization and adaptation strategies.

4. Discuss the concept of brand equity and why it is important.

5. List the steps in the process for developing new products and how each should be performed.

6. Describe the product life cycle and how it can be used to manage existing products.

7. List the major objectives of a company's pricing strategies.

8. Summarize the basic concepts and tools needed to set prices.

Profits Galore at the 99 Cents Only Stores

There are 142 branches of the 99 Cents Only Stores operating in California, Nevada, and Arizona. These stores generated revenues of $667 million in 2001. As the name implies, each item sold in the stores is priced at 99¢. On average, an item costs 60¢, which translates to a gross margin of 40 percent —twice that of Wal-Mart's. Its profit margin is a healthy eight percent, also twice that of Wal-Mart's.

A typical 15,000-square-foot store stocks approximately 6,000 items. About 40 percent of these items are closeouts purchased from manufacturers or other retailers. The company's founder and CEO, David Gold, has mandated that 60 percent of the store inventory must be recognizable brand names, like Coca-Cola or Safeguard. Only two percent of the inventory is unbranded "trinkets," items that are purchased only one time by customers. In contrast, other dollar chains allow as much as 45 percent of their product offerings to fall within that category.

Much of the branded merchandise sold through the 99 Cents Only Stores is specially packaged by store personnel.

99 Cents Only Stores rely heavily on two aspects of the marketing mix to ensure success. These are the product and pricing mixes. This chapter will discuss these two aspects of the marketing mix.

Introduction

Companies need to construct a marketing mix. Two major aspects of the marketing mix are the product mix and the pricing mix.

Product design involves the tangible aspects of a product. Product packages and warranties must be developed. Product brands can be national, private, or generic. When companies are marketing their products and services internationally, they must be familiar with the concepts of standardization and adaptation, and the advantages and disadvantages of those concepts. Brand equity—the value placed on a company's brand—is increasingly being used to determine the effectiveness of companies' product decisions.

New products can contribute greatly to the success of companies. They are developed for a number of reasons. In order to introduce successful new products, companies need to embrace a new product philosophy and follow a specific set of steps. Companies can use both internal and external sources for generating new product ideas. They will subject new product ideas to screening to see if they should be advanced to the next step of concept testing, where the basic idea of the product is presented to a sample of customers in order to obtain their feedback. The business analysis step involves projections of the potential profitability of the new product candidate. If these look good, the product can be physically developed. It is then subjected to both technical and market testing. Finally, the completed product is introduced to the market.

After new products are developed, they must be effectively managed. The product life cycle is the means often used to manage existing products. Companies must have in place a specific procedure for eliminating products that are not performing well.

In developing a pricing mix, firms will have to decide on their basic pricing objectives, that is, performance, prevention, maintenance, and survival. In order to achieve these objectives, decision makers must understand the concepts of demand and price elasticity. When pricing products to be sold internationally, companies need to cope with the concepts of transfer pricing and dumping. Retailers also need to pay close attention to markups and markdowns when developing their pricing strategies.

Guidelines for Developing the Marketing Mix

LEARNING OBJECTIVE 1
Explain how a marketing mix is developed.

The product or service being marketed and the markets to which it is directed are important factors that must be considered as a marketing mix is developed. Industrial products, for example, are not usually marketed through channels of distribution, but consumer products will ordinarily use such channels as wholesalers and retailers. If women prefer to buy perfume in department stores, then perfume had better be available in department stores. If men will not pay more than $39.95 for a certain type of shoes, then shoe stores should price this item below $39.95.

All elements of the marketing mix decision must be made together; they cannot be made separately. While a price of $10 for a product might generate a certain level of revenue, a price of $8 and an advertising expenditure of $100,000 might result in greater revenues. The point is that in considering two elements of the marketing mix—price *and* promotion—the company has improved its performance.

A company cannot use the same marketing mix forever; the mix must be modified over time as changes in the markets to which products and services are directed occur. For example, if customers now prefer to purchase a certain product at discount stores like Wal-Mart instead of at department stores, then channels of distribution should be changed to discount stores. This scenario is exactly what happened in Japan over the last decade as that economy stagnated. Japanese housewives would not buy on a price basis when the economy was robust; this was an admission that their husbands could not adequately provide for them. As the economy continued to be sluggish, many Japanese housewives switched buying from pricey department stores to lower-priced discounters.

reality
CHECK   *The next time you see a television advertisement for an automobile, jot down the elements of the marketing mix that were contained in the advertisement.*

Developing the Product Mix

product mix The combination of design, quality, brand name, package, warranty, and product line width and depth a company uses for its product lines

When executives put together a **product mix**—the combination of design, quality, brand name, package, warranty, and product-line width and depth—they need to make decisions about specific elements of products, provide a process for developing new products, and have a framework for managing existing products.

Product Elements

LEARNING OBJECTIVE 2
Describe the basic elements of a product.

product design The tangible aspects of a product, including materials, length, width, height, and hardness or softness

Product design refers to the tangible aspects of a product: its materials, shape, length, width, height, hardness or softness, and so on. These tangible aspects affect how a product looks and how it performs; they are important aspects in determining how well a product will be accepted in the marketplace.

Case in Point

DaimlerChrysler Relies on Product Design to Escape Performance Doldrums

When compared to the other major automobile makers such as Toyota, Nissan, Honda, General Motors, and Ford, the numbers for DaimlerChrysler in 2003 were not good. Its total market value ranked fourth, as did its operating profit as a percentage of revenues. It took DaimlerChrysler 28 hours to produce one vehicle—last among the Big Six—and its 311 defects per 100 vehicles produced also ranked last.

Much of DaimlerChrysler's decline has been blamed on its $36 billion acquisition of Chrysler in 1998, although having to pump in $7 billion to cope with losses occurring with its Japanese partner, Mitsubishi, didn't help either. While Mercedes automobiles are perceived as having "muscular engines, prestigious sedans, and leading-edge technology," Chrysler is viewed as having unpopular models, inefficient factories, and a weak brand image. The result: red ink at Chrysler, including an unexpected $1 billion loss in the second quarter of 2003 and an operating loss for the whole year. Overall, the acquisition of Chrysler is blamed for the $40 billion decrease in shareholder value since 1998, a catastrophe that has angered not only DaimlerChrysler shareholders but large asset-management firms like DWS and Deka Investment. These investment firms hold significant stakes in the company and are questioning how Chrysler's dismal performance justified Daimler's management team receiving $48 million in compensation in 2003.

In trying to cope with the Chrysler mess, Daimler will be forced to recognize and adjust to a new trend that is credited with driving sales of automobiles in the new millennium: design. Because of the significant increase in the number of models—up from 910 in the U.S. in 1995 to 1,314 in 2002—and the improvement in car quality as measured by the number of defects, models are viewed as "me too" by the car-purchasing consumer. How to differentiate one model from another? The answer appears to be through styling: "create a car with a strong personality. Get the proportions right—an elegantly curved shoulder line or an innovative grill—and you can add up to 1% to the sticker price and still outsell rivals." In order to get it right, companies are increasing design budgets, creating high-tech design studios, borrowing ideas from art, architecture, fashion, and furniture, using three-dimensional modeling software, and adapting designs emanating from individual star designers instead of from design committees. Top designers like BMW's Christopher Bangle and VW's Murat Guenak earn a million dollars annually and have access to the executive suite.

DaimlerChrysler has several models that rank high on design. The Chrysler 300C ($24,000) has a Bentley look to it and is part of Chrysler's effort to move the brand upscale. The Smart Roadster ($31,000), part of the Mercedes Smart super-mini series, is viewed as being "sassy, quick and light" and as a "great grandson of the MG." The 2004 Chrysler Crossfire was influenced by the design of the 1999 Audi TT. At the top of the list is the Mercedes-Berg SLR McLaren (priced at a whopping $450,000); it has a 626 horsepower engine and has "big, brutish, uncompromising power."

Source: Gail Edmondson and Kathleen Kervin, "Stalled," *Business Week,* September 29, 2003, pp. 54–56; Gail Edmondson, Chester Dawson and Kathleen Kervin, "Designer Cars," *Business Week,* February 16, 2004, pp. 56–61; and Gail Edmondson, "Daimler Fumbles Are Firing Up Europe's Shareholders," *Business Week,* April 19, 2004, p. 56.

Questions

1. Do you believe design is a more important factor in purchasing a car than performance or price? Why or why not?
2. Do you believe it is all right for top automobile designers to be making over a million dollars annually? Why or why not?
3. In view of Chrysler's poor performance, do you believe Daimler's management deserved to earn $48 million in 2003? Why or why not?

A **product's quality** is a function of its physical aspects. Some companies may offer different levels of quality for its products. For many years, Sears had three levels of quality for its Craftsman tools: good, better, and best. Often, if customers perceive that a product has high quality, the company can charge a higher price for it. On the other hand, Japanese car manufacturers, such as Honda and Toyota, were able to offer high-quality cars at lower prices, thereby

product's quality The physical aspects of a product that affect its level of performance

ensuring their success in the U.S. car market. Chrysler's trucks ranked lower on quality than did Ford's and General Motors', forcing the company to evaluate new models on quality while still in the design stage. The company added a vice president for quality who implemented this new policy.[1] Because of the problems Bridgestone-Firestone faced due to its tires shredding and causing automobile accidents, all its quality engineers now report to a vice president who, in turn, reports to the firm's CEO.[2]

The *name* placed on a brand is a critical element of its marketing mix. The wrong name can be a hindrance in getting the product accepted in the marketplace and can adversely affect sales and profits. The right name can have a positive effect on such objectives. There are a number of recommendations that companies need to follow when selecting **brand names.**

> Suggest the benefits of using the product (Gleem toothpaste, Spic'n Span cleaner, Beautyrest mattresses).
> Be short (Tide is a good example).
> Suggest excellence (Gold Medal flour).
> Be easy to spell (Manischewitz is *not* easy to spell).
> Not have geographical connotations; they may preclude mass-market acceptance because a local orientation is suggested (Lee Conshohocken Tires is an example; Conshohocken is a suburb of Philadelphia, where the company's tires are produced).
> Have an obvious meaning (Kreml and Drene were two hair-care products that violated this recommendation).

National brands are brands that carry the name placed on the product by the manufacturer, Procter & Gamble's Pampers and Crisco, for example. They may carry the name of the company, like Ford Explorer or Ford Taurus. **Private brands** carry the retailer's brand name, such as Talbot's women's clothes or Albertson's peanuts, cream cheeses, or canned vegetables. **Generic brands** do not carry a brand name; instead, the label designates the content of the package, such as white cake or tomato juice. National brands give the manufacturer the greatest level of control over marketing their product. Retailers benefit from carrying national brands because of the advertising and promotion dollars spent on the brand names by the manufacturers, which produce the name recognition in the marketplace that attracts consumers to the stores that are carrying these national brands.

Private and generic brands, however, are controlled by retailers; often the name of the retailer will be on the private brand. As retailers like Wal-Mart have gotten more powerful in the last twenty years, more private brands have appeared. Usually private brands carry lower prices than national brands. Because generics' prices are even lower than those of private brands, their sales normally increase during periods of economic downturns.

There are two types of packages. The **protective package** safeguards a product as it is transported from manufacturers to wholesalers to retailers. The **promotional package** is the one that encloses each unit of a product; it is the one that we see on retailer shelves that shouts at us "Buy me." Because some one-third of products may not be advertised, the promotional package takes over the promotional job. Successful packages often benefit the retailer or the consumer. For example, a package may enhance stackability of a product on the retailer's shelf and increase the length of time it can be stored at home before spoiling.

Packaging is expensive. In general, a package represents 25 percent of a product's total cost. For some products—beer, soft drinks, baby food, and frozen dinners—the cost of the package may exceed that of the contents. Because packaging materials

---

brand names The name placed on a brand

national brands Products that carry the brand name of the manufacturer

private brands Products that carry the brand name of the retailer

generic brands Products that do not have a brand name, but contain only an indication of their contents on the package

protective package The package that safeguards products as they are being transported

promotional package The package that encloses a product whose purpose is to help sell the product at the retail level

A supermarket aisle in Canton, China contains a wide variety of promotional packages.

contribute to the litter problem, the importance of disposable or recyclable packages has increased recently.

reality CHECK *Go to a supermarket and record how many different kinds of packages you see. What package elements did you use in your assessment?*

A **warranty** is an assurance or guarantee made by a seller to a buyer about the quality of the good or service the seller offers. It may be either spoken or written (an **express warranty**); an **implicit warranty** is neither spoken nor written but exists anyway because the Universal Product Code states that all goods are implicitly warranted to be at least fit for the ordinary purpose for which they are used. Warranties can benefit producers in a number of ways.

> They provide another persuasive element.
> They can differentiate one company's products from another's.
> They can generate repeat purchases.
> They lend credibility to the producer because they show that it believes in its product.
> They can pull customers away from competitors.
> They protect producers from unreasonable claims of customers.
> They limit costs of doing business. Such aspects of a warranty as duration, service problems, and freight reimbursement can be controlled.[3]
> They can be used to combat consumer concerns. In the aftermath of the shredding problem faced by Bridgestone-Firestone, the company began offering extended warranties of up to four years on its tires.[4]

Warranties can also benefit consumers. They assure product quality and value when they promise a certain level of performance for a long time. Warranties increase customers' self-confidence, reduce their feelings of risk about future ownership, and reduce the level of postpurchase dissonance that might exist.[5]

warranty An assurance made by a seller to a buyer about the quality of a product or service offered by the seller

express warranty An explicit warranty that is either written or spoken

implicit warranty An unwritten or unspoken warranty that exists because the Universal Product Code says that all goods are at least fit for the ordinary purpose for which they are used

LEARNING OBJECTIVE 3
Describe the differences between standardization and adaptation strategies.

standardization strategy Using the same product mix for international and domestic markets

Firms that are selling products to international markets have to decide whether they want to use a standardization or an adaptation strategy. A **standardization strategy** means using the same product mix (design, package, warranty, brand name, etc.) in overseas markets as in domestic markets. This strategy has a number of advantages, including not having to develop a new product mix and holding down R&D, production, and marketing costs. An **adaptation strategy** offers a different product mix to the various international markets than what is employed in the domestic market. Unlike the standardization strategy, it recognizes the needs and desires of consumers in those countries, but is more costly because higher R&D, production, and marketing costs are required to develop and market a variety of products.

adaptation strategy Using a different product mix for products sold internationally than those sold domestically

reality
CHECK
Scan the international articles in the most recent issues of Fortune, Business Week, *and* Forbes. *Are any of the companies pursuing a standardization or adaptation strategy?*

product width The number of different product lines a company is marketing

product depth The number of specific products or brands within a product line

A major decision is the number of products to produce and market. This decision involves both width and depth dimensions. **Product width** refers to the number of different lines, whereas **product depth** is the number of specific products (or brands) within each product line. Procter & Gamble has a number of product lines (width), including laundry and cleaning products, personal care, food, industrial, and medical. Some of these have relatively few brands (depth). At one time, there were only eight brands in the food line (Crisco, Crisco Oil, Jif, Pringles, etc.), but there were 22 in the personal care line (Coast, Ivory, Lava, Zest, Scope, Secret, Crest, Bounty, Pampers, etc.).

LEARNING OBJECTIVE 4
Discuss the concept of brand equity and why it is important.

brand equity The monetary value or worth of a brand

Companies are trying hard to maximize their **brand equity,** that is, the value or worth of their brands. Campbell Soup, Coca-Cola, General Electric, General Motors, Kellogg, Kodak, and Sara Lee are examples. Benefits from greater brand equity include improved balance sheets, better awareness of brands by consumers, company performance exceeding that of the stock market, above-average profitability and cash flows, and higher prices received when a company is sold to or acquired by another. Examples include Rolls Royce selling its brand name to Volkswagen for $66 million, General Electric getting additional annual revenues of $10 billion, and Rank Hovis McDougall reducing its debt ratio and, thus, having the capital needed to acquire Nabisco's British cereal operations.

What factors make up brand equity? Usually, past and projected future profits are emphasized. In predicting a brand's future profits, companies will use a variety of market and product measures. For example, brands that have higher market shares, are in a market experiencing rapid growth, have high levels of customer loyalty, and enjoy high levels of customer satisfaction are likely to be very profitable in years to come.

reality
CHECK
Which companies do you believe have the highest level of brand equity? Search the Internet under "brand equity" and find the most recent estimates of companies' brand equities. How well did you do?

Developing New Products

Why Develop New Products? Software giant Microsoft brought out Windows XP, a computer operating system that makes it easier to organize music files

Case in Point

Sony's Product Lines Are an Important Asset as It Considers Merger and Acquisition Possibilities

Sony's financial performance between 1998 and 2002 was mediocre. It was mainly caused by the poor performance of its electronics division, and the outlook for its media sector is not good either. Its consumer electronics divisions—TVs, DVDs, games, and camcorders—are very strong. Industry experts suggest that Sony should jettison some of its non-competitive products, such as computer peripherals, components, and chips, and either merge its entertainment section or spin it off.

A merger with MGM has been rumored; selling the division outright makes financial sense. It has been estimated that spinning off the entertainment sector could fetch as much as $17 billion, more than three times what Sony spent in the 1980s to acquire the music and film operation. Sony's trump card in any merger or acquisition decision is its vast array of entertainment products. It owns the rights to 3,500 movies, 35,000 episodes of TV shows, and 500,000 musical recordings, many of which involve top-flight artists like Michael Jackson. Some of Sony's recent movies have been box office successes, including *Spiderman, Spiderman 2, Men in Black, Stuart Little, Crouching Tiger, Hidden Dragon,* and *Black Hawk Down.* Making the entertainment division even more attractive is that it finally became profitable in 2002, after years of losses, due mainly to cost-cutting successes in film and TV production.

Source: Ronald Grover, Tom Lowry and Irene M. Kunii, "How Sony Could Sharpen Its Picture," *Business Week,* March 11, 2002, p. 80.

Questions

1. Should Sony get rid of its entertainment division? Why or why not?
2. Why are Sony's movies, TV shows, and musical recordings so valuable?
3. What problems might Sony encounter if it merged its entertainment operations?

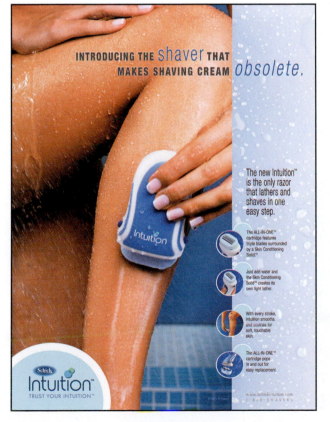

This Schick ad introduces its new product, the Intuition razor, by indicating the product's benefits to purchasers.

and obtain digital photos. Its *Xbox* home console established its presence in the video game market. And a new, bold venture into home networking was also being considered.[6] Not-so-successful Sunbeam—it filed for bankruptcy in February 2001—is also introducing a number of new products. CEO Jerry W. Levin realizes that without any new small appliance products to complement its Mr. Coffee coffeemakers and Oster blenders, Sunbeam's "prospects are bleak." Accordingly, a home electricity generator that is powered by fuel cells and the Thalia line of "smart" appliances—one of which is an alarm clock that downloads traffic reports from the Web—will be added.[7]

Why do Microsoft and Sunbeam and countless other firms around the world develop new products? There are a number of reasons. They develop and market new products in order to remain competitive. Many firms believe that they need to have at least 25 percent of their sales in five years accounted for by new products in order to keep up with competitors, who will also be bringing out new products in that time period. There is also the need to replace products that have been phased out. The new products will replace lost revenues and profits, keep the company name before present customers, and enable idle resources to be reemployed.

Many companies have a pronounced seasonal pattern of sales or production. Such peaks and valleys do not allow firms to operate efficiently. Thus, they will offer new products or services in the off-season in order to smooth out sales and production. An example would be an income tax service that decides to offer year-round financial advisory services.

Companies often have a large percentage of their revenues and profits accounted for by only a few products. If these start to be problematic, the firms will be in trouble. New products can be introduced to reduce the risk the companies are facing. Hershey Chocolate reduced its emphasis on chocolate products by branching out into macaroni, bakeries, restaurants, and coffee-brewing equipment.

Companies have discovered that new products developed from waste or by-products can boost revenues and profits. Many of the by-products from the oil-refining process can be used in plastics and pharmaceuticals. Meat packers make effective use of by-products in such products as Jell-O.

Exploiting new opportunities is another explanation for developing new products. A need that is not currently being met can be satisfied with a new product. Or, a competitive firm may stop marketing a product, leaving the door open for other companies to fill the void with new product offerings.

New Product Philosophy.   To develop new products, companies need to adhere to a basic philosophy. At the outset, they need to decide whether they want to be first in the market with new products or to employ a follow-the-leader strategy. First-mover companies have the advantage of maximizing potential revenues and profits because they have the market to themselves. However, they face high risk,

A new airport screening device searches for explosive residue by blowing particles from clothing.

because it is not known if the product will be successful. The follow-the-leader option allows companies to face reduced risks because they can wait to see if the new product will be successful. Revenues and profits obtained, however, may be lower because the first-in firm has the market to itself for some time. Management capabilities need to be considered. First-mover companies need to have skilled R&D operations, while follow-the-leader firms need to be adept at production (to lower the cost of the product and its price to the market) and marketing (to create demand in the market).

Chrysler tended to bring out new products in bunches instead of spreading them out over a number of years, causing industry analysts to worry about new product dry spells.[8] This failure suggests another basic philosophical principle for developing new products: They need to be developed on a continuous basis so that there are not lengthy periods with little or no revenues or profits coming in.

Developing new products is a time-consuming process. Some products can take two or even five years to get to the market. Many companies are trying to shorten the process because market tastes may change, other firms will have a better chance to bring out their new products, and important deadlines may not be met. On the other hand, companies must guard against rushing the development process, so that the product's quality is not jeopardized.

Companies need to realize that developing new products is a costly venture. At one extreme, it has been estimated that it costs between $1 billion and $2 billion to bring out a new automobile model. Firms should be wary of skimping on development expenditures so that the likelihood that the product will fail is not increased, but should be sure that each dollar expended is thoroughly justified.

A number of departments are involved in developing new products. Marketing, research and development, manufacturing, packaging, and finance usually have some new product responsibilities. Thus, some means must be in place to coordinate all of these activities.

Top management needs to support the new product process. They should communicate effectively the importance of new products to all areas of the firm and help to set objectives for them and the strategies for achieving the objectives, and set reasonable deadlines. Top executives, however, should not be involved on a day-to-day basis with the new product development process, as this may be viewed as putting too much pressure on the scientists and engineers working on the new products.

Companies should understand that not all of their new products will be successful; there will be failures because a firm may not know what competitors are doing, information about the market may be inaccurate, the market's tastes may change, the economy may go into a recession, and so on. Some high-profile, much-ballyhooed new products surprised their companies when they failed. Examples include the Ford Edsel, RCA videodisk camera, Eastman Kodak's disk camera, Polaroid's X-70 instamatic camera, and New Coke. Invariably, the reason for products failing is that they did not fulfill a need or desire in the market. However, the fear of failing does not keep firms from developing new-to-world products that are highly risky but, if successful, can generate huge profits for years.

The rate at which new products fail is debatable. Failure rates from 20 to 98 percent have been reported, depending on the types of products and industries studied. As mentioned above, some failures are acceptable. However, there are severe downsides when the failure rate gets excessive. The company's reputation suffers. Valuable and scarce resources are poorly allocated and have to be reallocated. Customers who did like the product may begin purchasing from a competitor. Revenues and profits will decline.

Like the rate of new product failure, what constitutes new product failure is not always agreed on. Does a product fail if it does not reach a certain level of profit or stays on the market less than a year? Should a product be considered a failure if it does not achieve a particular market share or level of revenues? Because of these different standards, it is best to consider a product successful if it obtains all or most of the objectives set for it by the company developing it and bringing it to market.

LEARNING OBJECTIVE 5
List the steps in the process for developing new products and explain how each should be performed.

EXHIBIT 9.1

Steps in the New Product Development Process

external source A source for new products that is located outside of a company

lead users High-profile firms in an industry that are good sources for new industrial products because their business methods are often emulated by other firms in the industry

technology transfer The adoption by one company for the development of new products of a technology that originated with another company

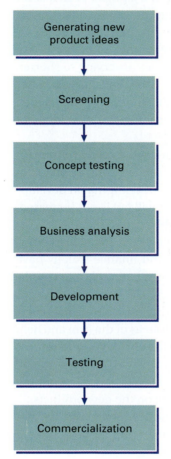

Steps in the New Product Development Process. Exhibit 9.1 shows the steps required to develop new products, steps that if performed correctly will increase the likelihood that new products will be successful.

GENERATING NEW PRODUCT IDEAS. Companies can look externally or internally for potential new products. The market may be the most important **external source.** Its new product needs should be carefully ascertained. **Lead users**—the large, high-profile firms in an industry whose business methods are often emulated by other companies—are especially good sources for new product ideas for industrial markets. Other companies' new products should be considered, as well as technology in other industries, because about 50 percent of new product ideas come via **technology transfer** from one company to another.

Patent offices are good sources for new product ideas. Individual patents can provide specific possibilities, and the analysis of patents over time can yield important new product trends. Scientific and professional meetings are an external source that is often overlooked. At such meetings, there is often an exchange of information that may suggest fruitful areas for further consideration.

Independent inventors can be a viable source for new products. Many of the truly significant inventions of the twentieth century were developed by individual inventors such as Frank Whittle (jet engine), Chester Carlson (photocopying), and Edwin Land (Polaroid instant camera). However, companies are well advised to have a structured procedure for dealing with such individuals in order to minimize some of the legal problems that may occur involving ownership, method of payment, and so on. The developer of the modern carburetor accused one of the car companies in the early 1900s of stealing his idea. One of the three developers of the automatic inoculation gun absconded with the idea.

Universities often have a unit that is responsible for developing new product ideas that can then be licensed to outside companies. One of the most successful is the one at Cambridge University in the United Kingdom. Venture teams, R&D personnel, the marketing department, and company employees are examples of the **internal sources** for new product ideas. **Venture teams** are temporary units formed to come up with new product ideas. They are made up of individuals from various departments who are highly regarded for their creativity.

internal sources Sources for new products that are located within a firm

venture team A temporary group that a company establishes to come up with new product ideas

The marketing department can be an important source of new product ideas. Marketing research people can uncover new product needs when they analyze markets. Sales personnel should be looking for new product possibilities when they call on their customers or potential customers. Brand managers need to be thinking of modifications for their products.

In general, internal sources are probably better for firms practicing a follow-the-leader strategy and firms interested in developing products that are similar to present offerings. External sources are more appropriate for firms attempting to be out first with new products or those developing ones that are significantly different from current offerings.

reality CHECK   *In the four most recent issues of* Business Week, *read the "Science and Technology" section. Determine if any of the articles indicate the source of the new product ideas.*

Once sources have been identified for new products, the new product ideas must be generated. Most companies use some form of **brainstorming,** in which participants offer new product ideas they think will be appropriate for their firm. The major component of this process is that no one is allowed to critique favorably or unfavorably any suggestion made. This restriction exists so that the free flow of new product ideas will not be hindered. Evaluation of the new product idea occurs in the screening stage of the new product development process.

brainstorming Considering potential new product ideas in a group setting

SCREENING. Once a list of new product ideas has been developed, **screening** occurs. The purpose of this step is to identify those offerings that have the best chance of being commercially successful. In this regard, it is desirable to avoid two mistakes: selecting products that will fail and rejecting those that would have been successful. The latter error is probably more dangerous, because there is little likelihood that a product idea, once rejected, will be reconsidered. On the other hand, the few offerings that are considered to be feasible come under close scrutiny later in the process, so there is the possibility that potential failures may be weeded out then. However, it is better if products that will not pass muster at subsequent steps are weeded out during the screening step, because steps further down the line require a much greater expenditure of time and money than are needed in the screening step. In the pharmaceutical industry, it is estimated that only one out of 5000 drug ideas is ever commercialized.[9] Obviously, it is better if the 4999 that are not marketed were dismissed during the screening stage.

screening The step in the new product development process in which new product ideas are subjected to an initial evaluation

In the screening process, new product candidates are evaluated on criteria the company believes predict success:

- The product meets a specific, significant need of the market.
- The product is superior to products already on the market.
- The product allows the use of current channels of distribution.
- The R&D department has the capability to develop the new product.
- The product can be brought to the market in less than two years.
- The necessary financial resources to develop and market the product are available.

If the candidate product successfully passes the screening hurdle, it moves to the next step: concept testing.

CONCEPT TESTING. In **concept testing,** the general notion of the new product and how it can benefit customers is presented to a sample of customers in order to get their reactions. The main objective is to find out how likely it is that the market

concept testing Presenting the general idea of a new product to a sample of the market in order to get its reaction

focus group A small group of consumers that is representative of the market for a new product and provides companies with reactions to new product concepts

would purchase the new product if it were available. Also, it is important to get some idea of the price customers would be willing to pay. Often, the new product idea is presented to members of a **focus group.** These are individuals who are representative of the market to which the new product will be directed. Focus group sessions usually last about two hours and are directed by a focus group leader who is skilled at getting information from the participants. As in brainstorming, the leader will not comment either negatively or positively on participants' comments, because this would tend to shut off their participation. Compensating participants, providing snacks, and giving adequate breaks are other important aspects of effectively conducting focus groups.

It is usually not desirable that the company have developed a physical prototype for the focus group to view. Prototypes cost a lot of money, so firms will wait to develop them later in the new product development process, when they are surer that the product will be successful. A former president of the OI corporation, a maker of testing equipment, has stated that the cost of even the simplest prototype would be a minimum of $50,000, so OI would never develop one early on in the new product development process. Viable options to prototypes include holograms and computer-aided design (CAD).

business analysis The step in the new product development process in which a new product's potential profits are estimated

BUSINESS ANALYSIS.   The **business analysis** step is used to predict how potentially profitable the new product candidate will be. This primarily involves an estimate of how many units of the product are likely to be sold. That figure can be combined with various estimates of price to forecast revenues. Estimated costs can then be subtracted from revenues to arrive at a forecast of profits. Throughout this step, decision makers consider the length of time needed to obtain the expected level of profits and how much risk is involved.

break-even formula The calculation that tells a company the number of units a new product needs to sell in order for it to cover the cost of development and the expected profit

Many of the above factors are incorporated into a calculation frequently used by companies in the business analysis stage. The **break-even formula** tells the company the number of units a new product needs to sell in order to cover the cost of developing the new product and providing the company with its desired level of profit. The calculation is

$$Q = \frac{DC + p}{P - CPU}$$

where
$$\begin{aligned}
Q &= \text{quantity} \\
DC &= \text{development cost} \\
p &= \text{desired level of profit} \\
P &= \text{product's price} \\
CPU &= \text{cost per unit}
\end{aligned}$$

Let's assume that the development costs for a new product are $500,000, the company wants a $100,000 profit, the suggested price is $20, and the cost per unit is estimated to be $14. When the data are put into the break-even formula, we see that 100,000 units must be sold in order to cover the development costs and provide the firm with its desired $100,000 in profit.

$$Q = \frac{\$500,000 + \$100,000}{\$20 - \$14}$$

$$Q = \frac{\$600,000}{\$6}$$

$$Q = 100,000$$

In making this calculation, it is helpful to understand that because the price exceeds the cost per unit by $6, every time a unit is sold, the development cost plus desired profit figure is reduced by $6; thus, in this example, it takes 100,000 units to totally "eliminate" the development cost and the profit desired. Once the company knows this figure, it can estimate how long it will take to sell that number of units and how likely it is that that number of units can be sold.

Two aspects of risk—how new the product is to the market and to the company's existing products—are dealt with in Exhibit 9.2. There, six classes of products are evaluated in terms of risk. The least risky are cost reductions; the most risky are new-to-world products. However, most companies will look not only at risk, but will include potential profit as well. These two variables are included in Exhibit 9.3.

Exhibit 9.4 (on p. 322) presents six aspects of new products that affect the potential level of acceptance and the speed at which it is achieved. **Relative advantage** refers to how much better than competitive products the new offering is. **Compatibility** involves the extent to which purchasers of new products can continue to operate as they have in the past or how much differently they have to operate than they are used to. Products that are *complex* are likely to be less well received in the market than those that are easy to use. Canasta was a card game introduced in the 1950s that never caught on, because the rules of play were so complicated. The level of purchases of personal computers increased greatly as they became easier to operate. **Communicability** refers to how easy or difficult it is to convey the product's benefits to the intended market. Products whose benefits can be easily demonstrated, such as a powerful vacuum cleaner picking up nails and coins as well as dust, are more likely to be accepted in the market than those whose benefits are not easy to communicate. As the cost of new products goes down, market acceptance will increase. When four-function, handheld calculators cost $300, market acceptance was low. As their price dropped to as low as $4 to $5, purchases increased dramatically. Demand was not great for VCRs when they cost $1000; it zoomed as price dropped into the $200 range. Many consumers are skeptical about new products; they do not want to purchase them without first trying them out. Products that have **divisibility** allow consumers to do this. Many bank customers were wary of using automated teller machines (ATMs) when they were first introduced; they felt they would make mistakes or that their cards would be destroyed or not returned. In order to deal with this concern, many banks allowed customers to practice using ATMs located in their lobbies, with help available if needed.

DEVELOPMENT. A company's research and development (R&D) department has the primary responsibility for the physical **development** of the new product. It is staffed primarily by scientists and engineers, who bring their technical expertise to the new product development process. It is their responsibility to turn a new product idea into a finished product within time and budget constraints.

Facilities for R&D may be located at company headquarters or at a separate location to better stimulate the creativity of R&D personnel. Companies that have a lot of business overseas

EXHIBIT 9.2

Risk of Types of New Products

(Risk increases from bottom left to top right)

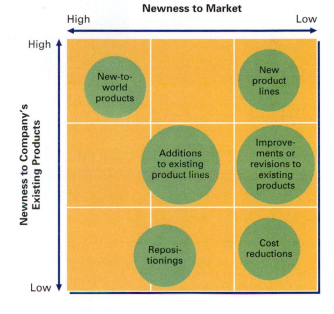

relative advantage How much better than competitive products a new product is

compatibility The extent to which a new product allows consumers to operate as they have in the past

communicability The ease with which it is possible to convey the benefits of a new product to the market

divisibility The aspect of a new product that enables consumers to try it in a piecemeal manner without having to purchase the entire product

EXHIBIT 9.3

The Relationship Between Risk and Profitability

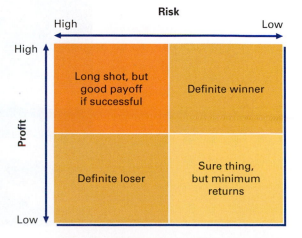

EXHIBIT 9.4

Six Aspects of New Products That Affect Their Level of Acceptance and the Speed at Which It Occurs

Low	Relative advantage	High
Low	Compatibility	High
Complex	Complexity	Simple
Low	Communicability	High
High	Cost	Low
Low	Divisibility	High

Left: Low level of acceptance and Low rate of speed
Right: High level of acceptance and High rate of speed

development The step in the new product development process in which the design of the new product is finalized (p. 321)

applied research Research designed to achieve a specific objective

basic research Research whose aim is to obtain knowledge with no specific, immediate payoff in mind

Technicians inspect computer discs at an R&D facility in Taiwan.

often have an R&D facility in another country to take advantage of the scientific personnel there. Another plus: Sometimes the R&D results occurring in overseas R&D locations can be transferred back to the United States for application to the domestic market. Such was the case with the European R&D operation of Ford Motor Company and the Ford Escort, which was developed initially for the European market.

Companies have to decide on R&D budgets and allocate dollars to specific projects. A major decision is how much to spend on applied and basic research. **Applied research** has as its objective the solving of specific problems. For example, a pharmaceutical firm might be developing specific drugs to help cure cancer. **Basic research** is research for the capturing of knowledge now, with no immediate payoff expected, although a payoff down the road is hoped for. The same firm that

is trying to come up with a cure for cancer might have scientists in the Amazon jungle in Brazil examining tropical plants to increase their knowledge in the hope that there might be a scientific payoff later.

When downturns in the economy occur, companies often reduce their R&D budgets. This decision often hurts companies in the future, because their subsequent new product development efforts will suffer. This mistake was not made by Texas Instruments during the semiconductor industry's deepest slump ever. Instead of cutting back, it tapped its $5 billion in cash to bring out a new generation of computer chips that will enhance its position in digital signal processors (DSPS) and analog chips. William J. McClean, president of IC Insights, says that "companies that spend money in the downturn gain market share in the upturn." Intel CEO Craig R. Barrett believes that successful companies are those that spend their way out of recessions, not save their way. STMicroelectronics, a European chip maker, followed this strategy and became the third largest company in the industry in 2002, up from 14th in 1995.[10]

Legal and ethical issues can affect R&D. For example, stem cell and cloning research that is being conducted by doctors and pharmaceutical companies around the world has the potential to revolutionize medicine. However, these practices are highly controversial, particularly in the United States. Public opinion and laws governing the conduct of this research vary widely between the United States and Europe. As a result, advances in this area of R&D are likely to be made abroad before they are made in the United States.

It is important that there be close coordination between marketing and R&D personnel throughout the development process; marketing should not simply hand off the product concept to R&D and then withdraw from the process. This cooperation will ensure that R&D will develop a product that is in tune with what the market wants. What can happen when there is not close cooperation occurred at Chrysler: The different product development teams did not communicate with each other so each team purchased different parts (windshield wipers, corrosion protection, etc.) for their models, and so needlessly increased the cost of the cars.[11]

The development process needs to be accelerated so products reach markets faster. This will provide first-mover advantages, preempt competitors, and relate to the market's needs and desires before they change. Because Japanese dealers were clamoring to have Honda's Fit, a car shaped like a loaf of bread, in showrooms earlier than expected, the company felt compelled to accelerate the new product development process so that the car was delivered three months earlier than planned. The Fit became the best-selling car in Japan—more popular than even the Toyota Corolla.[12]

While the benefits from accelerating the new product development process are substantial, companies should not be too hasty. One study of 195 industrial manufacturing companies analyzed the design phase of the new product development process. Firms that did not make detailed drawings had only 52.7 percent successful new products, compared to 71.4 percent for those that did. Firms that eliminated some of the seven design steps were not as successful with their new products as firms that performed a greater number of steps.[13]

Some companies will use informal methods of developing new products. Called **skunk works,** these refer to R&D people being allowed to devote a portion of their time to projects they would like to work on. Skunk works at Honda involve a four-foot-tall humanoid robot that can climb stairs, and one in North Carolina where work is being done on a business jet made from composites and powered by a Honda fan engine.[14] The famous Post-it® Notes (3M Company) were developed by a scientist working in his spare time.

skunk works R&D personnel being allowed to use their time to develop new products in which they are interested

technical testing Subjecting a new product to a physical evaluation that measures its ability to perform up to expectations

TESTING. Two types of testing are required. There is technical testing and market testing. **Technical testing** involves subjecting the product to physical evaluation that indicates its ability to meet the market's expectation of performance. Examples include simulating heat and rain on a new roofing material to estimate its useful life, trying out new medicines on a sample of patients, subjecting tires to sharp objects to see if they can withstand punctures, and driving new prototype automobiles in the summer in Death Valley to determine how well they will perform in hot weather climates. The results of technical testing enable companies to place warranties on their products and develop advertising campaigns built around product performance. Products that fail physical tests will either have to undergo further development or will be dropped. New medical drugs often run into problems when being tested. In other words, they do not perform well enough. For example, Oxford Glycosciences had a major product, Zavesca (for Gaucher's disease), fail a trial run with patients, and Powderject had to withdraw a vaccine for tuberculosis.[15]

market testing Marketing a product on a limited basis to help decide which marketing mix should be used when it is commercialized

Companies used to employ **market testing** to measure the level of customer acceptance of a new product. These results would determine whether the product would be introduced to the market or dropped. Today, a change in thinking has occurred. Firms will no longer subject a product to market testing unless they are sure that it will be accepted by the market; it is too expensive to allow a product to get that far in the new product development process unless management is sure that the product will be successful. Instead, companies will use market testing to decide how to more effectively commercialize the product. That is, what prices to charge, what channels of distribution to use, what advertisements will be most appropriate, and so on.

test markets Cities that mirror the entire U.S. market so that companies use them to market their products on a limited basis to develop a marketing mix for the commercialization stage

Test markets are cities that mirror the larger U.S. market on factors believed important in the sale of the new product, such as income, age, and ethnicity. Frequently used test market cities are Tulsa, Indianapolis, Phoenix, and Dallas. In order to find out which of two prices, for example, would result in the most revenue, a firm would choose two test markets and sell the product at a different price in each city. This process is called test marketing.

While the use of test marketing is helpful in developing the new product's marketing mix, there are several downsides. They are time consuming and expensive, often requiring more than six months and close to $1 million. Perhaps even more important, they tip off the competition, allowing them to get their products out before the test market is even completed. This happened to such well-known products as Mrs. Butterworth's syrup and Head and Shoulders shampoo. Competitors can also bias the test market results by, for example, charging a lower price that they know they can't sustain, thereby lowering the sales of the product in the test market and discouraging the company from introducing the product. Because of these problems, some companies are using **simulated test markets.** Consumers in shopping malls would be exposed to an advertisement for a product and would then take the product home. They would be called after having had the opportunity to use the product and asked to rate it. Simulated test markets can be accomplished more quickly and at lower costs than test markets, and they eliminate the possibility of competitor interference.

simulated test markets An alternative to test markets that offers speed, lower cost, and less competitor interference

commercialization Strategies employed to introduce a new product and to monitor its performance

COMMERCIALIZATION. **Commercialization** refers to the strategies used to introduce a new product to the market as well as the methods used to track its progress. The new product's marketing mix will be finalized based on the results of market testing. Its quality, warranties, price, promotion, and channels of distribution will be put into play with the expectation that they will enable the product to be successful.

The timing of the new product's introduction needs to be decided. Some products will be introduced to all geographical segments of the market at the same time. Some will be introduced on a rollout basis, that is, to the various geographical markets on a sequential basis. A rollout strategy provides the opportunity for marketers to fix problems that might arise before they can affect the entire market. A problem arises when new products are not available in stores when scheduled. This situation is especially disturbing to customers when the company has used preintroduction announcements to ballyhoo the new product. Customer expectations are not met, and they may refuse to buy the product when it is available, as well as other products that the offending company markets.

Early progress of the product must be tracked. The results will allow marketers to decide if expected future sales appear to be significant enough to warrant the product still being produced and marketed. The number of triers of the product, the percentage of those who are repeat purchasers, the frequency of the purchase, and the average purchase quantity can be used to predict the number of units sold in the future.

It is especially important that marketers of new products closely monitor innovators. **Innovators** are defined as the first 2.5 percent of adopters of new products. Innovators are quite receptive to new products (they are venturesome), but more importantly, they are respected for their opinions and are sought out by other potential adopters for these opinions. If innovators are passing on negative comments about the new product, companies need to know this as soon as possible so they can make proper adjustments in the product's marketing strategies.

innovators The first 2.5 percent of adopters of new products who are respected for their opinions and are sought out for these opinions by the market

Managing Existing Products

LEARNING OBJECTIVE 6
Describe the product life cycle and how it can be used to manage existing products.

Product Life Cycle. As a basis for managing a firm's existing products, it is helpful to understand the product life cycle (PLC). Exhibit 9.5 shows that the PLC is broken down into four stages over time and includes the curves that represent both revenues and profits. During the **introduction stage,** revenues increase from zero and continue to increase during the **growth stage.** A slower level of increase occurs during the beginning of the **maturity phase,** reaches its high point during the middle of this stage, then begins to drop. Revenues continue to drop during the **decline stage.** Low levels of profit exist during the introduction stage—sometimes there are

introduction stage The first phase of the product life cycle in which revenues and profits are low but begin to increase

growth stage The second stage of the product life cycle in which revenues increase rapidly and profits are maximized

maturity stage The third stage of the product life cycle in which profits drop and revenues are maximized

decline stage The fourth step of the product life cycle in which profits and revenues continue to fall

EXHIBIT 9.5

The Product Life Cycle

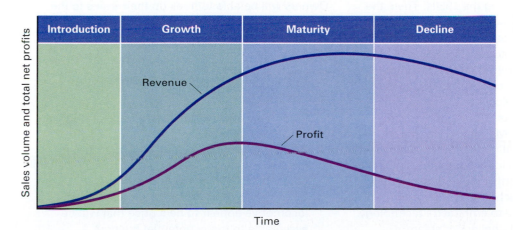

losses—and increase rapidly during the growth phase, reaching their peak during the latter portion, and dropping throughout the maturity and decline stages.

Two factors determine a company's marketing mixes over the PLC: the market and competition. During the introduction phase, purchasers come chiefly from the **primary market,** those purchasers whose needs and desires are the most compatible with the offering's features and benefits. These individuals view the product or service as satisfying their needs and desires and tend to be relatively insensitive to efforts by competitors to change their purchasing habits. Thus, the primary market can also be viewed as that market segment that exhibits very strong brand loyalty over the entire cycle.

In the growth period, the product or service begins to make significant inroads into the **secondary market**—that market segment in which the features and benefits of the product or service are not quite as congruent with the purchaser's needs and desires as they are in the primary market. It is very critical for the offering's success that it gain acceptance in the secondary market, since this segment tends to be much larger than the primary market.

Because there is not a 100 percent compatibility of needs and desires with the offering's features and benefits, the secondary market can be persuaded to purchase the offering only if it is made more attractive in some way. This may involve either a modification in the product or service, or some change in the marketing mix, such as lower price for lower quality, increased advertising expenditures, and so on. During the maturity period, purchases are made up of continued repeat purchases by the loyal primary market, first-time purchases by the balance of the secondary market, and repeat purchases on the part of the secondary market that has already tried the product or service.

A significant aspect of the maturity period is that the primary market accounts for a relatively small percentage of total purchases. The great majority of purchases

primary market The segment of the market for new products whose needs and desires are the most compatible with a new product's features and benefits

secondary market The market for a new product whose needs and desires are not as congruent with the new product's features and benefits as those of the primary market

---

Technology and Business

Electric Toy Trains Make a Comeback

Electric model trains used to be one of the United States' most popular toys. And Lionel was the largest toy electric train company in the world, selling 3 million engines and freight cars annually during the 1950s. Then, the company changed hands, lost its focus, and began producing plastic trains instead of the heavy, metal ones enthusiasts were used to owning. For over 30 years, the company just barely stayed in business as kids switched their affection to slot cars and space toys. In 1995, Wellspring Associates LLC, in partnership with rock star Neil Young, purchased Lionel and hired Richard N. Maddox, a lifelong train enthusiast, as CEO. The total market for toy trains is about $1 billion a year, but Lionel competes only in the large train segment, worth $250 million annually.

In an effort to get as much of this market as possible, Lionel has decided to emphasize technology. New models, like the $1800 Challenger steam locomotive, will be offered. A wireless remote control is available; it can control the sounds and speeds of up to 99 trains at the same time. Whistle sounds and commands from engineers have been created. Owners will be able to hook up their trains to the Internet in order to have problems diagnosed and can have new sounds and functions downloaded.

Source: Jeff Green, "The Toy-Train Company That Thinks It Can," *Business Week,* December 4, 2000, pp. 64–69.

Questions

1. Do you believe that the technology strategy of Lionel will be effective?
2. Do you believe that producing plastic trains instead of metal ones was the only reason Lionel barely managed to stay in business?
3. Does a price of $1800 for Challenger steam locomotive appear to be a price that will be acceptable to many potential buyers?

are from the secondary market, who are receptive to modifications in marketing tactics and strategies by competitors designed to influence their purchase allegiance. These tactics may be a major factor in causing a product or service to enter the decline stage.

During the decline period, the secondary market is essentially lost to other firms. Thus, sales volume drops markedly and sales are concentrated chiefly in the primary market, as they were during the introduction period. Not all products slide into the decline stage. In fact, companies often try to prevent this from happening as soon as possible. Procter & Gamble has been quite successful in doing this; Ivory soap and Crest toothpaste have been around for one hundred years and fifty years, respectively.

There are few, if any, competitors in the introduction phase, often because many companies are waiting to see how well the new product does. However, once they see revenues increasing during the growth phase, more of them will enter the market. More competitors are added during the early portion of the maturity stage, but as sales start to falter, they start to withdraw from the market. Their withdrawal is hastened during the decline stage, often leaving the original company facing only a handful of competitors.

Because the primary market dominates in the introduction stage and there are few competitors, companies' marketing mixes in the first stage of the PLC may not need to be as aggressive as they will need to be in the subsequent phases. Prices can be high on the one or few basic models offered, promotional expenditures can be relatively low, few distributors will be required, and warehousing and trucking operations will be leased. Because of the increasing importance of the secondary market and the influx of more competitors, a more aggressive marketing mix will usually be employed during the growth and maturity phases: lower prices, increasing level of promotion and distributors, and ownership of warehousing and trucking facilities. In recognition of a return to dominance by the primary market and a shakeout of competitors during the decline phase, companies will shrink the level of their marketing mix so that it often mirrors what is employed during the introduction stage.

reality CHECK   *In what stage of the product life cycle would you place personal computers? What criteria did you use to make your decision?*

Product Elimination.   The performance of many products eventually becomes so poor in the decline stage that they have to be considered for **product elimination.** In fact, companies often find that a large percentage of their products provide them with only a small percentage of their total revenues. This is called the **20/80 principle:** around 20 percent of a company's products will account for about 80 percent of its revenues, and, conversely, 80 percent of its products will generate only 20 percent of its revenues. Thus, these 80 percent of the company's products are primary candidates to be considered for elimination.

> **product elimination** The process whereby poorly performing products are dropped
>
> **20/80 principle** The idea that a small percentage of a company's products accounts for a large percentage of its revenues

Some companies have benefited greatly from their product elimination efforts. A small candy company dropped 796 of its 800 products, yet became one of the most profitable firms in the industry. Hunt Foods' sales increased eightfold over the decade that it was discarding 27 of 30 product lines. American Optical freed up additional executive time, dropped its inventory level, and made resources available for more-promising products. One year after its product elimination effort, Shaklee's net profits doubled. Chrysler dropped its 18-year-old Jeep Cherokee, a product that had numerous defects and an obsolete design, and replaced it with the Jeep Liberty, which was expected to help rejuvenate its sales.[16]

Successful product elimination programs subject all products to a periodic analysis—at least once a year. Because of the great number of products many companies have and the large amount of data needed for each, computer involvement is a must. The process for analyzing products needs to be formalized in writing. And a definite sequence of steps needs to be identified.

1. *Periodically monitor products.* This step involves collecting comprehensive data for each product, including product revenues in units and dollars, costs associated with each product, market share, inventory levels, and prices charged. From these data it is possible to compute important performance measures for products. For example, dollar revenues can be matched against costs to determine product profitability.

2. *Assess product performance.* The data collected from the monitoring step should be used to assess product performance. This means comparing how the product is doing with the objectives established for it. Thus, its actual return on investment would be compared to the desired return, and so on. Even though a product's performance may exceed the levels established for it, management should be wary of developments that suggest future problems, such as declining sales, introduction of a superior competitive product, and price declines required.

3. *Elimination or retention decision.* After assessing the product's performance, management must decide whether to eliminate or retain the product. Most products will undoubtedly be retained. Those that fail to achieve a large number of their most important objectives, especially profit, should probably be dropped. This assumes that management cannot develop strategies that will make the product's performance acceptable.

EXHIBIT 9.6

Implementing the Elimination and Retention Decisions

Factors to Consider When a Product Is to Be Eliminated
When should the product be eliminated?
To what other products will the freed-up resources be assigned? When should they be reassigned?
Should the current inventory be sold before the product is eliminated?
Should customers be notified about the elimination? When should the notice go out?
What should the notice say?
Should orders be filled after the day for elimination?
Are any laws or contractual agreements being violated?
Should customers be allowed to return units of the unsold product?

Strategies to Consider When a Product Is to Be Retained
Should the price be increased or decreased?
Should the promotional budget be increased or decreased?
Should the product be modified or should the quality be improved?
Should the channels of distribution be changed?
Should the advertising media used be changed?
Should the product be marketed to new market segments?
Should different modes of transportation be used?
Should the sales force effort for the product increase or decrease?

4. *Implement the elimination or retention decision.* If management decides to drop a product, that decision must be implemented in an orderly way that considers both the firm's and its customers' interests. Exhibit 9.6 lists the most important factors to consider.

When management decides to retain a product, it must then consider strategies that will improve its performance. These strategies are also listed in Exhibit 9.6. These are marketing mix alternatives. It is obvious that some of them involve a *decrease* in marketing effort for the retained product. Decreased marketing support is frequently an effective strategy for a product whose revenues will not drop greatly as a result of the reduced support. In some cases, greater profit will result because the sales decline is less than the decreased cost involved.

Developing the Pricing Mix

Once a company has put together its product mix, its executives can turn their attention to formulating the pricing mix. Their first consideration is to decide on the objectives they want the pricing mix to achieve.

LEARNING OBJECTIVE 7
List the major objectives of a company's pricing strategies.

Pricing Objectives

Maximizing net profit is the most important **performance objective.** Some companies are more concerned with the assets needed to obtain that profit and will, as a result, stipulate a return-on-investment target. Still others will use price to secure a particular market share. Japanese companies, especially automobile and consumer electronics firms, will price low in overseas markets to gain a foothold with the expectation that adequate profits will eventually follow. Intel engaged in steep price cuts in 2001 in an effort to gain a bigger share of the $81 billion PC chip market.

Firms will often have a **prevention objective**—keeping other firms from entering their market. For example, setting a low price will cause a potential competitor to be reluctant to enter because the low price needed to be competitive may not allow a potentially entering firm enough profit. Another prevention objective is to deter unfavorable government action. High prices may be suspect because they are viewed as causing consumers to pay too much. Low prices may be condemned because larger companies will supposedly use them to drive smaller competitors out of business, because they can't sustain them for long periods of time.

A **maintenance objective** may be employed to maintain the current competitive situation. In this case, price reductions will offset competitors' price cuts, increases in their promotional effort, or their introduction of a new product. Lower prices for wholesalers encourage them to maintain the same relationship with their suppliers. Occasionally, marketers have a **survival objective.** In this case, pricing strategies will allow a firm to remain in business. Mazda used $500 rebates to dealers and customers in the 1970s to survive after seeing its sales plummet due to the low mileage its models were getting and higher gasoline prices that were being charged.

performance objective A pricing objective designed to achieve a certain level of profit, revenues, or market share

prevention objective A pricing objective designed to keep other firms from entering the market

maintenance objective A pricing objective involving the desire to retain the current market or competitive situation

survival objective A pricing objective related to a firm remaining in business

reality CHECK *Glance through your favorite magazine looking for ads for automobiles. Can you calculate how much money the buyer would save over four or five years if he or she paid low or no interest?*

EXHIBIT 9.7

A Demand Schedule

Price	Quantity Demanded
$20	1
$18	2
$16	3
$14	4
$12	5
$10	6
$ 8	7
$ 6	8
$ 4	9
$ 2	10

EXHIBIT 9.8

Calculation of Total Revenues

Price	×	Quantity Demanded	=	Total Revenue
$20	×	1	=	$20
$18	×	2	=	$36
$16	×	3	=	$48
$14	×	4	=	$56
$12	×	5	=	$60
$10	×	6	=	$60
$ 8	×	7	=	$56
$ 6	×	8	=	$48
$ 4	×	9	=	$36
$ 2	×	10	=	$20

Pricing Concepts

LEARNING OBJECTIVE 8
Summarize the basic concepts and tools needed to set prices.

Demand is the number of units of a product that will be purchased at various prices. In general, more units of a product will be purchased at lower prices because a buyer can purchase more units of a product when the price is lower. For example, if a man has $80 to spend for shoes, he can buy four pairs if the price is $20 a pair. He could buy five pairs if a price of $16 a pair were charged. Thus, we can see that at the lower price of $16, more pairs of shoes can be bought (five) than at the higher price of $20 (four).

In order to be able to make intelligent pricing decisions for their products, marketers must have some idea of the number of units that would probably be purchased for a number of likely prices (see Exhibit 9.7). The demand schedule indicates the quantity of units that will be purchased for a number of prices. This same information can also be graphed. The graph is called a demand curve and was illustrated in Chapter 1. A demand curve provides the same information as a demand schedule: It indicates the number of units that will be purchased for each price. It is just a different way of expressing the same relationships.

The price that will maximize total revenue is important. In order to determine it, it is necessary to calculate the total revenue existing for each price and quantity. This is found by multiplying each price by its corresponding quantity (see Exhibit 9.8). There, we can see that total maximum revenue of $60 is found at two prices, $10 and $12.

The price that maximizes total revenue may not be the price that maximizes net profit, however. To discover this, marketers must estimate the costs required to produce and market the various quantities involved, then subtract them from total revenues.

Setting Prices for New Products

There are several steps that need to be taken in order to set prices on new products.

1. Decide on a basic pricing objective. This usually suggests either a high or a low price. For example, an objective to keep out competition necessitates a low price. An objective of securing a fast return on a product's investment usually means a relatively high price.

2. Estimate the total cost per unit for the product at various levels of demand. The product should probably not be priced below this floor.

3. Find out what the competition's prices are for similar products. These prices indicate, to some extent, an upper limit on the price that can be established.

4. Determine the extent to which the product is distinctive from competitive products. The more distinctive the product, the higher the price that can be charged; the less distinctive, the lower the price possible.

5. Find out how much marketing support will be provided the product in the form of advertising budget, speed of delivery, effort to be exerted by the sales

Case in Point

McDonald's Offers a $1-Item Menu

Until the third quarter of 2002, McDonald's had always posted a profit. However, for the third quarter of that year, company officials announced a loss.

At about the same time, a cutback in the number of international stores being opened and the closing of some 175 outlets already in place was indicated. It was well known that the world's largest fast-food chain was having problems with customer service. Many customers had complained about having to wait too long for orders and rude and incompetent personnel.

In the middle of 2002, McDonald's began offering a $1-item menu. For several years prior, one of the company's major competitors, Wendy's, had had a very successful 99¢ "Super Value Menu." Included on McDonald's $1-item menu were

Hot 'n Spicy McChicken
Big 'n Tasty
Two pies
Sundae (caramel or fudge)
Side salad
Medium soft drink
Medium fries
Snack size fruit/yogurt parfait

The first two items—Hot 'n Spicy McChicken and the Big 'n Tasty—were only temporarily $1 items; they ordinarily sold for about $2. The other items included on the $1-item menu had been priced around or a little more than $1.

There were no "big ticket" items on Wendy's 99¢ "Super Value Menu." All had cost about $1 or slightly higher. They included

Chili Chips 'n Cheese
Crispy Chicken Nuggets
Jr. Bacon Cheeseburger
Jr. Cheeseburger Deluxe
French fries (medium)
Soft drink (medium)
Frosty dairy dessert (small)
Chili (small)
Sour cream & chives potato
Side salad
Caesar side salad

Questions

1. Which low-priced menu—Wendy's or McDonald's—do you believe will be more successful?
2. Will offering a number of items for $1 overcome customer dissatisfaction about the level of service McDonald's is providing?
3. Does the fact that the items on Wendy's "Super Value Menu" are priced at 99¢ give it an advantage over McDonald's, which prices its items at $1? Or is this a disadvantage?

---

force, and so on. The greater this level of effort, the higher the price that can be justified. The lower the level of support, the lower the price.

6. Estimating demand involves a decision as to how many units are likely to be sold at various prices. Competitor prices, distinctiveness of the product, and level of marketing effort affect demand.

Changing Prices for Existing Products

Whether a demand curve is elastic or inelastic is important in deciding whether a product's price should be raised or lowered.

An **elastic demand** curve represents the situation where the market is very responsive to a product's price. Exhibit 9.9a (on p. 332) shows an elastic demand curve that tends toward the horizontal. With an elastic demand for a product, price decreases are desirable, but not price increases. At a price of $10, four units will be sold, yielding total revenue of $40 ($10 × 4 = $40). Decreasing the price to $9, however, increases total revenue to $72 ($9 × 8 = $72). Note that increasing the price with an elastic demand curve will lower total revenue. In Exhibit 9.9a, we see that increasing the price from $9 to $10 would reduce total revenue from $72 to $40.

elastic demand A combination of prices and quantities demanded that indicates that the market is very responsive to prices

Wal-Mart price signs indicate the company's emphasis on low prices and its assumption that the demand for its products is elastic.

inelastic demand A combination of prices and quantities for a product that indicates that the market is not very responsive to a product's prices

The concepts are reversed if the curve for a product represents **inelastic demand,** that is, the situation where the market is not very responsive to a product's prices. Exhibit 9.9b shows an inelastic demand curve that tends toward the vertical. With an inelastic demand curve for a product, price increases are desirable, but not price decreases. At a price of $5 and a demand of five units, total revenue is $25. When the price is increased to $10, total revenue increases to $40 ($10 × 4 = $40). However, a price decrease would result in lower total revenue, $40 at a price of $10 versus $25 at a price of $5.

reality CHECK *Visit a local supermarket and list those products for which you believe the demand is inelastic or elastic.*

EXHIBIT 9.9

Elastic and Inelastic Demand Curves

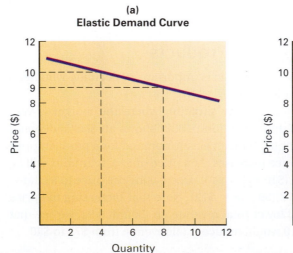

(a)
Elastic Demand Curve

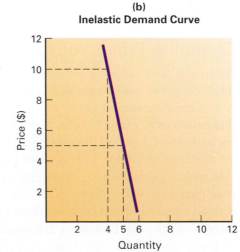

(b)
Inelastic Demand Curve

Pricing Decisions for Products Sold Internationally

There are two special pricing considerations for companies that are selling their products in international markets. **Transfer prices** are the prices a U.S. company will charge its overseas subsidiaries which will, in turn, sell the product in the foreign market. While the U.S. firm is interested in setting a transfer price that will maximize total profits, it also has to be concerned with taxes. This is because there are two taxing authorities that have to be recognized: those in the United States and those in the foreign country where the subsidiary is located.

transfer price The price a U.S. company charges its overseas subsidiary

Dumping occurs when a company sells a product in an international market at a price below its cost. Why would a firm do this when it is losing money on each product sold? Because the low price will enable it to gain market share at the expense of domestic competitors and other international competitors. Once these competitors have withdrawn from the market, the firm employing a dumping strategy can raise its prices to where it is making acceptable profits. Dumping is resented for this reason and often results in complaints to the World Trade Organization, which can order dumping stopped and can assess penalties for violation of the order.

dumping The practice of selling a product in foreign markets for less than its cost

Retailers' Pricing Decisions

Markup is the difference between what a retailer pays for a product and the price at which the product is sold. This difference must cover the expenses the retailer

markup The difference between what a retailer pays for a product and the price at which it is sold

---

Global Business

Fuji Film Accused of Dumping in the U.S. Market

In the late 1990s, Kodak was attempting to turn around poor operating results. The company, led by George M.C. Fisher, appeared to be on the right track—until it had to confront steep price cuts in the domestic market unveiled by its major competitor, Japan's Fuji Film. Fuji cut prices as much as 50 percent—to 25 percent of what it charged in Japan—resulting in an increase of sales for Fuji and a drop of sales of 11 percent for Kodak in the U.S. market. Additionally, Kodak's market share dropped on its home turf, a situation made worse by the market in the U.S. contracting due to heavy purchases by consumers of disposable cameras. Industry analysts predicted that within two years, Fuji's success in the U.S. would enable it to wrest the #1 spot from Kodak. In 1997, Kodak's global market share was 40 percent, versus 35 percent for Fuji.

Kodak responded to Fuji's pricing strategies by accusing the Japanese firm of dumping. Fuji had already lost a dumping case in 1994, when Kodak convinced the U.S. government that Fuji was selling photo paper in the United States at one-fourth of the price it charged in its home market. Fuji invested $1 billion in new manufacturing facilities in Greenwood, South Carolina, consisting of a paper plant operation and a color film plant that started production in late 1997.

Kodak maintained that Fuji's dumping strategy is aided by the fact that Fuji has a virtual monopoly in the Japanese market, where it has a 70 percent market share, giving it solid control of distribution and pricing.

Fuji countered Kodak's claims with the explanation that it does not compete in the U.S. market solely on price; it pointed to its high quality film that is being increasingly successful with professional photographers, and the heavy use of free samples.

Source: Geoffrey Smith, "A Dark Kodak Moment," *Business Week*, August 4, 1997, pp. 30–31.

Questions

1. Why would Fuji spend $1 billion to build new manufacturing facilities in South Carolina?
2. Should a firm be accused of dumping in an international market when its price covers all of its costs for that product but its price is much lower than domestic competitors' prices?
3. Should Fuji's 70 percent market share in Japan be used against it when Kodak accuses Fuji of dumping in the U.S. market?

EXHIBIT 9.10

Common Markup Percentages
on Cost and Price

EXHIBIT 9.10

Common Markup Percentages
on Cost and Price

Markup Percentage on Cost (%)	Equivalent Markup Percentage on Price (%)
10	9
20	16.7
25	20
30	23
33.3	25
40	28.6
50	33.3
60	37.5
75	43
100	50

has in selling the product as well as the profit the retailer desires. Markup can be expressed three different ways: as an absolute figure, as a percentage of cost, and as a percentage of price.

Let's assume that a retailer paid $10 for a dress and put a price of $15 on it. As an absolute figure, the markup is $5, that is, the difference in the cost of the item and its price ($15 − $10 = $5). As a percentage of cost, the markup is 50 percent ($5 markup/$10 cost = 50 percent). As a percentage of price, the markup is 33.3 percent ($5 markup/$15 selling price = 33.3 percent).

Each and every markup percentage figured on cost will have a unique and corresponding percentage when figured on the price. In the above example, the markup figured on cost of 50 percent is equivalent to a markup on selling price of 33.3 percent. Exhibit 9.10 provides a number of the most commonly used markup percentages. In practice, most retailers figure the markup on the selling price, not on cost.

Markup is an important concept for retailers because it is closely related to profit. The markup has to be sufficiently large to cover the expenses of operating the store and provide an acceptable rate of profit. Most retailers either apply a similar markup percentage for all products received or use different percentages for related groups of products. Jewelry and furniture, for example, generally carry higher markups than clothing or food items.

The danger of mechanically applying a markup percentage to merchandise is that the resulting price may not be the best one as far as maximizing profits is con-

Ethics in Business

Companies Charge Fees Because They Can't Raise Prices

In deflationary periods, periods with falling prices, companies find it difficult to raise prices or even maintain them. So they often resort to charging fees for a variety of services performed that they ordinarily would not charge for. Often, these charges are in fine print, causing some business observers to label them hidden charges.

It has been estimated that banks and other financial services firms take in an extra $50 billion annually from charging fees for various services. This amount results from bank customers paying extra for bounced checks and using automated teller machines. Credit card companies rake in $20 billion a year from such charges as late payment fees.

The wireless, long-distance, and cable company industries generate $33 billion a year from fees for setup, change of service, service termination, directory assistance, regulatory assessment, number portability, and cable hookup and equipment. Overall, fees add 20 percent to the cost of wireless, 15 percent to the cost of long distance, and 5 percent to cable and satellite bills.

Airlines take in $17 billion annually by charging fees. Airport security fees, landing fees, fuel surcharges, paper ticket fees, overweight baggage fees, and fees for changing a reservation (usually costing about $100) are examples. Some airlines are charging extra for food.

Retailers are getting into the act. Target and Best Buy force customers to pay 15 percent of a product's price for returning expensive electronic items (called a restocking fee). And so are state governments with $2.6 billion in new income for driving-without-a-license fines, court filing fees, and late-bar-closing fees.

What are the results of these policies? They make it almost impossible for consumers to compare prices. Consumers become frustrated and angry. "Stealth" inflation occurs, making it more difficult to develop economic policy. Companies spend a lot of time contriving new and even more complicated ways to charge fees.

Source: Emily Thornton, "Fees! Fees! Fees!" *Business Week*, September 29, 2003, pp. 99–104.

Questions

1. Do you think restocking fees are ethical?
2. Do you think companies should be allowed to charge fees when they find it difficult to raise prices?
3. Should airlines be charging customers for meals during a flight?

cerned. Expressed another way, the resulting price does not recognize demand. Retailers tend to price on the basis of standard markups because it is easy and simplifies record keeping and inventory control.

Very frequently retailers realize that they have put too high a price on some merchandise or they find that seasonal products like toys have not sold by the end of the season. In either case, the retailer marks down the items, lowers their prices, and hopes to move them.

A **markdown** is usually expressed as a percentage of the selling price. All of us at one time or another have been in stores and have seen signs advertising 20 percent off or 50 percent off, and so on. Most retailers do not have an effective markdown policy. They tend to start off with a low markdown and then increase it even more later if the product does not sell. But this is a mistake because it jeopardizes the selling of the item, and even if the item is sold, it may take a long time to sell it. The best policy is to make the first markdown high enough to move the merchandise quickly.

> **markdown** A reduction in price used by retailers to sell products that have not already sold

Careers in Brand Management

Many manufacturers of packaged consumer goods, such as Procter & Gamble (Tide, Crisco, Pampers, etc.), Lever Brothers, Pillsbury, and General Mills, are organized on a brand management basis. Brand managers develop the entire marketing program for a specific brand or group of brands. Sometimes called product managers, they will establish goals for their products and the strategies for achieving them. They will decide on product quality and the product's package and guarantees. Advertising, sales promotion, channels of distribution, and logistics decisions will have to be set for each product. Prices are established for each product and then adjusted according to market conditions, the state of the economy, and the prices competitors are charging.

In order to effectively manage their products, brand managers must work closely with various areas of marketing, especially sales, marketing research, and advertising. Production, finance, and research and development are nonmarketing areas with which they also need to interface. Customers, advertising agencies, and channels of distribution are external constituencies that receive a lot of brand managers' attention.

Before becoming a brand manager, it is normal that four to five years would have been spent as an assistant brand manager. It is common for brand managers to be earning about $75,000 a year.

Summary

LEARNING OBJECTIVE 1
Explain how a marketing mix is developed.

A company's marketing mix—its products or services and their prices, promotion, and distribution—must recognize the type of product or service involved and the markets to which they are directed. Marketing mixes need to be different for different products and must be modified over time.

LEARNING OBJECTIVE 2
Describe the basic elements of a product.

In developing a product, companies must decide on its design, quality, brand name, package, and warranty, as well as how many product lines will be offered (product width) and the number of brands or products in each line (product depth).

LEARNING OBJECTIVE 3
Describe the differences between standardization and adaptation strategies.

In marketing products overseas, a standardization (same marketing mix as that used domestically) can be employed, or an adaptation approach (different marketing mix in foreign market).

LEARNING OBJECTIVE 4
Discuss the concept of brand equity and why it is important.

Brand equity refers to the value or worth of a brand. The benefits from having a high level of brand equity include improved balance sheets, better awareness of brands by customers, and better prices when a company is acquired by another.

LEARNING OBJECTIVE 5
List the steps in the process for developing new products and how each should be performed.

Firms use a number of sequential steps to develop new products. In generating ideas for new products, they consider both internal and external sources. During screening, potential new products are evaluated on criteria the firm believes influence new product success, such as whether they meet a specific market need. Concept testing involves a sample of customers being introduced to the general notion of a new product and how it can benefit them. As business analysis is conducted, firms predict the likely profitability of the candidate. In developing a new product, firms should ensure that all required steps are carefully performed and the marketing department continues to be involved. Testing involves both technical testing to see how well a product's physical properties will respond to various stimuli and market testing to measure the level of customer demand. Commercialization refers to the strategies used to introduce the new product and the methods whereby its performance is tracked.

LEARNING OBJECTIVE 6
Describe the product life cycle and how it can be used to manage existing products.

The product life cycle consists of the introduction, growth, maturity, and decline stages of a product. Using the concepts of primary and secondary markets and the competitive landscape, companies can formulate marketing mix strategies over the PLC.

LEARNING OBJECTIVE 7
List the major objectives of a company's pricing strategies.

Besides maximizing profits, firms expect their products' prices to generate market share, prevent other firms from entering the market, maintain the current competitive situation, or even permit them to survive in a particular market, among others.

LEARNING OBJECTIVE 8
Summarize the basic concepts and tools needed to set prices.

In setting prices for their products, companies must know what objectives they want to achieve, the level of demand and its elasticity, the product's cost per unit, competitors' prices, how distinctive the product is from existing ones, and how much marketing support the product will receive.

Chapter Questions

1. What are some of the principles that should be recognized as companies select brand names?
2. What are the two major purposes of packaging? Can you think of any others?
3. Distinguish between express and implicit warranties.
4. Which strategy for developing products for overseas markets do you believe will be the most effective, standardization or adaptation?
5. What should be top management's role in the new product development process? What should it not do?
6. Are you comfortable with how the text defines product failure? Is there a better way?
7. What are the advantages and disadvantages of companies developing prototypes for their new products?
8. How would you describe the product life cycle? Indicate how it can help a company manage its current products.
9. Carefully distinguish between the primary market and the secondary market. Why are they important in formulating a strategy for managing existing products?
10. Should there be any restrictions on the ability of a company to pull products off the market? Why or why not?
11. Why is elasticity or inelasticity an important pricing concept?
12. What are the various ways markup can be measured?

Interpreting Business News

Ford Motor Company recently announced its intention to develop a new range of small, mass-market cars for emerging markets in Asia and South America. The cars would also be sold in Europe. The development and marketing of these cars is based on the following strategies:

Ford will develop a new global platform with sufficient flexibility to allow for regional differences in tastes.

No new product development funds would be required. The capital needed would be taken from Ford's annual product development budget of $6 to $7 billion. It was estimated that the new platform would require about $1 billion.

The development budget figures are based on Ford being able to continue wringing cost savings out of its team value management program, which relies on the identification of waste and employing less costly ways of obtaining raw materials and parts from suppliers.

Ford will be able to sell the car at a price in Asia and South America that is much less than the $10,000 currently charged European consumers.

1. What concepts discussed in this chapter are illustrated by this Interpreting Business News?
2. What are the advantages and disadvantages of Ford's strategy?
3. Are there other regions of the world in which the new vehicles might be sold?
4. Do you think that Ford's new cars will be successful? Why or why not?

Large food processors, such as General Mills, H.J. Heinz, and Hershey Foods, are reducing the number of products they sell through food retailers. Three factors explain this decision. First, the processors believe that they can increase profits by trimming product lines that are not selling well and are beset by higher commodity prices. (Prices of soybean oil and cheese increased 70 percent and 80 percent, respectively, in 2003.) Heinz estimated that this strategy increased its operating income to $1.38 billion in 2003, up 17.5 percent over that obtained in 2002. Second, large retailers like Wal-Mart are pressuring their suppliers to only provide them with fast-moving products. Third, large-scale food retailers—Albertson's, Kroger, Safeway—are increasing the number of private label products they develop and stock, leaving less shelf space for processors' brands. (Robert Berner, Diane Brady and Wendy Zellner, "There Goes the Rainbow Crunch," *Business Week*, July 19, 2004, p. 38).

1. What concepts discussed in this chapter are referred to in this Interpreting Business News?
2. Why would food retailers want to market their own private label products?
3. Which participant in the supply chain appears to have the most power?

Web Assignments

1. Go to the websites for Sony, McDonald's, and DaimlerChrysler. Compare the information contained on them about the products they offer and their prices. Which website offers the most information about the products? Do any discuss any new products that are being worked on? Are there any mentions of products being discontinued? Is product quality emphasized? How?
2. Return to the websites in assignment 1. Is there much information on these websites about the firms' prices? Do they appear to be using price as a major competitive weapon? Are price reductions being emphasized as a way of keeping and attracting customers?

Portfolio Projects

Exploring Your Own Case in Point

This chapter provides guidelines for developing a company's product mix and pricing mix. Answer these key questions about your selected company's product and pricing mixes.

1. How important are new products and services for your selected company? Can you identify any significant technological breakthroughs that it has developed?
2. How much does your company spend annually on research and development? Does it appear to emphasize basic or applied research?
3. Do you believe the demand for your company's products or services is elastic or inelastic? Does it vary according to types of products or services?

Starting Your Own Business

You will need to develop product and pricing mixes for your startup company. Drawing upon what you have learned in this chapter, answer the following.

1. Describe the level of quality for your products or services.
2. Describe the packaging for your products.
3. What warranties or guarantees will you offer for your products or services?
4. Develop (or describe) your trademark or logo.
5. Develop a step-by-step approach for arriving at the prices you will initially charge for your products or services. Be sure to consider the costs of your products or services, competitor prices, and the amount of marketing support you will provide each product.

Test Prepper

You've read the chapter, studied the key terms, and the exam is any day now. Think you are ready to ace it? Take this sample test to gauge your comprehension of chapter material. You can check your answers at the back of the book.

True/False Questions

Please indicate if the following statements are true or false:

_____ 1. Industrial products are not usually marketed through channels of distribution.

_____ 2. Marketing mixes need to be modified over time.

_____ 3. Product design involves the intangible aspects of products.

_____ 4. National brands are developed by and marketed by retailers.

_____ 5. For some products, the cost of the package may exceed the cost of the contents.

_____ 6. An implicit warranty is an unspoken or unwritten warranty.

_____ 7. A standardization strategy for marketing products to international markets has the advantage of holding down R&D, production, and marketing costs.

_____ 8. Product depth refers to the number of product lines a company has.

_____ 9. In comparison to follow-the-leader companies, first movers incur more risk when they bring out a new product.

_____ 10. Demand is an indication of the number of units that will be purchased at various prices.

Multiple-Choice Questions

Choose the best answer.

_____ 1. The major function of business analysis in the new product development process is to

   a. initially screen new product ideas.
   b. estimate potential profitability of the new product idea.
   c. estimate potential market share of the new product.
   d. develop a new product prototype.
   e. generate a list of new product ideas.

_____ 2. Which of the following is the type of new product that involves the greatest level of risk?

   a. Cost reductions

   b. Repositionings
   c. New product lines
   d. Additions to existing product lines
   e. New-to-world products

_____ 3. Which of the following refers to the extent to which a new product enables customers to try it on a limited basis without the product having to be purchased?

   a. Compatibility
   b. Relative advantage
   c. Complexity
   d. Divisibility
   e. Communicability

_____ 4. A 25 percent markup on cost is equivalent to which percentage markup on retail?

   a. 10 percent
   b. 20 percent
   c. 30 percent
   d. 33.3 percent
   e. 50 percent

_____ 5. If a new product has a development cost of $100,000, a desired profit of $20,000, a price of $10, and a cost per unit of $6, its break-even quantity is

   a. 10,000 units.
   b. 20,000 units.
   c. 30,000 units.
   d. 40,000 units.
   e. 50,000 units.

_____ 6. The first 2.5 percent of individuals to adopt a new product are called

   a. the late majority.
   b. the early majority.
   c. innovators.
   d. laggards.
   e. early adopters.

_____ 7. Profits for products are usually the highest during which stage of the product life cycle?

   a. Growth
   b. Introduction
   c. Maturity
   d. Decline
   e. Extension

_____ 8. An example of an internal interface for brand managers is

    a. R&D.
    b. customers.
    c. advertising agencies.
    d. channels of distribution.
    e. suppliers.

_____ 9. The step in the new product development process that involves the strategies employed to introduce a new product and monitor its performance is

    a. business analysis.
    b. concept testing.

    c. testing.
    d. commercialization.
    e. screening.

_____ 10. Which is the most important performance objective of companies' pricing strategies?

    a. Maximize net profit.
    b. Deter unfavorable government action.
    c. Keep firms from entering the market.
    d. Maintain the current competitive situation.
    e. Maximize market share.

Want more questions? Visit the student website at **http://college.hmco.com/business/student/** (select Gaspar, *Introduction to Business*) and take the ACE quizzes for more practice.

10

Developing the Promotion and Distribution Mixes

| Introduction

| **The Promotion Mix**
Advertising
Sales Promotion
Personal Selling
Publicity

| **The Distribution Mix**
Channels of Distribution
Logistics

| **Careers in Promotion**

| **Careers in Distribution**

Learning Objectives

After studying this chapter, you should be able to

1 Explain the concept of integrated marketing promotion.

2 List ways to improve the effectiveness of trade shows.

3 Discuss the sales force's main responsibilities.

4 Discuss the ways in which sales personnel can conduct themselves ethically.

5 Distinguish between the channels of distribution for consumer products and for industrial products.

6 Describe and give the advantages of using nonstore retailers in channels of distribution.

7 Explain the difference between materials management and physical distribution.

8 Compare the advantages and disadvantages of the five modes of transportation.

Getting into the Online Equine Game

Debra Smith decided to start a home-based business to supplement her husband's income. She had a long-time interest in horses, having owned several and having ridden in various horse shows.

As a rider and a caretaker for her horses, she had to drive 70 miles to purchase suitable equine equipment and supplies. This inconvenience caused her to consider opening a similar store in her hometown. However, this plan was shelved when she discovered she would need at least a $50,000 investment for inventory and yearly rent for a storefront would cost an additional $20,000. Consequently, Debra decided to operate an online equine business.

This option would require her to develop an appropriate website. While she had some idea as to what the website should include, she knew that she would need the services of a website expert to deal with the technical aspects of site development. Another requirement would be the availability of an 800-number so customers could call toll-free to place orders. Debra also realized that she would have to provide customers the option of ordering with credit cards.

Because of limited resources, Debra could not afford to advertise in such publications as *Horse and Rider, Western Horsemen,* and *Equine.* Even a 1/8-page, black-and-white ad was beyond her reach. Instead, she decided to take out small classified ads in these publications. On average, these would cost around $100 for 25–30 words. Another option she was exploring was the use of direct mail, whereby she would send a small brochure featuring her products to readers of the various equine magazines. She would pay these publications for their subscription lists and then incur the cost of the four-page brochure, the envelope, and postage. Debra also believed that she could promote her business by dropping off the brochures at various horse barns and horse shows.

Transportation and storage were the two most pressing logistics decisions. Since space was limited in their one-bedroom apartment, she decided to minimize inventory by ordering from equine suppliers only when she herself had received an order and having the supplier ship the merchandise directly to her customer. She planned on repackaging any bulk products she received into specific orders for her customers as soon as possible, so inventory would not accumulate. After considering costs and reliability, she decided to ship via UPS. This decision would require her to take special precautions with some of her cleaning and grooming products, as they were considered to be "hazmat" (hazardous materials) products.

Debra was surprised as to how much time and money she had to devote to promoting her products and transporting and storing them. After putting together a game plan for dealing with these responsibilities, she was still not sure she was on the right track. This chapter covers the promotion and logistics areas of marketing and provides information that would be helpful to Debra.

Introduction

Companies need to develop a promotion mix to help sell their products and services. They will have to determine the emphasis that will be placed on advertising, sales promotion, personal selling, and publicity. Advertising is nonpersonal communication through media (newspapers, magazines, television, radio, etc.) for which payment is made. Sales promotion is the nonpersonal form of promotion (trade shows, sweepstakes, samples, coupons, etc.) that does not involve measured media. Personal selling involves the use of a sales force to sell products and services. Publicity refers to items about a company and its products or personnel that appear in mass media. The advantages and disadvantages of each of these promotion tools and the markets to which companies' products and services are sold will largely determine the role each element plays in the promotion mix.

Companies' distribution mixes consist of decisions about channels of distribution and logistics. Channels of distribution involve the use of such intermediaries as wholesalers and retailers to market products and services to businesses and consumers and governments. A major decision for companies is whether they wish to use channels or bypass them and go direct to the end customer. Companies that are using channels must decide on the specific types of wholesalers and retailers to use and must develop a program for ensuring their cooperation in pushing their products.

Logistics consist of materials management (the inward flow of unfinished goods into a firm) and physical distribution (the outward flow of finished products to customers). Logistics also involves decisions about transportation (pipelines, water, rail, trucks, and air transportation), storage (types of warehouses, where to locate them, operations), customer service levels, whether to outsource, and special requirements for logistical operations within international markets.

The Promotion Mix

Companies promote their products and services for a variety of reasons. The major one is to stimulate demand, that is, to generate revenues. Other reasons include

- Making customers aware of and getting them to try new products
- Encouraging repeat purchases
- Getting customers to increase their purchase levels
- Retaining customers
- Providing information
- Facilitating channel of distribution support
- Responding to competitors' promotional efforts

promotion mix The configuration of advertising, sales promotion, personal selling, and publicity used to market products and services

A major responsibility for marketers is to put together a **promotion mix.** This involves deciding how much emphasis to place on each promotion element—advertising, sales promotion, personal selling, and publicity—developing a budget for each, and determining a promotion plan. To determine a promotion plan requires deciding when a promotion effort will occur and coordinating it with other parties involved, such as advertising agencies and media. There are four drivers that undergird the design of a promotion mix.

- The strengths and weaknesses in terms of control, feedback, and cost of each promotional alternative in relation to the objectives sought must be evaluated. Control is the extent to which an organization can be sure that the promotion effort has been carried out as planned. Feedback from the market concerns the effectiveness of the promotion. Cost is generally determined as cost-per-prospect reached.
- Different products and services require different promotion mixes. For example, advertising is emphasized in the marketing of consumer products, whereas personal selling predominates in the marketing of industrial goods.
- Promotion mixes need to be revised periodically to accommodate changes in the market and the competition.
- Promotion decisions need to be made in an integrated manner.

LEARNING OBJECTIVE 1
Explain the concept of integrated marketing promotion.

Integrated marketing promotion means that a company will consider the role of all relevant promotion alternatives when developing the promotion mix, employ those that provide the best opportunity for achieving the company's promotion objectives, and then coordinate the activities required to put into motion the agreed-on promotion mix. For example, for advertisers marketing books, *NewsMax*, a news and opinion magazine containing advertising, offers an integrated promotional effort, consisting of a variety of promotion options. An ad for a book or publishing house that runs in the magazine will reach 300,000 readers and the hosts of every major radio and television talk show. Additionally, NewsMax.com has 6 million visitors per month, and it offers options of banner headline ads and side links. Other promotion options include e-mail campaigns that can be directed to 200,000 opt-in subscribers and run as advertorials; a public relations network that can secure guest appearances for a book's author or editor on CNN, Fox News, MSNBC, and most radio talk shows; and *NewsMax*'s online store, which streamlines the order process for interested customers.

integrated marketing promotion The consideration of all relevant promotion alternatives when developing a promotion mix, employing those that provide the best opportunity for achieving the company's promotion objectives, and coordinating the activities required to put into motion the agreed-on promotion mix

reality CHECK *Choose any of the icon companies—Sony, DaimlerChrysler, or McDonald's—and indicate the different ways you are aware of that company uses to promote its products.*

Advertising

Advertising is nonpersonal communication through media for which payment is made. The major types of media and the percentage of total media expenditures ($233 billion) for each in 2001 are shown in Exhibit 10.1.

Direct mail, which allows for the greatest selectivity in reaching a target market, led all media in advertising expenditures (19.3 percent). Personal letters, booklets, and brochures can reach very specific market segments. For example, a letter soliciting the purchase of a new book about growing roses could be directed to retired men who have an avid interest in gardening and who live in the Southeast. The names and addresses of these individuals can be obtained from list brokers who have available hundreds of different lists. The most severe limitations in using direct mail are the public's distaste for junk mail and the difficulty in getting and maintaining good mailing lists. The latter problem was encountered by a firm that purchased a list of 2000 contractors located in the Southwest. Six hundred of them proved to be invalid. They were returned with such notations from the post office as "addressee no longer here" and "addressee unknown."

advertising Nonpersonal communications through media for which payment is made

direct mail A type of advertising that uses personal letters, booklets, and brochures to reach very specific market segments

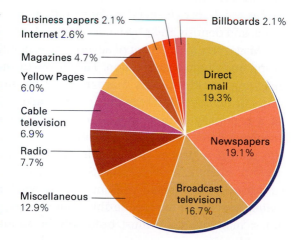

Business papers 2.1%
Internet 2.6%
Magazines 4.7%
Yellow Pages 6.0%
Cable television 6.9%
Radio 7.7%
Miscellaneous 12.9%
Billboards 2.1%
Direct mail 19.3%
Newspapers 19.1%
Broadcast television 16.7%

EXHIBIT 10.1

Percentage of Advertising Expenditures Accounted for by Various Media Sources

Source: "2002 Marketing Fact Book," *Marketing News,* July 8, 2002, p.15.

Newspapers (19.1 percent of total advertising expenditures) offer a flexible means of advertising. They can be chosen to cover a local market or several urban centers. Since almost everyone reads newspapers, they are an effective means of

closing time The time prior to publication by which an advertisement must be submitted

cooperative advertising Shared advertising costs by a company and a retailer carrying its products

reaching general markets. **Closing time,** the time prior to publication by which advertising copy must be submitted, seldom exceeds three days for newspapers. Thus, a firm can submit, withdraw, or modify copy up to three days before the advertising is scheduled to be printed. Newspapers are also an excellent means of providing retailer support, such as **cooperative advertising** agreements, in which the firm and its retailer share advertising costs.

However, the life of a newspaper advertisement is very short. There is little opportunity for the reader to get repeated exposure to a single advertisement. Although improvements have been made, newspapers are largely unable to offer the fine reproductions of photos and graphics found in magazines, especially for color ads.

Broadcast TV (16.7 percent of advertising expenditures) got about one-sixth of total advertising expenditures in 2001. This medium can be very effective because viewers of advertisements use two senses—sight and hearing—while exposed to the ads. However, television ads are expensive and they offer little audience selectivity. The latter disadvantage has been effectively exploited by cable television (6.9 percent of media expenditures), which offers programs designated for specific audiences. Examples include the History Channel, Travel Channel, ESPN, Food Channel, and Cartoon Network. Cable television has been successful in pulling viewers from broadcast TV.

Radio (7.7 percent of advertising expenditures) has short closing times; advertising copy can be submitted or changed minutes before it is scheduled for broadcast. Radio provides a high degree of selectivity in terms of geographical coverage and market segment appeal at a low cost, primarily because individual stations are able to focus on specific groups through their programming; for example, all-news stations or country-and-western music stations. The availability of portable radios and car radios allows the advertiser to reach an audience anywhere, especially those on the move.

Telephone directories, like the yellow pages (6.0 percent of advertising expenditures), are a medium that is very effective for local businesses. Telephone directories are a convenient source for people who need specific products or services, such as car repair, dry cleaners, tax preparation, apartments, attorneys, jewelry, insurance, and dentists and physicians.

Magazines (4.7 percent of advertising expenditures) provide high-quality color, print, and photo reproduction. They allow the advertiser to be highly selective in reaching specific markets. Magazines can be chosen to reach different geographic areas or demographic segments of the market. *Southern Living* is one illustration of a regionally focused magazine. *Cycling, Jogging,* and *Skiing* are examples of magazines directed toward specific sports segments. Magazines have a longer life than newspapers and provide the opportunity for repeated exposure to an advertisement in a single issue. Since magazines are often passed along to family and friends, a single advertisement may reach a very large readership. Unfortunately, magazines are less flexible than newspapers in terms of publication deadlines; magazine copy must ordinarily be submitted eight weeks or more prior to publication.

Internet advertising represented only 2.6 percent of advertising expenditures in 2001. However, it is expected on a global basis to reach $28 billion in 2007, almost triple the expenditures in 2001 ($10.3 billion). This projected increase is based on the explosion in purchases of personal computers for home use and an increase in consumers using credit cards over the Internet. Internet advertising has a major advantage—its extremely low cost. Major online advertising expenditures are for conventional (84 percent), rich media (12 percent), and streaming (5 percent).[1]

Business newspapers like *The Wall Street Journal, Financial Daily,* and *Barrons* accounted for advertising expenditures of $4.5 billion in 2001 (2.1 percent of advertising expenditures). Companies that advertise in business papers believe they are an effective means to reach other businesses.

Billboards (2.1 percent of advertising expenditures) offer intensity of coverage in a specific geographic market and are, therefore, an excellent medium to promote widely used consumer products and services, such as liquor and banking. They can reinforce messages presented in other media. A good opportunity exists for the viewer to be repeatedly exposed to the advertising message. Since billboards are directed to a mobile audience, the message is limited to a few words. Some communities and states in the United States have banned billboards or have severely restricted where they can be. France has banned billboards nationwide. Such measures are enacted because billboards are viewed as dangerous—drivers' attention is diverted—or unsightly—they detract from the scenery along roads.

A major development in advertising is an increasing effort to target newly recognized subcultures, such as gays, lesbians, African Americans, Hispanics, Asian Americans, children, and older Americans.

A billboard promotes a not-for-profit organization.

Sales Promotion

Sales promotion is the nonpersonal form of promotion that does not involve measured media, the advertising media just discussed. It does, however, include a wide assortment of other alternatives. Some of the most important of these are listed in Exhibit 10.2 (on p. 346). This exhibit shows that some sales promotions are appropriate for consumer markets, some for wholesalers and retailers (trade), and some for both markets.

Many people are surprised to learn that the annual spending in the United States for sales promotions exceeds that for advertising by a factor of three. A number of changes in the business situation explain why.

- Sales promotion became more respectable. Formerly, top executives resisted sales promotion efforts because they believed that they cheapened the product. Recent successful uses of sales promotions, however, have reduced this reluctance.
- Better-trained individuals have been put in charge of sales promotion efforts. Coupled with an upgrading of the top sales promotion position, to include broader responsibilities of a planning nature, additional reliance on sales promotion effort has occurred.
- Many companies have adopted a brand manager type of marketing organization. Brand managers are frequently under pressure to show immediate

sales promotion A nonpersonal form of promotion that does not involve measured media

EXHIBIT 10.2

Major Sales Promotion Techniques

Technique	Used For	
	Industrial Buyers	Consumers
Allowance	X	
Contest	X	X
Coupon		X
Cross coupon		X
Deal	X	X
End display	X	
Incentive	X	X
In-pack		X
Mail-in		X
P-O-P (Point-of-Purchase)	X	
Premium		X
Purchase with purchase		X
Samples	X	X
Sponsorship	X	X
Sweepstakes		X
Trade shows	X	

results. Since sales promotion programs can be implemented more quickly than advertising, as well as produce results more quickly, sales promotions many times tend to be preferred over advertising.

The above factors that explain the increasing popularity of sales promotions are essentially internal, that is, occur within companies. In addition to these internal reasons, a number of external developments are also important.

- The number of new brands, especially consumer brands, has increased. This brand proliferation means that sales promotions will be used to obtain limited retail shelf space.
- Competitors are turning to sales promotion. When this happens, companies are left with little choice but to accelerate their own sales promotion efforts.
- During economic recessions, sales promotions can be used to reduce inventory and improve a company's liquidity. Also, sales promotion techniques that involve price reductions in recessionary periods tend to be effective.
- The size and aggressiveness of such retailers as chain supermarkets, drug stores, and discount houses have increased. These and other large retailers have been putting more pressure on manufacturers for support and allowances.

allowances Concessions offered to retailers in exchange for services rendered

Allowances are concessions offered to retailers in exchange for services rendered. Examples include free goods, displays, advertising, and purchase discounts. Cosmetics manufacturers frequently provide department stores with advertising allowances when the department stores feature the manufacturers' products in local newspaper ads.

contests A form of sales promotion in which a prize is awarded for a competition

Contests are competitions for which prizes are awarded. They can be directed to retailers or consumers. Retailer sales personnel, for example, can be given prizes for selling specified quantities of a manufacturer's products. Cosmetics manufacturers frequently use contests to obtain increased sales for their products by sales personnel in department stores. Sports quizzes, crossword puzzles, and jingles are examples of contests targeting consumers.

Coupons are certificates that allow customers to receive a cash refund or a free product at the time of purchase. All of us at one time or another have probably redeemed coupons in supermarkets to receive 8¢, 10¢, 20¢, 50¢, or $2 off the price of some product. Coupons are frequently used to get consumers to switch brands or to try new products.

coupons Certificates that allow consumers to receive a cash refund or a free product at the time of purchase

Cross coupons involve having a coupon printed on an item or enclosed within the item's package that provides a discount on a different item. In many instances, the two products involved are related. For example, a coupon for chip dip may be included on a bag of potato chips. Or a coupon for pretzels may be found on soft drink cartons. Cross couponing can be used by two different manufacturers in the same promotion.

cross coupons Coupons printed on an item or enclosed within the item's package that provide a discount on a different item

Deals are inducements offered to retailers and consumers to purchase a certain quantity of a product. The "buy six, get one free" type of promotion is an example. For instance, if we buy six bottles of a soft drink, we get another one at no additional charge. Retailers may get a case of potato chips free if they purchase ten cases.

deals Inducements offered to retailers and consumers to purchase a certain quantity of a product

Displays are provided by manufacturers to retailers. They consist of a wide range of materials for holding merchandise. They can be placed at a variety of locations in a store. Frequently used locations are at checkout areas, entranceways, the middle of wide aisles, and the end of aisles. Displays are probably effective because they stimulate the purchase of impulse items. It has been estimated that about half of all merchandise purchased in supermarkets is bought on impulse.

displays Materials for holding merchandise sold in a retail store

Incentives can be offered to either retail salespeople or consumers. **Incentives** are rewards made available for a specified performance. Merchandise, travel, and cash are types of rewards generally provided. An **in-pack** is a premium that is enclosed with a product. One of the most familiar in-packs are the toys that are included in the boxes of Cracker Jack. Potential Cracker Jack inserts are now test marketed among children who evaluate their acceptability. **Mail-ins** consist of premiums provided to consumers once the consumer has requested them by mail. Proof of purchase is often required. For example, consumers may be told to cut out the brand name on a package of cereal and send it to the company to receive their premium.

incentives Rewards offered to retail salespeople or consumers for specified performance

in-pack A premium enclosed with a product

mail-ins Premiums provided to consumers once the consumer has requested them by mail

P-O-P (point of purchase) materials are provided to retailers by manufacturers to help them promote sales. They include a wide range of options, including banners, counter cards, signs, and display racks. In most instances, these are provided free to retailers, but sometimes a cost may be levied. **Premiums** consist of merchandise that is offered to consumers as an incentive to buy a product. Star Wars posters, beanie babies, decorated glasses, and Harry Potter memorabilia are some well-known examples. A **purchase with purchase** allows consumers to buy one product if they purchase another product. Hallmark Cards, for instance, offered consumers an 80-page holiday cookbook for $1.50 if they purchased at least $5 worth of Hallmark merchandise.

P-O-P Point-of-purchase materials provided to retailers to help them promote sales

premiums Merchandise offered to consumers as an incentive to buy a product

purchase with purchase An incentive that allows consumers to buy a product if they first purchase another product

Samples are free merchandise that are provided to retailers or consumers. The hope is that if consumers are involved, they will try the product, like it, and continue to purchase it. Most samples are smaller than the normal size of the product. Some examples of consumer products for which sampling is frequently done are food items (chips, hot dogs, crackers, etc.), where in many cases the sampling is done in retail food stores, and soap, liquid detergents, and deodorants, which may be sent directly to consumers' homes. Manufacturers sometimes will provide retailers with samples with the expectation that the product will sell well and the retailer will want to stock it on a regular basis.

samples Free merchandise that is provided to retailers or consumers

sponsoring Underwriting the cost of an event

Sponsoring some type of event can be an effective sales promotion alternative for either consumer or industrial products. In recent years, sponsoring sporting events has become increasingly attractive. In 2002, $9.4 billion was spent on sponsorship in North America; about two-thirds of that figure was spent on sports. The rest was allocated to entertainment, tours and attractions, festivals, fairs, annual events, causes, and the arts. Worldwide, about $25 billion was devoted to sponsorships—about 40 percent in North America, 30 percent in Europe, 17 percent in the Asia Pacific region, and 9 percent in South America. The industry most likely to be involved with sponsorships was nonalcoholic beverages, followed by banks, automotive, telecommunications, beer, packaged goods, retailers, airlines, insurance, and credit cards.[2] These industries are well represented in Exhibit 10.3, which shows the top ten U.S. sponsors.

Sponsorship can involve enormous sums. The professional golfer Tiger Woods earns $30 million a year endorsing such products as Buick cars. And not to be outdone, Lebron James, the high school basketball player drafted by the NBA, picked up $110 million in endorsements before even playing one game—$90 million of it from Reebok.

sweepstakes Chances for a consumer to win a prize or money, such as through a drawing

Sweepstakes involve a chance factor, such as a drawing or lucky number. Proof of purchase is usually not required or is optional so that lottery laws are not violated. Two famous and heavily promoted sweepstakes are those conducted by *Readers Digest* and Publishers Clearing House. Dell Computer Corporation used a sweepstakes in an effort to increase its 8.4 percent market share in the U.S. personal computer market. During July, any purchaser of a Dell PC would have a chance to win $50,000. Competitors were expected to retaliate. Hewlett-Packard decided to offer its own sweepstakes of three $2,000 shopping sprees.[3]

trade shows Shows where companies have the opportunity to display their products

Trade shows, where companies can display their products, are the major sales promotion strategy for firms marketing industrial products. Around $20 billion annually is spent on trade shows. By 2008, it is expected that around 2 million companies will be exhibiting at more than 6000 trade shows that will be attended by 125 million people.[4] Trade shows offer a number of important advantages, but in order to maximize these, exhibitors at trade shows need to recognize and employ several guidelines. Trade shows can speed up the selling process; they can get products to the market in less time.[5] Trade shows are attended by prospects who come with an open mind, actively seeking information. Trade shows allow prospects to actually

EXHIBIT 10.3

Top Ten U.S. Sponsors

Company	Amount (in millions)
Anheuser-Busch Co.	$215–$220
Philip Morris Co.	$190–$195
Pepsico	$190–$195
General Motors Corp.	$165–$170
Coca-Cola Co.	$130–$135
DaimlerChrysler AG	$105–$110
Nike	$105–$110
Eastman Kodak Co.	$90–$95
Ford Motor Co.	$75–$80
McDonald's Corp.	$75–$80

Source: "IEG Sponsorship Report," *Marketing News*, July 8, 2002, p. 23.

see the product. Products can be demonstrated at trade shows. Prospects can actually try out products in which they are interested.

Trade shows provide immediacy. If a prospect becomes interested in a product, he or she has someone right there who can answer questions. In addition, since competitor products are frequently displayed at trade shows, prospects can make meaningful comparisons right there. Trade shows can attract large numbers of first-time attendees, many of whom might be new prospects for exhibitors' products. Exhibitors at trade shows from the communications industry found that 44 percent of visitors to their booths were first-time attendees; 36 percent of computer companies' trade-show-booth visitors were first-timers.[6]

Trade shows are not as expensive as other ways to promote products. It has been estimated that the cost of contacting one prospect at a trade show is only one-third the cost of a sales call. Data and Securities group calculated that it costs $625 to get one sale from a trade show prospect, compared to $1117 through other means.[7]

Trade shows generate sales, so a company may get a large percentage of its annual sales from one trade show. For example, Azanda is a semiconductor firm that provides high-tech data traffic management services for public telephones and other industries. Exhibiting at the Networld + Interop 2002 conference in Las Vegas, it generated three new customers worth $3 to $5 million in annual sales.[8]

LEARNING OBJECTIVE 2
List ways to improve the effectiveness of trade shows.

In order to make a trade show exhibit successful, companies need to

- Promote their presence at the trade show to customers and prospects. Information about their company, the products that will be on display, where in the exhibit hall the exhibit will be located, and any receptions open to attendees needs to be communicated before the trade show begins. Iomega Corporation, which makes computer drives, used its logo and telephone number on 400 local cabs, a compelling exhibit booth, and a preshow promotion for its exhibit at the Comdex Computer trade show in Las Vegas.[9] A graphics design firm gave away bags of popcorn at its trade show. The irresistible smell drew hundreds of prospects to its booth.
- Generate *leads*, that is, companies that may purchase the exhibitor's products.
- Qualify all leads. This means the ones most likely to purchase must be separated from those unlikely to purchase.
- Follow up good leads—and soon after the trade show. This usually takes the form of a sales call being made on those prospects that look most promising. Surprisingly, it has been estimated that 70 percent of exhibitors fail to follow up on their leads.
- Set objectives for the trade show. The number of visitors, number of sales leads, number of units and dollar value of sales, and profit are examples of objectives. When companies evaluate trade shows, they need to determine if these objectives have been achieved.
- Make last-minute checks including seeing that the merchandise to be displayed has arrived, the accompanying sales literature also has been received, and booth personnel know their assigned times and stations.

reality CHECK *Make a list of the various facilities in your hometown or city that you believe would be appropriate for hosting a trade show. What factors did you use to develop your list?*

Personal Selling

personal selling Using a sales force to sell products and services

Personal selling is the use of a sales force to sell products and services. In 2001, there were slightly more than 16 million salespeople in the United States and almost half of these were females. It is important for a company to understand what a salesperson does. Exhibit 10.4 indicates the four major responsibilities for sales personnel and the components of each.

LEARNING OBJECTIVE 3
Discuss the sales force's main responsibilities.

Before salespeople can begin to plan sales presentations, they must acquire information about their company, the product sold, the competition, and their prospective customers. Salespeople must understand the basic objectives, philosophies, operations, and policies of their company, especially those that pertain to the selling job. For example, salespeople must know how much credit can be extended to customers and how long deliveries will take. It is helpful if they can tell customers how much time will be involved in processing orders.

Product knowledge is crucial to success in selling. Complete information about the products handled, including sizes, styles, colors, durability, and so on, is necessary. Salespeople must also know why and how their products are different from competitors' products. The sales force must be able to tell customers about the benefits they will obtain from using their company's products and about after-the-sale service available. They must know the product prices and the discounts from these prices.

Salespeople do a better job when they have knowledge about their company's competitors, especially their products, prices, differences between competitors' products and theirs, strategies of competitors' sales forces, benefits stressed for competing products, and changes in competitors' marketing strategies. There are many sources of information that a sales force can use to keep abreast of the competition. Annual reports and newspaper and magazine articles are excellent sources. Customers are an invaluable source of information about competitors. Trade fairs and competitors' advertisements frequently are useful.

The more knowledge salespeople have about their customers, the better job they will be able to do. A sales force must know the needs and desires of the market so that it can show how these needs and desires can be satisfied by the products being sold. Those who make the purchase decision should be identified. The extent to which customers are satisfied with current offerings should be determined.

Once the sales force has the information necessary for successful selling, it is ready to develop plans for making presentations to prospects and customers.

EXHIBIT 10.4

Salesperson's Responsibilities

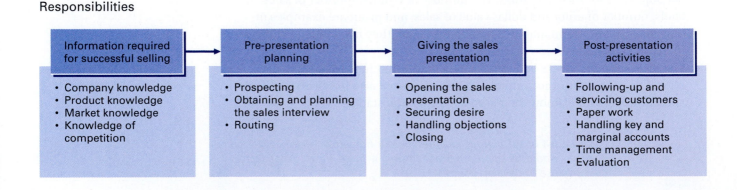

Prospecting, getting the sales interview, planning the sales presentation, and effective routing are important aspects of prepresentation planning. Prospecting allows the sales force to make effective use of time, increases the sales volume obtained, and increases compensation. **Prospecting** refers to a ranking of possible customers according to their potential sales volume and the likelihood of their purchasing the product. That likelihood is a result of a number of factors, including how closely the product's benefits satisfy needs and desires, how satisfied a prospect is with current products, and so on. A customer who has a potential sales volume of $20,000 and a probability of purchasing of .7 is a better prospect than one who has a potential sales volume of $10,000 and a probability of purchasing of .3 ($20,000 × .7 = $14,000; $10,000 × .3 = $3000).

prospecting Ranking of possible customers according to their potential sales volume and the likelihood of their purchasing the product

Many successful salespeople are in the habit of making appointments before sales calls, as up to 40 percent of all sales calls fail to identify a potential buyer. Thus, the smart salesperson sets up a sales interview in advance. This significantly reduces the possibility of not having a prospect with whom to talk. With the sales interview established and prospecting accomplished, the actual sales presentations can be planned. Products to be presented can be decided on, as well as product features and benefits that best satisfy customer needs and desires. Sales personnel use features to develop benefits. Benefits are what sell products and are emphasized in the presentation (see Exhibit 10.5). Then, the salesperson develops an outline of the presentation or a word-by-word presentation. The latter is more likely to be used in formal presentations to buying committees of large companies.

While planning the presentation, the salesperson also considers which audiovisual aids to use and when in the presentation they should appear. Audiovisual aids often increase the effectiveness of a presentation. Popular examples of audiovisual aids include overhead projectors, slides, movies, and PowerPoint presentations.

Effective routing involves the sequence in which customers and prospects will be contacted. Which streets or highways to be traveled, how long it will take to get from one customer to the next, and how long to stay with each customer are factors to be considered. In developing the route, a salesperson tries to reduce the travel time because it will result in lower travel costs for the company and more selling time. More selling time should increase sales volume and the salesperson's compensation.

EXHIBIT 10.5

Features and Benefits of an Attaché Case

General Feature	Specific Feature	General Benefit	Specific Benefit
Dimensions	12" by 20" inside dimensions	Convenience	Can put two regular-sized file folders side by side
Dimensions	5" deep	Convenience	Will accommodate books, thick reports, toilet articles, pocket-sized calculator, and pocket-sized tape recorder
Dimensions	5" by 12½" by 20½" outside dimensions	Convenience	Will fit under seat in airplane
Weight	1 lb	Comfort	Easy to carry
Materials	Aluminum construction	Durability	Will last 10 years
Price	$75	Cost savings	Costs only $7.50 per year, or about 2¢ a day
Attachments	Combination lock	Security	Protects valuable papers

In making sales presentations, the salesperson wants to obtain the prospect's attention, interest, desire, and conviction in order to make a sale. Handling objections and using successful closing techniques are also important. The major way that attention and interest can be obtained is by showing the prospect how the product can satisfy her or his most important needs. For example, a salesperson might say, "How would you like your company to save $200,000 a year producing your cotton towels? Our new machinery can obtain these savings for you."

Desire and conviction lead the prospect closer to making a favorable buying decision. Providing facts and figures is often a good way to secure desire and conviction. Using testimonials of satisfied customers helps. Demonstrating the product and getting prospects to use the product or to consider how they would use it are other successful approaches. Visual aids can also help obtain desire and conviction.

The professional salesperson is rarely disturbed by customer objections because from experience he or she knows what to expect and can handle the objections. Objections tend to be minimized if the salesperson has done a good job of offering products that satisfy a prospect's needs and desires. An effective way to handle objections is to agree with the objection—if it is valid—and then try to turn it into an advantage. An insurance salesperson, for example, might say, "I agree that the cost of our life insurance is 10 percent higher than the industry average, but we are providing much better coverage and 25 percent higher retirement benefits."

closing Efforts by a salesperson designed to get a prospect to purchase a product or service

Successful **closing** means that the prospect has decided to purchase. A number of techniques are helpful in successful closing (see Exhibit 10.6).

The salesperson's job does not end with closing a sale. There are a number of postpresentation activities that must be performed. Customers need to be followed up and served. Customers should be contacted periodically so that the sales force can determine if they are satisfied with the product. If they are not satisfied, corrective measures should be taken so that customers will not be lost. Customer complaints and returned goods should be cheerfully and promptly handled. Any credit problems should be taken care of quickly. The salesperson should ensure that installation, repair, and servicing obligations are fulfilled.

Most salespeople consider the task of keeping records an unnecessary evil. In many companies, it takes up a large percentage of their total time, often accounting for as much as one-fourth of the working day. The sales force must keep some records. Management has to know on whom the sales force called; what was

EXHIBIT 10.6

Tips for Successful Closing

- Don't be afraid to ask for the order. Try to close during the presentation as well as at the end.
- Look for closing signals from the prospect, such as questions about price, installation, repairs, and so on. These indicate a favorable disposition toward buying.
- Secure the prospect's agreement on product features and benefits.
- Review major product benefits prior to asking for the order.
- Reduce the number of alternative choices for the prospect.
- Use guarantees and warranties to aid closing.
- Analyze past presentations in order to determine which closing techniques work best in various selling situations.

Source: Richard T. Hise, *Effective Salesmanship,* The Dryden Press, Hinsdale, Illinois, 1980, pp. 261–264.

purchased; the reasons given if a sale did not occur; and expenses incurred, such as travel, food, and lodging. Many firms are trying to reduce the amount of paperwork for their salespeople by giving them more home-office clerical help and by computerizing the processing and analysis of data so that the salespeople will have more time for actual selling and better and more timely information.

It is possible to identify **key accounts** from a salesperson's records. These accounts make up that small nucleus of customers that accounts for a large percentage of a company's revenues and profit, or they are the customers who have above-average sales volume and profits. A customer may also be considered a key account if in the future it is likely to experience substantial growth in revenue or profit. Since key accounts are critical to a firm's success, they must receive plenty of attention from the sales force.

key accounts Accounts that represent a large percentage of a company's revenues and profits

Effective management of time is a key variable in separating the successful salesperson from the mediocre one. Good time management enables the salesperson to reduce the amount of time spent on unprofitable activities so that more time can be devoted to direct contact with customers and prospects. Reducing travel time and waiting time, better routing, making appointments in advance, and making use of unproductive times are important aspects of time management. As a starting point in effectively managing their time, salespeople need to know how they are actually spending their time. Exhibit 10.7 provides a convenient way for sales personnel to keep track of time on a daily basis.

The challenge of keeping good records in order to more effectively manage the sales force has been made easier with the use of computer-assisted sales programs (CASPs). CASPs are used in a wide variety of sales programs. These include redesigning sales territories, sales forecasting, analyzing accounts, order status reporting, personalizing literature send-outs, routing, generating competitor databases, checking inventory levels, and evaluating sales force performance. Benefits from using CASPs have been significant: *Sales and Marketing Management* reported companies using CASPs enjoyed a 43 percent increase in productivity as measured by closing ratios, call frequencies, account management, lead follow-up and tracking, and number of sales force calls made. Specific companies have benefited greatly. Typical is the experience of Hewlett-Packard. Their CASP initiative centered on providing the sales force with laptop computers. Selling time was increased by 27 percent. Productivity rose 10 percent. The number of inquiries rose by 27 percent, and the time to process inquiries was reduced from six weeks to one week. Sales personnel reported improved morale, an enhanced sense of professionalism, better control, and better preparation.[10]

EXHIBIT 10.7

Daily Time Record

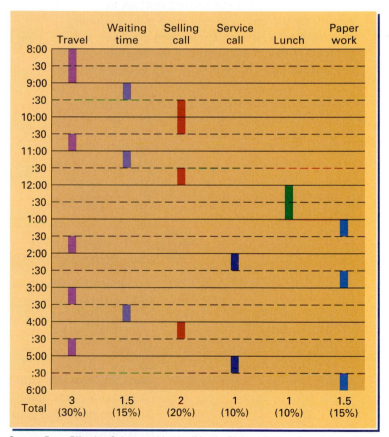

Source: From *Effective Salesmanship* 1st edition by Richard T. Hise. Copyright © 1980. Reprinted with permission of South-Western, a division of Thomson Learning: **www.thomsonrights.com**. Fax 800 730–2215.

reality CHECK *Glance through a recent issue of* Sales and Marketing Management. *What sales force responsibilities are discussed in the various articles?*

Ethics in Business

The Use of Incentives by Pharmaceutical Companies

The sales rep of a large pharmaceutical company walked into a doctor's office in New Jersey with samples of a new osteoporosis drug. The doctor said, "The last rep offered me a trip to Florida. What do you have?" The sales rep could not offer a trip to Florida, but was empowered to give free tickets to a Broadway play, free sample products, $1000 if the doctor attended the company's next educational lecture, and $200 if the doctor would prescribe the new medicine to the next six patients who "fit the drug's profile."

Selling pharmaceuticals is a daily exercise in ethical judgment. Salespeople walk the line between the common business practice of buying a prospect's time with a free meal and bribing doctors to prescribe the drugs. They sell in an industry highly criticized for its sales and marketing practices, but find themselves in the middle of the age-old chicken-or-egg question: Are doctors to blame for the escalating extravagancy of pharmaceutical marketing, or is it the industry's responsibility to decide the boundaries? In 2000, it was estimated that pharmaceutical firms allocated around $720 million on event spending. Pfizer led the way with $135 million, $86 million for such giveaways as pens, coffee mugs, shirts, and umbrellas. Companies' spending for marketing often exceeds what they spend for research and development. Every freebie given away contributes to the skyrocketing prescription prices.

Sales reps are important to doctors. They provide them with up-to-date information about new medicines—information that they often could not obtain from other sources. However, the receipt of this information has to be based on trust that the information provided is accurate. The quickest way to destroy a relationship is to provide bad information! Salespeople learn quickly that a precious relationship with a client will diminish if trust is even slightly broken.

Source: From "Doctoring Sales," *Sales & Marketing Management* by Erin Strout. Copyright 2001 by VNU Business Publications USA. Reproduced with permission of VNU Business Publications USA via Copyright Clearance Center.

Questions

1. Should pharmaceutical firms be allowed to give doctors incentives for recommending their products?
2. Who is at fault for the escalating extravagancy of pharmaceutical marketing programs, doctors or pharmaceutical firms?
3. What do you think of the fact that pharmaceutical firms may spend more on their marketing efforts than they spend on R&D?

LEARNING OBJECTIVE 4
Discuss the ways in which sales personnel can conduct themselves ethically.

Salespeople need to treat customers and potential customers ethically. Failure to do so will bring reproach on the salespeople, their companies, and the selling profession. It will also result in lost orders, declining sales, and shrinking profits. In addition, restrictive legislation is likely to result. A code of ethics for the selling profession includes

> Don't misrepresent your purpose.
> Call on prospects who can benefit from purchasing your product.
> Don't promise what you can't deliver.
> Don't disparage competitors' products.
> Answer all questions truthfully.
> Make sure customers are satisfied.
> Handle legitimate complaints and returns promptly and cheerfully.
> Observe all laws affecting selling.

Think of the last time a salesperson tried to sell you a product or service. Was there anything that the salesperson did or said that you felt was unethical?

Publicity

Publicity refers to items about a company, its products, or its personnel that appear in the mass media. The mass media that carry the publicity are not paid for carrying the information. Publicity can be negative, as well as positive. As a result, most large companies in the United States have established **public relations** departments. These departments put out press releases and use other means directed to the news media that cast the company, its products, or its personnel in a favorable light, and also undertake efforts to combat unfavorable publicity that has occurred.

The public relations department is keenly aware of the various publics with which a firm must be concerned. These include consumers, consumer groups, the general public, various levels of government, labor unions, and stockholders. Early public relations efforts in the United States focused on attempts to obtain legislation favorable to business (lobbying). The next phase in the evolutionary process involved the use of planned publicity to generate interest in the company and its products. The public relations department developed stories about its company, employees, and products and attempted to get news media to run them. Currently, public relations departments are stressing the value of research prior to launching public relations campaigns.

Publicity plays an important role in the promotion mix. Because competitors are often using the same advertising and similar sales promotion techniques, publicity offers the general advantage of promotion differentiation, that is, "an opportunity to shine by coming up with a program that takes the product out of competitive sameness and places it on a very special pedestal for the customer to view."[11]

Publicity can contribute to the marketing effort in a number of ways. If you are not sure who the best prospects are for a new product, a public relations effort across a wide variety of media is an inexpensive way to determine who the best prospects are. Publicity can be economically directed to those hard-to-get-to peripheral markets. For example, a photograph or news release could be sent to all specialized newspapers in the United States catering to Spanish-speaking individuals.

Customers are frequently skeptical of product claims. They are likely to be less skeptical if the product carries the endorsement of an objective third party. Third party endorsements are essentially achieved by having the implied approval of the media in which an editorial appears; the editorial provides the product with legitimacy. When people interested in a product see a news feature on it, they frequently get in touch with the company. Thus, good sales leads are provided. And sales calls are more than likely to result in orders if the prospect has seen something favorable about the salesperson's company.

Public relations personnel can help to establish individuals in a company as experts in various fields. The media may then turn to these experts when they need technical information. Customers tend to view companies with experts as being bigger and better.

Minor products frequently do not warrant the use of advertising, personal selling, or sales promotion. News releases or photos may generate sales for a minor product and help to elevate it to a better competitive position. Public relations departments can get interviews for their companies' top executives, or get them speaking engagements. These opportunities allow executives to straighten out misunderstandings, articulate company policies, and discuss company products.

Publicity helps to stretch a company's promotional dollars through the use of reprints. These can be disseminated to the various publics that concern an organization, and can also be distributed to individuals within the company who can

publicity News items about a company, its products, or its personnel that appear in the mass media

public relations Press releases and other efforts directed to the news media that portray a company, its products, or its personnel in a favorable light or combat unfavorable publicity

benefit from them. Sales literature should not be distributed only to the prospects and customers; it should also be given to public relations personnel who can disperse it among the company's various publics.[12]

The Distribution Mix

distribution mix The channels of distribution and logistics operations a company uses to move its products to its customers

The **distribution mix** refers to the channels of distribution and logistics operations a company uses to move its products to its customers.

Channels of Distribution

LEARNING OBJECTIVE 5
Distinguish between the channels of distribution for consumer products and for industrial products.

Wholesalers and retailers are the major channels of distribution a company can employ in developing its mix of channels of distribution. The way in which they are used often depends on the type of product involved. Exhibit 10.8 shows the usual channels of distribution for consumer products.

About 50 percent of all consumer products flow through wholesalers and retailers to reach consumers. Around 45 percent move only through retailers. What about the other 5 percent? The other 5 percent do not use channels of distribution; they go *directly* from the manufacturer to the consumer. Companies like Amway, Mary Kay Cosmetics, and Avon use a direct strategy to sell their products.

reality CHECK   *Think about your most recent five or six visits to a supermarket. What did you like and dislike about these experiences?*

The channels of distribution options for industrial goods are also indicated in Exhibit 10.8. Eighty percent of industrial goods go directly from the manufacturer to the industrial buyer, such as other manufacturers, processors, construction firms, and so on. In other words, they do not use channels. Only 20 percent of industrial goods involve the use of distribution channels (wholesalers) to reach the industrial buyer customer.

EXHIBIT 10.8

Typical Distribution Channels for Consumer and Industrial Products

Why would a company not use distribution channels? Companies that want to retain control over the marketing effort for their products would elect a direct strategy, especially if they themselves have the required marketing skills. A direct strategy is more costly than an indirect one. For example, salespeople need to be hired, trained, and paid. Thus, companies pursuing a direct strategy need to have sufficient funds to support this option. Customer preferences are an important variable, also. Some—like many industrial buyers—want to purchase directly from manufacturers. They want to talk face-to-

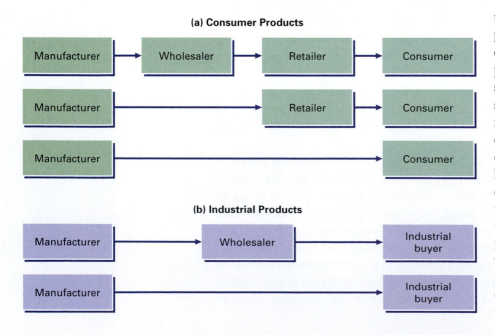

(a) Consumer Products

Manufacturer → Wholesaler → Retailer → Consumer

Manufacturer → Retailer → Consumer

Manufacturer → Consumer

(b) Industrial Products

Manufacturer → Wholesaler → Industrial buyer

Manufacturer → Industrial buyer

face with the manufacturer's purchasing department so they know the buyer's preferences, what they are willing to pay, when they expect delivery, and so on. Perishable products tend to go direct because of the spoilage factor.

Developing a channel strategy is very important. One channel expert says that the "wrong decision will cost you business. And lots of it."[13] What should be considered as this decision is contemplated? Customer preferences are important. In fact, the first step is to "uncover how the customers want to buy."[14] Companies often use the same channel strategies as the competition under the assumption that they are effective. How much money is available is an important consideration. Once the overall strategy is in place, companies must select specific channel companies to carry their products. The following should guide their decisions:

> How financially sound are the candidate companies?
> Are they experienced in carrying the types of products the firm needs marketed?
> Does their physical coverage of the market dovetail with what the manufacturer requires?
> Do they have a solid reputation?
> How likely is it that they will aggressively sell our product?
> How willing are they to carry inventories?

With firms wanting to sell their products overseas, it is often quite difficult to get answers to these questions. Fortunately, firms can turn to the U.S. government for help, especially the U.S. Department of Commerce. Such help is usually low cost or even free. Exhibit 10.9 lists the major government sources available.

Companies frequently need to change their channels of distribution. For example, beef jerky accounts for most of the sales of meat snacks and is experiencing a 30

EXHIBIT 10.9

U.S. Government Sources for Information About International Channels of Distribution

- **New Product Information Service.** U.S. firms get worldwide publicity and distributors can seek them out.
- **Trade Opportunities Program (TOP).** Department of Commerce matches product interests of foreign firms with U.S. firms.
- **Foreign Traders Index (FTI).** Data file on more than 140,000 importers, agents, and distributors.
- **Agent/Distributor Service (A/DS).** Locates foreign firms with compatible product interests that are willing to entertain proposals by U.S. firms.
- **World Traders Data Report (WTDR).** Provides profiles of foreign agents and brokers as well as a narrative report.
- **Economic Bulletin Board.** A personal, computerized bulletin board that is an online source for overseas agents and distributors.
- **Matchmaker trade delegations.** U.S. Department of Commerce missions to foreign countries designed to introduce U.S. exporters to prospective agents and distributors.
- **Customized sales survey.** Custom-tailored research service that provides firms with specific information about agents and distributors for their specific products in selected countries.
- **Multi-State/Catalog Exhibition Program.** Through catalogs, helps small- and medium-sized U.S. firms that are infrequent exporters to line up foreign agents and distributors.

percent growth rate. Much of the growth is the result of the industry expanding beyond gas stations into such new outlets as supermarkets, convenience stores, discounters like Kmart, and Blockbuster.[15] Ford's growth strategy has involved acquiring an impressive array of luxury cars, including Jaguar, Volvo, Land Rover, Aston Martin, and Lincoln. In a distinct break with tradition, Ford has decided to sell all five luxury brands in one dealership. While there will be separate sales departments, the service and back-office functions will be combined.[16]

If firms start off using channels of distribution, they often need to eventually change over to a direct strategy. This is because they may be dissatisfied with the effort put forth by the channels they have selected or they may have improved their own marketing skills. Another factor is cost; at some level of revenues, it may be less costly to go direct than it is to keep using channels. For example, assume a manufacturer is using agents and paying them a 10 percent commission. It estimates that it would require a $100,000 investment to recruit and train a sales force and the cost, pay, and expenses of maintaining the sales force would be 6 percent of sales. At what level of revenue should the firm switch from an indirect to a direct strategy? The equation below shows that, at least for this example, this is $2,500,000.

$$0.10x = 0.06x + \$100,000$$
$$0.04x = \$100,000$$
$$x = \$2,500,000$$

If revenues go beyond $2,500,000, it would be less costly to go direct. Let's see what the cost would be for both options if revenues were $3,000,000.

Indirect: (0.10) $(\$3,000,000) = \$300,000$
Direct: (0.06) $(\$3,000,000) + \$100,000 = \$280,000$

At revenues of $3,000,000, it would cost the firm $20,000 less to go direct.

In order to gain the cooperation of channels, manufacturers need to offer a number of concessions to them. They should be provided with salable products for which there is a strong demand. Demand can often be increased by allocating funds to help channels advertise or by manufacturers doing the advertising themselves. Manufacturers should sell products to distributors at a fair price so that when they are resold by distributors, distributors can earn a fair profit. Manufacturers should furnish distribution channels information about markets. On-time delivery and emergency shipments need to be provided. Allowing for consignment sales is helpful; these enable channels of distribution to delay paying for goods until they have sold them.

Channels of distribution are important segments of the U.S. economy. There are about 850,000 wholesaler operations in the United States doing over $4 trillion of business annually. The 3 million retailers have about $2.5 trillion in revenues yearly. Channels of distribution make significant contributors to economic well-being. They may reduce the cost of getting products to consumers—and the price consumers pay—because they are specialists who can perform various marketing functions, like transportation and storage, very efficiently. They take large lots of products, break them down into smaller lots, and move them on to other channel members (**dispersion**). The opposite is **concentration:** pooling small lots into larger ones, which are then moved to other channel members. They create **place utility** by transporting products to locations that are convenient for customers. They create **time utility** by storing products until customers want to purchase them. Because of their excellent knowledge of markets, they act as important sources of information.

dispersion The channel of distribution function involving the breaking down of large lots into smaller lots

concentration The channel of distribution function involving the pooling of small lots into larger ones

place utility The satisfaction for customers created when products are transported to locations that are convenient for them

time utility The satisfaction for customers created by products being stored until customers want to purchase them

Wholesalers.
Merchant wholesalers account for almost 80 percent of wholesaler revenues. **Merchant wholesalers** purchase merchandise, thus taking legal title to it, and resell it. Some merchant wholesalers provide a full range of services.

- **Regular wholesalers** provide a full range of services such as carrying inventories, providing promotion, and extending credit. They generally carry consumer goods and are independently owned firms.
- **Industrial distributors** are wholesalers that operate in the industrial goods market. They tend to specialize in a limited line of products and may specialize in the kinds of markets they reach.
- **Rack jobbers** are regular wholesalers who specialize in selling nonfood items, such as toys, records, and houseware items, to retailers. They stock the product for the retailers and mark the prices. Generally, they sell on **consignment** to retailers, which means that the retailers do not have to pay for merchandise until it is sold.

Others provide limited services.

- **Drop shippers** are limited-service wholesalers that take title to merchandise but do not take physical possession. The manufacturer performs the transportation and storage function.
- **Cash-and-carry wholesalers** do not extend credit to their purchasers and do not provide purchasers with transportation. Purchasers come to the establishment of cash-and-carry wholesalers, choose the merchandise they want, pay cash for the orders, and arrange for delivery.
- **Truck wholesalers** are limited-function wholesalers who generally sell perishable or semiperishable products. Carrying limited stock, they make frequent calls on their customers. Also called wagon jobbers, they tend to service food retailers, restaurants, and hotels.

Manufacturers' sales branches and sales offices are often established by firms separate from their manufacturing operations. These branches and offices enable the manufacturer to perform the wholesaling function and are often established when the manufacturer decides not to use wholesalers for all or part of the firm's product lines. **Sales branches** carry inventories of products and customer orders are filled from these inventories. **Sales offices** do not carry inventories. Both sales branches and sales offices serve as offices for salespeople in that territory.

Agents, brokers, and commission merchants do not purchase products for resale. They perform various services for which they are paid a commission. **Selling agents** sell all of a specified line or the entire output for their principals. They usually do not sell competing lines for firms that are in competition with their principals. They generally perform the entire range of marketing functions and are given control over the terms of the sale and pricing. Selling agents are used instead of a company's own sales force. They are paid a commission.

Manufacturers' agents, unlike selling agents, do not handle a manufacturer's total output or single product line. They are not given control over the terms of the sale and pricing. Manufacturers' agents are widely used in distributing industrial goods. They are paid a commission. **Brokers** bring buyers and sellers together to consummate a transaction. They represent either the buyer or the seller but not both. They usually have limited authority over the terms of the sale, such as extending credit and establishing price. They are paid a commission. Brokers are important in the sale of many kinds of food products.

merchant wholesalers Wholesalers that purchase merchandise and resell it

regular wholesalers Wholesalers that provide a full range of services

industrial distributors Wholesalers that handle industrial products and may specialize in a limited line of products and markets to which the products are sold

rack jobbers Regular whole-salers that sell nonfood items to retailers

consignment An arrangement whereby retailers do not have to pay for merchandise until they sell it

drop shippers Limited-service wholesalers that take title to merchandise but do not take physical possession

cash-and-carry wholesalers Limited-service wholesalers that do not provide their customers with credit or transportation

truck wholesalers Limited-service wholesalers that sell limited lines of perishable or semiperishable products to retailers

sales branches Wholesale operations that carry inventories that are established by manufacturers

sales offices Wholesale operations that do not carry inventories that are established by manufacturers

selling agents Wholesalers that represent a client and sell all the client's specific line or entire output and are given control over the terms of sale and pricing

manufacturers' agents Wholesalers that are not given control over the terms of sale and pricing because they sell only part of a client's output or product line

brokers Wholesalers with limited authority over the terms of sale; they bring buyer and seller together and are important in the sale of food products

commission merchants Sellers that have power over prices and terms of sale and specialize in providing transportation and arranging delivery for agricultural products

Commission merchants take physical possession of products and usually are granted broad powers over prices and terms of sale. The major services they provide are transportation and arranging delivery. They are most likely to be used in marketing agricultural products and are paid a commission.

Retailers.   There are four basic types of retailer organizations in the United States: stores, mail order, automatic vending, and direct selling. About two-thirds of U.S. retailers are stores and they account for around 90 percent of total retail sales.

STORES.   **Department stores** are large stores that sell a wide variety of merchandise organized into separate departments. In each line there is usually a wide assortment. The buyer for each department manages that department. Thus, buyers not only purchase merchandise for their departments—their major function—but they also supervise clerks, engage in inventory control, arrange for sales (markdowns), plan promotional campaigns, and so on. Department stores offer a wide variety of services to their customers. Some examples include luncheon rooms, gift wrapping, delivery, nurseries, beauty consultants, and charge accounts.

department stores Large stores that sell a wide variety of merchandise organized into separate departments

The traditional department store emphasizes the sale of soft goods, such as men's wear, women's wear, children's clothing, and household items like curtains, blankets, and sheets. Other lines of merchandise commonly carried include china, gourmet foods, cameras, luggage, tobacco products, shoes, jewelry, and cosmetics. In the past, many department stores carried appliances and sporting goods, but because of increased competition, they have dropped these lines.

Most department store buyers prefer to deal directly with manufacturers and thus bypass wholesalers. Because of their large size, they are often able to get good prices and favorable terms of sale.

discount stores Stores that emphasize the sale of hard goods at low prices with low levels of service at inexpensive locations

Discount stores appeared in the United States after World War II in response to consumer demand for low prices. In order to achieve these low prices, discount operators located in inexpensive buildings, used inexpensive fixtures, employed few clerks, and offered few services. Their main merchandise line was hard goods, such as washers, dryers, television sets, and radios. They tended to sell major brand names so that promotional costs could be minimized and consumers could easily see the price savings offered.

In recent years discount operations have moved to better locations, improved the quality of their interiors, and have begun to offer some services, such as credit and delivery. These actions have resulted in higher operating expenses and illustrate a phenomenon called the **wheel of retailing,** which means that low-cost retailers gain a competitive advantage when getting started by offering few services so that low prices can be charged. Once they become established, they add services that increase their costs and their prices. Thus, they become vulnerable to new forms of competition that stress low prices. Wal-Mart is the leading discounter in the United States and one of the largest global companies in terms of revenues ($245 billion in 2002).

wheel of retailing The process by which low-cost retailers begin offering services that increase their prices, making them vulnerable to new, low-cost retailers

Supermarkets are large food stores that sell dry goods, frozen foods, meat, and fresh fruit and vegetables. They frequently have 30,000 or more square feet of selling area and stock as many as 10,000 different items. Supermarkets have added many nonfood items, including toys and games, housewares, drugs, books and magazines, plants and flowers, and clothing. Supermarkets emphasize self-service. Because self-service allows them to hire fewer clerks, they reduce their costs and are able to charge lower prices.

supermarkets Large food stores that sell a wide variety of food and nonfood items

Convenience stores are small-sized food stores that sell a limited line of grocery items such as milk, bread, pastries, soft drinks, and ice cream. They tend to keep long hours. In fact, many such operations stay open 24 hours a day. Because these

convenience stores Small-sized stores that sell limited lines of food and nonfood items

Cookies by Design is an example of a small specialty store.

long hours provide a convenience to shoppers, convenience stores tend to charge high prices.

Specialty stores carry a broad assortment of merchandise in a single merchandise line. Examples are candy stores, women's clothing stores, shoe stores, sporting goods stores, flower shops, and toy stores. Generally, their prices are relatively high because they offer a wide variety of services, such as free alterations, and because they are specialists in their merchandise line. The Gap, Old Navy, Home Depot, Toys 'R' Us, Auto Zone, Office Max, Barnes & Noble, Talbot's, and Ross's are examples of successful specialty stores. When a single specialty store dominates its industry, it is called a **category killer.**

> **specialty stores** Stores that carry a broad assortment in a single merchandise line

> **category killer** A store that dominates its segment of the retailing industry

---

LEARNING OBJECTIVE 6
Describe and give the advantages of using nonstore retailers in channels of distribution.

NONSTORE RETAILING.   Nonstore retailing involves direct selling, direct marketing, and automatic vending. **Direct selling,** sometimes called door-to-door selling, consists of companies having salespeople call on customers in their homes or offices. Vacuum cleaners, encyclopedias, magazines, cosmetics, brushes, and clothing, such as business attire for executives, are examples of products that are sold this way. Companies that use direct selling often encounter three major disadvantages. First, salespeople's salaries, commissions, and expenses are often a high percentage of sales, sometimes as large as 50 percent. Second, salespeople's turnover can be very high. For some direct selling companies, it can be 100 percent in a year. Third, many consumers are reluctant to purchase from direct salespeople because of some of their deceptive practices.

> **direct selling** Nonstore retailing involving salespeople calling directly on customers in their homes or offices

Direct marketing uses the telephone and nonpersonal media to promote products and services. Customers can purchase by mail, telephone, or Internet. Catalog marketing, direct-response marketing, telemarketing, television home shopping, and online retailing are different types of direct marketing. In **catalog marketing,**

> **direct marketing** Using telephone and nonpersonal media to promote products and services

> **catalog marketing** Offering consumers sales of merchandise from catalogs containing information about products from which they can order

consumers examine catalogs containing information about merchandise and then order via mail, telephone, or Internet. This is a convenient means of shopping for people who cannot get out of the house easily or who do not want to bother shopping. Of course, there are several disadvantages in purchasing from catalogs, including an inability to inspect the merchandise, having to wait at least several days to receive purchases, and running a risk of being dissatisfied. Spiegel, J.C. Penny, Land's End, and J. Crew are several of the well-known catalog marketers.

direct-response marketing Using various media to ask consumers to purchase products

In **direct-response marketing,** a retailer uses various advertising media to ask consumers to purchase its product. A television ad, for example, may ask viewers to purchase paint to cover dents and scratches on cars. A magazine or newspaper advertisement may promote a new book that can be purchased by mailing a filled-out coupon or calling an 800 number. Direct mail literature requesting purchase can be sent directly to consumers' homes.

telemarketing Using the telephone to promote the sales of products and achieve other marketing objectives

Telemarketing involves companies using the telephone to request that customers purchase their products or services. Frequently, telemarketing will be used in conjunction with other marketing efforts, like direct mail, to generate sales. It can also be used to ensure that customers are satisfied with their purchases. Because many people find telemarketing calls annoying, legislation was passed in 2003 allowing consumers to be removed from telemarketers' lists.

television home shopping Shopping from television cable channels that do not have regular programming, but instead promote products

Television home shopping refers to shopping on television cable channels that do not have regular programming but promote products, often 24 hours a day. Interested viewers can order by calling an 800 number and paying with a credit card. Jewelry, clothing, housewares, and electronics are the most popular items sold. The Home Shopping Network and QVC are the major players in this type of nonstore retailing.

online retailing Making products and services available to consumers through computer connections

Online retailing makes products and services available to consumers through computer connections. A wide variety of companies in several industries, such as airlines and stock brokerage firms, sell products and services online. The major problem with online retailing is security. Many people do not want to reveal their credit card numbers or other personal information. Others are annoyed with unsolicited efforts to sell them products online—spamming.

> reality
> **CHECK**
> *Have you purchased any product or service over the Internet? What did you like and dislike about this experience?*

automatic vending Retailers dispensing convenience-type merchandise in machines

Automatic vending consists of using vending machines to dispense convenience-type merchandise at numerous locations. Candy, cigarettes, sandwiches, soups, chewing gum, and postage stamps are examples of products sold extensively through vending machines. Although their convenient location is beneficial to users, they are often a source of frustration if they malfunction. Automatic vending is frequently a high-cost sales method. Expenses can often be as high as 40 percent of sales.

The nonstore retailing options are more popular in some countries than in the United States. Mail order, automatic vending, and direct selling have grown at a significantly slower pace in the United States during the last decade than in Japan. Germans spend a higher percentage of their income on mail-order products than do Americans.

Logistics

In the early 1980s, Wal-Mart had operating costs amounting to 22 percent of revenues. The company began an aggressive effort to reduce these costs. They were successful; in only a decade, these costs had dropped to 14 percent of revenues. By being a low-cost retailer, Wal-Mart was able to employ an everyday low-pricing strategy (EDLP) that helped the company become the largest firm in the world in 2002, with revenues of about $254 billion annually.

How was this drastic reduction in costs achieved? Operating the logistics function more efficiently was a major contributor. Transportation and inventory costs were significantly pared and suppliers were forced to operate more efficiently. Heavy use of computers and satellite technology undergirded the entire cost reduction effort.

LEARNING OBJECTIVE 7
Explain the difference between materials management and physical distribution.

Exhibit 10.10 provides an important overview of what logistics is all about. There, we see that **logistics** has two main components. **Materials management** is the movement of raw materials, in-process materials, and semifinished goods *to a* manufacturer from a supplier. The manufacturer will either store the goods and then move them into the production process or move them immediately into the production process. Once the finished goods have been produced, they will be sent to the customers—**physical distribution.** Thus, materials management deals with the inward flow of components goods, whereas physical distribution involves the outward flow of finished goods. Logistics is the totality of the inward and outward flows.

> **logistics** The materials management and physical distribution activities of a firm
>
> **materials management** The movement of raw materials, in-process materials, and semifinished goods to a manufacturer from a supplier
>
> **physical distribution** The movement of finished goods from manufacturers to their customers

reality CHECK *The next time you visit a supermarket, drug store or mass merchandiser like Wal-Mart, see what examples of physical distribution you can identify.*

Logistics involves two main responsibilities: transportation and storage.

Transportation. The five major modes of transportation that a firm can choose from are pipeline, water, rail, truck, and air. Each alternative has advantages and disadvantages that should be considered. The advantages and disadvantages must be related to the kinds of products a company is shipping and the service requirements of customers. Each mode should also be evaluated on the basis of cost.

LEARNING OBJECTIVE 8
Compare the advantages and disadvantages of the five modes of transportation.

Natural gas and petroleum are moved through pipelines. Pipelines are very inexpensive forms of transportation, but they are not as cheap as barges. Barges transport heavy, nonperishable items such as coal, iron ore, and grain on navigable rivers, the Great Lakes, and the St. Lawrence Seaway. Freighters are used for shipping similar goods to overseas markets. Although water transportation is the cheapest, it is also the slowest. Railroads are used primarily for the shipment of bulky goods that are low in value in relation to their weight, such as coal, sand, and agricultural products. However, other products like automobiles and chemicals are also frequently transported by railroad. The major advantages of flexibility and speed encourage many manufacturing firms to ship a large percentage of their products by truck. Although the cost may be higher than by rail, the flexibility and speed of trucks are so important in providing good customer service that trucks are used anyway. It should be pointed out, however, that the railroad cost advantages usually exist on longer hauls and that the shipment by truck for short distances (300 miles or less) may cost less than rail.

EXHIBIT 10.10

Overview of the Logistics Function

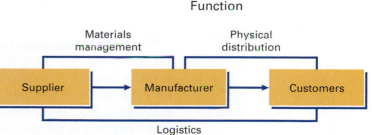

A railroad freight center.

common carriers Trucks not owned by shippers on which they can ship their products for a fee

private carriers Trucks owned and operated by shippers

A major decision that companies must make is whether to use **common carriers,** trucks not owned by shippers on which they can ship their products for a fee, or **private carriers,** their own fleet of trucks. Usually, the most significant factor in this decision is not the cost, but the extent to which the companies are satisfied with the level of customer service provided by the available common carriers. If shipments consistently arrive late and in poor condition, firms may be forced to invest in their own fleets. When the company owns its own fleet, it retains control over the transportation function. Thus, it can give the type and level of customer service it wants. It also has more flexibility in its operations. For example, it can ship when it wants and where it wants.

Air transportation is the fastest mode of transportation available. It is also the most expensive. As a result, high-value items like industrial machinery and automobile parts are frequently shipped by air. Because of the speed factor, perishable items like cut flowers, strawberries, and asparagus are shipped via airfreight. Many companies use air transportation to make emergency shipments to important customers. The extra cost is justified because of the good will that results. Because of the speed of service, companies shipping by air usually obtain a competitive advantage because they can provide better customer service. Samsonite Corporation used airfreight to ship luggage from its Denver plant to dealers in Chicago, Los Angeles, and San Francisco. Merchandise got to dealers quicker, dealers did not have to carry as much inventory, and out-of-stock situations could be minimized.

reality CHECK *Go to your college or university's library and skim through the most recent issues of five business periodicals. How many advertisements involved the five modes of transportation?*

Once the transportation mode has been selected, the shipper must determine the routes that the transportation mode should take. For example, truck routing involves decisions on when customers should receive deliveries, in what order the customer should receive the deliveries, and which roads should be used. Routing may have a number of objectives. Routes should be developed that minimize the times required to get shipments to customers. Total distance traveled should be reduced. This means that the shipper will incur a lower cost for transporting goods. Routes are often established to ensure that larger customers get better service.

The size of the shipment is an important logistics decision. Customers prefer smaller shipments because they do not want to invest heavily in storage facilities. On the other hand, shippers prefer larger shipments because they can take advantage of the quantity discounts offered by common carriers. If a shipper has its own trucks, it prefers to ship them full because it is probably going to incur much the same costs (fuel, drivers' pay) regardless of how full the truck is. Another advantage to the shipper of large shipments is that they may help to reduce the size of the warehousing space required.

Many companies are plagued with what is commonly called the **small-order problem,** that is, when a high percentage of orders shipped are made up of only a few pieces or lightweight pieces. What can shippers do about this problem? One possibility is to delay shipments until customer requirements in a particular geographic area become large enough to fill a truck or railroad car. Another possibility is to eliminate all paperwork from small orders by having customers telephone in their orders. Another alternative is to charge more for small orders. All of these alternatives, however, adversely affect customer service, which may hurt sales.

small-order problem The problem of a shipment that contains only a few pieces or lightweight pieces

Storage.   Companies need warehouses to store products until they can be released to customers. They can either own **private warehouses** that they have purchased or built or rent space in **public warehouses.** Owning a warehouse has some major advantages. The warehouse will be configured to allow for the most cost-efficient storage and handling of the company's products. The company will control the entire storage operation, assuring careful handling. There are tax advantages associated with private warehouses. The owner gains a sense of pride and can make a favorable impression on customers. The downsides of a private warehouse include the initial investment, land and construction, and the loss of flexibility, what to do if the present location is no longer appropriate.

private warehouses Warehouses owned (purchased or constructed) by a firm

public warehouses Warehouses not owned by the company that leases space in them

There are several benefits of using public warehouses. No initial investment for land and construction is needed. The user gains flexibility; space can be rented in warehouses that have locations that can best serve customers, and peak and off-season fluctuations in space requirements can be accommodated. Public warehouses often provide a wide variety of services, such as combining orders, providing special packages, and storing different types of products contained in barrels, drums, rolls, and cylinders. There is little risk that public warehouses will become obsolete, since they need to be kept up-to-date so that users can be obtained and retained. A **bonded warehouse** can be used by companies to obtain financing. In a bonded warehouse arrangement, the user's inventory, which is used as collateral to obtain a loan, is sequestered in a specific location and the bonded warehouse assures the lender that the level of inventory is stored at the facility.

bonded warehouse A public warehouse that leases space to users to store products that the user offers as collateral for loans

Managing inventory levels at storage sites is a primary logistics responsibility. Most companies today are trying to reduce their levels of inventory or eliminate inventory altogether to reduce or eliminate costs associated with the inventories, which can be substantial unless controlled. In order to improve warehousing productivity, the following are recommended:

Emphasize the effective use of cubic space, not only square-footage space.
Locate fast-moving items close to the shipping dock.
Locate products requiring similar handling close to one another.
Group smaller shipments into larger shipments.

An L.L. Bean catalog warehouse uses conveyors and computers to store and move merchandise.

Determine the percentage of sales accounted for by different types of products.

Use computers to improve information flow and accuracy.

Use automated, computer-driven retrieval systems to handle goods instead of relying exclusively on people and forklift trucks. Once the acquisition costs of these systems are recovered, companies will enjoy much lower operating costs.

Providing adequate levels of customer service at the lowest possible cost is a main responsibility of logistics management. This can be achieved by ensuring that orders are received on time, the time required to process orders is minimized, emergency and out-of-stock shipments are provided, frequent and small-size shipments are made, and that the status of orders is made available to customers. Such concessions to customers increase a company's costs, but the company hopes that increases in revenue will occur because the improved level of customer service will result in obtaining more customers and retaining a higher percentage of them. Academy is a large retailer of sporting goods and apparel located primarily in Texas. The company was experiencing significant growth, so it felt expansion into Louisiana, New Mexico, and Oklahoma was justified. The problem was that many of these stores would be greater than 300 miles from the Houston headquarters—300 miles being the greatest distance its current logistics system could replenish inventory within 24 hours. A new, $6 million logistics operation was developed in order to overcome this obstacle to expansion.

A main trend in logistics management is for companies to outsource all or part of their logistics operations to third parties. These specialized third parties may be able to perform these operations more efficiently than manufacturers, reducing their costs. Manufacturers also benefit because they are freed to concentrate more on their core competencies—activities they are skilled at doing, such as R&D, production, and marketing.

International Challenges. When a company decides to begin selling its products overseas, it encounters a new set of variables that affect its logistics operations. In countries like Italy and Japan, there will be more distribution layers than in the United States. Often, these wholesalers and retailers will be small inefficient operations. These factors result in more complicated and costly logistic operations. Poor logistics infrastructures are frequently the norm; bridges, tunnels, roads, ports, railroads, and airports may be of poor quality. Foreign buyers are more likely to accept longer delivery times than domestic customers, but once the buyer and seller agree on delivery dates and times, buyers expect deliveries to be on time. Because buyers may be separated from sellers by thousands of miles—making it difficult to deal with the various problems that may arise—international buyers demand that orders received are complete (no items missing), accurate (the correct products are received), and in good condition (not broken).

The greater distance required for international shipments results in sellers having to put more emphasis on the package designed to protect products in transit.

Technology and Business

Logistics Relies on Technology to Cut Cost and Provide Better Levels of Customer Service

Over the last fifty years, the logistics industry has relied on technology to cut costs and provide higher levels of customer service. The 1950s saw the advent of **containerization,** in which shipments are put in trailer-sized containers, usually 40 x 8 x 8 feet. The containers can then be moved from one type of transportation to another without having to have their contents unloaded and reloaded. In this intermodal transport, containers can be shipped via truck, train, airplane, or ocean-going vessel and moved from one to the other. Huge container cranes were developed that allow heavy containers to be loaded on or off ships without capsizing them. Containerization reduces handling costs, spoilage, and pilferage.

Slip sheets have been replacing more expensive wooden pallets that were prone to damage and were hard to keep track of. Stretch film wrappers help stabilize loads. Huge oil tankers carry millions of gallons of oil at low cost per gallon. Satellite tracking devices allow companies to keep track of where their trucks are, enable deliveries to be diverted to better service customers when last-minute needs arise, and monitor the safety of trucks, such as engine temperatures.

Technology has improved warehouse operations. Forklift trucks can quickly and effectively move inventory into storage areas or out to leading docks, as can mechanized conveyor belts. State-of-the-art automated inventory retrieval systems in concert with computers allow for overhead, safe, and rapid retrieval of products to fill customer orders. Computers are also used in electronic data interchange (EDI) systems where supplier and customer computers link up to automatically reorder products that are needed on a regular basis. Bar codes enable inventory levels to be maintained and shipments to be tracked.

The terrorist attack on the United States on September 11, 2001, has created security concerns. The bad news is that bombs, such as a small, low-yield nuclear device, can be hidden in containers and gotten into the United States through a port. It would be exorbitantly expensive and time-consuming to hand-check the tens of thousands of containers that arrive in the United States each week. The good news is that scanner devices have been developed that allow the monitoring of entire container contents without the containers having to be opened.

Questions

1. What are the advantages of the use of technology applications to the logistics areas of firms' operations?
2. What are intermodal shipments?
3. Have you seen any examples of stretch film wrappers in use?

The greater distances increase the logistics costs for international shipments. Whereas truck and rail shipments dominate domestic shipments, air and water are the most important for international shipments. Shipments by air account for only 1 percent of all international shipments, but represent 20 percent of their value. High-value perishable items and those that need to quickly reach customers, like cut flowers, personal computers, and emergency machine parts, are examples of goods that are usually transported on airplanes.

Companies beginning to market their products overseas are tempted to use the same logistics strategies in the international markets as employed in the domestic market. In so doing, they can begin operating quickly in foreign countries and can probably minimize their logistics costs. However, the differences encountered in overseas markets suggest that such a decision should be reached only after a great deal of thought.

Companies selling products overseas usually have to engage the services of a **freight forwarder.** Freight forwarders act as an agent for companies shipping products to international customers. They arrange for moving products to domestic ports or airports, negotiate with ships or airlines to transport products, expedite clearing

containerization The placement of products in trailer-sized containers that can be shipped by rail, air, ship, or truck

freight forwarder Agents that perform a wide variety of services for companies shipping products to international customers

Case in Point

McDonald's Good at Distribution—But Problems Elsewhere

Although Jim Cantalupo had retired as chairperson and CEO of McDonald's in 2001 after 26 years of service, he was reappointed to the top spot in December 2002. The main reason for his return was to help the company deal with a plague of recent problems.

McDonald's lost $344 million in the last quarter of 2002—the first time since its first year of operation, 1965, that it had suffered a loss. Its return on capital and revenue growth were declining. During 2002, same-store sales in the United States dropped every month; they had been stagnant for 10 years. On a measure of customer satisfaction developed by the University of Michigan, McDonald's brought up the rear in the fast-food industry and even ranked below airlines and the IRS. The company's value has dropped $20 billion; the stock fell to a ten-year low at $14; and its last new product success, Chicken McNuggets, was twenty years ago.

Unlike most fast-food firms, McDonald's emphasizes the real estate side of its operations. It owns the land and buildings of many of its franchise operations. Thus it collects rent, which accounts for about 10 percent of its annual revenues.

Anice Meyer, a restaurant sector analyst at Credit Suisse First Boston, has covered McDonald's for a decade. She believes that "McDonald's knows infrastructure. They are excellent at building supply lines and they are excellent at picking locations—building stores here and overseas. The system is flawless. Once they become penetrated and mature, however,

and they have some competition, they are not as good at generating sales gains per store. That is Wendy's territory." Increased fast-food competition, a lack of innovation, and poor marketing have been cited by other analysts as reasons for McDonald's declining performance.

In an effort to deal with McDonald's problems, Cantalupo has put into play a number of strategies.

- New products, such as the Grilled Chicken Flatbread and different salads with Newman's Own dressings, are offered.
- A system for grading the performance of all 13,000 U.S. restaurants will be introduced.
- The number of new store openings will be reduced.
- 700 underperforming stores will be closed.
- Getting more people into existing stores will be emphasized.
- Simplification of operations, eliminating some menu items, reducing the number of value meals, and paring the number of shelf-keeping units in the kitchens, will be employed in an effort to improve the level of customer service.

Source: Grainger David, "Can McDonald's Cook Again?" *Fortune*, April 14, 2003, pp. 120–129.

Questions

1. Do you agree with McDonald's decision to rehire Cantalupo?
2. Do you believe his recommended strategies will pay off?
3. What else should Cantalupo do?

---

customs in both the United States and the foreign country, negotiate storage arrangements, and most importantly, take care of all the confusing and time-consuming documentation (paperwork) needed to complete an international shipment.

Careers in Promotion

Advertising managers are responsible for their companies' advertising programs. They direct and coordinate the activities of the other advertising specialists, decide on the size of the advertising budget, choose the ads to be used and the media where they will appear, and select which advertising agency, if any, is to be used. Copywriters write the ads to be used. Artists and layout directors select photos, develop illustrations, and decide on the kind of type to be used for print ads. Production managers get the ad printed, filmed for television, or recorded for radio. Many advertising jobs are available in advertising agencies, which perform the advertising functions for their clients. Account executives generate business for the ad agency by identifying prospects, analyzing their advertising requirements, and developing a presentation as to how the ad agency proposes to carry out the advertising program for the client. Ad agency media directors negotiate contracts for advertising space (print media) and time (television or radio), negotiate the cost, and schedule the ads.

Salespeople call on prospects and existing customers and show how the company's or client's products or services can satisfy their needs and desires. If successful, these prospects and customers will purchase these products and services. Salespeople seek out new business, plan how they will spend their time, make their presentations, follow up with and service their customers, and fill out required reports.

Effective salespeople can easily earn $50,000 to $60,000 or more a year. Many are compensated through a combination of salary and bonus (commission). Starting salaries are around $30,000. Most sales personnel are given a car allowance, as well as funds for food and lodging when they travel to call on prospects and customers. The top spot in personal selling is the sales manager, the individual who is responsible for managing all the salespeople in a company. These individuals can earn well over $100,000 a year, plus bonus, depending on how well the sales force performs. If you like to be on your own and want to be well rewarded for your effort, selling may be the career for you.

Public relations (PR) personnel help their organizations build and maintain a favorable public image. The image of an organization has implications for its public acceptance, prosperity, even its continued existence. Manufacturing firms, insurance companies, government agencies, museums, colleges and universities, hospitals, and public utilities are all organizations that employ public relations personnel. In addition, public relations consulting firms and advertising agencies seek and use PR personnel.

Journalism, communications, and marketing are especially appropriate majors for PR careers. Some organizations, however, want a background in a technical field related to the organization's business. Some examples are biology, accounting, chemistry, and engineering. Public relations personnel need considerable communication skills, both verbal and written, and must be able to deal effectively with people. Some related experience is generally desired as well; writing or working for a local newspaper or television or radio station. Individuals in public relations need to have a good personality, self-confidence, and enthusiasm.

The demand for public relations personnel is expected to increase as fast as the national average for all occupations. Entry-level personnel were drawing an annual salary of around $25,000, with more experienced people earning about $42,500.

Careers in Distribution

The demand for young men and women in the retailing sector has traditionally been good and is expected to continue. Starting salaries are around $30,000 and the potential for rapid promotion and accompanying higher compensation, $50,000 to $60,000, is excellent.

Starting positions in department stores and discount chains are usually at the assistant buyer level. Most assistant buyers will be rotated through various departments, where they will check invoices on products received, keep stock records, and help supervise sales clerks. Buyers will purchase products for their departments, often by making buying trips to Dallas, New York, or San Francisco, even Milan or Paris. Merchandise managers supervise a number of buyers and are also responsible for merchandising. General merchandising managers are usually located at headquarters and supervise a number of merchandise managers. For supermarkets, discount stores, and drug stores, the store manager position is critical. Men and women holding these positions prepared for them by serving as assistant managers, following six months or so of training across a variety of departments. Store mangers are very well compensated, often earning in excess of $100,000 annually.

As firms continue to emphasize supply chain management, individuals with an interest and expertise in logistics will continue to be in demand. Specific positions available are in traffic management, customer service, cost analysis, warehousing, and inventory control. Entry-level positions usually involve starting as a supervisor of a loading or unloading dock. Opportunities can also be found with transportation carriers—railroads, trucking, airlines, water carriers, and pipelines—and in public warehousing. Two career paths exist. On the marketing side, specialists are responsible for selling the company's services to clients, like manufacturers or passengers in the cases of railroads and airlines. On the operations side, specialists are needed for scheduling, pricing, information gathering, deliveries, and inventory management.

Logistics personnel are needed by local, state, and federal governments. Transportation planning, economic analysis, research, urban studies, and accident investigation are some of the career paths available. Good opportunities in logistics are also available in the military. Starting salaries in logistics average about $30,000 to $35,000. The first tier of logistics managers earn about $65,000. Directors' salaries are about $90,000, and vice presidents of logistics' salaries often approach $150,000.

Summary

LEARNING OBJECTIVE 1
Explain the concept of integrated marketing promotion.

Integrated marketing promotion means that a company will consider the role of all relevant promotion alternatives when developing a promotion mix, employ those that provide the best opportunity for achieving the company's promotion objectives, and coordinate the activities required to put into motion the agreed-on promotion mix.

LEARNING OBJECTIVE 2
List ways to improve the effectiveness of trade shows.

Trade shows' effectiveness can be improved by companies' promoting their presence at trade shows before they are held; generating leads at trade shows for their products or services; qualifying these leads; following up on these qualified leads; making sure the merchandise to be displayed has arrived, sales literature has been received, and booth personnel know their assigned times and stations; establishing objectives that the trade show is to achieve; and determining if these objectives have been achieved.

LEARNING OBJECTIVE 3
Discuss the sales force's main responsibilities.

Sales personnel need knowledge about their company and its products, markets, and competitors. Their pre-presentation planning activities include prospecting, obtaining and planning the sales interview, and routing. When giving the sales presentation, they need to be able to handle objections and to close. Post-presentation activities include following up and servicing customers, doing paperwork, handling key and marginal accounts, managing their time, and evaluating their performance.

LEARNING OBJECTIVE 4

Discuss the ways in which sales personnel can conduct themselves ethically.

A code of ethics for the selling profession includes not misrepresenting their purpose, calling on prospects who can benefit by purchasing their product, not promising what the company can't deliver, not disparaging competitors' products, answering all questions truthfully, making sure customers are satisfied, handling all complaints and returns promptly and cheerfully, and observing all laws affecting selling.

LEARNING OBJECTIVE 5

Distinguish between the channels of distribution for consumer products and for industrial products.

Fifty percent of all consumer products move from manufacturers through wholesalers, then to retailers before reaching the consumer. Another 45 percent flow from manufacturers to retailers and then on to consumers. Five percent flow directly from manufacturers to consumers, bypassing wholesalers and retailers. Eighty percent of industrial products go directly from manufacturers to industrial buyers. The other 20 percent flow through wholesalers before reaching the industrial buyer.

LEARNING OBJECTIVE 6

Describe and give the advantages of using nonstore retailers in channels of distribution.

Automatic vending, direct marketing, and direct selling are the major types of nonstore retailing. Automatic vending provides consumers with convenient locations to purchase products. Direct marketing involves soliciting potential buyers to purchase a product or service and allowing them to do so in the comfort of their own homes or offices. Direct selling where salespeople call on customers in their homes or offices also allows customers to purchase from home or office. Convenience is a major advantage of nonstore retailers.

LEARNING OBJECTIVE 7

Explain the difference between materials management and physical distribution.

Materials management is the movement of raw materials, in-process materials, and semifinished goods to a manufacturer from a supplier. Physical distribution involves the flow of finished products from manufacturers to their customers.

LEARNING OBJECTIVE 8

Compare the advantages and disadvantages of the five modes of transportation.

Pipelines and water transportation possess the advantage of low cost. Rail can move a wide variety of industrial and consumer goods inexpensively. Truck transportation offers shippers speed and flexibility. Air transportation is the fastest but the most expensive.

Chapter Questions

1. Do you think it is ethical for communities to outlaw billboards because they can ruin the scenery along major roads?

2. What advantages exist for companies that choose to exhibit their products at trade shows?

3. What are the four major responsibilities for salespeople? Which do you believe is the most important? Why?

4. What is prospecting? Why is it important?

5. Do you believe it is all right for salespeople in the pharmaceutical industry to give doctors free samples of their products? Why or why not?

6. Improvement in productivity is mentioned as a benefit of CASP programs. How would sales force productivity be measured?

7. Do you agree with the code of ethics presented in the chapter for the selling profession? Are there any other ethical aspects that should be included?

8. Do you believe it is ethical for companies to have public relations departments whose major objective is to have the company and its personnel and products portrayed in a favorable light?

9. What are the major ways that publicity can contribute positively to a company's marketing effort?

10. Carefully distinguish between advertising and sales promotion. What factors explain the increased use of sales promotion by companies?

11. What are the factors that would encourage a company to use channels of distribution? Why, instead, would they prefer to go direct?

12. Discuss the contributions that brokers make to the U.S. economy.

13. Why do you think nonstore forms of retailing may be more important in some foreign countries than in the United States?

14. Identify the major difference between companies' materials management and physical distribution operations.

15. Distinguish between private warehouses and public warehouses. What are the advantages of each for companies that need to store their products?

16. Besides the opportunity to store their products, why are bonded warehouses used by companies?

17. What advantages do companies obtain from using freight forwarders for their international shipments?

Interpreting Business News

Some significant changes in the ways companies are allocating advertising dollars are discussed in an article written by Anthony Bianco, "The Vanishing Mass Market," *Business Week*, July 12, 2004, pp. 61–67. A major shift in marketing strategies and in the roles played by various media are causing the allocation shifts.

Firms are moving away from a mass-market strategy to a more targeted effort. That is, they are developing products and services and the accompanying promotional programs for specific segments of mass markets. Some firms are even narrowing the focus to individual customers. The media shifts include a significant increase in the importance of cable television channels, a decreasing audience share for the major networks (down 48%), a surge in the number of special interest consumer magazines, and the increasing importance of such advertising venues as telemarketing, direct mail, e-mail, in-store displays, and product placement.

The result of these changes is that many companies are spending less on advertising, increasing instead the level allocated to cable TV and the Internet, and less to network TV, and pumping more funds into in-store displays, telemarketing, direct mail, e-mail, and product placement.

1. Do you believe the trends indicated above justify the significant shifts in advertising expenditures? Why or why not?

2. What factors besides those indicated should companies have considered before deciding to shift their promotional dollars?

3. What is meant by product placement?

Fortune (April 14, 2003) carried an article about Gap, one of America's top clothing retailers, with 2002 revenues of $14.5 billion.

In the 1990s, this company started to experience problems. Per-store sales declined every month for 29 months. Profits dropped significantly, well below the $1 billion it took 30 years to reach. Debt jumped to $3.4 billion and was downgraded to junk status.

Paul Pressler, formerly the director of theme parks at Disney, was hired as Gap's new CEO. After visiting one of the company's distribution centers in Fishkill, New York, he and Old Navy's president, Jenny Ming, dropped in on the 34th and Broadway Gap and Old Navy stores at 11:00 P.M. While watching boxes of clothing arrive from the Fishkill distribution center, Pressler expressed concern that a lot of unopened boxes were left sitting around. Mr. Pressler asked the stores' night managers why they didn't move merchandise directly from trucks to the stores' sales floors. According to him, "Every product that is not sitting in front of the customer is a bad use of capital. Some people see boxes. I see dollar bills."

1. What major principles of logistics management are emphasized?

2. Will Mr. Pressler's background at Disney be helpful in forming logistics strategies for Gap?

Web Assignments

Go to the website of Sony. Study carefully any mention of this company's promotion and distribution mixes.

1. Notice to what extent Sony is dependent on advertising to generate revenues. Can you determine the percentage of revenues Sony devotes to advertising?

2. How reliant on sales promotion is Sony? What kind of sales promotion options does it appear to emphasize?

3. What kinds of channels of distribution are employed? What kinds of wholesalers does Sony use? Or, are its products distributed directly to retail stores? What types of retail stores carry Sony's products?

4. How important is logistics to Sony? Can you determine if Sony uses its own warehouses or public warehouses, or does it try to avoid having to carry inventory by moving products directly to retailers? Can you determine what percentage of Sony's revenues are accounted for by its logistics activities?

Portfolio Projects

Exploring Your Own Case in Point

This chapter discusses four aspects of the promotion mix: advertising, sales promotion, personal selling, and publicity. You were also introduced to channels of distribution and logistics, the two major components of a company's distribution mix. By answering the following questions, you will gain a better understanding about the promotion and distribution operations of your selected company.

1. What type of promotion does your company emphasize? Does it vary by product or service? Can you tell how much your selected company spends on promotion? Does the company reveal specific expenditures for advertising, sales promotion, personal selling, and publicity?

2. Does your company employ a specific public relations firm? If so, can you tell what it does for your company?

3. What channels of distribution does your company use? Do these channels appear to vary depending on the type of product or service?

4. What modes of transportation does your company use? Can you tell what the company's total logistics costs are?

Starting Your Own Business

This chapter provides information you need to know to effectively promote and distribute your products and services. Use the concepts contained in this chapter to deal with the following concerns.

1. Develop an overall promotion budget and a budget for each of the promotion options (advertising, sales promotion, personal selling, and publicity) you will be using. Decide how many promotional dollars should be allocated for each product or service.

2. Determine what advertising media you want to use. What major appeals will you use to promote your products or services?

3. Decide where you will store your inventory—at home or in a warehouse. How much inventory will you want to carry? How will you ship your products to your customers?

Test Prepper

You've read the chapter, studied the key terms, and the exam is any day now. Think you are ready to ace it? this sample test to gauge your comprehension of chapter material. You can check your answers at the back of the book.

True/False Questions

Please indicate if the following statements are true or false:

_____ 1. Personal selling is more important than advertising in promoting consumer products.

_____ 2. Cable television offers a better opportunity to target a selective audience than broadcast television.

_____ 3. More dollars are spent annually in the United States for advertising than are spent on sales promotion.

_____ 4. Contests are competitions for which prizes are awarded.

_____ 5. Trade shows are an important way to promote industrial products.

_____ 6. A salesperson has closed successfully when the prospect has decided to purchase.

_____ 7. Favorable publicity for a company is often effective because it is viewed as providing an objective, third-party endorsement.

_____ 8. A manufacturer-industrial buyer channel is an example of a distribution channel often used to market consumer products.

_____ 9. Materials management and logistics are components of physical distribution.

_____ 10. Air transportation is the fastest mode of transportation and is also the most expensive.

Multiple-Choice Questions

Choose the best answer.

_____ 1. Which of the following is the most important reason for companies to promote their products or services?

    a. To generate revenues
    b. To make customers aware of their new products
    c. To encourage repeat purchases
    d. To retain customers
    e. To get customers to try new products

_____ 2. The type of advertising that allows a company the best opportunity to selectively reach a target market is

    a. newspapers.
    b. radio.
    c. direct mail.
    d. broadcast television.
    e. magazines.

_____ 3. Certificates that allow customers to receive a cash refund or a free product at the time of purchase are

    a. displays.
    b. in-packs.
    c. sponsorships.
    d. coupons.
    e. POP.

_____ 4. The cost of contacting a prospect at a trade show is which fraction of the cost of a sales call?

    a. 1/8
    b. 1/4
    c. 1/3
    d. 1/2
    e. 2/3

_____ 5. Which of the following is *not* one of the four major responsibilities for salespeople?

    a. Acquiring necessary information
    b. Prepresentation planning
    c. Giving the sales presentation
    d. Prospecting
    e. Postpurchase activities

_____ 6. A manufacturer is using agents to sell their products. The agents receive a 12 percent commission. If the manufacturer invested $200,000 in developing a sales force and incurred expenses of 8 percent of sales in maintaining the sales force, at what level of revenues would the cost of using agents and going direct be equal?

    a. $1 million
    b. $2 million
    c. $3 million
    d. $4 million
    e. $5 million

_____ 7. Which of the following is *not* considered to be a type of nonstore retailing?

    a. Direct selling
    b. Catalog marketing

c. Direct-response marketing
d. Automatic vending
e. Manufacturers' agents

_____ 8. Which of the following is *not* a mode of transportation?

a. Pipeline
b. Water
c. Rail
d. Air
e. Public warehouse

_____ 9. Which of the following is *least* likely to be an advantage of using public warehouses?

a. An investment in land and construction is not necessary.
b. There is flexibility in being able to choose in which facility to store products.
c. Public warehouses provide users with a wide variety of services.

d. There is little risk that public warehouses will become obsolete.
e. Much control over the operational aspect of storage is obtained.

_____ 10. Which of the following is the most important reason why companies would want to store their products in a bonded warehouse?

a. A reduction in the level of inventory can be achieved.
b. The inventory stored can be used to obtain financing.
c. The user achieves a high level of flexibility.
d. Inventory can be quickly shifted to another location.
e. The user can take advantage of the automated materials handling equipment provided by the bonded warehouse.

Want more questions? Visit the student website at **http://college.hmco.com/business/student/** (select Gaspar, *Introduction to Business*) and take the ACE quizzes for more practice.

Accounting

CHAPTER 11
Accounting for Decision Making

CHAPTER 12
Financial Reporting

PART FOUR

How do investors decide what companies are the better investments? How do bankers decide whether to lend money to a loan applicant? How do managers within a company keep track of operations and determine if profits are going up or down? The answer to all three questions is accounting information. Accounting is the language of business. Accounting is the recording, summarizing, and reporting of the economic activities and events of an organization.

Accounting generates information used by people outside and inside the firm to make important decisions. Outside the firm, financial statements are used by investors and lending institutions to make investment and loan decisions, respectively. Within the firm, the accounting information system contributes to developing a sound organizational structure, ensuring that employees are held responsible for their actions, and to maintaining cost-effective business operations. Chapter 11 provides an overview of the accounting information system, the importance of internal controls, and some accounting career options.

Chapter 12 focuses on the purpose of financial reporting. Accounting will determine whether the revenues of a firm exceed its expenses, thus resulting in a profit. Alternatively, accounting will determine whether expenses exceed revenues, thus resulting in a loss. The most important output of the accounting information system is the set of financial statements. They include the income statement, statement of retained earnings, balance sheet, and statement of cash flows. Together, the four financial statements represent a business firm in financial terms. These statements provide information that people need to make effective business decisions.

11

Accounting for Decision Making

| Introduction

Accounting Information System

Management Accounting

Financial Accounting and External Users of Accounting Information

Accounting Literature: Generally Accepted Accounting Principles

Information Role of the Accounting Information System Within the Management Information System

Accounting for International Trade

International Information Flow

International Accounting Standards Board

International Financial Reporting Standards

International Auditing and Assurance Standards Board

International Standards on Auditing

Importance of Ethical Accounting Practices

Can Ethics Be Taught?

Role of Professional Organizations

| **Computer Crime**

| **Internal Control**

Types of Controls

Role of the Auditor

Foreign Corrupt Practices Act

Computer Security of Accounting Information

Computer Contingency Planning for Accounting Information

| **Careers in Accounting**

Learning Objectives

After studying this chapter, you should be able to

1. Explain the function of the accounting information system.

2. Describe how the AIS fits within the management information system.

3. Briefly recount accounting issues associated with international business, such as the importance of International Accounting Standards and International Standards on Auditing.

4. Discuss the importance of ethical accounting practices.

5. List a few examples of computer crime.

6. Explain the importance of internal controls.

Is It Possible to Stop Cyber Crime?

Companies lose billions of dollars each year as a result of cyber crimes, also referred to as electronic crimes or e-crimes. *Cyber* is short for cyberspace, the electronic medium of computer networks in which online communication takes place. There are numerous news stories regarding electronic crimes and the related costs to companies. Although control techniques and other security policies and procedures are critical to the deterrence of electronic crimes, detection and resolution of successful or attempted electronic crimes are also of critical importance. Not only the cost, but also the embarrassment of such crimes is something that all companies wish to avoid.

A well-designed accounting system can enhance a firm's abilities to detect and resolve electronic crimes. Is it possible to stop all criminal activity with controls and security techniques? No, even the best internal control system cannot be expected to stop every type of criminal activity. Even if a system was perfectly designed, it must still be operated by fallible human beings. For example, passwords may be set up to prevent unauthorized access to the system. Unfortunately, some employees have been known to sticky-note their passwords to their monitors, so that they don't forget their passwords. While this helps overcome forgetfulness, it also provides an easy way for an unauthorized person to gain access to the system.

Introduction

Accounting is the language of business. **Accounting** is the recording, summarizing, and reporting of the economic activities and events of an organization. Accounting generates information used by people inside and outside the firm to make important decisions. For example, a financial institution like a bank may use accounting information to decide whether to lend money to a loan applicant. The lending institution—an external user—must predict whether the applicant can pay back the loan; this decision depends on reliable accounting information contained in financial reports. Within the firm, business managers use accounting information to make decisions that contribute to the success of the firm. For business managers, timely and accurate accounting information is essential for managing and controlling company operations. The accounting information system contributes to developing a sound organizational structure, to ensuring that employees are held responsible for their actions, and to maintaining cost effective business operations.

> **accounting** The recording, summarizing, and reporting of the economic activities and events of an organization

Accounting Information System

LEARNING OBJECTIVE 1
Explain the function of the accounting information system.

The **accounting information system (AIS),** like all systems, has specific objectives, inputs, processes, outputs, and controls. A typical AIS has two principal objectives: to provide all the financial information needed internally by management for business decision making and to provide financial information to various external users concerned with the financial activities of the organization.

> **accounting information system (AIS)** A business system that provides all the financial information needed to internal management for their business decision making and to external users who are concerned with the financial activities of the organization

Management Accounting

management accounting
The component of the accounting information system that provides the financial information needed internally by business managers for efficient and effective decision making

The component of the accounting information system that provides information to management is referred to as **management accounting.** Management accounting is strictly concerned with the information needs of management, the only internal user of accounting information. Although internal information requirements may vary substantially between organizations, management accounting in most business firms includes similar kinds of financial analysis—for example, cost-volume-profit analysis, capital budgeting, and inventory planning. Specific steps in performing these types of analyses are virtually standardized. Additionally, most business firms use similar types of internal documents and reports, such as sales invoices, purchase orders, receiving reports, and budgets. There are widely accepted guidelines on how these internal documents and reports should be prepared.

Like other areas of business, technological innovation has had a profound effect on how management accounting tasks are performed. For example, specialized software is available to assist management accountants in performing many of the different types of financial analysis. Specialized hardware devices such as bar code readers may be used to help keep track of inventory. Telecommunications systems allow purchase orders to be placed electronically. Despite these technological advances, standard costing and variance analysis are done in much the same way today as they were in decades past. Of course, computers have reduced the time required to do such tasks. The competitive nature of the marketplace drives all functions within a business firm, including accounting, to become more efficient and productive. Using the latest technology is an essential ingredient for successful business operations, including accounting.

Financial Accounting and External Users of Accounting Information

financial accounting The component of the accounting information system that provides financial information needed by external users such as investors and lenders

The component of the accounting information system that supplies information to external users is **financial accounting.** External users of accounting information

In preparation for the holiday sales just prior to Easter Sunday, a worker in a field harvests buttercup blossoms to be added to the flowers inventory.

can be categorized into two major groups: organizations that require or expect information to be reported and organizations that receive information on an as-needed basis.

The first group includes organizations that require information to be reported to them. Federal, state, and local government agencies require business firms to report specific types of information, usually on a regular basis. The Social Security Administration, for example, requires regular reporting of payroll information, including the amount of social security taxes withheld from the employees and matched by the employer. The Internal Revenue Service (IRS) requires the filing of an annual tax return as well as the submission of other financial information, like federal income tax withholdings from employees' pay, throughout the year. The government requires publicly traded corporations to provide annual financial statements to stockholders. This information is filed with the Securities and Exchange Commission (SEC) on Form 10-K. The same financial statements are widely used by other external users for a variety of purposes.

In addition to government units that require certain information to be reported, numerous other external users of accounting information may not require but may expect certain information to be provided to them. For example, a business firm may wish to borrow money from a financial institution so that the firm can expand operations. The financial institution will probably ask the firm to provide certain financial information, typically the most recent financial statements. If the firm is publicly traded, then the statements are already prepared for stockholder use. The financial statements will enable the lender to assess the borrowing firm's ability to meet its financial obligations, specifically the ability to pay back the loan. Naturally, the lender will likely assess other factors as well, such as management's competence and general economic conditions. However, the financial statements, or information derived from them, may be the most important factor in the lender's loan decision. Other external groups that use accounting information include credit-rating agencies, suppliers, employees, and customers. Exhibit 11.1 (on p. 382) lists external users and the type of information with which they are typically concerned.

In many cases external accounting information is prepared in a specific format. For example, the IRS requires tax-related information to be prepared on specific IRS forms and according to specific procedures.

Accounting Literature: Generally Accepted Accounting Principles

The financial statements of publicly traded companies must be prepared according to **generally accepted accounting principles (GAAP).** GAAP are the guidelines by which financial statements are prepared and are primarily developed by the Financial Accounting Standards Board (FASB).

The FASB issues **Statements of Financial Accounting Standards (SFAS),** which provide the procedures for dealing with specific accounting problems. Guidance for treating accounting problems is provided in a number of places. Exhibit 11.2 (on p. 382) lists the primary sources of authoritative accounting literature.

Determining the appropriate accounting treatment for a particular transaction or event is sometimes a complex process requiring careful research. This research process is carried out by the accounting information system. GAAP is constantly evolving. Consequently, financial accountants in the AIS must be careful to stay abreast of current developments.

There are basically three fields of work for accountants: in the AIS of a business firm, in a public accounting firm, or in the AIS of a government entity or other

generally accepted accounting principles (GAAP) The principles by which financial statements are prepared

Statements of Financial Accounting Standards (SFAS) Statements issued by the Financial Accounting Standards Board that are part of the highest level of generally accepted accounting principles

EXHIBIT 11.1

External Users of Accounting Information

External User	Information Required or Expected
Government units	The IRS, for example, requires an annual tax return.
Lenders	Financial statement information, specifically information concerning the firm's ability to meet financial obligations.
Suppliers	Financial statement information, specifically information regarding ability to pay back purchases made on credit. Also, the supplier will receive financial documents from the firm.
Credit-rating agencies	Similar to information required by lenders and vendors. Lenders and suppliers often purchase the credit-worthiness assessments made by credit-rating agencies.
Investors	Financial statements as well as personal information regarding stock and dividend transactions.
Customers	Billing statements, sales invoices, amounts owed, account status, date due, and product information.
Employees	Individuals expect payment of wages and specific payroll information, such as payroll deductions for social security, insurance, etc. Employee groups, such as labor unions, may want aggregate information such as profits, payroll expenses, and pension funding and liability.

EXHIBIT 11.2

Authoritative Accounting Literature

Highest Level of Accounting Authority
Nonsuperseded sections of the Accounting Research Bulletins issued by Committee on Accounting Procedures
Nonsuperseded sections of the APB Opinions issued by the Accounting Principles Board
Statements of Financial Accounting Standards issued by the FASB
Interpretations issued by the FASB
Statements and Interpretations of the Governmental Accounting Standards Board for government units

Next Level of Accounting Authority
AICPA Industry Accounting Guides
AICPA Statements of Position
FASB and GASB technical bulletins
Industry accounting practices
AICPA Accounting Interpretations

Lower Level of Accounting Authority
Guidelines published by SEC and other regulatory agencies
FASB and GASB Concept Statements
APB Statements
AICPA Issues Papers
Minutes of the FASB Emerging Issues Task Force
Other professional association statements
Accounting textbooks, reference books, and articles written by recognized authorities in the field

not-for-profit organization. Most of the examples in this book are oriented toward the AIS of a business firm; however, the concepts are applicable to any type of organization. Accountants who work in the public accounting field are licensed by the state or states in which they work. The license is designated Certified Public Accountant (CPA). The licensing requirements include passing a rigorous exam and acquiring a certain amount of work experience. Accountants in industry, government, or public accounting may attain the CPA designation; however, public accounting is the field most closely associated with CPAs because it is a professional requirement. Other notable professional designations are the CMA, Certified Management Accountant; CIA, Certified Internal Auditor; and CFE, Certified Fraud Examiner.

CPAs in public accounting, like the financial accountants who work in a firm's AIS, pay close attention to developments in GAAP. Public accountants are called *external* or *independent accountants* because they are not employees of the business firm but independent contractors hired to provide specialized services, such as auditing, taxation, and consulting services, to the business firm. When CPAs provide audit services, they render an opinion as to whether the financial statements prepared by a firm's financial accountants are done according to GAAP.

reality CHECK *When have you been the recipient of information from an AIS?*

Information Role of the Accounting Information System Within the Management Information System

LEARNING OBJECTIVE 2
Describe how the AIS fits within the management information system.

The AIS provides the financial information needed internally by management and externally by users such as government agencies and stockholders. However, not all information needed by management or external users is financial. For example, a manufacturing company's management may plan to introduce a new product, but should first do marketing research to determine whether consumers will wish to purchase the new product. Tastes and preferences of consumers are essential pieces of information that the marketing system must obtain for management's decision-making purposes. Thus, while the AIS provides crucial information, it does not provide all the information needed by management.

The **management information system (MIS)** provides all the information, financial and nonfinancial, needed by management for its decision-making purposes. Therefore, the MIS can be thought of as a collection of all the organization's information sources. These information sources are based on functional areas; that is, the AIS is concerned with financial information, the marketing system is concerned with marketing-related information, and so forth. An example of MIS composition is illustrated in Exhibit 11.3 (on p. 384).

Each of the MIS components generates specific types of information. For example, marketing provides information associated with marketing research, customer relations, sales, product development, advertising, distribution, and public relations. Human resources provides information associated with recruiting, job descriptions, employee retention, and training and development.

Another key role of the AIS is to provide financial services to the other functional systems. Services of the AIS include financial record keeping and various types of financial analysis. For example, the AIS receives sales information, typically on sales invoices, from marketing and then records the sales amounts, maintains customer accounts, bills customers, tracks inventory movement, and provides related

management information system (MIS)
A business system that provides all the information, financial and nonfinancial, needed by management for decision making

EXHIBIT 11.3

Components of the Management Information System

reports, such as aging of accounts receivable and sales analyses, by product, by customer, or by salesperson. In the case of the personnel system, the AIS handles a number of critical record-keeping chores. The AIS maintains the payroll files, which include information on employee pay rates, federal income tax withholding rates, social security tax, and other deductions. The AIS processes the paychecks that are ultimately distributed by the other departments.

reality CHECK *In your most recent job, what interactions did you have with accounting information and how did that affect your job?*

Accounting for International Trade

LEARNING OBJECTIVE 3
Briefly recount accounting issues associated with international business, such as the importance of International Accounting Standards and International Standards on Auditing.

As far back as recorded history, peoples of the world have been engaged in global commerce. For as long as international trade has occurred, accounting has been necessary to record and report the results. International operations are increasingly important to all types of business firms. Many multinational firms are either expanding international operations or becoming part of other multinational firms via mergers or acquisitions. As a result, more firms than ever before are providing products and services to customers around the globe.

Peculiarities of international trade have periodically led to specialized accounting treatment. For example, during the seventeenth century, in Elizabethan England, expanding overseas business opportunities led to a new type of corporate entity. Merchants faced various difficulties, including pirates; long, dangerous journeys to transport goods; and frequent hostilities between trading nations. Consequently, trade was an expensive undertaking, filled with risk. In order to benefit from the business opportunities, merchants joined together to share the risks and increase productivity.

East India Company The first joint-stock company, which was given its charter by Queen Elizabeth in 1600 and achieved fame for engaging in international trade in the early days of the British Empire

In 1600 the first joint-stock company, the **East India Company,** was given its charter by Queen Elizabeth. The charter provided the legal right to be one corporate body to about 220 "adventurers." The charter also provided for corporate succession with power to admit and expel members; to receive, hold and grant property; to sue and be sued in the corporate name; and to use a common seal. Funds were collected from a broad array of investors, including earls, dukes, merchants, and tradespeople. Management directed business operations and ensured that shareholders received their portion of the profits.

East India Company transactions led to awkward reporting problems. The accountants and auditors of that time period complained of the difficulty in keeping accounts up-to-date. The most difficult accounting problem resulted when operations of several voyages overlapped in the same time period. Much to its own confusion and embarrassment, the firm was unable to segregate the accounting for the activities of individual trading voyages.

Business firms today are unlikely to need armed ships to fight off pirates, but international trade still has its problems, such as tariffs, language barriers, cultural differences, and incompatible equipment standards. The accounting information system provides crucial information to management for evaluating the viability of a firm's international operations. Additionally, the AIS provides information to external entities concerned with the firm's international activities.

International Information Flow

Multinational firms have no choice but to comply with the rules and regulations of the countries in which they operate. Furthermore, multinational firms must take into account the international organizations that define and restrict the flow of information, including accounting information, between nations. Several major organizations are shown in Exhibit 11.4.

International Accounting Standards Board

The **International Accounting Standards Board (IASB)** issues **International Financial Reporting Standards (IFRS),** which build on **International Accounting Standards (IAS).** The current structure and organization of the International Accounting Standards Board came about as a result of a strategy review undertaken by its predecessor body, the Board of the International Accounting Standards Committee. IASB publishes its standards in a series of pronouncements called International Financial Reporting Standards. The IASB has also adopted the body of standards issued by the Board of the International Accounting Standards Committee. Those pronouncements continue to be designated International Accounting Standards.

International Accounting Standards Board (IASB) A London-based organization that issues International Accounting Standards

International Financial Reporting Standards (IFRS) Accounting standards issued by the International Accounting Standards Board that have three goals: Increasing harmonization of accounting standards and disclosures to meet the needs of the global market; providing an accounting basis for underdeveloped or newly industrialized countries to follow as the accounting profession emerges in those countries; and increasing the compatibility of domestic and international accounting requirements

International Accounting Standards (IAS) Accounting standards issued by the Board of the International Accounting Standards Committee, and subsequently adopted by the International Accounting Standards Board

EXHIBIT 11.4

International Organizations Concerned with Transborder Data Flow

Council of Europe (COE)	Chiefly concerned with protection of personal privacy. Composed of 21 western European countries and based in Strasbourg, France.
Organization for Economic Cooperation and Development (OECD)	Set up guidelines to facilitate unrestricted transborder data flow among countries that maintain appropriate domestic privacy legislation, while warning member countries of the potential for imposed sanctions if their privacy laws are inadequate. Composed of 19 western European countries plus Australia, Canada, Japan, the United States, and New Zealand.
Intergovernmental Bureau of Information (IBI)	Assists member countries in acquiring benefits from transborder data flow technology. Considered an importers' advocate. Membership in the IBI is less than 40 countries, which are primarily from the Middle East, Latin America, Africa, and Europe. Based in Rome.
International Telecommunications Union (ITU)	Mandate includes assistance for third-world countries that are establishing and maintaining communications networks. Part of the United Nations. Includes over 160 countries.
United Nations Educational, Scientific, and Cultural Organization (UNESCO)	Originally founded to establish a global bibliographic system to facilitate exchange of information. Emphasis changed to restrictions on information flow; consequently, the United Kingdom and the United States withdrew from UNESCO.

The IASB is an independent, privately funded accounting standard-setter based in London. Board members come from nine countries and have a variety of functional backgrounds. The Board is committed to developing, in the public interest, a single set of high-quality, understandable, and enforceable global accounting standards that require transparent and comparable information in general purpose financial statements. In addition, the Board cooperates with national accounting standard-setters to achieve convergence in accounting standards around the world. The IASB represents over 100 worldwide accounting and financial organizations, from over 80 counties. Most projects require a minimum of three years from formation to standard issuance. Each IASB member has one vote on technical and other matters. The publication of a Standard, Exposure Draft, or final SIC Interpretation requires approval by 8 of the board's 14 members.

International Financial Reporting Standards

The objectives of international standards include

- Increasing harmonization of accounting standards and disclosures to meet the needs of the global market
- Providing an accounting basis for developing or newly industrialized countries to follow as the accounting profession emerges in those countries
- Increasing the compatibility of domestic and international accounting requirements

The rapid growth in international capital markets and cross-border mergers and acquisitions, as well as other international developments, has created pressures for harmonization of accounting standards beyond those contemplated at the formation of IASB. Arthur Wyatt, chairperson of the IASB, indicated that harmonization is no longer merely a philosophical notion about which to argue but rather is essential to global trade and commerce.

The goal of the IASB is to formulate and publish standards to be observed in the presentation of audited financial statements and to promote their worldwide acceptance and observance, that is, to achieve internationally recognized or harmonized standards of accounting and reporting. These standards are designed to reflect the needs of the professional and business communities throughout the world.

International standards have been created in broad terms. The standards are not definitive or detailed enough to cause problems in the application of accounting practice in the United States, given the level of detail and specificity to which the United States has become accustomed. The international standards encompass the most frequently encountered business transactions. Accounting issues such as joint ventures, inventory, and depreciation are addressed in the standards. A partial list of international accounting standards is provided in Exhibit 11.5.

Each country's accounting rules and regulations are a result of the cultural, economic, political, and legal systems of that country. These four factors have the potential to restrict economic development and international trade. The acceptance and implementation of international accounting standards has been impeded by these cultural and ethnic differences. The IASB seeks to resolve these differences in a manner that benefits everyone.

The international standards often provide two or more options for the selection of accounting methods. The number and variety of accounting choices were reviewed and reduced under a project titled "The Comparability and Improvements Project." This program was designed to revise current international accounting standards to permit fewer alternative accounting treatments for the same

EXHIBIT 11.5

Selected International Accounting Standards

IAS 1	Presentation of Financial Statements
IAS 2	Inventories
IAS 7	Cash Flow Statements
IAS 8	Net Profit or Loss for the Period, Fundamental Errors, and Changes in Accounting Policies
IAS 10	Events After the Balance Sheet Date
IAS 11	Construction Contracts
IAS 12	Income Taxes
IAS 14	Segment Reporting
IAS 15	Information Reflecting the Effects of Changing Prices
IAS 16	Property, Plant, and Equipment
IAS 17	Leases
IAS 18	Revenue
IAS 19	Employee Benefits
IAS 20	Accounting for Government Grants and Disclosure of Government Assistance
IAS 21	The Effects of Changes in Foreign Exchange Rates
IAS 22	Business Combinations
IAS 23	Borrowing Costs
IAS 24	Related Party Disclosures
IAS 26	Accounting and Reporting by Retirement Benefit Plans
IAS 27	Consolidated Financial Statements
IAS 28	Investments in Associates
IAS 29	Financial Reporting in Hyperinflationary Economies
IAS 30	Disclosures in the Financial Statements of Banks and Similar Financial Institutions
IAS 31	Financial Reporting of Interests in Joint Ventures
IAS 32	Financial Instruments: Disclosure and Presentation
IAS 33	Earnings per Share
IAS 34	Interim Financial Reporting
IAS 35	Discontinuing Operations
IAS 36	Impairment of Assets
IAS 37	Provisions, Contingent Liabilities, and Contingent Assets
IAS 38	Intangible Assets
IAS 39	Financial Instruments: Recognition and Measurement
IAS 40	Investment Property
IAS 41	Agriculture

transaction. The revised standards provide better implementation guidelines, resulting in more uniform interpretation by accountants, auditors, and standards-setting boards across the globe. Starting in 2005, the European Union requires International Financial Reporting Standards in the consolidated financial statements of virtually all publicly traded companies. IFRS are becoming more visible in the United States, which may have much to gain from the acceptance of these standards. Currently, foreign companies wishing to sell securities in the United States must reconcile their financial statements to United States generally accepted accounting principles, thereby increasing the costs of raising capital in the United States. The use of international standards may be the most cost-efficient and cost-effective method of utilizing international capital markets. At this time, however, the Securities Exchange Commission requires that financial statements either be based on U.S. GAAP or be reconciled to U.S. GAAP. This requirement has been unacceptable to some business firms. For example, until 1994, there were no German-based firms listed on any U.S. stock exchange because they had been unwilling to comply with U.S. accounting standards.

Many U.S. companies are already in compliance with international standards. For many accounting issues there is no significant difference between U.S. GAAP and IFRS. Where significant differences exist, the IASB is working with the Financial Accounting Standards Board and the Government Accounting Standards Board to reconcile differences and move toward harmonization.

The international standards are gaining increased acceptance, with over 40 countries permitting or requiring use of IFRS. Additionally, many developing countries that have insufficient resources to develop domestic standards may choose to adopt the international standards, and thus facilitate their national economic progress.

Worldwide acceptance of the IFRS will ultimately be determined by the International Organization of Securities Commissions (IOSCO) and the individual securities commissions that make up the IOSCO. Over 60 securities regulatory agencies worldwide, including the SEC, are members of IOSCO. A major objective of IOSCO is to facilitate cross-border securities offerings and multiple listings without compromising the financial statement information provided.

International Auditing and Assurance Standards Board

International Auditing and Assurance Standards Board (IAASB) The board that works to improve the uniformity of auditing practices and related services throughout the world by issuing pronouncements on a variety of audit and assurance functions and by promoting their acceptance worldwide

International Federation of Accountants (IFAC) An organization of national professional accountancy organizations that represent accountants employed in public practice, business and industry, the public sector, and education, as well as some specialized groups that interface frequently with the profession

International standards on auditing are issued by the **International Auditing and Assurance Standards Board (IAASB),** a committee of the International Federation of Accountants. The IAASB, previously called the International Audit Practices Committee, works to improve the uniformity of auditing practices and related services throughout the world by issuing pronouncements on a variety of audit and assurance functions and by promoting their acceptance worldwide.

The **International Federation of Accountants (IFAC)** was established in 1977. IFAC is an organization of national professional accountancy organizations that represent accountants employed in public practice, business and industry, the public sector, and education, as well as some specialized groups that interface frequently with the profession. Currently, it has 156 member bodies in 114 countries, representing 2 million accountants. The IFAC's structure and operations provide for representation of its diverse member organizations. The IFAC strives to develop the profession and harmonize its standards worldwide to enable accountants to provide services of consistently high quality in the public interest.

The IAASB's mission is to foster internationally recognized standards of auditing. The major objective of these standards is the development of uniform auditing practices and procedures across countries. However, the implementation of or adherence to the international standards is left up to standard-setters in individual countries; the IAASB has no enforcement mechanism of its own.

International Standards on Auditing

International Standards on Auditing (ISAs) The basic principles and essential procedures for auditing, along with related guidance in the form of explanatory and other material

International Standards on Auditing (ISAs) contain basic principles and essential procedures for auditing, along with related guidance in the form of explanatory and other material. The basic principles and essential procedures are to be interpreted in the context of the explanatory and other material that provide guidance in their application. ISAs cannot override national regulations or pronouncements governing the audit of financial information in a particular country. In the United States, compliance with domestic auditing standards usually results in compliance with the international standards. Where significant differences exist between U.S. and international standards, the U.S. standards-setters will give consideration to the differences with a purpose of achieving harmonization. Exhibit 11.6 lists the International Standards on Auditing.

EXHIBIT 11.6

International Standards on Auditing

100	Assurance Engagements
120	Framework of International Standards on Auditing
200	Objective and General Principles Governing an Audit of Financial Statements
210	Terms of Audit Engagements
220	Quality Control for Audit Work
230	Documentation
240	The Auditor's Responsibility to Consider Fraud and Error in an Audit of Financial Statements
240A	Fraud and Error
250	Consideration of Laws and Regulations in an Audit of Financial Statements
260	Communications of Audit Matters with Those Charged with Governance
300	Planning
310	Knowledge of the Business
320	Audit Materiality
400	Risk Assessments and Internal Control
401	Auditing in a Computer Information Systems Environment
402	Audit Considerations Relating to Entities Using Service Organizations
500	Audit Evidence
501	Audit Evidence—Additional Considerations for Specific Items
505	External Confirmations
510	Initial Engagements—Opening Balances
520	Analytical Procedures
530	Audit Sampling and Other Selective Testing Procedures
540	Audit of Accounting Estimates
545	Auditing Fair Value Measurements and Disclosures
550	Related Parties
560	Subsequent Events
570	Going Concern
580	Management Representations
600	Using the Work of Another Auditor
610	Considering the Work of Internal Auditing
620	Using the Work of an Expert
700	The Auditor's Report on Financial Statements
710	Comparatives
720	Other Information in Documents Containing Audited Financial Statements
800	The Auditor's Report on Special Purpose Audit Engagements
810	The Examination of Prospective Financial Information
910	Engagements to Review Financial Statements
920	Engagements to Perform Agreed-Upon Procedures Regarding Financial Information
930	Engagements to Compile Financial Information

Effective and efficient functioning of the global marketplace requires uniformity in accounting and auditing standards. At this time, businesspeople, financiers, and investors must take into consideration the differences that exist. Such differences substantially curtail the development of international business activity. Harmonization of standards has the potential of benefiting economic activity around the globe.

reality CHECK　　*How do people around the world benefit from international accounting standards?*

Importance of Ethical Accounting Practices

LEARNING OBJECTIVE 4
Discuss the importance of ethical accounting practices.

Ethical accounting practices are a key component of a country's economy. In general, ethical behavior is necessary to build trust. Trust is an essential ingredient for economic activity to occur. Without trust that a product will work, who would buy it? Without trust that an employer will pay employees for their work, who would go to work? Without trust that the accounting information in financial statements is reliable, who would invest in a company's stock? Without trust that the accounting information in financial statements is reliable, who would loan money to a company?

If accountants fail to do their jobs in an ethical manner, then investors are negatively affected. How can investors make sound investment decisions if accounting information in company financial statements is unreliable? Without reliable accounting information, determining the value of a company's stock is virtually impossible. This was a major reason that the stock market declined in 2001 and 2002. Investor confidence was shaken by corporate scandals and questionable accounting practices at firms such as Enron, Global Crossing, and WorldCom. Investors were uncertain as to how reliable any company's financial statements were.

In the case of Enron, the company created limited partnerships allegedly for the purpose of reducing liabilities. In this way, the company was able to shift assets and boost profits, at least in the short run. Many people were given a false impression of the company's financial situation. Using accounting information to mislead people is a violation of generally accepted accounting principles. Ultimately, the courts were called on to decide the guilt or innocence of persons charged with fraud and other crimes. Former CEO of Enron Jeffrey Skilling became a defendant in a lawsuit alleging he knowingly endorsed deceptive and misleading financial statements. In February 2004, the former CEO was indicted on 35 counts of fraud, conspiracy, filing false statements to auditors, and insider trading.

To help restore investor confidence after Enron and other financial scandals, the U.S. Congress passed the Sarbanes-Oxley Act in July 2002. The new law increased prison sentences for fraud and established the Public Company Accounting Oversight Board to oversee auditors of

Enron employees move out personal items after the energy company declared bankruptcy.

publicly traded companies. Ultimately, however, laws and regulations are insufficient to fully restore public confidence. Public confidence can only be restored and maintained by trust in the people involved. In this case, that would be the accountants and businesspeople who provide financial reports to the public. For this reason, ethical accounting practices are of paramount importance to a nation's economic success.

Investors are not the only people hurt by unreliable accounting information. Lending institutions such as banks base loan decisions on the financial reports provided by accountants. If the information is unreliable, then loans are made under false pretenses. Consequently, the loan may not be repaid. This hurts not only the lender but also all other borrowers. The interest charged on all loans must be increased to compensate for the loans that are not repaid. Companies that borrow money must pass along these higher costs by increasing prices charged to their customers.

When unreliable accounting information results in corporate failures and reorganizations, many employees lose their jobs. When Enron began shutting down its offices, many employees lost not only their jobs but also their savings for retirement. In addition, Enron was a very large company that purchased products and services from many other companies. These suppliers lost an important customer.

The bottom line is that ethical accounting practices are essential to countless people, including investors, lenders, employees, suppliers, and customers. In the history of the world, the United States is unique. Compared to people in other countries, Americans enjoy more freedom, more wealth that is more evenly distributed, and more opportunity. The accounting profession has played a key role in the United States' success story. The accounting profession has made essential contributions to efficient operations of business firms, to the functioning of the capital market system, and to the growth of the economy in general. All this depends on accountants doing their job according to the highest standards of ethics and personal integrity.

Ethics in accounting and business directs businesspeople to abide by a code of conduct that facilitates and encourages public confidence in their products and services. Many companies have an ethics code to guide their employees in how they conduct business. In addition, business and accounting organizations, such as the Institute of Internal Auditors (IIA), the American Institute of CPAs (AICPA), and the Institute of Management Accountants (IMA), recognize their professional responsibility by providing ethical guidelines to their members.

In a speech to the Yale Club in New York City, AICPA president Barry Melanchon stated that the accounting profession must take care of its most priceless asset, its reputation. He said that the profession's leadership must act to preserve a legacy of honor and integrity for future generations of CPAs. The profession must build on its traditional values such as a rigorous commitment to integrity.[1]

Article III in the Principles of the AICPA Code of Professional Conduct states: "To maintain and broaden confidence, members should perform all professional responsibilities with the highest sense of integrity. . . . Integrity is an element of character fundamental to professional recognition. It is the quality from which public trust derives and the benchmark against which a member must ultimately test all decisions."[2] The accounting professional must be skilled at implementing moral judgments so that he or she can consider the welfare of those affected by his or her actions.

In an issue of *Strategic Finance,* the journal of the Institute of Management Accountants, James Brackner, a member of the Institute's Committee on Ethics, stated:

Case in Point

McDonald's Works to Improve Health

After considering health concerns regarding cooking oil, McDonald's indicated that it would remove about 48 percent of trans fatty acids (TFAs) from most fried foods as part of its worldwide movement to get rid of TFAs in cooking oil. McDonald's maintains this change won't alter the taste of the foods. In cooperation with long-time oil supplier Cargill, McDonald's said it has come up with a better cooking oil that is much lighter on TFA levels while cutting saturated fat by 16 percent. This increases polyunsaturated fat, the good fat, by 167 percent, according to the company.

TFAs are found in hydrogenated or partly hydrogenated vegetable oils, those that are solidified to form margarine or shortenings. The typical shopper is hard pressed to avoid them. Trans fats are found in almost all processed foods and baked goods. McDonald's U.S. restaurants began cooking with the new-formula oil in 2002, with non-U.S. restaurants following suit in 2003. In addition to fries, McDonald's will deep-fry Chicken McNuggets, Filet-O-Fish, hash browns, and crispy chicken sandwiches in the oil. Overall, the fat-gram level will stay the same at 26 grams for a large order of fries. The calorie count remains the same, 540 in a large order of fries.

Margo Wootan, director of nutrition policy at the Center for Science in the Public Interest, said that this was a good step forward toward reducing the artery-clogging fat in fried foods and helping Americans to reduce their risk of heart disease.

The cooking oil change may have an impact on the fast-food industry, which has been slow to discover nutritious alternatives that people really want to eat. While fast-food chains have tested low-fat and even fat-free versions of their products, slow sales bumped them off permanent menus.

Source: Jennifer Waters, "McDonald's Loses 'Bad' Fat in Fries,"**CBS.MarketWatch.com,** September 3, 2002.

Questions

1. Altering restaurant operations, such as changing cooking oil, is a costly undertaking. Do you think the decision to change cooking oil will lead to higher or lower profits?
2. Was the decision the correct ethical decision, regardless of the effect on corporate profits?

The universities are responding with an increased emphasis on ethical training for decision making. For the most part, however, they ignore the teaching of values. For moral or ethical education to have meaning, there must be agreement on the values that are considered "right."[3]

In Chapter 1 of *Ethical Issues in the Practice of Accounting*, Michael Josephson listed the Ten Universal Values. They were

Honesty	Caring
Integrity	Respect for others
Promisekeeping	Responsible citizenship
Fidelity	Pursuit of excellence
Fairness	Accountability[4]

Can Ethics Be Taught?

People sometimes ask, *Can ethics be taught?* At some point in life, ethics must be taught. People are not born with innate desires to be ethical or to be concerned with the welfare of others. The role of the family embraces teaching children a code of ethical behavior that includes respect for parents, siblings, and others. The family bears the chief responsibility for ensuring that children will receive the necessary education and moral guidance to become productive members of society. The basic values such as honesty, self-control, concern for others, respect for legitimate authority, fidelity, and civility must be passed from one generation to the next—a fundamental process of the family.

Theodore Roosevelt, the twenty-sixth president of the United States, emphasized the importance of ethics education: "To educate a person in mind and not in morals is to educate a menace to society."[5] Cal Thomas made the following assessment: "If we want to produce people who share the values of a democratic culture, they must be taught those values and not be left to acquire them by chance."[6] American Accounting Association president G. Peter Wilson said that in the classroom, educators need to increasingly emphasize the value of integrity, which has long been a mainstay of accountants' reputation.[7]

Role of Professional Organizations

Specific responsibilities of the accounting profession are expressed in the various codes of ethics set forth by major organizations such as the American Institute of CPAs. The AICPA's first principle of professional conduct states: "In carrying out their responsibilities as professionals, members should exercise sensitive professional and moral judgments in all their activities."[8] A profession is based on three fundamental components.

- A generally accepted body of knowledge
- A widely recognized standard of attainment
- An enforceable code of ethics

A code of ethics is a crucial element in forming a profession. Ethics codes are fundamental to major accounting professional organizations, such as the American Institute of CPAs, the Institute of Internal Auditors, and the Institute of Management Accountants. Exhibit 11.7 shows the introduction to the Code of Ethics of the Institute of Internal Auditors.

EXHIBIT 11.7

Introduction to the Code of Ethics of the Institute of Internal Auditors

The purpose of The Institute's Code of Ethics is to promote an ethical culture in the profession of internal auditing.

Internal auditing is an independent, objective assurance and consulting activity designed to add value and improve an organization's operations. It helps an organization accomplish its objectives by bringing a systematic, disciplined approach to evaluate and improve the effectiveness of risk management, control, and governance processes.

A code of ethics is necessary and appropriate for the profession of internal auditing, founded as it is on the trust placed in its objective assurance about risk management, control, and governance. The Institute's Code of Ethics extends beyond the definition of internal auditing to include two essential components:

1. Principles that are relevant to the profession and practice of internal auditing;
2. Rules of Conduct that describe behavior norms expected of internal auditors.

These rules are an aid to interpreting the Principles into practical applications and are intended to guide the ethical conduct of internal auditors.

The Code of Ethics together with The Institute's *Professional Practices Framework* and other relevant Institute pronouncements provide guidance to internal auditors serving others. "Internal auditors" refers to Institute members, recipients of or candidates for IIA professional certifications, and those who provide internal auditing services within the definition of internal auditing.

Source: From Institute of Internal Auditors **www.theiia.org.** Copyright © 2004 by The Institute of Internal Auditors, 247 Maitland Avenue, Altamonte Sprints, FL 32710, USA. Reprinted with permission.

A key reason for having ethical guidelines is not to provide a cookbook solution to every practice-related problem, but to aid in the decision-making process for situations that involve ethical questions. Businesspeople will encounter novel situations in their jobs and will need ethical guidelines to handle them effectively. Ethics codes are necessary to provide such guidance. To aid its 100,000 members in resolving ethical dilemmas, the Institute of Management Accountants recently established an ethics hotline. Ethics counselors offer confidential advice, solace, and comfort to management accountants who may have no other place to turn for help.

reality CHECK   *How would you describe your values? Have you ever been confronted with an ethical dilemma in the workplace?*

Computer Crime

LEARNING OBJECTIVE 5
List a few examples of computer crime.

computer crime The use of computers to perpetrate or facilitate illegal activity

Lack of ethics naturally manifests itself in undesirable behavior. The latest technology is often used to commit crimes. **Computer crime** involves the use of computers to perpetrate or facilitate illegal activity. The average computer crime has been estimated to cost $600,000, while the average white-collar crime is estimated to cost only $23,500. The average armed robbery is estimated to cost even less, only $250. To make matters worse, statistics show that the higher the dollar amount of a crime, the lower its probability of prosecution.

The increased use of the computer to maintain financial records has led to more opportunities for computer crime. Estimates of computer fraud losses are several billion dollars per year. One of the most highly publicized crimes was the Equity Funding fraud, in which nonexistent insurance policy records were added to the customer master file of the firm. Allegedly, this was done by carrying out "unscheduled" file updating that was not part of the normal data-processing operations.

A second well-known computer crime concerned Pacific Telephone. The perpetrator was able to manipulate the system by taking advantage of the following system shortcomings:

> Account numbers and passwords that were shown on printouts were not adequately controlled.
> Equipment was allowed to be shipped to locations not normally used by the firm.
> Computerized purchasing procedures were available to personnel who had no need to know the procedures.

The online computer system of the state of Colorado was used to make unauthorized modifications to the driving records of persons convicted of violations. The modifications were made to enhance the insurability of the persons involved. The online computer system of the University of Southern California (USC) was used to make unauthorized changes to course grades. At both places, the state of Colorado and USC, unauthorized modifications were made by authorized operators, not by the persons whose records were changed.

The rail firm Penn Central Railroad once discovered that nearly 400 railcars had been "misplaced." The computer system had been modified in such a way that missing railcars would go unnoticed.

reality CHECK   *Do you know anyone who has been a victim of computer crime? Has your computer ever been infected by a computer virus?*

Internal Control

LEARNING OBJECTIVE 6
Explain the importance of internal controls.

A few generations ago, most businesses were owned and operated by one person. Under that form of business, the control structure was very simple. The owner-operator maintained firsthand knowledge of all aspects of the business. In other words, he or she kept an eye on things so that nothing was stolen or lost. Today the dominant form of business is the corporation, in which the owners, that is, the stockholders, rely on professional managers to operate the firm. Professional managers rely on the accounting information system to supply them with the financial information they need to make effective decisions. To ensure the accuracy and reliability of this information, a system of **internal controls** is established. Internal controls prevent dishonest persons from doing wrong, but just as importantly, prevent honest persons from being the subject of suspicion and false accusation.

internal controls A system of rules and procedures designed to ensure the accuracy and reliability of financial and accounting information

Types of Controls

The **internal control structure** is designed to prevent errors, or unintentional misrepresentations, and irregularities, or intentional misrepresentations, from occurring and to identify errors and irregularities after they occur so that corrective action may be taken. Thus, controls can be categorized as preventive controls or as feedback controls. Both categories of accounting controls are essential in a company's control structure.

Preventive controls are a type of internal control whose purpose it is to prevent mistakes or intentional misrepresentations from occurring in the accounting data. Segregation of related organizational functions, or separation of duties, is an example of a preventive control. This control involves assigning the tasks related

internal control structure A set of devices and procedures designed to prevent unintentional errors and intentional irregularities from occurring and to identify errors and irregularities after they occur so that corrective action may be taken

preventive controls A type of internal control whose purpose it is to prevent mistakes or intentional misrepresentations from occurring in the accounting data

Bottled milk is inspected by a factory worker of food company Parmalat Calisto Tanzi, located in Collecchio, Italy. In 2004, Italian prosecutors investigated a multibillion-euro fraud at the company.

to a particular transaction among two or more employees. In particular, the physical custody of an asset should be kept separate from the record-keeping function. For example, the person who is responsible for writing checks for disbursements should not be assigned the task of reconciling the bank account. Other preventive controls include

- Hiring competent and ethical employees
- Written policies and procedures
- Physical security of firm assets
- Appropriate management supervision
- Adequate documents and records

feedback controls A type of internal control that reports the occurrence of mistakes or intentional misrepresentations after they have occurred, so that corrective action can be taken

Feedback controls are a type of internal control that reports the occurrence of mistakes or intentional misrepresentations after they have occurred, so that corrective action can be taken. Feedback controls are effective only if they include the following characteristics:

- Benefits exceed costs of operating the controls.
- Deviations from the benchmark (e.g., budget or standards) are reported on a timely basis.
- Relevant and understandable information is provided.
- The manager takes action in a timely manner.

Examples of feedback or administrative accounting systems include credit control, production quality control, and internal audit.

Role of the Auditor

The success of any organization depends on an effective control structure. Since management is responsible for achieving a company's goals and objectives, it is responsible for the adequacy of the company's control structure. The independent auditor, on the other hand, has a responsibility to evaluate these controls and to report any material weaknesses noted to management.

Auditing standards require that the auditor obtain knowledge about the client's internal control structure. Audit effectiveness is improved with better audit planning and more precise assessment of control risk. Auditing standards define the relationship between internal control structure and assessing control risk and financial statement assertions.

The accounting information system and its control structure are the foundation on which financial information is gathered, verified, and disseminated. The independent auditor must develop a thorough understanding of the client's control structure and system. Understanding, testing, and evaluating accounting information systems has become more difficult due to the general complexity of systems, as well as to their increasing computerization. Auditors must possess a clear understanding of the impact of electronic data processing on the audit process. Statements on Auditing Standards No. 48, "The Effects of Computer Processing on the Examination of Financial Statements," states:

> The auditor should consider the methods the entity uses to process accounting information in planning the audit because such methods influence the design of the accounting system and the nature of the internal accounting control procedures. The extent to which computer processing is used in significant accounting applications, as well as the complexity of that processing, may also influence the nature, timing, and extent of audit procedures.[9]

Computerized accounting information systems have several inherent advantages over manual systems. The advantages include

- Reducing human error caused by fatigue or carelessness
- Processing transactions in a consistent fashion
- No dishonest or disloyal motivations on the part of the computer

On the other hand, computer systems have certain disadvantages. These include

- Lack of judgment
- Some users' assumption that computers are always correct
- Less segregation of duties and functions
- The audit trail being more difficult to follow because it is hidden or fragmented
- Greater potential for tampering with data to cause unauthorized actions
- Easier access to information concentrated in computerized files
- Easier loss of information electronically (A few keystrokes can erase whole files.)

Auditors must be aware of these advantages and disadvantages when planning the examination of a computerized accounting system.

If all employees were totally competent and ethical, then internal controls would be virtually unnecessary. However, no matter how effective the hiring function of the personnel system, some employees will be less than ideal. Furthermore, even well-intentioned employees will occasionally make mistakes due to fatigue or carelessness.

Foreign Corrupt Practices Act

The U.S. Congress passed the Foreign Corrupt Practices Act (FCPA) in 1977. The law prohibits any U.S. firm, including any officer, director, or employee, from using "the mails or any means or instrumentality of interstate commerce corruptly in furtherance of an offer, payment, promise to pay, or authorization of the payment of any money, or offer, gift, promise to give, or authorization of the giving of anything of value to"

> A foreign official
> A foreign political party
> An official of a foreign political party
> A candidate for foreign political office
> Any person who will in turn give the money (etc.) to one of the aforesaid
>   individuals or entities for purposes of influencing a decision or act in
>   order to assist in obtaining or retaining business or directing business to
>   a person.

Penalties for conviction of such acts include fines or imprisonment.

The FCPA amended the Securities Exchange Act of 1934 by requiring public companies to devise and maintain a system of internal accounting control sufficient to provide reasonable assurance that

- Transactions are executed in accordance with management's general or specific authorization.
- Transactions are recorded as necessary (I) to permit preparation of financial statements in conformity with generally accepted accounting principles or any other criteria applicable to such statements, and (II) to maintain accountability for assets.
- Access to assets is permitted only in accordance with management's general or specific authorization.
- The recorded accountability for assets is compared with the existing assets at reasonable intervals and appropriate action is taken with respect to any differences.

These objectives were originally taken from Statements on Auditing Standards No. 1 (SAS No. 1), Section 320.28, and were incorporated in Section 13(b) of the 1934 Act. Consequently, the management and employees of a public company may be civilly and criminally liable under the federal securities laws for failing to maintain a sufficient internal control structure.

Computer Security of Accounting Information

From watching movies and television shows, you might think that the greatest threat to computer security is intentional sabotage or unauthorized access to data or equipment. For most organizations this is simply not reality. There are five basic threats to security.

> Natural disasters
> Dishonest employees
> Disgruntled employees
> Persons external to the organization
> Unintentional errors and omissions

The extent to which each of these threats is actually realized is shown in Exhibit 11.8.

EXHIBIT 11.8

Threats to Computer Security of Accounting Information

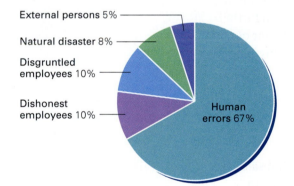

External persons 5%
Natural disaster 8%
Disgruntled employees 10%
Dishonest employees 10%
Human errors 67%

Unintentional errors and omissions cause the great majority of the problems concerning computer security. Errors and omissions are particularly prevalent in systems of sloppy design, implementation, and operation. On the other hand, if the systems development process is done properly, errors and omissions will be minimized. An effective internal control structure is an integral part of any reliable information system.

A key to computer security and the success of any control structure is the people of the organization. Systems development is most effective when the users are involved and most likely to fail when they are not. To develop effective computer security, management should consider the following positive steps:

1. Design controls and security techniques to ensure that all access to and use of the information system can be traced back to the user.

2. Restrict access by users to the parts of the system directly related to their jobs.

3. Conduct periodic security training.

4. Assign an individual or committee to administer system security in an independent manner.

5. Clearly communicate and consistently enforce security policies and procedures.

A primary motive for a well-designed set of internal controls is to support the fiscal management capabilities of the firm's officers and employees. Inadequate internal controls can severely hinder the fiscal management capabilities of officers and employees and place them in a position where they may be unduly tempted to become engaged in questionable activities and accounting practices. Chaotic accounting and fiscal management conditions resulting from inadequate controls place officers and employees under unnecessary conditions of stress. This can be expected to impair their mental well-being and task effectiveness. Assuming that officers and employees are honest, strong controls should be provided to guard them from suspicion and false accusations.

Computer Contingency Planning for Accounting Information

A company should safeguard critical accounting information from loss, destruction, theft, and other threats by creating a comprehensive **computer contingency plan.** The computer contingency plan should have the following component plans:

Emergency
Backup
Recovery
Test
Maintenance

The emergency plan describes actions to be taken immediately after a disaster. An important aspect of this plan is the preparation of a contingency organization chart showing the name of the contingency manager and primary contingency coordinators. The responsibilities of the contingency manager and contingency coordinators should be explained clearly.

The next part of a computer contingency plan is the preparation of a backup plan. This document is an important element necessary for recovery. The selection of a backup alternative requires careful planning. The company should consider the following alternatives: utilization of data-processing service bureaus, another company's computers, or a vendor's computers. To ensure a compatible computer is available on short notice, a mutually agreeable contract between the company and the other organization providing backup facilities should be prepared.

The third part of a computer contingency plan is the preparation of a recovery plan. The firm should assess its ability to restore critical accounting information within an acceptable time period. A competent recovery team is a significant part of any recovery plan. The names, telephone numbers, specific assignments, special or alternative training needs, and other essential information of all team members must be shown on the recovery plan. A section should indicate which recovery team members are responsible for establishing the timetable for the recovery operation and who decides if outside, temporary personnel are needed to complete the

computer contingency plan
A comprehensive plan of action designed to safeguard critical accounting information from loss, destruction, theft, and other threats

In the aftermath of Hurricane Charley, which smashed across Florida in August 2004, a business owner inspects the remains of his office building.

recovery on schedule. Also, the recovery plan should include procedures for coping with the nonavailability of data-processing personnel.

After the occurrence of a disaster, even if the firm has an excellent recovery plan, it may take a few days before the backup site can begin processing accounting information. Such a delay requires the company to focus its efforts on processing those computerized accounting jobs essential to the survival of the organization. Consequently, the recovery team must prioritize accounting applications that must be processed at the expense of all others. By identifying those accounting applications deemed critical and by further evaluating the resources required to sustain those critical accounting applications, decisions are more easily made regarding alternative work locations, schedules, backup facilities, software needs, data preparation needs, personnel needs, security, and documentation requirements.

The fourth part of a computer contingency plan is testing the plan. Numerous potential problems can be eliminated by developing a test strategy. The most effective way to determine if the contingency plan works is to conduct simulations of actual disasters. Test results should be reviewed by individuals who took part in the test. The results of the review should be utilized to identify any flaws in the contingency plan.

The fifth and final component of a computer contingency plan is maintenance of the plan. An organization should ensure procedures are devised to keep the contingency plan current. Any necessary changes based on the simulated disasters should be integrated into the documented plan. A plan of action should be prepared for the implementation of changes to ensure even greater protection from disasters.

The computer contingency plan is a corrective control. The contingency plan is not designed to prevent disasters from occurring, but when disaster strikes, the presence of a computer contingency plan enables a company to quickly restore its capabilities to process critical accounting information and to provide services and products for its customers efficiently and effectively. Preparation of such a plan forces a company to prioritize accounting applications into critical and noncritical categories. Thus, the company will be better prepared to continue processing critical accounting information.

 What internal controls have you seen used in the jobs you have had?

Careers in Accounting

Accounting is a field of great diversity and great opportunity. Accounting careers are available in public accounting, industry, and the government and not-for-profit areas. Public accounting firms are staffed by Certified Public Accountants (CPAs). CPAs are licensed by the state in which they work. Basic requirements to become a CPA include passing the CPA exam and obtaining work experience. CPA firms offer three types of services to their clients: auditing and other assurance services, tax-planning and compliance services, and management consulting services.

Accountants who work for industry firms are called management accountants. All types of industry firms need management accountants, from manufacturing companies like General Motors to technology firms like Microsoft to retail firms like Wal-Mart to movie studios like Universal. Fast-food restaurant chains need accountants. Rock bands need accountants.

Government and not-for-profit organizations need accountants. In the federal government, accounting graduates can work in a number of places, such as the

Internal Revenue Service, the Comptroller General's Office, the Central Intelligence Agency, or the Federal Bureau of Investigation. State governments and city governments need accountants to keep track of funds and how they are spent. Not-for-profit organizations such as the Red Cross, the United Way, and the March of Dimes need accountants to keep track of contributions received and how they are spent.

Accountants perform a variety of tasks, such as preparing financial statements and recording business transactions, analyzing costs and efficiency gains from new technologies, developing strategies for mergers and acquisitions, creating and using information systems to track financial performance, developing tax strategies, and helping manage health care. Accountants keep track of the sales revenues coming into the firm. They maintain records of property, equipment, inventories, receivables, payroll, shares of stock, production costs, overhead, and profit. Consequently, accountants get the big picture; they learn how the business functions. Accountants work with people in all areas of the firm, from marketing to finance to production. Accounting is a people-oriented job. The accounting field offers exciting and challenging work that is constantly evolving. Accountants learn about all aspects of a business; consequently, many CEOs and CFOs have accounting as their background.

Many accountants start their careers in public accounting and then move on to jobs in industry or the government or not-for-profit sector. The skills acquired in one field of work are generally transferable to other fields.

Accounting jobs are expected to increase in future years. The increased demand for accountants is partly due to the increasing complexity of corporate transactions and to the growth in the government sector.

Ethics in Business

How Do You Measure Success?

A popular story recounts a meeting that took place at the Edgewater Beach Hotel in Chicago in 1923. Attending this meeting were nine of the richest men in the world at that time:

Charles Schwab, president of the world's largest independent steel company

Samuel Insull, president of the world's largest utility company

Howard Hopson, president of the world's largest gas firm

Arthur Cutten, the world's greatest wheat speculator

Richard Whitney, president of the New York Stock Exchange

Albert Fall, member of the president's Cabinet

Leon Frazier, president of the Bank of International Settlements

Jessie Livermore, the world's greatest speculator in the stock market

Ivar Kreuger, head of the company with the most widely distributed securities in the world

Twenty-five years later,

Charles Schwab had died in bankruptcy, having lived on borrowed money for five years before his death.

Samuel Insull had died virtually penniless after spending some time as a fugitive from justice.
Howard Hopson was insane.
Arthur Cutten had died overseas, broke.
Richard Whitney had spent time in Sing-Sing prison.
Albert Fall was released from prison so that he could die at home.
Leon Fraizer, Jessie Livermore, and Ivar Kreuger had each died by suicide.

Measured by wealth and power, these men achieved success, at least temporarily. Making a lot of money may be an acceptable goal, but money most assuredly does not guarantee a truly successful life.

Many people consider fame and fortune when they measure success. In reality, a quality life is measured by strength of character and personal integrity, not by fame and fortune. In his testimony at the congressional hearing on accounting and business ethics in July 2002, Truett Cathy, founder of Chik-Fil-A, quoted Solomon: "A good name is more desirable than great riches; to be esteemed is better than silver or gold." How do *you* measure success?

Source: From K. T. Smith and L. M. Smith, 2003. *Business and Accounting Ethics,* Copyright © 2003. Used by permission of Dr. K. T. Smith and Dr. L. M. Smith.

Summary

LEARNING OBJECTIVE 1

Explain the function of the accounting information system.

Accounting is the language of business. It is the recording, summarizing, and reporting of the economic activities and events of an organization. Accounting generates information used by persons within the firm and external to the firm in their decision making. The accounting information system (AIS), like all systems, has specific objectives, inputs, processes, outputs, and controls. A typical AIS's objectives are to provide all the financial information needed internally by management for business decision making and to provide financial information to various external users concerned with the financial activities of the organization.

LEARNING OBJECTIVE 2

Describe how the AIS fits within the management information system.

The management information system (MIS) provides all the information, financial and nonfinancial, needed by management for decision making. The MIS can be thought of as a collection of all the organization's information sources, including the AIS and systems related to marketing, human resources, production, data processing, and so on.

LEARNING OBJECTIVE 3

Briefly recount accounting issues associated with international business, such as the importance of International Accounting Standards and International Standards on Auditing.

For as long as international trade has occurred, accounting has been necessary to record and report the results. International operations are increasingly important to all types of business firms. Many multinational firms are either expanding international operations or becoming part of other multinational firms via mergers or acquisitions. As a result, more firms than ever before are providing products and services to customers around the globe.

The International Accounting Standards Board issues International Accounting Standards (IASs). The objectives of IASs include increasing harmonization of accounting standards and disclosures to meet the needs of the global market, providing an accounting basis for underdeveloped or newly industrialized countries to follow as the accounting profession emerges in those countries, and increasing the compatibility of domestic and international accounting requirements.

International standards on auditing are issued by the International Auditing and Assurance Standards Board, a committee of the International Federation of Accountants. International Standards on Auditing contain basic principles and essential procedures for auditing, along with related guidance in the form of explanatory and other material.

LEARNING OBJECTIVE 4

Discuss the importance of ethical accounting practices.

Ethical accounting practices are essential to countless people, including investors, lenders, employees, suppliers, and customers. In the history of the world, the United States is unique. Compared to people in other countries, Americans enjoy more freedom, more wealth that is more evenly distributed, and more opportunity. The accounting profession has played a key role in the United States' success story. The accounting profession has made essential contributions to efficient operations of business firms, to the functioning of the capital market system, and to the growth of the economy in general. All this depends on accountants doing their jobs according to the highest standards of ethics and personal integrity.

Most companies have an ethics code to guide their employees in how they conduct business. Likewise, business and accounting organizations provide ethical guidelines to their members. Both accounting educators and professional organizations can help guide future and current accountants in the proper ways to conduct business.

LEARNING OBJECTIVE 5

List a few examples of computer crime.

The increased use of computers to maintain financial records has led to more opportunities for computer crimes, which are estimated to cost several billions of dollars annually. Computer crimes can include such things as creating false records, misusing account numbers and passwords, altering shipping and purchasing documents to create fraudulent sales or for purposes of theft, modifying criminal records, and modifying school grades.

LEARNING OBJECTIVE 6

Explain the importance of internal controls.

The success of any organization depends on an effective control structure. Internal control structures should be designed to prevent unintentional errors and intentional irregularities from occurring and to identify errors and irregularities after they occur so that corrective action may be taken. Thus, controls can be categorized as preventive controls or as feedback controls. Both categories of accounting controls are essential in a company's control structure.

Chapter Questions

1. What is accounting?
2. List some of the external users of accounting information and the specific types of information they require.
3. What is the function of generally accepted accounting principles?
4. Briefly describe the history of the East India Company.
5. Contrast management accounting with financial accounting.
6. Describe the role of the management information system (MIS) and the role of the accounting information system within the MIS.
7. What causes accounting rules and regulations to be different among countries?
8. Can ethics be taught?
9. What is the role of an internal control structure?
10. International trade has been around a long time. How do you think the world would be different if there had never been international trade?
11. The East India Company faced some peculiar problems. Contrast problems faced by the East India Company with problems faced by modern corporations.
12. Examine the list of International Accounting Standards in Exhibit 11.5. Pick one and describe why you think this information would be useful to stockholders.
13. Describe the advantages and disadvantages of computerized processing of accounting information.
14. What are the components of a computer contingency plan for accounting information? Describe a situation or event in which a business firm would have major problems if it did not have a contingency plan.

Interpreting Business News

1. A news story recounted the questionable accounting practices and financial collapses of major corporations such as Enron, WorldCom, and other firms. Do you think accounting rules can be developed and applied in a way that will prevent future corporate failures?
2. In a news article regarding the Foreign Corrupt Practices Act (FCPA), the writer said that the FCPA hurt the ability of U.S. firms to compete with non-U.S. firms. For example, U.S. companies find it difficult to compete in countries where bribery is a common business practice. The writer said that the time had come for Congress to repeal the FCPA so that U.S. firms would be better able to compete in the global marketplace. What do you think?
3. A news story described how a hurricane wiped out homes and businesses on the U.S. Gulf Coast. How do you think the firms with a computer contingency plan fared compared to those without a plan?

Web Assignments

1. Go to the website for the International Federation of Accountants and from there, go to the webpage for the International Auditing and Assurance Standards Board. What are International Auditing Practice Statements (IAPSs)? List several of the topics covered by IAPSs.
2. Use a Web search tool to investigate accounting ethics. List and briefly describe some websites that concern accounting ethics.
3. McDonald's is the world's leading food service retailer. Go to the website for MacDonald's, **www.mcdonalds.com.** How many restaurants does the firm have? In how many countries is the firm located? How many customers are served each day?

Portfolio Projects

Exploring Your Own Case in Point

In this chapter, the role of accounting is explained. Accounting information is necessary for decision making by people within and outside a business firm. Answering the questions below will help you better understand the role of accounting in your selected company's operations.

1. Who uses the financial accounting information produced by your company's accounting department? Who uses the management accounting information produced by your company's accounting department?

2. What is the chief product or service associated with your company? What department in the company produces the product or service? What type of accounting information does it need to do its job effectively?

3. What sorts of internal controls might your company use to ensure that company resources are not stolen or wasted? Why are auditors interested in internal controls?

Starting Your Own Business

After reading this chapter, you should have a basic understanding of the role of accounting. Even if you will be hiring someone to keep the books of your startup company, you will need to be able to speak about accounting to people both inside and outside your firm. Answer the following questions about accounting in your startup company.

1. Describe the objectives, inputs, processes, outputs, and controls of the accounting system in your startup company.

2. What are some internal controls that your company will use to help ensure that company resources are not stolen or wasted? What measures can you take to help prevent computer crime from being committed against your company?

Test Prepper

You've read the chapter, studied the key terms, and the exam is any day now. Think you are ready to ace it? Take this sample test to gauge your comprehension of chapter material. You can check your answers at the back of the book.

True/False Questions

Please indicate if the following statements are true or false:

_____ 1. One objective of a typical accounting information system is to provide all the financial information needed internally by management for business decision making.

_____ 2. One objective of a typical accounting information system is to provide financial information to various external users concerned with the financial activities of the organization.

_____ 3. When CPAs provide audit services, they render an opinion as to whether the financial statements prepared by a firm's financial accountants are prepared according to generally accepted accounting principles.

_____ 4. The management information system provides only financial information to management; the management information system does not deal with nonfinancial information.

_____ 5. Objectives of international standards include increasing the diversity of accounting standards and disclosures to meet the needs of U.S. investors.

_____ 6. Effective and efficient functioning of the global marketplace requires uniformity in accounting and auditing standards.

_____ 7. Many companies have an ethics code to guide their employees in how they conduct business.

_____ 8. Adherence to the standards set by the International Auditing and Assurance Standards Board is mandatory for all members of the International Federation of Accountants.

_____ 9. In contrast to a computerized accounting information system, a manual accounting system has several inherent advantages, such as reducing human error caused by fatigue or carelessness.

_____ 10. The internal control provisions of the Foreign Corrupt Practices Act are not limited to the detection or prevention of foreign bribery, and they affect all public companies that are involved in international trade. The provisions do not apply to public companies that are involved in strictly domestic trade.

Multiple-Choice Questions

Choose the best answer.

_____ 1. The accounting information system, like all systems, has all of the following *except* specific

   a. objectives.
   b. inputs.
   c. processes.
   d. outputs.
   e. technology.

_____ 2. External groups that use accounting information do *not* include

   a. credit-rating agencies.
   b. vendors.
   c. management.
   d. customers.
   e. lending institutions.

_____ 3. Reports or documents generated for management accounting purposes include all of the following *except*

   a. sales invoices.
   b. purchase orders.
   c. inventory reports.
   d. tax returns.
   e. capital budgets.

_____ 4. The _____ issues International Accounting Standards.

   a. United Nations Committee on Finance and Taxation
   b. International Accounting Standards Board
   c. American Institute of CPAs
   d. Institute of Management Accountants
   e. International Federation of Accountants

_____ 5. Unlike the East India Company in the 1600s, business firms today are unlikely to need armed ships to fight off pirates, but international trade still has its problems, which include all of the following *except*

   a. tariffs.
   b. language barriers.

c. cultural differences.
d. incompatible equipment standards.
e. a common currency.

_____ 6. All of the following are disadvantages of computerized accounting information systems *except*

a. they lack judgment.
b. some users assume they are always correct.
c. they reduce human error caused by fatigue or carelessness.
d. they present a potential for tampering with data.
e. information can be lost electronically.

_____ 7. Accounting rules and regulations are a result of various systems of each country that do not include.

a. cultural
b. economic
c. political
d. legal
e. engineering

_____ 8. The average computer crime has been estimated to cost $ _____, while the average white-collar crime is estimated to cost $ _____.

a. 600,000; 23,500
b. 100,000; 50,000
c. 23,500; 40,000
d. 10,000; 100,000
e. 1,000; 50,000

_____ 9. Preventive controls do *not* include

a. hiring competent and ethical employees.
b. feedback controls.
c. written policies and procedures.
d. physical security of firm assets.
e. segregation of related organizational functions.

_____ 10. CPA firms offer all of the following types of services to their clients *except*

a. auditing and other assurance services.
b. tax planning services.
c. management consulting services.
d. inventory planning services.
e. tax compliance services.

Want more questions? Visit the student website at **http://college.hmco.com/business/student/** (select Gaspar, *Introduction to Business*) and take the ACE quizzes for more practice.

Financial Reporting

| Introduction

| The Purpose of Financial Reporting

| The Four Financial Statements

Income Statement

Statement of Retained Earnings

Balance Sheet

Statement of Cash Flows

Relationships Among Financial Statements

| Auditing the Financial Statements

External or Financial Statement Audit

Audit Steps

Audit Evidence

Impact of Computerization

| Foreign Currency Translation

Current Rate Method

Temporal Rate Method

| The Impact of Technology

American Institute of CPAs Top Ten
Technologies

Accounting and Auditing Resources
on the Web

| Careers in Accounting

Learning Objectives

After studying this chapter, you should be able to

1 Explain the role of financial reporting.

2 Define the components of the four
financial statements.

3 Describe the contribution of auditing
to the usefulness of financial reporting.

4 Explain the steps in foreign currency
translation, a necessary element in
financial reporting of multinational
business firms.

5 Discuss the impact of technology, particularly resources on the Web, on
accounting.

Does a Company Benefit from Setting Up a Website?

Providing financial information to government regulators is a requirement for publicly traded corporations in the United States and many other countries. This helps ensure reliable financial reporting and is helpful to investors and other users of the financial statements. Many companies have set up websites to promote their business activities, and many companies provide financial statement information on the Web.

Research by Dr. Shirley Hunter at the University of Houston at Clear Lake investigated the impact of setting up a website on business firms located in emerging market countries such as India, Indonesia, and South Africa. She found that business firms in those countries do receive a positive benefit from setting up a corporate website. The website can be useful for providing general information about the company, as well as specific financial statement information.[1]

Introduction

Accounting information is used by people, both within and outside the firm, to evaluate the success or failure of the firm. The managers of a business firm decide how the firm will operate. Decisions such as the following must be made:

- What goods or services will be sold by the firm
- What price the firm will charge for its goods or services
- In what geographic locations the firm will be situated
- From what suppliers (vendors) the firm will acquire its inventory
- What employees to hire
- How the firm will market its products
- What type of assets the firm should acquire for use in operations
- How the firm will finance its operations

This chapter examines how accounting information is organized and reported to help make these decisions. As the opening vignette illustrates, financial reports are also used to communicate information to interested parties outside the firm.

The Purpose of Financial Reporting

LEARNING OBJECTIVE 1
Explain the role of financial reporting.

Accounting will determine whether the revenues of a firm exceed its expenses, thus resulting in a profit. Alternatively, accounting will determine whether expenses exceed revenues, thus resulting in a loss. Naturally, the managers want the firm to make a profit. The primary goal of the firm is to increase the wealth of the firm's owners, that is, investors. Investors buy stock and thereby become part owners of a corporation. In general, stock increases in value when a corporation is profitable. Thus, a firm with a record of profitability that is consistently reporting a solid net income on its financial statements is preferred by investors. As a practical matter, the current price of a company's stock is dependent on investor expectations of the future earnings of the company. Usually the best predictor of future earnings is past earnings.

Do you or anyone you know own any stock? If so, do you follow the stock price?

The Four Financial Statements

LEARNING OBJECTIVE 2

Define the components of the four financial statements.

Accounting is called the language of business because it provides information that people need to make effective business decisions. The most important output of the accounting information system is the set of **financial statements.** These accounting reports include the income statement, the statement of retained earnings, the balance sheet, and the statement of cash flows. Together, these four statements represent a business firm in financial terms. Each statement corresponds to a specific date or a designated time period, such as a year. If you were a manager or an investor, what would you like to know about the firm at the end of a time period? There are four essential questions that are answered by the four financial statements. These are shown in Exhibit 12.1.

> **financial statements** The income statement, statement of retained earnings, balance sheet, and statement of cash flows, which together represent a business firm in financial terms

Income Statement

The **income statement** is also referred to as the statement of operating results or the statement of earnings. This accounting report shows the firm's revenues, expenses, and net income or net loss for the period. The income statement for Cathy's Candy Company is shown in Exhibit 12.2 (on p. 410). Cathy's Candy Company, the parent firm, owns other firms that are its subsidiaries. To provide a full accounting of all the resources that Cathy's Candy Company controls, the amounts shown on the financial statements include figures for both Cathy's Candy Company and its subsidiaries. Most firms' financial statements show the consolidation of the parent firm and its subsidiary firms. That is the reason the word *consolidated* is used in the title.

> **income statement** The accounting report that shows the firm's revenues, expenses, and net income or net loss for a period

EXHIBIT 12.1

Fundamental Financial Questions and Answers

Question	How to Find the Answer	Which Financial Statement Shows This Information
How much did the firm earn or lose from operations during the period?	Revenues − expenses ———————— Net income (or net loss)	Income statement (also referred to as statement of operating results or statement of earnings)
In what way did the firm's retained earnings change during the period?	Beginning retained earnings + net income (or − net loss) − dividends ———————— Ending retained earnings	Statement of retained earnings
What is the firm's financial position at the end of the period?	Assets − liabilities ———————— Owners' equity	Balance sheet (also referred to as statement of financial position)
What amount of cash was generated and spent during the period?	Operating cash flows + investing cash flows + financing cash flows ———————— Increase (or decrease) in cash during the period	Statement of cash flows

EXHIBIT 12.2

Cathy's Candy Company
Consolidated Statement of Income

Revenue and Expenses	Year Ended Dec. 31, 2004 ($ millions)	% of Sales	Year Ended Dec. 31, 2003 ($ millions)	% of Sales
1. Net sales revenue	27,162	100.0	19,524	100.0
2. Expenses				
3. Cost of goods sold	15,954	58.7	12,063	61.8
4. Advertising expense	1,257	4.6	525	2.7
5. Depreciation expense	978	3.6	807	4.1
6. Other operating expenses	4,974	18.3	3,570	18.3
7. Interest expense	42	0.2	12	0.1
8. Earnings before income tax	3,957	14.6	2,547	13.0
9. Income tax expense	1,482	5.5	960	4.9
10. Net income	2,475	9.1	1,587	8.1

fiscal year An accounting period of 12 months, which may or may not end on December 31

The data shown on the income statement is for the years ended December 31, 2004, and December 31, 2003. A **fiscal year** is an accounting period of 12 months, which may or may not end on December 31. The majority of business firms use an accounting period that ends with the low point in their annual operations. Most often, that low point is December 31.

The Cathy's Candy Company income statement reports operating results for two accounting years, 2004 and 2003. The income statement shows more than one year's data to reveal the company's trends for sales and net income. During 2003, Cathy's Candy Company increased net sales from $19.5 billion to over $27 billion (see line 1). Net income rose from $1,587 million to $2,475 million (line 10). This upward trend in net income was good news for the firm's managers and investors.

Net Income. For business purposes, net income is determined as follows:

Total revenues and gains − total expenses and losses = net income

net income The amount of income after subtracting expenses and losses from revenues and gains

The word *net* indicates the result after a subtraction has occurred. Thus, **net income** is the amount of income after subtracting expenses and losses from the revenues and gains. During 2004, Cathy's Candy Company had net sales of $27,162 million (line 1). To determine net sales, the firm first subtracted from total sales the goods that Cathy's Candy Company received from customers who returned merchandise.

Total sales − sales returns from customers = net sales revenue

cost of goods sold The cost to a firm of the products sold by the firm to its customers

Cost of Goods Sold. The second item on the income statement is cost of goods sold (line 3), which is also referred to as cost of sales. **Cost of goods sold** is the cost to Cathy's Candy Company of the products the firm sold to its customers. Cost of goods sold is the biggest expense of merchandising firms such as Sears, Best Buy, and Kroger. Other major expenses include advertising, depreciation, other operating expenses, and interest on debt. Advertising (line 4) is a firm's expenditures to promote its business in magazines and newspapers, on TV and the Web, and in other media. Depreciation (line 5) is the firm's expense for using buildings, equipment, and other depreciable assets.

The fifth item on the income statement (line 6) is other operating expenses. This is a broad category for other expenses directly associated with the Cathy's Candy Company operations, which consist of selling candies. Interest expense (line 7) is the expense associated with debt. Earnings before income tax (line 8) amounted to $3,957 million in 2004 and $2,547 million in 2003. Income tax expense (line 9) reduced net income (profits) by $1,482 million in 2004 and $960 million in 2003. Cathy's Candy Company earned $2,475 million in 2004 and $1,587 million in 2003 after paying all expenses.

Cathy's Candy Company's income statement shows percentages for the amounts of each item. Each amount was divided by net sales revenue. Thus, in 2004, depreciation expense was computed to be 3.6 percent of net sales (978/27,162); in 2003, depreciation was 4.1 percent of net sales (807/19,524). Is this a good trend or a bad trend? This is a good trend. The proportionate expense of buildings, equipment, and other depreciable assets increased at a lower rate than revenues. This contributed to a higher **profit margin** in 2004 than in the previous year, 9.1 versus 8.1 percent.

profit margin The ratio of net income to net sales

The Financial Accounting Standards Board requires that in addition to net income, business firms report an income amount called comprehensive income. Comprehensive income includes net income plus several additional items. There is some debate among financial statement users whether comprehensive income is helpful for making financial decisions.

Statement of Retained Earnings

The Cathy's Candy Company **statement of retained earnings** is shown in Exhibit 12.3. As shown on the income statement, the firm earned net income of $2,475 million in 2004. This amount from the income statement also appears on the statement of retained earnings (line 2). Thus, net income is the link between the income statement and the statement of retained earnings. The net income in each year increases retained earnings.

statement of retained earnings The financial statement that shows the change in retained earnings from the beginning of the period to the end of the period

When a firm has net income, the board of directors must decide whether to pay a cash dividend to the owners, that is, the stockholders. In both 2004 and 2003, Cathy's Candy Company declared dividends (line 3). Dividends decrease retained earnings. As shown, the ending balance in one year (2003) becomes the starting balance in the subsequent year (2004).

EXHIBIT 12.3

Cathy's Candy Company
Consolidated Statement of Retained Earnings

Retained Earnings	Year Ended Dec. 31, 2004 ($ millions)	Year Ended Dec. 31, 2003 ($ millions)
1. Balance, beginning of year	7,176	5,826
2. Net income for the year	2,475	1,587
3. Less cash dividends declared	(288)	(237)
4. Balance, end of year	9,363	7,176

Balance Sheet

The **balance sheet** of Cathy's Candy Company is shown in Exhibit 12.4. The balance sheet is dated December 31, 2004, the last day of the firm's accounting period. A balance sheet provides a "snapshot" of a firm's financial position at a designated point in time (12 midnight on the balance sheet date). This is different from the other three accounting reports, which are period statements that account for events that occur throughout the year.

The balance sheet is also referred to as the **statement of financial position.** The balance sheet shows three types of accounts: assets, liabilities, and owners' equity. Corporations designate owners' equity as stockholders' equity because the stockholders are the owners.

EXHIBIT 12.4

Cathy's Candy Company
Consolidated Balance Sheet

Balance Sheet Elements	Dec. 31, 2004 ($ millions)	Dec. 31, 2003 ($ millions)
Assets		
Current assets		
1. Cash	1,710	2,745
2. Accounts receivable	1,153	1,199
3. Inventory	2,000	1,000
4. Prepaid expenses	750	546
5. Total current assets	5,613	5,490
Long-term assets: property and equipment		
6. Leasehold improvements	3,120	2,538
7. Equipment	4,803	3,708
8. Land and buildings	1,218	663
9. Total property and equipment	9,141	6,909
10. Accumulated depreciation	(3,513)	(2,814)
11. Net property and equipment	5,628	4,095
12. Intangibles and other assets	648	423
13. Total assets	11,889	10,008
Liabilities		
Current liabilities		
14. Notes payable, short-term	274	255
15. Accounts payable	2,053	1,250
16. Accrued expenses payable	1,965	1,217
17. Income taxes payable	367	251
18. Total current liabilities	4,659	2,973
Long-term liabilities		
19. Long-term debt	1,488	1,488
20. Other long-term liabilities	1,023	795
21. Total long-term liabilities	2,511	2,283
Stockholders' equity		
22. Common stock	1,194	765
23. Retained earnings	9,363	7,176
24. Treasury stock	(5,706)	(3,030)
25. Other equity	(132)	(159)
26. Total stockholders' equity	4,719	4,752
27. Total liabilities and stockholders' equity	11,889	10,008

Assets. **Assets** are the economic resources owned by the firm. They are categorized into current assets and long-term assets. **Current assets** are those that will be used up, sold, or converted to cash within the year or the normal operating cycle if longer than one year. Current assets for Cathy's Candy Company include cash, accounts receivable, inventory, and prepaid expenses. Accounts receivable (line 2) is the amount owed to the firm by customers. Prepaid expenses (line 4) designates prepayments for items such as rent, insurance, and advertising.

Property and equipment is the chief category of long-term assets. The total cost of property and equipment owned by the firm on December 31, 2004, was $9,141 million (line 9). This property and equipment was partially used up, as shown by the accumulated depreciation of $3,513 million (line 10). **Depreciation** is the accounting process of allocating an asset's cost to expense over the asset's useful life. The net value, also called book value, of property and equipment at December 31, 2004, is $5,628 million (line 11).

Liabilities. **Liabilities** are the debts or economic obligations of the firm. Like assets, liabilities are categorized into current and long-term. Debts that are payable within one year or within the firm's normal operating cycle if more than one year are designated **current liabilities.**

Owners' Equity. **Owners' equity** is the residual interest in the assets of the firm after subtracting the liabilities. Owners' equity, also called stockholders' equity in the case of a corporation, is simple to calculate. The **accounting equation** for owners' equity is

Assets − liabilities = owners' equity

The amount of total liabilities is subtracted from the amount of total assets. Owners' equity for Cathy's Candy Company (line 26) is $4,719 million on December 31, 2004. Owners' equity consists of common stock, retained earnings, treasury stock, and other equity. Common stock consists of millions of shares that the firm has sold to stockholders, which amounts to $1,194 million for Cathy's Candy Company on December 31, 2004.

assets The economic resources owned by the firm

current assets The assets that will be used up, sold, or converted to cash within the year or the firm's normal operating cycle if more than one year

depreciation The accounting process of allocating an asset's cost to expense over the asset's useful life

liabilities The debts or economic obligations of the firm

current liabilities The firm's obligations that are payable within one year or within the firm's normal operating cycle if more than one year

owners' equity The residual interest in the assets of the firm after subtracting the liabilities; also called stockholders' equity

accounting equation Assets = liabilities + owners' equity

The owner of a gift baskets store stands next to her inventory of specialty foods and candies.

For Cathy's Candy Company, the largest component of owners' equity is retained earnings, $9,363 million (line 23) on December 31, 2004. Treasury stock (line 24) is the common stock that Cathy's Candy Company previously issued but has now repurchased from stockholders and holds in its treasury. The amount for treasury stock is shown in parentheses because it is a negative amount of owners' equity. The final item, other equity, is a collection of miscellaneous equity accounts.

Statement of Cash Flows

statement of cash flows The financial statement that presents cash inflows (receipts) and outflows (payments) under three categories of business activities: operating activities, investing activities, and financing activities

The **statement of cash flows** for Cathy's Candy Company is shown in Exhibit 12.5. The statement of cash flows presents cash inflows (receipts) and outflows (payments) under three categories of business activities: operating activities, investing activities, and financing activities.

Operating Activities. Operating activities include sales that result in cash receipts from customers. They also include purchases of inventory that result in cash payments to suppliers. In addition, the firm disburses cash for expenses such as employee wages, rent, and advertising. Operating activities are the most critical of the three categories of business activities; they are the heart and soul of any business firm. For 2004, Cathy's Candy Company's largest cash inflow from operating activities was cash received from customers, $27,162 million (line 1).

EXHIBIT 12.5

Cathy's Candy Company
Consolidated Statement of Cash Flows

Cash Flows	Year Ended Dec. 31, 2004 ($ millions)	Year Ended Dec. 31, 2003 ($ millions)
From operating activities		
1. Cash received from customers	27,162	19,521
2. Cash received from interest revenue	1	9
3. Cash paid to suppliers and employees	(21,570)	(16,011)
4. Cash paid for interest expense	(42)	(12)
5. Cash paid for income tax expense	(1,482)	(960)
6. Net cash provided by operating activities	4,069	2,547
From investing activities		
7. Sales of short-term investments	1	522
8. Purchases of long-term investments	(1)	(9)
9. Purchases of property and equipment	(2,391)	(1,395)
10. Acquisition of other assets	(84)	(57)
11. Net cash used for investing activities	(2,475)	(939)
From financing activities		
12. Borrowing on notes payable	3	132
13. Borrowing on long-term debt	1	1,485
14. Issuance of common stock	271	90
15. Purchase of treasury stock	(2,676)	(1,779)
16. Cash dividends paid	(228)	(237)
17. Net cash used for financing activities	(2,629)	(309)
18. Other	0	(9)
19. Net increase (decrease) in cash	(1,035)	1,299
20. Cash at beginning of year	2,745	1,455
21. Cash at end of year	1,710	2,745

Investing Activities.   Investing activities include sales and purchases of long-term assets that are used in business operations. This is the second most critical of the three categories of business activities. For the year ended December 31, 2004, Cathy's Candy Company's largest cash outflow from investing activities was $2,391 million for the purchase of property and equipment (line 9).

Financing Activities.   Financing activities include borrowing, issuing stock, purchasing treasury stock, and paying cash dividends. For 2004, the largest financing cash flow was a $2,676 million purchase of treasury stock.

The chief aim of the statement of cash flows is to ascertain why the amount of cash changed during the year. The amount of the change can be readily determined by calculating the difference between cash at the beginning of the year and cash at the end of the year. For 2004, the net decrease in cash of $1,035 million is the difference between the start of the year figure, $2,745 million (December 31, 2003/January 1, 2004), and the end of the year figure, $1,710 million (December 31, 2004). Thus, Cathy's Candy Company ends the year with $1,710 million in cash (line 21 of Exhibit 12.5 and line 1 of Exhibit 12.4).

Relationships Among Financial Statements

Exhibit 12.6 illustrates the relationships among the four financial statements. Understanding these relationships will help you in making more effective business

EXHIBIT 12.6

Cathy's Candy Company Relationships Among Financial Statements

Income Statement—For the Year Ended December 31, 2004
(Details Given in Exhibit 12.2)

Revenues	27,162
Total Expenses	24,687
Net Income	2,475

Statement of Retained Earnings—For the Year Ended December 31, 2004
(Details Given in Exhibit 12.3)

Retained Earnings, Beginning of the Year	7,176
Net Income	2,475
Cash Dividends	(288)
Retained Earnings, End of the Year	9,363

Balance Sheet—December 31, 2004
(Details Given in Exhibit 12.4)

ASSETS	
Cash	1,710
All Other Assets	10,179
Total Assets	11,889
LIABILITIES	
Total Liabilities	7,170
STOCKHOLDERS' EQUITY	
Common Stock	1,194
Retained Earnings	9,363
Other Equity	(5,838)
Total Liabilities and Stockholders' Equity	11,889

Statement of Cash Flows—For the Year Ended December 31, 2004
(Details Given in Exhibit 12.5)

Net Cash Flows Provided by Operating Activities	4,069
Net Cash Flows Used for Investing Activities	(2,475)
Net Cash Flows Provided by Financing Activities	(2,629)
Net Increase (Decrease) in Cash	(1,035)
Beginning Cash	2,745
Ending Cash	1,710

Case in Point

DaimlerChrysler: Accounting for Costs and Benefits of Technology and Innovation

Using the latest technology is often essential to a business firm's ability to compete in the marketplace. Before a company adopts new technology, the company must first assess the costs and benefits of doing so. Accountants in a business firm are often called upon to assimilate information regarding the costs of incorporating new technologies and to estimate the potential revenues that the new technologies will help generate. These costs and revenues ultimately will have an impact on a company's financial performance, which will then be reflected in the financial statements.

Technological expertise, speed, and flexibility have made DaimlerChrysler a driving force behind progress in the automotive industry. Around 28,000 employees are working worldwide on the research and development of technical innovations. DaimlerChrysler registers around 2,000 patents every year. Improving technology is considered essential in the face of an increasingly tough global competition. With the initiative "Energy for the Future," DaimlerChrysler is illustrating its commitment to the environment as a part of its social responsibility to promote sustainable mobility.

At the annual Environmental Press Conference held in Stuttgart, Germany, DaimlerChrysler presented the world's first synthetic diesel fuel, which does not affect the CO_2 balance in the atmosphere during driving.

The world's first commercial fleet test with fuel cell vehicles—30 Mercedes-Benz city buses with fuel cell drive in ten European cities—are the CUTE and ECTOS projects, both supported by the European Commission.

Source: DaimlerChrysler website: **http://www.daimlerchrysler.com**, October 1, 2003.

Questions

1. Is use of new technology an important issue in the auto industry?
2. Is it essential that a business firm adopt every new technology that is developed?
3. How can a company determine if a new technology should be used or not used in company operations?

decisions. For example, the net income figure is shown on both the income statement and the statement of retained earnings. Retained earnings are shown on the statement of retained earnings and the balance sheet. Cash is shown on the balance sheet and the statement of cash flows.

reality CHECK   *If you were to prepare financial statements for yourself, what would they look like?*

Auditing the Financial Statements

LEARNING OBJECTIVE 3
Describe the contribution of auditing to the usefulness of financial reporting.

People who rely on financial statements are very concerned about the validity of the reports they receive. The management of a firm has the primary responsibility for designing its accounting information system (AIS). A key concern for a firm's management is the reliability and integrity of the reports produced by the AIS. Many business firms have a separate internal audit function charged with the responsibility of ensuring that the internal control structure, especially that related to the AIS, is operating effectively. In the case of publicly traded companies, users of its annual financial statements (such as investors) need some form of assurance that the statements do not contain material misstatements, either intentional or unintentional. Assurance is provided by the independent external auditor who examines the firm's financial statements and provides an audit opinion indicating whether those statements are fairly presented according to generally accepted accounting principles.

The two major categories of auditing are **internal auditing** and **external auditing.** There are two primary types of internal audits: the management, also called operational, audit, and the internal control audit.

The first the **management** or **operational audit** is concerned with evaluating the economy and efficiency with which scarce resources are utilized. Internal auditors often review all aspects of operations performed in a firm to determine whether any improvements can be made in departmental operations. The efficient utilization of resources by the various departments and their accomplishment of established objectives are evaluated by internal auditors in their performance of a management audit.

The second type of internal audit deals with the evaluation of internal controls. **Internal control structure** comprises those policies and procedures established to provide reasonable assurance that established objectives will be achieved. In performing an audit of internal controls, internal auditors review the internal control structure, which includes the control environment, the accounting system, and control procedures, and test specific controls to determine whether they are operating as anticipated. A key objective of an internal control audit is to ensure that the internal control structure is sound and provides a reasonable degree of assurance about the integrity of information output, such as the financial statements, by the accounting system, and that the firm's assets are safeguarded. The internal control structure audit is especially important as a result of the Sarbanes-Oxley Act of 2002.

A compliance audit can be performed by internal, external, or governmental auditors, depending on the constituency being served. A **compliance audit** has the objective of ensuring that the organization is in compliance with laws, rules, regulations, or contractual agreements. These rules and regulations are typically those that have been established by some governmental institution. For example, the Government Accounting Office (GAO) and the Department of Defense (DOD) auditors review the operations of governmental agencies and defense contractors, respectively. Internally, management might charge internal auditors with the responsibility of ensuring that the organization is in compliance with regulations established by the Environmental Protection Agency (EPA).

internal auditing Chiefly concerned with evaluating the economy and efficiency with which scarce resources are utilized, but may include other objectives such as evaluating the effectiveness of internal controls

external auditing Auditing of a firm's financial statements by an independent external auditor who is a certified public accountant

management or **operational audit** The audit done to evaluate the economy and efficiency with which scarce resources are utilized

internal control structure The control environment, the accounting system, and the control procedures that help ensure the integrity of information output and the safety of the firm's assets

compliance audit The audit done to ensure that the organization is in compliance with laws, rules, regulations, and contractual agreements

External or Financial Statement Audit

External or financial statement audits must be conducted by independent **Certified Public Accountants (CPAs).** External audits are required of all publicly traded companies. The external auditor must maintain his or her independence by having no material financial interest or stake in the outcome of the audit. In conducting a financial statement audit, CPAs must comply with Generally Accepted Auditing Standards (GAAS). Furthermore, CPAs must abide by the AICPA code of ethics in the conduct of all their activities.

Certified Public Accountants (CPAs) Accountants licensed by the state to provide accounting services, including external audits of a business firm's financial statements

Audit Steps

All audits are characterized by the following common set of steps: (1) plan the audit, (2) obtain and evaluate evidence, (3) arrive at an opinion, and (4) communicate audit results. Obtaining evidence to support the audit opinion involves the application of a series of audit procedures to verify the accuracy of assertions being made by the firm being audited, also called the auditee. For financial statement

audits, these assertions are representations made in the financial statements relating to the auditee's income, expenses, assets, and liabilities. Audit procedures for financial statement audits include reconciling bank accounts, obtaining confirmations of accounts receivable from customers of the company, and physically counting inventory. For a financial statement audit, these procedures are applied with the objective of ensuring

- The existence of assets and liabilities and occurrence of income and expenses
- The completeness of the financial statements (all assets, liabilities, income, and expenses are accounted for)
- Proper valuation of assets, liabilities, income, and expenses
- That the auditee owns the assets and is obligated to the extent of the liabilities shown
- That all financial statement items are properly presented and all disclosure regulations have been followed

In internal control audits, the assertions being made by the firm being audited pertain to the proper operation of controls. In compliance audits, the firm being audited is asserting that certain rules, regulations, laws, or contractual agreements have been complied with.

Audit Evidence

Evidence obtained as a result of applying audit procedures must then be evaluated so that the auditor can determine whether the assertions being made by the auditee conform to established criteria. For publicly held corporations, established criteria refer to generally accepted accounting principles that are issued by the Financial Accounting Standards Board (FASB). For audits of government entities, pronouncements of the Governmental Accounting Standards Board (GASB) constitute established criteria. Ascertaining the degree of correspondence between assertions being made by the auditee and established criteria requires the auditor to exercise professional judgment, which usually takes years to acquire.

On the basis of the audit evidence obtained regarding the degree of correspondence between assertions and established criteria, the auditor formulates an audit opinion, which is then communicated to interested parties. In financial statement audits, this communication occurs in the audit report that accompanies the financial statements in the annual report of the audited firm. Exhibit 12.7 (on p. 420) shows the audit report for DaimlerChrysler Corporation. The auditor also issues a separate, more detailed report internally to the audited firm. For operational or internal control audits, management would typically be the sole recipient of the auditor's report detailing the findings and conclusions of the audit.

Impact of Computerization

The audit process described above applies to both manual and computer-based systems. With the ever-increasing sophistication of computer-based accounting systems, auditors have had to significantly modify their audit procedures to adapt to the changing technology. Computer-based accounting systems are quite different from manual systems in many respects. Although information technology advances have made it more difficult for the auditor to examine accounting systems, these advances also provide opportunities for the auditor to conduct a significantly more effective and efficient audit than could be performed without them.

NBA star Yao Ming of the Houston Rockets shows off his McDonald's jersey, after being selected as global spokesman for the restaurant company. Looking on are Ronald McDonald and NBA Commissioner David Stern.

Computers can process accounting transactions with incredible speed, accuracy, and reliability. The computer will process the one thousandth transaction exactly as it did the first transaction. However, the accuracy and reliability of computer processing is a function of the accuracy and reliability of the program, or software, that drives the computer processing. The negative effects of computerization from an auditing standpoint are

Decreased visibility of transaction processing
Existence of data in computer-readable form only
Diminished audit trail
Extreme consequences of program errors
Inability of the computer to exercise logic

One problem caused by computerization is that the processing of transactions is no longer easily visible to the auditor. In manual auditing, the auditor can physically observe the recording of a sales transaction in the sales journal and its subsequent posting to the ledger. However, the computer's posting of a transaction to the appropriate computer files cannot be as readily observed, and the auditor has to rely on secondary means to observe exactly how the computer processes transactions. For example, the auditor could examine a trace produced by a special program that can track the sequence of steps performed by the computer.

A second problem caused by computer processing of accounting transactions is that the data cannot be viewed without the assistance of the computer. Data magnetically stored on a computer disk can only be viewed using software that either displays it on a screen or sends it to a printer. Again, this method of viewing

EXHIBIT 12.7

Audit Report for DaimlerChrysler Corporation

The Supervisory Board DaimlerChrysler AG:

We have audited the accompanying consolidated balance sheets of Daimler-Chrysler AG and subsidiaries ("DaimlerChrysler") as of December 31, 2003 and 2002, and the related consolidated statements of income (loss), changes in stockholders' equity, and cash flows for each of the years in the three-year period ended December 31, 2003. These consolidated financial statements are the responsibility of DaimlerChrysler's management. Our responsibility is to express an opinion on these consolidated financial statements based on our audits.

We conducted our audits in accordance with generally accepted auditing standards in the United States of America. Those standards require that we plan and perform the audit to obtain reasonable assurance about whether the financial statements are free of material misstatement. An audit includes examining, on a test basis, evidence supporting the amounts and disclosures in the financial statements. An audit also includes assessing the accounting principles used and significant estimates made by management, as well as evaluating the overall financial statement presentation. We believe that our audits provide a reasonable basis for our opinion.

In our opinion, the consolidated financial statements referred to above present fairly, in all material aspects, the financial position of DaimlerChrysler as of December 31, 2003 and 2002, and the results of their operations and their cash flows for each of the years in the three-year period ended December 31, 2003, in conformity with generally accepted accounting principles in the United States of America.

As described in Note 1 to the consolidated financial statements, DaimlerChrysler changed its method of accounting for stock-based compensation in 2003. As described in Notes 1, 2 and 11 to the consolidated financial statements, Daimler-Chrysler also adopted the required portions of FASB Interpretation No. 46 (revised December 2003), "Consolidation of Variable Interest Entities—an interpretation of ARB No. 51", in 2003. As described in Note 11 to the consolidated financial statements, DaimlerChrysler adopted Statement of Financial Accounting Standards No. 142, "Goodwill and Other Intangible Assets," in 2002.

Stuttgart, Germany
February 18, 2004

KPMG Deutsche Treuhand-Gesellschaft
Aktiengesellschaft
Wirtschaftsprüfungsgesellschaft

Wiedmann	Krauß
Wirtschaftsprüfer	Wirtschaftsprüfer

Source: DaimlerChrysler Annual Report 2003, p.113. **http://www.daimlerchrysler.com/Projects/c2c/ channel/documents/228297_dcag_gb_hv_2003.pdf**

accounting data is in contrast to manual accounting, where the auditor can open a ledger and directly observe the accounting data.

For manual systems, distinct links exist between source documents for an account cycle, their entry in a journal, the subsequent posting to a ledger, the entry in a trial balance, and the eventual amount displayed in a financial statement, such as the income statement or the balance sheet. This link from source document to financial statement entry is referred to as the **audit trail.** The audit trail is the connection between a source document like a sales invoice and the transaction's

audit trail The connection between a source document used to support an accounting transaction and the financial statements

ultimate disposition on the financial statements. Auditors follow the audit trail to find support for the figures shown on the financial statements.

In computer-based accounting systems, the audit trail is substantially diminished and much harder for the auditor to follow. In most computerized accounting transaction processing systems, the journal is eliminated; transactions are directly posted into permanent computer files—ledger accounts—when transactions are created and processed. Further, in online systems, source data is often directly keyed into the computer; no paper source document exists. Another problem with online systems is that the balances in ledger accounts are overwritten when they are updated; no record is maintained of the balance before the transaction was processed, unless the previous statement of the account is printed out or copied to a computer file.

Computer processing tends to make much of transaction processing invisible; consequently, an audit trail must be created by forcing the generation of documentation regarding the specific operating steps carried out by a computer program. For example, an online transaction processing system can be made to generate an error listing for invalid transactions, rather than merely signaling to the data entry operator that the transaction is invalid. Thus, the generation of documentation regarding key steps taken by the computer system during data input, processing, and output results in an audit trail that permits the tracing of transaction processing.

The quality of information processed and output by computer systems depends heavily on the quality of the computer programs that process the data input into transaction processing systems. A computer program replete with errors will inevitably compromise the integrity of the data within that transaction processing cycle. This problem is compounded by the inability of the computer to recognize illogical operations unless programmed to do so. The computer will blindly perform whatever functions the software demands of it, regardless of how illogical those operations might be (e.g., hours worked by one person of 400 for a week instead of 40). All of this indicates that the auditor must be concerned about verifying the validity of computer programs and of the controls relating to their development and modification.

Problems caused by computerization explain why a high degree of computer-related knowledge is required on the part of the auditor. Information technology advances have been occurring at a very rapid pace, and keeping up with recent developments is often a formidable task.

The complexities of computer processing of accounting data often result in greater difficulty for the auditor examining the computer-based accounting system. However, information technology advances also allow the auditor to harness the power of the computer in performing audit procedures. Sophisticated computer audit techniques, although difficult to implement, result in a very efficient and effective audit. Computer-based controls, which can be built into applications when they are initially created, can be designed to ensure that transactions meet a number of objectives (e.g., weekly hours worked should be less than or equal to 60). The computer will unerringly check *every* transaction for compliance with the transaction controls.

A computer's speed in processing accounting transactions also benefits the execution of computer audit procedures. Audit procedures such as randomly selecting transactions for detailed examination can easily be performed with the computer. Unlike in manual auditing, computer-generated random numbers could be used to select transactions. To the extent that control checks are performed by the computer, the auditor can be assured that those checks will be consistently and reliably carried out, much more so than if humans were performing the same control checks.

 Can you audit your personal financial information to be sure there are no mistakes in your bank records, credit card records, paychecks, and so on?

Foreign Currency Translation

> LEARNING OBJECTIVE 4
>
> Explain the steps in foreign currency translation, a necessary element in financial reporting of multinational business firms.

Many U.S. companies have multinational operations, with foreign subsidiaries around the globe. For example, McDonald's Corporation has over 30,000 restaurants; over half of these are outside the United States.

When a U.S. corporation owns more than 50 percent of the voting stock of a foreign company, a parent-subsidiary relationship exists, and the parent company is usually required to prepare consolidated financial statements. Before this can be done, the financial statements of the foreign subsidiary must be recast using U.S. generally accepted accounting principles. Next, the foreign accounts must be remeasured (translated) from the foreign currency into U.S. dollars. To make the translation, the first step is to identify three currencies.

- Currency of books and records (CBR). The CBR is the currency in which the foreign financial statements are denominated.
- Functional currency (FC). The FC is the currency in which the subsidiary generally buys, sells, borrows, and repays.
- Reporting currency (RC). The RC is the currency in which the consolidated financial statements are denominated.

A man makes a cash withdrawal from an unusual ATM machine at the Dusit Zoo in Bangkok, Thailand.

There are basically three approaches to currency translation: the temporal rate method, the current rate method, and the use of both methods. The following three rules are used to determine the method of translation:

Rule 1.   If the FC is hyperinflationary (i.e., 100 percent cumulative inflation within three years), then ignore the FC and remeasure the CBR into the RC using the temporal rate method.

Rule 2.   If the CBR is different from the FC, then remeasure the CBR into the FC using the temporal rate method.

Rule 3.   Translate from the FC into the RC using the current rate method.

The rules must be sequentially applied, stopping when the subsidiary's financial statements have been converted into the parent's reporting currency (RC). For example, when the functional currency (FC) is hyperinflationary, then Rule 1 applies; that is, the financial statements that are denominated in the CBR are translated into the RC using the temporal rate method, and Rules 2 and 3 aren't used. A second example is the case in which the CBR is British pounds, the FC is Dutch guilders (not hyperinflationary), and the RC is U.S. dollars; then Rule 1 is skipped and Rule 2 is applied. This translates the CBR (pounds) into the FC (guilders) using the temporal rate method. Since the FC (guilders) is not the RC (dollars), Rule 3 is then applied to translate the FC (guilders) into the RC (dollars) using the current rate method. A third example is when the CBR is the same as the FC; Rule 3 is applied directly.

Current Rate Method

When the current rate method is used, all assets and liabilities are translated using the current rate (i.e., exchange rate on the balance sheet date). Owners' equity and dividends are translated at historical rates (exchange rate at the time the asset was acquired, liability incurred, or element of paid-in capital was issued or reacquired). Income statement items can be translated using the average exchange rate (the average of the exchange rate at the beginning of the accounting period and the current rate).

Temporal Rate Method

When the temporal rate method is used, the objective is to measure each subsidiary transaction as though the transaction had been made by the parent. Monetary items like cash, receivables, inventories carried at market, payables, and long-term debt are remeasured using the current exchange rate. Other items, like prepaid expenses, inventories carried at cost, fixed assets, and stock, are remeasured using historical exchange rates.

Exhibit 12.8 (on p. 424) provides an example of how a foreign firm's financial statements would be translated from British pounds to U.S. dollars using the current rate method.

reality CHECK *Why do you think multinational business firms have to deal with foreign currency translation?*

The Impact of Technology

LEARNING OBJECTIVE 5
Discuss the impact of technology, particularly resources on the Web, on accounting.

Not long ago, an advance in information technology turned the world upside down. This new technology was quickly put to use in every advanced country. Consequently, the cost of information declined to only a tiny percentage of its previous cost. Soon, average citizens had more information in their homes than wealthy persons once had in their costly personal libraries. The new technology facilitated the rapid spread of knowledge. News about events in one place would be almost instantly communicated to distant locations. Information that had once been carefully controlled and monitored by governments and powerful organizations was now in the hands of nearly everyone. Ordinary people suddenly had power that they had not previously experienced. The new technology played a key role in the reshaping of the political structure of some of Europe's most powerful countries. Intense conflicts occurred. New approaches to government and business enterprise were necessary to deal with the new technology.

What was this new technology? The invention that shook the world was not the computer, but movable type. On a printing press invented by Johann Gutenberg in 1455, a book was produced mechanically for the first time in history. Almost everyone has heard of the Gutenberg Bible, but most people probably do not realize how modern printing, starting with the Gutenberg Bible, radically changed the course of history.

Advances in information technology profoundly affect the operations of the accounting information system and financial reporting. How will the world of tomorrow be different from that of today? Shakespeare called the future the

EXHIBIT 12.8

Foreign Currency Translation Using the Current Rate Method

ADJUSTED TRIAL BALANCE
In British Pounds (BP)
December 31, 2004

	Debit	Credit
Cash	10,000	
Accounts Receivable	35,000	
Inventory	105,000	
Equipment	60,000	
Accum. Dep.		10,000
Accounts Payable		35,000
Bonds Payable		50,000
Revenues		120,000
General Expenses	108,000	
Depreciation Expense	8,000	
Dividends	4,000	
Common Stock		62,000
Paid-in Capital in Excess of Par		44,000
Retained Earnings		9,000
Total	330,000	330,000

Exchange Rates:

	1 BP = $____
Current Exchange Rate	0.520
Average Exchange Rate	0.490
At July 31, 2004	0.505
At June 30, 2001	0.470

Other: All common stock was issued on June 30, 2001 (i.e., 6/30/01).
Dividends were declared and paid on July 31, 2004.
Translated Retained Earnings at 12/31/04 was: $5,500

TRANSLATION FROM BRITISH POUNDS TO U.S. DOLLARS
CURRENT RATE METHOD

Debits:	BP's	Exchange Rates	U.S. $'s
Cash	10,000	0.520	5,200
A/R	35,000	0.520	18,200
Inventory	105,000	0.520	54,600
Fixed Assets	60,000	0.520	31,200
General Expenses	108,000	0.490	52,920
Depreciation Exp.	8,000	0.490	3,920
Dividends (7/31/04)	4,000	0.505	2,020
Total	330,000		168,060
Credits:			
Accum. Depreciation	10,000	0.520	5,200
A/P	35,000	0.520	18,200
Bonds Payable	50,000	0.520	26,000
Revenues	120,000	0.490	58,800
Common Stock (6/30/01)	62,000	0.470	29,140
Paid-in Cap. (6/30/01)	44,000	0.470	20,680
Retained Earnings	9,000	n.a.	5,500
Cum. Transl. Adjustment			4,540
Total	330,000		168,060

Technology and Business

Timeline of Major Events Regarding Accounting and Information Processing

1455	Johann Gutenberg invents movable type.
1494	Luca Pacioli writes first book on double-entry accounting.
1629	Appointment of auditors to examine the accounts of Massachusetts Bay Colony.
1700s	Accountants trained through apprenticeships in counting houses.
1790s	New York Stock Exchange established.
1830s	Charles Babbage develops analytic engine, the forerunner of the electronic computer.
1883	First college accounting course offered at the University of Pennsylvania.
1887	American Association of Public Accountants formed.
1896	New York is first state to pass CPA legislation.
1919	National Association of Cost Accountants formed.
1930s	Securities Acts of 1933 and 1934 require filing and public disclosure of audited financial statements to the SEC.
1940	Institute of Internal Auditors formed.
1946	The first electronic computer, ENIAC, is constructed at the University of Pennsylvania.
1958	In response to Soviet technological advances, the United States forms the Advanced Research Projects Agency (ARPA), with the Department of Defense, to develop U.S. prominence in science and technology applicable to the military.
1969	ARPANET, the forerunner of the Internet, established with four nodes: UCLA, Stanford, UC–Santa Barbara, and University of Utah.
1970	First applications of electronic data interchange (EDI) made.
1973	Financial Accounting Standards Board (FASB) established. International Accounting Standards Committee (IASC) established.

1980s	Widespread use of microcomputers, particularly for word processing and spreadsheet applications, occurs.
1984	Internet host computers exceed 1000.
1990s	Advancements in hardware and software made. The PC is helpful in virtually every accounting task, from financial analysis to audit examinations to tax research to communications.
1991	Tim Berners-Lee, working at CERN in Geneva, develops a hypertext system to provide efficient information access. He posts the first computer code of the World Wide Web in a relatively innocuous newsgroup, alt.hypertext.
1994	Pizza Hut sells pizza on its website. First Virtual, the first cyberbank, is opened.
1997	Business-to-business (B2B) e-commerce begins.
1999	Most large corporations provide financial reports on the Web, referred to as Internet financial disclosure or electronic financial reporting.
2003	Internet host computers, computers with a registered IP address, exceed 150 million. Users in over 150 countries are connected.
2004	Tim Berners-Lee knighted by Queen Elizabeth for contributions to Internet development, specifically for inventing the World Wide Web.

Questions

1. Considering the major historical events affecting accounting and information processing, which one or two would you consider the most profound?
2. The use of the Web has revolutionized business. With what firms have you done e-business?
3. With what firms would you like to do e-business if they had an e-business website?

"undiscovered country." What will the undiscovered country of accounting and information processing look like? Just a few decades ago, could anyone have predicted the impact of the Web on business and e-commerce?

Improvements will continue to be made in basic computer applications such as spreadsheet, database, word processing, and communication software. Microcomputer power as measured by processing speed, storage capacity, and portability will continue advancing. Are there limits to what technology can accomplish? Before the invention of microcomputers and spreadsheet software, few could have predicted their impact on the accounting profession.

Our world is changing. International trade and technological advances have dramatically shaped our modern culture. There have been periods of rapid change throughout recorded history. Like the invention of the printing press, the computer and the Internet are having a profound impact on how people communicate, work, and relax.

Information technology has dramatically altered the business world, especially in accounting. The accumulation, storage, and processing of vast amounts of financial data once required armies of "number-crunchers." Now the number-crunching is turned over to computers. Accountants are able to focus on other aspects of their role in the firm, such as financial analysis, operational auditing, internal control evaluation, and managerial planning.

American Institute of CPAs Top Ten Technologies

The Information Technology Division of the American Institute of CPAs identified technologies expected to have an impact on accounting or business in general. On an overall basis, the top ten technologies were listed as follows:[2]

1. Information security. The hardware, software, processes, and procedures in place to protect an organization's information systems from internal and external threats. They include firewalls, antivirus procedures, password management, patches, locked facilities, Internet protocol strategy, and perimeter control.

2. Business information management. The process of capturing, indexing, storing, retrieving, searching, and managing documents electronically, including knowledge and database management (XML, PDF, and other formats). Business information management brings to fruition the promise of the "paperless office."

3. Application integration. The ability of different operating systems, applications, and databases to "talk" to each other and for information to flow freely regardless of application, language, or platform.

4. Web services. Applications that use the Internet as their infrastructure and access tool, including both Web-enabled and Web-based applications. Examples include Java applications, Microsoft's .Net initiative, and today's Application Service Providers (ASPs) and business portals.

5. Disaster recovery planning. The development, monitoring, and updating of the process by which organizations plan for the continuity of their business in the event of a loss of business information resources due to impairments such as theft, virus infestation, weather damage, accidents, or other malicious destruction.

6. Wireless technologies. The transfer of voice or data from one machine to another via the airwaves without physical connection. Examples include cellular, satellite, infrared, Bluetooth, wireless (WiFi), 3G, and two-way paging.

7. Intrusion detection. Software or hardware solutions that list and track successful and unsuccessful log-in attempts on a network, such as Tripwire. Intrusion detection capabilities are being built into many of today's firewall applications.

8. Remote connectivity. Technology that allows a user to connect to a computer from a distant location outside of the office. Examples would include Remote Access Services (RAS), Windows Terminal Server (WTS), Citrix, MangoMind, and PCAnywhere.

9. Customer relationship management. Managing all customer touch points, including call center technologies, e-commerce, data warehousing, and all other technologies used to facilitate communications with customers and prospects.

10. Privacy. Today, more and more personal information is being collected and converted to digital formats. This information must be protected from unauthorized use by those with access to the data. Privacy is a business issue, as well as a technology issue, because of state, federal, and international regulations.

Source: Copyright © 2003 by the American Institute of Certified Public Accountants, Inc. Reprinted with permission.

Accounting and Auditing Resources on the Web

The Internet, specifically the World Wide Web, has become an extremely useful research tool. The Web can be used to find valuable information about many subjects. Also, various authorities can be easily consulted both by their postings to the Web and through tools made available on the Web.

Regarding financial reporting and other accounting issues, the Web is especially useful for staying informed of current developments and resolving technical issues. Since organizations responsible for creating accounting and auditing standards maintain websites, the Web now presents a convenient way to keep up-to-date on technical developments. Accounting and auditing issues can be resolved by searching sites that provide accounting and auditing-related information, researching sites that contain authoritative pronouncements, submitting questions to specialists, or posting questions to online forums.

Exhibit 12.9 (on p. 428) lists accounting and auditing websites in six categories: financial accounting, auditing, international accounting and auditing, research and publications, accounting organizations, search and Web technology tools, and other. The websites are also listed, with their respective links, on the Web (**http://acct.tamu.edu/smith/acctwebs.htm**), along with several additional sites that may be of interest.

Websites Related to Financial Accounting. The following websites will be useful for investigating topics pertaining to financial accounting. Staying up-to-date regarding generally accepted accounting principles (GAAP) can be challenging. Rule 203 of the American Institute of CPAs Code of Professional Conduct specifies the organizations that establish GAAP. These include the Financial Accounting Standards Board (FASB) for private business firms, the Governmental Accounting Standards Board (GASB) for state and local government entities, and the Federal Accounting Standards Advisory Board (FASAB) for federal government entities. For each of these organizations, the highest level of GAAP is called Category A, second highest Category B, and so on. For example, regarding FASB, Category A GAAP are the FASB Statements of Financial Accounting Standards, together with Accounting Research Bulletins and Accounting Principles Board Opinions that are not superseded by action of the FASB.

FINANCIAL ACCOUNTING STANDARDS BOARD (**www.fasb.org**). This site is helpful for following the FASB and Emerging Issues Task Force (EITF) activities. The Publications section contains summaries of all FASB Statements (Category A GAAP). These

EXHIBIT 12.9

Accounting and Auditing Resources on the Web

Financial Accounting	
Financial Accounting Standards Board	www.fasb.org
Governmental Accounting Standards Board	www.gasb.org
Federal Accounting Standards Advisory Board	www.fasab.gov
Securities and Exchange Commission	www.sec.gov
Auditing	
AICPA Audit and Attest Standards	www.aicpa.org/members/div/auditstd/index.htm
GAO Governmental Auditing Standards	www.gao.gov/govaud/ybk01.htm
Sarbanes-Oxley Act	www.sarbanes-oxley.com
Public Company Accounting Oversight Board	www.pcaob.com
Office of Management and Budget (OMB)	www.whitehouse.gov/omb/
International Accounting and Auditing	
International Accounting Standards Board (IASB)	http://www.iasb.org/
International Federation of Accountants (IFAC)	www.ifac.org
Research and Publications	
CPA Journal (award-winning professional journal)	www.cpaj.com
AuditNet (free audit programs)	www.auditnet.org
ITAudit (focus on information technology)	www.theiia.org/itaudit
Accounting Organizations	
American Institute of CPAs	www.aicpa.org
New York State Society of CPAs	www.nysscpa.org
Texas Society of CPAs	www.tscpa.org
Institute of Internal Auditors	www.theiia.org
American Accounting Association	http://aaahq.org
Institute of Management Accountants	www/imanet.org
Association of Certified Fraud Examiners	www.cfenet.com
Financial Executives Institute	www.fei.com
Other	
Quotations on Ethics (cool quotes & movie clips)	acct.tamu.edu/smith/ethics/quotes.htm
Ancient Accountants at Work	acct.tamu.edu/smith/ethics/history.htm
Star Wars: Accounting Implications	acct.tamu.edu/smith/starwars/starwars.htm

Note: Links to the websites listed above can be directly accessed at **http://acct.tamu.edu/smith/acctwebs.htm.**

online summaries are the same as those inside the printed standards. The Emerging Issues Task Force section, found under the Technical Projects link, provides a summary of current issues the EITF has discussed and indicates if a consensus was reached. EITF consensus positions are Category C GAAP. This link also provides access to the Technical Inquiry Service. This section contains an online form that allows you to submit questions about FASB literature and projects. The site provides a wealth of information about the FASB's and EITF's projects. These include meeting agendas, exposure drafts, press releases, a quarterly plan of technical items under review, and e-mail addresses for contacting the FASB board members and staff.

GOVERNMENTAL ACCOUNTING STANDARDS BOARD (**www.gasb.org**). The GASB establishes financial reporting standards applicable to state and local government entities. This website's Publications section contains summaries of the three categories of GAAP: GASB Statements (Category A); GASB Interpretations (Category A); and GASB Concept Statements (Category E). The site has other items related to the GASB's activities: exposure drafts, news agendas for board meetings, and the GASB's Technical Project Plan, which details the project's objectives and status. The Performance Measures section has extensive information about reporting on service efforts and accomplishments. The Communication section provides the email addresses and phone extensions for the GASB board members and staff.

FEDERAL ACCOUNTING STANDARDS ADVISORY BOARD (http://www.fasab.gov/). At its October 1999 meeting, the AICPA Council adopted a resolution recognizing the Federal Accounting Standards Advisory Board (FASAB) as the body designated to establish generally accepted accounting principles (GAAP) for federal government entities. This website provides the FASAB standards and concepts.

SECURITIES AND EXCHANGE COMMISSION (www.sec.gov). Accountants involved with public companies will find several useful links in the Current SEC Rulemaking section of this website. The Proposed Rule link lists rule proposals related to accounting and other matters the SEC regulates. Comments on the proposals may be submitted by e-mail. The Final Rule section lists final rules currently available. The site also contains the most recently issued pronouncements, such as Staff Accounting Bulletins. New Bulletins are listed in this section. Concept and Interpretative Releases as well as Policy Statements can be found here.

Websites Related to Auditing.

The following websites are useful for researching current issues pertaining to auditing standards:

AICPA AUDIT AND ATTEST STANDARDS (www.aicpa.org/members/div/auditstd/index.htm). This site distributes information about the pronouncements of the Auditing Standards Board (ASB). The Technical Activities and Publications section includes summaries of recently issued Statements on Auditing Standards (SASs) and Statements on Standards for Attestation Engagements (SSAEs), as well as interpretations of SASs and SSAEs. The site also provides a wealth of information about the ASB's activities. For example, there are highlights of each ASB meeting, as well as *In Our Opinion,* a quarterly publication of the Audit and Attest Standards Team. Finally, interested parties can obtain exposure drafts and other documents of interest to auditors, such as the AICPA's *Audit Issues in Revenue Recognition* paper.

GAO GOVERNMENTAL AUDITING STANDARDS (www.gao.gov/govaud/ybk01.htm). Government Auditing Standards, that is, the "Yellow Book," contains standards for audits of government organizations, programs, activities, and functions and for audits of government assistance received by contractors, not-for-profit organizations, and other nongovernment organizations. The complete Yellow Book text is available at this site. In February 1997, the Advisory Council on Government Auditing Standards endorsed an issue-by-issue approach to revising individual standards. The approach continues the practice of exposing all revisions to public comment. Since the exposure drafts and recently issued standards are available on this website, it is valuable for keeping current on changes to the Yellow Book. For example, Government Auditing Standard Amendment 2 was available electronically two months prior to printed copies. In addition to tracking changes to the Yellow Book, this site also makes it easy to follow the actions of the Advisory Council, since it carries meeting highlights and notices of forthcoming meetings.

Sarbanes-Oxley Act (http://www.sarbanes-oxley.com). This website allows firms to stay abreast of the proposed and final rules and regulations issued by the SEC to implement the Sarbanes-Oxley Act (SOA). Key provisions of the SOA were

- Establishes a Public Company Accounting Oversight Board consisting of five full-time members to set "auditing, quality control, ethics, independence and other standards relating to the preparation of audit reports"
- Limits the types of consulting services audit firms can provide to their public company audit clients
- Requires retention of audit work papers necessary to support the audit report for seven years
- Requires auditors to report on internal control, perform tests of compliance with SEC rules and regulations, perform concurring partner reviews, and rotate lead and concurring partners at least every five years
- Prohibits audit firms from auditing public companies whose CEO, CFO, controller, or equivalent worked for the audit firm during the preceding year

Public Company Accounting Oversight Board (www.pcaob.com). The Public Company Accounting Oversight Board will perform annual peer reviews of audit firms with 100 or more public company audit clients, and every three years will review all other firms with public company audit clients. The board has the authority to investigate and discipline public company auditors. The website contains all the latest information on standard setting and quality review. The site also includes news and current events and links to a technical forum and a management forum.

Office of Management and Budget (www.whitehouse.gov/omb). Under the Grants Management link, this site provides the full text of OMB Circular A–133, *Audits of States, Local Governments, and Non-Profit Organizations*. This circular establishes uniform audit requirements for nonfederal entities that administer federal awards and implements the Single Audit Act Amendments of 1996. It also provides the March 2000 Compliance Supplement, which identifies existing important compliance requirements that the federal government expects to be considered as part of an audit required by the 1996 amendments. Since auditors are required to follow the provisions of OMB Circular A–133 and the Compliance Supplement, this site is very useful in tracking changes to these important documents.

Websites Related to International Accounting and Auditing. The following websites are useful for researching current issues pertaining to international accounting and auditing:

International Accounting Standards Board (www.iasb.org). The IASB issues International Financial Reporting Standards (IFRS). The IASB's website provides a detailed summary of these standards. The site also provides information on IASB's projects and news releases, as well as on its structure and operation. This site will be very interesting to those who are following the harmonization of international and U.S. accounting standards. There is even a quiz to test your knowledge of international standards.

International Federation of Accountants (www.ifac.org). Those with an interest in international auditing standards and the harmonization of standards will find this site very interesting. The International Auditing and Assurance Standards Board (IAASB) is a committee of the International Federation of Accountants (IFAC) that works to improve the uniformity of auditing practices and related services throughout the world by issuing pronouncements on a variety of audit and assur-

The International Accounting Standards Board website offers information about the international standard-setting process.

Copyright © IASCF. Reprinted with permission of International Accounting Standards Committee Foundation.

ance functions and by promoting their acceptance worldwide. The IFAC site lists exposure drafts, committee activities, and task forces that address special topics.

Websites Related to Accounting Research and Publications.

Websites such as the FASB provide a means of submitting technical questions to their staff. The Web can be used in three other ways for conducting research into accounting and auditing issues: (1) accessing authoritative literature, (2) posting questions to online forums, and (3) searching sites that catalog online accounting and auditing resources. The following websites are useful for researching various topics such as ethics, GAAP, auditing issues, professional associations, continuing professional education (CPE), and current practice-related issues:

CPA JOURNAL (**www.cpaj.com**). The *CPA Journal* is a refereed journal published by the New York State Society of CPAs, with a circulation of approximately 38,000. It is a nationally prominent journal widely circulated among accounting practitioners in public accounting, industry, and government, as well as among accounting faculty and students. The journal previously received the Anbar Golden Page Award as the number one practical journal in the accounting and finance category. Over 400 magazines and journals were evaluated for this award by the U.K.-based electronic database of journals published in English. The *CPA Journal* website includes software downloads, Internet resources, and online archives of past issues going back to 1989. The archives can be searched based on key words.

AUDITNET (**www.auditnet.org**). AuditNet provides a great deal of electronic audit-related information. Kaplan's Audit Resource List (KARL) contains links to more than 950 Web resources for auditors. Auditor's Sharing Audit Programs (ASAP) contains over 150 audit programs that you can freely use and modify. Information is easy to locate through the site's cleanly organized menu or search engine.

ITAudit (www.theiia.org/itaudit). This site focuses on information technology (IT) for auditors. Features include a forum that publishes IT audit-related articles. Also available at ITAudit are

> An excellent reference library that provides links and additional information
>
> A bulletin board that allows registered users to post messages
>
> A Yellow Pages section that provides an extensive database of IT products, services, and resources of interest to audit professionals
>
> A jobs section, which is the Audit Career Center for the Institute of Internal Auditors (IIA). The Career Center helps match organizations that have position openings with IIA members seeking new opportunities.

Websites Related to Accounting Organizations. The following websites are useful for obtaining information pertaining to various professional accounting organizations:

AMERICAN INSTITUTE OF CPAS (www.aicpa.org). The AICPA is the premier national professional association for public accounting in the United States. The AICPA and its predecessors have been serving the accounting profession since 1887. Its mission is to provide members with the resources, information, and leadership that enable them to provide valuable services in the highest professional manner, to benefit the public as well as employers and clients.

NEW YORK STATE SOCIETY OF CPAS (www.nysscpa.org). The New York State Society of CPAs (NYSSCPA) was incorporated in 1897. The NYSSCPA is one of the largest state accounting organizations in the nation and currently has over 30,000 members. Among its purposes are

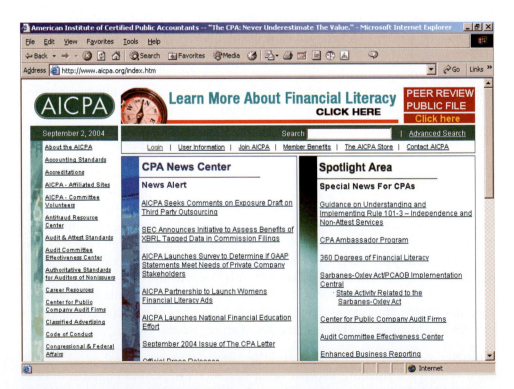

The American Institute of CPAs website lists a number of functions and services carried out by this prominent accounting organization.

> To cultivate, promote, and disseminate knowledge and information concerning certified public accountants
>
> To establish and maintain high standards of integrity, honor, and character among certified public accountants
>
> To furnish information regarding accountancy and the practice and methods thereof to its members and the general public

The Professional Library section of the NYSSCPA website contains summaries of FASB and GASB pronouncements and exposure drafts.

THE TEXAS SOCIETY OF CERTIFIED PUBLIC ACCOUNTANTS (www.tscpa.org). The TSCPA is a not-for-profit, voluntary, professional organization representing Texas CPAs. TSCPA has 20 local chapters statewide and 27,000 members, one of the largest in-state memberships of any CPA organization in the nation. The society is committed to serving the public interest with programs that advance the highest standards of ethics and practice within the CPA profession.

THE INSTITUTE OF INTERNAL AUDITORS (www.theiia.org). Established in 1941, the IIA serves more than 70,000 members from more than 100 countries in internal auditing, governance and internal control, IT audit, education, and security. The IIA is the world's leader in certification, education, research, and technological guidance for the internal auditing field.

AMERICAN ACCOUNTING ASSOCIATION (http://aaahq.org). The American Accounting Association promotes worldwide excellence in accounting education, research, and practice. Founded in 1916 as the American Association of University Instructors in Accounting, its present name was adopted in 1936. The association is a voluntary organization of people interested in accounting education and research.

INSTITUTE OF MANAGEMENT ACCOUNTANTS (www.imanet.org). The IMA is the leading professional organization devoted exclusively to management accounting and financial management. The IMA helps members stay abreast of the changes affecting the management accounting and financial management professions. The IMA provides new insights and ideas in these evolving fields and provides ethical guidance as well. The website offers resources such as continuing education; on-line issues of the IMA's journal, *Strategic Finance* (formerly *Management Accounting*); and information about the IMA's certification program.

ASSOCIATION OF CERTIFIED FRAUD EXAMINERS (www.cfenet.com). The Association of Certified Fraud Examiners, established in 1988, is based in Austin, Texas. The 25,000-member professional organization is dedicated to educating qualified individuals (Certified Fraud Examiners) who are trained in the highly specialized aspects of detecting, investigating, and deterring fraud and white-collar crime. Each member of the association designated a Certified Fraud Examiner (CFE) has earned certification after an extensive application process and on passing the uniform CFE examination.

FINANCIAL EXECUTIVES INSTITUTE (www.fei.org). The Financial Executives Institute is a professional association for senior-level financial executives, representing 15,000 individuals. The FEI provides peer networking opportunities, information on current events, and professional development services to chief financial officers, vice presidents of finance, controllers, treasurers, tax executives, and educators. This is done through an Internet community, 86 chapters, and 9 technical committees. Membership is limited to individuals holding senior management positions

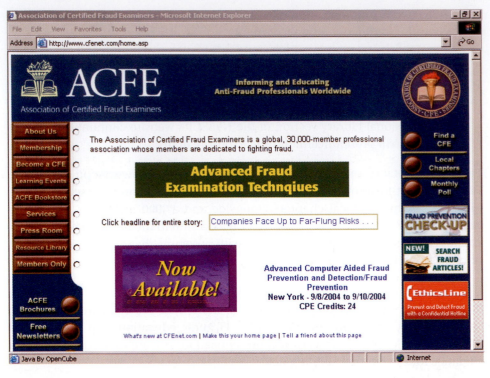

The website of the Association of Certified Fraud Examiners provides lots of useful information about the organization and its activities.
www.CFEnet.com, The Association of Certified Fraud Examiners, Austin, Texas. Reprinted with permission.

similar to those listed above, but other finance professionals may join if they meet certain criteria.

Other Websites

QUOTATIONS ON ETHICS (acct.tamu.edu/smith/ethics/quotes.htm). This website provides a number of incisive quotes regarding ethics. Categories include historically famous Americans, leadership, friendship, national character, personal integrity, and inspiration and faith. Also on the website are pertinent movie clips from *Star Wars* and *Braveheart*.

ANCIENT ACCOUNTANTS AT WORK (acct.tamu.edu/smith/ethics/history.htm). This website offers a humorous look at ancient accountants along with links to authentic accounting history websites, such as Luca Pacioli, the Father of Accounting.

STAR WARS: ACCOUNTING IMPLICATIONS (acct.tamu.edu/smith/starwars/starwars.htm). This humor website delves into the accounting implications of one of the greatest movie series of all time. The great battle is between those who use "the Force" for good and their antagonists who tap into the "dark side." The battle is fought using various futuristic devices such as handheld light sabers, robots, and massive star destroyers. Both sides are limited by their resources. This is where accounting plays a key role. In the centers of power, on Coruscant and numerous other worlds, the accountants are hard at work keeping track of production, inventory, cash flow, personnel, operating expenditures, and other financial matters.

 *How have technology and the Internet made your college studies different from those of your parents?*

Careers in Accounting

A good place to obtain information about careers in accounting is from the professional accounting organizations, such as the American Institute of CPAs, the Institute of Internal Auditors, the Institute of Management Accountants, and the Association of Certified Fraud Examiners. In fact, several accounting organizations offer student memberships at discounted membership dues.

The American Institute of CPAs offers a Student Affiliate Membership for $35 per year, starting as early as your freshman year in college and going through to the end of graduate school. Membership is also available to recent college graduates who are in the workforce and who have not yet passed the CPA exam. Student Affiliate Membership in the AICPA includes a subscription to the *Journal of Accountancy*, a subscription to *The CPA Letter*, a newsletter, access to the AICPA website (**www.aicpa.org**), access to a student web page (**www.aicpa.org/nolimits**), discounts on publications, software, professional development courses, and conferences, self-assessment and career tools, and more.

The Institute of Internal Auditors offers a student membership for $30 per year (regular dues are $115 per year). Student membership is available to full-time students who are studying internal auditing or related courses at colleges and universities. IIA student membership benefits include career networking opportunities with other members, a subscription to *Internal Auditor* magazine, a subscription to *Auditwire* (the association's newsletter), access to the twice-monthly e-magazine *ITAudit Forum*, access to the Audit Career Center (including the IIA Resume Service), and more.

Becoming a student member of a major professional organization can help you start building a career as you gain opportunities to learn more about the accounting profession and to meet with accounting professionals.

Summary

LEARNING OBJECTIVE 1
Explain the role of financial reporting.

Accounting provides critical information to business managers within the firm and to interested parties outside the firm. Within the firm, managers use accounting information to make decisions regarding the operations of the firm. Accounting will determine whether the revenues of the firm exceed its expenses, thus resulting in a profit. Alternatively, accounting will determine whether expenses exceed revenues, thus resulting in a loss. Naturally the managers want the firm to make a profit.

make effective business decisions. The most important output of the accounting information system is the set of financial statements. These accounting reports include the income statement, statement of retained earnings, balance sheet, and statement of cash flows. The income statement shows the firm's revenues, expenses, and net income or loss for a period. The statement of retained earnings shows the change in retained earnings from the beginning to the end of the year. The balance sheet provides a snapshot of the firm's financial position. The statement of cash flows presents receipts and payments for operating, investing, and financing activities.

LEARNING OBJECTIVE 2
Define the components of the four financial statements.

Accounting is called the language of business because accounting provides the information that people need to

LEARNING OBJECTIVE 3
Describe the contribution of auditing to the usefulness of financial reporting.

A key concern of investors who rely on the integrity of the financial statements is the validity of the reports they receive. The firm's management is also concerned about the reliability and integrity of the reports produced by the AIS. Both internal auditing and external auditing help provide the assurances needed by decision makers who rely on financial statements.

LEARNING OBJECTIVE 4

Explain the steps in foreign currency translation, a necessary element in financial reporting of multinational business firms.

Most large U.S. companies have multinational operations, with foreign subsidiaries around the globe. When a U.S. corporation owns more than 50 percent of the voting stock of a foreign company, a parent-subsidiary relationship exists. The parent company is usually required to prepare consolidated financial statements. Before this can be done, the financial statements of the foreign subsidiary must be recast using U.S. generally accepted accounting principles (GAAP).

LEARNING OBJECTIVE 5

Discuss the impact of technology, particularly resources on the Web, on accounting.

Advances in information technology have dramatically altered the business world, especially in accounting. The accumulation, storage, and processing of vast amounts of financial data once required armies of "number-crunchers." Now the number-crunching is turned over to computers. Accountants are able to focus on other roles in the firm, such as financial analysis, operational auditing, internal control evaluation, and managerial planning.

Websites can be helpful for researching financial reporting and other accounting issues. Websites are available for obtaining information on financial accounting, auditing, international accounting and auditing, research and publications, accounting organizations, and other issues. Knowing where to go can save considerable time and effort in conducting research on the Web.

Chapter Questions

1. Who uses accounting information and for what purpose?
2. List some of the decisions that business managers must make.
3. What are the components of the income statement?
4. What are the components of the statement of retained earnings?
5. What are the components of the balance sheet?
6. What are the components of the statement of cash flows?
7. List the four essential questions that are answered by the four financial statements.
8. Who conducts an external audit and who benefits from the audit?
9. Contrast external auditing with internal auditing.
10. Describe the basic steps in an audit.
11. How has computerization affected auditing?
12. What is the audit trail?
13. What is foreign currency translation and why is it necessary?
14. Give an example of how an accountant might use the Web to help on the job.
15. Briefly describe the origin of the Internet.

Interpreting Business News

1. In a news article about the advances in information technology, the writer predicted everyone in the world would have access to the Internet within a decade. Do you think this is likely? How might this affect a firm's business operations?
2. In a news story about a company going bankrupt, the writer suggested that the auditors had failed in doing their job. Are business failures the result of poor auditing?
3. People sometimes say that the world is shrinking. Thanks to improved communications and transportation technologies, the world doesn't seem as large as it once did. A news article about international trade predicted that global commerce would increase dramatically in the coming year. Do you think international trade will increase? Will that be good or bad for U.S. companies?

Web Assignments

1. Sony Corporation is a leading manufacturer of audio, video, communications, and information technology products for the consumer and professional markets. Sony's music, motion picture, television, computer entertainment, and online businesses make the firm one of the most comprehensive entertainment companies in the world. Go to the website of Sony Corporation (**sony.com**). Where is the firm's worldwide headquarters? Where is the firm's U.S. headquarters (Sony Corporation of America)? What were Sony's worldwide sales? U.S. sales? How many people are employed by Sony?

2. Use a Web search tool and investigate auditing. List and briefly describe some websites that concern auditing.

3. The American Institute of Certified Public Accountants (AICPA) is the premier national professional association for accountants in the United States. The AICPA and its predecessors have been serving the accounting profession since 1887.

Its mission is to provide members with the resources, information, and leadership that enable them to provide valuable services in the highest professional manner to benefit the public as well as employers and clients. Go to the AICPA website (**http://www.aicpa.org**). What are the requirements for becoming a Certified Public Accountant (CPA)? What are the different sections on the CPA exam?

 # Portfolio Projects

Exploring Your Own Case in Point

In this chapter we describe the purpose of financial reporting and present the four financial statements. Answering these questions will help you better understand the role of financial reporting by your company.

1. Go to your company's website and locate the financial reports. What was the amount of your company's total assets for the most current year? What was the amount of your company's profit (net income) for the most current year?

2. On the auditor's report, find the name of the audit firm that audited your company's financial statements. Did the auditor's report indicate whether the auditor followed generally accepted auditing standards? In the auditor's report, does the audit opinion state whether your company was in compliance with generally accepted accounting principles?

3. Is your company engaged in international trade? Do the financial statements indicate a foreign exchange gain or loss? If so, how much was it?

Starting Your Own Business

After reading this chapter, you should be able to make some plans regarding your startup company's financial statements.

1. What financial statements does your company need to prepare? Regarding the balance sheet, what sorts of assets would your company need? What sorts of liabilities would your company incur? Prepare a proposed starting balance sheet for your company based on this information.

2. Regarding the income statement, what sort of revenues would you expect your company to generate in its first year of operations? What sort of expenses would you expect to incur? Prepare a forecasted income statement for your company's first year of operations based on this information.

3. The chapter describes notable advances in information technology and how they affect accounting. How would you use current information technology in your company, particularly with regard to the accounting system?

Test Prepper

You've read the chapter, studied the key terms, and the exam is any day now. Think you are ready to ace it? Take this sample test to gauge your comprehension of chapter material. You can check your answers at the back of the book.

True/False Questions

Please indicate if the following statements are true or false:

_____ 1. Accounting is called the language of business because accounting provides the information that people need to make effective business decisions.

_____ 2. The balance sheet is also referred to as the statement of operating results or the statement of earnings.

_____ 3. A fiscal year is an accounting period of 12 months, which may or may not end on December 31.

_____ 4. External audits must be conducted by either independent Certified Public Accountants (CPAs) or internal auditors.

_____ 5. The audit trail is the connection between a source document (e.g., a sales invoice) and the transaction's ultimate disposition on the financial statements.

_____ 6. Over half of McDonald's Corporation's restaurants are outside the United States.

_____ 7. When a U.S. corporation owns 25 percent or more of the voting stock of a foreign company, a parent-subsidiary relationship exists, and the parent company is usually required to prepare consolidated financial statements.

_____ 8. Since organizations responsible for creating accounting and auditing standards maintain websites, the Web now presents a convenient way to keep up-to-date on technical developments.

_____ 9. The Sarbanes-Oxley Act established the Public Company Accounting Oversight Board.

_____ 10. The American Institute of CPAs is the premier national professional association for public accounting in the United States.

Multiple-Choice Questions

Choose the best answer.

_____ 1. The primary goal of a firm is to

a. increase tax revenues to the government.

b. increase the wealth of the firm's owners, that is, investors.

c. reduce dependence on foreign imports.

d. provide job security to all employees.

e. develop multinational operations.

_____ 2. The financial statements do *not* include a(n)

a. statement of retained expenses and future cash flows.

b. income statement.

c. statement of retained earnings.

d. balance sheet.

e. statement of cash flows.

_____ 3. _____ is the biggest expense of merchandising firms such as Sears, Best Buy, and Kroger.

a. Utility expense

b. Depreciation expense

c. Cost of goods sold

d. Income tax expense

e. Advertising

_____ 4. All audits are characterized by a common set of steps. These steps do *not* include

a. arrive at an opinion.

b. plan the audit.

c. obtain and evaluate evidence.

d. investigate competitor pricing.

e. communicate results.

_____ 5. The negative effects of computerization from an auditing standpoint do *not* include

a. the existence of data in computer-readable form only.

b. an increased visibility of transaction processing.

c. a diminished audit trail.

d. extreme consequences of program errors.

e. the inability of the computer to exercise logic.

_____ 6. The _____ is the currency in which the financial statements of a foreign subsidiary are denominated.

a. functional currency

b. currency of books and records

c. reporting currency

d. global currency

e. dollar

_____ 7. The _____ is the currency in which the foreign subsidiary generally buys, sells, borrows, and repays.

a. functional currency

b. currency of books and records

c. reporting currency

d. global currency

e. dollar

_____ 8. The _____ is the currency in which the consolidated financial statements are denominated.

a. functional currency

b. currency of books and records

c. reporting currency

d. global currency

e. dollar

_____ 9. The website for the _____ contains the Yellow Book of standards for audits of government organizations, programs, activities, and functions.

a. Sarbanes-Oxley Act

b. AICPA Audit and Attest Standards

c. Federal Accounting Standards Advisory Board

d. GAO Governmental Auditing Standards

e. Office of Management and Budget

_____ 10. Starting in the _____, many corporations began providing their financial statements on the Web.

a. 1950s

b. 1970s

c. 1980s

d. 1990s

e. 2000s

Want more questions? Visit the student website at **http://college.hmco.com/business/student/** (select Gaspar, *Introduction to Business*) and take the ACE quizzes for more practice.

Finance

You need money to buy and sell goods and services, save for large purchases, invest for retirement in old age, and give to worthy charitable causes. While you use money every day, how much do you really know about it? Who makes it? How is it controlled in the country? How do businesses use it to invest in the production of their products? What role do banks and other financial institutions play? What kinds of financial instruments are available to you for investment? Is there a risk that you could lose your money when you invest in different financial instruments? Can time change the value of money? These and many other questions are related to the study of finance.

Finance is applicable to all areas of business enterprise—an advertising campaign in marketing, the equipment needed to assemble a product, the wages that should be paid to employees, legal matters of intellectual property rights, and the application of accounting data to business decisions. Whenever money is involved in a business, government, or personal decision, principles of finance apply.

We divide our discussion of finance into the perspective of the firm or individual—microlevel, and of the economy—macrolevel. Chapter 13 covers the financial management of the firm, including investing in individual firms. Here we consider how companies both raise funds for investment and evaluate how best to invest those funds. For private firms owned by stockholders, the goal of financial managers is to maximize the value of their common stock or equity. Investors that purchase the debt and equity of firms seek to evaluate how well financial managers are performing their duties. Investors want to know not only how much they might earn on debt and equity securities but also how much risk they are taking.

CHAPTER 13
Financial Management of the Firm and Investment Management

CHAPTER 14
Understanding the Financial System, Money, and Banking

CHAPTER 15
Personal Financial Planning

PART FIVE

Chapter 14 looks at the bigger picture of the financial system as a whole. The financial system comprises financial markets, institutions, and instruments. Government plays an important role in financial systems through monetary policy and regulation. On the one hand, finance is an international subject of keen interest to countries all around the world. On the other hand, financial systems affect the lives of individuals and the success of business firms in all those countries.

Chapter 15 covers important principles of personal financial planning. You should begin financial planning as early as possible in your career. Financial planning involves gathering all your financial and personal data, analyzing that data, and creating a financial plan for the future. Periodically, you need to review the plan and make necessary changes as your environment and financial conditions change. This chapter provides information to assist you right now as a college student and to help you plan for future years.

441

13

Financial Management of the Firm and Investment Management

| Introduction

Key Financial Concepts
Owners Versus Managers
Accounting Profits Versus Economic Profits
Role of the Financial Manager
Time Value of Money and Interest Rates

Firm Financial Decision Making
Net Present Value and Capital Budgeting Decisions
Sources of Funds and Financing Decisions
Managing Cash Within the Firm
Matching Assets and Liabilities

The Role of Investment Managers
Balancing Returns and Risks
Measuring Returns
Counting the Risks
Managing Investment Risks
Making Investment Choices

Careers in Financial and Investment Management

Learning Objectives

After studying this chapter, you should be able to

 1 Explain how financial managers fit into the organizational structure of a firm and what their role is.

2 Use the time value of money to differentiate between present values and future values of money.

3 Apply net present value analyses to the basic capital budgeting decisions facing financial managers.

4 Identify the sources of funds and their usage in financing decisions.

5 Describe different types of investment managers and the services they provide investors.

 6 Give details of how to measure investment returns and what investment risks confront investors.

7 Provide sound advice on how to manage investment risks and make investment choices.

What is the Firm's Future Profitability?

DaimlerChrysler, McDonald's, Sony, and other companies make decisions today that will affect their future success. Financial managers are involved in this decision-making process by evaluating the future potential profit prospects of their firms' products and services. For example, before DaimlerChrysler produces a new model automobile, it must project future sales revenues, costs of production, sales costs, taxes, and so on, to estimate net cash flows over time for the new car. These future net cash flows are used to decide whether to produce the car, how many cars to produce, and whether financing from a bank or another source is needed to begin production. Typically, financial managers compare the future net cash flows over time of all products and services within the firm, rank them in terms of profitability, and then choose those that will tend to increase the value of the firm's stock price. Of course, nobody can know the future with certainty. There is always risk associated with their decisions; namely, that the firm will fail in reaching forecast net cash flows. For this reason financial managers are constantly monitoring the profitability of the firm's products and services. Their main goal is to make decisions that maximize profit for the firm and, at the same time, minimize the risk that profit goals will not be achieved.

Introduction

Financial management and investment management are concerned with analyzing the returns and risks of firms. Imagine that you work for a firm as a financial manager, and you must decide which of five new products should be produced. Information from marketing, production, and accounting departments in the firm has been used to make detailed projections of revenues and operating costs for each product over the next five years. Your job is to use this information to rank the profitability of each product. After ranking the products, you must make a decision as to which products are acceptable and which should be rejected. Your analyses and decisions will influence the future of the firm for years to come. Also, many employees in the firm will be affected. What financial tools can you utilize to analyze the profitability of each product? How does risk come into play and possibly change your ranking of products? These questions are central to the process of making capital budgeting decisions.

After successfully ranking the five new products and deciding on their feasibility, financial managers must raise the funds needed to begin production. How should acceptable projects be financed? Should you use internal funding by relying on retained earnings? What if retained earnings are not sufficient to cover the start-up costs of a number of new products? In this case you may well opt to seek external funding. If so, should you use debt or equity funds? What are the costs of these external sources of funds? How can you decide what mix of debt and equity to use? These financing decisions are separate, or independent, of the capital budgeting decisions.

Unlike financial managers who work within the firm, investment managers are external to the firm. Their job is to evaluate how well financial managers within the firm are handling the capital budgeting and financing decisions. Later, as the new products are actually produced and sold in the marketplace, investment managers monitor the success of each product. This information is used to make buy-or-sell decisions about the firms' debt and equity securities that it issued to raise funds. Stock and bond prices tend to rise if the firm's products prove to be profitable.

On the other hand, unprofitable products lower stock and bond prices, which depend on cash flows. Indeed, excessive losses on products can raise the risk of firm failure or bankruptcy. Thus, the stakes are high for financial managers, not to mention investment managers advising clients on purchases and sales of the firms' outstanding securities.

Key Financial Concepts

Owners Versus Managers

treasurer The financial manager responsible for managing cash, raising funds, and maintaining contacts with the financial marketplace

controller The financial manager responsible for accounting, financial statements, and tax payments

agency costs The costs that occur when managers as agents of the firm are in conflict with the shareholders as principals

Except for in small firms, owners and managers are different people. Owners hold shares of common stock issued by the firm that entitle them to its net profits. Also, owners have voting power to control the important decisions of the firm. Through voting rights, owners can remove managers who do not seek to increase the value of the common stock. The board of directors is elected by shareholders to represent their interests in the firm. The board typically includes both members of top management and executives from outside the firm. The separation of ownership and management in business firms ensures that firms can exist beyond the natural lives of managers or owners. New managers are regularly appointed by the board.

The Chief Financial Officer (CFO) is the highest-ranking financial manager. The treasurer and controller are key financial managers who report to the CFO. The **treasurer** is responsible for managing cash, raising funds, and maintaining contacts with the financial marketplace. The **controller** is responsible for accounting, financial statements, and tax payments. Many other financial managers work with these top executives to fulfill their duties. Exhibit 13.1 shows how financial managers fit into the organizational structure of a firm.

EXHIBIT 13.1

The Role of Financial Managers in Business Firms

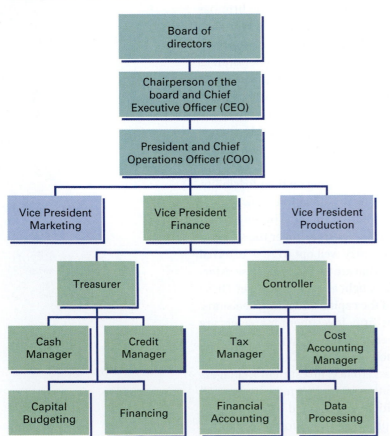

Sometimes managers make decisions that are advantageous to their own personal goals, rather than the goals of shareholders. As an example, managers could act to engage in empire building by seeking mergers and acquisitions to increase the size of the firm. Since they now manage more assets, the managers could justify increasing their own salaries. However, the larger size of the firm may not increase the value of the firm's common stock. In effect, managers as agents of the firm are in conflict with the shareholders as principals. Principal–agent conflicts are called **agency costs.** These costs can be reduced if the managers hold shares in the firm. For this reason many times firms offer managers stock options as compensation instead of increased salaries. Stock options give managers shares of the firm that they can buy at a specified price. As the price of a firm's common stock rises, the value of stock options rises. Let's say you are a manager of a firm and hold stock options on 1000 shares at a price of $30 per share. If share prices rise to $50 in the financial market, you can buy shares for $30 from the firm and turn around and sell them for $50 in the market for a profit of $20 per share, or $20,000 for all 1000 shares. Hence, stock options are valuable to managers and help align their interests with those of shareholders.

Accounting Profits Versus Economic Profits

Suppose that a firm has positive net income after taxes. From an accounting perspective, it is profitable. However, if the level of accounting profits is below other similar, or peer, firms in its industry, we can infer that the managers are not doing a good job. Another problem for a firm could be that profits are earned but only at the cost of taking excessive risks. It could be that the firm was lucky to make any profits! It is likely in these situations that the value of the firm's common stock would decline. Here we see that stock values are a way to measure **economic profits.** Only if accounting profits lead to higher share values do they have economic value. The treasurer and controller work together to turn accounting profits into economic profits by seeking to maximize the share values of the firm and, therefore, the wealth of shareholders.

economic profits Higher stock prices due to earning higher accounting profits or reducing the riskiness of profits

Role of the Financial Manager

LEARNING OBJECTIVE 1
Explain how financial managers fit into the organizational structure of a firm and what their role is.

Financial managers have two basic functions in business firms—the *administration of assets* and the *acquisition of funds*. The administration of assets involves evaluating different investment opportunities or projects facing the firm. Firms must consider whether the products or services they produce and sell are profitable. Alternative investment projects are compared to one another in the process of **capital budgeting.** For example, McDonald's has a variety of hamburger and chicken sandwiches, and each of its products must be profitable in order to be sold in its restaurants to consumers. If capital budgeting analyses reveal that a product is unprofitable, it must be discontinued or the value of McDonald's common stock could fall. Investors holding stock in the firm expect that only profitable investments will be undertaken by the firm.

capital budgeting The process of comparing or ranking the profitability of alternative investment projects within a firm

Acquisition of funds by financial managers involves raising funds in the financial marketplace to pay for profitable investment projects selected by capital budgeting decisions. For example, if a particular type of hamburger is more profitable than other sandwiches at McDonald's, it would be reasonable to increase its production and sales. To do this, the firm may need to obtain a bank loan, issue debt in the marketplace, or issue new common stock to raise funds for increased investment in inventory, advertising, labor, equipment, and other expenditures. What types of funds should the firm raise, debt or equity funds? Which source is least costly to the firm? These are **financing decisions,** as outlined in Exhibit 13.2.

financing decisions The choice made between internal and external funding and between debt and equity funds to finance the firm's investment projects

EXHIBIT 13.2

Capital Budgeting Decisions and Financing Decisions

Capital Budgeting Decisions	Financing Decisions
Administration of funds	Acquisition of funds
Investment in projects inside the business firm	Getting bank loans
	Issuing debt and equity

It is generally true that capital budgeting decisions are *separate* from financing decisions. That is, financial managers initially select the investment projects with highest potential economic value. Other managers raise required funds needed to purchase assets, pay for labor, and cover other investment costs. If earnings from an investment project exceed its costs, it is considered a feasible investment project that will increase economic profits and related share values.

A crucial aspect of this kind of capital budgeting analysis that complicates matters is that earnings and costs normally occur over time. How do we compare the total earnings and total costs in this case? Do we simply add up the earnings over time and do the same for costs? As we will see in the next section, simply adding up the earnings and costs over time does not consider that fact that the value of money changes over time. Let's take a closer look at the relationship between money and time.

reality
CHECK   *If you were offered stock options for excellent job performance at a company, would you work harder than otherwise?*

Time Value of Money and Interest Rates

LEARNING OBJECTIVE 2
Use the time value of money to differentiate between present values and future values of money.

Money is worth less tomorrow than it is today. The main reason is that inflation causes goods and services to cost more tomorrow than they do today. In 1960, you could buy a McDonald's hamburger for 25 cents. Today, the price of the same hamburger is about 80 cents. Rising costs of food, labor, equipment, land, buildings, and so on, have caused the price of a hamburger to increase. Another reason that money declines in value over time is that people would rather spend it now than later. Suppose you were given a choice between a dollar received today and a dollar received one year from now. If there were no inflation over the next year, which dollar would you want? Most people would say that the dollar today is worth more to them than the dollar tomorrow. If they had the dollar today, they would have more options for spending the money than if they received the dollar in one year. The difference in the values of the dollar in this case is due to the time preference for consumption. Simply put, people prefer to consume now rather than later, all else being the same.

Now consider the situation that arises when one person wants to borrow money from another person. The lender transfers money to the borrower and gives up some current consumption. The lender can only use the money for consumption in the future, after the borrower repays the loan. Due to the lender's **time preference for consumption,** the borrower must pay the lender an additional amount called **interest** as compensation for the declining time value of the money. Suppose $100 is borrowed for one year, there is no inflation, and the interest charged by the lender is $2, due to the time preference for consumption. In this case the rate of interest is 2 percent ($2/$100 = 0.02), which is known as the **real rate of interest.** The real rate of interest is known to be fairly constant over time, as the time preference for consumption does not change much over time.

The lender still has the problem of inflation decreasing the purchasing power of his or her money over time. When he or she later gets the money back from the borrower, the lender faces the problem that the money will buy less than before. Prices of goods and services generally rise over time. As protection against inflation—the rising prices of goods and services—the lender will demand additional interest from the borrower. This rate of interest will be equal to the expected rate of inflation over

time preference for consumption The desire by people to consume goods and services now rather than in the future

interest The amount that a borrower must pay a lender in addition to the principal value, as compensation for the declining time value of money

real rate of interest The interest rate charged by lenders on loans to borrowers for forgoing present consumption for future consumption the next year. If people expect the general level of prices to increase by 3 percent over the next year, the total interest rate charged by the lender will be

Nominal interest rate = real interest rate + expected inflation rate

In our example, the nominal interest rate would be 5 percent (2 percent real rate + 3 percent inflation rate). The nominal interest rate is also known as the **stated interest rate,** or simply the *interest rate* in the everyday financial news. The total amount repaid by the borrower to the lender after one year equals $100 principal plus $5 interest (0.05 × $100), or $105: $100 today is worth $105 in one year. If there were no inflation in the world, that is, if prices of goods and services remained constant over time, the nominal interest rate would equal the real rate of interest. Also, if our expectations about the future rate of inflation change, the nominal interest rate will change. If we thought that inflation would rise at a 4 percent rate over the next year in the previous example, then the nominal interest rate would be 6 percent, and $100 today would be worth $106 in one year. Indeed, changes in interest rates are usually due to changing inflation expectations.

So far, we have assumed that there is no risk that loan principal and interest would not be repaid by the borrower. However, what if there were a risk that the borrower would not pay the lender back? When firms borrow money from a bank, the bank will assess the **default risk** of borrowing firms, which is the chance that the firm will go bankrupt and be unable to pay back the loan. If the loan defaults, the bank could lose its principal and promised interest. To compensate for potential losses due to default risk, the bank (lender) will demand additional interest from the firm (borrower). This added interest is known as a **default risk premium.** Continuing our earlier example, let's assume that the lender demands an additional 5 percent default risk premium from the borrower. Now the total interest rate charged by the lender would be

Nominal interest rate = real interest rate + expected inflation rate
+ default risk premium

nominal interest rate The rate of interest quoted in the financial news comprising the real rate of interest plus the expected inflation rate

stated interest rate The nominal interest rate, also referred to simply as the *interest rate* in the everyday financial news

default risk The chance that a borrower will go bankrupt and be unable to pay back a debt

default risk premium The added interest rate charged by lenders due to the default risk of the borrower

To "Keep America Rolling" after the events of 9/11, General Motors began offering zero percent financing to car buyers. The low promotional interest rate triggered similar competitive financing deals from other car makers, which stimulated car sales and production. While lowering costs for customers, the low rates decreased the cash flows and profits of automobile manufacturers.

Technology and Business

The Time Value of Money: How Money Grows

Money declines in value over time. Simply put, a dollar next year is not worth as much as a dollar today. The reason is that the prices of goods and services generally rise over time due to inflation. Higher prices mean that your purchasing power declines over time. Returning to our example, a business borrows $100 from a bank at a 10 percent rate of interest. The future value of the $100 is $100 × (1 + 0.10) = $110.

What if you wanted to know the future value of $100 two years from now. Let's assume that the riskless rate of interest and default premium stay the same in both the first and second years. So the nominal rate of interest is 10 percent. In the first year the bank makes a loan at the beginning of the year for $100 and is repaid $110 at the end of the year. Assume further that the bank takes this $110 and lends it out to another firm in the second year. At the end of the second year the bank would have $110 + (0.10 × $110) = $110 + $11 = $121. After two years the initial investment of $100 has grown to a value of $121. We can write this example in mathematical terms.

$$\$100 \times (1 + 0.10) \times (1 + 0.10) = \$121$$

or, more generally,

Present value $\times (1 + r) \times (1 + r)$ = future value

Dividing both sides by $(1 + r)^2$, we can see that

Present value = future value/$(1 + r)^2$

That is,

$$\$100 = \$121/(1.10)^2$$
$$= \$121/1.21$$

An interesting result with regard to the above loan is that we have more interest on the loan than 10 percent per year. If we made 10 percent in year one and 10 percent in year two, the total interest would be $10 + $10 = $20. But the total profit is $21, not $20. What happened? How did the bank earn an extra $1? Looking at the equations, we see that this extra $1 is the 10 percent interest earned in year two on the $10 interest earned in year one. The bank has earned interest on interest. This *compound interest* is otherwise known as the *force of interest*.

To understand more about compound interest, imagine that we extended the loan agreement to 20 years. Using the same example,

$$\text{Future value} = \$100 \times (1 + r)^{20}$$
$$= \$100 \times (1 + 0.10)^{20}$$
$$= \$672.75$$

which is the future value of $100 in 20 years using a 10 percent rate of return. Given that the initial principal was $100, the total interest paid is $572.75. If only 10 percent per year were earned on the $100 principal value of the loan each year, the total interest would have been only $200 ($10 per year × 20 years). The difference between $572.75 and $200 is the compound interest earned on the loan. In other words, $372.75 was earned simply due to the force of interest. This example is used to construct Exhibit 13.5, which shows how interest grows over time.

Compound interest causes borrowers to pay more in interest payments than otherwise. Alternatively, lenders that invest small amounts today can realize large total returns in the future. This fact is an important reason why investing money today can drastically change future consumption. People invest money today by forgoing consumption now. In doing so, they gain higher future levels of consumption from the force of interest.

Questions

1. Assume that you borrowed $100 from a bank at a rate of interest of 6 percent for two years. What will be the total amount that you will pay back to the bank?
2. In the previous example, how much interest will you pay and how much of this interest payment is compound interest?
3. What if you borrowed the $100 for five years instead of only two years. Now what answers do you get for total amount paid, total interest paid, and amount of compound interest?

So, we would get a nominal interest rate of 10 percent (2 + 3 + 5 percent). The total payment of principal and interest would rise from $105 to $110 [$100 + (0.10 × $100) = $100 + $10] due to default risk. If there were no default risk, the nominal interest rate would be only 5 percent, which is known as the **riskless rate of interest.** The risky interest rate is 10 percent, as it is made up of the sum of the riskless rate of interest and the default premium (5 + 5 percent).

We can restate the above loan agreement between lender and borrower in a different way. The bank is making an investment of $100 that will earn an expected profit of $10 after one year. The rate of return on this investment is

Rate of return = profit/investment cost

In our example the rate of return is the rate of interest, or 10 percent ($10 profit/$100 investment). This required rate of return by the bank on the loan is due to the time preference for consumption, expected inflation, and default risk. The **future value** of the $100 investment or loan is $110. Alternatively, the **present value** of the future $110 principal and interest is $100. We can write these concepts in equation form.

Present value × nominal interest rate = future value

In our example, that is

$$\$100 \times 0.10 = \$110$$

or

Present value = future value/discount rate
$$\$100 = \$110/(1 + 0.10)$$

Notice that the nominal interest rate is referred to as the **discount rate** when it is used to convert future values back to present values. You can now see that interest rates connect present values to future values of money, and vice versa. Exhibit 13.3 summarizes different terms for and components of the nominal interest rate.

For more details about the time value of money, including mathematical equations, see the box "The Time Value of Money: How Money Grows." Exhibit 13.4 (on p. 450) shows how $100 invested today and earning 10 percent each year will grow in value over 20 years. The value of money grows at an increasing rate over time. Compound interest causes money to grow faster than a simple linear rate. **Compound interest** is interest earned on previous interest paid. This makes it attractive for banks, individuals, and others to invest money for longer periods of time than one year. The longer money is invested, the more it grows.

reality CHECK *Do you save some of your money for the future? Would you save more if the interest rate earned on your savings were very high?*

riskless rate of interest The interest rate charged by lenders in the case that the borrower has no default risk

rate of return The ratio of profit on an investment to the cost of the investment

future value The value of a dollar in the future, which is less than its value today

present value The value today of money to be received in the future

discount rate Any rate used in present value calculations to convert money from its future value to its present value

compound interest Interest that is earned on previous interest, also known as the force of interest

EXHIBIT 13.3

What's in an Interest Rate?

Nominal interest rate	=	riskless interest rate	+	default risk premium
Other Names: • Stated interest rate • Interest rate • Discount rate • Rate of return		**Components:** Real interest rate **+** expected inflation rate ↑ Time preferences for consumption ↑ Rising prices of goods and services		The risk of not being paid back

Firm Financial Decision Making

Financial managers manage the assets of the firm by using capital budgeting and manage the liabilities of the firm by making financing decisions. To make capital budgeting decisions, they must take into account the time value of money by finding the net present value of future profits. To make financing decisions, they must consider alternative sources of funds, including retained earnings, debt, and common stock. They must also manage the cash held by the firm.

Net Present Value and Capital Budgeting Decisions[1]

LEARNING OBJECTIVE 3
Apply net present value analyses to the basic capital budgeting decisions facing financial managers.

Let's expand on our bank loan example to demonstrate how financial managers make capital budgeting decisions. Suppose that Sony borrows $100 million for one year from a bank at a 10 percent interest rate. Sony uses the money to purchase materials and labor to build a new product to be sold in the marketplace. Let's assume that the new product is a high-tech television with a clearer screen than current televisions have, which consumers would like. The new television is estimated to generate net profits (after material, labor, marketing, and other costs) of $120 million by the end of the year. This investment project has some amount of risk. That is, it is possible that Sony will have a lower or higher net profit than $120 million. A very bad scenario is a net profit of $80 million, while a very good scenario is a net profit of $160 million. However, the expected or average net profit is $120 million. **Risk** is defined here as variability of profit. Higher variability means more risk, say, a range of net profits from $40 million to $160 million, and less variability implies less risk, say, a range of net profits from $90 million to $110 million.

risk The variability of profits over time, with higher risk implying more variability

Since the investment's average net profit is $120 million, and the investment's cost is $100 million, we might quickly conclude that the investment's economic profit is $20 million. Jumping to this simple answer would be a mistake! The $100 million cost is incurred at time 0 (now), whereas the $120 million net profit is realized at time 1 (one year from now). There is a difference in the timing of project costs and project profits. To figure out the economic profit of the new product, we must compare cash flows in present value terms at time 0 (now). Using our present value formula and the notation r for the interest rate, we have

Present value of net profit = $120 million$/(1 + r)$

But what do we use for r in this equation? We might use the interest rate of 10 percent on the bank loan of $100 million. Jumping to this simple solution would be another mistake! The bank priced the loan at 10 percent based on the risk of Sony going bankrupt. Sony needs to do the same thing as the bank. It should consider the risk of the investment project and demand a rate of return that takes into account the real rate of interest, the inflation rate, and the project risk. But how does Sony know what this rate of return should be?

The best way to get the rate of return, or r, is to think about alternative investments that the $100 million could buy. Sony's shareholders might be able to earn, say, 15 per-

EXHIBIT 13.4

The Future Value of $100 Using a 10 Percent Interest Rate

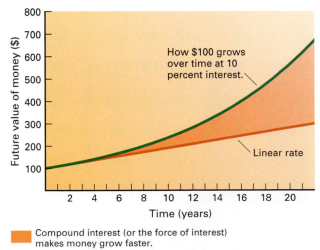

Compound interest (or the force of interest) makes money grow faster.

cent if they were given the $100 million to invest in securities in the financial marketplace. Remember that the goal of any firm is to increase the value of shareholder wealth. If shareholders demanded 15 percent as a minimum rate of return, then the project should earn at least this much. This alternative rate of return of 15 percent is referred to as the **opportunity cost** of the investment funds, that is, the rate of return that could be earned by investing in something other than the new television. Using 15 percent as the rate of return in the denominator of our equation, we get

opportunity cost The alternative rate of return that can be earned by an investor if a security or investment project is not selected

$$\text{Present value of net profit} = \$120 \text{ million}/(1 + 0.15)$$
$$= \$104.35 \text{ million}$$

The 15 percent opportunity cost is used here as the discount rate to convert future values to present values. Another term for the opportunity cost is the **required rate of return** that shareholders demand as a minimum rate of return on an investment. Now we can get the expected economic profit of this investment project.

required rate of return The opportunity cost that investors demand as a minimum rate of return on their investment

$$\textbf{Net present value (NPV)} = \text{present value of cash flows} - \text{investment cost}$$
$$= \$104.35 \text{ million} - \$100 \text{ million} = \$4.35 \text{ million}$$

net present value (NPV) The net profit on a product or service of a firm calculated as the present value of cash flows minus the cost of the investment

where cash flows are defined as net profit here. This capital budgeting analysis reveals that the project is acceptable. Because the net present value is greater than zero, it will increase shareholder wealth. If the NPV were zero, the project would still be acceptable to shareholders, as it would earn 15 percent, which is the opportunity cost to shareholders of using the $100 million to invest in securities. If the NPV were negative, it would have a negative economic profit and, therefore, would reduce the value of the firm's stock price. For a more detailed capital budgeting example in which the project has a life of more than one year, see the box "Capital Budgeting Decisions for Multiple-Year Investments."

Sony borrowed $100 million to build a new television and expected that on average it would earn a net profit of $120 million one year from now. But Sony's total return on this investment will not be equal to the $20 million accounting profits. Instead, due to discounting future net profits at the opportunity cost of capital (the minimum required rate of return of shareholders), the net present value reveals that Sony will earn only $4.35 million. While still profitable in economic terms, the project is less profitable than accounting profits would suggest.

These capital budgeting principles can be applied to any investment project that a firm is considering. Normally, firms have a variety of projects that they are evaluating. Projects can be ranked by their NPVs. Again, all NPVs greater than or equal to zero are feasible, or acceptable, investments. Those projects with NPVs less than zero are not feasible and should be rejected. Exhibit 13.5 reviews capital budgeting principles. Six projects are ranked by the present value of their cash flows. It is assumed that the investment cost is $100 for each project. Exhibit 13.5 shows which projects are acceptable and which should be rejected. Now it is up to financial managers to raise the money needed to finance the investment cost of the feasible projects.

EXHIBIT 13.5

Selecting Acceptable Capital Budgeting Projects

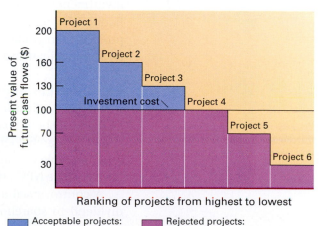

reality CHECK *Assume that you are assigned to do a net present value analysis of an investment project for a firm. What data do you think would be the most difficult to obtain?*

Technology and Business

Capital Budgeting Decisions for Multiple-Year Investments

Let's consider a capital budgeting decision in which a firm is considering purchasing a machine for $100. The financing costs of the machine are not relevant to the investment decision process; instead, we must use the opportunity cost of this $100 to determine the discount rate (and not the interest cost of the $100 from a bank or other lender of funds). The machine provides a stream of net profits, or cash flows, over a period of five years. After five years the machine can be sold for its salvage value of $50. Assume that the opportunity cost of the $100 investment is 16 percent. The cash flows earned on the machine and the associated present value of each cash flow are

Year	Cash Flow	Present Value
1	$10	$10/(1.16) = $8.62
2	$10	$10/(1.16)^2 = $7.43
3	$10	$10/(1.16)^3 = $6.41
4	$10	$10/(1.16)^4 = $5.52
5	$10 + $50	($10 + $50)/(1.16)^5 = $28.57
	(salvage value)	Total present value = $56.55

The NPV for this investment is $56.55 (present value of cash flows) − $100 (investment cost) = − $43.45. Clearly, this investment should be rejected.

This example allows us to review key capital budgeting concepts. If we simply added up the cash flows, we would get $100, which is equal to the investment cost of $100. But this mistaken approach does not take into account the time value of money. The $10 earned each year on the project is falling in present value terms. This trend is reasonable because a dollar tomorrow is worth less than a dollar today. Also, the force of interest gets larger over time. We receive $60 in year 5, but it is only worth $28.57 in present value dollars. The force of interest has more than halved its value after only five years!

Questions

1. What is the correct discount rate to use for future cash flows on an investment project?
2. If you use a higher discount rate, will this make a project more or less profitable in net present value terms?
3. Would you rather see high cash flow on an investment project in early years or in later years? Why?

Sources of Funds and Financing Decisions

LEARNING OBJECTIVE 4
Identify the sources of funds and their usage in financing decisions.

Firms can acquire funds to invest in projects from a variety of sources. If a firm had high profits (i.e., net income after taxes) and only a few positive net present value investment projects, it could probably rely only on retained earnings from profits to finance the projects. However, many times firms have more profitable investment projects than available retained earnings are capable of financing. In this case debt and equity financing are needed.

Retained Earnings.   Net income after taxes minus dividends equals retained earnings. If a firm has no profitable projects after conducting capital budgeting analyses, it should pay out all of its earnings to shareholders as **dividends.** In this situation shareholders are better off taking dividends and investing this money in other possible investments. However, if a number of the firm's investment projects have positive NPVs, then it should retain earnings to finance them.

A controversial area in making financing decisions is whether to pay out a dividend to shareholders. Suppose that shareholders like to periodically, say,

dividend Income paid to common shareholders from a firm's net income after taxes

quarterly, receive some of the firm's earnings in the form of a dividend. A simple reason for this shareholder behavior is that shareholders want to consume some of their earnings over time, as opposed to receiving all of their earnings years in the future and consuming their income later. Even if the firm has profitable projects available to it, shareholders likely will want the firm to pay out some proportion of its earnings as dividends. Some firms pay out a fixed dividend each quarter, while others pay out a fixed proportion of their retained earnings to shareholders. For example, if a firm had $1 million in net income after taxes and a 30 percent dividend payout policy, it would pay $300,000 in dividends and have $700,000 in retained earnings.

More than 50 percent of a firm's assets are typically financed with retained earnings. In this way, firms grow from within using internal earnings, as opposed to using external sources of funds like debt and equity to expand their asset size. We can infer that large firms were highly profitable in the past, which allowed them to invest retained earnings in land, buildings, equipment, and other real assets. Obviously, firms that have higher retained earnings are able to grow faster than other firms.

Many times, successful firms are growing so fast that retained earnings are not sufficient to keep up with the costs of filling rising orders for their goods and services. In this case, firms must turn to external financing to raise more funds to pay for production costs. The major forms of external financing are debt and equity.

Debt. The largest source of external finance for most firms is debt. In a debt contract, borrowers promise to pay back to lenders the loan (or principal) at a later time known as the *maturity date*. Also, debtors must pay interest to lenders. Debt funds can be obtained from bank loans and debt issues in the financial marketplace. Bank loans are the most important type of debt financing, especially for small- and medium-sized businesses and for short-term loans of less than one year. Debt issues can be used to acquire short-term and long-term funds. **Commercial paper** is the most common type of short-term debt issue. Larger, well-known firms have greater access to commercial paper financing than smaller firms. **Bonds** are used as a long-term source of funds; 5, 10, 20, and 30 years are typical maturities. Like commercial paper, bonds are sold in the financial marketplace. Today, firms can issue commercial paper and bonds on a global scale. Bonds issued outside a firm's home country are known as **Eurobonds;** bonds issued by a U.S. firm in Japan are Eurobonds. The global bond market has grown rapidly in the last 10 to 20 years, allowing firms to finance their international expansion into other countries.

Which form of debt should a firm use? This financing decision is governed by the length of the investment project. A one-year project should be financed with a one-year debt. Since it is short-term in nature, bank loans and commercial paper are recommended. Small- and medium-sized firms primarily rely on bank loans to meet short-term financing needs. Larger firms can more readily use commercial paper financing. A five-year project, such as the capital budgeting example of a five-year machine (shown in the "Capital Budgeting for Multiple-Year Investments" box), should be financed with five-year bonds. The bonds can be sold publicly to anyone who wants to purchase them or privately to large financial institutions.

Debt financing is cheaper than equity financing due to the tax deductibility of interest payments on debt. By contrast, dividends paid on equity are not tax deductible. Let's see how tax deductibility lowers debt costs. The following data show how interest tax deductions lower the firm's income taxes:

commercial paper Short-term, unsecured debt securities normally issued by large, financially sound firms to raise funds

bonds Long-term debt securities issued by firms to raise funds to finance long-term capital budgeting projects, such as land, buildings, and equipment

Eurobonds Bonds that are issued outside a firm's home country

	No Interest Deductions Allowed	Interest Deductions Allowed
Net income before interest and taxes	$1000	$1000
minus interest payments on debt	0	−200
Net income before taxes	$1000	$800
minus income taxes (at 30%)	−300	−240
Net income after taxes	$700	$560
minus interest payments on debt	−200	
Net income after taxes	$500	

Notice that net income after taxes, or the bottom line, is higher with interest deductions allowed than with no interest deductions. The income tax savings make up the entire difference. Income taxes are $300 with no interest deductions but only $240 with interest deductions. The $60 tax savings increase the bottom line and, therefore, go to the shareholders of the firm. In effect, interest tax deductions transfer funds from the government to the shareholders. It pays for shareholders to have the firm use debt finance. Does this mean that firms should keep increasing debt financing until they wipe out all of their taxes? This financing strategy would maximize income tax savings, and shareholders would increase their wealth from this tax gain. Unfortunately, as a firm increases its use of debt finance, there is the rising problem of not being able to cover debt payments and going bankrupt. If net income before interest and taxes falls below interest payments at any point in time, debt payments cannot be met, and the firm will be in default. Default risk is a major hazard of using too much debt. As firms borrow more and more money using bank loans, commercial paper, and bonds, they will find that lenders will require higher interest rates on debt. This higher interest rate is required as compensation for the increasing default risk that lenders face on the debt. Also, firms may well reach a limit on debt usage at some point. Lenders logically will not supply any more credit to the firm due to extremely high default risk.

When a firm defaults on its debt, debt holders will demand immediate payment. To protect itself from creditors (lenders), the firm can file for **bankruptcy**. Bankruptcy is a legal remedy that affords the firm some amount of protection from creditors and others to whom it owes money. A court is appointed to oversee bankruptcy proceedings. The judge in charge of the court generally seeks to manage creditor claims in an orderly manner. Many times, the judge will merge a bankrupt firm with a healthy firm. If this happens, it is likely that debt holders will not experience any losses. If no merger can be arranged, the judge could rule to liquidate all of the firm's assets. In this outcome creditors can lose money. If the total debt payments due are $5 million but the liquidation value of the assets is $3 million, debt holders will lose $2 million. The judge will review creditor claims and use proceeds from the liquidation of assets to pay creditors.

In bankruptcy, so-called **secured creditors** are paid before unsecured creditors. Secured creditors have claim to specific assets that were previously pledged as collateral on debt in the event of default on debt. Unsecured creditors are paid the remainder of liquidated assets. Many times unsecured creditors can lose all or some portion of their principal and the interest due to them. This brings up an important aspect of debt finance. Unsecured debt holders will require the firm to pay them higher interest rates on debt finance, while secured debt holders will offer the firm lower interest rates on debt due to their lower default or credit risk.

bankruptcy A legal remedy afforded to firms that default on their debt that provides some amount of protection from creditors and others to whom it owes money

secured creditors Creditors to whom proceeds of a firm's liquidation due to bankruptcy are paid before other unsecured creditors

How can you determine the amount of default risk on commercial paper and long-term bonds issued by different firms? *Moody's* as well as *Standard & Poor's* rating services assign letter grades to publicly issued debt that represent estimates of the chance a firm could default. Debt issues assigned one of the top four grades—AAA, AA, A, and BBB—are considered to be **investment grade** in the sense that they have low default risk. Debt issues of firms that are rated below investment grade—BB, B, CCC, CC, and C—are known as **junk bonds.** These lower-rated debt securities have higher default risk. Of course, bond ratings influence the interest rate at which firms can borrow in the financial marketplace. Normally, bond ratings below investment grade have higher interest costs of debt. To get investment grade credit ratings, firms need to have good profitability, low to moderate levels of debt usage, and sound business practices.

investment grade Bonds with lower default risk that are rated in the top four letter grades by Moody's and Standard & Poor's rating services

junk bonds Bonds with higher default risk that are rated below the top four letter grades by Moody's and Standard & Poor's rating services

Common Stock.

Shareholders obtain ownership claims on the firm's assets and associated earnings on assets by holding common stock. **Common stock** differs from debt in the following ways:

- Common stockholders have voting rights.
- Common stock has no maturity date.
- Common stock pays dividends instead of interest.

common stock Securities issued by firms that represent ownership claims on the earnings of the firm

Dividends differ from interest in that there is no promised amount that must be paid to shareholders. Additionally, if the firm does not pay a dividend on common stock, there is no default risk as with interest on debt. Unlike debt issues that require the firm to repay the lender's initial loan amount (or principal) on the maturity date, the firm does not pay back to the stockholders their investment on common stock. Instead, shareholders can sell their shares of common stock in the financial marketplace.

Suppose that a firm issues 300,000 shares of stock at a par value of $10 per share. This stock issuance would raise $3 million of equity capital for the firm, which the firm would not have to pay back in the future. However, the firm may well pay shareholders dividends every three months. Shareholders also can make profits on their investment by selling the stock for more than the purchase price. If a shareholder bought some of the shares for $30 and the market price of the shares rose to $50, they could be sold for a **capital gain** of $20 on each share. Another difference between debt issues and common stock is that, in the event of default and bankruptcy, shareholders are paid after all debt holders and court costs. This means that shareholders will have greater losses than debt holders in bankruptcy and are likely to lose their entire investment in the firm.

capital gain The difference between the purchase price and sales price of a real or financial asset

Each share of stock typically gives the owner one vote. When major issues come up at meetings of the board of directors that will affect the future of the firm, a shareholder vote is taken to determine which alternative course of action will be taken. Will the firm merge with another firm or not? Should the firm pay higher or lower dividends? What about the prospect of making a large investment in a new technology or product? All of these decisions would likely involve a vote by the shareholders. In the voting process, shareholders have the right to transfer their vote to another shareholder by means of a **proxy.** Any shareholder can solicit proxy votes from other shareholders by mail. If a shareholder were able to control over 50 percent of the total possible votes by owning common stock and obtaining proxy votes, he or she would effectively be able to control the firm with respect to a particular decision.

proxy The transfer of voting rights from the owner of common stock to someone else

Another interesting aspect of common stock is the **preemptive right.** If a firm issues new stock, existing shareholders can maintain their proportionate

preemptive right The right of shareholders to maintain their proportionate ownership of a firm's outstanding stock if new shares are issued by the firm

ownership of the firm. For example, if you owned 10 percent of the outstanding stock of the firm and the firm issued 100 new shares, you would have a preemptive right to purchase 10 of these new shares to maintain your 10 percent ownership proportion.

If there are only a few shareholders in a firm (such as in a typical small business), the shareholders can easily use their voting power to control the firm's decisions. Such small business firms are referred to as **closely held firms** and generally do not trade their common stock in the financial marketplace. However, if there are many shareholders, such as in large corporate enterprises, ownership is diluted among so many people that it is difficult for individual shareholders to control the firm's decisions. In these **publicly held firms,** the common stock is widely traded in financial markets.

There are advantages and disadvantages of being a publicly held firm. One advantage is that such firms can raise large amounts of equity funds by making public issues of common stock shares. Another advantage is that the large potential number of buyers of the stock in the financial marketplace enables firms to sell shares at the highest price possible. Of course, firms want to issue stock at high prices to raise as much money as possible per share of stock. A disadvantage of a firm's being publicly held is that shareholders have difficulty controlling managers in the firm. In other words, publicly held firms are more prone to principal–agent conflicts, or agency costs, than closely held firms. In closely held, small businesses, the owners are also the managers in many cases, and this avoids agency costs.

An **initial public offering (IPO)** is the first time a firm issues stock to the public in financial markets. IPOs are exciting because many new shareholders are invited into the firm as owners. With greater access to equity financing, the IPO signals a major turning point in the firm's development. Now the firm can grow faster than when it was closely held. Later issues of stock are referred to as **seasoned issues.**

Another type of new equity is *venture capital*. Suppose that a small business needs start-up capital to produce a new product. Venture capitalists are investors in

closely held firms Firms that are owned by a relatively small number of shareholders who do not openly trade their shares

publicly held firms Firms in which there are many shareholders who openly trade their shares in the financial marketplace

initial public offering (IPO) The first time a firm issues stock to the public in financial markets

seasoned issues Stock issues by a firm that are not initial public offerings

Google filed initial public offering (IPO) plans in January 2004. Here we see co-founders Larry Page (left) and Sergey Brin at their company's headquarters in Mountain View, California. The company planned to issue 25.7 million shares for between $108 and $135 per share, which would raise about $3.4 billion of new equity funds. The massive IPO created quite a stir among investors, thereby stimulating interest in the firm and its common stock shares.

the local community who will purchase equity in the small business in exchange for not only voting power but direct control of its day-to-day operations. Normally, the original owner can buy out the venture capitalists within the next five years or so and regain control of the firm. Venture capitalists many times were successful small business people and offer expertise that is valuable in getting the new product off the ground and making it a profitable capital budgeting project. Local banks and organizations are good places to get references to local venture capitalists, otherwise known as *angels*.

Financing Mix.   Which forms of finance should a firm use to pay for acceptable investment projects? Most experts would agree that there is a "pecking order" in terms of the financing used.

- First, and most important, is retained earnings. Most new projects to purchase assets are financed from the profits on previous projects. In effect, shareholders are reinvesting their earnings in the firm in the hopes that new projects will increase the price of common stock. If the price of the common stock rises, shareholders can earn a capital gain as the market price of stock exceeds the initial purchase price.

- Second, debt is used to finance assets. Due to interest tax deductions, it is cheaper than issuing new equity. Also, the many forms of debt finance enable firms to acquire large amounts of funds to meet their needs in paying for capital budgeting projects.

- Third, and last, common stock is used by firms. Because of its higher cost and voting implications, shareholders prefer to use retained earnings, rather than new stock issues, to provide equity financing. However, if the firm has many acceptable investment projects, it may be necessary to issue common stock to raise additional funds.

Firms generally seek some optimal mix of retained earnings, debt, and common stock. The optimal financing mix is where total financing costs are at a minimum. By lowering total financing costs, the firm can increase its profitability and, therefore, the value of its common stock.

Managing Cash Within the Firm

Another important function of financial managers is cash management. Cash management encompasses not only the cash held by the firm but also the assets that are readily convertible to cash or require cash payment in the near future. Total cash receipts minus total cash payments at any point in time is **net cash flow.** Corporate treasurers seek to maintain sufficient net cash flow to pay for unexpected bills. Excessive cash flow over this amount is wasteful because the extra funds could be invested in productive assets. Thus, there is an opportunity cost of excess or idle cash.

net cash flow Total cash receipts minus total cash payments at any point in time

   Net working capital is equal to total current assets minus total current liabilities. These accounts represent short-term uses and sources of cash. Current assets include cash, short-term securities, inventory, and accounts receivables, that is, products and services sold previously under trade credit terms that allow customers to pay within 30 to 90 days. Like cash, managers do not want to have excessive levels of inventory and accounts receivables. However, some amount of these current assets is needed to fill customer orders and attract new orders for products and services. Short-term securities can be readily converted into cash and are a good

net working capital Total current assets minus total current liabilities

factoring The sale of accounts receivables to a financial institution that then collects payments by customers

lock box system A way for firms to speed the collection of payments from customers, who submit payments to local post offices, where the payments are picked up by local banks and forwarded to the firm's bank

trade credit A credit system that allows a firm to buy goods and services from another firm and pay within 30 to 90 days from the date of purchase

source of cash if net cash flow becomes negative. Accounts receivables can be quickly converted to cash using **factoring.** A financial institution that buys accounts receivables from a firm is a factor. In this case customers pay the factor instead of the firm.

Of course, many times customers pay in cash on receipt of a product or service. If a firm's sales are on a national or international level, a problem arises in consolidating all of the cash payments as quickly as possible in a centralized bank account. A popular way to do this is to use a **lock box system.** Customers make payments to post office boxes in local postal service facilities, and the payments are regularly collected by local banks in the area. Cash is then wired by local banks via computer telecommunications equipment to a settlement bank in which the cash is concentrated. Since the settlement bank typically is the disbursing agent to make bill payments, it can compare cash inflows and cash outflows to get net cash flow at any moment.

Current liabilities are short-term debts, accrued wages and other accrued expenses (such as taxes), and accounts payables. Accounts payables come about as the firm purchases materials used in the production of products or services. It is common practice for supplier firms to offer the producing firm trade credit terms that allow the firm to pay the supplier within 30 to 90 days from the date of purchase. **Trade credit** gives the firm time to make products and services and sell them in the marketplace. Cash inflows on sales can then be used to meet cash outflows on current liabilities. In general, financial managers seek to pay bills as late as possible without missing a payment deadline.

Sometimes a discounted price on purchased materials (for example, 2 percent lower cost) is allowed if the firm promptly pays within 10 or 15 days of the date of purchase. Timely payment of bills is cost efficient if the discount can be obtained. However, because cash inflows from sales occur later, the firm likely will need some debt financing to cover the early payment for materials. Financial managers must weigh the benefits of trade discounts versus the costs of debt financing.

Matching Assets and Liabilities

A basic principle of financial management is to match the maturities of assets and liabilities. As discussed previously, if the firm is going to invest in a machine with a life of five years, it should finance this investment with five-year bonds. Shorter-life assets, such as inventory that is held for, say, 30 days on average before it is sold, should be financed with 30-day bank loans or commercial paper.

What if you did not do this? Let's assume that you financed a five-year machine with a one-year bank loan. At the end of the year, you would have to ask the bank for another loan. But what if the firm's financial condition had deteriorated during the year? Under these circumstances, the bank may well not want to renew the loan. Cut off from another loan, the firm would have to pay off the old loan out of cash and near-cash assets. If the firm could not access enough cash to make the interest and principal payments on the debt, it could default and end up in bankruptcy.

Another reason to match the maturities of assets and liabilities is that net cash flows in each month or quarter can be planned out in advance. Using five-year bonds to finance a five-year machine allows the financial manager to better understand net cash flows for each period in the future.

reality CHECK *If you owned some common stock of a company, what percentage of your earnings would you wish to receive in dividend payments versus capital gains? How would this affect the company's sources of funds and related financing decisions?*

The Role of Investment Managers

LEARNING OBJECTIVE 5
Describe different types of investment managers and the services they provide investors.

Investment managers provide a variety of services for individual, business, and government participants in the financial markets. Financial managers in firms benefit from the services of **investment bankers.** These investment specialists assist firms seeking to raise funds by means of either debt or equity. Many times an investment bank will purchase the bonds or stocks directly from the firm, which is known as **underwriting.** Subsequently, they turn around and try to sell the underwritten securities for a higher price in the financial marketplace. Investment bankers earn revenues from service fees for professional advice, as well as from the difference between the buying and selling prices for securities. Because a merger or acquisition of another firm normally involves raising funds, investment bankers work closely with client firms in this process. A merger or acquisition is an expensive venture and so is a lucrative source of revenues for investment banks.

Securities issued by firms are purchased in the financial marketplace by individuals and large institutions. **Brokers** assist investors purchasing and selling financial securities. They earn service fees for making securities transactions. By being members of national and regional stock exchanges, they have representatives on the trading floor standing ready to execute buy-and-sell orders of securities for their customers. There are three kinds of brokerage firms.

- *Full-service firms* do more than fill buy-and-sell orders for securities. They have large research departments to analyze firms' profitability and risk. Also, they employ market experts to help advise clients on investment decisions. Full-service brokerage firms can offer clients comprehensive financial planning services that include savings and retirement, estate management, tax advice, corporate services, and so on. You can even combine a brokerage account with a checking account and credit card in an **asset management account.**

- *Discount brokerage firms* tend to have lower-cost services than full-service firms and put more emphasis on executing buy-and-sell orders. Today, some of these firms are adding research and financial services, but these services are limited.

- *Online brokerage firms* are low-cost, computer-electronic communications providers of security trading services. Their websites offer research and other informational content that is useful to investors. Their disadvantage is that there is no personal adviser to ask questions of and get recommendations from.

All three types of brokerage firms make most of their revenues from commissions earned on buy-and-sell transactions ordered by investors.

Dealers are firms that buy and sell securities but do so from an inventory of stocks, bonds, or other financial assets that they hold. For example, if you want to buy some shares of stock, the dealer will sell you shares that it owns. If you want to sell some shares, the dealer will buy them. The dealer seeks to make a profit not only on commission charges but also on the difference between the price it paid to buy securities and the price at which it sells them.

Brokers and dealers are different from other investment managers in that they will buy and sell individual bonds and stocks for customers. Special types of orders are allowed. For example, a **limit order** can be placed that sets a specific buy-or-sell price to execute a transaction. If the price moves up to a certain level, the securities

investment bankers Investment managers who assist firms seeking to raise debt or equity funds from the financial marketplace

underwriting The purchase of securities from a firm by an investment bank, which then seeks to sell the securities at a higher price in the financial marketplace

brokers Investment managers who execute buy-and-sell orders for securities and earn commissions on this service

asset management account An investment account that combines brokerage, checking, and credit card services

dealers Investment managers who buy and sell securities for customers and hold inventories of stocks, bonds, or other financial assets

limit order A securities transaction that sets a specific buy-or-sell price to execute a buy-or-sell order for a security

Ethics in Business

Trust in Investment Services

Imagine that you called a stockbroker and paid her or him to provide you with research about the investment prospects of DaimlerChrysler, McDonald's, and Sony. The data in the broker's report produced for you overviewed the return and risk prospects for all three firms' stocks in the next year. One problem: the report is biased by the fact that the broker has favorable business relationships with these three firms. The broker may be offering financial services to these firms and may even hold stock in its dealer activities in the stock market. What if CEOs and other top executives in these firms received lower brokerage costs with this broker than other investors?

Naturally, these conflicts of interest are cheating the everyday investor seeking brokerage services. In the last few years, numerous cases of illegal or irregular trading practices have surfaced in the financial news. Charles R. Schwab, CEO of the brokerage firm bearing his name, observed that these kinds of widely publicized abuses have shaken investors' trust in the investment community. How can people be sure that investment managers are not subject to conflicts of interest? His recommendation to President Bush and the Securities Exchange Commission was to require that a code of conduct be implemented. To ensure ethical practices by investment professionals, CEOs and some key investment managers would have to sign a document assuring that controls over potential conflicts of interest were in place and describe what those controls are. Personal certification of ethical investment conduct by leaders in financial services firms is an important step to restoring investor trust. In Schwab's view, open disclosure of information and accountability are the keys to gaining back investors' confidence.

In October 2002, the SEC voted to propose rules implementing ethics-related provisions of the new 2002 Sarbanes-Oxley Act. Consistent with this act, the proposed rules require public companies to disclose whether the company has adopted a code of ethics for the company's principal executive officer and senior financial officers. If a company has not adopted such a code, it must explain why it has not done so. According to the SEC, the proposed rules would define a code of ethics as a codification of standards that are reasonably necessary to deter wrongdoing and to promote

Honest and ethical conduct, including the ethical handling of actual or apparent conflicts of interest between personal and professional relationships

Avoidance of conflicts of interest, including disclosure to an appropriate person or persons identified in the code of any material transaction or relationship that reasonably could be expected to give rise to such a conflict

Full, fair, accurate, timely, and understandable disclosure in reports and documents that a company files with, or submits to, the SEC and in other public communications made by the company

Compliance with applicable governmental laws, rules, and regulations

Prompt internal reporting of code violations to an appropriate person or persons identified in the code

Accountability for adherence to the code

According to the SEC, a company would be required to disclose in its annual report whether it has a code of ethics.

Source: Charles R. Schwab, "Remaking the Market: My Investors, My Responsibility," *The Wall Street Journal,* November 5, 2002, p. A22.

Questions

1. Suppose that a stockbroker received a large number of sell orders for a stock. The stockbroker realized that this large volume of sell orders would cause the stock price to decline. Is it ethical for the broker to sell any shares of stock they own before selling the customers' orders?

2. Do you think that stockbrokers should include in their code of ethics, under the new 2002 Sarbanes-Oxley Act, something to prevent them from "stepping in front" of customers' stock buy-and-sell orders?

3. Would you trust a securities firm that has no code of ethics?

---

institutional investors Large financial institutions, including insurance companies, pension funds, and investment companies, that trade securities in financial markets

will be automatically sold to lock in a profit. Or, if the price moves down to some specified level, the securities will be automatically sold to prevent a large loss. Brokers and dealers seek to move quickly to execute trades for customers at the best prices they can obtain.

Lastly, managers of large **institutional investors** play a major role in the investment world. Insurance companies invest funds from policies they sell to customers in financial securities. Pension funds invest the savings of individuals intended for their retirement years in securities. And, investment companies, also called mutual funds, offer customers a tremendous variety of alternative securities.

The Securities Exchange Commission (SEC) regulates the securities markets in the United States. Its duties include making sure that investors receive fair pricing and ethical securities practices by brokers, dealers, and financial institutions. Occasionally, unethical activities occur, such as when a dealer is recommending to investors to buy a stock of which it holds a large amount. The SEC and other securities regulators in countries around the world face a constant challenge in making sure that all investors are treated equitably and fairly.

reality CHECK *What if you learned that some investors were able to buy stocks that you could not buy? Is this fair? Ethical?*

Balancing Returns and Risks

LEARNING OBJECTIVE 6
Give details of how to measure investment returns and what investment risks confront investors.

A guiding principle in investment finance is that security returns are directly related to risks. As the risk of loss increases on a security, investors will demand a higher rate of return as compensation for risk bearing. Suppose you were comparing two securities: one security was low risk and the other was high risk. What if both securities offered a 10 percent rate of return? Why take extra risk for the same return? Everyone would choose the low-risk security. Exhibit 13.6 graphically illustrates the traditional **risk-return trade-off.** Securities that lie on or near the line are substitutable in that their return per unit risk is the same. Importantly, knowing whether a security has a high or low return is not sufficient information to evaluate it. You must know the return per unit risk to compare two or more securities with one another.

What types of securities should any particular investor purchase? The answer to this question depends on the investor's risk preference. Investors who cannot tolerate high risk, like retired investors, should seek securities that lie in the low return-risk region of the line in Exhibit 13.6. Those investors seeking higher-risk securities, like young college graduates, should focus on the high return-risk region of the line. Investment managers need to carefully gauge the risk preferences of their clients to advise them on the most appropriate securities to purchase. How do you feel about risk? Where would you be on the return-risk line in Exhibit 13.6?

risk-return trade-off The basic finance principle that higher returns can only be earned by taking more risk

EXHIBIT 13.6

The Risk-Return Trade-off for Investment Securities

Trade-off: To get a higher return, you must take more risk.

Measuring Returns

The return on an investment is measured by its gain or loss. We earlier considered a bank making a loan (or investment) of $100 that earned a profit (or return) of $10 after one year. The rate of return on this investment was $10/$100 = 0.10, or 10 percent. Let's extend these concepts to the return on a share of common stock. Suppose you buy a share of stock for $20. You later receive a dividend payment of $2 and sell the stock for $23. The dividend return ($2) plus the capital gain return ($23 − $20 = $3) equals the total return ($5). We can now calculate the rate of return on the stock.

$$\text{Rate of return on stock} = \frac{(\text{sales price} - \text{purchase price}) + \text{dividends}}{\text{purchase price}}$$

Using this formula, we get

$$\text{Rate of return on stock} = \frac{(\$23 - \$20) + \$2}{\$20}$$

$$= \frac{\$5}{\$20}$$

$$= 0.25 \qquad \text{or 25 percent}$$

Here the capital gains rate of return, or yield, is $3/$20 = 0.15, or 15 percent. The dividend yield is $2/$20 = 0.10, or 10 percent. The sum of the *capital gains yield* and *dividend yield* is the rate of return on the stock. Most firms keep dividends fairly stable over time and only cut them in the event of abnormally low net income after taxes. Thus, we can infer that rates of return on stocks change primarily due to changing prices over time. Exhibit 13.7 shows how to read stock market quotations of prices and dividends for a firm in the newspaper.

How can an investor determine if a particular stock will pay a good rate of return? To assess expected returns on a stock, it is necessary to estimate the future profitability of the issuing firm. Profitable firms can pay healthy dividends and can attract investors to buy their stock. Increased demand for a stock by investors will increase its share prices. Another important aspect for investors to evaluate is the risk of the firm. Are its profits stable or volatile over time? Do the firm's revenues fall so low at times that it could default on its debt and go bankrupt? Consider two firms A and B with net incomes after taxes over a five-year period as follows:

	Year 1	Year 2	Year 3	Year 4	Year 5	Average Profit
Firm A	$10	$10	$10	$10	$10	$50/5 years = $10/year
Firm B	$10	$14	$6	$12	$8	$50/5 years = $10/year

While firms A and B have equal average profitability, investors would not consider these two firms to have equal risk. Firm B has more unstable profits than firm A. For this reason investors would not pay as high a price for B compared to A. We can infer that firms with less risk will have higher share prices, holding average profitability the same. In summary, firms can increase their share prices by both increasing profits *and* reducing risk.

EXHIBIT 13.7

How to Read Stock Market Quotations in the Newspaper

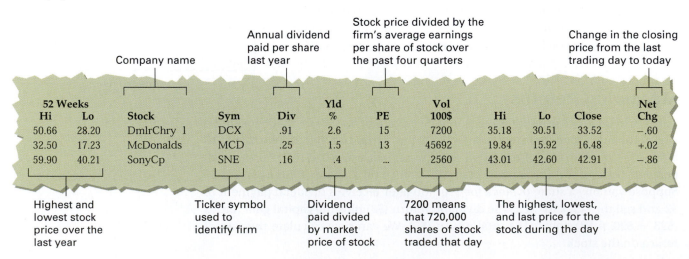

52 Weeks		Stock	Sym	Div	Yld %	PE	Vol 100$	Hi	Lo	Close	Net Chg
Hi	Lo										
50.66	28.20	DmlrChry 1	DCX	.91	2.6	15	7200	35.18	30.51	33.52	−.60
32.50	17.23	McDonalds	MCD	.25	1.5	13	45692	19.84	15.92	16.48	+.02
59.90	40.21	SonyCp	SNE	.16	.4	...	2560	43.01	42.60	42.91	−.86

Company name

Annual dividend paid per share last year

Stock price divided by the firm's average earnings per share of stock over the past four quarters

Change in the closing price from the last trading day to today

Highest and lowest stock price over the last year

Ticker symbol used to identify firm

Dividend paid divided by market price of stock

7200 means that 720,000 shares of stock traded that day

The highest, lowest, and last price for the stock during the day

Let's next consider how to calculate the rate of return on a bond. Bonds pay returns in the form of interest **coupon payments** and capital gains. Suppose that an investor buys a one-year bond for $950. When the bond matures at the end of one year, it will pay the investor a **principal, or par, value** of $1000. At the end of the year, the investor will also be paid a coupon of $100. The coupon rate of return is $100/$1000 = 0.10, or 10 percent. However, the coupon rate is not the total rate of return, or **yield,** on the bond due to the capital gain of $50 = $1000 − $950. The rate of return on this bond is

> **coupon payments** Interest paid to bondholders by a firm on its outstanding debt
>
> **principal**, or **par, value** The amount paid back by a firm on each bond on its maturity date
>
> **yield** The total return on a bond, including the capital gains and coupon interest paid

$$\text{Rate of return on bond} = \frac{(\text{par value} - \text{purchase price}) + \text{coupons}}{\text{purchase price}}$$

As before, after plugging in the data,

$$\text{Rate of return on bond} = \frac{(\$1000 - \$950) + \$100}{\$950}$$

$$= \frac{\$150}{\$950}$$

$$= 0.158 \quad \text{or } 15.8 \text{ percent}$$

Another way to solve for the bond's yield is to use the time value of money. Referring back to the present value equation, we can link the present value of the bond to its future coupon payments and principal value.

$$\text{Present value} = \frac{\text{future value}}{(1 + r)}$$

where r is the bond's yield.

$$\$950 = \frac{\$100 + \$1000}{(1 + r)}$$

Using some algebra, we have $(1 + r) = \$1100/\$950 = 1.158$. Once again, we get $r = 0.158$, or 15.8 percent.

From this example, we see that higher coupon payments and capital gains increase the rate of return on a bond. An important assumption here is that the risk of the bond does not change. If the risk of the bond were to increase, say due to increased default risk, the price of the bond could fall. However, unlike stocks, bonds have a maturity date, and on this date they pay the promised principal, or par, a value of $1000 in this case. If the investor sells the bond before it matures, the increasing risk of the bond would result in a lower price and lower capital gain. It makes sense in this situation for the investor *not* to sell the bond and instead wait for it to mature and receive the $1000 par value. On the other hand, if the bond's risk of default is relatively high, rather than wait until maturity, it would be prudent to sell the bond and avoid larger potential losses that could occur in bankruptcy. Since most bonds have low chances of default, investors normally hold bonds to maturity and receive the par value.

Counting the Risks

Higher bond and stock returns mean higher risks. What kinds of risk do investors face on securities? This topic attracts intense study in the field of investment finance. We know that default risk, which is also termed credit risk, concerns the chance that a firm's earnings will not be sufficient to meet its debt payments. However, there are many other risks that confront investors as they attempt to make buy-and-sell decisions on different securities.

market risk The risk of an individual firm's stock prices going down in value as bond market prices move down, and vice versa

Market risk relates to the tendency of an individual firm's bond and stock prices to be affected by movements in the entire financial market. The Standard & Poor's 500 (S&P 500) index represents the average return on the 500 largest U.S. firms' stocks. When this average market index goes up or down, it is generally true that most U.S. firms' stock prices likewise fall or rise. Otherwise known as *systematic risk*, this risk cannot be avoided by the investor. Likewise, the bond market as a whole can systematically go up and down as interest rates change over time. This **interest rate risk** is another type of market risk that the investor cannot control.

interest rate risk The risk of bond prices moving down as the general level of interest rates moves up, and vice versa

Case in Point

Market Risk and the Stock Performance of DaimlerChrysler, McDonald's, and Sony

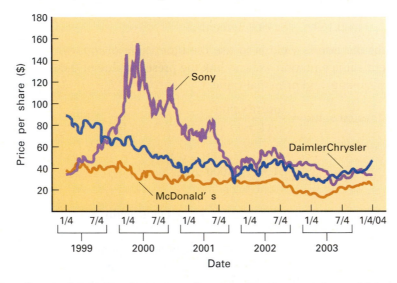

The above graph gives the stock price performance of DaimlerChrysler, McDonald's, and Sony from January 1999 to July 2004. Here we see that Sony's stock price has been much more volatile than the other two firms over time. The price rose dramatically in 1999 due to an economic boom at that time. However, Sony's stock price declined thereafter and lost all of the gains of 1999. One problem for Sony has been that the Japanese economy has had difficulties in recent years. Thus, market risk caused Sony's stock price to fall from about $150 per share in early 2000 to about $25 by mid-2004.

Over this same time period, McDonald's and DaimlerChrysler also experienced a decrease in share price, but the decline was much less dramatic. Nonetheless, the stock prices of McDonald's and DaimlerChrysler fell by more than one-half in this time period. Again, the best assessment of the reason for the decline is market risk. In the U.S. stock market, the Standard & Poor's 500 Index (representing the largest 500 U.S. firms) declined from around 1600 to about 1000 from early 2000 to mid-2004. The main reason for the general stock market decline was an

economic recession, which was less severe in the United States and Europe than in Japan. Consequently, McDonald's and DaimlerChrysler's stocks were exposed to less negative market risk than Sony's. Finally, in the second half of 2003 and early 2004, the stock prices of all three stocks increased as an economic recovery began to take hold. We can conclude that the general economy in a country or region is a powerful factor that can affect systematically stock prices of companies.

Questions

1. Why did Sony's stock price rise dramatically in 1999?
2. Why did Sony's stock price fall in 2000 and the years thereafter?
3. Did market risk affect the share prices of McDonald's and DaimlerChrysler? Briefly explain in what ways.
4. Look up these stock prices on Yahoo Finance (**http://finance.yahoo.com**). How have the stocks performed in recent months?

Investors use the levels of interest rates on government bonds, known as Treasury securities in the United States, to monitor interest rate risk. As movements in interest rate levels become more volatile, bond prices increasingly fluctuate. In general, when interest rates go up, bond prices go down, and vice versa.

Liquidity risk concerns the problem of selling a security quickly for a fair market price. Some bonds and stocks are illiquid in the sense that an investor must substantially lower the sales price to attract a buyer. Bonds and stocks issued by large firms tend to be more liquid than those issued by smaller firms.

Tax risk is the exposure of earnings from an investment to government taxation. Dividend and coupon payments are subject to income taxes, which are typically higher than capital gains taxes. Investors in high tax brackets may well be expected to seek investments with lower dividend and coupon payments and higher capital gains. Bonds issued by state and local governments, known as **municipal securities,** pay coupon interest payments that are exempt from income taxes. Again, investors in high tax brackets can be expected to purchase these securities.

Firm-specific risk encompasses any risk that faces the individual firm that is not related to market, liquidity, and tax risks. Examples are default risk, competition from other firms in the industry, legal actions against the firm, agency problems between managers and shareholders, scandals that damage the firm's reputation, technological adaptability of the firm, management competence, and marketing effectiveness. These are firm-specific risks that pertain to how the firm manages its business activities.

Reinvestment risk arises when an investor receives a payment on a security and decides to buy other securities with the proceeds. The problem is that the new securities may have lower earning power than the old securities. Dividend and coupon payments can be difficult to always reinvest at good rates of return. When interest rates are rising, coupons can be reinvested at higher interest rates than previously. Alternatively, in recent years interest rates have fallen to historically low levels, which means that coupons are reinvested in low-earning bonds. Also, dividends can be reinvested in stocks when the S&P 500 index is rising. However, if the stock market as a whole is experiencing falling prices, reinvesting dividends in stocks would result in capital losses. These same concepts apply to payments of bond principal or sales of stocks and bonds. Reinvestment risk can work for or against an investor.

Total risk is the sum of the aforementioned risks. A convenient way to measure this risk is to look at the volatility of rates of return on a security. Exhibit 13.8 shows the rates of return for two securities over time. Because security 1 has higher volatility than security 2, it has more total risk than security 2.

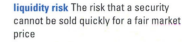

How much risk would you take if you invested your money in stocks and bonds? Would this risk change as you got older?

Managing Investment Risks[2]

LEARNING OBJECTIVE 7
Provide sound advice on how to manage investment risks and make investment choices.

Tip 1: Do Not Entirely Avoid Risk. A misguided solution to managing these different kinds of investment risk is to simply avoid them. For example, a person could keep all of his or her savings in a bank checking account. While the

---

liquidity risk The risk that a security cannot be sold quickly for a fair market price

tax risk The exposure of earnings from an investment to government taxation, including income and capital gains taxes

municipal securities Debt securities issued by state and local governments to raise funds, with coupon payments that are exempt from federal income taxes

firm-specific risk Any risk that is particular to an individual firm and not related to market, liquidity, and tax risks that affect all firms

reinvestment risk The risk an investor faces when payments on high-earning securities are received and are subsequently used to buy other securities that have lower earnings

total risk The sum of all risks associated with a security, which can be measured as the volatility of the security's price over time

EXHIBIT 13.8

Total Risk and Volatility of Rates of Return

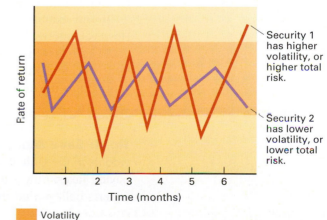

Security 1 has higher volatility, or higher total risk.

Security 2 has lower volatility, or lower total risk.

Volatility

rate of return is low, at least the money is safe from loss. This investment strategy is more common than you might think. Unfortunately, it is seriously flawed. The main problem is the opportunity cost of savings. Most investments earn higher returns than checking accounts. The lost earnings by saving in checking accounts are a high cost to pay for safety. Also, in the end, financial safety would be better served by investing in riskier types of securities with higher rates of return.

Tip 2: Invest for Long Periods of Time. In Figure 13.4 we showed that $100 invested in a loan for 20 years at a 10 percent interest rate would grow to about $673. If the loan were made at a 15 percent interest rate, the $100 would grow to about $1637. Our money more than doubled by increasing the interest rate from 10 to 15 percent, even though the interest rate only increased by one-half, or 5 percent. If the loan rate were 2 percent, the total after 20 years would only be about $149. Now imagine that these were alternative payoffs on your investments in stocks and bonds. Which amount would you rather earn? Confirming Tip 1, we can readily see that investing money at low interest rates does not lead to later financial security.

Not only does investing over a long period of time allow your returns to multiply, but it also actually lowers risk. Investing for short periods of time raises risk. If you bought some stock and planned to sell it in one year, you could suffer large losses if the entire stock market went down over the next year. Also, a sudden increase in interest rates could cause bond values to go down, resulting in short-term capital losses. By investing for the long term, investors smooth out their earnings on stocks and bonds. Short-term movements in the prices of financial assets become irrelevant to investors. Exhibit 13.9 shows that, although short-term security earnings can be volatile, the long-term trend in security earnings is relatively stable.

EXHIBIT 13.9

Short-Run Volatility and the Long-Run Trend in Stock Returns

Tip 3: Invest Regularly Over Time. Another way to manage investment risk is to regularly purchase securities. In the above example we assumed that $100 was invested for 20 years. At 10 percent interest we would get about $673. What if we invested $100 every year for 20 years? Now we would have $5727.50 after 20 years. By saving and investing on a consistent basis from year to year, the total sum earned is dramatically increased.

This example has important implications for our aging society. Many people think that they have to make a lot of money to gain financial security in their old age or retirement years. In reality, the best way to ensure that you have enough money in your retirement is to regularly save and invest. Even modest savings every month that are invested in the financial marketplace will grow to sizable totals in later life.

In our example we assumed that the investor could always earn 10 percent. However, interest rates move up and down over time, so the $100 invested each year could earn less than or more than 10 percent. While this is true, by investing regularly over time, in the end we can earn a long-run, *average* interest rate of 10 percent. This is the interest rate that corresponds to the long-run trend in returns over time (see Exhibit 13.9).

Tip 4: Save More to Earn More. Today, the average savings rate for individuals in the United States is about 4 percent of disposable income. That is, after paying taxes, only 4 in 100 dollars is invested in the financial marketplace. Most experts believe that this savings rate is too low. If people saved 10 percent, their earnings from investments in securities would likely lead to financial security after about 20 to 30 years. What if their disposable income were $40,000? A 10 percent savings rate per year would mean that they would save and invest $4000 each year. Over 20 years, by investing these savings regularly over time as recommended in Tip 3, this level of investment would yield $229,100. Assuming that the savers paid off a home valued at $100,000 over this 20 years and accumulated $20,000 in other savings, their **total net worth** would be around $350,000. If they saved for 40 years instead of 20 years, their total net worth would rise to $1,770,370 + $100,000 + $20,000 = $1,890,370. These rough figures reveal that a sure way to earn more is simply to save and invest more.

> **total net worth** The sum of the market values of all financial and real assets owned, including cash, bonds, stocks, land, buildings, and other property
>
> **diversification** Buying different financial and real assets whose prices or values have different patterns of movement up and down over time, such that the total risk or volatility is reduced for the entire portfolio of assets

Tip 5: Diversify Securities. **Diversification** is a powerful tool used to decrease investment risk.[3] It is important to recognize that diversification cannot increase investment returns, only decrease risk per unit return. Let's see how diversification works to decrease risk. Exhibit 13.10 shows the same two securities, labeled 1 and 2, as in Exhibit 13.8. Both securities are fairly risky over time, with security 1 having more volatile price movements over time than security 2. Consider what would happen if we combined these two assets into a portfolio (labeled P). Portfolio P has 50 percent of our money invested in security 1 and 50 percent in security 2. The average rate of return is represented by the dark line in Exhibit 13.10. The volatility of portfolio P is much less than that of security 1 or security 2. Thus, diversification reduces risk.

Diversification is more than simply buying different assets. Instead, investors need to purchase assets that have different patterns of returns or prices over time. What if we had a third security, security 3, with the same price pattern over time as security 1? In this case, a portfolio comprising securities 1 and 3 would not decrease risk; that is, the average price pattern would look the same as that of security 1. On the other hand, assume that yet another security, security 4, had a price pattern that was the exact opposite of security 1. That is, when the price of security 1 rose, the price of security 4 would fall by the same amount. If we made a portfolio of securities of 1 and 4, it would look like a flat line, with no price movements at all. In this case diversification would have eliminated *all* price risk. To diversify risk means to buy different assets with different patterns of returns or prices over time.

Making Investment Choices

Market participants have a wide variety of stocks, bonds, and real estate investment opportunities from which to choose. Exhibit 13.11 shows a graph of different stocks (labeled S1, S2, etc.) and long-term bonds (B1, B2, etc.) that an investor can purchase. Using diversification, the investor can combine these assets to form portfolios that have lower risk than the individual assets. The curve labeled *EF* represents the portfolios of stocks and bonds that have the lowest risk. For rational investors who do not like risk (i.e., are risk averse), we can say

EXHIBIT 13.10

How Diversification Can Reduce Total Risk

Portfolio P, composed of security 1 plus security 2, has lower risk, or volatility, than either security alone.

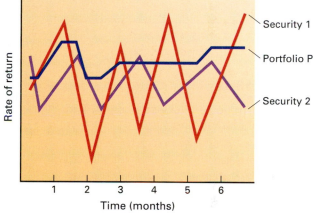

Harry Markowitz is seen here in Tokyo in 1990, after hearing news that he had been awarded the Nobel Prize in Economics for his contributions on investment diversification.

efficient frontier The set of portfolios of assets that has minimum risk over a range of expected returns

EXHIBIT 13.11

Efficient Frontier of Investment Opportunities

Combinations or portfolios of bonds and stocks that have minimum risk for any given return.

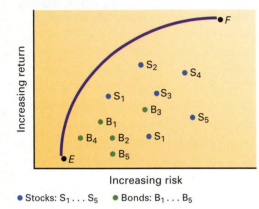

● Stocks: $S_1 \ldots S_5$ ● Bonds: $B_1 \ldots B_5$

EXHIBIT 13.12

Market Portfolio M, Riskless Asset Z, and the Capital Market Line

All investors will invest in some combination of riskless asset Z and market portfolio M, which is the capital market line. This line gives the highest return-risk trade-off.

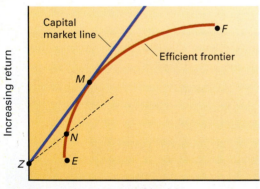

Increasing risk

market portfolio The portfolio of assets that investors should purchase to earn the highest return-risk trade-off

capital market line The line that shows the return-risk trade-off available to investors, who have a choice between a riskless asset and the market portfolio

exchange traded funds (ETFs) Diversified portfolios of securities offered by the American Stock Exchange that can be bought and sold as individual stocks can be

that portfolios on curve *EF* are optimal. These portfolios are efficient in the sense that they minimize risk for any given level of return. For this reason the curve *EF* is called the **efficient frontier.**

One possibility that is missing in Exhibit 13.11 is that an investor will seek to entirely avoid risk. For example, if an extremely risk-averse investor desired to avoid risk, she or he could put her or his money in a bank deposit account. While very safe, the rate of return, or interest earned, on a bank account is minimal. This riskless rate of return is shown as the point labeled *Z* on the *Y* axis in Exhibit 13.11. Asset Z has no risk but has a minimum rate of interest. Another example of a riskless asset is short-term government debt securities, such as U.S. Treasury bills.

Suppose that the investor can choose between riskless asset Z and a risky portfolio on the efficient frontier *EF*. If she or he put 50 percent of her or his money in asset Z and 50 percent in a portfolio lying on the curve *EF*, which portfolio would be the best one to choose?

Exhibit 13.12 gives the solution. Looking at the graph, we see that the highest return per unit risk is achieved by investing in portfolio M. This portfolio is obtained by finding the line just tangent to the curve *EF*, the solid line in Exhibit 13.12. If you picked portfolio N, you can readily see that the dashed line *ZN* is below the solid line *ZM*. All investors will pick the same optimal portfolio, portfolio M. Portfolio M is named the **market portfolio** due to this rather startling finding.

What kinds of assets are contained in portfolio M? In theory, all assets in the world are contained in M. In practice, studies have found that portfolios with only 30 to 50 stocks and bonds are fairly good approximations for portfolio M. Many people use broad stock indexes, such as the Standard & Poor's 500 index or the Dow Jones World Stock index, to estimate portfolio M. Three-month or one-year U.S. Treasury bills are used to estimate the riskless rate at point Z.

In choosing investments, investors who are extremely risk averse should put all of their money in a bank account or in U.S. Treasury bills (point Z in Exhibit 13.12). Investors seeking considerable levels of risk should put all of their money in market portfolio M. Investors wanting some balance between these two points should divide their money so they will be somewhere along the line *ZM*. The investors' risk preferences determine where they will lie on the line *ZM*. The line *ZM* is known as the **capital market line.**

Investors do not have to work to find the highest earning stocks. All they need to do is properly diversify by purchasing market portfolio M. Nowadays it is quite easy to buy portfolio M. For example, investment companies sell a wide variety of stock index portfolios. Also, **exchange traded funds (ETFs)** that represent a diversified portfolio of securities on the American Stock Exchange offer stocks to investors. These innovations in financial markets allow investors to readily achieve return-risk levels on the capital market line.

   *How would you invest your retirement money to maximize the returns per unit risk? Is your investment portfolio diversified?*

Careers in Financial and Investment Management

Financial and investment managers are responsible for collecting, analyzing, and reporting financial information within their organizations. They are involved in capital budgeting, financing, and investment decisions. Business, economics, and mathematics courses are most useful in terms of educational training. All large organizations in both private and government sectors of the economy hire financial or investment managers in various roles. Small- and medium-sized firms will utilize fewer finance professionals than large firms, but it is still common for them to hire individuals in selected finance roles. Some people seek self-employment in financial services. Examples of self-employment options are financial and investment consultants, stockbrokers, insurance brokers, and property consultants.

Exhibit 13.1 listed the primary roles of financial managers in business organizations.

- *Treasurers* and *finance officers* oversee financial goals and budgets, including capital budgeting decisions, financing decisions, cash management, and mergers and acquisitions.

- *Controllers* are responsible for preparing financial reports, such as income statement and balance sheet information, cash flow analyses, and pro forma or future revenues and expenses. They often participate in accounting, audit, and budget activities within the organization.

- *Cash managers* put together details of the cash movements within the organization. Cash collections and disbursements are monitored and projected to anticipate cash problems. Recommendations for capital budgeting and financing decisions may be offered.

- *Credit managers* are involved in all credit decisions, such as raising funds using bank loans and debt issues, evaluating the credit risk of bonds and firms, and monitoring past-due accounts receivables.

According to the U.S. Department of Labor (**http://stats.bls.gov/oco/ocos010. htm**), the average earnings of selected financial managers in 2002 were vice president of finance, $183,500; treasurer, $150,600; assistant vice president–finance $141,300; controller or comptroller, $134,300; director, $130,600; assistant treasurer, $111,900; assistant controller or comptroller, $115,500; manager, $84,500; and cash manager, $64,700.

Financial institutions also hire financial and investment managers in various areas, including lending, mortgages, trusts, operations, electronic financial services, and investments. Government financial managers must be knowledgeable about government regulations and budgeting procedures. Also, health care financial managers must understand specific aspects of health care insurance and relevant government regulations. According to 2003 data collected by the U.S. Department of Labor (**http://www.bls.gov/bls/blswage.htm**), average incomes in industries employing the largest numbers of financial and investment managers were financial managers ($130,230); accountants and auditors ($60,600); bank loan officers ($55,210); personal financial advisors ($66,740); and network and computer systems administrators ($55,970). Of course, these are average figures, and ranges of salaries and wages can vary considerably depending on firm size and individual responsibilities.

Summary

LEARNING OBJECTIVE 1

Explain how financial managers fit into the organizational structure of a firm and what their role is.

In this chapter we have reviewed the roles of financial managers and investment managers. Firms rely on financial managers to make capital budgeting decisions and raise funds to finance the production and sale of products and services. Their main goal is to turn accounting profits into economic profits, as measured by higher common stock prices. Agency costs arise when managers undertake activities that benefit themselves but do not increase common stock prices.

LEARNING OBJECTIVE 2

Use the time value of money to differentiate between present values and future values of money.

To perform capital budgeting analyses, it is necessary to understand the time value of money. Simply put, a dollar received tomorrow is worth less than a dollar received today. Interest rates link future values to present values. The main components of nominal interest rates are the real interest rate, inflation rate, and default risk premium. When money is invested for more than one period, it can grow at an increasing rate over time.

LEARNING OBJECTIVE 3

Apply net present value analyses to the basic capital budgeting decisions facing financial managers.

To evaluate alternative products or services, financial managers need to calculate the net present value (NPV) of earnings over time. The NPV is the present value of future earnings minus the initial investment cost of the product or service. If an investment project has an NPV greater than or equal to zero, it is considered acceptable. Such projects have economic value in the sense of increasing or not changing the value of common stock.

LEARNING OBJECTIVE 4

Identify the sources of funds and their usage in financing decisions.

Once acceptable products and services are identified by capital budgeting analyses, financial managers must acquire the necessary funds to pay for their initial investment costs. Most funds are generated internally by profits in the form of retained earnings. Retained earnings are affected by the firm's dividend policy. If shareholders demand high dividend payments, retained earnings will likely be inadequate to finance acceptable projects. In this case the firm must seek external financing, including bank loans or the issuance of bonds and stocks in the financial marketplace. Debt financing, or bank loans and bonds, tends to be lower cost than equity financing, or common stock, due to the tax deductability of interest payments. Financial managers attempt to use an optimal mix of sources of funds that minimizes their overall cost.

LEARNING OBJECTIVE 5

Describe different types of investment managers and the services they provide investors.

Investment managers seek to buy and sell securities issued by firms to make a profit for their clients. Brokers and dealers execute the buy-and-sell orders of the public for a service fee. Investment bankers help firms issue their bonds and stocks. Also, institutional investors assist in securities transactions for individuals, businesses, and the government.

LEARNING OBJECTIVE 6

Give details of how to measure investment returns and what investment risks confront investors.

A fundamental concept in investment analysis is the risk-return trade-off. Higher risk securities require higher expected returns as compensation to investors for bearing risk. The rate of return on a share of common stock is comprised of a dividend yield and a capital gains yield. The rate of return on a bond is the sum of the coupon rate plus the capital gain yield. Since returns must be balanced against risks, investors need to carefully evaluate security risks. Total risk includes market risk, interest rate risk, liquidity risk, tax risk, firm-specific risk, and reinvestment risk.

LEARNING OBJECTIVE 7

Provide sound advice on how to manage investment risks and make investment choices.

To properly manage these risks and earn fair returns, some important investment tips are to not entirely avoid risk, invest for long periods of time, invest regularly over time, save more to earn more, and diversify in different securities. Modern portfolio management suggests that investors should purchase securities that together reduce risk. Given the existence of a riskless rate of return, all investors should purchase the same market portfolio to maximize their returns per unit of risk. Stock market indexes are believed to be a good proxy for the market portfolio. Mutual funds offer a number of different stock market indexes that investors can readily purchase.

Chapter Questions

1. What are the main responsibilities of the CFO, treasurer, and controller in a firm?
2. Do financial managers and shareholders always work together to maximize share prices? How can financial managers be motivated to accomplish this firm goal?
3. Are accounting profits and economic profits the same thing? Explain.
4. How is people's time preference for consumption related to the real interest rate?
5. If the real rate of interest is 2 percent and the expected inflation rate is projected to be 5 percent over the next year, what should the nominal interest rate be?
6. A bank makes a loan for $1000 to a firm at an interest rate of 8 percent. How much did the firm have to pay back if the loan was due or matured in one year? What if the firm paid back the loan in two years? (Hint: Convert present values to future values using the interest rate. See "The Time Value of Money: How Money Grows" to figure out the answer for two years.)
7. Assume you invest $1000 in a bond that pays 8 percent per year. Draw a graph with future value on the Y axis and time in years on the X axis. Show how compound interest, or the force of interest, would increase the future value of the bond after 1, 5, 10, 15, and 20 years. (Hint: See "The Time Value of Money: How Money Grows" and use the future value equation. You will need a calculator to compute your answer. The power function can be used to enter the number of years.)
8. Assume that your firm invests in a machine costing $100 at time 0 (now). One year from now, the machine is sold and the net profit from its operation is estimated to be $120. Why is the economic profit *not* equal to $20?
9. Do financing decisions affect capital budgeting decisions? For example, if a firm borrowed some money from a bank to finance building a new product, how would the interest rate on the loan affect the discount rate used in capital budgeting analyses? How should firms determine the correct discount rate to use in capital budgeting analyses?
10. What is the process of capital budgeting? Which projects should be accepted versus rejected? What is the net present value (NPV)?
11. In "Capital Budgeting Decisions for Multiple-Year Investments," we presented a capital budgeting analysis of a firm evaluating the purchase of a machine for $100. Instead of using an opportunity cost of 16 percent in the analysis, use an opportunity cost of funds of 6 percent. What is the present value of cash flows for the machine? What is the net present value (NPV)? (Hint: Use a calculator to do your work.)
12. What are the main sources of financing to pay for acceptable capital budgeting projects? How do dividends affect the use of these financing sources?
13. Differentiate between the following different types of debt: commercial paper, bonds, and Eurobonds.
14. Why is debt a lower-cost form of external finance than equity for a firm?
15. A firm has income before interest expenses of $1000. It has interest payments of $400 and a tax rate of 25 percent. What is the net income before taxes? Net income after taxes? How much was the tax savings on interest payments due to their tax deductability? Who gets these tax savings?
16. What is investment grade debt? Is it lower or higher risk than junk bonds? If a firm defaults on its debt, why would it want to file for bankruptcy?
17. What is an initial public offering of stock by a firm? Why is this a significant event?
18. How are securities brokers and dealers alike? How do they differ from one another? What do investment bankers do?
19. Write the basic formulas for the rate of return on a stock and the rate of return for a bond. What is the difference between dividend versus interest payments?
20. There are many risks involved in investing in bonds and stocks. What is market risk? Liquidity risk? Tax risk? Firm-specific risk? Reinvestment risk?
21. List five basic tips for making sound investment decisions.
22. Draw a picture of the efficient frontier, market portfolio, and capital market line. How does the existence of a riskless asset like government securities affect investment decisions for market participants?

Interpreting Business News

1. Assume that you read that interest rate declines in recent months have increased borrowing by firms. It is expected that the new debt funds will be used by firms to expand production. Some experts believe that the low-cost debt will have a beneficial effect on firms' profits. Other experts worry that increased debt burdens will increase bankruptcy risk among firms. Why might these experts be right?
2. Yesterday, a firm announced a new compensation scheme for top executives in the firm. The new scheme will reduce salaries and wages and increase the use of stock options to motivate top executives to boost the firm's profitability. Why do you think that top management would become

more sensitive to the needs of shareholders in the future?

3. Recent news reports make the argument that the high inflation rate in the last few years is increasing the yields on bonds. Bond prices have fallen to five-year lows and have become attractive to investors. Not only are coupon payments high, but if interest rates decline in the future, bondholders would stand to gain healthy capital gains. Do you think it is a good time to buy bonds?

4. The two candidates for president of the United States have different proposals for tax reform. One candidate wants higher corporate income taxes and higher capital gains taxes. The other candidate proposes lower corporate income taxes and lower capital gains taxes. How would these different tax proposals affect firms' usage of debt and equity to finance their capital budgeting projects?

5. Recent data indicate that few investors in the United States invest in bonds and stocks in different countries. This "home bias," or lack of international investment, by U.S. investors could lower their diversification and increase their risk. Why do people tend to prefer buying bonds and stocks of companies that are in their home country?

Web Assignments

1. Use a Web browser to search on the key words *Sony* and *bond issue*. Pick one bond issue and describe what capital budgeting projects are being financed with the debt funds. What is the size of

the bond issue? When will the bond issue mature? What is the interest rate?

2. Go to the corporate website for McDonald's and find the most recent reports on global results. What are the highlights noted at the beginning of the report? Did McDonald's economic value increase lately?

3. Go to the DaimlerChrysler website and find the most recent consolidated balance sheet, which can be found in the annual report. Go to the section of the balance sheet entitled "Liabilities and stockholders' equity." Using the U.S. dollar figures (quoted there in millions of dollars), what is the amount of stockholders' equity and liabilities? How much of stockholders' equity is retained earnings? How much of liabilities is financial liabilities, or debt? What does this information tell you about how DaimlerChrysler finances its operations?

4. Go to a Web browser and search on the key words "one-year interest rates" and "U.S. government debt." Now draw a graph with rate of return on the Y axis and risk on the X axis. Use the one-year interest rate as the riskless interest rate on the Y axis. Assume that the average rate of return on the stock market is 10 percent. Plot this market portfolio in return-risk space. Finally, draw the capital market line connecting the riskless rate and the market portfolio. Given your risk preference, where on the capital line would you be? (Hint: A very conservative investor would be at the riskless rate, while a high-risk investor would prefer to be at the market portfolio.)

Portfolio Projects

Exploring Your Own Case in Point

In this chapter, you learned how firms evaluate their investment projects as well as how investors evaluate firms in this regard. To better understand the financial management of your firm, answer the following questions.

1. What are some recent capital budgeting projects in the news about your company?

2. After reviewing the consolidated balance sheet for the firm, give a short description of how your firm finances its operations. Using a recent income statement, how much of net income after taxes did your firm pay out in dividends to shareholders?

3. Use the Internet to find the stock price per share for your firm over time. What has been the capital

gain yield on the stock over the past year? What was the dividend per share paid by the firm over the past year? Use the stock price per share and dividend per share information to compute the rate of return on the stock over the past year.

Starting Your Own Business

After reading this chapter, you should be able to update your business plan with financial information regarding your capital budgeting plans for initial production.

1. What is the initial long-term investment cost of production (i.e., expenses for equipment, property, and other fixed assets)?

2. Give annual estimates over the next five years for:

a. Revenues

b. Operating costs (total of inventory, labor, utility bills, etc.)

c. Depreciation and amortization (of equipment and property)

d. Taxes (assume 25 percent unless you have a more accurate estimate)

e. Net income after taxes

f. Net cash flow (net income after taxes plus non-cash charges such as depreciation and amortization)

3. Discount back your net cash flows using a 15 percent discount rate or cost of capital. To do this, divide the first year's net cash flow by 1.15, divide the second year's net cash flow by $(1.15)^2$, year 3 by $(1.15)^3$, year 4 by $(1.15)^4$, and year 5 by $(1.15)^5$. Now add up these discounted net cash flows for the five years to get the total present value of net cash flows. Subtract from this total present value the investment cost in question 1. Did you get a positive or negative net present value (NPV)? Should you invest in this new business? Do you think that a different discount rate than 15 percent should be used due to the riskiness of your new business?

Test Prepper

You've read the chapter, studied the key terms, and the exam is any day now. Think you are ready to ace it? Take this sample test to gauge your comprehension of chapter material. You can check your answers at the back of the book.

True/False Questions

Please indicate if the following statements are true or false:

_____ 1. The highest-ranking financial manager is the chief executive officer.

_____ 2. Only if accounting profit leads to higher share values is economic profit earned.

_____ 3. The time preference for consumption does not change much over time and is related to the real rate of interest.

_____ 4. If there were no default risk, the nominal interest rate would equal the risky rate of interest.

_____ 5. To figure out the economic profit of a new product, we must compare cash flows in present value terms at time 0 (now).

_____ 6. If the minimum rate of return on an investment project is 15 percent, then this is the interest rate that should be used in finding present values of the project's future cash flows.

_____ 7. Bonds are a short-term source of funds for firms.

_____ 8. Lower-rated debt securities are known as junk bonds.

_____ 9. Factoring is when customers make payments to post office boxes in local postal facilities.

_____ 10. Firm-specific risk encompasses any risk that faces the individual firm that is not related to market, liquidity, and tax risks.

Multiple-Choice Questions

Choose the best answer.

_____ 1. You are a manager of a firm that owns stock options on 1000 shares at a price of $20 per share. If the market price of the shares rises to $30, assuming that you sell the shares, you will earn a profit of

    a. $1,000.
    b. $10,000.
    c. $20,000.
    d. $30,000.
    e. $100,000.

_____ 2. If the real rate of interest is 2 percent, and the expected inflation rate is 5 percent, then the nominal interest rate is

    a. 2 percent.
    b. 3 percent.
    c. 5 percent.
    d. 7 percent.
    e. 10 percent.

_____ 3. The chance that a firm will go bankrupt and be unable to pay back a loan from a bank is known as the

    a. nominal interest rate.
    b. inflation rate.
    c. default risk.
    d. market risk.
    e. loan risk.

_____ 4. Assume a firm invests $100 at an annual rate of return of 20 percent (0.20). The future value of this $100 in one year is

    a. $20.
    b. $80.
    c. $100.
    d. $110.
    e. $120.

_____ 5. The nominal interest rate contains the

    a. stated interest rate and the real interest rate.
    b. required rate of return, the stated interest rate, and the inflation rate.
    c. real interest rate, the expected inflation rate, and the default risk premium.
    d. riskless rate of interest and the real interest rate.
    e. compound interest and the discount rate.

_____ 6. In evaluating investment projects using capital budgeting principles, projects that are acceptable investments have

    a. only positive net present values (NPVs).
    b. only negative NPVs.
    c. only zero NPVs.
    d. positive and zero NPVs.
    e. negative and zero NPVs.

_____ 7. Assume a firm has a 30 percent tax rate. Also assume that the same firm has $100 of interest payments on debt. If it has $200 of net income before interest and taxes, the firm's net income after taxes is

a. $30.
b. $40.
c. $70.
d. $100.
e. $140.

_____ 8. In the voting process, shareholders have the right to transfer their votes to another shareholder by means of a(n)

a. proxy.
b. preemptive right.
c. capital gain.
d. dividend.
e. agency cost.

_____ 9. Which of the following assists investors purchasing and selling financial securities?

a. Investment bankers
b. Underwriters
c. Brokers
d. Dealers
e. Institutional investors

_____ 10. You buy a share of stock of a firm for $10. One year later you sell the share of stock for $12. Also you received a dividend during the year of $1. The rate of return on the stock is

a. 10 percent.
b. 20 percent.
c. 25 percent.
d. 30 percent.
e. 40 percent.

Want more questions? Visit the student website at **http://college.hmco.com/business/student/** (select Gaspar, *Introduction to Business*) and take the ACE quizzes for more practice.

14

Understanding the Financial System, Money, and Banking

| Introduction

| **The Financial System**
Components of the Financial System
Structure of Financial Systems
Financial Systems and the Economy

| **Money and Banking**
What Is Money?
Central Banks and Monetary Policy
Monetary Policy Framework

| **Financial Institutions**
Depository Institutions
Nondepository Institutions
Managing a Financial Institution

| Careers in the Financial System

Learning Objectives

After studying this chapter, you should be able to

1. Define the components of financial systems and understand the benefits of financial intermediation.

2. Contrast different kinds of financial systems around the world and state how regulation can protect the safety and soundness of financial systems.

3. Understand how the health of the financial system affects the productivity of the economy, including the roles of the IMF and the World Bank.

4. Overview the history of money and why money matters to the economy.

5. Explain what central banks do to control money and achieve economic goals.

6. Compare the different types of financial institutions as well as their roles in the economy.

The Large Bank Merger Wave

Numerous large bank mergers in recent years promise to change the financial systems in the United States, Europe, Japan, and other countries around the world. For example, the largest U.S. bank was formed in 2003 when Bank of America, the third largest U.S. bank, and FleetBoston, the seventh largest U.S. bank, agreed to merge. This merger was followed by the announcement of another mega-merger between Wells Fargo and Bank One in January 2004. Other large U.S. merger deals that took place in recent years were First Chicago–Bank One, Wells Fargo–Norwest, Bank of America–NationsBank, Citigroup–Travelers Group, and Chase Manhattan–J.P. Morgan. Megabank mergers are not unique to the United States. In Europe, some of the mergers that have taken place in recent years are Banque Indosuez–Credit Agricole in France, Credit Suisse–Swiss Volksbank and Union Bank of Switzerland–Swiss Bank Corporation in Switzerland, Generale Bank–Fortis Group in Belgium, and the cross-Atlantic ocean merger between Deutsche Bank in Germany and Bankers Trust in the United States. Other European banks are growing fast through mergers, including Spain's Banco Santander Central Hispano, Royal Bank of Scotland, the Dutch banks ING and ABN Amro Holding, the U.K. banking organizations Barclay and HSBC Holdings, and France's BNP Paribas. In Japan the government mandated the consolidation of 21 large banks and many insurance and brokerage firms into only seven financial-holding companies. In 1999 the largest bank in the world was created by the merger of the Industrial Bank of Japan, Dai-ichi Kangyo Bank, and Fuji Bank—it has over one trillion dollars in assets!

What will be the impact of this bank merger wave on the world financial system? Will it have good or bad effects on business firms, consumers, and investors? How will it affect the development of different countries? These are intriguing questions, but the answers will take some time to be fully revealed. One thing is certain: the next few decades are going to be an interesting and challenging period in the history of the financial world.

Introduction

Smoothly functioning financial systems are a prerequisite to a productive economy with profitable firms, good employment opportunities, and wages and salaries that allow people to enjoy a decent standard of living. Payments for goods and services are efficiently handled. Savings of the public are channeled to profitable investments. The growth of savings from profitable investments creates new wealth. It is obvious that for a nation to be prosperous, a competitive financial system is needed.

The Great Depression in the United States in the 1930s made it painfully clear that no country can afford not to protect the safety and soundness of its financial system. So many financial institutions failed and so much turmoil existed in financial markets that people lost confidence in the financial system altogether. The breakdown of financial systems around the world at that time destroyed the payments system and access to credit funds. The result was widespread business failures, millions of lost jobs, and societal upheaval.

Throughout the twentieth century, countries sought to foster safe and sound financial systems. However, overly regulated financial systems did not lead to competitive financial firms. Too much government protection of commercial banks led to problems. Banks gradually became unable to provide the quality and types of financial services demanded by the public. Other financial service firms, such as securities firms, grew in importance, and banks began to shrink in influence. In recent years, financial systems around the world have been in the process of deregulation. Previous barriers to expanding into various kinds of financial services and into other geographic areas are being removed. In the United States, Europe, and Japan, recent deregulation has allowed banks, securities firms, and insurance companies to join together into single, conglomerate financial services firms called *financial holding companies*. In the United States, geographic deregulation now allows banks to freely move across state lines, while Europe has adopted similar changes allowing any financial service firm to move across national borders in the 25-member European Union countries. Due to deregulation, a wave of mergers and other changes is causing the formation of mega-institutions that are truly global in scale. These transcontinental financial institutions will offer many new finance careers in the years ahead.

One of the most important regulators in financial systems are the central banks of different countries. Central banks, such as the Federal Reserve (or Fed) in the United States, not only regulate financial firms but can control the amount of money in circulation, the levels of interest rates, and general economic conditions, such as the growth of output and jobs in the nation. Can central bank activities affect you? Let's assume that you work for a small business that produces and sells pizza. Your business finances the purchase of dough, meats, cheese, and sauce by borrowing funds from a local bank. On the evening news, you hear that the Fed increased the money supply and decreased the level of interest rates. What will be the impact of this news on your pizza sales? Your bank financing? Your profitability over the next year? Lately, the pizza business has been slower than normal. Will times get better due to the Fed's actions? Due to the birth of a child in your family, you have been thinking of buying a new house. How will the Fed's actions affect your home purchase decision? Will the cost of the house be affected? Events within our financial system have direct effects on our personal lives.

The Financial System

LEARNING OBJECTIVE 1
Define the components of financial systems and understand the benefits of financial intermediation.

In this section we discuss the components of the financial system, including the principal kinds of financial instruments, financial markets, and financial institutions. We overview different possible financial system structures, government regulation to promote safety and soundness and public confidence, and how financial systems affect the economy.[1]

Components of the Financial System

financial system The financial marketplace, including financial instruments, financial markets, and financial institutions

Financial systems are comprised of three basic components: financial instruments, financial markets, and financial institutions.

Financial Instruments. Financial instruments are bought and sold and, therefore, priced in financial markets. Financial instruments can be classified as debt, equity, or derivative securities. They can also be classified as money market instruments or capital market instruments.

Money market instruments are short-term securities having maturities of less than one year. Investors, business firms, and others use this market for liquidity adjustment in the sense of temporarily parking funds for use in the near future for paying bills or making other investments. If they held large amounts of money in cash form, there would clearly be an opportunity cost in terms of lost interest earnings. Suppose that a corporate treasurer has $1 million of excess cash that could earn 5 percent in a money market instrument. The opportunity cost of holding this cash for an entire year is $50,000. Clearly, the corporate treasurer would want to purchase money market instruments with excess cash holdings.

money market instruments Short-term securities that have maturities less than one year

Capital market instruments are long-term securities with maturities exceeding one year. Unlike the money market instruments, the main role of these instruments is long-run investment and risk taking. Not surprisingly, long-run returns in the capital market are considerably higher than in the money market. For example, suppose that your grandmother invested $1000 in 1929 in the money market. By 1991 this investment would return about $11,000, which seems like a fairly good result. However, $1000 invested in stocks would grow to $675,000 in this same period of time. The money market is not the best place to invest savings for the long run.

capital market instruments Long-term securities that have maturities more than one year

Trading in money and capital market securities can take place in either organized exchanges or over-the-counter (OTC) exchanges. **Organized exchanges** characteristically have a physical location, such as the New York Stock Exchange, Chicago Board of Trade, London International Financial Futures Exchange, Frankfurt Stock Exchange, Tokyo Stock Exchange, Hong Kong Stock Exchange, Mexican Stock Exchange, and many others. **Over-the-counter (OTC) exchanges** do not have a physical location; instead, they are telecommunications and computer networks that electronically trade securities. A good example is Nasdaq, the world's largest electronic stock market, which transmits real-time quote and trade data via communications equipment and computers to more than 1.3 million users in 83 countries. An interesting development in recent years is electronic communications networks (ECNs), which provide services to Nasdaq and other exchanges, in addition to offering Internet trading of securities (e.g., Instinet, Bloomberg Tradebook, Nextrade).

organized exchanges Securities exchanges that have a physical location

over-the-counter (OTC) exchanges Securities exchanges that do not have a physical location, due to the use of telecommunications and computer networks

The Chicago Board of Trade (CBOT) trading pits fill with traders before the opening bell in the morning. The CBOT is one of the world's largest markets for futures and options contracts on stocks, bonds, currencies, and commodities.

Case in Point

Are the Golden Arches Turning Red?

McDonald's has a global appetite for using debt. The following summarizes its borrowing from banks and the financial markets through bonds:

Currency Denomination of Debt	2001 (in millions of U.S. dollars)	2002 (in millions of U.S. dollars)
Total U.S. dollars	3828.7	3457.1
Total Euros	2354.6	2632.5
Total British pounds	849.1	1338.7
Total other European currencies	335.8	393.3
Total Japanese yen	811.9	900.4
Total other Asia/Pacific currencies	617.6	871.5
Total other currencies	26.4	21.1
Total debt obligations	8,824.1	9,614.6

With total assets in 2002 of about $24 billion, McDonald's was financing about 40 percent of its investments with debt funds. Common stockholders contributed another $1.8 billion, the book value of common stock on the balance sheet, to finance the firm. Credit is a major source of money used to maintain McDonald's operations, and it acquires credit on a global scale by tapping international debt markets and banks around the world.

Why borrow so much money? Is it bad? After all, if the firm earned healthy profits on retail food sales, there would seem to be enough money to pay for goods and services needed to produce and sell its hamburgers, French fries, and other products. However, this common reasoning has two major flaws. First, investment in land, buildings, and equipment is so expensive that the costs must be spread out over a long time. By borrowing money using 5-, 10-, 15-, and even 30-year long-term bonds and paying out a fixed amount on the debt every month, the high costs of fixed plant and equipment can be distributed over time and paid gradually. Otherwise, the firm would have to wait a long time to accumulate a large enough amount of profits before it could grow into new facilities and expand its physical units. Most of this kind of long-term debt is covered by issuing bonds into the financial marketplace. Second, there are timing problems in the payments for raw materials and labor services and the receipt of sales. Farmers must be paid for meat, potatoes, vegetables, and so on. Transportation firms must be paid for shipping. Distribution firms bill for their warehousing and management services. These and other expenses all take place before a single hamburger is sold at a retail facility. In fact, as sales increase, the gap between expenses and revenues increases. Thus, most successful businesses need to finance these working capital expenses. For this short-term financing need, firms normally use bank loans.

Source: Financial statements for McDonald's, **http://www.mcdonalds.com/corporate/investor/financialinfo/investorpub/financial**.

Questions

1. What are the top four countries from which McDonald's acquired its debt?
2. Why does McDonald's need to finance up to 40 percent of its assets with debt?
3. What kinds of assets are financed with long-term bonds versus bank loans?

With increased usage of electronic trading by organized exchanges over time, the differences between organized and OTC markets have been gradually diminishing. For instance, the NYSE's SuperDOT system is an electronic system used to place orders for stocks that are listed as trading on the NYSE. Of course, ECNs are a technological innovation that is reducing the transactions costs of buying and selling securities, not to mention allowing more global movement of investment funds.

With a few clicks of the mouse on a computer screen, professional and individual investors can easily make securities transactions. *Market orders* are executed at the prevailing market price determined by supply and demand forces, while *limit orders* are executed at a set price (e.g., the highest or lowest price at which a person is willing to buy or sell, respectively). An automated trading system scans the network for matching orders and either immediately executes the order or posts the order for later execution or cancellation.

Financial Markets. Financial markets can be classified as public versus private and primary versus secondary. In the public market a security is offered for sale to virtually any buyer, whereas a private sale is available only to selected buyers. In the corporate bond market it is common for firms to privately issue their bonds to large institutional buyers, such as life insurance companies and pension funds. The **primary market** is the initial sale of a security in the financial marketplace, in contrast to the trading of outstanding issues in the secondary market. The **secondary market** is much larger than the primary market in terms of trading volume. Nonetheless, the primary market can be quite interesting when a firm issues equity for the first time in public securities markets (i.e., an initial public offering or IPO) or when firms issue a large amount of debt to finance a major expansion.

primary market The initial sale of a security in the financial marketplace

secondary market The trading of outstanding securities in the financial marketplace

Financial Institutions. **Financial institutions** are privately owned firms that provide payment, deposit, credit, securities, and other services. Like any firm, they seek to maximize the value of their common stock shares. Unlike other nonfinancial firms, they are heavily regulated due to their importance in the national economy. Many financial institutions act as intermediaries that channel savings of individuals to investments of business firms.

financial institutions Privately owned firms that provide financial services

Exhibit 14.1 illustrates the process of **financial intermediation** in the financial system. Small savings of individuals are pooled in various financial institutions in exchange for indirect securities (e.g., bank accounts, insurance policies, and pension fund plans). Subsequently, institutions invest savings in the direct securities (e.g., loans, bonds, and common stock) issued by business firms. Savers gain the benefits of convenience, record and safekeeping services, alternative investment options, and financial expertise. Business firms benefit from payments services, debt and equity supplies of funds, and financial expertise.

financial intermediation The process of pooling individuals' savings in financial institutions that channel them to business firms

While financial intermediation has obvious benefits for both savers and business firms, its implications for the institutions themselves are quite complex. Small, safe, short-term savings are converted by institutions into large, risky, and

EXHIBIT 14.1

The Process of Financial Intermediation

long-term investments. In so doing, institutions bear various risks, including the following:

- Credit risk. The probability that loans to business firms will not be paid
- Price risk. The change in values of long-term securities as interest rates change in the financial marketplace
- Liquidity risk. The possibility of running short of cash to meet needs of savers or investors
- Operational risk. The problem of producing and delivering financial services that customers want
- Strategic risk. The challenge of competing with other financial service firms
- Regulatory risk. The need to comply fully with many regulations and laws
- Reputation risk. The possibility that public confidence in the safety and soundness of an institution will be lost

Financial intermediation not only has effects at the microlevel of individuals, business firms, and financial institutions, but it can have important effects on the economy as a whole too. For example, assuming that financial institutions successfully allocate funds to high-profit firms, total production by the business sector is greater than otherwise. In turn, greater productivity by the business sector leads to higher employment and better wages and salaries for workers. It is easy to see that **allocational efficiency** is important for any country.

Financial intermediation can yield operational efficiency and market efficiency benefits, too. Competition among financial institutions implies that they must operate at minimum cost to maximize profits. **Operational efficiency** results in low-cost basic financial services, better quality services, and innovation of new financial services. Likewise, in competitive financial markets, institutions must accurately price financial assets and liabilities, including deposits, loans, and securities. By ensuring that all information is rapidly reflected in prices, **market efficiency** is improved.

In sum, financial intermediation enhances allocational, operational, and market efficiency in financial markets and the general economy. By channeling public savings to investment, it tends to encourage saving and, consequently, boosts investment also. Higher saving and investment leads to increased wealth and a higher standard of living for society. Given that the ultimate benefit of a smoothly-functioning financial system is a higher standard of living, it is important to consider how best to design the structure of a financial system.

allocational efficiency The transfer of savings to the most profitable investments in the economy

operational efficiency Producing financial services at low cost for individuals, businesses, and the government

market efficiency The ability of prices of stocks, bonds, and other assets to rapidly reflect publicly available information

reality CHECK   *What kinds of financial instruments do you own? What financial institutions do you use? What about your parents?*

Structure of Financial Systems

LEARNING OBJECTIVE 2
Contrast different kinds of financial systems around the world and state how regulation can protect the safety and soundness of financial systems.

Financial systems can be classified into market-oriented systems and bank-centered systems. **Bank-centered systems,** as in Japan and Germany, are dominated by banking institutions as opposed to securities firms. The dominant role of banks enables them to develop close relationships with their client firms. Such close relationships allow banks to obtain a great deal of private information about client firms that is valuable in better understanding lending risks. Also, the reduced ability of firms to use public markets to issue debt means that banks have some degree of monopoly power and extract higher loan rates (for example) from firms.

bank-centered systems Financial systems that are dominated by banks

Tokyo businessmen walking past the Bank of Japan, which implemented record-low interest rates to fight chronic economic problems over the past 15 years.

By contrast, **market-oriented systems,** as in the United States and Great Britain, have larger securities markets that offer firms an alternative source of debt financing to compete with bank credit. With alternative sources of credit available to them, firms can borrow at more competitive, lower loan rates. One drawback of securities-based systems is that it is more difficult for banks to get private information about firms. Due to the lack of this valuable information, it is possible that lending decisions are less well informed than they would be otherwise. Bankers may well be expected to reduce lending due to greater information uncertainty. In general, countries' financial systems lie on a continuum between all-banks and all-securities markets. The best system for a particular country is likely to be a balance of these two types of systems.

Financial systems are shaped by government regulation. Because they can influence the economy and government seeks to foster a strong economy, financial institutions and markets are heavily regulated around the world. Regulation seeks both to protect the safety and soundness of the financial system and foster a competitive environment that delivers the financial services that meet the needs of the public. Unfortunately, the goals of safety and soundness and competition in the financial system tend to conflict with one another. As more regulatory restrictions are placed on financial institutions and markets to increase safety and soundness, the financial system's ability to operate normally and reach free market solutions to problems is reduced. Competition results in an increased quantity and quality of financial services for the public, in addition to new services that result from financial innovation. However, competition can lead to more failures of financial institutions. Regulators must trade off the goals of safety and soundness and increased competitiveness in establishing regulatory policies.

A difficult problem for many institutions is a sudden loss of *public confidence,* which can trigger a run on institutional deposits and funds and create a liquidity crisis. In 1984, the eighth-largest bank in the United States at that time, Continental Illinois, suffered losses on foreign loans as well as oil and gas loans. Within days

market-oriented systems Financial systems that have large securities markets

of news stories about the losses, a global run on its deposits took place. Faced with uncertainty about the bank's solvency, large depositors around the world immediately withdrew their funds from the bank. For this reason, government regulators were prompted to close Continental Illinois and lend money to the bank to enable it to pay out large sums of cash to cover deposit withdrawals. After the liquidity crisis subsided, regulators divided up the bank and merged it with other healthy institutions. Continental Illinois demonstrates that public confidence is paramount to the viability of financial institutions.

One way to reduce the risk of deposit runs and thereby preserve public confidence and protect the safety and soundness of the financial system is for the government to provide **deposit insurance.** For example, in the United States, each deposit account is insured up to $100,000 by the Federal Deposit Insurance Corporation (FDIC), a government agency that protects small depositors. Banks pay the FDIC a premium, or fee, to obtain deposit insurance. By pooling these premiums, the FDIC raises funds to cover losses by insured banks. If a bank fails, deposit insurance covers the losses of most depositors with small checking and savings accounts. Typically, a failed bank is merged overnight with a healthy bank by the FDIC. The next day most customers of the failed bank likely will not even know that anything has happened. Of course, some observant customers may notice the new bank name posted on the outside of the bank's building.

> **deposit insurance** A guarantee on deposits that protects them from losses due to the failure of a bank or other depository institution

While deposit insurance reduces the likelihood of depositor panics and associated runs on institutions, it introduces what is known as **moral hazard risk,** the risk that managers of insured institutions will not manage their risks in a prudent way. The reason for this is that, if an institution fails due to excessive risk-taking, the government pays the depositor losses. Knowing that the FDIC rather than the bank itself pays for losses, managers of banks might act irresponsibly and seek to invest in high-risk investments in the hope of earning high returns or profits. This "go-for-broke" approach to management is a dangerous potential side effect of deposit insurance.

> **moral hazard risk** The risk that managers of insured institutions will take excessive risk and act imprudently

In the event that depositor losses exceed the funds held by the government insurance agency, then the taxpaying public must pay the losses. Indeed, in the United States the sudden failure of numerous depository institutions in the early 1980s resulted in taxpayers footing the bill for about $200 billion in losses! Many experts believe that these losses were in large due to deposit insurance that encouraged the institutions to take unreasonable risks. Despite the problems that arise due to moral hazard risk, deposit insurance is crucial to maintaining public confidence in banks and thereby contributes to the safety and soundness of banks.

There are four ways regulation can protect the government and taxpayers from financial institution losses, including losses due to moral hazard risk. First, insured institutions must pay deposit insurance premiums to the insurance agency to build up a reserve to cover losses. As an institution takes more risk in its loans and securities activities, it must pay higher deposit insurance premiums.

Second, institutions must have adequate equity capital on their balance sheets to absorb unexpected losses on loans and securities. The 1988 Basle Agreement set international capital regulations for banks, and similar regulations have been implemented for other types of financial institutions in many countries. As institutions take more risk, under the Basle Agreement standards, they must increase their equity capital positions on their balance sheets. Thus, shareholders of institutions increasingly bear more of the risk of losses as they engage in risky financial market behaviors. Due to this risk, shareholders will seek to reduce bank risk-taking.

Third, regulators conduct on-site exams of institutions to evaluate their safety and soundness. Examiners visit institutions, talk with employees, evaluate credit records and other financial activities, and obtain firsthand information about their performance. Institutions identified as relatively risky can have sanctions drawn against them in the form of restrictions on risky activities. For example, a bank could be forced to sell risky securities or certain loans.

Fourth, and last, regulators can establish rules concerning permissible activities of financial institutions. After the Great Depression, strict regulations were put into place in the United States that essentially separated banks, securities firms, and insurance companies. By restricting their asset powers, competition between different kinds of financial institutions was reduced, and this decreased the number of financial institution failures.

However, regulatory barriers among banks, securities firms, and insurance companies have gradually eroded over time. Each type of financial firm found ways to get around restrictions. For example, banks began offering securities services outside the United States and, therefore, avoided U.S. regulations prohibiting such services. Securities firms started offering short-term, money market accounts to their customers that were similar to deposit accounts at banks. Another force for change was rising competition among financial institutions on a global level. These changes eventually led to the deregulation of financial institutions' asset powers. In the European Union, recent financial deregulation under the Second Banking Coordination Directive of 1988 and the establishment of the single market for financial services in 1993 allow individual institutions to offer a full menu of financial services, including bank deposits and loans as well as securities and insurance services. In the United States, the **Financial Services Modernization Act** of 1999 similarly deregulated the financial services powers of banking institutions to include securities and insurance activities. Moreover, due to economic and financial crises in the 1990s, the *Japanese Big Bang* led to deregulation that likewise allowed the formation of financial supermarkets comprising banks, securities firms, and insurance companies. A financial institution that offers all three types of financial services is known as a **financial holding company.**

> **Financial Services Modernization Act** Legislation passed in 1999 that allows banks, securities firms, and insurance companies to freely compete with one another

Structural reforms due to financial deregulation around the world in the 1990s continue today and are transforming financial systems. One implication of these changes is the ability of financial institutions to take new financial risks and earn higher returns. Another implication is that institutions are more diversified than in the past in the sense of offering a wider variety of financial services to customers. Finally, another important change is the formation of mega-institutions that are extremely large in size. As noted in the opening vignette, in 1999 three large Japanese banks merged to form the world's first trillion-dollar bank, named Mizuho Holdings. With $1.2 trillion in total assets, Mizuho exceeded Deutsche Bank's $735 billion in assets in that year. Large mergers are also occurring in the United States and Europe.

> **financial holding company** A conglomerate financial services firm that can offer its customers banking, securities, and insurance services

Most of the **consolidation movement** in financial institutions is taking place on a continental basis in the United States, Europe, and Asia. Intercontinental, or across-the-water, consolidation has been limited so far. However, certainly the next merger wave will involve the formation of international institutions that are truly global in nature.

> **consolidation movement** The wave of mergers and acquisitions among financial institutions that has been sweeping the world in recent years

reality CHECK *Is the bank in which you have deposits insured by the government? Why should you check this?*

Financial Systems and the Economy

LEARNING OBJECTIVE 3
Understand how the health of the financial system affects the productivity of the economy, including the roles of the IMF and the World Bank.

Financial systems are an essential building block to a healthy economy. During the U.S. Great Depression, the world economy suffered an unprecedented collapse. In the United States between 1929 and 1932, the Dow Jones Industrial Average (DJIA) stock market index, representing the 30 largest U.S. firms, declined from a high of 381 to a low of 41. Unemployment surged to more than 25 percent. The financial market panic spilled over to the banking sector, as more than 5000 banks failed, many due to runs on their deposits by the public. Bank regulators were overwhelmed by the failures. Many banks were closed and their assets and deposits frozen until regulators had time to deal with the problems. Depositors commonly waited more than five years to get their deposits out of closed banks, and many depositors were lucky to eventually get back 50 cents for each dollar of deposits!

Most experts agree that one of the main reasons for the depth and duration of the Depression was the massive failures of financial institutions, particularly commercial banks. By disrupting the financial intermediation process, payments for goods and services in the economy broke down, access to credit for business firms and consumers decreased, and valuable relationships between firms and banks were lost. It was a harsh lesson showing that our financial system plays an important role in the real economy. Businesses need banks and other financial institutions to acquire investment funds to purchase working capital as well as plant and equipment. Cut off from capital funds, business firms must rely entirely on profits from sales to finance their growth. Also, business firms need the financial expertise of financial institutions to assist them in merger and acquisition decisions and other important financial matters. Finally, businesses and consumers need banks to assist in payments for goods and services. The payments system is essential to a successful economy.

More recent episodes of financial crises have occurred in Japan, Mexico, Russia, Finland, Sweden, Turkey, Argentina, and a number of emerging Asian countries. In financial crises, banks and other institutions can suffer losses, depositors can lose their funds, and financial markets can become volatile. Another significant problem is that relationships between lenders and borrowers are damaged. Since large firms typically utilize many alternative sources of finance, they are less affected by problems with specific lenders than small firms. Normally, small firms depend entirely on banks for financing. If the bank-firm relationship is broken, small firms can be cut off from credit and forced to reduce their business activities.

Timely intervention by the national government, as well as international agencies such as the International Monetary Fund (IMF) and the International Bank for Reconstruction and Development (IBRD or World Bank), can reduce the ill effects of financial crises. In this way permanent damage to the economy from which it would take many years to recover can be limited.

The IMF and the World Bank were established in 1944 as agencies of the United Nations. These public institutions were set up to promote international monetary stability and international trade. The IMF monitors exchange rates, makes short-term loans to countries experiencing financial difficulties, and lends technical assistance to countries also. The World Bank offers long-term loans to countries for development purposes. Up through today, it has loaned more than $200 billion to over 100 countries.

More than 180 countries are members of the IMF, and as members they support it with monetary contributions. In the 1980s and 1990s, the IMF increasingly became a lending institution. When financial crises occur in emerging market countries that are in the early stages of economic development, the IMF serves the role of lender of last resort by making loans to reduce currency panics and assisting troubled banks. It also steps in as a mediator between debtor countries experiencing financial crises and creditor countries and banks worried about their investments in those countries.

The World Bank seeks to help the poorest countries improve their standard of living. Some of their main missions are health (e.g., fight against the spread of HIV/AIDS), educational quality and access, social development, poverty reduction, environmental protection, private business formation, and economic reforms leading to stability and future productivity. Together, the World Bank and the IMF are the world's largest sources of development and emergency assistance to poorer countries.

reality CHECK *What do you think are the five most important needs of developing countries to assist them in their future success?*

Money and Banking

We use money everyday to make purchases of goods and services. Here we discuss different kinds of money and how money has changed over time. Any government can control the amount of total money in public hands through the establishment of a central bank. An important aspect of central bank management of money supplies is known as *monetary policy*, which attempts to use money to influence the economic productivity of the country. Since money can affect peoples' lives and businesses' success, money matters.

What Is Money?

Money takes many forms. Most people immediately think of coins and paper currency because they can purchase goods and services with them. Indeed, the most basic characteristic of money is its use as a medium of exchange. Without money, we would be forced to barter to make exchanges. For example, if we produced shoes but wanted bread to eat, we would have to negotiate a trade of shoes for bread with a baker. Money frees us of barter negotiations and enables us to easily make payments for goods or services. In making payments, we use money to assign the value of each good and service that is produced; that is, money is a **unit of account.** Another important characteristic of money is that it normally does not perish or deteriorate over reasonable periods of time. A loaf of bread must be exchanged immediately or it would lose value due to spoiling. However, money is a **store of value** that can be saved and used at a convenient time in the future. Lastly, money can used to record the amount of interest and principal owed on debt. In this respect money is a **standard of deferred payment.**

unit of account The function of money to serve as means for valuing of goods and services

store of value The function of money to retain its value over time

standard of deferred payment The function of money to be employed in recording the amount of debt payments

LEARNING OBJECTIVE 4
Overview the history of money and why money matters to the economy.

Coins and Paper Money. The history of money is a fascinating subject with close relationships to the economic and political power of countries. Ancient money used by the Egyptians in 2500 B.C. was made of metal rings. The Lydians are believed to be the first Western civilization to have minted coins in 700

commodity money Coins that are made out of precious metals

B.C. as a way to facilitate their widespread trade activities. The Greeks and Romans expanded the use of coins, especially coins made of precious metals that increased their store-of-value property. This so-called **commodity money** had the drawback of being heavy and difficult to divide into smaller pieces. In Europe, the Spanish 8-reale (or eightreale) was popular in the eighteenth century because it could be split into pieces; half a coin equaled four bits and a quarter of a coin was two bits, terms that are still used today when referring to a half or quarter dollar. In China the weight problem was solved by paper money issued during the Tang Dynasty (618–907 A.D.).

Paper money spread to Europe and was commonly printed by banks. By the nineteenth century, a large number of banks issued their own notes in Europe and in the United States. It became necessary to back paper currency with gold, silver, or government securities to ensure its value. Currencies traded at different exchange rates, depending on the likelihood that the notes could be redeemed at a particular issuing bank and the cost of making the transaction. Trustworthiness of banks was critical to the value of paper currency. However, problems with the printing of thousands of different paper currencies by many different banks led to government control of currency and coin issuance at the close of the nineteenth century in most countries. The history of money then entered a period in which the national currencies of each government in the world were created. Money became a symbol of national sovereignty and identity during this period.

fiat money Money that is valuable because the government deems it so

gold standard Backing of money with gold at a fixed exchange rate per ounce of gold

The next important event in the history of money was the 1913 establishment of the Federal Reserve System in the United States and the resultant rise of the dollar as a major world currency. Shortly thereafter, World War I broke out, leading to unstable precious metal prices. Many countries were forced to drop gold, silver, and other backing of paper currency. Money was instead backed by the fiat, or law, of the national government. **Fiat money** was legal tender to purchase goods and services because the government deemed it to be.

Many governments used money to meet the political goals of stimulating economic growth and providing employment for citizens. Economic activity could be increased by merely printing more money. With more money in their hands, people purchased more goods and services and the economy would benefit, at least for a while. This political use of money was not without its pitfalls. Excess supplies of money could cause inflation. That is, when the supply of money exceeds the demand for goods and services, the prices of goods and services can rise. For example, if we doubled the amount of money in a country but the production of goods and services stayed the same, the price of all goods and services would rise approximately twofold, holding constant other factors such as external trade.

Today there are around 150 different national currencies in the world. Currencies of large industrial nations are known as hard currencies, as opposed to the soft currencies of other countries. The 1999 introduction of the European euro is interesting due to the fact that the euro is a regional currency.

Gold and Dollar Standards. Inflation problems with printing fiat money led to repeated attempts to return to a **gold standard** for money. For example, in 1934 the conversion rate was 35 U.S. dollars for 1 ounce of gold. In 1944, the Bretton Woods agreement set up a global currency system with the dollar pegged at a fixed rate of exchange to gold, and 43 other countries fixed their currencies to the dollar.

Thus, after World War II, the U.S. dollar became a standard of value for all world currencies. One hope of pegging currency values of countries to the dollar was it would prevent governments from issuing too much currency and causing inflation. In 1971, the Bretton Woods agreement broke down as the United States moved away from pegging the dollar to gold. While the dollar continued to be important in denominating the value of other currencies, many countries allowed their currencies to float, or vary, in world markets to one degree or another. In the remaining part of the twentieth century, the breakdown of the world monetary system in 1971 led to problems of wide fluctuations in currency values, periodic inflation, and occasional economic stagnation.

The European Euro.

In many ways, these problems set the stage for the largest monetary event since the emergence of the dollar as the **numeraire currency,** or currency benchmark, in the world. In 1999, 12 European countries formed the European Monetary Union (EMU). The EMU introduced the **euro** as a new currency to replace the currencies of the 12 member countries. In 2002, euro coins and notes were distributed for the first time. The euro was an immediate success and quickly became the second most important currency in the world, ahead of the Japanese yen. For countries using the euro, problems of currency fluctuations, inflation, and related economic downturns should be substantially reduced. For the individual European consumer or businessperson, it means not having to always be converting one currency to another as he or she travels or conducts business between countries. Frequent currency exchanges are expensive and time consuming.

numeraire currency A currency that serves as a benchmark for all other currencies in the world

euro The new currency issued in 2002 by the 12 countries in the European Monetary Union

Hard Currencies.

Together, the dollar, euro, and yen account for around 60 percent of the world economy. In effect, the dollar, euro, and yen describe three currency areas of the world that lend monetary stability to each respective regional economy. The British pound sterling is another example of a leading world currency. These so-called **hard currencies** are used by emerging market countries to peg the values of their **soft currencies.** For example, Argentina for many years pegged their peso currency value to the U.S. dollar, wherein the value of the peso was kept within a set range of values per dollar. Thus, **currency pegging** is a way for emerging market countries to enhance their monetary stability. However, it should be recognized that, while each hard currency is fairly stable within its own region of the world, its value can fluctuate considerably against the other hard currencies. Thus, currency risk is still a major factor in international trade and finance, even between large industrial countries.

hard currencies Currencies that are relatively stable in value, are issued by large industrial countries, and include the U.S. dollar, Japanese yen, European euro, and British pound sterling

soft currencies Currencies that are issued by emerging market countries whose economies are developing

currency pegging The currency of a country that is kept within a fixed range of values relative to a hard currency

currency risk The fluctuation in a country's currency value relative to other currencies in the world

Currency risk can have serious effects on inflation, economic production, and employment in countries. For example, in 1994 the value of the Mexican peso dropped suddenly due to panic by the public. Mexican firms and the government were experiencing difficulties in making debt payments. The possibility of debt default raised fears among people that the peso would fall in value relative to the U.S. dollar. Runs on banks occurred as citizens attempted to exchange their pesos for dollars. The massive selling pressure on the peso caused its value to collapse. The peso was no longer a store of value, which greatly damaged its acceptability as money among the public. In 1998, Russia faced similar problems after the government defaulted on its outstanding debt. The Russian ruble fell suddenly in value and the dollar replaced it as a currency among many citizens. Today, payments can be made in either rubles or dollars in many places in Russia, and holders of large quantities of rubles tend to favor the dollar due to its being a more stable store of value.

Even normal currency risk can be fairly important over five- to ten-year periods of time. Suppose that at one point in time it cost you $30 to purchase a pair of shoes made in Indonesia; three years later the same pair of shoes cost $50 because the value of the dollar gradually decreased compared to the Indonesian rupiah. Such currency movements can and often do affect international trade and finance.

electronic money The use of computers, equipment, and electronic communications to make payments, including credit cards, stored value cards, debt cards, wire transfers, and Internet payments

Electronic Money.   Another form of money is **electronic money,** which is increasingly replacing coin and paper currency. Some of the most popular types of electronic money are listed below.

- *Credit cards* allow people to borrow money on demand from financial institutions in order to pay for goods and services. Credit cards issued by such firms as Mastercard, Visa, and American Express can be used in many countries around the world. A U.S. citizen on vacation in Japan purchasing Sony products would be billed in yen, and international banks would convert the yen debt to U.S. dollars at the prevailing U.S. dollar/yen exchange rate. Assuming that 100 yen equal $1, a debt of 3000 yen would be converted to $30 (3000 yen divided by 100 yen/$1). Credit card companies charge interest rates on outstanding balances, which customers must pay back on a monthly basis. Banks get information from different sources to evaluate the creditworthiness of potential customers and aggressively market their credit cards by mail, phone, and promotions.

- *Stored value cards* have a magnetic strip that records the money value of the card to be used in paying subway and toll road fees. Once the value of the card is used up, it can be reloaded.

- *Debit cards* or *smart cards* have a computer chip that records the money value of the card. As people use the card, it adjusts the balance remaining. Like stored value cards, the money held in debit cards can be reloaded. However, debit cards can be used at more locations than stored value cards, such as grocery stores, gasoline stations, and restaurants.

- *Wire transfers* can be used to make large-denomination payments or tranfers, especially in international business transactions. In the United States, the Clearing House Interbank Payments System (CHIPS) and the Fed wire provide wire services for banks, businesses, and government. Also, the Society for Worldwide Interbank Financial Telecommunications (SWIFT) is a major supplier of international wire transfers.

- *Internet payments* can be made by means of online deposit and investment accounts that permit digital transfers of funds to pay monthly bills, pay for goods and services, and buy and sell securities. Even home mortgage loans can now be arranged over the Internet. Specialized Internet banks have emerged in some cases. However, most banks have Internet websites from which customers can access and move their money.

The advantages of electronic money are speed, convenience, low transactions costs, automated record keeping, and increased control of funds. However, there are some disadvantages. Unlike coins and paper money, electronic money is not always accepted by business firms. Credit cards are most widely accepted but can be rejected as payment by some business firms. Many times the user must prove his or her identity to access electronic money. Also, some people express confusion in terms of deciding what forms of electronic money are most appropriate to meet their needs. The most serious concern is safety. If information about a person's electronic money or physical cards is lost or stolen, money can be remotely and rapidly removed from a person's account. The security and privacy of electronic money are paramount to its future success.

Ethics and Identity Theft. Unfortunately, identity theft is a growing problem due to the increased use of electronic money. A major ethical and criminal problem, identity thieves steal credit cards, debt and ATM cards, mail, bank accounts, social security numbers, and so on, in an effort to take your money. They can also assume your identity, open new bank and credit card accounts, and even steal borrowed money in your name. How does this happen? Surprisingly, there are many avenues through which thieves obtain important information, including simple everyday transactions such as writing a check, charging tickets to a concert, doing income tax returns on your computer, calling home on your cell phone, charging some purchase for which a carbon copy is created at the point of purchase, ordering new checks, applying for a credit card, or giving your social security number to people other than your employer, insurance agents, and others who have a legal right to such personal information. Of course, you can protect yourself by being vigilant with your private information and annually checking your credit rating (see Exhibit 14.2). Shred credit card applications that come in the mail to prevent someone from rummaging through the garbage. Destroy carbon copies that are made in a credit card purchase yourself. Update virus protection on your computer and use a firewall to prevent hackers from getting private information. Be careful in telephone conversations and in mail correspondence to protect important information. If you do become a victim of identity theft, call the Federal Trade Commission's (FTC) Identity Theft Hotline toll-free at 1-877-IDTHEFT (438-4338). Counselors will take your complaint and advise you on how to deal with the credit-related problems that could result. In addition, the FTC, in conjunction with banks, credit grantors, and consumer advocates, has developed the ID Theft Affidavit to help

EXHIBIT 14.2

Credit Bureau Contact Information

The FTC recommends that you order a credit report from each of the three major credit bureaus once a year.

> **Equifax: www.equifax.com**
> To order your report, call 800-685-1111.
> To report fraud, call 800-525-6285
> TDD 800-255-0056 or write
> P.O. Box 740241, Atlanta, GA 30374-0241.
>
> **Experian: www.experian.com**
> To order your report, call 888-EXPERIAN (397-3742).
> To report fraud, call 888-EXPERIAN (397-3742) or
> TDD 800-972-0322 or write
> P.O. Box 9532, Allen, TX 75013.
>
> **TransUnion: www.transunion.com**
> To order your report, call 800-888-4213.
> To report fraud, call 800-680-7289 or
> TDD 877-553-7803; fax 714-447-6034; email **fvad@transunion.com;** or
> write Fraud Victim Assistance Department, P.O. Box 6790, Fullerton, CA 92634-6790.

victims of ID theft restore their good names. The FTC's website, **http://www.ftc.gov/bcp/conline/pubs/credit/idtheft.htm,** contains detailed instructions on forms and steps to take if you become a victim. The FTC puts your information into a secure consumer fraud database where it can be used to help other law enforcement agencies and private entities in their investigations and victim assistance.

**reality
CHECK**   *What forms of money do you use? How do you keep your money secure from theft?*

Central Banks and Monetary Policy

LEARNING OBJECTIVE 5
Explain what central banks do to control money and achieve economic goals.

Central banks are government entities that conduct the country's monetary policy, supervise and regulate its financial institutions, maintain the stability of its financial system, and provide certain financial services needed by the government, the public, financial institutions, and foreign institutions. The U.S. Federal Reserve System, the European Central Bank, and the Bank of Japan are examples of central banks.

Setting monetary policy is the most important role of central banks. Because it has major implications to the world economy, many times central banks from different countries hold joint meetings to discuss monetary policy. The objective of monetary policy is to achieve productivity of the business sector, employment of citizens, stable prices of goods and services (or low inflation), and international trade and commerce. Because monetary policy is so important to the economy, it can affect the future success or failure of business firms as well as the everyday lives of most people in a country. Here we focus on the Federal Reserve System, or Fed, for purposes of illustration. However, the discussion is equally relevant to most central banks of large industrial countries, which are similar in structure and operation.

The Fed has a seven-member Board of Governors headed by a chairperson who oversees policy issues. The Fed's most powerful method of influencing the financial and economic systems is **open market operations** involving the purchase and sale of government securities from banks. The Federal Open Market Committee (FOMC), made up of the seven board members and five Fed district bank presidents, regularly meets to discuss open market operations. If the Fed purchases government securities from banks, the amount of cash, or so-called **bank reserves,** held by banks increases as new funds are transferred from the Fed to the banks. These new reserves can be used by banks to make loans to their customers. Alternatively, the Fed can sell securities to banks in exchange for cash, so that bank reserves and the amount of loans banks can make decrease.

The Fed can influence interest rates by increasing or decreasing the cash reserves held by banks. The reason for this is that banks constantly lend money to one another throughout the day. Banks that are short on cash borrow reserves from other banks with excess reserves. The rate that banks charge one another for these reserves is known as the **federal funds rate.** If the Fed purchases securities from banks and there is an increase in the supply of cash reserves held by banks, the interest rate that banks charge one another in the money market tends to decrease. Alternatively, if the Fed sells securities to banks and decreases banks' reserves, the greater scarcity of reserves causes banks to charge a higher federal funds rate. Notice that the federal funds rate is essentially the price of so-called federal funds set by banks that are borrowing and lending these funds. This pricing mechanism is no different from prices set by grocery stores for apples as determined by buyers and sellers of apples. As the supply of apples increases, holding demand constant,

open market operations The purchase and sale of government securities from banks by the central bank to control bank reserves and federal funds rates

bank reserves The amount of cash held by commercial banks

federal funds rate The interest rates that banks charge one another for borrowing money

the price of the apples must decrease. However, if the supply of apples decreases, all else the same, the price of apples must increase. By buying or selling government securities from banks, the Fed can directly affect bank reserves and the federal funds rate, or the price of those reserves.

A Closer Look at Open Market Operations.

Exhibit 14.3 shows how money and interest rates are affected by open market operations. The vertical axis of the graph shows the federal funds rate. The horizontal axis shows the quantity of money supplied or demanded by banks. The supply of money is directly under the control of the central bank via open market operations and therefore is drawn as a vertical line. This vertical line moves to the right as money supply is increased and moves to the left as money supply is decreased. The demand for money is downward sloping. The reason for this shape is that interest rate levels change banks' demand for federal funds. At lower federal funds rates, banks will demand more money, as these funds can be obtained at low cost to the bank. However, higher federal funds rates increase the cost of obtaining funds and will cause banks to demand less money.

Now let's see how Exhibit 14.3 can be used to better understand open market operations. Consider what would happen if there were an increase in money supply from quantity S_1 to S_2, which can be implemented by the Fed's open market operation purchases of securities from banks. It is clear that a higher money supply reduces the federal funds rate from i_1 to i_2. In this case the Fed is essentially increasing the amount of cash reserves held by banks. The lowering of interest rates is logical because now banks have more reserves to lend, and interest rates represent the price of money. The lowering of federal funds rates means a lower cost of funds for banks. Banks can pass these lower costs along to borrowers by offering loans at lower interest rates. So, lower federal funds rates lead to lower loan rates. And, lower loan rates tend to increase bank loans, as borrowers are willing to seek credit at banks.

Why would the Fed increase the money supply and lower money market interest rates? It is important to recognize that the federal funds rate is a benchmark interest rate that affects other interest rates in the money and capital markets. As the federal funds rate moves up or down, the interest rates on bonds and bank loans likewise move up and down. In our example in Exhibit 14.3, the lower federal funds rate could potentially stimulate business activity, as business firms would be attracted by the lower interest rates available at banks to borrow money needed to produce goods and services. Many individuals buying cars, houses, and other goods that require debt financing would be beneficially affected by lower interest costs of borrowed funds also. Alternatively, the Fed could sell government securities in open market operations, decrease the money supply in banks, increase interest rates, and slow down business or economic activity. It should be apparent that open market operations by central banks can have powerful effects on business firms and individuals in particular and the economy in general.

EXHIBIT 14.3

Monetary Policy and the Relationship Between Money Supply and Interest Rates

Central banks lower interest rates by increasing the money supply.

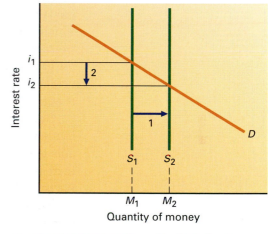

D = Money demand curve M = Quantity of money
S = Money supply curve i = Interest rate

Why Money Matters.

The well-known **quantity theory** provides insight into how monetary policy affects the economy as a whole. In this theory, an *equation of exchange* can be written that links the financial system on the left-hand side and the economy on the right-hand side.

quantity theory The notion that money matters to the real economy as expressed in the equation of exchange

$$MV = PQ$$

where M = the money supply in the country, V = the velocity of money (i.e., the average number of times that a dollar changes hands per year), P = the average price level of goods and services in the economy, and Q = the quantity of goods and services sold. If we consider the rate of change in these variables over time, we can rewrite the equation as follows:

$$m + v = p + q$$

where m = the rate of growth of the money supply, v = the rate of change of the velocity of money (normally considered to be zero), p = the rate of change in the prices of goods and services, known as the *inflation rate*, and q = the rate of growth of the real economy. An important implication of this equation is that the money growth rate on the left-hand side is linked to the economic growth rate on the right-hand side. Not only does an increase in the money supply tend to decrease interest rates, as already shown in Exhibit 14.3, but it also increases the funds available to the public to buy goods and services and thereby stimulates business production. In short, money matters!

As an example, assume that the velocity of money v is zero and that the growth rate of money m is 5 percent. If the inflation rate p is 2 percent, we know that the growth rate of the economy q will be 3 percent. The central bank could increase the growth rate of the economy to 4 percent by increasing the growth rate of money to 6 percent, where we have assumed that the inflation rate will stay at 2 percent.

Notice that rate of growth of the economy will increase in response to money growth as long as the inflation rate does not increase. We can measure the rate at which prices are rising by rearranging the equation as $p = m - q$, where $v = 0$. Here we see that if the growth rate of money implemented by the central bank exceeds the growth rate of the economy, as measured by change in the gross national product, then inflation, an increase in the average prices of goods and services, will occur.

One problem in the equation of exchange is that money supply growth does not immediately result in growth of the economy. We know that there are long and variable lags between changes in money supply and increases in productivity; that is, increases in the money supply today will take some amount time before they affect the growth of the economy. Some economists have argued that, given this lag is unpredictable, monetary policy should simply establish a fixed growth rate of money and not change it. However, because money does matter to the economy and monetary policy seeks to achieve economic goals, some amount of fine tuning of the money supply is typically used to speed up or slow down the economy. If the economy is growing faster or slower than desired, the Fed can decrease or increase money supply growth rates in an effort to maintain more stable economic growth over time. The downside of fine tuning the money supply is that this type of discretionary monetary policy can cause higher inflation. For example, if the money supply is increased today but for some reason the growth rate of the economy does not increase in the future, then "too much money will be chasing too few goods" and we will have an increase in inflation. Since it is generally true that central banks around the world seek to maintain low and stable prices by controlling inflation rates, it is common to set a fixed range of money growth, say, 3 to 5 percent, and fine-tune only within this target range.

Definitions of Money.   In the 1950s, central banks began classifying money into different types. The following definitions of money have developed over the years:

- M1. Money that can be readily spent by the public, including cash (coins and paper currency) and checking accounts (third-party drafts on funds held in banks). Demand deposits are checking accounts that pay no interest to customers, whereas NOW (negotiable order of withdrawal) accounts are interest-bearing checking accounts.
- M2. M1 plus all small savings and time deposits in banks worth less than $100,000. Short-term assets held by small investors in money market mutual funds (to be discussed later) are also included in M2.
- M3. M2 plus large-time deposits in banks worth more than $100,000, which are normally deposited by business firms.
- L. M3 plus short-term money securities with maturities less than one year.

Of these monetary aggregates, M1 and M2 are most closely watched by central banks. The reason for this is that M1 and M2 represent money held by consumers that can be spent on goods and services in the economy. Since consumer spending drives production by firms, M2 is a good measure of money to use in monetary policy.

The "moneyness" of a particular type of money is dependent on how fast it can be spent by consumers. Money held in M1 is immediately spendable, while L is made up of short-term money market securities that must first be sold and converted to cash before they can be spent. However, since money market securities are highly liquid, we can think of L as near-money.

Monetary Policy Framework

Exhibit 14.4 shows a picture of the **monetary policy** framework, including policy tools, operating targets, intermediate targets, and economic goals. The Fed can use **policy tools,** such as open market operations, the discount rate, and reserve requirements, to directly control day-to-day **operating targets,** namely, the federal funds rate and bank reserves. Open market operations are the most powerful and frequently used policy tool. If these operations are not successful in achieving

monetary policy A central bank framework for using policy tools to affect operating targets, intermediate targets, and economic goals

policy tools The tools that the central bank uses to implement monetary policy, such as open market operations, the discount rate, and reserve requirements

operating targets The everyday targets that the central bank seeks to achieve using its policy tools, namely, the federal funds rate and bank reserves

EXHIBIT 14.4

How Monetary Policy Works

The Fed can use open market operations to buy securities from banks, lower discount rates, or lower reserve requirements to decrease the Fed funds rate and increase bank reserves. Over time these changes would tend to lower long-term interest rates, increase bank credit, and increase the money supply. These monetary changes would stimulate productivity and increase employment.

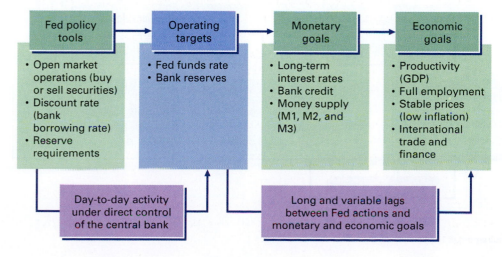

discount rate The interest rate at which banks can borrow from the central bank's discount window

operating targets, the Fed can change the **discount rate,** which is the rate at which banks can borrow from its discount window. A lower discount rate will increase bank borrowing from the Fed. As banks borrow funds, there is an increase in the supply of bank reserves, which lowers the federal funds rate. The discount window also enables the Fed to act as *lender of last resort* to institutions in times of financial crisis. Banks experiencing depositor runs can turn to the discount window for cash.

reserve requirements The percentage of transactions deposits that must be held by banks in cash form and not loaned out

Another monetary policy tool is **reserve requirements.** While infrequently used to change the level of bank reserves, they can have a large effect when needed. For example, referring to Exhibit 14.5, suppose that the Federal Reserve buys $100 million of securities from Bank 1. If the bank has a reserve requirement of 10 percent, it must retain $10 million in cash reserves (10 percent) but can lend the remaining $90 million out to its customers. Now assume that borrowers who receive this $90 million make purchases of goods and services and that these funds end up in Bank 2. As shown in Exhibit 14.5, Bank 2 must carry reserves of $9 million (or 10 percent) but can lend $81 million. This process continues until the original $100 million of *hot money* expands as follows:

$$D = R/rr$$

where D = transactions deposits (or checking accounts), R = bank reserves (or cash balances in the bank), and rr = bank reserve requirements. Notice that, due to banks lending money to customers, the money supply eventually expands by $1 billion = $100 million/0.10. The creation of money through bank credit means that small changes in reserve requirements can have a large effect on the money supply. If the Fed reduced rr to 0.08, the money supply as measured by D would expand to $1.25 billion, for an increase of $250 million!

The link between bank reserves, credit, and deposits is important because it means that changes in the federal funds rate will also affect short-term bank loans. Lower federal funds rates allow banks to make lower rate loans, and vice versa as federal funds rates increase. As already mentioned, the federal funds rate is consid-

EXHIBIT 14.5

How Central Banks and Commercial Banks Create Money

The Fed can increase the money supply (as measured by bank deposits) by buying securities from banks. Here we see that $100 million of new or hot money in Bank 1 expands to $90 million in Bank 2. This process will continue with Bank 2 lending $81 million, which would end up as deposits at Bank 3, and so on. Due to the 10 percent reserve requirement, the final increase in the money supply would be $100 million/0.10 = $1 billion. A lower reserve requirement would result in an even greater increase in the money supply than $1 billion.

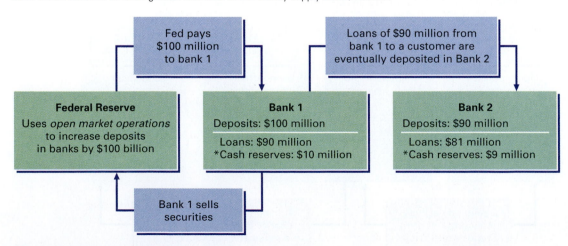

*Reserve requirement is 10 percent.

ered a benchmark interest rate. Other short-term interest rates in the money market are likewise affected by federal funds rate movements. Through the federal funds rate, the Fed maintains direct control of money market rates.

The causal link between policy tools and broader monetary and economic goals (shown in Exhibit 14.4) is less direct. Key monetary goals are the **intermediate targets** of money supply, long-term interest rates, and bank credit. A number of market forces can weaken the Fed's control over these monetary goals. For example, while higher demand deposits immediately increase M1, the effect on M2 (small savings deposits of consumers) and M3 (large savings deposits of business firms) can be delayed for some months. Also, bank credit may not expand as much as anticipated in the transactions deposits equation due to other factors, such as a slowdown in the economy. Additionally, changes in money market (short-term) rates should affect capital market (long-term) rates, but the timing is difficult to precisely predict. The Fed might push down money market interest rates in an attempt to stimulate firms to borrow money and get the economy moving in a period of recession. However, in times of recession, many firms do not want to borrow money due to low sales revenues. Firms will not increase borrowing until they feel confident that sales revenues are increasing. In this case monetary policy tools and related operating targets are less effective than would be desired by the Fed as it seeks to jump-start the economy and stimulate increased credit and output. The dynamic aspects of these events make the amount and timing of policy tool changes uncertain to some degree. Of course, the Fed is constantly monitoring the effects of using policy tools on operating targets and their delayed impacts on monetary as well as economic goals.

Economic goals are the final outcomes of monetary policy, including productivity (or output growth), employment, stable prices (or low inflation), and international trade. The news media regularly reports information on gross national product and industrial production as common measures of productivity. Unemployment rates, inflation rates, and export and import figures are frequently mentioned in the news also. Importantly, from the equation of exchange, we know that money matters in the sense that it can affect productivity in the economy. Stimulating productivity normally tends to increase jobs and trade.

Sometimes the economic goals of output, full employment, stable prices, and international trade can conflict with one another. As an example of economic trade-offs, higher inflation normally means less unemployment, whereas lower inflation is associated with higher unemployment. We would prefer to have both lower inflation and lower unemployment, but these economic goals often trade off against one another. Thus, if the Fed implements monetary policies to lower inflation, it could do so at the cost of higher unemployment.

International trade and finance can conflict with other economic goals also. If the Fed uses a higher interest rate to slow down business activity, because currency values and interest rates tend to be inversely related to one another, the value of the U.S. dollar would fall over time. The lower value of the dollar would stimulate exports by U.S. firms. For example, suppose that Volkswagen in Europe wanted to purchase steel from the United States. As the U.S. dollar falls, European buyers can purchase more steel per euro than previously. In effect, the prices of U.S. goods and services fall in foreign currency terms. Increased production in the United States to meet rising export demand would offset to some degree the negative effect of higher interest rates on slowing production by U.S. firms. These and other potential conflicts in monetary and economic goals suggest that the Fed must prioritize competing goals and regularly monitor progress in achieving key goals.

intermediate targets The primary monetary targets in the financial marketplace, which are money supply, long-term interest rates, and bank credit

economic goals The aims of monetary policy, including productivity, employment, stable prices, and trade

Can the Fed's monetary policy actions affect you? Recall the scenario in the introductory part of the chapter. You work for a small pizza business. Also, you are considering the purchase of a new home due to the birth of a child. An evening news report indicates that the Fed increased the money supply and lowered interest rates. These lower interest rates will allow your business to borrow money from the local bank at a lower cost than before. If the Fed's actions tend to increase economic activity, pizza sales will likely increase in the near future. With higher income, you could afford to buy the new home. Also, lower interest rates might allow you to get a larger house than you had previously thought possible due to lower monthly mortgage payments. If you and others are encouraged to buy homes by the lower interest rate on borrowed funds, home builders will benefit in terms of sales and more jobs for employees. Also, many consumer durable products go into new homes, such as refrigerators, ovens, and furniture. Firms making these products would experience increased sales and jobs also. Workers earning higher incomes can use their money to buy groceries, which is good for grocery stores and farmers. Central banks can have a powerful effect on the lives of you and many other people.

Balancing Monetary and Economic Goals.   Throughout the post–World War II period from 1945 to 1979, central banks generally sought to increase output, or productivity, as measured by the growth of gross national product. The GNP represents the total value of goods and services produced by a country in a specific time period. Also, maximum sustainable employment and wage rates were key areas of concern. These economic policies mean that keeping interest rates relatively low and stable was the primary concern of central banks. Given the terrible economic conditions during the Great Depression, this emphasis on a healthy business sector was certainly reasonable.

The top portion of Exhibit 14.6a shows how central banks maintained low and stable interest rates using monetary policy. If the demand for money increased, causing a rightward shift in the demand curve D, higher interest rates would be prevented by central bank actions to increase the money supply and bring federal funds rates back into the target interest rate range i^*. This policy was successful for many years, until repeated increases in the money supply periodically caused inflation to increase. Recall that $p = m - q$ from the equation of exchange, so increases in the growth rate of money greater than increases in the growth rate of productivity (or real economic output) result in higher inflation rates. Higher levels of inflation are difficult for most business firms to manage. Prices or costs of labor and materials increase more rapidly than normal at such times. A major problem is that business firms must increase the sales prices of their goods and services to keep up with the rising costs and maintain their profit margins between costs and revenues. But raising the prices of goods and services can cause a firm's sales to slow down, as some customers choose not to make purchases at higher prices. In this inflationary business environment, it is difficult for managers to make plans for sales and production. In sum, business conditions become very uncertain and unpredictable.

A second problem associated with inflation is that interest rates increase as inflation rates increase. In fact, the nominal interest rate stated in financial news is composed of the real rate of interest plus the inflation rate. This simple relationship is known as the *Fisher effect*. The real rate of interest is determined by people's time preferences for consumption. In other words, people with money have a choice of either spending (consuming) their money or lending their money to others. Borrowers must pay lenders a rate of interest in order to entice or encourage them to lend money. This is the real rate of interest. The Fisher effect says that, as inflation rates increase, lenders want higher interest rates to enable them to earn enough

EXHIBIT 14.6

Monetary Policy Choices

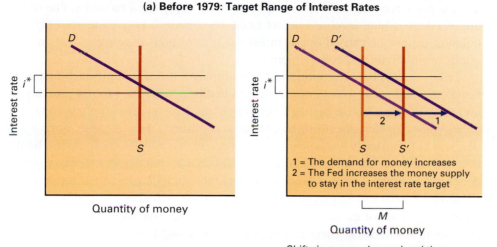

(a) Before 1979: Target Range of Interest Rates

1 = The demand for money increases
2 = The Fed increases the money supply
   to stay in the interest rate target

Shifts in money demand and then
money supply keep interest rates
in the target range.

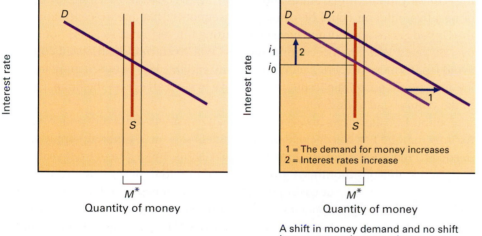

(b) After 1979: Target Range of Money Supply

1 = The demand for money increases
2 = Interest rates increase

D = Money demand curve M = Quantity of money
S = Money supply curve i = Interest rate level

A shift in money demand and no shift
in money supply causes interest rates
to rise and target range of money
supply to be maintained.

interest to later pay the rising prices of goods and services. Let's say that the real rate
of interest is 2 percent and is fairly constant over time, which is generally true. Now,
if the inflation rate increases from 3 to 4 percent, the nominal interest rate will
increase from 5 to 6 percent. Importantly, as inflation increases and pushes up
nominal interest rates, business firms are less likely to borrow funds from banks
and others. The higher cost of money has similar negative effects on business firms
as do the higher costs of labor and goods; interest costs are expenses that can lower
profits. Generally speaking, high inflation rates disrupt normal business operations. Many business firms fail due to difficulties in keeping down their operating
costs of labor, goods, and borrowed funds.

Due to the problem of inflation disrupting businesses, causing failures, and
slowing economic growth, in 1979 central banks changed their monetary policy and
made fighting inflation the primary economic goal. The bottom portion of Exhibit
14.6b illustrates this policy. A target range of money supply M^* was set, and if the
demand for money increased, interest rates were allowed to increase as determined

by market forces. Unfortunately, due to increases in the demand for money at that time, interest rates shot up to over 15 percent by 1980. Oddly, while attempting to bring down inflation rates and related interest rates, Fed monetary policy pushed interest rates even higher! This unexpected result triggered a recession due to the unprecedented high level of interest rates. The lesson learned was that fighting inflation cannot be carried out as in Exhibit 14.6 without keeping an eye on economic productivity and employment.

Today, central banks around the world employ a balanced approach to monetary policy that seeks to foster both economic productivity (or interest rate targeting) and price stability (or money supply targeting). The relative emphases on these policy goals can shift according to economic conditions. For example, since inflation was at historically low levels in the 1990s and early 2000s, most central banks targeted interest rates more aggressively than money supply in monetary policy decisions. In Japan, inflation has been so low for over a decade that it has become negative; in other words, prices are falling. Stock prices, real estate prices, wages of employees, costs of goods and services, and so on, have experienced dramatic declines in some cases. These falling prices are causing Japanese monetary policy makers to worry that the economy will slip into a depression unless it can be revived. With no reason to worry about inflation, the Japanese central bank is following a monetary policy of keeping interest rates down—close to zero—and increasing the money supply to stimulate the economy. In the early 2000s, a slowing economy in the United States and Europe raised concerns that a similar episode of negative inflation could be coming. Consequently, like Japan, central banks in the United States and Europe have been cutting interest rates to levels not seen in over 50 years. Will Japan's economy recover? Will Western industrialized countries avoid Japan's recent experience? With long and variable lags between monetary policy actions and economic results, we will have to keep an eye on the financial press in the years ahead to find out.

Exhibit 14.7 illustrates how economic goals can affect monetary policy choices. Assume that the Fed has decided that the target range of M1 money supply growth needed to maintain a healthy growth rate of GNP is 3 to 5 percent per year. However, in the previous month M1 grew at a rapid rate that placed it above the target range at point Z. At its next meeting, the Board of Governors could consider three alternative monetary strategies for getting back within its M1 target range. Point A implies a rapid decrease in money supply to immediately get back within the M1 target range. This aggressive monetary strategy is consistent with policy that seeks to control inflation as a priority. At the other extreme, if inflation were not a major concern, point C could be used. This less aggressive monetary strategy would allow the Fed to gradually work toward its M1 target range, thereby enabling it to focus more attention on target interest rates and related GDP and employment goals than point A. The intermediate approach at point B would balance inflation goals and GDP or employment goals. This example demonstrates that central bank monetary policy must take into consideration current and expected economic conditions when making monetary policy and strategy decisions.

Fiscal Policy Versus Monetary Policy. Rather than use monetary policy, the government can implement

EXHIBIT 14.7

Monetary Policy Strategy: Inflation Versus Interest Rate Targeting

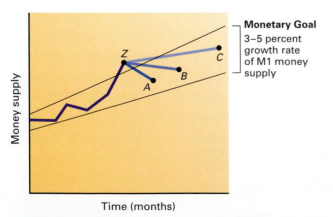

A = Aggressive control of money supply to fight inflation
B = Moderate approach balancing inflation targets and interest rate targets
C = Less control of money supply to target interest rates

fiscal policies to achieve economic goals. **Fiscal policies** involve government spending and taxation. The severity of economic downturns can be decreased by letting the federal government play a more active role by means of fiscal policy. During recessions with slow economic activity, government can increase spending or cut taxes to put people back to work and stimulate consumer spending and business activity. During the Great Depression, U.S. president Franklin Roosevelt implemented fiscal spending to get the economy going again. The success of these ideas in terms of shortening the depression led to wide popularity around the world of the use of fiscal policy to reach economic goals that continues today.

fiscal policies The use of government spending and taxation to stimulate or slow down the growth rate of the economy

One problem with fiscal policy is that it is difficult to implement in a timely way. For example, assume that we are seeking to stimulate the economy during a recession. While the executive and legislative branches of the government may agree that tax cuts are needed to stimulate the economy, political differences between members of different political parties in the country can slow down or even disallow passage of tax-cut laws. By the time tax cuts are made, the economy may have already begun to rebound and the tax cuts may no longer be needed. Indeed, in this case the fiscal stimulus may require the central bank to use more restrictive monetary policy to dull or offset the incorrectly timed fiscal effect on the economy.

Another problem is that sometimes fiscal policy is simply not politically feasible. Imagine being a political leader trying to convince voters that you want to increase taxes or cut government programs to slow down the economy. This political platform would surely decrease your chances of being elected by voters.

For this reason monetary policy, rather than fiscal policy, is most commonly used to affect economic conditions. Not surprisingly, central bank decisions and speeches of central bank officials capture the attention of the financial press almost daily. Nonetheless, there are times when government action through fiscal policy is needed to work alongside monetary policy to achieve desired economic goals. Particularly in severe economic downturns, government fiscal policy can play a positive role and complement monetary policy efforts to stimulate an economic recovery.

reality CHECK   *How has monetary policy affected you over the past year?*

Financial Institutions

LEARNING OBJECTIVE 6
Compare the different types of financial institutions as well as their roles in the economy.

Financial institutions are generally private firms that seek to maximize the value of their share prices. In serving as financial intermediaries channeling public savings to investment, they can be classified as depository or nondepository. Depository institutions are those financial firms that offer deposit services to the public and therefore are important to the payments system. Nondepository institutions offer various securities management and insurance services that are essential to a well-functioning financial system. Exhibit 14.8 lists some of the largest financial institutions in the world.

There are a number of unique aspects of financial institutions that make them distinct from nonfinancial firms.

- *Separation of finance and commerce.* Most countries do not allow financial firms to cross over into nonfinancial activities; that is, finance and commerce are separated sectors of the economy. Banks are not allowed to manufacture

EXHIBIT 14.8

Largest Financial Institutions in the World

Commercial Banks	Insurance Companies
1. Mizuho Holdings, Japan	1. Allianz, Germany
2. Citigroup, U.S.	2. ING Group, Netherlands
3. Deutsche Bank, Germany	3. AXA, France
4. Sumitomo Mitsui Banking Corporation, Japan	4. Nippon Life Insurance, Japan
	5. American International Group, U.S.
5. UBS, Switzerland	
6. BNP Paribas, France	**Securities Firms**
7. JP Morgan Chase, U.S.	1. Morgan Stanley Dean Witter Discover, U.S.
8. HSBC, U.K.	2. Merrill Lynch, U.S.
9. Bayerische Hypo-und Vereinsbank, Germany	3. Credit Suisse First Boston, U.S.
	4. Nomura Securities, Japan
10. Bank of America, U.S.	5. Lehman Brothers Holdings, U.S.

Source: Staff, *Global Finance,* October 2002, p. 69; "Swiss Re, Sigma No,"
http://www.internationalinsurance.org/default.htm, June 2001.

and sell nonfinancial products and services, such as computers or airline services. It should be mentioned, however, that some countries allow firms to engage in both finance and commerce. For example, Germany permits *universal banking* enabling commercial banks to have nonfinancial operations.

- *Regulation.* Due to their importance to the national economy in terms of allocating financial capital to business firms and consumers, financial institutions are heavily regulated at the federal and state levels. Some examples of federal regulators are: United States—Federal Reserve System, Federal Deposit Insurance Corporation (FDIC), and Securities and Exchange Commission; Japan—Ministry of Finance (MOF) and Bank of Japan (BOJ); Germany—Deutsche Bundesbank; and United Kingdom—Bank of England. These regulatory agencies have excellent websites with information about their respective financial systems.

- *Financial assets and liabilities.* Financial firms have relatively small fixed assets—land, buildings, and equipment—due to the fact that almost all their assets and liabilities are financial in nature. Since the value of financial contracts is greatly affected by movements in interest rates, the profitability of financial firms is sensitive to interest rate changes. Generally speaking, high interest rates in financial markets tend to lower profits of financial institutions, while low interest rates tend to increase their profits.

- *Low equity capital.* Financial institutions have little equity capital and high use of debt or financial leverage compared to nonfinancial firms. Most nonfinancial firms finance their assets using between 30 to 50 percent debt; by contrast, financial firms typically use 90 percent or more debt. With less than 10 percent equity capital on their balance sheets, financial firms must be careful not to have large unexpected losses. This small margin for mistakes in operations has resulted in the *reserve for losses.* The reserve for losses account is intended to absorb expected losses on loans, securities, and so on. Only unexpected losses over and above the reserve for losses are absorbed by equity capital. The reserve for losses is found in the capital section of the balance sheet alongside equity and long-term debt.

- *Private information.* Financial institutions are considered to be special in that they obtain a lot of private information about individuals and businesses. Imagine being able to view all the checks or payments made by a person or business. You would be privy to a great deal of **inside information** about the person or business that others do not have. Since this information enables institutions like commercial banks to better understand and evaluate the probability of being repaid in a loan agreement, many experts believe that financial institutions are unique. With this private, or inside, information, institutions can signal others without this information by means of the loans they make and the prices and conditions they set on loans, for example. In providing signaling services about the credit quality or earning potential of firms in the economy, institutions serve to increase allocational and market efficiency in the financial system.

inside information Private information about individuals or business firms obtained by financial institutions

Depository Institutions

Because they are central to the payments system in the economy, **depository institutions** are foundational to the financial system. Deposits of individuals, business firms, and government are pooled and channeled to investment into business, consumer, agricultural, and real estate loans in communities. Depository institutions are made up of commercial banks and thrift institutions, with the latter institutions consisting of savings and loan associations, mutual savings banks, cooperative banks, and credit unions. In terms of total assets, commercial banks ($5,522 billion) are much larger in size than savings institutions ($1,408 billion) and credit unions ($589 billion).

depository institutions Financial institutions that hold deposit accounts of individuals, business firms, and government

Of course, due to deposit insurance, depository institutions are more heavily regulated by the government than nondepository institutions. The government is a stakeholder in depository institutions in the sense that their failure means that insured depositors must be paid by the government insurance agency, the FDIC in the United States. If the insuring agency does not have sufficient funds to cover the losses of depository institutions, then the public must pay the losses through higher taxes. Clearly, the failure of depository institutions is more serious than the failure of nonfinancial firms, whose losses are borne by the creditors and shareholders of such firms but not the taxpaying public.

Commercial Banks. Among depository institutions, **commercial banks** are dominant in most countries.[2] Historically, commercial banks focused their attention on business customers, with emphases on commercial loans. Prior to the Great Depression, banks were relatively unregulated and could offer most financial services demanded by business customers. Due to the large numbers of failures of banks in the United States and other countries during the Great Depression, laws were passed to severely restrict the financial activities of banks. In general, banks, securities firms, and insurance firms were separated and not allowed to compete with one another. It was not until the 1980s that deregulation of the financial system began to take place around the world. Deregulation relaxed previous restrictions on

commercial banks The most dominant type of depository institution that takes public deposits of funds and channels these savings to loans and investments

- The interest rates that depository institutions can offer to depositors
- The geographic location of offices in a country or region
- The financial services that can be produced and delivered to customers

By the year 2000, most of the deregulation had become effective.

At the present time, due to deregulation, rapid changes in the structure of the financial system are taking place. In effect, we are reverting back to the preregulation days prior to the Great Depression—a sort of "back-to-the-future" change in regulatory policy and financial systems. For banks, the changes have meant the purchase of securities and insurance firms to expand their services into those areas. Also, banks have been increasing in size through mergers and acquisitions. Larger banks are needed to compete on a national and global level.

Recent changes in the banking industry are causing the following:

- A decline of the traditional banking model in which banks collect deposits and make loans
- An increase in nontraditional banking services including securities, insurance, electronic payments services, Internet banking, and so on
- Cross-selling to customers by first offering deposit accounts and loans to them and then following up by selling other financial services
- A blurring of the definition of a bank to encompass the wide variety of services banks can now offer customers
- More emphasis on initially identifying customer needs and then designing products and services to meet those needs

These trends are causing banks to diversify into new financial services. At the same time, banks must carefully consider which services to offer by identifying market or customer demand for services. Also, the bank must have personnel with the necessary expertise to competently deliver those services.

A controversy that arises with the formation of large, multiservice banks is whether they will be viable or able to survive in the long run. Proponents argue that diversification into a variety of financial services will reduce the risk of banks. Also, modern banks will be better able to meet the convenience needs of customers by offering one-stop financial supermarket shopping. On the other hand, opponents argue that banks should specialize by concentrating on fewer, specific types of financial services. By specializing, banks can take advantage of management expertise and avoid coordination problems involved in managing a firm that is spread out over a wide assortment of financial services. Should banks put all their eggs in one basket or not? Is diversifying or specializing the best strategy?

Savings and Loan Associations and Mutual Savings Banks.

thrift institutions Depository institutions that are primarily home lenders

Known also as cooperative banks and building and loan associations in some countries, these so-called **thrift institutions** are primarily home lenders. In the early 1900s they offered savings accounts and made home loans to individuals, who normally could not obtain financial services from commercial banks. By promoting thriftiness among individuals and contributing to the development of communities, these institutions became an important part of the financial system. Unfortunately, many thrifts had problems with adapting to the deregulation of financial services that led to many failures and mergers in the 1980s and 1990s. Today, while they are still involved in consumer finance and home lending, their role is diminished due to competition from banks and other financial service firms in their traditional product areas. As part of the structural changes in the banking industry, many of these thrifts have opted to become subsidiaries of banking organizations.

Credit Unions.

credit unions Not-for-profit thrift institutions that have members with a common bond, such as employer, religious group, and educational institution

These thrift institutions are consumer-oriented like other thrifts but are different due to their not-for-profit organization status. There are no shareholders of such firms; instead, the depositors and borrowers are the owners. Because they are not-for-profit organizations, they pay no state or federal income taxes and can use volunteer labor. To retain their not-for-profit status, they can only sell financial services to customers who satisfy a common bond requirement. Some typical examples of a common bond are employer, religious group, and educational institution. **Credit unions** are most active in small consumer loans for furniture,

Technology and Business

Online Banking

Internet-based financial services are increasing at banks and thrifts. These so-called *Internet banks* have no physical location and offer customers the convenience of banking around the clock from their home, workplace, mobile phone, and other locations. For example, Sony recently opened an online bank in cooperation with Sumitomo Mitsui Banking in Japan and J.P. Morgan Chase in the United States. Sony is not new to financial services, with operations in insurance, leasing, and credit financing through Sony Finance International. Sony's online banking accounts offer customers deposit services including bill payments, and are linked to other financial services, such as investments, loans, and so on. Eventually, Sony hopes to link its financial services to its electronic products, such as video games, to allow customers doing online video gaming to access their money online too.

If you are thinking about using online banking services with a company, it is important to know if they are legitimate and if your money is protected by deposit insurance. The Federal Deposit Insurance Agency (FDIC) offers the following tips for safe Internet banking. Learn to avoid costly surprises and even scams.

- Read important information about the bank on its website. Most websites contain information such as the official name and address of the bank's headquarters, the history of the bank, and its FDIC insurance coverage.
- Protect yourself from fraudulent websites. Be careful not to be fooled by copycat websites that deceptively use a name or web address very similar to that of a legitimate financial institution. The perpetrator wants to get you to give personal information about yourself and your financial assets, such as your account number and

password. With this information in hand, he or she can access your bank account and steal your money. When you access an Internet bank website, make sure that the address is correct.
- Confirm that the Internet bank is an FDIC-insured depository institution. The words *Member FDIC* or *FDIC Insured* should appear somewhere on the website. If you are not sure, go to the FDIC's website; select "Is My Bank Insured?"; enter the institution's official name, city, and state; and click "Find My Institution." If your bank cannot be found at this website, contact the FDIC by e-mail or telephone. If your bank is located outside the United States, contact the appropriate government insurance agency to make sure your bank has deposit insurance.
- Be aware that many times the name of an online bank is different from its main office at a particular physical location. If you hold deposits at both the Internet bank and the traditional bank, your deposits at the two banks are insured for the $100,000 limit available from one bank. If you have less than $100,000 in total at both banks, there is no need to worry about insurance coverage.

Note that only deposits are FDIC insured. If you have investment accounts, pension funds, or other financial assets at a depository institution, these assets are not insured against potential loss.

Questions

1. Do you use the Internet to do your banking with a local bank? If so, why do you like this financial service? If not, why might you use it in the future?
2. How could you make sure that your Internet banking is secure and safe?
3. Do you think that Internet banking will increase in the future? Why?

autos, vacations, and so on. They tend to be relatively small depository institutions, although there are some large, multibillion-dollar credit unions.

Nondepository Institutions

Financial service firms that do not hold deposit accounts are considered to be nondepository institutions. These institutions play an important role in financing the long-term investment needs of business firms. Also, they provide a number of important financial contracts that contribute to the financial security of businesses and consumers. Unlike depository institutions, they are not major participants in the money market but do play a major role in the capital market. They pool together the long-term savings of the country and allocate these funds to capital investments in land, buildings, and equipment. Since these long-term savings are not insured by the government, nondepository institutions are not as heavily regulated as depository institutions. Exhibit 14.9 gives the sizes of different nondepository financial institutions. Here we see that private pension funds are the largest nondepository institution, followed by life insurance and mutual funds, which are similar in size. Securities firms and other insurance companies like property-casualty insurance firms are relatively small compared to the other types of nondepository institutions.

insurance companies Financial institutions that offer various kinds of protection from financial losses to individuals and business firms

Insurance Companies.   Historically, **insurance companies** are one of the most successful financial institutions. Their success proves that people and business firms are risk averse and are willing to pay money to protect themselves from financial losses. There are two types of insurance companies: life insurance companies and property-casualty companies. Together, they represent the third largest group of institutions, behind banks and pension funds.

Life insurance companies offer three basic types of financial protection to their customers: death, old age or retirement, and medical. In each case an insurance policy is sold to customers that promises specific benefits to the individual or their beneficiaries. Policyholders must pay monthly premiums to maintain their insurance coverage. Premiums are invested by the life insurance company in bonds, stocks, and real estate. The largest share of funds is invested in bonds. The reason for this investment strategy is that life insurance companies are able to use actuarial science to accurately predict such items as death rates. While it is difficult to predict when a single person will die, for large groups of people it is possible to estimate the number of individuals who will die in any given year. With this knowledge in hand, the life insurance company seeks to invest its funds in capital market instruments that offer predictable cash flows over time to meet policyholder death benefits. In this regard, bonds paying fixed interest payments over time are clearly superior to stocks and real estate. Given relatively stable liabilities in the form of death benefits, in addition to stable cash flows from bonds, life insurance companies are able to consistently earn fair profits and, therefore, tend to have low failure rates.

term insurance An insurance policy that offers a lump sum death benefit to policyholders

whole life insurance An insurance policy that offers both a term policy plus a type of savings account that increases in cash value over time as premiums are paid

annuity A type of savings plan offered by insurance companies that offers either a lump sum death benefit or a steady stream of cash payments to beneficiaries over time

Three of the most popular life insurance policies are term insurance, whole life or permanent insurance, and an annuity. **Term insurance** offers a lump sum death benefit to policyholders and is quite inexpensive to obtain. **Whole life insurance** offers both a term policy plus a type of savings account that increases in cash value over time as premiums are paid. An **annuity** is a savings plan that offers either a

EXHIBIT 14.9

Total Asset Sizes of Different Kinds of U.S. Nondepository Institutions, 2003

Type of Nondepository Institution	Total Asset Size (billions of dollars)
Private pension funds	$7,936
Mutual funds	$3,587
Life insurance	$3,358
Securities firms	$1,376
Other insurance	$ 925

Source: "Flow of Funds Statements," Board of Governors of the Federal Reserve System, Washington, DC, **http://www.federalreserve.gov/releases/Z1/Current.**

lump sum death benefit or a steady stream of cash payments to beneficiaries over time. Many times group life insurance policies are sold to business firms and government agencies to offer to their employees at more competitive premium rates than an individual could negotiate with the life insurance company. Additionally, life insurance companies offer **medical insurance** that covers most costs associated with doctor, hospital, and pharmacy drug expenses. Because the cost of medical insurance can be high, most people co-insure through their employer under *group insurance plans;* for example, your employer would pay $1000 of your monthly premium and you would pay $400, for a total of $1400. You can see that purchasing medical insurance on your own would be much more expensive.

Property-casualty insurance companies provide policies to protect property, such as homes, buildings, vehicles, and other capital assets. Auto insurance, fire insurance, theft insurance, workers' compensation insurance, crop and hail damage insurance, and environmental insurance are some of the most popular property-casualty policies.

Life insurance and property-casualty companies can be classified as stock versus mutual organizations. *Stock organizations* have separate owners and policyholders. In *mutual organizations* there are no stockholders, so the policyholders are considered the owners. Whereas dividends are paid to stockholders in stock organizations, they are paid to policyholders in the form of lower premiums in mutual organizations.

Pension Funds.

Pension funds are a relative newcomer among financial institutions, but their growth since 1950 has been phenomenal. Most individuals seek to retire from work later in life. A typical retirement age is 65. On retirement, one must live on savings accumulated during one's working years. Pension funds are the primary source of savings for most people.

Many firms have matching programs in which, for every dollar saved by a person in the pension fund, the firm will put a second dollar in the fund. Another incentive to save in pension funds is that the contributions to the plan are not taxable. If a person made $1000 before taxes, and then put $50 in her or his pension fund, the firm would put another $50 into the fund, and the taxable income for the person would now be $950. The reduction in taxes is $50 times the tax rate of the person; a 30 percent tax rate would mean a $15 tax savings.

Pension funds take the savings of individuals and invest them in stocks, bonds, and real estate. This brings up a further incentive to save in pension funds; namely, earnings on the investments are not taxed by the government. When funds are eventually taken out of the pension plan on retirement, individuals must pay income taxes. However, because taxes are deferred for so long, the tax burden on retirement savings is quite small. If you do not like to pay taxes, put your money in a retirement account.

What kinds of retirement plans are there? The example above is a **defined contribution plan,** which is the most common type of pension plan in the United States today. Historically, the most popular pension plan was the **defined benefit plan.** In this plan the employer promises to pay out a specified amount of monthly pay to an employee on his or her retirement. For instance, the firm might pay 70 percent of the average of the employee's last 10 years' annual wages and salary. These so-called **public pension plans** are often offered by government entities at the federal, state, and local level. Because they are backed by the taxing power of government, they are relatively safe. However, private firms that offer these plans expose their employees to the risk that they will fail and be unable to meet defined benefit payments to retirees. For this reason, **private pension plans** offered by firms are normally defined contribution plans.

medical insurance An insurance policy that covers most costs associated with doctor, hospital, and pharmacy drug expenses

property-casualty insurance Insurance policies to protect property, such as homes, buildings, vehicles, and other capital assets

pension funds Financial institutions that offer various kinds of retirement savings plans to individuals

defined contribution plan A type of pension plan in which the employee sets aside a portion of her or his paycheck in a savings plan and the employer provides matching funds in many cases

defined benefit plan A type of pension plan in which the employer promises to pay out a specified amount of monthly pay to an employee upon his or her retirement

public pension plans Pension plans offered by federal, state, and local government that are backed by the taxing power of the government

private pension plans Pension plans offered by private firms to employees

Carole Lee volunteers at the Retired Senior Volunteer Program in Cleveland as a long-time social worker and health educator.

The main risk that retirees face is inflation. Inflation erodes the purchasing power of their savings. By definition, inflation is an increase in the prices of goods and services. When people are in their working years, wage levels tend to rise as inflation increases and workers thereby maintain their purchasing power. If wage levels did not rise as inflation increased, people would find that they could not purchase as many goods and services as before. In effect, they would become poorer even though their annual income was the same. With no wages from a job, retirees must protect themselves from inflation by investing in assets that grow over time in value. Since stocks have higher long-run rates of return than bonds and real estate, stocks dominate pension investment portfolios.

However, once a person retires, it is prudent to reduce the share of investments in stocks and increase proportionately investments in bonds. The reason for this is that stock prices are relatively volatile, whereas bonds offer more stable cash flow payments. Retirees need the steady income of bonds to maintain their standard of living. Nonetheless, some amount of stock investments is still warranted due to the fact that people are living longer nowadays and must protect their income from inflation for 10, 20, or 30 years after retirement. In sum, the mix of stocks and bonds in a pension plan portfolio changes over time, with higher proportions of stocks in a person's younger years and higher proportions of bonds in retirement years.

Some other common pension plans in the United States are social security, individual retirement accounts (IRAs), and self-employment plans known as Keogh plans. Social security taxes are levied on all U.S. citizens' wages. As contributors to social security, U.S. citizens are entitled to social security benefits on retirement. It is important to note that the social security program is an **unfunded pension plan** in the sense that taxes collected by the government are simply passed through to retirees, rather than invested in an account for an individual as in the case of a **funded pension plan.** An IRA is a funded pension plan that allows individuals to save for their future retirement outside of an employer-sponsored plan. A Keogh plan allows self-employed persons, such as small business employees and owners, to save for their retirement.

unfunded pension plan A pension plan that pays retirees from cash flows or taxes instead of from funds set aside over time in a savings plan

funded pension plan A pension plan that pays retirees from their funds set aside in a savings plan during their working years

Social security taxes are a controversial issue due to the aging of the so-called baby boom generation born after the end of World War II in 1945. Given that social security is an unfunded pension plan, as increased numbers of baby boomers retire, the tax paid by working individuals must increase. However, due to low birth rates over the last 30 years in the United States as well as in many major industrial countries around the world, the number of working people is decreasing relative to the number of retired people. Of course, this means that the social security tax rate will have to be increased to pay retiree benefits in the years to come. At some point, working individuals will not be able to bear the high taxes, with the result that pension benefits will have to be cut. To offset this risk, the U.S. government is encouraging individuals to invest savings by giving tax incentives. For example, if you put $1000 in an IRA, this money cannot be taxed by the government until you later withdraw the money in your retirement years. This is a big tax break. If you had a 20 percent income tax rate, you would have avoided $200 in taxes. Keogh plans and defined contribution pension plans are eligible for similar income tax breaks. A Roth IRA allows you to pay taxes now but not later; that is, the $1000 income in the previous example would be taxed at your current income tax rate, say 20 percent, so that you can put $800 of this income in a Roth IRA that will not be taxed when you withdraw the funds in retirement years. If you have a low tax rate now, the Roth IRA may be a better choice than a standard IRA.

Investment Companies. Firms that offer investors unit shares of ownership in portfolios of stocks, bonds, real estate, and money market securities are known as **investment companies.** These firms pool the savings of thousands of customers, issue unit shares of ownership to their customers, and invest the savings in securities portfolios. Actively managed funds employ professional investment managers to choose the securities and seek to maximize the return per unit risk for their customers. Passively managed funds invest in well-defined securities portfolios, such as market indexes like the Standard & Poor's 500 index, comprised of the largest 500 firms' common stocks in the United States, or high quality corporate bonds in a bond index. Actively managed funds charge customers higher fees than passively managed funds due to the higher costs of professional investment managers. In these funds, portfolio managers seek to pick the highest-earning investment securities per unit of risk for their customers.

investment companies or **mutual funds** Financial institutions that pool the savings of thousands of customers, issue unit shares of ownership to their customers, and invest the savings in securities portfolios

Investment companies, sometimes called **mutual funds,** have been extremely successful due to the many advantages that they offer customers. Most customers benefit from lower transactions costs, financial expertise, diversification in a large number of different securities, international investment, convenient access via 800 telephone numbers and Internet accounts, and accurate record keeping. Funds can be easily and rapidly transferred from one type of security to another. In general, customers have tremendous control over how their savings are invested at any moment in time. Most mutual fund shares are owned by households, with pension funds and banks a distant second and third, respectively.

The large number of these mutual funds and the incredible variety of investment options can be a confusing experience for all but the most knowledgeable investor. However, some good rules of thumb to follow in using investment companies are

- Choose three to five different investment companies to spread your savings across a number of different investment management teams.
- Spread your savings across different kinds of securities, with a target mix of stocks, bonds, and money market securities; for example, 50, 40, and 10 percent, respectively.
- Rebalance your mix of investments every year or two. Over time, if the value of stocks increases faster than bonds and money market securities, your

percentage ownership of stocks will be higher than the targeted amount of 50 percent. Sell off some stocks and buy bonds and money market securities until you get back to your target mix of securities.

You might have noticed that rebalancing sells securities that have increased in value more than others and buys securities that have increased in value less than others. In this way, investors can benefit from selling high and buying low. By spreading savings across a wide variety of securities and different investment companies, investors can achieve a reasonable degree of portfolio diversification. Portfolio diversification is beneficial in that it tends to decrease the risk or volatility of earnings from investments. Given that most investors are risk averse, portfolio diversification is a rational response to the fact that stocks and bonds can be risky investments. Some pension funds, such as Enron's private pension plan, invested all of employees' savings in only Enron stock. When the company failed, many employees lost all of their savings. Clearly, this investment strategy was severely flawed because it did not take advantage of the risk-reducing benefits of portfolio diversification.

Institutional Investors.   Today, insurance companies, pension funds, and investment companies are major institutional investors that can have powerful effects on financial markets around the world. If these institutional investors decide that a firm is risky and sell its bonds and stocks, the firm will immediately suffer from lower bond and stock prices, which translate into higher costs of debt and equity funds. Institutional investors can affect even countries, as they move funds from one country to the other in search of higher returns per unit risk. Large outflows of investment funds from a country can result in slower business sector growth, lower employment and wages, and a lower standard of living.

Some experts believe that these large investors have increased market volatility. Herd behavior can occur at times. For example, when many institutions began selling stocks at the same time on October 19, 1987, the stock market fell 24 percent in one day. Known as Black Monday, billions of dollars of wealth were wiped out in a matter of hours. Rapid movements of prices have caused stock exchanges to implement **circuit breakers** that act like speed bumps, stopping or slowing down trading when security prices fall too rapidly for buy orders to keep up with sell orders of securities from institutional traders.

circuit breakers Temporarily stopping or slowing down the trading of stocks and bonds by a securities exchange

Managing a Financial Institution

Financial institutions manage a two-stage production process (see Exhibit 14.1). In stage one, deposits and savings of the public are obtained by issuing indirect securities of various kinds, such as deposit accounts, insurance policies, pension plans, and unit shares of ownership. In stage two, the funds acquired in stage one are loaned or invested. The difference between total revenues on loans and investments and total costs of funds is net income before taxes. If we divide net income after taxes by total assets, we get the return on assets (ROA). This financial ratio is a good indicator of how well managers utilized the institution's assets to generate profits. A typical ROA among financial institutions is about 1 percent. By dividing net income after taxes by total equity, we get the return on equity (ROE). This profit measure is closely watched by the institution's common shareholders. While financial institutions seek to maximize both of these profit measures, ROE is relatively more important than ROA, as shareholders ultimately control privately-owned institutions.

In order to maximize profit, institutions can either increase revenues or minimize costs. In this respect, interest revenues and interest costs are typically much larger than noninterest revenues like service fees and noninterest costs like labor, equipment, and real estate expenses. The **net interest margin** is the difference between interest revenues and interest costs divided by total assets. Because interest revenues and interest costs are so large, as interest rates go up or down, the net interest margin can change. If interest rates go up and cause interest costs and interest revenues to rise, but interest costs rise more than interest revenues, then net profit margin will decrease. Alternatively, as interest rates rise, if interest revenues increase more than interest costs, the net profit margin will increase. The sensitivity of institutions' profitability to interest changes is known as **gap risk.** Since changes in interest rates can immediately affect their profitability, financial institutions seek to reduce gap risk.

Another key source of revenues and costs is **credit risk.** Credit risk is the chance that promised interest and principal on debt will not be paid. Institutions seek to make loans to customers or invest in debt securities that offer revenues adequate to offset the costs of losses from default or nonpayment. To do this, they charge higher interest rates on loans and debt securities that have higher credit risk than other investments. If a riskless debt security paid an interest rate of 5 percent and a loan was made with sufficient credit risk to require a **risk premium** of 4 percent, the total interest rate charged on the loan would be 9 percent. Institutions can also offset losses from credit risk by securing loans with collateral, such as inventory purchased with funds from the loan. If debt is secured and default on promised payments occurs, the institution can seize the collateral as payment. Finally, to manage credit risk, institutions normally set aside some amount of funds to cover anticipated losses in any quarter. It is common sense that, if an institution makes thousands of investments in risky debt instruments, some debt contracts will default. As mentioned earlier, institutions set aside a **reserve for losses** that can be used to absorb anticipated losses without affecting profitability. If losses due to credit risk exceed loan loss reserves, however, these unanticipated losses will need to be absorbed by equity, thereby lowering the equity value of the institution. Of course, if equity is wiped out by large, unanticipated debt losses, the institution is bankrupt.

Capital risk is the chance that unanticipated losses will exceed the institution's level of equity capital on its balance sheet. A bankrupt institution is closed by regulatory officials and subsequently merged with a healthy institution in most cases. The merger of a failed institution can occur literally overnight. Indeed, only the most observant customers might notice the change in the name of the institution the next morning. Most institutional failures come about due to excessive credit risk. Regulations require that institutions maintain reasonable levels of equity capital to absorb unanticipated losses. Consequently, as institutions increase their credit risk, regulators will require institutions to increase their equity capital.

Financial institutions earn profits by managing risks. Those institutions that can earn the highest return per unit risk will have the highest stock prices. Like other private firms, the ultimate goal of financial institutions is to maximize stock prices. Failure to do so will result in shareholder losses, not to mention potential replacement of managers and loss of customers.

net interest margin A profit measure for financial institutions that equals the difference between interest revenues and interest costs divided by total assets

gap risk The sensitivity of a financial institution's profitability due to changes in interest changes

credit risk The chance that promised interest and principal on debt will not be paid

risk premium The added interest rate that must be paid on risky debt and equity securities in addition to the riskless rate of interest, such as the U.S. government debt interest rate

reserve for losses Funds set aside by financial institutions to absorb anticipated losses without affecting profitability

capital risk The chance that unanticipated losses will exceed the institution's level of equity capital on its balance sheet and cause bankruptcy

reality CHECK *Do your parents have a defined benefit or defined contribution pension plan? Which one would you prefer to have?*

Careers in the Financial System

Job opportunities in the financial system can be found in financial institutions and regulatory agencies. Private financial institutions offer a wide variety of career opportunities. Because their customers are extremely diverse, they need to hire people with all kinds of different professional skills. A wide variety of jobs are available in banks, thrifts, insurance companies, pension funds, and investment companies. Jobs in the public financial sector are available in a number of regulatory agencies, including the Federal Reserve System, Federal Deposit Insurance Corporation, Comptroller of the Currency, Securities Exchange Commission, and state-level banking, securities, and insurance regulatory bodies.

Most financial careers require good accounting skills as a prerequisite. Also, a general business studies education is essential to be able to understand how businesses work and to communicate with customers from various types of business enterprises. Most institutional managers require analytical and mathematical skills obtained in finance studies, not to mention interpersonal skills to work effectively with others. Because it is difficult to gain in-depth expertise in all areas of finance, it is important to work in teams many times. Also, because financial institutions are private firms, jobs are available in management, marketing, computer, and other traditional business disciplines.

Finance professionals regularly point out that helping businesses grow and prosper through meeting their financial needs is a rewarding experience. Also, many bankers, insurance agents, pension managers, investment analysts, financial advisors, and securities brokers are well respected due to their valuable contributions to improving business, education, and public service in their communities.

Summary

LEARNING OBJECTIVE 1

Define the components of financial systems and understand the benefits of financial intermediation.

Financial systems are composed of financial instruments (bonds and stocks), financial markets (money and capital markets as well as organized and over-the-counter markets), and financial institutions (depository and nondepository institutions). In financial systems, savings are channeled to investments via financial intermediation. In this process, allocative efficiency, operational efficiency, and market efficiency can lead to greater productivity in the economy. Of course, higher productivity in the business sector means more jobs, higher wages, greater wealth, and a higher standard of living for citizens of a country.

LEARNING OBJECTIVE 2

Contrast different kinds of financial systems around the world and state how regulation can protect the safety and soundness of financial systems.

Financial systems can be classified as market-oriented as in the United States, or bank-centered, as in Germany and Japan. In both cases government regulation plays an important role in maintaining the safety and soundness of the financial system. During the Great Depression, the failures of large numbers of banks and other financial institutions substantially worsened the economic downturn. Deposit runs on banks due to widespread panic by the public was a terrible episode that affected countries around the world. Over the past two decades, financial crises have broken out in Japan, Mexico, Russia, Finland, Sweden, Turkey, Argentina, and a number of emerging Asian countries. National government, as well as international agencies such as the International Monetary Fund and the World Bank, can play a vital role in preventing or diminishing the negative effects of financial crises. The goal is to limit permanent damage to a country's economy and foster recovery and steady growth.

LEARNING OBJECTIVE 3

Understand how the health of the financial system affects the productivity of the economy, including the roles of the IMF and the World Bank.

The financial system is an essential building block to a healthy economy. As such, regulation in the areas of deposit insurance, equity capital rules, on-site examinations, and restrictions on asset powers have been implemented. Deposit insurance is crucial to maintaining public confidence and preventing bank runs, but comes at the cost of moral hazard risk. In recent years the asset powers of financial institutions have been deregulated in the United States, Europe, Japan, and other countries to allow banks, securities firms, and insurance companies to compete with one another. This deregulation triggered a consolidation movement marked by mergers that is creating mega-institutions that are global in scale.

LEARNING OBJECTIVE 4

Overview the history of money and why money matters to the economy.

In the money and banking section, we overviewed the history of money, including coins, paper money, and emergence of the U.S. dollar as a numeraire (benchmark) currency in world currency markets. Instability of currency values later led to the European euro in 1999. Problems with currency risk can affect economic conditions in countries as well as business firms attempting to make payments in international trade.

LEARNING OBJECTIVE 5

Explain what central banks do to control money and achieve economic goals.

The quantity theory and related equation of exchange show that money matters in the sense that it can impact economic output and inflation. Central banks have the ability to control money supplies and, in turn, impact the macroeconomy through monetary policy. The monetary policy framework of central banks consists of tools (open market operations, discount rates, and reserve requirements), operating targets (federal funds rates and bank reserves), intermediate targets (long-term interest rates, money supply, and bank credit), and economic goals (output, employment, inflation, and international trade). Another way for government to affect the macroeconomy is through fiscal policies of taxation and spending. Unfortunately, many times it is not possible to stimulate or slow down the economy using fiscal policy, due to the political difficulties of making changes in tax rates and government spending. For this reason, monetary policy is a superior approach to affecting economic conditions in most instances. Not surprisingly, the financial press regularly contains news about what the central bank is doing in the financial markets.

LEARNING OBJECTIVE 6

Compare the different types of financial institutions as well as their roles in the economy.

Financial firms differ from nonfinancial firms due to heavy regulation, large quantities of financial assets and liabilities on their balance sheets, low levels of equity capital, and the knowledge of private information about firms and individuals. The latter information explains why many experts consider financial firms to be special. Financial institutions can be classified as depository institutions—banks and thrifts, including savings and loan associations, mutual savings banks, and credit unions—and nondepository institutions—insurance companies, pension funds, and investment companies. Depository institutions are foundational to the economy due to their pivotal role in the payments system. Nondepository institutions are repositories of private savings that are pooled and then invested in long-run capital projects in the business sector. Big institutional investors can have a powerful influence on capital flows to business firms and even countries.

Chapter Questions

1. What are the three major components of a financial system?
2. What is financial intermediation? Discuss the efficiency benefits of this process to the economy as a whole.
3. How does the Japanese financial system differ from the U.S. financial system? What are the advantages and disadvantages of the Japanese financial system?
4. List and briefly discuss four ways that regulation can be used to protect the safety and soundness of financial systems.
5. What is the Financial Services Modernization Act of 1999? Are similar changes to financial systems occurring in Europe and Japan?
6. How did the large number of bank failures during the Great Depression affect the economy of the United States at that time?
7. Distinguish between the different roles of the IMF and the World Bank.
8. Describe three important characteristics of money. Why did the world change from commodity money to fiat money?
9. Give three examples of electronic money. Why is this form of money gradually replacing paper money?

10. The quantity theory proposes the equation of exchange to show the relationship between the financial system and the economy. Use this equation to explain how the growth rate of money can affect the inflation rate and the growth rate of the real economy.

11. The monetary policy framework consists of policy tools, operating targets, intermediate targets, and economic goals. What are each of these components? Do any of the economic goals conflict with one another at times?

12. If the central bank wants to lower the federal funds rate, how can it hit this operating target using open market operations? The discount rate? Reserve requirements?

13. If increasing economic productivity is the main goal, what should be the main focus of monetary policy? What if controlling inflation is the main goal? Today, which goal is more important to central banks around the world?

14. Compare the different kinds of depository institutions, including commercial banks, savings and loan associations, and credit unions. What "back-to-the-future" changes have been occurring in the banking industry in recent years?

15. Compare the different kinds of nondepository institutions, including insurance companies, pension funds, and investment companies. How are defined contribution pension plans different from defined benefit plans? If a person is using investment companies to manage her or his retirement savings in a defined contribution plan, what are three good rules of thumb to follow?

Interpreting Business News

1. What does the following news quote mean? "While some people saving for retirement have moved to the sidelines in the money market, they will eventually have to return to the capital market."

2. Suppose that depositors of a failed large bank were bailed out by the FDIC. How could this government rescue of insured depositors potentially lead to greater risks at the bank in the future?

3. Some countries in South America have begun pegging their currency to the European euro. How could you know the value of these South American currencies?

4. The Federal Reserve used open market operations to lower the federal funds rate. How exactly does the Fed do this?

5. Due to concern about inflation, the central bank is expected to tighten control of the money supply. Why would this help to slow down inflation?

Web Assignments

1. Go to the website for the Board of Governors of the Federal Reserve System (**http://www.federalreserve.gov**). Look for information about the Fed and check into who the members of the Board are. Now click back to the home page and check the breaking news items. Pick one of those items and briefly summarize the news story.

2. Go to the FDIC website (**http://www.fdic.gov**). Look for questions and answers about deposit insurance. Summarize the information there on deposit insurance coverage.

3. Go to the website for the central bank in a country other than the United States. What are the key areas of monetary policy that are being discussed at the present time for that country?

4. Go to the website of a major financial institution in the world. You might pick a name from the newspaper. What kinds of financial services does it provide?

5. Go the website for the Federal Trade Commission (**http://www.ftc.gov/bcp/conline/pubs/credit/idtheft.htm**) and find out more about identity theft. What steps should you take if you are a victim of this ethical and criminal problem in today's society? How has electronic money affected this problem?

Portfolio Projects

Exploring Your Own Case in Point

In this chapter, you learned that financial systems affect both individuals and business firms in important ways. Answering the following questions will help you gain insights into how your firm is influenced by financial news events.

1. How are current monetary policies affecting your company in its home country? In your answer, consider intermediate monetary targets, including money supply, long-term interest rates, and bank credit.

2. How are current economic conditions affecting your company in its home country? Will the monetary policy goals of the central bank with regard to the economy be beneficial to your company?

3. What sources of debt does your firm use? (*Hint:* You might find this information by searching the annual report for the firm or accounting information available from the Internet at **http://finance.yahoo.com/**.)

Starting Your Own Business

After reading this chapter, you should update your business plan to address questions concerning your financial resources.

1. What internal sources of start-up (or seed) capital financing are available to you? (*Hint:* These capital funds are needed to purchase equipment, property, and other fixed expenses.)

2. Can you use credit cards to help finance initial working capital needs, especially inventory and wage costs?

3. Contact your local Small Business Development Center (SBDC). Does it know some local angels and banks that might offer financing for your new business? What kinds of financing are available from these sources?

Test Prepper

You've read the chapter, studied the key terms, and the exam is any day now. Think you are ready to ace it? Take this sample test to gauge your comprehension of chapter material. You can check your answers at the back of the book.

True/False Questions

Please indicate if the following statements are true or false:

_____ 1. Money market instruments are short-term securities with maturities less than five years.

_____ 2. An over-the-counter exchange does not have a physical location.

_____ 3. Credit risk deals with the change in value of long-term securities as interest rates change in the financial marketplace.

_____ 4. Japan and Germany have bank-centered financial systems, as opposed to market-oriented systems.

_____ 5. The Financial Services Modernization Act of 1999 deregulated the financial services powers of banking institutions to include securities and insurance activities.

_____ 6. A total of 20 countries in the European Monetary Union have adopted the euro as their currency.

_____ 7. Open market operations by the Federal Reserve involve the purchase and sale of government securities.

_____ 8. Fiscal policies involve government spending and taxation.

_____ 9. Term insurance provides a lump sum benefit to policyholders and is quite inexpensive to obtain.

_____ 10. Portfolio diversification is beneficial in that it tends to increase returns to investors.

Multiple-Choice Questions

Choose the best answer.

_____ 1. Which of the following is *not* a component of the financial system?

a. Financial instruments including money market instruments
b. Financial instruments including capital market instruments
c. Financial markets
d. Financial mathematics
e. Financial institutions

_____ 2. The initial sale of a security in the financial marketplace takes place in the

a. direct market.
b. indirect market.
c. primary market.
d. secondary market.
e. open market.

_____ 3. By ensuring that all information is reflected in prices, _____ is improved.

a. allocational efficiency
b. operational efficiency
c. market efficiency
d. regulatory efficiency
e. financial efficiency

_____ 4. In the United States, each deposit account at a commercial bank is insured by the Federal Deposit Insurance Corporation up to

a. $10,000.
b. $20,000.
c. $50,000.
d. $100,000.
e. $500,000.

_____ 5. Money is all of the following *except*

a. a unit of account.
b. a store of value.
c. a standard of deferred payment.
d. a fixed asset.
e. a medium of exchange.

_____ 6. If the Federal Reserve increases the money supply, assuming all else remains the same, we would expect

a. interest rates to increase.
b. interest rates to decrease.
c. interest rates to stay the same.
d. higher unemployment.
e. lower unemployment.

_____ 7. The equation of exchange can be written as

a. $m + v = p + q$.
b. $m + p = v + q$.
c. $m = p$.
d. $v = q$.
e. $v = p$.

_____ 8. Which of the following is *not* a final economic goal of monetary policy?

    a. Productivity

    b. Employment

    c. Stable prices

    d. International trade

    e. Bank credit

_____ 9. Which of the following is *not* a depository institution?

    a. Commercial banks

    b. Savings and loan associations

    c. Investment companies

    d. Mutual savings banks

    e. Credit unions

_____ 10. A pension plan that pays out a specified amount of monthly pay to an employee on his or her retirement is a

    a. defined contribution plan.

    b. defined benefit plan.

    c. term plan.

    d. life insurance plan.

    e. premium plan.

ACE self-test

Want more questions? Visit the student website at **http://college.hmco.com/business/student/** (select Gaspar, *Introduction to Business*) and take the ACE quizzes for more practice.

15

Personal Financial Planning

❚ **Introduction**

❚ **The Purpose of Personal Financial Planning**

❚ **Key Concepts**
Computing Net Worth
Setting Financial Goals
Evaluating Spending Patterns
Identifying Your Stage in Life
Turning to Experts

❚ **Managing Income**
Budgeting
The Envelope Budget
Checkbook Management
Financial Planning Software
Web Resources
Insurance

❚ **Living on One Income**

❚ **Investing**
Managing Investments
Fixed-Income Investments
Equity Investments
Your Home

❚ **Retirement and Estate Planning**
Social Security
IRAs and 401(k) Plans
A Will

❚ **Tax Planning**

❚ **Ethics of Financial Planning**
Giving
Repaying Debts
Paying Taxes
Providing for Your Family
Planning for Future Needs
Keep Money in Perspective

❚ **Careers in Personal Financial Planning**

Learning Objectives

After studying this chapter, you should be able to

1. Explain the purpose of personal financial planning.

2. Define concepts such as net worth.

3. Describe the budgeting process.

4. Explain the key considerations in deciding to live on one income.

5. Describe how to make wise investments, including an evaluation of risk and return.

6. List retirement and estate planning considerations.

7. Identify the goals of tax planning.

8. State the ethical issues associated with personal financial planning.

How Much of a Risk-Taker Are You?

Making financial plans requires that you assess how much of a risk-taker you really are. Some people prefer to take no risks with their savings and investments. Others are willing to take very high risks. Most people are somewhere in the middle. Good financial planning will enable you to make investments that fit your risk preferences. For example, you can invest in low yield, but very secure bank certificates of deposit (CDs). Alternatively, you can invest in corporate stocks, whose returns are not secure but are potentially much higher than a bank CD.

Money invested in a bank CD might yield a fixed interest return of 3 percent per year for five years. The same money invested in the stock market, such as an index mutual fund, might yield the stock market's historical average return of 11 percent per year. However, the stock market offers no guaranteed return. In fact, it could be even less than the bank CD. There have been time periods when the stock market had very negative returns and other periods when it had very high returns. Almost everyone agrees that investments in the stock market should have a long-term time frame of at least several years.

Introduction

Personal financial planning should begin as early as possible in your career. Financial planning is both a process and an attitude that will hopefully become a habit. Financial planning involves gathering all your financial and personal data, analyzing that data, and creating a financial plan for the future. Next, you must take action and follow the plan. Periodically, you need to review the plan and make necessary changes as your environment and financial conditions change. This chapter provides information to assist you right now as a college student and to help you plan for future years.

The Purpose of Personal Financial Planning

LEARNING OBJECTIVE 1
Explain the purpose of personal financial planning.

The purpose of **personal financial planning** is to meet current and future financial needs through a combination of effective planning and implementation of those plans. Americans spend much of their lives earning money, but they rarely spend any time planning how to use their accumulated wealth. Many people reach age 65 financially unprepared for retirement. Some college students think that financial planning is unnecessary, or at least something that can be put off for years without negative consequences. This is not true. Developing financial planning skills and good spending habits at an early age will pay huge dividends in later years.

personal financial planning Planning that enables a person to meet current and future financial needs

Personal financial planning takes time and effort, and it can be complicated and frustrating. Financial planning may not make you wealthy, but lack of planning is equivalent to planning for failure. Planning will almost certainly result in your being better off than if you had not planned, and will, we hope, result in your life being fuller and happier. Your financial success is worth some time and effort. Plan today for your financial well-being.

Key Concepts

LEARNING OBJECTIVE 2
Define concepts such as net worth.

Personal financial planning requires some fundamental knowledge. Key concepts include how to compute net worth, how to set financial objectives, how to evaluate spending patterns, how to identify your stage in life, and from whom to seek expert advice.

Computing Net Worth

Preparing a personal balance sheet is necessary to determine how much money you now have, so you can estimate how much more you will need to reach your short-term and long-term financial goals. Preparing a **personal balance sheet** enables you to identify what you own, your assets, and what you owe, your liabilities. Assets are listed in order of liquidity, and liabilities are listed in order of claim. The difference between the two, assets minus liabilities, is your **net worth.** Several other terms that you need to know in order to properly complete and analyze your personal balance sheet include the following:

personal balance sheet A balance sheet that lists what an individual owns (assets) and what she or he owes (liabilities)

net worth The difference between what an individual owns (assets) and what she or he owes (liabilities)

appreciating assets Assets that have the possibility of increasing in value over their lifetime

depreciating assets Assets that usually decrease in value over their lifetime

portfolio of assets All the assets an individual possesses

return on your portfolio Cash generated from an individual's investments and the annual increase in the fair market value of the investment instruments, such as stocks and bonds

- *Appreciating assets* are assets that have the possibility of increasing in value over their lifetime.
- *Depreciating assets* are assets that usually decrease in value over their lifetime. *Diversification* is allocating your money among many different types of assets rather than concentrating it in one asset. Diversification reduces the danger that you will lose the overall value of your investments.
- *Portfolio of assets* includes all the assets you possess.
- *Return on your portfolio* includes both the cash generated from your investments and the annual increase in the fair market value of investment instruments, such as stocks and bonds.

A sample personal balance sheet form is provided in Exhibit 15.1. Assets are basically those things that you own or will eventually own once they are paid for. Examples of the most common types of assets include cash, houses, stocks, bonds, and cars.

liquidity How easily an asset can be converted into cash

Liquidity refers to how easily as asset can be converted into cash. Personal assets, such as a house or car, are much less liquid than stocks or bonds. In other words, the less liquid an asset is, the longer it usually takes to sell and thus provide you with its market value in cash. A good idea is to evaluate whether your assets are those that you believe will appreciate in value or those that won't. There is an obvious advantage in having assets that will go up in value as opposed to having assets that will either maintain value or decrease in value. A house is often considered an appreciating asset, but today it may just maintain its value or even decrease in value.

Liabilities are items that represent a future outlay of cash. Exhibit 15.1 lists some of the more common liabilities. Don't forget to include liabilities connected to assets on which you still owe money. For instance, you might still owe half the value of your auto. In this situation, include the unpaid portion of your auto loan (the part you are still paying off) under car loans in the liability section of your personal balance sheet, and the fair market value of the car in the asset section.

EXHIBIT 15.1

Personal Balance Sheet

Assets	
Cash in bank checking account	$ _____
Other bank accounts	$ _____
Money market accounts	$ _____
House	$ _____
Cars	$ _____
Furnishings and appliances	$ _____
Clothing, jewelry, and art	$ _____
Stocks, bonds, and other securities	$ _____
Cash value of insurance and annuities	$ _____
Retirement savings, such as IRAs or employee savings plans	$ _____
Other	$ _____
Total assets	$ _____

Liabilities	
Taxes owed	$ _____
Mortgage loans	$ _____
Alimony or child support owed	$ _____
Credit card debt	$ _____
Car loans	$ _____
Education loans	$ _____
Any unpaid bills	$ _____
Other debt	$ _____
Total liabilities	$ _____
Personal net worth (total assets − total liabilities)	$ _____

Once you have totaled your assets and liabilities, you are ready to calculate your net worth by subtracting your total liabilities from your total assets. Your net worth is a snapshot of your financial standing at a particular point in time. By comparing your yearly snapshots, you'll be able to determine your financial progress.

After preparing your personal balance sheet, you should consider the composition of your individual assets and liabilities. Are your assets made up of clothes, furniture, or other depreciating assets? Wouldn't you be better off if you acquired assets that are likely to appreciate, such as stocks or real estate? However, if you invest only in real estate and real estate values decrease, then your assets lose money instead of appreciating. The way to reduce the risk that your assets won't appreciate is to have several different types of appreciating assets. Diversification is critical. If one type of asset doesn't go up in value, perhaps another type of asset will.

After computing your personal net worth, you have a good idea of your present financial condition. Are you satisfied or dissatisfied with your present condition? In either case, knowing where you are enables you to make plans for the future. If your personal net worth is a negative amount, then your top-priority financial goal should be to pay off some debts. If your net worth is only a small positive number, that is, assets barely exceeding liabilities, then a financial emergency could put you in a precarious situation. A primary financial goal should be to increase your net worth by decreasing your liabilities, increasing your appreciable assets, or both.

Setting Financial Goals

financial success Having enough money to pay for one's living expenses and at the same time saving enough to meet future financial needs

independently wealthy Having enough money so that it is no longer necessary to work to pay for living expenses

wealth An abundance of worldly possessions

Have you set any financial goals? Do you want to be a financial success? **Financial success** means having enough money to pay for one's living expenses, and at the same time saving enough to meet future financial needs. Do you want to be independently wealthy? To be **independently wealthy** means that you have enough money that you no longer need to work to pay for your living expenses. Ultimately, at some point in your life, you will probably no longer be able to work. You will then live on your investments, pension, government transfer payments, or charity.

Wealth is defined as an abundance of worldly possessions. Wealth can also be defined as the amount of money necessary for personal contentment. Are you wealthy? Some people do not consider themselves wealthy even though they have millions of dollars. The amount of money necessary to be considered financially successful or independently wealthy varies greatly among individuals. Real success involves many dimensions, not just money. The greatest success is measured by character and personal integrity, not fame and fortune. Even so, a person of character and personal integrity should strive to be a financial success. Financial success enables a person to provide for his or her own needs and to help others. Financial success does not usually happen overnight, but it can happen for anyone who is willing to make good plans and stick to them.

The starting point in achieving financial success is to know and accept where you are today. If you are in poor financial condition, don't give up. The productive

A retired shipping clerk volunteers his time to care for infants in the neonatal intensive care unit at Oklahoma University Medical Center Children's Hospital. If he had not been financially prepared for retirement, he would have been unable to donate his time to this excellent cause.

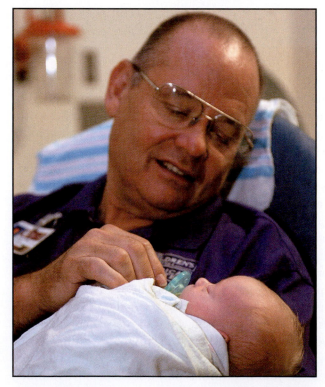

thing to do is make plans that will improve your situation. On the other hand, you may not be in bad shape, but with proper planning, you may be able to improve an already good situation. This improvement is achieved by acquiring financial knowledge and resolving to take control of your own financial future.

A lack of financial knowledge stops most people from ever changing their financial situation. Knowledge is obtained by reading and studying. Some helpful hints for improving your financial situation include the following:

Accept your current situation as a starting point and realize that you can change it for the better with the right kind of knowledge.

Realize that only you can improve your financial situation. No broker, money manager, or relative can put more effort and dedication into changing your financial situation than you can. Take control of your own financial future.

Read enough financial literature to feel confident about the financial decisions you have to make. Know what you're doing. Some people may get the hang of it after reading only one book. However, other people may need to read several books and to talk with several consultants before they are sure of what they are doing.

You are probably set in the way you spend money. If so, then you may need to change your spending habits. This change is much easier said than done. You can easily make purchases on a credit card that charges 15 percent annual interest, even when you don't have money in the bank; waiting to make purchases until after you have accumulated the necessary funds requires discipline. You must develop budgetary discipline to succeed financially. Discipline is a good habit to have for managing any area of your life, but it is indispensable in the financial area.[1]

Acquiring financial knowledge and understanding is the first step to improving your financial position. The next step is implementing the new information so that you can achieve financial success.

To stay motivated and to keep your financial plans on track, you should establish clear goals. Exhibit 15.2 provides a short list of possible goals. Each goal you select should be ranked as short-term or long-term. Those in the short-term column should be achieved first, while those in the long-term column should be achieved second. You will need to achieve certain short-term goals on your way to some particular long-term achievement. Furthermore, many goals will be interrelated, like having children and financing their education. Without stated goals, you will expend effort without a purpose. If you lack a purpose, you may wind up achieving nothing.

The acquisition of wealth begins when your monthly income exceeds your monthly expenses. At that point you can invest the excess in different financial mechanisms that earn you money.

Evaluating Spending Patterns

Personal spending patterns vary dramatically, chiefly because people have many different goals and objectives. These goals and objectives are somewhat related to demographic characteristics, such as age and educational background, and personal characteristics. For example, some people are frugal, while others are spendthrifts bogged down in excessive mortgages, personal loans, and other debts.

EXHIBIT 15.2

Examples of Personal Goals

Possible Goals	Short-Term	Long-Term
Minimize your debt.	_____	_____
Pay off college loans.	_____	_____
Build an emergency fund.	_____	_____
Buy a house.	_____	_____
Make home improvements.	_____	_____
Buy a vacation home.	_____	_____
Buy a new car.	_____	_____
Have children.	_____	_____
Finance children's education.	_____	_____
Buy major luxury items.	_____	_____
Buy new furniture or appliances.	_____	_____
Enjoy an expensive vacation.	_____	_____
Take time off from work.	_____	_____
Start your own business.	_____	_____
Retire early.	_____	_____
Live in style after retirement.	_____	_____
Other.	_____	_____

Education plays a key role in determining a person's spending patterns. In general, college-educated people earn more and spend more than less-educated people. As a result, many consumer product companies gear their marketing to those households with college-educated inhabitants.

People with college educations tend to invest for their future more than those who have not attended college. People without college educations generally have less money to invest after immediate needs are met. In addition, college graduates spend about twice as much on entertainment as nongraduates do. College graduates account for 60 percent of clothing sales. College graduates allocate 6 percent of their budgets to health care, compared to barely 4 percent of the less-educated person's budget. College graduates spend roughly five times the amount on education that non-college graduates spend.

Personal spending patterns vary tremendously among different people. Your own spending pattern is affected by many factors, including your age, your education, your household income, your personal tastes, and your stage in life. For example, older people spend more money on medicine, drugs, and doctors. Lower-income households spend a larger percentage of their income on food and other necessities. The percentage of spending on automotive products and services increases as income increases.

Other factors affecting your spending pattern may include your marital status, the number of children, place of residence, sex, race, moral and religious beliefs, and cultural background. Young, unmarried people spend a larger percentage of income on recreation and clothing. Family priorities shift to educational needs when children reach certain ages. Members of certain religious groups donate a significant amount of earnings to their church, synagogue, or other charitable causes.

Your spending pattern will change as your financial goals and objectives change. Spending money in a way that generates the highest quality of life, given both your own desires and the money you have, is an art based on sound financial principles. Learning how to allocate your financial resources in a way that provides for a quality lifestyle now and in the future is the key to financial success. Financial success results from planning, not from worrying about the use of your financial resources.

Identifying Your Stage in Life

Identifying your stage in life helps in effective financial planning. Different stages usually have different financial needs. The American Institute of Certified Public Accountants (AICPA) identified five stages in an average person's life.

Stage one. Employed, before marriage. With little responsibility to others, the single person can afford to take risks. Long-term growth is one objective during this phase. Clothing and recreation are important. Insurance generally is not relevant.

Stage two. Married, before children. This is a time to begin accumulating assets, despite heavy pressure to spend on other things. Careful budgeting is essential. Furnishings for the home are important. Insurance becomes a factor, although perhaps not a substantial one.

Stage three. Married, with precollege children. Insurance protection becomes very important. Income may increase significantly, but so does the need to spend. Budgeting becomes even more important. So does tax planning. Concern about future college costs begins.

Stage four. The empty nest. Earning power may be at its peak. Risk avoidance becomes important; investment strategy tends toward building up capital. Travel may become more important.

Stage five. Retirement. A steady, comfortable income is now a concern. Investment strategy must be balanced. There is greater freedom, but risk must be limited because the time necessary to recover from a disaster is no longer there.

Spending patterns differ at the various stages of life. You need to consider your stage as you plan your budget. If you are a typical college student, you are about to enter stage one.

Turning to Experts

King Solomon wrote, "Plans fail for lack of counsel, but with many advisors they succeed."[2] That bit of wisdom is particularly appropriate for personal financial planning. No one can singlehandedly keep track of all aspects of financial planning. A team effort is required. Depending on your personal goals and financial objectives, you may need advice from several different experts, such as stockbrokers, insurance agents, lawyers, bankers, and accountants.

Solomon wrote that our lives are like a morning mist, here and gone so quickly. Make the most of where and when you are.

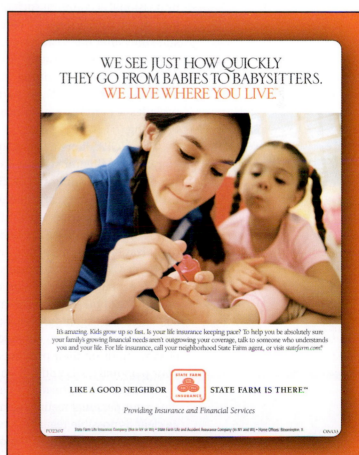

Traditionally, financial planning advice has been sought from established professionals, such as accountants, insurance agents, and stockbrokers. In addition to these traditional financial advisors, a new category of professionals includes people who specialize strictly in financial planning. The industry's largest trade group, the International Association of Financial Planners (IAFP), recommends that you have a short meeting with your prospective planner at which time you discuss the following:

The planner's background, including education and experience.

The planner's references, including clients you can call.

The planner's competence in different kinds of investments, tax-advantaged vehicles, insurance, and tax strategies. He or she need not be a specialist in all of these areas, but should be sufficiently familiar with them to deliver a comprehensive plan.

Who will actually work with you or supervise and coordinate the efforts of those who will develop your plan.

The degree of individualization you will receive. Are all recommendations arrived at independently through a detailed study based on research of your particular situation?

The planner's method of compensation. Most professionals base their fees on the complexity of your circumstances and amount of time spent on your affairs. The three basic methods of compensation for financial planners are fee only, fee and commission, and commission only.

Certified public accountants (CPAs) constitute one group of traditional financial advisors who are particularly well suited to financial planning. The most prestigious professional accounting society is the American Institute of CPAs (AICPA). All members of the AICPA must be certified public accountants. CPAs are licensed by each state only after they pass a rigorous exam and meet a work experience requirement.

The AICPA recommends that its members who have a professional interest in personal financial planning join the Personal Financial Planning (PFP) division. Additionally, the AICPA, as part of its Continuing Professional Education division, provides a Certificate of Educational Achievement Program in Personal Financial Planning.

Personal Financial Specialist (PFS) A specialty designation awarded by the American Institute of CPAs to a CPA after he or she meets designated requirements

The AICPA offers a specialty designation, **Personal Financial Specialist (PFS).** To qualify, a CPA must meet six requirements, including passing a one-day examination, having a minimum of 250 hours of experience in personal financial planning in each of the three years immediately preceding the initial application, and providing six references from other professionals and clients. Exhibit 15.3 lists three prominent financial planning specialist designations and the addresses of the sponsoring organizations. For more information, you may contact these organizations.

While CPAs and other professionals offer high-quality services, they also are relatively expensive. Depending on the complexity of your financial situation, you may either obtain financial planning services from experts or do the planning yourself. Insurance agents and stockbrokers generally offer free financial advice, but you must be cautious when considering their recommendations. Typically, they receive commissions on their products. Be sure that their recommendations are based on your personal goals and not on which products provide the highest commissions.

If you decide to turn to an expert financial planner for help, be prepared to discuss your personal feelings and concerns without withholding any information. Be as clear as possible regarding your financial goals. You have the right to clear explanations for any recommendations from your financial planner. Ask questions. Don't take any actions without a thorough understanding of the possible consequences.

EXHIBIT 15.3

Financial Planning Specialist Designations

Designation	Sponsoring Organization
Certified Financial Planner (CFP)	Certified Financial Planner Board of Standards 1700 Broadway, Suite 2100 Denver, CO 80290 **http://www.cfp.net**
Chartered Financial Consultant (ChFC)	American College Student Services 270 Bryn Mawr Bryn Mawr, PA 19010 **http://www.amercall.edu**
CPA, Personal Financial Specialist (PFS)	American Institute of Certified Public Accountants 1211 Avenue of the Americas New York, NY 10036 **http://www.aicpa.org**

reality CHECK *What is your net worth? Do you have any short-term or long-term plans to improve your net worth?*

Managing Income

LEARNING OBJECTIVE 3
Describe the budgeting process.

Managing income requires planning and controlling the use of your financial resources so that you can meet current and future financial needs. Managing income includes budgeting, checkbook management, use of financial planning software, locating information on the Web, and acquiring appropriate insurance.

Budgeting

A cash flow budget is necessary to gain control of your finances and ultimately to achieve financial success. The motivation for maintaining and sticking to a budget is that it enables you to cover all your bills by paying according to a cash management agenda and to have some money left over for savings and investment. Proper saving and wise investments will enable you to prepare for your future needs. **Cash flow** is the term used to describe the flow of money into and out of your accounts—cash inflows and outflows. A **cash flow budget** shows what came in and what went out of your bank account during the selected time period. Cash inflows, or sources of cash, include resources such as employment and investment income. Cash outflows, or uses of cash, include purchases of necessities and other items, charitable contributions, and tax payments. **Net cash inflow** is the excess of total cash inflows over total cash outflows.

Preparing a cash flow budget begins with an evaluation of your historical expenses. You can start by filling out the worksheet in Exhibit 15.4 (on p. 528) with figures from the previous year to produce a cash flow budget for that year.

Second, prepare a projected cash flow budget for the coming year based on your prior year's figures, but make adjustments for any anticipated changes in income and expenses for the coming year. Exhibit 15.5 shows some estimated expenses as

cash flow The flow of money into (inflows) and out of (outflows) accounts

cash flow budget A budget that shows what cash came in and what went out during a selected time period

net cash inflow The excess of total cash inflows over total cash outflows

EXHIBIT 15.4

Cash Flow Budget

Cash Inflows	
Wages or salary	$_____
Spouse's wages or salary	$_____
Interest and dividends	$_____
Rent and royalty income	$_____
Other	$_____
Total cash inflows	$_____

Cash Outflows	
Rent or mortgage payments	$_____
Food	$_____
Clothing	$_____
Utilities	$_____
Eating out	$_____
Furniture and appliances	$_____
Recreation	$_____
Gas for car	$_____
Car payments	$_____
Car repairs	$_____
Car insurance	$_____
Doctor bills	$_____
Medicine	$_____
Interest expense	$_____
Household repairs	$_____
Life and disability insurance	$_____
Education (tuition)	$_____
Day care	$_____
Taxes (income, property, etc.)	$_____
Other	$_____
Total cash outflows	$_____
Net cash inflow (outflow)	$_____

a percentage of your net income. These are, of course, only estimates, and depend ultimately on your personal circumstances and tastes.

If your cash flow budget for last year shows a net cash outflow, try to reduce various cash outflow accounts as you prepare your projected cash flow budget for next year. Exhibit 15.6 (on p. 530) suggests ways to cut expenses. Other possibilities include reducing the balance on your credit cards by taking out loans at much lower rates in order to pay them off. After paying off your credit card debt, it is good advice for most people never again to accumulate debt on credit cards. If you use credit cards, be sure to pay off your balance each month.

When your monthly cash inflows exceed your monthly cash outflows, you are on your way to investing for the future. However, before you begin investing, you need an emergency liquid fund, or savings cushion—for example, six months' living expenses—in order to cope with unanticipated future expenses. If last year's

EXHIBIT 15.5

Estimated Expenses as a Percentage of Net Income

Expenses	Single with No Children	Single with Children	Married with Children	Married with No Children
Housing	20	22	25	23
Loan payments	10	5	5	7
Food	9	12	12	12
Recreation	10	7	5	10
Child care	0	6	5	0
Auto or transit	6	7	7	5
Utilities and phone	5	6	6	5
Clothing	5	4	4	4
Savings	5	5	5	5
Pension	5	5	5	5
Health	3	4	4	5
Education	5	3	3	3
Gifts and contributions	10	10	10	10
Vacation	5	2	2	4
Insurance	1	1	1	1
Other	1	1	1	1

cash budget shows a net cash inflow, calculate how long it will take to accumulate your savings cushion. Consider any decreases in expenses that might allow you to achieve your savings cushion faster.

To determine monthly figures for cash inflow and cash outflow, divide amounts on the projected annual cash budget by 12. Keep accurate records of cash inflows and cash outflows to determine if your monthly cash budget is working. If your budget is not matching up with your actual cash inflows and outflows, then you should consider making appropriate adjustments to your budget.

To achieve financial success, you must control your cash inflows and outflows. Financial planning experts can help you determine how to manage your finances, but financial planning experts can never totally replace the need for your personal involvement in the financial planning process. Furthermore, outside experts have less at stake if your financial plans fail. And even if the expert's advice is perfect, ultimately it is up to you to see that those plans are implemented. If your recreation expenses are budgeted at $100 per month, then you must limit your spending to that amount.

The Envelope Budget

An **envelope budget** is a very simple but effective budgeting system. You take envelopes and write the name of each of your expenditures on them, such as your car payment, house payment, food, and recreation. At the beginning of each month, when you receive your paycheck, you write checks for each of the envelopes.

You mail the house payment and car payment checks to the lenders. You also mail the checks for the utility and telephone bills. The other checks are cashed when payments are required and the cash is used to buy gas, food, and necessities. Any cash left over after the first purchase is replaced in the appropriate envelope.

envelope budget A budgeting system in which money is placed in envelopes labeled as rent, car payment, food, and so on

EXHIBIT 15.6

Simple Methods to Cut Expenses

Method	Monthly Savings
Subscribe to newspapers and magazines rather than buying them on newsstands.	$10
Buy food in larger quantities.	$40
Use newspaper and magazine coupons.	$10
When vacationing, stay in less expensive hotels.	$20
Increase insurance deductibles.	$20
Fill up with self-serve gas.	$10
Do your own laundry.	$30
Pay off credit cards faster.	$20
Prepare your own tax return.	$75 to $225 (per year)
Return recyclable bottles.	$5
Bring lunch to work.	$100
Quit smoking and drinking alcoholic beverages.	$100 to $150
Don't buy it just because it's on sale.	$5 to $100
Mow your own yard.	$20 to $40
Have an interest-bearing checking account.	$10 to $30
Learn to do some plumbing and basic household repairs.	$30 to $40
Avoid impulse buying.	$15 to $30

Any amount remaining at the end of the month is transferred to your savings and investment envelope. Thanks to the envelope system, you know how much you have left to spend for any item in your budget at any given time. The major advantage of the envelope approach to budgeting is that it physically divides funds among your individual budget items. Additionally, it allows you to readily ascertain the status of any budget item—what funds are currently available for each item.

Checkbook Management

Owning a checking account is essential for managing personal finances. Each check provides a record of purchases and of paid bills, and the financial record provided by your checkbook is an invaluable tool for financial planning purposes. To use a checkbook effectively, you should adhere to the following guidelines:

Enter all checks written on and all deposits made to your account immediately. Never postpone recording checks or deposits. Procrastination leads to inaccurate records.

Reconcile your bank statement as soon as possible after the statement is received, usually once a month.

Always pay your bills at the proper time. If you receive a bill before the due date, you may wish to postpone payment until that time in order to maintain access to your money for as long as possible. On the other hand, if small amounts are involved, it probably isn't worth delaying payment and possibly forgetting to pay on time. Always pay on time. To ensure that each check is issued on a timely basis, mark the payment due date on your calendar.

EXHIBIT 15.7

Jacob Lawrence
Bank Reconciliation Statement

Balance per the bank statement, July 31, 2005	$2000
Add: Deposit in transit	900
Bank error, check drawn by Jean Deaux charged to the account of Jacob Lawrence	110
Less: Outstanding checks	
Number 96, $35	
Number 102, $25	
Number 108, $40	
Number 110, $20	(120)
"True" cash balance, July 31, 2005	$2890
Balance per the books, July 31, 2005	$2500
Add: Note collected by the bank	395
Error made in recording check number 103	55
Interest earned	15
Less: Bank charges	(20)
NSF check	(55)
"True" cash balance, July 31, 2005	$2890

File all receipts for bills paid by check. The receipt and check may be needed for future use, such as to document a tax deduction. A file system should be established for storing these records; such a system ensures that you have the necessary information for resolving any discrepancy that might arise regarding a past payment and for preparing your tax returns. The file system also helps you to track your expenditures over time, to make any corrections necessary to your cash flow budget, and to gain better control over your cash flows.

The **bank statement** sent to you periodically, usually once a month, shows the bank's record of disbursements and receipts concerning your checking account. You should reconcile the statement with your records (your checkbook) in order to verify the accuracy of your records and to discover if any errors have been made by the bank. The bank's record of your checking account and your record of your checking account will differ because of erroneous entries made either by you or by the bank, and because of differences in timing when transactions are recorded by you and by the bank. Timing differences may occur, for example, if you write a check and deduct it from your balance, but the bank does not process the check and subtract it from your account balance before preparing your statement. Exhibit 15.7 provides an example of a **bank reconciliation.** The goal of the bank reconciliation is to find the "true" cash balance in your checking account and to enable you to discover any errors made either by you or by the bank.

Start with the bank's record of your checking account balance. Add any deposits and subtract any checks written that are recorded in your checkbook but that are not shown on the bank statement. Second, adjust the bank's balance for any errors made by the bank. Bank errors are much less likely than your errors. The resulting number is the true cash balance in your checking account.

bank statement A statement of the bank's record of disbursements from and receipts to a checking account

bank reconciliation A bank reconciliation is an analysis that resolves differences between your checkbook's cash balance and the bank statement's cash balance. The result is the "true" cash balance in your checking account

To ensure the accuracy of the true cash balance based on the bank balance, you must update your checkbook balance for items recorded by the bank but not recorded by you. Begin with the checking account balance shown in your checkbook. Subtract any bank charges and checks that you deposited that were returned for nonsufficient funds (NSF). If you have an interest-bearing checking account, add any interest earned to your checkbook balance. If there are no errors in your checkbook records, the resulting number also should be your "true" cash balance and match the earlier calculation. All items that affect "balance per the books" must be recorded in your checkbook register.

An alternative approach to finding the balance of your checking account is to add to the bank's record of your checking account balance, shown on the bank statement, any deposits made; then subtract any checks you have written that the bank has not yet processed, and that are therefore not on the bank statement. This procedure does not permit you to discover any errors made by the bank and should, therefore, be used in conjunction with a bank reconciliation to find the "true" cash balance.

Financial Planning Software

personal financial planning (PFP) software Software that facilitates financial planning with features such as a computerized checkbook, budget forms, and a net worth report

Personal financial planning (PFP) software is among the most popular software packages. Many PFP packages are available, offering a wide variety of features and carrying an equally wide variety of price tags. Most, however, cost from less than $50 to about $200. The most basic packages provide a computerized checkbook, automatically calculate the checkbook balance, and print checks. More advanced programs provide for budgeting and preparing a net worth report (personal balance sheet).

The majority of PFP software packages are written for the IBM PC and PC-compatible computers, although some are also available for the Apple Macintosh (Mac) or both the IBM PC and Mac. Information on specific software can be obtained from local computer software retailers, computer vendors, software mail order companies, industry publications, and current users of such software.

Prior to purchasing any type of software, you should see a demonstration of the software on a computer system similar to the one you own. If at all possible, talk to people who are currently using the software; ask them about any problems they have encountered.

A typical PFP program is *Quicken* by Intuit Software of Palo Alto, CA (**www.intuit.com**). *Quicken* provides for checking, budgeting, general accounting, and single-entry bookkeeping. Support is provided by manual, online, and telephone. *Quicken* allows for importing and exporting data from and to spreadsheet software, such as Microsoft *Excel,* and features a menu-driven system, a help screen, and customization of accounts.

PFP software should be able to perform calculations quickly and should include a reference manual with an index. A program's budget report should show the time period covered, expense accounts with actual and budgeted amounts, and the difference between actual and budgeted amounts. PFP software can compute totals for specific accounts, such as payments to the telephone company. To use PFP software successfully, you must consistently enter data into the program on a timely basis.

An alternative to using personal financial planning software programs is to design your own financial planning reports using a spreadsheet program. Among all software, spreadsheet programs are second only to word processing programs in popularity.

Popular spreadsheet programs include *Excel* by Microsoft Corporation and *Quattro Pro* by Corel Corporation. If you already use a spreadsheet program, then you can easily type in the worksheets described earlier in the chapter:

Personal Balance Sheet (Exhibit 15.1)
Personal Goals (Exhibit 15.2)
Cash Flow Budget (Exhibit 15.4)
Bank Reconciliation Statement (Exhibit 15.7)

By creating your own financial planning reports, you can customize them to your individual needs. For example, you can add or delete items to the example of a personal balance sheet previously provided. You may even wish to type your checkbook register into a spreadsheet file to facilitate computing the current balance in your account.

Whether you choose to create your own report forms using a spreadsheet program or to use a personal financial planning program, a computerized approach to financial planning offers several advantages over a manual approach.

Calculations are rapidly and accurately made.
Reports can be efficiently prepared and printed.
Updates and changes can be easily made.
Computerized applications facilitate what-if analysis.

Computer software can help you gain control of your finances by improving record keeping and facilitating report preparation, such as a personal balance sheet preparation. But buying a computer and software won't solve all your financial problems. You still have to stick to your budget, whether it is prepared using pencil and paper or using computer software and printer.

E*Trade offers a variety of financial planning resources on its website.

Reprinted with permission of E*Trade Financial

Web Resources

Many websites are available to assist you with financial planning. A dozen of the most useful sites are briefly described below.

Bank of America (**http://www.bankofamerica.com**) is one of the largest financial institutions in the United States. Its website provides online banking services, and an entire area of the website is devoted to personal finance. The personal finance page has links to resources like mortgage solutions, retirement planning, home equity loans, and credit card debt. Bank of America's website is massive and has a wealth of information related to financial planning.

Century 21 (**http://www.century21.com**) is one of the country's top real estate corporations. The Century 21 website is geared toward providing information about purchasing and selling a home. Features of this website include an online mortgage application, an office locator, and many tips on how to handle the transactions of buying or selling a home.

CNBC (**http://www.cnbc.com**) is a major financial news network on television. Its website tracks all of the important financial and headline news of the day and has many user-friendly features. Some of these features are a personalized portfolio tracker, stock quotes, investment research material, and many links to other financial websites.

E*Trade (**http://www.etrade.com**) is one of the largest online investing services available on the Web. E*Trade's Portfolio Manager lets you create portfolios for all the investments you want to track, whether you hold them at E*Trade or elsewhere. E*Trade offers online investing in stocks, options, bonds, IPOs, and over 5200 mutual funds. E*Trade provides real-time quotes and customizable charts on thousands of stocks. E*Trade also offers banking services.

Fannie Mae (**http://www.fanniemae.com**) provides a steady stream of mortgage funds to the United States' homebuyers by purchasing home loans from a myriad of financial institutions. The website is mainly devoted to providing mortgage information and giving links to potential homebuyers. Some of the features of the website are property listings, links to sites where mortgages can be applied for, and information on mortgage businesses.

Fidelity Investments (**http://www.fidelity.com**) is one of the United States' premier brokerages. Its website provides resources for managing a portfolio, online trading, and planning for the future.

Freddie Mac (**http://www.freddiemac.com**) is very similar to Fannie Mae in its business. Much of its website is also devoted to mortgage information. Resources are available pertaining to mortgage planning and to obtaining a home loan. Much of this information overlaps with that of Fannie Mae.

The U.S. Department of Housing and Development (HUD, **http://www.hud. gov**) strives to provide every American with affordable housing. Its website provides links for buying a HUD home, applying for public housing, and a wealth of information with regard to purchasing or selling a house.

Intuit Corporation's website (**www.intuit.com**) provides a link to a number of financial calculators (**http://www.intuitadvisor.com/intuit/vortal/gtf/financalc_draw.gtf**). Among the financial calculators provided on the website are

- Home affordability calculator
- Investment yield calculator
- Mortgage qualification calculator
- Savings goal—monthly deposit calculator
- Rent versus buy calculator

Morningstar (**http://www.morningstar.com**) is a financial information service that provides investors with lots of valuable information. Much of the site can be personalized to track your own investment portfolio. In addition, you can sign up for a premium membership to obtain exclusive analyst reports, stock picks, and other resources.

Quicken (**http://www.quicken.com**) provides online and software applications to help people manage their finances. The website provides investment information, loan information, software support, and tax planning help. Quicken is one of the most trusted names in personal finance management.

Wells Fargo (**http://www.wellsfargo.com**) is a large bank that provides a range of services on its website. This site also has a personal finance section filled with investment, mortgage, and financial planning pages. Wells Fargo has many features that allow you to personalize them by signing up for an online account.

Yahoo! Finance (**www.finance.yahoo.com**) provides a wealth of investment research material, stock quotes, analyst reports, and other financial information that allows you to manage your own portfolio. In addition, it has links to many of the other financial information services and institutions.

Insurance

insurance An arrangement in which an individual pays a fee (premium) and in return, if the individual suffers a designated loss, the insurance company compensates him or her

In addition to saving the equivalent of six months of living expenses in liquid investments like a passbook savings account, money market mutual fund, or bank money market deposit account, you should acquire insurance to shield you from financial setbacks. In general, **insurance** is an arrangement in which you pay a fee (premium) and in return, if you suffer a designated loss, the insurance company compensates you. Most insurance policies include a **deductible,** which is the amount of the loss that you must pay. The insurance company pays the amount of loss that exceeds the deductible. Your safety net of insurance should include health, disability, life, property and casualty, and automobile coverage.

Insurance is the expense that many people dislike the most. However, you should protect yourself from loss before you begin to invest for gain. Insurance is an indispensable component in managing your financial affairs.

Health. Health insurance coverage is essential. If your employer-provided health insurance offers insufficient coverage, you should obtain additional major medical coverage independently. Group insurance may be available from an affiliation other than your employer, for example, from professional societies, labor unions, religious groups, or college alumni associations.

Health maintenance organizations (HMOs) are prepaid health care plans that provide medical care, but you must use HMO member doctors and not other doctors, as is possible with a private carrier. A variation on the HMO concept is a Preferred Provider Organization (PPO). With a PPO, hospitals and doctors agree to provide a company's employees with health services at a discounted rate.

Disability. Disability insurance provides income if you become sick or injured and are unable to work. The younger and more active you are, the more coverage needed. A 32-year-old male has a six-and-one-half times greater risk of being disabled for three months or longer than he does of dying during his working years. Since social security disability insurance does not protect all of your income, you should have enough disability insurance to cover the difference between your monthly expenses and all the income you will receive from other sources if you are disabled.

Avoid a disability insurance policy that contains an "any occupation" clause, since benefits stop if you take another job to earn money. The policy should have an "own occupation" clause that allows you to work part-time. Make sure the policy is also guaranteed renewable. You can save on your premiums by choosing a policy with a longer waiting period, two or three months, for benefits.

Life. The amount and type of coverage you need depends on your obligations to others and the amount of risk you are willing to assume. You need more life insurance when you marry, have children, or incur debt. Your need for life insurance diminishes as you fund your children's education and your net worth increases. A typical person needs from $200,000 to $2 million coverage, around 5 to 10 years' worth of income. There are a variety of life insurance products.

- Term insurance provides no-frills insurance protection and does not include a savings element. Term insurance is relatively inexpensive when you are young, but premiums increase with age.
- Permanent insurance (or cash-value or ordinary life) has higher premiums than term insurance in the early years of coverage. These extra premiums go into a fund that builds cash value. Later, these earnings can offset insurance

deductible The amount of a loss that an individual must pay before an insurance arrangement compensates him or her

Insurance is a critical component of effective financial planning.

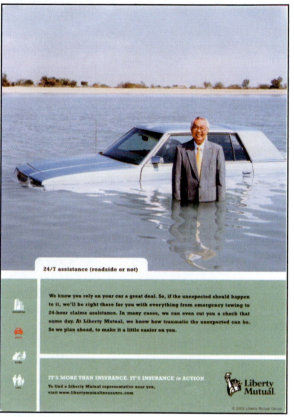

24/7 assistance (roadside or not)

We know you rely on your car a great deal. So, if the unexpected should happen to it, we'll be right there for you with everything from emergency towing to 24-hour claims assistance. In many cases, we can even cut you a check that same day. At Liberty Mutual, we know how traumatic the unexpected can be. So we plan ahead, to make it a little easier on you.

IT'S MORE THAN INSURANCE. IT'S INSURANCE *in* ACTION
To find a Liberty Mutual representative near you, visit www.libertymutualinsurance.com

Liberty Mutual.

premiums. In general, you should buy permanent insurance only if you can maintain the policy for at least 20 years.

- Whole life insurance provides protection for an insured's entire life, and the premiums remain the same for the life of the policy. It does include a savings element. Any premiums paid in excess of administrative expenses (commissions, selling, and marketing expenses) and mortality costs are added to accumulated cash values that earn interest.

- Variable life insurance is a permanent insurance contract with level premiums. The cash reserve is maintained in a separate account and the policyholder determines how it is to be invested (equity funds, bond funds, or money market funds). The death benefits vary with the investment return in the separate account, but the death proceeds cannot be less than the policy's original face amount.

- Universal life insurance is flexible premium insurance that includes monthly renewable term insurance and an investment component. Administrative expenses are deducted from each premium payment, and any remainder is added to the policy's accumulated cash value. This type of insurance defers current income taxes on policy earnings. If interest rates drop significantly, your premiums will rise.

- Universal variable life insurance combines the flexible features of universal life and variable life policies. You may be able to invest in stocks.

- Single-premium life insurance involves paying a one-time premium for a specified amount of life insurance protection. Earnings on the investment grow and are tax-deferred as long as they are not withdrawn or borrowed.

Property and Casualty. Property and casualty insurance coverage should include 100 percent of the replacement cost of your home and belongings. If you are a renter, then you will need insurance that covers only your belongings. If you have to file a claim after a fire or theft, you will need valid evidence of what was in your home. Videotape or photograph the contents of your home or have an inventory prepared of your household goods. Store such evidence *outside* of your home, for example, in a safe deposit box.

Automobile. In addition to insurance on your home and belongings in your home, you will need automobile insurance. Automobile insurance is a necessary expense that comes with owning a car. It includes coverage for damages to your car (collision and comprehensive) and for damages your car causes to others (liability), both car repairs and bodily injury.

Shop around for insurance and compare products of different companies. Ask the agent about his or her commissions. An insurance agent is in the business to make money and may sell you the insurance that gives the most commissions and not necessarily the best performance. Consider buying a policy directly from the insurer without sales commissions.

reality
CHECK *Do you have a budget? Do you have insurance?*

Living on One Income

LEARNING OBJECTIVE 4
Explain the key considerations in deciding to live on one income.

This section addresses an issue that confronts many working couples when one wage earner, either involuntarily or voluntarily, no longer has a job. Involuntarily losing a job may result from being laid off or your firm going out of business. Voluntarily quitting a job may result from a conscious decision, such as a couple deciding that one of the two should stay home full-time to care for children.

Can two live as cheaply as one? No, but most families that want to live on one wage earner's income can probably do so. Many people erroneously believe that two incomes are essential to afford the basic needs of a modern family. The fact is that the financial benefits of a second income are often exaggerated. The disadvantages of a two-income family are numerous: day-care costs, hectic schedules, fast-food diets, restaurant meals, and paid housekeepers. If you would like to consider living on one income, then you may benefit from the following strategies:

First, identify the items on which you spend your money. Make a record of all your purchases for a month or two. Most people are amazed at how the little things add up. If you have an up-to-date cash flow budget, then you can skip this step.

Second, identify all the expenses associated with the second job, such as child care, commuting, work clothes, business lunches, and so on. Deduct these expenses from the second job's income. In addition, remember to deduct taxes and other withholdings. How much is left? That's the amount by which you have to cut your expenses in order to live on one income. There are several areas in which you may be able to save money.

You can help minimize your automobile expenses by keeping your car well maintained. A car that is properly cared for should last at least ten years. When you have to replace your vehicle, consider buying a used car. Shop very carefully. Search the classified ads. Car dealers typically have a substantial markup above what individual sellers would charge for a similar car. Prior to purchase, be sure to have the car inspected by a dependable mechanic.

Is it possible for you to cut your clothing costs? The average family of four spends over $2500 annually on clothes. The key to cutting this amount is to use what you have. Most people have closets full of clothes, but they are unable to resist buying unnecessary additional items. When new clothes are needed, begin your shopping at discount stores and wait for sales at other stores.

Mother and sons work together to minimize back-to-school shopping expenses.

The average family of four spends about $800 per month on food. There are several ways this amount can be reduced without sacrificing nutritional quality, variety, or dining pleasure. The first step is to identify the places that provide the most economical prices for basic food items. Check out the warehouse stores and farmers' markets, as well as supermarkets in your locale. The second step is to prepare meals at home. Typically, the cost of home-prepared meals is one-fourth or less of the expense of convenience or prepared foods. If you think your time is too valuable to spend cooking, consider that many simple meals require only ten minutes of hands-on preparation. The third step is to consider planting a small garden. A garden and a chest freezer can help cut your food bill by several hundred dollars per year. For many people, gardening also serves as an enjoyable and relaxing hobby.

Have you purchased any exercise equipment? Do you use it? Millions of people have stored their exercise bikes, step machines, and treadmills in the closet or garage. Likewise, health club memberships typically go unused. Walking and biking are two good examples of cheap but effective exercise.

Americans spend small fortunes on recreational items and activities, which usually involve sitting, listening, and watching. Entertainment is generally an expensive, indolent activity. Instead of paying to sit through a movie or a sports event, you might visit a free or inexpensive attraction in your area. Go to early movies or rent the movie. Take a Frisbee to the park. Visit a historical site. Go to the lake or beach. You may want to begin a productive hobby such as painting, sewing, woodworking, writing, or baking. Recreation does not have to be passive or unproductive.

The biggest single expenditure for most people is their house. To become a one-income family, you may consider moving to a smaller house with a lower mortgage payment. Before buying a house, you should examine as many houses as possible. If you can visit 25 to 50 houses, not only will you be more likely to get a bargain, but you'll be more likely to get the ideal home with the features you want. When financing a home mortgage, you are usually better off with the shortest possible term, such as 15 years, instead of the traditional 30 years.

At home, you should minimize your utility bills. Some utility companies offer free energy audits. Air conditioning and heating bills can be reduced by ensuring that doors and windows are properly sealed. Natural gas is the most economical energy source for heat-generating devices such as stoves, ovens, and hot water heaters. You can reduce your water bill by installing specially-designed shower heads and toilets that minimize water use. These items usually pay for themselves in less than a year.

See how much a second income brings in after all its costs are deducted; then ask yourself if a second income is really necessary. Do you want to live on one income? If it is financially feasible and you are willing to make the required lifestyle changes, you can do it.

reality
CHECK   *Would you want to live on one income if you were married? Why or why not?*

Investing

LEARNING OBJECTIVE 5
Describe how to make wise investments, including an evaluation of risk and return.

Setting aside money on a monthly basis is the best way to accumulate wealth. Saving money and investing it should become a habit. When you consider any investment, remember that risk and return are a trade-off. As a rule, higher rewards are earned only by riskier investments.

Practically speaking, **investment risk** can be defined as the probability that you will lose all or part of your investment. In general, the greater the potential return on an investment, the higher the risk. How well a person predicts the future is an important factor in determining the risk involved. The further in the future a return is expected, the greater the risk involved, since it is hard to predict the future with any degree of certainty. The shorter the time horizon, the less the uncertainty involved, so the lower the risk. The more variable the rate of return, the greater the uncertainty.

Many people are risk averse, meaning that they prefer investments with low risk. How much risk can you tolerate? The greater the risk involved, the greater the potential compensation, but also the greater the chances of loss. Insured certificates of deposit (CDs) and T-bills are the least risky investments and have low levels of uncertainty. Exploratory drilling for oil and futures contracts are risky investments; they involve a great amount of uncertainty. Exhibit 15.8 shows a number of possible investments and their relative risk.

Managing Investments

Investing today to accumulate money for future needs is at the heart of financial planning. An important consideration before deciding if you should manage all or part of your investments is whether you have the time necessary to do so. Managing your own investments requires that you read and analyze daily all information that concerns your investments. Being your own investment manager requires time and a sound basis for your investment decisions.

You must decide how to divide your money among stocks, bonds, real estate, money market funds, and other investment instruments. This process is called **asset allocation.** The amount you decide to put into each type of investment has much to do with individual goals and objectives. Asset allocation can have a major impact on your total portfolio return. Asset allocation is more critical than specific stock selections. A diversified portfolio is one asset allocation strategy, and a diversified portfolio enables you to withstand market volatility with less risk.

A key consideration in developing your portfolio is your **time horizon.** Your time horizon refers to the number of years you have to achieve your financial plan. Developing your portfolio requires you to consider your time horizon, where you are now and where you want to be in the future, and your reasons for investing. These considerations are determined by your age, annual income, family make-up, future financial obligations, and need for liquidity. For example, the portfolio allocations of a newly married couple in their twenties with no children, a couple in their early forties with two teenagers soon to be entering college, and a single individual at age 55 should be substantially different because of their different time horizons and financial goals.

Equity investments should be allocated among the major sectors of the economy. These sectors include the automotive, banking, computer, energy, industrial, pharmaceutical, retail, and utility industries. If you are employed by a firm in one industry, don't be afraid of investing in competitive companies that you know are well managed. Be cautious about investing too much in your employer's stock. If the company in which you work fails, you could lose both your job and your investment.

investment risk The probability that an individual will lose all or part of an investment

EXHIBIT 15.8

Investments and Relative Risk

Highest Risk/ Highest Return

- Exploratory drilling
- Production funds
- Commodity futures
- Collectibles
- Undeveloped land
- Investment real estate
- Put and call options
- Junk bonds
- Oil and gas participation
- Precious metals
- Common stocks
- Mutual funds
- Corporate bonds
- Variable life insurance
- Variable annuities
- Municipal bonds
- Government securities
- Non-variable annuities
- Homes
- Money market funds
- Treasury bills
- Certificates of deposit
- Guaranteed life insurance
- Series EE and HH bonds
- Savings accounts
- Checking accounts
- Cash

Lowest Risk/ Lowest Return

asset allocation The process of dividing one's money among stocks, bonds, real estate, money market funds, and other investment instruments

time horizon The number of years an individual has to achieve her or his financial plan

Global Business

Buying Stock in Multinational Companies Is a Way to Diversify Your Investment Portfolio

Diversification is an important risk reduction strategy for investors. Investing in companies in different industries is one example of diversification. For example, you could invest in manufacturing, retail, technology, and service companies. Consequently, if manufacturing companies had a poor year from an investment standpoint but other industry groups had a good year, your investment portfolio might still have an overall positive return. Investing in companies located around the world is another type of diversification. You could invest in companies that have their corporate headquarters in various countries, such as Sony in Japan, McDonald's in the United States, and BMW in Germany. Of course, investing in U.S.-based companies that have global operations would still provide some level of international diversification.

Coca-Cola is a U.S.-based company with corporate headquarters in Atlanta, Georgia. Coke has operations in almost 200 countries. Thus, even if profits from Coca-Cola's U.S. operations declined, profits from Coke's non-U.S. operations might be increasing. As a result, Coke's stock price could go up, even while one geographic area of operation was not doing well.

Questions

1. Suppose you have decided to invest in three company stocks: Sony, McDonald's, and BMW. How much of $10,000 would you invest in each company? Why?
2. If you added a fourth company, Coca-Cola, how much would you invest in each of the four companies? Why?

mutual fund A pool of commingled funds contributed by many investors and managed by a professional fund advisor in exchange for a fee

Since you may lack the time or expertise to manage an investment portfolio, you may wish to consider managed investments. Managed investments include mutual funds, unit investment trusts, and real estate investment trusts. A **mutual fund** is a pool of commingled funds contributed by many investors and managed by a professional fund advisor in exchange for a fee. Mutual funds are available to meet a wide range of investment objectives, and there are about 11,000 mutual funds for investors to choose from. To meet different investor needs, mutual funds specialize in municipal bonds, money markets, growth stocks, small company stocks, gold stocks, foreign stocks, business sectors, indexes, and other specializations.

unit investment trust (UIT) A type of closed-end mutual fund that allows investors to lock in relatively high yields

A **unit investment trust (UIT)** is a type of closed-end mutual fund that allows you to lock in relatively high yields. A UIT is established when an investment company acquires various bonds and then sells units of that portfolio to the general public. UITs may consist of tax-exempt or taxable bonds. The UIT offers a method of locking in current interest rates (as with other fixed-income investments). However, the investment is subject to interest-rate risk and default risk like other fixed-rate investments. Default risk is usually low because of the diversification in the portfolio, but interest-rate risk is ever-present. Another problem with UITs is that they are not very liquid. An advantage of UITs is that they offer diversification to a small investor who may be unable to acquire enough individual bonds to be adequately diversified.

real estate investment trust (REIT) A trust that invests in real estate rather than stocks and securities

A **real estate investment trust (REIT)** invests in real estate rather than stocks and securities. Although real estate is not very liquid, a real estate investment trust allows your real estate investment to be liquid. Almost like mutual funds, many REITs are traded on one of the major stock exchanges. An REIT is generally required by tax laws to distribute 90 percent of its taxable income as dividends or lose its tax-advantage status.

Fixed-Income Investments

A **fixed-income investment** is one in which you invest an initial amount of money (principal), collect interest on that initial amount, and receive back the initial amount when the security matures. Fixed-income investments are generally low risk, as shown in Exhibit 15.8, but the return on these investments is also typically rather low. There are two chief dangers associated with fixed-income investments: interest rate risk and default risk. **Interest rate risk** is the risk that interest rates will rise, resulting in a decrease in the value of the investment. Default risk is the danger that the borrower will default either on interest or on principal payments.

> **fixed-income investment** An investment in which an individual invests an initial amount of money (principal), collects interest on that initial amount, and receives back the initial amount when the security matures

> **interest rate risk** The risk that interest rates will rise, resulting in a decrease in the value of the investment

The most popular of all fixed-income investments is U.S. Treasury obligations. Treasury securities are backed by the full faith and credit of the U.S. government and, therefore, offer the investor both maximum safety of principal and a guaranteed yield. The yield is typically less than that of a corporate bond, but Treasury securities have virtually no default risk. However, they are subject to interest rate risk.

Treasury Securities. The most popular Treasury securities for individual investors are Treasury bills, Treasury notes, and Treasury bonds. Treasury bills have maturities up to and including one year. Treasury notes mature in one to ten years, while Treasury bonds range in maturity from 10 to 30 years.

U.S. Savings Bonds. Savings bonds are another popular fixed-income investment. Savings bonds are sold at a discount from their face value. They are highly liquid investments, although if they are cashed in before maturity, there is a reduction in the rate of interest earned. Interest from Series EE bonds offers the tax advantage of being exempt from federal income tax until they are cashed in or until maturity.

Corporate Bonds. Corporate bonds are another form of fixed-income investment. Compared to government-backed securities, they carry a greater element of risk. The level of risk depends chiefly on the quality of the corporation issuing the bonds. Consequently, there is great diversity in risk level.

Municipal Bonds. Municipal bonds are issued by state and local governments and offer relatively low risk. Also, they feature significant tax advantages, since they are exempt from federal income tax.

Other Fixed-Income Investments. Other fixed-income investments are customer accounts provided by banks and savings and loan institutions. From lowest to highest level of return, the three most popular types of customer accounts are savings accounts, money market accounts, and certificates of deposit (CDs). Risk is extremely low and liquidity is high. Consequently, return is relatively low for each of these types of accounts. Insurance companies issue another kind of fixed-income investment called an annuity. An annuity is sold by an insurance company to an investor, who is guaranteed a fixed return for a certain period of time—10 years, 20 years, or the life of the investor.

Equity Investments

Equity investments are investments in corporate stocks. Stocks in companies publicly traded on exchanges such as the New York Stock Exchange and the NASDAQ are highly liquid. The *Wall Street Journal* is the best-known source of information

Case in Point

Financial Information Available to Investors on the Web Regarding Sony Corporation

Stock Market Symbol: SNE

Last Trade: $34.93

Trade Time: 4:00 PM ET

Change: +0.33

Prev Close: $34.60

Open: $35.00

1y Target Est: $37.00

Day's Range: $34.77 – 35.14

52wk Range: $31.86 – 43.67

Volume: 520,100 shares

Avg Vol (3m): 433,681 shares

Market Capitalization: $32.27 Billion

P/E Ratio: 31.13

Earnings Per Share: $1.122

Dividend & Yield: $0.2258 (0.65%)

Source: Yahoo! Finance, **http://finance.yahoo.com,** August 24, 2004.

Questions

1. What is Sony's P/E ratio?
2. How many years will it take for current earnings per share to equal the current stock price?
3. Relatively speaking, does that seem like a long time or short time?
4. What might this imply about the average investor's expectations as to whether Sony's earnings will increase or decrease in the future?

on daily stock prices, although most major newspapers also publish daily highs, daily lows, closing prices, and net change from the previous closing price for individual stocks. The *Wall Street Journal* and the *New York Times* stock market listings also provide the highest and lowest price of each stock during the past 52 weeks, the dividend amount (with corresponding yield percentage), and volume of shares traded.

A number of websites, such as Yahoo! Finance (**http://finance.yahoo.com**), provide stock quotes. Many websites that allow you to maintain a personalized page will also allow you to track a personalized portfolio of stocks on your page. For example, Yahoo! will allow quotes to be maintained for several stocks and for several indexes of your choosing on a "My Yahoo!" page, along with other personalized news and services. Stock price services such as these are usually delayed from 15 minutes to an hour and are provided by various news sources. Many sites will also allow you to review historical charts and graphs of these stocks.

Stock market investments range from very high risk to very low risk. Some stocks provide relatively high dividend yields (dividend amount divided by market price of the stock), while others provide no dividends. **Growth stocks** are those that provide low, if any, dividends, but do offer long-term capital appreciation. In other words, the price of the stock is expected to increase over time. Wal-Mart has been an example of a growth stock.

Income stocks are those that offer little opportunity for capital appreciation but provide relatively high dividends. Most utility companies, such as Philadelphia Electric or Texas Utilities, are considered income stocks. Many companies provide some dividends and are considered combination growth and income stocks. Stocks of automobile manufacturing companies, for example, provide both substantial dividends and opportunities for capital appreciation. A company's board of directors typically sets the dividend policy on the basis of the desires of the management, the stockholders, and applicable laws and regulations. Value stocks include stodgy old utilities and industrial firms such as Allstate, John Deere, Alcoa, Duke Power, Philip Morris, and Caterpillar. **Value stocks** represent companies that are

growth stocks Stocks that provide low, if any, dividends, but do offer potential long-term capital appreciation

income stocks Stocks that offer little opportunity for capital appreciation but provide relatively high dividends

value stocks Stocks of companies that are considered relatively low risk, have expected but limited growth potential, and generally pay modest dividends

considered relatively low risk, have expected but limited growth potential, and generally pay moderate dividends. About 200 value-oriented mutual funds disappeared during the Internet boom, when technology stocks were very popular. In the aftermath of the technology stock bust, value stocks regained some popularity.

Stocks continually rise and fall in price. If you are bothered by an investment that constantly fluctuates in value, then the stock market is not for you. Sometimes stock prices fall dramatically, as happened in the stock market crash of October 1987, when the market dropped 508 points, or 26 percent, in one day. In the following years, however, stock prices increased dramatically, greatly offsetting the 1987 downturn. They then plunged in late summer of 1990 as a result of the invasion of Kuwait and the sharp increase in oil prices. NASDAQ first closed over 2000 on July 16, 1998. In March 2000, NASDAQ went above 5000 when the tech bubble reached its zenith. Only one year later, the NASDAQ was down to the 1600 level. The market had a significant drop after the September 11, 2001, terrorist attack.

Over the past 65 years, common stocks have returned an average of 12 percent annually. One of the keys to successfully investing in stock is to maintain a balanced portfolio of stocks. Stocks themselves should be only one component in your total portfolio of savings and investments. Let us assume that stocks represent 50 percent of all of your savings and investments. The other 50 percent of your total portfolio may consist of Treasury securities, bank CDs, and real estate. The 50 percent invested in stock should be allocated among different types of stock, possibly three or more different types of mutual funds.

A recommended approach to acquiring a balanced portfolio is to invest in a mutual fund, especially an index fund. Instead of acquiring individual shares of stock, you may purchase shares of a mutual fund, which itself is made up of shares of many different companies. Some basic investment guidelines to follow are

> Determine your investment goals and your risk tolerance level.
> Set your target-level annual return for the next three years.
> Decide how much you can afford to invest each year.
> Keep track of your investment performance.

One final consideration in making equity investments is your purchasing strategy. A popular approach is called **dollar cost averaging.** This method seems to work well and is extremely simple. You ignore price trends and invest a fixed amount at regular intervals. Thus, some shares will be acquired at relatively high prices and some shares at low prices.

dollar cost averaging An investment approach where the investor ignores price trends and invests a fixed amount at regular intervals

The opposite of the dollar cost averaging approach is the **market timing approach.** In market timing, you attempt to purchase shares when their price is low and to sell when their price is high. Many investment firms offer market timing services. Some are much more successful than others. If you use a market timing service, be sure to investigate the past performance of the service.

market timing approach An investment strategy where the investor attempts to purchase shares when their price is low and to sell when their price is high

Your Home

Home ownership remains the great American dream. Thanks to mortgage loans, the dream has become reality for many Americans. A mortgage loan supplies the cash many people need to purchase a home. The loan is usually repaid over a long period of time, usually 15 or 30 years. **Mortgage** is defined as a claim on property, given to a person who has loaned money in case the money is not repaid when due.

mortgage A claim on property, given to a person or institution that has loaned money in case the money is not repaid when due

The term *mortgage* has historically carried an implication of servitude. It is derived from an old French word meaning "death pledge," or pledge payable on death. The term *amortize* is also derived from an old French word, which meant "to deaden." The idea of amortizing a loan over a long time period is to deaden the pain of the debt. Mortgage lenders have an important responsibility to ensure that borrowers can afford their American dream. Not only does this benefit the borrower, but it also ensures the lender a profitable repayment of the loan. Consequently, all parties to a mortgage loan benefit.

Is a home a good investment? Home prices increased at a double-digit pace during the 1970s. In later years, home prices fell in areas like Texas, Louisiana, California, and Oklahoma. In recent years, home prices have increased in some areas and decreased in others. Either way, homeowners can benefit in several ways from owning a home.

Paying off a real estate loan, a mortgage, builds equity that can sometimes be used as collateral for financing other purchases. Home mortgage interest and property tax are two of the tax breaks remaining in U.S. tax laws. Homeowners can still deduct mortgage interest and property tax from other taxable income.

In light of recent market conditions, you should consider a home as a living expense and not as an investment. Financial instruments generally make better investments than property during periods of low inflation. Financial planners recommend paying off mortgage debt as quickly as possible when the home-value appreciation rate is low. Why? The only way to build equity when the home is not appreciating is to reduce the debt on the house. Consequently, the 15-year mortgage is widely used because it builds equity about seven times faster than the traditional 30-year mortgage.

How much can you afford to pay for a home? Most lenders have general rules regarding the maximum loan amount. The National Association of Realtors uses the method shown below.

1. Calculate the borrower's gross monthly income. To do this, divide the borrower's yearly salary before any deductions by 12. If the borrower's spouse works, do the same for that salary.

In April 2004, the median house price in the United States rose to $176,000.

2. Deduct monthly payments on long-term debts (e.g., car loans) from gross monthly income.

3. Multiply that figure (gross monthly income minus long-term debt payments) by 0.32. The resulting amount is the monthly payment that the borrower can afford, according to most lending guidelines, with a down payment of 10 percent or more.

4. Determine the average real estate tax in the area. Real estate taxes on an average home can vary substantially, from several hundred to several thousand dollars annually. Add 2 to 4 percent for annual insurance premiums, which also may vary substantially. Divide the total by 12 to calculate monthly costs for taxes and insurance. The average monthly cost for taxes and insurance on a $100,000 home would be about $200.

5. Subtract the monthly cost of taxes and insurance from the monthly payment computed in step 3. The resulting figure is how much the borrower can afford to pay for a mortgage each month.

Let's consider the case of Lawrence and Doris McDonald, who have a combined gross income of $48,000 per year, a monthly car payment of $280, and savings of $20,000. The McDonalds' gross monthly income is $4000; subtracting the

$280 car payment leaves $3720. Multiplying that by 0.32 reveals that the family can afford $1190.40 in monthly payments. After subtracting estimated taxes and insurance costs of $200, a total of $990.40 is left for a mortgage principal and interest payment.

Assume that the McDonalds plan to obtain a 30-year, 10-percent, fixed-rate mortgage. A 30-year, 10-percent, fixed-rate mortgage on $110,000 yields mortgage principal and interest payments of $972.39. That amount is just under the maximum the McDonalds can pay, $990.40, which was previously calculated.

Closing costs average about 4 percent of the mortgage amount on a new mortgage with 2 points. Points are finance charges that are calculated by the lender at closing. Each point equals 1 percent of the loan amount. For example, 2 points on a $110,000 loan equals $2200. Typically, points paid are inversely related to the interest rate charged on the loan. Consequently, the McDonalds must set aside $4400 of their $20,000 savings, leaving $15,600 for a down payment. They can thus afford to purchase a $125,000 house, putting $15,000 down (a little more than 12 percent), and have enough income to qualify for a mortgage on the remaining $110,000 cost of the house. A number of realty, bank, and title company Web pages offer mortgage calculators to give you a quick idea of what monthly payments may be on a certain home given the down payment and total cost of the house. Keep in mind that these calculators are helpful, but will not consider all of the costs that come with home ownership, and may not reflect the interest rate that you will actually obtain from your lender.

There are other considerations in purchasing a home. Property insurance will need to be obtained, and the difference in homeowner's insurance and renter's insurance may be substantial. If a down payment is made that is less than 20 percent of the price of the home, mortgage insurance will also have to be purchased. There are also regular maintenance costs, and depending on the size of your new home, utility costs may increase. Homeowner's association fees and property taxes should also be considered when determining the cost of purchasing a home.

reality CHECK *Have you made any investments? Do you prefer high-risk or low-risk investments?*

Retirement and Estate Planning

LEARNING OBJECTIVE 6
List retirement and estate planning considerations.

The earlier you start to plan for retirement, the better you can solidify your financial position. You'll need a solid nest egg of retirement investments to allow you to grow old gracefully. When many people reach retirement age, they are financially unprepared; yet they may live 20 to 30 percent of their entire life span after retirement.

Most people assume that they will need about 80 percent of their preretirement income to live comfortably in their later years. In your retirement years, some of your expenses, such as taxes, will fall; other expenses, such as medical expenses, will increase.

Social Security

The average American works at least 40 hours a week, and every two weeks or once a month gets paid for the work she or he has done. Your gross pay is reduced by a number of deductions such as federal income tax withholdings, social security, health insurance premiums, and contributions to your retirement plan. When you look at your paycheck, you are concerned primarily with the bottom line, what's called net pay or take-home pay—what's left over after all deductions.

Social security is one of the most significant deductions from your gross pay. Since social security tax is a major deduction, you should know how it is computed and what benefits it provides. Virtually every working individual has social security tax withheld from his or her paycheck. The social security tax was established to fund a government program that provides for the economic security and social welfare of the U.S. worker and his or her family.

The social security tax is also known as the Federal Income Contribution Act (FICA) tax. The FICA tax rate in 2004 was 15.3 percent, of which the Medicare portion was 2.9 percent; thus, the social security portion was 12.4 percent. This tax amount is divided equally between the employee and the employer. The employee has 6.2 percent of gross earnings withheld from his or her pay for social security. The company or employer is responsible for paying the remaining 6.2 percent. The social security tax is applied to every dollar earned up to a maximum amount called the base amount. In 2002, this base amount was $84,900. The Medicare portion of 2.9 percent is applied to all earnings (i.e., no maximum amount); one-half of this amount is paid by the employer and one-half by the employee. Benefits that a worker may expect to receive after paying the employee's portion of the FICA tax during working years fall into four categories:

> Old age or disability benefits paid to the individual worker
> Benefits paid to the dependents of a retired or disabled worker
> Benefits paid to surviving family members of a deceased worker
> Lump-sum death payments

social security A government program that provides for the economic security and social welfare of the U.S. worker and his or her family

IRAs and 401(k) Plans

For most retired persons, social security benefits are insufficient to cover all living expenses. You should set aside additional funds, such as individual retirement accounts like IRAs and employer-sponsored plans like 401(k)s. Individual retirement accounts may be set up at a bank or other financial institution, including Web firms such as E*Trade. Depending on your earnings situation, contributions to a regular IRA account may be tax deductible. Employer-sponsored 401(k) plans typically include an employee deduction and an employer-matching component. For example, a 401(k) plan may include a 6 percent deduction from the employee, which is matched by a 3 percent contribution from the employer. The money in the 401(k) plan is usually tax-deferred until retirement.

A Will

No one should be without a will. The will is a key vehicle of transfer at death, and its preparation is often the first step taken by people in planning the disposition of their estates. A will is a set of written instructions prepared under legal rules that direct how a person's property will be disposed of at death. Everybody needs a properly executed will, and a copy of the will should be kept outside the safe deposit box. If the only copy is inside the box, it may be impossible for the heirs or executors to get at it without a lot of time-consuming legal rigmarole.

 When will you start planning for retirement?

Tax Planning

LEARNING OBJECTIVE 7
Identify the goals of tax planning.

Benjamin Franklin said that two things are certain: death and taxes. Nearly everyone faces the income tax, whether as an individual concerned with this major deduction from pay or as a businessperson concerned with this significant expense to the firm. You should pay what is legally due but not a dollar more, and it is likely that your payment can be reduced if you plan and organize. Planning purposefully and keeping thorough records helps you in nontax ways also.

Most Americans must file a tax return each year and must maintain accounting records to supply data for the tax return. Accounting records include the taxpayer's customary financial records, as well as specialized records and data as may be necessary to support entries on a tax return. The law does not specify the type of records a taxpayer should maintain, so they need not be elaborate or formal. A simple system should facilitate prompt entries as income is received and as payments for deductible expenses are made.

Failure to maintain adequate records may increase your tax liability and may result in penalties. The Tax Court sustained a negligence penalty against a taxpayer who claimed certain business deductions but did not have the necessary documents to back them up. The taxpayer had maintained only a partial log for business expenses, and the court decided that some of the claimed expenses were questionable.

Keep copies of completed tax returns in a safe place. Taking time to accumulate, record, summarize, and retain the appropriate tax information can help reduce your taxes and increase your personal wealth. There are many home finance software packages that will interface with tax preparation software. This is a good way for some people to track expenses, keep a budget, and maintain tax information.

On a final note, keep in mind that tax laws change. Whenever this occurs, review the changes to see how they affect your current situation and your plans for the future.

reality CHECK *Why should you do tax planning?*

Ethics of Financial Planning

LEARNING OBJECTIVE 8
State the ethical issues associated with personal financial planning.

Whatever the source of ethical values, whether from religious principle, history and literature, or personal observation, there are some basic ethical guidelines that are essential to civilized society. No nation survives for long without citizens who share common values such as courage, devotion to duty, respect for other people's lives and property, respect for the law, and a willingness to sacrifice personal interests for a greater cause. When considering both personal and social responsibilities, the following are five ethical uses for money: giving, repaying debts, paying taxes, providing for one's family, and planning for future needs. These activities require wise money management and financial planning. In practicing these uses of money, one should feel that his or her actions are carrying out ethical duties and not merely pursuing self-interest.

Giving

Americans are among the most generous people in the world, and Internal Revenue Service statistics reveal that low-income Americans give as much to charity as those in high-income brackets. The recipients include churches, schools, and other not-for-profit organizations that provide valuable services to the society at large. By including planned giving in your budget, you are able to help others on a regular basis and enjoy the personal satisfaction of knowing you can live on less than you earn. Moreover, research has shown that people who focus on the needs of others are happier than those who think only of themselves.

Repaying Debts

In general, debt should be avoided, but it is sometimes necessary to finance the purchase of a major item such as a home or a car. If people could not be trusted to repay their debts, then there would be no credit available and the whole economy would be drastically affected. Repaying your debts helps ensure that credit is available to others and allows society as a whole to enjoy a higher standard of living. Repaying debts enhances your credit rating and ensures that credit will be available if needed in the future.

Paying Taxes

Western tradition holds that citizens should support legitimate governments and bear a portion of the overall social responsibility. Without tax revenues, governments could not function, and programs such as national defense, aid to the poor, maintenance of the transportation system, public education, and repayment of the public debt would all come to a halt. Society benefits from all these government activities, and you benefit from meeting your social responsibilities and fulfilling your ethical duties. On the other hand, failure to pay the proper amount of taxes may result in penalties and interest charges, and tax evasion is a criminal offense.

An adult volunteer plays a game with students in a Head Start class in Hopkinsville, Kentucky.

Providing for Your Family

Well-considered financial planning enables a family to identify appropriate financial objectives and to facilitate their accomplishment. If people fail to provide for their families, society as a whole suffers, both from the burden of supporting more people and from the effects of such examples of financial irresponsibility. Many social problems, such as the high proportion of women and children living in poverty, child abuse, teenage gang activity, and crime in general, have grown out of the failure of individuals to provide for their own families.

Planning for Future Needs

Setting money aside for a rainy day and investing wisely are considered morally worthy actions. Saving should be an element of everyone's budget. Long-term financial planning includes setting aside funds on a regular basis to provide for future needs such as retirement or children's college expenses. Savings are also necessary to meet unexpected financial demands such as home or car repairs.

Managing money wisely is personally rewarding. Good money management enables you to meet your family's financial needs as well as to help others. You will enhance your children's lives, not merely by giving them things but by teaching them through example how to handle money. Virtually everyone knows that money does not bring lasting happiness. Attaining wealth for no reason but to be rich would be utter folly, but managing money to achieve appropriate goals and objectives is true wisdom.

Keep Money in Perspective

Who has not heard the old adage, money can't buy everything? Most people agree that relationships to other people are more important than money. On the other hand, how many people occasionally place their jobs ahead of their spouses, children, relatives, and friends? Where you spend your time is the true indicator of what you value most. Workaholics often lose track of their priorities. Anyone who sacrifices important personal relationships for career or monetary advancement has made a tragic error in judgment.

Near the end of life, has anyone ever looked back and said, "I wish I had spent two more hours each day at work"? Certainly not! Regrets usually involve the lack of time spent with aging parents, children, and spouses. Remember that money is merely a means to an end, not an end in itself. Money is required for the acquisition of food, clothing, shelter, and other necessary items. If you have a lot of money, then you can purchase nonessential items, such as caviar for food, mink coats for clothing, and large mansions for housing. However, no matter how rich you are, you will never have more than 24 hours a day to live. Everyone is equally poor or rich in that regard. How you spend your time is ultimately connected to how truly successful you are. Managing your money wisely will enable you to spend your time in a more useful manner, such as with family and friends.

Don't waste your time or your money! A primary advantage of good financial planning is that the money you make will be used more efficiently. And if your money is used more efficiently, then you can work fewer hours to achieve the same quality of life than if your money is not used efficiently. Set realistic financial goals that can be achieved without sacrificing important personal relationships.

For a married person, financial planning must be a team effort with his or her spouse. Building a good marriage requires spending time with your spouse, and part of that time should focus on financial planning. Spending time together is essential for a couple to remain close; good financial planning will enable you to spend more time together as a married couple without worrying about finances. A major cause of marital problems is disagreement over money; not necessarily the lack of it, but how it is spent. If you are married, spend time with your spouse discussing financial goals and objectives.

Personal financial planning revolves around your entire family. You must teach your children about money and consult older children when making financial decisions that have an impact on them, such as how much you can afford to contribute toward their college expenses.

reality CHECK   *What do you want to do with the money you make?*

Careers in Personal Financial Planning

Accounting professionals are frequently involved in providing financial planning services to business firms and individuals. The American Institute of CPAs has established a credential for CPAs who specialize in personal financial planning (PFP). The Personal Financial Specialist (PFS) credential only is granted to CPAs with significant PFP experience who want to demonstrate their knowledge, skill, and experience by earning this exclusive credential.

CPAs should obtain the PFS credential if they are involved in PFP services for the following reasons. First, the PFS credential enhances the CPA's image as a competent and trustworthy financial advisor. Second, the PFS credential engenders a greater level of confidence from current and potential clients. Third, the PFS credential shows commitment to continuously improving PFP skills and expertise, resulting in increased professional competency. Fourth, the PFS credential makes the CPA a member of a community of CPA financial planners with related interests and practices. Last, the PFS credential meets the minimum competency requirement in almost all states for becoming a Registered Investment Advisor.

Summary

LEARNING OBJECTIVE 1
Explain the purpose of personal financial planning.

Personal financial planning enables you to meet current and future financial needs by a combination of effective planning and implementation of those plans. Americans spend much of their lives earning money, but they rarely spend any time planning how to use their accumulated wealth. Developing financial planning skills and good spending habits at an early age will pay huge dividends in later years.

LEARNING OBJECTIVE 2
Define concepts such as net worth.

Personal financial planning requires some fundamental knowledge. Key concepts include how to compute net

worth, how to set financial objectives, how to evaluate spending patterns, how to identify your stage in life, and from whom to seek expert advice.

LEARNING OBJECTIVE 3
Describe the budgeting process.

Managing income requires planning and controlling the use of your financial resources so that you can meet current and future financial needs. Managing income includes budgeting, checkbook management, use of financial planning software, locating information on the Web, and acquiring appropriate insurance.

LEARNING OBJECTIVE 4
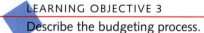
Explain the key considerations in deciding to live on one income.

Can two live as cheaply as one? No, but most families that want to live on one wage earner's income can probably do so. Many people erroneously believe that two incomes are essential to afford the basic needs of a modern family. The fact is that the financial benefits of a second income are often exaggerated.

LEARNING OBJECTIVE 5
Describe how to make wise investments, including an evaluation of risk and return.

Setting aside money on a monthly basis is the best way to accumulate wealth. Saving money and investing it should become a habit. When you consider any investment, remember that risk and return are a trade-off. As a rule, higher rewards are earned only by riskier investments.

LEARNING OBJECTIVE 6
List retirement and estate planning considerations.

The earlier you start to plan for retirement, the better you can solidify your financial position. You'll need a solid nest egg of retirement investments to allow you to grow old gracefully. When many people reach retirement age, they are financially unprepared; yet they may live 20 to 30 percent of their entire life span after retirement.

LEARNING OBJECTIVE 7
Identify the goals of tax planning.

Most Americans must file a tax return each year and must maintain accounting records to supply data for the tax return. Accounting records include the taxpayer's customary financial records, as well as specialized records and data as may be necessary to support entries on a tax return.

LEARNING OBJECTIVE 8
State the ethical issues associated with personal financial planning.

Virtually everyone knows that money does not bring lasting happiness. Attaining wealth for no reason but to be rich would be utter folly, but managing money to achieve appropriate goals and objectives is true wisdom.

Chapter Questions

1. What is the purpose of personal financial planning?
2. Describe the components of a personal balance sheet and how to calculate net worth.
3. Define liquidity.
4. Describe the five stages in life and how they affect your financial needs.
5. Prepare your cash flow budget (use the worksheet provided in Exhibit 15.4). Do you have a net cash inflow or net cash outflow?
6. What is an envelope budget?
7. How can computer software help you gain control of your finances?
8. Describe some of the Web resources that can assist you with financial planning.
9. What are some basic types of insurance?
10. Define investment risk.
11. What is asset allocation? Why is diversification important?
12. Describe the two purchasing strategies for making equity investments: dollar cost averaging and market timing. Which method do you recommend and why?
13. Why should you have a will?
14. What are the five ethical uses of money?
15. Use the information about Jacob Lawrence's checkbook below and prepare a bank reconciliation for him.

Date	Check No.	Item	Check	Deposit	Balance
9/1					$ 525
4	622	Abe's Country Grocery	$ 19		506
9		Dividends received		$ 116	622
13	623	Dependable Tire Co.	43		579
14	624	ExxonMobil Oil Co.	58		521
18	625	Cash	50		471
26	626	Grace Bible Church	25		446
28	627	Bent Tree Apartments	275		171
30		Paycheck		1800	1971

(continued)

Jacob's September bank statement shows the following:

	Amount	
Balance		$525
Add: Deposits		116
Deduct checks:		
Number 622	$19	
Number 623	43	
Number 624	68*	
Number 625	50	(180)
Other charges:		
Printed checks	$ 8	
Service charge	12	(20)
Balance		$441

*This is the correct amount for check number 624.

Interpreting Business News

1. News articles have indicated that in the long term, the stock market has provided better returns to investors than fixed-rate investments such as CDs and U.S. Treasury securities. If this is true, why would a person not invest in the stock market?
2. News articles have identified some companies as environmentally friendly. Would you recommend investing in those companies? Why or why not?
3. Some news reporters are predicting that Asia, particularly China, will be the place where most economic growth will occur in the future. If this is true, would it be wise to invest in the stocks of China-based corporations? Why or why not?

Web Assignments

1. Use a Web search tool like Yahoo.com and find information on personal financial planning software. Prepare a one-page report. Describe some of their features. Use at least two Web sources. Cite your sources, including their Web addresses, in your report.
2. Pick five major corporations. Search the Web for information about each firm's stock. How would you categorize the stock in terms of growth, income, or value? If you had to pick one in which to invest, which would you pick and why?
3. Search the Web for information about work–life balance. How does this relate to keeping money in perspective?

Portfolio Projects

Exploring Your Own Case in Point

In this chapter we present the purpose of personal financial planning. Financial planning involves gathering all your financial and personal data, analyzing that data, and creating a financial plan for the future. Answering the questions below will relate your personal financial planning to your selected company.

1. Locate your company's financial reports. The net worth of a company is the stockholders' equity, which is calculated by subtracting total liabilities (debts) from total assets (resources). What is your company's net worth? You can calculate your personal net worth by subtracting your total liabilities from your total assets. What is your net worth?
2. Examine the financial performance of your company. Do you think your company would be a good short-term investment? Long-term investment?
3. Assume that you just inherited $100,000. How much would you invest in your selected company? Why?

Starting Your Own Business

After reading this chapter, you should realize that if you start your own company, personal financial planning is even more important than if you work for someone else.

1. What is your current net worth? What are your personal financial goals? How would starting your own company affect your net worth? Would having your own company help you achieve your personal financial goals?
2. How would having your own company affect your retirement and estate planning? Would you feel more secure or less secure?
3. What are some things you want to do with the money you make? Do you think you will make more or less money by starting your own company? Do you see possible advantages to having your own company, even if you make less money?

Test Prepper

You've read the chapter, studied the key terms, and the exam is any day now. Think you are ready to ace it? Take this sample test to gauge your comprehension of chapter material. You can check your answers at the back of the book.

True/False Questions

Please indicate if the following statements are true or false:

_____ 1. Net worth is the difference between your assets and your liabilities.

_____ 2. The purpose of personal financial planning is to meet current and future financial needs through a combination of effective planning and implementation of those plans.

_____ 3. Liabilities are items that represent a past outlay of cash.

_____ 4. To stay motivated and to keep your financial plans on track, you should probably not establish clear goals.

_____ 5. Financial planning advice can be obtained from several different experts, such as stockbrokers, insurance agents, lawyers, bankers, and accountants.

_____ 6. Having a checking account is not essential for managing personal finances.

_____ 7. The goal of the bank reconciliation is to find the "true" cash balance in your checking account and to enable you to discover any errors made either by you or by the bank.

_____ 8. As a rule, higher rewards are earned only by riskier investments.

_____ 9. Failure to maintain adequate records may increase your tax liability and result in penalties.

_____ 10. Repaying debts enhances your credit rating and ensures that credit will be available if needed in the future.

Multiple-Choice Questions

Choose the best answer.

_____ 1. _____ refers to how easily an asset can be converted into cash.
   a. Neutrality
   b. Convertibility
   c. Liquidity
   d. Equalization
   e. Diversification

_____ 2. In general, college-educated people _____ than less-educated people.
   a. earn more and spend less
   b. earn about the same but spend more
   c. earn less and spend more
   d. earn more and spend more
   e. earn less and spend less

_____ 3. According to the AICPA, the last stage in an average person's life is
   a. employment.
   b. marriage.
   c. empty nest.
   d. retirement.
   e. death.

_____ 4. _____ is the term used to describe the flow of money into and out of your accounts, that is, cash inflows and outflows.
   a. Financial derivatives
   b. Cash flow
   c. Warp flow
   d. Liquid flow
   e. Asset flow

_____ 5. _____ life insurance provides no-frills insurance protection and does not include a savings element. This type of insurance is relatively inexpensive when you are young, but premiums increase with age.
   a. Term
   b. Whole
   c. Disability
   d. Variable
   e. Permanent

_____ 6. All of the following are disadvantages of a two-income family *except*
   a. day-care concerns.
   b. hectic schedules.
   c. fast-food diets.
   d. higher income.
   e. paid housekeepers.

_____ 7. _____ can be defined as the probability that you will lose all or part of your investment.
   a. Hedging risk
   b. Bad luck
   c. Investment risk

d. Interest rate risk
e. Default risk

_____ 8. A _____ portfolio is one asset allocation strategy, and will enable you to withstand market volatility with less risk.

a. diversified
b. liquid
c. venerable
d. utility
e. value

_____ 9. The _____ tax was established to fund a government program that provides for the economic security and social welfare of the U.S. worker and his or her family.

a. income
b. property
c. social security
d. welfare
e. IRA

_____ 10. All of the following can be considered ethical uses for money *except*

a. providing for one's family.
b. repaying debts.
c. charitable giving.
d. evading taxes.
e. planning for future needs.

Want more questions? Visit the student website at **http://college.hmco.com/business/student/** (select Gaspar, *Introduction to Business*) and take the ACE quizzes for more practice.

Managing Business Operations, Management Information Systems, and the Digital Enterprise

CHAPTER 16
Managing Business Operations

CHAPTER 17
Management Information Systems

CHAPTER 18
The Digital Enterprise

PART SIX

Part Six comprises three independent but interrelated chapters. In the first two chapters, two business functions are presented, operations management and management information systems. In the third chapter, the impact of information technology on businesses is explored.

Chapter 16, "Managing Business Operations," deals with questions such as, What will demand be? How can products and services be improved? How much capacity will be needed? How can productivity be improved? How is quality defined? What is a satisfactory location for a facility? How much inventory should the business have?

Chapter 17, "Management Information Systems," deals with questions such as, What is the difference between data and information? What are the roles that computer hardware and software, databases, and telecommunications networks play in making management information systems a crucial business function? How do information systems support managers—operational, middle, and senior— and other business functions—marketing, operations, accounting, finance, and human resources? How are information systems developed? How are management information systems created to support global business efforts? How are security, accuracy, and reliability maintained in management information systems?

Chapter 18, "The Digital Enterprise," deals with questions such as, What is the information technology infrastructure that is making possible the creation of digital enterprises? What are the roles that enterprise resource planning systems, supply chain management, and e-businesses play in the emergence of digital enterprises?

16

Managing Business Operations

| Introduction

| **What Is Operations Management?**

Goods and Services

Operations Management and Competitiveness

Historical Development of Operations Management

| **What Do Operations Managers Do?**

| **Design Decisions**

Product

Process

Capacity

Location

Layout

| **Planning Decisions**

Production Rate

Material Requirements

Purchasing

Inventory

| **Control Decisions**

Scheduling

Quality

| **Careers in Operations Management**

Learning Objectives

After studying this chapter, you should be able to

1. Explain what operations management is.

2. Compare manufacturing operations and service operations.

3. Evaluate the impact of operations management on the competitiveness of a business organization.

4. Describe the historical development of operations management.

5. Discuss what operations managers do.

6. Identify the design decisions about product, process, capacity, location, and layout.

7. Illustrate the planning decisions about production rate, material requirements, purchasing, and inventory.

8. Outline the control decisions about scheduling and quality.

Operations Management Is a Powerful Competitive Weapon

Toyota Motor Corporation, one of the most successful companies in the world, is scrambling to overhaul itself. After nearly doubling its revenue in the past decade and redefining competition in key parts of the auto industry, Toyota suddenly finds itself confronting mushrooming quality problems. At the same time, Toyota has launched a worldwide campaign to simplify its production systems.

Toyota's next big goal is to expand its share of the global market from 10 percent now to 15 percent over the next decade. That would make Toyota roughly the same size as the current number-one automaker, General Motors. But there are signs that the company's ambitious growth agenda is straining human and technical resources and undercutting one of Toyota's most critical strategic advantages: operations management in general and quality in particular. The marriage of efficient production to an obsessive concern for quality has helped Toyota establish a reputation for bullet-proof reliability that remains a huge competitive advantage.

Source: *The Wall Street Journal*, August 4, 2004, pp. A1 and A2.

Introduction

In this chapter we take a look at *operations*, the business function responsible for the production of goods and services. We first define *operations management*, list the similarities and differences between producing goods and producing services, motivate the competitive impact of good operations management (as in the case of Toyota Motor Corporation), and provide the historical evolution of operations management. Then, we explore the decisions that operations managers make in regard to designing, planning, and controlling production operations. Next we describe in detail the nature and challenges of these decisions. We close the chapter with an overview of jobs in operations management.

What Is Operations Management?

LEARNING OBJECTIVE 1
Explain what operations management is.

Production is the creation of goods or services. Examples of goods are automobiles, televisions, and computers. Examples of services are health care, entertainment, and consulting. For convenience and when appropriate, in this chapter we will use the word *product* to encompass goods or services. A **production system** is the system that businesses use to produce products. When the company produces mostly goods, the production system is typically called a *manufacturing system*. When the company produces mostly services, the production system is commonly called a *service system*. For example, the production system of DaimlerChrysler would be called a manufacturing system, and the production system of the M.D. Anderson Cancer Center, a service system.

production The creation of goods or services

production system The system that businesses use to produce products

A production system can be modeled as a system that takes inputs and creates outputs via a transformation process. Exhibit 16.1 illustrates this model.

In this model, the *inputs* include materials, land, labor, machines and equipment, energy, and information. The *outputs* represent the desired goods or services. And the *transformation process* may consist of one or more of the following transformations:

- Physical, as in manufacturing
- Locational, as in transportation
- Informational, as in consulting
- Psychological, as in entertainment
- Physiological, as in health care
- Exchange, as in retailing
- Storage, as in warehousing

At DaimlerChrysler, for example, the transformation process is physical, and the outputs are automobiles; at McDonald's, the transformation process is physical and exchange, and the outputs are the items in their menu; and at M.D. Anderson Cancer Center, the transformation process is physiological, and the outputs are healthy patients. Some of the inputs for DaimlerChrysler are steel, glass, plastics, production facilities, engineers, and workers. Some of the inputs for McDonald's are meat, bread, vegetables, spices, buildings, cooking equipment, and personnel. Some of the inputs for the M.D. Anderson Cancer Center are medical supplies and drugs, hospitals, doctors, nurses, staff, medical equipment, and laboratories. In all three cases, additional inputs are energy and information—car designs for DaimlerChrysler, recipes for McDonald's, and medical protocols for the M.D. Anderson Cancer Center.

operations management The management of the direct resources that are involved in the production system of a business organization

Operations management is the management of the direct resources that are involved in the production system of a business organization. Until recently, operations management was mostly applied in manufacturing firms and was called *manufacturing management* or *production management*. To include applications in service industries, the name was changed to *production and operations management* or just *operations management*. Following current practice, we will use the term *operations management* to include the management of both manufacturing systems and service systems.

Businesses exist because their products add value to society. In other words, for a company to succeed, the price of its outputs has to exceed the cost of its inputs. This difference between prices and costs represents the value added by the firm. And given that operations management deals with managing the direct resources in the production system, this business function is naturally positioned to help companies maximize the value they add to their products.

 Can you think of a company where operations management is the most important function? When you go to your favorite restaurant, where do you see operations management in action?

EXHIBIT 16.1

A Production System Model

Goods and Services

LEARNING OBJECTIVE 2
Compare manufacturing operations and service operations.

Most business organizations produce and sell products that involve a combination of goods and services. In some combinations, the value of the goods dominates the value of the services, for example, buying a computer with a warranty. In some other combinations, the value of the services dominates the value of the goods, for example, buying a tailor-made suit. Exhibit 16.2 presents more examples of several goods and services combinations.

Hence, you should keep in mind that sometimes organizations that are called service organizations may also provide goods, and organizations that are called manufacturing organizations may also provide services.

Regardless of the specific combination of goods and services that a company produces, it is important to keep in mind that from an operations management perspective, there are several characteristics that differentiate goods from services. Although some of the differentiating characteristics are obvious, others are not.

Customer Contact. In the case of goods, there is no contact required between the customer and the good being produced. In the case of services, there is typically some contact required between the customer and the service being provided. For example, compare buying a gallon of milk at a supermarket with getting a haircut at a barbershop. In fact, the degree and type of contact between the customer and the service can be classified as follows:

Constant physical contact, as in getting a haircut
Constant communication, as in getting help from 911
Sporadic physical contact, as in medical services
Sporadic communication, as in legal services

Customer Participation. In the case of goods, the customer does not participate in the production of goods. In the case of services, frequently the customer participates in the delivery of the services. For example, compare buying a computer at a local store with buying groceries at a supermarket. The degree of customer participation in services can be low, as in taking a cruise, or high, as in attending college.

Inventory. Manufacturers may produce goods in anticipation of demand, hence creating inventory to be sold in the future. For example, a toy manufacturer

EXHIBIT 16.2

Examples of Goods and Services Combinations

Business	Percentage Goods	Percentage Services
Supermarket	95	5
Car manufacturer	90	10
Fast-food restaurant	50	50
Hotel	10	90
Consulting	5	95

may produce and inventory toys from January to October, when demand is low, with the expectation of selling them in the high-demand holiday season. Service organizations, on the other hand, cannot inventory services. For example, empty rooms in a hotel when demand is low cannot be inventoried for when demand is high. If a shoe manufacturer cannot sell a pair of shoes in a given week, the shoes can be kept and sold the next week. If a commercial airline cannot sell an available seat on a particular flight, the seat cannot be stored and sold later. Once the plane leaves, the use of the seat on that particular flight is lost forever.

Tangibility.   Goods are physical objects that can be touched; services are intangible. As a consequence, managing operations in service systems is more complex than in manufacturing systems. In particular, it is more difficult to measure productivity and quality in services than in goods. For example, a manufacturer of soft drinks will have an easier time measuring the productivity of a production line, say, in cans per hour, than a clinic measuring the productivity of a doctor, say, in patients per hour. While each can of soft drink produced is identical to each other, each patient is obviously different from each other. At the same time, the same manufacturer could easily establish methods for measuring quality in the soft drinks produced, but it would be inherently more difficult to measure the quality of health care provided by the doctor.

 When you rent a movie, how much of what you are getting is goods and how much is services? When you buy clothes from a store, how much of what you are getting is goods and how much is services?

Operations Management and Competitiveness

LEARNING OBJECTIVE 3
Evaluate the impact of operations management on the competitiveness of a business organization.

In free market economies, all businesses face competitors in both the domestic and international arenas. And as research has shown, good operations management should play a pivotal role in helping a company stay ahead of its competitors.[1] Businesses compete mostly along three dimensions: *price*, *quality*, and *time*.

Price.   Since price and demand are intimately related, and for a company to be profitable the price of a product has to exceed its production cost, good operations management should lead to production costs that allow the firm to set competitive prices and hence attract customer demand.

Quality.   Because products are created by the production system, good operations management should lead to quality products that conform to the specifications that customers require.

Time.   Competition among businesses has evolved from price only, to price and quality, to price, quality, and time. After lowering prices and improving quality as much as possible, businesses have found that time is an increasingly crucial dimension by which they can differentiate themselves from their competitors. Time-based competition encompasses getting new products to market quicker, as well as delivering existing products faster and with greater reliability. Good operations management should lead to a production system that quickly accommodates new products and, at the same time, can produce existing products in competitive lead times.

Sometimes the competitive dimensions price or cost, quality, and time are complementary, and sometimes they lead to trade-offs. When they are complementary, we may find that a company, by improving its quality—say, reducing the number of defective products from 10 to 5 percent—also improves its production cost, as defective products lead to waste, and its production time, as defective products need to be reworked and hence increase the lead time. When they lead to trade-offs, we may find a company where improving one dimension yields negative consequences in another dimension. For example, improving quality may lead to a higher cost, or decreasing time may lead to a higher cost and lower quality. Whether the competitive dimensions are complementary or lead to trade-offs is dependent on the situation of each firm and it is the subject of more advanced material.

reality CHECK *In what way is operations management helping FedEx be a competitive company? In what way is operations management helping Coca-Cola be a competitive firm?*

Historical Development of Operations Management

LEARNING OBJECTIVE 4
Describe the historical development of operations management.

Production systems are as old as mankind. The Great Wall of China, the Egyptian pyramids, the Greek Parthenon, and the aqueducts and roads of the Roman Empire are all proof of human ingenuity organized for production. However, the way ancient people produced products was quite different from the modern factory system. Production was done by highly skilled workers using simple, flexible tools. These workers spent many years in apprenticeship programs, learning all the intricacies of producing goods or providing services. Items were produced in small quantities and according to customer specifications. Even so, no two products were the same. This type of production system is called **craft production** because of the craftsmanship involved, or the **cottage system** because products were produced in homes or cottages. Craft production had major shortcomings. Because products were produced by skilled workers who custom-fitted parts, production was slow and expensive. And when one of the parts failed, the replacement for that part had to be custom-made. Another disadvantage was that production costs did not decrease with volume—there were no *economies of scale*—and hence there was no incentive for companies to expand their operations.

craft production or **cottage system** Production done by highly skilled workers using simple, flexible tools, where items were produced in small quantities and according to customer specifications

The Industrial Revolution that started in England in the 1700s forever changed the cottage approach to production. In 1764, James Watt invented the steam engine, which substituted machine power for human power. The 1776 publication of Adam Smith's *The Wealth of Nations* promoted the **division of labor,** in which an operation, such as assembling an automobile, is divided up into a series of many small tasks, and workers assigned to one task. Unlike craft production, where each worker was responsible for doing many tasks and thus required skill, with the division of labor the tasks were so narrow that virtually no skill was required. Consequently, the factories of the late 1700s had available machines and a way of planning and controlling the work of production workers.

division of labor The idea of dividing production operations into a series of many small tasks, where workers are assigned to perform one of these tasks

The Industrial Revolution spread from England to the rest of Europe and eventually to the United States. In 1800, American inventor Eli Whitney introduced the concept of *interchangeable parts* to President Thomas Jefferson with a demonstration in which he selected musket parts at random, assembled them, and then fired the musket. The approach prevalent at that time was to handcraft every musket with its customized parts. By the middle 1800s, the old cottage system of producing products had been replaced by the factory system, but vast improvements to factories were yet to come.

The *scientific management movement* brought widespread changes to the management of factories. The movement was led by an efficiency engineer and inventor, Frederick Taylor, who is referred to as the father of scientific management. Taylor believed in a science of management based on the analysis and improvement of work methods and on economic incentives. He studied work methods in great detail to identify the best method for performing each job. Taylor believed that scientific laws govern the maximum daily output of a worker, that it is management's job to discover and use these laws for planning the operation of a production system, and that it is the worker's job to execute management's plan without any worker input. Besides Taylor, there were other pioneers that contributed to the scientific management era. Frank Gilbreth developed motion studies, Lillian Gilbreth (Frank's wife) performed fatigue studies, and Henry Gantt created a scheduling chart called the *Gantt chart*. Of special interest, Taylor, a devout Quaker, requested "cussing lessons" from an earthy foreman to help him communicate with workers; Frank Gilbreth defeated younger champion bricklayers in bricklaying contests by using his own principles of motion economy; and Gantt won a presidential citation for his application of the Gantt chart to shipbuilding during World War I.[2]

In 1913, Henry Ford designed his Model T Ford to be produced on an *assembly line,* where men stood still while the car moved. The assembly line concept combined two key elements: interchangeable parts and division of labor. Before the assembly line was introduced in August of 1913, each auto chassis was assembled by one worker in about 12.5 hours. After the assembly line was in its final form, with each worker performing a small unit of work and the chassis being moved mechanically, the average labor time per chassis was reduced to 93 minutes. It has been said that all Models T were painted black because black paint dried the fastest. Besides achieving great success with his assembly line, Ford popularized assembly lines as

Assembly line in 1932 at the Ford Motor Company plant in Dearborn, Michigan.

an efficient way to produce large volumes of products at low cost. This popularity later extended to other industries in the United States and the rest of the world.

Between World War I and World War II, the *human relations movement* emerged, emphasizing the importance of the human element in job design. Notable in this movement was the work from 1927 to 1932 of Elton Mayo at the Hawthorne, Illinois, plant of the Western Electric Company. His studies, known as the *Hawthorne studies,* revealed that in addition to the physical and technical aspects of work, worker motivation is a critical factor for improving productivity. These types of results led to the creation in business organizations of personnel management and human resources departments.

The lessons learned with the logistics and operational problems in World War II, such as deploying enormous quantities of manpower, supplies, planes, ships, and other resources in an extremely challenging environment, led to the development and utilization of complex mathematical techniques and tools known as *operations research* or *management science.* Some of these techniques have been used successfully to manage operations and have brought scientific rigor to operations management by replacing intuitive decision-making for large complex problems with a systematic approach that identifies the best alternative through quantitative and qualitative analysis.

In the late 1950s and 1960s, scholars began to write textbooks dealing with operations management, and operations became a legitimate functional area within business organizations. In the 1980s research demonstrated the importance of using operations as a key strategic ingredient for achieving competitive advantage.[3] During the 1970s and 1980s, several Japanese companies started the "quality revolution" and time-based management, hence enlarging the competitive dimensions from cost to cost, quality, and time.

reality CHECK   *Do you think that some kind of operations management was used during the construction of the Egyptian pyramids? Do you think that operations management was used in the design of Microsoft products such as Excel and Word? Give concrete examples.*

What Do Operations Managers Do?

LEARNING OBJECTIVE 5
Discuss what operations managers do.

Operations managers make decisions regarding the *design, planning,* and *control* of the production system. **Design decisions** are the decisions related to creating the products and the production system itself. For example,

- What products should the company offer?
- How should the products be produced?
- What should be the capacity of the production system?
- Where should the production system be located?
- What should be the layout of the production system?

design decisions Decisions related to creating the products and the production system itself

Planning decisions are the decisions related to preparing the production system for production. For example,

- How should the production rate be determined?
- What are the materials required for a given production plan?
- How should suppliers be selected?
- What are appropriate inventory levels?

planning decisions Decisions related to preparing the production system for production

control decisions Decisions made once the production system is producing

Control decisions are the decisions made once the production system is producing. For example,

- What should be the production sequence of different work orders at different workstations?
- How should product quality be controlled?

Design decisions have long-term implications and are typically made using a time horizon of years. Planning decisions have medium-term implications and are typically made using a time horizon of months. Controlling decisions have short-term implications and are typically made using a time horizon of weeks.

reality CHECK *In two business organizations that you know well, identify the operations manager. Examples of business organizations that you may know well are your local bank, car dealership, or supermarket.*

Design Decisions

LEARNING OBJECTIVE 6
Identify the design decisions about product, process, capacity, location, and layout.

Given the long-term implications of design decisions, operations managers need to exercise extreme care when making them. For example, changing the location of one of the manufacturing plants of DaimlerChrysler could be an expensive proposition. Similarly, changing the layout of the M.D. Anderson Cancer Center is not a trivial task.

Product

From a business perspective, successful product designs can only be achieved with the full cooperation of all the business functions involved. Lack of cooperation can lead to undesirable consequences, such as products that are useful for customers but too expensive to produce or products that incorporate the latest technology but are too difficult for customers to use.

From an operations management perspective, there are several issues, tools, and concepts that need to be considered when designing products. We will first look at designing goods.

Design for Manufacturing. Products should be designed with the firm's manufacturing capabilities in mind. A great engineering design is useless if the company cannot produce the product.

Design for Assembly. A good product design should not only consider how the product will be manufactured, but also how the product will be assembled. The main focus of this effort is to reduce the number and complexity of the parts that make up the product, as well as to simplify the assembly steps and methods.

Design for Recycling. Because of environmental concerns, a good product design should also take into account the possibility of disassembling the product for recycling of materials and components. In fact, an emerging idea in manufacturing is to **remanufacture products,** where components of old products are removed and used in new products. Examples of products with remanufactured components are automobiles, computers, and telephones.

remanufactured products New products in which the components of old products are being reused

Northeast Lamp Recycling, Inc. in East Windsor, Connecticut, annually recycles thousands of fluorescent light tubes to be used in new products.

Robust Designs. Products that perform well under a wide variety of conditions are said to have **robust designs.** Thus the more designers can build robustness into a product, the better it will hold up, leading to higher customer satisfaction. A product where robustness has increased by leaps and bounds is videocassette recorders.

robust design Design that allows products to perform well under a wide variety of conditions

Modular Designs. Production of a wide variety of products by using a low number of components is made possible by modular designs. For customers, they offer a great product selection. For the operations manager, there are only a limited number of components to deal with. For example, Ford Motor Company recently announced an integrated global product plan in which the number of basic vehicle platforms has been reduced by 50 percent, while the number of parts common to different vehicles is increased to 50 percent. Better yet, customers will have more distinct and unique vehicles because model variations per platform are being increased by 45 percent.[4]

Quality Function Deployment. Quality function deployment (QFD) is a technique for translating the voice of the customer, the customer's needs and wants, into the product design. Before QFD, companies struggled with translating the ordinary language that customers use to the technical language that designers use. In addition, QFD is not only a useful tool for linking customer requirements to technical specifications, but it also facilitates internal cooperation among marketing, engineering, and operations. Although most of the initial applications of QFD were in manufacturing organizations, QFD has also been applied with success in service organizations. For example, Euro Disney in Paris used QFD principles for its service design.[5]

The design of goods has been studied and developed over the years and can be described precisely; however, the design of services has not received as much attention.[6] Two major issues in service design are the level of customer contact and participation and the level of service customization. If the level is low on both counts, then the design of the service, such as getting gas at a gas station using the self-service lane, is similar to the design of goods. If the level is high on both counts, then the design of the service, such as using a real estate agent to buy a house, will be customer dependent. Companies sometimes do not need to design new products but just to redesign existing ones. For example, as market needs have evolved over time, McDonald's has redesigned its initial product offerings to include salads, chicken, fish, burritos, ice cream, meals for children, breakfast meals, and many other options in addition to hamburgers.

Process

project process A process where the product is produced in low volumes with high levels of customization

Operations managers can design their production systems by combining one or more of the following process types: *project, job, batch, line,* and *continuous.* As Exhibit 16.3 shows, the best choice depends on the volume and customization level of the product. When looking at processes, it is instructive to look at the flow of materials in the case of manufacturing systems or at the flow of customers in the case of service systems.

EXHIBIT 16.3

Process Types

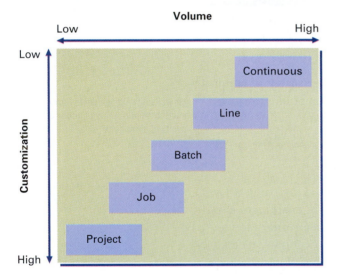

A **project process** is used when the product is produced in low volumes and requires a high level of customization. Examples of project processes are expanding the Miami International airport, building a new subway for Athens, Greece, and developing Windows XP. Project processes require a unique sequence of operations and typically create one-of-a-kind products made specifically to customer order. Professional services such as legal, medical, and architectural services are classified as project processes. Project processes are said to have no flow of materials or customers. For example, when building the new subway in Athens, Greece, the product being produced—the subway—did not flow in the sense that all resources came and went to the place where the subway was being built, but the subway itself never moved.

A **job process** is used when the product is produced in relatively low volumes and at relatively high levels of customization. Examples of job processes are hand-tailored clothing, a gourmet restaurant, an automotive repair shop, and special delivery mail. A job process, compared to a project process, offers a lower degree of customization but a higher production volume. In a job process, as in a project process, products are made-to-order and hence they are not produced ahead of time; but unlike in a project process products are produced several at a time instead of just a few or one at a time. These orders of several made-to-order units are usually called *jobs;* hence the name job process. Job processes do experience a flow of products from one production resource to another. For example, at an automotive repair shop, a car being repaired could flow from the electrical area to the body shop area to the tire alignment and balancing area. Because the flow from job to job will be different, it is said that job processes lead to *intermittent flow.* As another example of a job process, a patient who arrives at the emergency room of a hospital may next flow to an operating room, then to intensive care, and then to regular care.

job process A process where the product is produced in relatively low volumes with relatively high levels of customization

batch process A process where the product is produced at medium volumes and customization levels

A **batch process** is used when the product is produced at medium volumes and customization levels. Examples of batch processes are movie theaters, commercial airlines, furniture manufacturers, and bakeries. A batch process, when compared to a job process, offers less customization and hence less product variety but a higher production volume because of the narrower range of products that are offered. That is, the number of units being produced in a *batch* is markedly larger than the number of units being produced in a *job*. In a batch process, product variety is achieved by an assemble-to-order strategy instead of the make-to-order strategy utilized in project and job processes. Another important difference between job and batch processes is that frequently there could be several jobs concurrently being produced in a job process, while batches are produced one at a time. Although batches, like jobs, flow from one production resource to another, in batch processes, unlike in job processes, dominant flow paths emerge. For example, in a furniture company that manufactures chairs, tables, and desks, all batches of, say, chairs will tend to follow the same flow path.

A **line process** involves a relatively high production volume and a relatively low product customization. Examples of line flow are a cafeteria, a car oil-change shop, an automobile manufacturer, and a car wash facility. In a line process, production orders are not necessarily directly linked to customers orders, as in the case of project, job, and batch processes. Production is done under a make-to-stock strategy, and hence customer orders are filled using an inventory of finished goods. Because the products in a line process are highly standardized, production resources are organized around each product, and products flow linearly from one production resource to another. The assembly line used by Henry Ford to produce his Model T automobiles represents a pioneering application of the line process notion.

line process A process where the product is produced at a relatively high volume with relatively low product customization

A **continuous process** produces products in very large volumes but with very little customization. Examples of organizations using continuous processes are oil refineries, chemical plants, electricity producers, and paper companies. It has been argued that emergency services organizations such as ambulance companies, police departments, and fire stations are also examples of service systems using continuous processes. The process is called *continuous* because the goods or services flow continuously. Hence, while the products produced in the project, job, batch, and line processes can be measured in discrete units such as buildings, repaired cars, manufactured desks, and assembled computers, the products produced in continuous processes have to be measured in continuous units such as gallons, pounds, and time. The major advantage of continuous processes is the economies of scale that can be achieved by the very large production volumes. The major disadvantage is that they are very inflexible. Once the process has been designed and set to produce a particular product, say, gasoline, it is virtually impossible to change the process to produce a different product, say, steel. The process may be able to produce a different grade of gasoline, but the product will still have to be gasoline. Compare this to a company that uses a job process to produce windmills, elevators, and overhead cranes, which obviously are very different products.

continuous process A process where the product is produced in very large volumes but with very little customization

Capacity

Designing the production system to have the right capacity is extremely important for two reasons. First, if a company has too much capacity, this may lead to an excessive level of finished goods inventory, which is very risky and costly, or it may lead to unacceptable levels of idleness in the production system, which is also very costly. Imagine staffing an emergency room with five physicians when two are adequate. On the other hand, if a company has not enough capacity, then it will be losing customers to the competition or will have to permanently subcontract the needed capacity with potentially serious financial and quality consequences. The second reason for the importance of capacity is that adding or reducing capacity implies major capital expenditures.

EXHIBIT 16.4

Basic Strategies for Capacity Increases

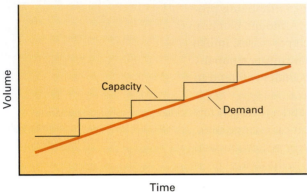

First Strategy: Lead Demand

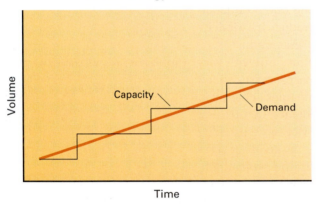

Second Strategy: Match Demand

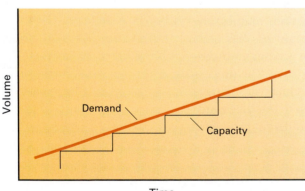

Third Strategy: Lag Demand

In simple terms, **capacity** is the capability of the production system measured in units of input or output per unit time. When the product line is relatively homogeneous, units of output per unit time are used to express capacity. For example, DaimlerChrysler could measure the capacity of one of its plants by the number of vehicles that can be assembled in a week, and Sony could measure the capacity of one of its manufacturing shops by the number of televisions that can be produced in a day. When the product line is diverse, units of input are preferred. For example, the capacity of a hospital can be measured by the number of beds, the capacity of a restaurant by the number of tables, and the capacity of a hotel by the number of rooms.

Capacity can be added in response to demand increases and decreases according to three basic strategies: *lead demand*, *match demand*, and *lag demand*. Exhibit 16.4 illustrates the three basic strategies when demand is increasing at a steady pace.

Lead demand strategy. The company uses capacity to keep its market share, as a weapon to prevent expansion from competitors, or to steal customers from capacity-constrained competitors. This is an aggressive but risky strategy.

Match demand strategy. The firm settles for a balance between risk and return. Capacity is only increased to keep up with demand.

Lag demand strategy. The company uses a conservative wait-and-see approach. It is only when the increases in demand have materialized that capacity is added. While this is a low-risk strategy, it could also lead to reductions in market share.

A widely used tool in capacity decisions is a *decision tree*. To illustrate the use of the decision tree, consider a company that is planning to launch a new product, but is unsure of the market response. The demand for the new product could be high, medium, or low. A marketing study indicates that the probability of high demand is .3, the probability of medium demand is .5, and the probability of low demand is .2. The company can design the production system to have enough capacity to satisfy the high demand level, the medium demand level, or the low demand level. We will respectively refer to these designs as the *high-capacity*, *medium-capacity*, and *low-capacity* designs. A financial study has been conducted to evaluate the profitability of the different demand-capacity combinations. The results of the study are presented in Exhibit 16.5.

With the high-capacity design and high-demand scenario, the company would get a profit of $250,000. With the high-capacity design and low-demand scenario, the company would experience a loss of $35,000. Should the company design the production system for high, medium, or low capacity? This capacity design decision can be represented as the decision tree in Exhibit 16.6.

Each capacity design option is represented by a tree branch; the square represents the decision point; and the nodes represent the randomness in the demand

capacity The capability of the production system measured in units of input or output per unit time

lead demand strategy A strategy where capacity is increased before demand increases

EXHIBIT 16.5

Profit for the Different Capacity-Demand Combinations

Design Decision	High Demand	Medium Demand	Low Demand
High capacity	$250,000	$ 50,000	($35,000)
Medium capacity	$100,000	$100,000	($10,000)
Low capacity	$ 80,000	$ 80,000	$80,000

match demand strategy A strategy where capacity is increased as demand increases (p.568)

lag demand strategy A strategy where capacity is increased after demand increases (p.568)

level. A decision tree compares the three alternative capacity designs by calculating their expected values. For example, the expected value of the high-capacity design is calculated as

$$\$250,000(.3) + \$50,000(.5) + (-\$35,000)(.2) = \$93,000$$

The expected values of the medium- and low-capacity designs are calculated similarly.

Medium-capacity design: $\$100,000(.3) + \$100,000(.5) + (-\$10,000)(.2)$
                          $= \$78,000$

Low-capacity design: $\$80,000(.3) + \$80,000(.5) + \$80,000(.2)$
                       $= \$80,000$

Because the high-capacity design has the greatest expected value, the decision tree analysis recommends that the company should select the high-capacity design.

Location

Another important design decision that operations managers have to make is the geographic location of the production system. According to a survey, when making location decisions for manufacturing systems, operations managers generally look at five dominant factors.

Favorable labor climate
Proximity to markets
Quality of life
Proximity to suppliers and resources
Proximity to the parent company's other facilities[7]

A favorable labor climate was selected by 76 percent of the respondents as a dominant factor in location decisions, and this is especially true of labor-intensive industries such as furniture, textiles, and consumer electronics. The labor climate is a function of wages, worker availability, worker productivity, attitudes toward work, and union strength.

Proximity to markets was voted by 55 percent of the respondents as a dominant factor in facility location. This factor is more important for heavy or bulky products where transportation costs are particularly high. For example, manufacturers of food, paper, plastics, and metals are usually located close to their markets.

Quality of life includes quality schools, good recreational facilities, cultural events, and attractive natural surroundings. Approximately 35 percent of

EXHIBIT 16.6

Example of a Decision Tree for a Capacity Decision

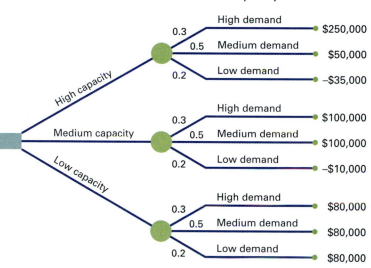

High capacity	High demand 0.3	$250,000
	Medium demand 0.5	$50,000
	Low demand 0.2	–$35,000
Medium capacity	High demand 0.3	$100,000
	Medium demand 0.5	$100,000
	Low demand 0.2	–$10,000
Low capacity	High demand 0.3	$80,000
	Medium demand 0.5	$80,000
	Low demand 0.2	$80,000

respondents included quality of life as a major factor in locating their companies. Most of these respondents were executives in high-tech industries.

Proximity to suppliers and resources was chosen by 31 percent of the respondents as a major factor in location decisions. Most of these respondents work in companies where inputs are heavy, bulky, or perishable. For example, food companies would locate near farms, and paper businesses would locate near forests.

Proximity to the parent company's other facilities received a 25 percent vote from respondents in the survey. Good candidates for this factor would be companies that own multiple facilities, where some manufacturing plants supply materials to other manufacturing plants.

When it comes to service systems, *proximity to customers* is without question the dominant factor in location decisions, since with few exceptions, customers are not willing to travel long distances to obtain services. Other important factors in service facility locations are operating costs, competitors, environment, support systems, and transportation. Service businesses such as warehousing and distribution tend to locate where *operating costs* are the lowest. Some service companies favor locations that are close to their *competitors*. For example, fast-food restaurants and car dealerships are usually located near each other. In fact, fast-food chains such as McDonald's, Burger King, and Wendy's find that locations within 1 mile of each other stimulate sales. The *environment* can play a fundamental role for service businesses such as skiing, where they have to be close to snow areas, or recreational parks, where the climate must be good most of the year for the business at hand. An example of the last situation would be the area around Orlando, Florida, where a cluster of entertainment parks is located. *Support systems* are another factor in location decisions for service firms where as in the case of big medical centers, they attract doctor's offices, pharmacies, and hotels. For service companies such as mail order companies, *transportation* becomes an essential ingredient, and they tend to locate in areas with an excellent transportation network.

Layout

Layout decisions involve the best physical arrangement of activity centers, where activity centers can be anything that consumes space: a person or group of people, chairs and desks, machines, stairways, aisles, storage rooms, workstations, and so on. The objective of layout decisions is to facilitate the flow of materials, people, and information. As a first step in the layout decision, the operations manager must address the following four issues:

- Activity centers to be included in the layout. For example, should the company have a centralized storage room or several smaller, decentralized storage rooms?
- Amount of space to be allocated to activity centers. Not enough space leads to reduced productivity, lack of privacy, and potential health and safety problems. Too much space leads to reduced productivity and higher costs.
- Configuration of activity centers. The physical placement of machines and workers at a production stage or workstation can have a significant impact on efficiency and materials flow. A similar argument can be made for the configuration of a maternity ward at a hospital.
- Placement of activity centers in relation to each other. Activity centers with frequent interactions or movements of people and materials should be located next to each other, assuming there are no technical constraints.

The second step in the layout decision is the selection of one of the following three basic types of layout: *fixed-position* layout, *process-oriented* layout, and *product-*

oriented layout. In a **fixed-position layout,** the product stays in one place, while the workers, materials, and equipment come to the product for manufacturing or service operations. This layout minimizes the movement of the product and often times is the only feasible option. Examples of production systems that use fixed-position layouts are manufacturing ships; building highways, bridges, dams, and houses; and mining and oil exploration. Notice that fixed-position layouts go hand in hand with project processes.

A **process-oriented layout** organizes the different activity centers by function. For example, in Exhibit 16.7a, the layout for a furniture manufacturer has been decided by grouping people, materials, machines, and equipment according to the functions they provide: office, cutting, drilling, sanding, gluing, painting, and packaging. As another example, in Exhibit 16.7b, the layout for an emergency room has also been organized by function: admissions, triage, laboratory, radiology, surgery, pharmacy, and beds.

In both layouts the goods and customers, respectively, will only visit those activity centers that are needed. That is, in the furniture manufacturing process, some goods will require painting and some other goods will not require painting. Similarly, in the emergency room, some patients will require surgery while some others will not. Both job processes and batch processes lead to process-oriented layouts.

A **product-oriented layout** is one where production resources are dedicated to products. For example, another furniture manufacturer, instead of grouping all cutting machines in a cutting area, all drilling machines into a drilling area, and so on, could consider a product-oriented layout such as the one in Exhibit 16.8, where the different machines are assigned to product families, say, desks, chairs, and tables, according to their production requirements.

fixed-position layout A layout where the product stays in one place, while the workers, materials, and equipment come to the product for manufacturing or service operations

process-oriented layout A layout where the different activity centers are organized by function

EXHIBIT 16.7

Examples of a Process-Oriented Layout

A Furniture Manufacturer

Painting	Packaging
Sanding	Gluing
Cutting	Drilling
Office	

An Emergency Room

Surgery	Beds
	Pharmacy
Laboratory	Radiology
Admissions	Triage

product-oriented layout A layout where production resources are dedicated to products

EXHIBIT 16.8

Example of a Product-Oriented Layout for a Furniture Manufacturer

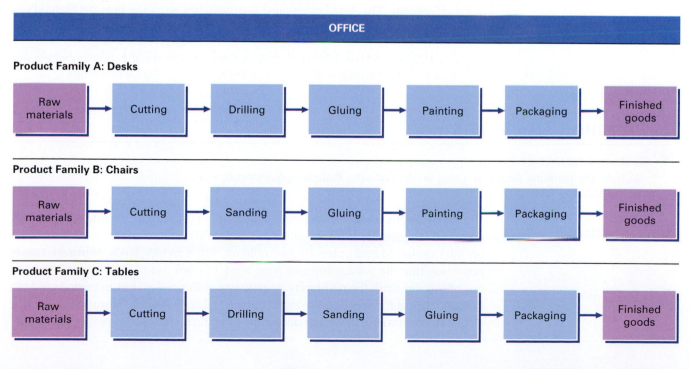

Technology and Business

McDonald's Looks for Competitive Advantage with Its New High-Tech Kitchen Layout

In its half century of corporate existence, McDonald's has revolutionized the restaurant industry by inventing the limited-menu fast-food restaurant. Its first innovation, the introduction of indoor seating in the 1950s, was a strategic issue of facility layout, as was its second, drive-through windows introduced in the 1970s. Its third innovation, adding breakfast to the menu in the 1980s, was a product strategy; its fourth, adding play areas in the 1990s, was again a layout decision.

Now, in 2000, McDonald's is reaching for its fifth major innovation, and, not surprisingly, it is a new layout to facilitate a mass customization process. This time the corporation is banking on the radical redesign of the kitchens in its 13,500 North American outlets. Dubbed the "Made for You" kitchen system, sandwiches are now assembled to order and production levels are controlled by computers. The new layout is intended to improve the taste of food by ensuring it is always freshly made, and to facilitate the introduction of new products. It is being introduced at a pace of 900 stores per month.

Under the new restaurant design, no food is prepared in advance except the meat patty, which is kept hot in a cabinet. To shorten the total production process to 45 seconds, some steps were eliminated and some shortened. For instance, the company developed a toaster that browns buns in 11 seconds instead of 30. Bread suppliers had to change the texture of the buns so they could withstand the additional heat. Workers also figured out they could save two seconds if condiment containers were repositioned to apply mustard to sandwiches with one motion instead of two.

The payoff for the layout change? McDonald's will save $100 million per year because only the meat, and no longer the bun or other ingredients, will be discarded when sandwiches do not sell fast enough. The company is banking that with the new layout, new standards of efficiency and happier customers will provide a competitive advantage.

Source: From Jay Heizer and Barry Render, *Operations Management*, 7th Edition, © 2004. Adapted by permission of Pearson Education, Inc., Upper Saddle River, NJ.

Questions

1. Does McDonald's new high-tech kitchen layout belong to one of the three basic types of layouts?
2. In what ways can McDonald's new high-tech kitchen layout be improved?

Notice that line processes and continuous processes would require product-oriented layouts. The Technology and Business box explains how McDonald's is looking for a competitive advantage by using a new high-tech kitchen layout.

reality CHECK *How would you describe the design decisions at a company where you recently worked? Do you think the design was appropriate?*

Planning Decisions

LEARNING OBJECTIVE 7
Illustrate the planning decisions about production rate, material requirements, purchasing, and inventory.

Design decisions impose constraints on planning decisions. For example, a plant designed to assemble 100 computers per hour will certainly place an upper bound on the number of computers to assemble on, say, a weekly basis. However, this is not to say that the production rate from week to week has to be the same. In periods of low demand, the plant may operate one shift per day; but in periods of high demand, the plant may operate three shifts per day. Therefore, planning decisions, although constrained by design decisions, offer the operations manager the opportunity to make adjustments in the production system such that demand is satisfied in the most efficient and effective way.

Production Rate

One of the fundamental challenges that all businesses face is matching production and demand rates for the product that they offer. This challenge is especially hard when product demand exhibits a rate that varies significantly from month to month. This type of demand rate pattern is called *seasonal demand*. Examples of products with seasonal demand are toys, air conditioners, and computers. In matching production and demand rates, companies can try to modify the demand rate pattern by using several options: *pricing, advertising and promotion*, and *back ordering*. These options primarily pertain to the marketing function; as such, they will only be touched on briefly here.

Pricing is used to reduce the peaks and valleys in seasonal demand. For example, airlines and hotels increase prices in high-demand seasons and lower prices in low-demand seasons. Advertising and promotion are done in such a way as to increase demand in typically slow periods, and sometimes even to shift demand from peak periods to slack periods. For example, automobile and computer manufacturers offer rebates in periods of slow demand. This may entice a customer to buy a computer when he was not thinking of buying one or may push a customer to buy an automobile earlier than she had planned. **Back ordering** represents a shift of demand from demand peak times to demand slack times. In this case, the customer is willing to wait for the product in return for a financial incentive, usually in the form of a discount.

back ordering An option where the customer is willing to wait for the product in return for a financial incentive

To complement these three options, operations managers can modify the production rate by using one or more of the following alternatives: *hiring or firing workers, overtime or undertime*, and *subcontracting*. Hiring or firing workers is utilized in varying degrees in different industries. Some industries will do everything they can before reducing their workforce, while in other industries increases and decreases of the workforce are carried out routinely. Overtime or undertime is an alternative where for the most part, the workforce remains stable, and changes in the production rate are achieved by asking workers to work more time—overtime—or less time—undertime. A third alternative for increasing the production rate is to **subcontract** some of the products being produced. The subcontractor may produce the whole product or some of its components. Computer manufacturers usually subcontract most of the computer components. Secretarial and catering help is typically obtained by subcontracting.

subcontract An option where products are produced by a third party

Given a demand rate pattern and using the above three alternatives, the operations manager needs to decide on the production rate strategy that will match demand at minimum cost. There are two extreme production rate strategies: *chase* and *level*. In the **chase strategy**, adjustments to the production rate come exclusively from changes in the workforce by hiring and firing workers. In the **level strategy**, the workforce remains stable, and adjustments to the production rate are achieved by using overtime, undertime, and subcontracting. In practice, these two strategies are rarely used but serve as a comparison point. Most successful strategies incorporate elements of the chase and level strategies and are called **hybrid strategies.** Exhibit 16.9 (on p. 574) presents an example of a chase strategy, and Exhibit 16.10 (on p. 574) presents an example of a level strategy. In these examples, each worker can produce 20 units per month while working in regular time and 10 units per month while working in overtime.

chase strategy An extreme strategy where production rate adjustments come exclusively from hiring and firing workers

level strategy An extreme strategy where the workforce remains stable and production rate adjustments come from overtime or undertime, and subcontracting

hybrid strategy A strategy that combines the chase and level strategies in different degrees

EXHIBIT 16.9

Example of a Chase Strategy

Month	Demand (units)	Workforce (workers)	Regular Time Production (units)
1	200	10	200
2	200	10	200
3	300	15	300
4	500	25	500
5	400	20	400
6	200	10	200

In the chase strategy, the workforce varies from a low of 10 workers to a high of 25 workers. In the level strategy, the workforce stays at 10 workers, and the production rate is increased by asking workers to work overtime in months 3 to 5 and by subcontracting the production of 200 units in month 4 and 100 units in month 5.

Material Requirements

Once the production rate strategy has been decided, it is time to estimate the materials that are required to support the strategy. For example, if the units being produced are automobiles and we are planning to produce 20 automobiles next month, then we need to estimate all the materials that would be required by such a production plan. Such estimation is not easy, especially when one considers the number of components that go into a car, which can easily run in the tens of thousands. Fortunately, in the 1960s, a computer-based technique called **material requirements planning (MRP)** was developed to perform such a complex estimation task.

MRP has been used successfully in manufacturing and service systems. To illustrate the logic of MRP, consider a company that produces an office chair. The sequence in which the chair is assembled is called the **bill of material.** Exhibit 16.11 contains the bill of material with three levels for the office chair.

Suppose that the production rate strategy calls for the production of 100 office chairs in month 1 and 200 chairs in month 2, and that months 1 and 2 comprise

material requirements planning (MRP) A computer-based technique for calculating the materials required by a production plan

bill of material A graphical representation of the sequence in which products are assembled

EXHIBIT 16.10

Example of a Level Strategy

Month	Demand (units)	Workforce (workers)	Regular Time Production (units)	Overtime Production (units)	Subcontracted Production (units)	Total Production (units)
1	200	10	200	0	0	200
2	200	10	200	0	0	200
3	300	10	200	100	0	300
4	500	10	200	100	200	500
5	400	10	200	100	100	400
6	200	10	200	0	0	200

EXHIBIT 16.11

Bill of Material for an Office Chair

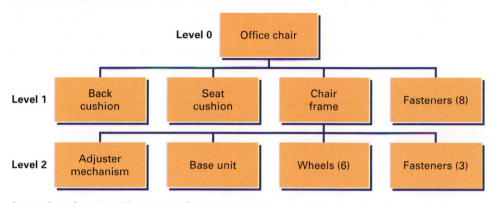

Source: From *Operations Management: Concepts in Manufacturing and Services,* 2nd edition by Markland, Vickery, and Davis. Copyright © 1998. Reprinted with permission of South-Western, a division of Thomson Learning: **www.thomsonrights.com**. Fax 800 730-2215.

exactly 4 weeks each. Once the production rate strategy is broken down into weeks, it is called the **master production schedule.** The master production schedule for office chairs is provided in Exhibit 16.12.

In addition, suppose that there are currently on hand 22 back cushions, 52 seat cushions, 50 chair frames, 970 fasteners, 4 adjuster mechanisms, 77 base units, and 900 wheels. Lastly, assume that it takes one week to assemble the office chair and the chair frame, and it takes two weeks to produce the other components.

Using MRP logic, the operations manager would estimate the requirements for chair frames as in Exhibit 16.13. The number of chair frames requested comes directly from the master production schedule for office chairs; that is, if 25 office chairs will be produced during week 1, then 25 chair frames will be requested at the beginning of week 1. In turn, given that there are currently 50 chair frames on hand, no chair frames will be required until the beginning of week 3. And because it takes one week to assemble chair frames, the 25 chair frames that are required at the

master production schedule A schedule where the production rate strategy is broken down into weeks

EXHIBIT 16.12

Master Production Schedule for Office Chairs

Week	Production (chairs)
1	25
2	25
3	25
4	25
5	50
6	50
7	50
8	50

EXHIBIT 16.13

Requirements for Chair Frames and Wheels

Chair Frames	0	1	2	3	4	5	6	7	8
				Week					
Requested		25	25	25	25	50	50	50	50
On hand	50	50	25	0	0	0	0	0	0
Required		0	0	25	25	50	50	50	50
Ordered		0	25	25	50	50	50	50	0

Wheels	0	1	2	3	4	5	6	7	8
				Week					
Requested		0	150	150	300	300	300	300	0
On hand	900	900	900	750	600	300	0	0	0
Required		0	0	0	0	0	300	300	0
Ordered		0	0	0	300	300	0	0	0

beginning of week 3 should be ordered for assembly at the beginning of week 2. The numbers in the other cells are calculated similarly.

The estimation of the requirements for wheels is more involved and is also done in Exhibit 16.13. Given that six wheels are used in each chair frame, when the orders to assemble 25 chair frames are released at the beginning of weeks 2 and 3, a request for 150 wheels will be triggered at those points in time; and when the orders to assemble 50 chair frames are released at the beginning of weeks 4 to 7, requests for 300 wheels will be issued. The other calculations in Exhibit 16.13 should now be apparent. Of course, the requirements for all of the other components of the office chair, listed on its bill of material, would be estimated with the same logic.

Purchasing

purchasing The business function responsible for the acquisition of goods and services

Purchasing is responsible for the acquisition of goods and services needed by a business organization. The relevance of purchasing can be easily understood when one considers that in manufacturing systems, approximately 60 percent of the finished goods cost comes from purchased materials and services, and in service systems such as retail and wholesale firms, this percentage can be as high as 90 percent. Operations managers make purchasing decisions in regard to *outsourcing*, *value analysis*, and *supplier selection*.

outsourcing Buying goods and services from outside sources rather than producing them in-house

Outsourcing refers to buying goods and services from outside sources rather than producing them in-house. A useful tool in outsourcing decisions is called *break-even analysis*. Let P denote the unit purchase price, C the in-house unit variable production cost, F the in-house fixed production cost, and N the number of units that are needed. Then the total cost when buying the items, $TC(B)$, can be expressed as

$$TC(B) = PN$$

and the total cost of producing the items in-house, $TC(P)$, can be expressed as

$$TC(P) = F + CN$$

Notice that if there exists a value of N, say N^*, such that $TC(B) = TC(P)$, then N^* is given by

$$PN^* = F + CN^*$$

or

$$N^* = F/(P - C)$$

Therefore, if the number N of units needed is less than N^*, then the company should outsource the item; if the number N of units needed is more than N^*, then the company should produce the item in-house; otherwise, the company is indifferent regarding outsourcing or producing the item in-house. For example, if a firm is facing a buying price of $100 per unit, in-house variable production costs of $75 per unit, and in-house fixed production costs of $10,000, then

$$N^* = 10,000/(100 - 75) = 400$$

Hence for volumes lower than 400 units, the firm should outsource the item; for volumes higher than 400 units, the firm should produce the item in-house; and for a volume of exactly 400 units, the firm is indifferent regarding outsourcing the item or producing the item in-house.

value analysis An examination of the function that each purchased part serves, done in order to find lower-cost alternatives

Value analysis is a disciplined effort to examine the *function* that each purchased part serves, in order to find lower-cost alternatives. The effort is done in groups that include representatives from operations, engineering, marketing, and accounting. Questions asked by the group include

• What is the function performed by the part?

- Does the function performed by the part add value to the product?
- Are there alternative sources for the part?
- Can the part's specifications be relaxed to lower its cost without affecting the function performed?
- Can the part be combined with another part?

Obviously, value analysis should not be performed every time a part is ordered. Instead, it should be applied periodically to large-dollar-volume parts that offer the highest savings potential.

Supplier selection involves evaluating the different sources of supply, and takes into account the following factors:

> *Price.* Is the supplier offering a price that is competitive?
>
> *Quality.* A supplier may charge a higher price, but the quality of its product may also be higher. Higher quality leads to lower production costs due to less waste and disruptions.
>
> *Service.* If the part fails, what is the supplier willing to do?
>
> *Location.* Nearby suppliers may lead to lower transportation costs and faster response time.
>
> *Flexibility.* How easily can the supplier handle changes in production volumes of the part or in its design?

One recent trend in supplier selection is to look at suppliers as partners instead of as adversaries. Maintaining good relations with suppliers has become a new source of competitive advantage. Hence companies are establishing long-term relationships with fewer suppliers that can provide high-quality parts, can deliver the parts quickly and reliably, and can be relatively flexible in modifications of production specifications and delivery schedules. Another important trend in supplier selection is globalization. As international trade barriers fall, it is getting easier and more attractive to get parts from international sources. Some of the risks and challenges that accompany this trend are

- Dealing with different languages and cultures
- Having to use additional modes of transportation
- Facing exchange rate fluctuations
- Managing with different time zones and very long procurement times

Inventory

Inventories are omnipresent. All companies have them and need them. The decision for the operations manager is one of balancing: if inventories are too low, business operations could be disrupted or customers could be lost; if inventories are too high, the associated monetary investment will translate into high financial costs and a risky position for the firm, thus impacting negatively on the organization's market stock price. To achieve an appropriate inventory level, the operations manager needs to consider the following inventory costs:

- **Ordering cost** is the cost that is incurred every time an order is placed to procure more items. In order to minimize ordering costs, one would try to place infrequent but large procurement orders. When the item is produced in-house instead of purchased, ordering costs are also called *setup costs,* alluding to the setup times that are typically needed to produce a batch of products. For example, when an ice cream company has finished producing an order of 200 gallons of chocolate ice cream, it would incur a setup cost when cleaning the process to run a different ice cream flavor, say vanilla.

- **Holding cost** is the cost resulting from keeping one unit in inventory for a given time period, typically one year. Holding cost includes, among other

supplier selection An evaluation of different supply sources in order to select one or more

ordering cost The cost that is incurred every time an order is placed to procure more items

holding cost The cost resulting from keeping one unit in inventory for a given time period, usually a year

Case in Point

Operations Management Is a Powerful Competitive Weapon

Toyota Motor Corporation has long been recognized as one of the most successful companies in the world. Toyota nearly doubled its revenue in the past decade and redefined competition in key areas of the auto industry. However, Toyota suddenly finds itself plagued with increasing quality problems and having to launch a world-wide program to simplify its production systems.

On the agenda, Toyota has as its next big goal to increase its share of the global market from 10% to 15% in the next decade. If achieved, Toyota would become approximately the same size No. 1 auto maker General Motors is today. Such an ambitious goal is tough,

straining Toyota's human and technical resources and undercutting one of Toyota's most critical strategic advantages: operations management in general and quality in particular. The marriage of efficient production systems to an obsessive concern for quality has helped Toyota establish a reputation for bullet-proof reliability that remains a huge competitive advantage.

Source: *The Wall Street Journal,* August 4, 2004, pages A1 and A2.

Questions

1. Do you agree with Toyota's ethics policy for procurement and purchasing?
2. In what ways could Toyota's ethics policy for procurement and purchasing be improved?

---

interest cost The cost that is incurred by having money invested in inventory

costs, the cost of operating the storage facility; the cost of insuring the items; the cost of depreciation, obsolescence, deterioration, spoilage, breakage, and pilferage of the items; and the *interest cost*. The **interest cost** represents the expense that is incurred by having the money invested in inventory. For example, if a company asks for a bank loan in order to keep in inventory one unit of an item valued at $20,000, and the interest rate for the loan is 10 percent per year, then the interest cost would be ($20,000)(0.10) = $2000 per year. Interest cost is frequently the major component of holding cost. The holding cost typically ranges between 20 and 40 percent of an item's value. In order to minimize holding costs, one would try to place small but frequent procurement orders.

To illustrate how an operations manager can find an appropriate inventory level, we will consider a basic inventory model. In this model, the following assumptions are made:

- Demand for the item is known and constant.
- The ordered units are received all at once.
- The cost of the item is independent of the number of units ordered.

Let us use the following notation:

D = annual demand for the item (in units per year)
O = ordering cost ($ per order)
h = annual holding cost as a percentage
V = item's value ($ per unit)
$H = hV$ = annual holding cost in dollars ($ per unit per year)
Q = quantity procured in each order (units)
N = number of orders per year
L = average inventory level (units)
AOC = annual ordering cost ($ per year)
AHC = annual holding cost ($ per year)
$TAC = AOC + AHC$ = total annual ordering and holding cost ($ per year)

Then

$$N = D/Q \quad \text{and} \quad L = Q/2$$

For example, if the annual demand for an item is $D = 600$ units and the quantity procured in each order is $Q = 30$ units, then the number of orders per year would be $N = D/Q = 600/30 = 20$, and the average inventory level will be $L = Q/2 = 30/2 = 15$ units.

We now have that

$$AOC = ON = OD/Q$$
$$AHC = HL = HQ/2$$
$$TAC = OD/Q + HQ/2$$

The operations manager would like to find the value of Q that minimizes TAC. Because $L = Q/2$, the operations manager is also implicitly finding the value of L that minimizes TAC.

For example, if the annual demand for an item is $D = 600$ units, the ordering cost is $O = \$90$ per order, the annual holding cost is $h = 30$ percent of the item's value, the item's value is $V = \$100$, and the item is sold in boxes of 10 units, then to find the value of Q that minimizes TAC, the operations manager would perform the calculations presented in Exhibit 16.14. In these calculations, $H = hV = (0.30)(100) = 30$. When the number of boxes procured per order is 1 and thus the number of units procured per order is 10, we can calculate the following:

$$N = D/Q = 600/10 = 60$$
$$L = Q/2 = 10/2 = 5$$
$$AOC = ON = (90)(60) = \$5400$$
$$AHC = HL = (30)(5) = \$150$$
$$TAC = AOC + AHC = \$5400 + \$150 = \$5550$$

The other calculations in Exhibit 16.14 are performed similarly.

Observe that the minimum TAC is $\$1800$, which is achieved by $L = 30$ units, resulting from procuring 6 boxes per order or, equivalently, procuring 60 units per order. Any average inventory level lower or higher than 30 units will lead to higher total annual ordering and holding costs. The operations manager has thus found an inventory level that is not too low or too high. Of special interest is that the minimum TAC occurs when the AOC and the AHC are equal, or balanced, in our example at $\$900$ each. This is always the case in this model.

reality CHECK *What do you think would happen if companies stopped carrying inventory?*

EXHIBIT 16.14

Finding the Optimal Inventory Level

Number of Boxes Procured per Order	Quantity Procured in Each Order Q	Number of Orders per Year N	Average Inventory Level L	Annual Ordering Cost AOC	Annual Holding Cost AHC	Total Annual Ordering and Holding Cost TAC
1	10	60	5	$5400	$ 150	$5550
2	20	30	10	$2700	$ 300	$3000
3	30	20	15	$1800	$ 450	$2250
4	40	15	20	$1350	$ 600	$1950
5	50	12	25	$1080	$ 750	$1030
6	60	10	30	$ 900	$ 900	$1800
7	70	9	35	$ 771	$1050	$1821
8	80	8	40	$ 675	$1200	$1875
9	90	7	45	$ 600	$1350	$1950
10	100	6	50	$ 540	$1500	$2040

Control Decisions

LEARNING OBJECTIVE 8
Outline the control decisions about scheduling and quality.

Once the operations manager has designed the production system and its products and has planned the production rate and the materials required along with their supply sources, as well as the inventory levels, he or she still has to make two major control decisions: *scheduling* and *quality.*

Scheduling

scheduling Allocating available production resources to tasks, jobs, orders, activities, or customers in a given time period

Scheduling decisions allocate available production resources to tasks, jobs, orders, activities, or customers in a given time period. The capacity design decision constrains the production rate decision, which in turn restricts the scheduling decision. A production schedule indicates what is to be done, when, by whom, and with what resources. Scheduling decisions vary with the type of process: project, job, batch, line, and continuous. In this introductory treatment, we consider the scheduling decision only for job processes.

One of the most widely used scheduling tools is known as the *Gantt chart,* first proposed by Henry Gantt in 1917. Exhibit 16.15 illustrates a scheduling decision for a job process using a Gantt chart.

In this example, there are fours jobs A, B, C, and D that have to be scheduled in three work centers I, II, and III. The route stipulates the sequence in which jobs need to visit the work centers, as well as the machine hours required at each work center. For instance, first job D needs to go to work center I and be processed for three hours; next job D needs to go to work center III and be processed for two hours; and finally job D needs to go to work center II and be processed for one hour. The decision that the operations manager faces is how to schedule the jobs in the work centers so that all jobs are finished as soon as possible. The Gantt chart for the case where jobs are scheduled in the order A, B, C, D is

- Job A is scheduled at work center I for hours 1 and 2, then at work center II for hours 3 to 5, and then at work center III for hours 6 to 9.
- Job B is scheduled at work center III for hours 1 and 2, then at work center II for hours 6 and 7 (because hours 1 and 2 are not feasible, and hours 3 to 5 are already assigned to job A), and then at work center I for hours 8 and 9.
- Job C is scheduled at work center II for hours 8 to 10 (because job C requires three hours, hence hours 1 and 2 are not sufficient and hours 3 to 7 are already assigned to jobs A and B), then at work center III for hour 11, and then at work center I for hours 12 to 14.
- Job D is scheduled at work center I for hours 3 to 5 (because hours 1 to 2 are already assigned to job A), then at work center III for hours 12 and 13 (because hours 1 to 5 are not feasible, hours 6 to 9 are already assigned to job A, hour 10 is not sufficient, and hour 11 is already assigned to job C), and then at work center II for hour 14.

According to this first schedule, all four jobs can be finished in 14 hours.

Now consider the second Gantt chart where jobs were scheduled in the order D, C, B, A. This second schedule is superior because all jobs are finished in 13 hours. The operations manager would keep trying different job schedules in order to find the one schedule where all jobs are finished as soon as possible.

Variations of the Gantt chart can also be used for scheduling decisions in project and batch processes.

EXHIBIT 16.15

Example of a Scheduling Decision for a Job Process

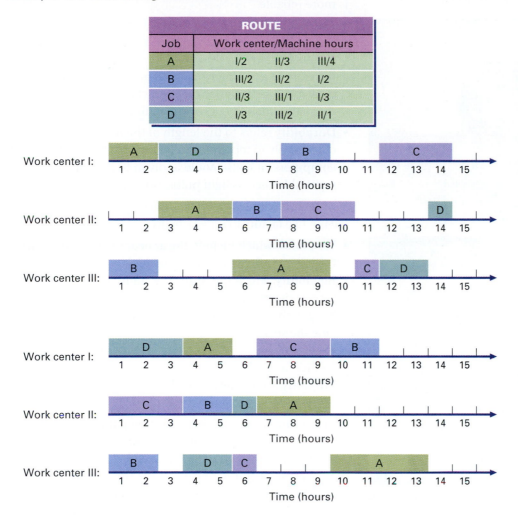

Quality

Quality is the ability of a product to meet or exceed customers' expectations. Quality can be viewed on two additional dimensions: *quality of design* and *quality of conformance*. **Quality of design** refers to the excellence of the intention of designers to include or exclude features in a product. In terms of design, a Rolex watch would have a higher quality of design than a Timex watch, and of course the prices of these watches would reflect this difference. The quality of design is mostly associated with the marketing function. **Quality of conformance** is the degree to which the product conforms to the intent of the designers. In terms of conformance, we would say that a Rolex watch has a lower quality of conformance than a Timex watch if the Rolex watch did not conform to the designer's specifications and the Timex watch did. The quality of conformance is mostly associated with the operations function.

The three dimensions of quality apply equally to goods and services. However, the factors that customers use to judge quality in goods are different from those they use for services. In the case of goods, customers look at the following three factors, which add a future time dimension:

- **Reliability** refers to length of time in between failures of the item. For example, if under similar usage conditions copy machine A breaks down on average

quality The ability of a product to meet or exceed customers' expectations

quality of design The excellence of the intention of designers to include or exclude features in a product

quality of conformance The degree to which the product conforms to the intent of the designers

reliability (of an item) The length of time between failures of an item

Marcelo Vieria, a Brazilian coffee farmer, leads a new generation of coffee farmers in controlling the quality of the coffee blends that his company markets worldwide.

maintainability (of an item) The ease and speed with which an item can be repaired

durability (of an item) The length of an item's life

tangibles (of service) The appearance of the service facilities, equipment, and personnel

reliability (of service) The ability to perform the service dependably and accurately

responsiveness (of service) The willingness to provide the service

assurance (of service) The ability to convey trust and confidence

empathy (of service) The flexibility in adapting the service to meet individual needs

quality control A set of activities aimed at ensuring that the production system is producing products that conform to design specifications

every six months and copy machine B breaks down on average every nine months, then the second copy machine is more reliable.

- **Maintainability** refers to the ease and the speed with which the item can be repaired. For example, if all repairs for copy machine A take a long time and require the work of a company technician, while all repairs for copy machine B can be done quickly by the user, then the maintainability of copy machine B is better.

- **Durability** refers to the length of the item's life. This could apply to repairable items such as automobiles and computers, and also could apply to items that are not repairable such as light bulbs, tires, and car batteries.

   When it comes to services, customers consider the following five factors to judge quality:

- **Tangibles,** which include the appearance of the service facilities, equipment, and personnel
- **Reliability,** which measures the ability to perform the service dependably and accurately
- **Responsiveness,** which measures the willingness to provide the service
- **Assurance,** which refers to the ability to convey trust and confidence
- **Empathy,** which measures the flexibility in adapting the service to meet individual needs[8]

   For example, on a visit to a doctor, patients would judge service quality by asking, am I comfortable in the doctor's office (tangibles)? Is the doctor qualified to help me (reliability)? Is the doctor happy to see me (responsiveness)? Can I trust this doctor (assurance)? Is the doctor interested in me individually or is the doctor helping me just as an average patient (empathy)?

   The quality of conformance is in the realm of the operations manager. The operations manager needs to decide the best way to control quality of conformance, which is commonly called *quality control*. **Quality control** is the set of activities aimed at ensuring that the production system is producing products that conform to design specifications. One of the most widely used tools for quality control is the *process control chart*, or simply the *control chart*.

   In order to understand the philosophy behind control charts, it is necessary to first introduce the concepts of *normal variation* and *abnormal variation*. If we were, for example, to compare our signatures on the checks that we wrote in the past six months, we would see that from check to check, there would be normal variations in the way we signed our name. Even though we are the ones signing the checks and we should know how to sign our name, because we are not perfectly consistent, our signatures will exhibit these normal variations. On the other hand, if we saw a document where somebody had forged our signature and compared that signature with our real signature, then we should see an abnormal variation between the forged signature and our real signature. Similarly, because the people and the processes in the production system are not perfectly consistent, products can exhibit normal variations but sill conform to specifications. At the same time, products that exhibit abnormal variations would not conform to specifications. When the production system is producing products with normal variations, we say it is an **in-control production system;** when the production system is producing products with abnormal variations, we say it is an **out-of-control production system** and we should perform any necessary adjustments to bring it in control.

By means of the **control chart,** the operations manager can help the production system operators to detect when product variations are normal and when they are abnormal. For example, one of the design specifications for a box of detergent is that it must contain 48 ounces. Using historical data and statistical analysis, the operations manager has determined that when the production system is in control and a random sample of ten boxes is taken, the average number of ounces per box is 48 (although individual boxes may contain more or fewer ounces per box). However, due to normal variations in the filling process, some samples could have an average as high as 48.3 ounces, called the *upper control limit,* or as low as 47.7 ounces, called the *lower control limit.* The resulting control chart is presented in Exhibit 16.16.

In this example, operators would be instructed to

- Take a random sample of ten boxes every hour and calculate the average weight per box. If in the sample at 8 A.M. the weights for the ten boxes were 47.8, 48.1, 47.4, 48.2, 47.5, 47.9, 47.6, 47.8, 47.8, and 47.9, then the average weight per box is 47.8 ounces.
- Plot the average weight on the control chart.
- If the average weight is not equal to 48 ounces but falls within the upper and lower control limits, then the production system is in control and no adjustments are needed.
- If the average weight falls outside the upper or lower control limits, then the production process is out of control and any necessary adjustments to bring it in control should be performed.

In Exhibit 16.16, the production system was in control from 8 until 10 A.M. and went out of control between 10 and 11 A.M. Thus the system should be checked to identify any needed repairs in order to bring it back in control.

in-control production system The production system where products produced exhibit normal variations

out-of-control production system The production system where products produced exhibit abnormal variations

control chart A chart used to detect if the production system is in control or out of control

EXHIBIT 16.16

An Example of a Control Chart

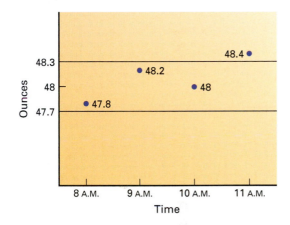

reality
CHECK *How would you define quality in a soft drink, a watch, and a hotel?*

Careers in Operations Management

The operations function offers an exciting career path with plenty of job opportunities. Forty percent of *all* jobs are in operations management.[9] When asked what he liked about his job, one operations manager responded, "In my job, I'm doing the main job of business—making products for customers. Being involved in the process of producing products and services is something tangible that I can grab on to and understand. Every day is interesting because there is such variety of things that I do, from solving problems related to quality to installing a new robotic machine. And there are plenty of opportunities for dealing with people, from suppliers, to our personnel, to customers. After being here, I don't think that I could handle a job that deals in intangibles like debits and credits."[10]

There are several career paths for manufacturing and service operations, differentiating between line and staff positions. *Line* positions have direct responsibility for producing the product. *Staff* positions provide support to line positions. The titles below are only suggestive.

Operations Management Careers in Manufacturing—Line

- Corporate Vice President of Manufacturing
- Divisional Manager of Production
- Plant Manager
- Vice President of Materials Management
- Project Manager

Operations Management Careers in Manufacturing—Staff

- Director of Quality
- Materials Manager
- Production Scheduler
- Performance Improvement Manager
- Project Manager/Consultant (internal or external)
- Purchasing Agent

Operations Management Careers in Services—Line

- Corporate Vice President of Operations
- Divisional Manager of Operations
- Administrative Head
- Department Supervisor
- Facilities Manager
- Branch or Store Manager

Operations Management Careers in Services—Staff

- Quality Supervisor
- Materials Manager
- Staff Scheduler
- Performance Improvement Manager
- Project Manager/Consultant (internal or external)
- Purchasing Agent[11]

The following are samples of specific job descriptions:

> *Plant manager.* Division of *Fortune 100* company seeks plant manager for plant located in the upper Hudson Valley area. This plant manufactures loading dock equipment for commercial markets. The candidate must be experienced in plant management, including expertise in production planning, purchasing, and inventory management.
>
> *Quality manager.* Several openings exist in our small package processing facilities in the Northeast, Florida, and Southern California for quality managers. These highly visible positions require extensive use of statistical tools to monitor all aspects of service timeliness and workload measurement.
>
> *Process improvement consultant.* An expanding consulting firm is seeking consultants to design and implement lean production and cycle time reduction plans in both service and manufacturing processes. Our firm is currently working with an international bank to improve its back office operations as well as with several manufacturing firms.[12]

Summary

LEARNING OBJECTIVE 1
Explain what operations management is.

Operations management is the management of the direct resources in the production system of a business organization. Production is the creation of goods or services, and a production system is the system that businesses use to produce products. The production system of a company that produces mostly goods is called a manufacturing system, and the production system of a company that produces mostly services is called a service system. Operations management is naturally positioned to help companies maximize the value that they add to their products.

LEARNING OBJECTIVE 2
Compare manufacturing operations and service operations.

Most business organizations produce and sell products that entail a combination of goods and services. However, from an operations management perspective, considering customer contact, customer participation, inventory, and tangibility can differentiate goods and services.

LEARNING OBJECTIVE 3
Evaluate the impact of operations management on the competitiveness of a business organization.

Good operations management can help businesses compete along the dimensions of price, quality, and time. Good operations management leads to production costs that allow firms to set competitive prices that attract customer demand. Since products are created by the production system, good operations management yields quality products that will satisfy customers' requirements. Good operations management is conducive to getting new products to market quickly and to delivering current products promptly and reliably.

LEARNING OBJECTIVE 4
Describe the historical development of operations management.

The history of operations management is rich and inspiring. From craft production, to division of labor, to the Industrial Revolution, to scientific management, to assembly lines, to operations research and management science, to the quality revolution and time-based management, human ingenuity has always been present in efforts to organize for production.

LEARNING OBJECTIVE 5
Discuss what operations managers do.

Operations managers make decisions regarding the design, planning, and control of the production system. Design decisions deal with the creation of products and the production system itself. Planning decisions involve preparing the production system for production. Control decisions are made once the production system is producing.

LEARNING OBJECTIVE 6
Identify the design decisions about product, process, capacity, location, and layout.

Products should be designed with manufacturing, assembly, recycling, and modularity considerations, among others. Process designs include job, batch, line, and continuous processes. Capacity decisions should lead to a level that is neither too high nor too low. Capacity can be added by leading, matching, or lagging demand. Decision trees are widely used tools in capacity decisions. The location decision typically is influenced by factors such as a favorable labor climate, proximity to markets, quality of life, proximity to suppliers and resources, and proximity to the parent company's other facilities. The layout decision entails configuring and placing activity centers to optimize their operation. The operations manager may adopt a fixed-position, process-oriented, or product-oriented layout.

LEARNING OBJECTIVE 7
Illustrate the planning decisions about production rate, material requirements, purchasing, and inventory.

One of the fundamental challenges that all businesses face is matching production and demand rates for the product that they offer. Pricing, advertising and promotion, and back ordering can modify the demand rate pattern. The production rate can be modified by hiring or firing workers, by using overtime or undertime, and by subcontracting. The chase strategy and the level strategy are two extreme production rate strategies; the most successful strategies are called hybrid strategies and incorporate elements of the chase and level strategies. Material requirements planning (MRP) is a computer-based technique that is used to estimate the materials that are required to support the selected production rate strategy. Concepts utilized by MRP are bill of material and master production schedule. The purchasing decision includes whether to outsource goods and services, value analysis to provide a cost justification of the function that each purchased part serves, and the evaluation of suppliers based on price, quality, service, location, and flexibility. The inventory decision consists of finding an inventory level at which the sum of the ordering cost and the holding cost is minimized.

LEARNING OBJECTIVE 8

Outline the control decisions about scheduling and quality.

Scheduling decisions allocate available production resources to tasks, jobs, orders, activities, or customers in a given period. A production schedule indicates what is to be done, when, by whom, and with what resources.

Scheduling decisions for job processes can be analyzed via a Gantt chart. Quality is the ability of a product to meet or exceed customers' expectations. There is also quality of design and quality of conformance, and for operations managers these three dimensions hold for both goods and services. However, the factors that customers use to judge quality in goods are different from those they use to judge quality in services. Operations managers mostly deal with quality of conformance. Quality control is the set of activities aimed at ensuring that the production system is achieving quality of conformance. One of the most widely used tools for quality control is the process control chart.

Chapter Questions

1. What is operations management?
2. Compare the production of goods with the production of services.
3. How can operations management help businesses compete?
4. What are the milestones in the historical development of operations management?
5. What are the decisions that operations managers make?
6. What is the relationship between the product and process design decisions?
7. What are the advantages of simultaneously considering the capacity, location, and layout decisions?
8. What is the production rate planning decision?
9. What is the material requirements planning decision?
10. What is the quality control decision?
11. Consider the capacity example using decision trees. What capacity design would you recommend if the probabilities of high, medium, and low demand respectively, are .2, .4, and .4?
12. Consider the material requirements example. Estimate the requirements for seat cushions, base units, and fasteners.
13. Consider the outsourcing example. If the in-house variable production cost is $80, for what volume should the company outsource the item?
14. Consider the inventory example. If the annual demand increases from 600 units to 1200 units, find the procurement quantity and its associated average inventory level that minimize the total annual ordering and holding cost.
15. Consider the scheduling example. Find two more schedules.

Interpreting Business News

1. It has been said that one of the major forces behind the success of Japanese car manufacturers is their excellent operations management. Based on the design, planning, and control decisions presented in this chapter, offer at least three reasons in support of this statement.
2. The productivity of service industries tends to be lower than the productivity of manufacturing industries. Why do you think this is the case? (Hint: Read the section "Goods and Services" again.)
3. The costs of health care are escalating in most world economies. Explain how operations management could help contain these costs. (Hint: Use the design, planning, and control decisions presented in this chapter.)

Web Assignments

1. One of the student and professional organizations for operations management is called *APICS: The Educational Society for Resource Management*. Visit its website at **www.apics.org** and learn more about operations management, student membership, and the APICS certification program for operations managers. What does it take to become certified?
2. Use a search engine to look for operations management jobs. What kinds of things do the jobs have in common? Comment on the differences between manufacturing-related and service-related jobs.
3. Use a search engine to search for undergraduate and graduate programs in operations management. Describe the kinds of courses involved in this program of study.

Portfolio Projects

Exploring Your Own Case in Point

After reading this chapter, you should be ready to answer several fundamental questions about the company that you have decided to study in depth.

1. What percentage of the value in your company's products comes from goods and what percentage comes from services?

2. What process type(s) does it use? How is its production capacity measured?

3. Where is the company located? What is its layout?

4. What scheduling decisions does it face? How does it define quality?

Starting Your Own Business

After reading this chapter, consider these operational aspects of your startup.

1. Of the products that you plan to offer, which are mostly goods and which are mostly services?

2. What is going to be your business strategy in terms of price, cost, and quality?

3. What type of production process are you going to use? What is going to be the capacity of your business? Where is your business going to be located and what is going to be its layout?

4. How are you going to decide on your production rate? Will you need to use MRP? Which items will be produced in-house and which items will be outsourced? How are you going to select your suppliers? How will inventory be managed? What schedules will be needed and how is quality going to be defined and controlled?

Test Prepper

You've read the chapter, studied the key terms, and the exam is any day now. Think you are ready to ace it? Take this sample test to gauge your comprehension of chapter material. You can check your answers at the back of the book.

True/False Questions

Please indicate if the following statements are true or false:

_____ 1. The production system of a law firm is an example of a service system.

_____ 2. Watching a movie at a movie theater would be an example of a storage transformation process.

_____ 3. Operations management is the management of the indirect resources that are involved in the production system of a business organization.

_____ 4. Services are tangible and goods are not.

_____ 5. The three dimensions where operations management can help businesses compete are cost, quality, and service.

_____ 6. The Industrial Revolution introduced a type of production system called the cottage system.

_____ 7. Planning decisions have medium-term implications and are typically made using a time horizon of months.

_____ 8. A project process is used when the product is produced in low volumes and requires a high level of customization.

_____ 9. To achieve an appropriate inventory level, the operations manager needs to consider ordering and holding costs.

_____ 10. Quality of design and quality of conformance are synonymous concepts.

Multiple-Choice Questions

Choose the best answer.

_____ 1. A production system can be modeled as a system that takes inputs and creates outputs via a transformation process. In this model, some of the inputs include

a. materials, land, and labor.
b. the desired goods or services.
c. location, information, and exchange.
d. machines, equipment, and storage.
e. information, money, and people.

_____ 2. Goods and services can be differentiated along all the following characteristics

a. customer contact and knowledge.
b. inventory and work-in-process.
c. customer contact and participation.
d. quality of design and conformance.
e. price and cost.

_____ 3. The assembly line concept combined two key elements:

a. analysis and improvement of work methods.
b. skilled workers and custom-fitted parts.
c. interchangeable parts and division of labor.
d. unskilled workers and specialized parts.
e. craft production and the cottage system.

_____ 4. When designing goods, products that perform well under a wide variety of conditions are said to have a

a. good design for manufacturing.
b. good design for assembly.
c. good design for recycling.
d. robust design.
e. modular design.

_____ 5. A job process is used when the product is produced

a. in relatively low volumes and at relatively high levels of customization.
b. at medium volume and customization levels.
c. in low volumes and at high levels of customization.
d. in relatively high volumes and at relatively low levels of customization.
e. in very large volumes but with very little customization.

_____ 6. Consider the capacity example using decision trees. What would be the expected value of the medium-capacity design if the demand outcomes for high, medium, and low demand, respectively, changed to $100,000, $50,000, and $0?

a. $78,000

b. $55,000
c. $50,000
d. $62,000
e. $41,000

_____ 7. A product-oriented layout is one where

    a. the product stays in one place, while the workers, materials, and equipment come to the product for manufacturing or service operations.

    b. the different activity centers are organized by function.

    c. the product stays in one place.

    d. production resources are dedicated to products.

    e. the different activities are organized by cost center.

_____ 8. Consider the production rate example. If the demand in the second month changed from 200 to 250 units and a level strategy was used, in Exhibit 16.10 the regular time production in the second month would change to

    a. 250 units.

    b. 50 units.

    c. 100 units.

    d. 10 workers.

    e. It would not change.

_____ 9. Consider the material requirements example. If the bill of material for the chair were redesigned to include eight wheels

instead of six wheels, in Exhibit 16.13 the number of requested wheels for week 7 would change to

    a. 150.

    b. 8.

    c. 900.

    d. 400.

    e. 137.

_____ 10. Consider the control chart in Exhibit 16.16. We know that the system went out of control between 10 and 11 A.M. because

    a. the average weights for the samples taken at 8, 9, and 11 A.M. were all different from the design specification of 48 ounces per box.

    b. the average weights for the samples taken at 8, 9, 10, and 11 A.M. are all different.

    c. the average weight for the first sample at 8 A.M. is less than 48 ounces, and the average weight for the last sample at 11 A.M. is more than 48 ounces.

    d. the average weights for the samples taken at 10 and 11 A.M. are different.

    e. the average weights for the samples taken at 8, 9, and 10 A.M. are all within the lower and upper control limits, and the average weight for the sample taken at 11 A.M. is higher than the upper control limit of 48.3 ounces.

Want more questions? Visit the student website at **http://college.hmco.com/business/student/** (select Gaspar, *Introduction to Business*) and take the ACE quizzes for more practice.

17

Management Information Systems

| Introduction

| **What Are Management Information Systems?**
  Computer Hardware
  Computer Software
  Databases
  Telecommunications Networks

| **Classification of Information Systems**
  Information Systems for Operations Managers
  Information Systems for Middle Managers
  Information Systems for Senior Managers
  Marketing Information Systems
  Production Information Systems
  Accounting Information Systems
  Financial Information Systems
  Human Resources Information Systems

| **Developing Information Systems**

| **Global Information Systems**

| **Information Systems Controls**

| **Careers in Information Systems**

Learning Objectives

After studying this chapter, you should be able to

1. Explain what management information systems are.

2. Describe the roles that computer hardware, computer software, databases, and telecommunications networks play in management information systems.

3. Classify information systems by the organizational level they support and by the business function they serve.

4. Identify the activities involved in the development of information systems.

5. Discuss how global companies are configuring their information systems.

6. Illustrate what businesses can do to assure the security and accuracy of their information systems.

Management Information Systems at the Boeing Company

In the mid-1980s, the Boeing Company invested in three-dimensional computer-aided design/computer-aided manufacturing (CAD/CAM) technology for strategic reasons. By the end of that decade, a single strategy for applying this capability emerged after numerous pilot programs were conducted. The pilot programs clearly demonstrated the benefits of modeling airplane parts as three-dimensional solids in the computer-aided three-dimensional interactive application (CATIA) system. Developed by Dassault Systemes of France and marketed by IBM in the United States, CATIA, along with several Boeing-created applications, allowed Boeing engineers to simulate the geometry of an airplane design on the computer without the costly and time-consuming investment of using physical mockups.

Studies at Boeing showed that part interference, incidents of assembly parts overlapping each other, and difficulty in properly fitting parts together in aircraft final assembly are the most pervasive problems in manufacturing airplanes. By 1989, the Boeing engineering organization was confident that it could significantly reduce the costly rework caused by part interference and fit problems by digitally preassembling the airplane on the computer. The improved accuracy in part design and assembly, as well as the instantaneous communications capability of this technology, convinced Boeing that the significant investment required to implement it would more than pay for itself in the long run by improving the quality of airplane designs and reducing the cycle time required to introduce new airplanes into the marketplace.

The opportunity to apply the new CAD/CAM approach, as well as other new engineering and manufacturing ideas, came in 1990 with the launch of the Boeing 777 twin jet. The 777 program established design-build teams to develop each element of the airplane's airframe or system. Under this approach, all of the different specialties involved in airplane development—designers, manufacturing representatives, toolers, engineers, financers, suppliers, customers, and others—worked jointly to create the airplane's parts and systems. Based at the same location, team members worked concurrently, sharing their knowledge rather than applying their skills sequentially. Communication among the program's 238 design-build teams was accomplished by using sophisticated computers linked by the largest mainframe installation of its kind in the world, consisting of eight IBM mainframe computers. This computer network consisted of mainframes and workstation installations in Seattle, Washington; Wichita, Kansas; Philadelphia; Japan; and other locations.

Central to the digital design approach was the CATIA system. From the beginning of the 777 program, the three key participants in the system—Boeing, Dassault Systemes ,and IBM—developed a working-together agreement signed by their respective chief executive officers. The three companies made a commitment in the agreement to deliver products and services on schedule to the 777 program computer users. But the basic CAD/CAM technology provided by the CATIA system was not enough. The possibilities this technology provided required Boeing to rethink the entire process of designing and building an airplane, in order to leverage these capabilities to their maximum extent. The company found that several enhancements to the CATIA system were required in order to allow engineers to productively design an entire airplane using these new processes. Boeing applications enhanced the CATIA system in three major areas: data management, user productivity, and visualization. Each of these major enhancements was required to deal with the size and scale of productively managing the millions of 777 airplane parts modeled on CATIA.

Once all of the computing applications were in place, Boeing engineers and designers were able to use the three-dimensional digital software to see parts as solid images and then simulate the assembly of those parts on the screen, easily correcting misalignments and other fit or interference problems. In June 1995, the Boeing 777 Division was recognized for its innovative application of computing technology to the 777 when it won the top spot in the manufacturing category of the annual Computerworld Smithsonian Awards. The awards honor the world's most creative and innovative use of information technology that benefits society. By earning top honors in the category, the Boeing computing and design application earned a place in history in the Smithsonian Institution's permanent research collection.[1]

Introduction

As illustrated in the vignette about Boeing, one of the key ingredients for business success is information. In fact, it is well known that sometimes the differentiating factor between organizations that lead and organizations that follow in an industry is the way in which information is managed. This chapter deals with *management information systems*, systems that use information technology to manage information in a business organization. We first define management information systems and describe in detail the resources used by this business function. We then present a classification of information systems in business. Next, we take a detailed look at the process of developing information systems, at the configuration strategies for information systems that global companies are using, and at the controls needed to assure the security and accuracy of information systems. The chapter closes with a brief discussion of career paths in management information systems.

What Are Management Information Systems?

LEARNING OBJECTIVE 1
Explain what management information systems are.

data Facts about events or attributes of things, places, or people

information Data that have been transformed to be meaningful and valuable to specific users

Data are collections of facts, events, or attributes of entities such as things, places, or people. Examples of data are the ages of the citizens of a given country, the maximum daily temperatures of a city for the last ten years, and the amount spent by each customer in a given year at a particular McDonald's restaurant. **Information** is data that have been transformed to be meaningful and valuable to specific users. For example, the data on the ages of the citizens of a given country could be transformed into the average age by gender, and hence become information for public health officials. As a second example, the data on the maximum daily temperatures of a city for the last ten years could be transformed into the average maximum daily temperature for the last ten years, and thus become weather information. And as a third example, the data on the amount spent by each customer in a given year at a particular McDonald's restaurant could be transformed into average daily or weekly sales information.

An **information system** is a system that converts data into information. Some information systems use computers, and some information systems do not use computers. We will concentrate on *computer-based* information systems. **Management information systems (MISs)** are the systems that manage the direct resources needed for creating, storing, and distributing information in a business organization. The direct resources that MISs manage include computer hardware, computer software, databases, and telecommunications networks.

information system A system that converts data into information

management information systems The systems that manage the direct resources needed for creating, storing, and distributing information in a business organization

reality CHECK *Can you think of some applications of management information systems in your college or university?*

Computer Hardware

LEARNING OBJECTIVE 2
Describe the roles that computer hardware, computer software, databases, and telecommunications networks play in management information systems.

A modern computer system includes a central processing unit, primary storage, secondary storage, input devices, output devices, and communication devices. The **central processing unit (CPU)** manipulates numbers, letters, and symbols and controls the other elements of the computer system. In turn, the CPU consists of two units: the **arithmetic-logic unit,** which performs arithmetic operations (addition, subtraction, multiplication, and division) and comparison operations (for example, 7 is greater than 3), and the **control unit,** which transmits electronic signals to the other components of the computer system to perform needed operations.

central processing unit (CPU) The computer hardware element that controls other elements of a computer system

arithmetic-logic unit The part of the CPU that performs arithmetic and logic operations

control unit The part of the CPU that transmits electronic signals to the other components of a computer system to perform needed operations

Computer storage capacity is measured in *bytes*. In the computer, the number 1 represents the presence of an electronic/magnetic signal and the number 0 represents the absence of the signal. A **bit** is a binary 0/1 digit representing one of these two mutually exclusive states and is the smallest unit of data in a computer system. A **byte** is a string of eight bits that the computer stores as a unit. A byte can store a number, letter, or symbol. For example, under the ASCII binary coding standard, the letter *A* is represented by the byte 01000001; each of the eight positions is a bit and each position takes a value equal to either 0 or 1. A **kilobyte** is a unit of computer storage capacity equal to 1000 bytes (really 1024). A **megabyte** is equal to 1 million bytes, a **gigabyte** is equal to 1 billion bytes, and a **terabyte** is equal to 1 trillion bytes. A **petabyte** is equal to 1000 terabytes, and an **exabyte** is equal to 1 million terabytes. Five megabytes can hold the text of the entire works of Shakespeare. Ten terabytes would hold the Library of Congress. Five exabytes would hold all the words ever spoken by human beings on this planet.

bit A binary 0 or 1 digit representing the presence or absence of an electronic or magnetic signal in a computer

byte A string of eight bits, representing a number, letter, or symbol, that the computer stores as a unit

kilobyte One thousand bytes

megabyte One million bytes

gigabyte One billion bytes

terabyte One trillion bytes

petabyte One thousand terabytes

exabyte One million terabytes

Primary storage stores the operating system that manages the operation of the computer and all or part of a software program that is being executed, as well as the data that are being used by the program. Primary storage includes *random access memory (RAM)*, whose contents are lost when the computer is turned off, and *read-only memory (ROM)*, whose contents are not lost when the computer is turned off. Typically, ROM contains software programs burned in by the computer manufacturer.

primary storage The computer system component that stores the operating system and all or part of a software program that is being executed, as well as the data that are being used by the program

Secondary storage is used to store large quantities of data outside the computer and retains its contents when the computer is turned off. The most important technologies for secondary storage are *magnetic disks* and *optical disks.*

Magnetic disks can be floppy disks or hard disks. Floppy disks offer convenience because they are inexpensive and portable, but they typically store only 1 to 3 megabytes and they have a slow access rate. Hard disks offer storage capacities

secondary storage The computer system component that stores large quantities of data outside the computer and retains its contents when the computer is turned off

measured in gigabytes and a faster access rate, but they are much more expensive than floppy disks and not as portable.

Optical disks can be compact disks (CDs) or digital video disks (DVDs). CDs store up to 660 megabytes and can be compact disk–read-only memory (CD-ROM), which is read-only storage, compact disk–recordable (CD-R), which can record data only once, and compact disk–rewritable (CD-RW), which can record data many times. DVDs are the same size as CDs but have a much higher storage capacity. DVDs can store a minimum of 4.7 gigabytes. DVDs are used to store multimedia applications and movies, and like CDs, they can also be read-only, recordable, and rewritable.

In 1999 the amount of information created and stored was

- 240 terabytes on paper
- 427 petabytes on film
- 83 terabytes on optical disks (music and data CDs/DVDs)
- 1.693 exabytes on magnetic disks (camcorder and data tapes)

for a total of 2.1 exabytes. We have clearly gone from an era with little information to an era with "too much" information.

People interact with computers via the input and output devices. **Input devices** are used to collect and transform data into an electronic form that the computer can use. The two most common input devices are the keyboard and the computer mouse. Other input devices are pen-based input such as in PDAs, audio input such as voice recognition, and optical scanning such as desktop scanners and bar-coding scanners. **Output devices** display the information processed by the computer to the user. The principal output devices are video monitors and printers.

The last element of modern computer systems is **communications devices,** which provide connections between the computer and other computers via telecommunications networks.

Modern computers can be classified as *mainframe computers, midrange computers, microcomputers,* and *supercomputers.* **Mainframe computers** are large, fast, and powerful computers. They can process millions of instructions per second and have large primary storage capacity. They are used for very large business applications such as those at international banks, airlines, and major corporations.

Midrange computers are medium-sized computers capable of serving the needs of many business organizations. Midrange computers can be used as *minicomputers* in systems at factories, universities, and research laboratories, or they can be used as *servers* providing software and related resources for other computers over a network.

Microcomputers are computers that satisfy the needs of individual users. Microcomputers can be used as *personal computers (PCs)* in the laptop or desktop versions or as *workstations,* which have more powerful mathematic and graphical capabilities than personal computers. For example, workstations are used for computer-aided design by engineers and for portfolio analysis by investment bankers.

Supercomputers are extremely powerful computers specifically designed for applications requiring complex calculations at a very high speed. They have been traditionally used for scientific work such as global weather forecasting and computational cosmology and astronomy, and for military research on defense systems and classified weapons. Supercomputers are now starting to be used in business for massive manipulations of data such as those required by data mining, described later in the Databases section of this chapter. Deep Blue, the computer that defeated world chess champion Garry Kasparov in 1997, was a supercomputer manufactured by IBM.

The speed at which computers operate has been increasing at an unprecedented rate. The speed has evolved from *milliseconds,* thousandths of a second, to

input devices Computer system devices such as the keyboard or mouse that are used to collect and transform data into an electronic form that the computer can use

output devices Computer system devices such as video monitors or printers that are used to display the information processed by the computer for users

communications devices Computer system devices that provide connections between the computer and other computers via telecommunications networks

mainframe computers Large, fast, and powerful computers that are used for very large business applications

midrange computers Computers that are medium-sized and capable of serving the needs of many business organizations

microcomputers Computers that satisfy the needs of individual users

supercomputers Extremely powerful computers specifically designed for applications requiring complex calculations at a very high speed

microseconds, millionths of a second, to *nanoseconds*, billionths of a second, to *picoseconds*, trillionths of a second. To provide some perspective on these speeds, consider that if a person could take one step per nanosecond, the person would circle the earth about 20 times in one second.[2]

Computer Software

Software is the entire set of programs, procedures, and related documentation associated with a system. Thus **computer software** is the detailed instructions that control the operation of a computer system. A **software program** is a specific set of statements to direct and control computer hardware. The creation of software programs is called *programming*, and the individuals who perform this task are called *programmers*. Computer software can be *system software* or *application software*. **System software** is a set of software programs that manage and support the operations of the computer system. Programmers who write system software are called *system programmers*. **Application software** is a set of software programs that direct the computer to perform an information-processing task specified by end users. Programmers who write application software are called *application programmers*. The end user interacts with the application software, the application software interacts with the system software, and the system software interacts with the computer hardware. The most well-known type of system software is the *operating system*. An **operating system** is the software program that manages and controls the activities of the computer. The operating system helps the computer to operate in the most efficient way. For example, the operating system allocates primary storage for programs, controls the printer, schedules the execution of different programs, and keeps track of who is using the computer system. The most popular operating systems are Windows in its 98, NT, Me, 2000, and XP versions; Unix; Linux; and Mac OS. Other types of system software are performance monitors, security monitors, and system utilities.

software The entire set of programs, procedures, and related documentation associated with a system

computer software The detailed instructions that control the operation of a computer system

software program A specific set of statements to direct and control computer hardware

system software The set of software programs that manage and support the operations of a computer system

application software The set of software programs that direct the computer to perform an information-processing task specified by end users

operating system The software program that manages and controls the activities of the computer

In November 2002, an employee walks by the Earth Simulator in Yokohama, southeast of Tokyo, Japan. The Earth Simulator is the fastest supercomputer in the world, running 35.6 trillion calculations per second.

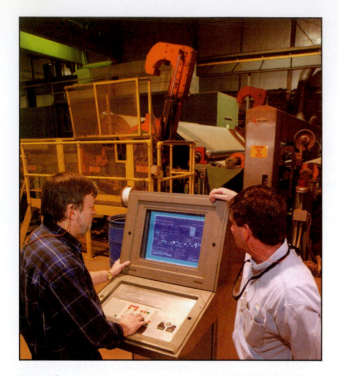

United Corrstack, Inc. production manager Ronald Johnson (left) and mill manager Art McLaughlin using a management information system at their Reading, Pennsylvania plant.

One way of classifying application software is as *general-purpose* or *application-specific*. **General-purpose software** is programs that perform common information processing jobs for end users. Examples of general-purpose software are word processors such as Microsoft Word and WordPerfect, electronic spreadsheets such as Microsoft Excel and Lotus 1-2-3, and presentation graphics such as Microsoft PowerPoint and Lotus Freelance Graphics. **Application-specific software** is programs that support specific applications for end users in business and other fields. Examples of application-specific software are investment analysis programs, accounting programs, and sales management programs.

Application software is created by using one or more *programming languages*. A **programming language** is the tool that the programmer uses to develop the sets of instructions that constitute a software program. Programming languages have evolved through four generations. The first generation of programming languages was **machine languages,** all programming instructions had to be written using binary code. Machine languages are difficult and error-prone. For example, to compute the sum of two numbers as expressed by the formula $A = B + C$, the machine language instructions would be

$$\begin{array}{ll} 1010 & 11001 \\ 1011 & 11010 \\ 1100 & 11011^3 \end{array}$$

Assembler languages are the second generation of programming languages. **Assembler languages** use translator programs called *assemblers* to convert symbolic instructions into machine language. For example, to compute the sum of two numbers as expressed by the formula $A = B + C$, assembler language instructions would be

$$\begin{array}{l} \text{LOD B} \\ \text{ADD C} \\ \text{STR A}^4 \end{array}$$

High-level languages are the third generation of programming languages. **High-level languages** use translator programs called *compilers* to convert statements, which are more like natural language, into machine language. When compiled, each statement in a high-level language generates several machine language instructions. Widely used high-level languages are FORTRAN, COBOL, BASIC, Pascal, C, and C++. For example, to compute the sum of two numbers as expressed by the formula $A = B + C$, the respective BASIC and COBOL statements would be

$$\begin{array}{l} A = B + C \\ \text{COMPUTE } A = B + C^5 \end{array}$$

Fourth-generation languages consist of a variety of programming languages that are less procedural than earlier programming languages and are very close to human languages. Procedural languages have to specify the sequence of steps that tell the computer what to do and how to do it. Fourth-generation languages allow the user to indicate the results she or he wants, and then the computer determines the series of instructions that will achieve the desired result. For example, to com-

general-purpose software The set of software programs that perform common information processing jobs, such as word processing, for end users

application-specific software The set of software programs that support specific applications, such as investment analysis, for end users in business and other fields

programming language The tool that a programmer uses to develop the sets of instructions that constitute a software program

machine languages First-generation programming languages where all programming instructions had to be written using binary code

assembler languages Second-generation programming languages that convert symbolic instructions into machine language

high-level languages Third-generation programming languages that convert natural-language-like statements into machine language

fourth-generation languages Programming languages that are less procedural than earlier programming languages and are very close to human languages

pute the sum of two numbers as expressed by the formula $A = B + C$, a fourth-generation language statement would be

SUM THE NUMBERS B AND C[6]

Databases

From a computer hardware perspective, a bit is the most elementary data element. However, from a logical perspective, the most basic data element that can be observed and manipulated is a **character,** which can be a number, a letter, or another symbol. A **field** is a grouping of characters. For example, the grouping of letters in a person's name forms a field that could be called the *name field,* the grouping of numbers in a person's social security number forms a field that could be called the *SSN field,* and the grouping of numbers in a person's salary forms a field that could be called the *salary field.* A **record** is a collection of related fields. For example, if for two employees we have

Name field: John Smith   Name field: Guadalupe Garcia
SSN field: 137-47-2239   SSN field: 932-11-4567
Salary field: $35,0000   Salary field: $50,000

then the collection of the first three fields would constitute the payroll record of the first employee and the collection of the second three fields would constitute the payroll record of the second employee. It is said that a record represents a set of *attributes,* characteristics or qualities, that describe an *entity,* an object, person, place, or event. Hence in the payroll record example, the entity is the employee and the attributes are the name, social security number, and salary.

A **file** is a group of related records. Thus the collection of payroll records for all employees in a business organization constitute the payroll file. Files are also called *tables.* A **database** is a group of related files and represents the highest level in the

character The most basic data element—a number, letter or other symbol—that can be observed and manipulated

field A grouping of characters

record A collection of related fields

file A group of related records

database A group of related files that represents the highest level in the data hierarchy

Oracle Corporation is the largest supplier of databases in the world.
Reprinted with permission of Oracle Corporation.

database management system The software for creating and maintaining a database

operational database A database used to support the day-to-day operations in a firm

data warehouse A database used for various businesses' analyses that contains current and historical data from various operational databases

data mining Systematic searching for patterns and trends in business activities that can be exploited by managers to gain competitive advantage

data marts Subsets of a data warehouse that contain data for a certain group of users

telecommunication The communication of information by electronic means over some distance

telecommunications networks Collections of computer hardware and software arranged to transmit information from one place to another

communications channels The physical means by which information is transmitted

twisted-pair wire Copper wires twisted in pairs

coaxial cable Sturdy copper or aluminum wire wrapped with spacers to insulate it

fiber-optic cable Thousands of hair-thin glass fiber filaments wrapped in a protective cover

analog signal An electromagnetic signal of a continuous waveform that can handle voice communications

digital signal An electromagnetic signal of a discrete waveform that can handle data communications

modem A device that translates digital signals into analog signals and vice versa

communications processors Devices that support the transmission and reception of information in a telecommunications network

multiplexer A communications processor that enables a single communications channel to carry simultaneous information transmissions from multiple sources

data hierarchy. For example, a personnel database would include, among others, the payroll file and the benefits file. The purpose of databases is to store and manage data using one location and to organize the data in such a way that it can provide data for many applications. A **database management system** is software for creating and maintaining a database and for easily extracting data from a database.

Databases can be *operational databases* or *data warehouses*. An **operational database** is a database used to support the day-to-day operations of a firm. Examples of operational databases are personnel databases, customer databases, and inventory databases. Operational databases are also called *transaction databases* and *production databases*. A **data warehouse** is a database that contains current and historic data from the various operational databases and is used for a variety of business analyses. One of the most successful uses of data warehouses is *data mining*. **Data mining** is the systematic search for patterns and trends in business activities that can be exploited by managers to gain competitive advantage. **Data marts** are subsets of a data warehouse that contain data for a certain group of users.

Telecommunications Networks

Telecommunication is the communication of information by electronic means over some distance. **Telecommunications networks** are collections of computer hardware and software arranged to transmit information from one place to another. The essential components of a telecommunications network are communications channels, communications processors, communications software, computers, and input and output devices.

Communications channels are the physical means by which information is transmitted. The most common media used for telecommunications channels are *twisted-pair wire, coaxial cable,* and *fiber-optic cable.* **Twisted-pair wire** consists of copper wires twisted in pairs. It is the oldest communication medium and the one used in traditional telephone lines. **Coaxial cable** consists of sturdy copper or aluminum wire wrapped with spacers to insulate it. It allows high-speed data transmission and is also used for cable television. **Fiber-optic cable** consists of thousands of hair-thin glass fiber filaments wrapped in a protective cover. Its transmission rate is approximately 60 times greater than coaxial cable and 3000 times greater than twisted-pair wire. The cost of fiber-optic cable is higher than the cost of coaxial cable, which in turn is higher than the cost of twisted-pair wire.

In a telecommunications network, information travels as an electromagnetic signal that can be of two types. An **analog signal** is a continuous waveform that can handle voice communications. A **digital signal** is a discrete waveform that transmits data coded as 0-bits and 1-bits, which are represented by on/off electric pulses. Most computers communicate with digital signals. Traditional telephone lines use analog signals, while modern telephone lines use digital signals. For computers to communicate via traditional telephone lines, a device called a *modem* is necessary. Modem is an abbreviation for modulation/demodulation. A **modem** translates digital signals into analog signals and vice versa.

Modems are the most common type of communications processors; other types are *multiplexers, switches,* and *routers.* **Communications processors** support the transmission and reception of information in a telecommunications network. A **multiplexer** is a communications processor that enables a single communications channel to carry simultaneous information transmissions from multiple sources. Switches and routers are communications processors that interconnect different telecommunications networks, and for this reason they are called *internetwork processors.*

Telecommunications software provides a variety of communications support services such as establishing transmission speed, detecting and correcting transmission errors, and protecting the network from unauthorized users. Telecommunications software may reside in computers and in communication processors.

There are three basic types of network structures or *topologies*, which are illustrated in Exhibit 17.1. The **star network** consists of a host computer connected to several, typically smaller computers. This topology is used when some processing must be centralized and some can be performed locally. Because all communications among computers in the network must pass through the host computer, this topology is vulnerable to problems in the host computer. In a **bus network,** there is no host computer and all computers in the network share the same communications channel—twisted-pair wire, coaxial cable, or fiber-optic cable. One advantage of the bus network is that if one of the computers in the network fails, the other computers in the network are not affected. One disadvantage of the bus network is that the communications channel can only handle one message at a time; if two computers attempt to send a message at the same time, a "collision" occurs and the messages need to be resent. Consequently, as traffic in the network increases, performance will degrade. A **ring network** is similar to a bus network in that there is no

telecommunications software The software that provides a variety of communications support services such as establishing transmission speed and protecting the network from unauthorized users

star network A network topology where a host computer is connected to several, typically smaller computers and all communications among computers in the network must pass through the host computer

bus network A network topology where all computers in the network share the same communications channel and there is no host computer

ring network A network topology similar to a bus network but where the communications channel forms a closed loop and hence information is passed from one computer to the next one in the ring in only one direction

EXHIBIT 17.1

The Three Basic Types of Network Topologies

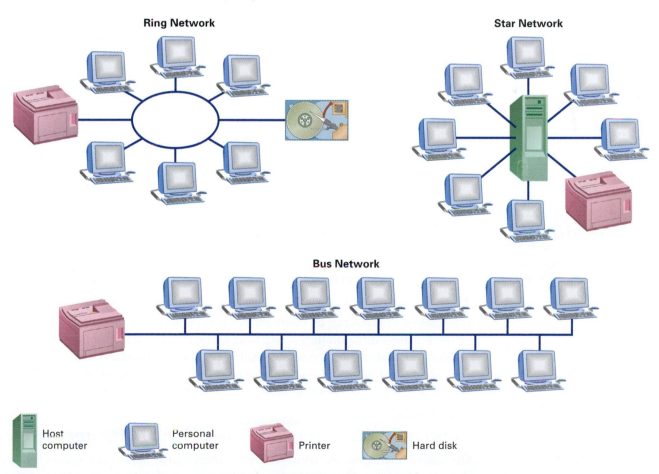

Ring Network

Star Network

Bus Network

Host computer Personal computer Printer Hard disk

Source: James O'Brien, *Introduction to Information Systems: Essentials for the Internetworked Enterprise,* 9th edition (New York: McGraw-Hill/Irwin) 2000, p. 157.

host computer and any two computers in the network can communicate with each other. However, the communications channel forms a closed loop, and hence information is passed from one computer to the next one in the ring in only one direction.

Telecommunications networks can be classified by their geographic coverage as *local area networks* and *wide area networks*. **Local area networks (LANs)** provide connectivity within a limited physical area such as an office, a building, a manufacturing plant, or several buildings in close proximity. An example of a LAN is provided in Exhibit 17.2.

local area network (LAN) A network that provides connectivity within a limited physical area such as an office, a building, or several buildings in close proximity

EXHIBIT 17.2

Example of a Local Area Network

Source: James O'Brien, *Introduction to Information Systems: Essentials for the Internetworked Enterprise,* 9th edition (New York: McGraw-Hill/Irwin) 2000, p. 144.

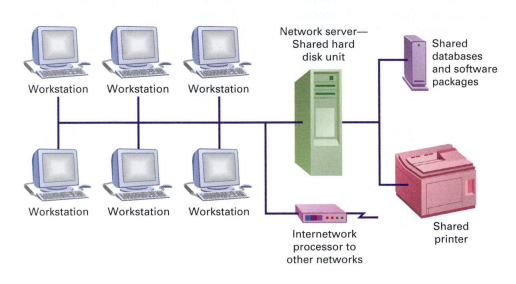

wide area network (WAN) A network that provides connectivity over large distances, sometimes from one continent to another

Wide area networks (WANs) provide connectivity over large distances. The WAN of one of the major oil companies connects its offices in the United States, Canada, Europe, Africa, Asia, and Australia.

reality CHECK — *When you use your credit card, what is the role that is played by computer hardware and software, databases, and telecommunications networks?*

Classification of Information Systems

LEARNING OBJECTIVE 3
Classify information systems by the organizational level they support and by the business function they serve.

Information systems can be classified by the organizational level they support and by the business function they serve. Thus in the first classification, we would have information systems for operational managers, middle managers, and senior managers. And in the second classification we would have information systems for marketing, production, accounting, finance, and human resources.

Information Systems for Operations Managers

Operations managers are concerned with short-range plans such as weekly production schedules. They direct the use of resources and the performance of tasks according to procedures and within budgets and schedules they establish for employees under their span of control. Information systems for operations managers are called **operational-level systems** because they monitor the elementary activities and transactions of the business organization. For example, they are used to keep track of payroll, sales orders, materials receipts, cash deposits, and credit decisions. Operational-level systems help answer questions such as, What is the inventory of a particular material? When was a certain vendor paid? How many overtime hours did each employee work in a given day? Operational-level systems are central to business survival. A prolonged failure of these systems could paralyze a firm. They are also major feeders of information for the other types of information systems.

operational-level systems Information systems for operations managers that monitor the elementary activities and transactions of a business organization

Information Systems for Middle Managers

Middle managers develop medium-range plans and specify the policies, procedures, and business goals for their business subunits. They allocate the resources and monitor the performance of their organizational subunits, including departments, divisions, and project teams. Information systems for middle managers can be *managerial information systems* or *decision-support systems*. **Managerial information systems** help middle managers to plan, control, and make routine decisions. They provide answers to routine questions that have been prespecified and have a predefined procedure in place to obtain the answers. For example, a managerial information system for DaimlerChrysler could compare the sales of its different dealers in a sales region by product line and by month.

managerial information systems Information systems for middle managers that help them plan, control, and make routine decisions

Decision-support systems combine data with sophisticated mathematical models and data analysis tools to help middle managers make non-routine decisions. Decision-support systems address problems where the procedure for arriving at a solution cannot be specified in advance. They use information from operational-level systems and from managerial information systems. In addition,

decision-support systems Information systems for middle managers that combine data with sophisticated models and data analysis tools help them make non-routine decisions

Aiesha Clark, call center representative at New Jersey Manufacturing Insurance Company, uses an operational-level information system to handle existing customer callers in Trenton, New Jersey.

they use information from external sources, such as interest rates and pricing from competitors. For example, a decision-support system could help Sony decide on its optimal product mix: How many units of each product should be produced monthly for next year? As another example, McDonald's could use a decision-support system to predict the effect of a promotion strategy on its market share. Decision-support systems contain a variety of models to analyze data, and they can condense large amounts of data into a format that is useful for middle managers. These systems are interactive and have user-friendly software. Using a decision-support system involves four basic types of analytical modeling activities: what-if analysis, sensitivity analysis, goal-seeking analysis, and optimization analysis.

what-if analysis A modeling activity in a decision-support system where the value of one or more variables is changed to observe the effect on one or more other variables of interest

In **what-if analysis,** the value of one or more variables is changed to observe the effect on one or more other variables of interest. For example, the user may change the value of production lot sizes to observe the effect on production lead times.

sensitivity analysis A modeling activity in a decision-support system where what-if analysis is used repeatedly to establish a range where the variables of interest do not change

In **sensitivity analysis,** the what-if analysis is used repeatedly to establish a range where the variables of interest do not change. For example, we may use sensitivity analysis to conclude that as long as the price of a product is in the range $150 to $200, the sales level of the product will not change. Thus we may say that the sales level for this product is insensitive to prices in the range $150 to $200.

goal-seeking analysis A modeling activity in a decision-support system where a target for a variable or variables of interest is set and then the values of other variables are changed until the target is achieved

In **goal-seeking analysis,** a target for the variables of interest is set and then the values of other variables are changed until the target is achieved. For example, we may specify a sales level of $10 million dollars, and then the values of prices and advertising budgets would be changed until the sales level is reached.

optimization analysis A modeling activity in a decision-support system that tries to find the optimal, maximum or minimum, value of one or more variables by changing the values of one or more other variables, which are typically subject to constraints

Optimization analysis finds the optimal, maximum or minimum, value of one or more variables by changing the values of one or more other variables, which are typically subject to constraints. For example, we may find the production levels of different products such that the total profit is maximized, where the production levels are constrained by production capacity and demand. Optimization analysis relies on sophisticated mathematic techniques such as linear and nonlinear programming.

Information Systems for Senior Managers

Senior mangers are concerned with strategic issues and long-term trends inside the firm and in the external environment. These managers develop overall organizational goals and objectives to assure that the company can survive and be successful in a competitive environment. The information systems for senior managers are called **executive information systems,** and they support non-routine, unstructured decisions requiring judgment, evaluation, and insight. Executive information systems combine the features of managerial information systems and decision-support systems, but they tend to make less use of analytical modeling. Instead they filter, compress, and track critical data and employ the most-advanced graphics software to minimize the time and effort required from senior managers. For example, senior managers of DaimlerChrysler could use an executive information system to assist them in answering the questions, Should we launch a new product line? What is the competition doing? Should we sell one of our business units? Should we consolidate or expand our existing manufacturing facilities? Executive information systems have *drill down* capabilities, which allow senior managers to access related information at lower levels of detail.

executive information systems Information systems for senior managers that support nonroutine, unstructured decisions requiring judgment, evaluation, and insight

Marketing Information Systems

Marketing is the business function that plans, promotes, and sells current products in existing markets and, at the same time, develops new products and new markets to better serve present and potential customers. **Marketing information systems** are information systems that provide information for supporting the major components of the marketing function. For operational managers, marketing information systems can help with locating prospective customers, processing sales orders, tracking sales orders, and providing customer service support. For middle managers, marketing information systems can assist with market research and performance, sales and product management, advertising and promotion, and pricing decisions. For senior managers, marketing information systems can monitor the performance of competitors' products, predict sales trends affecting current products, and signal opportunities for new products.

marketing information systems
Information systems that provide information to support the major components of the marketing function

Production Information Systems

Production is the business function that is responsible for the creation of goods and services. **Production information systems** are information systems that help a company develop, plan, execute, and control this production. For operations managers, production information systems can help with processing production orders, monitoring inventory levels, tracking production orders, managing quality control charts, and supervising maintenance schedules. For middle managers, production information systems facilitate the analysis of production costs and required resources and materials, the estimation of the optimal reorder points and lot sizes for an inventory system, and the determination of the optimal production levels for a given time horizon. For senior managers, production information systems assist with plant location and layout decisions, strategic capacity needs, and product and process design.

production information systems
Information systems that help a company develop, plan, execute, and control the production of goods and services

Accounting Information Systems

The accounting function records and reports the flow of funds in a business organization. **Accounting information systems** perform legal and historical record keeping, and produce financial statements. Accounting information systems are the oldest and most widely used information systems in business. For operations managers, accounting information systems help track money owed to the firm, accounts receivable, and money owned by the firm, accounts payable; they also help with order processing, inventory control, and payroll. For middle managers, accounting information systems assist in preparing budgets, calculating profitability per product and product line, and analyzing financial statements. For senior managers, accounting information systems provide long-range forecasts of the company's financial performance and investment and cash needs and estimates of the impact of mergers and acquisitions.

accounting information systems
Information systems that perform legal and historical record keeping and produce financial statements

Financial Information Systems

The finance function deals with the acquisition of financial assets and the allocation of these assets to maximize the market value of the firm. **Financial information systems** support decisions regarding the financing of a business organization and the allocation of financial resources within the organization. For operations managers, financial information systems keep track of cash, stocks, bonds, and other financial assets. For middle managers, financial information systems help

financial information systems
Information systems that support decisions regarding the financing of a business organization and the allocation of financial resources within the organization

with determining the firm's portfolio of investments, allocating financial resources to competing projects, and forecasting cash deficits or surpluses. For senior managers, financial information systems assist in developing an optimal financing plan for the business by using forecasts of the economy, business operations, interest rates, types of financing available, and stock and bond prices.

Human Resources Information Systems

human resources information systems Information systems that support planning for meeting personnel needs, developing employees to their full potential, and controlling personnel policies and programs

The human resources function involves recruiting, placing, evaluating, compensating, and developing the employees of a business organization. **Human resources information systems** support planning for meeting personnel needs, developing employees to their full potential, and controlling personnel policies and programs. For operations managers, human resources information systems assist with recruiting, workforce planning and scheduling, skills assessment, performance evaluations, payroll control, and benefits administration. For middle managers, human resources information systems help with labor cost analysis and budgeting, turnover analysis, training effectiveness, career matching, compensation effectiveness and equity analysis, and benefits preference analysis. For senior managers, human resources information systems support workforce planning and tracking, succession planning, performance appraisal systems, contract costing, and salary forecasting.

reality CHECK *If you were or are employed by a business organization, what was your interaction with the human resources information system?*

Developing Information Systems

LEARNING OBJECTIVE 4
Identify the activities involved in the development of information systems.

information systems development The activities involved in the creation of an information system

systems analysis The identification of what the information system should do

feasibility study A study to determine if the proposed solution of a business problem is feasible organizationally, economically, technically, and operationally

Information systems are created to solve business problems or to improve business operations. The activities involved in the creation of an information system are called **information systems development.** These activities can be grouped by stages as systems analysis, systems design, programming, testing, conversion, and production and maintenance.

Systems analysis consists of defining the problem, identifying its causes, specifying the solution, and identifying the information needed to achieve the solution. Systems analysis describes *what* the information system should do. One of the major activities in systems analysis is a **feasibility study** to determine if the proposed solution is feasible in four major categories:

Organizational. Can the organization handle the changes introduced by the information system?
Economic. Is the information system a good investment?
Technical. Can the firm's information systems specialists handle the technology required by the information system?
Operational. Will the information system be accepted by its users?

information requirements The details of who needs what information, where, when, and how

systems design The description of how the information system will meet the information needs identified by the systems analysis

The most challenging activity in systems analysis is determining the **information requirements,** which are a detailed statement of who needs what information, where, when, and how.

Systems design details how the information system will meet the information needs identified by the systems analysis. Systems design entails designing the user interface, the structure of the database to be used by the information system, and the programs and procedures needed by the information system. The final product of systems design is called **system specifications,** which specify the computer hardware, computer software, databases, telecommunications networks, and end users and information systems staff that will be needed by the information system.

Programming entails translating the system specifications into software programs. These programs could be created in-house, outsourced, or purchased as commercially available software packages.

Testing involves making sure that the information system will produce the desired results. The first level of testing is **unit testing** and consists of verifying that each individual program is working properly. The second level of testing is **system testing** and involves determining if the individual programs will function together as planned. The third level of testing is **acceptance testing,** which users and managers do in order to certify that the information system is ready to be used in a production setting.

Conversion is the process of moving from the current situation to the new one where the information system is in use. There are four conversion strategies: *parallel*, *phased*, *pilot*, and *plunge*. In the **parallel conversion strategy,** the old system and the new system are in operation until users agree that the new system is functioning properly. The **phased conversion strategy** introduces the new system in stages, either by function or by organizational units. The **pilot conversion strategy** operates the new system using a subset of users, and once it proves to be fully functional, the new system is installed for all users. The **plunge conversion strategy** calls for completely replacing the old system by the new system on an agreed-on day.

Once the conversion is completed and the system is being used, the system is said to be in **production.** For systems that are in production, any changes to a system in order to correct errors, meet new requirements, or improve its operation are called **maintenance.**

reality CHECK *It is a common practice for software companies to release a beta version of their software before the software is commercialized. From an information systems development perspective, what function do beta versions serve?*

Global Information Systems

LEARNING OBJECTIVE 5
Discuss how global companies are configuring their information systems.

Globalization is here to stay, and as business organizations enter the international arena, they need to configure their information systems to support their new endeavors. The four basic configuration strategies for information systems are *centralized, duplicated, decentralized*, and *networked*. The four organizational structures for conducting business globally are *domestic exporter, multinational, franchiser*, and *transnational*.

In a **centralized configuration strategy,** the development and operation of all information systems is done at a home base. In a **duplicated configuration strategy,** the development of all information systems is done at a home base, but the operation of these systems is handed over to autonomous business units at foreign locations. In the **decentralized configuration strategy,** each autonomous business

---

system specifications The specifications of the computer hardware, computer software, databases, telecommunications networks, and people resources that will be needed by the information system

programming Translating the system specifications into software programs

testing Making sure that the information system will produce the desired results

unit testing Verifying that each individual program is working properly

system testing Verifying that individual programs will function together as planned

acceptance testing Verifying that the information system is ready to be used in a production setting; done by managers and end users

conversion The process of moving from an old information system to a new information system

parallel conversion strategy The conversion strategy where an old information system and a new information system are in operation until users agree that the new system is functioning properly

phased conversion strategy The conversion strategy where a new information system is introduced in stages, either by function or by organizational units

pilot conversion strategy The conversion strategy where a new information system is operated using a subset of users and, once it proves to be fully functional, is installed for all users

plunge conversion strategy The conversion strategy where a new information system replaces at once an old information system on an agreed-on day

production The information systems development stage when the conversion is completed and the new information system is being utilized by end users

maintenance The information systems development stage when the production system is being changed to correct errors, meet new requirements, or improve its operation

centralized configuration strategy The strategy where the development and operation of all information systems is done at a home base

Case in Point

Information Systems Development at McDonald's

In 1991, McDonald's began its first campaign to collect daily sales data from its restaurants via an electronic register, or point-of-sale (POS) system. But rather than turning to a system from outsiders, McDonald's decided to cook up one of its own.

Most of McDonald's fast-food restaurant competitors—and most retailers, for that matter—use packaged POS software, as those systems are not usually viewed as strategic. McDonald's was convinced that by building its own system, it could save money. This belief led to a long-term internal development effort that culminated with McDonald's spinning off its POS development effort as a separate business backed by eMac Digital—a technology incubator supported by McDonald's and venture capitalists Accel-KKR. After some initial franchisee resistance, the POS system became a standard for McDonald's American restaurants. While McDonald's is currently looking to upgrade this now-outdated POS system, it remains at the heart of the company's restaurant operations.

POS systems play a key role in automating the interaction between retailers and their customers. When these systems electronically capture the details of each purchase, they not only yield sales totals but also information on what has been used from on-hand inventory. At an aggregate level, POS data can indicate to managers the products that are selling well and the products that are not moving, as well as when the load in operations reaches peaks and valleys. According to Carl Dill, who was McDonald's chief information officer from 1982 to 1998 and oversaw the development of the POS system, McDonald's wanted to use the system to improve its relationship with its suppliers and to gain a better understanding of product demand.

The software that McDonald's developed, called PC POS, is a two-part system. The first part consists of the actual POS terminals used at the counter and drive-through window. These terminals provide "software functionality for cash registers" says Dill, "like taking orders, communicating to cooking operations, and giving change." The second part to the system is the back-end "in-store processor" or ISP. The ISP helps turn POS data into information that can be used to better manage the restaurant. The ISP sends information via modem to McDonald's corporate headquarters and some of its partners—including Martin-Brower and Perlman-Rocque, companies that distribute everything from food to trash bags to the clothes worn by McDonald's crews—to drive store replenishment. The information sent back to McDonald's headquarters is collected in databases and then transferred to the burger giant's IBM mainframe systems. This information, when aggregated, provides a number of ways for executives to track restaurant performance, measuring metrics such as the time from when orders were placed to when they were cleared from the system. The ISP also provides restaurant managers with software to manage employees' schedules. "The process of doing that—it used to take 8 to 12 hours a week for an assistant manager just to schedule the crew—was shaved down to 2 hours," says Dill. The system also automated inventory management and reordering of nonfood supplies, such as napkins, bathroom soap, and crew uniforms—things that previously had been done on paper. Dill estimates that the ISP saved each restaurant manager 30 hours a week in paperwork.

"We developed something good for all our restaurants," says Dill. "But it was hard to get licensees to commit to it." Some franchisees already had established relationships with other POS vendors, and many were concerned about how much of their data would be sent back to McDonald's corporate headquarters, according to Dill. "There was always a concern about Big Brother looking over their shoulder," Dill says.

Now McDonald's is looking to a newer system and this time it is looking outside the company. This way the fast-food giant can now focus on hamburgers instead of cooking up its own code.

Source: "McDonald's Wants It Their Way," by Sean Gallagher, *Baseline*, at **www.baselinemag.com**, July 2, 2003.

Questions

1. What problems was the POS system going to solve?
2. Was the development of the POS system a success?
3. What would you propose to make it easier for franchisees to commit to the POS system?

unit at a foreign location develops and operates its own information systems. In the **networked configuration strategy,** the development and operation of information systems is done in an integrated and coordinated way across all business units.

A **domestic exporter** is an organizational structure where there is a heavy centralization of corporate activities in the home country. International sales are achieved by using agency agreements and subsidiaries. Examples of companies with this organizational structure are Texas Instruments, Caterpillar, and Otis Elevators. In a **multinational company,** financial management and control are concentrated at a home base, but other business functions such as production, sales, and marketing are decentralized in business units in other countries. Examples of multinational firms are General Motors, Intel, and DaimlerChrysler. A **franchiser** is an organizational structure where a product is created, designed, financed, and initially produced in the home country, but for product-specific reasons, typically cost or product perishability, relies heavily on foreign personnel for further production, marketing, and human resources. Examples of franchising companies are McDonald's, Coca-Cola, and Mrs. Fields Cookies. Key activities in a **transnational company** are neither centralized in the parent company nor decentralized so that each subsidiary can carry out its own tasks on a local basis. Instead, the resources and activities are dispersed but specialized, so as to be both efficient and flexible in an interdependent network. Examples of transnational companies are Nestlé, Citicorp, and Sony.

Domestic exporters tend to adopt a centralized configuration strategy for their information systems. Multinational companies rely on decentralized configuration strategies. Franchisers typically develop information systems at the home base, and then replicate them around the world; thus they use the duplicated configuration strategy. Transnational firms, given the interdependence of their units, prefer the networked configuration strategy.[7]

reality CHECK *Why would it make sense for a company like McDonald's to develop its information systems at its home base and then replicate them around the world?*

duplicated configuration strategy The strategy where the development of all information systems is done at a home base, but the operation of these systems is handed over to autonomous business units at foreign locations (p. 605)

decentralized configuration strategy The strategy where each autonomous business unit at a foreign location develops and operates its own information systems (p. 605)

networked configuration strategy The strategy where the development and operation of information systems is done in an integrated and coordinated way across all business units

domestic exporter An organizational structure where there is heavy centralization of corporate activities in the home country of origin

multinational company An organizational structure where financial management and control are concentrated at a home base, but other business functions such as production, sales, and marketing are decentralized to business units in other countries

franchiser An organizational structure where a product is created, designed, financed, and initially produced in the home country, but for product-specific reasons, relies heavily on foreign personnel for further production, marketing, and human resources

transnational company An organizational structure where the resources are dispersed in various countries, but each business unit in each country is specialized, so as to form an efficient, flexible, and independent network

"Ronald McDonald" greets a Ukranian woman shortly after McDonald's opened its first restaurant in Kiev. McDonald's is a franchiser that uses the duplicated configuration strategy for its global information systems.

Information Systems Controls

LEARNING OBJECTIVE 6
Illustrate what businesses can do to assure the security and accuracy of their information systems.

information systems controls The policies, procedures, and technical measures used to protect information systems and to assure the accuracy and reliability of these systems

systems controls Controls to monitor the accuracy and security of the input, processing, storage, and output activities

Information systems controls are the policies, procedures, and technical measures used to protect information systems and to assure the accuracy and reliability of these systems. Information systems controls consist of system controls, procedural controls, and facility controls. **Systems controls** monitor the accuracy and security of the input, processing, storage, and output activities. Input controls include passwords and other security codes, formatted data entry screens, and audible error signals. Processing controls identify errors in arithmetic or logical operations, as well as assure that data are not lost and are processed. Output controls ensure that information products are correct and complete and are available to authorized users in a timely manner. Access to the online output of computer networks is usually controlled by security codes that determine which users can receive what information. Storage controls protect the data resources of an organization. Typically, a multilevel password system is used to protect databases. At the first level, the password allows users to *read* information from a file in the database; at the second level, the password allows users to *change* information in the file; and at the third level, the password allows users to *create* or *delete* files in the database.

computer monitoring Using computers to monitor the productivity of employees while they work

Ethics in Business

Computer Monitoring

Computer monitoring is the use of computers to monitor the productivity of employees while they work. Supposedly, computer monitoring is done so employers can collect productivity data about their employees to increase the efficiency and quality of service. However, computer monitoring has been criticized as unethical because it monitors individuals, not just work, and is done continually, thus violating workers' privacy and personal freedom. For example, in an airline reservations firm, the reservations agent may be timed on the number of seconds he or she takes per caller to make an airline reservation, the time between calls, and the number and length of breaks taken. In addition, the reservation agent's conversation with the customer may be monitored.

Computer monitoring has been criticized as an invasion of the privacy of employees because, in many cases, they do not know that they are being monitored or how the monitored information is being used. Critics also say that an employee's right of due process may be harmed by the improper use of collected data to make personnel decisions. Since computer monitoring increases the stress on employees who must work under constant electronic surveil-

lance, it has also been blamed for causing health problems among monitored workers. Finally, computer monitoring has been blamed for robbing workers of the dignity of their work. In effect, some people say that computer monitoring creates an "electronic sweatshop," where workers are forced to work at a hectic pace under poor working conditions.

Political pressure is building to outlaw computer monitoring in the workplace. For example, public advocacy groups, labor unions, and many legislators are pushing for action at the state and federal levels in the United States. The proposed laws would regulate computer monitoring and protect the worker's right to know and right to privacy. In the meantime, lawsuits by monitored workers against employers are increasing. So computer monitoring of workers is one ethical issue that will not go away.

Source: Adapted from James O'Brien, *Introduction to Information Systems,* 9th Edition, McGraw-Hill/Irwin, 2000. Copyright © 2000 by The McGraw-Hill Companies, Inc. Reprinted with permission.

Questions

1. Discuss when computer monitoring may be ethical and when it may not.
2. Should computer monitoring be regulated by laws?

Procedural controls ensure the accuracy and integrity of computer and network operations and of systems development activities. Procedural controls include standard operating procedures and documentation, authorizations for systems development and program changes requests, and disaster recovery plans. **Facility controls** protect an organization's computing facilities from loss or destruction. Facility controls can take the form of identification badges, electronic door locks, burglar alarms, security police, closed-circuit TV, fire detection and extinguishing systems, fireproof storage vaults for the protection of files, emergency power systems, electromagnetic shielding, and controls for temperature, humidity, and dust.

procedural controls Controls to ensure the accuracy and integrity of computer and network operations and of systems development activities

facility controls Controls to protect an organization's computing facilities from loss or destruction

reality
CHECK
What is your school doing to assure the security of its information systems?

Careers in Information Systems

Advances in information technology have created rewarding and challenging job opportunities in management information systems. These opportunities are available in any business sectors that are supported by an information infrastructure. According to the Career Center at Texas A&M University, examples of business sectors using information technology include financial institutions, the oil and gas industries, retail organizations, government entities, colleges and universities, consulting companies, the energy sector, and manufacturing firms. The Career Center at Texas A&M University also lists the following job positions in management information systems:.

Programmer. Programmers meet with clients or end users to determine their business needs. Then, they translate the required business needs into code, or a language that can be understood by the computer. Programmers are also responsible for testing the program and fixing any bugs. Finally, these individuals publish a user's manual including detailed documentation about the program. Programmers should be problem solvers and should be familiar with a variety of programming languages. Programming opportunities are available in almost all organizations.

Database Administrator. With the incredible increase in computer technology, businesses are in need of experts to manage the storage and retrieval of data. This is the goal of database administrators. They determine the most efficient manner to store, organize, maintain, and retrieve records of information. They also analyze how to maintain the security of the database. Data is a strategic tool for businesses, and database administrators develop the best way to utilize this resource to its fullest advantage.

Systems Analyst and Business Analyst. Systems analysts and business analysts act as liaisons between the user and the programmer. They assess the user's needs and develop a detailed design that represents the best solution for the existing problems. Systems analysts are more involved in technical projects, while business analysts focus on analyzing a business process. These analysts may also conduct a cost-benefit comparison that will assist in the decision-making process regarding a proposal for the new or enhanced system. The analyst will communicate the design to a programmer, who will build the program. The analyst will assist in testing and implementing the program, as well as in training the users and documenting the program. Systems analysts may be involved in both hardware and software design.

Networking Specialist. Technology has allowed for new ways to communicate and to share information that is stored within different computer systems. A networking specialist develops the tools necessary to create and maintain this communication. These individuals are responsible for hardware and software design used to create tools such as local area networks or wide area networks.

Consultant. Consulting firms provide systems or information technology services to their clients. Consultants will advise clients on the design of new systems and will assist in the installation of such systems.

Summary

LEARNING OBJECTIVE 1
Explain what management information systems are.

Management information systems are the systems that manage the direct resources needed for creating, storing, and distributing information in a business organization. The direct resources that MISs manage include computer hardware, computer software, databases, and telecommunications networks.

LEARNING OBJECTIVE 2
Describe the roles that computer hardware, computer software, databases, and telecommunications networks play in management information systems.

Computer hardware is the major physical aspect of MISs. Modern computer systems include a central processing unit, primary and secondary storage, input and output devices, and communication devices. Modern computers can be classified as mainframe computers, midrange computers, microcomputers, and supercomputers. Computer software is the detailed instructions that control the operation of a computer system. The two major kinds of computer software are system software and application software. A database is a group of related files and represents the highest level in the data hierarchy. The two major types of databases are operational databases and data warehouses. Telecommunications networks are collections of computer hardware and software arranged to transmit information from one place to another. Telecommunications networks can be classified by their geographical coverage as local area networks or wide area networks.

LEARNING OBJECTIVE 3
Classify information systems by the organizational level they support and by the business function they serve.

Information systems (ISs) can be classified by the organizational level they support: as ISs for operations

managers, ISs for middle managers, and ISs for senior managers. ISs can also be classified by the business function that they serve as marketing ISs, production ISs, accounting ISs, financial ISs, and human resources ISs.

LEARNING OBJECTIVE 4
Identify the activities involved in the development of information systems.

The activities involved in the development of information systems are systems analysis, systems design, programming, testing, conversion, production, and maintenance. The four conversion strategies when moving from a current system to a new system are called parallel, phased, pilot, and plunge.

LEARNING OBJECTIVE 5
Discuss how global companies are configuring their information systems.

Domestic exporters tend to follow a centralized configuration strategy for their information systems. Multinational companies typically adopt decentralized configuration strategies. Franchisers usually use a duplicated configuration strategy. Transnational firms prefer the networked configuration strategy.

LEARNING OBJECTIVE 6
Illustrate what businesses can do to assure the security and accuracy of their information systems.

Businesses use system controls that monitor the accuracy and security of the input, processing, storage, and output activities. Firms also institute procedural controls that ensure the accuracy and integrity of computer and network operations and of systems development activities. Companies further establish facility controls that protect the organization's computing facilities from loss or destruction.

Chapter Questions

1. What are management information systems?
2. What are two classifications of information systems?
3. What are the major activities in developing information systems?
4. How are global firms configuring their information systems?
5. What are information systems controls?
6. What is the relationship between computer hardware and computer software?
7. Who decides what are data and what is information?
8. Discuss the evolution of programming languages.
9. What is the difference between an operational database and a data warehouse?
10. What are the advantages and disadvantages of using twisted-pair wire, coaxial cable, and fiber-optic cable as media for telecommunications channels?
11. Under what circumstances would you recommend a star network, a bus network, and a ring network?
12. When would you use what-if analysis, sensitivity analysis, goal-seeking analysis, and optimization analysis?
13. How would you go about creating an executive information system?
14. What are the most important stages in information systems development and why?
15. How would you economically justify information systems controls?

Interpreting Business News

1. Information technology now accounts for more than 40 percent of total business expenditures on capital equipment in the United States. Whether this investment has translated into genuine productivity gains remains open to debate. For over a decade, researchers have been trying to quantify the benefits from information technology investments by analyzing data collected at the economy level, industry level, firm level, and information systems application level. The results of these studies have been mixed and the term *productivity paradox* was coined to describe such findings. Why do you think the results of the research studies have been mixed? How can organizations determine the business value of their information systems?

2. There has been a lot of talk lately in business organizations about ethics in information systems and any related legislation. Do you think that ethics in information systems can or should be legislated? How can organizations ensure that their information systems are used in an ethical manner?

3. Business information technology is evolving at an unprecedented pace that can be described by what is called *Moore's law*. In 1965, Gordon Moore, cofounder of Intel, made the following prediction: Given that the number of transistors per square inch on integrated circuits has doubled every year since the integrated circuit was invented, this trend will continue for the foreseeable future. In subsequent years, the pace slowed down a bit, but data density has doubled approximately every 18 months, and this is the current definition of Moore's law, which Moore himself has blessed. Most experts, including Moore himself, expect Moore's law to hold for at least another two decades. How can organizations develop an information technology structure that can support their goals when business conditions and technologies are changing so rapidly?

Web Assignments

1. One of the student and professional organizations for management information systems is called *AITP: The Association of Information Technology Professionals*. Visit its website at **www.aitp.org** and learn more about management information systems, student membership, and the AITP certification program for information technology professionals. What does it take to become certified?

2. Use a search engine to search for management information systems jobs. What do the jobs have in common? Where are the jobs located?

3. Use a search engine to search for undergraduate and graduate programs in management information systems. Describe the kinds of courses involved in this program of study.

Portfolio Projects

Exploring Your Own Case in Point

After reading this chapter, you can better understand the management information systems function of the company that you have selected to research.

1. What computer hardware and software, databases, and telecommunications networks does your company use?

2. Does your company have information systems for operational, middle, and senior managers? If so, how are these systems used? Does it have information systems for marketing, production, accounting, finance, and human resources? If so, how are these systems used?

3. What has been your company's experience in developing information systems? Does it have global information systems in place?

4. What information systems controls does your company use? What is its organizational structure for its management information systems business function?

Starting Your Own Business

After reading this chapter, you will be in a better position to plan for the information systems needs of your startup company.

1. What computer hardware and software, databases, and telecommunications networks will be needed by your business?

2. What information systems will your managers (operational, middle, and senior) need?

3. How will the information systems needed by your managers be developed?

4. What controls will you have in place to protect your management information systems?

Test Prepper

You've read the chapter, studied the key terms, and the exam is any day now. Think you are ready to ace it? Take this sample test to gauge your comprehension of chapter material. You can check your answers at the back of the book.

True/False Questions

Please indicate if the following statements are true or false:

_____ 1. Data are information that has been transformed to be meaningful and valuable to specific users.

_____ 2. An information system is a system that converts data into information.

_____ 3. Mainframe computers are extremely powerful computers specifically designed for applications requiring complex calculations at a very high speed.

_____ 4. An operating system is the software program that manages and controls the activities of the computer.

_____ 5. A data warehouse is the systematic search for patterns and trends in business activities that can be exploited by managers to gain competitive advantage.

_____ 6. A bus network is similar to a star network in that there is no host computer and any two computers in the network can communicate with each other.

_____ 7. In sensitivity analysis, the what-if analysis is used repeatedly to establish a range where the variables of interest do not change.

_____ 8. Production information systems perform legal and historical record keeping and produce financial statements.

_____ 9. In information systems development, testing involves making sure that the information system will produce the desired results.

_____ 10. Procedural controls monitor the accuracy and security of the input, processing, storage, and output activities.

Multiple-Choice Questions

Choose the best answer.

_____ 1. Management information systems are the systems that manage the

   a. direct resources needed for creating, storing, and distributing information in a business organization.

   b. direct resources needed for creating, storing, and distributing data in a business organization.

   c. indirect resources needed for creating, storing, and distributing information in a business organization.

   d. indirect resources needed for creating, storing, and distributing data in a business organization.

   e. computers only.

_____ 2. A petabyte is equal to

   a. 1000 bytes.
   b. 1000 kilobytes.
   c. 1000 megabytes.
   d. 1000 gigabytes.
   e. 1000 terabytes.

_____ 3. Word processors such as Microsoft Word and WordPerfect, electronic spreadsheets such as Microsoft Excel and Lotus 1-2-3, and presentation graphics programs such as Microsoft PowerPoint and Lotus Freelance Graphics are examples of

   a. operating software.
   b. general-purpose software.
   c. application-specific software.
   d. programming software.
   e. database software.

_____ 4. Programming languages that use translator programs called compilers to convert programming statements, which are more like natural language, into machine language are called

   a. fourth-generation languages.
   b. third-generation languages.
   c. high-level languages.
   d. assembler languages.
   e. machine languages.

_____ 5. A record is a collection of

   a. related files.
   b. related fields.
   c. files.
   d. databases.
   e. operational databases.

_____ 6. A modem translates

  a. digital signals into analog signals and vice versa.
  b. digital signals into electrical signals.
  c. analog signals into electrical signals.
  d. multiplex signals via switches.
  e. multiplex signals via routers.

_____ 7. The star network consists of

  a. several computers that are connected and share the same communications channel.
  b. a host computer connected to several, typically smaller computers.
  c. several computers that are connected and do not share the same communications channel.
  d. several computers that are connected and together form a closed loop.
  e. several computers that are connected and share the same communications channel but have no host computer.

_____ 8. _____ networks provide connectivity over long distances.

  a. Star
  b. Bus

  c. Ring
  d. Local area
  e. Wide area

_____ 9. Information systems that combine data with sophisticated mathematical models and data analysis to help middle managers make non-routine decisions are called

  a. operational-level systems.
  b. managerial information systems.
  c. executive information systems.
  d. decision-support systems.
  e. production information systems.

_____ 10. Each autonomous business unit at a foreign location develops and operates its own information system in a

  a. centralized configuration strategy.
  b. duplicated configuration strategy.
  c. networked configuration strategy.
  d. decentralized configuration strategy.
  e. transnational configuration strategy.

Want more questions? Visit the student website at **http://college.hmco.com/business/student/** (select Gaspar, *Introduction to Business*) and take the ACE quizzes for more practice.

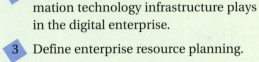

The Digital Enterprise

18

| Introduction

| Information Technology Infrastructure for the Digital Enterprise

| Enterprise Resource Planning Systems
  Benefits and Costs of ERP Systems
  ERP Software Vendors
  Implementing ERP Systems

| Supply Chain Management
  Economic Impact of Supply Chain Management
  Supply Chain Management Strategies

| E-Business
  Electronic Payment Systems
  Opportunities and Challenges

| Careers in the Digital Enterprise
  Information Technology Infrastructure for the Digital Enterprise
  ERP Systems
  Supply Chain Management
  E-Business

Learning Objectives

After studying this chapter, you should be able to

1. Explain what the digital enterprise is.

2. Describe the role that the new information technology infrastructure plays in the digital enterprise.

3. Define enterprise resource planning.

4. Compare the five major vendors of enterprise resource planning software.

5. Evaluate the two major strategies for implementing enterprise resource planning systems.

6. Illustrate supply chain management.

7. Outline the roles that ERP systems, supply chain management, and e-business play in the emergence of the digital enterprise.

Dangers of the Digital Enterprise

They were just a few short lines of code, but they provided a big wake-up call for anyone using a computer. The recent back-to-back hits by the Blaster and SoBig viruses ended a long lull in high-profile attacks on computer systems. The chaos they created was an unpleasant reminder that computer networks and the Internet—now so vital to a company's business—are still vulnerable to intrusions.

What's more, virus outbreaks are only the most visible evidence of computers' vulnerability. Sophisticated thieves can steal customers' credit card numbers out of vast databases, industrial spies can tap e-mails and other communications for sensitive corporate secrets, and unscrupulous or negligent employees—not to mention malevolent hackers—can sabotage critical computer systems. "The attacks are getting more frequent, and they are more complex," says Robert A. Clyde, chief technology officer at security-software maker Symantec, Corporation, of Cupertino, California.[1]

Introduction

LEARNING OBJECTIVE 1
Explain what the digital enterprise is.

business processes The unique ways in which companies organize, coordinate, and execute activities, information, and knowledge in order to produce goods or services

digital enterprise A business organization where all major business processes and relationships with suppliers, customers, employees, managers, and shareholders are digitally enabled

Business processes are the unique ways in which companies organize, coordinate, and execute activities, information, and knowledge in order to produce goods or services. A **digital enterprise** is a business organization where all major business processes and relationships with suppliers, customers, employees, managers, and shareholders are digitally enabled. Cisco Systems, Procter & Gamble, and Dell are examples of digital enterprises in the making. Furthermore, nearly all other firms, especially larger and traditional firms such as DaimlerChrysler and Sony, are being driven in the digital enterprise direction by the synergy of the following independent but interrelated developments:

- New information technology infrastructures that include *intranets, extranets,* and the *Internet*
- New business software for integrating business processes across a firm known as *enterprise resource planning*
- New market forces leading to the integration of business organizations across their supply chains, which has been termed *supply chain management*
- New opportunities for businesses to interact electronically with customers and other businesses that have been called *e-business*

In this chapter, we explore these developments and their synergies, emphasizing their contribution to the digital integration of enterprises with their suppliers, customers, employees, managers, and shareholders. Whereas legal and ethical issues are a concern to every organization, e-businesses must be particularly interested in security, as illustrated by the virus problems narrated in the vignette. We finish the chapter with a presentation of career opportunities in digital enterprises.

 What digital enterprises do you interact with?

Information Technology Infrastructure for the Digital Enterprise

LEARNING OBJECTIVE 2
Describe the role that the new information technology infrastructure plays in the digital enterprise.

Internetworking is the linking of separate networks into an interconnected network, where each network retains its own identity. The **Internet** is an international network of networks containing hundreds of thousands of private and public networks in more than 150 countries. The Internet is an example of internetworking, and it is the world's largest and most widely used network, with an estimated 500 million users and growing. The use of the Internet jumped twelve-fold between 1996 and 2000, while TV viewing barely went up at all.[2]

The Internet was created by the U.S. Department of Defense to link scientists and university professors around the world. To connect to the Internet, individuals need the services of an *Internet service provider*. An **Internet service provider (ISP)** is a business organization with a permanent connection to the Internet that sells temporary connections to subscribers. The Internet can also be accessed through online service companies such as America Online (AOL) and Microsoft Network (MSN). The Internet is extremely flexible. Networks can be added or removed with ease, and if a network in the Internet fails, the rest of the Internet can continue to operate without any problems. Using special technology and communications standards, any two computers linked to the Internet can communicate with each other, even using regular telephone lines, regardless of where the computers are located—next door or around the world. Business organizations and individuals can use the Internet to exchange text messages, graphical displays, sound, and video. In short, the Internet provides the primary information technology platform for the digital enterprise.

The Internet capability called the *World Wide Web* is one of the reasons the Internet has become so popular in such a short period of time. The **World Wide Web (WWW or www)** is a system with universally accepted standards for displaying, formatting, storing, and retrieving information in a networked environment. In the World Wide Web, information is stored and displayed on electronic pages, called **webpages,** that may contain text, graphics, sound, animations, and video. Webpages can be accessed by any type of computer and can be linked to other webpages, independently of where the other webpages are located. In order to access the linked webpages, one simply has to click on a highlighted word or button on the viewed webpage. The collection of all the World Wide Web pages maintained by an individual or business organization is called a **website.** The design and management of websites has generated multiple job and business opportunities. A **webmaster** is the person in charge of a firm's website.

Connectivity in the Internet is achieved by the *Transmission Control Protocol/Internet Protocol (TCP/IP)*. The TCP/IP was developed by the U.S. Department of Defense in 1972 as a reference model for any two computers to communicate, even if the computers had different hardware and software platforms. To access a website, the user has to specify a **uniform resource locator (URL),** which represents the address of a resource on the Internet. For example, the URL for Texas A&M University is **http://www.tamu.edu.** The first four characters, *http*, are an abbreviation for **hypertext transport protocol,** which is a communications standard used to transfer webpages on the World Wide Web. The characters *www.tamu.edu* represent the domain name, which identifies the Web server storing the webpages of Texas A&M University. A **search engine** is a tool for locating websites on the Internet. Search engines contain software that looks for webpages

---

internetworking The linking of separate networks into an interconnected network, where each network retains its own identity

Internet An international network of networks containing hundreds of thousands of private and public networks in more than 150 countries

internet service provider (ISP) A business organization with a permanent connection to the Internet that sells temporary connections to subscribers

World Wide Web (WWW or www) A system with universally accepted standards for displaying, formatting, storing, and retrieving information in a networked environment

webpage An electronic page where information is stored and displayed on the World Wide Web, and that may contain text, graphics, sound, animations, and video

website The collection of all the World Wide Web pages maintained by an individual or business organization

webmaster The person in charge of a firm's website

uniform resource locator (URL) The address of a resource on the Internet

hypertext transfer protocol (http) A communications standard used to transfer webpages on the World Wide Web

search engine A tool for locating websites on the Internet containing the search terms or key words. Popular search engines are Yahoo!, Google, and AltaVista.

Telecommunications networks can be classified as *intranets* and *extranets*. An **intranet** is an internal network in a business organization that is used by employees to collaborate, share information, and access internal websites. An **extranet** is a network that links the intranet resources of a company with other organizations outside the company. For example, extranets allow customers and suppliers of a firm to access the firm's selected intranet websites. Organizations can establish private extranets among themselves or use the Internet as the connecting medium. In the latter case, security can be achieved by a *virtual private network*. A **virtual private network (VPN)** is a secure network that uses the Internet as its main backbone network, but relies on a *network firewall*. A **network firewall,** or simply a firewall, is a computer that uses security software to screen all network traffic for passwords and other security codes and permits only authorized transmissions in and out of the network. A firewall is a gatekeeper computer system that protects a company's intranets from unauthorized users. For example, a virtual private network enables DaimlerChrysler to use the Internet to build secure intranets among its manufacturing plants and corporate offices and to maintain secure extranets with its suppliers and customers.

Telecommunications networks can also be classified as *client/server networks*, on the basis of the role that each computer plays in the network. A **client/server network** is a telecommunications network where some computers are "clients" and some computers are "servers." The **clients** are personal computers or workstations that provide user interfaces and perform some processing on an application. The **servers** are midrange or mainframe computers that perform most of the processing on an application, all computations, and database management. The most common client/server network is known as a *three-tier network*. In a **three-tier client/server network,** the user interface resides on personal computers or workstations, the system and application software reside on midrange computers, and the database resides on mainframe computers. Client/server networks have become the predominant information architecture for the digital enterprise.

reality CHECK   *Can you think of the information technology infrastructure behind Amazon.com?*

intranet An internal network in a business organization that is used by employees to collaborate, share information, and access internal websites

extranet A network that links the intranet resources of a company with other organizations

virtual private network (VPN) A secure network that uses the Internet as its main backbone network, but relies on a network firewall for security

network firewall A computer that uses security software to screen all network traffic for passwords and other security codes and permits only authorized transmission in and out of the network

client/server network A telecommunications network where some computers are "clients" and some computers are "servers"

clients Personal computers or workstations in a client/server network that provide user interfaces and perform some processing on an application

servers Midrange or mainframe computers in a client/server network that perform most processing on an application, all computations, and database management

three-tier client/server network A client/server network where the user interface resides on personal computers or workstations, the system and application software reside on midrange computers, and the database resides on mainframe computers

Enterprise Resource Planning Systems

LEARNING OBJECTIVE 3
Define enterprise resource planning.

Many modern businesses are organized by functional area: accounting, finance, marketing, operations, and human resources, among others. While this form of organization has reduced the complexity in business management, it has also naturally induced the problem of *information fragmentation*. **Information fragmentation** refers to the situation where the information of a business organization does not reside in a single repository, but instead is spread across functional areas, business units, regions, factories, and offices. The problem of information fragmentation is exacerbated by information systems that typically do not "talk" to each other, and consequently, lead to decisions that have to be made using

information fragmentation The situation in a business organization where the information does not reside in a single repository, but instead is spread across functional areas, business units, regions, factories, and offices

outdated and partial information. If a company's information is fragmented, its business is fragmented.[3]

Enterprise resource planning (ERP) systems, sometimes simply called *enterprise systems*, offer a solution to the problem of information fragmentation. The idea behind ERP systems is simple.

- Store all information in a single database.
- Represent each business function by a module.
- Design and build the ERP system as a collection of business processes, not business functions.

The anatomy of an ERP system is presented in Exhibit 18.1.

Notice that because there is a single database, the information used for decision making is always up-to-date and because there is only one system, the modules for each business function are guaranteed by design to "talk" to each other. **ERP systems** are then software packages designed to integrate the majority of a firm's business processes, execute all transactions related to the firm's business processes that are being integrated, store each piece of data only once in an enterprise-wide database, allow access to data and information in real time, and

EXHIBIT 18.1

Anatomy of an ERP System

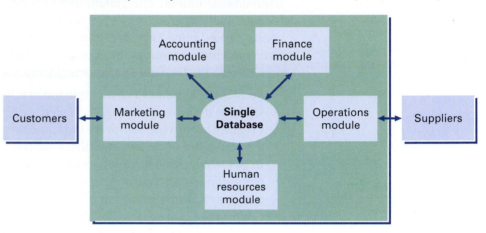

operate in a client/server environment, whether traditional or Web-based. Notice that ERP systems digitalize the business processes of the firm. Any or all information systems that the ERP system replaces are called **legacy systems.**

Examples of business processes for different business functions that are supported by ERP systems are

> *Marketing.* Order processing, pricing, shipping, billing, sales management, sales planning
>
> *Operations.* Inventory management, purchasing, shipping, production planning, materials requirements planning, plant and equipment maintenance
>
> *Accounting and finance.* Accounts payable, accounts receivable, cash management, product-cost accounting, cost-center accounting, asset management, general ledger, financial reporting
>
> *Human resources.* Personnel administration, time accounting, payroll, personnel planning and development, benefits accounting, applicant tracking, travel and expense reporting

To address the globalization trends of businesses, some ERP systems are *multilanguage, multicurrency,* and *multinational.* **Multilanguage** refers to the ability of ERP software to be in multiple languages. For example, one company sells an ERP system that can simultaneously operate in more than 30 different languages. When the user launches the ERP system, he or she has the option of selecting the language in which he or she will interact with the system. **Multicurrency** refers to the ability of ERP software to handle multiple currencies. For example, a Japanese user of Sony's ERP system is able to view Sony's profit and loss statement in yens, while a

ERP systems Software packages designed to integrate the majority of a firm's business processes, execute all transactions related to the firm's business processes being integrated, store each piece of data only once in an enterprise-wide database, allow access to data and information in real time, and operate in a client/server environment, traditional or Web-based

legacy systems Any and all information systems that an ERP system replaces

multilanguage A property of ERP systems to simultaneously operate in multiple languages

multicurrency A property of ERP systems to handle multiple currencies

multinational A property of ERP systems to handle the accounting standards of multiple countries

U.S. user is able to see the same statement in U.S. dollars. **Multinational** refers to the ability of ERP software to handle the accounting standards of multiple countries. For example, DaimlerChrysler's ERP system follows the U.S. accounting standards in its U.S. subsidiaries, and follows the Mexican accounting standards in its Mexico subsidiaries. ERP systems are now being used in more than 100 countries and by virtually all major industries, which include oil and gas; telecommunications; pharmaceutical; utilities; automotive; high tech and electronics; engineering and construction; consumer products; chemicals; retail; consulting and professional services; banking; media; metal, paper, and wood products; public sector; and health care.

For example, suppose a salesperson for a U.S. computer manufacturer is accessing an ERP system from Paris via the Internet to prepare a quote for a customer. The salesperson enters some basic information about the customer's requirements into the ERP system using her or his laptop computer. The ERP system automatically produces a formal contract, in French, specifying the product's configuration, price in French francs or Euros, and delivery date. When the customer accepts the terms in the contract, the sales representative keys this information into the ERP system. The system automatically

- Verifies the customer's credit limit and, if it is approved, records the order.
- Updates the sales and production plan.
- Creates a bill of materials for the order and executes a materials requirement plan.
- Schedules the shipment, identifying the best routing, and, working backward from the delivery date, reserves the necessary materials from inventory.
- Orders any needed parts from suppliers and schedules final assembly at the company's factory in Taiwan.
- Credits the salesperson's payroll account with the corresponding commission in French francs or Euros, and his or her travel account with the expense of the sales call.
- Calculates the actual product cost and profitability in U.S. dollars and updates the divisional and corporate balance sheets, the accounts-payable and accounts-receivable ledgers, the cost-center accounts, and the corporate cash levels.

In short, the ERP system performs nearly every business transaction resulting from the sale.[4]

Benefits and Costs of ERP Systems

A recent survey of 163 companies representing a wide range of industries and the public sector in Australia, France, Germany, Spain, the United Kingdom, and the United States examined the effects of ERP systems. It determined the benefits achieved by these organizations; the number in parentheses represents the percentage of the companies in the survey that achieved that particular benefit.

Improved financial management (70 percent). Financial and general managers can exert tighter financial control, make better predictions about financial performance, and assess better the implications of operational changes on key performance metrics.

Faster, more accurate transactions (69 percent). Highly integrated, accurate databases result in reduced IT costs, improved data quality, and better customer service. Accurate transactions are an intermediate benefit that enables other business objectives.

Better managerial decision-making (63 percent). Managers supported by efficient decision-making capabilities are able to make better, faster decisions that are aligned with the organization's strategies.

Improved inventory and asset management (60 percent). Consistent, tightly integrated systems allow organizations to provide better service and reduce costs through efficiencies such as better asset management or inventory reductions.

Ease of expansion or growth and increased flexibility (55 percent). ERP systems enable a more agile, flexible organization. They position an organization for growth and enable easier integration of newly acquired entities.

Use of fewer physical resources and improved logistics (54 percent). By streamlining logistics and minimizing the associated physical resources, organizations can attain increased operational efficiency and cost reduction.

Cycle time reduction (53 percent). Shortening cycle time enables an organization to be more nimble, cut costs, and improve its responsiveness to employees and customers.

Improved customer service and retention (47 percent). Integrated customer information allows organizations to serve their customers faster and more effectively, thereby increasing customer satisfaction, loyalty, and retention.

Headcount reduction (40 percent). Through greater systems and operational efficiencies enabled by ERP software, organizations can minimize their support staff and thereby reduce costs.

Increased revenue (36 percent). Integrated business processes can enable a firm to offer new products or exploit new channels, thus creating new opportunities to generate revenue.[5]

The cost of an ERP system includes several components.

- The cost of the ERP software, which is related to the size of the company that it must serve
- The cost of the additional hardware that is typically needed to run the ERP software
- The cost of the consultants that are needed to install and configure the ERP software
- The cost of training employees to use the ERP system[6]

A large company may spend from $50 million to $500 million U.S. dollars for an ERP system. For example, Allied Signal, a manufacturer with annual sales of $14.5 billion U.S. dollars, is implementing an ERP system in its Turbocharging Systems Division, which encompasses 18 sites in 11 countries and 9 languages. Such an implementation might cost $30 million U.S. dollars in ERP software license fees, $200 million U.S. dollars in consulting fees, plus millions of more U.S. dollars for additional hardware and training. In addition, the implementation may take four to six years. A midsized company may spend from $10 million to $20 million U.S. dollars implementing an ERP system, and it may take one to two years to finish the implementation.

reality CHECK *When you buy a ticket from a commercial airline via its website, you are interacting with its ERP system. Why do you think this is the case?*

ERP Software Vendors

LEARNING OBJECTIVE 4
Compare the five major vendors of enterprise resource planning software.

The largest five ERP software vendors in increasing order of market share are Baan, J.D. Edwards, PeopleSoft, Oracle, and SAP. This number may be reduced: PeopleSoft has been in the process of merging with J.D. Edwards, and Oracle announced a hostile takeover of PeopleSoft. Other ERP software vendors include but are not limited to Great Plains, Lawson, QAD, Ross Systems, and Systems Union.

Baan was founded in the Netherlands in 1978. Baan's ERP market share is approximately 4 percent and its 1998 revenues where roughly $750 million U.S. dollars. Baan has over 3000 clients in 5000 sites worldwide. Baan was thrust into the international ERP software spotlight when it won the Boeing Company ERP engagement in 1994.

J.D. Edwards recently introduced its multiplatform software, OneWorld, which was designed to gradually replace its previous ERP product. Reportedly, OneWorld is designed for between 5 and 500 users. In 1997, J.D. Edwards commanded about 7 percent of the ERP market, mostly concentrating in midsized companies. In 1998, its ERP revenues were $979 million U.S. dollars. J.D. Edwards is a U.S. company.

PeopleSoft was founded in 1987 and went public in 1992. PeopleSoft is the third-largest ERP software vendor. In 1997, its share of the ERP market was 7 percent, and in 1998 its revenues exceeded $1.3 billion U.S. dollars. PeopleSoft's ERP system can be scaled to accommodate from 10 to 500 users. PeopleSoft has become known for having the broadest human resources module. In many cases, firms have adopted the human resources module from PeopleSoft and the other modules from other ERP vendors. In some cases, the quality of its human resources module led some clients to adopt the rest of PeopleSoft's ERP modules. PeopleSoft is a U.S. company.

Oracle is the second-largest supplier of ERP software in the world; however, it is perhaps best known for its database system and not its ERP software. Oracle was founded in 1977 in the United States. Oracle's ERP applications were developed for the U.S. market in 1989 and for the international market in 1993. In 1997, Oracle announced that it was going to market to specific industries and improve the international characteristics of its software. Oracle's ERP market share in 1997 was 13 percent, and its 1998 ERP revenues were $2.4 billion U.S. dollars. Oracle's ERP software can accommodate over 1,000 users. Oracle's reputation in ERP systems is for developing a product that can be easily interfaced with modules of other ERP systems. Oracle was the first ERP vendor to make its ERP system compatible with the Internet.

The largest market share for ERP software is held by Systems, Applications, and Products in Data Processing (SAP, which is pronounced S-A-P), with estimates ranging from 40 to 60 percent. Five former IBM analysts founded SAP in 1972 in Mannheim, Germany, because they wanted to develop and market standard software that would integrate business processes, to process data interactively and have it available in real time, and to have users to work with data on a computer screen, and not with voluminous printed output.

In 1979, SAP released its first commercial ERP software, called R/2, which operated on mainframe computers and integrated financial and operational data into a single database. In 1994, SAP released its next generation ERP software, called R/3, which exploited the increasingly popular client/server architecture. Specifically, SAP R/3 was implemented using a three-tier client/server network. In 1997, SAP's revenues exceeded $5 billion U.S. dollars, and by 2002 its revenues reached $8 billion U.S. dollars. SAP is known for spending about 20 percent of its sales income on research and development. In 2002, SAP had more than 28,000 employees and more than 12,000 customers in 107 countries, and had sold more than 22,000 installations of its ERP software. Reportedly, SAP R/3 can be scaled for between 25 and 1000 users. The client/server-based SAP R/3 is being gradually transitioned to a Web-based architecture called mySAP.com.

ERP firms do not implement all the software that they sell; instead, they work with a wide variety of partners that do so. For example, SAP has four types of partners. *Alliance* partners like Accenture and Deloitte & Touche provide professional services. *Platform* partners like IBM and Hewlett-Packard provide hardware. *Technology* partners like Microsoft and Oracle provide operating systems and database systems. And *complementary* partners like FedEx and UPS provide tools that run with R/3. The approach used by SAP, and soon copied by other ERP software vendors, was to share a major portion of the implementation revenues with its partners. In Europe, its plan was to share 80 percent of the revenues with implementation partners, while in the United States, its plan was to share 90 percent, in order to generate market share.

Because the modules of some ERP software vendors are better than the modules of other ERP software vendors, some companies have decided to buy different modules from different ERP software vendors. For example, a company may decide to buy the accounting module from SAP, the operations module from Baan, the human resources module from PeopleSoft, and the finance module from Oracle. In ERP systems jargon, such a company is said to follow a **best-of-breed approach.** When a company adopts all the required modules from a single ERP software vendor, such a company is said, again in ERP systems jargon, to follow a **monolithic approach.** The advantage of a best-in-breed approach is that the company is getting the best modules in the market; the disadvantage is that developing interfaces among the modules from different ERP software vendors can turn into a nightmare. The advantage of the monolithic approach is that the ERP software vendor designed all the modules to seamlessly interface with each other, and if there are problems with the ERP software, then there is only one vendor to deal with. The disadvantage is that not all modules from one vendor are necessarily the best in the market. An example of a company that adopted the best-in-breed approach is Dell; an example of a company that adopted the monolithic approach is CITGO Petroleum Corporation.[7]

best-of-breed approach An approach for implementing an ERP system where the modules of the system are from different ERP software vendors

monolithic approach An approach for implementing an ERP system where all the modules of the system are from a single ERP software vendor

reality CHECK *If your school has ERP software, do you know which vendor supplied it?*

SAP is the largest vendor of ERP systems in the world.

Implementing ERP Systems

LEARNING OBJECTIVE 5
Evaluate the two major strategies for implementing enterprise resource planning systems.

The two major strategies used by companies to implement ERP systems are called the *phased* and the *big bang* strategies. In the **phased strategy,** modules are implemented one at a time and, if it is the case, one location at a time. For example, CITGO Petroleum Corporation used the phased strategy when it implemented its SAP R/3 system. It implemented the finance module at its Lake Charles oil refinery and then at its Corpus Christi oil refinery. Then it implemented the human resources module at its Lake Charles oil refinery, and later at its Corpus Christi oil refinery. The phased strategy is similar to the phased conversion strategy for information systems presented in Chapter 17.

In the **big-bang strategy,** all required modules are implemented at once and, if it is the case, at all locations. In the case of Quantum, this meant implementing at once 17 modules of Oracle ERP at 23 sites around the world. The big-bang strategy is similar to the plunge conversion strategy for information systems presented in Chapter 17.

There are several advantages and disadvantages of the phased and big-bang strategies.

> *Interfaces.* Because it replaces legacy systems all at once, the big-bang strategy does not require temporary interfaces, while the phased strategy does.
>
> *Risk.* In the phased strategy, implementation team members participate in phases as different modules are implemented. In the big-bang strategy, the entire implementation team tackles the project at roughly the same time. As a result, some have argued that the phased strategy is more risky because not all team members will be involved and coordinated at the same time. In addition, with the big-bang strategy, there are no legacy systems to go back to. Knowing that there is no return makes it easier to not

phased strategy A strategy for implementing an ERP system where modules are implemented one at a time and, if it is the case, one location at a time

big-bang strategy A strategy for implementing an ERP system where all required modules are implemented at once and, if it is the case, at all locations

Zack Nofal is the owner of a CITGO gas station in Nashville, Tennessee. CITGO Petroleum Corporation took more than four years and spent more than $100 million U.S. to implement its ERP system.

look back and yields a commitment to the ERP system that might not otherwise be possible. At the same time, the big-bang strategy may end up being riskier than the phased strategy because if the system fails, the whole company could get paralyzed. For example, this is what happened to Cisco Systems, Inc. when it implemented its ERP system.

Time. Because the big-bang strategy handles design, development, testing, and implementation of all modules simultaneously, it generally takes less time.

Cost. If all goes well, the big-bang strategy costs less because there is limited if any work on legacy systems and temporary interfaces.

Resources. Whereas the big-bang strategy requires substantial one-time resource use, the phased strategy can spread those peak resource requirements over multiple phases.

Learning. In a phased implementation, knowledge gained in one phase can be transferred to other phases. As a result, modules can be implemented by increasingly more experienced people as design, development, and testing issues are fed back to the project team.

Results. In the phased strategy, the successful implementation of one module can be used to show the rest of the organization that the ERP system works. In this scenario, the "easiest" modules should be implemented first.

Lag. With the big-bang strategy, there can be a very long period of time between when the system is being designed, developed, and tested and when the system can be used in production. Consequently, some team members may grow restless, and this may have an impact on the team's morale and productivity.[8]

reality CHECK *Do you think that the phased implementation strategy is better for certain types of business organization? Which types, and why?*

Supply Chain Management

LEARNING OBJECTIVE 6
Illustrate supply chain management.

A **supply chain** encompasses all the activities associated with the flow and transformation of finished goods from the raw material stage through to the end user, together with the corresponding flows of monetary funds and information. These activities are typically performed by different business organizations identified as suppliers, manufacturers, distributors, and retailers. An example of a simple supply chain is presented in Exhibit 18.2 (on p. 626).

Supply chain management is the management of all the activities in the supply chain, in order to minimize the total costs of the chain and to maximize the value to the end user. Supply chain management cuts through most business functions and across several business organizations. Consequently, it leads to the integration of various business processes in the business organizations that are members of the supply chain. ERP systems have been used with enormous success to integrate most business processes within a company, and have become the backbone of most supply chain management efforts. Therefore, ERP systems, in combination with supply chain management, are leading to firms that are digitally enabling their business processes and relationships with other members of the supply chain.

supply chain All activities associated with the flow and transformation of finished goods from the raw material stage through to the end user, together with the corresponding flows of monetary funds and information

supply chain management (SCM) The management of all activities in the supply chain, in order to minimize the total costs of the chain and to maximize the value to the end user

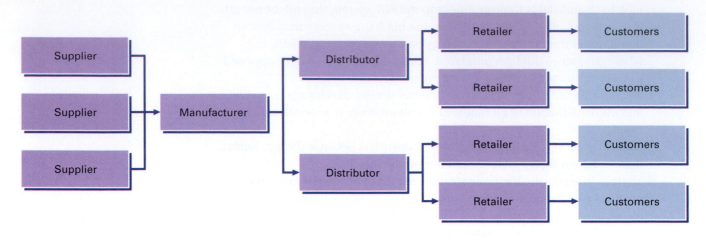

EXHIBIT 18.2

A Simple Supply Chain

If integration of the various business functions within a firm is the key concept behind ERP systems, then integration of the various firms in a supply chain is the fundamental notion behind supply chain management. A well-known classical example of the lack of information integration in a supply chain is the so-called *bullwhip effect*. When examining the demand for Pampers disposable diapers, Procter & Gamble executives noticed that even though retail sales of the product were relatively uniform, the distributors' orders placed to the manufacturer fluctuated much more than retail sales. In turn, the manufacturer's orders to suppliers fluctuated even more.[9] This increase in variability from lower to higher in the supply chain is what is called the **bullwhip effect**. A graphical representation of the bullwhip effect is shown in Exhibit 18.3.

bullwhip effect The property of supply chains where demand increases in variability as it travels up in the supply chain

EXHIBIT 18.3

The Bullwhip Effect

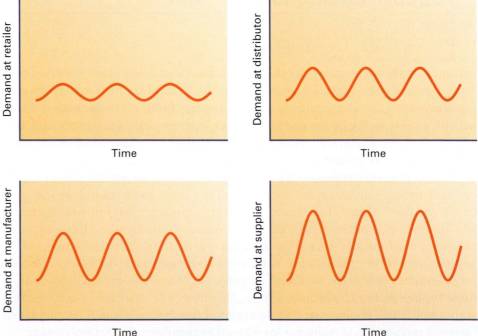

Economic Impact of Supply Chain Management

Supply chain management is about minimizing the total costs in the chain and maximizing the value to the end user. In turn, the economic impact of supply chain management is significant because for both goods and services, supply chain costs as a fraction of sales are often considerable, as shown in Exhibit 18.4.

Of greater importance is the impact on profit of reductions in supply chain costs. Consider a firm whose supply chain costs represent 50 percent of sales, other variable costs represent 20 percent of sales, and fixed costs represent 25 percent of sales. Then, on sales of $100, profit would be $5, or 5 percent of sales. This calculation is illustrated in Exhibit 18.5 in the column labeled "Base Case." Now, if supply chain management reduced the supply chain costs by 2 percent, from $50 to $49, then profit would increase to $6, or 6 percent of sales. This calculation is illustrated in Exhibit 18.5 in the column labeled "Reducing Supply Chain Costs." On the other hand, if sales increased from $100 to $120, then profit would also increase to $6, or 6 percent of sales. This calculation is illustrated in Exhibit 18.5 in the column labeled "Increasing Sales." Therefore, the economic impact on profit of reducing supply chain costs by 2 percent is equivalent to increasing sales by 20 percent. Clearly, the leverage on profit provided by reducing supply chain costs is enormous.

EXHIBIT 18.4

Examples of Supply Chain Costs as a Percentage of Sales

Industry	Supply Chain Costs (% of sales)
Automobile	67
Food	60
Lumber	61
Paper	55
Petroleum	79
Transportation	62
All industries	52

Source: From Jay Heizer and Barry Render, *Operations Management,* 7th Edition, © 2004. Adapted by permission of Pearson Education, Inc., Upper Saddle River, NJ.

Supply Chain Management Strategies

There are four basic supply chain management strategies: *few versus many suppliers, vertical integration, virtual collaboration,* and *bypassing.* In the many suppliers option, suppliers respond to a "request for quotation" from the company, and the contract usually goes to the lowest bidder. This is a common approach when products are commodities and suppliers compete aggressively with one another. It also places the burden of meeting the buyer's demands on the supplier. This strategy obviously does not lead to long-term partnering with the suppliers.

In the few suppliers option, rather than looking for short-term attributes, such as low cost, the firm is looking for a long-term relationship with a few dedicated suppliers. Long-term suppliers are more likely to understand the broad objectives of the procuring firm and the end customer. Using few suppliers can create value by allowing suppliers to have economies of scale and a learning curve that yields both lower transactions costs and lower production costs.

Vertical integration is a supply chain management strategy in which one supply chain member develops the ability to perform the function that another supply chain member has been performing. This may happen by internal efforts or by acquisition. For example, Ford Motor Company integrated vertically when it decided to manufacture its own car radios. In this case, a manufacturer decided to perform the function of one of its suppliers by internal efforts. As a second example, if DaimlerChrysler were to purchase the supplier of radios for its cars, then DaimlerChrysler would be integrating vertically by acquisition. In both examples, because Ford Motor Company and DaimlerChrysler are manufacturers and are "downstream" in the supply chain from their car radio suppliers, it is said that their

EXHIBIT 18.5

Economic Impact on Profit of Reducing Supply Chain Costs Versus Increasing Sales

	Base Case	Reducing Supply Chain Costs	Increasing Sales
Sales	$100	$100	$120
Supply chain costs	$ 50	$ 49	$ 60
Other variable costs	$ 20	$ 20	$ 24
Fixed costs	$ 25	$ 25	$ 30
Profit	$ 5	$ 6	$ 6

vertical integration A supply chain management strategy where one supply chain member develops the ability to perform the function that another supply chain member has been performing

backward vertical integration A form of vertical integration where the supply chain member that develops the ability to perform the function that another supply chain member has been performing is "downstream" from that supply chain member

forward vertical integration A form of vertical integration where the supply chain member that develops the ability to perform the function that another supply chain member has been performing is "upstream" from that supply chain member

virtual collaboration A supply chain management strategy where companies form a supply chain to provide goods or services on demand

bypassing A supply chain management strategy where one member of the supply chain eliminates the functions performed by another member of the chain

vertical integration was **backward.** If DaimlerChrysler decided to acquire all of its car dealers, which are "downstream" in the supply chain from DaimlerChrysler, then it would be said that its vertical integration was **forward.**

Virtual collaboration is a supply chain management strategy where companies form a supply chain to provide goods or services on demand. The apparel business provides a traditional example of virtual collaboration. The designers of clothes seldom manufacture their designs; rather, they license the manufacture. In turn, the manufacturer may rent a loft, lease sewing machines, and contract for labor. The result is a supply chain that has low overhead, remains flexible, and can respond rapidly to market. A contemporary case of virtual collaboration is the semiconductor industry, exemplified by Visioneer in Palo Alto, California. This firm subcontracts almost everything: Software is written by several partners, hardware is manufactured by a subcontractor in Silicon Valley, printed circuit boards are made in Singapore, and plastic cases are made in Boston, where units are also tested and packaged for shipment.

Bypassing is a supply chain management strategy where one member of the supply chain eliminates the functions performed by another member. Dell provides the best example of bypassing with its direct sales to customers model. In this case, distributors and retailers are bypassed by the manufacturer. The Dell supply chain has only three stages: suppliers, manufacturer, and customers, as shown in Exhibit 18.6.

Because Dell is in direct contact with its customers, it has been able to finely segment them and analyze the needs and profitability of each segment. Close contact with its customers and an understanding of

EXHIBIT 18.6

The Dell Supply Chain

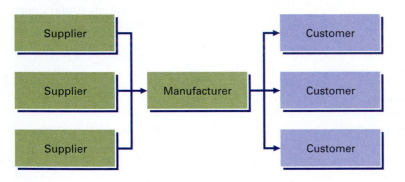

tact with its customers and an understanding of customers' needs also allows Dell to develop better demand forecasts. To further improve the match between supply and demand, Dell makes an active effort to steer customers in real time, on the phone or via the Internet, toward PC configurations than can be built given the components available. Dell was established in 1984, and by 1998 it had grown into a $12 billion U.S. dollars company. Since 1993, Dell has experienced earnings growth of more than 65 percent per year. Its earnings growth is anticipated to be more than 30 percent per year over the next five years. Dell has attributed a significant part of its success to superb supply chain management and its direct sales to customers model.

reality CHECK   *How does supply chain management affect you as a consumer?*

E-Business

LEARNING OBJECTIVE 7
Outline the roles that ERP systems, supply chain management, and e-business play in the emergence of the digital enterprise.

e-business The process of buying and selling goods and services electronically

E-business is the process of buying and selling goods and services electronically. E-business involves transactions that use networks, the Internet, and other digital technologies. If ERP systems provide the links among the different business functions in a business organization, and supply chain management provides the links

Case in Point

Supply Chain Management at DaimlerChrysler

Some companies, either emboldened by a higher strategic vision or forced by necessity, have invested in real-time information systems to streamline manufacturing and distribution. For example, the Mopar Parts group at DaimlerChrysler Corporation distributes spare parts to Chrysler, Dodge, and Jeep dealers in the United States. The group handles some 280,000 different parts procured from 3000 suppliers and processes more than 220,000 dealer orders per day. The distribution chain includes four national distribution centers and 15 regional warehouses.

Traditionally, Mopar's order processing system would first try to fill orders from the dealer's nearest regional warehouse; that resulted in an 89.5 percent fill rate the first day. Orders that could not be filled regionally were bumped up to the central warehouses, which would try to fill the remaining orders. By the end of the second day, 92 percent of orders were filled.

Next, the system would try to fill orders from other regional warehouses; then inventory planners would check for parts in transit or would special-order them from suppliers and express-ship them to dealers. Still, after five working days, 2.5 percent of orders remained unfilled—a small percentage, but given the huge number of orders, an expensive gap for Mopar and an inconvenience for too many customers.

To improve the situation, Mopar implemented a supply chain system from SeeCommerce of Palo Alto, California, two years ago. A group of applications known collectively as SeeChain extracts parts supply information from Mopar's ERP system, organizes the information, and generates reports and notices. Users can also search information at will.

Armed with more timely information and better analytical tools, planners can anticipate parts requirements and spot shortages before they happen, so needed parts are more likely to be available at the regional warehouses when they are needed. At the same time, orders move through the system faster; if an order cannot be filled at the regional warehouse, inventory managers can use the system to locate the parts more quickly. The result is that 98.5 percent of orders are now filled in three to five days. It is only a small percentage improvement, but one that translates into big bottom-line results. Mopar estimates it saves $10 million annually in transportation costs alone because it makes fewer rush shipments to fill dealer requests, and millions more in reduced inventory levels.

Source: "Does Everyone Have the Same View in Your Supply Chain? Not Sharing Real-Time Data Can Wreak Havoc Unless Software Ties It Together," Larry Tuck, *Frontline Solutions,* July 2002. Reprinted with permission of the author.

Questions

1. Describe how DaimlerChrysler is managing its supply chain to improve business operations.
2. Explain the role that enterprise resource planning is playing in DaimlerChrysler's supply chain management efforts.

among the firms that are members of a supply chain, e-business provides the links between the end users and the supply chain and between a firm and the firms and other entities with which it does business. DaimlerChrysler uses an ERP system to integrate its business processes. It uses supply chain management, where its ERP system is the backbone, to minimize the total costs of the chain and to maximize the value to the end user. It uses e-business to buy goods and services electronically from its many vendors, some of which are members of the supply chain and some of which, like insurance organizations and health care providers for its employees, are not. And it uses e-business to sell electronically its automobiles to Daimler-Chrysler dealers and customers. If one adds the efforts of DaimlerChrysler to digitally enable its relationships with its shareholders, then obviously this company is being driven in the digital-enterprise direction.

One way in which e-business transactions can be classified is by the nature of the participants in the electronic transaction. **Business-to-consumer (B2C) e-business** involves selling goods and services to individual consumers.

business-to-consumer (B2C) e-business
The e-business that involves selling goods and services to individual consumers

Global Business

Global Supply Chains

When companies enter growing global markets such as eastern Europe, China, South America, or even Mexico, expanding their supply chains becomes a strategic challenge. Quality production in those areas may be a challenge, just as distribution systems may be less reliable, suggesting higher inventory levels than would be needed in one's home country. Tariffs and quotas may block non-local companies from doing business. Moreover, both political and currency risk remain high in much of the world.

So the development of a successful strategic plan for supply chain management requires innovative planning and careful research. Supply chains in a global environment must be

- Flexible enough to react to sudden changes in parts availability, distribution or shipping channels, import duties, and currency rates
- Able to use the latest computer and transmission technologies to schedule and manage the shipment of parts in and finished products out
- Staffed with local specialists to handle duties, trade, freight, customs, and political issues

McDonald's planned for a global supply chain challenge six years in advance of its opening in Russia. Creating a $60 million U.S. dollars "food town," it developed independently-owned supply plants in Moscow to keep its transportation costs and handling times low and its quality and customer service levels high. Every component in this food chain—meat plant, chicken plant, bakery, fish plant, and lettuce plant—is closely monitored to make sure that all the supply chain's links are strong.

Firms like Ford Motor Company and the Boeing Company also face global procurement decisions. Ford's Mercury has only 227 suppliers worldwide, a small number compared to the 700 involved in previous models. Ford has set a trend of developing a global network of fewer suppliers that provide the lowest cost and highest quality regardless of home country. So global is the production of the Boeing 777 that officials from the company proclaim, "The Chinese now make so many Boeing parts that when Boeing planes fly to China, they are going home."

Source: From Jay Heizer and Barry Render, *Operations Management*, 7th Edition, © 2004. Adapted by permission of Pearson Education, Inc., Upper Saddle River, NJ.

Questions

1. Discuss the advantages and disadvantages of global supply chains.
2. List three global supply chains that you think are particularly successful.

---

business-to-business (B2B) e-business The e-business that involves selling goods and services among businesses

consumer-to-consumer (C2C) e-business The e-business that involves consumers selling goods and services to other consumers

Amazon.com, which sells books, software, and music to individual consumers, is an example of B2C e-business. **Business-to-business (B2B) e-business** involves selling goods and services among businesses. Milpro.com, Milacron's website for selling cutting tools, grinding wheels, and metal working fluids to more than 100,000 small machining businesses, is an example of B2B e-business. **Consumer-to-consumer (C2C) e-business** involves consumers selling goods and services to other consumers. For example, eBay, the giant Web auction site, allows people to sell their goods to other consumers by auctioning the merchandise off to the highest bidder.

Another way of classifying e-business is in terms of the participant's physical connection to the Internet. Until recently, almost all e-business transactions took place over wired networks. Now, cell phones and other wireless, handheld digital devices are Internet-enabled so that they can be used to send e-mail or access websites. Companies are rushing to offer new sets of web-based products and services that can be accessed by these wireless devices. For example, in Great Britain, customers of Virgin Mobile can use their cell phones to browse Virgin's website and purchase compact disks, wine, TV sets, and washing machines. Subscribers to Japan's NTT DoCoMo Internet cell phone service can send and receive e-mail, tap into online news, purchase airplane tickets, trade stocks, and browse through restaurant guides, linking websites that have been redesigned to fit into tiny

Employees at Amazon.com's distribution warehouse in Seattle, Washington, fill orders for the Christmas season.

screens. The use of handheld devices for purchasing goods and services has been termed **mobile commerce** or simply **m-commerce.**

Electronic Payment Systems

An **electronic payment system** is the use of digital technologies to pay for goods and services electronically. Electronic payment systems for e-business include *digital credit cards*, *digital cash*, *digital wallets*, and *digital checks*.

A **digital credit card** extends the functionality of regular credit cards to protect the information transmitted among customers, merchant sites, and processing banks. Digital credit cards provide mechanisms for authentication of the purchaser's credit card to make sure it is valid and arrange for the bank that issued the card to deposit money for the amount of the purchase into the seller's bank account.

Digital cash, also called electronic cash or e-cash, is currency represented in electronic form that moves outside the normal network of money (paper currency, coins, checks, and credit cards). Users are supplied with client software and can exchange money with another e-cash user over the Internet or with a retailer accepting e-cash. ECoin and InternetCash.com are examples of digital cash services.

A **digital wallet** is software that stores credit card and owner identification information and provides these data automatically during e-business transactions. The digital wallet enters the shopper's name, credit card number, and shipping information automatically when invoked to complete the purchase. Gator and America Online's Quick Checkout are examples of a digital wallet.

Digital checking extends the functionality of regular checking accounts so that they can be used for online shopping payments. Digital checks are less expensive than credit cards and much faster than traditional paper-based checking. Digital

mobile commerce or **m-commerce** The use of handheld devices for purchasing goods and services over the Internet

electronic payment system A system that uses digital technologies to pay for goods and services electronically

digital credit card An electronic payment system that extends the functionality of regular credit cards to protect the information transmitted among customers, merchant sites, and processing banks

digital cash An electronic payment system that represents currency in an electronic form that moves outside the normal network of money

digital wallet An electronic payment system that stores credit card and owner identification information and provides these data automatically during e-business transactions

digital checking An electronic payment system that extends the functionality of existing checking accounts so that they can be used for online shopping payments

checks are encrypted with a digital signature that can be verified and used for payments in e-business transactions. Examples of digital checking systems are CHEXpedite and Achex.

Opportunities and Challenges

Although e-business offers organizations a wealth of new opportunities, it also presents managers with a series of challenges. First, many new e-business models have yet to prove enduring sources of profit. Digitalization of business processes for e-business requires far-reaching organizational change. The legal environment for e-business has not yet solidified, and companies pursuing e-business must be vigilant about security.

Unproven business models. Not all companies are making money doing e-business. Hundreds of retail dotcom firms, including Garden.com, Productopia.com, and Pets.com, have closed their doors. Dotcom stock prices collapsed after many of these companies failed to generate enough revenue to sustain their costly marketing campaigns, information technology infrastructures, and staff salaries; they lost money on every sale they made.

Far-reaching organizational changes. E-business requires careful orchestration of the firm's divisions, production sites, and sales offices, as well as closer relationships with customers, suppliers, and other business partners in its network of value creation. Essential business processes must be redesigned and more closely integrated, especially those for supply chain management. Given that supply chain management requires aligning the business practices and behaviors of the different companies in the supply chain, then e-business requires for these companies well-defined policies and procedures for sharing data with the other members of the supply chain, including specifications for the type, format, level of precision, and security of data to be exchanged. The digitally-enabled enterprise must transform the way it conducts business to act rapidly and with precision.

Legal issues. Laws governing e-business are still being written. Legislatures, courts, and international agreements are just starting to settle questions about the legality and force of e-mail contracts, the role of electronic signatures, and the application of copyright laws to electronically copied documents. Moreover, the Internet is global, and it is used by individuals and organizations in hundreds of different countries. If a product were offered for sale in Mexico via a server in Spain, and the buyer lived in France, whose law would apply? The legal and regulatory environment for e-business has not been fully established.

Security. E-business transactions, including e-mail, pass through many computer systems on the Internet before reaching their destination. This information can be monitored, captured, and stored at any of these points along the route. Valuable data may be intercepted, such as credit card numbers and names, private personnel data, marketing plans, sales contracts, product development and pricing data, negotiations between companies, and other data that might be of value to the competition.

 How has e-business changed some of the companies you do business with? What roles do ERP systems and supply chain management play when you buy something online?

Ethics in Business

Information Technology and Privacy

Privacy is the condition of being left alone, free from surveillance or interference from other individuals or organizations, including the state. Information technology and systems threaten individual claims to privacy by making the invasion of privacy cheap, profitable, and effective.

The claim to privacy is protected in the U.S., Canadian, and German constitutions in a variety of different ways, and in other countries through various statutes. In the United States, the claim to privacy is protected primarily by the First Amendment guarantees of freedom of speech and association, the Fourth Amendment protections against unreasonable search and seizure of one's personal documents or home, and the guarantee of due process.

Due process has become a key concept in defining privacy rights. Due process requires that a set of rules or laws exist that clearly define how information about individuals will be treated and what appeal mechanisms are available. Perhaps the best statement of due process in record keeping is given by the Fair Information Practices Doctrine developed in the early 1970s.

Most U.S. and European privacy law is based on a regime called *Fair Information Practices,* first set forth in a report written in 1973 by the U.S. federal government (U.S. Department of Health, Education, and Welfare). The **Fair Information Practices (FIP)** are a set of principles governing the collection and use of information about individuals. The five FIP principles are

> There should be no personal record systems whose existence is secret.
> Individuals have rights of access to, inspection of, review of, and amendment to systems that contain information about them.
> There must be no use of personal information for purposes other than those for which it was gathered, without prior consent.
> Managers of systems are responsible for and can be held accountable and liable for the damage done by systems.
> Governments have the right to intervene in the information relationships among private parties.

FIP forms the basis of several federal statutes that set forth the conditions for handling information about individuals in such areas as credit reporting, education, financial records, newspaper records, and electronic communication. The Privacy Act of 1974 has been the most important of these federal statutes, regulating the federal government's collection, use, and disclosure of information. At present, most U.S. federal privacy laws apply only to the federal government and regulate very few areas of the private sector.

Efforts are under way to develop appropriate legislation to protect the privacy of Internet users. The Federal Trade Commission (FTC) has made a series of recommendations to the U.S. Congress for online privacy protection, issuing its own set of FIP principles in 1998. The FTC's FIP restate and extend the original FIP to provide guidelines more appropriate for privacy protection in the age of the Internet. Core principles specify that websites must disclose their information practices before collecting data and that consumers must be allowed to choose how information about them will be used for secondary purposes—purposes other that those supporting the immediate transaction.

In the United States, privacy law is enforced by individuals who must sue agencies or companies in court to recover damages. European countries and Canada define privacy in a similar manner to the United States, but they have chosen to enforce their privacy laws by creating privacy commissions or data protection agencies to pursue complaints brought by their citizens.

Source: From Kenneth C. Laudon and Jane P. Laudon, *Essentials of Management Information Systems: Managing the Digital Firm,* 5th Edition, © 2003. Adapted by permission of Pearson Education, Inc., Upper Saddle River, NJ.

Questions

1. Explore the advantages and disadvantages of the way privacy law is enforced in the United States and the way it is enforced in European countries and Canada.
2. Analyze the five FIP principles. Which principles would you change or delete and why?

privacy The condition of individuals of being left alone, free from surveillance or interference from other individuals or organizations, including the state

fair information practices (FIP) A set of principles governing the collection and use of information about individuals

Careers in the Digital Enterprise

Most job opportunities in the digital enterprise are in the same catgories as the sections of this chapter. There are some that combine two of these categories.

Information Technology Infrastructure for the Digital Enterprise

The Career Center at Texas A&M University lists the following job description in Web development: Organizations are increasingly using the World Wide Web for a diverse set of business purposes. Websites are used for marketing, sales, communications, public relations, and training, to name just a few. Careers in Web development involve the design and maintenance of such sites. Web developers typically work with a client to determine the needs of the organization. The Web developer will then design a prototype, usually using multiple applications and interfaces. The design will be tested and technical documentation is written for the program. Positions in Web development require creativity. The majority of positions are found at companies that specialize in Web development and multimedia creations, but some large corporations hire Web developers for in-house design as well. The array of organizations seeking Web developers is extremely diverse. These organizations may include publishing firms, electronic game companies, educational institutions, marketing firms, government agencies, and many more.

ERP Systems

The job opportunities in ERP systems commonly fall into three categories. First, one may find a job as a developer, consultant, or trainer for one of the ERP software companies like SAP, Oracle, PeopleSoft, J.D. Edwards, and Bann. Developers design or identify the best practices for business processes and then create the code to execute these processes. Consultants can specialize in the technical or functional areas. For example, one may become a consultant in the information technology infrastructure needed to successfully run an ERP system; SAP calls this type of consultant a *basis consultant*. One may also become a consultant in one of the functional areas like accounting, human resources, or logistics. Finally, one may work as a trainer for users of the ERP software.

A second category of job opportunities in ERP systems is becoming a consultant for one of the professional services firms that are alliance partners to the ERP software company. For example, one may work as a PeopleSoft expert at Accenture or Deloitte & Touche. These consulting jobs may also be in technical or functional areas.

A third category of job opportunities in ERP systems is working for a company that is implementing or has implemented an ERP system. In this company, one may work as a developer, technical or functional consultant, or trainer. The Oracle ERP implementation by Cisco Systems was completed with the help of the professional consulting services firm KPMG. ERP systems expertise could lead to a job with the Oracle ERP group or the Cisco Systems group, or the KPMG group.

Supply Chain Management

The Career Center at Texas A&M University indicates that demand for professionals in this area is rapidly growing as firms are realizing the improved efficiency and profitability resulting from supply chain management. According to the same career center, a job in supply chain management involves one or more of the following, depending on the size of the business organization:

- Providing an uninterrupted flow of materials, supplies, and services required to operate the organization
- Developing productive working relationships with external constituents, such as vendors and retailers, and internal departments, such as marketing, accounting, operations, and MISs
- Analyzing and negotiating contracts with suppliers, manufacturers, or distributors
- Integrating information technology into the supply chain to improve profitability

Industries in which supply chain management graduates are hired include communications, consulting, financial institutions, government, health care, hospitality, manufacturing, retail, and transportation. Examples of companies recruiting for supply chain management graduates are Accenture, Dell, Delloite & Touche, Ford Motor Company, Frito Lay, IBM, Johnson & Johnson, Motorola, Nestlé, and Nokia Telecommunications.

E-Business

The Bureau of Labor Statistics at the U.S. Department of Labor reports that in order to remain competitive, firms will continue to install sophisticated computer networks and set up more complex Internet and intranet sites. Keeping these sites running smoothly is essential to almost every organization. Firms will be more than willing to hire managers who can accomplish that. The security of computer networks will continue to increase in importance as more business is conducted over the Internet. Organizations need to understand how their systems are vulnerable and how to protect their infrastructure and Internet sites from hackers, viruses, and other acts of cyber terrorism. As a result, there will be a high demand for managers proficient in computer security issues.

Due to the explosive growth of e-business and the ability of the Internet to create new relationships with customers, the role of managers in this field will continue to evolve in the future. They will continue to become more vital to their companies and the environments in which they work. The expansion of e-business will spur the need for managers in this field with both savvy and technical proficiency.

Summary

LEARNING OBJECTIVE 1

Explain what the digital enterprise is.

Business processes are the unique ways in which companies organize, coordinate, and execute activities, information, and knowledge in order to produce their goods or services. The digital enterprise is a business organization in which all major business processes and relationships with suppliers, customers, employees, managers, and shareholders are digitally-enabled.

LEARNING OBJECTIVE 2

Describe the role that the new information technology infrastructure plays in the digital enterprise.

The Internet is an international network of networks containing hundreds of thousands of private and public networks all over the world. The Internet capability called the World Wide Web is one of the reasons why the Internet has become so popular in such a short period of time. An intranet is an internal network in a business organization that is used by employees to collaborate, share information, and access internal websites. An extranet is a network that links the intranet resources of a company with other organizations. A virtual private network is a secure network that uses the Internet as its main backbone network and relies on a network firewall. A client/server network is a telecommunications network where some computers are "clients" and some computers are "servers." Client/server networks, virtual private networks, and extranets have become the predominant information architecture for the digital enterprise.

LEARNING OBJECTIVE 3
Define enterprise resource planning.

Enterprise resource planning refers to computer software that integrates the majority of a firm's business processes, executes all transactions related to the integrated business processes, stores each piece of data only once in an enterprise-wide database, allows access to data and information in real time, and operates in a traditional or Web-based client/server environment. Twenty years of experience with ERP systems demonstrates that these systems produce benefits such as improved financial management, better managerial decision making, improved inventory and asset management, and faster, more accurate business transactions. ERP systems are useful for the globalization trends in businesses by offering multilanguage, multicurrency, and multinational capabilities. ERP systems have been implemented in more than 100 countries, in most major industries, and in companies of all sizes.

LEARNING OBJECTIVE 4
Compare the five major vendors of enterprise resource planning software.

The five largest ERP software vendors in increasing order of market share are Baan, J.D. Edwards, PeopleSoft, Oracle, and SAP. Baan and SAP are based in Europe, while the other three vendors are based in the United States. Baan became well known when it sold its software to the Boeing Company in 1994. J.D. Edwards' market niche has been midsized companies. PeopleSoft's strength is in human resources. Oracle's reputation in ERP systems has been built around developing a product that can be easily interfaced with modules of other ERP systems. SAP is currently the major player in ERP systems, with a market share estimated around 40 to 60 percent. SAP is known for spending about 20 percent of its sales income on research and development.

LEARNING OBJECTIVE 5
Evaluate the two major strategies for implementing enterprise resource planning systems.

The two major strategies for implementing ERP systems are the phased strategy and the big-bang strategy. In the phased strategy, modules are implemented one at a time, and for companies with multiple locations, modules are implemented one location at a time. In the big-bang strategy, all required modules are implemented at once, and for firms with multiple locations, modules are implemented at all locations at once.

LEARNING OBJECTIVE 6
Illustrate supply chain management.

Supply chain management is the management of all activities in the supply chain, in order to minimize the total costs of the chain and to maximize the value to the end users of the chain. Using ERP systems as a backbone, supply chain management fosters the integration of business processes across the different firms that constitute the supply chain. Supply chain management has had a significant business impact and has led to several strategies, such as optimizing the number of suppliers, vertical integration, virtual collaboration, and bypassing.

LEARNING OBJECTIVE 7
Outline the roles that ERP systems, supply chain management, and e-business play in the emergence of the digital enterprise.

E-business is the process of buying and selling goods and services electronically. E-business transactions use computer networks, the Internet, and other digital technologies. E-business transactions can be business-to-consumer (B2C), business-to-business (B2B), and consumer-to-consumer (C2C). E-business transactions typically take place over wired networks, but lately these transactions are also taking place via wireless devices in what is called mobile commerce. E-business uses electronic payment systems such as digital credit cards, digital cash, digital wallets, and digital checks. It offers to companies unprecedented business opportunities and, at the same time, challenges related to unproven business models, far-reaching organizational changes, legal issues, and security.

ERP systems provide a digital link among functions within a firm. Relying for the most part on ERP systems, supply chain management provides a link among the firms that are members of a supply chain. E-business provides the digital link between the end users and the supply chain, and between a firm and the firms with which it does business. The synergy among ERP systems, supply chain management, and e-business has made possible the emergence of the digital enterprise.

Chapter Questions

1. What is a business process?
2. What is a digital enterprise?
3. What is the Internet?
4. What is the relationship among intranets, extranets, and virtual private networks?
5. What is a three-tier client/server network?
6. What is an ERP system?
7. Discuss the benefits and costs of ERP systems.
8. Who are the five major vendors of ERP software?
9. What is the difference between the best-of-breed and the monolithic approaches?
10. What are the advantages and disadvantages of the phased and big-bang strategies?
11. What is supply chain management?
12. What are the four basic supply chain management strategies?
13. What is e-business?
14. What are the most common types of electronic payment systems in e-business?
15. What are some of the challenges and opportunities of e-business?

Interpreting Business News

1. The *Wall Street Journal* and magazines such as *Business Week* have published numerous stories about companies that experienced great success or great failure when implementing an ERP system. What do you think are the major determinants of success or failure for companies that have implemented an ERP system?
2. Experiences of companies such as Dell and Wal-Mart show that supply chain management yields substantial savings for the entire supply chain, but at the same time, those savings are not uniform across the companies in the supply chain. How do you think those savings should be allocated among the members of the supply chain?
3. Over the past five years, e-business showed great promise for a lot of companies, but was not able to deliver on that promise for several companies. Why do you think this was the case?

Web Assignments

1. One of the student and professional organizations for supply chain management is called *Council of Logistics Management*. Visit its website at **www.clm1.org** and learn more about supply chain management, student membership, and certification programs for supply chain management professionals. What does it take to become certified?
2. Use a search engine to look for enterprise resource planning jobs. What do the jobs have in common?
3. Use a search engine to look for undergraduate and graduate programs in supply chain management. Describe the kinds of courses involved in this program of study.

Portfolio Projects

Exploring Your Own Case in Point

After reading this chapter, answering the questions below should help you understand whether the company that you have elected to investigate is on its way to becoming a digital firm.

1. Does your company use a virtual private network? Has it implemented an enterprise resource planning system? If so, which ERP software vendor did it use?
2. Identify the companies that are members of your company's supply chain. Has your company used one of the four supply chain management strategies?
3. Is your company engaged in e-business? If so, is it doing B2C and/or B2B? What forms of electronic payment does it use?

Starting Your Own Business

After reading this chapter, you should be more comfortable deciding on the following elements of your business plan.

1. Should an enterprise resource planning system be used in your firm?
2. What is your supply chain management strategy?
3. Will your business engage in B2C and B2B transactions? Will you be using an electronic payment system?

Test Prepper

You've read the chapter, studied the key terms, and the exam is any day now. Think you are ready to ace it? Take this sample test to gauge your comprehension of chapter material. You can check your answers at the back of the book.

True/False Questions

Please indicate if the following statements are true or false.

_____ 1. Business processes are the unique ways in which companies organize, coordinate, and execute activities, information, and knowledge in order to produce goods or services.

_____ 2. A digital enterprise is a business organization where some of the major business processes are digitally enabled.

_____ 3. An intranet is a network that links the extranet resources of a company with other organizations.

_____ 4. Enterprise resource planning systems offer a solution to the problem of information fragmentation.

_____ 5. Three of the major ERP software vendors are Oracle, Microsoft, and SAP.

_____ 6. A company is following a best-of-breed approach when it adopts all its required modules from a single ERP software vendor.

_____ 7. A well-known example of the lack of information integration in a supply chain is the so-called bullwhip effect.

_____ 8. Two of the four basic supply chain management strategies are horizontal integration and virtual collaboration.

_____ 9. An electronic payment system is the use of digital technologies to pay for goods and services electronically.

_____ 10. One of the challenges of e-business is security, because e-business transactions, including e-mail, pass through many computer systems on the Internet before they reach their destination.

Multiple-Choice Questions

Choose the best answer.

_____ 1. A business organization where all major business processes and relationships with suppliers, customers, employees, managers, and shareholders are digitally enabled is called a(n)

a. virtual enterprise.
b. networked enterprise.
c. digital enterprise.
d. modern enterprise.
e. e-enterprise.

_____ 2. The Internet capability that is one of the reasons why the Internet has become so popular in a short period of time is the

a. World Wide Web.
b. International Web.
c. Electronic Web.
d. Networked Web.
e. Digital Web.

_____ 3. The type of network that has become the predominant information architecture for the digital enterprise is the

a. local area network.
b. wide area network.
c. virtual network.
d. client/server network.
e. virtual private network.

_____ 4. All of the following are ideas behind ERP systems *except*

a. storing all information in a single database.
b. representing each business function by a module.
c. designing the ERP system as a collection of business processes, not business functions.
d. keeping information protected by a firewall.
e. building the ERP system as a collection of business processes, not business functions.

_____ 5. To address the globalization trends of businesses, ERP systems are

a. sold only to international companies.
b. multilanguage, multicurrency, and multinational.
c. very easy to implement.
d. based on English as a universal language.
e. simplified with the use of one base currency.

_____ 6. Benefits achieved by companies that have implemented an ERP system include all of the following *except*

    a. improved financial management.
    b. cycle time reduction.
    c. faster, more accurate transactions.
    d. higher inventory costs.
    e. better managerial decision-making.

_____ 7. The supply chain management strategy followed by Dell, with its direct sales to customers model, is an example of

    a. few suppliers.
    b. bypassing.
    c. virtual collaboration.
    d. vertical integration.
    e. many suppliers.

_____ 8. ERP systems have become the backbone of most supply chain management efforts because

    a. ERP systems have been used with great success to integrate most business processes within a company.
    b. ERP systems allow the separate management of each business function.
    c. ERP systems always minimize the total costs of the chain.

    d. ERP systems focus on the manufacturer as the most important member of the supply chain.
    e. ERP systems seek to achieve the bullwhip effect.

_____ 9. A digital wallet

    a. is the use of digital technologies to pay for goods and services electronically.
    b. extends the functionality of credit cards to protect information transmitted electronically.
    c. is software that stores credit card and owner identification information and provides that data automatically during e-business transactions.
    d. is currency represented in electronic form.
    e. extends the functionality of checking accounts so they can be used for online shopping.

_____ 10. All of the following are e-business challenges *except*

    a. unproven business models.
    b. far-reaching organizational changes.
    c. security.
    d. the difficulty of going global.
    e. legal issues.

Want more questions? Visit the student website at **http://college.hmco.com/business/student/** (select Gaspar, *Introduction to Business*) and take the ACE quizzes for more practice.

Appendix:
Case in Point Company Profiles

DaimlerChrysler AG

Company Profile

Headquarters:	DaimlerChrysler AG and DaimlerChrysler Corporation
	70546 Stuttgart Auburn Hills
	Germany Michigan, USA
Phone:	+ 49-711-170 +1-248-576-5741
	Fax: + 49-711-17-94022
Website:	**www.daimlerchrysler.com/**

Divisions/Business Fields: Automotive

Stock Exchanges: New York, Frankfurt

Ticker Symbol: DCX

Incorporated: November 1, 1998

Major Divisions:

Mercedes Car Group [Brands: Maybach, Mercedes Benz, and Smart]
Chrysler Group [Brands: Chrysler, Dodge, and Jeep]
Commercial Vehicles [Brands: Freightliner, Mercedes-Benz, Setra, Sterling Trucks, Western Star Trucks, and Fuso]
Services [DaimlerChrysler Bank]

The Board of Management (as of October 1, 2004):

Prof. Jürgen E. Schrempp, Chairman of the Board of Management
Dr. Eckhard Cordes, Mercedes Car Group
Gunther Fleig, Human Resources & Labor Relations Director
Dr. Manfred Gentz, Finance & Controlling
Dr. Rudiger Grube, Corporate Development
Prof. Jürgen Hubbert, Executive Automotive Council
Thomas LaSorda, Chief Operating Officer, Chrysler Group
Andreas Renschler, Commercial Vehicles
Thomas W. Sidlik, Global Procurement & Supply
Bodo Uebber, Services
Dr. Thomas Weber, Research & Technology
Dr. Dieter Zetsche, Chrysler Group

Strategic partners: Mitsubishi Motor Corporation and Hyundai Motor Company

Major Competitors: General Motors Corporation, Toyota Motors, Ford Motor Company, Volkswagen, BMW, Honda Motors, Nissan Motors, Peugeot Citroen

CORPORATE MISSION

"DaimlerChrysler is unique in the automotive industry: Our product portfolio ranges from small cars to sports cars and luxury sedans; and from versatile vans to heavy-duty trucks or comfortable coaches. We are extremely well positioned worldwide with our strong passenger-car and commercial-vehicle brands, and have products in nearly every market and market segment.

We aim to convince our customers with our exciting automobiles, attractive and economical commercial vehicles, and tailored financial and other automotive services. With our innovative technology, we intend to make the traffic of tomorrow even safer, as well as more economical and environment-friendly.

And by implementing this strategy, we intend to create lasting value for our shareholders. To these ends we focus our global resources and the knowledge, experience, and energy of our employees."

HISTORICAL PERFORMANCE

	1998	1999	2000	2001	2002	2003
Revenues (million euros)	130,122	148,243	160,278	150,386	147,368	136,437
Net income (million euros)	4,820	5,746	7,894	(662)	4,718	448
Ave. shares outstanding (millions)	959.3	1,002.9	1,003.2	1,003.2	1,008.3	1,012.7
Net income (loss): euros per share	5.03	5.73	7.87	(0.66)	4.68	0.44
Cash dividend per share (euros)	2.35	2.35	2.35	1.00	1.50	1.50
Share Price (Frankfurt: in euros)	83.60	77.00	44.74	48.35	29.35	37.34
MSCI World Index (automobiles)						
Average number of employees	433,939	463,561	449,594	379,544	370,677	370,648

BRIEF HISTORY

DaimlerChrysler AG—the fifth-largest automaker in the world, with a global market share of 9 percent—is the product of the November 1998 merger of Daimler-Benz AG of Germany and Chrysler Corporation of the United States. A truly global company with manufacturing facilities in 34 countries and sales on all continents, DaimlerChrysler has a global strategy, a global workforce, a global shareholder base, globally known brands, and leading-edge technology. Yet, 47 percent of its total revenues come from the United States, 6 percent from Canada and Mexico combined, 17.5 percent each from Germany and other European Union countries, and the balance of 12 percent from the rest of the world. DaimlerChrysler sold 4.3 million passenger cars and commercial vehicles in 2003. The Mercedes Car Group dominates vehicle sales with some 40 percent of total sales followed by the Chrysler Group with 38 percent and Commercial Vehicles with 22 percent. Vehicle financing is a growing and important support component of vehicle sales.

The origins of Daimler-Benz go back to the mid-1880s when, unknown to each other, Karl Benz and Gottlieb Daimler (who lived some 60 miles apart around Stuttgart, Germany) both developed small and fast-running internal combustion engines that were used to power Benz's first car in 1885 and Daimler's in 1886. In 1900, Daimler's need for financial resources to manufacture high-performance cars led to his meeting with Austro-Hungarian businessman Emil Jellinek, who offered to provide financing if Daimler named the vehicle after Jellinek's beloved daughter—Mercedes. A series of subsequent events led to a merger between Daimler and Benz in 1926. They formed Daimler-Benz Aktiengesellschaft to manufacture cars under the brand name Mercedes-Benz. Daimler-Benz's focus was on leading-edge technology and long-term global market share often at the expense of short-term profits. Mercedes-Benz's strategy was to sell its vehicles as an "investment" in quality, reliability, and luxury. In the mid-1980s, Daimler-Benz embarked on a diversification strategy that involved three acquisitions: Motoren und Turbinen-Union (MTU)—a manufacturer of aircraft engines and diesel motors for tanks and ships (in 1985); Dornier—a manufacturer of spacecraft systems, commuter planes, and medical equipment (in 1985); and AEG—a manufacturer of turbines, robotics, household appliances, and data processing (in 1986). In the mid-1990s, ABB (Asea Brown Boveri), a Swedish-Swiss engineering and construction company of international repute, teamed up with Daimler-Benz to form ABB Daimler-Benz Transportation, which became the world's largest rail system provider.

The origins of Chrysler Corporation can be traced to 1920, when Walter Percy Chrysler resigned (because of policy differences) from his position as president of Buick division of General Motors and went on to restore Maxwell Motor Corporation to solvency. Because of his huge success in turning around Maxwell Motors, the company was renamed Chrysler Corporation. To achieve economies of scale in production, Walter Chrysler acquired Dodge Brothers Corporation in 1928—a car manufacturer in Detroit. Furthermore, to meet the needs of the lower-end consumer market, Chrysler developed the Plymouth and DeSoto divisions within Chrysler. During World War II, Chrysler diverted its attention from cars to the manufacture of B-29 bomber engines and anti-aircraft guns and tanks. Success in this area later led Chrysler to become the prime contractor for NASA's Saturn booster rocket. Unfortunately, Chrysler Corporation was unable to adjust to the aftereffects of the 1973 oil shock, which created a huge demand for well-built, fuel-efficient cars. In 1979, the U.S. government decided to rescue Chrysler through a loan guarantee in exchange for the company's promises of management change and restructuring of operations. As president, Lee Iacocca successfully steered Chrysler Corporation through these turbulent times and implemented a process of cost control, disinvestment, and new product introduction.

In their quest to grow and maintain their global presence—in light of stiff competition from Japan and South Korea and excess automotive production capacity worldwide—Daimler-Benz and Chrysler came to one conclusion. They realized that a Daimler-Benz-Chrysler merger would complement (in terms of product lines and geographical coverage) each other and also bring about synergies that could result in billions of dollars in cost savings while at the same time extending their global reach. After months of negotiations, Daimler-Benz and Chrysler agreed to merge and form DaimlerChrysler AG in May 1998. This merger of equals (hence two corporate headquarters) resulted in the formation of three automotive divisions: Mercedes-Benz passenger cars; the Chrysler Group; and Commercial Vehicles. Furthermore, in 1999 DaimlerChrysler Aerospace merged with France's Aerospatiale Matra and Spain's CASA to become a part (30 percent ownership) of European Aeronautic Defense and Space Company (EADS)—the largest aerospace firm in Europe and the second largest in the world. In order to boost its presence in Asia where DaimlerChrysler has less than five percent market share of the automotive market, the company formed an alliance with Mitsubishi Motors Corporation of Japan in early 2000 by acquiring a 34 percent stake in that company. In addition, Daimler-

Chrysler acquired a 10.5 percent stake in Hyundai Motors of South Korea, which it resold in August 2004. It now works with Hyundai as a strategic partner on a project-by-project basis.

CHALLENGES AHEAD

With DaimlerChrysler shares losing about two-thirds of their value since the merger, one could argue whether or not the deal was a mistake. Industry analysts have raised several issues. First, can a luxury automobile manufacturer (Daimler-Benz) effectively integrate its operations with mass-market manufacturers to produce Chairman Jürgen Schrempp's "Welt AG"—a truly global company? Second, can the relatively weak brand image of Chrysler and quality problems at Mitsubishi be overcome by infusing new manufacturing techniques (for example,

onsite outsourcing), sharing of parts, and pooling of purchasing to reduce cost and improve quality at the same time? Finally, what will be DaimlerChrysler's strategy to effectively meet the Lexus-Toyota (the benchmark for automotive quality and service) challenge in the world market? While sustained profitability has been a challenge for DaimlerChrysler since the merger in 1998, positive developments especially at the Chrysler division provide hope for a better future.

Sources: **www.daimlerchrysler.com/dccom** (Home; Daily News; Investor Relations; Top Stories; Special Reports); and Jay P. Pedersen, Ed., DaimlerChrysler, *International Directory of Company Histories,* [Chicago: St. James Press, c 2000] Vol. 34, pp. 128–137.

McDonald's Corporation

COMPANY PROFILE

Headquarters: McDonald's Plaza
Oak Brook, Illinois 60523

Phone: 630-623-3000
Fax: 630-623-5004

Website: **www.mcdonalds.com**

Industry: Fast-food restaurants

Stock Exchanges: New York, Midwest, Frankfurt, Munich, Paris, Tokyo, Zurich, Geneva, Basel

Ticker Symbol: MCD

Founded: March 2, 1955

Major Divisions:
McDonald's
Boston Market Restaurants
Chipotle Mexican Grill
Donatos Pizza Chain
Various international divisions

Management (as of November 23, 2004):
Chairman and Chief Executive Officer—James A. Skinner
Senior Chairman—Fred L. Turner
Vice Chairman—Vacant
President and Chief Operating Officer—Michael Roberts
Executive Vice President and Chief Financial Officer—Matthew H. Paull
Executive Vice President, Global Human Resources—Stanly R. Stein
Executive Vice President, Strategy and Business Development—Mats Lederhausen
Global Chief Marketing Officer—Larry Light
Vice President, Marketing—Kay Napier

Major Competitors: Wendy's, Burger King, Jack-in-the-Box, and various regional and local hamburger operations

HISTORICAL PERFORMANCE

	1997	1998	1999	2000	2001	2002	2003
Revenues (billion dollars)	11.41	12.42	13.26	14.24	14.87	15.41	17.14
Net income (billion dollars)	1.60	1.55	1.95	1.98	1.64	0.89	1.47
Number of employees (thousands)	267	284	314	364	395	413	418
Shares outstanding (millions)	1,371	1,356	1,351	1,305	1,281	1,268	1,262
Price per share (year end, dollars)	23.88	38.41	40.31	34.00	26.47	16.08	24.83
Dividends per share (dollars)	0.16	0.18	0.20	0.22	0.23	0.24	0.40

BRIEF HISTORY

McDonald's restaurants have been in existence since the 1930s. The original hamburger stands were introduced by brothers Dick and Mac McDonald in San Bernardino, California. In 1954, salesman Ray Kroc took exclusive distributorship of a five-spindled milkshake maker called Multimixer after he heard and saw how the McDonald brothers ran eight Multimixers simultaneously to serve a large number of customers efficiently. He then decided to investigate McDonald's operations.

Impressed with the simplicity of the hamburger operation—they sold only hamburgers, cheeseburgers, French fries, milkshakes, soft drinks, and apple pie—Kroc was able to convince the owners to allow him to take the restaurants nationwide (hoping to sell eight Multimixers at each McDonald's outlet) through franchising agreements. Most of the early locations were on corner lots in suburban locations. Thirty-four restaurants were in existence by 1958; sixty-seven more opened in 1959. But real growth occurred in the 1960s, spurred by the increasing popularity of the automobile and the greater number of people living in the suburbs.

In 1961, McDonald's sold out to Kroc for $2.7 million. In 1965, McDonald's went public with a share of common stock selling for $22.50. If a person had purchased 100 shares at that time, that investment of $2,250 would have been worth $1.8 million by the turn of the century.

In 1968, the company opened its 1,000th restaurant. By 1988, it had 10,000 outlets. By 1997, 23,000 restaurants were in existence due to an aggressive expansion program that averaged opening 2,500 restaurants annually. In 2002, the company was operating around 27,000 restaurants worldwide and sales reached $15.41 billion. The company also had mini-restaurants located inside Wal-Marts and Chevron stores.

In February 1998, McDonald's announced its first move outside its traditional product lines by obtaining a minority interest in Chipotle Mexican Grill restaurants. Other such acquisitions soon followed: Donatos Pizza chain and the 750-unit Boston Market restaurants.

Global Expansion

In 1967, McDonald's opened its first restaurant outside the United States—in British Columbia, Canada. By the early 1990s, it had 3,600 operations in 58 countries. In 2002, 53 percent of its 27,000 restaurants were located outside the United States in 120 countries, and these overseas operations accounted for 60 percent of sales and 50 percent of profits.

Products

The main products of McDonald's have been hamburgers, cheeseburgers, French fries, and soft drinks. However, over the years, the company has added a number of new products—some that proved to be successful and some that did not:

- 1965 Fish sandwich. Still on McDonald's menu.
- 1973 McMuffin. This breakfast sandwich was the catalyst for McDonald's to add a full breakfast menu five years later. The company now accounts for around one-fourth of all breakfasts eaten outside the home.
- 1983 Chicken McNuggets. A huge success, they are still on McDonald's menu.
- 1987 Ready-to-eat salads.
- 1991 McLean Deluxe sandwich. A 91 percent fat-free burger, it was dropped in 1996.
- 1990s Fried chicken, pasta, fajitas, and pizza. All were failures.
- 1996 Arch Deluxe and Deluxe burgers. Targeted to adults, they never caught on.
- 1998 McFlurry desserts. Caught on and are still around.

Technology

The efficient operations of the early McDonald's is what attracted Kroc. Each worker's steps were designed to ensure maximum efficiency. This saved preparation time, which reduced costs and allowed McDonald's to sell its hamburgers at 50 percent of what competitors were charging.

When Kroc was operating the first McDonald's in Des Plaines, Illinois (outside of Chicago), he was faced with mushy French fries. He solved the problem by using an electric fan to dry potatoes that had been cut and placed in cold water and then blanched. Kroc also had to adapt the McDonald's building to northern weather; furnaces had to be installed and inadequate ventilation had to be dealt with.

In the 1960s, McDonald's continued to emphasize technology. Under the leadership of Fred Turner, president and chief administrative officer, McDonald's determined the optimum number of hamburger patties that should be in a box and also began using presliced hamburger buns in order to save preparation time.

In 1975, McDonald's opened its first drive-thru window. This method of delivering products now accounts for half of the company's sales. In the 1980s, when McDonald's began adding urban sites, it was forced to develop new architectural styles. In 1979, Braille menus were brought out; they were reintroduced in March of 1992. Clamshell cookers, able to cook both sides of a hamburger at the same time, were invented.

In 1998, a major technological effort was undertaken. The "Made for You" system was introduced to provide customers with "fresher, hotter food" and enabled consumers to request special orders. The system relied on its flexibility to allow for easier introduction of new items. Eventually introduced into all restaurants, the system cost $25,000 per unit.

Promotion

Kroc viewed promotion as an investment that would be repaid many times over. The famous golden arches logo was introduced in 1962. Aggressive advertising was the norm for the hamburger industry in the 1980s, resulting in the "burger wars." Because of this situation, companies were forced to slash their prices. Nevertheless, McDonald's sales and market share improved.

Its 1988 Olympic Games tie-in promotion, "When the U.S. wins, you win," was a huge success. The 1996 55-cent Big Mac promotion proved disastrous because customers did not know that they had to purchase the sandwich with full-price fries and drinks. In 1997, McDonald's fired its ad agency of 15 years, Leo Burnett, because of the failure of the nostalgic "My McDonald's" campaign. It was replaced by BDD Needham, who had developed the very successful "You Deserve a Break Today" campaign in the 1970s.

The company scored a huge success with its Teenie Beanie Baby promotion; virtually overnight, 80 million were acquired. A 10-year alliance with Disney proved fruitful in the late 1990s. McDonald's promoted such Disney movies as *101 Dalmatians, Flubber, Mulan, Armageddon,* and *A Bug's Life.*

During the 1990s and in the first years of the twenty-first century, McDonald's annual advertising budget averaged $1.5 billion.

Ethics

McDonald's has tried to operate in a socially responsible manner since its founding. Ray Kroc believed strongly in "giving something back into the community where you do business." In 1974, the company opened its first Ronald McDonald's House in Philadelphia to provide a "home away from home" for families of children who were patients in nearby hospitals. By 1986, one hundred other Ronald McDonald Houses were in existence. During the 1980s, in order to fill a labor shortage, McDonald's became the first U.S. firm to hire retirees. In 1990, it purchased $100 million worth of recycled prod-

ucts and promised to do the same each year. Recycled products are found in its chairs, tables, table tops, eating counters, table columns, waste containers, cartons, packaging materials, and bathroom tissue papers. In conjunction with the U.S. Environmental Defense Fund, it has developed an aggressive effort to reduce solid waste. One notable effort: wrapping hamburgers in paper instead of plastic resulted in a 90 percent decrease in waste.

CHALLENGES AHEAD

A slower level of growth in revenues and a sharp decline in net income in 2002 are significant concerns for McDonald's management. Too rapid an expansion in the number of foreign restaurants had to be dealt with by cutting back on the number of new foreign openings and the elimination of poorly performing foreign restaurants. Terrorist incidents and the threat of them at several foreign sites were also major concerns.

Continuing complaints about poor and slow service got management's attention. Toughening competition from other hamburger and fast-food chains is a problem the company has grappled with in the past and one that will undoubtedly continue in the future as these competitors attempt to attack the leader in the industry. A proposed hike in the minimum wage would increase the company's operating costs and could potentially deflate its profit margins. Effective management of non-burger operations will have to be a priority.

A major problem that will have to be dealt with is the increasingly negative image of fast food. This industry is being blamed for much of the increase in obesity in the United States. McDonald's is often cited as the major offender. The company has responded by introducing four "premium" salads containing grilled or crispy chicken. However, this may not be sufficient to eliminate McDonald's and other fast-food companies as the scapegoats for America's poor eating habits and sedentary life style.

Source: **www.mcdonalds.com/corp/invest/pub/financial/**; *Mergent Industrial Manual,* 2003; *Security Owners Stock Guide,* Standard & Poors, July 2004; *Hoover's Billion Dollar Directory,* 1997; and *Hoover's Masterlist of Major U.S. Companies,* 2001.

Sony Corporation

COMPANY PROFILE

Headquarters: 6-7-35 Kitashinagawa
Shinagawa-ku
Tokyo 141-0001 Japan

Phone: +03 5448-2111
Fax: +03 5448-2244

Website: **www.world.sony.com**

Industries: Consumer electronics, music, movies and television, computer entertainment, and insurance

Stock Exchanges: Tokyo, Osaka, Nagoya, Fukuoka, Sapporo, New York, Pacific, Chicago, Toronto, London, Paris, Frankfurt, Dusseldorf, Brussels, Vienna, and Zurich

Ticker Symbol: SNE

Founded: May 7, 1946

Major Divisions:
Sony Electronics Inc.
Sony Music Entertainment Inc.
Sony Pictures Entertainment Inc.
Sony Computer Entertainment America Inc.
Other activities [Insurance and Banking]

Corporate Executive Officers (as of September 1, 2004):
Nobuyuki Idei, Chairman and Group Chief Executive Officer
Kunitake Ando, President

Howard Stringer, Vice Chairman and Chief Operating Officer of Entertainment Business Group

Shizuo Takashino, Executive Deputy President and Chief Operating Officer of IT & Mobile Solutions Network Company and Professional Solutions Network Company

Ken Kutaragi, Executive Deputy President and Chief Operating Officer of Game Business Group, Home Electronics Network Company, and Semiconductor Solutions Network Company

Ryoji Chubachi, Executive Deputy President and Chief Operating Officer of Micro Systems Network Company

Fujio Nishida, Executive Vice President, Marketing and Corporate Communications

Takao Yuhara, Senior Vice President, Finance and Investor Relations

Nobuyiki Oneda, Senior Vice President, Corporate Planning & Control, Accounting and Information Systems

Yasunori Kirihara, Senior Vice President, Corporate Human Resources

Major Competitors: Matsushita Electric Corporation, Nintendo Co. Ltd., Motorola Inc., AOL Time Warner, Dell Computer Corporation, IBM Corporation, Intel Corporation, Microsoft Corporation, and The Walt Disney Company.

HISTORICAL PERFORMANCE

	2000	2001	2002	2003	2004
Revenues (million yen)	6,686,661	7,314,824	7,578,258	7,473,633	7,496,391
Net income (million yen)	121,835	16,754	15,310	115,519	88,511
Ave. shares outstanding (millions)	453.6	919.6	919.7	922.4	926.4
Net income (loss): yen per share	131.7	19.28	16.67	118.21	90.88
Cash dividend per share (yen)	25.00	25.00	25.00	25.00	25.00
Share Price (Tokyo: in yen)	14,500	8,900	6,700	4,200	4,360
Average number of employees	189,700	N/A	N/A	161,100	162,000

BRIEF HISTORY

Sony was founded by former naval lieutenant Akio Morita and defense contractor Masaru Ibuka. Morita, a weapons researcher, first met Ibuka during World War II while developing a heat-seeking missile-guidance system and a night-vision gun scope. In May 1946, the two men established a partnership with $500 in borrowed capital and registered their company as the Tokyo Tsushin Kogyo Kabushiki Kaisha (Tokyo Telecommunications Engineering Corporation) or TTK. Morita and Ibuka started their company in a crude facility on a

hill in southern Tokyo, and that is where they developed their first consumer product: a rice cooker, which failed commercially. In its first year, TTK registered a profit of $300 on sales of less than $7,000.

In 1950, TTK introduced the first Japanese tape recorder, and although initial demand for the tape recorder was low, customers such as the Academy of Art in Tokyo ended up purchasing so many that TTK was soon forced to move to a larger building in Shinagawa. TTK began mass production of transistor radios in 1955, and that same year the company went public. The TTK transistor radio was named Sony, which resulted from the combination of two words. One is "sonus" in Latin, which is the root of such words as "sound" and "sonic." The other is "sonny," meaning little son. The second word was selected because the company was started by two young men, both of whom were full of energy and passionate about what they were creating. In 1958, the rising popularity of the Sony radios led Morita and Ibuka to change the name of their company to Sony Kabushiki Kaisha (Sony Corporation).

Sony announced in 1960 that it had developed a transistorized television. That same year, Sony established a trade office in New York City and another in Switzerland. During the early 1960s, Sony engineers continued to introduce new, miniaturized products based on the transistor, including an AM/FM radio and a videotape recorder. By 1968, Sony had developed new color-television technology called Sony Trinitron, which used one electron gun for more accurate beam alignment and one lens for better focus. This technology produced a clearer image than conventional three-gun, three-lens sets. Also in 1968, Sony entered the record business through a joint venture with CBS, Inc.

Sony developed its first VCR for the consumer market, the Betamax, in 1975. Matsushita Electric developed a separate VCR format called VHS (video home system). Matsushita launched a vigorous marketing campaign to convince customers and other manufacturers not only that VHS was superior but also that Betamax would soon be obsolete. Although Betamax was generally considered a technically superior product, the VHS format grew in popularity and gradually displaced Betamax as a standard format.

But Sony's luck was about to change. In 1979, Morita personally oversaw the development of a compact cassette tape player called the Walkman. The entire development program took only five months from start to finish, and the product's success is now legendary—Walkman even became the generic term for similar devices produced by Sony's competitors.

Another groundbreaking result of Sony's commitment to research and development was a machine that used a laser to reproduce music recorded digitally on a small plastic disk. The compact disc (or CD) player, introduced by Sony in 1982, eliminated much of the noise common to conventional, analog phonograph records. Sony developed the CD in association with the Dutch electronics firm Philips. Because Philips had developed the most advanced laser technology, this company represented an ideal partner for Sony, which led in the pulse-code technology that made digital sound reproduction possible. By the mid-1990s, the CD format had virtually replaced phonograph systems as the recording medium of choice.

Early in the 1980s, Morita began ceding some of his duties to Sony's president, Norio Ohga, a young opera student who had been hired 30 years earlier to improve Sony's first tape recorders. During Ohga's tenure from 1982 to 1995, Sony was transformed from an electronics company into a total entertainment company through the establishment of the music, movies, and gaming businesses. In 1985, Sony introduced its 8mm video camera. Two years later, Sony purchased CBS Records (at that time the largest producer of records and tapes in the world) for $2 billion. Sony sought further diversification in U.S. entertainment companies and in 1989 made headlines around the world when it bought Columbia Pictures Entertainment, Inc., from Coca-Cola for $3.4 billion. Columbia provided Sony with an extensive film library and a strong U.S. distribution system.

Sony unexpectedly entered the video game market in the mid-1990s, making an immediate splash. The development of the Sony PlayStation had actually begun in the late 1980s as a joint project with game giant Nintendo Co., Ltd. But when Nintendo pulled out of the project in 1992, Sony decided to develop the new game console on its own. When introduced, the PlayStation was an immediate and huge success, and by 1998, it had grabbed about 40 percent of the worldwide video game market. In 1997, Sony surprised many observers by entering the crowded and low-margin personal computer business. That year, through a partnership with Intel, Sony began selling its VAIO line of PCs.

In April 1995, Ohga ascended to the chairmanship of Sony and Morita was made an honorary chairman. Nobuyuki Idei, a 34-year veteran of Sony, became the company's new president. During 1999, a year that saw the passing of company cofounder, Morita (the other founder, Ibuka, died in 1997), Idei launched a sweeping reorganization to position the company for the future—in Sony's vision statement, "the network era of the 21st century." For Idei, the key to Sony was a historic shift in focus: hardware had traditionally driven product development, but Idei instead wanted software development and services to drive hardware design. Perhaps the first example of such an approach came with the 2000 introduction of the Sony PlayStation 2, featuring enhanced graphics, processing power, DVD, and broadband capabilities. Sony continued to face competition in the game field from Nintendo, and faced the prospect of a new competitor, Microsoft Corporation, which was also planning a fall 2001 release of its XBox machine.

CHALLENGES AHEAD

In June 2000, Idei was named chairman and CEO of Sony, while Kunitake Ando, who had headed the VAIO unit, was named president and COO. The new team faced myriad challenges in the rapidly changing high-tech world of the early twenty-first century. One example was in Sony's music business, which was being rocked by the industry-wide threat of the rampant and unauthorized downloading of digital music files over the

Internet. Sony joined other music giants in suing Napster, the most obvious threat. Sony also entered into a joint venture with Vivendi Universal, S.A., to develop an online subscription service that would allow music downloads through what was called "virtual jukebox." Such a service was part of a new push by Sony into broadband delivery of the audio and video material owned by its content arms. With its aggressive moves in the areas of games, networking, and delivery of digital content, Sony is almost certain to remain a frontrunner in the ever-broadening field of consumer electronics and related platforms and services.

Source: **www.world.sony.com**; Jay P. Pedersen, editor, "Sony Corporation," *International Directory of Company Histories*, Chicago: St. James Press, 2000, Vol. 40, p. 404–410.

Glossary

20/80 principle The idea that a small percentage of a company's products accounts for a large percentage of its revenues (Ch 9)

360-degree feedback Full-circle evaluation of an employee by supervisor, peers, subordinates, and so on (Ch 6)

absolute advantage The ability of one country to produce a good or service more efficiently than another (Ch 2)

acceptance testing Verifying that the information system is ready to be used in a production setting; done by managers and end users (Ch 17)

accounting The recording, summarizing, and reporting of the economic activities and events of an organization (Ch 11)

accounting equation Assets = liabilities + owners' equity (Ch 12)

accounting information system (AIS) A business system that provides all the financial information needed to internal management for their business decision making and to external users who are concerned with the financial activities of the organization (Ch 11)

accounting information systems (AIS) Information systems that perform legal and historical record keeping and produce financial statements (Ch 17)

acquisitions Purchase of established firms abroad with the goal of utilizing the existing production, marketing, and distribution networks and of having instant access to foreign markets that fit the purchasing firm's global strategy; The purchase of one firm by another for a price that is paid to the purchased firm's owner(s) (Ch 2; Ch 4)

adaptation strategy Using a different product mix for products sold internationally than those sold domestically (Ch 9)

advertising Nonpersonal communications through media for which payment is made (Ch 10)

affirmative action The principle that some groups of employees should receive a degree of preference in the employment relationship (Ch 6)

agency costs The costs that occur when managers as agents of the firm are in conflict with the shareholders as principals (Ch 13)

agents People working for the owners of the business (Ch 3)

allocational efficiency The transfer of savings to the most profitable investments in the economy (Ch 14)

allowances Concessions offered to retailers in exchange for services rendered (Ch 10)

analog signal An electromagnetic signal of a continuous waveform that can handle voice communications (Ch 17)

angels Venture capitalists who are wealthy individuals and who likely were previously successful small business people (Ch 4)

annuity A type of savings plan offered by insurance companies that offers either a lump sum death benefit or a steady stream of cash payments to beneficiaries over time (Ch 14)

antitrust policies Government laws designed to break up monopolies and control monopoly abuses by business (Ch 1)

applicant pool The pool of people applying for a particular job or jobs (Ch 6)

application software The set of software programs that direct the computer to perform an information-processing task specified by end users (Ch 17)

application-specific software The set of software programs that support specific applications, such as investment analysis, for end users in business and other fields (Ch 17)

applied research Research designed to achieve a specific objective (Ch 9)

appreciating assets Assets that have the possibility of increasing in value over their lifetime (Ch 15)

arithmetic-logic unit The part of the CPU that performs arithmetic and logic operations (Ch 17)

assembler languages Second-generation programming languages that convert symbolic instructions into machine language (Ch 17)

asset allocation The process of dividing one's money among stocks, bonds, real estate, money market funds, and other investment instruments (Ch 15)

asset management account An investment account that combines brokerage, checking, and credit card services (Ch 13)

assets The economic resources owned by the firm (Ch 12)

assurance (of service) The ability to convey trust and confidence (Ch 16)

asymmetry of corporate information An imbalance among different people regarding information or what's going on at a corporation (Ch 3)

attitudes Consistent ways of acting that determine what, why, and how consumers purchase goods and services (Ch 8)

audit trail The connection between a source document used to support an accounting transaction and the financial statements (Ch 12)

authority Legitimate power within an organization over certain matters (Ch 5)

autocratic style A top-down approach to management where all decisions are made by the top manager with little if any input from employees or subordinates (Ch 7)

automatic vending Retailers dispensing convenience-type merchandise in machines (Ch 10)

B2B Business-to-business electronic commerce (Ch 1)

B2C Business-to-consumer electronic commerce (Ch 1)

back ordering An option where the customer is willing to wait for the product in return for a financial incentive (Ch 16)

backward vertical integration A form of vertical integration where the supply chain member that develops the ability to perform the function that another supply chain member has been performing is "downstream" from that supply chain member (Ch 18)

balance sheet The financial statement that provides a "snapshot" of a firm's financial position at a designated point in time (12 midnight on the balance sheet date) (Ch 12)

bandwidth The amount of data and other information that can be transferred in a second via the Internet (Ch 1)

bank reconciliation A bank reconciliation is an analysis that resolves differences between your checkbook's cash balance and the bank statement's cash balance. The result is the "true" cash balance in your checking account (Ch 15)

bank reserves The amount of cash held by commercial banks (Ch 14)

bank statement A statement of the bank's record of disbursements from and receipts to a checking account (Ch 15)

bank-centered systems Financial systems that are dominated by banks (Ch 14)

bankruptcy A legal remedy afforded to firms that default on their debt that provides some amount of protection from creditors and others to whom it owes money (Ch 13)

bargaining unit The specifically defined group of employees eligible for union representation (Ch 6)

barriers to competition Barriers that arise when certain legal restrictions (patent protection, licensing, and tariffs) that reduce the level of competition are imposed on an industry (Ch 1)

basic research Research whose aim is to obtain knowledge with no specific, immediate payoff in mind (Ch 9)

batch process A process where the product is produced at medium volumes and customization levels (Ch 16)

benefits The nonwage or nonsalary portion of employee compensation, such as health and life insurance (Ch 6)

best-of-breed approach An approach for implementing an ERP system where the modules of the system are from different ERP software vendors (Ch 18)

big-bang strategy A strategy for implementing an ERP system where all required modules are implemented at once and, if it is the case, at all locations (Ch 18)

bill of material A graphical representation of the sequence in which products are assembled (Ch 16)

bit A binary 0 or 1 digit representing the presence or absence of an electronic or magnetic signal in a computer (Ch 17)

board of directors The governing board of a corporation which generally must have at least three members (Ch 3)

bonded warehouse A public warehouse that leases space to users to store products that the user offers as collateral for loans (Ch 10)

bonds Long-term debt securities issued by firms to raise funds to finance long-term capital budgeting projects, such as land, buildings, and equipment (Ch 13)

brainstorming Considering potential new product ideas in a group setting (Ch 9)

brand equity The monetary value or worth of a brand (Ch 9)

brand name The name placed on a brand (Ch 9)

break-even formula The calculation that tells a company the number of units a new product needs to sell in order for it to cover the cost of development and the expected profit (Ch 9)

brokers Wholesalers with limited authority over the terms of sale; they bring buyer and seller together and are important in the sale of food products; Investment managers who execute buy-and-sell orders for securities and earn commissions on this service (Ch 10; Ch 13)

bullwhip effect The property of supply chains where demand increases in variability as it travels up in the supply chain (Ch 18)

bus network A network topology where all computers in the network share the same communications channel and there is no host computer (Ch 17)

business analysis The step in the new product development process in which a new product's potential profits are estimated (Ch 9)

business codes of ethics Formal written documents adopted by businesses regarding ethical conduct standards (Ch 3)

business cycles The up- and downswings in real GNI, GNP, or GDP levels over time (Ch 1)

business ethics The principles governing whether certain business practices are morally acceptable especially when they have a detrimental impact on consumers, investors, or employees; The application of ethical standards to business situations (Ch 1; Ch 3)

business judgment rule The requirement that corporate directors and officers act in good faith and exercise at least an ordinary prudent person's judgment in making business decisions (Ch 3)

business processes The unique ways in which companies organize, coordinate, and execute activities, information, and knowledge in order to produce goods or services (Ch 18)

business risks Internal and external risks of losses that can severely cripple a business or even cause bankruptcy (Ch 4)

businesses Those organizations that try to create value for the customer (Ch 1)

business-to-business (B2B) e-business The e-business that involves selling goods and services among businesses (Ch 18)

business-to-business market The market where businesses purchase goods and services from other businesses (Ch 8)

business-to-consumer (B2C) e-business The e-business that involves selling goods and services to individual consumers (Ch 18)

bypassing A supply chain management strategy where one member of the supply chain eliminates the functions performed by another member of the chain (Ch 18)

byte A string of eight bits, representing a number, letter, or symbol, that the computer stores as a unit (Ch 17)

C corporation A legal entity that is chartered under state law (Ch 4)

capacity The capability of the production system measured in units of input or output per unit time (Ch 16)

capital budgeting The process of comparing or ranking the profitability of alternative investment projects within a firm (Ch 13)

capital gain The difference between the price paid to purchase a share of stock and the money received when it is sold; The difference between the purchase price and sales price of a real or financial asset (Ch 4; Ch 13)

capital goods Finished goods like machinery and equipment that can be used as inputs for further production of goods and services (Ch 1)

capital market instruments Long-term securities that have maturities more than one year (Ch 14)

capital market line The line that shows the return-risk trade-off available to investors, who have a choice between a riskless asset and the market portfolio (Ch 13)

capital risk The chance that unanticipated losses will exceed the institution's level of equity capital on its balance sheet and cause bankruptcy (Ch 14)

capitalism The economic system that is based on private property rights, the free market system, the pursuit of self-interest, the freedom to choose, and the ability to borrow money (Ch 1)

cash flow The flow of money into (inflows) and out of (outflows) accounts (Ch 15)

cash flow budget A budget that shows what cash came in and what went out during a selected time period (Ch 15)

cash-and-carry wholesalers Limited-service wholesalers that do not provide their customers with credit or transportation (Ch 10)

catalog marketing Offering consumers sales of merchandise from catalogs containing information about products from which they can order (Ch 10)

category killer A store that dominates its segment of the retailing industry (Ch 10)

central processing unit (CPU) The computer hardware element that controls other elements of a computer system (Ch 17)

centralized configuration strategy The strategy where the development and operation of all information systems is done at a home base (Ch 17)

centralized organization An organization where relatively little delegation of authority occurs and authority is concentrated at the top (Ch 5)

Certified Public Accountants (CPAs) Accountants licensed by the state to provide accounting services, including external audits of a business firm's financial statements (Ch 12)

chain of command The lines of authority or reporting relationships that exist within an organization (Ch 5)

chaos theory The theory based on the assumption that organizations are multifaceted and complex and operate in a disorderly business environment (Ch 7)

character The most basic data element—a number, letter or other symbol—that can be observed and manipulated (Ch 17)

charismatic leaders Energetic transformational leaders who are often considered heroes by the organization in their pursuit of a rosy vision for the future (Ch 7)

chase strategy An extreme strategy where production rate adjustments come exclusively from hiring and firing workers (Ch 16)

chief executive officer (CEO) The top officer of a corporation (Ch 3)

chief financial officer (CFO) The top corporate financial officer (Ch 3)

circuit breakers Temporarily stopping or slowing down the trading of stocks and bonds by a securities exchange (Ch 14)

client/server network A telecommunications network where some computers are "clients" and some computers are "servers" (Ch 18)

clients Personal computers or workstations in a client/server network that provide user interfaces and perform some processing on an application (Ch 18)

closely held firms Firms that are owned by a relatively small number of shareholders who do not openly trade their shares (Ch 13)

closing Efforts by a salesperson designed to get a prospect to purchase a product or service (Ch 10)

closing time The time prior to publication by which an advertisement must be submitted (Ch 10)

coaxial cable Sturdy copper or aluminum wire wrapped with spacers to insulate it (Ch 17)

command, or planned, economic system The economic system in which the ownership and control of the factors of production are totally in government hands (Ch 1)

commercial banks The most dominant type of depository institution that takes public deposits of funds and channels these savings to loans and investments (Ch 14)

commercial paper Short-term, unsecured debt securities normally issued by large, financially sound firms to raise funds (Ch 13)

commercialization Strategies employed to introduce a new product and to monitor its performance (Ch 9)

commission merchants Sellers that have power over prices and terms of sale and specialize in providing transportation and arranging delivery for agricultural products (Ch 10)

committee authority The right of committees to run an organization (Ch 5)

commodity money Coins that are made out of precious metals (Ch 14)

common carriers Trucks not owned by shippers on which they can ship their products for a fee (Ch 10)

common market or single market A market formed when member countries of a customs union remove all barriers to the movement of capital and labor within the customs union (Ch 2)

common stock Securities issued by firms that represent ownership claims on the earnings of the firm (Ch 13)

communicability The ease with which it is possible to convey the benefits of a new product to the market (Ch 9)

communications channels The physical means by which information is transmitted (Ch 17)

communications devices Computer system devices that provide connections between the computer and other computers via telecommunications networks (Ch 17)

communications processors Devices that support the transmission and reception of information in a telecommunications network (Ch 17)

company credo A business philosophy that provides an ethical standard for a firm, as well as its managers and employees (Ch 4)

company unions Unions that are supported and dominated by the employer (Ch 6)

comparable worth The principle that men and women should be paid the same for comparable work (Ch 6)

comparative advantage The ability of one country that has an absolute advantage in the production of two or more goods (or services) to produce one of them relatively more efficiently than the other (Ch 2)

compatibility The extent to which a new product allows consumers to operate as they have in the past (Ch 9)

competitive competitor intelligence (CI) Information about competitors (Ch 8)

compliance audit The audit done to ensure that the organization is in compliance with laws, rules, regulations, and contractual agreements (Ch 12)

compound interest Interest that is earned on previous interest, also known as the force of interest (Ch 13)

computer contingency plan A comprehensive plan of action designed to safeguard critical accounting information from loss, destruction, theft, and other threats (Ch 11)

computer crime The use of computers to perpetrate or facilitate illegal activity (Ch 11)

computer monitoring Using computers to monitor the productivity of employees while they work (Ch 17)

computer software The detailed instructions that control the operation of a computer system (Ch 17)

concentration The channel of distribution function involving the pooling of small lots into larger ones (Ch 10)

concept testing Presenting the general idea of a new product to a sample of the market in order to get its reaction (Ch 9)

conceptual skills Abilities to think broadly and abstractly, to see the big picture (Ch 5)

confidentiality agreements Agreements by employees to keep confidential trade secrets or other sensitive information learned by working at a company (Ch 3)

consignment An arrangement whereby retailers do not have to pay for merchandise until they sell it (Ch 10)

consolidation movement The wave of mergers and acquisitions among financial institutions that has been sweeping the world in recent years (Ch 14)

consultative leadership The leader conferring with colleagues and employees before making the final decision (Ch 7)

Consumer Confidence Index An indicator that measures the self-assurance of consumers and is crucial in determining consumer spending habits that have a direct impact on business prospects and the economy (Ch 1)

consumer market People and households that purchase consumer products and services (Ch 8)

consumer-to-consumer (C2C) e-business The e-business that involves consumers selling goods and services to other consumers (Ch 18)

consumption The amount used by private domestic residents (Ch 1)

containerization The placement of products in trailer-sized containers that can be shipped by rail, air, ship, or truck (Ch 10)

contests A form of sales promotion in which a prize is awarded for a competition (Ch 10)

contingency approach to leadership An approach to management where managers study the environment in which their companies operate to determine the appropriate leadership style to adopt (Ch 7)

contingency planning Planning for change and for business dynamics that are subject to change (Ch 5)

contingency theories of leadership Theories that assert that leadership effectiveness is maximized when leaders make their behavior dependent on the characteristics of their followers and the business environment (Ch 7)

continuous process A process where the product is produced in very large volumes but with very little customization (Ch 16)

control chart A chart used to detect if the production system is in control or out of control (Ch 16)

control decisions Decisions made once the production system is producing (Ch 16)

control unit The part of the CPU that transmits electronic signals to the other components of a computer system to perform needed operations (Ch 17)

controller The financial manager responsible for accounting, financial statements, and tax payments (Ch 13)

controlling Measuring, monitoring, evaluating, and regulating an organization's progress toward meeting its goals (Ch 5)

convenience stores Small-sized stores that sell limited lines of food and nonfood items (Ch 10)

conversion The process of moving from an old information system to a new information system (Ch 17)

cooperative advertising Shared advertising costs by a company and a retailer carrying its products (Ch 10)

core competency The aspects of a company's operations that it is best at doing (Ch 8)

corporations Legal "persons," or entities, established for the purpose of doing business and distinct from their owners in terms of liability (Ch 3)

cost of goods sold The cost to a firm of the products sold by the firm to its customers (Ch 12)

counter trade A barter system of exchange in which trade between specific countries is conducted without the use of monetary transactions (Ch 2)

coupon payments Interest paid to bondholders by a firm on its outstanding debt (Ch 13)

coupons Certificates that allow consumers to receive a cash refund or a free product at the time of purchase (Ch 10)

covenants not to compete Agreements by employees not to compete with their former employer (Ch 3)

craft production or **cottage system** Production done by highly skilled workers using simple, flexible tools, where items were produced in small quantities and according to customer specifications (Ch 16)

creative destruction The competitive process of business success and failure, whereby small firms enter the marketplace to compete against existing larger firms and cause the failure of some of those existing firms (Ch 4)

credit risk The chance that promised interest and principal on debt will not be paid (Ch 14)

credit unions Not-for-profit thrift institutions that have members with a common bond, such as employer, religious group, and educational institution (Ch 14)

crisis planning Planning for very high-magnitude, unthinkable events (Ch 5)

cross coupons Coupons printed on an item or enclosed within the item's package that provide a discount on a different item (Ch 10)

culture The behavior patterns, beliefs, and institutions that underpin all human activities, explain much of our behavior, and create an awareness for learning, and vary by social grouping (Ch 1)

currency pegging The currency of a country that is kept within a fixed range of values relative to a hard currency (Ch 14)

currency risk The fluctuation in a country's currency value relative to other currencies in the world (Ch 14)

current assets The assets that will be used up, sold, or converted to cash within the year or the firm's normal operating cycle if more than one year (Ch 12)

current liabilities The firm's obligations that are payable within one year or within the firm's normal operating cycle if more than one year (Ch 12)

customer departmentalization Departmentalization according to potential customers of the organization (Ch 5)

customs union A group of free trade member countries that have adopted a common external tariff with nonmember countries (Ch 2)

data Facts about events or attributes of things, places, or people (Ch 17)

data marts Subsets of a data warehouse that contain data for a certain group of users (Ch 17)

data mining Systematic searching for patterns and trends in business activities that can be exploited by managers to gain competitive advantage (Ch 17)

data warehouse A database used for various business' analyses that contains current and historical data from various operational databases (Ch 17)

database Banks of information that companies have about their individual customers; A group of related files that represents the highest level in the data hierarchy (Ch 8; Ch 17)

database management system The software for creating and maintaining a database (Ch 17)

dealers Investment managers who buy and sell securities for customers and hold inventories of stocks, bonds, or other financial assets (Ch 13)

deals Inducements offered to retailers and consumers to purchase a certain quantity of a product (Ch 10)

decentralized configuration strategy The strategy where each autonomous business unit at a foreign location develops and operates its own information systems (Ch 17)

decentralized organization An organization where a significant amount of delegation of authority has occurred and authority is spread out (Ch 5)

decision-support systems Information systems for middle managers that combine data with sophisticated models and data analysis tools and help them make non-routine decisions (Ch 17)

decline stage The fourth step of the product life cycle in which profits and revenues continue to fall (Ch 9)

deductible The amount of a loss that an individual must pay before an insurance arrangement compensates him or her (Ch 15)

default risk The chance that a borrower will go bankrupt and be unable to pay back a debt (Ch 13)

default risk premium The added interest rate charged by lenders due to the default risk of the borrower (Ch 13)

defined benefit plan Retirement plans where the benefit is based on a formula and precisely known; A type of pension plan in which the employer promises to pay out a specified amount of monthly pay to an employee upon their retirement (Ch 6; Ch 14)

defined contribution plan Retirement plans where contributions are known but benefits may vary; A type of pension plan in which the employee sets aside a portion of her or his paycheck in a savings plan and the employer provides matching funds in many cases (Ch 6; Ch 14)

delegation The assignment by a manager of some of his or her authority or work to other employees (Ch 5)

demand curve The curve that shows the relationship between the quantity demanded and the price of a product or service for a particular customer, group of consumers, or even a whole country (It is downward sloping.) (Ch 1)

democratic style A bottom-up approach to management where management receives input from its members and major policies are accepted for implementation on the basis of majority vote (Ch 7)

department stores Large stores that sell a wide variety of merchandise organized into separate departments (Ch 10)

departmentalization The process of grouping jobs into coordinated units (Ch 5)

deposit insurance A guarantee on deposits that protects them from losses due to the failure of a bank or other depository institution (Ch 14)

depository institutions Financial institutions that hold deposit accounts of individuals, business firms, and government (Ch 14)

depreciating assets Assets that usually decrease in value over their lifetime (Ch 15)

depreciation The accounting process of allocating an asset's cost to expense over the asset's useful life (Ch 12)

depressions Long, severe economic downturns that are particularly damaging to a business economy (Ch 4)

design decisions Decisions related to creating the products and the production system itself (Ch 16)

development The step in the new product development process in which the design of the new product is finalized (Ch 9)

digital cash An electronic payment system that represents currency in an electronic form that moves outside the normal network of money (Ch 18)

digital checking An electronic payment system that extends the functionality of existing checking accounts so that they can be used for online shopping payments (Ch 18)

digital credit card An electronic payment system that extends the functionality of regular credit cards to protect the information transmitted among customers, merchant sites, and processing banks (Ch 18)

digital enterprise A business organization where all major business processes and relationships with suppliers, customers, employees, managers, and shareholders are digitally enabled (Ch 18)

digital era The period of transformation within our lifestyle to make the Internet and related technologies a part of our everyday lives (Ch 1)

digital signal An electromagnetic signal of a discrete waveform that can handle data communications (Ch 17)

digital wallet An electronic payment system that stores credit card and owner identification information and provides these data automatically during e-business transactions (Ch 18)

dilution of ownership control The loss of ownership control that occurs as more shareholders own stock, thereby reducing the percentage ownership of each individual shareholder (Ch 4)

direct mail A type of advertising that uses personal letters, booklets, and brochures to reach very specific market segments (Ch 10)

direct marketing Using telephone and nonpersonal media to promote products and services (Ch 10)

direct selling Nonstore retailing involving salespeople calling directly on customers in their homes or offices (Ch 10)

directing Guiding, motivating, and leading employees toward what an organization wishes to achieve (Ch 5)

direct-response marketing Using various media to ask consumers to purchase products (Ch 10)

disability insurance Protection offered by insurance companies against longer-term expenses resulting from a chronic medical condition that prevents a person from continuing to work (Ch 4)

discount rate Any rate used in present value calculations to convert money from its future value to its present value; The interest rate at which banks can borrow from the central bank's discount window (Ch 13; Ch 14)

discount stores Stores that emphasize the sale of hard goods at low prices with low levels of service at inexpensive locations (Ch 10)

dispersion The channel of distribution function involving the breaking down of large lots into smaller lots (Ch 10)

displays Materials for holding merchandise sold in a retail store (Ch 10)

disposable income The money left over after taxes are taken out of a person's paycheck (Ch 2)

distribution mix The channels of distribution and logistics operations a company uses to move its products to its customers (Ch 10)

diversification Buying different financial and real assets whose prices or values have different patterns of movement up and down over time, such that the total risk or volatility is reduced for the entire portfolio of assets; Allocating your money among many different types of assets rather than concentrating them in one asset (Ch 13; Ch 15)

dividend The portion of profits distributed to stockholders; Quarterly payments by the firm from net income after taxes to shareholders; Income paid to common shareholders from a firm's net income after taxes (Ch 1; Ch 4; Ch 13)

divisibility The aspect of a new product that enables consumers to try it in a piecemeal manner without having to purchase the entire product (Ch 9)

division of labor The idea of dividing production operations into a series of many small tasks, where workers are assigned to perform one of these tasks (Ch 16)

divisional organizational structure The structure of an organization with various divisions operating autonomously under a broad organizational framework (Ch 5)

dollar cost averaging An investment approach where the investor ignores price trends and invests a fixed amount at regular intervals (Ch 15)

domestic exporter An organizational structure where there is heavy centralization of corporate activities in the home country of origin (Ch 17)

double taxation of earnings The taxation of a corporation's profits plus the taxation of the dividends paid to shareholders from after-tax profits (Ch 4)

drop shippers Limited-service wholesalers that take title to merchandise but do not take physical possession (Ch 10)

dumping The practice of selling a product in foreign markets for less than its cost (Ch 9)

duplicated configuration strategy The strategy where the development of all information systems is done at a home base, but the operation of these systems is handed over to autonomous business units at foreign locations (Ch 17)

durability (of an item) The length of an item's life (Ch 16)

duty of fair representation The duty of a union to fairly represent all employees in its bargaining unit (Ch 6)

East India Company The first joint-stock company, which was given its charter by Queen Elizabeth in 1600 and achieved fame for engaging in international trade in the early days of the British Empire (Ch 11)

e-business The process of buying and selling goods and services electronically (Ch 18)

economic and monetary union A union formed when members of a common market agree to implement common social programs (on education, employee benefits and retraining, health care, etc.) and coordinated macroeconomic policies (such as fiscal and monetary policies) that would lead to the creation of a single regional currency and an apex central bank (Ch 2)

economic goals The aims of monetary policy, including productivity, employment, stable prices, and trade (Ch 14)

economic profits Higher stock prices due to earning higher accounting profits or reducing the riskiness of profits (Ch 13)

economic resources Land, labor, capital, and technology that are scarce (Ch 1)

economic transition The move from a command economic system to a capitalist economic system (in the direction of competitive, market-oriented economics) that is aimed at ending the inefficiencies of central planning (Ch 1)

economies of scale The reduction in cost per unit output that occurs as a firm mass-produces a product or service (Ch 4)

efficient frontier The set of portfolios of assets that has minimum risk over a range of expected returns (Ch 13)

elastic demand A combination of prices and quantities demanded that indicates that the market is very responsive to prices (Ch 9)

electronic money The use of computers, equipment, and electronic communications to make payments, including credit cards, stored value cards, debt cards, wire transfers, and Internet payments (Ch 14)

electronic payment system A system that uses digital technologies to pay for goods and services electronically (Ch 18)

embargoes Trade sanctions that are imposed on a country and that restrict trade with that country (Ch 2)

empathy (of service) The flexibility in adapting the service to meet individual needs (Ch 16)

employee empowerment A proactive approach to management where workers decide what, when, and how they will work to achieve corporate goals (Ch 7)

Employee Retirement Income Security Act (ERISA) A federal law passed in 1974 to regulate employer-defined benefit plans (Ch 6)

employer pay confidentiality rules Employer rules mandating that employees not speak to others about their pay (Ch 6)

employment-at-will Legal rule stating that an employer can fire an employee at any time for any reason, and an employee can quit at any time (Ch 6)

entrepreneur People with initiative who seize opportunities as they see them to get things done or make things happen, generally for profit; Anyone who starts, owns, or runs a small or large business (Ch 1; Ch 4)

envelope budget A budgeting system in which money is placed in envelopes labeled as rent, car payment, food, and so on (Ch 15)

environmental analysis A strategic scan by an organization for external threats and opportunities (Ch 5)

equal employment opportunity The principle that all groups of employees should be treated equally in the employment relationship (Ch 6)

Equal Employment Opportunity Commission (EEOC) The federal agency that administers U.S. employment discrimination laws (Ch 6)

Equal Pay Act A federal law passed in 1963 requiring equal pay for men and women doing equal work (Ch 6)

equity theory The theory that employees are motivated to work smart and contribute to the success of the firm as long as they believe that they are treated and compensated fairly relative to others with *similar* levels of education and professional experience (Ch 7)

ERP systems Software packages designed to integrate the majority of a firm's business processes, execute all transactions related to the firm's business processes being integrated, store each piece of data only once in an enterprise-wide database, allow access to data and information in real time, and operate in a client/server environment, traditional or Web-based (Ch 18)

estate plan A plan that seeks to reduce taxes on the family level and provide for an orderly transfer of wealth and leadership within a firm (Ch 4)

ethics Beliefs about what is right and wrong, what is morally acceptable and what is not (Ch 3)

euro The new currency issued in 2002 by the 12 countries in the European Monetary Union (Ch 14)

Eurobonds Bonds that are issued outside a firm's home country (Ch 13)

exabyte One million terabytes (Ch 17)

exchange rate The price of one currency compared with that of another currency (Ch 2)

exchange rate policy A policy of managing the country's exchange rate, to improve the country's balance of payments position (Ch 2)

exchange traded funds (ETFs) Diversified portfolios of securities offered by the American Stock Exchange that can be bought and sold as individual stocks can be (Ch 13)

executive information systems Information systems for senior managers that support nonroutine, unstructured decisions requiring judgment, evaluation, and insight (Ch 17)

Executive Order 11246 The presidential executive order mandating affirmative action in employment by large federal government contractors (Ch 6)

expectancy theory The theory that an individual will be motivated to work hard to achieve a coveted reward, provided the prospect of receiving that reward is reasonable, or the individual will not bother at all (Ch 7)

export-import business A relatively low-risk operation, that involves penetrating foreign markets (by exporting) or importing merchandise (of all kinds) at competitive prices for domestic consumption (Ch 2)

exports Goods or services that are sold to citizens abroad (Ch 2)

express warranty An explicit warranty that is either written or spoken (Ch 9)

external auditing Auditing of a firm's financial statements by an independent external auditor who is a certified public accountant (Ch 12)

external recruiting Considering individuals outside the organization as candidates for the job (Ch 6)

external source A source for new products that is located outside of a company (Ch 9)

extranet A network that links the intranet resources of a company with other organizations (Ch 18)

extrinsic motivation Motivation for which the reward is obtained as a consequence of the activity (Ch 7)

facility controls Controls to protect an organization's computing facilities from loss or destruction (Ch 17)

factoring The sale of accounts receivables to a financial institution that then collects payments by customers (Ch 13)

factory system A method of mass production in which raw materials, machinery, and labor are brought together in large volumes in one location to produce goods less expensively than in dispersed locations (Ch 1)

fair information practices (FIP) A set of principles governing the collection and use of information about individuals (Ch 18)

Fair Labor Standards Act (FLSA) A federal law passed in 1938 regulating employee wages and work hours (Ch 6)

feasibility study A study to determine if the proposed solution of a business problem is feasible organizationally, economically, technically, and operationally (Ch 17)

federal funds rate The interest rates that banks charge one another for borrowing money (Ch 14)

feedback controls A type of internal control that reports the occurrence of mistakes or intentional misrepresentations after they have occurred, so that corrective action can be taken (Ch 11)

fiat money Money that is valuable because the government deems it so (Ch 14)

fiber-optic cable Thousands of hair-thin glass fiber filaments wrapped in a protective cover (Ch 17)

field A grouping of characters (Ch 17)

file A group of related records (Ch 17)

financial accounting The component of the accounting information system that provides financial information needed by external users such as investors and lenders (Ch 11)

financial holding company A conglomerate financial services firm that can offer its customers banking, securities, and insurance services (Ch 14)

financial information systems Information systems that support decisions regarding the financing of a business organization and the allocation of financial resources within the organization (Ch 17)

financial institutions Privately owned firms that provide financial services (Ch 14)

financial intermediation The process of pooling individuals' savings in financial institutions that channel them to business firms (Ch 14)

financial managers Managers in charge of the money side of an organization (Ch 5)

Financial Services Modernization Act Legislation passed in 1999 that allows banks, securities firms, and insurance companies to freely compete with one another (Ch 14)

financial statements The income statement, statement of retained earnings, balance sheet, and statement of cash flows, which together represent a business firm in financial terms (Ch 12)

financial success Having enough money to pay for one's living expenses and at the same time saving enough to meet future financial needs (Ch 15)

financial system The financial marketplace, including financial instruments, financial markets, and financial institutions (Ch 14)

financing decisions The choice made between internal and external funding and between debt and equity funds to finance the firm's investment projects (Ch 13)

firm concentration ratios The percentage of total industry output that can be accounted for by the four largest firms and so a measure of the sellers' market power (Ch 1)

firm-specific risk Any risk that is particular to an individual firm and not related to market, liquidity, and tax risks that affect all firms (Ch 13)

first mover The company that is first into a market with a new product or service (Ch 8)

first-line managers Managers who are directly responsible for supervising and working with employees and getting the work done (Ch 5)

fiscal policy A government policy of using expenditures and taxation to guide the economy to meet economic goals (related to output, employment, inflation, and the exchange rate); The use of government spending and taxation to stimulate or slow down the growth rate of the economy (Ch 2; Ch 14)

fiscal year An accounting period of 12 months, which may or may not end on December 31 (Ch 12)

fixed exchange rate system The system in which a country pegs (fixes) its currency value (formally or de facto) at a fixed rate to a major currency or a basket of currencies (Ch 2)

fixed-income investment An investment in which an individual invests an initial amount of money (principal), collects interest on that initial amount, and receives back the initial amount when the security matures (Ch 15)

fixed-position layout A layout where the product stays in one place, while the workers, materials, and equipment come to the product for manufacturing or service operations (Ch 16)

flexible, or cafeteria, benefit plans Plans giving employees considerable choice in picking the benefits they want (Ch 6)

flextime The flexible daily work hours chosen by employees in consultation with their supervisors in addition to core time, the daily period during which all employees are expected to be at work to facilitate interactive communication and workflow (Ch 7)

floating exchange rate system The system in which currency values are determined by the demand for and supply of currencies in a foreign exchange market (Ch 2)

focus group A small group of consumers that is representative of the market for a new product and provides companies with reactions to new product concepts (Ch 9)

forced distribution methods Performance appraisals requiring a defined ranking of performance into different levels (Ch 6)

Foreign Corrupt Practices Act The federal law prohibiting U.S. companies doing business overseas from making payments to foreign officials to influence their discretionary decisions (Ch 3)

foreign direct investment (FDI) An overseas investment in plant and equipment to produce goods or services for local consumption or for exports (Ch 2)

foreign exchange markets Financial centers where a network of international banks and currency traders (people who buy, sell, or speculate on currencies) transact business (Ch 2)

forward vertical integration A form of vertical integration where the supply chain member that develops the ability to perform the function that another supply chain member has been performing is "upstream" from that supply chain member (Ch 18)

fourth-generation languages Programming languages that are less procedural than earlier programming languages and are very close to human languages (Ch 17)

franchise An authorization by a corporation to individuals that allows them to participate as an owner-manager of a branch entity of the corporate firm (Ch 4)

franchiser An organizational structure where a product is created, designed, financed, and initially produced in the home country, but for product-specific reasons, relies heavily on foreign personnel for further production, marketing, and human resources (Ch 17)

franchising The practice in which a firm is obligated to provide specialized equipment and service support (e.g., training, product, price, promotion, and distribution strategy), and at times even some seed money, in return for an annual fee from the franchisee (Ch 2)

free market system The economic system in which consumers demand certain goods and services and are willing to pay a price based on their budget, and producers are willing to supply the goods and services on the basis of a price that will cover their costs and provide a profit margin (Ch 1)

free trade area An area in which two or more countries agree to eliminate all barriers to trade such as tariffs, quotas, and nontariff barriers like border restrictions, while at the same time they keep their own external tariffs (usually within WTO guidelines) against nonmembers (Ch 2)

free trade regime A system in which imports and exports of goods or services take place voluntarily, without government restrictions and based on a principle of free markets (Ch 2)

free-rein style An approach to management where employees are given complete freedom to perform their jobs the way they want within company rules and objectives (Ch 7)

freight forwarder Agents that perform a wide variety of services for companies shipping products to international customers (Ch 10)

functional departmentalization Departmentalization based on the functions performed by that unit (Ch 5)

functional organizational structure The structure of an organization around certain functions such as marketing, finance, and so on (Ch 5)

funded pension plan A pension plan that pays retirees from their funds set aside in a savings plan in during their working years (Ch 14)

future value The value of a dollar in the future, which is less than its value today (Ch 13)

gainsharing plans Plans for sharing company productivity gains or savings with the responsible work group (Ch 6)

gap risk The sensitivity of a financial institution's profitability due to changes in interest changes (Ch 14)

general managers Managers who coordinate and supervise more-specialized managers (Ch 5)

general partners Partners who run the partnership's business and who are liable for its actions (Ch 3)

general-purpose software The set of software programs that perform common information processing jobs, such as word processing, for end users (Ch 17)

generally accepted accounting principles (GAAP) The principles by which financial statements are prepared (Ch 11)

generic brands Products that do not have a brand name, but contain only an indication of their contents on the package (Ch 9)

geographic departmentalization Departmentalization based on the geographic areas or locations served by the organization (Ch 5)

gigabyte One billion bytes (Ch 17)

globalization The process of integrating the market for goods and services worldwide; The process of eliminating trade, investment, cultural, and even political barriers across countries, which in turn could lead to freer movement of goods, services, labor, capital, technology, and companies across international borders (Ch 1; Ch 2)

goals The aims that guide the future direction of a firm (Ch 4)

goal-seeking analysis A modeling activity in a decision-support system where a target for a variable or variables of interest is set and then the values of other variables are changed until the target is achieved (Ch 17)

gold standard Backing of money with gold at a fixed exchange rate per ounce of gold (Ch 14)

golden parachute agreements Severance payment agreements, often fairly lucrative, to be received by corporate executives if their corporation is acquired (Ch 3)

good faith bargaining The duty of employers and unions to bargain with each other honestly (Ch 6)

government expenditure The amount spent by the government; The purchase of goods and services by government to serve the needs of the general public (Ch 1; Ch 2)

government markets Local, state, and federal purchasers of goods and products (Ch 8)

gross domestic product (GDP) The total dollar value of all final goods and services produced each year within a country's borders (Ch 1)

gross national income (GNI) The expenditures that make up GNP and are equal to the income that the factors of production (land, labor, capital, and technology) receive (Ch 1)

gross national product (GNP) The value of all final goods and services produced in an economy and measured at current prices over a given time period, usually a year (Ch 1)

growth stage The second stage of the product life cycle in which revenues increase rapidly and profits are maximized (Ch 9)

growth stocks Stocks that provide low, if any, dividends, but do offer potential long-term capital appreciation (Ch 15)

hard currencies Currencies that are relatively stable in value, are issued by large industrial countries, and include the U.S. dollar, Japanese yen, European euro, and British pound sterling (Ch 14)

Hawthorne effect The principle that when employees are given autonomy to control their work environment, they become more motivated, and this has a positive impact on employee morale, job satisfaction, and productivity (Ch 7)

Hawthorne Studies Studies conducted by a group of engineers at the Hawthorne plant of Western Electric Company in Chicago in 1925 to determine the impact of changing light intensity on worker productivity (Ch 7)

health insurance Protection offered by insurance companies against the high costs of medical treatment, such as doctor and dentist visits, vision care, prescription drugs, and major medical procedures (Ch 4)

Herzberg's motivation-hygiene theory The theory that job satisfaction and dissatisfaction are not part of the same spectrum (Ch 7)

high-level languages Third-generation programming languages that convert natural-language-like statements into machine language (Ch 17)

holding cost The cost resulting from keeping one unit in inventory for a given time period, usually a year (Ch 16)

home business A small business that is operated out of a household address, rather than out of a business office or factory (Ch 4)

human relations skills Abilities to get along and deal effectively with people (Ch 5)

human resources information systems Information systems that support planning for meeting personnel needs, developing employees to their full potential, and controlling personnel policies and programs (Ch 17)

human resources managers Managers who manage the people part of an organization (Ch 5)

hybrid strategy A strategy that combines the chase and level strategies in different degrees (Ch 16)

hygiene factors Factors that influence the work environment which determine job dissatisfaction (Ch 7)

hypertext transfer protocol (http) A communications standard used to transfer webpages on the World Wide Web (Ch 18)

hypothesis Marketing researchers' idea as to what is the cause of a problem (Ch 8)

imperfect competition The industry market structure where the industry's output of goods or services is supplied by a relatively small number of firms and price is largely determined by market forces (Ch 1)

implicit warranty An unwritten or unspoken warranty that exists because the Universal Product Code says that all goods are at least fit for the ordinary purpose for which they are used (Ch 9)

imports Goods or services that are purchased from abroad (Ch 2)

incentives Rewards offered to retail salespeople or consumers for specified performance (Ch 10)

income statement The accounting report that shows the firm's revenues, expenses, and net income or net loss for a period (Ch 12)

income stocks Stocks that offer little opportunity for capital appreciation but provide relatively high dividends (Ch 15)

incomes policies Strategies based on wage and price controls that are used by governments to curb inflation and at the same time maintain employment and keep economic output stable (Ch 2)

in-control production system The production system where products produced exhibit normal variations (Ch 16)

increasing shareholder wealth Increasing dividends and stock prices (Ch 1)

independent outside directors Outside directors who do not have any financial or other relationship with the corporation beyond their service as a director (Ch 3)

independently wealthy Having enough money so that it is no longer necessary to work to pay for living expenses (Ch 15)

industrial distributors Wholesalers that handle industrial products and may specialize in a limited line of products and markets to which the products are sold (Ch 10)

inelastic demand A combination of prices and quantities for a product that indicates that the market is not very responsive to prices (Ch 9)

inflation The rate of price level increase in an economy from one period to another (monthly, quarterly, or annually) (Ch 2)

information Data that have been transformed to be meaningful and valuable to specific users (Ch 17)

information fragmentation The situation in a business organization where the information does not reside in a single repository, but instead is spread across functional areas, business units, regions, factories, and offices (Ch 18)

information managers Managers who manage computer and other information systems within an organization (Ch 5)

information requirements The details of who needs what information, where, when, and how (Ch 17)

information system A system that converts data into information (Ch 17)

information systems controls The policies, procedures, and technical measures used to protect information systems and to assure the accuracy and reliability of these systems (Ch 17)

information systems development The activities involved in the creation of an information system (Ch 17)

initial public offering (IPO) The first public sale by a firm of its common stock; The first time a firm issues stock to the public in financial markets (Ch 4; Ch 13)

innovation planning Planning to instill more of an entrepreneurial spirit into an organization (Ch 5)

innovators The first 2.5 percent of adopters of new products who are respected for their opinions and are sought out for these opinions by the market (Ch 9)

in-pack A premium enclosed with a product (Ch 10)

input devices Computer system devices such as the keyboard or mouse that are used to collect and transform data into an electronic form that the computer can use (Ch 17)

inputs Factors of production (land, labor, capital, and technology), that is, commodities or services that are used by firms in their production processes (Ch 1)

inside directors Corporate board of directors members employed full-time by the company, for example, the CEO or other corporate officers (Ch 3)

inside information Private information about individuals or business firms obtained by financial institutions (Ch 14)

insider trading Stock trading based on material nonpublic information (Ch 3)

institutional investors Large, professionally managed sources of capital; Large financial institutions, including insurance companies, pension funds, and investment companies, that trade securities in financial markets (Ch 3; Ch 13)

instructional-based programs Teaching and learning approaches to employee development (Ch 6)

insurance An arrangement in which an individual pays a fee (premium) and in return, if the individual suffers a designated loss, the insurance company compensates him or her (Ch 15)

insurance companies Financial institutions that offer various kinds of protection from financial losses to individuals and business firms (Ch 14)

insurance premium A payment to an insurance company on a monthly or periodic basis for insurance coverage (Ch 4)

integrated marketing promotion The consideration of all relevant promotion alternatives when developing a promotion mix, employing those that provide the best opportunity for achieving the company's promotion objectives and coordinating the activities required to put into motion the agreed-on promotion mix (Ch 10)

interest The amount that a borrower must pay a lender in addition to the principal value, as compensation for the declining time value of money (Ch 13)

interest cost The cost that is incurred by having money invested in inventory (Ch 16)

interest rate risk The risk of bond prices moving down as the general level of interest rates moves up, and vice versa; The risk that interest rates will rise, resulting in a decrease in the value of the investment (Ch 13; Ch 15)

intermediate targets The primary monetary targets in the financial marketplace, which are money supply, long-term interest rates, and bank credit (Ch 14)

internal auditing Chiefly concerned with evaluating the economy and efficiency with which scarce resources are utilized, but may include other objectives such as evaluating the effectiveness of internal controls (Ch 12)

internal control structure A set of devices and procedures designed to prevent unintentional errors and intentional irregularities from occurring and to identify errors and irregularities after they occur so that corrective action may be taken; The control environment, the accounting system, and the control procedures that help ensure the integrity of information output and the safety of the firm's assets (Ch 11; Ch 12)

internal controls A system of rules and procedures designed to ensure the accuracy and reliability of financial and accounting information (Ch 11)

internal recruiting Considering present employees as candidates for available jobs (Ch 6)

internal sources Sources for new products that are located within a firm (Ch 9)

International Accounting Standards (IAS) Accounting standards issued by the Board of the International Accounting Standards Committee, and subsequently adopted by the International Accounting Standards Board (Ch 11)

International Accounting Standards Board (IASB) A London-based organization that issues International Accounting Standards (Ch 11)

International Auditing and Assurance Standards Board (IAASB) The board that works to improve the uniformity of auditing practices and related services throughout the world by issuing pronouncements on a variety of audit and assurance functions and by promoting their acceptance worldwide (Ch 11)

International Federation of Accountants (IFAC) An organization of national professional accountancy organizations that represent accountants employed in public practice, business and industry, the public sector, and education, as well as some specialized groups that interface frequently with the profession (Ch 11)

International Financial Reporting Standards (IFRS) Accounting standards issued by the International Accounting Standards Board that have three goals: Increasing harmonization of accounting standards and disclosures to meet the needs of the global market; providing an accounting basis for underdeveloped or newly industrialized countries to follow as the accounting profession emerges in those countries; and increasing the compatibility of domestic and international accounting requirements (Ch 11)

international joint venture A business that is jointly owned (implies shared equity) and operated by two or more firms (usually one from the host country and the other from another country) that pool their resources (capital, technology, and management) to penetrate host country markets, generate (and share) profits, and share the commercial risk (Ch 2)

international markets Markets for products and services that exist in foreign countries (Ch 8)

international skills Abilities to understand foreign cultures, markets, politics, languages, and so on (Ch 5)

International Standards on Auditing (ISAs) The basic principles and essential procedures for auditing, along with related guidance in the form of explanatory and other material (Ch 11)

international trade The import or export of goods or services from or to other countries by individuals, firms, or governments (Ch 2)

Internet An international network of networks containing hundreds of thousands of private and public networks in more than 150 countries (Ch 18)

internet service provider (ISP) A business organization with a permanent connection to the Internet that sells temporary connections to subscribers (Ch 18)

internetworking The linking of separate networks into an interconnected network, where each network retains its own identity (Ch 18)

intranet An internal network in a business organization that is used by employees to collaborate, share information, and access internal websites (Ch 18)

intrapreneur A person within a large corporation who takes the responsibility to develop a new product through innovation and risk taking (Ch 4)

intrinsic motivation Motivation for which the reward is provided by the activity itself (Ch 7)

introduction stage The first phase of the product life cycle in which revenues and profits are low but begin to increase (Ch 9)

inventory Unsold goods in stock (Ch 1)

investment The amount spent by private firms on new plant and equipment for future production and profit (Ch 1)

investment bankers Investment managers who assist firms seeking to raise debt or equity funds from the financial marketplace (Ch 13)

investment companies or **mutual funds** Financial institutions that pool the savings of thousands of customers, issue unit shares of ownership to their customers, and invest the savings in securities portfolios (Ch 14)

investment grade Bonds with lower default risk that are rated in the top four letter grades by Moody's and Standard & Poor's rating services (Ch 13)

investment risk The probability that an individual will lose all or part of an investment (Ch 15)

investors Those who have a financial stake in a business, small or large, and expect to receive a return on their invested capital (Ch 1)

job analysis A systematic evaluation of the elements and requirements needed for a job (Ch 6)

job description A list of the duties of the job, working conditions, responsibilities, people to be supervised, and so on (Ch 6)

job enlargement The practice where employees are assigned to manage and run related tasks that lead to job enrichment (Ch 7)

job evaluation The process of determining the relative worth of different jobs (Ch 6)

job process A process where the product is produced in relatively low volumes with relatively high levels of customization (Ch 16)

job redesign Redefining jobs to keep employees satisfied and to enhance their creativity and performance (Ch 7)

job rotation Periodically shifting employees from one job to another; The practice where employees are periodically moved through different operations in a company to break job monotony and to provide employees the opportunity to learn different skills and obtain a feel for all the operations of the company (Ch 5; Ch 7)

job specialization Organizational activities are broken down into specific tasks and different people designated to perform those tasks (Ch 5)

job specification A detailed listing of the individual qualifications needed for a job (Ch 6)

junk bonds Bonds with higher default risk that are rated below the top four letter grades by Moody's and Standard & Poor's rating services (Ch 13)

just cause provision The labor contract provision stating that an employer can only fire or discharge an employee for a legitimate business reason (Ch 6)

key accounts Accounts that represent a large percentage of a company's revenues and profits (Ch 10)

kilobyte One thousand bytes (Ch 17)

knowledge- or **skill-based pay** Pay for individuals for having or obtaining specific knowledge or skills (Ch 6)

knowledge workers Employees whose jobs require formal and advanced schooling (Ch 1)

labor arbitration The resolution of a labor dispute by a neutral outside third party (Ch 6)

labor organization Any sort of employee organization that deals with the employer about working conditions (Ch 6)

lag demand strategy A strategy where capacity is increased after demand increases (Ch 16)

laissez faire The economic doctrine that advocates total government inaction in business, so businesses are free to do what and as they please (Ch 1)

Landrum Griffin Act A federal law of 1959 regulating internal union activities (Ch 6)

lead demand strategy A strategy where capacity is increased before demand increases (Ch 16)

lead users High-profile firms in an industry that are good sources for new industrial products because their business methods are often emulated by other firms in the industry (Ch 9)

leadership The art of motivating employees to enhance their performance in order to achieve corporate goals ethically (Ch 7)

leadership style The behavior that top managers exhibit when dealing with their employees and professional staff (Ch 7)

learning Acquiring information, preferences, and habits that determine what, why, and how consumers purchase goods and services (Ch 8)

legacy systems Any and all information systems that an ERP system replaces (Ch 18)

level strategy An extreme strategy where the workforce remains stable and production rate adjustments come from overtime or undertime, and subcontracting (Ch 16)

liabilities The debts or economic obligations of the firm (Ch 12)

liability insurance Insurance coverage of employees under worker compensation laws that require employers to pay health and disability costs to injured employees and of liability losses in court decisions against a firm (Ch 4)

licensing The practice by governments of selecting investors to operate certain types of businesses, thereby restricting entry into those businesses and reducing competition; The practice in which a company or individual provides the foreign partner the technology (patented technology, copyright, process, trademark, etc.) to manufacture and sell products or services for an annual license fee (Ch 1; Ch 2)

life insurance Protection offered by insurance companies intended to pay a death benefit to a beneficiary (e.g., a family member or friend) (Ch 4)

lifetime value (LTV) The future value of a customer based on recency, frequency, and dollar amount of past purchases (Ch 8)

limit order A securities transaction that sets a specific buy-or-sell price to execute a buy-or-sell order for a security (Ch 13)

limited liability The principle that shareholders are not generally liable for the debts or actions of the corporation (Ch 3)

limited liability company (LLC) A type of corporation that combines the corporate advantage of limited liability protection with the personal taxation of a partnership or S corporation (Ch 4)

limited partners Partners whose liability is limited to the amount of money they invested in the partnership and who generally aren't involved in running the business (Ch 3)

line authority The right to achieve organizational goals by being part of an organization's direct chain of command (Ch 5)

line process A process where the product is produced at a relatively high volume with relatively low product customization (Ch 16)

liquidity How easily an asset can be converted into cash (Ch 15)

liquidity risk The risk that a security cannot be sold quickly for a fair market price (Ch 13)

local area network (LAN) A network that provides connectivity within a limited physical area such as an office, a building, or several buildings in close proximity (Ch 17)

lock box system A way for firms to speed the collection of payments from customers, who submit payments to local post offices, where the payments are picked up by local banks and forwarded to the firm's bank (Ch 13)

logistics The materials management and physical distribution activities of a firm (Ch 10)

machine languages First-generation programming languages where all programming instructions had to be written using binary code (Ch 17)

mail-ins Premiums provided to consumers once the consumer has requested them by mail (Ch 10)

mainframe computers Large, fast, and powerful computers that are used for very large business applications (Ch 17)

maintainability (of an item) The ease and speed with which an item can be repaired (Ch 16)

maintenance The information systems development stage when the production system is being changed to correct errors, meet new requirements, or improve its operation (Ch 17)

maintenance objective A pricing objective involving the desire to retain the current market or competitive situation (Ch 9)

managed floating exchange rate system A floating exchange rate system in which the values of some currencies are partly determined by active government intervention (central bank purchases and sales of their own currencies) (Ch 2)

management The process of planning, organizing, directing, and controlling an organization's resources in the manner most effective for it to achieve its goals (Ch 5)

management accounting The component of the accounting information system that provides the financial information needed internally by business managers for efficient and effective decision making (Ch 11)

management by objective (MBO) A top-down approach to management that requires full collaboration of employees right down the line to be a success (Ch 7)

management information system (MIS) A business system that provides all the information, financial and nonfinancial, needed by management for decision making; The systems that manage the direct resources needed for creating, storing, and distributing information in a business organization (Ch 11; Ch 17)

management or **operational audit** The audit done to evaluate the economy and efficiency with which scarce resources are utilized (Ch 12)

managerial information systems Information systems for middle managers that help them plan, control, and make routine decisions (Ch 17)

managers People involved in the management of organizations (Ch 5)

manufacturers' agents Wholesalers that are not given control over the terms of sale and pricing because they sell only part of a client's output or product line (Ch 10)

maquiladoras The Maquiladora program allowed factories (primarily on the Mexican border to the U.S.) to temporarily import supplies, parts, machinery, and equipment necessary to produce goods and services in Mexico duty-free, as long as the output was exported back to the United States (Ch 2)

markdown A reduction in price used by retailers to sell products that have not already sold (Ch 9)

market clearing, or **equilibrium, price** The price at which supply will equal demand (Ch 1)

market domination A strategy of either acquiring competitors or colluding with them to control product prices and prevent new competitors from entering the market (Ch 1)

market efficiency The ability of prices of stocks, bonds, and other assets to rapidly reflect publicly available information (Ch 14)

market portfolio The portfolio of assets that investors should purchase to earn the highest return-risk trade-off (Ch 13)

market risk The risk of an individual firm's stock prices going down in value as bond market prices moves up, and vice versa (Ch 13)

market segmentation The breakdown of target consumers into categories on the basis of age, gender, education, ethnic background, or other criteria to determine the products or services that could be made to suit the segments' specific needs (Ch 1)

market share The percentage of total units sold of a product or service divided into the number of units of that product sold by a specific company (Ch 8)

market structure The organization of an industry determined by the level of competition within the industry (Ch 1)

market testing Marketing a product on a limited basis to help decide which marketing mix should be used when it is commercialized (Ch 9)

market timing approach An investment strategy where the investor attempts to purchase shares when their price is low and to sell when their price is high (Ch 15)

market value The price of a company's stock multiplied by the number of shares of the stock (Ch 8)

marketing The determination of the needs and desires of markets so that products and services can be developed, priced, promoted, and distributed to these markets in order to satisfy the market's needs and desires and the organization's objectives (Ch 8)

marketing environment Areas outside the firm (competition, technology, economy, legal and political arenas, and culture) that companies need to monitor and react to (Ch 8)

marketing information systems (MIS) Systems that continually monitor, with heavy use of computers, a company's market, competition, customers, products, and marketing operations in order to determine if problems exist; Information systems that provide information to support the major components of the marketing function (Ch 8; Ch 17)

marketing managers Managers in charge of developing firm marketing strategies (Ch 5)

marketing mix The combination of products or services, prices, promotion, and distribution used to market products or services to specific markets over a specific period of time (Ch 8)

marketing research The process whereby marketers are provided with information so that effective marketing decisions can be made (Ch 8)

market-oriented systems Financial systems that have large securities markets (Ch 14)

markup The difference between what a retailer pays for a product and the price at which it is sold (Ch 9)

Maslow's hierarchy of needs The principle that physiological needs are basic and must be satisfied before a person is motivated to satisfy higher levels of needs that have more subtle origins (Ch 7)

master production schedule A schedule where the production rate strategy is broken down into weeks (Ch 16)

match demand strategy A strategy where capacity is increased as demand increases (Ch 16)

Material Requirements Planning (MRP) A computer-based technique for calculating the materials required by a production plan (Ch 16)

materials management The movement of raw materials, in-process materials, and semifinished goods to a manufacturer from a supplier (Ch 10)

matrix organizational structure The structure of an organization around team project situations where employees report to more than one manager (Ch 5)

maturity stage The third stage of the product life cycle in which profits drop and revenues are maximized (Ch 9)

medical insurance An insurance policy that covers most costs associated with doctor, hospital, and pharmacy drug expenses (Ch 14)

megabyte One million bytes (Ch 17)

merchant wholesalers Wholesalers that purchase merchandise and resell it (Ch 10)

mergers and acquisitions The process of identifying, valuing, and taking over a foreign firm to meet a company's growth objectives (Ch 2)

merit pay plans Pay plans that compensate individuals on the basis of their individual contribution to the organization (Ch 6)

microbusiness A small business with fewer than five employees (Ch 4)

microcomputers Computers that satisfy the needs of individual users (Ch 17)

middle managers Managers who implement the decisions, policies, and strategies of the top managers (Ch 5)

midrange computers Computers that are medium-sized and capable of serving the needs of many business organizations (Ch 17)

mission statement Statements spelling out the basic purpose of the enterprise (Ch 5)

mixed economic system The economic system that exhibits elements of both the capitalist and the command economic systems (Ch 1)

mobile commerce or **m-commerce** The use of handheld devices for purchasing goods and services over the Internet (Ch 18)

modem A device that translates digital signals into analog signals and vice versa (Ch 17)

modified rebuy The buying decision for organizations that involves the consideration of different suppliers for an item previously bought on a straight rebuy basis (Ch 8)

monetary policy A policy followed by the central bank (the Fed in the United States) to control the money supply in an economy, and hence to manage inflation, economic growth, employment, and the exchange rate; A central bank framework for using policy tools to affect operating targets, intermediate targets, and economic goals (Ch 2; Ch 14)

money market instruments Short-term securities that have maturities less than one year (Ch 14)

monolithic approach An approach for implementing an ERP system where all the modules of the system are from a single ERP software vendor (Ch 18)

monopoly The industry market structure where there is essentially a single supplier of goods or services that has the power to set prices (Ch 1)

Montana Wrongful Discharge from Employment Act A law in the state of Montana outlawing the doctrine of employment-at-will (Ch 6)

moral hazard risk The risk that managers of insured institutions will take excessive risk and act imprudently (Ch 14)

mortgage A claim on property, given to a person or institution that has loaned money in case the money is not repaid when due (Ch 15)

motivation The drive to achieve a goal in life (Ch 7)

motivation factors Factors such as the job itself, responsibility, and advancement which determine job satisfaction (Ch 7)

motive A specific need or desire that arouses an individual and directs his or her behavior toward achieving a goal (Ch 7)

multicurrency A property of ERP systems to handle multiple currencies (Ch 18)

multilanguage A property of ERP systems to simultaneously operate in multiple languages (Ch 18)

multinational A property of ERP systems to handle the accounting standards of multiple countries (Ch 18)

multinational company An organizational structure where financial management and control are concentrated at a home base, but other business functions such as production, sales, and marketing are decentralized to business units in other countries (Ch 17)

multinational enterprises Firms that have a home base in one country, but own and control plants (factories) or other businesses in one or more foreign countries (Ch 2)

multiplexer A communications processor that enables a single communications channel to carry simultaneous information transmissions from multiple sources (Ch 17)

municipal securities Debt securities issued by state and local governments to raise funds, with coupon payments that are exempt from federal income taxes (Ch 13)

mutual fund A pool of commingled funds contributed by many investors and managed by a professional fund advisor in exchange for a fee (Ch 15)

national brands Products that carry the brand name of the manufacturer (Ch 9)

National Labor Relations Act (NLRA) A federal law of 1935 establishing employee right to unionize (Ch 6)

National Labor Relations Board (NLRB) The federal agency with regulatory authority over U.S. labor laws (Ch 6)

needs analyses Assessments of an organization's job-related needs and the abilities of the current workforce (Ch 6)

negative reinforcement Reprimanding of an employee by a manager to reduce unacceptable behavior (Ch 7)

net cash flow Total cash receipts minus total cash payments at any point in time (Ch 13)

net cash inflow The excess of total cash inflows over total cash outflows (Ch 15)

net exports Exports minus imports of goods and services (Ch 1)

net income The amount of income after subtracting expenses and losses from revenues and gains (Ch 12)

net interest margin A profit measure for financial institutions that equals the difference between interest revenues and interest costs divided by total assets (Ch 14)

net present value (NPV) The net profit on a product or service of a firm calculated as the present value of cash flows minus the cost of the investment (Ch 13)

net working capital Total current assets minus total current liabilities (Ch 13)

net worth The difference between what an individual owns (assets) and what she or he owes (liabilities) (Ch 15)

network firewall A computer that uses security software to screen all network traffic for passwords and other security codes and permits only authorized transmission in and out of the network (Ch 18)

network organizational structures Organizational structures of organizations where the organization contracts out most functions except administration (Ch 5)

networked configuration strategy The strategy where the development and operation of information systems is done in an integrated and coordinated way across all business units (Ch 17)

new economy An economy largely driven by developments in information technology and the Internet (Ch 1)

new tasks Brand-new, first-time purchasing decisions for organizations that require a great deal of information gathering and evaluation (Ch 8)

niche marketing strategy The plan of a company to direct different products and services to different market segments (Ch 8)

nominal GNI, GNP, or GDP Economic output measured in current prices (Ch 1)

nominal interest rate The rate of interest quoted in the financial news comprising the real rate of interest plus the expected inflation rate (Ch 13)

Norris–La Guardia Act New Deal legislation of 1932 limiting employer rights (Ch 6)

North American Industry Classification System (NAICS) The use of two, three, four, and five digits to classify industries and subindustries in the United States, Canada, and Mexico (Ch 8)

not-for-profit organizations Organizations whose primary objective is to provide goods and services to society without the goal of making a profit (Ch 1)

numeraire currency A currency that serves as a benchmark for all other currencies in the world (Ch 14)

objective evaluation methods Performance appraisals based on specific and clear criteria such as sales mode (Ch 6)

objectives Goals or targets that companies and their marketing departments establish and try to achieve (Ch 8)

off-duty conduct statutes State laws protecting in various degrees employee off-duty conduct (Ch 6)

oligopoly The industry market structure where a few producers of almost identical products cater to the needs of the whole market (Ch 1)

online retailing Making products and services available to consumers through computer connections (Ch 10)

open market operations The purchase and sale of government securities from banks by the central bank to control bank reserves and federal funds rates (Ch 14)

operating system The software program that manages and controls the activities of the computer (Ch 17)

operating targets The everyday targets that the central bank seeks to achieve using its policy tools, namely, the federal funds rate and bank reserves (Ch 14)

operational database A database used to support the day-to-day operations in a firm (Ch 17)

operational efficiency Producing financial services at low cost for individuals, businesses, and the government (Ch 14)

operational plans Very short-term (less than one year) plans formulated for achieving organizational strategic goals (Ch 5)

operational-level systems Information systems for operations managers that monitor the elementary activities and transactions of a business organization (Ch 17)

operations management The management of the direct resources that are involved in the production system of a business organization (Ch 16)

operations managers Managers in charge of the production of goods and services (Ch 5)

opportunity cost The alternative rate of return that can be earned by an investor if a security or investment project is not selected (Ch 13)

optimization analysis A modeling activity in a decision-support system that tries to find the optimal, maximum or minimum, value of one or more variables by changing the values of one or more other variables, which are typically subject to constraints (Ch 17)

ordering cost The cost that is incurred every time an order is placed to procure more items (Ch 16)

organization A grouping of two or more people working together to achieve certain ends (Ch 5)

organization chart A diagram depicting an organization's structure (Ch 5)

organizational analysis A strategic scan by an organization of its own strengths and weaknesses (Ch 5)

organizational structure Specified positions within an organization and the ways they interrelate with each other (Ch 5)

organized exchanges Securities exchanges that have a physical location (Ch 14)

organizing Setting up organizational structures to carry out strategic plans (Ch 5)

orientation The process of introducing new employees to the organization (Ch 6)

out-of-control production system The production system where products produced exhibit abnormal variations (Ch 16)

output devices Computer system devices such as video monitors or printers that are used to display the information processed by the computer for users (Ch 17)

outputs A wide array of useful goods or services that are either consumed or used for further production in business (Ch 1)

outside directors Corporate board of directors members not employed full-time by the company (Ch 3)

outsourcing Buying goods and services from outside sources rather than producing them in-house (Ch 16)

over-the-counter (OTC) exchanges Securities exchanges that do not have a physical location, due to the use of telecommunications and computer networks (Ch 14)

owners' equity The residual interest in the assets of the firm after subtracting the liabilities; also called stockholders' equity (Ch 12)

par value The initial value of stocks issued by a firm (Ch 4)

parallel conversion strategy The conversion strategy where an old information system and a new information system are in operation until users agree that the new system is functioning properly (Ch 17)

participative management A management approach where employees participate in the management decision-making process as well as in the operation of the company (Ch 7)

partnership agreement An agreement spelling out the organizational details of a partnership (Ch 3)

partnerships Unincorporated businesses run by two or more individuals (Ch 3)

part-time work Work that is permanent and in which the employee agrees with the firm's management to work for less than the normal 40 hours per week (Ch 7)

patents Awards to companies or individuals by governments to protect their inventions (intellectual property) by providing exclusive rights to the owner to produce the goods (e.g., pharmaceutical products) or services (e.g., software or operating systems) for a set period of time, thereby preventing others from doing so during that time period (Ch 1)

Pension Benefit Guaranty Corporation (PBGC) The federal agency administering the defined benefit plan insurance program (Ch 6)

pension funds Financial institutions that offer various kinds of retirement savings plans to individuals (Ch 14)

perception The awareness of cues or stimuli from the physical surroundings that affect what, why, and how consumers purchase goods and services (Ch 8)

performance appraisals Formal evaluations of the effectiveness of employees' job performance (Ch 6)

performance objective A pricing objective designed to achieve a certain level of profit, revenues, or market share (Ch 9)

personal balance sheet A balance sheet that lists what an individual owns (assets) and what she or he owes (liabilities) (Ch 15)

personal financial planning Planning that enables a person to meet current and future financial needs (Ch 15)

personal financial planning (PFP) software Software that facilitates financial planning with features such as a computerized checkbook, budget forms, and a net worth report (Ch 15)

Personal Financial Specialist (PFS) A specialty designation awarded by the American Institute of CPAs to a CPA after he or she meets designated requirements (Ch 15)

personal selling Using a sales force to sell products and services (Ch 10)

petabyte One thousand terabytes (Ch 17)

phased conversion strategy The conversion strategy where a new information system is introduced in stages, either by function or by organizational units (Ch 17)

phased strategy A strategy for implementing an ERP system where modules are implemented one at a time and, if it is the case, one location at a time (Ch 18)

physical distribution The movement of finished goods from manufacturers to their customers (Ch 10)

piece-rate system A compensation method where employees are paid on the basis of the number of units they produce (Ch 7)

pierce the corporate veil The situation where creditors of a corporation are able to break down the legal wall separating the corporation and its shareholders and reach the assets of its shareholders (Ch 3)

pilot conversion strategy The conversion strategy where a new information system is operated using a subset of users and, once it proves to be fully functional, is installed for all users (Ch 17)

place utility The satisfaction for customers created when products are transported to locations that are convenient for them (Ch 10)

planning Establishing organizational goals and deciding how best to get them achieved (Ch 5)

planning decisions Decisions related to preparing the production system for production (Ch 16)

plunge conversion strategy The conversion strategy where a new information system replaces at once the old information system on an agreed-on day (Ch 17)

policy tools The tools that the central bank uses to implement monetary policy, such as open market operations, the discount rate, and reserve requirements (Ch 14)

political union The union created when member countries of an economic and monetary union work closely with each other to arrive at common defense and foreign policies and behave as a single country (Ch 2)

P-O-P Point-of-purchase materials provided to retailers to help them promote sales (Ch 10)

portfolio of assets All the assets an individual possesses (Ch 15)

positioning Endowing a new or existing product or service with attributes deemed important by a market so that the market perceives the offering as superior to competitive products on these attributes (Ch 8)

positive reinforcement Giving of rewards by managers to try to strengthen employees' good behavior (Ch 7)

preemptive right The right of shareholders to maintain their proportionate ownership of a firm's outstanding stock if new shares are issued by the firm (Ch 13)

preliminary investigation The step in the marketing research process wherein companies try to get some idea as to what is the cause of a problem (Ch 8)

premiums Merchandise offered to consumers as an incentive to buy a product (Ch 10)

present value The value today of money to be received in the future (Ch 13)

prevention objective A pricing objective designed to keep other firms from entering the market (Ch 9)

preventive controls A type of internal control whose purpose it is to prevent mistakes or intentional misrepresentations from occurring in the accounting data (Ch 11)

price elastic demand The demand where a small change in the price will have a significant impact on the quantity demanded of a product or service (Ch 1)

price elastic supply The supply where a small change in the price will bring about significant increases in the quantity of a product or service supplied by the producer (Ch 1)

price inelastic demand The demand where significant increases in the price of a product or service will have little effect on the quantity of the product or service demanded (Ch 1)

price inelastic supply The supply where a large change in the price will have little impact on the quantity of a good or service supplied by the producer (Ch 1)

primary drives Instinctive or unlearned motives like hunger, thirst, and sex that direct behavior that is vital to survival (Ch 7)

primary market The segment of the market for new products whose needs and desires are the most compatible with a new product's features and benefits; The initial sale of a security in the financial marketplace (Ch 9; Ch 14)

primary storage The computer system component that stores the operating system and all or part of a software program that is being executed, as well as the data that are being used by the program (Ch 17)

principal, or par, value The amount paid back by a firm on each bond on its maturity date (Ch 13)

principals Owners—shareholders—of a business (Ch 3)

privacy The condition of individuals of being left alone, free from surveillance or interference from other individuals or organizations, including the state (Ch 18)

private brands Products that carry the brand name of the retailer (Ch 9)

private carriers Trucks owned and operated by shippers (Ch 10)

private pension plans Pension plans offered by private firms to employees (Ch 14)

private warehouses Warehouses owned (purchased or constructed) by a firm (Ch 10)

privatization The process of selling state enterprises to private entrepreneurs (Ch 1)

procedural controls Controls to ensure the accuracy and integrity of computer and network operations and of systems development activities (Ch 17)

process-oriented layout A layout where the different activity centers are organized by function (Ch 16)

product departmentalization Departmentalization based on the products or services sold (Ch 5)

product depth The number of specific products or brands within a product line (Ch 9)

product design The tangible aspects of a product, including materials, length, width, height, and hardness or softness (Ch 9)

product differentiation A strategy that firms employ to make their product seem different from those of their competitors (Ch 1)

product elimination The process whereby poorly performing products are dropped (Ch 9)

product life cycle theory The theory that explains the different stages—introduction, growth, maturity, and decline—that a product goes through before it fades away (Ch 1)

product mix The combination of design, quality, brand name, package, warranty, and product line width and depth a company uses for its product lines (Ch 9)

product width The number of different product lines a company is marketing (Ch 9)

product's quality The physical aspects of a product that affect its level of performance (Ch 9)

production The creation of goods or services; The information systems development stage when the conversion is completed and the new information system is being utilized by end users (Ch 16; Ch 17)

production information systems Information systems that help a company develop, plan, execute, and control the production of goods and services (Ch 17)

production system The system that businesses use to produce products (Ch 16)

productivity The dollar output of goods and services per dollar input of labor (Ch 1)

product-oriented layout A layout where production resources are dedicated to products (Ch 16)

profit The difference between revenue (income or sales) and expenditure (cost of goods or services sold) (Ch 1)

profit margin A company's profit divided by its revenues; The ratio of net income to net sales (Ch 8; Ch 12)

profit sharing plans Pay plans that give employees some share of overall company profits (Ch 6)

programming Translating the system specifications into software programs (Ch 17)

programming language The tool that a programmer uses to develop the sets of instructions that constitute a software program (Ch 17)

project process A process where the product is produced in low volumes with high levels of customization (Ch 16)

promotion mix The configuration of advertising, sales promotion, personal selling, and publicity used to market products and services (Ch 10)

promotional package The package that encloses a product whose purpose is to help sell the product at the retail level (Ch 9)

property insurance Protection purchased from an insurance company against property losses due to fire, water and wind damage, lightning, crime, and so on (Ch 4)

property-casualty insurance Insurance policies to protect property, such as homes, buildings, vehicles, and other capital assets (Ch 14)

prospecting Ranking of possible customers according to their potential sales volume and the likelihood of their purchasing the product (Ch 10)

protection The government practice imposing trade barriers (e.g., tariffs) to shield domestic producers from international competition (Ch 2)

protective package The package that safeguards products as they are being transported (Ch 9)

proxy The transfer of voting rights from the owner of common stock to someone else (Ch 13)

psychographics The analysis and understanding of the consumer's mind to identify consumer likes, dislikes, or preferences and develop commercials that manipulate the recipient's mind to create a need for certain new goods or services (Ch 1)

psychological factors Learning, perception, motives, attitudes, and self-concept that affect what, why, and how consumers purchase goods and services (Ch 8)

public pension plans Pension plans offered by federal, state, and local government that are backed by the taxing power of the government (Ch 14)

public relations Press releases and other efforts directed to the news media that portray a company, its products, or its personnel in a favorable light or combat unfavorable publicity (Ch 10)

public warehouses Warehouses not owned by the company that leases space in them (Ch 10)

publicity News items about a company, its products, or its personnel that appear in the mass media (Ch 10)

publicly held firms Firms in which there are many shareholders who openly trade their shares in the financial marketplace (Ch 13)

purchase with purchase An incentive that allows consumers to buy a product if they first purchase another product (Ch 10)

purchasing The business function responsible for the acquisition of goods and services (Ch 16)

purchasing power parity (PPP) The purchasing power of an international dollar, which will have the same purchasing power in any country as the U.S. dollar has in the United States (Ch 1)

pure competition The industry market structure where there are a large number of suppliers that produce essentially identical products, which are sold at a price determined by the market (Ch 1)

quality The ability of a product to meet or exceed customers' expectations (Ch 16)

quality control A set of activities aimed at ensuring that the production system is producing products that conform to design specifications (Ch 16)

quality of conformance The degree to which the product conforms to the intent of the designers (Ch 16)

quality of design The excellence of the intention of designers to include or exclude features in a product (Ch 16)

quantitative restrictions (QRs) Quotas that limit the amount of imports that can come into a country (Ch 2)

quantity theory The notion that money matters to the real economy as expressed in the equation of exchange (Ch 14)

rack jobbers Regular wholesalers that sell nonfood items to retailers (Ch 10)

rate of return The ratio of profit on an investment to the cost of the investment (Ch 13)

real estate investment trust (REIT) A trust that invests in real estate rather than stocks and securities (Ch 15)

real GNI, GNP, or GDP Economic output measured on an inflation-adjusted basis (Ch 1)

real rate of interest The interest rate charged by lenders on loans to borrowers for forgoing present consumption for future consumption (Ch 13)

recessions Relatively brief slowdowns, or contractions, in economic activity within a business cycle (Ch 4)

record A collection of related fields (Ch 17)

recruiting Attracting qualified job applicants (Ch 6)

reference Someone who can provide information about a job applicant's suitability for a job (Ch 6)

reference groups Groups to which consumers belong or would like to belong to that affect what, why, and how they purchase goods and services (Ch 8)

regular wholesalers Wholesalers that provide a full range of services (Ch 10)

reinforcement theory The theory that is based on the principle that rewarding good behavior will lead to continued good performance, while penalizing unacceptable behavior will lead to reducing unacceptable conduct (Ch 7)

reinforcer Any consequence that strengthens a specific behavior (Ch 7)

reinvestment risk The risk an investor faces when payments on high-earning securities are received and are subsequently used to buy other securities that have lower earnings (Ch 13)

relationship marketing Developing long-lasting, profitable relations with customers (Ch 8)

relative advantage How much better than competitive products a new product is (Ch 9)

reliability The consistency with which a product is produced or a service rendered (Ch 8)

reliability (of an item) The length of time in between failures of an item (Ch 16)

reliability (of service) The ability to perform the service dependably and accurately (Ch 16)

remanufactured products New products in which the components of old products are being reused (Ch 16)

replacement charts Charts outlining possible replacements for key personnel (Ch 6)

required rate of return The opportunity cost that investors demand as a minimum rate of return on their investment (Ch 13)

research study design A comprehensive plan for testing an hypothesis, that includes planning the sample and collecting data (Ch 8)

reserve for losses Funds set aside by financial institutions to absorb anticipated losses without affecting profitability (Ch 14)

reserve requirements The percentage of transactions deposits that must be held by banks in cash form and not loaned out (Ch 14)

responsibility Accountability within an organization for certain matters (Ch 5)

responsiveness (of service) The willingness to provide the service (Ch 16)

restricted stock Corporate stock that has some restrictions on it, for example, regarding when it can be sold (Ch 3)

retained earnings The portion of profits not distributed as dividends but reinvested back into the company to generate additional profits in the future (Ch 1)

return on assets A company's profit divided by the assets used to obtain that profit (Ch 8)

return on owners' equity A company's profit divided by the amount of assets contributed to the company by its owners (Ch 8)

return on your portfolio Cash generated from an individual's investments and the annual increase in the fair market value of the investment instruments, such as stocks and bonds (Ch 15)

revenue The sum of the quantities of all goods or services sold times their price (Ch 1)

right-to-work laws Laws allowing workers represented by unions the right to be employed without paying dues to the union (Ch 6)

ring network A network topology similar to a bus network but where the communications channel forms a closed loop and hence information is passed from one computer to the next one in the ring only in only one direction (Ch 17)

risk The probability that the business will fail; The variability of profits over time, with higher risk implying more variability (Ch 1; Ch 13)

risk premium The added interest rate that must be paid on risky debt and equity securities in addition to the riskless rate of interest, such as the U.S. government debt interest rate (Ch 14)

risk profile The potential loss that entrepreneurs are willing to take in a business (Ch 2)

riskless rate of interest The interest rate charged by lenders in the case that the borrower has no default risk (Ch 13)

risk-return trade-off The basic finance principle that higher returns can only be earned by taking more risk (Ch 13)

robust design Design that allows products to perform well under a wide variety of conditions (Ch 16)

Rule FD The federal fair disclosure rule prohibiting selective disclosure of corporate information to certain parties (Ch 3)

S corporation A hybrid form of corporation that has limited liability but is taxed as a partnership and therefore avoids double taxation of earnings; also known as a Subchapter S corporation (Ch 4)

salary Monies paid to employees for fulfilling job responsibilities (Ch 6)

sales branches Wholesale operations that carry inventories that are established by manufacturers (Ch 10)

sales offices Wholesale operations that do not carry inventories that are established by manufacturers (Ch 10)

sales promotion A nonpersonal form of promotion that does not involve measured media (Ch 10)

samples Free merchandise that is provided to retailers or consumers (Ch 10)

Sarbanes-Oxley Act Federal corporate governance legislation increasing the duties and liabilities of corporate officers and directors (Ch 3)

scheduling Allocating available production resources to tasks, jobs, orders, activities, or customers in a given time period (Ch 16)

scientific management Figuring out and using the best way of getting a job done by dissecting the work into its logical components (Ch 7)

screening The step in the new product development process in which new product ideas are subjected to an initial evaluation (Ch 9)

search engine A tool for locating websites on the Internet (Ch 18)

seasoned issues Stock issues by a firm that are not initial public offerings (Ch 13)

secondary drives Motives that are acquired through learning, such as a work ethic (Ch 7)

secondary market The market for a new product whose needs and desires are not as congruent with the new product's features and benefits as those of the primary market; The trading of outstanding securities in the financial marketplace (Ch 9; Ch 14)

secondary storage The computer system component that stores large quantities of data outside the computer and retains its contents when the computer is turned off (Ch 17)

secured creditors Creditors to whom proceeds of a firm's liquidation due to bankruptcy are paid before other unsecured creditors (Ch 13)

selection Choosing the best individual from the applicant pool (Ch 6)

self-concept The combination of self-image, ideal image, looking-glass self, and real self that determines what, why, and how consumers purchase goods and services (Ch 8)

self-managing teams Employee-formed teams that make wide range of decisions, including traditional management choices (Ch 7)

selling agents Wholesalers that represent a client and sell all the client's specific line or entire output and are given control over the terms of sale and pricing (Ch 10)

seniority Longevity on the job (Ch 6)

sensitivity analysis A modeling activity in a decision-support system where what-if analysis is used repeatedly to establish a range where the variables of interest do not change (Ch 17)

separation of ownership and control The fact that the shareholders of major corporations generally do not have much control with respect to the corporation (Ch 3)

servant leadership The leader creating a work environment that induces participants to function at their best (Ch 7)

servers Midrange or mainframe computers in a client/server network that perform most processing on an application, all computations, and database management (Ch 18)

share of wallet The percentage of a customer's spending on a product or service category that is obtained by a specific company's product or service (Ch 8)

shareholder model of business governance The business governance model operating from the premise that the purpose of the business is to maximize financial returns to shareholders (Ch 3)

shareholder proposal process The process by which shareholders make proposals a number of months before a firm's annual meeting, so that they can be included in the company's annual proxy materials (Ch 3)

shortage The amount of a good or service that will not be available when the price of the good or service is set below the equilibrium price (Demand will exceed supply.) (Ch 1)

short-swing profits Stock trading profits made by corporate insiders within a six-month period (Ch 3)

simulated test markets An alternative to test markets that offers speed, lower cost, and less competitor interference (Ch 9)

six sigma initiatives Organizational initiatives seeking to limit defects to 3.4 per million (Ch 5)

skills inventory A data bank listing skills, experiences, and aspirations of present employees (Ch 6)

skunk works R&D personnel being allowed to use their time to develop new products in which they are interested (Ch 9)

small business A firm with fewer than 500 employees that is typically owned and managed by the same person and serves a niche market (Ch 4)

small-order problem The problem of a shipment that contains only a few pieces or lightweight pieces (Ch 10)

social class structure The social level in a society that affects what, why, and how consumers purchase goods and services (Ch 8)

social security A government program that provides for the economic security and social welfare of the U.S. worker and his or her family (Ch 15)

societal responsibility model of business governance The business governance model operating from the premise that a purpose of business is to benefit society at large (Ch 3)

sociological factors Group-related variables that affect what, why, and how consumers purchase goods and services (Ch 8)

soft currencies Currencies that are issued by emerging market countries whose economies are developing (Ch 14)

software The entire set of programs, procedures, and related documentation associated with a system (Ch 17)

software program A specific set of statements to direct and control computer hardware (Ch 17)

sole proprietorships Individually operated unincorporated businesses (Ch 3)

span of control The number of employees directly reporting to, or being supervised by, a given manager (Ch 5)

specialization of labor Grouping employees to work on assigned tasks on the basis of their specific skills and factory demand (Ch 1)

specialty stores Stores that carry a broad assortment in a single merchandise line (Ch 10)

sponsoring Underwriting the cost of an event (Ch 10)

stable currency A currency with a value that does not fluctuate wildly (Ch 2)

staff authority The right to provide advice, support, and special expertise within an organization (Ch 5)

stakeholder company A business that takes into consideration the interests of all its partners, including its customers, management, employees, suppliers, and society (Ch 1)

stakeholder model of business governance The business governance model operating from the premise that the purpose of businesses is to benefit all groups with a meaningful stake in them (Ch 3)

standard of deferred payment The function of money to be employed in recording the amount of debt payments (Ch 14)

standardization strategy Using the same product mix for international and domestic markets (Ch 9)

star network A network topology where a host computer is connected to several, typically smaller computers and all communications among computers in the network must pass through the host computer (Ch 17)

state enterprises Government-owned firms that produce goods and services, generally in command and mixed economic systems (Ch 1)

stated interest rate The nominal interest rate, also referred to simply as the *interest rate* in the everyday financial news (Ch 13)

statement of cash flows The financial statement that presents cash inflows (receipts) and outflows (payments) under three categories of business activities: operating activities, investing activities, and financing activities (Ch 12)

statement of financial position Another name for the balance sheet (Ch 12)

statement of retained earnings The financial statement that shows the change in retained earnings from the beginning of the period to the end of the period (Ch 12)

Statements of Financial Accounting Standards (SFAS) Statements issued by the Financial Accounting Standards Board that are part of the highest level of generally accepted accounting principles (Ch 11)

stock options A type of compensation that gives managers the right to buy common shares of stock at a predetermined price; The right to buy company stock at a predetermined price (Ch 4; Ch 6)

stock price The market value of a share of stock issued by a firm (Ch 4)

store of value The function of money to retain its value over time (Ch 14)

straight rebuy A routine purchasing situation for organizations that requires little or no time or effort to conclude (Ch 8)

strategic alliances Marriages of convenience between two or more firms that do not involve the creation of a separate entity with joint ownership (nonequity arrangements) and in which the firms stand to gain through cooperation with each other for specific purposes and for a given period of time (Ch 2)

strategic goals Long-term goals related to an organization's mission statement (Ch 5)

strategies More detailed descriptions of how a goal can be achieved; Ways that companies use to achieve their objectives; (Ch 4; Ch 8)

strategy formulation The formulation of the approach to achieving strategic goals (Ch 5)

structured interviews Interviews where all job applicants are asked a specific set of questions (Ch 6)

subcontract An option where products are produced by a third party (Ch 16)

subjective evaluation methods Performance appraisals based on less-well-defined criteria (Ch 6)

subsidiaries New facilities built and operated overseas by MNEs that require large investment of capital given the fact that these new establishments are tailored to the exact needs of the MNEs (Ch 2)

succession planning Planning related to choosing successors for top organization executives (Ch 5)

supercomputers Extremely powerful computers specifically designed for applications requiring complex calculations at a very high speed (Ch 17)

supermarkets Large food stores that sell a wide variety of food and nonfood items (Ch 10)

supplier selection An evaluation of different supply sources in order to select one or more (Ch 16)

supply chain All activities associated with the flow and transformation of finished goods from the raw material stage through to the end user, together with the corresponding flows of monetary funds and information (Ch 18)

supply chain management (SCM) The management of all activities in the supply chain, in order to minimize the total costs of the chain, and to maximize the value to the end user (Ch 18)

supply curve The curve that shows that the relationship between the quantity supplied and the price of a product or service (It is upward sloping.) (Ch 1)

supravoting shares Shares of a corporation's stock that have superior voting rights (Ch 3)

surplus The amount of a good or service that will not be sold when the price of the good or service is set above the equilibrium price (Supply will exceed demand.) (Ch 1)

survival objective A pricing objective related to a firm remaining in business (Ch 9)

sustainable competitive advantage (SCA) A strategy that gives a firm a significant edge over competition and can be maintained over an extended length of time (Ch 8)

sweepstakes Chances for a consumer to win a prize or money, such as through a drawing (Ch 10)

system software The set of software programs that manage and support the operations of a computer system (Ch 17)

system specifications The specifications of the computer hardware, computer software, databases, telecommunications networks, and people resources that will be needed by the information system (Ch 17)

system testing Verifying that individual programs will function together as planned (Ch 17)

systems analysis The identification of what the information system should do (Ch 17)

systems controls Controls to monitor the accuracy and security of the input, processing, storage, and output activities (Ch 17)

systems design The description of how the information system will meet the information needs identified by the systems analysis (Ch 17)

tactical plans Shorter-term (one to three years) plans formulated for achieving organizational strategic goals (Ch 5)

Taft-Hartley Act A federal law of 1947 cutting back on the power of labor unions (Ch 6)

takeover bid An offer made by another company to acquire a company (Ch 3)

tangibles (of service) The appearance of the service facilities, equipment, and personnel (Ch 16)

target group A population segment whose members have more or less similar consumption habits (Ch 1)

tariffs Taxes on imports that raise the price of imports and consequently enable domestic competitors to raise prices as well; Taxes on imports (Ch 1; Ch 2)

tax risk The exposure of earnings from an investment to government taxation, including income and capital gains taxes (Ch 13)

technical skills Specific skills needed to perform a specialized task (Ch 5)

technical testing Subjecting a new product to a physical evaluation that measures its ability to perform up to expectations (Ch 9)

technology The development of new products and processes (Ch 8)

technology transfer The adoption by one company for the development of new products of a technology that originated with another company (Ch 9)

telecommunication The communication of information by electronic means over some distance (Ch 17)

telecommunications networks Collections of computer hardware and software arranged to transmit information from one place to another (Ch 17)

telecommunications software The software that provides a variety of communications support services such as establishing transmission speed and protecting the network from unauthorized users (Ch 17)

telecommuting An employee's working at home for family or physical reasons while being "virtually" at work with the help of current information technology (Ch 7)

telemarketing Using the telephone to promote the sales of products and achieve other marketing objectives (Ch 10)

television home shopping Shopping from television cable channels that do not have regular programming, but instead promote products (Ch 10)

terabyte One trillion bytes (Ch 17)

term insurance An insurance policy that offers a lump sum death benefit to policyholders (Ch 14)

test markets Cities that mirror the entire U.S. market so that companies use them to market their products on a limited basis to develop a marketing mix for the commercialization stage (Ch 9)

testing Making sure that the information system will produce the desired results (Ch 17)

theory or **law of demand** The statement, which appears to hold, that consumers will buy more when prices fall and less when prices increase (Ch 1)

theory or **law of supply** The statement, which appears to hold, that producers will be willing to sell more when prices rise and less when prices fall (Ch 1)

Theory X The theory that is based on the distrustful vision of human nature in general and employees in particular (Ch 7)

Theory Y The theory that is based on the positive view of employees (Ch 7)

three-tier client/server network A client/server network where the user interface resides on personal computers or workstations, the system and application software reside on midrange computers and the database resides on mainframe computers (Ch 18)

thrift institutions Depository institutions that are primarily home lenders (Ch 14)

time horizon The number of years an individual has to achieve her or his financial plan (Ch 15)

time preference for consumption The desire by people to consume goods and services now rather than in the future (Ch 13)

time utility The satisfaction for customers created by products being stored until customers want to purchase them (Ch 10)

time-and-motion studies Studies that measure the time taken to conduct each subactivity of a job in order to determine the best approach to performing the total job efficiently (Ch 7)

top managers The people who run organizations (Ch 5)

total net worth The sum of the market values of all financial and real assets owned, including cash, bonds, stocks, land, buildings, and other property (Ch 13)

total risk The sum of all risks associated with a security, which can be measured as the volatility of the security's price over time (Ch 13)

total satisfaction The postpurchase response in which the customer has no dissatisfaction at all with the product or service accompanying the product (Ch 8)

trade credit A credit system that allows a firm to buy goods and services from another firm and pay within 30 to 90 days from the date of purchase (Ch 13)

trade policy Government policy implemented primarily through changes in tariff rates or quotas with the objective of encouraging exports or discouraging imports (Ch 2)

trade shows Shows where companies have the opportunity to display their products (Ch 10)

transactional leadership The leader providing followers rewards for good performance or reprimanding followers for unacceptable performance (Ch 7)

transfer price The price a U.S. company charges its overseas subsidiary (Ch 9)

transformational leadership The leader gaining the trust of and inspiring followers to work jointly to achieve the leader's vision for the organization and to benefit the members of the organization (Ch 7)

transnational company An organizational structure where the resources are dispersed in various countries, but each business unit in each country is specialized, so as to form an efficient, flexible, and independent network (Ch 17)

treasurer The financial manager responsible for managing cash, raising funds, and maintaining contacts with the financial marketplace (Ch 13)

truck wholesalers Limited-service wholesalers that sell limited lines of perishable or semiperishable products to retailers (Ch 10)

twisted-pair wire Copper wires twisted in pairs (Ch 17)

Type Z firm An ideal U.S. firm that combines the best practices of U.S. and Japanese management systems and would advocate lifetime employment, a more specialized career path, collective decision making with corresponding responsibilities for its outcomes, and gradual pay increases along with great concern for the welfare of all employees (Ch 7)

underwriting The purchase of securities from a firm by an investment bank, which then seeks to sell the securities at a higher price in the financial marketplace (Ch 13)

undifferentiated strategy The plan of a company to make the same product and service available to all segments of a market (Ch 8)

unethical behavior Behavior that is either illegal or morally unacceptable to the larger community (Ch 3)

unfunded pension plan A pension plan that pays retirees from cash flows or taxes instead of from funds set aside over time in a savings plan (Ch 14)

uniform resource locator (URL) The address of a resource on the Internet (Ch 18)

unit investment trust (UIT) A type of closed-end mutual fund that allows investors to lock in relatively high yields (Ch 15)

unit of account The function of money to serve as means for valuing of goods and services (Ch 14)

unit testing Verifying that each individual program is working properly (Ch 17)

value analysis An examination of the function that each purchased part serves, done in order to find lower-cost alternatives (Ch 16)

value stocks Stocks of companies that are considered relatively low risk, have expected but limited growth potential, and generally pay modest dividends (Ch 15)

venture capitalists Investors in small business firms seeking higher-risk and higher-return business opportunities by purchasing equity ownership positions (Ch 4)

venture team A temporary group that a company establishes to come up with new product ideas (Ch 9)

vertical integration A supply chain management strategy where one supply chain member develops the ability to perform the function that another supply chain member has been performing (Ch 18)

vestibule training Employee training provided in a simulated environment close to the actual work situation (Ch 6)

virtual collaboration A supply chain management strategy where companies form a supply chain to provide goods or services on demand (Ch 18)

virtual private network (VPN) A secure network that uses the Internet as its main backbone network, but relies on a network firewall for security (Ch 18)

vision, or mission, statement A statement that illuminates the main goals of an enterprise (Ch 4)

voluntary restraints Self-imposed export quotas on specific sensitive products (autos, steel, etc.), to a specific country or countries for a set period of time (Ch 2)

wage and salary surveys Data collection on prevailing wages and salaries within an industry or geographic area (Ch 6)

wages Monies paid to employees for time worked (Ch 6)

warranty An assurance made by a seller to a buyer about the quality of a product or service offered by the seller (Ch 9)

wealth An abundance of worldly possessions (Ch 15)

webmaster The person in charge of a firm's website (Ch 18)

webpage An electronic page where information is stored and displayed on the World Wide Web, that may contain text, graphics, sound, animations, and video (Ch 18)

website The collection of all the World Wide Web pages maintained by an individual or business organization (Ch 18)

what-if analysis A modeling activity in a decision-support system where the value of one or more variables is changed to observe the effect on one or more other variables of interest (Ch 17)

wheel of retailing The process by which low-cost retailers begin offering services that increase their prices, making them vulnerable to new, low-cost retailers (Ch 10)

whistleblowers Employees who inform the appropriate authorities about an employer's wrongdoing (Ch 3)

whole life insurance An insurance policy that offers both a term policy plus a type of savings account that increases in cash value over time as premiums are paid (Ch 14)

wide area network (WAN) A network that provides connectivity over large distances, sometimes from one continent to another (Ch 17)

work-based programs Programs that tie employee development activities directly to task performance (Ch 6)

working capital Money needed to pay the short-run expenses of producing a product or service, including raw materials, variable production costs, and labor (Ch 4)

work-life programs Employment programs and policies aimed at meeting the needs of employees, especially those with young children (Ch 7)

work-share programs Jobs that are permanent and in which two compatible employees with similar professional background split a job (Ch 7)

World Wide Web (WWW or www) A system with universally accepted standards for displaying, formatting, storing, and retrieving information in a networked environment (Ch 18)

yellow dog contract Employment contract where employee agrees not to join a union (Ch 6)

yield The total return on a bond, including the capital gains and coupon interest paid (Ch 13)

Test Prepper Answers

Chapter 1

True/False Questions: 1. True, 2. False, 3. True, 4. False, 5. False, 6. False, 7. False, 8. False, 9. True, 10. False.

Multiple-Choice Questions: 1. d, 2. d, 3. d, 4. e, 5. c, 6. d, 7. d, 8. d, 9. d, 10. e.

Chapter 2

True/False Questions: Answers: 1. False, 2. True, 3. True, 4. True, 5. True, 6. False, 7. True, 8. False, 9. True, 10. False.

Multiple-Choice Questions: 1. d, 2. d, 3. d, 4. d, 5. c, 6. e, 7. e, 8. b, 9. c, 10. d.

Chapter 3

True/False Questions: 1. False, 2. True, 3. False, 4. False, 5. True, 6. True, 7. False, 8. True, 9. True, 10. False.

Multiple-Choice Questions: 1. d, 2. b, 3. c, 4. e, 5. a, 6. d, 7. b, 8. e, 9. b, 10. e.

Chapter 4

True/False Questions: 1. True, 2. True, 3. False, 4. True, 5. True, 6. False, 7. False, 8. True, 9. True, 10. True.

Multiple-Choice Questions: 1. b, 2. c, 3. e, 4. d, 5. a, 6. e, 7. a, 8. c, 9. e, 10. a.

Chapter 5

True/False Questions: 1. False, 2. False, 3. True, 4. True, 5. True, 6. False, 7. False, 8. True, 9. False, 10. True.

Multiple-Choice Questions: 1. c, 2. d, 3. b, 4. e, 5. b, 6. d, 7. c, 8. b, 9. a, 10. a.

Chapter 6

True/False Questions: 1. False, 2. True, 3. True, 4. False, 5. False, 6. True, 7. True, 8. False, 9. True, 10. False.

Multiple-Choice Questions: 1. c, 2. e, 3. a, 4. b, 5. d, 6. e, 7. b, 8. d, 9. b, 10. a.

Chapter 7

True/False Questions: 1. False, 2. True, 3. False, 4. False, 5. True, 6. True, 7. False, 8. False, 9. True, 10. False.

Multiple-Choice Questions: 1. e, 2. c, 3. b, 4. d, 5. a, 6. a, 7. b, 8. e, 9. d, 10. c.

Chapter 8

True/False Questions: 1. True, 2. True, 3. False, 4. True, 5. True, 6. True, 7. False, 8. True, 9. True, 10. True.

Multiple-Choice Questions: 1. b, 2. a, 3. e, 4. a, 5. b, 6. b, 7. c, 8. d, 9. a, 10. b.

Chapter 9

True/False Questions: 1. True, 2. True, 3. False, 4. False, 5. True, 6. True, 7. True, 8. False, 9. True, 10. True.

Multiple-Choice Questions: 1. b, 2. e, 3. d, 4. b, 5. c, 6. c, 7. a, 8. a, 9. d, 10. a.

Chapter 10

True/False Questions: 1. False, 2. True, 3. False, 4. True, 5. True, 6. True, 7. True, 8. False, 9. False, 10. True.

Multiple-Choice Questions: 1. a, 2. c, 3. d, 4. c, 5. d, 6. e, 7. e, 8. e, 9. e, 10. b.

Chapter 11

True/False Questions: 1. True, 2. True, 3. True, 4. False, 5. False, 6. True, 7. True, 8. False, 9. False, 10. False.

Multiple-Choice Questions: 1. e, 2. c, 3. d, 4. b, 5. e, 6. c, 7. e, 8. a, 9. b, 10. d.

Chapter 12

True/False Questions: 1. True, 2. False, 3. True, 4. False, 5. True, 6. True, 7. False, 8. True, 9. True, 10. True.

Multiple-Choice Questions: 1. b, 2. a, 3. c, 4. d, 5. b, 6. b, 7. a, 8. c, 9. d, 10. d.

Chapter 13

True/False Questions: 1. False, 2. True, 3. True, 4. False, 5. True, 6. True, 7. False, 8. True, 9. False, 10. True.

Multiple-Choice Questions: 1. b, 2. d, 3. c, 4. e, 5. c, 6. d, 7. c, 8. a, 9. c, 10. d.

Chapter 14

True/False Questions: 1. False, 2. True, 3. False, 4. True, 5. True, 6. False, 7. True, 8. True, 9. True, 10. False.

Multiple-Choice Questions: 1. d, 2. c, 3. c, 4. d, 5. d, 6. b, 7. a, 8. e, 9. c, 10. b.

Chapter 15

True/False Questions: 1. True, 2. True, 3. False, 4. False, 5. True, 6. False, 7. True, 8. True, 9. True, 10. True.

Multiple-Choice Questions: 1. c, 2. d, 3. d, 4. b, 5. a, 6. d, 7. c, 8. a, 9. c, 10. d.

Chapter 16

True/False Questions: 1. True, 2. False, 3. False, 4. False, 5. False, 6. False, 7. True, 8. True, 9. True, 10. False.

Multiple-Choice Questions: 1. a, 2. c, 3. c, 4. d, 5. a, 6. b, 7. d, 8. e, 9. d, 10. e.

Chapter 17

True/False Questions: 1. False, 2. True, 3. False, 4. True, 5. False, 6. False, 7. True, 8. False, 9. True, 10. False.

Multiple-Choice Questions: 1. a, 2. e, 3. c, 4. c, 5. b, 6. a, 7. b, 8. e, 9. d, 10. d.

Chapter 18

True/False Questions: 1. True, 2. False, 3. False, 4. True, 5. False, 6. False, 7. True, 8. False, 9. True, 10. True.

Multiple-Choice Questions: 1. c, 2. a, 3. d, 4. d, 5. b, 6. d, 7. b, 8. a, 9. c, 10. d.

Notes

Chapter 1

1. D. Quinn Mills, *Wheel, Deal, and Steal: Deceptive Accounting, Deceitful CEOs, and Ineffective Reform* (Englewood Cliffs, NJ: Prentice-Hall, 2003).
2. P. T. Ellsworth, *The International Economy*, 3rd ed. (New York: Macmillan Co., 1964), pp. 181–214.
3. Peter Drucker, "The Next Society—A Survey of the Future," *The Economist*, November 3, 2001, pp. 1–20.
4. W. Michael Cox, "Schumpeter—In His Own Words," *Economic Insights*, Federal Reserve Bank of Dallas, vol. 6, no. 3, p. 1.
5. Joseph A. Schumpeter, *Business Cycles: A Theoretical, Historical, and Statistical Analysis of the Capitalist Process* (New York: McGraw-Hill, 1939), p. 223.
6. U.S. Census Bureau, 2001 data.
7. Zuliu Hu and Mohsin S. Khan, "Why Is China Growing so Fast," *Economic Issues*, no. 8, International Monetary Fund, 1997.
8. Oleh Havrylyshyn and Donal McGettigan, "Privatization in Transition Countries," *Economic Issues*, no. 18, International Monetary Fund, 1999.
9. U.S. Census Bureau, *Statistical Abstract of the United States* (Washington, DC: U.S. Department of Commerce, 2002).
10. "Untangling E-Economics," *The Economist*, A Survey of the New Economy, September 23, 2000, p. 6.
11. Don Tapscott and David Agnew, "Governance in the Digital Economy," *Finance & Development*, December 1999, pp. 34–37.
12. Thomas F. Siems, "B2B E-Commerce: Why the New Economy Lives," *Southwest Economy*, Federal Reserve Bank of Dallas, July–August 2001, pp. 1–3.
13. "B2B E-Commerce: Why the New Economy Lives," p. 5
14. Peter Drucker, "The Guru's Guide," *Business 2.0*, no. 8, October 2001, p. 68.
15. "Untangling E-Economics," p. 19.
16. "Getting Better All the Time: A Survey of Technology and Development," *The Economist*, November 10, 2001.

Chapter 2

1. Paul A. Samuelson and Willam D. Nordhaus, *Economics*, 12th ed. (New York: McGraw-Hill, 1985), pp. 77–88.
2. Bela Balassa, *The Theory of Economic Integration* (Homewood, IL.: Irwin, 1961), p. 2.
3. John McCormick, *Understanding the European Union: A Concise Introduction* (New York: Palgrave Macmillan, 1999), pp. 13, 230–232.
4. David E. O'Connor, *The Global Economy: A Resource Guide for Teachers* (Storrs, CT: Center for International Business Education and Research (CIBER), University of Connecticut, 2000).
5. Aaron Bernstein, *Sweatshops*: "Finally, Airing the Dirty Linen," *Business Week*, June 23, 2003, pp. 100–101.
6. Daniel Litvin, *Empires of Profit: Commerce, Conquest and Corporate Responsibility* (New York & London: Thomson Texere, 2003).

Chapter 3

1. Daniel Akst, "Look Underground, and Unemployment is Low," *New York Times*, September 7, 2003, sec. 3, p. 4.
2. See, e.g., Anthony Bimico, William Symonds, and Nanette Byunes, "The Rise and Fall of Dennis Koslowski," *Business Week*, December 23, 2002, p. 65.
3. Rosanna Ruiz, "Watkins, 2 Others Share Time Honor," *Houston Chronicle*, December 23, 2002, p. 1.
4. Matthew Swibel, "Corporate Cover," *Forbes Magazine*, December 9, 2002, pp. 164–66.
5. Kathleen Allen, *Entrepreneurship for Dummies*, pp. 209–211 (2001).
6. Nicholas Varchaver, "Who's the King of Delaware?" *Fortune Magazine*, May 13, 2002, pp. 125–126. For information about incorporating and generally doing business in Delaware, visit the website **www.state.de.us/dedo.**
7. Proxy Statement, Surewest Communications, Roseville, California, April 5, 2002, p. 9.
8. Tucker Carlson, "Artful Dodgers," *Reader's Digest*, September 2002, pp. 47–48; Phyllis Plitch, "Stanley Holders Barely Approve Controversial Tax-Haven Plan," *Wall Street Journal*, May 10, 2002, at B2.
9. "GE Announces Corporate Governances Changes," General Electric Corporation Press Release, November 7, 2002.
10. Milton Friedman, *Capitalism and Freedom* (Chicago: University of Chicago Press, 1962), p. 133.
11. John A. Byrne, "The Collapse of Arthur Andersen," *Business Week*, Aug. 12, 2002, pp. 51–56.
12. Ben White, "ImClone's Waksol Gets Maximum Jail Sentence," Washington Post.com, June 11, 2003.
13. David Leonhardt, "Options Payday: Raking It In, Even as Stocks Sag," *New York Times*, Dec. 29, 2002, sec. 3, pp. 1, 10.
14. Ibid.
15. Ibid.
16. Ibid.
17. Arthur Levitt, Jr., "A Call to Action," *Bloomberg Personal Finance*, March 2002, p. 13.
18. Bill Deener, "Cost to Stay Public Soars for Small Companies," *Dallas Morning News*, July 25, 2003, sec. D, p. 1.
19. Matthew Harper and Ari Weinberg, "Schering Aims to Move Past Disclosure Flap," Forbes.com, September 9, 2003.
20. "Blackwell Gives Keynote at Labor Day Celebration," *ILR Connections*, Cornell University, ILR School, Winter 2003.
21. Coca-Cola Corporation website, Corporate Governance section, **www2.coca-cola.com/investors/governance/index.html.**
22. Amy Cortese, "The New Accountability: Tracking the Social Costs," *New York Times*, March 24, 2002, sec. 3 (Business), p. 4.
23. Ibid.
24. Isabelle Maigrian and David A. Ralston, "Corporate Social Responsibility in Europe and the U.S.: Insights from Businesses' Self-Presentations," *Journal of International Business Studies*, vol. 33 (2002), p. 503.
25. "Lattee and Paintbrush To Go," *New York Times*, September 7, 2003, sec. 3, p. 2.
26. Atlantic Stewardship Bank website, **www.asbnow.com/tithing.htm** (accessed June 3, 2004).
27. Gretchen Morgenson, "It's Time for Investors to Start Acting Like Owners," *New York Times*, March 24, 2002, sec. 3 (Business), p. 1.
28. McDonald's Corporation website, **www.mcdonalds.com/corporate/diversity/suppliers/suppliers.html** (accessed June 3, 2004).
29. Nordstrom Corporation website, **http://about.nordstrom.com/aboutus.**
30. "Ethics in Action. Getting It Right," *Selections* (The Magazine of the Graduate Management Admission Council), Fall 2002, p. 25.
31. Nordstrom Corporation website, **http://nordstrom.newjobs.com/employment.html.**
32. "Ethics in Action," supra note 30, p. 26.
33. Ibid. p. 27.

34. DaimlerChrysler Corporations 2002 Environmental Report, **www.daimlerchrysler.de/environ/report2002/editorial_e.htm.**

35. Britta Waller, "Siding with Sarah," *Sky Magazine* (Delta Airlines Magazine), August 2002, p. 61.

36. "Trial and Error," *Economist Magazine*, June 22, 2002, p. 65.

37. Carrick Mollenkamp and Betsy McKay, "Augusta Membership Controversy Ensnares Over Two Dozen Firms," *Wall Street Journal*, December 19, 2002, p. A10.

38. Lee Enterprises, Incorporated, 2002 Annual Report; Lee Enterprises, Incorporated, Code of Business Conduct and Ethics, **www.lee.net/governance/code.**

39. Mike France, "The Mea Culpa Defense," *Business Week,* August 26, 2002, pp. 77–78.

40. Laura M. Franze, "The Whistleblower Provisions of the Sarbanes-Oxley Act of 2002," *Insights: The Corporate and Securitites Law Advisor,* December 2002, p. 12.

41. Melinda Ligos, "Boot Camp on Ethics Ask the 'What Ifs?' " *New York Times,* January 5, 2003, sec. 3 (Business), p. 12.

42. Ibid.

43. Daniel Actman, "Enron Professor of Economics Has a New Ring Now," *New York Times,* February 3, 2002, sec. 3 (Business), p. 7; Liz Wiken, "Indicted, Convicted Keep Edifices at Harvard, Koslowski Hall," December 10, 2002, Bloomberg News Archive, **www.bloomberg.com.**

Chapter 4

1. For further reading on creative destruction, see Joseph A. Schumpeter, *The Theory of Economic Development* (Cambridge, MA: Harvard University Press, 1934). See also Joseph A. Schumpeter, *Capitalism, Socialism, and Democracy* (New York: Harper & Row, 1942).

2. For further information on small business firms, see Zolten J. Acs, ed., *Are Small Firms Important? Their Role and Impact* (Boston: Kluwer, 1999).

3. Visit the U.S. Small Business Administration website at **www.sba.gov.**

4. For further information on small business planning, see the following resources: Justin G. Longenecker, Carlos W. Moore, and J. William Petty, *Small Business Management* (Cincinnati, OH: South-Western, 2003); Norman M. Scarborough and Thomas W. Zimmerer, *Effective Small Business Management*, 7th ed. (Englewood Cliffs, NJ: Prentice-Hall, 2003); and *The Entrepreneur Magazine Small Business Advisor* (New York: Wiley, 1995).

Chapter 5

1. Patrick McGeehan, "Goldman Chief Apologizes for Remarks About Firm," **www.nytimes.com,** February 9, 2003.

2. Ibid.

3. Ibid.

4. Research presentation by Professor Michael A. Hitt, Texas A&M University, College Station, TX, March 3, 2003.

5. Jeffrey E. Garten, "Listen Up, Execs: Playing It Safe Won't Cut It," *Business Week*, March 3, 2003, p. 28.

6. Ibid.

7. Whirlpool Corporation, **www.whirlpoolcorp.com.** Reprinted with permission of Whirlpool Corporation.

8. "Whirlpool Corporation to Acquire Polar S.A., Poland's Leading Home Appliance Manufacturer," company news release, **www.whirlpoolcorp.com,** March 20, 2002.

9. Ben Dolven, "Hubble Bubble, Toil and Trouble," *Far Eastern Economic Review* (Dow Jones), February 23, 2003, pp. 30–32.

10. The Sears handshake, **www.whirlpoolcorp.com/about/history,** July 30, 2004.

11. Ben Dolven, "Hubble Bubble," pp. 30–32.

12. Jack Welch, *Straight From the Gut,* 2001, pp. 407–429.

13. Ibid., p. 426.

14. Julian Birkinshaw, "The Paradox of Corporate Entrepreneurship," *Strategy & Business* (Booz Allen Hamilton) 50 (Spring 2003): 46–57.

15. Art Kleiner, "The Man Who Saw the Future," *Strategy & Business* (Booz Allen Hamilton) 50 (Spring 2003): 26–31.

16. John Tagliabue, "U.S. Brands Abroad Are Feeling Global Tensions," *New York Times*, March 15, 2003, p. B3.

17. Russ Banham, "Solid Continuity Plans," *NYSE Magazine* (New York Stock Exchange), September 1, 2002, pp. 33–36.

18. Randy Starr, Jim Newfrock, and Michael Delurey, "Enterprise Resilience: Managing Risk in the Networked Economy," *Strategy & Business* (Booz Allen Hamilton) 50 (Spring 2003): 70–78.

19. Michael S. Dell and Patricia R. Olsen, "Executive Life: The Boss, More Fun Than School," *New York Times*, March 9, 2003, sec. 3, p. 12.

20. Ibid.

21. Dell Corporation Website, **www.dell.com,** September 25, 2003.

22. Robert K. Cooper and Ayman Sawaf, *Executive EQ*, 1997, p. 87.

23. Richard Neustadt, "Presidential Power and the Modern President," **alphs.fdu.edu/Peabody/neustadt.html,** September 25, 2003.

24. "The Spirit of St. Louis," *The Economist*, March 9, 2002, p. 17.

25. Greg Brve, *Six Sigma For Managers*, 2002; Ronald D. Snee and Roger W. Hoerl, *Leading Six Sigma*, 2003.

26. Diane Brady, "Crashing GE's Glass Ceiling," *Business Week*, July 28, 2003, p. 77.

27. Daniel Goleman, *Emotional Intelligence: Why It Matters More Than IQ*, 1995.

Chapter 6

1. Marcie Alboher Nusbaum, "Lawyers Push to Keep the Office at Bay," *New York Times*, September 7, 2003, sec. 3, p. 13.

2. "The Times They Are A-Changin,**"** Copyright © 1963 by Warner Bros. Inc. Copyright renewed by Special Rider Music. All rights reserved. International copyright secured. Reprinted by permission.

3. For a more extensive discussion of this whole dynamic, see Peter F. Drucker, "Knowledge-Worker Productivity: The Biggest Challenge," *California Management Review* 41 (1999): 79–94.

4. J. Bonasia, "HR Role Becoming More Strategic," *Investor's Business Daily*, September 30, 2002, p. A8.

5. Jeffrey Pfeffer, "Seven Practices of Successful Organizations," *California Management Review* 40 (1998): 100.

6. Ibid., p. 101.

7. Mary Williams Walsh, "The Biggest Company Secret; Workers Challenge Employer Policies on Pay Confidentiality," *New York Times*, July 28, 2000, p. C1.

8. "Enron Fallout: Bush Focuses on Protecting Pensions, Shareholders," **www.newsmax.com/archieves/articles/2002,** Friday, January 11, 2002.

9. Guest Lecture, John Greenwald, "Rank and Fire," June 11, 2001, *Time Magazine* online edition-tabs, **www.time.com.**

10. *Coppage v. Kansas*, 236 U.S. 1 (1915).

11. Horace G. Wood, *Master and Servant*, sec. 134 (1877).

12. 29 U.S.C., sec. 158(a)(2) (2000).

13. 29 U.S.C., sec. 152(5) (2000).

14. 29 U.S.C., sec. 158(d) (2000).

15. 42 U.S.C., sec. 12102(2) (2000).

16. *PGA Tour, Inc. v. Martin*, 532 U.S.–661 (2001).

17. Montana Statutes Annotated, secs. 39-2-901, 39-2-904 (2000).
18. "The Supreme Court's Wise Decision," *Business Week*, July 7, 2003, p. 112.
19. "Statement from Microsoft in Response to the Supreme Court's Ruling in the University of Michigan Affirmative Action Case," June 23, 2003 **http://www.microsoft.com/presspass/press/2003/jun03/06-23DiversityJudgmentStatementPR.asp,** accessed July 27, 2004.
20. Sana Siwolop, "A Legal Tightrope for Employers After Attacks," *New York Times*, October 24, 2001, p. C6.
21. EEOC Files Post-9/11 National Origin Discrimination Suit Against Chromalloy Castings Tampa Corportion, EEOC press release, September 30, 2002.

Chapter 7

1. Joel Stein, "Just Say Om," *Time*, August 4, 2003, p. 48.
2. Abraham H. Maslow, *Motivation and Personality* (New York: Harper & Row, 1954).
3. Douglas McGregor, *The Human Side of Enterprise* (New York: McGraw-Hill, 1960).
4. William Ouchi, *Theory Z* (Reading, MA: Addison-Wesley, 1981).
5. William Dyer, *Team Building* (Reading, MA: Addison-Wesley, 1987).
6. Reprinted from *Managing Cultural Differences*, Philip R. Harris and Robert T. Moran, p. 109. Copyright © 1996, with permission from Elsevier.
7. M. Fenton-O'Creevy, "Employee Involvement and the Middle Manager: Antecedents of Resistance and Support," *Human Resource Management Journal* 11(1) (2001); M. Fenton-O'Creevy, "Employee Involvement and the Middle Manager: Evidence from a Survey of Organizations," *Journal of Organizational Behavior* 19(1) (1998).
8. "Service Industries Go Global: Skilled White-Collar Jobs Are Starting to Migrate to Lower-Cost Centers Overseas," *Financial Times*, August 20, 2003, p. 11.
9 Pete Engardio, Aaron Bernstein, and Manjeet Kriplani, "Is Your Job Next?" *Business Week*, February 3, 2003, pp. 50–60.
10. S. D. Friedman and J. H. Greenhaus, *Work and Family—Allies or Enemies?* (New York: Oxford University Press, 2000).
11. N. Millard, A. Bryson, and J. Forth, *All Change at Work? British Employee Relations, 1980–1998: Portrayed by the Workplace Employee Relations Survey* (London: Routledge, 2000).
12. "World's Most Respected Companies Report," *Financial Times*, January 20, 2004.
13. Warren G. Bennis and Robert J. Thomas, *Geeks and Geezers: How Era, Values, and Defining Moments Shape Leaders* (Cambridge, MA: Harvard Business School Press, 2002).
14. J. M. Burns, *Leadership* (New York: Harper & Row, 1978).
15. Bernard Bass, *Leadership and Performance Beyond Expectations* (New York: Free Press, 1985).
16. Jane M. Howell and Bruce J. Avolio, "The Ethics of Charismatic Leadership," *Academy of Management Executive* 6(2) (1992).
17. R. L. Hughes, R. C. Ginnett, and G. J. Curphy, *Leadership: Enhancing the Lessons of Experience* (Chicago: Irwin, 1996).
18. P. Hersey and K. H. Blanchard, "Life Cycle Theory of Leadership," *Training and Development Journal* 23 (1969): pp. 26–34.
19. V. H. Vroom and P. W. Yetton, *Leadership and Decision Making* (Pittsburg, PA: University of Pittsburg Press, 1973).
20. F. E. Fiedler, *A Theory of Leadership Effectiveness* (New York. McGraw-Hill, 1967).
21. R. J. House and G. Fressler, "The Path-Goal Theory of Leadership: Some Post Hoc and A Priori Tests," in *Contingency Approaches to Leadership*, ed. J. G. Hunt and L. L. Larson (Carbondale: Southern Illinois University Press, 1974).
22. Margaret J. Wheatley, *Leadership and the New Science: Learning About Organization From an Orderly Universe* (San Francisco, CA: Berrett-Koehler, 1994).
23. "The Best (& Worst) Managers of the Year," *Business Week*, January 13, 2003, pp. 58–92.
24. John Kotter, *A Force for Change: How Leadership Differs from Management* (New York: Free Press, 1990).

Chapter 8

1. Mel Mandell, "Web-Based Market Research Works!" *World Trade*, November 2001, pp. 52, 54.
2. Kerry Capell, "Novartis' Marketing Doctor," *Business Week*, March 5, 2001, p. 56.
3. Alex Taylor III, "Can the Germans Rescue Chrysler?" *Fortune*, April 30, 2001, pp. 106–112.
4. Bruce Johnson, "Taking a Global View of Your Value Chain," *World Trade*, September 2001, pp. 46–48.
5. "The Tech Slump Doesn't Scare Michael Dell," *Business Week*, April 16, 2001, p. 48.
6. *Sales and Marketing Management, 2001 Survey of Buying Power*.
7. World Bank, *2002 World Development Indicators*.
8. *2002 World Development Indicators*.
9. "They Snoop to Conquer," *Business Week*, October 28, 1996, pp. 172–176.
10. Rebecca Piirto Heath, "Competition Intelligence," *Marketing Tools*, July–August 1996, pp. 53–59.
11. Ibid.
12. "They Snoop to Conquer."
13. *2002 World Development Indicators*.
14. Michael Arndt, "Prices Just Keep Plunging," *Business Week*, October 21, 2001, pp. 38–39.
15. Dan Carney, "A Different Kind of Trustbuster," *Business Week*, April 16, 2001, pp. 66, 68.
16. Lara L. Sowinski, "Sketchers Puts Its Best Foot Forward," *World Trade*, November 2001, pp. 34, 36.
17. Christine Tierney, "Michelin Rolls," *Business Week*, September 30, 2002, pp. 58–62.
18. Karen Bannan, "Sole Survivor," *Sales and Marketing Management*, July 2001, pp. 36–41.
19. Eric Nee, "Refocusing Compaq," *Fortune*, March 9, 2001, pp. 128–134.
20. Elana Harris, "Standing Tall," *Sales and Marketing Management*, December 2000, pp. 76–84.
21. Amy Barrett, "DuPont's Big Remake May Need a Remix," *Business Week*, October 30, 2000, pp. 84–86.
22. Ibid.
23. Taylor, "Can the Germans Rescue Chrysler?"
24. "The Tech Slump Doesn't Scare Michael Dell."
25. Anthony Bianco, "Unleashed," *Business Week*, April 9, 2001, pp. 58–70.
26. Taylor, "Can the Germans Save Chrysler?"
27. Bannan, "Sole Survivor."
28. Stanley Homes, "Boeing Attempts a U-Turn at High Speed," *Business Week*, April 16, 2001, pp. 126–128.
29. Joann Muller, "Kmart's Last Chance," *Business Week*, March 11, 2002, pp. 68–69, and "Kmart's Bright Idea," *Business Week*, April 9, 2001, pp. 50–52.
30. William Symonds, "A Fresh Face Could Do Wonders for Gillette," *Business Week*, November 6, 2000, p. 52.
31. Stephanie Anderson Forest, "Can an Outsider Fix J.C. Penny?" *Business Week*, February 12, 2001, pp. 56–58.
32. Stephanie Anderson Forest, "Don't Tell Kohl's There Is a Slowdown," *Business Week*, February 12, 2001, p. 62.

33. Brian Grow, "Saks Fights Off the Ravages of Age," *Business Week,* September 9, 2002, pp. 70–72.

34. Christopher Palmeri, "Mattel: Up the Hill Minus Jill," *Business Week,* April 9, 2001, pp. 53–54.

35. Grow, "Saks Fights Off the Ravages of Age."

36. Lara L. Sowinski, "Pernod Ricard Toasts Its U.S. Distribution Partners," *World Trade,* August 2002, pp. 24–25.

37. Ronald. Grover and Top Lowry, "How Sony Could Sharpen Its Picture," *Business Week,* March 11, 2002, p. 80.

38. Arnold Maltz, "Why You Outsource Dictates How," *T&D,* March 1995, pp. 73–80.

39. Taylor, "Can the Germans Save Chrysler?"

40. Charles Wesley Ortan, "A Fine Kettle of Fish," *World Trade,* October 2001, pp. 74–76.

41. H. Parker Smith, "Is Your Product D.U.M.B. Enough to Take Overseas?" *World Trade,* February 2001, pp. 30–32.

42. John Teets, "Divide and Conquer," *Chief Executive,* April 1995, pp. 50–53.

43. Ibid.

44. Katherine Morrall, "The Children's Market Has Plenty of Appeal," *Bank Marketing,* February 1995, pp. 45–51.

45. Roberta Maynard, "Rich Niches," *Nation's Business,* November 1993, pp. 39–47.

46. Chris Roush, "Managed Care, Niche by Niche," *Business Week,* June 13, 1994, p. 72.

47. Ron Chepesiuk, "Finding the Right Niche," *Editor & Publisher,* February 5, 1994, pp. 14–15, 33.

48. Stuart Kahan, "Contracting or Expanding, Firms Narrow Their Focus," *Practical Accountant,* April 1994, pp. 19–21.

49. Francis J. Gouillart and Fredrick D. Sturdivant, "Spend a Day in the Life of Your Customer," *Harvard Business Review,* January–February 1999, pp. 116–125.

50. Fredrick F. Reichheld, "Learning from Customer Defections," *Harvard Business Review,* March–April 1996, pp. 56–69.

51. Rahul Jacob, "Why Some Customers Are More Equal Than Others," *Fortune,* September 19, 1994, pp. 215–224.

52. Erika Rasmusson, "Wanted: Profitable Customers," *Sales and Marketing Management,* May 1999, pp. 28–34.

53. Larry Selden and Geoffrey Colvin, "Will This Customer Sink Your Stock?" *Fortune,* September 30, 2002, pp. 127–132.

54. Ibid.

55. Michelle Colin, "Newelizing Rubbermaid," *Forbes,* May 31, 1999, p. 118.

56. Thomas O. Jones and W. Earl Sasser Jr., "Why Satisfied Customers Defect," *Harvard Business Review,* November–December 1995, pp. 88–89.

57. Patricia Sellers, "Keeping the Burgers You Already Have," *Fortune,* Autumn–Winter 1993, pp. 56–58.

58. Gouillart and Sturdivant, "Spend a Day in the Life of Your Customer."

59. Ibid.

60. Steven E. Prokesch, "Competing on Customer Service: An Interview with British Airways' Sir Colin Marshall," *Harvard Business Review,* November–December 1995, pp. 101–112.

61. B. Joseph Pine II, Don Peppers, and Martha Rogers, "Do You Want To Keep Your Customers Forever?" *Harvard Business Review,* March–April 1995, pp. 103–114.

62. R. Whiteley, *The Customer Driven Company* (Boston: Addison-Wesley, 1991).

63. Alan Silver, "Measuring Your Customer Service," *Industrial Distribution,* May 1976, p. 115.

64. Jacob, "Why Some Customers Are More Equal Than Others."

65. Sellers, "Keeping the Burgers You Already Have."

66. Prokesch, "Competing on Customer Service."

67. Jacob, "Why Some Customers Are More Equal Than Others."

68. Gouillart and Sturdivant, "Spend a Day in the Life of Your Customer."

69. Paula Lyon Andruss, "So You Want to Be a CEO?" *Marketing News,* January 29, 2001, pp. 1, 11.

Chapter 9

1. Alex Taylor III, "Can the Germans Rescue Chrysler?" *Fortune,* April 30, 2001, pp. 106–112.

2. David Welch, "Meet the New Face of Firestone," *Business Week,* April 30, 2001, pp. 64–65.

3. James U. McNeal and Richard T. Hise, "An Examination of Written Warranties on Routinely Purchased Supermarket Items," *Akron Business and Economic Review,* Fall 1986, pp. 20–30.

4. Welch, "Meet the New Face of Firestone."

5. McNeal and Hise, "An Examination of Written Warranties."

6. Jay Greene, "The House That Microsoft Is Building," *Business Week,* July 22, 2002, p. 40.

7. Charles Haddad, "Sunbeam's Sole Ray Of Hope," *Business Week,* February 19, 2001, p. 62.

8. Taylor, "Can the Germans Rescue Chrysler?"

9. Catherine Arnst, "The Birth of a Cancer Drug," *Business Week,* July 9, 2001, pp. 95–102.

10. Andrew Park and Irene M. Kunii, "A Downturn Well Spent," *Business Week,* July 22, pp. 64–65.

11. Taylor, "Can the Germans Rescue Chrysler?"

12. Alex Taylor III, "Honda Goes Its Own Way," *Fortune,* July 22, 2002, pp. 149–152.

13. Richard T. Hise, Larry O'Neal, James U. McNeal, and A. Parasuraman, "The Effect of Product Design Activities on Commercial Success Levels of New Industrial Products," *Journal of Product Innovation Management,* March 1989, pp. 43–50.

14. Taylor, "Honda Goes Its Own Way."

15. *Financial Times,* November 12, 2002.

16. Taylor, "Can the Germans Rescue Chrysler?"

Chapter 10

1. *Marketing News,* July 8, 2002.

2. Ibid.

3. Cliff Edwards, "Everyone Loves A Freebie—Except Dell's Rivals," *Business Week,* July 22, 2002, p. 36.

4. Danielle Harris, "The Shows Will Go On," *Sales and Marketing Management,* May 8, 2000, p. 85.

5. Ibid.

6. *Marketing News,* July 8, 2002.

7. Harris, "The Shows Will Go On."

8. Deborah L. Vencie, "Trade Show Magic," *Marketing News,* November 11, 2002, p. 4.

9. Harris, "The Shows Will Go On."

10. Richard T. Hise and Edward l. Reid, "Improving the Performance of the Industrial Sales Force in the 1990s," *Industrial Marketing Management,* October 1994, pp. 273–279.

11. Philip Kotler and William Mindak, "Marketing and Public Relations," *Public Relations Journal,* October 1978, p. 16.

12. Daniel S. Roher, "A Public Relations Primer for the Marketing Manager," *Public Relations Journal,* September 1973, pp. 15–16.

13. Lambeth Hochwald, "Tuning In the Right Channel," *Sales and Marketing Management,* March 2000, pp. 66–74.

14. Ibid.
15. Bethany McLean, "Beef Jerky Gets a Healthy Makeover," *Fortune,* March 5, 2001, p. 54.
16. Joann Muller and David Welch, "Ford's Gamble on Luxury," *Business Week,* March 5, 2001, pp. 69–70.

Chapter 11

1. Barry Melanchon, AICPA President, Speech to the Yale Club in New York City, September 4, 2002.
2. American Institute of CPAs, "Code of Professional Conduct," American Institute of CPAs website, **http://www.aicpa.org/about/ code/index.htm,** September 26, 2003.
3. James W. Brackner, "History of Moral and Ethical Education," *Strategic Finance,* July 1992, p. 22.
4. Michael S. Josephson, in Chapter 1 of *Ethical Issues in the Practice of Accounting,* ed.: W. S. Albrecht (Cincinnati, OH: South-Western Publishing), 1992, pp. 14–17.
5. T. Roosevelt, Famous Quotations website, **http://quotes.teleman-age.ca/quotes.nsf,** September 26, 2003.
6. Cal Thomas, *The Death of Ethics in America* (Dallas, TX: Word Books, 1988).
7. G. P. Wilson, American Accounting Association President, Fall Address to the Membership, August 2002.
8. American Institute of CPAs, "Code of Professional Conduct. "
9. American Institute of CPAs, *Statement on Auditing Standards No. 48, The Effects of Computer Processing on the Examination of Financial Statements* (New York: AICPA, 1984).

Chapter 12

1. Shirley Hunter, "The Effect of Electronic Disclosure on the Valuation of Emerging Market Firms," Texas A&M University Working Paper, 2004.
2. AICPA, "Information Security Leads AICPA 2003 Top Ten Technologies List," press release, New York, American Institute of CPAs, January 2, 2003.

Chapter 13

1. For further discussion of capital budgeting, see Stewart C. Myers and Richard A. Brealey, *Principles of Corporate Finance,* 7th ed. (New York: McGraw-Hill/Irwin, 2003); and George W. Gallinger and Jerry B. Poe, *Essentials of Finance: An Integrated Approach,* 3rd ed. (Englewood Cliffs, NJ: Prentice-Hall, 2002).
2. For more detailed discussion on investment and portfolio management, see Edwin J. Elton, Martin J. Gruber, Stephen J. Brown, and William N. Goetzmann, *Modern Portfolio Theory and Investment Analysis,* 6th ed. (New York: Wiley, 2003).
3. See Harry Markowitz, *Portfolio Selection: Efficient Diversification of Investments* (New York: Wiley, 1959).

Chapter 14

1. For more information on the components of financial systems, see Jeff Madura, *Financial Markets and Institutions,* 6th ed. (Cincinnati, OH: South-Western College/International Thomson, 2003); and Peter S. Rose, *Money and Capital Markets,* 8th ed. (New York: McGraw-Hill/Irwin, 2003).
2. For further reading about banks and how they are managed, see Benton E. Gup and James W. Kolari, *Banking, Financial Services, and the Management of Risk,* 3rd ed. (New York: Wiley, 2005); and

Timothy W. Koch and S. Scott McDonald, *Bank Management,* 5th ed. (Cincinnati, OH: South-Western College/International Thomson, 2003).

Chapter 15

1. L. M. Smith and D. L. Crumbley, *Keys to Personal Financial Planning,* 3rd ed. (Hauppauge, NY: Barron's Educational Series, 2002).
2. Jewish Virtual Library, **http://www.us-israel.org/jsource/Bible/ Proverb31.html,** March 5, 2004.

Chapter 16

1. Robert H. Hayes and Steven C. Wheelwright, *Restoring Our Competitive Edge: Competing Through Manufacturing* (New York: Wiley, 1984).
2. Mark M. Davis, Nicholas J. Aquilano, and Richard B. Chase, *Fundamentals of Operations Management,* 3rd ed. (New York: McGraw-Hill/Irwin, 1999), pp. 15–16.
3. Hayes and Wheelwright, *Restoring Our Competitive Edge;* Wickham Skinner, *Manufacturing: The Formidable Competitive Weapon* (New York: Wiley, 1985).
4. Richard Schroeder, *Operations Management: Contemporary Concepts and Cases* (New York: McGraw-Hill/Irwin, 2000), p. 48.
5. Robert E. Markland, Shawnee K. Vickery, and Robert A. Davis, *Operations Management: Concepts in Manufacturing and Services,* 2d ed. (Cincinnati, OH: South-Western College Publishing, 1995), p. 185.
6. Robert G. Murdick, Barry Render, and Roberta S. Russel, *Service Operations Management* (Needham Heights, MA: Allyn & Bacon, 1990), p. 92.
7. Markland, Vickery, and Davis, *Operations Management,* pp. 229–230.
8. Leonard L. Berry and A. Parasuraman, *Marketing Services* (New York: Free Press, 1991), pp. 117–123.
9. Jay Heizer and Barry Render, *Operations Management,* 6th ed. (Englewood Cliffs, NJ: Prentice-Hall, 2001), p. 10.
10. Norman Gaither, *Production and Operations Management,* 6th ed. (Orlando, FL: Dryden, 1994), p. 4.
11. Martin K. Starr, *Operations Management: A Systems Approach* (Danvers, MA: Boyd & Fraser, 1996), pp. 31–32.
12. From Jay Heizer and Barry Render, *Operations Management,* 7th Edition, © 2004. Adapted by permission of Pearson Education, Inc., Upper Saddle River, NJ.

Chapter 17

1. "Computing & Design/Build Processes Help Develop the 777," **http://www.boeing.com/commercial/777family/pf/pf_computing .html,** June 25, 2004. All rights reserved. Copyright © Boeing Management Company. Reprinted with permission.
2. James O'Brien, *Introduction to Information Systems: Essentials for the Internetworked Enterprise,* 9th ed. (New York: McGraw-Hill/Irwin, 2000), pp. 64–65.
3. Ibid., pp. 116–119.
4. Ibid., pp. 116–119.
5. Ibid., pp. 116–119.
6. Ibid., pp. 116–119.
7. From Kenneth C. Laudon and Jane P. Laudon, *Essentials of Management Information Systems: Managing the Digital Firm,* 5th Edition, © 2003. Adapted by permission of Pearson Education, Inc., Upper Saddle River, NJ.

Chapter 18

1. "How to Find Your Weak Spots," *Wall Street Journal*, September 29, 2003, p. R3.
2. "Numbers Are What You Make of Them," *Kiplinger's*, May 2003, p. 18.
3. Thomas H. Davenport, "Putting the Enterprise into the Enterprise System," *Harvard Business Review*, July–August 1998, pp. 120–131.
4. Ibid.
5. From "The Return of Enterprise Solutions: The Director's Cut," Thomas H. Davenport, Jeanne G. Harris, and Susan Cantrell, Institute for High Performance Business, Accenture, 2002, www.accenture.com.
6. Joseph A. Brady, Ellen F. Monk, and Bret J. Wagner, *Concepts in Enterprise Resource Planning*, Course Technology, Thompson Learning, Boston, MA, 2001.
7. Adapted from *Enterprise Resource Planning Systems: Systems, Life Cycle, Electronic Commerce, and Risk*, by Daniel E. O'Leary, 2000. Reprinted with the permission of Cambridge University Press.
8. Adapted from *Enterprise Resource Planning Systems: Systems, Life Cycle, Electronic Commerce, and Risk*, by Daniel E. O'Leary, 2000. Reprinted with the permission of Cambridge University Press.
9. David Simchi-Levi, Philip Kaminsky, and Edit Simchi-Levi, *Designing and Managing the Supply Chain: Concepts, Strategies, and Case Studies* (New York: McGraw-Hill/Irwin, 2000).

Photo Credits

Chapter 1

p. 5, AP/Wide World; p. 20, Queen Esther Productions, Inc./Redux Pictures; p. 26, AP/Wide World; p. 35, AP/Wide World.

Chapter 2

p. 54, AP/Wide World; p. 64, AP/Wide World; p. 82, AP/Wide World.

Chapter 3

p. 109, AP/Wide World; p. 110, AP/Wide World.

Chapter 4

p. 131, AP/Wide World; p. 137, © Wyatt McSpadden; p. 143, AP/Wide World.

Chapter 5

p. 164, AP/Wide World; p. 169, XINHUA/ AP/Wide World; p. 185, AP/Wide World.

Chapter 6

p. 197, AP/Wide World; p. 199, AP/Wide World; p. 211, AP/Wide World; p. 215, AP/Wide World.

Chapter 7

p. 243, © Bob Daemmrich/Stock, Boston; p. 251, © Jim Pickerell/Stock Connection/IPN; p. 256, AP/Wide World.

Chapter 8

p. 276, © Najlah Feanny/CORBIS/SABA; p. 285, AP/Wide World; p. 288, Reprinted with permission of Unilever Bestfoods; p. 300, Reprinted with permission of Smith Barney, a subsidiary of Citigroup Global Markets, Inc. Photo by Corbis Images.

Chapter 9

p. 313, AP/Wide World; p. 315, Reprinted with permission of Energizer; p. 316, AP/Wide World; p. 322, AP/Wide World; p. 332, The Hawk Eye/AP/Wide World.

Chapter 10

p. 345, The Town Talk/AP/Wide World; p. 361, AP/Wide World; p. 364, AP/Wide World; p. 366, © Kevin Fleming/CORBIS.

Chapter 11

p. 380, AP/Wide World; p. 390, AP/Wide World; p. 395, © Max Rossi/Reuters/CORBIS; p. 399, *Sarasota Herald-Tribune*/AP/Wide World.

Chapter 12

p. 413, AP/Wide World; p. 418, © Jim Young/Reuters/CORBIS; p. 419, AP/Wide World; p. 422, AP/Wide World.

Chapter 13

p. 447, AP/Wide World; p. 456, AP/Wide World; p. 467, AP/Wide World.

Chapter 14

p. 479, AP/Wide World; p. 483, AP/Wide World; p. 488, © William Whitehurst/CORBIS; p. 508, AP/Wide World.

Chapter 15

p. 522, AP/Wide World; p. 525, Copyright State Farm Mutual Automobile Insurance Company, 2003. Used by Permission; p. 535, Reprinted with permission of the Liberty Mutual Group 2004; p. 537, AP/Wide World; p. 544, © Chris Daniels/CORBIS; p. 548, Kentucky New Era/AP/Wide World.

Chapter 16

p. 562, Ford Motor Co./AP/Wide World; p. 565, AP/Wide World; p. 582, AP/Wide World.

Chapter 17

p. 595, AP/Wide World; p. 596, Reading Eagle/AP/Wide World; p. 601, AP/Wide World; p. 607, AP/Wide World.

Chapter 18

p. 624, *The Tennessean*/AP/Wide World; p. 631, AP/Wide World.

Name Index

Accenture, 623, 635
Acs, Zolten J., N2
Actman, Daniel, N2
Adamson, James B., 294
ADM, 77
Agnew, David, N1
Air France, 18
Akst, Daniel, N1
Albrecht, W. S., N5
Allen, Kathleen, N1
Allianz, 502
Allied Stores, 130
ALPKEM Corporation, 146
AltaVista, 618
Amazon.com, 36, 37, 630
American Accounting Association, 433
American Eagle Outfitters, 26
American Express, 170, 296, 490
American Institute of CPAs (AICPAs), 391,
        393, 426–427, 435, 525, 526, 550, N5
American International Group, 502
American Optical, 327
American Standard, 285
America Online (AOL), 288, 617
Amtrak, 18
Anaheim Angels, 164
Ancient Accountants at Work, 434
Andersen Corporation, 117
M.D. Anderson Cancer Center, 557, 558
Ando, Kunitake, A7
Andruss, Paula Lyon, N4
Anheuser-Busch, 348
Aquilano, Nicholas J., N5
Armour, Stephanie, 218
Armstrong, C. Michael, 96
Arndt, Michael, N3
Arnst, Catherine, N4
Arthur Andersen, 23, 95, 117, 120, 254
Association of Certified Fraud Examiners, 433
Atlantic Stewardship Bank, 113–114
AT&T, 96, 298
AuditNet, 431
Auditor's Sharing Audit Programs (ASAP), 431
Augusta National Golf Club, 117–118
Autobytel.com, 36, 277
Automatic Data Processing Corporation, 196
Aventis, 78
Avolio, Bruce J., N3
A&W All American Food Restaurants, 79
AXA, 502

Baan, 621–623, 634
Bain & Company, 300
Balassa, Bela, N1
Bangle, Christopher, 311
Banham, Russ, N2
Bank of America, 477, 502, 533
Bank of Japan, 54, 483
Bank One, 477
Bannan, Karen, N3
Barbakow, Jeffrey C., 107
Barrett, Amy, N3
Barrett, Colleen, 253

Barrett, Craig R., 323
Barrons, 345
Bartmess, Pat, 150
Bass, Bernard, N3
Baum, Herbert M., 285
Bayerische Hypo-und Vereinsbank, 502
Beard, Shane, 136
Bear Stearns, 23
Becker, Gary S., 134
Begley, Charlene T., 184, 253
Bennis, Warren B., N3
Benz, Karl, A2
Beradino, Joseph, 254
Berkshire Hathawy, 23, 259
Berners-Lee, Tim, 3
Bernstein, Aaron, N1, N3
Berry, Leonard L., N5
Best Buy, 334
Best Western, 145
A Better Life Foundation, 38
Bianco, Anthony, N3
Bimico, Anthony, N1
BioCosmetics Research Labs, 297
Birkinshaw, Julian, N2
Black, Lisa, 218
Blackwell, Ron, 112
Blanchard, K. H., N3
BleetBank, 477
BMW, 80, 259
BNP Paribas, 502
Bob's Valley Market, 150
Boeing, 77, 294, 591–592
Boeri Sports USA, 276
Bonasia, J., N2
Bondarev, Anatoly, 275
Botts, William W., 146–147
Bove, Jose, 29
Bower, Marvin, 254
BP, 80
Brackner, James W., 391–392, N5
Brady, Diane, N2
Brady, Joseph A., N6
Branson, Richard, 258
Bravo, Rose Marie, 255
Brealey, Richard A., N5
Brennan, Robert E., 120
Bridgestone-Firestone, 295, 312
Brin, Sergey, 456
British Airways, 298, 301–302
British Petroleum, 82
Brown, Stephen J., N5
Browne, John, 258
Brve, Greg, N2
Bryson, A., N3
Buffet, Warren, 23–24, 253, 257, 258
Burger King, 78
Burns, J. M., N3
Bush, George W., 178
Byrne, John A., 254, N1
Byunes, Nanette, N1

California Public Employees Retirement
    System (CalPERS), 109

Cambridge University, 318
Campbell Soup, 296
Cantalupo, Jim, 368
Cantrell, Susan, N6
Capell, Kerry, N3
CARE, 40
Cargill, 77
Carlson, Chester, 318
Carlson, Tucker, N1
Carnegie, Andres, 165
Carney, Dan, N3
Caterpillar, 607
Cavanagh, Richard E., 107
Century 21, 533
Chase, Richard B., N5
Chase Manhattan, 477
Chepesiuk, Ron, N4
Chevrolet, 288
Chicago Board of Trade, 479
Chrysler, 294, 311, 312, 317, 323, 327
Cisco Systems, 259, 616, 634
CITGO Petroleum Corporation, 623
Citicorp, 607
Citigroup, 23, 82, 96, 477, 502
Clark, Aiesha, 601
Clinical Development Corporation, 146
Clyde, Robert A., 616
CMS Research Corporation, 146
CNCB, 533
Coca-Cola Company, 28–30, 80, 84–85,
        112–114, 118, 137, 149, 180, 259, 288,
        348, 540, 607
Cohen, Laurie P., 96
Colin, Michelle, N4
Colvin, Geoffrey, N4
Conagra, 77
Conklin, Michelle, 218
Continental Airlines, 130
Cookies by Design, 361
Cooper, Cynthia, 95
Cooper, Robert K., N2
Aldoph Coors Company, 118
Corel Corporation, 532
Cortese, Amy, N1
Cox, W. Michael, N1
CPA Journal, 431
Credit Suisse First Boston, 23, 502
Crumbley, D. L., N5
Curphy, G. J., N3
Cutten, Arthur, 401

Daft, Donald, 28
da Gamma, Vasco, 66
Daimler, Gottlieb, A2
DaimlerChrysler Corporation, 28, 61, 79–82,
        115–117, 259, 296, 311, 348, 416, 464,
        557, 558, 568, 607, 618, 620, 627–629,
        A1 – A3, N2
Davenport, Thomas H., N6
Davis, Mark M., N5
Davis, Robert A., N5
Dawson, Chester, 311
Deener, Bill, N1

Deere & Company, 300
Dell, Michael S., 165, 171, 172, 174, 176, 177, 258, 277, N2
Dell Computer Corporation, 36, 120, 171, 173–174, 176, 177, 259, 277, 294, 348, 623, 628, 635
Deloitte & Touche, 623, 635
Delurey, Michael, N2
Department of Commerce, 134
Department of Defense (DOD), 417, 617
Department of Housing and Development (HUD), 534
Department of Labor, 134, 212, 469, 635
DeRocco, Emily Stover, 154
Deutsche Bank, 502
Dill, Carl, 606
Director's Video, 138
Disney, 259, 565
Doctors Without Borders, 25
Dolven, Ben, N2
Domino's Pizza, 78
Douglas, William O., 3–4
Drucker, Peter F., 4, 244, N1, N2
Dukes, Betty, 215
Duncan, Herschel Mills, 149
Duncan, Mills, 137
Duncan Coffee Company, 137, 149
Du Pont, 259
Dyer, William, N3
Dylan, Bob, 195, 218

Eastern Airlines, 130
East India Company, 384
Eastman Kodak Co., 333, 348
eBay, 20, 36, 294
Ebeling, Thomas, 276
Eckert, Robert A., 295
ECS, 249
Edmondson, Gail, 311
Edmund Scientific, 141
Edwards, Cliff, N4
Edwards, J. D., 621-622, 634
Eisner, Michael, 258
Eli Lilly, 78
Ellsworth, P. T., N1
Elton, Edwin J., N5
Emerson Electric Company, 182
Engardio, Pete, N3
Enron Corporation, 3, 23, 95, 100, 104, 105, 108, 117, 120, 207, 254, 390
Enterprise Rent-A-Car Corporation, 200
Environmental Protection Agency (EPA), 417
Equifax, 491
E*Trade, 533–534
European Central Bank, 54
Experian, 491
Exxon Mobil, 82, 259, 294

Fairfield University, 120
Fall, Albert, 401
Fannie Mae, 534
Fastsigns, 136
Federal Accounting Standards Advisory Board, 429
Federal Deposit Insurance Corporation (FDIC), 484, 505, 512
Federal Trade Commission (FTC), 491, 633
Federated Department Stores, 130
FedEx, 623
Fenton-O'Creevy, M., N3
Feuerstein, Aaron, 116
Fichera, Sal, 197
Fidelity Investments, 299, 534

Fiedler, F. E., N3
Financial Accounting Standards Board (FASB), 388, 418, 427–428
Financial Daily, 345
Financial Executives Institute, 433–434
Financial Times, 40, 253
Financial Times Global 500, 40
Fiorina, Carly, 253, 256, 258
First Chicago Bank, 477
Fisher, George M. C., 333
Flex-Time Lawyers, 195
Food and Drug Administration, 287
Ford, Henry, 165, 562
Ford, William, 258
Ford Motor Company, 22, 80, 312, 562, 565, 627, 635
Forest, Stephanie Anderson, N3
Forster, Julie, 301
Forth, J., N3
France, Mike, N2
Frankfurt Stock Exchange, 479
Franklin, Benjamin, 547
Franze, Laura M., N2
Fraser, Sheila, 418
Frazier, Leon, 401
Fressler, G., N3
Friedman, Milton, 102, N1
Friedman, S. D., N3
Frito Lay, 635
Fuji Film, 333
Fukui, Takeo, 258
Fuller, Doug, 199

Gaither, Norman, N5
Gallagher, Sean, 606
Gallinger, George W., N5
Gantt, Henry, 562, 580
Garlic Company, 50
Garten, Jeffrey E., N2
Gasparino, Charles, 96
Gates, Bill, 96, 165, 253, 257, 258
General Analysis Corporation, 146
General Electric, 77, 80, 82, 101, 103, 107, 114, 121, 168–169, 182, 183, 253, 257, 259, 286–287, 298, 314
General Motors Corporation, 121, 211, 259, 312, 348, 557, 607
Gerstner, Louis V., Jr., 254, 258
Gettelfinger, Ron, 211
Ghosn, Carlos, 258
Gilbert, Peter M., 107
Gilbreth, Frank, 562
Gilbreth, Lillian, 562
Gillette, 294
Gilmartin, Raymond, 108
Ginnett, R. C., N3
GlaxoSmithKline, 172, 249
Global Crossing, 23, 38, 390
Goetzmann, William N., N5
Gold, David, 309
Goldman Sachs, 23, 163
Goleman, Daniel, N2
Goodwill Industries, 4
Goodyear, 295
Google, 456, 618
Gouillart, Francis J., N4
Government Accounting Office (GAO), 417
Government Accounting Standards Board (GASB), 388, 418, 428–429
Green, Jeff, 326
Greenberg, Jack M., 301
Greene, Jay, N4
Greenhaus, J. H., N3

Greenspan, Alan, 258
Greenwald, John, N2
Greyhound, 130
Gross, William H., 114
Grove, Andrew S., 165
Grover, Ronald, 315, N4
Grow, Brian, N4
Gruber, Martin J., N5
Grubman, Jack, 95, 96
Guenak, Murat, 311
Gup, Benton E., N5

Haddad, Charles, N4
Haier, 167
Hallmark Cards, 347
Harper, Matthew, N1
Harris, Danielle, N4
Harris, Elana, N3
Harris, Jeanne G., N6
Harris, Philip R., N3
Hassan, Fred, 253
Hauser, Marc, 276
Havrylyshyn, Oleh, N1
Hayes, Robert H., N5
HealthSouth, 23
Heath, Rebecca Piirto, N3
Heizer, Jay, 572, 630, N5
Hersey, P., N3
Hershey Chocolate, 316
Herzberg, Frederick, 237–238
Hewlett-Packard, 348
Hire.com, 171
Hise, Richard T., 352, 353, N4
Hitt, Michael A., N2
Hochwald, Lambeth, N4
Hoerl, Roger W., N2
Holiday Inn, 145
Home Depot, 30, 129
Homes, Stanley, 278, N3
The Home Shopping Network, 362
Honda Motor Company, 240, 259, 311–312, 323
Hong Kong Stock Exchange, 479
Hopson, Howard, 401
House, R. J., N3
Howell, Jane M., N3
HSBC, 502
Hu, Zuliu, N1
Hughes, Howard, 254
Hughes, R. L., N3
Hunt, J. G., N3
Hunter, Shirley, 408, N5
Hunt Foods, 327
Hyundai Motor Company, 28, 61, 79–81

IBM, 80, 82, 118, 259, 635
Ibuka, Masaru, 187
Idei, Nobuyuki, 258, A7
ImClone, 23, 287
Immelt, Jeffrey, 168–169, 258
Infosys, 37, 246
ING Group, 502
Institute of Internal Auditors (IIA), 391, 393, 433, 435
Institute of Management Accountants, 393, 433
Intel Corporation, 77, 129–130, 165, 298, 607
Internal Revenue Service (IRS), 381
International Accounting Standards Board (IASB), 385–386, 430
International Association of Financial Planners (IAFP), 526

International Auditing and Assurance Standards Board (IAASB), 388
International Federation of Accountants (IFAC), 388, 430–431
International Monetary Fund (IMF), 7, 8, 55, 66, 486
International Organization of Securities Commissions (IOSCO), 388
Intuit Corporation, 534
Iomega Corporation, 349
I-2 Technologies, 20

J. Crew, 362
Jacob, Rahul, N4
Jefferson, Thomas, 561
Jiffy Lube International, 145
Jobs, Steve, 258
John Deere, 298
Johnson, Bruce, N3
Johnson, Lyndon B., 220
Johnson & Johnson, 82, 115, 259, 285, 635
SC Johnson Company, 116–117
Jones, Thomas O., N4
Josephson, Michael S., 392, N5
Jung, Andrea, 253

Kahan, Stuart, N4
Kaminsky, Philip, N6
Kampouris, Emmanuel, 285
Kaplan's Audit Resource List (KARL), 431
Kauffaman, Michael, 302
Kervin, Kathleen, 311
Key Corp, 297
KFC, 78, 79
Khan, Mohsin S., N1
Kia, 80
Kissinger, Henry, 178
Kleiner, Art, N2
Kmart, 294, 358
Koch, Timothy W., N5
Kohl's, 294
Kolari, James W., N5
Koslowski, Dennis, 95, 120
Kotler, Philip, N4
Kotter, John, N3
Kraft Foods, 179
Krawcheck, Sallie, 253
Kreiger, Ivar, 401
Kriplani, Manjeet, N3
Kroc, Ray, A5
Kropf, Susan, 253
Kunii, Irene M., 315, N4
Kutaragi, Ken, 262

La Bella Madonna, 141
Laboratory Automation, 146
Laird, Melvin R., 178
Land, Edwin, 318
Lands' End Corporation, 174, 362
Lang, Leslie, 199
Larson, L. L., N3
LaRussa, Tony, 164
Laudon, Jane P., 633, N5
Laudon, Kenneth C., 633, N5
Lay, Kenneth, 108, 207, 254
Lee Enterprises, Incorporated, 119, N2
Lehman Brothers Holdings, 23, 502
Leonhardt, David, N1
Levin, Jerry W., 315
Levitt, Arthur, Jr., 108, N1

Lewis, Demetris, 143
LG Electronics, 166, 167
Ligos, Melinda, N2
Lillian Vernon, 141
Lionel, 326
Lipton, 296
Litvin, Daniel, N1
Livermore, Jessie, 401
London International Financial Futures Exchange, 479
Longenecker, Justin G., N2
Long John Silver's, 79
L'Oreal, 259
Lowe's, 129
Lowry, Tom, 315, N4
Lucent Technologies, 23
Lufthansa Airlines, 80
Luna, Harry, 138

R. H. Macy, 130
Maddox, Richard N., 326
Madura, Jeff, N5
Maigrian, Isabelle, N1
Mail Boxes Etc., 145
Malden Mills, 116
Maltz, Arnold, N4
Mandell, Mel, N3
Markland, Robert E., N5
Markowitz, Harry, 467, N5
Marriott, 285
Marshall, Colin, 300, 301
Mary Kay Cosmetics, 289–290
Maslow, Abraham H., 236–237, N3
MasterCard, 490
Maxwell Communication, 130
Maynard, Roberta, N4
Mayo, Elton, 235, 563
Maytag Corporation, 166
Mazda, 80, 329
McClean, William J., 323
McCormick, John, N1
McDonald, Dick, A4
McDonald, Mac, A4
McDonald, S. Scott, N5
McDonald's Corporation, 21, 28, 29, 61, 78–79, 145, 146, 219, 301, 331, 368, 392, 420, 445, 464, 480, 558, 572, 606, 607, A3–A5
McGeehan, Patrick, 96, N2
McGettigan, Donal, N1
McGregor, Douglas, 238, 239, N3
McKay, Betsy, N2
McKinsey & Company, 254, 277
McLean, Bethany, N5
McNeal, James U., N4
Melanchon, Barry, 391, N5
Mercedes Benz, 27, 78
Merck, 78, 108
Merrill Lynch, 23, 96, 249, 502
Mexican Stock Exchange, 479
Meyer, Anice, 368
MGM, 315
Michelin, 295
Microsoft Corporation, 80, 82, 96, 129–130, 220, 246, 253, 259, 314–315, 532, 623
Microsoft Network (MSN), 617
Millard, N., N3
Mills, D. Quinn, 3, 23, N1
Minarcek, Andrea, 218
Mindak, William, N4
Ming, Yao, 419
Mitsubishi Motors, 79, 311
Mizuho Holdings, 502

Mollenkamp, Carrick, N2
Monk, Ellen F., N6
Montgomery, Donna Mae, 141
Moody's, 455
Moore, Carlos W., N2
Moran, Robert T., N3
J. P. Morgan Chase, 23, 502, 505
Morgan Stanley, 23, 242
Morgan Stanley Dean Witter Discover, 502
Morgenson, Gretchen, 96, N1
Morita, Akio, A7
Morningstar, 534
Morrall, Katherine, N4
Motorola Corporation, 182, 635
Mrs. Field's Cookies, 607
Muller, Joann, N3, N5
Murdick, Robert G., N5
Murdoch, Rupert, 258
Murris, Timothy J., 287–288
Myers, Stewart C., N5

Nabisco, 314
Nardelli, Bob, 169
Narivaha, Jay, 301
Nasdaq, 479
National Association of Realtors, 544
National Public Radio, 21
NationsBank, 477
Natural Nectar, 297
Nee, Eric, N3
Nelson, Emily, 96
Nestlé, 259, 607, 635
Netstock Direct Corporation, 171
Neustadt, Richard, N2
Newfrock, Jim, N2
New Jersey Manufacturing Insurance Company, 601
New York Stock Exchange, 101, 479
New York Times, 542
Nike, 348
99 Cents Only Stores, 309
Nippon Life Insurance, 502
Nixon, Richard M., 178
Nofal, Zack, 624
Nokia Telecommunications, 635
Nomura Securities, 502
Nordhaus, William D., N1
Nordstrom Corporation, 114, 115
Norwest, 477
Novi, 136
Nusbaum, Marcie Alboher, N2

O'Brien, James, 608, N5
Occupational Information Network (O*NET), 154
Oceanography International Corporation (OIC), 146
O'Connor, David E., N1
Office of Management and Budget, 430
Ohga, Norio, A7
O.I. Corporation, 146
Oklahoma University Medical Center Children's Hospital, 522
O'Leary, Daniel E., N6
Olsen, Patricia R., N2
Olympia & York, 130
Omidyar, Pierre, 20
O'Neal, Larry, N4
O'Neill, Stan, 253
Opinion Research Corporation, 300
Oracle, 20, 621–623, 634
Ortan, Charles Wesley, N4
Otis Elevators, 607

Ouchi, William, 239–240, N3
Owen-Jones, Lindsay, 258
Oxford Glycosciences, 324

Pacific Investment Management Company (PIMCO), 114
Pacific Telephone, 394
Page, Larry, 456
Palmeri, Christopher, N4
Pan Am, 130
Parasuraman, A., N4, N5
Park, Andrew, N4
Parsons, Dick, 253
Paulson, Henry M., 163
Penn Central Railroad, 394
J.C. Penney, 294, 362
PeopleSoft, 621–623, 634
Peppers, Don, N4
Pepsico, 296, 348
Pernod Ricard, 295
Petty, J. William, N2
Pfeffer, Jeffrey, N2
Pfizer, 82, 169–170, 172, 180, 354
Philip Morris, 348
Pine, B. Joseph, II, N4
Pitofsky, Robert, 288
Pizza Hut, 78, 79
Poe, Jerry B., N5
Popeye's, 78
Porsches, 62–63
Powell, Colin L., 178
PricewaterhouseCoopers, 3, 253
Procter & Gamble, 259, 327, 626
Prokesch, Steven E., N4
Provera, Marco Tronchetti, 258
Public Broadcasting System, 21
Public Company Accounting Oversight Board, 390–391, 430
Publishers Clearing House, 348

Quaker State, 285
Quantrell Enterprise, 143
Quicken, 534
Quotations on Ethics, 434
QVC, 362

RadioShack, 145
Ralston, David A., N1
Rank Hovis McDougall, 314
Rasmusson, Erika, N4
Reader's Digest, 348
Red Cross, 40
Reed, John, 96
Reflections on Vintage Clothing, 137–138
Reichheld, Fredrick F., 300, N4
Reid, Edward I., N4
Render, Barry, 572, 630, N5
Rice, Condoleeza, 178
Richard, Bernice, 137–138
Richard, Patrick, 295
Rigas, John, 253
Rite Aid, 23
Ritz Carlton Hotel, 178, 298, 302
Rodgers, William P., 178
Rodriguez, Margaret, 128
Rogers, Martha, N4
Roher, Daniel S., N4
Roosevelt, Theodore, 393, N5
Rose, Peter S., N5
Roush, Chris, N4
Royal Bank of Canada, 299
Royal Dutch/Shell Group, 82, 112–113, 259

Ruiz, Rosanna, N1
Rumsfeld, Donald H., 178
Russel, Roberta S., N5

Saks Fifth Avenue, 294, 295
Salomon Smith Barney, 95
Salvation Army, 4, 5
Samsonite Corporation, 364
Samuelson, Paul A., N1
SAP, 20, 246, 621, 623, 634
Sasser, W. Earl, Jr., N4
Sawaf, Ayman, N2
Scarborough, Norman M., N2
Schering-Plough Corporation, 111
Schiffman, John T., 297
Schlumberger, 300
Schrempp, Juergen E., 81, 258, 277, 296
Schroeder, Jim, 277
Schroeder, Richard, N5
Schumpeter, Joseph A., 129, N1, N2
Schwab, Charles, 401, 460
Sears, Roebuck & Company, 166, 174, 311
Securities and Exchange Commission (SEC), 111, 121, 381, 388, 429, 460, 461, 512
Selden, Larry, N4
Sellers, Patricia, N4
Service Corps of Retired Executives (SCORE), 136
Shakespeare, William, 423, 425
Shell, 80
Siemens Corporation, 166, 167, 259
Siems, Thomas F., N1
Silver, Alan, N4
Simchi-Levi, David, N6
Simchi-Levi, Edith, N6
Siwolop, Sana, N3
Skilling, Jeffrey, 207, 390
Small Business Development Centers (SBDCs), 136
Smith, Adam, 561
Smith, Batchelder, & Rugg, 297
Smith, Debra, 341
Smith, Geoffrey, 333
Smith, Geri, 278
Smith, H. Parker, N4
Smith, Jack, 258
Smith, K. T., 401
Smith, L. M., 401, N5
Smith, Orin, 278
SNCF, 18
Snee, Ronald D., N2
Sony Corporation, 61, 80, 185–187, 259, 262, 283, 295, 315, 464, 505, 607, 619, A6 – A8
Southwest Airlines, 196, 259, 286
Southwestern Bell Yellow Pages, 302
Sowinski, Lara L., N3, N4
Spiegel, 362
Spitzer, Eliot, 3, 23
Spokane Farmers Market, 131
Standard & Poor's, 455
Stanley Works Corporation, 100
Starbucks Corporation, 113, 278
Starr, Martin K., N5
Starr, Randy, N2
Star Wars: Accounting Implications, 434
State Farm, 298, 525
Stein, Joel, N3
Stern, David, 419
Stewart, Martha, 95, 287
STMicroelectronics, 323
Stoff, Michael, 136
Strout, Erin, 354

Sturdivant, Fredrick D., N4
Subway, 78
Sumitomo Mitsui Banking Corporation, 502, 505
Sunbeam Corporation, 104, 315
Sun Microsystems, 120, 296
Swibel, Matthew, N1
Symonds, William, N1, N3
Sytel, 131

Taco Bell, 79, 298
Tagliabue, John, N2
Tapscott, Don, N1
Target Stores, 113, 334
Tata Consulting Services, 37, 78
Tate & Lyle, 113
Taylor, Alex, III, N3, N4
Taylor, Frederick W., 231, 235, 562
Technical Assistance Research Programs, 301
Teets, John, N4
Tenet Healthcare Corporation, 107
Tennessee Valley Authority, 18
Texaco, 130
Texas A&M University, 30, 609, 617, 634
Texas Instruments, 182, 285, 607
Texas Society of Certified Public Accountants, 433
Thomas, Cal, 393, N5
Thomas, Robert J., N3
Thompson, Carletta, 131
Thornton, Emily, 334
3M, 259, 323
Tierney, Christine, 295, N3
Time Warner, 288
Tokyo Stock Exchange, 479
Toyota Motor Corporation, 179, 253, 259, 311–312, 557, 578
Toys R' Us, 296
TransUnion, 491
Travelers Group, 477
Truman, Harry S., 212
Tuck, Larry, 629
Tyco Corporation, 95, 120

UBS Warburg, 23, 502
UNICEF, 25
United Auto Workers (UAW) Union, 211
United Nations, 40
United Way, 40
Unsull, Samuel, 401
UPS, 623
U.S. Army, 173
U.S. Census Bureau, 26–27, N1
U.S. Small Business Administration, 132–134, 136, 146, 150, 153, 154
US Bancorp Piper Jaffray, 23

Varchaver, Nicholas, N1
Vencie, Deborah L., N4
Vickery, Shawnee K., N5
Vieria, Marcelo, 582
Vinchel, 275
Virgin Mobile, 630
Visa, 490
Visioneer, 628
Volkswagen, 314
Volvo, 80
Vroom, V. H., N3

Wade, Mark, 113
Wagner, Bret J., N6

Wagoner, Rick, 211
Waller, Britta, N2
Wall Street Journal, 345, 541–542
Wal-Mart Corporation, 30, 82, 109, 204, 215, 259, 332, 360, 362–363, 542
Walsh, Mary Williams, N2
Walton, Sam, 165, 258
Warren, Peg, 197
Waters, Jennifer, 392
Watkins, Sherron, 95
Weill, Sanford I., 96, 259–260
Weinberg, Ari, N1
Welch, David, N4, N5
Welch, Jack, 168, 169, 236, 253, 257, 258, N2
Wells Fargo, 477, 534
Wellspring Associates LLC, 326
Western Electric Company, 235, 563
Western Union Corporation, 187
Weyerhaeuser Sawmill, 300

Wheatley, Margaret J., N3
Wheelwright, Steven C., N5
Whirlpool Corporation, 165–167
White, Ben, N1
Whiteley, R., N4
Whitman, Meg, 20, 253
Whitney, Eli, 561
Whitney, Richard, 401
Whittle, Frank, 318
Wiedeking, Wendelin, 258
Wiken, Liz, N2
Wilson, G. Peter, 393, N5
Wipro, 37
Wood, Horace G., N2
Woods, Tiger, 348
Wootan, Margo, 392
World Bank, 7–8, 66, 69–70, 486, 487, N3
WorldCom Corporation, 23, 38, 95, 104, 107, 390

World Trade Organization (WTO), 8, 55, 67
World Vision, 25
William Wrigley Corporation, 100, 103
Wyatt, Arthur, 386

Xerox Corporation, 299

Yahoo!, 3, 618
Yahoo! Finance, 534
Yetton, P. W., N3
Young, Neil, 326
Yuhara, Takao, 185
Yum! Brands, 79
Yun, Jong Yong, 258

Zeevo, 171
Zimmerer, Thomas W., N2

Subject Index

Abnormal variation, 582–583
Acceptance testing, 605
Accounting. *See also* Financial statements
  careers in, 35, 400–401
  ethics in, 390–393
  explanation of, 379
  foreign currency translation and, 422–423
  impact of technology on, 423–427
  internal controls and, 395–400
  international standards for, 386–388
  websites for information on, 427–434
Accounting information system (AIS)
  computerized, 396–397, 420–421
  design of, 416
  explanation of, 379, 396, 603
  financial accounting and, 380–382
  generally accepted accounting principles and, 381–383
  information role of, 383–384
  international trade and, 385
  management accounting and, 380
Acquisitions
  elements of, 103–104
  explanation of, 150
  international, 84–85
Adaptation strategy, 314
Advertising
  careers in, 368–369
  cooperative, 344
  explanation of, 341, 343
  types of media for, 343–344
Affirmative action
  explanation of, 219–220
  University of Michigan cases and, 220
Affirmative Action Act of 1986, 137
Age Discrimination Act of 1967, 215–216
Agency costs, 444
Agents, 103
AICPA Audit and Attest Standards, 429
Allocation efficiency, 482
Allowances, 346
Alternative-work policies, 252–253
Americans with Disabilities Act of 1990, 216–217
Analog signal, 598
Angels, 141, 150, 457
Annuities, 506–507
Antitrust policies, 7
Applicant pool, 199
Application integration, 426
Application software, 595
Application-specific software, 596
Applied research, 322
Appreciating assets, 520
Arithmetic-logic unit, 593
Assembler languages, 596
Assembly design, 564
Assembly lines, 562–563
Asset allocation, 539
Asset management accounts, 459
Assets
  appreciating, 520
  depreciating, 520
  explanation of, 413

managing maturity of, 458
  personal, 520, 521
  portfolio of, 520
Association of South East Asian Nations (ASEAN), 73–74
Assurance, of service, 582
Asymmetry of corporate information, 106
Attitudes, consumer, 280
Audio-visual aids, 351
Auditing
  evidence obtained by, 418–419
  external, 417
  of financial statements, 416–421
  impact of computerization on, 419–420
  internal, 417
  internal controls and, 396–397
  international standards for, 388–389
  steps for, 417–418
  websites related to, 429–434
Audit trail, 420–421
Authority, 176, 179
Autocratic leadership style, 259–260
Automatic vending, 362
Automobile industry, 63, 536
Automobile insurance, 536

Back ordering, 573
Balance sheets, 412–414, 520
Bandwidth, 35
Bank-centered systems, 482
Bank reconciliation, 531
Bank reserves, 492, 496
Bankruptcy, 153, 454
Banks. *See also* Depository institutions; Financial institutions; Financial systems
  central, 54–55, 478, 492–496, 500
  commercial, 496, 503–505
  deregulation of, 478, 485, 503–504
  mergers of, 477
  mutual savings, 504
Bank statement, 531, 532
Bargaining units, 209–210
Barriers to competition, 15
Basic research, 322
Batch process, 566–567
Behavior theory, 235–236
Benefits. *See* Employee benefits
Bermuda, 100, 102
Best-of-breed approach, 623
Big-bang strategy, 624–625
Billboards, 345
Bill of material, 574
Biotechnology, 9
Bit, 593
Board of directors, 101, 107–108
Bonded warehouses, 365–366
Bonds
  corporate, 541
  explanation of, 453
  issued by state and local governments, 465
  junk, 455
  municipal, 541

rate of return on, 463
  retirement and investment in, 508
  U.S. savings, 541
Brainstorming, 319
Brand equity, 309, 314
Brand management careers, 335
Brand names, 312
Brands, 312
Bretton Woods agreement, 488
Broadcast media, 344
Brokerage firms, 459
Brokers
  dealers vs., 459–460
  explanation of, 359, 459
Budgeting
  capital, 445, 449–452
  envelope, 530
  personal, 527–530
Bullwhip effect, 626
Business
  demand for goods and services and, 25–30
  digital era in, 35–38
  establishment of export-import, 77–78
  evolution of U.S., 5–8
  explanation of, 4–5
  family, 149–150
  for-profit, 4
  gross domestic product and, 31–32
  gross national income and, 30–31
  gross national product and, 30
  impact of economic systems on, 10–19
  not-for-profit, 4
  production of goods and services and, 19–20
  purchasing power parity and, 33, 34
  role of knowledge workers on, 8–9
  technological change and, 38–39
Business analysts, 609–610
Business careers. *See* Careers
Business codes of ethics, 119, 391, 393–394
Business cycles, 34, 152
Business environment. *See also* Globalization
  evaluation of, 51
  fiscal policy and, 53–54
  foreign exchange market and exchange rate and, 64–66
  global nature of, 56–61
  goals of economic management and, 52–53
  incomes policy and, 55
  international operations and, 76–85
  international trade and investment barriers and, 61–64
  monetary policy and, 54–55
  regional trading blocks and, 67–76
  trade and exchange rate policies and, 55–56
  trends in, 50–51
  World Trade Organization and, 66–67
Business ethics. *See also* Ethics, 23
  accounting and, 390–393
  breaches of, 119
  codes of, 119, 391, 393–394
  computer monitoring and, 608

corporate profits and, 23
entrepreneurship and, 148–149
explanation of, 117–118
fee charges and, 334
identity theft and, 491–492
investment services and, 460
pressures leading to questionable, 95–96
sales and, 354
training in, 120
universities and, 120
Business governance
  shareholder model of, 102–112
  societal responsibility model of, 116–117
  stakeholder model of, 112–116
Business information management, 426
Business judgment rule, 101
Business performance
  not-for-profit organizations and, 24–25
  profit and shareholder wealth and, 21–22
  stakeholder wealth and, 22–24
  unemployment and income inequalities
    and, 24
Business plans
  business ideas on, 140–141
  essential components of, 139–140
Business processes, 616
Business risk, 151–153
Business structures
  characteristics of, 97
  corporations as, 98–102
  partnerships as, 97–98
  sole proprietorships as, 97
Business-to-business (B2B) e-business, 37,
  38, 630
Business-to-business market, 281–282
Business-to-consumer (B2C) e-business, 37,
  38, 629–630
Bus network, 599
Bypassing, 628
Byte, 593

Cafeteria benefit plans, 205
Canada, 72–73, 213
Capacity
  design options for, 568–569
  explanation of, 567–568
Capital
  forms of, 20
  net working, 457–458
Capital budgeting
  explanation of, 445
  for multiple-year investments, 452
  net present value and, 449–451
Capital gains, 144, 455
Capital goods, 20
Capitalism
  competition in, 13–16
  demand, supply, and price in, 11–12
  explanation of, 10, 21
  private property and property rights in, 10,
    12–13
Capital market instruments, 479–481
Capital market line, 468
Capital risk, 511
Careers
  in accounting, 400–401, 435
  in brand management, 335
  in business, 39–40
  in digital enterprise, 634–635
  in distribution, 369–370
  in financial and investment management,
    469
  in governance, ethics, and social responsi-
    bility, 120–121
  in human resources management, 221

in information systems, 609–610
international, 85–87
in management, 187
in marketing, 302
in motivation and leadership, 263–264
in operations management, 583–584
overview of, 39–40
in promotion, 368–369
in small businesses, 154
Carter, Jimmy, 177
Cash-and-carry wholesalers, 359
Cash flow, 527–528, 530
Cash flow budget, 527, 528
Cash management, 457–458
Cash managers, 469
Casualty insurance, 536
Catalog marketing, 361–362
C corporations, 144
Central banks
  explanation of, 54–55, 478
  monetary policy and, 492–496, 500
Centralized configuration strategy, 605
Centralized organization, 177
Central processing unit (CPU), 593
Certificates of deposit (CDs), 519
Certified financial planners (CFPs), 527
Certified public accountants (CPAs), 383, 400,
  417, 526
Chain of command, 173
Chancery Court, 99
Chaos theory, 257
Character (data), 597
Charismatic leadership, 256
Chartered financial consultants (ChFCs), 527
Chase strategy, 573–574
Checkbook management, 530–532
Chief executive officers (CEOs)
  covenants not to compete and, 109–110
  explanation of, 101, 102
  focus and orientation of, 104, 105
  information access and, 106
Chief financial officers (CFOs), 102, 444
Chief marketing executives (CMEs), 277, 302
China, 17–19, 50
Circuit breakers, 510
Civil Rights Act of 1964, 215, 219
Clayton Act, 287
Client/server network, 618
Closely held firms, 456
Closing, 352
Closing time, 344
Coaxial cable, 598
Coins, 488
Collective bargaining, 210–212
Command economic system, 17
Commercial banks
  deregulation of, 503–504
  explanation of, 496, 503
  list of largest, 502
Commercialization, 324–325
Commercial paper, 453
Commission merchants, 360
Committee authority, 179
Commodity money, 488
Common carriers, 364
Common market, 68
Common stock
  explanation of, 100, 144, 543
  features of, 455–457
  owners vs. managers and, 444
Communicability, 321
Communications channels, 598
Communications processors, 598
Compact disks (CDs), 594
Company credo, 148

Comparable worth, 202
Comparative advantage theory, 59–60
Compatibility, 321
Compensation. See also Employee benefits
  contingent, 202–203
  explanation of, 201
  wages and salary as, 201–202
Competition
  barriers to, 15
  degrees of, 13–15
  imperfect, 14
  marketing intelligence programs and, 285
  monopolistic, 15–16
  operations management and, 560–561
  pure, 14
  time-based, 560–561
Competitor intelligence (CI), 285
Compliance audit, 417
Compound interest, 448
Computer-assisted sales programs (CASPs),
  353
Computer contingency planning, 399–400
Computer crime, 379, 394
Computers. See also Internet; Software;
    Technology; Websites
  accounting and, 396–400, 419–421
  hardware for, 593–594
  monitoring use of, 608
  speed of operation of, 594–595
  types of, 594
  vulnerability of, 616
Concentration, 358
Concept testing, 319–320
Conceptual skills, 186
Confidentiality agreements, 109–110
Configuration strategies, 605, 607
Conflicts of interest, 103–112
Conformance, quality of, 581
Consignment, 359
Consolidation movement, 477, 485
Consultants, 610
Consultative leadership, 260
Consumer Confidence Index, 25–26
Consumer market
  explanation of, 277–278
  psychological aspects of, 279–280
  sociological aspects of, 280–281
  statistics regarding, 278–279
Consumer Products Safety Act, 287
Consumers
  confidence of, 25–26
  demographics of, 26–27
  psychographics of, 27
Consumption, 446
Containerization, 367
Contests, 346–347
Contingency approach to leadership,
    256–257, 260–263
Contingency planning, 170
Continuous process, 567
Control chart, 583
Control decisions
  quality and, 581–583
  scheduling and, 580, 581
Controllers, 444, 469
Control unit, 593
Convenience stores, 360–361
Conversion, 605
Cooperative advertising, 344
Core competencies, 295
Corporate bonds, 541
Corporate veil, 100
Corporations
  board of directors for, 101
  characteristics of, 97, 144

Corporations *(continued)*
  classes of stock of, 100
  confidentiality agreements in, 109–110
  corporate veil and, 100
  ethical violations in, 117–119
  explanation of, 98–99, 143–144
  information access and, 105–106
  intrapreneurs in, 131
  investment orientation in, 104–105
  legislation related to, 110–111
  officers of, 102
  place of incorporation of, 99–100, 102
  shareholder model of business governance
      and, 102–112
  takeover bids and, 103–104
  types of, 144–145
Cost of goods sold, 410
Cottage system, 561
Counter trade, 63–64
Coupon payments, 463
Coupons, 347
Covenants not to compete, 109–110
Coworker dating, 218
Creative destruction, 129–130
Credit bureaus, 491
Credit cards, 490, 631
Credit managers, 469
Creditors, 114
Credit risk, 482, 511
Credit unions, 504–505
Crime, electronic, 379, 394
Crisis planning, 170
Cross coupons, 347
Cuba, 64
Cultural diversity
  business ethics and, 118
  explanation of, 27–28
  marketing and, 288
  in workforce, 218–220
Culture, 27, 280
Currency
  functional, 422
  hard, 489–490
  numeraire, 489
  reporting, 422
  soft, 489
  stable, 53
Currency of books and records (CBR), 422
Currency pegging, 489
Currency risk, 489
Currency translation, 422–424
Current assets, 413
Customer departmentalization, 176
Customer relationship management, 427
Customers
  analysis of, 298–299
  creating value for, 142
  handling objections of, 352
  quality factors for, 582
  satisfaction of, 299–300
  stakeholder model of business governance
      and, 115
Customer service
  explanation of, 300–302
  logistics issues and, 366, 367
Customs union, 68
Cybercrime, 379

Data analysis, 291
Database administrators, 609
Database management system, 598
Databases
  elements of, 597–598
  explanation of, 291–292, 597

Data marts, 598
Data mining, 598
Data warehouse, 598
Dating, coworker, 218
Dealers, 459–460
Deals, 347
Debit cards, 490
Debt
  decisions regarding, 453–455
  ethical handling of, 548
  financing investments with, 480
Decentralization, 177–178
Decentralized configuration strategy, 605,
    607
Decision-support systems, 601–602
Decision tree, 568–569
Decline stage, product, 325–326
Deductible, 535
Default risk, 447, 454–455, 540, 541
Default risk premium, 447
Defined benefit plans, 204, 507
Defined contribution plans, 204, 507, 509
Deflation, 286
Delaware, 99
Delegation
  centralization vs. decentralization and,
      177–178
  explanation of, 176–177
  organizational authority and, 179
  span of control and, 178–179
Demand
  in capitalist system, 11
  price elastic, 11, 331, 332
  price inelastic, 11, 332
  product, 330
  seasonal, 573
  theory of, 11
Demand curve, 11, 12
Democratic leadership style, 260–261
Demographics, 26–27
Departmentalization, 174–176
Department stores, 360
Deposit insurance, 484
Depository institutions. *See also* Banks;
      Financial institutions
  commercial banks, 503–504
  credit unions, 504–505
  explanation of, 503
  mutual savings banks, 504
  savings and loan associations, 504
Depreciating assets, 520
Depreciation, 413
Depressions, 152
Deregulation, bank, 478, 485, 503–504
Design decisions
  capacity, 567–569
  explanation of, 563
  layout, 570–572
  location, 569–570
  process, 566–567
  product, 564–566
Design quality, 581
Digital cash, 631
Digital checking, 631–632
Digital credit card, 631
Digital enterprise
  careers in, 634–635
  dangers of, 616
  e-business and, 628–632
  enterprise resource planning systems and,
      618–625
  explanation of, 616
  information technology infrastructure for,
      617–618
  supply chain management and, 625–628

Digital era. *See also* Information technology
      (IT)
  e-business and, 35–38
  explanation of, 35
  impact of, 38–39
Digital signal, 598
Digital wallet, 631
Dilution of ownership control, 144
Direct mail, 343
Direct marketing, 361–362
Direct response marketing, 362
Direct selling, 361
Disability insurance, 153, 535
Disaster recovery planning, 426
Discount brokerage firms, 459
Discount rate, 448, 496
Discount stores, 360
Dispersion, 358
Displays, 347
Disposable income, 54
Distribution careers, 369–370
Distribution channels
  explanation of, 342, 356–358
  retailers and, 360–362
  wholesalers and, 359–360
Distribution mix
  distribution channels and, 356–358
  explanation of, 342, 356
  logistics and, 362–368
  retailers and, 360–362
  wholesalers and, 359–360
Distributors, 114–115
Diversification, investment, 467, 540
Dividends
  explanation of, 22, 144
  paying out shareholder, 452–453
Divisional organizational structure, 180
Division of labor, 561
Dollar cost averaging, 543
Dollar standard, 488–489
Domestic importers, 607
Dotcoms, 3, 6, 38
Double taxation of earnings, 144
Drop shippers, 359
Due process, 633
D.U.M.B. strategy, 296
Duplicated configuration strategy, 605
Durability, 582
Duty of fair representation, 210

Earnings, retained, 22, 452–453
E-business
  background of, 35–38
  business-to-business, 37, 38, 630
  business-to-consumer, 37, 38, 629–630
  careers in, 635
  classification of, 629–631
  electronic payment systems and, 631–632
  explanation of, 628–629
  opportunities and challenges in, 632
  trends in, 36–37
Economic and monetary union, 68
Economic management
  goals for, 51–53
  policy tools for, 51, 53–56
Economic policies
  exchange rate, 55–56
  fiscal, 53–54
  incomes, 55
  monetary, 54–55, 497–500
  trade, 55, 56
Economic profits, accounting profits vs., 445
Economic resources, 10

Economic systems
  capitalist, 10–16
  command, 17
  mixed, 17–18
  in transition, 18–19
Economic transition, 18–19
Economies of scale, 130–131
Economy
  financial systems and, 486–487
  marketing and, 286–287
  new, 8
  underground, 95
Education, 136
Efficient frontier, 468
Elastic demand, 11, 331, 332
Electronic cash (e-cash), 631
Electronic crime, 79, 394
Electronic money
  advantages and disadvantages of,
      490–491
  explanation of, 490
  identity theft and, 491–492
  types of, 490, 631–632
Electronic payment systems, 631–632
E-mail, 96
Embargoes, 64
Employee benefits. *See also* Compensation
  explanation of, 203–204
  flexible, 205
  pension plans as, 204
  stock or stock options as, 204–205
Employee motivation. *See* Motivation
Employee performance
  job enrichment and, 248
  job redesign and, 248–249
  management by objective and, 244–245
  overview of, 243
  participative management and employee
      empowerment and, 246–247
  teams and, 245–246
Employee performance appraisals
  explanation of, 205
  frequency of, 208
  methods for, 206–208
Employee Retirement Income Security Act
    (ERISA), 204
Employees
  empowerment of, 246–247
  evaluation of, 205–208
  recruitment of, 199
  selection of, 200–201
  stakeholder model of business governance
      and, 115–116
Employer pay confidentiality rules, 202
Employment-at-will
  explanation of, 208, 213–214
  state courts and, 217
Empowerment, 246–247
Enterprise resource planning systems (ERP
    systems)
  benefits and costs of, 620–621
  careers in, 634
  explanation of, 618–620
  implementation of, 624–625
  software vendors of, 621–623
Entrepreneurs. *See also* Small businesses
  education and training of, 136
  explanation of, 20, 129, 135
  in information technology, 3
  personal qualities of, 135
  women as, 137–138
Envelope budget, 530
Environmental analysis, 165–166
Equal Credit Opportunity Act of 1975, 137
Equal employment opportunity, 219–220

Equal Employment Opportunity Commission
    (EEOC), 215, 220, 242
Equal Opportunity for Women in the
    Workplace Act of 1999, 137
Equal Pay Act, 202, 215
Equilibrium price, 12
Equity investments, 541–543
Equity theory, 233–234, 241–242
Estate plans, 153
Ethics. *See also* Business ethics
  explanation of, 117
  of financial planning, 547–550
  in universities, 120
  workplace, 218
Euro, 489
Eurobonds, 453
European Coal and Steel Community (ECSC),
    70
European Economic Community (EEC), 70
European Free Trade Association (EFTA), 70
European Monetary Union (EMU), 134–135,
    489
European Union (EU)
  function of, 70–71
  origins of, 69–70
  profile of countries in, 71
Exabyte, 593
Excel (Microsoft), 532
Exchange rate policy, 55–56
Exchange rates, 53, 65–66
Exchange traded funds (ETFs), 469
Executive information systems, 602
Executive Order 11246, 220
Expectancy theory, 233–234, 240–241
Export-import business, 77–78
Exports, 56, 58. *See also* Trade
Express warranties, 313
External accountants, 383
External auditing, 417
External recruitment, 199
External sources, 318
Extranet, 618
Extrinsic motivation, 230

Facility controls, 609
Factoring, 458
Factory system, 6
Fair Information Practices (FIP), 633
Fair Labor Standards Act (FLSA), 201, 209
Fair Packaging and Labeling Act, 287
Fait money, 488
Family and Medical Leave Act of 1993, 217
Family businesses, 149–150
Feasibility studies, 604
Federal fund rate, 492
Federal Income Contribution Act (FICA) tax,
    546. *See also* Social security
Federal Open Market Committee (FOMC),
    492
Federal Reserve System, 54, 488, 492, 493,
    495, 512
Federal Trade Commission Act, 287
Feedback controls, 396
Fees, ethics of, 334
Fiber-optic cable, 598
Field, 597
File, 597
Finance officers, 469
Financial accounting, 380–382
Financial decision making
  asset and liability management and, 458
  capital budgeting and, 445–446
  cash management and, 457–458
  common stock and, 455–457

debt and, 453–455
  financing mix and, 457
  net present value and capital budgeting
      decisions and, 449–451
  retained earnings and, 452–453
Financial holding companies, 478, 485
Financial information systems, 603–604
Financial institutions. *See also* Banks;
    Depository institutions
  careers in, 512
  consolidation movement in, 477, 485
  depository, 503–505
  deregulation of, 478, 485
  explanation of, 481–482
  legislation affecting, 485
  management of, 510–511
  nondepository, 505–510
  public confidence in, 483–484
  regulation of, 483–485
  unique aspects of, 501–503
Financial instruments
  capital market, 479–481
  explanation of, 478
  money market, 479
Financial intermediation, 481–482
Financial management
  accounting profits vs. economic profits
      and, 445
  careers in, 469, 550
  function of, 443–444
  time value of money and interest rates
      and, 446–448
Financial managers
  explanation of, 185
  owners vs., 44–445
  role of, 445–446
Financial markets, 481
Financial planners, 526, 527
Financial planning. *See* Personal financial
    planning (PFP)
Financial planning software, 532–533
Financial reporting, 408–409. *See also*
    Accounting
Financial Services Modernization Act, 485
Financial statements. *See also* Accounting
  auditing of, 416–421
  balance sheet, 412–414
  explanation of, 409
  income statement, 409–411
  relationships among, 415–416
  statement of cash flows, 414–415
  statement of retained earnings, 411
Financial success, 522–523
Financial systems
  economy and, 486–487
  financial institutions and, 481–482
  financial instruments and, 478–481
  financial markets and, 481
  overview of, 477–478
  regulation of, 483
  structure of, 482–485
Financing activities, 415
Firewall, 618
Firm concentration ratios, 14
Firm-specific risk, 465
First-line managers, 184
First-mover advantages, 298
Fiscal policy
  explanation of, 53–54, 501
  monetary policy vs., 500–501
Fiscal year, 410
Fisher effect, 498–499
Fixed exchange rate system, 65–66
Fixed-income investments, 541
Fixed-position layout, 571

Flexible benefit plans, 205
Flextime programs, 250
Floating exchange rate system, 656
Forced evaluation methods, 207
Foreign Corrupt Practices Act, 118, 119, 397–398
Foreign currency translation, 422–424
Foreign direct investment (FDI), 61
Foreign exchange markets, 65
Former Soviet Union countries, 18–19
For-profit businesses, 4–5
Fortune 500 companies, 40
401(k) plans, 546
Fourth-generation languages, 596–597
France, 18
Franchises
    advantages and disadvantages of, 146
    examples of, 146–147
    explanation of, 78–79, 143, 145–146, 607
Free enterprise system. See Capitalism
Free market system, 10. See also Capitalism
Free-rein leadership style, 260–262
Free trade area, 68
Free Trade Area of the Americas (FTAA), 75
Free trade regime, 58
Freight forwarder, 367–368
Full-service brokerage firms, 459
Functional currency (FC), 422
Functional departmentalization, 174
Functional organizational structure, 180
Funded pension plans, 508
Future value, 448, 449

Gainsharing plans, 203
Gantt chart, 562, 580-581
Gap risk, 511
Garlic production, 50
General Agreement on Tariffs and Trade (GATT), 8, 66–67. See also World Trade Organization (WTO)
Generally accepted accounting principles (GAAP), 381, 383, 388
General managers, 185
General partners, 98
General-purpose software, 596
Generic brands, 312
Geographic departmentalization, 176
Germany, 54, 76, 213
Gigabyte, 593, 594
Globalization
    adaptation and, 29
    effects on workers of, 56
    explanation of, 8, 66
    impact of information technology on, 38–39
    managerial skills and, 186
    post–World War II, 7–8
    rise of, 66–67
    small business and, 132, 133
Global Market Series Export Certificate Program, 77
Global Technology Network, 77
Goals
    on business plans, 139
    impact of leadership and motivation on, 228–229
    strategic, 165
Goal-seeking analysis, 602
Golden parachute agreements, 110
Gold standard, 488–489
Good faith bargaining, 210–211
Goods
    demand for, 25–27
    operations management and, 559–560
    production of, 19–20

Government, 86, 134–135. See also Regulation
Governmental Auditing Standards, 429
Government expenditure, 53
Government market, 282–283
Gratz v. Bollinger, 220
Great Britain, 6, 213, 252
Great Depression
    financial system and, 477, 486
    labor-management relations and, 209
    manufacturing during, 7
Gross domestic product (GDP)
    economic policies and, 53–55
    explanation of, 31, 286
    nominal, 31, 32
    real, 31, 32, 52
    small business shares of, 130
Gross national income (GNI)
    explanation of, 30–31
    nominal, 31
    real, 31
    in world economies, 33, 34
Gross national product (GNP), 30–31
Group insurance plans, 507
Growth stage, product, 325
Growth stocks, 542
Grutter v. Bollinger, 220

Hard disks, 593–594
Hawthorne effect, 235–236
Hawthorne studies, 232–233, 235–236, 563
Health insurance, 153, 203–204, 507, 535
Health maintenance organizations (HMOs), 535
Herzberg's motivation-hygiene theory, 232–233, 237–238
Hierarchy of needs, 232–233, 236–237
High-level languages, 596
Holding cost, 577–578
Home businesses, 132, 137
Home ownership, 543–545
Homeowner's insurance, 545
Hong Kong, 17–18
Human relations skills, 186
Human resources information systems, 604
Human resources management. See also Labor-management relations
    careers in, 221
    demand forecasts and, 197–198
    employee benefits and, 203–205
    employee selection and, 200–201
    employment-at-will and, 213–214
    equal employment opportunity and affirmative action and, 219–220
    federal legislation impacting, 214–217
    feedback and performance appraisal and evaluation and, 206–208
    job analysis and, 197
    needs analysis and, 205
    orientation and, 201
    recruiting and, 199
    state regulation impacting, 217–218
    supply forecasts and, 198
    technology and, 196–197
    trends in, 195–196
    wages and salary and, 201–203
    workforce development and, 205–206
    workplace diversity and, 218–220
Human resources managers, 184–185
Hybrid strategies, 573
Hygiene factors, 237
Hypertext transport protocol, 617
Hypotheses, 290

Identity theft, 491–492
Immigrant-owned businesses, 138–139
Imperfect competition, 14
Implicit warranties, 313
Imports, 56. See also Trade
Incentives, 347, 354
Income
    disposable, 54
    management of personal, 527–536
    minimization of inequalities in, 24
    in United States, 279
    in various countries, 284
Incomes policies, 55
Income statements, 409–411
Income stocks, 542
In-control production system, 583
Independent accountants, 383
Independently wealthy, 522
Independent outside directors, 101
India, 18, 36–37
Individual retirement accounts (IRAs), 508, 509, 546
Industrial distributors, 359
Industrial Revolution, 6, 561
Inelastic demand, 11, 332
Inflation
    explanation of, 52, 286, 446
    monetary policy and, 498–500
    rate of, 446–447
    retirees and, 508
Information fragmentation, 618
Information managers, 185
Information requirements, 604
Information security, 426
Information systems. See also Management information systems
    careers in, 609–610
    classification of, 600–604
    controls for, 608–609
    development of, 604–605
    explanation of, 593
    global, 605, 607
Information technology (IT). See also Technology
    accounting and, 423–427
    careers in, 634
    developments in, 4, 20, 35
    digital enterprise and, 617–618
    dotcoms collapse and, 3, 6, 38
    e-business and, 35–38
    entrepreneurs in, 3
    globalization and, 38–39
    knowledge workers and, 8–9
    privacy and, 427, 608, 633
    small businesses and, 133
Initial public offering (IPO), 150, 456
Innovation, in small business, 130–131
Innovation planning, 169–170
Innovators, 325
In-pack incentives, 347
Input devices, 594
Inputs, 19, 558
Inside directors, 101
Inside information, 503
Insider trading, 111
Institutional investors
    explanation of, 460–461, 510
    shareholder proposals and, 109
Instructional-based programs, 206
Insurance
    automobile, 536
    casualty, 536
    deposit, 484
    disability, 153, 535
    explanation of, 534–535

health, 153, 203–204, 507, 535
homeowner's, 545
liability, 152–153
life, 506, 535–536
property, 152, 536, 545
renter's, 545
term, 506
Insurance companies, 502, 506–507
Insurance premiums, 152
Interest
compound, 448
explanation of, 446
tax deductions on, 453–454
Interest cost, 578
Interest-rate risk, 464–465
Interest rates
money supply and, 493
nominal, 447–448
real, 446
riskless, 448
stated, 447
Intermediate targets, 497
Intermittent flow, 566
Internal auditing, 417
Internal controls
computer contingency planning and,
399–400
computer security of accounting information and, 398
explanation of, 395
feedback, 396
Foreign Corrupt Practices Act and, 397–398
preventive, 395
role of auditor in, 396–397
structure of, 395
types of, 395–396
Internal control structure, 417
Internal recruitment, 199
Internal sources, 318
International business
accounting standards for, 386–388
careers in, 85–87
channels of distribution and, 357
export-import, 77–78
foreign currency translation and, 422–423
joint ventures and strategic alliances and,
79–80
licensing and franchising and, 78–79
logistics operations for, 366–368
mergers and acquisitions and, 84–85
multinational enterprises and, 80–85
overview of, 76
subsidiaries and, 85
International Financial Reporting Standards
(IFRS), 385, 387
International joint ventures, 79–80
International markets
explanation of, 283–284
products for, 314, 333
strategies for, 296
International skills, 186
International Standards on Auditing (ISAs),
388–390
International trade. *See* Trade; Trade policy
Internet. *See also* Websites; World Wide Web
advertising on, 344
e-business and, 35–38
explanation of, 617
globalization and, 38–39
information for small business on, 134, 136
origins of, 3
researching international business opportunities using, 86
Internet payments, 490
Internet service provider (ISP), 617

Internetworking, 617
Internetwork processors, 598
Interviews, employment, 200
Intranet, 618
Intrapreneurs, 131
Intrinsic motivation, 230
Introduction stage, product, 325
Intrusion detection, 426
Invention, 130–131
Inventory
explanation of, 25, 559–560
management of, 365–366
optimal level of, 577–579
Investing activities, 415
Investment bankers, 459
Investment companies, 509–510
Investment grade, 455
Investment management
balancing returns and risks and, 461–465
careers in, 469
ethics and, 460
explanation of, 443
investment choices and, 467–469
managing risk and, 465–467
personal, 538–540
role of, 459–461
Investment risk, 539
Investments, 541–543
Investors
accounting information for, 390–391
explanation of, 21
institutional, 460–461

Japan, 63, 76, 247
Job analysis, 197
Job applications, 200
Job description, 197
Job enlargement, 248
Job enrichment, 248
Job evaluations, 202
Job process, 566
Job redesign, 248–249
Job rotation, 174, 248
Job satisfaction
job enrichment and, 248
job redesign and, 248–249
management by objective and, 244–245
participative management and employee
empowerment and, 246–247
teams and, 245–246
Job specialization, 173–174
Job specification, 197
Joint ventures, international, 79–80
Junk bonds, 455
Just cause provisions, 211

Keogh plans, 508, 509
Key accounts, 353
Kilobyte, 593
Knowledge-based pay, 203
Knowledge workers, 8–9

L, 495
Labor, 6, 19–20
Labor arbitration, 211
Labor-management relations
collective bargaining and, 210–212
decline of unions and, 212–213
historical background of, 208–210
international, 213
Labor unions
collective bargaining and, 210–212

company, 209
decline of, 212–213
organizing employees and electing,
209–210
in other countries, 213
representation elections in, 210
role of, 195
Lag demand strategy, 568, 569
Laissez-faire system, 7, 208
Land, 19
Landrum Griffin Act, 212, 213
Lanham Trademark Act, 287
Latin America, 74–75
Latin American Free Trade Association
(LAFTA), 74–75
Law of demand, 11. *See also* Demand
Law of supply, 11–12. *See also* Supply
Layout, 570–572
Lead demand strategy, 568
Leadership
careers in, 263–264
chaos theory and, 257
charismatic, 256
consultative, 260
contingency approach to, 256–257,
260–263
explanation of, 253–255
servant, 255
transactional, 255–256
transformational, 256
Leadership styles
autocratic, 259–260
democratic, 260–261
explanation of, 257–258
free-rein, 260–262
Lead users, 318
Learning, 279–280
Legacy systems, 619
Legal issues/legislation
for corporations, 110–111
for e-business, 632
for financial institutions, 485
for human resources management,
214–217
for marketing, 287
privacy and, 427, 608, 633
Level strategy, 573-574
Liabilities
explanation of, 413
managing maturity of, 458
personal, 520–521
Liability insurance, 152–153
Licensing, 15, 78
Life insurance
explanation of, 153, 203, 535
types of, 506–507, 535–536
Life insurance companies, 506–507
Lifetime value (LTV), 291
Limited liability, 98, 144
Limited liability company (LLC), 145
Limited partners, 98
Limit orders, 459, 481
Line authority, 179
Line process, 567
Liquidation risk, 482
Liquidity, 520
Liquidity risk, 465
Living standards, 58–59
Local area networks (LANs), 600
Location, 569–570
Location decisions, 569–570
Lock box system, 458
Logistics
careers in, 370
components of, 363

Logistics (continued)
explanation of, 342, 362–363
international challenges to, 366–368
storage and, 365–366
transportation and, 363–365

Machine languages, 596
Magazine advertising, 344
Mail-ins, 347
Mainframe computers, 594
Maintainability, of product, 582
Maintenance, 605
Maintenance objectives, 329
Managed floating exchange rate system, 65
Management. See also Human resources
        management
brand, 335
controlling function of, 182–183
directing function of, 182
explanation of, 163–164
organizing function of, 171–181
participative, 246–247
planning function of, 164–170
skills for, 186–187
Management accounting, 380
Management audits, 417
Management by objective (MBO), 244–245
Management information systems
accounting, 603
careers in, 609–610
classification of, 600
computer hardware for, 593–595
computer software for, 595–597
controls for, 608, 609
databases for, 597–598
development of, 604–605
example of, 591–592, 606
explanation of, 383–384, 592–593
financial, 603–604
global, 605, 607
human resources, 604
marketing, 603
for middle managers, 601–602
for operations managers, 601
production, 603
for senior managers, 602
telecommunications networks for, 598–600
Management process
controlling and, 182–183
directing and, 182
organizing and, 170–182
planning and, 164–170
Management science, 563
Managerial information systems, 601–602
Managers
areas for, 184–185
explanation of, 163–164
functions of, 183–184
levels of, 184
middle, 184, 601–602
operations, 601
senior, 602
Manufacturers' agents, 359
Manufacturing
design for, 564
during Great Depression, 7
operations management careers in, 584
post–World War II, 8
trends in, 195
Manufacturing system, 557
Maquiladoras, 84
Market clearing price, 12
Market domination, 7
Market efficiency, 482

Marketing
coordination between research and devel-
        opment and, 323
direct, 361–362
explanation of, 276
importance of, 276
objectives of, 292–294
overview of, 275
relationship, 292
Marketing environment
competition and, 285
culture and, 288
economy and, 286–287
explanation of, 284
laws and politics and, 287–288
technology and, 285–286
Marketing information systems (MIS),
        288–290, 603
Marketing managers, 185
Marketing mix
development of, 310
explanation of, 276, 309–310
pricing mix and, 329–335 (See also Pricing;
        Pricing mix)
product mix and, 310–329 (See also
        Product mix; Products)
Marketing research, 290–291, 319
Marketing strategies
explanation of, 294–296
niche, 296–298
undifferentiated, 296
Market orders, 481
Market-oriented financial systems, 483
Market portfolio, 468
Market risk, 464
Markets
business-to-business, 281–282
consumer, 277–281
government, 282–283
international, 283–284
primary, 326
secondary, 326
Market segmentation, 27
Market structure, 14–16
Market testing, 324
Market timing approach, 543
Markup, price, 333–335
Marshall Plan, 69
Maslow's hierarchy of needs, 232–233,
        236–237
Master production schedule, 575
Match demand strategy, 568, 569
Materials management, 363
Material requirements, 574–576
Material requirements planning (MRP), 574,
        575
Matrix organizational structure, 180
Maturity date, 453
Maturity stage, product, 325–327
McGregor's theories X and Y, 232–233,
        238–239
Medical insurance, 507
Medicare, 546
Meditation, 228
Megabyte, 593
Merchant wholesalers, 359
Mergers
bank, 477
elements of, 103
international, 85
Merit pay plans, 203
Mexico, 72–73
Microbusiness, 129. See also Small businesses
Microcomputers, 594
Middle managers, 184, 601–602

Midrange computers, 594
Minimum wage, 201
Mission statements, 139, 165
Mixed economic system, 17–18
Mobile commerce (m-commerce), 631
Modem, 598
Modified rebuy, 282
Modular designs, 565
M1, 495
Monetary policy
central banks and, 492–495
economic goals of, 497–500
explanation of, 54–55
fiscal policy vs., 500–501
framework for, 495–497
quantity theory and, 493–494
Money
commodity, 488
definitions of, 494–495
electronic, 490–492
Euro, 489
function of, 20, 487
gold and dollar standards, 488–489
hard currencies, 489–490
historical background of, 487–488
personal view of, 549–550
time value of, 446–448, 450
Money market instruments, 479
Monolithic approach, 623
Monopolistic competition, 15–16
Monopoly, 14, 16
Montana Wrongful Discharge for
        Employment Act, 217
Moral hazard risk, 484
Mortgages, 543–544
Motivation, 229–230, 263–264
Motivational theories
behavior theory, 235–236
equity theory, 241–242
evolution of, 230, 232–234
expectancy theory, 240–241
Herzberg's motivation-hygiene theory,
        237–238
Maslow's hierarchy of needs, 236–237
McGregor's theories X and Y, 238–239
Ouchi's theory Z, 239–240
reinforcement theory, 242
Taylor's scientific management theory, 231,
        235
Motivation factors, 237
Motivation-hygiene theory, 232–233, 237–238
Motives, 229, 280
M3, 495
M2, 495
Multicurrency, 619–620
Multi Fiber Arrangement (MFA), 63
Multilanguage, 619
Multinational enterprises (MNEs)
background of, 81–82
careers in, 86
explanation of, 80–81, 607
function of, 82–83
list of largest, 82
mergers and acquisitions and, 84–85
subsidiaries and, 85
Multiplexer, 598
Municipal bonds, 541
Municipal securities, 465
Mutual funds, 509–510, 543
Mutual organizations, 507
Mutual savings banks, 504

Nanotechnology, 9
National brands, 312

National income accounts, 30
National Labor Relations Act (NLRA), 209, 210, 212
National Labor Relations Board (NLRB), 209, 210
Needs analysis, 205
Negative reinforcement, 242
Net cash inflow, 527
Net income, 410
Net interest margin, 511
Net present value (NPV), 451
Networked configuration strategy, 607
Network firewall, 618
Net working capital, 457–458
Networking specialists, 610
Network organizational structure, 180–181
Network structures, 599–600
Net worth, personal, 520–522
New economy, 8
Newspaper advertising, 343–345
New tasks, 282
Niche marketing strategy, 296–298
Nominal GDP, 31, 32
Nominal GNI, 31
Nominal GNP, 31
Nominal interest rate, 447–448
Nondepository institutions
    explanation of, 505–506
    institutional investors, 510
    insurance companies, 506–507
    investment companies, 509–510
    pension funds, 507–509
Nonstore retailing, 361–362
Normal variation, 582–583
Norris-LaGuardia Act, 209
North American Commission on Labor Cooperation, 213
North American Free Trade Agreement (NAFTA), 72–73, 75, 213
North American Industry Classification System (NAICS), 281–282
Not-for-profit organizations
    explanation of, 4, 21
    objectives of, 24–25
Numeraire currency, 489
Nutritional Labeling and Education Act, 287

Objective evaluation methods, 206
Objectives, 292–294
Occupational Safety and Health Act of 1970, 216
Occupations, 9. See also Careers
Off-duty conduct statutes, 217–218
Officers, corporate, 102
Offshoring, 249
Oligopoly, 15, 16
Online banking, 505
Online brokerage firms, 459
Online retailing, 362
Open market operations, 492
Operating activities, 414
Operating system, 595
Operating targets, 495
Operational audits, 417
Operational database, 598
Operational efficiency, 482
Operational-level systems, 601
Operational plans, 167
Operational risk, 482
Operations management
    careers in, 583–584
    competitiveness and, 560–561
    control decisions of, 564, 580–583
    design decisions of, 563–571

explanation of, 185, 557–558
    goods and services and, 559–560
    historical background of, 561–563
    planning decisions of, 563, 572–579
Operations research, 563
Opportunity cost, 451
Optical disks, 594
Optimization analysis, 602
Ordering cost, 577
Organizational analysis, 166
Organizational structure
    chain of command and, 173
    delegation and, 176–179
    departmentalization and, 174–176
    explanation of, 170–173
    job specialization and, 173–174
    types of, 180–181
Organizations
    centralized vs. decentralized, 177
    explanation of, 171–172
Organized exchanges, 479, 480
Orientation, 201
Ouchi's theory Z, 232–233, 239–240
Out-of-control production system, 583
Output devices, 594
Outputs, 19, 52, 558
Outside directors, 101
Outsourcing, 296, 366, 576
Over-the-counter (OTC) exchanges, 479, 480
Owners, managers vs., 444–445
Owners' equity, 413–414

Packaging, 312–313
Paper money, 488
Parallel conversion strategy, 605
Participative management, 246–247
Partnership agreements, 98
Partnerships, 97–98, 143
Part-time work, 195, 251
Par value, 144, 463
Patents, 15
Path-goal theory, 257
Pension Benefit Guaranty Corporation (PBGC), 204
Pension funds, 507–509
Pension plans
    explanation of, 204
    funded, 508
    types of, 507–508
    unfunded, 508, 509
Perception, 280
Performance appraisals. See Employee performance appraisals
Performance objectives, 329
Permanent insurance, 535–536
Personal balance sheet, 520
Personal financial planning (PFP)
    careers in, 550
    computing net worth and, 520–522
    ethics of, 547–550
    evaluating spending patterns and, 523–525
    identifying your stage in life and, 525
    income management and, 527–536
    investing and, 538–545
    living on one income and, 536–538
    purpose of, 519
    retirement and estate planning and, 545–546
    setting financial goals and, 522–523
    software for, 532–533
    tax planning and, 547
    using experts for, 525–527
    web resources for, 533–534
Personal financial specialists (PFSs), 526, 527, 550

Personal selling
    closings in, 352–353
    ethics and, 354
    explanation of, 342, 350
    features of, 350–351
    presentations in, 351–352
    record keeping for, 353
Personal spending, 523–525
Petabyte, 593
Pharmaceutical industry, 354
Phased conversion strategy, 605
Phased strategy, 624–625
Physical capital, 20
Physical distribution, 363
Piece-rate system, 235
Pilot conversion strategy, 605
Place utility, 358
Planned economic system. See Command economic system
Planning. See also Strategic planning
    contingency and crisis, 170
    explanation of, 164–165
    human resources, 197–198
    innovation, 169–170
    strategic formulation and, 165–166
    strategic goals and, 165
    strategic implementation and, 166–167
    succession, 168–169
Planning decisions
    explanation of, 572–573
    material requirements and, 574–576
    production rate and, 573–574
    purchasing and, 576–577
Plant managers, 584
Plunge conversion strategy, 605
Policy tools, 495
Political union, 68
P-O-P (point of purchase), 347
Portfolio of assets, 520
Positioning, 298
Positive reinforcement, 242
Preemptive right, 455–456
Preferred provider organizations (PPOs), 535
Preferred stock, 100
Pregnancy Discrimination Act of 1978, 216
Preliminary investigation, in marketing research, 290
Present value
    decisions regarding net, 449–451
    explanation of, 448
    net, 451
Prevention objectives, 329
Preventive controls, 395–396. See also Internal controls
Price elastic demand, 11
Price elastic supply, 12
Price inelastic demand, 11
Price inelastic supply, 12
Price risk, 482
Prices
    competitiveness and, 560
    seasonal demand and, 573
    transfer, 333
Pricing mix
    existing products and, 331–332
    objectives for, 329–330
    price-setting steps and, 330–331
    for products sold internationally, 333
    retailer markup and, 333–335
Primary drives, 230
Primary market, 326, 481
Primary storage, 593
Principals, 103
Principal value, 463
Privacy, 427, 608, 633

Private brands, 312
Private carriers, 364
Private pension plans, 507
Private property, 10, 12–13
Private warehouses, 365–366
Privatization, 18
Procedural controls, 609
Process, 566–567
Process improvement consultants, 584
Process-oriented layout, 571
Product departmentalization, 174–175
Product development
    aspects of new products, 321–323
    commercialization stage of, 324–325
    concept testing stage of, 319–321
    explanation of, 314–316
    idea generation for, 318–319
    philosophy of, 316–318
    screening stage of, 319
    steps in, 318–325
    testing stage of, 324
Product elimination programs, 327–329
Production
    explanation of, 557
    rate of, 573–574
    system, 605
Production information systems, 603
Production systems
    explanation of, 557–558
    historical background of, 561–563
    in-control, 583
    out-of-control, 583
Productivity, 24
Product life cycle
    explanation of, 13, 309
    product elimination and, 327–329
    stages in, 325–327
Product mix
    elements of, 310–314
    explanation of, 309
    management of existing products and, 325–329
    new product development and, 314–325
Product-oriented layout, 571–572
Product quality, 311–313
Products
    design of, 310, 311
    differentiation of, 15–16
    in international markets, 314
    introduction of new, 309
    pricing for new, 330–331 (See also Pricing mix)
    width and depth dimensions of, 314
Profit margin, 411
Profits
    ethics and, 23
    explanation of, 4
    maximization of, 21–22
Profit sharing plans, 203
Programmers, 609
Programming, 605
Programming language, 596
Project process, 566
Promotional packaging, 312–313
Promotion mix
    advertising and, 343–345
    explanation of, 341–343
    personal selling and, 350–354
    publicity and, 355–356
    sales promotion and, 345–349
Property-casualty insurance companies, 507
Property insurance, 152, 536, 545
Property rights, 12–13
Prospecting, 351

Protection, 61
Protective packaging, 312–313
Psychographics, 27
Psychological factors, of consumer markets, 279–280
Public accounting, 383
Publicity, 355–356
Publicly held firms, 456
Public pension plans, 507
Public relations, 355, 369
Public warehouses, 365–366
Purchase with purchase, 347
Purchasing
    explanation of, 576
    outsourcing and, 576
    planning decisions and, 576–577
    supplier selection and, 577
    value analysis and, 576–577
Purchasing power parity (PPP), 33, 34
Pure competition, 14, 16
Pure Food and Drug Act, 287

Quality
    competitiveness and, 560
    of conformance, 581
    control decisions related to, 581–583
    of design, 581
    explanation of, 581
Quality control, 582–583
Quality function deployment (QFD), 565–566
Quality managers, 584
Quantitative restrictions (QRs), 62–63. See also Quotas
Quattro Pro, 532
Quicken, 532
Quotas, 62–63

Rack jobbers, 359
Radio advertising, 344
Railroad era, 6–7, 38
Rate of return
    explanation of, 448
    measurement of, 461–463
    required, 451
Real estate, 543–545
Real estate investment trust (REIT), 540
Real GDP, 31, 32, 52
Real GNI, 31
Real GNP, 31
Real rate of interest, 446–447
Recessions, 152, 501
Record, 597
Recruitment, 147–148, 199
Recycling, 564
Reference groups, 280
References, job, 201
Regional integration
    Association of South East Asian Nations and, 73–74
    European Union and, 69–71
    in Latin America, 74–75
    North American Free Trade Agreement and, 72–73
    pros and cons of, 68–69
    stages of, 67–68
    in triad economies, 75–76
Regular wholesalers, 359
Regulation
    affecting human resources management, 217–218
    affecting marketing, 287–288
    of financial institutions, 483–485
Regulatory agency careers, 512

Regulatory risk, 482
Reinforcement theory, 233–234, 242
Reinforcers, 242
Reinvestment risk, 465
Relationship marketing, 292
Relative advantage, 321
Reliability, 301, 581–582
Remanufactured products, 564
Remote connectivity, 427
Renter's insurance, 545
Replacement charts, 198
Reporting currency (RC), 422
Reputation risk, 482
Required rate of return, 451
Research and development (R&D), 321–322
Research study design, 290–291
Reserve for losses, 511
Reserve requirements, 496
Responsibility, 176
Responsiveness, of service, 582
Restricted stock payments, 107
Résumés, 200
Retailing
    careers in, 369–370
    markup in, 333–335
    types of, 360–362
    wheel of, 360
Retained earnings, 22, 452–453
Retirement planning
    explanation of, 204, 545
    IRAs and 401(k) plans and, 546
    social security and, 545–546
    wills and, 546
Return on assets (ROA), 510
Return on equity (ROE), 510
Return on investments, 461–463
Return on portfolio, 520
Revenue, 21
Right-to-work laws, 212
Ring network, 599–600
Risk
    balancing returns and, 461
    capital, 511
    control of business, 151–153
    credit, 482, 511
    currency, 489
    default, 447, 454–455, 540, 541
    explanation of, 4–5, 449
    firm-specific, 465
    gap, 511
    interest rate, 464–465
    investment, 539
    liquidation, 482
    liquidity, 465
    managing investment, 465–468
    market, 464
    moral hazard, 484
    new product, 321
    operational, 482
    price, 482
    regulatory, 482
    reinvestment, 465
    reputation, 482
    strategic, 482
    systematic, 465
    tax, 465
    total, 465
Riskless rate of interest, 448
Risk premium, 511
Risk profile, 76
Risk-return trade-off, 461
Robinson-Patman Act, 287
Robust designs, 565
Roth IRAs, 509
Rule Fair Disclosure (Rule FD), 111

Salary, 201–202
Sales branches, 359
Sales offices, 359
Sales promotion
    explanation of, 341–342, 345–346
    types of, 346–349
Samples, 347
Sarbanes-Oxley Act, 110–111, 119–121, 390,
    430, 460
Savings and loan associations, 504
Scheduling, 580, 581
Scientific management, 231, 235, 562
S corporations, 98, 144–145
Screening, new product, 319
Search engine, 617–618
Seasonal demand, 573
Seasoned issues, 456
SEC Act of 1934, 111
Secondary drives, 230
Secondary market, 481
Secondary storage, 593
Secured creditors, 454
Securities Exchange Act of 1934, 397
Securities firms, 502
Security issues, 367, 426, 632
Selection, employee, 200–201
Self-actualization, 236
Self-concept, 280
Self-managing teams, 252
Selling agents, 359
Seniority, 202
Sensitivity analysis, 602
Separation of ownership and control, 103
September 11 terrorist attacks, 220, 367
Servant leadership, 255
Servers, 618
Service industry careers, 87
Services
    demand for, 25–27
    operations management and, 559–560
    operations management careers in, 584
    production of, 19–20
Service system, 557
Setup costs, 577
Shareholder model of business governance
    explanation of, 102–103
    separation of ownership and control and
        potential conflicts of interest and,
        103–112
Shareholder proposal process, 108–109
Shareholders
    rights of, 144
    stakeholder model of business governance
        and, 116
Shareholder wealth, 22
Share of wallet, 292
Sherman Antitrust Act, 287
Shortage, 12
Short-swing profits liability, 111–112
Silicon Valley, 3–4
Simulated test markets, 324
Single market, 68
Single-premium life insurance, 536
Situational leadership model, 256
Six sigma initiatives, 182–183
Skill-based pay, 203
Skills inventories, 198
Skunk works, 323
Small businesses. See also Entrepreneurs
    business plans for, 139–142
    careers in, 154
    causes of failure in, 153, 154
    creating value for, 142
    creative destruction and, 129–130
    ethical issues in, 148–149

ethnic and immigrant, 138–139
explanation of, 128–129
for family businesses, 149–150
globalization and, 132, 133
going public vs. staying private and,
    150–151
government support of, 134–135
hiring employees and, 147–148
in home, 132
importance of, 129
initial production and sales for, 142
invention and innovation in, 130–132
job opportunities in, 132
risk control in, 151–153
seed money for, 141–142
women in, 137–138
Small business organizations
    corporations as, 143–145
    franchises as, 145–147
    partnerships as, 143
    sole proprietorships as, 142–143
Small-order problem, 365
Social class structure, 281
Social security, 508, 509, 546
Societal responsibility model of business gov-
    ernance, 116–117
Sociological factors, of consumer markets,
    280–281
Software
    digital wallet, 631
    enterprise resource planning systems
        vendors, 621–623
    explanation of, 595
    for management information systems,
        595–597
    for personal financial planning, 532–533
    telecommunications, 599–600
Sole proprietorships
    explanation of, 97, 142–143
    woman-operated, 138
Southern Cone Common Market (Mercosur),
    75
Soviet Union. See Former Soviet Union coun-
    tries
Span of control, 178–179
Specialization of labor, 6
Specialty stores, 361
Sponsoring, 348
Stable currency, 53
Staff authority, 179
Stakeholder companies, 22–24
Stakeholder model of business governance
    business and local communities and,
        112–114
    creditors and, 114
    customers and, 115
    distributors and, 114–115
    employees and, 115–116
    explanation of, 112
    shareholders and, 116
    suppliers and, 114
Standardization strategy, 314
Standard of deferred payment, 487
Star Alliance system, 80
Star network, 599
Stated interest rate, 447
State enterprises, 17, 18, 24
Statement of cash flows, 414–415
Statement of financial position. See Balance
    sheet
Statement of retained earnings, 411
Statements of Financial Accounting
    Standards (SFAS), 381
Statements on Auditing Standards, 396, 398
State regulations, 217–218

Steel industry, 62
Stock options
    aligning financial interests and, 106–107,
        444–445
    employee, 204–205
    explanation of, 144
Stock organizations, 507
Stock price, 144
Stocks
    classes of, 100
    common, 100, 144, 444, 543
    growth, 542
    income, 542
    rate of return on, 462
    restricted, 107
    retirement and investment in, 508
    value, 542–543
Storage, 365–366
Stored value cards, 490
Stores, 360–361
Straight rebuy, 282
Strategic alliances, 80, 296
Strategic goals, 165
Strategic planning, 167–168
Strategic risk, 482
Strategies, business plan, 139–140
Strategy formulation, 165–166
Strategy implementation, 166–167
Structured interviews, 200
Subcontract, 573
Subcultures, 280
Subjective evaluation methods, 206–207
Subsidiaries, international, 85
Succession planning, 168–169
Summit of the Americas, 75
Supercomputers, 594
Supermarkets, 360
Suppliers, 114, 577
Supply, 11–12
Supply chain management
    careers in, 634–635
    economic impact of, 627
    example of, 629
    explanation of, 370, 625–626
    global, 630
    strategies for, 627–628
Supply chains, 37
Supply curve, 12
Supravoting shares, 100
Surplus, 12
Survival objectives, 329
Sustainable competitive advantage (SCA), 295
Sweepstakes, 348
System analysts, 609–610
Systematic risk, 465
Systems analysis, 604
Systems controls, 608
Systems design, 604–605
System software, 595
System specifications, 605
System testing, 605

Tactical plans, 166–167
Taft-Hartley Act, 212, 213
Takeover bids, 103–104
Tangibles, of service, 582
Target group, 27
Tariffs, 15, 62
Tax Court, 547
Taxes
    corporate, 98, 144
    responsibility to pay, 548
    role of, 53–54
Tax planning, personal, 547

Tax risk, 465
Taylor's scientific management theory, 231–235
TCP/IP (Transmission Control Protocol/Internet Protocol), 617
Teams
    guidelines to facilitate, 245–246
    self-managing, 252
Technical skills, 186
Technical testing, 324
Technology. *See also* Computers; Internet
    accounting and, 423–427
    human resource management and, 196–197
    for logistics operations, 367
    marketing and, 285–286
    for online banking, 505
    privacy issues and, 427, 608, 633
    production and, 20
    wireless, 38, 426
Technology transfer, 318
Telecommunication, 598
Telecommunications networks, 598–600, 618
Telecommuting, 252–253
Telemarketing, 362
Telephone Consumer Protection Act, 287
Telephone directory advertising, 344
Television advertising, 344
Television home shopping, 362
Terabyte, 593
Term insurance, 506, 535
Testing, 324, 605
Test markets, 324
Theory X (McGregor), 238–239
Theory Y (McGregor), 238–239
Theory Z (Ouchi), 232–233, 239–240
360-degree feedback, 207–208
Three-tier client/server network, 618
Thrift institutions, 504
Time-and-motion studies, 235
Time horizon, 539
Time management, 353
Time preference for consumption, 446
Time utility, 358
Time value of money, 446–448, 450
Top managers, 184
Total net worth, 467
Total risk, 465
Total satisfaction, 299–300
Trade
    absolute advantage in, 59
    accounting for, 384–385
    comparative advantage in, 59–60
    explanation of, 56
    licensing and, 78
    reasons for, 58–59
    regional integration and, 67–76 (*See also* Regional integration)
    by regions and industrialization, 60, 61
    small businesses and, 132
    trends in, 60–61
    World Trade Organization and, 66–67

Trade barriers
    counter trade as, 63–64
    embargoes as, 64
    explanation of, 61–62
    quotas as, 62–63
    tariffs as, 62
    voluntary restraints as, 63
Trade credit, 458
Trademark Counterfeiting Act, 287
Trade policy, 55
Trade shows, 348–349
Training, 120, 136, 391
Transactional leadership, 255–256
Transfer prices, 333
Transformational leadership, 256
Transformation process, 558
Transition economies, 18–19
Transnational companies, 607. *See also* Globalization; Multinational enterprises (MNEs)
Transportation modes, 363–365
Treasurers, 444, 469
Treasury securities, 541
Treaty of Asuncion of 1991, 75
Treaty of Montevideo of 1960, 74–75
Treaty of Rome of 1957, 70
Triad economies, 75–76
Truck wholesalers, 359
20/80 principle, 327
Twisted-pair wire, 598

Underground economy, 95
Underwriting, 459
Undifferentiated strategy, 296
Unemployment, 24
Unethical behavior, 117–118. *See also* Business ethics
Unfunded pension plans, 508, 509
Uniform resource locators (URLs), 617
Unions. *See* Labor unions
United States
    cultural diversity in, 28
    gross domestic product in, 31–32
    population in, 279
    trade in, 64, 72, 75–76
Unit investment trust (UIT), 540
Unit of account, 487
Unit testing, 605
Universal life insurance, 536
Universal Product Code, 313
Universities, 120
U.S. savings bonds, 541

Value stocks, 542–543
Variable life insurance, 536
Venture capitalists, 141, 150–151, 456–457
Venture teams, 318
Vertical integration, 627–628
Vestibule training, 206
Virtual collaboration, 628

Virtual private network (VPN), 618
Vision statement. *See* Mission statements
Voluntary restraints, 63
Vroom and Yetton model of leadership, 256

Wage and salary surveys, 201–202
Wages, 201–202
Wagner Act of 1935, 212
Warehouses, 365–366
WARN Act of 1988, 216
Warranties, 313
Wealth, 522
The Wealth of Nations (Smith), 561
Webmaster, 617
Webpage, 617
Web services, 426
Websites. *See also* Internet
    for accounting and auditing, 427–434
    explanation of, 617
    for financial planning, 533–534
    for researching international business opportunities, 86
    for small business information, 134, 154
What-if analysis, 602
Wheeler Lea Act, 287
Wheel of retailing, 360
Whole life insurance, 506, 536
Wholesalers, 359–360
Wide area networks (WANs), 600
Wills, 546
Wireless technology, 38, 426
Wire transfers, 490
Women
    in small business, 137–138
    in workforce, 218
Work-based programs, 205–206
Workforce
    development of effective, 205–208
    production rate and, 573
    women in, 218
Working capital, 141–142
Work-life programs
    explanation of, 249–250
    flextime, 250
    part-time work, 251
    self-managing teams, 252
    telecommuting, 252–253
    work-share, 251–252
Workplace
    computer monitoring in, 608
    coworker dating in, 218
    diversity in, 30, 218–220
    ethics in, 218
Work-share programs, 251–252
World Trade Organization (WTO), 8, 55, 67
World Wide Web, 3, 617. *See also* Internet; Websites

Yellow dog contracts, 209
Yellow pages, 344